FOURTH EDITION

MORALITY AND MORAL CONTROVERSIES

John Arthur, Editor

*Binghamton University—
State University of New York*

*- use this with news clips/current events f/o.
- issues can come from here or elsewhere.*

PRENTICE HALL, Upper Saddle River, New Jersey 07458

Library of Congress Cataloging-in-Publication Data

Morality and moral controversies / [edited by] John Arthur.—4th ed.
 p.   cm.
  ISBN 0–13–231143–7
  1. Ethics.   2. Social problems.   I. Arthur, John (date).
 BJ1025.M67   1996
 170—dc20

95–9659
CIP

Acquisitions editor: Ted Bolen
Editorial assistant: Meg McGuane
Editorial/production supervision
  and interior design: Linda B. Pawelchak
Copy editor: Kathyrn Beck
Cover design: Bruce Kenselaar
Manufacturing buyer: Lynn Pearlman
Cover illustration: Astromujoff/The Image Bank

© 1996, 1993, 1986, 1981, by Prentice-Hall, Inc.
Simon & Schuster/A Viacom Company
Upper Saddle River, New Jersey 07458

Printed in the United States of America
10 9 8 7 6 5 4 3

ISBN 0-13-231143-7

Prentice-Hall International (UK) Limited, *London*
Prentice-Hall of Australia Pty. Limited, *Sydney*
Prentice-Hall Canada Inc., *Toronto*
Prentice-Hall Hispanoamericans, S.A., *Mexico*
Prentice-Hall of India Private Limited, *New Delhi*
Prentice-Hall of Japan, Inc., *Tokyo*
Simon & Schuster Asia Pte. Ltd., *Singapore*
Editors Prentice-Hall do Brasil, Ltda., *Rio de Janeiro*

Contents

iii

Part II. Issues of Life and Death

Part III. Political Relationships

Part IV. Personal Relationships

Part V. Gender, Race, and Multiculturalism

Preface to the Fourth Edition

I have been very pleased with the reception the last edition of this book received and had not planned to make substantial revisions this soon. Two important considerations have persuaded me otherwise, however. First, Prentice Hall agreed to include along with the new edition a collection of articles and essays from *The New York Times*—something that I believe will be of real value to students and instructors alike. The collection includes, for example, a report on recent scientific findings on smoking and the nature of addiction, an essay on affirmative action's impact on women and Asians, and a discussion by Richard Rorty on educational diversity, among many others. The second consideration is the continuing growth and improvement in the materials available; each year, it seems, a significant number of excellent articles appear on familiar topics as well as on those that are not normally included in ethics classes. This new edition allows me to include thirty new articles, more than a third of the total.

The fourth edition includes many other important changes. First, a serious effort has been made to increase the presence of different cultural and racial perspectives, reflecting the growing interest in multiculturalism and diversity. I have also tried to expand the last edition's emphasis on articles that speak directly to one another so that the issues are developed in a coherent fashion by authors who explicitly criticize the positions and arguments of those who have gone before.

Part I, *Moral Theory,* has been reorganized and expanded to include discussions of human rights and relativism, including two new articles on rights in Africa, and a selection from David Hume's *Enquiry Concerning the Principles of Morals.* Also new are essays by well-known philosophers who are critical of traditional approaches to moral theory, including Friedrich Nietzsche and Alison Jaggar. Part II, *Issues of Life and Death,* includes new essays on violence (including violence in sports), animal rights, and abortion.

Part III, *Political Relationships,* has undergone significant revisions. Although I have kept many of the same topics—property, free speech, paternalism and drugs, legal authority, and civil disobedience continue as major themes—seven new essays expand and deepen these discussions into new areas that are of real concern to students. Both smoking and alcohol addiction are now discussed in the section on liberty, and welfare has its own section, which, along with new essays on property and economic justice, gives far more opportunities to probe questions of economic justice, property rights, work, effort and desert, and the distribution of medical care.

The selections in Part IV, *Personal Relationships,* now include a pair of essays on date rape, along with the earlier readings on personal relationships such as homosexuality, adultery, surrogacy, baby selling, and adult children's duties to parents.

Part V, *Gender, Race, and Multiculturalism,* is entirely new. It includes, in addition to new essays on sexual equality and gender, others that focus on racism, assimilation, and integration. Readings then turn to problems of individual identity and the politics of difference, multiculturalism, and the relevance of evolutionary biology for feminism. Part V concludes with a debate about affirmative action, followed by a discussion of free speech, pornography, and the multicultural curriculum.

I have again included various study aids. Each essay begins with a general introduction outlining what students can expect to find in the reading. A series of review and discussion questions ends each essay. They are designed to test students' understanding of the basic arguments presented in the essay and to provoke discussion by suggesting possible lines of criticism and interesting comparisons with other essays or legal opinions in the text. In addition to these study aids, I have now added a new section at the beginning of the book entitled "Reading and Writing Philosophy" that will guide students in their efforts to understand what they are reading as well as in writing philosophy papers. I've also written a "Peer Review Form" to help instructors improve students' writing.

In selecting this material I have been especially careful to strike what I hope is the right balance between philosophical sophistication and the needs of typical undergraduates. Many of the essays were written by women and others not traditionally included in philosophy texts. I have also expanded the range of topics in the hope that the book will be of interest to all students and teachers, without sacrificing the clarity and rigor for which philosophy is known.

Special thanks to the reviewers of this edition: Deni Elliott, University of Montana; David Haslett, University of Delaware; and Joseph Kupfer, Iowa State University; and to the production editor, Linda B. Pawelchak.

Reading and Writing Philosophy

John Arthur

I. READING PHILOSOPHY

Students sometimes find philosophy difficult to read. Occasionally that may be because the philosopher, however profound, is a bad writer; more often, the issues are subtle and abstract, and therefore difficult, or the writing style is unfamiliar. Here are some suggestions that will help you understand what you are reading.

Think of a philosophy essay as an attempt to get you to either change your beliefs on an issue or to acquire new ones. Sometimes an author accomplishes this by giving you new information (facts and figures, historical data, etc.) or by describing subtle features of human experience; other times, a writer may provide a unifying theoretical perspective that helps you to understand more deeply aspects of human practices that otherwise seem confusing and incoherent. But whatever strategy or method is employed, it is typical in philosophy to be presented with *reasons* and *arguments*. The key, then, is to assess the argument that, the author claims, should lead to a change in belief about some specific topic, such as abortion, or to a new, deeper understanding of morality in general.

Step 1: Identify the Argument Structure

Your first step should be to *skim* the material to get a general sense of the author's intentions. Begin with the title: what does it tell you about the subject of the paper or the viewpoint the author is taking? Next you should read the first and last paragraphs, along with the section headings. What problem is the author addressing? What seems to be the main point? Who is the author responding to? Also consider *why* you are reading the material for this course: remember that the readings have been chosen because of their contribution to the larger issues under consideration.

After you have a general sense of what the author is trying to do, read the essay more closely. Your basic task, as I said, is to understand exactly what the author is advocating, and why. To identify this argumentative structure, it is helpful to keep in mind three questions: (1) What is the author's main conclusion or thesis? (2) What are the assumptions or premises the author relies on? And (3) what are the steps in the writer's argument from those assumptions to the conclusion? In thinking about these questions, remember that it is important to interpret authors charitably, in their best light. Ask yourself why a thoughtful person might take this position. Try seeing things through the author's eyes.

Begin, then, by considering the essay's over-all thesis. Is this thesis stated explicitly, or do you have to make a charitable guess on the basis of scattered comments made throughout the reading? You should already know this from your initial skimming. It is often useful to think about what you are reading in connection with other essays or theories you have been discussing.

Next, you should focus on the author's reasoning or *argument,* keeping in mind that the author is claiming you must accept the conclusion based on your acceptance of the *premises*. These premises are the grounds on which the conclusion rests: if you accept them, it is claimed, then you should also accept the conclusion. It is also important to keep in mind that the author may be giving a series or chain of arguments, with one conclusion providing the premise for another argument, leading eventually to the final conclusion. If so, then that chain needs to be identified as part of the structure.

In assessing the essay, keep in mind that arguments can take many structural forms. Often analogies are used, so that, for example, affirmative action might be defended by comparing society with an unfair race. Other times, appeals will be made to general principles that the author believes are true and that, she thinks, would establish the conclusion. Or a writer may criticize positions of others, trying to uncover weaknesses such as questionable generalizations, doubtful assumptions, or bad analogies. Other authors might argue that the opposing position leads to absurd or unacceptable results. Clearly, then, it is not easy to understand a philosophy article; the text must be read very carefully to uncover its argumentative structure. It may also require interpretation on your part, since few writers are clear on every point. You will have to read the text very carefully, line by line. Reading aloud can help; taking notes as you read is almost always a must.

Ultimately, if the author has done a good job of writing the essay, and you have done a good job reading it, you should be able to outline the essay, or explain it to yourself or someone else in your own words. Until you can do that, you have not really understood what you have read.

Step 2: Critically Evaluate What You Have Read

The next step is to *evaluate* the author's argument or position. You must think about the structure or form of argument you have just uncovered—its general principles, analogies, new information, and attacks on other's arguments, as well as how accurately the author has described human experience and practices.

To begin, recall that authors make certain *assumptions* that, they claim, provide the grounds or premises for the *conclusion* they wish to reach. These premises are taken for granted in the belief that readers will agree. This might be because the premises are so unobjectionable that defending them seems unnecessary. But some assumptions may indeed be quite controversial. In that case, while the rest of the argument may be faultless, you should remain unpersuaded. So you must ask: Do I find the writer's assumptions plausible? Are they controversial? Do I have reason to doubt one or more of them? Do other authors you have studied dispute them? If the premises are controversial, did the author defend them? Was the defense successful? You should also ask whether there are exceptions or *counter examples* to the general principles on which the author relies. Or whether accepting the author's premises would lead down a *slippery slope* to unacceptable consequences. Also ask yourself: Is the author inconsistent in some way, holding a position in one context that is incompatible with another position in another context? Does the argument depend on *equivocation,* in the sense that a key term is used in one way in one context but another way elsewhere?

Assuming you were to accept the premises, the next question is whether the argument or arguments are *sound*. Do the premises, in other words, really establish the conclusion? Is there a logical gap in the argument? Does the writer rely on a bad analogy, for example? Is the position the author is attacking correctly described, or has the author created a *straw man* and merely attacked *it?* Has the author created a *false dilemma* by arguing that there are only two alternatives when, in fact, there are others? Are there other factors that the author does not consider which weaken the position?

Finally, you may also want to ask if there are changes you think the author could—and should—have made to establish the position. If you found a weakness in one of the author's premises, for example, you should also consider how it could be defended and whether you would then find it acceptable. Could other objections you have raised be "fixed" so that the conclusion would, in fact, follow? How?

II. WRITING A PHILOSOPHY PAPER

Knowing how to read philosophy effectively is an immense help in writing a good philosophy paper; but, alas, it is only the first step. The task of writing a paper usually forces students to criticize what they have read. Before doing that, however, you obviously must understand the material you plan to discuss (back to *Reading Philosophy*). It is critical that your writing be as clear as possible. You would not want to make the same mistakes in your arguments that you have found others making! Here then are some suggestions about how to proceed in writing a philosophy paper. They are not a recipe that must always be followed, but they are helpful, particularly if you have not had much experience at it.

First, do not hide the ball; give the reader all the help you can in understanding what you want to say. It's a good idea to say in the *first paragraph* what your general goal for the paper is and how you plan to accomplish it. Normally, philosophy papers have a thesis: they defend or attack a certain position. Your task, therefore, is to convince the reader that your thesis is correct and to do this by stating good reasons why this is so. Occasionally, you may write a paper that compares or contrasts two different positions or authors, or perhaps simply analyzes the view of one writer; but, even here, you will be trying to show that your interpretation is correct by giving evidence from the texts. So always state, at the beginning, what you intend to accomplish by describing your thesis or outlining the authors or positions you intend to analyze or compare.

In writing your paper, keep in mind the *outline* of your argument; if *you* cannot give a clear outline of the paper, then how is anybody else supposed to follow it? Be very clear at each step along the way just what you are trying to establish and how you are trying to do it. Never be tempted by the old excuse "I understand what I mean; I just can't say it." Until you can say it, or better still put it on paper, you don't *really* understand it. That's why writing is often difficult—and important.

Avoid logical errors, of which, as we have already seen, there are many varieties, including straw man, equivocation, false dilemma, and questionable analogy. Other possible mistakes to keep in mind are these: Do not *beg the question* by assuming the truth of your conclusion in your premises. Do not commit an *ad hominem* by attacking the person instead of the person's position. Do not appeal to emotion instead of reason. Do not express controversial opinions without supporting your position.

You should also consider what you take to be the most important *objections to your own view*. How might somebody who disagrees respond to your paper? Is that response a serious one that you should address? How might you best answer the objection? It's always better to acknowledge an objection (and so get credit for seeing it) even if you cannot respond completely. Be honest in your paper. If you cannot adequately answer an objection, you might still conclude that the balance of reasons supports your position, despite its admitted weaknesses. Nothing says you cannot admit that there are problems with your argument.

Finally, be sure to provide the reader with an overview, near the end, of your major points. Summarize your main thesis and the major arguments you used to defend it. If you compared different authors, summarize the important similarities and differences you uncovered.

Now for some practical suggestions. First, after you are finished with the first draft, confirm that the paper is well organized by reoutlining it. Second, *never pass in a paper that you have not rewritten completely at least once.* When rewriting, ask of each sentence and paragraph: Why is it there? Could I express my idea more clearly? Remember too that other students can be of immense help here; let them read and comment on the paper, explain to them what your basic argument is. If you cannot explain it to them, how is a reader going to understand it? The actual writing, however, must of course be your own; and you must always give credit for others' ideas if you use them. Third, the handling of references is easiest done by mentioning the author of the book or article, date, and page in the text, as follows: (Smith, 1988 at 2), and then giving a full bibliographical reference at the end. Give the actual author—not the editor—of the book from which the quotation was taken. Finally, never, ever pass in a paper with silly grammatical, spelling, or other errors. There is no excuse for this. A paper represents your mind; you do not want it, or you, to seem superficial, sloppy, confused, or dull.

In the attempt to improve one's writing, it is especially helpful when people review each other's work critically—useful both for the person doing the reviewing and for the paper's author. It is especially important then to rewrite the paper in light of comments and criticisms. (Studies show that students learn a great deal from discussing ideas outside the formal classroom, whether with other students or with faculty.) A *peer review* is a very useful mechanism in that it encourages such discussions as well as helps to improve the writing of both the reviewer and the writer. On the next page is a peer review form that my students and I have found useful.

PEER REVIEW OF PAPERS

Author of essay under review:_____

Reviewer:_____

Here are some guidelines that will help you in evaluating other students' papers as well as in improving your own work based on the peer evaluation you will receive. In doing your peer review, comment on each of these questions. Feel free also to give any additional comments you think will be helpful.

1. Do the title and introductory paragraph give a clear sense of the paper's topic as well as a sense of the author's approach or general conclusion? If not, how could the author have done better?
2. Is the paper's organizational structure reasonably clear? Does the author develop the position in a way that makes sense?
3. Are some of the sentences unclear, requiring you to try to figure out what the author is saying? (Be sure, if you are forced to pause, that it is not because the point is a subtle one rather than because the sentence is unclear.) Explain.
4. Does the paper have grammar or punctuation that distract you? Underline the places where you find this problem, indicating anything you think might help the author correct the errors, such as general patterns or consistent mistakes you have noticed.
5. Are there spelling or word usage problems that detract from the paper? If so, underline them and explain your comments in the margin.
6. At the conclusion, first indicate what you found to be the paper's greatest strength(s). Then, outline how it could be improved: Has the author understood the material being discussed? If not, where does the paper need improvement? Are there specific places where you think the author's argument or position needs to be better substantiated? Does the author make questionable assumptions? Does the author fail to address possible problems with the paper? Are there errors in reasoning? If so, indicate that in the margin or at the end of the paper. What objections should be considered? What other issues might the author have addressed? Is there too much summary of other people's position and not enough of the author's ideas? Has the author provided grounds for the conclusions or merely offered personal opinion?

When you receive your paper from the reviewer, you should consider very carefully all the comments. If the reviewer had problems understanding a sentence, try reading the sentence aloud and ask yourself if *you* think it is clear. If not, then you have probably not yet developed the ideas you want to express clearly enough in your own mind. Consider other writing problems in the same way, asking yourself why the reader was confused, found the organization unclear, objected to punctuation, grammar, or whatever. Think about all the objections the reviewer has raised. Do they have merit? Can you fix them?

Finally, you should rewrite your paper from scratch, thinking not only about how you can correct the problems identified in the peer review but how you can make other improvements as well. Rewriting is a critical step; it is here that you will make the most progress. Always remember: *No paper is ever so good that it cannot be improved by rewriting.*

Opening Case

Killing on a Lifeboat:

The Queen v. Dudley and Stephens

Legal cases are a fertile ground for moral and philosophical reflection; and because they involve real people being held to account for their actions, judicial opinions also illustrate how important, difficult, and yet inevitable philosophical questions can be. Few cases make these points better than this one. It raises many of the troubling problems that will be discussed in much greater detail later in the text, including the morality of killing, the aims of punishment, the moral basis of law, the importance of fairness, and the philosophical basis of morality. The case concerns four sailors adrift in a lifeboat. After 20 days with little food or water, two of them—Dudley and Stephens—killed the youngest member of their party, a boy 17 or 18 years old, in order to eat him. Details of their ordeal are given in the jury's verdict, followed by the court's decision about whether or not the two committed murder.

Indictment for the murder of Richard Parker on the high seas with in the jurisdiction of the Admiralty.

At the trial before Huddleston, B., at the Devon and Cornwall Winter Assizes, November 7, 1884, the jury, at the suggestion of the learned judge, found the facts of the case in a special verdict which stated "that on July 5, 1884, the prisoners, Thomas Dudley and Edward Stephens, with one Brooks, all able-bodied English seamen, and the deceased also an English boy, between seventeen and eighteen years of age, the crew of an English yacht, a registered English vessel, were cast away in a storm on the high seas 1600 miles from the Cape of Good Hope, and were compelled to put into an open boat belonging to the said yacht. That in this boat they had no supply of water and no supply of food, except two 11b. tins of turnips, and for three days they had nothing else to subsist upon. That on the fourth day they caught a small turtle, upon which they subsisted for a few days, and this was the only food they had up to the twentieth day when the act now in question was committed. That on the twelfth day the remains of the turtle were entirely consumed, and for the next eight days they had nothing to eat. That they had no fresh water, except such rain as they from time to time caught in their oilskin capes. That the boat was drifting on the ocean, and was probably more than 1000 miles away from land. That on the eighteenth day, when they had been seven days without food and five without water, the prisoners spoke to Brooks as to what should be done if no succour came, and suggested that some one should be sacrificed to save the rest, but Brooks dissented, and the boy, to whom they were understood to refer, was not consulted. That on the 24th of July, the day before the act now in question, the prisoner Dudley proposed to Stephens and Brooks that lots should be cast who should be put to death to save the rest, but Brooks refused to consent, and it was not put to the boy, and in point of fact there

Reprinted from *Law Reports, Queen's Bench Division*, vol. 14 (1884–1885)(London: William Clowes and Sons, 1885), pp. 273–88.

was no drawing of lots. That on that day the prisoners spoke of their having families, and suggested it would be better to kill the boy that their lives should be saved, and Dudley proposed that if there was no vessel in sight by the morrow morning that boy should be killed. That next day, the 25th of July, no vessel appearing, Dudley told Brooks that he had better go and have a sleep, and made signs to Stephens and Brooks that the boy had better be killed. The prisoner Stephens agreed to the act, but Brooks dissented from it. That the boy was then lying at the bottom of the boat quite helpless, and extremely weakened by famine and by drinking sea water, and unable to make any resistance, nor did he ever assent to his being killed. The prisoner Dudley offered a prayer asking forgiveness for them all if either of them should be tempted to commit a rash act, and that their souls might be saved. That Dudley, with the assent of Stephens, went to the boy, and telling him that his time was come, put a knife into his throat and killed him then and there; that the three men fed upon the body and blood of the boy for four days; that on the fourth day after the act had been committed the boat was picked up by a passing vessel, and the prisoners were rescued, still alive, but in the lowest state of prostration. That they were carried to the port of Falmouth, and committed for trial at Exeter. That if the men had not fed upon the body of the boy they would probably not have survived to be so picked up and rescued, but would within the four days have died of famine. that the boy, being in a much weaker condition, was likely to have died before them. That at the time of the act in question there was no sail in sight, nor any reasonable prospect of relief. That under these circumstances there appeared to the prisoners every probability that unless they then fed or very soon fed upon the boy or one of themselves they would die of starvation. That there was no appreciable chance of saving life except by killing some one for the others to eat. That assuming any necessity to kill anybody, there was no greater necessity for killing the boy than any of the other three men. But whether upon the whole matter by the jurors found the killing of Richard Parker by Dudley and Stephens be felony and murder the jurors are ignorant, and pray the advice of the Court thereupon, and if upon the whole matter the Court shall be of opinion that the killing of Richard Parker be felony and murder, then the jurors say that Dudley and Stephens were each guilty of felony and murder as alleged in the indictment."

The learned judge then adjourned the assizes until the 25th of November at the Royal Courts of Justice. On the application of the Crown they were again adjourned to the 4th of December, and the case ordered to be argued before a Court consisting of five judges.

Dec. 4. *Sir H. James, A.G. (A. Charles, Q.C., C. Mathews, and Danckwerts, with him), appeared for the Crown [and] A. Collins, Q.C. (H.Clark, and Pyke, with him), for the prisoners. . . .*

Sir H. James, A.G., **for the Crown:** . . . With regard to the substantial question in the case—whether the prisoners in killing Parker were guilty of murder—the law is that where a private person acting upon his own judgment takes the life of a fellow creature, his act can only be justified on the ground of self-defence—self-defence against the acts of the person whose life is taken. This principle has been extended to include the case of a man killing another to prevent him from committing some great crime upon a third person. But the principle has no application to this case, for the prisoners were not protecting themselves against any act of Parker. If he had had food in his possession and they had taken it from him, they would have been guilty of theft; and if they killed him to obtain this food, they would have been guilty of murder. . . .

A. Collins, Q.C., **for the prisoners:** . . . Lord Bacon gives the instance of two shipwrecked persons clinging to the same plank and one of them thrusting the other from it, finding that it will not support both, and says that this homicide is excusable through unavoidable necessity and upon the great universal principle of self-preservation, which prompts every man to save his own life in preference to that of another, where one of them must inevitably perish. It is true that Hale's Pleas of the Crown, p. 54, states distinctly that hunger is no excuse for theft, but that is on the ground that there can be no such extreme necessity in this country. In the present case the prisoners were in circumstances where no assistance could be given.

The essence of the crime of murder is intention, and here the intention of the prisoners was only to preserve their lives. . . .

Dec. 9. The judgment of the Court *(Lord Coleridge, C.J., Grove* and *Denman, JJ., Pollock* and *Huddleston, BB.)* **was delivered by** *Lord Coleridge, C.J.:* . . . The two prisoners, Thomas Dudley and Edwin Stephens, were indicted for the murder of Richard Parker on the high seas on the 25th of July in the present year. They were tried before my Brother Huddleston at Exeter on the 6th of November, and, under the direction of my learned Brother, the jury returned a special verdict, the legal effect of which has been argued before us, and on which we are not to pronounce judgment.

The special verdict as, after certain objections by Mr. Collins to which the Attorney General yielded, it is finally settled before us is as follows. [His Lordship read the special verdict as above set out.] From these facts, stated with the cold precision of a special verdict, it appears sufficiently that the prisoners were subject to terrible temptation, to sufferings which might break down the bodily power of the strongest man, and try the conscience of the best. Other details yet more harrowing, facts still more loathsome and appalling, were presented to the jury, and are to be found recorded in my learned Brother's notes. But nevertheless this is clear, that the prisoners put to death a weak and unoffending boy upon the chance of preserving their own lives by feeding upon his flesh and blood after he was killed, and with the certainty of depriving *him* of any possible chance of survival. The verdict finds in terms that "if the men had not fed upon the body of the boy they would *probably* not have survived," and that "the boy being in a much weaker condition was *likely* to have died before them." They might possibly have been picked up next day by a passing ship; they might possibly not have been picked up at all; in either case it is obvious that the killing of the boy would have been an unnecessary and profitless act. It is found by the verdict that the boy was incapable of resistance, and, in fact, made none; and it is not even suggested that his death was due to any violence on his part attempted against, or even so much as feared by, those who killed him. Under these circumstances the jury say that they are ignorant whether those who killed him were guilty of murder, and have referred it to this Court to determine what is the legal consequence which follows from the facts which they have found. . . .

There remains to be considered the real question in the case—whether killing under the circumstances set forth in the verdict be or be not murder. The contention that it could be anything else was, to the minds of us all, both new and strange, and we stopped the Attorney General in his negative argument in order that we might hear what could be said in support of a proposition which appeared to us to be at once dangerous, immoral, and opposed to all legal principle and analogy. . . .

Is there, then, any authority for the proposition which has been presented to us? Decided cases there are none. . . .

The American case cited by my Brother Stephen in his Digest, from Wharton on Homicide, in which it was decided, correctly indeed, that sailors had no right to throw passengers overboard to save themselves, but on the somewhat strange ground that the proper mode of determining who was to be sacrificed was to vote upon the subject by ballot, can hardly, as my Brother Stephen says, be an authority satisfactory to a court in this country. . . .

We are dealing with a case of private homicide, not on imposed upon men in the service of their Sovereign and in the defence of their country. Now it is admitted that the deliberate killing of this unoffending and unresisting boy was clearly murder, unless the killing can be justified by some well-recognised excuse admitted by the law. It is further admitted that there was in this case no such excuse, unless the killing was justified by what has been called "necessity." But the temptation to the act which existed here was not what the law has ever called necessity. Nor is this to be regretted. Though law and morality are not the same, and many things may be immoral which are not necessarily illegal, yet the absolute divorce of law from morality would be of fatal consequence; and such divorce would follow if the temptation to murder in this case were to be held by law an absolute defence of it. It is not so. To preserve one's life is generally speaking a duty, but it may be the plainest and the highest duty to sacrifice it. War is full of instances in which it is a man's duty not to live, but to die. The duty, in case of shipwreck, of a captain to his crew, of the crew to the passengers, of soldiers to women and children, as in the noble case of the *Birkenhead;* these duties impose on men the moral necessity, not of the preservation, but of the sacrifice of their lives for others, from which in no country, least of all, it is to be hoped, in England, will men ever shrink, as indeed, they have not shrunk. It is not correct, therefore, to say that there is any absolute or unqualified necessity to preserve one's life. . . .

It is not needful to point out the awful danger of admitting the principle which has been contended for. Who is to be the judge of this sort of necessity? By what measure is the comparative value of lives to be measured? Is it to be strength, or intellect, or what? It is plain that the principle leaves to him who is to profit by it to determine the necessity which will justify him in deliberately taking another's life to save his own. In this case the weakest, the youngest, the most unresisting, was chosen. Was it more necessary to kill him than one of the grown men? The answer must be "No." . . .

It is quite plain that such a principle once admitted might be made the legal cloak for unbridled passion and atrocious crime. There is no safe path

for judges to tread but to ascertain the law to the best of their ability and to declare it according to their judgment; and if in any case the law appears to be too severe on individuals, to leave it to the Sovereign to exercise that prerogative of mercy which the Constitution has intrusted to the hands fittest to dispense it.

It must not be supposed that in refusing to admit temptation to be an excuse for crime it is forgotten how terrible the temptation was; how awful the suffering; how hard in such trials to keep the judgment straight and the conduct pure. We are often compelled to set up standards we cannot reach ourselves, and to lay down rules which we could not ourselves satisfy. But a man has no right to declare temptation to be an excuse, though he might himself have yielded to it, nor allow compassion for the criminal to change or weaken in any manner the legal definition of the crime. It is therefore our duty to declare that the prisoners' act in this case was wilful murder, that the facts as stated in the verdict are no legal justification of the homicide; and to say that in our unanimous opinion the prisoners are upon this special verdict guilty of murder.[1]

The Court then proceeded to pass sentence of death upon the prisoners.[2]

NOTES

1. My brother Grove has furnished me with the following suggestion, too late to be embodied in the judgment but well worth preserving: "If the two accused men were justified in killing Parker, then if not rescued in time, two of the three survivors would be justified in killing the third, and of the two who remained the stronger would be jus-tified in killing the weaker, so that three men might be justifiably killed to give the fourth a chance of surviving."—C.

2. This sentence was afterwards commuted by the Crown to six months' imprisonment.

REVIEW AND DISCUSSION QUESTIONS

1. Describe what happened on the lifeboat, the legal issue, and why the court made the decision it did.

2. In finding Dudley and Stephens guilty of murder, the court says that there was "temptation" but not "necessity" and, moreover, that there is no "absolute or unqualified necessity to preserve one's life." Do you agree?

3. Assess the court's contention that to find Dudley and Stephens innocent would set a dangerous precedent.
4. Is it reasonable to apply standard moral and legal principles to a case such as this, or are morality and law inapplicable in such extreme circumstances?
5. An earlier case suggests the survivors should have drawn straws. Do you agree? Explain.
6. Should the survivors have considered questions such as whether they had families, were old or sick, performed socially useful jobs, or were convicted criminals? Why or why not?
7. Is it *realistic* for law to demand that people sit idly by, doing nothing, while they wait to die? Is it *just* for the law to demand that?

Part I _____
MORAL THEORY

1

Individual Conscience and Religious Authority

The two essays in this section consider the connections between moral conscience and other features of human life. The first reading explores the nature of conscience by focusing on the conflicts between duty and sympathetic concern for others. The second asks about possible connections between morality and religion and concludes with a discussion of the "social" nature of morality and conscience along with the role of moral education.

The Conscience of Huckleberry Finn

Jonathan Bennett

Sometimes a situation will arise in which a person feels a conflict between doing the right thing and sympathy for those who may be hurt as a result of meeting morality's demands. Here, Jonathan Bennett graphically illustrates this conflict in three surprising and fascinating examples: Huck Finn's conflict over whether to free his slave friend Jim; Nazi commander Himmler's feelings for the Jews and the duty he felt to kill them; and Jonathan Edwards's attitudes toward fallen people, who he thought were doomed to live in hell, and the justice of the wrathful God who condemns them. Bennett uses these examples to explore the relations between duty and sympathy as well as the wisdom of relying on our feelings when they conflict with duty. Jonathan Bennett is professor of philosophy at Syracuse University.

Jonathan Bennett, "The Conscience of Huckleberry Finn," *Philosophy,* 49 (April 1974). © 1974 by the Royal Institute of Philosophy. Reprinted by permission of the author and Cambridge University Press.

In this paper,[1] I shall present not just the conscience of Huckleberry Finn but two others as well. One of them is the conscience of Heinrich Himmler. He became a Nazi in 1923; he served drably and quietly, but well, and was rewarded with increasing responsibility and power. At the peak of his career he held many offices and commands, of which the most powerful was that of leader of the S.S.—the principal police force of the Nazi regime. In this capacity, Himmler commanded the whole concentration-camp system, and was responsible for the execution of the so-called 'final solution of the Jewish problem'. It is important for my purposes that this piece of social engineering should be thought of not abstractly but in concrete terms of Jewish families being marched to what they think are bath-houses, to the accompaniment of loud-speaker renditions of extracts from *The Merry Widow* and *Tales of Hoffman,* there to be choked to death by poisonous gases. Altogether, Himmler succeeded in murdering about four and a half million of them, as well as several million gentiles, mainly Poles and Russians.

The other conscience to be discussed is that of the Calvinist theologian and philosopher Jonathan Edwards. He lived in the first half of the eighteenth century, and has a good claim to be considered America's first serious and considerable philosophical thinker. He was for many years a widely-renowned preacher and Congregationalist minister in New England; in 1748 a dispute with his congregation led him to resign (he couldn't accept their view that unbelievers should be admitted to the Lord's Supper in the hope that it would convert them); for some years after that he worked as a missionary, preaching to Indians through an interpreter; then in 1758 he accepted the presidency of what is now Princeton University, and within two months died from a smallpox inoculation. Along the way he wrote some first-rate philosophy: his book attacking the notion of free will is still sometimes read. Why I should be interested in Edwards' conscience will be explained in due course.

I shall use Heinrich Himmler, Jonathan Edwards and Huckleberry Finn to illustrate different aspects of a single theme, namely the relationship between *sympathy* on the one hand and *bad morality* on the other.

All that I can mean by a 'bad morality' is a morality whose principles I deeply disapprove of. When I call a morality bad, I cannot prove that mine is better; but when I here call any morality bad, I think you will agree with me that it is bad; and that is all I need.

There could be dispute as to whether the springs of someone's actions constitute a *morality,* I think, though, that we must admit that someone who acts in ways which conflict grossly with our morality may nevertheless have a morality of his own—a set of principles of action which he sincerely assents to, so that for him the problem of acting well or rightly or in obedience to conscience is the problem of conforming to those principles. The problem of conscientiousness can arise as acutely for a bad morality as for any other: rotten principles may be as difficult to keep as decent ones.

As for 'sympathy': I use this term to cover every sort of fellow-feeling, as when one feels pity over someone's loneliness, or horrified compassion over his pain, or when one feels a shrinking reluctance to act in a way which will bring misfortune to someone else. These feelings must not be confused with *moral judgments.* My sympathy for someone in distress may lead me to help him, or even to think that I ought to help him; but in itself it is not a judgment about what I ought to do but just a feeling for him in his plight. We shall get some light on the difference between feelings and moral judgments when we consider Huckleberry Finn.

Obviously, feelings can impel one to action, and so can moral judgments; and in a particular case sympathy and morality may pull in opposite directions. This can happen not just with bad moralities, but also with good ones like yours and mine. For example, a small child, sick and miserable, clings tightly to his mother and screams in terror when she tries to pass him over to the doctor to be examined. If the mother gave way to her sympathy, that is to her feeling for the child's misery and fright, she would hold it close and not let the doctor come near; but don't we agree that it might be wrong for her to act on such a feeling? Quite generally, then, anyone's moral principles may apply to a particular situation in a way which runs contrary to the particular thrusts of fellow-feeling that he has in that situation. My immediate concern is with sympathy in relation to bad morality, but not because such conflicts occur only when the morality is bad.

Now, suppose that someone who accepts a bad morality is struggling to make himself act in accordance with it in a particular situation where his sympathies pull him another way. He sees the struggle as one between doing the right, conscientious thing, and acting wrongly and weakly, like the mother who won't let the doctor come near her sick, frightened baby. Since we don't accept this person's morality, we may see the situation very differently, thoroughly disapproving of the action he regards as the right one, and endorsing the action which from his point of view constitutes weakness and backsliding.

Conflicts between sympathy and bad morality won't always be like this, for we won't disagree with every single dictate of a bad morality. Still, it can happen in the way I have described, with the agent's right action being our wrong one, and vice versa. That is just what happens in a certain episode in chapter 16 of *The Adventures of Huckleberry Finn,* an episode which brilliantly illustrates how fiction can be instructive about real life.

Huck Finn has been helping his slave friend Jim to run away from Miss Watson, who is Jim's owner. In their raft-journey down the Mississippi River, they are near to the place at which Jim will become legally free. Now let Huck take over the story:

Jim said it made him all over trembly and feverish to be so close to freedom. Well, I can tell you it made me all over trembly and feverish, too, to hear him, because I begun to get it through my head that he was most free—and who was to blame for it? Why, me. I couldn't get that out of my conscience, no how nor no way. It hadn't ever come home to me, before, what this thing was that I was doing. But now it did; and it stayed with me, and scorched me more and more. I tried to make out to myself that I warn't to blame, because I didn't run Jim off from his rightful owner; but it warn't no use, conscience up and say, every time: 'But you knowed he was running for his freedom, and you could a paddled ashore and told somebody.' That was so—I couldn't get around that, no way. That was where it pinched. Conscience says to me: 'What had poor Miss Watson done to you, that you could see her nigger go off right under your

eyes and never say one single word? What did that poor old woman do to you, that you could treat her so mean? . . . ' I got to feeling so mean and so miserable I most wished I was dead.

Jim speaks of his plan to save up to buy his wife, and then his children, out of slavery; and he adds that if the children cannot be bought he will arrange to steal them. Huck is horrified:

Thinks I, this is what comes of my not thinking. Here was this nigger which I had as good as helped to run away, coming right out flat-footed and saying he would steal his children—children that belonged to a man I didn't even know; a man that hadn't ever done me no harm.

I was sorry to hear Jim say that, it was such a lowering of him. My conscience got to stirring me up hotter than ever, until at last I says to it: 'Let up on me—it ain't too late, yet—I'll paddle ashore at first light, and tell.' I felt easy, and happy, and light as a feather, right off. All my troubles was gone.

This is bad morality all right. In his earliest years Huck wasn't taught any principles, and the only ones he has encountered since then are those of rural Missouri, in which slaveowning is just one kind of ownership and is not subject to critical pressure. It hasn't occurred to Huck to question those principles. So the action, to us abhorrent, of turning Jim in to the authorities presents itself clearly to Huck as the right thing to do.

For us, morality and sympathy would both dictate helping Jim to escape. If we felt any conflict, it would have both these on one side and something else on the other—greed for a reward, or fear of punishment. But Huck's morality conflicts with his sympathy, that is, with his unargued, natural feeling for his friend. The conflict starts when Huck sets off in the canoe towards the shore, pretending that he is going to reconnoitre, but really planning to turn Jim in:

As I shoved off, [Jim] says: 'Pooty soon I'll be a-shout'n for joy, en I'll say, it's all on accounts o' Huck I's a free man . . . Jim won't ever forgit you, Huck; you's de bes' fren' Jim's ever had; en you's de only fren' old Jim's got now.'

I was padding off, all in a sweat to tell on him; but when he says this, it seemed to kind of take the tuck all out of me. I went along slow then, and I warn't right down certain whether I was glad I started or whether I warn't. When I was fifty yards off, Jim says:

'Dah you goes, de ole true Huck; de on'y white genlman dat ever kep' his promise to ole Jim.' Well, I just felt sick. But I says, I *got* to do it—I can't get *out* of it.

In the upshot, sympathy wins over morality. Huck hasn't the strength of will to do what he sincerely thinks he ought to do. Two men hunting for runaway slaves ask him whether the man on his raft is black or white:

I didn't answer up prompt. I tried to, but the words wouldn't come. I tried, for a second or two, to brace up and out with it, but I warn't man enough—hadn't the spunk of a rabbit. I see I was weakening; so I just give up trying, and up and says: 'He's white.'

So Huck enables Jim to escape, thus acting weakly and wickedly—he thinks. In this conflict between sympathy and morality, sympathy wins.

One critic has cited this episode in support of the statement that Huck suffers 'excruciating moments of wavering between honesty and respectability'. That is hopelessly wrong, and I agree with the perceptive comment on it by another critic, who says:

The conflict waged in Huck is much more serious: he scarcely cares for respectability and never hesitates to relinquish it, but he does care for honesty and gratitude—and both honesty and gratitude require that he should give Jim up. It is not, in Huck, honesty at war with respectability but love and compassion for Jim struggling against his conscience. His decision is for Jim and hell: a right decision made in the mental chains that Huck never breaks. His concern for Jim is and remains irrational. Huck finds many reasons for giving Jim up and none for stealing him. To the end Huck sees his compassion for Jim as a weak, ignorant, and wicked felony.[2]

That is precisely correct—and it can have that virtue only because Mark Twain wrote the episode with such unerring precision. The crucial point concerns reasons, which all occur on one side of the conflict. On the side of conscience we have principles, arguments, considerations, ways of looking at things:

'It hadn't ever come home to me before what I was doing'

'I tried to make out that I warn't to blame'
'Conscience said "But you knowed . . . "'—I couldn't get around that'
'What had poor Miss Watson done to you?'
'This is what comes of my not thinking'
'children that belonged to a man I didn't even know'.

On the other side, the side of feeling, we get nothing like that. When Jim rejoices in Huck, as his only friend, Huck doesn't consider the claims of friendship or have the situation 'come home' to him in a different light. All that happens is: 'When he says this, it seemed to kind of take the tuck all out of me. I went along slow then, and I warn't right down certain whether I was glad I started or whether I warn't.' Again, Jim's words about Huck's 'promise' to him don't give Huck any reason for changing his plan: in his morality promises to slaves probably don't count. Their effect on him is of a different kind: 'Well, I just felt sick.' And when the moment for final decision comes, Huck doesn't weigh up pros and cons: he simply *fails* to do what he believes to be right—he isn't strong enough, hasn't 'the spunk of a rabbit'. This passage in the novel is notable not just for its finely wrought irony, with Huck's weakness of will leading him to do the right thing, but also for its masterly handling of the difference between general moral principles and particular unreasoned emotional pulls.

Consider now another case of bad morality in conflict with human sympathy, the case of odious Himmler. Here, from a speech he made to some S.S. generals, is an indication of the content of his morality:

What happens to a Russian, to a Czech, does not interest me in the slightest. What the nations can offer in the way of good blood of our type, we will take, if necessary by kidnapping their children and raising them here with us. Whether nations live in prosperity or starve to death like cattle interests me only in so far as we need them as slaves to our Kultur; otherwise it is of no interest to me. Whether 10,000 Russian females fall down from exhaustion while digging an antitank ditch interests me only in so far as the antitank ditch for Germany is finished.[3]

But has this a moral basis at all? And if it has, was there in Himmler's own mind any conflict between morality and sympathy? Yes there was. Here is more from the same speech:

... I also want to talk to you quite frankly on a very grave matter ... I mean ... the extermination of the Jewish race ... Most of you must know what it means when 100 corpses are lying side by side, or 500, or 1,000. To have stuck it out and at the same time—apart from exceptions caused by human weakness—to have remained decent fellows, that is what has made us hard. This is a page of glory in our history which has never been written and is never to be written.

Himmler saw his policies as being hard to implement while still retaining one's human sympathies—while still remaining a 'decent fellow'. He is saying that only the weak take the easy way out and just squelch their sympathies, and is praising the stronger and more glorious course of retaining one's sympathies while acting in violation of them. In the same spirit, he ordered that when executions were carried out in concentration camps, those responsible 'are to be influenced in such a way as to suffer no ill effect in their character and mental attitude'. A year later he boasted that the S.S. had wiped out the Jews

without our leaders and their men suffering any damage in their minds and souls. The danger was considerable, for there was only a narrow path between the Scylla of their becoming heartless ruffians unable any longer to treasure life, and the Charybdis of their becoming soft and suffering nervous breakdowns.

And there really can't be any doubt that the basis of Himmler's policies was a set of principles which constituted his morality—a sick, bad, wicked *morality*. He described himself as caught in 'the old tragic conflict between will and obligation'. And when his physician Kersten protested at the intention to destroy the Jews, saying that the suffering involved was 'not to be contemplated', Kersten reports that Himmler replied:

He knew that it would mean much suffering for the Jews. ... 'It is the curse of greatness that it must step over dead bodies to create new life. Yet we must cleanse the soil or it will never bear fruit. It will be a great burden for me to bear.'

This, I submit, is the language of morality.

So in this case, tragically, bad morality won out over sympathy. I am sure that many of Himmler's killers did extinguish their sympathies, becoming 'heartless ruffians' rather than 'decent fellows'; but not Himmler himself. Although his policies ran against the human grain to a horrible degree, he did not sandpaper down his emotional surfaces so that there was no grain there, allowing his actions to slide along smoothly and easily. He did, after all, bear his hideous burden, and even paid a price for it. He suffered a variety of nervous and physical disabilities, including nausea and stomach-convulsions, and Kersten was doubtless right in saying that these were 'the expression of a psychic division which extended over his whole life'.

This same division must have been present in some of those officials of the Church who ordered heretics to be tortured so as to change their theological opinions. Along with the brutes and the cold carcerists, there must have been some who cared, and who suffered from the conflict between their sympathies and their bad morality.

In the conflict between sympathy and bad morality, then, the victory may go to sympathy as in the case of Huck Finn, or to morality as the case of Himmler.

Another possibility is that the conflict may be avoided by giving up, or not ever having, those sympathies which might interfere with one's principles. That seems to have been the case with Jonathan Edwards. I am afraid that I shall be doing an injustice to Edwards' many virtues, and to his great intellectual energy and inventiveness; for my concern is only with the worst thing about him—namely his morality, which was worse than Himmler's.

According to Edwards, God condemns some men to an eternity of unimaginably awful pain, though he arbitrarily spares others—'arbitrarily' because none deserve to be spared:

Natural men are held in the hand of God over the pit of hell ... ; they have deserved the fiery pit, and are already sentenced to it; and God is dreadfully provoked, his anger is as great towards them as to those that are actually suffering the executions of the fierceness of his wrath in hell; the devil is waiting for them, hell is gaping for them, the flames gather and flash about them, and would fain lay hold on them . . . ; and . . . there are no means within reach that can be any security to them. . . . All that preserves them is the mere arbitrary will, and uncovenanted unobliged forebearance of an incensed God.4

Notice that he says 'they have deserved the fiery pit.' Edwards insists that men *ought* to be condemned to eternal pain; and his position isn't that this is right because God wants it, but rather that God wants it because it is right. For him, moral standards exist independently of God, and God can be assessed in the light of them (and of course found to be perfect). For example, he says:

They deserve to be cast into hell; so that . . . justice never stands in the way, it makes no objection against God's using his power at any moment to destroy them. Yea, on the contrary, justice calls aloud for an infinite punishment of their sins.

Elsewhere, he gives elaborate arguments to show that God is acting justly in damning sinners. For example, he argues that a punishment should be exactly as bad as the crime being punished: God is infinitely excellent; so any crime against him is infinitely bad; and so eternal damnation is exactly right as a punishment—it is infinite, but, as Edwards is careful also to say, it is 'no more than infinite.'

Of course, Edwards himself didn't torment the damned; but the question still arises of whether his sympathies didn't conflict with his *approval* of eternal torment. Didn't he find it painful to contemplate any fellow-human's being tortured for ever? Apparently not:

The God that holds you over the pit of hell, much as one holds a spider or some loathsome insect over the fire, abhors you, and is dreadfully provoked; . . . he is of purer eyes than to bear to have you in his sight; you are ten thousand times so abominable in his eyes as the most hateful venomous serpent is in ours.

When God is presented as being as misanthropic as that, one suspects misanthropy in the theologian. This suspicion is increased when Edwards claims that 'the saints in glory will . . . understand how terrible the sufferings of the damned are; yet . . . will not be sorry for [them].'5 He bases this partly on a view of human nature whose ugliness he seems not to notice:

The seeing of the calamities of others tends to heighten the sense of our own enjoyments. When the saints in glory, therefore, shall see the doleful state of the damned, how will this heighten their sense of the blessedness of their own state. . . . When they shall see how miserable others of their fellow-creatures are . . . ; when they shall see the smoke of their torment, . . . and hear their dolorous shrieks and cries, and consider that they in the mean time are in the most blissful state, and shall surely be in it to all eternity; how they will rejoice!

I hope this is less than the whole truth! His other main point about why the saints will rejoice to see the torments of the damned is that it is *right* that they should do so:

The heavenly inhabitants . . . will have no love nor pity to the damned. . . . [This will not show] a want of a spirit of love in them . . . ; for the heavenly inhabitants will know that it is not fit that they should love [the damned] because they will know then, that God has no love to them, nor pity for them.

The implication that *of course* one can adjust one's feelings of pity so that they conform to the dictates of some authority—doesn't this suggest that ordinary human sympathies played only a small part in Edwards' life?

Huck Finn, whose sympathies are wide and deep, could never avoid the conflict in that way; but he is determined to avoid it, and so he opts for the only other alternative he can see—to give up morality altogether. After he has tricked the slave-hunters, he returns to the raft and undergoes a peculiar crisis:

I got aboard the raft, feeling bad and low, because I knowed very well I had done wrong, and I see it warn't no use for me to try to learn to do right; a body that don't get *started* right when he's little, ain't got no show—when the pinch comes there ain't nothing to back him up and keep him to his work, and so he gets beat. Then I thought a minute, and says to myself, hold on—s'pose you'd a done right and give Jim up; would you feel better than what you do now? No, says I, I'd feel bad—I'd feel just the same way I do now. Well, then, says I, what's the use of you learning to do right, when it's troublesome to do right and ain't no trouble to do wrong, and the wages is just the same? I was stuck. I couldn't answer that. So I reckoned I wouldn't bother no more about it, but after this always do whichever come handiest at the time.

Huck clearly cannot conceive of having any morality except the one he has learned—too late, he thinks—from his society. He is not entirely a prisoner of that morality, because he does after all reject it; but for him that is a decision to relinquish morality as such; he cannot envisage revising his morality, altering its content in face of the various pressures to which it is subject, including pressures from his sympathies. For example, he does not begin to approach the thought that slavery should be rejected on moral grounds, or the thought that what he is doing is not theft because a person cannot be owned and therefore cannot be stolen.

The basic trouble is that he cannot or will not engage in abstract intellectual operations of any sort. In chapter 33 he finds himself 'feeling to blame, somehow' for something he knows he had no hand in; he assumes that this feeling is a deliverance of conscience; and this confirms him in his belief that conscience shouldn't be listened to:

It don't make no difference whether you do right or wrong, a person's conscience ain't got no sense, and just goes for him *anyway*. If I had a yaller dog and didn't know no more than a person's conscience does, I would poison him. It takes up more room than all the rest of a person's insides, and yet ain't no good, nohow.

That brisk, incurious dismissiveness fits well with the comprehensive rejection of morality back on the raft. But this is a digression.

On the raft, Huck decides not to live by principles, but just to do whatever 'comes handiest at the time'—always acting according to the mood of the moment. Since the morality he is rejecting is narrow and cruel, and his sympathies are broad and kind, the results will be good. But moral principles are good to have, because they help to protect one from acting badly at moments when one's sympathies happen to be in abeyance. On the highest possible estimate of the role one's sympathies should have, one can still allow for principles as embodiments of one's best feelings, one's broadest and keenest sympathies. On that view, principles can help one across intervals when one's feelings are at less than their best, i.e.

through periods of misanthropy or meanness or self-centredness or depression or anger.

What Huck didn't see is that one can live by principles and yet have ultimate control over their content. And one way such control can be exercised is by checking of one's principles in the light of one's sympathies. This is sometimes a pretty straightforward matter. It can happen that a certain moral principle becomes untenable—meaning literally that one cannot hold it any longer—because it conflicts intolerably with the pity or revulsion or whatever that one feels when one sees what the principle leads to. One's experience may play a large part here: experiences evoke feelings, and feelings force one to modify principles. Something like this happened to the English poet Wilfred Owen, whose experiences in the First World War transformed him from an enthusiastic soldier into a virtual pacifist. I can't document his change of conscience in detail; but I want to present something which he wrote about the way experience can put pressure on morality.[6]

The Latin poet Horace wrote that it is sweet and fitting (or right) to die for one's country—*dulce et decorum est pro patria mori*—and Owen wrote a fine poem about how experience could lead one to relinquish that particular moral principle. He describes a man who is too slow donning his gas mask during a gas attack—'As under a green sea, I saw him drowning,' Owen says. The poem ends like this:

In all my dreams, before my helpless sight
He plunges at me, guttering, choking, drowning.
If in some smothering dreams you too could pace
Behind the wagon that we flung him in,
And watch the white eyes writhing in his face,
His hanging face, like a devil's sick of sin;
If you could hear, at every jolt, the blood
Come gargling from the froth-corrupted lungs,
Obscene as cancer, bitter as the cud
Of vile, incurable sores on innocent tongues,—
My friend, you would not tell with such high zest
To children ardent for some desperate glory,
The old Lie: Dulce et decorum est
Pro patria mori.

There is a difficulty about drawing from all this a moral for ourselves. I imagine that we agree in our rejection of slavery, eternal damnation, genocide, and uncritical patriotic self-abnegation; so we shall agree that Huck Finn, Jonathan Edwards, Heinrich Himmler, and the poet Horace would have done well to bring certain of their principles under severe pressure from ordinary human sympathies. But then we can say this because we can say that all those are bad moralities, whereas we cannot look at our own moralities and declare them bad. This is not arrogance: it is obviously incoherent for someone to declare the system of moral principles that he accepts to be bad, just as one cannot coherently say of anything that one *believes* it but it is *false*.

Still, although I can't point to any of my beliefs and say 'That is false', I don't doubt that some of my beliefs *are* false; and so I should try to remain open to correction. Similarly, I accept every single item in my morality—that is inevitable—but I am sure that my morality could be improved, which is to say that it could undergo changes which I should be glad of once I had made them. So I must try to keep my morality open to revision, exposing it to whatever valid pressures there are—including pressures from my sympathies.

I don't give my sympathies a blank cheque in advance. In a conflict between principle and sympathy, principles ought sometimes to win. For example, I think it was right to take part in the Second World War on the Allied side; there were many ghastly individual incidents which might have led someone to doubt the rightness of his participation in that war; and I think it would have

been right for such a person to keep his sympathies in a subordinate place on those occasions, not allowing them to modify his principles in such a way as to make a pacifist of him.

Still, one's sympathies should be kept as sharp and sensitive and aware as possible, and not only because they can sometimes affect one's principles or one's conduct or both. Owen, at any rate, says that feelings and sympathies are vital even when they can do nothing but bring pain and distress. In another poem he speaks of the blessings of being numb in one's feelings: 'Happy are the men who yet before they are killed/Can let their veins run cold,' he says. These are the ones who do not suffer from any compassion which, as Owen puts it, 'makes their feet/Sore on the alleys cobbled with their brother.' He contrasts these 'happy' ones, who 'lose imagination', with himself and others 'who with a thought besmirch/Blood over all our soul.' Yet the poem's verdict goes against the 'happy' ones. Owen does not say that they will act worse than the others whose souls are besmirched with blood because of their keen awareness of human suffering. He merely says that they are the losers because they have cut themselves off from the human condition:

> By choice they made themselves immune
> To pity and whatever moans in man
> Before the last sea and the hapless stars;
> Whatever mourns when many leave these shores;
> Whatever shares
> The eternal reciprocity of tears.

NOTES

1. This paper began life as the Potter Memorial Lecture, given at Washington State University in Pullman, Washington, in 1972.

2. M. J. Sidnell, 'Huck Finn and Jim,' *The Cambridge Quarterly,* vol. 2, pp. 205–206.

3. Quoted in William L. Shirer, *The Rise and Fall of the Third Reich* (New York, 1960), pp. 937–938. Next quotation: ibid., p. 966, All further quotations relating to Himmler are from Roger Manwell and HeinrichFraenkel, *Heinrich Himmler* (London, 1965), pp. 132, 197, 184 (twice), 187.

4. Vergilius Ferm, ed., *Puritan Sage: Collected Writings of Jonathan Edwards* (New York, 1953), p. 370. Next three quotations: ibid., p. 366, p. 294 ('no more than infinite'), p. 372.

5. This and the next two quotations are from "The End of the Wicked Contemplated by the Righteous: or, The Torments of the Wicked in Hell, no Occasion of Grief to the Saints in Heaven," from *The Works of President Edwards* (London, 1817), vol. IV, pp. 507–8, 511–12 and 509, respectively.

6. Extracts from "Dulce et Decorum Est" and "Insensibility" are from *The Collected Poems of Wilfred Owen,* ed. by C. Day Lewis. © Chatto & Windus Ltd. 1946, 1963. Reprinted by permission of The Owen Estate, Chatto & Windus Ltd., and New Directions Publishing Corporation.

REVIEW AND DISCUSSION QUESTIONS

1. Describe the examples Bennett uses to illustrate how feelings and duty may conflict.
2. How does Bennett characterize the relationship between morality and sympathy? In light of his examples, do you agree with the role he gives to each?
3. Why does Bennett think Edwards's morality was worse than Himmler's?
4. Besides sympathy, what means are available to criticize our own or others' moral principles?

Religion, Morality, and Conscience

John Arthur

What is morality? Does it need religion in some way? Or is it purely social? In this essay, John Arthur first discusses, and then rejects, three ways it has been thought that morality depends on religion: (1) that without religious motivation, people could not be expected to do the right thing; (2) that religion is necessary to provide guidance to people in their search for the correct course of action; and (3) that religion is essential for there even to be a right and a wrong. Arthur then considers another conception of morality, suggested by John Dewey, which claims that "morality is social." He concludes with some brief comments on the importance of these reflections for moral deliberation and for education. John Arthur is professor of philosophy and director of the Program in Philosophy, Politics, and Law at Binghamton University, State University of New York.

The major issue that I address in this paper is the nature of the connections, if any, between morality and religion. I will argue that although there are a variety of ways the two can be connected, in fact religion is not necessary for morality. Nonetheless, I argue, there are important respects in which the two are related, both historically and from the perspective of individuals. In the concluding section I look briefly at the various respects in which morality is "social" and the implications of that fact for how we understand moral thinking and education. First, however, I want to say something about the subjects: Just what are we referring to when we speak of morality and of religion?

1. MORALITY AND RELIGION

A useful way to approach the first question—the nature of morality—is to ask what it would mean for a society to exist without a moral code. How would people without a morality think and behave? What would such a society look like? First, it seems clear that such people would never feel guilt or resentment. For example, the notions that I ought to remember my parent's anniversary, that he has a moral responsibility to help care for his children after the divorce, that she has a right to equal pay for equal work, and that discrimination on the basis of race is unfair would be absent in such a society. Notions of duty, rights, and obligations would not be present, except perhaps in the legal sense; concepts of justice and fairness would also be foreign to these people. In short, people would have no tendency to evaluate or criticize the behavior of others, nor to feel remorse about their own behavior. Children would not be taught to be ashamed when they steal or hurt others, nor would they be allowed to complain when others treat them badly. (People might, however, feel regret at a decision that didn't turn out as they had hoped; but that would only be because their expectations were frustrated, not because they feel guilty.)

Such a society lacks a moral code. What, then, of religion? Is it possible that a society such as the one I have described would have religious beliefs? It seems clear that it is possible. Suppose every day these same people file into their place of worship to pay homage to God (they may believe in many gods or in one all-powerful creator of heaven and earth). Often they can be heard praying to God for help in dealing with their problems and thanking Him for their good fortune. Whenever a disaster befalls them, the people assume that God is angry with them; when things go well they believe He is pleased. Frequently they give sacrifices to God, usually in the form of money spent to build beautiful temples and churches. These practices might also be institutionalized, in the sense that certain people are assigned important leadership roles and specific texts are taken as authoritative.

To have a moral code, then, is to tend to evaluate (perhaps without even expressing it) the behavior of others and to feel guilt at certain actions when we perform them. Religion, on the other hand, involves beliefs in supernatural power(s) that created and perhaps also control nature, the tendency to worship and pray to those supernatural forces or beings, and the presence of leadership structures and authoritative texts. The practices of morality and religion are different. One involves

our attitudes toward various forms of behavior (lying and killing, for example), typically expressed using the notions of rules, rights, and obligations. The other, religion, typically involves prayer, worship, beliefs about the supernatural, institutional forms, and authoritative texts.

We come, then, to the central question: What is the connection, if any, between a society's moral code and its religious beliefs? Many people have felt that morality is in some way dependent on religion or religious truths. But what sort of "dependence" might there be? In what follows, I distinguish various ways in which one might claim that religion is necessary morality, arguing against those who claim morality depends on religion. I will also suggest, however, some other important ways in which the two are related.

2. RELIGIOUS MOTIVATION AND GUIDANCE

One possible role which religion might play in morality relates to motives people have. Religion, it is often said, is necessary so that people will DO right. Typically, the answer begins with the important point that doing what is right often has costs: refusing to shoplift or cheat can mean people go without some good or fail a test; returning a billfold means they don't get the contents. Religion is therefore said to be necessary in that it provides motivation to do the right thing. God rewards those who follow His commands by providing for them a place in heaven or by ensuring that they prosper and are happy on earth. He also punishes those who disobey. Others emphasize less self-interested ways in which religious motives may encourage people to act rightly. Since God is the creator of the universe and has ordained that His plan should be followed, they point out, it is important to live one's life in accord with this divinely ordained plan. Only by living a moral life, it is said, can people live in harmony with the larger, divinely created order.

The first claim, then, is that religion is necessary to provide moral motivation. The problem with that, of course, is that religious motives are far from the only ones people have. For most of us, a decision to do the right thing (if that our decision) is made for a variety of reasons: "What if I get caught? What if somebody sees me—what will he or she think? How will I feel afterwards? Will I regret it?" Or maybe the thought of cheating just doesn't occur. We were raised to be decent people, and that's what we are—period. That's much more important than whatever we might gain from stealing or cheating, let alone hurting another person. So it seems clear that many motives for doing the right thing have nothing whatsoever to do with religion. Most of us, in fact, do worry about getting caught, being blamed, and being looked down on by others. We also may do what is right just because it's right, or because we don't want to hurt others or embarrass family and friends. To say that we need religion to act morally is mistaken; indeed, it seems to me that many of us, when it really gets down to it, don't give much of a thought to religion when making moral decisions. All those other reasons are the ones that we tend to consider, or we just don't consider cheating and stealing at all. So far, then, there seems to be no reason to suppose that people can't be moral yet irreligious at the same time.

Another argument that religion is necessary to morality focuses on moral knowledge rather than on people's motives. However much people may want to do the right thing, according to this view, we cannot ever know for certain what is right without the guidance of religious teaching. Our own understanding is inadequate to this task; morality involves immensely complex and difficult problems, and so we must consult religious revelation for help.

Again, however, this argument fails. Just consider what we would need to know in order for religion to provide moral guidance. First, we must be sure that there is a God. And, there's the question of which of the many religions is true. How can anybody be sure his or her religion is the right one? Even if we can somehow convince ourselves that, for instance, the Judeo-Christian God is the real one, we still need to find out just what it is He wants us to do. Revelation comes in at least two forms, and not even Christians agree which form is real. Some hold that God tells us what he wants by providing us with His words: the Ten Com

mandments are an example. Many even believe, as evangelist Billy Graham once said, that the entire *Bible* was written by God using thirty-nine secretaries. Others doubt that every word of the *Bible* is literally true, believing instead that it is merely an account, written by human beings, of the historical events in history whereby God revealed Himself. On this view, revelation is not understood to be statements made by God but rather is seen as His acts, such as leading His people from Egypt, testing Job, and sending His son as an example of the ideal life. The *Bible* is not itself revelation, on this second view; it's the historical account of it.

If we are to use revelation as a moral guide, however, we must first know what is to count as revelation—words given us by God, historical events, or both? But even supposing that we could somehow answer those questions, the problems of relying on revelation are still not over since we still must interpret that revelation. Some feel, for example, that the *Bible* justifies various forms of killing, including war and capital punishment, on the basis of such statements as "an eye for an eye." Others, emphasizing such sayings as "Judge not lest ye be judged" and "Thou shalt not kill," believe the *Bible* demands absolute pacifism. How are we to know which interpretation is correct? It is likely, of course, that the answer people give to such religious questions will itself be influenced by their moral beliefs. But it is not a happy conclusion for those wishing to rest morality on revelation to discover that their understanding of revelation is itself dependent on their moral views.

So rather than providing a short-cut to moral understanding, looking to revelation for guidance often creates more questions and problems. And since religious beliefs will sometimes be influenced by moral ones, it seems simpler to address complex moral problems such as abortion, capital punishment, and affirmative action directly than to seek answers in revelation.

3. THE DIVINE COMMAND THEORY

It may seem that we have not yet gotten to the heart of the matter. Even if religion is not necessary for moral motivation or guidance, it is often claimed, religion is necessary in another more fundamental sense. According to this view, religion is necessary for morality because without God there could BE no right or wrong. God, in other words, provides the foundation or bedrock on which morality is founded. This idea was expressed by Bishop R. C. Mortimer:

God made us and all the world. Because of that He has an absolute claim on our obedience. . . . From [this] it follows that a thing is not right simply because we think it is. It is right because God commands it.[1]

What Bishop Mortimer has in mind can be seen by comparing moral rules with legal ones. Legal statutes, we know, are created by legislatures, and if there had been no statute passed requiring that people limit the speed they travel, then there would be no such legal obligation. Without the statutory "commands" of the legislature, law simply would not exist. The view defended by Mortimer, often called the *divine command theory,* is therefore that God has the same relation to moral law as the legislature does to statutes. Without God's commands there would be no moral rules, just as without a legislature there would be no statutes.

A related feature of the divine command theory is that only it can explain the objective difference between right and wrong. This point was forcefully argued by F. C. Copleston in a 1948 British Broadcasting Corporation radio debate with Bertrand Russell.

Copleston: . . . The validity of such an interpretation of man's conduct depends on the recognition of God's existence, obviously. . . . Let's take a look at the Commandant of the [Nazi] concentration camp at Belsen. That appears to you as undesirable and evil and to me too. To Adolph Hitler we suppose it appeared as something good and desirable. I suppose you'd have to admit that for Hitler it was good and for you it is evil.

Russell: No, I shouldn't go so far as that. I mean, I think people can make mistakes in that as they can in other things. If you have jaundice you see things yellow that are not yellow. You're making a mistake.

Copleston: Yes, one can make mistakes, but can you make a mistake if it's simply a question of reference to a feeling or emotion? Surely Hitler would be the only possible judge of what appealed to his emotions.

Russell: . . . you can say various things about that; among others, that if that sort of thing makes that sort of appeal to Hitler's emotions, then Hitler makes quite a different appeal to my emotions.

Copleston: Granted. But there's no objective criterion outside feeling then for condemning the conduct of the Commandant of Belsen, in your view. . . . The human being's idea of the content of the moral law depends certainly to a large extent on education and environment, and a man has to use his reason in assessing the validity of the actual moral ideas of his social group. But the possibility of criticizing the accepted moral code presupposes that there is an objective standard, that there is an ideal moral order, which imposes itself. . . . It implies the existence of a real foundation of God.[2]

Against those who, like Bertrand Russell, seek to ground morality in feeling, Copleston argues that there must be a more solid foundation if we are to be able to claim truly that the Nazis were evil. God, according to Copleston, is able to provide the objective basis for the distinction, which we all know to exist, between right and wrong. Without divine commands at the root of human obligations, we would have no real reason for condemning the behavior of anybody, even Nazis. Morality, Copleston thinks, would then be nothing more than an expression of personal feeling.

To begin assessing the divine command theory, let's first consider this last point. Is it really true that only the commands of God can provide an objective basis for moral judgments? Certainly many philosophers have felt that morality rests on its own perfectly sound footing, be it reason, human nature, or natural sentiments. It seems wrong to conclude, automatically, that morality cannot rest on anything but religion; nor, or course, can we be certain that morality even needs such a foundation. And it is also possible, finally, that moral "objectivity" (whatever that means) really is a myth, and morality doesn't need such a foundation.

In addition to these problems with Copleston's argument, the divine command theory faces other problems as well. First, we would need to say much more about the relationship between morality and divine commands. Certainly the expressions "is commanded by God" and "is morally required" do not *mean* the same thing. People and even whole societies can use moral concepts without understanding them to make any reference to God. And while it is true that God (or any other moral being for that matter) would tend to want others to do the right thing, this hardly shows that being right and being commanded by God are the same thing. Parents want their children to do the right thing, too, but that doesn't mean parents, or anybody else, can make a thing right just by commanding it!

I think that, in fact, theists should reject the divine command theory. One reason is what it implies. Suppose we were to grant (just for the sake of argument) that the divine command theory is correct, so that actions are right just because they are commanded by God. The same, of course, can be said about those deeds that we believe are wrong. If God hadn't commanded us not to do them, they would not be wrong. (Recall the comparison made with the law that depends on the legislature having passed it.)

But now notice this. Since God is all-powerful, and since right is determined solely by His commands, is it not possible that He might change the rules and make what we now think of as wrong into right? It would seem that according to the divine command theory it is possible that tomorrow God will decree that virtues such as kindness and courage have become vices while actions that show cruelty and cowardice are the right actions. Rather than it being right for people to help each other out and prevent innocent people from suffering unnecessarily, it would then be right (God having changed His mind) to create as much pain among innocent children as we possibly can! To adopt the divine command theory commits its advocate to the seemingly absurd position that even the greatest atrocities might be not only acceptable but morally required if God were to command them.

Plato made a similar point in the dialogue Euthyphro. Socrates is asking Euthyphro what it is that makes the virtue of holiness a virtue, just as we have been asking what makes kindness and courage virtues. Euthyphro has suggested that holiness is just whatever all the gods love.

Socrates: Well, then, Euthyphro, what do we say about holiness? Is it not loved by all the gods, according to your definition?

Euthyphro: Yes.

Socrates: Because it is holy, or for some other reason?

Euthyphro: No, because it is holy.

Socrates: Then it is loved by the gods because it is holy: it is not holy because it is loved by them?

Euthyphro: It seems so.

Socrates: . . . Then holiness is not what is pleasing to the gods, and what is pleasing to the gods is not holy as you say, Euthyphro. They are different things.

Euthyphro: And why, Socrates?

Socrates: Because we are agreed that the gods love holiness because it is holy: and that it is not holy because they love it.[3]

But having claimed at first that virtues are merely what is loved by the gods, why would Euthyphro contradict this and agree that the gods love holiness because it's holy? One likely possibility is that Euthyphro believes that whenever the gods love something, they do so with good reason, not just arbitrarily. The gods are pleased or displeased for some reason. To deny this and say that it is simply the gods' love that makes holiness a virtue would mean that the gods have no basis for their attitudes, that they are arbitrary. It's far from clear, however, that a religious person would want to say that God is arbitrary in that way. Furthermore, if we say that it is simply God's loving something that makes it right, then what sense would it make to say God wants us to do right? All that could mean, it seems, is that God wants us to do what He wants us to do—He would have no reason for wanting it. Similarly "God is good" would mean little more than "God does what He pleases." The divine command theory seems to have led us to the result that God is morally arbitrary and that His wishing us to do good or His being just mean nothing more than that He does what He does and wants whatever He wants. Religious people who reject that consequence would also, I am suggesting, have reason to reject the divine command theory.

This now raises another problem, however. If God approves kindness because it is a virtue and hates the Nazis because they were evil, then it seems that God discovers morality rather than inventing it. So haven't we then identified a limitation on God's power, since He now, being a good God, must love kindness and command us not to be cruel? Without the divine command theory, in other words, what is left of God's omnipotence?

But why, we may ask, is such a limitation on God unacceptable? It is not at all clear that God really can do anything. Can He, for example, destroy Himself? Or make a rock so heavy that He cannot lift it? Or create a universe that was never created by Him? Many have thought that God cannot do these things, but also that His inability to do them does not constitute a serious limitation on His power since these are things that cannot logically be done. Christianity's most influential theologian, Thomas Aquinas, wrote in this regard that "whatever implies contradiction does not come within the scope of divine omnipotence, because it cannot have the aspect of possibility. Hence, it is more appropriate to say that such things cannot be done than that God cannot do them."[4] Aquinas thus rejects the view that there is nothing that God cannot do.

How, then, ought we to understand God's relationship to morality if we reject the divine command theory? Can religious people consistently maintain their faith in God the Creator and yet deny that what is right is right because He commands it? I think the answer to this is "yes." Making cruelty good is not like making a universe that wasn't made, of course. It's a moral limit on God rather than a logical one. But why suppose that God's limits are only logical?

Furthermore, there still remains a sense in which God could change morality even if we reject the divine command theory. If we assume— plausibly, I think—that morality depends in part on how we reason, what we desire and need, and the circumstances in which we find ourselves, then morality will still be under God's control since God could have constructed us or our environment very differently. Suppose, for instance, that he created us so that we couldn't be hurt by others, didn't care about freedom, and weren't influenced by other's suffering. Or perhaps our natural environment were different so that we never lacked for anything we wanted. If God had created either nature or us that way, then it seems likely our morality might also be different in important ways from the one we now think correct. In that sense, then, morality depends on God whether or not one supports the divine command theory.

4. "MORALITY IS SOCIAL"

I have argued here that religion is not necessary in providing moral motivation or guidance, nor should the religious person subscribe to the divine command theory and claim God necessary for there to be morality. In this last section, I want first to look briefly at how religion and morality sometimes do influence each other. Then I will consider briefly the important ways in which morality might correctly be thought to be "social."

Nothing I have said so far means that morality and religion are independent of each other. But in what ways are they related, assuming I am correct in claiming morality does not *depend* on religion? First, of course, we should note the historical influence religions have had on the development of morality as well as on politics and law. Many of the important figures in the abolitionist and civil rights movements were religious leaders, as are many current members of the pro-life movement. The relationship is not, however, one-sided: morality has also influenced religion, as the current debate within the Catholic church over the role of women, abortion, and other social issues shows. In reality, then, it seems clear that the practices of morality and religion have historically each exerted an influence on the other.

But just as the two practices have shaped each other historically, so, too, do they interact at the individual level. I have already suggested how people's understanding of revelation, for instance, is often shaped by morality as they seek the best interpretations of revealed texts. Whether a work of art, a legal statute, or a religious text, interpreters regularly seek to place them in the best light—to make them the best they can be, which requires that they bring moral judgment to the task of religious interpretation and understanding.

The relationship can go the other direction as well, however, as people's moral views are shaped by both their religious training and their current religious beliefs. These relationships are often complex, hidden even from ourselves, but it does seem clear that our views on important moral issues, from sexual morality and war to welfare and capital punishment, are often influenced by our religious outlook. So not only are religious and moral practices and understandings historically linked, but, for many religious people, the relationship extends to the personal level—to their understanding of moral obligations as well as their sense of who they are and their vision of who they wish to be.

Morality, then, is influenced by religion, just as religion is affected by morality; morality is a social practice shaped by other social practices. But morality's social character extends deeper even than that, I want to argue. Consider the following comments from John Dewey about the origins of morality and conscience taken from an article he titled "Morality is Social":

In language and imagination we rehearse the responses of others just as we dramatically enact other consequences. We foreknow how others will act, and the foreknowledge is the beginning of judgment passed on action. We know *with* them; there is conscience. An assembly is formed within our breast which discusses and appraises proposed and performed acts. The community without becomes a forum and tribunal within, a judgment-seat of charges, assessments and exculpations. Our thoughts of our own actions are saturated with the ideas that others entertain about them. . . . Explicit recognition of this fact is a prerequisite of improvement in moral education. . . . Reflection is morally indispensable.[5]

Dewey is suggesting four important senses in which morality is social. First, of course, he assumes that we possess a socially acquired language within which we think about our choices and possible responses to them by the world, including other people. Second, morality is social in that it governs relationships among people, defining our responsibilities to others and theirs to us. Morality provides the standards on which we rely in gauging our interactions with family, lovers, friends, fellow citizens, and even strangers. Third, morality is social in the sense that we are, in fact, subject to criticism by others for our actions. We discuss with others what we should do and often hear from them concerning whether our decisions were acceptable. Blame and praise are central features of morality.

Besides these points, however, Dewey also wants to make another, less obvious yet in some ways more important one about morality's social character. This fourth point depends on appreciating the fact that thinking from the moral point of view, as opposed to the selfish one, for instance, demands that we reject our subjective perspective in favor of the perspective of others and envision how they might respond to various choices we might make. Far from being private and unrelated to others, moral conscience is in that sense "public." To consider a decision from the moral perspective requires envisioning what Dewey terms an "assembly of others" that is "formed within our breast." Conscience therefore cannot be distinguished from the social: it already brings with it the perspective of the other. "Is this right?" and "What would this look like to others?" are not separable questions.

It is important not to confuse Dewey's point here, however. He is not saying that what is right is finally to be decided by the actual reactions of others or even by society as a whole. To the contrary, it is always possible that members of one's society might in fact approve an action that is incompatible with the dictates of conscience, despite the fact that conscience is "social" in his sense. Conscience, understood as the voice of an "assembly" of others within each of us, cannot be reduced to the expected reaction of any particular individual or group. The assembly Dewey is describing is in fact much closer to what might be called an "ideal" assembly than any particular individual or group. It is always possible that any such actual reaction, including even society as a whole, might be judged wrong when subjected to the voice of one's conscience. Morality is therefore *inherently* social; it depends on socially learned language, is learned from interactions with others, governs our interactions with others, and, even more importantly, it demands by its very nature that we envision others' points of view as well as our own. Morality is deeply and thoroughly social. But conscience also looks beyond actual members of society, depending instead on our powers of "imagination" and our capacity to occupy, self-critically, the positions of others.6

Viewed in this light, God might play a role in moral reflection that closely mirrors what I am terming, following Dewey, "conscience." It is unlikely, for instance, that the religious person would distinguish God's reaction to the morality of an action from the reaction dictated by conscience, and indeed quite plausible that conscience might feature, along with the reactions of others, the imagined reaction of God as well. Other people remain necessary since, as I have argued, it is often an open question as to just what God's reaction would be; revelation's meaning, then, is subject to interpretation that itself relies on moral judgment.

This leads to my final point, about moral education. If Dewey is correct, then it seems clear there is an important sense in which morality not only can be taught but must be. Besides early moral training, moral thinking, as well as conscience itself, depends on our ability to imagine others' reactions. "What would somebody (including, perhaps, God) think if this got out?" expresses more than a concern with being embarrassed or punished; it is also the voice of conscience and of morality itself. That means, then, that listening to others, reading about what others think and do, and reflecting on our actions and whether we could defend them to others are part of the practice of morality itself. Morality cannot exist without the broader, social perspective introduced by others, and this social nature ties it, in that way, to public discussion, both actual and imagined. "Private" moral reflection taking place independently of the social world would be no moral reflection at all. Moral education is therefore not only possible but essential.

NOTES

1. R. C. Mortimer, *Christian Ethics* (London: Hutchinson's University Library, 1950), pp. 7–8.
2. This debate was broadcast on the Third Program of the British Broadcasting Corporation in 1948.
3. Plato, *Euthyphro,* trans. H. N. Fowler (Cambridge, MA: Harvard University Press, 1947).
4. Thomas Aquinas, *Summa Theologica,* Part I, Q. 25, Art. 3.
5. John Dewey, "Morality Is Social" in *The Moral Writings of John Dewey,* rev. ed. ed. James Gouinlock (Amherst, NY: Prometheus Books, 1994), pp. 182–4.
6. Animals pose an interesting problem for this conception of morality. Is it wrong to torture animals only because other *people* could be expected to disapprove? Or is it that the animal itself would disapprove? Or, perhaps, our duty to animals rests on sympathy and compassion, whereas human moral relations are as Dewey describes them, resting on morality's inherently social nature?

REVIEW AND DISCUSSION QUESTIONS

1. How does Arthur respond to those who argue that morality is necessary for moral motivation?
2. Arthur denies that morality is necessary for moral understanding or knowledge. Why does he think that?
3. How does the analogy with a legal system suggest that God may be necessary for there to be a right and wrong?
4. Why does Arthur reject the divine command theory?
5. In what ways are morality and religion connected, according to Arthur?
6. "Morality is social," said John Dewey. What did he mean by that?

7. What is the significance of Dewey's idea for moral education? What would Dewey probably have thought about a class in ethics?

8. In footnote 6, Arthur raises the problem of human's obligations to animals. How would you be inclined to answer the questions he asks there?

9. "Without God, everything is permitted" said a character in *The Brother Karamazov*. What do you think he meant? How, in light of this reading, could you respond to that statement?

2
Classical Moral Theories

Selections in Section 2 are from five of the most important works on moral theory in the history of philosophy. They range from Aristotle's *Nicomachean Ethics,* published more than two thousand years ago, to Mill's classic work *Utilitarianism,* written in the last century. Each of them raises important questions, still alive today, about the foundations on which morality rests, its ultimate purpose or justification, the test for right and wrong, and the ideal or best way of life.

Nicomachean Ethics

Aristotle

Aristotle (384–322 B.C.) was born in Stagira, a town near Macedonia. He went to Athens when he was seventeen years old and studied with Plato at the Academy for twenty years. When Plato died, Aristotle left Athens and traveled to Macedonia, where he tutored the young heir to the throne—who was later to become known as Alexander the Great. In 334 B.C., Aristotle returned to Athens and founded his own school, the Lyceum. When Alexander died in 323, there was strong, anti-Macedonian feeling in Athens, and Aristotle left for Chalcis, where he died the next year at sixty-two.

Aristotle studied and wrote about an astonishing range of subjects. No single person, it is often said, has ever founded and advanced so many fields of learning. Aristotle wrote separate treatises on physics, biology, logic, psychology, ethics, metaphysics, aesthetics, literary criticism, and political science. In the Middle Ages, he was known simply as "The Philosopher."

In this selection, taken from *Nicomachean Ethics,* Aristotle begins with a discussion of the study of ethics and of human nature and then turns to the nature of *eudainomonia*—that is, well-being or happiness. To understand happiness, it is necessary to understand the natural purpose or function of man, which Aristotle describes as activity in accordance with reason. In that sense, happiness is also an excellent, specifically virtuous activity. Virtues, he argues, are those habits and traits that allow people to live well in communities, and true happiness is not, contrary to popular opinion, merely a pleasure. Nor is happiness to be found in economic wealth, although living a virtuous and happy life requires at least some wealth and certainly brings pleasure to the one who is able to achieve it. Turning finally to the nature of the virtues, Aristotle first distinguishes intellectual from moral virtue, arguing that while intellectual virtues can be taught, moral virtues must be acquired through habit and require a certain sort of community if they are to be realized. Using examples such as courage and liberality, he argues that moral virtues can best be understood as a mean between extremes.

From *Nicomachean Ethics*, trans. James E. C. Weldon (1892).

BOOK I

Every art and every scientific inquiry, and similarly every action and purpose, may be said to aim at some good. Hence the good has been well defined as that at which all things aim. But it is clear that there is a difference in ends; for the ends are sometimes activities, and sometimes results beyond the mere activities. Where there are ends beyond the action, the results are naturally superior to the action.

As there are various actions, arts, and sciences, it follows that the ends are also various. Thus health is the end of the medical art, a ship of shipbuilding, victory of strategy, and wealth of economics. It often happens that a number of such arts or sciences combine for a single enterprise, as the art of making bridles and all such other arts as furnish the implements of horsemanship combine for horsemanship, and horsemanship and every military action for strategy; and in the same way, other arts or sciences combine for others. In all these cases, the ends of the master arts or sciences, whatever they may be, are more desirable than those of the subordinate arts or sciences, as it is for the sake of the former that the latter are pursued. It makes no difference to the argument whether the activities themselves are the ends of the action, or something beyond the activities, as in the above-mentioned sciences.

If it is true that in the sphere of action there is some end which we wish for its own sake, and for the sake of which we wish everything else, and if we do not desire everything for the sake of something else (for, if that is so, the process will go on ad infinitum, and our desire will be idle and futile), clearly this end will be good and the supreme good. Does it not follow then that the knowledge of this good is of great importance for the conduct of life? Like archers who have a mark at which to aim, shall we not have a better chance of attaining what we want? If this is so, we must endeavor to comprehend, at least in outline, what this good is, and what science or faculty makes it its object. . . .

As every science and undertaking aims at some good, what is in our view the good at which political science aims, and what is the highest of all practical goods? As to its name there is, I may say, a general agreement. The masses and the cultured classes agree in calling it happiness, and conceive that "to live well" or "to do well" is the same thing as "to be happy." But as to what happiness is they do not agree, nor do the masses give the same account of it as the philosophers. The former take it to be something visible and palpable, such as pleasure, wealth, or honor; different people, however, give different definitions of it, and often even the same man gives different definitions at different times. When he is ill, it is health, when he is poor, it is wealth; if he is conscious of his own ignorance, he envies people who use grand language above his own comprehension. Some philosophers, on the other hand, have held that, besides these various goods, there is an absolute good which is the cause of goodness in them all. [These were members of Plato's school of thought.] It would perhaps be a waste of time to examine all these opinions; it will be enough to examine such as are most popular or as seem to be more or less reasonable.

. . . Men's conception of the good or of happiness may be read in the lives they lead. Ordinary or vulgar people conceive it to be a pleasure, and accordingly choose a life of enjoyment. For there are, we may say, three conspicuous types of life, the sensual, the political, and, thirdly, the life of thought. Now the mass of men present an absolutely slavish appearance, choosing the life of brute beasts, but they have ground for so doing because so many persons in authority share the tastes of Sardanapalus. [A half legendary ruler of ancient Assyria, whose name to the Greeks stood for the extreme of Oriental luxury and extravagance.] Cultivated and energetic people, on the other hand, identify happiness with honor, as honor is the general end of political life. But this seems too superficial an idea for our present purpose; for honor depends more upon the people who pay it than upon the person to whom it is paid, and the good we feel is something which is proper to a man himself and cannot be easily taken away from him. Men too appear to seek honor in order to be assured of their own goodness. Accordingly, they seek it at the hands of the sage and of those who know them well, and they seek it on the ground of their virtue; clearly then, in their judgment at any rate, virtue is better than honor. Perhaps then we might look on virtue rather than honor as the end of political life. Yet even this idea appears not quite complete; for a man may possess virtue and yet be asleep or inactive throughout life, and not only so, but he may experience the greatest calamities and misfortunes. Yet no one would call such a life a life of happiness, unless he were maintaining a paradox. But we need not dwell further on this subject, since it is sufficiently discussed in popular philosophical treatises. The third life is the life of thought. . . .

The life of money making is a life of constraint; and wealth is obviously not the good of which we are in quest; for it is useful merely as a means to something else. It would be more reasonable to take the things mentioned before—sensual pleasure, honor, and virtue—as ends than wealth, since they are things desired on their own account. Yet these too are evidently not ends, although much argument has been employed to show that they are. . . .

But leaving this subject for the present, let us revert to the good of which we are in quest and consider what it may be. For it seems different in different activities or arts; it is one thing in medicine, another in strategy, and so on. What is the good in each of these instances? It is presumably that for the sake of which all else is done. In medicine this is health, in strategy victory, in architecture a house, and so on. In every activity and undertaking it is the end, since it is for the sake of the end that all people do whatever else they do. If then there is an end for all our activity, this will be the good to be accomplished; and if there are several such ends, it will be these.

Our argument has arrived by a different path at the same point as before; but we must endeavor to make it still plainer. Since there are more ends than one, and some of these ends—for example, wealth, flutes, and instruments generally—we desire as means to something else, it is evident that not all are final ends. But the highest good is clearly something final. Hence if there is only one final end, this will be the object of which we are in search; and if there are more than one, it will be the most final. We call that which is sought after for its own sake more final than that which is sought after as a means to something else; we call that which is never desired as a means to something else more final than things that are desired both for themselves and as means to something

else. Therefore, we call absolutely final that which is always desired for itself and never as a means to something else. Now happiness more than anything else answers to this description. For happiness we always desire for its own sake and never as a means to something else, whereas honor, pleasure, intelligence, and every virtue we desire partly for their own sakes (for we should desire them independently of what might result from them), but partly also as means to happiness, because we suppose they will prove instruments of happiness. Happiness, on the other hand, nobody desires for the sake of these things, nor indeed as a means to anything else at all. . . .

Perhaps, however, it seems a commonplace to say that happiness is the supreme good; what is wanted is to define its nature a little more clearly. The best way of arriving at such a definition will probably be to ascertain the function of man. For, as with a flute player, a sculptor, or any artist, or in fact anybody who has a special function or activity, his goodness and excellence seem to lie in his function, so it would seem to be with man, if indeed he has a special function. Can it be said that, while a carpenter and a cobbler have special functions and activities, man, unlike them, is naturally functionless? Or, as the eye, the hand, the foot, and similarly each part of the body has a special function, so may man be regarded as having a special function apart from all these? What, then, can this function be? It is not life; for life is apparently something that man shares with plants; and we are looking for something peculiar to him. We must exclude therefore the life of nutrition and growth. There is next what may be called the life of sensation. But this too, apparently, is shared by man with horses, cattle, and all other animals. There remains what I may call the active life of the rational part of man's being. Now this rational part is twofold; one part is rational in the sense of being obedient to reason, and the other in the sense of possessing and exercising reason and intelligence. The active life too may be conceived of in two ways, [In other words, life may be taken to mean either the mere possession of certain faculties or their active exercise.] either as a state of character, or as an activity; but we mean by it the life of activity, as this seems to be the truer form of the conception.

The function of man then is activity of soul in accordance with reason, or not apart from reason. Now, the function of a man of a certain kind, and of a man who is good of that kind—for example, of a harpist and a good harpist—are in our view the same in kind. This is true of all people of all kinds without exception, the superior excellence being only an addition to the function; for it is the function of a harpist to play the harp, and of a good harpist to play the harp well. This being so, if we define the function of man as a kind of life, and this life as an activity of the soul or a course of action in accordance with reason, and if the function of a good man is such activity of a good and noble kind, and if everything is well done when it is done in accordance with its proper excellence, it follows that the good of man is activity of soul in accordance with virtue, or, if there are more virtues than one, in accordance with the best and most complete virtue. But we must add the words "in a complete life." For as one swallow or one day does not make a spring, so one day or a short time does not make a man blessed or happy. . . .

Our account accords too with the view of those who hold that happiness is virtue or excellence of some sort; for activity in accordance with virtue is virtue. But there is plainly a considerable difference between calling the supreme good possession or use, a state of mind, or an activity. For a state of mind may exist without producing anything good—for example, if a person is asleep, or in any other way inert. Not so with an activity, since activity implies acting and acting well. As in the Olympic games it is not the most beautiful and strongest who receive the crown but those who actually enter the combat, for from those come the victors, so it is those who act that win rightly what is noble and good in life.

Their life too is pleasant in itself. For pleasure is a state of mind, and whatever a man is fond of is pleasant to him, as a horse is to a lover of horses, a show to a lover of spectacles, and, similarly, just acts to a lover of justice, and virtuous acts in general to a lover of virtue. Now most men find a sense of discord in their pleasures, because their pleasures are not all naturally pleasant. But the lovers of nobleness take pleasure in what is naturally pleasant, and virtuous acts are naturally pleasant. Such acts then are pleasant both to these

persons and in themselves. Nor does the life of such persons need more pleasure attached to it as a sort of charm; it possesses pleasure in itself. For, it may be added, a man who does not delight in noble acts is not good; as nobody would call a man just who did not enjoy just action, or liberal who did not enjoy liberal action, and so on. If this is so, it follows that acts of virtue are pleasant in themselves. They are also good and noble, and good and noble in the highest degree, for the judgment of the virtuous man on them is right, and his judgment is as we have described. Happiness then is the best and noblest and pleasantest thing in the world. . . .

Still it is clear, as we said, that happiness requires the addition of external goods; for it is impossible, or at least difficult, to do noble deeds with no outside means. For many things can be done only through the aid of friends or wealth or political power; and there are some things the lack of which spoils our felicity, such as good birth, wholesome children, and personal beauty. For a man who is extremely ugly in appearance or low born or solitary and childless can hardly be happy; perhaps still less so, if he has exceedingly bad children or friends, or has had good children or friends and lost them by death. As we said, then, happiness seems to need prosperity of this kind in addition to virtue. For this reason some persons identify happiness with good fortune, though others do so with virtue. . . .

It is reasonable then not to call an ox or a horse or any other animal happy; for none of them is capable of sharing in this activity. For the same reason no child can be happy, since the youth of a child keeps him for the time being from such activity; if a child is ever called happy, the ground of felicitation is his promise, rather than his actual performance. For happiness demands, as we said, a complete virtue and a complete life. And there are all sorts of changes and chances in life, and the most prosperous of men may in his old age fall into extreme calamities, as Priam did in the heroic legends. [The disastrous fate of Priam, king of Troy, was part of the well-known Homeric tales.] And a person who has experienced such chances and died a miserable death, nobody calls happy. . . .

Now the events of chance are numerous and of different magnitudes. Small pieces of good fortune or the reverse do not turn the scale of life in any way, but great and numerous events make life happier if they turn out well, since they naturally give it beauty and the use of them may be noble and good. If, on the other hand, they turn out badly, they mar and mutilate happiness by causing pain and hindrances to many activities. Still, even in these circumstances, nobility shines out when a person bears with calmness the weight of accumulated misfortunes, not from insensibility but from dignity and greatness of spirit.

Then if activities determine the quality of life, as we said, no happy man can become miserable; for he will never do what is hateful and mean. For our idea of the truly good and wise man is that he bears all the chances of life with dignity and always does what is best in the circumstances, as a good general makes the best use of the forces at his command in war, or a good cobbler makes the best shoe with the leather given him, and so on through the whole series of the arts. If this is so, the happy man can never become miserable. I do not say that he will be fortunate if he meets such chances of life as Priam. Yet he will not be variable or constantly changing, for he will not be moved from his happiness easily or by ordinary misfortunes, but only by great and numerous ones; nor after them will he quickly regain his happiness. If he regains it at all, it will be only over a long and complete period of time and after great and notable achievement.

We may safely then define a happy man as one who is active in accord with perfect virtue and adequately furnished with external goods, not for some chance period of time but for his whole lifetime. . . .

Inasmuch as happiness is an activity of soul in accordance with complete or perfect virtue, it is necessary to consider virtue, as this will perhaps be the best way of studying happiness. . . .

BOOK II

Virtue then is twofold, partly intellectual and partly moral, and intellectual virtue is originated and fostered mainly by teaching; it therefore demands experience and time. Moral virtue on the other hand is the outcome of habit. From this fact it is clear that moral virtue is not implanted in us by nature, for a law of nature cannot be altered by habituation. Thus a stone, that naturally tends to fall downwards, cannot be habituated or trained to rise upwards. It is neither by nature then nor in defiance of nature that virtues are implanted in us. Nature gives us the capacity of receiving them, and that capacity is perfected by habit.

Again, if we take the various natural powers which belong to us, we first possess the proper faculties and afterwards display the activities. It is obviously so with the senses. Not by seeing frequently or hearing frequently do we acquire the sense of seeing or hearing; on the contrary, because we have the senses we make use of them; we do not get them by making use of them. But the virtues we get by first practicing them, as we do in the arts. For it is by doing what we ought to do when we study the arts that we learn the arts themselves; we become builders by building and harpists by playing the harp. Similarly, it is by doing just acts that we become just, by doing temperate acts that we become temperate, by doing brave acts that we become brave. The experience of states confirms this statement, for it is by training in good habits that lawmakers make the citizens good. This is the object all lawmakers have at heart; if they do not succeed in it, they fail of their purpose; and it makes the distinction between a good constitution and a bad one.

Again, the causes and means by which any virtue is produced and destroyed are the same. It is by our actions in dealing between man and man that we become either just or unjust. It is by our actions in the face of danger and by our training ourselves to fear or to courage that we become either cowardly or courageous. It is much the same with our appetites and angry passions. People become temperate and gentle, others licentious and passionate, by behaving in one or the other way in particular circumstances. In a word, moral states are the results of activities like the states themselves. It is our duty therefore to keep a certain character in our activities, since our moral states depend on the differences in our activities. So the difference between one and another training in habits in our childhood is not a light matter, but important, or rather, all-important.

Our present study is not, like other studies, purely theoretical in intention; for the object of our inquiry is not to know what virtue is but how to become good, and that is the sole benefit of it. We must, therefore, consider the right way of performing actions, for it is acts that determine the character of the resulting moral states.

That we should act in accordance with right reason is a common general principle, which may here be taken for granted. . . .

The first point to be observed is that in matters we are now considering deficiency and excess are both fatal. It is so, we see, in questions of health and strength. Too much or too little gymnastic exercise is fatal to strength. Similarly, too much or too little meat and drink is fatal to health, whereas a suitable amount produces, increases, and sustains it. . . .

It is not enough to state merely that virtue is a moral state, we must also describe the character of that moral state. . . .

It must be laid down then that every virtue or excellence has the effect of producing a good condition of that of which it is a virtue or excellence, and of enabling it to perform its function well. Thus the excellence of the eye makes the eye good and its function good, as it is by the excellence of the eye that we see well. Similarly, the excellence of the horse makes a horse excellent and good at racing, at carrying its rider and at facing the enemy.

If then this is universally true, the virtue or excellence of man will be such a moral state as makes a man good and able to perform his proper function well. We have already explained how this will be the case, but another way of making it clear will be to study the nature or character of this virtue.

Now in everything, whether it is continuous or divisible, it is possible to take a greater, a smaller, or an equal amount, and this either absolutely or in relation to ourselves, the equal being a mean between excess and deficiency. By the mean in respect of the thing itself, or the absolute mean, I understand that which is equally distinct from both extremes; and this is one and the same thing for everybody. By the mean considered relatively to ourselves I understand that which is neither too much nor too little; but this is not one thing, nor is it the same for everybody. Thus if 10 be too much and 2 too little we take 6 as a mean in respect of the

thing itself; for 6 is as much greater than 2 as it is less than 10, and this is a mean in arithmetical proportion. But the mean considered relatively to ourselves must not be ascertained in this way. It does not follow that if 10 pounds of meat be too much and 2 be too little for a man to eat, a trainer will order him 6 pounds, as this may itself be too much or too little for the person who is to take it; it will be too little e.g. for Milo [the famous Crotoniate wrestler], but too much for a beginner in gymnastics. It will be the same with running and wrestling; the right amount will vary with the individual. This being so, everybody who understands his business avoids alike excess and deficiency; he seeks and chooses the mean, not the absolute mean, but the mean considered relatively to ourselves.

Every art then performs its function well, if it regards the mean and refers the works which it produces to the mean. This is the reason why it is usually said of successful works that it is impossible to take anything from them or to add anything to them, which implies that excess or deficiency is fatal to excellence but that the mean state ensures it. Good artists too, as we say, have an eye to the mean in their works. But virtue, like Nature herself, is more accurate and better than any art; virtue therefore will aim at the mean;—I speak of moral virtue, as it is moral virtue which is concerned with emotions and actions, and it is these which admit of excess and deficiency and the mean. Thus it is possible to go too far, or not to go far enough, in respect of fear, courage, desire, anger, pity, and pleasure and pain generally, and the excess and the deficiency are alike wrong; but to experience these emotions at the right times and on the right occasions and towards the right persons and for the right causes and in the right manner is the mean or the supreme good, which is characteristic of virtue. Similarly there may be excess, deficiency, or the mean, in regard to actions. But virtue is concerned with emotions and actions, and here excess is an error and deficiency a fault, whereas the mean is successful and laudable, and success and merit are both characteristics of virtue.

It appears then that virtue is a mean state, so far at least as it aims at the mean.

On the other hand, there are many different ways of going wrong; for evil is in its nature infinite. [It] is easy to miss the mark but difficult to hit it. And so by reasoning excess and deficiency are characteristics of vice and the mean as a characteristic of virtue.

Virtue then is a state of deliberate moral purpose consisting in a mean that is relative to ourselves, the mean being determined by reason, or as a prudent man would determine it. . . .

But not every action or every emotion admits of a mean. There are some whose very name implies wickedness, as, for example, malice, shamelessness, and envy among the emotions, and adultery, theft, and murder among the actions. All these and others like them are marked as intrinsically wicked, not merely the excesses or deficiencies of them. It is never possible then to be right in them; they are always sinful. Right or wrong in such acts as adultery does not depend on our committing it with the right woman, at the right time, or in the right manner; on the contrary it is wrong to do it at all. It would be equally false to suppose that there can be a mean or excess of deficiency in unjust, cowardly or licentious conduct. . . .

There are then three dispositions, two being vices, namely, excess and deficiency, and one virtue, which is the mean between them; and they are all in a sense morally opposed. Thus the brave man appears foolhardy compared with the coward, but cowardly compared with the foolhardy. Similarly, the temperate man appears licentious compared with the insensible man but insensible compared with the licentious; and the liberal man appears extravagant compared with the stingy man but stingy compared with the spendthrift. The result is that the extremes each denounce the mean as belonging to the other extreme; the coward calls the brave man foolhardy, and the foolhardy man calls him cowardly; and so on in other cases. . . .

That is why it is so hard to be good; for it is always hard to find the mean in anything; anybody can get angry—that is easy—and anybody can give or spend money, but to give it to the right person, to give the right amount of it, at the right time, for the right cause and in the right way, this is not what anybody can do, nor is it easy. That is why goodness is rare, praiseworthy and noble. One who aims at the mean must begin by departing from the extreme, for of the two extremes one is more wrong than the other. . . . We must also note the weakness to which we are ourselves particularly prone, since different natures tend in different ways; and we may ascertain what our tendency is by observing our feelings of pleasure and pain. Then we must drag ourselves away towards the opposite extreme; for by pulling ourselves as far as possible from what is wrong we shall arrive at the mean.

In all cases we must especially be on our guard against the pleasant, or pleasure, for we are not impartial judges of pleasure. . . .

Undoubtedly this is a difficult task, especially individual cases. It is not easy to determine the right matter, objects, occasion and duration of anger. Sometimes we praise people who are deficient in anger, and call them gentle, and at other times we praise people who exhibit a fierce temper as high spirited. It is not however a man who deviates a little from goodness, but one who deviates a great deal, whether on the side of excess or of deficiency, that is blamed; for he is sure to call attention to himself. It is not easy to decide in theory how far and to what extent a man may go before he becomes blameworthy, but neither is it easy to define in theory anything else in the region of the senses; such things depend on circumstances, and our judgment of them depends on our perception.

REVIEW AND DISCUSSION QUESTIONS

1. What is the end or function of human beings, according to Aristotle?
2. What is happiness, according to Aristotle? Why is it the supreme good?
3. Why does Aristotle reject the pursuit of money or pleasure as the key to happiness?
4. Explain Aristotle's understanding of the nature of virtue and its connection with habit.
5. Explain the theory of the virtues as a mean between extremes. Give examples of the virtues.
6. Do you agree that happiness (or well-being) and virtue are connected? If not, what is the basis of happiness?

Leviathan

Thomas Hobbes

Thomas Hobbes was born in 1588 when the approach of the Spanish Armada was threatening Britain. "Fear and I were born twins," he would later say, emphasizing his conviction that the need for security was the foundation of society and the basis of political obligation. He lived during a critical and difficult period of English history, which included struggles over the traditional authority of the church and emerging role of modern science. He also saw radical political change, including the absolutism of the Stuart monarchy, the English civil war, Cromwell, and the restoration of monarchy. He died just before Constitutional government won its final victory. Hobbes served as tutor for Charles II, who gave Hobbes a pension after Charles was restored to throne. Hobbes was sent into exile, condemned in the House of Commons, and, even after he died, his books were burned at Oxford. He was suspected of atheism, and, perhaps most importantly, he rejected the divine basis of political authority. God, he said, is beyond rational understanding; we can only know he exists as the first cause of the universe. Hobbes lived until the age of ninety-one, enjoying a life of travel, study, polemical controversy, and literary and philosophical activity. He was personally temperate, lively, and a loyal friend; he played tennis until the age of seventy-five and attributed his lifelong good health to exercise and singing in bed. He wrote on a variety of subjects, but his most famous work by far is *Leviathan*, published in 1691.

Hobbes was heavily influenced by the new, Galilean scientific method and thought that physical laws could account for human behavior, just as they do all other phenomena. He sought to understand man (and politics) in accord with the new scientific methods.

Just before the selection reprinted here, Hobbes argued that the world, including human beings, is comprised of material particles. Minds, he argued, are therefore no different from bodies; human "motion" such as walking, speaking, and other acts are caused by our desires, appetites, and aversions. Turning to politics and morality, Hobbes next discusses how reason and the human condition induce people to leave a "state of nature" and agree to be ruled by a common power strong enough to enforce our contracts and ensure peace. Morality is, therefore, a form of convention, agreed to by all in order to avoid the war of all against all. Without an agreement, and the threat of harm imposed by the sovereign, there can be neither morality nor justice. Power and threats are the necessary bases of all obligations.

THE FIRST PART: OF MAN

Good. Evil. . . . . Whatsoever is the object of any man's appetite or desire, that is it which he for his part calleth *good:* and the object of his hate and aversion, *evil;* and of his contempt, *vile* and *inconsiderable.* For these words of good, evil, and contemptible, are ever used with relation to the person that useth them: there being nothing simply and absolutely so; nor any common rule of good and evil, to be taken from the nature of the objects themselves; but from the person of the man, where there is no commonwealth; or, in a commonwealth, from the person that representeth it; or from an arbitrator or judge, whom men disagreeing shall by consent set up, and make his sentence the rule thereof. . . .

Deliberation.   When in the mind of man, appetites, and aversions, hopes, and fears, concern-

From Thomas Hobbes, *Leviathan* (1691).

ing one and the same thing, arise alternately; and divers good and evil consequences of the doing, or omitting the thing propounded, come successively into our thoughts; so that sometimes we have an appetite to it; sometimes an aversion from it; sometimes hope to be able to do it; sometimes despair, or fear to attempt it; the whole sum of desires, aversions, hopes and fears continued till the thing be either done, or thought impossible, is that we call DELIBERATION. . . .

The Will.   In *deliberation,* the last appetite, or aversion, immediately adhering to the action, or to the omission thereof, is that we call the WILL; the act, not the faculty, of *willing.* And beasts that have *deliberation,* must necessarily also have *will.* The definition of the *will,* given commonly by the Schools, that it is a *rational appetite,* is not good. For if it were, then could there be no voluntary act against reason. For a *voluntary act* is that, which proceedeth from the *will,* and no other. But if instead of a rational appetite, we shall say an appetite resulting from a precedent deliberation, then the definition is the same that I have given here. *Will* therefore *is the last appetite in deliberating.* . . .

By this it is manifest, that not only actions that have their beginning from covetousness, ambition, lust, or other appetites to the thing propounded; but also those that have their beginning from aversion, or fear of those consequences that follow the omission, are *voluntary actions.* . . .

Felicity.   *Continual success* in obtaining those things which a man from time to time desireth, that is to say, continual prospering, is that men call FELICITY; I mean the felicity of this life. For there is no such thing as perpetual tranquility of mind, while we live here; because life itself is but motion, and can never be without desire, nor without fear, no more than without sense. . . .

Of the Natural Condition of Mankind as Concerning Their Felicity and Misery

Men by Nature Equal.   Nature hath made men so equal, in the faculties of the body, and mind; as that though there be found one man sometimes manifestly stronger in body, or of quicker mind than another; yet when all is reckoned together, the difference between man, and man, is not so consider-

able, as that one man can thereupon claim to himself any benefit, to which another may not pretend, as well as he. For as to the strength of body, the weakest has strength enough to kill the strongest, either by secret machination, or by confederacy with others, that are in the same danger with himself.

And as to the faculties of the mind, setting aside the arts grounded upon words, and especially that skill of proceeding upon general, and infallible rules, called science; which very few have, and but in few things; as being not a native faculty, born with us: nor attained, as prudence, while we look after somewhat else, I find yet a greater equality amongst men, than that of strength. For prudence, is but experience; which equal time, equally bestows on all men, in those things they equally apply themselves unto. That which may perhaps make such equality incredible, is but a vain conceit of one's own wisdom, which almost all men think they have in a greater degree, than the vulgar; that is, than all men but themselves, and a few others, whom by fame, or for concurring with themselves, they approve.

From Equality Proceeds Diffidence.   From this equality of ability, ariseth equality of hope in the attaining of our ends. And therefore if any two men desire the same thing, which nevertheless they cannot both enjoy, they become enemies; and in the way to their end, which is principally their own conservation, and sometimes their delectation only, endeavor to destroy, or subdue one another. And from hence it comes to pass, that where an invader hath no more to fear, than another man's single power; if one plant, sow, build, or possess a convenient seat, others may probably be expected to come prepared with forces united, to dispossess, and deprive him, not only of the fruit of his labour, but also of his life, or liberty. And the invader again is in the like danger of another.

From Diffidence War.   And from this diffidence of one another, there is no way for any man to secure himself, so reasonable, as anticipation; that is, by force, or wiles, to master the persons of all men he can, so long, till he see no other power great enough to endanger him: and this is no more than his own conservation requireth, and is generally allowed. Also because there be some, that taking pleasure in contemplating their own power in the acts of conquest, which they pursue farther than their security requires; if others, that otherwise would be glad to be at ease within modest bounds, should not by invasion increase their power, they would not be able, long time, by standing only on their defence, to subsist. And by consequence, such augmentation of dominion over men being necessary to a man's conservation, it ought to be allowed him.

Again, men have no pleasure, but on the contrary a great deal of grief, in keeping company, where there is no power able to over-awe them all. For every man looketh that his companion should value him, at the same rate he sets upon himself: and upon all signs of contempt, or undervaluing, naturally endeavors, as far as he dares, (which amongst them that have no common power to keep them in quiet, is far enough to make them destroy each other), to extort a greater value from his contemners, by damage; and from others, by the example.

So that in the nature of man, we find three principal causes of quarrel. First, competition; secondly, diffidence; thirdly, glory.

The first, maketh men invade for gain; the second, for safety; and the third, for reputation. The first use violence, to make themselves masters of other men's persons, wives, children, and cattle; the second, to defend them, the third, for trifles, as a word, a smile, a different opinion, and any other sign of undervalue, either direct in their persons, or by reflection in their kindred, their friends, their nation, their profession, or their name.

Out of Civil States, There Is Always War of Every One Against Every One.

Hereby it is manifest, that during the time men live without a common power to keep them all in awe, they are in that condition which is called war; and such a war, as is of every man, against every man. For WAR, consisteth not in battle only, or the act of fighting; but in a tract of time, wherein the will to contend by battle is sufficiently known: and therefore the notion of *time,* is to be considered in the nature of war; as it is in the nature of weather. For as the nature of foul weather, lieth not in a shower or two of rain; but in an inclination thereto of many days together: so the nature of war, consisteth not in actual fighting; but in the known disposition thereto, during all the time there is no assurance to the contrary. All other time is PEACE.

The Incommodities of Such a War.

Whatsoever therefore is consequent to a time of war, where every man is enemy to every man; the same is consequent to the time, wherein men live without other security, than what their own strength, and their own invention shall furnish them withal. In such condition, there is no place for industry; because the fruit thereof is uncertain: and consequently no culture of the earth; no navigation, nor use of the commodities that may be imported by sea; no commodious building; no instruments of moving, and removing, such things as require much force; no knowledge of the face of the earth; no account of time; no arts; no letters; no society; and which is worst of all, continual fear, and danger of violent death; and the life of man, solitary, poor, nasty, brutish, and short.

It may seem strange to some man, that has not well weighed these things; that nature should thus dissociate, and render men apt to invade, and destroy one another: and he may therefore, not trusting to this inference, made from the passions, desire perhaps to have the same confirmed by experience. Let him therefore consider with himself, when taking a journey, he arms himself, and seeks to go well accompanied; when going to sleep, he locks his doors; when even in his house he locks his chests; and this when he knows there be laws, and public officers, armed, to revenge all injuries shall be done him; what opinion he has of his fellow-subjects, when he rides armed; of his fellow citizens, when he locks his doors; and of his children, and servants, when he locks his chests. Does he not there as much accuse mankind by his actions, as I do by my words? But neither of us accuse man's nature in it. The desires, and other passions of man, are in themselves no sin. No more are the actions, that proceed from those passions, till they know a law that forbids them: which till laws be made they cannot know: nor can any law be made, till they have agreed upon the person that shall make it.

It may peradventure be thought, there was never such a time, nor condition of war as this; and I believe it was never generally so, over all the world: but there are many places, where they live so now. For the savage people in many places of America, except the government of small families, the concord whereof dependeth on natural lust, have no government at all; and live at this day in that brutish manner, as I said before. Howsoever, it may be perceived what manner of life there would be, where there were no common power to fear, by the manner of life, which men that have formerly lived under a peaceful government, use to degenerate into, in a civil war.

But though there had never been any time, wherein particular men were in a condition of war one against another; yet in all times, kings, and persons of sovereign authority, because of their independency, are in continual jealousies, and in the state and posture of gladiators; having their weapons pointing, and their eyes fixed on one another; that is, their forts, garrisons, and guns upon the frontiers of their kingdoms; and continual spies upon their neighbours; which is a posture of war. But because they uphold thereby, the industry of their subjects; there does not follow from it, that misery, which accompanies the liberty of particular men.

In Such a War Nothing Is Unjust. To this war of every man, against every man, this also is consequent; that nothing can be unjust. The notions of right and wrong, justice and injustice have there no place. Where there is no common power, there is no law: where no law, no injustice. Force, and fraud, are in war the two cardinal virtues. Justice, and injustice are none of the faculties neither of the body, nor mind. If they were, they might be in a man that were alone in the world, as well as his senses, and passions. They are qualities, that relate to men in society, not in solitude. It is consequent also to the same condition, that there be no propriety, no dominion, no *mine* and *thine* distinct; but only that to be every man's, that he can get: and for so long, as he can keep it. And thus much for the ill condition, which man by mere nature is actually placed in; though with a possibility to come out of it, consisting partly in the passions, partly in his reason.

The Passions That Incline Men to Peace. The passions that incline men to peace, are fear of death; desire of such things as are necessary to commodious living; and a hope by their industry to obtain them. And reason suggesteth convenient articles of peace, upon which men may be drawn to agreement. These articles, are they, which otherwise are called the Laws of Nature: whereof I shall speak more particularly [below].

Of the First and Second Natural Laws, and of Contracts

Right of Nature What. The RIGHT OF NATURE, which writers commonly call *jus naturale,* is the liberty each man hath, to use his own power, as he will himself, for the preservation of his own nature; that is to say, of his own life; and consequently, of doing any thing, which in his own judgment, and reason, he shall conceive to be the aptest means thereunto.

Liberty What. By LIBERTY, is understood, according to the proper signification of the word, the absence of external impediments: which impediments, may oft take away part of a man's power to do what he would; but cannot hinder him from using the power left him, according as his judgment, and reason shall dictate to him.

A Law of Nature What. Difference of Right and Law. A LAW OF NATURE, *lex naturalis,* is a precept or general rule, found out by reason, by which a man is forbidden to do that, which is destructive of his life, or taketh away the means of preserving the same; and to omit that, by which he thinketh it may be best preserved. . . .

Naturally Every Man Has Right to Every Thing. The Fundamental Law of Nature. And because the condition of man, as hath been declared [above], is a condition of war of every one against every one; in which case every one is governed by his own reason; and there is nothing he can make use of, that may not be a help unto him, in preserving his life against his enemies; it followeth, that in such a condition, every man has a right to every thing; even to one another's body. And therefore, as long as this natural right of every man to every thing endureth, there can be no security to any man, how strong or wise soever he be, of living out the time, which nature ordinarily alloweth men to live. And consequently it is a precept, or general rule of reason, *that every man, ought to endeavor peace, as far as he has hope of obtaining it; and when he cannot obtain it, that he may seek, and use, all helps, and advantages of war. . . .*

The Second Law of Nature. From this fundamental law of nature, by which men are commanded to endeavor peace, is derived this second law; *that a man be willing, when others are so too, as far-forth, as for peace, and defence of himself he shall think it necessary, to lay down this right to all things; and be contented with so much liberty against other men, as he would allow other men against himself.* For as long as every man holdeth this right, of doing any thing he liketh; so long are all men in the condition of war. But if other men will not lay down their right, as well as he; then there is no reason for anyone to divest himself of his: for that wereto expose himself to prey, which no man is bound to, rather than to dispose himself to peace. . . .

Not All Rights Are Alienable. Whensoever a man tranferreth his right, or renounceth it; it is either in consideration of some right reciprocally transferred to himself; or for some other good he hopeth for thereby. For it is a voluntary act: and of the voluntary acts of every man, the object is some *good to himself.* And therefore there be some rights, which no man can be understood by any words, or other signs, to have abandoned, or transferred. As first a man cannot lay down the right of resisting them, that assault him by force, to take away his life; because he cannot be understood to aim thereby, at any good to himself. The same may be said of wounds, and chains, and imprisonment; because there is no benefit consequent to such patience; as there is to the patience of suffering another to be wounded, or imprisoned. . . .

Covenants of Mutual Trust, When Invalid. If a covenant be made, wherein neither of the parties perform presently, but trust one another; in the condition of mere nature, which is a condition of war of every man against every man, upon any reasonable suspicion, it is void; but if there be a common power set over them both, with right and force sufficient to compel performance, it is not void. For he that performeth first, has no assurance

the other will perform after; because the bonds of words are too weak to bridle men's ambition, avarice, anger, and other passions, without the fear of some coercive power; which in the condition of mere nature, where all men are equal, and judges of the justness of their own fears, cannot possibly be supposed. And therefore he which performeth first does but betray himself to his enemy; contrary to the right, he can never abandon, of defending his life, and means of living. . . .

Covenants Extorted by Fear Are Valid. Covenants entered into by fear, in the condition of mere nature, are obligatory. For example, if I covenant to pay a ransom, or service for my life, to an enemy; I am bound by it: for it is a contract, wherein one receiveth the benefit of life; the other is to receive money, or service for it; and consequently, where no other law, as in the condition of mere nature, forbiddeth the performance, the covenant is valid. . . .

Of Other Laws of Nature

The Third Law of Nature, Justice. From that law of nature, by which we are obliged to transfer to another, such rights, as being retained, hinder the peace of mankind, there followeth a third; which is this, *that men perform their covenants made:* without which, covenants are in vain, and but empty words; and the right of all men to all things remaining, we are still in the condition of war.

Justice and Injustice What. And in this law of nature, consisteth the fountain and original of JUSTICE. For where no covenant hath preceded, there hath no right been transferred, and every man has right to every thing; and consequently, no action can be unjust. But when a covenant is made, then to break it is unjust: and the definition of INJUSTICE, is no other than *the not performance of covenant.* And whatsoever is not unjust, is *just.*

Justice and Propriety Begin With the Constitution of Commonwealth. But because covenants of mutual trust, where there is a fear of not performance on either part, as hath been said in the former chapter, are invalid; though the original of justice be the making of covenants; yet injustice actually there can be none, till the cause of such fear be taken away; which while men are in the natural condition of war, cannot be done. Therefore before the names of just, and unjust can have place, there must be some coercive power, to compel men equally to the performance of their covenants, by the terror of some punishment, greater than the benefit they expect by the breach of their covenant; and to make good that propriety, which by mutual contract men acquire, in recompense of the universal right they abandon: and such power there is none before the erection of a commonwealth. . . .

Justice Not Contrary to Reason.   The fool hath said in his heart, there is no such thing as justice; and sometimes also with his tongue: seriously alleging, that every man's conservation, and contentment, being committed to his own care, there could be no reason, why every man might not do what he thought conduced thereunto. He does not therein deny, that there are covenants; and that they are sometimes broken, sometimes kept; but he questioneth whether injustice, taking away the fear of God, may not sometimes stand with that reason, which dictateth to every man his own good. . . .

[I say that] in a condition of war, wherein every man to every man, for want of a common power to keep them all in awe, is an enemy, there is no man who can hope by his own strength, or wit, to defend himself from destruction without the help of confederates; where every one expects the same defence by the confederation, that any one else does: and therefore he which declares he thinks it reason to deceive those that help him, can in reason expect no other means of safety than what can be had from his own single power. He therefore that breaketh his covenant, and consequently declareth that he thinks he may with reason do so, cannot be received into any society, that unite themselves for peace and defence, but by the error of them that receive him; nor when he is received, be retained in it, without seeing the danger of their error; which errors a man cannot reasonably reckon upon as the means of his security: and therefore if he be left, or cast out of society he perisheth; and if he live in society, it is by the errors of other men, which he could not foresee, nor reckon upon; and consequently against the reason of his preservation. . . .

THE SECOND PART: OF COMMONWEALTH

Of the Causes, Generation, and Definition of a Commonwealth

The End of Commonwealth, Particular Security. The final cause, end, or design of men, who naturally love liberty, and dominion over others, in the introduction of that restraint upon themselves, in which we see them live in commonwealths, is the foresight of their own preservation, and of a more contented life thereby; that is to say, of getting themselves out from that miserable condition of war, which is necessarily consequent, as hath been shown, to the natural passions of men, when there is no visible power to keep them in awe, and tie them by fear of punishment to the performance of their covenants, and observation of those laws of nature set down [above].

Which Is Not to Be Had from the Law of Nature. For the laws of nature, as *justice, equality, modesty, mercy,* and, in sum, *doing to others, as we would be done to,* of themselves, without the terror of some power, to cause them to be observed, are contrary to our natural passions, that carry us to partiality, pride, revenge, and the like. And covenants, without the sword, are but words, and of no strength to secure a man at all. Therefore notwithstanding the laws of nature (which every one hath then kept, when he has the will to keep them, when he can do it safely) if there be no power erected or not great enough for our security; every man will, and may lawfully rely on his own strength and art, for caution against all other men. . . . For if we could suppose a great multitude of men to consent in the observation of justice, and other laws of nature, without a common power to keep them all in awe; we might as well suppose all mankind to do the same; and then there neither would be, nor need to be any civil government, or commonwealth at all; because there would be peace without subjection. . . .

The Generation of a Commonwealth. The Definition of a Commonwealth.   The only way to erect such a common power, as may be able to defend them from the invasion of foreigners, and the injuries of one another, and thereby to secure them in such sort, as that by their own industry, and by the fruits of the earth, they may nourish themselves and live contentedly; is, to confer all their power and strength upon one man, or upon one assembly of men, that may reduce all their wills, by plurality of voices, unto one will: which is as much as to say, to appoint one man, or assembly of men, to bear their person; and every one to own, and acknowledge himself to be author of whatsoever he that so beareth their person, shall act, or cause to be acted, in those things which concern the common peace and safety; and therein to submit their wills, every one to his will, and their judgments, to his judgment. This is more than consent, or concord; it is a real unity of them all, in one and the same person, made by covenant of every man with every man, in such manner, as if every man should say to every man, *I authorize and give up my right of governing myself, to this man, or to this assembly of men, on this condition, that thou give up thy right to him, and authorize all his actions in like manner.* This done, the multitude so united in one person, is called a COMMONWEALTH, in Latin CIVITAS. This is the generation of that great LEVIATHAN, or rather, to speak more reverently, of that *mortal god,* to which we owe under the *immortal God,* our peace and defence. For by this authority, given him by every particular man in the commonwealth, he hath the use of so much power and strength conferred on him, that by terror thereof, he is enabled to form the wills of them all, to peace at home, and mutual aid against their enemies abroad. And in him consisteth the essence of the commonwealth; which, to define it, is *one person, of whose acts a great multitude, by mutual covenants one with another, have made themselves every one the author, to the end he may use the strength and means of them all, as he shall think expedient, for their peace and common defence.*

Sovereign, and Subject, What. And he that carrieth this person, is called SOVEREIGN, and said to have *sovereign power;* and every one besides, his SUBJECT.

Of the Liberty of Subjects Liberty, What. LIBERTY, or FREEDOM, signifieth, properly, the absence of opposition; by opposition, I mean external impediments of motion; and may be applied no less to irrational, and inanimate creatures, than to rational. For whatsoever is so tied, or environed, as it cannot move but within a certain space, which space is determined by the opposition of some external body, we say it hath not liberty to go further. And so of all living creatures, whilst they are imprisoned, or restrained, with walls, or chains; and of the water while it is kept in by banks, or vessels, that otherwise would spread itself into a larger space, we use to say, they are not at liberty, to move in such manner, as without those external impediments they would. But when the impediment of motion, is in the constitution of the thing itself, we use not to say; it wants the liberty; but the power to move; as when a stone lieth still, or a man is fastened to his bed by sickness.

What It Is to Be Free. And according to this proper, and generally received meaning of the word, a FREEMAN, *is he that in those things, which by his strength and wit he is able to do, is not hindered to do what he has a will to....* So when we *speak freely,* it is not the liberty of voice, or pronunciation, but of the man, whom no law hath obliged to speak otherwise than he did. Lastly, from the use of the word *free-will,* no liberty can be inferred of the will, desire, or inclination, but the liberty of the man; which consisteth in this, that he finds no stop, in doing what he has the will, desire, or inclination to do.

Fear and Liberty Consistent. Fear and liberty are consistent; as when a man throweth his goods into the sea for *fear* the ship should sink, he doth it nevertheless very willingly, and may refuse to do it if he will: it is therefore the action of one that was *free:* so a man sometimes pays his debt, only for *fear* of imprisonment, which because nobody hindered him from detaining, was the action of a man at *liberty.* And generally all actions which men do in commonwealths, for *fear* of the law, are actions, which the doers had *liberty* to omit.

Liberty and Necessity Consistent. Liberty, and *necessity* are consistent: as in the water, that hath not only *liberty,* but a *necessity* of descending by the channel; so likewise in the actions which men voluntarily do: which, because they proceed from their will, proceed from *liberty;* and yet, because every act of man's will, and every desire, and inclination proceedeth from some cause, and that from another cause, in a continual chain, whose first link is the hand of God the first of all causes, proceed from *necessity*. So that to him that could see the connexion of those causes, the *necessity* of all men's voluntary actions, would appear manifest.

REVIEW AND DISCUSSION QUESTIONS

1. Hobbes is often described as a "psychological egoist." What might that mean, given his understanding of human nature and motivation?
2. How does Hobbes understand happiness?
3. Describe the "state of nature." When does Hobbes think it would arise? What would life be like under it?
4. What are the "laws of nature"?
5. Explain how all of morality, not just politics, may be understood as an agreement for mutual advantage.
6. How does Hobbes respond to the "fool" who claims that justice is contrary to reason and that a rational person would act unjustly?
7. What is freedom, according to Hobbes? Do people have both freedom and free will? Explain.
8. Does Hobbes think morality applies in a state of war? Evaluate his answer, as you understand it. Why do you agree or disagree?

An Enquiry Concerning the Principles of Morals

David Hume

David Hume (1711–1776) was a towering figure of the Scottish Enlightenment. He lived in Edinburgh where he wrote on a wide array of subjects including epistemology, history, religion, science, ethics, and politics. Hume attended Edinburgh University until he was about fifteen. By the age of twenty-eight, he had already published his massive, critical study of knowledge and morality titled *A Treatise of Human Nature*. Deeply disappointed by the book's reception, which, he wrote, "fell dead born from the press," Hume rewrote it as *An Enquiry Concerning Human Understanding* (1748) and *An Enquiry Concerning the Principles of Morals* (1751), excerpts of which are reprinted here. Hume himself described his *Enquiry* as "incomparably the best" of all his writings. He subsequently published *Political Discourses* (1752) and *History of England* (1754), which won him wide acclaim.

Hume was an amiable, moderate man whose company was widely sought. His philosophy, however, was radically critical. Taking his lead from modern science, especially Newton, Hume sought

From David Hume, *An Enquiry Concerning the Principles of Morals* (1751).

to use the tools of philosophical empiricism to understand human knowledge, religion, morality, and politics. As an empiricist, Hume believed that anything that can be present to the mind (which he termed *perceptions*) are either impressions or ideas. *Impressions* occur whenever we feel an emotion or have an image of an external object; *ideas* are present whenever we reflect on impressions we have had. Ideas are therefore weaker than impressions, and all of our ideas are derived from sense impressions.

Rejecting the views of other Scottish philosophers, including his teacher, Francis Hutcheson, that human beings have a distinct "moral sense" enabling them to perceive right and wrong, Hume contends instead that morality rests finally on sentiment or feeling. It is, he argues, utility that provides the foundation for the two cardinal virtues of benevolence and justice. The social contract, he claims, is a myth that gets in the way of a clear understanding of the true origins of morality. Justice, for example, is best understood entirely instrumentally, as a means to promote utility.

OF THE GENERAL PRINCIPLES OF MORALS

There has been a controversy started of late, much better worth examination, concerning the general foundation of Morals; whether they be derived from Reason, or from Sentiment; whether we attain the knowledge of them by a chain of argument and induction, or by an immediate feeling and finer internal sense; whether, like all sound judgment of truth and falsehood, they should be the same to every rational intelligent being; or whether, like the perception of beauty and deformity, they be founded entirely on the particular fabric and constitution of the human species.

The ancient philosophers, though they often affirm, that virtue is nothing but conformity to reason, yet, in general, seem to consider morals as deriving their existence from taste and sentiment. On the other hand, our modern enquirers, though they also talk much of the beauty of virtue, and deformity of vice, yet have commonly endeavoured to account for these distinctions by metaphysical reasonings, and by deductions from the most abstract principles of the understanding. . . .

It must be acknowledged, that both sides of the question are susceptible of specious arguments. Moral distinctions, it may be said, are discernible by pure *reason*: else, whence the many disputes that reign in common life, as well as in philosophy, with regard to this subject: the long chain of proofs often produced on both sides; the examples cited, the authorities appealed to, the analogies employed, the fallacies detected, the inferences drawn, and the several conclusions adjusted to their proper principles. Truth is disputable: not taste: what exists in the nature of things is the standard of our judgement; what each man feels within himself is the standard of sentiment. . . .

On the other hand, those who would resolve all moral determinations into sentiment, may endeavor to show, that it is impossible for reason ever to draw conclusions of this nature. To virtue, say they, it belongs to be *amiable* and vice *odious*. This forms their very nature or essence. But can reason or argumentation distribute these different epithets to any subjects, and pronounce beforehand, that this must produce love, and that hatred? Or what other reason can we ever assign for these affections, but the original fabric and formation of the human mind, which is naturally adapted to receive them?

The end of all moral speculations is to teach us our duty; and, by proper representations of the deformity of vice and beauty of virtue, beget correspondent habits, and engage us to avoid the one, and embrace the other. But is this ever to be expected from inferences and conclusions of the understanding, which of themselves have no hold of the affections or set in motion the active powers of men? . . .

What is honourable, what is fair, what is becoming, what is noble, what is generous, takes possession of the heart, and animates us to embrace and maintain it. What is intelligible, what is evident, what is probable, what is true, procures only the cool asset of the understanding; and gratifying a speculative curiosity, puts an end to our researches.

Extinguish all the warm feelings and prepossessions in favour of virtue, and all disgust or aversion to vice: render men totally indifferent towards these distinctions; and morality is no longer a practical study, nor has any tendency to regulate our lives and actions.

These arguments on each side (and many more might be produced) are so plausible, that I am apt to suspect, they may, the one as well as the other, be solid and satisfactory, and that *reason* and *sentiment* concur in almost all moral determinations and conclusions. The final sentence, it is probable, which pronounces characters and actions amiable or odious, praiseworthy or blameable; that which stamps on them the mark of honour or infamy, approbation or censure; that which renders morality an active principle and constitutes virtue our happiness and vice our misery; it is probable, I say, that this final sentence depends on some internal sense or feeling, which nature has made universal in the whole species. For what else can have an influence of this nature? But in order to pave the way for such a sentiment, and give a proper discernment of its object, it is often necessary, we find, that much reasoning should precede, that nice distinctions be made, just conclusions drawn, distant comparisons formed, complicated relations examined, and general facts fixed and ascertained. . . .

But though this question, concerning the general principles of morals, be curious and important, it is needless for us, at present, to employ farther care in our researches concerning it. For if we can be so happy, in the course of this enquiry, as to discover the true origin of morals, it will then easily appear how far either sentiment or reason enters into all determinations of this nature. In order to attain this purpose, we shall endeavor to follow a very simple method: we shall analyse that complication of mental qualities, which form what, in common life, we call Personal Merit: we shall consider every attribute of the mind, which renders a man an object either of esteem and affection, or of hatred and contempt; every habit or sentiment or faculty, which, if ascribed to any person, implies either praise or blame, and may enter into any panegyric or satire of his character and manners. . . .

We shall begin our enquiry on this head by the consideration of the social virtues, Benevolence and Justice. The explication of them will probably give us an opening by which the others may be accounted for.

OF BENEVOLENCE

Part I

It may be esteemed, perhaps, a superfluous task to prove, that the benevolent or softer affections are estimable; and wherever they appear, engage the approbation and good-will of mankind. The epithets *sociable, good-natured, humane, merciful, grateful, friendly, generous, beneficent,* or their equivalents, are known in all languages, and universally express the highest merit, which *human nature* is capable of attaining. Where these amiable qualities are attended with birth and power and eminent abilities, and display themselves in the good government or useful instruction of mankind, they seem even to raise the possessors of them above the rank of *human nature,* and make them approach in some measure to the divine. Exalted capacity, undaunted courage, prosperous success; these may only expose a hero or politician to the envy and ill-will of the public: but as soon as the praises are added of humane and beneficent; when instances are displayed of lenity, tenderness or friendship; envy itself is silent, or joins the general voice of approbation and applause. . . .

[N]o qualities are more intitled to the general good-will and approbation of mankind than beneficence and humanity, friendship and gratitude, natural affection and public spirit, or whatever proceeds from a tender sympathy with others, and a generous concern for our kind and species. These wherever they appear seem to transfuse themselves, in a manner, into each beholder, and to call forth, in their own behalf, the same favourable and affectionate sentiments, which they exert on all around.

Part II

We may observe that, in displaying the praises of any humane, beneficent man, there is one circumstance which never fails to be amply insisted on, namely, the happiness and satisfaction, derived to society from his intercourse and good offices. To his parents, we are apt to say, he endears himself by his pious attachment and duteous care still more than by the connexions of nature. His children never feel his authority, but when employed for their advantage. With him, the ties of love are consolidated by beneficence and friendship. The ties of friendship approach, in a fond observance of each obliging office, to those of love and inclination. His domestics and dependants have in him a sure resource; and no longer dread the power of fortune, but so far as she exercises it over him. From him the hungry receive food, the naked clothing, the ignorant and slothful skill and industry. Like the sun, an inferior minister of providence he cheers, invigorates, and sustains the surrounding world.

If confined to private life, the sphere of his activity is narrower; but his influence is all benign and gentle. If exalted into a higher station, mankind and posterity reap the fruit of his labours.

As these topics of praise never fail to be employed, and with success, where we would inspire esteem for any one; may it not thence be concluded, that the utility, resulting from the social virtues, forms, at least, a *part* of their merit, and is one source of that approbation and regard so universally paid to them?

Upon the whole, then, it seems undeniable, *that* nothing can bestow more merit on any human creature than the sentiment of benevolence in an eminent degree; and *that* a *part*, at least, of its merit arises from its tendency to promote the interests of our species, and bestow happiness on human society. We carry our view into the salutary consequences of such a character and disposition; and what ever has so benign an influence, and forwards so desirable an end, is beheld with complacency and pleasure. The social virtues are never regarded without their beneficial tendencies, nor viewed as barren and unfruitful. The happiness of mankind, the order of society, the harmony of families, the mutual support of friends, are always considered as the result of their gentle dominion over the breasts of men. . . .

OF JUSTICE

Part I

That Justice is so useful to society, and consequently that *part* of its merit, at least, must arise from that consideration, it would be a superfluous undertaking to prove. That public utility is the *sole*

origin of justice, and that reflections on the beneficial consequences of this virtue are the *sole* foundation of its merit; this proposition, being more curious and important, will better deserve our examination and enquiry.

Let us suppose that nature has bestowed on the human race such profuse *abundance* of all *external* conveniences, that, without any uncertainty in the event, without any care or industry on our part, every individual finds himself fully provided with whatever his most voracious appetites can want, or luxurious imagination wish or desire. His natural beauty, we shall suppose, surpasses all acquired ornaments: the perpetual clemency of the seasons renders useless all clothes or covering; the raw herbage affords him the most delicious fare; the clear fountain, the richest beverage. No laborious occupation required: no tillage: no navigation. Music, poetry, and contemplation form his sole business: conversation, mirth, and friendship his sole amusement.

It seems evident that, in such a happy state, every other social virtue would flourish, and receive tenfold increase; but the cautious, jealous virtue of justice would never once have been dreamed of. For what purpose make a partition of goods, where every one has already more than enough? Why give rise to property, where there cannot possibly be any injury? Why call this object mine, when upon the seizing of it by another, I need but stretch out my hand to possess myself to what is equally valuable? Justice, in that case, being totally useless, would be an idle ceremonial, and could never possibly have place in the catalogue of virtues.

We see, even in the present necessitous condition of mankind, that, wherever any benefit is bestowed by nature in an unlimited abundance, we leave it always in common among the whole human race, and make no subdivisions of right and property. Water and air, though the most necessary of all objects, are not challenged as the property of individuals; nor can any man commit injustice by the most lavish use and enjoyment of these blessings. In fertile extensive countries, with few inhabitants, land is regarded on the same footing. . . .

Again; suppose, that, though the necessities of human race continue the same as at present, yet the mind is so enlarged, and so replete with friendship and generosity, that every man has the utmost tenderness for every man, and feels no more concern for his own interest than for that of his fellows; it seems evident, that the use of justice would, in this case, be suspended by such an extensive benevolence, nor would the divisions and barriers of property and obligation have ever been thought of. Why should I bind another, by a deed or promise, to do me any good office, when I know that he is already prompted, by the strongest inclination, to seek my happiness, and would, of himself, perform the desired service; except the hurt, he thereby receives, be greater than the benefit accruing to me? In which case, he knows, that, from my innate humanity and friendship, I should be first to oppose myself to his impudent generosity. Why raise land marks between my neighbour's field and mine, when my heart has made no division between our interests; but shares all his joys and sorrows with the same force and vivacity as if originally my own? Every man, upon this supposition, being a second self to another, would trust all his interests to the discretion of every man; without jealousy, without partition, without distinction. And the whole human race would form only one family; where all would lie in common, and be used freely, without regard to property; but cautiously too, with as entire regard to the necessities of each individual as if our own interests were most intimately concerned.

In the present disposition of the human heart, it would, perhaps, be difficult to find complete instances of such enlarged affections; but still we may observe, that the case of families approaches towards it; and the stronger the mutual benevolence is among the individuals, the nearer it approaches; till all distinction of property be, in a great measure, lost and confounded among them. Between married persons, the cement of friendship is by the laws supposed so strong as to abolish all division of possessions; and has often, in reality, the force ascribed to it. . . .

To make this truth more evident, let us reverse the foregoing suppositions; and carrying everything to the opposite extreme, consider what would be the effect of these new situations. Suppose a society to fall into such want of all common necessaries, that the utmost frugality and industry cannot preserve the greater number from perish-

ing, and the whole from extreme misery; it will readily, I believe, be admitted, that the strict laws of justice are suspended, in such a pressing emergence, and give place to the stronger motives of necessity and self-preservation. Is it any crime, after a shipwreck, to seize whatever means or instrument of safety one can lay hold of, without regard to former limitations of property? Or if a city besieged were perishing with hunger; can we imagine, that men will see any means of preservation before them, and lose their lives, from a scrupulous regard to what, in other situations, would be the rules of equity and justice? The use and tendency of that virtue is to procure happiness and security, by preserving order in society: but where the society is ready to perish from extreme necessity, no greater evil can be dreaded from violence and injustice; and every man may now provide for himself by all the means, which prudence can dictate, or humanity permit. . . .

Suppose likewise, that it should be a virtuous man's fate to fall into the society of ruffians, remote from the protection of laws and government; what conduct must he embrace in that melancholy situation? He sees such a desperate rapaciousness prevail; such a disregard to equity, such contempt of order, such stupid blindness to future consequences, as must immediately have the most tragical conclusion, and must terminate in destruction to the greater number, and in a total dissolution of society to the rest. He, meanwhile, can have no other expedient than to arm himself, to whomever the sword he seizes, or the buckler may belong: To make provision of all means of defence and security: And his particular regard to justice being no longer of use to his own safety or that of others, he must consult the dictates of self-preservation alone, without concern for those who no longer merit his care and attention. . . .

Thus, the rules of equity or justice depend entirely on the particular state and condition in which men are placed, and owe their origin and existence to that utility, which results to the public from their strict and regular observance. Reverse, in any considerable circumstance, the condition of men: Produce extreme abundance or extreme necessity: Implant in the human breast perfect moderation and humanity, or perfect rapaciousness and malice: By rendering justice totally *useless,* you thereby totally destroy its essence, and suspend its obligation upon mankind.

The common situation of society is a medium amidst all these extremes. We are naturally partial to ourselves, and to our friends; but are capable of learning the advantage resulting from a more equitable conduct. Few enjoyments are given us from the open and liberal hand of nature; but by art, labour, and industry, we can extract them in great abundance. Hence the ideas of property become necessary in all civil society: Hence justice derives its usefulness to the public: And hence alone arises its merit and moral obligation. . . .

Were the human species so framed by nature as that each individual possessed within himself every faculty, requisite both for his own preservation and for the propagation of his kind: Were all society and intercourse cut off between man and man, by the primary intention of the supreme Creator: It seems evident, that so solitary a being would be as much incapable of justice, as of social justice and conversation. . . .

But suppose the conjunction of the sexes to be established in nature, a family immediately arises; and particular rules being found requisite for its subsistence, these are immediately embraced; though without comprehending the rest of mankind within their prescriptions. Suppose that several families unite together into one society, which is totally disjoined from all others, the rules, which preserve peace and order, enlarge themselves to the utmost extent of that society; but becoming then entirely useless, lose their force when carried one step farther. But again suppose, that several distinct societies maintain a kind of intercourse for mutual convenience and advantage, the boundaries of justice still grow larger, in proportion to the largeness of men's views, and the force of their mutual connexions. History, experience, reason sufficiently instruct us in this natural progress of human sentiments, and in the gradual enlargement of our regards to justice, in proportion as we become acquainted with the extensive utility of that virtue.

Part II

If we examine the *particular* laws, by which justice is directed, and property determined; we shall still be presented with the same conclusion. The good of mankind is the only object of all these laws and regulations. Not only is it requisite, for the peace and interest of society, that men's possessions should be separated; but the rules, which we follow, in making the separation, are such as can best be contrived to serve farther the interests of society. . . . Render possessions ever so equal, men's different degrees of art, care, and industry will immediately break that equality. Or if you check these virtues, you reduce society to the most extreme indigence; and instead of preventing want and beggary in a few, render it unavoidable to the whole community. The most rigorous inquisition too is requisite to watch every inequality on its first appearance; and the most severe jurisdiction, to punish and redress it. But besides, that so much authority must soon degenerate into tyranny, and be exerted with great partialities; who can possibly be possessed of it, in such a situation as is here supposed? Perfect equality of possessions, destroying all subordination, weakens extremely the authority of magistracy, and must reduce all power nearly to a level, as well as property.

We may conclude, therefore, that, in order to establish laws for the regulation of property, we must be acquainted with the nature and situation of man; must reject appearances, which may be false, though specious; and must search for those rules, which are, on the whole, most *useful* and *beneficial*. Vulgar sense and slight experience are sufficient for this purpose; where men give not way to too selfish avidity, or too extensive enthusiasm.

Who sees not, for instance, that whatever is produced or improved by man's art or industry ought, for ever, to be secured to him, in order to give encouragement to such *useful* habits and accomplishments? That the property ought to also descend to children and relations, for the same *useful* purpose? That it may be alienated by consent, in order to beget that commerce and intercourse, which is so *beneficial* to human society? And that all contracts and promises ought carefully to be fulfilled, in order to secure mutual trust and confidence, by which the general *interest* of mankind is so much promoted?

Examine the writers on the laws of nature; and you will always find, that, whatever principles they set out with, they are sure to terminate here at last, and to assign, as the ultimate reason for every rule which they establish, the convenience and necessities of mankind. . . .

What is man's property? Anything which it is lawful for him, and for him alone, to use. *But what rule have we by which we can distinguish these objects?* Here we must have recourse to statutes, customs, precedents, analogies, and a hundred other circumstances; some of which are constant and inflexible, some variable and arbitrary. But the ultimate point, in which they all professedly terminate, is the interest and happiness of human society. Where this enters not into consideration, nothing can appear more whimsical, unnatural, and even superstitious, than all or more of the laws of justice and of property.

Those who ridicule vulgar superstitions, and expose the folly of particular regards to meats, days, places, postures, apparel, have an easy task; while they consider all the qualities and relations of the objects, and discover no adequate cause for that affection or antipathy, veneration of horror, which have so mighty an influence over a considerable part of mankind. A Syrian would have starved rather than taste pigeon: an Egyptian would not have approached bacon: But if these species of food be examined by the senses of sight, smell, or taste, or scrutinized by the sciences of chemistry, medicine, or physics, no difference is ever found between them and any other species, nor can that precise circumstance be pitched on, which may afford a just foundation for the religious passion. A fowl on Thursday is lawful food; on Friday abominable: Eggs in this house and in this diocese, are permitted during Lent; a hundred paces farther, to eat them is a damnable sin. This earth or building, yesterday was profane; today, by the muttering of certain words, it has become holy and sacred. . . .

But there is this material difference between *superstition* and *justice*, that the former is frivolous, useless, and burdensome; the latter is absolutely requisite to the well-being of mankind and existence of society. When we abstract from this circumstance (for it is too apparent ever to be overlooked) it must be confessed, that all regards to right and property, seem entirely without foundation, as much as the grossest and most vulgar superstition. Were the interests of society nowise concerned, it is as unintelligible why another's articulating certain sounds implying consent, should

change the nature of my actions with regard to a particular object, as why the reciting of a liturgy by a priest, in a certain habit and posture, should dedicate a heap of brick and timber, and render it, thenceforth and for ever, sacred.

These reflections are far from weakening the obligations of justice, or diminishing anything from the most sacred attention to property. On the contrary, such sentiments must acquire new force from the present reasoning. For what stronger foundation can be desired or conceived for any duty, than to observe, that human society, or even human nature, could not subsist without the establishment of it; and will still arrive at greater degrees of happiness and perfection, the more inviolable the regard is, which is paid to that duty? . . .

All birds of the same species in every age and country, built their nests alike: In this we see the force of instinct. Men, in different times and places, frame their houses differently: Here we perceive the influence of reason and custom. A like inference may be drawn from comparing the instinct of generation and the institution of property.

How great soever the variety of municipal laws, it must be confessed, that their chief outlines pretty regularly concur; because the purposes, to which they tend, are everywhere exactly similar. In like manner, all houses have a roof and walls, windows and chimneys; though diversified in their shape, figure, and materials. The purposes of the latter, directed to the conveniences of human life, discover not more plainly their origin from reason and reflection, than do those of the former, which points all to a like end. . . .

The convenience, or rather necessity, which leads to justice is so universal, and everywhere points so much to the same rules, that the habit takes place in all societies; and it is not without some scrutiny, that we are able to ascertain its true origin. The matter, however, is not so obscure, but that even in common life we have every moment recourse to the principle of public utility, and ask, *What must become of the world, if such practices prevail? How could society subsist under such disorders?* Were the distinction or separation of possessions entirely useless, can any one conceive, that it ever should have obtained in society?

Thus we seem, upon the whole, to have attained a knowledge of the force of that principle here insisted on, and can determine what degree of esteem or moral approbation may result from reflections on public interest and utility. The necessity of justice to the support of society is the sole foundation of that virtue; and since no moral excellence is more highly esteemed, we may conclude that this circumstance of usefulness has, in general, the strongest energy, and most entire command over our sentiments. . . .

WHY UTILITY PLEASES

Part I

It seems so natural a thought to ascribe to their utility the praise, which we bestow on the social virtues, that one would expect to meet with this principle everywhere in moral writers, as the chief foundation of their reasoning and enquiry. In common life, we may observe, that the circumstance of utility is always appealed to; nor is it supposed, that a greater eulogy can be given to any man, than to display his usefulness to the public, and enumerate the services, which he has performed to mankind and society. . . . A building, whose doors and windows were exact squares, would hurt the eye by that very proportion; as ill adapted to the figure of a human creature, for whose service the fabric was intended. What wonder then, that a man, whose habits and conduct are hurtful to society, and dangerous or pernicious to every one who has an intercourse with him, should, on that account, be an object of disapprobation, and communicate to every spectator the strongest sentiment of disgust and hatred. . . .

The social virtues must, therefore, be allowed to have a natural beauty and amiableness, which, at first, antecedent to all precept or education, recommends them to the esteem of uninstructed mankind, and engages their affections. And as the public utility of these virtues is the chief circumstance, whence they derive their merit, it follows, that the end, which they have a tendency to promote, must be some way agreeable to us, and take hold of some natural affection. It must please, either from considerations of self-interest, or from more generous motives and regards.

It has often been asserted, that, as every man has a strong connexion with society, and perceives the impossibility of his solitary subsistence, he becomes, on that account, favourable to all those habits or principles, which promote order in society, and insure to him the quiet possession of so inestimable a blessing. As much as we value our own happiness and welfare, as much must we applaud the practice of justice and humanity, by which alone the social confederacy can be maintained, and every man reap the fruits of mutual protection and assistance.

This deduction of morals from self-love, or a regard to private interest, is an obvious thought. . . . [Y]et is not this an affair to be decided by authority, and the voice of nature and experience seems plainly to oppose the selfish theory.

We frequently bestow praise on virtuous actions, performed in very distant ages and remote countries; where the utmost subtilty of imagination would not discover any appearance of self-interest, or find any connexion of our present happiness and security with events so widely separated from us.

A generous, a brave, a noble deed, performed by an adversary, commands our approbation; while in its consequences it may be acknowledged prejudicial to our particular interest. . . .

Usefulness is agreeable, and engages our approbation. This is a matter of fact, confirmed by daily observation. But, useful? For what? For somebody's interest, surely. Whose interest then? Not our own only: For our approbation frequently extends farther. It must, therefore, be the interest of those, who are served by the character of action approved of; and these we may conclude, however remote, are not totally indifferent to us. By opening up this principle, we shall discover one great source of moral distinctions.

Part II

. . . We have found instances, in which private interest was separate from public; in which it was even contrary: And yet we observed the moral sentiment to continue, notwithstanding this disjunction of interests. . . .

Have we any difficulty to comprehend the force of humanity and benevolence? Or to conceive, that the very aspect of happiness, joy, prosperity, gives pleasure; that of pain, suffering, sorrow, communicates uneasiness? The human countenance, says Horace, borrows smiles or tears from the human countenance. Reduce a person to solitude, and he loses all enjoyment, except either of the sensual or speculative kind; and that because the movements of his heart are not forwarded by correspondent movements in his fellow-creatures. The signs of sorrow and mourning, though arbitrary, affect us with melancholy; but the natural symptoms, tears and cries and groans, never fail to infuse compassion and uneasiness. And if the effects of misery touch us in so lively a manner; can we be supposed altogether insensible or indifferent towards its causes; when a malicious or treacherous character and behaviour are presented to us?

We enter, I shall suppose, into a convenient, warm, well-contrived apartment: We necessarily receive a pleasure from its very survey; because it presents us with the pleasing ideas of ease, satisfaction, and enjoyment. The hospitable, good-humoured, humane landlord appears. This circumstance surely must embellish the whole; nor can we easily forbear reflecting, with pleasure, on the satisfaction which results to every one from his intercourse and good-offices.

His whole family, by the freedom, ease, confidence, and calm enjoyment, diffused over their countenances, sufficiently express their happiness. I have a pleasing sympathy in the prospect of so much joy, and can never consider the source of it, without the most agreeable emotions.

He tells me, that an oppressive and powerful neighbour had attempted to dispossess him of his inheritance, and had long disturbed all his innocent and social pleasures. I feel an immediate indignation arise in me against such violence and injury.

But it is no wonder, he adds, that a private wrong should proceed from a man, who had enslaved provinces, depopulated cities, and made the field and scaffold stream with human blood. I am struck with horror at the prospect of so much misery, and am actuated by the strongest antipathy against its author.

In general, it is certain, that, wherever we go, whatever we reflect on or converse about, everything still presents us with the view of human happiness or misery, and excites in our breast a sympathetic movement of pleasure or uneasiness. In our serious occupations, in our careless amusements, this principle still exerts its active energy. . . . We surely take into consideration the happiness and misery of others, in weighing the several motives of action, and incline to the former, where no private regards draw us to seek our own promotion or advantage by the injury of our fellow-creatures. And if the principles of humanity are capable, in many instances, of influencing our actions, they must, at all times, have *some* authority over our sentiments, and give us a general approbation of what is useful to society, and blame of what is dangerous or pernicious. The degrees of these sentiments may be the subject of controversy; but the reality of their existence, one should think, must be admitted in every theory or system. . . . Sympathy, we shall allow, is much fainter than our concern for ourselves, and sympathy with persons remote from us much fainter than that with persons near and contiguous; but for this very reason it is necessary for us, in our calm judgments and discourse concerning the characters of men, to neglect all these differences, and render our sentiments more public and social. Besides, that we ourselves often change our situation in this particular, we every day meet with persons who are in a situation different from us, and who could never converse with us were we to remain constantly in that position and point of view, which is peculiar to ourselves. The intercourse of sentiments, therefore, in society and conversation, makes us form some general unalterable standard, by which we may approve or disapprove of characters and manners. And though the heart takes not part entirely with these general notions, nor regulates all its love and hatred by the universal abstract differences of vice and virtue, without regard to self, or the persons with whom we are more intimately connected; yet have these moral differences a considerable influence, and being sufficient, at least for discourse, serve all our purposes in company, in the pulpit, on the theatre, and in the schools.

Thus, in whatever light we take this subject, the merit, ascribed to the social virtues, appears still uniform, and arises chiefly from that regard, which the natural sentiment of benevolence engages us to pay to the interests of mankind and society. . . .

Were it doubtful, whether there were any such principle in our nature as humanity or a concern for others, yet when we see, in numberless instances, that whatever has a tendency to promote the interests of society, is so highly approved of, we ought thence to learn the force of the benevolent principle; since it is impossible for anything to please as means to an end, where the end is totally indifferent. On the other hand, were it doubtful, whether there were, implanted in our nature, any general principle of moral blame and approbation, yet when we see, in numberless instances, the influence of humanity, we ought hence to conclude, that it is impossible, but that everything which promotes the interest of society must communicate pleasure, and what is pernicious gives uneasiness. But when these different reflections and observations concur in establishing the same conclusion, must they not bestow an undisputed evidence upon it? . . .

CONCLUSION

. . . It is sufficient for our present purpose, if it be allowed, what surely, without the greatest absurdity cannot be disputed, that there is some benevolence, however small, infused into our bosom; some spark of friendship for human kind; some particle of the dove kneaded into our frame, along with the elements of the wolf and serpent. Let these generous sentiments be supposed ever so weak; let them be insufficient to move even a hand or finger of our body, they must still direct the determinations of our mind, and where everything else is equal, produce a cool preference of what is useful and serviceable to mankind, above what is pernicious and dangerous. A *moral distinction,* therefore, immediately arises; a general sentiment of blame and approbation; a tendency, however faint, to the objects of the one, and a proportionable aversion to those of the other. . . .

Avarice, ambition, vanity, and all passions vulgarly, though improperly, comprised under the denomination of *self-love,* are here excluded from our theory concerning the origin of morals, not because they are too weak, but because they have not a proper direction for that purpose. The notion of morals implies some sentiment common to all mankind, which recommends the same object to general approbation, and makes every man, or most men, agree in the same opinion or decision concerning it. It also implies some sentiment, so universal and comprehensive as to extend to all mankind, and render the actions and conduct, even of the persons the most remote, an object of applause or censure, according as they agree or disagree with that rule of right which is established. . . .

When a man denominates another his *enemy,* his *rival,* his *antagonist,* his *adversary,* he is understood to speak the language of self-love, and to express sentiments, peculiar to himself, and arising from his particular circumstances and situation. But when he bestows on any man the epithets of *vicious* or *odious* or *depraved,* he then speaks another language and expresses sentiments, in which he expects all his audience to concur with him. He must here, therefore, depart from his private and particular situation, and must choose a point of view, common to him with others; he must move some universal principle of the human frame, and touch a string to which all mankind have an accord and symphony. If he mean, therefore, to express that this man possesses qualities, whose tendency is pernicious to society, he has chosen this common point of view, and has touched the principle of humanity, in which every man, in some degree, concurs. While the human heart is compounded of the same elements as at present, it will never be wholly indifferent to public good, nor entirely unaffected with the tendency of characters and manners. And though this affection of humanity may not generally be esteemed so strong as vanity or ambition, yet, being common to all men, it can alone be the foundation of morals, or of any general system of blame or praise. . . .

What more, therefore, can we ask to distinguish the sentiments, dependent on humanity, from those connected with any other passion, or to satisfy us, why the former are the origin of morals, not the latter? Whatever conduct gains my approbation, by touching my humanity, procures also the applause of all mankind, by affecting the same principle in them; by what serves my avarice or ambition pleases these passions in me alone, and affects not the avarice and ambition of the rest of mankind. There is no circumstance of conduct in any man, provided it have a beneficial tendency, that is not agreeable to my humanity, however remote the person; but every man, so far removed as neither to cross nor serve my avarice and ambition, is regarded as wholly indifferent by those passions. The distinction, therefore, between these species of sentiment being so great and evident, language must soon be moulded upon it, and must invent a peculiar set of terms, in order to express those universal sentiments of censure or approbation, which arise from humanity, or from views of general usefulness and its contrary. Virtue and Vice become then known; morals are recognized; certain general ideas are framed of human conduct and behaviour; such measures are expected from men in such situations. This action is determined to be conformable to our abstract rule; that other, contrary. And by such universal principles are the particular sentiments of self-love frequently controlled and limited. . . .

One principal foundation of moral praise being supposed to lie in the usefulness of any quality or action, it is evident that reason must enter for a considerable share in all decisions of this kind; since nothing but that faculty can instruct us in the tendency of qualities and actions, and point out their beneficial consequences to society and to their possessor. In many cases this is an affair liable to great controversy: doubts may arise; opposite interests may occur; and a preference must be given to one side, from very nice views, and a small overbalance of utility. This is particularly remarkable in questions with regard to justice; as is, indeed, natural to suppose, from that species of utility which attends this virtue. Were every single instance of justice, like that of benevolence, useful to society; this would be a more simple state of the case, and seldom liable to great controversy. But as single instances of justice are often pernicious in their first and immediate tendency, and as the advantage to society results only from the observance of the general rule, and from the concurrence and combination of several persons in the same equitable conduct; the case here becomes more intricate and involved. The various circumstances of society; the various consequences of any practice; the various interests which may be proposed; these, on many occasions, are doubtful, and subject to great discussion and inquiry. The object of municipal laws is to fix all the questions with regard to justice: the debates of civilians; the reflections of politicians; the precedents of history and public records, are all directed to the same purpose. And a very accurate *reason* or *judgement* is often requisite, to give the true determination, amidst such intricate doubts arising from obscure or opposite utilities.

But though reason, when fully assisted and improved, be sufficient to instruct us in the pernicious or useful tendency of qualities and actions; it is not alone sufficient to produce any moral blame or approbation. Utility is only a tendency to a certain end; and were the end totally indifferent to us, we should feel the same indifference towards the means. It is requisite a *sentiment* should here display itself, in order to give a preference to the useful above the pernicious tendencies. This sentiment can be no other than a feeling for the happiness of mankind, and a resentment of their misery; since these are the different ends which virtue and vice have a tendency to promote. Here therefore reason instructs us in the several tendencies of actions, and *humanity* makes a distinction in favour of those which are useful and beneficial. . . .

REVIEW AND DISCUSSION QUESTIONS

1. What is the basic philosophical question that Hume wants to solve? What method does he use to solve it?
2. What does Hume mean by *benevolence* or *humaneness?*
3. What is justice, according to Hume? What imaginary situations does he use to explain its meaning and importance?
4. Explain Hume's position on the nature and importance of property.
5. How does Hume respond to the "selfish theory"?

6. What is the role of reason in Hume's theory?

7. Hume distinguishes between the "private and particular situation" and the moral point of view "common to him with others." In light of that, explain how Hume's view might be described as an "ideal observer" theory.

8. How might Hume argue that a person's moral position is mistaken or wrong?

9. Compare Hume's view of people's psychological motivation with the view of Hobbes. Which view do you think is the more accurate?

10. It is sometimes said that Hume's account of justice is defective because he focuses on only the total amount of happiness and ignores the fact that our feelings of approval are also influenced by how the happiness or utility is distributed. Do you agree? Explain.

The Fundamental Principles of the Metaphysic of Morals

Immanuel Kant

Immanuel Kant lived his entire life within a few miles of Koningsberg, in East Prussia, where he was born in 1724. Kant never married and was a man of remarkable organization and regularity of habits; it is even said that people would set their clocks based on his afternoon walks. Like Hobbes, he lived a long and very productive life, dying in 1804 at the age of eighty. Kant's writing has had and continues to have an immense impact on all areas of philosophy from epistemology and ethics to metaphysics and political theory.

Rejecting both Aristotle, who believed it necessary to study closely human psychology in order to understand morality, and Hume, who believed sentiment and feeling were at the root of morality, Kant argues that morality and moral duties are based solely on reason. To be genuinely worthy, Kant argues, one must not just act *in accordance with* duty; one must also act for *duty's sake*. To do the right thing out of selfish motives (for fear of getting caught, for example) would not be to act for the sake of duty and therefore would not evidence the kind of value that actions done purely for the sake of duty do.

How then is one to know what duty requires? Reacting against Hume's emphasis on sentiment and the consequences of actions as a test of morality, Kant argues that reason provides the foundation on which duty rests. An action is right, he claimed, if it conforms to a moral rule that any agent must follow if he is to act rationally. That rule, which distinguishes right from wrong, is what Kant calls the *categorical* (that is, exceptionless) *imperative;* an imperative that Kant expressed as requiring that a person must never perform an act unless he or she can consistently will that the maxim of that act become a universal law. In this way, Kant argues, the categorical imperative comprises the heart of the distinction between right and wrong—a distinction that any rational being can comprehend and act on.

Kant also speaks of a second formulation of the categorical imperative that he felt was equivalent to the one previously mentioned. The second formulation states that one must act so as to treat

From *The Fundamental Principles of the Metaphysic of Morals* (1785), trans. Thomas K. Abbott (1873).

people as ends in themselves, never merely as means. That second version, then, looks at actions from the perspective of the victim rather than the agent. Kant concludes with a brief discussion of what he termed the "kingdom of ends" as well as of human dignity and autonomy.

THE GOOD WILL

Nothing can possibly be conceived in the world, or even out of it, which can be called good without qualification, except a *good will*. Intelligence, wit, judgment, and the other talents of the mind, however they may be named, or courage, resolution, perseverance, as qualities of temperament, are undoubtedly good and desirable in many respects; but these gifts of nature may also become extremely bad and mischievous if the will which is to make use of them, and which, therefore, constitutes what is called *character,* is not good. It is the same with the *gifts of fortune*. Power, riches, honor, even health, and the general well-being and contentment with one's condition which is called *happiness,* inspire pride, and often presumption, if there is not a good will to correct the influence of these on the mind, and with this also to rectify the whole principle of acting, and adapt it to its end. The sight of a being who is not adorned with a single feature of a pure and good will, enjoying unbroken prosperity, can never give pleasure to an impartial rational spectator. Thus a good will appears to constitute the indispensable condition even of being worthy of happiness.

There are even some qualities which are of service to this good will itself, and may facilitate its action, yet which have no intrinsic unconditional value, but always presuppose a good will, and this qualifies the esteem that we justly have for them, and does not permit us to regard them as absolutely good. Moderation in the affections and passions, self-control, and calm deliberation are not only good in many respects, but even seem to constitute part of the intrinsic worth of the person; but they are far from deserving to be called good without qualification, although they have been so unconditionally praised by the ancients. For without the principles of a good will, they may become extremely bad; and the coolness of a villain not only makes him far more dangerous, but also directly makes him more abominable in our eyes than he would have been without it.

A good will is good not because of what it performs or effects, not by its aptness for the attainment of some proposed end, but simply by virtue of the volition—that is, it is good in itself, and considered by itself is to be esteemed much higher than all that can be brought about by it in favor of any inclination, nay, even of the sum-total of all inclinations. Even if it should happen that, owing to special disfavor of fortune, or the niggardly provision of a stepmotherly nature, this will should wholly lack power to accomplish its purpose, if with its greatest efforts it should yet achieve nothing, and there should remain only the good will (not, to be sure, a mere wish, but the summoning of all means in our power), then, like a jewel, it would still shine by its own light, as a thing which has its whole value in itself. Its usefulness or fruitlessness can neither add to nor take away anything from this value. It would be, as it were, only the setting to enable us to handle it the more conveniently in common commerce, or to attract to it the attention of those who are not yet connoisseurs, but not to recommend it to true connoisseurs, or to determine its value. . . .

To be beneficent when we can is a duty; and besides this, there are many minds so sympathetically constituted that, without any other motive of vanity or self-interest, they find a pleasure in spreading joy around them, and can take delight in the satisfaction of others so far as it is their own work. But I maintain that in such a case an action of this kind, however proper, however amiable it may be, has nevertheless no true moral worth, but is on a level with other inclinations, for example, the inclination to honor, which, if it is happily directed to that which is in fact of public utility and accordant with duty, and consequently honorable, deserves praise and encouragement, but not esteem. For the maxim lacks the moral import, namely, that such actions be done *from duty,* not from inclination. Put the case that the mind of that philanthropist was clouded by sorrow of his own, extinguishing all sympathy with the lot of others, and that while he still has the power to benefit others in distress, he is not touched by their trouble because he is absorbed with his own; and now suppose that he tears himself out of this dead insensibility and performs the action without any inclination to it, but simply from duty, then . . . has his action its genuine moral worth. . . . It is just in this that the moral worth of the character is brought out which is incomparably the highest of all, namely, that he is beneficent, not from inclination, but from duty. . . .

THE FIRST PROPOSITION OF MORALITY

We have then to develop the notion of a will which deserves to be highly esteemed for itself, and is good without a view to anything further. . . . [Consider] that it is always a matter of duty that a tradesman should not overcharge an inexperienced purchases; and wherever there is much commerce the prudent tradesman does not overcharge, but keeps a fixed price of everyone, so that a child buys of him as well as any other. Men are thus honestly served, but this is not enough to make us believe that the tradesman acted from duty and from principles of honesty: his own advantage required it. Accordingly the action was done neither from duty nor from direct inclination, but merely with a selfish view. . . .

On the other hand, it is a duty to maintain one's life; and, in addition, everyone also has a direct inclination to do so. But on this account the often anxious care which most men take for it has no intrinsic worth, and their maxim has no moral import. They preserve their life *as duty requires,* no doubt, but not *because duty requires.* On the other hand, if adversity and hopeless sorrow have completely taken away the relish for life; if the unfortunate one, strong in mind, indignant at his fate rather than desponding or dejected, wishes for death, and yet preserves his life without loving it—not from inclination of fear, but from duty—then his maxim has a moral worth.

To be beneficent when we can is a duty; and besides this, there are many minds so sympathetically constituted that, without any other motive of vanity or self-interest, they find a pleasure in spreading joy around them, and can take delight in the satisfaction of others so far as it is their own

work. But I maintain that in such a case an action of this kind, however proper, however amiable it may be, has nevertheless no true moral worth, but is on a level with other inclinations. For the maxim lacks the moral import, namely, that such actions be done *from duty,* not from inclination. Put the case that the mind of a philanthropist was clouded by sorrow of his own, extinguishing all sympathy with the lot of others, and that while he still has the power to benefit others in distress, he is not touched by their trouble because he is absorbed with his own; and now suppose that he tears himself out of this dead sensibility, and performs the action without any inclination to it, but simply from duty—then does his action have a genuine moral worth. Further still; if nature has put little sympathy in the heart of this or that man; if he, supposed to be an upright man, is by temperament cold and indifferent to the sufferings of others, perhaps because in respect of his own he is provided with a special gift of patience and fortitude, and supposes, or even requires, that others should have the same—and such a man would certainly not be the meanest product of nature—but would he not still find in himself a source from whence to give himself a far higher worth than that of a good natured temperament would be? Unquestionably. It is just in this that the moral worth of character is brought out which is incomparably the highest of all, namely, that he is beneficent, not from inclination, but from duty. . . .

It is in this manner, undoubtedly, that we are to understand those passages of Scripture in which we are commanded to love our neighbour, even our enemy. For love, as an affection, cannot be commanded, but beneficence for duty's sake may. This is *practical* love, and not *pathological*—a love that is seated in the will, and not in the propensities of feeling—in principles of action and not of tender sympathy; and it is this love alone which can be commanded.

THE SECOND AND THIRD PROPOSITIONS OF MORALITY

The second proposition is: That an action done from duty derives its moral worth, *not from the purpose* which is to be attained by it, but from the maxim by which it is determined, and therefore does not depend on the realization of the object of the action, but merely on the *principle of volition* by which the action has taken place, without regard to any object of desire. It is clear from what precedes that the purposes which we may have in view in our actions, or their effects regarded as ends and springs of the will, cannot give to actions any unconditional or moral worth. In what, then, can their worth lie if it is not to consist in the will and in reference to its expected effect? It cannot lie anywhere but in the *principle of the will* without regard to the ends which can be attained by the action. . . .

The third proposition, which is a consequence of the two preceding, I would express thus: *Duty is the necessity of acting from respect for the law.* I may have *inclination* for an object as the effect of my proposed action, but I cannot have *respect* for it just for this reason that it is an effect and not an energy of will. Similarly, I cannot have respect for inclination, whether my own or another's; I can at most, if my own, approve it; if another's, sometimes even love it, that is, look on it as favorable to my own interest. It is only what is connected with my will as a principle, by no means as an effect—what does not subserve my inclination, but overpowers it, or at least in case of choice excludes it from its calculation—in other words, simply the law of itself, which can be an object of respect, and hence a command. Now an action done from duty must wholly exclude the influence of inclination, and with it every object of the will, so that nothing remains which can determine the will except objectively the *law,* and subjectively *pure respect* for this practical law, and consequently the maxim[1] that I should follow this law even to the thwarting of all my inclinations.

Thus the moral worth of an action does not lie in the effect expected from it, nor in any principle of action which requires to borrow its motive from this expected effect. For all these effects—agreeableness of one's condition, and even the promotion of the happiness of others—could have been also brought about by other causes, so that for this there would have been no need of the will of a rational being; whereas it is in this alone that the supreme and unconditional good can be found. The pre-eminent good which we call moral can

therefore consist in nothing else than *the conception of law* in itself, *which certainly is only possible in a rational being,* in so far as this conception, and not the expected effect, determines the will. This is a good which is already present in the person who acts accordingly, and we have not to wait for it to appear first in the result.

THE SUPREME PRINCIPLE OF MORALITY: THE CATEGORICAL IMPERATIVE

But what sort of law can that be the conception of which must determine the will, even without paying any regard to the effect expected from it, in order that this will may be called good absolutely and without qualification? As I have deprived the will of every impulse which could arise to it from obedience to any law, there remains nothing but the universal conformity of its actions to law in general, which alone is to serve the will as a principle, that is, I am never to act otherwise than so *that I could also will that my maxim should become a universal law.* Here, now, it is the simple conformity to law in general, without assuming any particular law applicable to certain actions, that serves the will as its principle, and must so serve it if duty is not to be a vain delusion and a chimerical notion. The common reason of men in its practical judgments perfectly coincides with this, and always has in view the principle here suggested. Let the question be, for example: May I when in distress make a promise with the intention not to keep it? I readily distinguish here between the two significations which the question may have: whether it is prudent or whether it is right to make a false promise? The former may undoubtedly often be the case. I see clearly indeed that it is not enough to extricate myself from a present difficulty by means of this subterfuge, but it must be well considered whether there may not hereafter spring from this lie much greater inconvenience than that from which I now free myself, and as, with all my supposed *cunning,* the consequences cannot be so easily foreseen but that credit once lost may be much more injurious to me than any mischief which I seek to avoid at present, it should be considered whether it would not be more *prudent* to act herein according to a universal maxim, and to make it a habit to promise nothing except with the intention of keeping it. But it is soon clear to me that such a maxim will still only be based on the fear of consequences. Now it is a wholly different thing to be truthful from duty, and to be so from apprehension of injurious consequences. In the first case, the very notion of the action already implies a law for me; in the second case, I must first look about elsewhere to see what results may be combined with it which would affect myself. For to deviate from the principle of duty is beyond all doubt wicked; but to be unfaithful to my maxim of prudence may often be very advantageous to me, although to abide by it is certainly safer. The shortest way, however, and an unerring one, to discover the answer to this question whether a lying promise is consistent with duty, is to ask myself, Should I be content that my maxim (to extricate myself from difficulty by a false promise) should hold good as a universal law, for myself as well as for others; and should I be able to say to myself, "Every one may make a deceitful promise when he finds himself in a difficulty from which he cannot otherwise extricate himself"? Then I presently become aware that, while I can will the lie, I can by no means will that lying should be a universal law. For with such a law there would be no promises at all, since it would be in vain to allege my intention in regard to my future actions to those who would not believe this allegation, or if they over-hastily did so, would pay me back in my own coin. Hence my maxim, so soon as it should be made a universal law, would necessarily destroy itself.

I do not, therefore, need any far-reaching penetration to discern what I have to do in order that my will may be morally good. Inexperienced in the course of the world, incapable of being prepared for all its contingencies, I only ask myself: Canst thou also will that thy maxim should be a universal law? If not, then it must be rejected, and that not because of a disadvantage accruing from it to myself or even to others, but because it cannot enter as a principle into a possible universal legislation, and reason extorts from me immediate respect for such legislation. I do not indeed as yet *discern* on what this respect is based (this the philosopher may inquire), but at least I understand

this—that it is an estimation of the worth which far outweighs all worth of what is recommended by inclination, and that the necessity of acting from pure respect for the practical law is what constitutes duty, to which every other motive must give place because it is the condition of a will being good *in itself,* and the worth of such a will is above everything.

Thus, then, without quitting the moral knowledge of common human reason, we have arrived at its principle. And although, no doubt, common men do not conceive it in such an abstract and universal form, yet they always have it really before their eyes and use it as the standard of their decision. Here it would be easy to show how, with this compass in hand, men are well able to distinguish, in every case that occurs, what is good, what bad, conformably to duty or inconsistent with it. . . .

IMPERATIVES: HYPOTHETICAL AND CATEGORICAL

Everything in nature works according to laws. Rational beings alone have the faculty of acting according *to the conception* of laws, that is according to principles, *i.e.,* have a *will.* Since the deduction of actions from principles requires *reason,* the will is nothing but practical reason. . . .

The conception of an objective principle, in so far as it is obligatory for a will, is called a command (of reason), and the formula of the command is called an Imperative.

All imperatives are expressed by the word *ought* [or *shall*], and thereby indicate the relation of an objective law of reason to a will, which from its subjective constitution is not necessarily determined by it (an obligation). . . .

Now all *imperatives* command either *hypothetically* or *categorically.* The former represent the practical necessity of a possible action as means to something else that is willed (or at least which one might possibly will). The categorical imperative would be that which represented an action as necessary of itself without reference to another end, that is, as objectively necessary. . . .

If now the action is good only as a means to *something else,* then the imperative is *hypothetical;* if it is conceived as good *in itself* and consequently as being necessarily the principle of a will which of itself conforms to reason, then it is *categorical.* . . .

Accordingly the hypothetical imperative only says that the action is good for some purpose, *possible or actual.* In the first case it is a *problematical,* in the second an *assertorial* practical principle. The categorical imperative which declares an action to be objectively necessary in itself without reference to any purpose, that is, without any other end, is valid as an *apodictic* (practical) principle. . . .

FIRST FORMULATION OF THE CATEGORICAL IMPERATIVE: UNIVERSAL LAW

When I conceive a hypothetical imperative, in general I do not know beforehand what it will contain until I am given the condition. But when I conceive a categorical imperative, I know at once what it contains. For as the imperative contains besides the law only the necessity that the maxims[2] shall conform to this law, while the law contains no conditions restricting it, there remains nothing but the general statement that the maxim of the action should conform to a universal law, and it is this conformity alone that the imperative properly represents as necessary.

There is therefore but one categorical imperative, namely, this: *Act only on that maxim whereby thou canst at the same time will that it should become a universal law.*

Now if all imperatives of duty can be deduced from this one imperative as from their principle, then, although it should remain undecided whether what is called duty is not merely a vain notion, yet at least we shall be able to show what we understand by it and what this notion means. . . .

Four Illustrations

We will now enumerate a few duties, adopting the usual division of them into duties to ourselves and to others, and into perfect and imperfect duties.

1. A man reduced to despair by a series of misfortunes feels wearied of life, but is still so far in possession of his reason that he can ask himself whether it would not be contrary to his duty to himself to take his own life. Now he inquires whether the maxim of his action could become a universal law of nature. His maxim is: From self-love I adopt it as a principle to shorten my life when its longer duration is likely to bring more evil than satisfaction. It is asked then simply whether this principle founded on self-love can become a universal law of nature. Now we see at once that a system of nature of which it should be a law to destroy life by means of the very feeling whose special nature it is to impel to the improvement of life would contradict itself, and therefore could not exist as a system of nature; hence that maxim cannot possibly exist as a universal law of nature, and consequently would be wholly inconsistent with the supreme principle of all duty.

2. Another finds himself forced by necessity to borrow money. He knows that he will not be able to repay it, but sees also that nothing will be lent to him unless he promises stoutly to repay it in a definite time. He desires to make this promise, but he has still so much conscience as to ask himself: Is it not unlawful and inconsistent with duty to get out of a difficulty in this way? Suppose, however, that he resolves to do so, then the maxim of his action would be expressed thus: When I think myself in want of money, I will borrow money and promise to repay it, although I know that I never can do so. Now this principle of self-love or of one's own advantage may perhaps be consistent with my whole future welfare; but the question now is, Is it right? I change then the suggestion of self-love into a universal law, and state the question thus: How would it be if my maxim were a universal law? Then I see at once that it could never hold as a universal law of nature, but would necessarily contradict itself. For supposing it to be a universal law that everyone when he thinks himself in a difficulty should be able to promise whatever he pleases, with the purpose of not keeping his promise, the promise itself would become impossible, as well as the end that one might have in view in it, since no one would consider that anything was promised to him, but would ridicule all such statements as vain pretenses.

3. A third finds in himself a talent which with the help of some culture might make him a useful man in many respects. But he finds himself in comfortable circumstances and prefers to indulge in pleasure rather than to take pains in enlarging and improving his happy natural capacities. He asks, however, whether his maxim of neglect of his natural gifts, besides agreeing with his inclination to indulgence, agrees also with what is called duty. He sees then that a system of nature could indeed subsist with such a universal law, although men (like the South Sea islanders) should let their talents rest and resolve to devote their lives merely to idleness, amusement, and propagation of their species—in a word, to enjoyment; but he cannot possibly will that this should be a universal law of nature, or be implanted in us as such by a natural instinct. For, as a rational being, he necessarily wills that his faculties be developed, since they serve him, and have been given him, for all sorts of possible purposes.

4. A fourth, who is in prosperity, while he sees that others have to contend with great wretchedness and that he could help them, thinks: "What concern is it of mine? Let everyone be as happy as Heaven pleases, or as he can make himself; I will take nothing from him nor even envy him, only I do not wish to contribute anything to his welfare or to his assistance in distress! Now no doubt, if such a mode of thinking were a universal law, the human race might very well subsist, and doubtless even better than in a state in which everyone talks of sympathy and good-will, or even takes care occasionally to put it into practice, but, on the other side, also cheats when he can, betrays the rights of men, or otherwise violates them. But although it is possible that a universal law of nature might exist in accordance with that maxim, it is impossible to *will* that such a principle should have the universal validity of a law of nature. For a will which resolved this would contradict itself, inasmuch as many cases might occur in which one would have need of the love and sympathy of others, and in which, by such a law of nature, sprung from his own will, he would deprive himself of all hope of the aid he desires.

These are a few of the many actual duties, or at least what we regard as such, which obviously fall into two classes on the one principle that we have laid down. We must be *able to will* that a maxim of our action should be a universal law. This is the canon of the moral appreciation of the action generally. Some actions are of such a character that their maxim cannot without contradiction be even *conceived* as a universal law of nature, far from it being possible that we should *will* that it *should* be so. In others, this intrinsic impossibility is not found, but still it is impossible to *will* that their maxim should be raised to the universality of a law of nature, since such a will would contradict itself. . . .

SECOND FORMULATION OF THE CATEGORICAL IMPERATIVE: HUMANITY AS END IN ITSELF

The will is conceived as a faculty of determining oneself to action *in accordance with the conception of certain laws*. And such a faculty can be found only in rational beings. The ends which a rational being proposes to himself at pleasure as *effects* of his actions are all only relative, for it is only their relation to the particular desires of the subject that gives them their worth, which therefore cannot furnish principles universal and necessary for all rational beings and every volition, that is to say practical laws. Hence all these relative ends can give only hypothetical imperatives. Supposing, however, that there were something *whose existence* has *in itself* an absolute worth, something which, being *an end in itself,* could be a source of definite laws, then in this and this alone would lie the source of a possible categorical imperative, i.e. a practical law. . . .

Now I say: man and generally any rational being exists as an end in himself, *not merely as a means* to be arbitrarily used by this or that will, but in all his actions, whether they concern himself or other rational beings, must be always regarded at the same time as an end. All objects of the inclinations have only a conditional worth; for if the inclinations and the wants founded on them did not exist, then their object would be without value. Thus the worth of any object which is *to be acquired* by our action is always conditional. Beings whose existence depends not on our will but on nature's, have nevertheless, if they are nonrational beings, only a relative value as means, and are therefore called *things;* rational beings, on the contrary, are called *persons,* because their very nature points them out as ends in themselves, that is, as something which must not be used merely as means, and so far therefore restricts freedom of action (and is an object of respect). These, therefore, are not merely subjective ends whose existence has a worth *for us* as an effect of our action, but *objective ends,* that is, things whose existence is an end in itself—an end, moreover, for which no other can be substituted, which they should subserve *merely* as means, for otherwise nothing whatever would possess *absolute worth; . . .*

If then there is a supreme practical principle or, in respect of the human will, a categorical imperative, it must be one which, being drawn from the conception of that which is necessarily an end for everyone because it is *an end in itself*, constitutes an objective principle of will, and can therefore serve as a universal practical law. The foundation of this principle is: *rational nature exists as an end in itself*. Man necessarily conceives his own existence as being so: so far then this is a *subjective* principle of human actions. But every other rational being regards its existence similarly, just on the same rational principle that holds for me: so that it is at the same time an objective principle, from which as a supreme practical law all laws of the will must be capable of being deduced. Accordingly the practical imperative will be as follows: *So act as to treat humanity, whether in thine own person or in that of any other, in every case as an end withal, never as means only.* We will now inquire whether this can be practically carried out. . . .

THE KINGDOM OF ENDS

The conception of the will of every rational being as one which must consider itself as giving in all the maxims of its will universal laws, so as to judge itself and its actions from this point of view—this conception leads to another which depends on it and is very fruitful, namely that of a *kingdom of ends*.

By a *kingdom* I understand the union of different rational beings in a system by common laws.

Now since it is by laws that ends are determined as regards their universal validity, hence, if we abstract from the personal differences of rational beings and likewise from all the content of their private ends, we shall be able to conceive all ends combined in a systematic whole (including both rational beings as ends in themselves, and also the special ends which each may propose to himself), that is to say, we can conceive a kingdom of ends, which on the preceding principles is possible.

For all rational beings come under the *law* that each of them must treat itself and all others *never merely as means,* but in every case *at the same time as ends in themselves*. Hence results a systematic union of rational beings by common objective laws, *i.e.*, a kingdom which may be called a kingdom of ends, since what these laws have in view is just the relation of these beings to one another as ends and means. It is certainly only an ideal.

A rational being belongs as a *member* to the kingdom of ends when although giving universal laws in it he is also himself subject to these laws. He belongs to it *as sovereign,* when while giving laws he is not subject to the will of any other.

A rational being must always regard himself as giving laws in a kingdom of ends which freedom of the will makes possible, whether it be as member or as sovereign. He cannot, however, maintain the latter position merely by the maxims of his will, but only in case he is a completely independent being without wants and with unrestricted power adequate to his will.

Morality consists then in the reference of all action to the legislation which alone can render a kingdom of ends possible. This legislation must be capable of existing in every rational being, and of emanating from his will, so that the principle of this will, is never to act on any maxim which could not without contradiction be also a universal law, and accordingly always so to act *that the will could at the same time regard itself as giving in its maxims universal laws*. If now the maxims of rational beings are not by their own nature coincident with this objective principle, then the necessity of acting on it is called practical obligation, *i.e., duty*. Duty does not apply to the sovereign in the kingdom of ends, but it does to every member of it and to all in the same degree.

The practical necessity of acting on this principle, i.e. duty, does not rest at all on feelings, impulses, or inclinations, but solely on the relation of rational beings to one another, a relation in which the will of a rational being must always be regarded as *legislative*. . . .

In the kingdom of ends everything has either Value or Dignity. Whatever has a value can be replaced by something else which is *equivalent;* whatever on the other hand is above all value, and therefore admits of no equivalent, has a dignity.

Whatever has reference to the general inclinations and wants of mankind has a *market value;* whatever without presupposing a want, corresponds to a certain taste, that is to a satisfaction in the mere purposeless play of our faculties, has a *fancy value;* but that which constitutes the condition under which alone anything can be an end in itself, this has not merely a relative worth, *i.e.,* value, but an intrinsic worth, that is, *dignity*.

Now morality is the condition under which alone a rational being can be an end in himself, since by this alone is it possible that he should be a legislating member in the kingdom of ends. Thus morality, and humanity as capable of it, is that which alone has dignity. Skill and diligence in labour have a market value; wit, lively imagination, and humour have a fancy value; on the other hand, fidelity to promises, benevolence from principle (not from instinct) have an intrinsic worth. Neither nature nor art contains anything which in default of these it could put in their place, for their worth consists not in the effects which spring from them, not in the use and advantage which they secure, but in the disposition of mind, that is the maxims of the will which are ready to manifest themselves in such actions, even though they should not have the desired effect. These actions also need no recommendation from any subjective taste or sentiment, that they may be looked on with immediate favour and satisfaction: they need no immediate propensities or feeling for them; they exhibit the will that performs them as an object of an immediate respect, and nothing but reason is required to *impose* them on the will; not to *flatter* it into them, which in the case of duties would be a contradiction. This estimation therefore shows that the worth of such a disposition is dignity, and places it infinitely above all value, with which it cannot for a moment be brought into comparison or competition without as it were violating its sanctity.

What then is it which justifies virtue or the morally good disposition, in making such lofty claims? It is nothing less than the privilege it secures to the rational being of participating in the giving of universal laws, by which it qualifies him to be a member of a possible kingdom of ends, a privilege to which he was already destined by his own nature as being an end in himself, and on that account legislating in the kingdom of ends; free as regards all laws of physical nature, and obeying those only which he himself gives, and by which his maxims can belong to a system of universal law, to which at the same time he submits himself. For nothing has any worth except what the law assigns it. Now the legislation itself which assigns the worth of everything, must for that very reason possess dignity, that is an unconditional incomparable worth, and the word *respect* alone supplies a becoming expression for the esteem which a rational being must have for it. *Autonomy* then is the basis of the dignity of human and of every rational nature. . . .

THE AUTONOMY OF THE WILL

Autonomy of the will is the property that the will has of being a law to itself (independently of any property of the objects of volition). The principle of autonomy is this: Always choose in such a way that in the same volition the maxims of the choice are at the same time present as universal law.

If the will seeks the law that is to determine it anywhere but in the fitness of its maxims for its own legislation of universal laws, and if it thus goes outside of itself and seeks this law in the character of any of its objects, then heteronomy always results. The will in that case does not give itself the law, but the object does so because of its relation to the will. This relation, whether it rests on inclination or on representations of reason, admits only of hypothetical imperatives: I ought to do something because I will something else. On the other hand, the moral, and hence categorical, imperative says that I ought to act in this way or that way, even though I did not will something else. . . .

The Concept of Freedom Is the Key That Explains the Autonomy of the Will

The will is a kind of causality belonging to living beings in so far as they are rational, and *freedom* would be this property of such causality that it can be efficient, independently of foreign causes determining it; just as physical necessity is the property that the causality of all rational beings has of being determined to activity by the influence of foreign causes. . . .

What else then can freedom of the will be but autonomy, that is, the property of the will to be a law to itself? But the proposition: The will is in every action a law to itself, only expresses the principle to act on no other maxim than that which can also have as an object itself as a universal law. Now this is precisely the formula of the categorical imperative and is the principle of morality, so that a free will and a will subject to moral laws are one and the same. . . .

Freedom Must Be Presupposed as a Property of the Will of All Rational Beings

It is not enough to predicate freedom of our own will, from whatever reason, if we have not sufficient grounds for predicating the same of all rational beings. For as morality serves as a law for us only because we are rational beings, it must also hold for all rational beings. Now I say every being that cannot act except under the idea of freedom is just for that reason in a practical point of view really free, that is to say, all laws which are inseparably connected with freedom have the same force for him as if his will had been shown to be free in itself by a proof theoretically conclusive. (I adopt this method of assuming freedom merely as an idea which rational being suppose in their actions, in order to avoid the necessity of proving it in theory. The form is sufficient for my purpose; for even though the speculative proof should not be made out, yet a being that cannot act except with the idea of freedom is bound by the same laws that would oblige a being who is actually free.) Now I affirm that we must attribute to every rational being which has a will that it has also the idea of freedom and acts entirely under this idea. For in such a being we conceive a reason that is practical, that is, has causality in reference to its objects. It must regard itself as the author of its principles independent on foreign influences. Consequently, as practical reason or as the will of a rational being it must regard itself as free, that is to say, the will of such a being cannot be a will of its own except under the idea of freedom. This idea must therefore in a practical point of view be ascribed to every rational being.

NOTES

1. A *maxim* is the subjective principle of volition. The objective principle (i.e., that which would also serve subjectively as a practical principle to all rational beings if reason had full power over the faculty of desire) is the practical law.

2. A *maxim* is a subjective principle of action, and must be distinguished from the objective principle, namely, practical law. The former contains the practical rule set by reason according to the conditions of the subject (often its ignorance or its inclinations), so that it is the principle on which the subject acts; but the law is the objective principle valid for every rational being, and is the principle which it *ought to act*—that is, an imperative.

REVIEW AND DISCUSSION QUESTIONS

1. What distinguishes acting from inclination and acting from duty? Which reflects genuine moral worth? Why?
2. How do hypothetical and categorical imperatives differ?
3. Describe the two versions Kant gives of the categorical imperative. Give an example of how the categorical imperative is applied.
4. What does Kant mean by a *maxim?*

5. Explain what Kant means by *autonomy*. Are persons autonomous?
6. Compare Kant's view of autonomy with Hobbes's view of freedom.
7. Explain how Kant would respond to Hume on the question of the role of emotions and "inclinations" in morality.

Utilitarianism

John Stuart Mill

John Stuart Mill (1806–1873) had an unusual life by almost any standard. His father, James Mill, who was a friend of the economist David Ricardo and the legal theorist John Austin, was among the most devoted followers of Jeremy Bentham, the utilitarian philosopher. James developed a plan for the education of his son, John Stuart, that included a rigorous tutoring program and the isolation of the boy from other children. Young John was a brilliant student. By the age of three, he had begun learning Greek. At eight, he learned Latin and pursued mathematics and history. By the age of twelve, he was studying logic and political economy, and at fifteen, he studied law at University College, London, with John Austin.

At twenty-four, Mill began a lifelong friendship and intellectual collaboration with Harriet Taylor. Although they were close companions, Harriet Taylor remained married for two decades. When her husband John Taylor died, she and John Stuart Mill were married. The two then withdrew from "insipid society" and the gossip they had endured for years; they lived happily for seven years until her death. Mill served briefly as a member of Parliament and died in France (where he had bought a house near the cemetery in which Harriet was buried).

Mill's influence has been tremendous; he wrote important books on logic, philosophy of science, and economics, as well as on ethics and political philosophy. *On the Subjection of Women* (see Section 15) remains a classic, as is *On Liberty,* his brilliant statement of the justification and limits of government (see Section 11). In the following selections from *Utilitarianism,* Mill explains utilitarian moral theory, responds to critics, and explores the theory's philosophical basis.

GENERAL REMARKS

On the present occasion, I shall attempt to contribute something towards the understanding and appreciation of the Utilitarian or Happiness theory, and towards such proof as it is susceptible of. It is evident that this cannot be proof in the ordinary and popular meaning of the term. Questions of ultimate ends are not amenable to direct proof. We are not, however, to infer that its acceptance or rejection must depend on blind impulse, or arbitrary choice. Considerations may be presented capable of determining the intellect either to give or withhold its assent to the doctrine; and this is equivalent of proof.

WHAT UTILITARIANISM IS

The creed which accepts as the foundation of morals *utility* or the *greatest happiness principle* holds that actions are right in proportion as they

From John Stuart Mill, *Utilitarianism* (1861).

tend to promote happiness, wrong as they tend to produce the reverse of happiness. By "happiness" is intended pleasure, and the absence of pain; by "unhappiness," pain, and the privation of pleasure. To give a clear view of the moral standard set up by the theory, much more requires to be said; in particular, what things it includes in the ideas of pain and pleasure, and to what extent this is left an open question. But these supplementary explanations do not affect the theory of life on which this theory of mortality is grounded—namely, that pleasure, and freedom from pain, are the only things desirable as ends; and that all desirable things (which are as numerous in the utilitarian as in any other scheme) are desirable either for the pleasure inherent in themselves, or as means to the promotion of pleasure and the prevention of pain.

Now such a theory of life excites in many minds, and among them in some of the most estimable in feeling and purpose, inveterate dislike. To suppose that life has (as they express it) no higher end than pleasure—no better and nobler object of desire and pursuit—they designate as utterly mean and groveling; as a doctrine worthy only of swine. . . .

[But it] is quite compatible with the principle of utility to recognize the fact, that some *kinds* of pleasure are more desirable and more valuable than others. It would be absurd that while, in estimating all other things, quality is considered as well as quantity, the estimation of pleasures should be supposed to depend on quantity alone.

If I am asked what I mean by difference of quality in pleasures, or what makes one pleasure more valuable than another merely as a pleasure, except its being greater in amount, there is but one possible answer. Of two pleasures, if there be one to which all or almost all who have experience of both give a decided preference, irrespective of any feeling of moral obligation to prefer it, that is the more desirable pleasure. If one of the two is, by those who are competently acquainted with both, placed so far above the other that they prefer it, even though knowing it to be attended with a greater amount of discontent, and would not resign it for any quantity of the other pleasure which their nature is capable of, we are justified in ascribing to the preferred enjoyment a superiority in quality, so far outweigh-

ing quantity as to render it, in comparison, of small account.

Now it is an unquestionable fact that those who are equally acquainted with, and equally capable of appreciating and enjoying, both, do give a most marked preference to the manner of existence which employs their higher faculties. Few human creatures would consent to be changed into any of the lower animals, for a promise of the fullest allowance of a beast's pleasures; no intelligent human being would consent to be a fool; no instructed person would be an ignoramus, no person of feeling and conscience would be selfish and base, even though they should be persuaded that the fool, the dunce, or the rascal is better satisfied with his lot than they are with theirs. They would not resign what they possess more than he for the most complete satisfaction of all the desires which they have in common with him. If they ever fancy they would, it is only in cases of unhappiness so extreme, that to escape from it they would exchange their lot for almost any other, however undesirable in their own eyes. A being of higher faculties requires more to make him happy, is capable probably of more acute suffering, and certainly accessible to it at more points, than one of an inferior type; but in spite of these liabilities, he can never really wish to sink into what he feels to be a lower grade of existence. We may give what explanation we please of this unwillingness: we may attribute it to pride, a name which is given indiscriminately to some of the most and to some of the least estimable feelings of which mankind are capable; we may refer it to the love of liberty and personal independence, an appeal to which was with the Stoics one of the most effective means for the inculcation of it; to the love of power, or to the love of excitement, both of which do really enter into and contribute to it: but its most appropriate appellation is a sense of dignity, which all human beings possess in one form or other, and in some, though by no means in exact, proportion to their higher faculties, and which is so essential a part of the happiness of those in whom it is strong, that nothing which conflicts with it could be, otherwise than momentarily, an object of desire to them. . . .

From this verdict of the only competent judges I apprehend there can be no appeal. On a question which is the best worth having of two pleasures, or which of two modes of existence is the most grateful to the feelings, apart from its moral attributes and from its consequences, the judgment of those who are qualified by knowledge of both, or, if they differ, that of the majority among them, must be admitted as final. And there need be the less hesitation to accept this judgment respecting the quality of pleasures, since there is no other tribunal to be referred to even on the question of quantity. What means are there of determining which is the acutest of two pains, or the intensest of two pleasurable sensations, except the general suffrage of those who are familiar with both? Neither pains nor pleasures are homogeneous, and pain is always heterogeneous with pleasure. What is there to decide whether a particular pleasure is worth purchasing at the cost of a particular pain, except the feelings and judgment of the experienced? When, therefore, those feelings and judgment declare the pleasures derived from the higher faculties to be preferable in kind, apart from the question of intensity, to those of which the animal nature, disjoined from the higher faculties, is susceptible, they are entitled on this subject to the same regard. . . .

Utilitarianism, therefore, could only attain its end by the general cultivation of nobleness of character, even if each individual were only benefited by the nobleness of others, and his own, so far as happiness is concerned, were a sheer deduction from the benefit. But the bare enunciation of such an absurdity as this last renders refutation superfluous. . . .

Though it is only in a very imperfect state of the world's arrangements that anyone can best serve the happiness of others by the absolute sacrifice of his own, yet so long as the world is in that imperfect state, I fully acknowledge that the readiness to make such a sacrifice is the highest virtue which can be found in man. I will add that in this condition of the world, paradoxical as the assertion may be, the conscious ability to do without happiness gives the best prospect of realizing such happiness as is attainable. For nothing except that consciousness can raise a person above the chances of life, by making him feel that, let fate and fortune do their worst, they have not power to subdue him. . . .

The utilitarian morality does recognize in human beings the power of sacrificing their own greatest good for the good of others. It only refuses to admit that the sacrifice is itself a good. A sacrifice which does not increase, or tend to increase, the sum total of happiness, it considers as wasted. . . .

The assailants of utilitarianism seldom have the justice to acknowledge, that the happiness which forms the utilitarian standard of what is right in conduct is not the agent's own happiness but that of all concerned. As between his own happiness and that of others, utilitarianism requires him to be as strictly impartial as a disinterested and benevolent spectator. In the golden rule of Jesus of Nazareth, we read the complete spirit of the ethics of utility. "To do as you would be done by," and "to love your neighbor as yourself," constitute the ideal perfection of utilitarian morality. As the means of making the nearest approach to this ideal, utility would enjoin, first, that laws and social arrangements should place the happiness or (as speaking practically, it may be called) the interest of every individual as nearly as possible in harmony with the interest of the whole; and, secondly, that education and opinion, which have so vast a power over human character, should so use that power as to establish in the mind of every individual an indissoluble association between his own happiness and the good of the whole, especially between his own happiness and the practice of such modes of conduct, negative and positive, as regard for the universal happiness prescribes; so that not only he may be unable to conceive the possibility of happiness to himself, consistent with the conduct opposed to the general good, but also that a direct impulse to promote the general good may be every individual one of the habitual motives of action, and the sentiments connected therewith may fill a large and prominent place in every human being's sentient existence. . . .

We not uncommonly hear the doctrine of utility inveighed against as a *godless* doctrine. If it be necessary to say anything at all against so mere an assumption, we may say that the question depends upon what idea we have formed of the moral character of the Deity. If it be a true belief that God desires, above all things, the happiness of his creatures, and that this was his purpose in their creation, utility is not only not a godless doctrine, but more profoundly religious than any other. If it be meant that utilitarianism does not recognize the revealed will of God as the supreme law of morals, I answer that a utilitarian who believes in the perfect goodness and wisdom of God necessarily believes that whatever God has thought fit to reveal on the subject of morals must fulfill the requirements of utility in a supreme degree. . . .

Again, defenders of utility often find themselves called upon to reply to such objections as this—that there is not time, previous to action, for calculating and weighing the effects of any line of conduct on the general happiness. This is exactly as if anyone were to say that it is impossible to guide our conduct by Christianity because there is not time, on every occasion on which anything has to be done, to read through the Old and New Testaments. The answer to the objection is that there has been ample time, namely, the whole past duration of the human species. During all that time mankind have been learning by experience the tendencies of actions; on which experience all the prudence as well as all the morality of life are dependent. The corollaries from the principle of utility, like the precepts of every practical art, admit of indefinite improvement, and, in a progressive state of the human mind, their improvement is perpetually going on. But to consider the rules of morality as improvable is one thing; to pass over the intermediate generalization entirely and endeavor to test each individual action directly by the first principle is another. It is a strange notion that the acknowledgment of a first principle is inconsistent with the admission of secondary ones. To inform a traveler respecting the place of his ultimate destination is not to forbid the use of landmarks and direction-posts on the way. . . .

There exists no moral system under which there do not arise unequivocal cases of conflicting obligation. These are real difficulties, the knotty points both in the theory of ethics and in the conscientious guidance of personal conduct. They are overcome practically, with greater or with less success, according to the intellect and virtue of the individual; but it can hardly be pretended that anyone will be the less qualified for dealing with them, from possessing an ultimate standard to which conflicting rights and duties can be referred. If utility is the ultimate source of moral obligations, utility may be invoked to decide between them when their de-

mands are incompatible. Though the application of the [utilitarian] standard may be difficult, it is better than none at all; while in other systems, the moral laws all claiming independent authority, there is no common umpire entitled to interfere between them; their claims to precedence one over another rest on little better than sophistry, and, unless determined, as they generally are, by the unacknowledged influence of consideration of utility, afford a free scope for the action of personal desires and partialities. We must remember that only in these cases of conflict between secondary principles is it requisite that first principles should be appealed to. There is no case of moral obligation in which some secondary principle is not involved; and if only one, there can seldom be any real doubt which one it is, in the mind of any person by whom the principle itself is recognized.

OF WHAT SORT OF PROOF THE PRINCIPLE OF UTILITY IS SUSCEPTIBLE

It has already been remarked that questions of ultimate ends do not admit of proof, in the ordinary acceptation of the term. To be incapable of proof by reasoning is common to all first principles; to the first premises of our knowledge, as well as to those of our conduct. But the former, being matters of fact, may be the subject of a direct appeal to the faculties which judge of fact—namely, our senses, and our internal consciousness. Can an appeal be made to the same faculties on questions of practical ends? Or by what other faculty is cognizance taken of them?

Questions about ends are, in other words, questions about what things are desirable. The utilitarian doctrine is, that happiness is desirable, and the only thing desirable, as an end; all other things being only desirable as means to that end. What ought to be required of this doctrine—what conditions is it requisite that the doctrine should fulfil—to make good its claim to be believed?

The only proof capable of being given that an object is visible, is that people actually see it. The only proof that a sound is audible, is that people hear it: and so of the other sources of our experience. In like manner, I apprehend, the sole evidence it is possible to produce that anything is desirable, is that people do actually desire it. If the end which the utilitarian doctrine proposes to itself were not, in theory and in practice, acknowledged to be an end, nothing could ever convince any person that it was so. No reason can be given why the general happiness is desirable, except that each person, so far as he believes it to be attainable, desires his own happiness. This, however, being a fact, we have not only all the proof which the case admits of, but all which it is possible to require, that happiness is a good: that each person's happiness is a good to that person, and the general happiness, therefore, a good to the aggregate of all persons. Happiness has made out its title as *one* of the ends of conduct, and consequently one of the criteria of morality.

But it has not, by this alone, proved itself to be the sole criterion. To do that, it would seem, by the same rule, necessary to show, not only that people desire happiness, but that they never desire anything else. Now it is palpable that they do desire things which, in common language, are decidedly distinguished from happiness. They desire, for example, virtue, and the absence of vice, no less really than pleasure and the absence of pain. The desire of virtue is not as universal, but it is as authentic a fact, as the desire of happiness. And hence the opponents of the utilitarian standard deem that they have a right to infer that there are other ends of human action besides happiness, and that happiness is not the standard of approbation and disapprobation.

The ingredients of happiness are very various, and each of them is desirable in itself, and not merely when considered as swelling an aggregate. The principle of utility does not mean that any given pleasure, as music, for instance, or any given exemption from pain, as for example health, is to be looked upon as means to a collective something termed happiness, and to be desired on that account. They are desired and desirable in and for themselves; besides being a means, they are part of the end. Virtue, according to the utilitarian doctrine, is not naturally and originally part of the end, but is capable of becoming so; and in those who live disinterestedly it has become so, and is desired and cherished, not as a means to happiness, but as part of their happiness.

To illustrate this further, we may remember that virtue is not the only thing originally a means, and which if it were not a means to anything else would be and remain indifferent, but which by association with what it is a means to comes to be desired for itself, and that too with the utmost intensity. What, for example, shall we say of the love of money? There is nothing originally more desirable about money than about any heap of glittering pebbles. Its worth is solely that of the things which it will buy; the desires for other things than itself, which it is a means of gratifying. Yet the love of money is not only one of the strongest moving forces of human life, but money is, in many cases, desired in and for itself; the desire to possess it is often stronger than the desire to use it, and goes on increasing when all the desires which point to ends beyond it, to be compassed by it, are falling off. It may, then, be said truly that money is desired not for the sake of an end, but as part of the end. From being a means to happiness, it has come to be itself a principal ingredient of the individual's conception of happiness. The same may be said of the majority of the great objects of human life: power, for example, or fame, except that to each of these there is a certain amount of immediate pleasure annexed, which has at least the semblance of being naturally inherent in them—a thing which cannot be said of money. . . .

It results from the preceding considerations that there is in reality nothing desired except happiness. Whatever is desired otherwise than as a means to some end beyond itself, and ultimately to happiness, is desired as itself a part of happiness, and is not desired for itself until it has become so. . . .

We have now, then, an answer to the question, of what sort of proof the principle of utility is susceptible. If the opinion which I have now stated is psychologically true—if human nature is so constituted as to desire nothing which is not either a part of happiness or a means of happiness—we can have no other proof, and we require no other, that these are the only things desirable. If so, happiness is the sole end of human action, and the promotion of it the test by which to judge of all human conduct; from whence it necessarily follows that it must be the criterion of morality, since a part is included in the whole. . . .

ON THE CONNECTION BETWEEN JUSTICE AND UTILITY

In all ages of speculation, one of the strongest obstacles to the reception of the doctrine that Utility or Happiness is the criterion of right and wrong, has been drawn from the idea of Justice. . . .

To throw light upon this question, it is necessary to attempt to ascertain what is the distinguishing character of justice, or of injustice: . . .

In the first place is mostly considered unjust to deprive anyone of his personal liberty, his property, or any other thing which belongs to him by law. Here, therefore, is one instance of the application of the terms just and unjust in a perfectly definite sense, namely, that it is just to respect, unjust to violate, the *legal rights* of any one. . . .

Secondly; the legal rights of which he is deprived, may be rights which *ought* not to have belonged to him; in other words, the law which confers on him these rights, may be a bad law. . . . When, however, a law is thought to be unjust, it seems to be regarded as being so in the same way in which a breach of law is unjust, namely, by infringing somebody's right; which, as it cannot in this case be a legal right . . . is called a moral right. We may say, therefore, that a second case of injustice consists in taking or withholding from any person that to which he has a *moral right*.

Thirdly, it is universally considered just that each person should obtain that (whether good or evil) which he *deserves;* and unjust that he should obtain a good, or be made to undergo an evil, which he does not deserve. . . . Speaking in a general way, a person is understood to deserve good if he does right, evil if he does wrong; and in a more particular sense, to deserve good from those to whom he does or has done good, and evil from those to whom he does or has done evil. . . .

Fourthly, it is confessedly unjust to *break faith* with any one: to violate an engagement, either express or implied, or disappoint expectations raised by our own conduct, at least if we have raised those expectations knowingly and voluntarily. . . .

Fifthly, it is, by universal admission, inconsistent with justice to be *partial*—to show favor or preference to one person over another in matters in which favor and preference do not apply. . . .

Among the many diverse applications of the term "justice" it is a matter of some difficulty to seize the mental link which holds them together. We must observe that it contains as yet nothing to distinguish that obligation [justice] from moral obligation in general. We do not call anything wrong unless we mean to imply that a person ought to be punished in some way or other for not doing it—if not by law, by the opinion of his fellow creatures; if not by opinion, by the reproaches of his own conscience. This seems the real turning point between morality and simple expediency. It is part of the notion of duty in every one of its forms that a person may rightfully be compelled to fulfill it. Duty is a thing which may be *exacted* from a person, as one exacts a debt. . . .

This, therefore, being the characteristic difference which marks off, not justice, but morality in general from the remaining provinces of expedience and worthiness, the character is still to be sought which distinguishes justice from other branches of morality. . . . In our survey of the various popular acceptations of justice, the term appeared generally to involve the idea of a personal right—a claim on the part of one or more individuals, light that which the law gives when it confers a proprietary or other legal rights. Whether the injustice consists in depriving a person of a possession, or in breaking faith with him, or in treating worse than he deserves, or worse than other people who have no greater claims—in each case the supposition implies two things: a wrong done, and some assignable person who is wronged. Injustice may also be done by treating a person better than others; but the wrong in this case is to the competitor, or are also assignable persons. It seems to me that this feature in the case—a right in some person, correlative to the moral obligation—constitutes the specific difference between justice and generosity or beneficence. Justice implies something which is not only right to do, and wrong not to do, but which some individual person can claim from us as his moral right. No one has a moral right to our generosity or beneficence because we are not morally bound to practice those virtues toward any given individual. . . .

We have seen that the two essential ingredients in the sentiment of justice are, the desire to punish a person who has done harm, and the knowledge or belief that there is some definite individual or individuals to whom harm has been done.

Now it appears to me, that the desire to punish a person who has done harm to some individual is a spontaneous outgrowth from two sentiments, both in the highest degree natural, and which either are or resemble instincts; the impulse of self-defence, and the feeling of sympathy.

It is natural to resent, and to repel or retaliate, any harm done or attempted against ourselves, or against those with whom we sympathize. The origin of this sentiment it is not necessary here to discuss. Whether it be an instinct or a result of intelligence, it is, we know, common to all animal nature; for every animal tries to hurt those who have hurt, or who it thinks are about to hurt, itself or its young. Human beings, on this point, only differ from other animals in two particulars. First, in being capable of sympathizing, not solely with their offspring, or, like some of the more noble animals, with some superior animal who is kind to them, but with all human, and even with all sentient beings. Secondly, in having a more developed intelligence, which gives a wider range to the whole of their sentiments, whether self-regarding or sympathetic. By virtue of his superior intelligence, even apart from his superior range of sympathy, a human being is capable of apprehending a community of interest between himself and the human society of which he forms a part, such that any conduct which threatens the security of the society generally, is threatening to his own, and calls forth his instinct (if instinct it be) of self-defence. The same superiority of intelligence, joined to the power of sympathizing with human beings generally, enables him to attach himself to the collective idea of his tribe, his country, or mankind, in such a manner that any act hurtful to them, raises his instinct of sympathy, and urges him to resistance.

The sentiment of justice, in that one of its elements which consists of the desire to punish, is thus, I conceive, the natural feeling of retaliation or vengeance, rendered by intellect and sympathy applicable to those injuries, that is, to those hurts, which wound us through, or in common with, society at large. This sentiment, in itself, has nothing moral in it; what is moral is, the exclusive subordination of it to the social sympathies, so as to wait on and obey their call. For the natural feeling would make us resent indiscriminately whatever any one does that is disagreeable to us; but when moralized by the social feeling, it only acts in the directions conformable to the general good: just persons resenting a hurt to society, though not otherwise a hurt to themselves, and not resenting a hurt to themselves, however painful, unless it be of the kind which society has a common interest with them in the repression of.

It is no objection against this doctrine to say that, when we feel our sentiment of justice outraged, we are not thinking of society at large or of any collective interest, but only of the individual case. It is common enough, certainly, though the reverse is commendable, to feel resentment merely because we have suffered pain; but a person whose resentment is really a moral feeling, that is, who considers whether an act is blamable before he allows himself to resent it—such a person, though he may not say expressly to himself that he is standing up for the interests of society, certainly does feel that he is asserting a rule which is for the benefit of others as well as for his own. If he is not feeling this, if he is regarding the act solely as it affects him individually, he is not consciously just; he is not concerning himself about the justice of his actions. This is admitted even by anti-utilitarian moralists. When Kant propounds as the fundamental principle of morals, "So act that thy rule of conduct might be adopted as a law by all rational beings," he virtually acknowledged that the interest of mankind collectively, or at least mankind indiscriminately, must be in the mind of the agent when conscientiously deciding on the morality of an act. To give any meaning to Kant's principle, the sense put upon it must be that we ought to shape our conduct by a rule which all rational beings might adopt *with the benefit of their collective interest.*

To recapitulate: the idea of justice supposes two things; a rule of conduct, and a sentiment which sanctions the rule. The first must be supposed common to all mankind, and intended for their good. The other (the sentiment) is a desire that punishment may be suffered by those who infringe the rule. There is involved, in addition, the conception of some definite person who suffers by the infringement; whose rights (to use the expression appropriated to the case) are violated by it. And the sentiment of justice appears to me to be, the animal desire to repel or retaliate a hurt or damage to oneself, or to those with whom one sympathizes, widened so as to include all persons, by the human capacity of enlarged sympathy, and the human conception of intelligent self-interest. From the latter elements, the feeling derives its morality; from the former, its peculiar impressiveness, and energy of self-assertion.

I have, throughout, treated the idea of a *right* residing in the injured person, and violated by the injury, not as a separate element in the composition of the idea and sentiment, but as one of the forms in which the other two elements clothe themselves. These elements are, a hurt to some assignable person or persons on the one hand, and a demand for punishment on the other. An examination of our own minds, I think, will show, that these two things include all that we mean when we speak of violation of a right. When we call anything a person's right, we mean that he has a valid claim on society to protect him in the possession of it, either by the force of law, or by that of education and opinion. If he has what we consider a sufficient claim, on whatever account, to have something guaranteed to him by society, we say that he has a right to it. If we desire to prove that anything does not belong to him by right, we think this done as soon as it is admitted that society ought not to take measures for securing it to him, but should leave him to chance, or to his own exertions. Thus, a person is said to have a right to what he can earn in fair professional competition; because society ought not to allow any other person to hinder him from endeavouring to earn in that manner as much as he can. But he has not a right to three hundred a year, though he may happen to be earning it; because society is not called on to provide that he shall earn that sum. On the contrary, if he owns ten thousand pounds three per cent, stock, he *has* a right to three hundred a year; because society has come under an obligation to provide him with an income of that amount.

To have a right, then, is, I conceive, to have something which society ought to defend me in the possession of. If the objector goes on to ask, why it ought? I can give him no other reason than general utility. If that expression does not seem to convey a sufficient feeling of the strength of the obligation, nor to account for the peculiar energy of the feeling, it is because there goes to the composition of the sentiment, not a rational only but also an animal element—the thirst for retaliation; and this thirst derives its intensity, as well as its moral justification, from the extraordinarily important and impressive kind of utility which is concerned. The interest involved is that of security, to everyone's feelings the most vital of all interests. . . .

We are continually informed that utility is an uncertain standard, which every different person interprets differently, and that there is no safety but in the immutable, ineffaceable, and unmistakable dictates of justice, which carry their evidence in themselves. [But] not only have different nations and individuals different notions of justice, but in the mind of one and the same individual, justice is not some one rule, principle, or maxim but many which do not always coincide in their dictates, and, in choosing between which, he is guided either by some extraneous standard or by his own personal predilections.

For instance, there are some who say that it is unjust to punish anyone for the sake of example to others. Others maintain the extreme reverse, contending that to punish persons who have attained years of discretion for their own benefit, is despotism and injustice since, if the matter is solely their own good, no one has a right to control their own judgment of it; but that they may justly be punished to prevent evil to others. . . .

To escape these and other difficulties, a favorite contrivance has been the fiction of a contract whereby at some unknown period all members of society engaged to obey the laws and consented to be punished for any disobedience to them, thereby giving to their legislators the right, which it is assumed they would not otherwise have had, of punishing them, either for their own good or for that of the society. This happy thought was considered to get rid of the whole difficulty and to legitimate the infliction of punishment, in virtue of another received maxim of justice—that is not unjust which is done with the consent of the person who is supposed to be hurt by it. I need hardly remark that, even if consent were not a mere fiction, this maxim is not superior in authority to others which it is brought in to supersede. It is, on the contrary, an instructive specimen of the loose and irregular matter in which supposed principles of justice grow up. . . .

Again, . . . how many conflicting conceptions of justice come to light in discussing the proper apportionment of punishment to offenses. [One is] an eye for an eye, a tooth for a tooth. [Others think] it should be measured by the moral guilt of the culprit, [or] what amount of punishment is necessary to deter the offense. To take another example, . . . in a cooperative industrial association is it just or not that talent or skill should give the title to superiour remuneration? On the negative side of the question it is argued that whoever does the best he can deserves equally well, and ought not in justice to be pun a position of inferiority for no fault of his own; that superior abilities have already advantages more than enough, in the admiration they excite, the personal influence they command, and the internal sources of satisfaction attending them, without adding to these a superior share of the world's goods; and that society is bound in justice rather to make compensation to the less favored for this unmerited inequality of advantages than to aggravate it. On the contrary side it is contended that society receives more from the efficient laborer; that, his services being more useful, society owes him the larger return for them; that a greater share of the joint result is ac-

tually his work, and not to allow his claim to it is a kind of robbery; that, if he is only to receive as much as others, he can only be justly required to produce as much, and to give a smaller amount of time and exertion, proportioned to his superior efficiency. Who shall decide between these appeals to conflicting principles of justice? Each, from his own point of view, is unanswerable; and any choice between them, on grounds of justice, must be perfectly arbitrary. Social utility alone can decide the preference. . . .

Has society been under a delusion in thinking that justice is a more sacred thing than policy, and that the latter ought only to be listened to after the former has been satisfied? By no means. . . . Justice is a name for certain classes of moral rules which concern the essential of human well being more nearly, and are therefore of more absolute obligation, than any other rules for the guidance of life. The moral rules which forbid mankind to hurt one another (in which we must never forget to include a wrongful interference with each other's freedom) are more vital to human well-being than any maxims, however important, which only point out the best mode of managing some department of human affairs. The moralities which protect every individual from being harmed by others, either directly or by being hindered in his freedom of pursuing his own good, are at once those which he himself has most at heart and those which he has the strongest interest in publishing and enforcing by word and deed. Now it is these moralities primarily which compose obligations of justice.

REVIEW AND DISCUSSION QUESTIONS

1. What does Mill mean in claiming that some pleasures are "higher" than others? What argument does Mill give for that conclusion?
2. Does Mill think people should appeal to utility directly, when deciding what to do, or should they rely on other standards and feelings? Explain.
3. Discuss Mill's "proof" of the utility principle.
4. Explain how Mill accounts for the apparent fact that people value and desire virtue for its own sake.
5. Explain the different forms of justice, indicating which features they share in common.
6. Describe the role of "sentiments" in Mill's theory of justice. How does he answer the charge that utilitarianism does not give an adequate account of justice?
7. Explain Mill's theory of rights.
8. How does Mill respond to those who argue that utilitarianism is a "godless" doctrine?

9. Describe how Mill understand's Kant's position, in relation to his own. Does Mill do justice to Kant on this score? Explain.

10. Contrast Mill's approach to ethics with the social contract theory. Why does Mill reject the social contract in favor of the utility principle?

11. How do Hume and Mill understand the idea of impartiality and its role in moral theory? How do Aristotle and Kant understand it? Which view of these theories seems most attractive? Why?

12. Philosopher Robert Nozick has raised an important question about value. Imagine, he suggests, that there existed an "experience machine" that would provide people any experience they want once they are hooked into it. Available experiences would include great pleasures, wonderful accomplishments, important relationships, or anything else that one wanted. The only catch, of course, is that it is all done via computers attached to the brain. The question, then, is whether there would be anything valuable that you would miss in the machine. What, other than the having of experiences, *is* valuable, if anything? How would Mill answer that question? What do you think the answer is?

3
Critical Perspectives

Essays in Section 3 are written by philosophers who are in different ways critical of the classical moral theories included in the last section. The first, by Friedrich Nietzsche, attacks the objectivity of ethics as well as the substance of traditional ethical thinking. Contrasting the morality of nobility to that of a slave, he describes the origins of the lower, slave morality in religion, weakness, and resentment. Though they differ on many points, the next two authors agree in criticizing many of the classical theorists for their emphasis on the ideal of impartiality. These doubts extend both to the possibility of such impartiality as well as the hope to find a universal basis of moral knowledge. One writer considers ethical theory from the feminist perspective, the other from a more social, communitarian standpoint. The section concludes with a constitutional case involving patriotism, free speech, and the right to burn the flag.

The Genealogy of Morals: An Attack

Friedrich Nietzsche

Friedrich Nietzsche was born in a small village in Saxony, Prussia, in 1844. His father died when Nietzsche was six. Nietzsche attended the University of Bonn, and later the University of Leipzig. He served during the war with Austria but was injured when thrown from a horse and was unable to complete his tour of duty. His health was poor, yet he was able to produce a large and important body of work. He spent years writing and trying to return to health. He became friends with Wagner. But, in 1889, Nietzsche became increasingly ill and soon went insane; the cause of his insanity is disputed. After spending time in a sanitarium, Nietzsche died in 1890.

Nietzsche's work has had a large impact, especially on the European continent. Nietzsche was impressed with classical Greek and Roman civilization and was deeply opposed to religion in general and to Christianity in particular. It is, he said, "the most fatal and seductive lie that has ever existed" and teaches a "morality of the paltry people." Nietzsche tirelessly attacked what he saw as the decadence of Europe at that time. In this essay, he discusses the origins and nature of English and Judeo-Christian moral teachings, contrasting them to the morality of nobility. It is in resentment, he claims, that one can see most clearly the origins of the morality of slaves.

From Friedrich Nietzsche, *The Birth of Tragedy and the Genealogy of Morals*, trans. Francis Golffing. Copyright © 1956 by Doubleday, a division of Bantam Doubleday Dell Publishing Group, Inc. Used by permission of Doubleday, a division of Bantam Doubleday Dell Publishing Group, Inc.

The English psychologists to whom we owe the only attempts that have thus far been made to write a genealogy of morals are no mean posers of riddles, but the riddles they pose are themselves, and being incarnate have one advantage over their books—they are interesting. What are these English psychologists really after? One finds them always, whether intentionally or not, engaged in the same task of pushing into the foreground the nasty part of the psyche, looking for the effective motive forces of human development in the very last place we would wish to have them found, e.g., in the inertia of habit, in forgetfulness, in the blind and fortuitous association of ideas: always in something that is purely passive, automatic, reflexive, molecular, and, moreover, profoundly stupid. . . . I do wish wholeheartedly that things may be otherwise with these men—that these microscopic examiners of the soul may be really courageous, magnanimous, and proud animals, who know how to contain their emotions and have trained themselves to subordinate all wishful thinking to the truth—any truth, even a homespun, severe, ugly, obnoxious, un-Christian, unmoral truth. For such truths do exist. . . .

All honor to the beneficent spirits that may motivate these historians of ethics! One thing is certain, however, they have been quite deserted by the true spirit of history. They all, to a man, think unhistorically, as is the age-old custom among philosophers. The amateurishness of their procedure is made plain from the very beginning, when it is a question of explaining the provenance of the concept and judgment good. "Originally," they decree, "altruistic actions were praised and approved by their recipients, that is, by those to whom they were useful. Later on, the origin of that praise having been forgotten, such actions were felt to be good simply because it was the habit to commend them." We notice at once that this first derivation has all the earmarks of the English psychologists' work. Here are the key ideas of utility, forgetfulness, habit, and, finally, error, seen as lying at the root of that value system which civilized man had hitherto regarded with pride as the prerogative of all men. This pride must now be humbled, these values devalued. Have the debunkers succeeded?

Now it is obvious to me, first of all, that their theory looks for the genesis of the concept good in the wrong place: the judgment good does not originate with those to whom the good has been done. Rather it was the "good" themselves, that is to say the noble, mighty, highly placed, and high-minded who decreed themselves and their actions to be good, i.e., belonging to the highest rank, in contradistinction to all that was base, low-minded and plebeian. It was only this *pathos of distance* that authorized them to create values and name them—what was utility to them? The notion of utility seems singularly inept to account for such a quick jetting forth of supreme value judgments. Here we come face to face with the exact opposite of that lukewarmness which every scheming prudence, every utilitarian calculus presupposes—and not for a time only, for the rare, exceptional hour, but permanently. The origin of the opposites *good* and *bad* is to be found in the pathos of nobility and distance, representing the dominant temper of a higher, ruling class in relation to a lower, dependent one. (The lordly right of bestowing names is such that one would almost be justified in seeing the origin of language itself as an expression of the rulers' power. They say, "This is that or that"; they seal off each thing and action with a sound and thereby take symbolic possession of it.) Such an origin would suggest that there is no *a priori* necessity for associating the word *good* with altruistic deeds, as those moral psychologists are fond of claiming. In fact, it is only after aristocratic values have begun to decline that the egotism-altruism dichotomy takes possession of the human conscience; to use my own terms, it is the herd instinct that now asserts itself. Yet it takes quite a while for this instinct to assume such sway that it can reduce all moral valuations to that dichotomy—as is currently happening throughout Europe, where the prejudice equating the terms *moral, altruistic,* and *disinterested* has assumed the obsessive force of an *idée fixe.*

Quite apart from the fact that this hypothesis about the origin of the value judgment *good* is historically untenable, its psychology is intrinsically unsound. Altruistic deeds were originally commended for their usefulness, but this original reason has now been forgotten—so the claim goes. How is such a forgetting conceivable? Has there ever been a point in history at which such deeds lost their usefulness? Quite the contrary, this usefulness has been apparent to every age, a thing that has been emphasized over and over again. Therefore, instead of being forgotten, it must have impressed itself on the consciousness with ever increasing clearness. The opposite theory is far more sensible, though this does not necessarily make it any the truer—the theory held by Herbert Spencer, for example, who considers the concept *good* qualitatively the same as the concepts *useful* or *practical*; so that in the judgments good and bad, humanity is said to have summed up and sanctioned precisely its unforgotten and unforgettable experiences of the *useful practical* and the *harmful impractical.* According to this theory, the *good* is that which all along has proved itself useful and which therefore may lay the highest claim to be considered valuable. As I have said, the derivation of this theory is suspect, but at least the explanation is self-consistent and psychologically tenable within its limits.

The clue to the correct explanation was furnished me by the question "What does the etymology of the terms for good in various languages tell us?" I discovered that all these terms lead us back to the same conceptual transformation. The basic concept is always *noble* in the hierarchical, class sense, and from this has developed, by historical necessity, the concept good embracing nobility of mind, spiritual distinction. This development is strictly parallel to that other which eventually converted the notions common, *plebeian, base* into the notion *bad.* Here we have an important clue to the actual genealogy of morals; that it has not been hit upon earlier is due to the retarding influence which democratic prejudice has had upon all investigation of origins. . . .

Granting that political supremacy always gives rise to notions of spiritual supremacy, it at first creates no difficulties (though difficulties might arise later) if the ruling caste is also the priestly caste and elects to characterize itself by a term which reminds us of its priestly function. In this context we encounter for the first time concepts of pure and *impure* opposing each other as signs of class, and here, too, *good* and *bad* as terms no longer referring to class, develop before long. . . . There is from the very start something unwholesome about such priestly aristocracies, about their way of life, which is turned away from action and swings between brooding and emotional explosions: a way of life which may be seen as responsible for the morbidity and neurasthenia of priests of all periods. Yet are we not right in maintaining that the cures which they have developed for their morbidities have proved a hundred times more dangerous than the ills themselves? Humanity is still suffering from the after-effects of those priestly cures. Think, for example, of certain forms of diet (abstinence from meat), fasting, sexual continence, escape "into the desert"; think further of the whole anti-sensual metaphysics of the priests, conducive to inertia and false refinement; of the self-hypnosis encouraged by the example of fakirs and Brahmans, where a glass knob and an *idée fixe* take the place of the god. And at last, supervening on all this, comes utter satiety, together with its radical remedy, nothingness—or God, for the desire for a mystical union with God is nothing other than the Buddhist's desire to sink himself in nirvana. Among the priests everything becomes more dangerous, not cures and specifics alone but also arrogance, vindictiveness, acumen, profligacy, love, the desire for power, disease. In all fairness it should be added, however, that only on this soil, the precarious soil of priestly existence, has man been able to develop into an interesting creature; that only here has the human mind grown both profound and evil; and it is in these two respects, after all, that man has proved his superiority over the rest of creation.

By now the reader will have got some notion how readily the priestly system of valuations can branch off from the aristocratic and develop into its opposite. An occasion for such a division is furnished whenever the priest caste and the warrior caste jealously clash with one another and find themselves unable to come to terms. The chivalrous and aristocratic valuations presuppose a strong physique, blooming, even exuberant health, together with all the conditions that guarantee its preservation: combat, adventure, the chase, the dance, war games, etc. The value system of the priestly aristocracy is founded on different presuppositions. So much the worse for them when it becomes a question of war! As we all know, priests are the most evil enemies to have—why should this be so? Because they are the most impotent. It is their impotence which makes their hate so violent and sinister, so cerebral and poisonous. The greatest haters in history—but also the most intelligent haters—have been priests. Beside the brilliance of priestly vengeance all other brilliance fades. Human history would be a dull and stupid thing without the intelligence furnished by its impotents. Let us begin with the most striking example. Whatever else has been done to damage the powerful and great of this earth seems trivial compared with what the Jews have done, that priestly people who succeeded in avenging themselves on their enemies and oppressors by radically inverting all their values, that is, by an act of the most spiritual vengeance. This was a strategy entirely appropriate to a priestly people in whom vindictiveness had gone most deeply underground. It was the Jew who, with frightening consistency, dared to invert the aristocratic value equations good/noble/powerful/beautiful/happy/favored-of-the-gods and maintain, with the furious hatred of the underprivileged and impotent, that "only the poor, the powerless, are good; only the suffering, sick, and ugly, truly blessed. But you noble and mighty ones of the earth will be, to all eternity, the evil, the cruel, the avaricious, the godless, and thus the cursed and damned!" . . . We know who has fallen heir to this Jewish inversion of values. . . . In reference to the grand and unspeakably disastrous initiative which the Jews have launched by this most radical of all declarations of war, I wish to repeat a statement I made in a different context *(Beyond Good and Evil),* to wit, that it was the Jews who started the slave revolt in morals; a revolt with two millennia of history behind it, which we have lost sight of today simply because it has triumphed so completely.

You find that difficult to understand? You have no eyes for something that took two millennia to prevail? . . . There is nothing strange about this: all long developments are difficult to see in the round. From the tree trunk of Jewish vengeance and hatred—the deepest and sublimest hatred in human history, since it gave birth to ideals and a new set of values—grew a branch that was equally unique: a new love, the deepest and sublimest of loves. From what other trunk could this branch have sprung? But let no one surmise that this love represented a denial of the thirst for vengeance, that it contravened the Jewish hatred. Exactly the opposite is true. Love grew out of hatred as the tree's crown, spreading triumphantly in the purest sunlight, yet having, in its high and sunny realm, the same aims—victory, aggrandizement, temptation—which hatred pursued by digging its roots ever deeper into all that was profound and evil. Jesus of Nazareth, the gospel of love made flesh, the "redeemer," who brought blessing and victory to the poor, the sick, the sinners—what was he but temptation in its most sinister and irresistible form, bringing men by a roundabout way to precisely those Jewish values and renovations of the ideal? Has not Israel, precisely by the detour of this "redeemer," this seeming antagonist and destroyer of Israel, reached the final goal of its sublime vindictiveness? Was it not a necessary feature of a truly brilliant politics of vengeance, a farsighted, subterranean, slowly and carefully planned vengeance, that Israel had to deny its true instrument publicly and nail him to the cross like a mortal enemy, so that "the whole world" (meaning all the enemies of Israel) might naively swallow the bait? And could one, by straining every resource, hit upon a bait more dangerous than this? What could equal in debilitating narcotic power the symbol of the "holy cross," the ghastly paradox of a crucified god, the unspeakably cruel mystery of God's self-crucifixion for the benefit of mankind? One thing is certain, that in this sign Israel has by now triumphed over all other, nobler values. . . .

The slave revolt in morals begins by rancor turning creative and giving birth to values—the rancor of beings who, deprived of the direct outlet of action, compensate by an imaginary vengeance. All truly noble morality grows out of triumphant selfaffirmation. Slave ethics, on the other hand, begins by saying no to an "outside," an "other," a non-self, and that no is its creative act. This reversal of direction of the evaluating look, this invariable looking outward instead of inward, is a fundamental feature of rancor. Slave ethics requires for its inception a sphere different from and hostile to its own. Physiologically speaking, it requires an outside stimulus in order to act at all; all its action is reaction. The opposite is true of aristocratic valuations: such values grow and act spontaneously, seeking out their contraries only in order to affirm themselves even more gratefully and delightedly. . . .

All this stands in utter contrast to what is called happiness among the impotent and oppressed, who are full of bottled-up aggressions. Their happiness is purely passive and takes the form of drugged tranquillity, stretching and yawning, peace, "sabbath," emotional slackness. Whereas the noble lives before his own conscience with confidence and frankness (*gennaios* "nobly bred" emphasizes the nuance "truthful" and perhaps also "ingenuous"), the rancorous person is neither truthful nor ingenuous nor honest and forthright with himself. His soul squints; his mind loves hide-outs, secret paths, and back doors; everything that is hidden seems to him his own world, his security, his comfort; he is expert in silence, in long memory, in waiting, in provisional self-depreciation, and in self-humiliation. A race of such men will, in the end, inevitably be cleverer than a race of aristocrats, and it will honor sharp-wittedness to a much greater degree, i.e., as an absolutely vital condition for its existence. . . .

The exact opposite is true of the noble-minded, who spontaneously creates the notion *good,* and later derives from it the conception of the *bad.* How ill-matched these two concepts look, placed side by side: the bad of noble origin, and the *evil* that has risen out of the cauldron of unquenched hatred! The first is a by-product, a complementary color, almost an afterthought; the second is the beginning, the original creative act of slave ethics. But neither is the conception of good the same in both cases, as we soon find out when we ask ourselves who it is that is really evil according to the code of rancor. The answer is: precisely the good

one of the opposite code, that is the noble, the powerful—only colored, reinterpreted, reenvisaged by the poisonous eye of resentment. And we are the first to admit that anyone who knew these "good" ones only as enemies would find them evil enemies indeed. For these same men who, amongst themselves, are so strictly constrained by custom, worship, ritual, gratitude, and by mutual surveillance and jealousy, who are so resourceful in consideration, tenderness, loyalty, pride and friendship, when once they step outside their circle become little better than uncaged beasts of prey. Once abroad in the wilderness, they revel in the freedom from social constraint and compensate for their long confinement in the quietude of their own community. They revert to the innocence of wild animals: we can imagine them returning from an orgy of murder, arson, rape, and torture, jubilant and at peace with themselves as though they had committed a fraternity prank—convinced, moreover, that the poets for a long time to come will have something to sing about and to praise. Deep within all these noble races there lurks the beast of prey, bent on spoil and conquest. This hidden urge has to be satisfied from time to time, the beast let loose in the wilderness. This goes as well for the Roman, Arabian, German, Japanese nobility as for the Homeric heroes and the Scandinavian vikings. The noble races have everywhere left in their wake the catchword "barbarian." And even their highest culture shows an awareness of this trait and a certain pride in it (as we see, for example, in Pericles' famous funeral oration, when he tells the Athenians: "Our boldness has gained us access to every land and sea, and erected monuments to itself *for both good and evil.*") This "boldness" of noble races, so headstrong, absurd, incalculable, sudden, improbable (Pericles commends the Athenians especially for their *rathumia*), their utter indifference to safety and comfort, their terrible pleasure in destruction, their taste for cruelty—all these traits are embodied by their victims in the image of the "barbarian," the "evil enemy," the Goth or the Vandal. The profound and icy suspicion which the German arouses as soon as he assumes power (we see it happening again today) harks back to the persistent horror with which Europe for many centuries witnessed the raging of the blond Teutonic beast (although all racial connection between the old Teutonic tribes and ourselves has been lost). . . . If it were true, as passes current nowadays, that the real meaning of culture resides in its power to domesticate man's savage instincts, then we might be justified in viewing all those rancorous machinations by which the noble tribes, and their ideals, have been laid low as the true instruments of culture. But this would still not amount to saying that the *organizers* themselves represent culture. Rather, the exact opposite would be true, as is vividly shown by the current state of affairs. These carriers of the leveling and retributive instincts, these descendants of every European and extra-European slavedom, and especially of the pre-Aryan populations, represent human retrogression most flagrantly. Such "instruments of culture" are a disgrace to man and might make one suspicious of culture altogether. One might be justified in fearing the wild beast lurking within all noble races and in being on one's guard against it, but who would not a thousand times prefer fear when it is accompanied with admiration to security accompanied by the loathsome sight of perversion, dwarfishness, degeneracy? And is not the latter our predicament today? What accounts for our repugnance to man—for there is no question that he makes us suffer? Certainly not our fear of him, rather the fact that there is no longer anything to be feared from him; that the vermin "man" occupies the entire stage; that, tame, hopelessly mediocre, and savorless, he considers himself the apex of historical evolution; and not entirely without justice, since he is still somewhat removed from the mass of sickly and effete creatures whom Europe is beginning to stink of today.

But to return to business: our inquiry into the origins of that other notion of goodness, as conceived by the resentful, demands to be completed. There is nothing very odd about lambs disliking birds of prey, but this is no reason for holding it against large birds of prey that they carry off lambs. And when the lambs whisper among themselves, "These birds of prey are evil, and does not this give us a right to say that whatever is the opposite of a bird of prey must be good?" there is nothing intrinsically wrong with such an argument—though the birds of prey will look somewhat quizzically and say, "*We* have nothing against these good lambs; in fact, we love them; nothing tastes better than a tender lamb."—To expect that strength will not manifest itself as strength, as the desire to overcome, to appropriate, to have enemies, obstacles, and triumphs, is every bit as absurd as to expect that weakness will manifest itself as strength. A quantum of strength is equivalent to a quantum of urge, will, activity, and it is only the snare of language (of the arch-fallacies of reason petrified in language), presenting all activity as conditioned by an agent—the "subject"—that blinds us to this fact. For, just as popular superstition divorces the lightning from its brilliance, viewing the latter as an activity whose subject is the lightning, so does popular morality divorce strength from its manifestations, as though there were behind the strong a neutral agent, free to manifest its strength or contain it. But no such agent exists; there is no "being" behind the doing, acting, becoming; the "doer" has simply been added to the deed by the imagination—the doing is everything. The common man actually doubles the doing by making the lightning flash; he states the same event once as cause and then again as effect. The natural scientists are no better when they say that "energy *moves*," "energy *causes*." For all its detachment and freedom from emotion, our science is still the dupe of linguistic habits; it has never yet got rid of those changelings called "subjects." The atom is one such changeling, another is the Kantian "thing-in-itself." Small wonder, then, that the repressed and smoldering emotions of vengeance and hatred have taken advantage of this superstition and in fact espouse no belief more ardently than that it is within the discretion of the strong to be weak, of the bird of prey to be a lamb. Thus they assume the right of calling the bird of prey to account for being a bird of prey. We can hear the oppressed, downtrodden, violated whispering among themselves with the wily vengefulness of the impotent, "Let us be unlike those evil ones. Let us be good. And the good shall be he who does not do violence, does not attack or retaliate, who leaves vengeance to God, who, like us, lives hidden, who shuns all that is evil, and altogether asks very little of life—like us, the patient, the humble, the just ones." Read in cold blood, this means nothing more than "We weak ones are, in fact, weak. It is a good thing that we do nothing for which we are not strong enough." But this plain fact, this basic prudence, which even the insects have (who, in circumstances of great danger, sham death in order not to have to "do" too much) has tricked itself out in the garb of quiet, virtuous resignation, thanks to the duplicity of impotence—as though the weakness of the weak, which is after all his essence, his natural way of being, his sole and inevitable reality, were a spontaneous act, a meritorious deed. This sort of person requires the belief in a "free subject" able to choose indifferently, out of that instinct of self-preservation which notoriously justifies every kind of lie. It may well be that to this day the subject, or in popular language the soul, has been the most viable of all articles of faith simply because it makes it possible for the majority of mankind—i.e., the weak and oppressed of every sort—to practice the sublime sleight of hand which gives weakness the appearance of free choice and one's natural disposition the distinction of merit. . . .

Let us conclude. The two sets of valuations, good/bad and good/evil, have waged a terrible battle on this earth, lasting many millennia; and just as surely as the second set has for a long time now been in the ascendant, so surely are there still places where the battle goes on and the issue remains in suspension. It might even be claimed that by being raised to a higher plane the battle has become much more profound. Perhaps there is today not a single intellectual worth his salt who is not divided on that issue, a battleground for those opposites. The watchwords of the battle, written in characters which have remained legible throughout human history, read: "Rome vs. Israel, Israel vs. Rome." No battle has ever been more momentous than this one. Rome viewed Israel as a monstrosity; the Romans regarded the Jews as *convicted* of hatred against the whole of mankind—and rightly so if one is justified in associating the welfare of the human species with absolute supremacy of aristocratic values. But how did the

Jews, on their part, feel about Rome? A thousand indications point to the answer. It is enough to read once more the Revelations of St. John, the most rabid outburst of vindictiveness in all recorded history. (We ought to acknowledge the profound consistency of the Christian instinct in assigning this book of hatred and the most extravagantly doting of the Gospels to the same disciple. There is a piece of truth hidden here, no matter how much literary skullduggery may have gone on.) The Romans were the strongest and most noble people who ever lived. Every vestige of them, every least inscription, is a sheer delight, provided we are able to read the spirit behind the writing. The Jews, on the contrary, were the priestly, rancorous nation par excellence, though possessed of an unequaled ethical genius; we need only compare with them nations of comparable endowments, such as the Chinese or the Germans, to sense which occupies the first rank. Has the victory so far been gained by the Romans or by the Jews? But this is really an idle question. Remember who it is before whom one bows down, in Rome itself, as before the essence of all supreme values—and not only in Rome but over half the globe, wherever man has grown tame or desires to grow tame: before three Jews and one Jewess (Jesus of Nazareth, the fisherman Peter, the rug weaver Paul, and Maria, the mother of that Jesus). This is very curious: Rome, without a doubt, has capitulated. It is true that during the Renaissance men witnessed a strange and splendid awakening of the classical ideal; like one buried alive, Rome stirred under the weight of a new Judaic Rome that looked like an ecumenical synagogue and was called the Church. But presently Israel triumphed once again, thanks to the plebeian rancor of the German and English Reformation, together with its natural corollary, the restoration of the Church—which also meant the restoration of ancient Rome to the quiet of the tomb. In an even more decisive sense did Israel triumph over the classical ideal through the French Revolution. For then the last political nobleness Europe had known, that of seventeenth- and eighteenth-century France, collapsed under the weight of vindictive popular instincts. A wilder enthusiasm was never seen. And yet, in the midst of it all, something tremendous, something wholly unexpected happened: the ancient classical ideal appeared incarnate and in unprecedented splendor before the eyes and conscience of mankind. Once again, stronger, simpler, more insistent than ever, over against the lying shibboleth of the rights of the majority, against the furious tendency toward leveling out and debasement, sounded the terrible yet exhilarating shibboleth of the "prerogative of the few." Like a last signpost to an *alternative* route Napoleon appeared, most isolated and anachronistic of men, the embodiment of the noble ideal. It might be well to ponder what exactly Napoleon, that synthesis of the brutish with the more than human, did represent. . . .

Was it all over then? Had that greatest conflict of ideals been shelved for good? Or had it only been indefinitely adjourned? Might not the smoldering fire start up again one day, all the more terrible because longer and more secretly nourished? Moreover, should we not wish for this event with all our hearts, and even help to promote it? If the reader at this point begins to develop his own train of thought, he is not likely soon to come to the end of it. . . .

It is no small discipline and preparation of the intellect on its road to final "objectivity" to see things for once through the wrong end of the telescope; and "objectivity" is not meant here to stand for "disinterested contemplation" (which is a rank absurdity) but for an ability to have one's pros and cons within one's command and to use them or not, as one chooses. It is of the greatest importance to know how to put the most diverse perspectives and psychological interpretations at the service of intellection. Let us, from now on, be on our guard against the hallowed philosophers' myth of a "pure, will-less, painless, timeless knower"; let us beware of the tentacles of such contradictory notions as "pure reason," "absolute knowledge," "absolute intelligence." All these concepts presuppose an eye such as no living being can imagine, an eye required to have no direction, to abrogate its active and interpretative powers—precisely those powers that alone make of seeing, seeing *something.* All seeing is essentially perspective, and so is all knowing. The more emotions we allow to speak in a given matter, the more different eyes we can put on in order to view a given spectacle, the more complete will be our conception of it, the greater our "objectivity." But to eliminate the will, to suspend the emotions altogether, provided it could be done—surely this would be to castrate the intellect, would it not?

REVIEW AND DISCUSSION QUESTIONS

1. Describe Nietzsche's view of "English psychologists" and moral philosophers, in particular their misunderstanding of history and of psychology.
2. What does Nietzsche mean by the *nobler values?*
3. Describe Nietzsche's view of "slave ethics." How is it connected with the priestly class?
4. What has been the role of Judaism and Christianity in the evolution of slave morality, according to Nietzsche?
5. Explain the role of resentment in Nietzsche's thinking.
6. What is the contrast between good and bad, on one hand, and good and evil, on the other? How are those two pairs related to Nietzsche's discussion of the noble and slave ethics.
7. What does Nietzsche understand "objectivity" to mean? How is it connected to the will?
8. How might Hume respond to Nietzsche?
9. Could Kant *prove* to Nietzsche that Nietzsche is mistaken? Explain, indicating whether you think the answer matters.
10. It is sometimes suggested there are two great motivations behind morality: (1) sympathy for others and (2) the desire to be able to defend one's actions to others in terms that they should accept. Explain how the classical theories of Section 2 might be said to exemplify that idea. Nietzsche would seem to take another view, however. Does he? Explain.

Feminist Ethics: Some Issues for the Nineties

Alison M. Jaggar

Beginning with a discussion of some of the objectives of feminist moral theory, Alison M. Jaggar goes on to discuss five different areas that have been the major focus of feminist ethics: equality and difference, impartiality, subjectivity, autonomy, and moral epistemology. Her conclusion is that feminist ethics, far from presenting a rigid orthodoxy, is full of controversy and excitement. And, she points out, the issues are not unique to feminists. Alison M. Jaggar is professor of philosophy at the University of Colorado at Boulder.

Feminist approaches to ethics are distinguished by their explicit commitment to re-thinking ethics with a view to correcting whatever forms of male bias it may contain. Feminist ethics, as these approaches are often called collectively, seeks to identify and challenge all those ways, overt but more often and more perniciously covert, in which western ethics has excluded women or rationalized their subordination. Its goal is to offer both practical guides to action and theoretical understandings of the nature of morality that do not, overtly or covertly, subordinate the interests of any woman or group of women to the interests of any other individual or group.

While those who practice feminist ethics are united by a shared project, they diverge widely in their views as to how this project may be accomplished. These divergences result from a variety of philosophical differences, including differing conceptions of feminism itself, a perennially contested concept. The inevitability of such disagreement means that feminist ethics cannot be identified in terms of a specific range of topics, methods or orthodoxies. For example, it is a mistake, though one to which even some feminists occasionally have succumbed, to identify feminist ethics with any of the following: putting women's interests first; focusing exclusively on so-called women's issues;

accepting women (or feminists) as moral experts or authorities; substituting "female" (or "feminine") for "male" (or "masculine") values; or extrapolating directly from women's experience.

Even though my initial characterization of feminist ethics is quite loose, it does suggest certain minimum conditions of adequacy for any approach to ethics that purports to be feminist.

1. Within the present social context, in which women remain systematically subordinated, a feminist approach to ethics must offer a guide to action that will tend to subvert rather than reinforce this subordination. Thus, such an approach must be practical, transitional and nonutopian, an extension of politics rather than a retreat from it. It must be sensitive, for instance, to the symbolic meanings as well as the practical consequences of any actions that we take as gendered subjects in a male dominated society, and it must also provide the conceptual resources for identifying and evaluating the varieties of resistance and struggle in which women, particularly, have tended to engage. It must recognize the often unnoticed ways in which women and other members of the underclass have refused co-operation and opposed domination, while acknowledging the inevitability of collusion and the impossibility of totally clean hands.

Reprinted by permission from *Journal of Social Philosophy*, 20, nos. 1–2 (Spring/Fall 1989) © 1989 *Journal of Social Philosophy*. Some notes and references omitted.

2. Since so much of women's struggle has been in the kitchen and the bedroom, as well as in the parliamentary chamber and on the factory floor, a second requirement for feminist ethics is that it should be equipped to handle moral issues in both the so-called public and private domains. It must be able to provide guidance on issues of intimate relations, such as affection and sexuality, which, until quite recently, were largely ignored by modern moral theory. In so doing, it cannot assume that moral concepts developed originally for application to the public realm, concepts such as impartiality or exploitation, are automatically applicable to the private realm. Similarly, an approach to ethics that is adequate for feminism must also provide appropriate guidance for activity in the public realm, for dealing with large numbers of people, including strangers.

3. Finally, feminist ethics must take the moral experience of all women seriously, though not, of course, uncritically. Though what is feminist will often turn out to be very different from what is feminine, a basic respect for women's moral experience is necessary to acknowledging women's capacities as moralists and to countering traditional stereotypes of women as less than full moral agents, as childlike or "natural." Furthermore, as Okin [1987], among others, has argued, empirical claims about differences in the moral experience of women and men make it impossible to assume that any approach to ethics will be unanimously accepted if it fails to consult the moral experience of women. Additionally, it seems plausible to suppose that women's distinctive social experience may make them especially perceptive regarding the implications of domination, especially gender domination, and especially well equipped to detect the male bias that has been shown to pervade so much of male-authored western moral theory.

On the surface, at least, these conditions of adequacy for feminist ethics are quite minimal—although I believe that fulfilling them would have radical consequences for ethics. I think most feminist, and perhaps even many nonfeminist,* philosophers would be likely to find the general statement of these conditions relatively uncontroversial, but that inevitably there will be sharp disagreement over when the conditions have been met. Even feminists are likely to differ over, for instance, just what are women's interests and when they have been neglected, what is resistance to domination and which aspects of which women's moral experience are worth developing and in which directions.

I shall now go on to outline some of these differences as they have arisen in feminist discussions of five ethical and meta-ethical issues. These five certainly are not the only issues to confront feminist ethics; on the contrary, the domain of feminist ethics is identical with that of nonfeminist ethics—it is the whole domain of morality and moral theory. I have selected these five issues both because I believe they are especially pressing in the context of contemporary philosophical debate, and because I myself find them especially interesting. As will shortly become evident, the issues that I have selected are not independent of each other; they are unified at least by recurrent concern about questions of universality and particularity. Nevertheless, I shall separate the issues for purposes of exposition.

1. EQUALITY AND DIFFERENCE

The central insight of contemporary feminism without doubt has been the recognition of gender as a sometimes contradictory but always pervasive system of social norms that regulates the activity of individuals according to their biological sex. Thus individuals whose sex is male are expected to conform to prevailing norms of masculinity, while female individuals are expected to conform to prevailing norms of femininity. In 1970, Shulamith Firestone began her classic *The Dialectic of Sex* with the words "Sex class is so deep as to be invisible" and, for the first decade of the contemporary women's movement, feminists devoted themselves to rendering "sex-class" or gender visible; to exploring (and denouncing) the

---

*"Nonfeminist" here refers to philosophers who do not make their feminist concerns explicit in their philosophical work; it is not intended to imply that such philosophers do not demonstrate feminist concern in other ways.

depth and extent of gender regulation in the life of every individual. Norms of gender were shown to influence not only dress, occupation and sexuality, but also bodily comportment, patterns of speech, eating habits and intellectual, emotional, moral and even physical development—mostly in ways that, practically and/or symbolically, reinforced the domination of men over women.

The conceptual distinction between sex and gender enabled feminists to articulate a variety of important insights. These included recognizing that the superficially nondiscriminatory acceptance of exceptional, i.e., "masculine," women is not only compatible with but actually presupposes a devaluation of "the feminine." The sex/gender distinction also enabled feminists to separate critical reflection on cultural norms of masculinity from antagonism towards actual men.

Useful as the concept of gender has been to feminism, however, more recent feminist reflection has shown that it is neither as simple nor as unproblematic as it seemed when feminists first articulated it. Some feminists have challenged the initially sharp distinction between sex and gender, noting that, just as sex differences have influenced (though not ineluctably determined) the development of gender norms, so gender arrangements may well have influenced the biological evolution of certain secondary sexual characteristics and even of that defining criterion of sex, procreation itself. Other feminists have challenged the distinction between gender and other social categories such as race and class. Recognizing that feminist claims about "women" often had generalized illicitly from the experience of a relatively small group of middle-class white women, feminists in the last ten years have emphasized that gender is a variable rather than a constant, since norms of gender vary not only between but also within cultures, along dimensions such as class, race, age, marital status, sexual preference and so on. Moreover, since every woman is a woman of some determinate age, race, class and marital status, gender is not even an independent variable; there is no concept of pure or abstract gender that can be isolated theoretically and studied independently of class, race, age or marital status. Neither, of course, can these other social categories be understood independently of gender.

Their increasingly sophisticated understandings of gender have complicated feminists' discussions of many moral and social issues. One of these is sexual equality. At the beginning of the contemporary women's movement, in the late 1960s, this seemed to be a relatively straightforward issue. The nineteenth century feminist preference for "separate spheres" for men and women had been replaced by demands for identity of legal rights for men and women or, as it came to be called, equality before the law. By the end of the 1960s, most feminists in the United States had come to believe that the legal system should be sex-blind, that it should not differentiate in any way between women and men. This belief was expressed in the struggle for an Equal Rights Amendment to the U.S. Constitution, an amendment that, had it passed, would have made any sex-specific law unconstitutional.

By the late 1970s and early 1980s, however, it was becoming apparent that the assimilationist goal of strict equality before the law does not always benefit women, at least in the short term. One notorious example was "no fault" divorce settlements that divided family property equally between husband and wife but invariably left wives in a far worse economic situation than they did husbands. In one study, for instance, ex-husbands' standard of living was found to have risen by 42% a year after divorce, whereas ex-wives' standard of living declined by 73%. This huge discrepancy in the outcome of divorce resulted from a variety of factors, including the fact that women and men typically are differently situated in the job market, with women usually having much lower job qualifications and less work experience. In this sort of case, equality (construed as identity) in the treatment of the sexes appears to produce an outcome in which sexual inequality is increased.

The obvious alternative of seeking equality by providing women with special legal protection continues, however, to be as fraught with dangers for women as it was earlier in the century when the existence of protective legislation was used as an excuse for excluding women from many of the more prestigious and better paid occupations. For instance, mandating special leaves for disability on account of pregnancy or childbirth promotes the perception that women are less reliable workers than men; recognizing "pre-menstrual syndrome" or post-partum depression as periodically disabling conditions encourages the perception that women are less responsible than men; while attempts to protect women's sexuality through legislation restricting pornography or excluding women from employment in male institutions such as prisons, perpetuate the dangerous stereotypes that women are by nature the sexual prey of men. This cultural myth serves as an implicit legitimation for the prostitution, sexual harassment and rape of women, because it implies that such activities are in some sense natural. In all these cases, attempts to achieve equality between the sexes by responding to perceived differences between men and women seem likely to reinforce rather than reduce existing differences, even differences that are acknowledged to be social rather than biological in origin.

Furthermore, a "sex-responsive," as opposed to "sex-blind," conception of equality ignores differences between women, separating all women into a single homogenous category and possibly penalizing one group of women by forcing them to accept protection that another group genuinely may need.

Sooner or later, most feminist attempts to formulate an adequate conception of sexual equality run up against the recognition that the baseline for discussions of equality typically has been a male standard. In Catharine MacKinnon's inimitable words:

Men's physiology defines most sports, their needs define auto and health insurance coverage, their socially designed biographies define workplace expectations and successful career patterns, their perspectives and concerns define quality in scholarship, their experiences and obsessions define merit, their objectification of life defines art, their military service defines citizenship, their presence defines family, their inability to get along with each other—their wars and rulerships—defines history, their image defines god, and their genitals define sex. [MacKinnon 1987:36]

Having once reached this recognition, some feminist theorists have turned away from debating the pros and cons of what MacKinnon calls the "single" versus the "double standard" and begun

speculating about the kinds of far-reaching social transformation that would make sex differences "costless." In discussions elaborating such notions as that of "equality as acceptance," feminists seem to be moving towards a radical construal of equality as similarity of individual outcome, equality of condition or effect, a conception quite at odds with traditional liberal understandings of equality as equality of procedure or opportunity.

While some feminists struggle to formulate a conception of sexual equality that is adequate for feminism, others have suggested that the enterprise is hopeless. For them, equality is an integral part of an "ethic of justice" that is characteristically masculine insofar as it obscures human difference by abstracting from the particularity and uniqueness of concrete people in their specific situations and seeks to resolve conflicting interests by applying an abstract rule rather than by responding directly to needs that are immediately perceived. Such feminists suggest that a discourse of responsibility or care may offer a more appropriate model for feminist ethics—even including feminist jurisprudence. Both of these suggestions remain to be worked out in detail.

The tangled debate over equality and difference provides an excellent illustration of one characteristic feature of contemporary feminist ethics, namely, its insistence that gender is often, if not invariably, a morally relevant difference between individuals. Given this insistence, the starting point of much feminist ethics may be different from that of modern moral theory: instead of assuming that all individuals should be treated alike until morally relevant grounds for difference in treatment can be identified, feminist theorists may shift the traditional burden of moral proof by assuming, until shown otherwise, that contemporary men and women are rarely "similarly situated." This leads into a related and equally crucial question for feminist ethics in the nineties, namely, how to characterize and evaluate impartiality.

2. IMPARTIALITY

In the modern western tradition, impartiality typically has been recognized as a fundamental value, perhaps even a defining characteristic of morality, distinguishing true morality from tribalism. Impartiality is said to require weighing the interests of each individual equally, permitting differentiation only on the basis of differences that can be shown to be morally relevant. Impartiality thus is linked conceptually with equality and also with rationality and objectivity, insofar as bias often has been defined as the absence of impartiality.

In the last few years, the preeminence traditionally ascribed to impartiality has been challenged both by feminist and nonfeminist philosophers. Nonfeminists have charged that an insistence on impartiality disregards our particular identities, constituted by reference to our particular projects and our unchosen relationships with others; and that it substitutes abstract "variables" for real human agents and patients. Williams [1973, 1981], for instance, has argued that the requirement of impartiality may undermine our personal integrity because it may require us to abandon projects that are central to our identity, and he also suggests that acting from duty may sometimes be less valuable than acting from an immediate emotional response to a particular other. MacIntyre [1981] and Sommers [1986] have argued that impartiality fails to respect tradition, customary expectations and unchosen encumbrances, and may require behavior that is morally repugnant.

While some of the moral intuitions that motivate the nonfeminist critics of impartiality certainly are shared by many feminists, other intuitions most likely are not. It is implausible to suppose, for instance, that most feminists would join Williams in applauding Gaugin's abandonment of his family in order to pursue his art, or that they would join Sommers in accepting without question the claims of customary morality on issues such as women's responsibilities. Instead, the feminist criticisms of impartiality tend to be both less individualistic and less conventionalist. They are quite varied in character.

Nell Noddings [1984] is one of the most extreme opponents of impartiality and her work has been influential with a number of feminists, even though the sub-title of her book makes it clear that she takes herself to be elaborating a feminine rather than a feminist approach to ethics. Noddings views the emotion of caring as the natural basis of morality, a view that would require impartiality to be expressed in universal caring. Noddings claims, however, that we are psychologically able to care only for particular others with whom we are in actual relationships, i.e., relationships that can be "completed" by the cared-for's acknowledgment of our caring. She concludes that pretensions to care for humanity at large are not only hypocritical but self defeating, undermining true caring for those with whom we are in actual relationship. Noddings' arguments, if valid, of course would apply indifferently to caring practised either by men or by women, and so the distinctively feminist interest of Noddings' work might seem to reside solely in her obviously debatable claim that women are "better equipped for caring than men" (97) and therefore less likely to be impartial. As we have noted already, however, feminist ethics is not committed to reproducing the moral practice even of most women and so feminist (and nonfeminist) moral theorists need to evaluate critically all of Noddings' arguments against impartiality, independently of whether her claims about "feminine" morality can be empirically confirmed.

A different criticism of impartiality has been made by those feminist philosophers who assert that, while impartiality is associated historically with individualism, it paradoxically undermines respect for individuality because it treats individuals as morally interchangeable [Code 1988; Sherwin 1987]. Many, though certainly not all, feminists claim that women are less likely than men to commit this alleged moral error because they are more likely to appreciate the special characteristics of particular individuals; again, however, feminist estimates of the soundness or otherwise of Code's and Sherwin's argument must be independent of this empirical claim.

Finally, at least one feminist has extended the claim that women need special protection in the law by recommending that feminist ethics should promote a double standard of morality, limiting moral communities on the basis of gender or perhaps gender solidarity. Susan Sherwin writes that feminists feel a special responsibility to reduce the suffering of women in particular; thus, "(b)y acknowledging the relevance of differences among people as a basis for a difference in sympathy and concern, feminism denies the legitimacy of a central premise of traditional moral theories, namely that all persons should be seen as morally equivalent by us" [Sherwin 1987:26 . . .]. However, since women and even feminists are not homogenous groups, as we have seen, this kind of reasoning seems to push the suggested double standard towards becoming a multiple moral standard—which Enlightenment theorists might well interpret as the total abandonment of impartiality and thus of morality itself.

A variety of responses seems to be available to the foregoing criticisms of impartiality. One alternative is to argue that the criticisms are unwarranted, depending on misrepresentation, misunderstanding and caricature of the impartialist position. If this response can be sustained, it may be possible to show that there is no real conflict between "masculine" impartialism and "feminine" particularism, "masculine" justice and "feminine" care. Another alternative is to bite the bullet of direct moral confrontation, providing arguments to challenge the intuitions of those who criticize impartiality as requiring courses of action that are morally repugnant or politically dangerous. Yet a third alternative may be to reconceive the concept of impartiality and the considerations appropriate for determining our responsibilities toward various individuals and groups. Feminist ethics must find a way of choosing between those or other options and evaluating the proper place of impartiality in ethics for the nineties.

3. MORAL SUBJECTIVITY

Related to the foregoing questions about impartiality are questions about how to conceptualize individuals, the subjects of moral theory. Feminists and nonfeminists alike have criticized the neo-Cartesian model of the moral self, a disembodied, separate, autonomous, unified, rational being, essentially similar to all other moral selves. Marx challenged the ahistoricism of this model; Freud challenged its claims to rationality; contemporary communitarians, such as Sandel and MacIntyre, challenge the assumption that individuals are "unencumbered," arguing instead that we are all members of communities from which we may be able to distance ourselves to some extent but which nevertheless are deeply constitutive of our identities; postmodernists have deconstructed the model to reveal fractured rather than unitary identities.

The gender bias alleged to contaminate each of the traditions mentioned above means that feminists cannot appropriate uncritically existing critiques of the neo-Cartesian moral self. Nevertheless, in developing their own challenges to this model of the self, feminist theorists often have paralleled and/or built on some nonfeminist work. . . .

Given this burgeoning literature, it is evident that a central concern for feminist ethics in the nineties must be to develop ways of thinking about moral subjects that are sensitive both to their concreteness, inevitable particularity and unique specificity, expressed in part through their relations with specific historical communities, and to their intrinsic and common value, the ideal expressed in Enlightenment claims about common humanity, equality and impartiality.

4. AUTONOMY

One aspect of this task is the rethinking of autonomy which, like impartiality (to which it is often conceptually connected), has been a continuing ideal of modern moral theory. (In addition, a closely related concept of autonomy has played a central role in the Cartesian epistemological tradition, which envisions the search for knowledge as a project of the solitary knower.) The core intuition of autonomy is that of independence or self legislation, the self as the ultimate authority in matters of morality or truth. In the Kantian tradition, where the ideal of autonomy is particularly prominent, moral autonomy has been elaborated in terms of disinterest, detachment from particular attachments and interests, and freedom from prejudice and self-deception [Hill 1987].

Contemporary feminists have had a mixed response to the modern ideal of moral autonomy. On the one hand, they have insisted that women are as autonomous in the moral and intellectual sense as men—as rational, as capable of a sense of justice, and so on; and they have also demanded political, social and economic autonomy for women through political representation, the abolition of sex discrimination and respect for women's choices on issues such as abortion. On the other hand, however, some feminists have questioned traditional interpretations of autonomy as masculine fantasies. For instance, they have explored some of the ways in which "choice" is socialized and "consent" manipulated. In addition, they have questioned the possibility of separating ourselves from particular attachments and still retaining our personal identity, and they have suggested that freeing ourselves from particular attachments might result in a cold, rigid, moralistic rather than a truly moral response [Noddings 1984]. Rather than guaranteeing a response that is purely moral, freeing ourselves from particular attachments might instead make us *incapable* of morality if an ineliminable part of morality consists in responding emotionally to particular others.

Feminist ethics in the nineties must find ways of conceptualizing moral agency, choice and consent that are compatible with the feminist recognition of the gradual process of moral development, the gendered social construction of the psyche, and the historical constraints on our options. This is one area in which some promising work by feminists exists already.

5. MORAL EPISTEMOLOGY AND ANTI-EPISTEMOLOGY

Enlightenment moral theory characteristically assumed that morality was universal—that, if moral claims held, they were valid at all times and in all places. However, the modern abandonment of belief in a teleological and sacred universe rendered the justification of such claims constantly problematic, and much moral theory for the last three centuries has consisted in attempts to provide a rational grounding for morality. At the present time, both the continental European tradition, especially but not only in the form of postmodernism, and the Anglo-American tradition, especially but not only in the form of communitarianism, have developed powerful challenges to the very possibility of the view that morality consists in universally valid rules grounded in

universal reason. The inevitable result of these skeptical challenges has been to reinforce normative and meta-ethical relativism.

Feminists are ambivalent about these challenges. On the one hand, many of the feminist criticisms of modern moral theory parallel the criticisms made by communitarianism and postmodernism. On the other hand, however, feminists are understandably concerned that their critique of male dominance should not be dismissed as just one point of view. It is therefore crucial for feminist ethics to develop some ways of justifying feminist moral claims. However, moral epistemology is an area in which feminists' critiques are better developed than their alternatives.

Feminist discussions of moral epistemology may be divided into two categories, each distinguished by a somewhat different view of the nature of morality. Feminists in the first category do not explicitly challenge the modern conception of morality as consisting primarily in an impartial system of rationally justified rules or principles, though few feminists would assert that it is possible to identify rules that are substantive, specific and hold in all circumstances. Those in the second category, by contrast, deny that morality is reducible to rules and emphasize the impossibility of justifying the claims of ethics by appeal to a universal, impartial reason. The contrast between these two groups of feminists is not as sharp as this initial characterization might suggest: for instance, both share several criticisms of existing decision procedures in ethics. But feminists in the former group are more hopeful of repairing those procedures, while feminists in the latter group seem ready to abandon them entirely.

Feminists in the latter group frequently claim to be reflecting on a moral experience that is distinctively feminine and for this reason they are often—incorrectly—taken to represent a feminist orthodoxy. They include authors such as Gilligan [1982], Noddings [1984], Baier [1987], Blum [1987], Ruddick [1989] and Walker [1989]. While there is considerable variation in the views of these authors, they all reject the view attributed to modern moral theorists that the right course of action can be discovered by consulting a list of moral rules, charging that undue emphasis on the epistemological importance of rules obscures the crucial role of moral insight, virtue and character in determining what should be done. A feminist twist is given to this essentially Aristotelian criticism when claims are made that excessive reliance on rules reflects a juridical-administrative interest that is characteristic of modern masculinity [Blum 1982] while contemporary women, by contrast, are alleged to be more likely to disregard conventionally accepted moral rules because such rules are insensitive to the specificities of particular situations [Gilligan 1982; Noddings 1984]. A morality of rule, therefore, is alleged to devalue the moral wisdom of women, as well as to give insufficient weight to such supposedly feminine virtues as kindness, generosity, helpfulness and sympathy.

Some feminists have claimed that "feminine" approaches to morality contrast with supposedly masculine rule-governed approaches in that they characteristically consist in immediate responses to particular others, responses based on supposedly natural feelings of empathy, care and compassion [Gilligan 1982; Noddings 1984] or loving attention [Murdoch 1970; Ruddick 1989]. However, apart from the difficulties of establishing that such a "particularist" approach to morality [Blum 1987] indeed is characteristically feminine, let alone feminist, attempts to develop a moral epistemology based on such responses face a variety of problems. First, they confront the familiar, though perhaps not insuperable, problems common to all moral epistemologies that take emotion as a guide to right action, namely, the frequent inconsistency, unavailability or plain inappropriateness of emotions. In other words, they face the danger of degenerating into a "do what feels good" kind of subjective relativism. In addition, it is not clear that even our emotional responses to others are not responses to them under some universal description and so in this sense general rather than particular—or, if indeed particular and therefore nonconceptual, then perhaps closer to animal than to distinctively human responses. It is further uncertain how these sorts of particular responses can guide our actions towards large numbers of people, most of whom we shall never meet. Finally, the feminist emphasis on the need for "contextual" reasoning opens up the obvious dangers of ad hocism, special pleading and partiality.

Not all feminists, of course, are committed to a particularist moral epistemology. Even some of those who take emotions as a proper guide to morality emphasize the intentionality of emotions and discuss the need for their moral education. Additionally, while most feminists criticize certain aspects of the decision procedures developed by modern moral theory, some believe it may be possible to revise and reappropriate some of these procedures. The main candidates for such revision are the methods developed by Rawls and Habermas, each of whom believes that an idealized situation of dialogue (which each describes differently) will both generate and justify morally valid principles. . . .

One possible alternative both to an unwelcome relativism and to what many feminists see as the pretensions of moral rationalism may be the development of a moral standpoint that is distinctively feminist. Sara Ruddick claims that such a standpoint can be found in maternal thinking [1989], but her work has been criticized by some feminists as ethnocentric and overvaluing motherhood. Even if the feminist standpoint were differently identified, however, problems would remain. Standpoint epistemology derives from Marx and, at least in its Lukacian version, it seems to require an objectivist distinction between appearance and reality that is quite alien to the social constructionist tendencies in much contemporary feminism.

The controversy in feminist moral epistemology currently is so sharp that Held [1984] has suggested abandoning the search for a "unified field theory" covering all domains of life activity. However, other authors have pointed to the danger that, if a supposedly feminine "ethic of care" were limited to the realm of personal life, as Kohlberg, for instance has suggested, it would be perceived as subordinate to the supposedly masculine "ethic of justice," just as, in contemporary society, the private is subordinate to the public.

CONCLUSION

Even such a limited survey as this should make it evident that feminist ethics, far from being a rigid orthodoxy, instead is a ferment of ideas and controversy, many of them echoing and deepening debates in nonfeminist ethics. The centrality of the issues and the liveliness of the on-going discussions suggest that the nineties will be a fruitful period for feminist ethics—and thus for ethics generally.

REFERENCES

Baier, Annette, "The Need for More Than Justice," *Science, Morality and Feminist Theory,* ed. Marsha Hanen and Kai Nielsen. Calgary: University of Calgary Press, 1987.

Blum, Lawrence, "Kant's and Hegel's Moral Rationalism: A Feminist Perspective," *Canadian Journal of Philosophy* 12:2 (June 1982).

Blum, Lawrence, "Particularity and Responsiveness," *The Emergence of Morality in Young Children,* eds. Jerome Kagan and Sharon Lamb. Chicago: University of Chicago Press, 1987.

Code, Lorraine, "Experience, Knowledge and Responsibility," *Feminist Perspectives in Philosophy,* eds. Morwenna Griffiths and Margaret Whitford. Bloomington and Indianapolis: Indiana University Press, 1988.

Gilligan, Carol, *In a Different Voice: Psychological Theory and Women's Development.* Cambridge, MA: Harvard University Press, 1982.

Held, Virginia, *Rights and Goods.* New York: The Free Press, 1984.

Hill, Thomas E., Jr., "The Importance of Autonomy," *Women and Moral Theory,* eds. Eva Feder Kittay and Diana T. Meyers. Totowa, NJ: Rowman and Littlefield, 1987.

MacIntyre, Alasdair, *After Virtue: A Study in Moral Theory.* London: Duckworth, 1981.

MacKinnon, Catharine A., *Feminism Unmodified: Discourses on Life and Law.* Cambridge, MA: Harvard University Press, 1987.

Murdoch, Iris, *The Sovereignty of Good.* London: Routledge & Kegan Paul, 1970.

Noddings, Nell, *Caring: A Feminine Approach to Ethics and Moral Education.* Berkeley: University of California Press, 1984.

Okin, Susan Moller, "Justice and Gender," *Philosophy and Public Affairs* 16:1 (Winter 1987).

Ruddick, Sara, *Maternal Thinking: Toward a Politics of Peace.* Boston: Beacon Press, 1989.

Sherwin, Susan, "A Feminist Approach to Ethics," *Resources for Feminist Research* 16:3, 1987. (Special issue on "Women and Philosophy.")

Sommers, Christina Hoff, "Filial Morality," *The Journal of Philosophy* 83:8 (August 1986).

Walker, Margaret, "Moral Understandings: Alternative 'Epistemology' for a Feminist Ethics," *Hypatia: A Journal of Feminist Philosophy* 4:2 (Summer 1989).

Williams, B., "Morality and the Emotions," *Problems of the Self.* Cambridge: Cambridge University Press, 1973.

Williams, B., "Persons, Character and Morality," "Moral Luck," and "Utilitarianism and Moral Self Indulgence," *Moral Luck.* Cambridge: Cambridge University Press, 1981.

REVIEW AND DISCUSSION QUESTIONS

1. What are the three conditions that various forms of feminist ethics have in common, according to Jaggar?
2. Describe the disputes that feminists have identified involving equality and difference.
3. Why have feminists often challenged the ideal of impartiality, according to Jaggar?
4. How have different feminists responded to the ideal of moral autonomy?
5. What are the two approaches feminists have taken toward moral epistemology?
6. Are feminists correct to attack impartiality, in your view? Explain.
7. Which of the traditional moral theories comes closest to Jaggar's conception of feminist ethics? How close is that theory?

Is Patriotism a Virtue?

Alasdair MacIntyre

In this essay, Alasdair MacIntyre argues that classical "liberal" moral theories such as utilitarianism and Kanteanism, which rest on familiar Enlightenment ideals of objectivity and impartiality, are deeply mistaken. Because such theories would have us judge actions from an impartial standpoint, it follows that patriotism, rather than being a virtue, would in fact be a moral vice since patriots are partial or biased in favor of their own nation. MacIntyre defends patriotism against this charge by questioning the adequacy of the liberal moral vision. Morality must finally rest, he claims, on the values found in the community in which people live rather than on the universal, cross-cultural norms of liberalism. The liberal vision should be replaced, he argues, by the patriot's willingness to exempt his or her nation's projects and practices from criticism. Such an exemption does not mean, however, that the patriot must support any particular policy or even government—but instead that he or she remains committed to the nation viewed as a historic project with a distinctive political and moral identity. Only through such a patriotic stance, he argues, can a satisfactory moral vision be supported, one that maintains the essentially historical connections that constitute a community's identity and provide people's lives with meaning. Alasdair MacIntyre is professor of philosophy at Duke University.

I.

. . . It is quite clear that there are large disagreements about patriotism in our society. And although it would be a mistake to suppose that there are only two clear, simple and mutually opposed sets of beliefs about patriotism, it is at least plausible to suggest that the range of conflicting views can be placed on a spectrum with two poles. At one end is the view, taken for granted by almost everyone in the nineteenth century, a commonplace in the literary culture of the McGuffey readers, that 'patriotism' names a virtue. At the other end is the contrasting view, expressed with sometimes shocking clarity in the nineteen sixties, that 'patriotism' names a vice. It would be misleading for me to suggest that I am going to be able to offer good reasons for taking one of these views rather than the other. What I do hope to achieve is a clarification of the issues that divide them.

A necessary first step is to distinguish patriotism properly so-called from two other sets of attitudes that are all too easily assimilated to it. The first is that exhibited by those who are protagonists of their own nation's causes because and only because, so they assert, it is their nation which is the champion of some great moral ideal. In the Great War of 1914–18 Max Weber claimed that Imperial Germany should be supported because its was the cause of *Kultur,* while Émile Durkheim claimed with equal vehemence that France should be supported because its was the cause of *civilization.* And here and now there are those American politicians who claim that the United States deserves our allegiance because it champions the goods of freedom against the evils of communism. What distinguishes their attitude from patriotism is twofold: first it is the ideal and not the nation which is the primary object of their regard; and secondly insofar as their regard for the ideal provides good reasons for allegiance to their country,

The Lindley Lecture, Department of Philosophy, University of Kansas (1984). © 1984 by the University of Kansas. Reprinted by permission.

it provides good reasons for anyone at all to uphold their country's cause, irrespective of their nationality or citizenship.

Patriotism by contrast is defined in terms of a kind of loyalty to a particular nation which only those possessing that particular nationality can exhibit. Only Frenchmen can be patriotic about France, while anyone can make the cause of *civilization* their own. But it would be all too easy in noticing this to fail to make a second equally important distinction. Patriotism is not to be confused with a mindless loyalty to one's own particular nation which has no regard at all for the characteristics of that particular nation. Patriotism does generally and characteristically involve a peculiar regard not just for one's own nation, but for the particular characteristics and merits and achievements of one's own nation. These latter are indeed valued as merits and achievements and their character as merits and achievements provides reasons supportive of the patriot's attitudes. But the patriot does not value in the same way precisely similar merits and achievements when they are the merits and achievements of some nation other than his or hers. For he or she—at least in the role of patriot—values them not just as merits and achievements, but as the merits and achievements of this particular nation. . . .

II.

The presupposition of the thesis [that patriotism is not a virtue] is an account of morality which has enjoyed high prestige in our culture. According to that account to judge from a moral standpoint is to judge impersonally. It is to judge as any rational person would judge, independently of his or her interests, affections and social position. And to act morally is to act in accordance with such impersonal judgments. Thus to think and to act morally involves a moral agent in abstracting him or herself from all social particularity and partiality. The potential conflict between morality so understood and patriotism is at once clear. For patriotism requires me to exhibit peculiar devotion to my nation and you to yours. It requires me to regard such contingent social facts as where I was born and what government ruled

over that place at that time, who my parents were, who my great-great-grandparents were and so on, as deciding for me the question of what virtuous action is—at least insofar as it is the virtue of patriotism which is in question. Hence the moral standpoint and the patriotic standpoint are systematically incompatible.

Yet although this is so, it might be argued that the two standpoints need not be in conflict. For patriotism and all other such particular loyalties can be restricted in their scope so that their exercise is always within the confines imposed by morality. Patriotism need be regarded as nothing more than a perfectly proper devotion to one's own nation which must never be allowed to violate the constraints set by the impersonal moral standpoint. This is indeed the kind of patriotism professed by certain liberal moralists who are often indignant when it is suggested by their critics that they are not patriotic. To those critics however patriotism thus limited in its scope appears to be emasculated, and it does so because in some of the most important situations of actual social life either the patriotic standpoint comes into serious conflict with the standpoint of a genuinely impersonal morality or it amounts to no more than a set of practically empty slogans. What kinds of circumstances are these? They are at least twofold.

The first kind arises from scarcity of essential resources, often historically from the scarcity of land suitable for cultivation and pasture, and perhaps in our own time from that of fossil fuels. What your community requires as the material prerequisites for your survival as a distinctive community and your growth into a distinctive nation may be exclusive use of the same or some of the same natural resources as my community requires for its survival and growth into a distinctive nation. When such a conflict arises, the standpoint of impersonal morality requires an allocation of goods such that each individual person counts for one and no more than one, while the patriotic standpoint requires that I strive to further the interests of my community and you strive to further those of yours, and certainly where the survival of one community is at stake, and sometimes perhaps even when only large interests of one community are at stake, patriotism entails a willingness to go to war on one's community's behalf.

The second type of conflict-engendering circumstance arises from differences between communities about the right way for each to live. Not only competition for scarce natural resources, but incompatibilities arising from such conflict-engendering beliefs may lead to situations in which once again the liberal moral standpoint and the patriotic standpoint are radically at odds. The administration of the *pax Romana* from time to time required the Roman *imperium* to set its frontiers at the point at which they could be most easily secured. . . . But this required infringing upon the territory and the independence of barbarian border peoples. A variety of such peoples—Scottish Gaels, Iroquois Indians, Bedouin—have regarded raiding the territory of their traditional enemies living within the confines of such large empires as an essential constituent of the good life; whereas the settled urban or agricultural communities which provided the target for their depredations have regarded the subjugation of such peoples and their reeducation into peaceful pursuits as one of their central responsibilities. And on such issues once again the impersonal moral standpoint and that of patriotism cannot be reconciled.

For the impersonal moral standpoint, understood as the philosophical protagonists of modern liberalism have understood it, requires neutrality not only between rival and competing interests, but also between rival and competing sets of beliefs about the best way for human beings to live. Each individual is to be left free to pursue in his or her own way that way of life which he or she judges to be best; while morality by contrast consists of rules which, just because they are such that any rational person, independently of his or her interests or point of view on the best way for human beings to live, would assent to them, are equally binding on all persons. Hence in conflicts between nations or other communities over ways of life, the standpoint of morality will once again be that of an impersonal arbiter, adjudicating in ways that give equal weight to each individual person's needs, desires, beliefs about the good and the like, while the patriot is once again required to be partisan.

Notice that in speaking of the standpoint of liberal impersonal morality in the way in which I have done I have been describing a standpoint whose truth is both presupposed by the political actions

and utterances of a great many people in our society and explicitly articulated and defended by most modern moral philosophers; and that it has at the level of moral philosophy a number of distinct versions—some with a Kantian flavour, some utilitarian, some contractarian. I do not mean to suggest that the disagreements between these positions are unimportant. Nonetheless the five central positions that I have ascribed to that standpoint appear in all these various philosophical guises: first, that morality is constituted by rules to which any rational person would under certain ideal conditions give assent; secondly, that those rules impose constraints upon and are neutral between rival and competing interests—morality itself is not the expression of any particular interest; thirdly, that those rules are also neutral between rival and competing sets of beliefs about what the best way for human beings to live is; fourthly, that the units which provide the subject-matter of morality as well as its agents are individual human beings and that in moral evaluations each individual is to count for one and nobody for more than one; and fifthly, that the standpoint of the moral agent constituted by allegiance to these rules is one and the same for all moral agents and as such is independent of all social particularity. What morality provides are standards by which all actual social structures may be brought to judgment from a standpoint independent of all of them. It is morality so understood allegiance to which is not only incompatible with treating patriotism as a virtue, but which requires that patriotism—at least in any substantial version—be treated as a vice.

But is this the only possible way to understand morality? As a matter of history, the answer is clearly 'No'. This understanding of morality invaded post Renascence Western culture at a particular point in time as the moral counterpart to political liberalism and social individualism and its polemical stances reflect its history of emergence from the conflicts which those movements engendered and themselves presuppose alternatives against which those polemical stances were and are directed. Let me therefore turn to considering one of those alternative accounts of morality, whose peculiar interest lies in the place that it has to assign to patriotism.

III.

According to the liberal account of morality *where* and *from whom* I learn the principles of morality are and must be irrelevant both to the question of what the content of morality is and to that of the nature of my commitment to it, as irrelevant as *where* and *from whom* I learn the principles and precepts of mathematics are to the content of mathematics and the nature of my commitment to mathematical truths. By contrast on the alternative account of morality which I am going to sketch, the questions of *where* and *from whom* I learn my morality turn out to be crucial for both the content and the nature of moral commitment.

On this view it is an essential characteristic of the morality which each of us acquires that it is learned from, in and through the way of life of some particular community. Of course the moral rules elaborated in one particular historical community will often resemble and sometimes be identical with the rules to which allegiance is given in other particular communities, especially in communities with a shared history or which appeal to the same canonical texts. But there will characteristically be some distinctive features of the set of rules considered as a whole, and those distinctive features will often arise from the way in which members of that particular community responded to some earlier situation or series of situations in which particular features of difficult cases led to one or more rules being put in question and reformulated or understood in some new way. Moreover the form of the rules of morality as taught and apprehended will be intimately connected with specific institutional arrangements. The moralities of different societies may agree in having a precept enjoining that a child should honor his or her parents, but what it is so to honor and indeed what a father is and what a mother is will vary greatly between different social orders. So that what I learn as a guide to my actions and as a standard for evaluating them is never morality as such, but always the highly specific morality of some highly specific social order. . . .

[It] is not just that I first apprehend the rules of morality in some socially specific and particularised form. It is also and correlatively that the goods by reference to which and for the sake of which any set of rules must be justified are also going to be goods that are socially specific and particular. For central to those goods is the enjoyment of one particular kind of social life, lived out through a particular set of social relationships and thus what I enjoy is the good of *this* particular social life inhabited by me and I enjoy it as what it is. It may well be that it follows that I would enjoy and benefit equally from similar forms of social life in other communities; but this hypothetical truth in no way diminishes the importance of the contention that my goods are as a matter of fact found *here,* among *these* particular people, in *these* particular relationships. . . .

It follows that *I* find *my* justification for allegiance to these rules of morality in *my* particular community; deprived of the life of that community, *I* would have no reason to be moral. But this is not all. To obey the rules of morality is characteristically and generally a hard task for human beings. Indeed were it not so, our need for morality would not be what it is. It is because we are continually liable to be blinded by immediate desire, to be distracted from our responsibilities, to lapse into backsliding and because even the best of us may at times encounter quite unusual temptations that it is important to morality that I can only be a moral agent because we are moral agents, that I need those around me to reinforce my moral strengths and assist in remedying my moral weaknesses. It is in general only within a community that individuals become capable of morality, are sustained in their morality and are constituted as moral agents by the way in which other people regard them and what is owed to and by them as well as by the way in which they regard themselves. . . .

Indeed the case for treating patriotism as a virtue is now clear. *If* first of all it is the case that I can only apprehend the rules of morality in the version in which they are incarnated in some specific community; and *if* secondly it is the case that the justification of morality must be in terms of particular goods enjoyed within the life of particular communities; and *if* thirdly it is the case that I am characteristically brought into being and maintained as a moral agent only through the particular kinds of moral sustenance afforded by my community, *then* it is clear that deprived of this community, I am unlikely to flourish as a moral agent. Hence my allegiance to the community and what it requires of me—even to the point of requiring me to die to sustain its life—could not meaningfully be contrasted with or counterposed to what morality required of me. Detached from my community, I will be apt to lose my hold upon all genuine standards of judgment. Loyalty to that community, to the hierarchy of particular kinship, particular local community and particular natural community, is on this view a prerequisite for morality. So patriotism and those loyalties cognate to it are not just virtues but central virtues. Everything however turns on the truth or falsity of the claims advanced in the three preceding if-clauses. . . . What we have here are two rival and incompatible moralities, each of which is viewed from within by its adherents as morality-as-such, each of which makes its exclusive claim to our allegiance. How are we to evaluate such claims?

One way to begin is . . . to focus attention on those accusations which the adherents of each bring against the rival position which the adherents of that rival position treat as of central importance to rebut. For this will afford at least one indication of the issues about the importance of which both sides agree and about the characterisation of which their very recognition of disagreement suggests that there must also be some shared beliefs. In what areas do such issues arise?

IV.

One such area is defined by a charge which it seems reasonable at least *prima facie* for the protagonists of patriotism to bring against liberal morality. The morality for which patriotism is a virtue offers a form of rational justification for moral rules and precepts whose structure is clear and rationally defensible. The rules of morality are justifiable if and only if they are productive of and partially constitutive of a form of shared social life whose goods are directly enjoyed by those inhabiting the particular communities whose social life is of that kind. Hence *qua* member of this or that particular community I can appreciate the justification for what morality requires of me from within the social roles that I live out in my community. By contrast, it may be argued, liberal

morality requires of me to assume an abstract and artificial—perhaps even an impossible—stance, that of a rational being as such, responding to the requirements of morality not *qua* parent or farmer or quarterback, but *qua* rational agent who has abstracted him or herself from all social particularity, who has become not merely Adam Smith's impartial spectator, but a correspondingly impartial actor, and one who in his impartiality is doomed to rootlessness, to be a citizen of nowhere. How can I justify to myself performing this act of abstraction and detachment?

The liberal answer is clear: such abstraction and detachment is defensible, because it is a necessary condition of moral freedom, of emancipation from the bondage of the social, political and economic *status quo*. For unless I can stand back from every and any feature of that *status quo,* including the roles within it which I myself presently inhabit, I will be unable to view it critically and to decide for myself what stance it is rational and right for me to adopt towards it. This does not preclude that the outcome for such a critical evaluation may not be an endorsement of all or some of the existing social order; but even such an endorsement will only be free and rational if I have made it for myself in this way. . . . Thus liberal morality does after all appeal to an overriding good, the good of this particular kind of emancipating freedom. And in the name of this good it is able not only to respond to the question about how the rules of morality are to be justified, but also to frame a plausible and potentially damaging objection to the morality of patriotism.

It is of the essence of the morality of liberalism that no limitations are or can be set upon the criticism of the social *status quo*. No institution, no practice, no loyalty can be immune from being put in question and perhaps rejected. Conversely the morality of patriotism is one which precisely because it is framed in terms of the membership of some particular social community with some particular social, political and economic structure, must exempt at least some fundamental structures of that community's life from criticism. Because patriotism has to be a loyalty that is in some respects unconditional, so in just those respects rational criticism is ruled out. But if so the adherents of the morality of patriotism have condemned themselves to a fundamentally irrational attitude—since to refuse to examine some of one's fundamental beliefs and attitudes is to insist on accepting them, whether they are rationally justifiable or not, which is irrational—and have imprisoned themselves within that irrationality. What answer can the adherents of the morality of patriotism make to this kind of accusation? The reply must be threefold.

When the liberal moralist claims that the patriot is bound to treat his or her nation's projects and practices in some measure uncritically, the claim is not only that at any one time certain of these projects and practices will be being treated uncritically; it is that some at least must be permanently exempted from criticism. . . . What then is exempted? The answer is: the nation conceived *as a project,* a project somehow or other brought to birth in the past and carried on so that a morally distinctive community was brought into being which embodied a claim to political autonomy in its various organized and institutionalised expressions. . . . What the patriot is committed to is a particular way of linking a past which has conferred a distinctive moral and political identity upon him or her with a future for the project which is his or her nation which it is his or her responsibility to bring into being. Only this allegiance is unconditional and allegiance to particular governments or forms of government or particular leaders will be entirely conditional upon their being devoted to furthering that project rather than frustrating or destroying it. Hence there is nothing inconsistent in a patriot's being deeply opposed to his country's contemporary rulers, or plotting their overthrow as Adam vot Trott did.

Yet although this may go part of the way towards answering the charge of the liberal moralist that the patriot must in certain areas be completely uncritical and therefore irrationalist, it certainly does not go all the way. For everything that I have said on behalf of the morality of patriotism is compatible with it being the case that on occasion patriotism might require me to support and work for the success of some enterprise of my nation as crucial to its overall project, crucial perhaps to its survival, when the success of that enterprise would not be in the best interests of mankind, evaluated from an impartial and an im-

personal standpoint. The case of Adam von Trott is very much to the point.

Adam von Trott was a German patriot who was executed after the unsuccessful assassination attempt against Hitler's life in 1944. Trott deliberately chose to work inside Germany with the minuscule, but highly placed, conservative opposition to the Nazis with the aim of replacing Hitler from within, rather than to work for an overthrow of Nazi Germany which would result in the destruction of the Germany brought to birth in 1871. But to do this he had to appear to be identified with the cause of Nazi Germany and so strengthened not only his country's cause, as was his intention, but also as an unavoidable consequence the cause of the Nazis. This kind of example is a particularly telling one, because the claim that such and such a course of action is "to the best interests of mankind" is usually at best disputable, at worst cloudy rhetoric. But there are a very few causes in which so much was at stake—and that this is generally much clearer in retrospect than it was at the time does not alter that fact—that the phrase has clear application: the overthrow of Nazi Germany was one of them.

How ought the patriot then to respond? Perhaps in two ways. The first begins by reemphasising that from the fact that the particularist morality of the patriot is rooted in a particular community and inextricably bound up with the social life of that community, it does not follow that it cannot provide rational grounds for repudiating many features of that country's present organized social life. The conception of justice engendered by the notion of citizenship within a particular community may provide standards by which particular political institutions are found wanting. . . . Yes, the liberal critic of patriotism will respond, this indeed may happen; but it may not and it often will not. Patriotism turns out to be a permanent source of moral danger. And this claim, I take it, cannot in fact be successfully rebutted. . . .

That the rational protagonist of the morality of patriotism is compelled, if my argument is correct, to concede this does not mean that there is not more to be said in the debate. And what needs to be said is that the liberal morality of impartiality and impersonality turns out also to be a morally dangerous phenomenon in an interestingly corresponding way. For suppose the bonds of patriotism to be dissolved: would liberal morality be able to provide anything adequately substantial in its place? What the morality of patriotism at its best provides is a clear account of and justification for the particular bonds and loyalties which form so much of the substance of the moral life. It does so by underlining the moral importance of the different members of a group acknowledging a shared history. Each one of us to some degree or other understands his or her life as an enacted narrative; and because of our relationships with others we have to understand ourselves as characters in the enacted narratives of other people's lives. Moreover the story of each of our lives is characteristically embedded in the story of one or more larger units. I understand the story of my life in such a way that it is part of the history of my family or of this farm or of this university or of this countryside; and I understand the story of the lives of other individuals around me as embedded in the same larger stories, so that I and they share a common stake in the outcome of that story and in what sort of story it both is and is to be: tragic, heroic, comic.

A central contention of the morality of patriotism is that I will obliterate and lose a central dimension of the moral life if I do not understand the enacted narrative of my own individual life as embedded in the history of my country. For if I do not so understand it I will not understand what I owe to others or what others owe to me, for what crimes of my nation I am bound to make reparation, for what benefits to my nation I am bound to feel gratitude. Understanding what is owed to and by me and understanding the history of the communities of which I am a part is on this view one and the same thing. . . .

In modern communities in which membership is understood only or primarily in terms of reciprocal self-interest, only two resources are generally available when destructive conflicts of interest threaten such reciprocity. One is the arbitrary imposition of some solution by force; the other is appeal to the neutral, impartial and impersonal standards of liberal morality. The importance of this resource is scarcely to be underrated; but how much of a resource is it? The problem is that some motivation has to be provided for allegiance to the standards of impartiality and impersonality which both has rational justification and can outweigh the

considerations provided by interest. Since any large need for such allegiance arises precisely and only when and insofar as the possibility of appeals to reciprocity in interests has broken down, such reciprocity can no longer provide the relevant kind of motivation. And it is difficult to identify anything that can take its place. The appeal to moral agents *qua* rational beings to place their allegiance to impersonal rationality above that to their interests has, just because it is an appeal to rationality, to furnish an adequate reason for so doing. And this is a point at which liberal accounts of morality are notoriously vulnerable. This vulnerability becomes a manifest practical liability at one key point in the social order.

Every political community except in the most exceptional conditions requires standing armed forces for its minimal security. Of the members of these armed forces it must require both that they be prepared to sacrifice their own lives for the sake of the community's security and that their willingness to do so be not contingent upon their own individual evaluation of the rightness or wrongness of their country's cause on some specific issue, measured by some standard that is neutral and impartial relative to the interests of their own community and the interests of other communities. And, that is to say, good soldiers may not be liberals and must indeed embody in their actions a good deal at least of the morality of patriotism. So the political survival of any polity in which liberal morality had secured large-scale allegiance would depend upon there still being enough young men and women who rejected that liberal morality. And in this sense liberal morality tends towards the dissolution of social bonds.

Hence the charge that the morality of patriotism can successfully bring against liberal morality is the mirror-image of that which liberal morality can successfully urge against the morality of patriotism. For while the liberal moralist was able to conclude that patriotism is a permanent source of moral danger because of the way it places our ties to our nation beyond rational criticism, the moralist who defends patriotism is able to conclude that liberal morality is a permanent source of moral danger because of the way it renders our social and moral ties too open to dissolution by rational criticism. And each party is in fact in the right against the other. . . .

REVIEW AND DISCUSSION QUESTIONS

1. Describe the two (mistaken) conceptions of patriotism that MacIntyre describes.
2. Describe what it is that "liberal" moral theories have in common, giving examples from other readings.
3. Explain MacIntyre's argument that patriotism (however defined) must be a vice from the perspective of liberal moral theory.
4. MacIntyre outlines an alternative to liberal morality (which is often termed *communitarianism*). Explain the three facts that, he claims, lead naturally to this moral theory as opposed to liberalism.
5. How does MacIntyre think patriotism should be understood?
6. MacIntyre argues that communitarian morality has an advantage over liberalism when people are asked to join the military and fight. Explain his argument.
7. How do you think a nation could identify its "historical project"? Can it be done without in some way invoking universal moral standards?
8. Is MacIntyre right in thinking that true patriotism does not rest in the commitment to one's country based on the values it stands for (freedom, for example)?
9. Might MacIntyre's view lead to ethical relativism and thus the conclusion that, for example, the Nazi's did not violate human rights? Explain.
10. Select one of the philosophers from the previous section and write a short essay explaining how you think that philosopher would respond to MacIntyre's discussion of the nature of morality and the role of impartiality.
11. Compare MacIntyre's position with Nietzsche's.

Flag Burning as Constitutionally Protected:

Texas v. *Johnson*

After burning the U.S. flag as an act of political protest, Gregory Lee Johnson was convicted of desecrating a flag in violation of Texas law. The state of Texas, after losing in lower courts, appealed to the U.S. Supreme Court, which had to decide whether Johnson's conviction was consistent with the First Amendment's protection of freedom of speech. By a narrow 5-to-4 vote, the Court again held that the Texas law was unconstitutional. Delivering the opinion of the Court, Justice Brennan argues that the state cannot "prescribe what shall be orthodox" by punishing symbolic actions like flag burning. The way to preserve the flag's special role in our national life, he argues, is not to punish those who feel differently about this symbol but to persuade them that they are wrong. In their separate dissents, Justice Rehnquist and Justice Stevens reject the idea that the flag is just another symbol, toward which it would be unconstitutional to require minimal respect.

57 L. W. 4770 (1989).

Justice Brennan: As in *Spence* [v. *Washington,* a 1974 case on expressive conduct], "[w]e are confronted with a case of prosecution for the express on of an idea through activity," and "[a]ccordingly, we must examine with particular care the interests advanced by [petitioner] to support its prosecution." . . . Johnson was not, we add, prosecuted for the expression of just any idea; he was prosecuted for his expression of dissatisfaction with the policies of this country, expression situated at the core of our First Amendment values.

Moreover, Johnson was prosecuted because he knew that his politically charged expression would cause "serious offense." If he had burned the flag as a means of disposing of it because it was dirty or torn, he would not have been convicted of flag desecration under this Texas law: federal law designates burning as the preferred means of disposing of a flag "when it is in such condition that it is no longer a fitting emblem for display." . . .

If we are to hold that a state may forbid flagburning wherever it is likely to endanger the flag's symbolic role, but allow it wherever burning a flag promotes that role—as where, for example, a person ceremoniously burns a dirty flag—we would be saying that when it comes to impairing the flag's physical integrity, the flag itself may be used as a symbol—as a substitute for the written or spoken word or a "short cut from mind to mind"—only in one direction. We would be permitting a state to "prescribe what shall be orthodox" by saying that one may burn the flag to convey one's attitude toward it and its referents only if one does not endanger the flag's representation of nationhood and national unity.

We never before have held that the government may ensure that a symbol he used to express only one view of that symbol or its referents. . . .

We are fortified in today's conclusion by our conviction that forbidding criminal punishment for conduct such as Johnson's will not endanger the special role played by our flag or the feelings it inspires. To paraphrase Justice [Oliver Wendell] Holmes, we submit that nobody can suppose that this one gesture of an unknown man will change our nation's attitude towards its flag. . . . Indeed, Texas's argument that the burning of an American flag " 'is an act having a high likelihood to cause a breach of peace,' " . . . and its statute's implicit assumption that physical mistreatment of the flag will lead to "serious offense," tend to confirm that the flag's special role is not in danger; if it were, no one would riot or take offense because a flag had been burned.

We are tempted to say, in fact, that the flag's deservedly cherished place in our community will be strengthened, not weakened, by our holding today. Our decision is a reaffirmation of the principles of freedom and inclusiveness that the flag best reflects, and of the conviction that our toleration of criticism such as Johnson's is a sign and source of our strength. Indeed, one of the proudest images of our flag, the one immortalized in our own national anthem, is of the bombardment it survived at Fort McHenry. It is the nation's resilience, not its rigidity, that Texas sees reflected in the flag— and it is that resilience that we reassert today.

The way to preserve the flag's special role is not to punish those who feel differently about these matters. It is to persuade them that they are wrong. "To courageous, self-reliant men, with confidence in the power of free and fearless reasoning applied through the processes of popular government, no danger flowing from speech can be deemed clear and present, unless the incidence of the evil apprehended is so imminent that it may befall before there is opportunity for full discussion. If there be time to expose through discussion the falsehood and fallacies, to avert the evil by the processes of education, the remedy to be applied is more speech, not enforced silence." . . . And, precisely because it is our flag that is involved, one's response to the flag-burner may exploit the uniquely persuasive power of the flag itself. We can imagine no more appropriate response to burning a flag than waving one's own, no better way to counter a flag-burner's message than by saluting the flag that burns, no surer means of preserving the dignity even of the flag that burned than by—as one witness here did—according its remains a respectful burial. We do not consecrate the flag by punishing its desecration, for in doing so we dilute the freedom that this cherished emblem represents.

Johnson was convicted for engaging in expressive conduct. The state's interest in preventing breaches of the peace does not support his conviction because Johnson's conduct did not threaten to disturb the peace. Nor does the state's interest in preserving the flag as a symbol of nationhood and national unity justify his criminal conviction for engaging in political expression. The judgment of the Texas Court of Criminal Appeals is therefore affirmed.

Justice Rehnquist, Dissenting: In holding this Texas statute unconstitutional, the court ignores Justice Holmes's familiar aphorism that "a page of history is worth a volume of logic." . . . For more than 200 years, the American flag has occupied a unique position as the symbol of our nation, a uniqueness that justifies a governmental prohibition against flag burning in the way respondent Johnson did here. . . .

In the First and Second World Wars, thousands of our countrymen died on foreign soil fighting for the American cause. At Iwo Jima in the Second World War, United States Marines fought hand-to-hand against thousands of Japanese. By the time the Marines reached the top of Mount Suribachi, they raised a piece of pipe upright and from one end fluttered a flag. That ascent had cost nearly 6,000 American lives. . . .

During the Korean War, the successful amphibious landing of American troops at Inchon was marked by the raising of an American flag within an hour of the event. . . .

The government is simply recognizing as a fact the profound regard for the American flag created by that history when it enacts statutes prohibiting the disrespectful public burning of the flag.

The court concludes its opinion with a regrettably patronizing civics lecture, presumably addressed to members of both houses of Congress, the members of the 48 state legislatures that enacted prohibitions against flag burning and the troops fighting under that flag in Vietnam who objected to its being burned: "The way to preserve the flag's special role is not to punish those who feel differently about these matters. It is to persuade them that they are wrong." . . .

The court's role as the final expositor of the Constitution is well established, but its role as a platonic guardian admonishing those responsible to public opinion as if they were truant school children has no similar place in our system of government. The cry of "no taxation without repre-

sentation" animated those who revolted against the English crown to found our nation—the idea that those who submitted to government should have some say as to what kind of laws would be passed. Surely one of the high purposes of a democratic society is to legislate against conduct that is regarded as evil and profoundly offensive to the majority of people—whether it be murder, embezzlement, pollution or flag burning.

Our Constitution wisely places limits on powers of legislative majorities to act, but the declaration of such limits by this court "is, at all times, a question of much delicacy, which ought seldom, if ever, to be decided in the affirmative, in a doubtful case." . . . Uncritical extension of constitutional protection to the burning of the flag risks the frustration of the very purpose for which organized governments are instituted. The court decides that the American flag is just another symbol, about which not only must opinions pro and con be tolerated, but for which the most minimal public respect may not be enjoined. The government may conscript men into the armed forces where they must fight and perhaps die for the flag, but the government may not prohibit the public burning of the banner under which they fight. I would uphold the Texas statute as applied in this case.

Justice Stevens, Dissenting: As the court analyzes this case, it presents the question whether the state of Texas, or indeed the federal government, has the power to prohibit the public desecration of the American flag. The question is unique. In my judgment, rules that apply to a host of other symbols, such as state flags, armbands or various privately promoted emblems of political or commercial identity, are not necessarily controlling. Even if flag burning could be considered just another species of symbolic speech under the logical application of the rules that the court has developed in its interpretation of the First Amendment in other contexts, this case has an intangible dimension that makes those rules inapplicable.

A country's flag is a symbol of more than "nationhood and national unity." . . . It also signifies the ideas that characterize the society that has chosen that emblem as well as the special history that has animated the growth and power of those ideas. The fleurs-de-lis and the tricolor both symbolized "nationhood and national unity," but they had vastly different meanings. The message conveyed by some flags—the swastika, for example—may survive long after it has outlived its usefulness as a symbol of regimented unity in a particular nation.

So it is with the American flag. It is more than a proud symbol of the courage, the determination and the gifts of nature that transformed 13 fledgling colonies into a world power. It is a symbol of freedom, of equal opportunity, of religious tolerance and of goodwill for other peoples who share our aspirations. The symbol carries its message to dissidents both at home and abroad who may have no interest at all in our national unity or survival.

The value of the flag as a symbol cannot be measured. Even so, I have no doubt that the interest in preserving that value for the future is both significant and legitimate. Conceivably that value will be enhanced by the court's conclusion that our national commitment to free expression is so strong that even the United States as ultimate guarantor of that freedom is without power to prohibit the desecration of its unique symbol. But I am unpersuaded. . . .

The case has nothing to do with "disagreeable ideas." . . . it involves disagreeable conduct that, in my opinion, diminishes the value of an important national asset.

The court is therefore quite wrong in blandly asserting that respondent "was prosecuted for his expression of dissatisfaction with the policies of this country, expression situated at the core of our First Amendment values." . . . Respondent was prosecuted because of the method he chose to express his dissatisfaction with those policies. Had he chosen to spray paint—or perhaps convey with a motion picture projector—his message of dissatisfaction on the facade of the Lincoln Memorial, there would be no question about the power of the government to prohibit his means of expression. The prohibition would be supported by the legitimate interest in preserving the quality of an important national asset. Though the asset at stake in this case is intangible, given its unique value, the same interest supports a prohibition on the desecration of the American flag.

The ideas of liberty and equality have been an irresistible force in motivating leaders like Patrick Henry, Susan B. Anthony and Abraham Lincoln, schoolteachers like Nathan Hale and Booker T. Washington, the Philippine Scouts who fought at Bataan, and the soldiers who scaled the bluff at Omaha Beach. If those ideas are worth fighting for—and our history demonstrates that they are— it cannot be true that the flag that uniquely symbolizes their power is not itself worthy of protection from unnecessary desecration.

I respectfully dissent.

REVIEW AND DISCUSSION QUESTIONS

1. What does Texas argue is the danger in allowing flag burning?
2. What is the "fixed star" in our constitutional system that Justice Brennan argues is at the heart of this issue?
3. Why, according to Justice Brennan, might allowing such political protests actually *increase* people's sense of patriotism?
4. Why does Justice Rehnquist think government is justified in prohibiting flag burning?
5. On what basis does Justice Stevens dissent?
6. How might it be argued that the preventing flag burning is *not* tantamount to establishing political orthodoxy?
7. Which position do you think Alasdair MacIntyre would probably support, given his understanding of the virtue of patriotism?
8. How might Nietzsche react to the issues raised in this case?

4
Relativism and Human Rights

Readings in Section 4 address two related issues: the nature of human rights and the claims of cultural and moral relativism. Authors take different perspectives, with some arguing for universal human rights and others defending the claim that they are culturally relative. The section concludes with a discussion of the nature of rights and the limits they place on governments committed to pursuing the "common good."

The African Context of Human Rights

Claude Ake

In this essay, Claude Ake argues that human rights, as understood by the West, are not of much importance from the perspective of modern Africa. In addition, argues Ake, an emphasis on rights will tend to retard economic and social development. Instead of the individual rights emphasized by Western liberalism, he concludes, Africa would benefit from a more socialist conception of collective or group rights. Claude Ake is professor of political science at the University of Port Harcourt, Nigeria.

Nobody can accuse Africa of taking human rights seriously. In a world which sees concern for human rights as a mark of civilized sensitivity, this indifference has given Africa a bad name. It is not unlikely that many consider it symptomatic of the rawness of life which has always been associated with Africa. I am in no position to say with any confidence why Africa has not taken much interest in human rights but I see good reasons why she should not have done so.

Before going into these reasons let us be clear what we are talking about. The idea of human rights is quite simple. It is that human beings have certain rights simply by virtue of being human. These rights are a necessary condition for the good life. Because of their singular importance, individuals are entitled to, indeed, required to claim them and society is enjoined to allow them. Otherwise, the quality of life is seriously compromised.

The idea of human rights, or legal rights in general, presupposes a society which is atomized and individualistic, a society of endemic conflict. It presupposes a society of people conscious of their separateness and their particular interests and anxious to realize them. The legal right is a claim which the individual may make against other members of society, and simultaneously an obligation on the part of society to uphold this claim.

The values implicit in all this are clearly alien to those of our traditional societies. We put less

From *Africa Today,* 34, nos. 1 & 2, 1987. Copyright © 1987 by Africa Today Associates. Reprinted by permission of the publisher.

emphasis on the individual and more on the collectivity, we do not allow that the individual has any claims which may override that of the society. We assume harmony, not divergence of interests, competition and conflict; we are more inclined to think of our obligations to other members of our society rather than our claims against them.

The Western notion of human rights stresses rights which are not very interesting in the context of African realities. There is much concern with the right to peaceful assembly, free speech and thought, fair trial, etc. The appeal of these rights is sociologically specific. They appeal to people with a full stomach who can now afford to pursue the more esoteric aspects of self-fulfillment. The vast majority of our people are not in this position. They are facing the struggle for existence in its brutal immediacy. Theirs is a totally consuming struggle. They have little or no time for reflection and hardly any use for free speech. They have little interest in choice for there is no choice in ignorance. There is no freedom for hungry people, or those eternally oppressed by disease. It is no wonder that the idea of human rights has tended to sound hollow in the African context.

The Western notion of human rights lacks concreteness. It ascribes abstract rights to abstract beings. There is not enough concern for the historical conditions in which human rights can actually be realized. As it turns out, only a few people are in a position to exercise the rights which society allows. The few who have the resources to exercise these rights do not need a bill of rights. Their power secures them. The many who do not have the resources to exercise their rights are not helped any by the existence of these rights. Their powerlessness dooms them.

The idea of human rights really came into its own as a tool for opposing democracy. The French Revolution had brought home forcefully to everyone the paradox of democracy, namely that its two central values, liberty and equality, come into conflict at critical points. There is no democracy where there is no liberty for self-expression or choice. At the same time there is no democracy where there is no equality, for inequality reduces human relations to subordination and domination. The French Revolution and Jean Jacques Rousseau revealed rather dramatically the paradoxical rela-

tion between these two central values of democracy by leaning heavily towards equality. They gave Europe a taste of what it would be like to take the idea of equality and the correlative idea of popular sovereignty seriously.

Bourgeois Europe was horrified. The idea of a popular sovereign insisting on equality and having unlimited power over every aspect of social life was unacceptable. For such power was a threat to the institution of private property as well as the conditions of accumulation. So they began to emphasize liberty rather than the collectivity. This emphasis was also a way of rejecting democracy in its pure form as popular sovereignty. That was the point of stressing the individual and his rights and holding that certain rights are inalienable. That was the point of holding that the individual could successfully sustain certain claims and certain immunities against the wishes of the sovereign or even the rest of society. It is ironical that all this is conveniently forgotten today and liberal democrats can pass as the veritable defenders of democracy.

CHANGING STATUS OF HUMAN RIGHTS IN AFRICA

Africa is at last beginning to take interest in human rights. For one thing, the Western conception of human rights has evolved in ways which have made it more relevant to the African experience, although its relevance still remains ambiguous. Because human rights is such an important part of the political ideology of the West, it was bound to register in Africa eventually. Human rights record is beginning to feature in Western decisions of how to relate to the countries and leaders of Africa. Western decisions on this score have been made with such cynical inconsistency that one wonders whether human rights record really matters to them at all. However, our leaders ever so eager to please are obliged to assume that it matters and to adjust their behavior accordingly. Also the authoritarian capitalism of Africa is under some pressure to be more liberal and thereby create political conditions more conducive to capitalist efficiency.

If these are the reasons why Africa is beginning to take more interest in human rights, they are by no means the reason why she ought to do so. The way I see it is that we ought to be interested in human rights because it will help us to combat social forces which threaten to send us back to barbarism. Because it will aid our struggle for the social transformation which we need to survive and to flourish. To appreciate this let us look at the historical conditions of contemporary Africa.

I hope we can all agree that for now, the most salient aspect of these conditions is the crisis. It has been with us for so long we might well talk of the permanent crisis. No one seems to know for sure what its character is but we know its devastating effects only too well. We Africans have never had it so bad. The tragic consequences of our development strategies have finally come home to us. Always oppressed by poverty and deprivation, our lives become harsher still with each passing day as real incomes continue to decline. We watch helplessly while millions of our people are threatened by famine and look pitifully to the rest of the world to feed us. Our social and political institutions are disintegrating under pressure from our flagging morale, our dwindling resources and the intense struggle to control them. What is the problem? I am not sure. But I am convinced that we are not dealing simply or even primarily with an economic phenomenon. There is a political dimension to it which is so critical, it may well be the most decisive factor.

This is the problem of democracy or the problem of political repression. A long time ago our leaders opted for political repression. Having abandoned democracy for repression, our leaders are delinked from our people. Operating in a vacuum, they proclaim their incarnation of the popular will, hear echoes of their own voices, and reassured, pursue with zeal, policies which have nothing to do with the aspirations of our people and which cannot, therefore, mobilize them. As their alienation from the people increases, they rely more and more on force and become even more alienated.

CONSEQUENCES OF THE PROBLEM OF DEMOCRACY

The consequences of this are disastrous. In the first place it means that there is no development. Political repression ensures that the ordinary people of Africa who are the object of development remain silent, so that in the end nobody really speaks for development and it never comes alive in practice. Development cannot be achieved by proxy. A people develops itself or not at all. And it can develop itself only through its commitment and its energy. That is where democracy comes in. Self-reliance is not possible unless the society is thoroughly democratic, unless the people are the end and not just the means of development. Development occurs, in so far as it amounts to the pursuit of objectives set by the people themselves in their own interest and pursued by means of their own resources.

Another consequence of repression is the brutalization of our people. Look around you. The willful brutalization of people occurring among us is appalling. Human life is taken lightly, especially if it is that of the underprivileged. All manner of inhuman treatment is meted out for minor offenses and sometimes for no offenses at all. Ordinary people are terrorized daily by wanton display of state power and its instruments of violence. Our prison conditions are guaranteed to traumatize. The only consensus we can mobilize is passive conformity arising from fear and resignation. As we continue to stagnate this gets worse.

Yet another disaster threatens us. I am referring to fascism. In all probability this is something which nobody wants. But we might get it anyway because circumstances are moving steadily in that direction. All the ingredients of fascism are present now in most parts of Africa: a political class which has failed even by its own standards, and which is now acutely conscious of its humiliation and baffled by a world it cannot control; a people who have little if any hope or sense of self-worth yearning for redeemers; a milieu of anomie; a conservative leadership pitted against a rising popular radicalism and poised to take cover in defensive radicalism. That is what it takes and it is there in plenty. If Africa succumbs it will be terrible—fascism has always been in all its historical manifestations.

It seems to me that for many African countries the specter of fascism is the most urgent and the most serious danger today. Unless we contain it effectively and within a very short time, then we are in a great deal of trouble.

If this analysis is correct, then our present agenda must be the task of preventing the rise of fascism. To have a chance of succeeding this task requires a broad coalition of radicals, populists, liberals and even humane conservatives. That is, a coalition of all those who value democracy not in the procedural liberal sense but in the concrete socialist sense. This is where the idea of human rights comes in. It is easily the best ideological framework for such a coalition.

AN AFRICAN CONCEPTION OF HUMAN RIGHTS

We have now seen the relevance of human rights in the African context. But on a level of generality which does not tell us very much and so does not really settle the question of the applicability of the Western concept of human rights. I do not see how we can mobilize the African masses or the intelligentsia against fascism or whatever by accepting uncritically the Western notion of human rights. We have to domesticate it, recreate it in the light of African conditions. Let me indicate very briefly how these conditions redefine the idea of human rights.

First, we have to understand that the idea of legal rights presupposes social atomization and individualism, and a conflict model of society for which legal rights are the necessary mediation. However, in most of Africa, the extent of social atomization is very limited mainly because of the limited penetration of capitalism and commodity relations. Many people are still locked into natural economies and have a sense of belonging to an organic whole, be it a family, a clan, a lineage or an ethnic group. The phenomenon of the legal subject, the largely autonomous individual conceived as a bundle of rights which are asserted against all comers has not really developed much especially outside the urban areas.

These are the conditions which explain the forms of consciousness which we insist on misunderstanding. For instance, ethnic consciousness and ethnic identity. It is the necessary consciousness associated with non-atomized social structures and mechanical solidarity. Ethnic consciousness will be with us as long as these

structural features remain, no matter how we condemn it or try to engineer it out of existence.

All this means that abstract legal rights attributed to individuals will not make much sense for most of our people; neither will they be relevant to their consciousness and living conditions. It is necessary to extend the idea of human rights to include collective human rights for corporate social groups such as the family, the lineage, the ethnic group. Our people still think largely in terms of collective rights and express their commitment to it constantly in their behavior. This disposition underlies the zeal for community development and the enormous sacrifices which poor people readily make for it. It underlies the so-called tribalist voting pattern of our people, the willingness of the poor villager to believe that the minister from his village somehow represents his share of the national cake, our traditional land tenure systems, the high incidence of cooperative labor and relations of production in the rural areas. These forms of consciousness remain very important features of our lives. If the idea of human rights is to make any sense at all in the African context, it has to incorporate them in a concept of communal human rights.

For reasons which need not detain us here some of the rights important in the West are of no interest and no value to most Africans. For instance, freedom of speech and freedom of the press do not mean much for a largely illiterate rural community completely absorbed in the daily rigors of the struggle for survival.

African conditions shift the emphasis to a different kind of rights. Rights which can mean something for poor people fighting to survive and burdened by ignorance, poverty and disease, rights which can mean something for women who are cruelly used. Rights which can mean something for the youth whose future we render more improbable every day. If a bill of rights is to make any sense, it must include among others, a right to work and to a living wage, a right to shelter, to health, to education. That is the least we can strive for if we are ever going to have a society which realizes basic human needs.

Finally, in the African context, human rights have to be much more than the political correlate of commodity fetishism which is what they are in the Western tradition. In that tradition the rights are not only abstract, they are also ascribed to abstract persons. The rights are ascribed to the human being from whom all specific determinations have been abstracted: the rights have no content just as individuals who enjoy them have no determination and so do not really exist.

All these problems which usually lurk beneath the surface appear in clear relief when we confront them with empirical reality. Granted, I have the freedom of speech. But where is this freedom, this right? I cannot read, I cannot write. I am too busy trying to survive. I have no time to reflect. I am so poor I am constantly at the mercy of others. So where is this right and what is it really? Granted, I have the right to seek public office. That is all very well. But how do I realize this right? I am a full-time public servant who cannot find the time or the necessary resources to put up the organization required to win office. If I take leave from my work, I cannot hold out for more than one month without a salary. I have no money to travel about and meet the voters, even to pay the registration fees for my candidature. If I am not in a position to realize this right, then what is the point of saying that I have it? Do I really have it?

In Africa liberal rights make less sense even as ideological representations. If rights are to be meaningful in the context of a people struggling to stay afloat under very adverse economic and political conditions, they have to be concrete. Concrete in the sense that their practical import is visible and relevant to the conditions of existence of the people to whom they apply. And most importantly, concrete in the sense that they can be realized by their beneficiaries.

To be sure, there are rights which are realizable and there are people in Africa who effectively realize their rights. However, the people who are in a position to realize their rights are very few. They are able to realize their rights by virtue of their wealth and power. The litmus test for rights is those who need protection. Unfortunately these are precisely the people who are in no position to enjoy rights. Clearly, that will not do in African conditions. People are not going to struggle for formalities and esoteric ideas which will not change their lives.

Therefore, a real need arises, namely, to put more emphasis on the realization of human rights. How is this to be? Not in the way we usually approach such matters: by giving more unrealizable rights to the powerless and by begging the powerful to make concessions to them in the name of enlightened self-interest, justice and humanity. That approach will fail us always. Rights, especially those that have any real significance for our lives are usually taken, not given—with the cooperation of those in power if possible, but without it if necessary. That is the way it was for other peoples and that is the way it is going to be in Africa.

The realization of rights is best guaranteed by the power of those who enjoy the rights. Following this, what is needed is the empowerment by whatever means, of the common people. This is not a matter of legislation, although legislation could help a little. It is rather a matter of redistributing economic and political power across the board. That means that it is in the final analysis a matter of political mobilization and struggle. And it will be a protracted and bitter struggle because those who are favored by the existing distribution of power will resist heartily.

CONCLUSION: HUMAN RIGHTS AND SOCIAL TRANSFORMATION

It is at this point that the ideal of human rights is fully articulated for it is now that we see its critical dialectical moment. Initially part of the ideological prop of liberal capitalism, the idea of human rights was a conservative force. It was meant to safeguard the interests of the men of property especially against the threatening egalitarianism of popular sovereignty. It was not of course presented as a tool of special interests but a universal value good for humanity. That went down well and it has been able to serve those who propagated it behind this mystification.

But ideas have their own dynamics which cannot easily be controlled by the people who brought them into being. In case of human rights, its dynamics soon trapped it in a contradiction somewhat to the dismay of its protagonists. Fashioned as a tool against democracy, the idea became an important source of legitimation for those seeking the expansion of democracy. But in Europe, this contradiction never fully matured. An agile and accommodating political class and unprecedented affluence saw to that.

In Africa, prevailing objective conditions will press matters much further particularly the question of empowerment. In all probability, the empowerment of people will become the primary issue. Once this happens, the social contradictions will be immensely sharpened and the idea of human rights will become an asset of great value to radical social transformation. I cannot help thinking that Africa is where the critical issues in human rights will be fought out and where the idea will finally be consummated or betrayed.

REVIEW AND DISCUSSION QUESTIONS

1. How does Ake describe Western conceptions of human rights?
2. Why does Ake think Africa should not focus on human rights?
3. What is the African conception of human rights? How does it differ from the Western conception?
4. What economic assumptions does Ake make in claiming that the Western conception of human rights is incompatible with economic development? Do you agree?

What's Culture Got to Do with It? Excising the Harmful Tradition of Female Circumcision

Editors, *Harvard Law Review*

Human rights are controversial: sometimes people disagree about particular rights; other times they doubt that such rights exist at all, claiming that morality and rights are relative to a particular culture. The author of this essay disputes the cultural relativist's skepticism about the existence of universal human rights, arguing instead that universal moral standards exist and, furthermore, that the African practice of female circumcision violates the human rights of African women. The author first explores the legal and philosophical basis for condemning the practice and then responds to each of the "traditionalist" cultural arguments offered in its defense. This article was written by Harvard Law School students and published in the *Harvard Law Review*.

The film was graphic and riveting. A baby girl was being administered to by a traditional medical practitioner. As he tattooed a lizard on the abdomen of the child, the little girl wailed plaintively: "Maami, maami, maami!"

But there was no 'maami' to rescue her. Marks had already been engraved on her cheeks which were covered by a black substance. As the traditional medical man worked, he would stop periodically to wash the area of operation with water from a nearby basin and he would inspect his work, oblivious to the wails of the child.

The tattoo completed to his satisfaction, the traditional practitioner then turned to the next task. He sharpened a crude, circular blade on a grinding stone which he had earlier washed off with water from the same basin. The girl was thrust to him with her chubby legs spread-eagled in front of him. He quickly grasped and excised her clitoris, a part of the external female genitalia.

The wailing that had taken place earlier was mild compared to the screams that erupted from the little girl's mouth at that point. Receiving the crying child, the mother looked at her baby apprehensively but also with some measure of pride. Her child, it would appear, had passed some milestone.[1]

This film of a traditional medicine man scarring and circumcising an infant girl does not depict a fictional event or a birth ritual performed centuries ago and long since discontinued. The videotaped event took place recently in Ajegunle, an impoverished community in Lagos, Nigeria. If all went "well" with the procedure, the little girl in the film will grow up blissfully unaware of the trauma and pain she experienced at such a tender age. She will be regarded in her village as a "normal" girl and a virtuous woman. When she is old enough, her parents will be offered the appropriate "bride price," and she will marry a man who will expect that she has been circumcised in accordance with this deeply entrenched tradition.

If complications develop, however, the little girl might become one of the thousands of African children who die annually from tetanus infections as a result of such procedures. If she survives, she may suffer severe hemorrhaging or experience dysuria (painful urination) and dysmenorrhoea (painful menstruation) due to pelvic congestion. By the time she is ready to bear children, scar tissue may block the birth canal or cause other complications during labor, possibly resulting in an intrauterine fetal death.

Despite the frequency and seriousness of these complications, the traditional practice of female circumcision has received scant attention from the Nigerian government or from the governments of the other twenty-five countries on the African continent where female circumcision is practiced. Policymakers remain indifferent to this "silent emergency that continues to menace at least eighty million women and young girls."[2] Although statistical data on morbidity and mortality from female circumcision is difficult to procure, the known side effects and complications are severe enough to merit government intervention. Due to the lack of authoritative governmental intervention, non-governmental organizations, such as the Inter-African Committee on Traditional Practices Affecting the Health of Women and Children (IAC), have undertaken concrete efforts to abolish female circumcision, as well as other harmful practices such as body scarring, early-childhood marriage, and nutritional taboos.

Informed by first-hand accounts of the personal experiences of women in Nigeria, this Note presents the devastating health consequences of female circumcision, but analyzes the practice primarily from a human rights perspective. It argues that, although human nature is necessarily defined by cultural contexts, the decisions regarding which customs will be preserved in the name of culture or tradition must be oriented toward the promotion and protection of universal human rights in order to have legitimacy in any contemporary society. Part I introduces the types of circumcision commonly practiced and discusses their post-operative effects. Part II presents and critiques the prevalent reasons for the continuation of the practice among certain ethnic groups in Nigeria. Part III argues for the legal eradication of female circumcision, and uses the Nigerian Constitution and selected international human rights instruments as a foundation. Part IV addresses the theory of cultural relativism as it applies to female circumcision and concludes that the promotion of universal human rights is not a mutually exclusive alternative to the maintenance of cultural identity and tradition.

I. TYPES OF CIRCUMCISION AND THEIR EFFECTS

The term "female circumcision" refers to several genital operations that entail incision, and usually removal, of part or all of the female external genitalia, which is composed of the clitoris and the clitoral prepuce, the labia majora (large lips of the vagina), and the labia minora (small lips of the vagina). Clitoridectomy, the form of female circumcision that is most comparable to its male counterpart, involves removal of the clitoral prepuce or tip of the clitoris. In Muslim countries, this "mild" form of circumcision is also known as "sunna," which means tradition. In excision, the entire clitoris and the labia minora are removed, which leaves the labia majora intact and the remainder of the vulva unsutured. In "pharonic circumcision" or infibulation, the sides of the labia majora are sewn together with thorns after the clitoris and the labia minora are removed. The woman's legs are then bound together from thigh to ankle for several weeks to allow scar tissue to form. Complete occlusion is prevented by inserting a splinter of wood or a matchstick, which preserves a small orifice through which urine and menstrual fluid can pass. Introcision refers to a procedure in which the perineum is cut to enlarge the vaginal opening. These "gishiri" cuts, typically performed in early childhood, are intended to facilitate sexual penetration of young girls in communities where child marriage is widely practiced.

Female circumcision is usually performed by "traditional surgeons," or "traditional birth attendants." In parts of northern Nigeria, the procedure may also be performed by the village barber, although typically the practitioner is a woman. The surgical instruments used include razor blades, iron knives, and pieces of cut glass, or similarly constructed home-made tools. Usually the operations are performed without anaesthesia and under conditions that are not sterile. Indeed, "[m]any of the traditional practitioners handle several babies in succession using the same blade." After the operation, the incision is treated daily with a native soap, palm oil, vaseline, kerosene, or even engine oil.

In Nigeria, the over 250 ethnic groups differ in their use of the methods described above. Similarly, there is widespread variation in the age at which the operation is performed. Regardless of the age at which circumcision is performed, the consequences of the operation are often more severe than expected. The degree of hygiene under which the operation is performed, the expertise of the practitioner, the general health of the girl or woman being circumcised, and the amount of struggling she does will all influence the outcome. Immediate effects can include intense pain, shock, hemorrhage, retention of urine and menstrual discharge, fever, tetanus, and genital infection. The girl or woman may die if a major blood vessel is cut and she cannot reach a medical facility equipped to deal with such emergencies.

For many women, however, the detrimental effects of circumcision do not immediately appear. Thus, the parents, patient, or medical practitioner may see no causal connection between the procedure and the post-operative ailments that can materialize intermittently during later years. These include reproductive tract infections that sometimes are severe enough to cause infertility, urinary tract infections, cysts, and the formation of obstructive genital scar tissue.

Inevitably, the consummation of marriage or the occasion of first intercourse is a painful ordeal for an infibulated woman. If the vaginal opening is too small for penetration, another incision must be made to enlarge the opening. The small opening and scar tissue create even more difficulties during childbirth. Obstructed labor may result in hemorrhaging, tearing of perineal tissue, and eventually a prolapsed uterus. For the baby, such a prolonged and difficult delivery is life-threatening; the infant may be stillborn, or if it survives, it may suffer brain damage from a lack of oxygen during the difficult delivery.

Female circumcision also inflicts psychological wounds. Indeed, it is traumatizing to read about, let alone experience, the suffering of a woman or young girl whose "life-giving canal is stitched up amid blood and fear and secrecy, while she is forcibly held down, and told that if she screams she will cause the death of her mother, or bring shame on her family." Although ceremonial circumcision is typically preceded by singing, dancing, and celebration, adolescent girls often suffer severe operative anxiety, experience traumatizing terror during the procedure, and feel betrayed afterwards by the mother or female relative who urged or forced them to undergo the operation.

II. JUSTIFYING FEMALE CIRCUMCISION IN NIGERIA

Proponents of female circumcision in Nigeria offer several reasons for the continuation of the practice.3 Such reasons include the maintenance of tradition, the promotion of social and political cohesion, the enhancement of fertility, the fulfillment of religious requirements, the prevention of promiscuity, the preservation of virginity, the maintenance of feminine hygiene, and the pursuit of aesthetics. Identical or closely related justifications are offered by those who adhere to the tradition throughout Africa.

A. Tradition

. . . Tradition—the reluctance to break with age-old practices that symbolize the shared heritage of a particular ethnic group—is the most frequent reason that diverse ethnic groups cling fiercely to a practice that inflicts significant pain and suffering on women and children.

In some communities, circumcision is the traditional ritual that confers full social acceptability and integration into the community upon females. The ability to identify with one's heritage and to enjoy recognition as a full member of one's ethnic group, with just claim to its social privileges and benefits, is very important to most African families. For many women and young girls, circumcision satisfies this deep-seated need "to belong" and ensures that they will not be ostracized. . . .

Although the maintenance of a group's cultural identity and the promotion of social and political cohesion are legitimate objectives, the right to belong—to contribute to and participate in one's community as a full member—should not be conditioned on a price of human suffering. Such a requirement puts women and young girls in the unjust position of having to jeopardize either their right to health and bodily integrity or the esteem privilege of social acceptance. . . .

B. The Enhancement of Fertility

In the Isoko and Urhobo communities of the Delta state, women are circumcised during the advanced stages of their first pregnancy. The legend behind the tradition of circumcising pregnant women is that if the first-born baby's head touches the clitoris during childbirth, the child will die. A related myth is that, if left uncircumcised, the clitoris will "cause symbolic or spiritual injury to the baby."

When confronted with the fact that uncircumcised women carry their babies to term and have normal, unobstructed deliveries, traditional birth attendants who perform clitoridectomies still insist that these procedures are a prerequisite to a safe delivery. When they are informed that medical reports confirm that circumcision often causes infertility and is even more dangerous during pregnancy, some traditional practitioners retort, "Modern doctors may say what they like. We have never experienced any problem whatsoever with this thing."4 Furthermore, they claim that "this is what our culture demands. It was handed over to us by our forefathers. We cannot afford not to circumcise our women."5

In light of the compelling veracity and force of the medical arguments against female circumcision, the above responses from adherents to the practice seem to be at odds with the facts. Moreover, their responses lead to one question: can ethnic groups that are genuinely concerned about cultural continuity afford to adhere to a tradition that endangers the fertility of women and young girls, the life-giving sources of society? Probably not.

C. Religion

Adherence to religious doctrine is another widely given but misplaced justification for female circumcision in Nigeria. The dominant formal religions practiced in Nigeria are Christianity and Islam. Although the Bible discusses male circumcision, neither Christian nor Islamic doctrine requires female circumcision. Religious leaders who advocate the practice seem to adopt an ill-conceived transitive rationale in which religious ideals are displaced onto the medical procedure. The argument begins with the premise that modesty and virginity are highly valued in traditional African societies and that the same virtues are prescribed by the Bible and the Koran. Next, proponents argue that female circumcision is intended to prevent promiscuity and to preserve the chastity of young girls until they marry by removing an organ that is believed to cause women to become over-sexed. Therefore, female circumcision is required by tradition, and more importantly in this context, by religious doctrine. Not surprisingly, those who insist that the practice is a religious requirement never cite textual verses that verify the alleged religious requirements.

Aside from the fact that the religious justification for female circumcision rests on an insufficient doctrinal foundation, the argument ultimately misuses religion as an instrument of fear, oppression, and exploitation. A religion that is authentic in the principles it represents "aims at truth, equality, justice, love and a healthy wholesome life for all people, whether men or women."[6] In contrast, the argument that circumcision is a religious requirement casts religion in the role of mandating mutilation, amputation, and infirmity of otherwise healthy female reproductive organs. The latter characterization is the complete antithesis of the ideals that religion should promote.

D. Preventing Promiscuity

In addition to the religious arguments in favor of chastity, advocates point to the prevention of promiscuity as a separate and distinct reason to continue the practice of female circumcision. Because the clitoris is believed to provoke women to make uncontrollable sexual demands on their husbands—demands that will drive a woman to seek extra-marital affairs if her husband does not meet them—removal of the clitoris is presumed to be beneficial for women and for society. This justification is flawed in that it incorrectly assumes that the sexual control and subjugation of women is beneficial to them and necessary for a harmonious society. It also implies that men have no responsibility or control over their own sexual behavior. Although the so-called promiscuous female certainly has multiple male partners in any traditional African society, custom does not dictate varying degrees of male circumcision, from circumcision in its mildest form to castration, as a means of ensuring male fidelity.

At best, the practice of circumcising women and young girls reinforces the mistaken notion that women should see their sexual impulses in terms of what suits men. In reality, female circumcision is a life-threatening form of subjugation when performed on women and a form of child abuse when performed on an infant or child. Superstition regarding the elimination of sexually promiscuous behavior is an unacceptable justification for subjugation and abuse.

E. Cleanliness and Aesthetics

Supporters of female circumcision also offer feminine hygiene and aesthetics as justifications for the practice. These arguments are no more persuasive than those based on the enhancement of fertility. Circumcision simply does not make women and young girls cleaner. To the contrary, circumcision's post-operative health consequences such as urine retention and the accumulation of menstrual blood in the vagina lead to discomfort, infection, and odors more offensive than those caused by normal hormonal secretions. Furthermore, the idea that circumcision makes the vulva aesthetically more appealing—that circumcision should be performed as a type of cosmetic surgery—is at best arbitrary, and at worst absurd. If, as the saying goes, "beauty is in the eye of the beholder," then the post-operative scarification that results can hardly be perceived universally as beautiful. The keloid stump that develops after the clitoris has been excised and the long scar that seals the vagina after infibulation are in fact, in the eyes of some individuals, extremely unattractive. This is not to say that Western notions of physical beauty should be the standard for the rest of the world, but instead to challenge the sincerity of those who insist that "true" conceptions of beauty and femininity necessarily exclude the woman who is not circumcised, excised, infibulated, or introcised.

III. THE LEGAL MANDATE TO ERADICATE FEMALE CIRCUMCISION

In any argument against a practice as deeply embedded in a culture as female circumcision is in Nigerian society, the strategic thrust of the argument should be based on texts that Nigeria has adopted and endorsed. Arguments and solutions based on such texts are likely to be heeded and enforced, because these texts were affirmatively—and in some instances democratically—approved by the Nigerian people. In contrast, suggestions that local traditions should be abandoned in order to comply with external norms are likely to be counterproductive and to elicit indignation and resistance to change. Thus, the Constitution of Nigeria, as well as international instruments endorsed by Nigeria, including the African Charter on Human and Peoples' Rights and the Convention on the Elimination of All Forms of Discrimination Against Women, can and should be drawn upon to provide the basis for a legal mandate to eradicate female circumcision.

A. The Constitution of Nigeria

Chapter IV of the Constitution of Nigeria delineates the "fundamental rights" of Nigerian citizens. It states that "[e]very person has a right to life, and no one shall be deprived intentionally of his life."7 Further, "[e]very individual is entitled to respect for the dignity of his person, and accordingly—no person shall be subjected to torture or to inhuman or degrading treatment."8 In light of the explicit language in these provisions, Nigerians need look no further than their own constitution for an injunction against female circumcision as a violation of women's and children's constitutional rights.

B. The African Charter on Human and Peoples' Rights

The practice of female circumcision also contravenes the spirit and substance of many international instruments to which Nigeria is a signatory. In 1983, Nigeria ratified the African Charter on Human and Peoples' Rights,9 which contains several articles that can be interpreted to proscribe female circumcision. Article 4 declares that "[e]very human being shall be entitled to respect for his life and the integrity of his person."10 Article 5 prohibits "[a]ll forms of exploitation and degradation of man particularly . . . torture, cruel, inhuman or degrading punishment and treatment."11 Article 16 proclaims that "[e]very individual shall have the right to enjoy the best attainable state of physical and mental health,"12 and article 18 requires the state to "ensure the elimination of every discrimination against women and also ensure the protection of the rights of the woman and the child as stipulated in international declarations and conventions."13

Significantly, the African Charter also recognizes the importance of African culture and tradition. Article 17 states that "[e]very individual may freely take part in the cultural life of his community. The promotion and protection of morals and traditional values recognized by the community shall be the duty of the State."14 In addition, article 29 establishes the duty "[t]o preserve and strengthen positive African cultural values in . . . relations with other members of the society."15 Although it is possible to construe these provisions as a directive to respect the tradition of female circumcision, such an interpretation flatly contradicts the tenor of the document's preamble.16 It strains logic to argue that, in the name of "tradition," a document whose purpose is to "promote and protect human and peoples' rights"17 would endorse a practice like female circumcision—a practice that results in the torture and mutilation of half of the population that the document aims to protect. Indeed, traditions to be preserved should be limited to those that embody "positive African cultural values."18

C. The Convention on the Elimination of All Forms of Discrimination Against Women

Nigeria has also ratified the Convention on the Elimination of All Forms of Discrimination Against Women (CEDAW). CEDAW is an important human rights instrument in the international anticircumcision campaign, because it calls for an end to both gender discrimination in general and to social and cultural customs based on the idea of the inferiority or superiority of either of the sexes. . . .

IV. ENGAGING THE TRADITIONALIST FEMALE'S CULTURAL ARGUMENT

. . . Part of the difficulty in engaging *the* Traditionalist Female is that she is not simply one woman who speaks with one voice. Instead, the Traditionalist Female represents several women who speak with myriad voices and who offer complex and sometimes conflicting explanations for their shared viewpoints. . . . The task is further complicated when *they* becomes *us,* and *us* is *we,* and *we* is the collective *me,* and *me* is *I,* an individual who feels a sense of attachment and responsibility as her sister's keeper. Based upon a belief in the persuasive power of global sisterhood, this Note endorses the culture of resistance to the ongoing practice of harmful traditions. It is from this perspective and this political stance that this Note respectfully engages, and attempts to understand, the Traditionalist Female. This Part addresses the proponents of female circumcision who invoke claims of cultural relativism and ethnocentrism in defense of the practice and is informed by actual personal observations of and conversations with Traditionalist Females in Nigeria (and their male counterparts).

The Nigerian Traditionalist Female argues that what is held to be a fundamental right at a given time in one society may be regarded as anti-social at a different time or in a different society. Moreover, those persons who are opposed to a particular practice or custom have no right to impose their value judgments on autonomous individuals who have different viewpoints and values. This relativist argument, however, is less convincing in the context of human rights. The premise that the morality and the personality of an individual are shaped by the culture and the history of a given society does not negate the philosophical theory that human rights, defined literally as the rights to which one is entitled simply by virtue of being human, are universal by definition. So although human nature is necessarily culturally relative in that it is determined to some extent by social rules and mores, human rights are universal entitlements that are grounded in cross-culturally recognized moral values.

Incidentally, the cultural argument advanced by the Traditionalist Female uncomfortably parallels the invocation of culture or ethnicity as a "defense" or excuse for violence, injustice, and a host of other social ills. When cast in this light, the cultural argument is patently offensive, but this misrepresentation is directly analogous to the Traditionalist Female's use of African culture to defend human rights abuses. There is nothing inherently "ethnic" or specifically Nigerian about injustice or violence, and this is also true for human rights abuses

that are unjust or violent, whether they take the form of arbitrary arrests and detention, torture, or the circumcision of girls and women. Thus, "culture" and "ethnicity" should not be used as defenses to human rights abuses, because "[c]ultural values and cultural practice are as legitimately subject to criticism from a human rights perspective as any structural aspect of a society."[19] Even well-established and ongoing cultural practices are subject to universal human rights limitations.

Of course, the cultural relativist will object to the theory of universal human rights, so it is important to examine what is meant by "culture" when it is used as a defense for harmful traditions. Most advocates of female circumcision appear to equate culture with history and tradition, but they fail to recognize the many ways in which their present actions and lifestyles reinforce a notion of culture that comprises not only the traditional, but the contemporary as well. This concept of culture, which this Note adopts, is a dynamic notion, not a static one. African culture incorporates things precolonial, colonial, and contemporary, as well as things social, economic, and political, and things both individual and collective. If culture is the group identifier and cohesive element that ethnocentrists profess it to be, culture must be inherently dynamic in order to bond several generations of an ethnic group.

Due to the dynamic nature of culture, changes must be channeled so that they do not result in the extinction of the traditional culture. On the other hand, practices, beliefs, and lifestyles passed down through several generations of an ethnic group need to be re-examined periodically in light of contemporary values and knowledge, in order to ascertain whether the customs deserve to be perpetuated. During the discussions that preceded the drafting of the African Charter, several African leaders commented on the ability to "find inspiration in those . . . traditions that are good and positive" and the desire to reflect "traditions which deserve to be preserved . . . in order to complete the global international effort made to reinforce respect for human rights."[20] Perhaps the best reason to maintain a given traditional practice is that the original justifications for its existence continue to validate its persistence today. This paradigm lends a sense of contemporary legitimacy to those traditional practices that have been preserved.

One custom that is still readily apparent in Nigerian society today is the tendency of Yoruba women to kneel and men to prostrate as a sign of respect when greeting an elder. Another custom involves mothers suspending their babies on their backs in a pouch of wrapped cloth in a manner which enables them to carry out their work routines while they maintain constant physical association with the child. Traditional engagement and wedding ceremonies, which frame the marriage not only as a contract between the two individuals, but also as a contract between the families of the marrying pair, are also customary. Each of these customs, although it manifests adherence to traditional beliefs and lifestyles, also has contemporary legitimacy because of its practical utility and because it reinforces shared values in modern society in a manner that is neither physically nor mentally injurious.

Conversely, those practices that have neither factual, historical validity nor contemporary legitimacy in terms of societal values, and that furthermore inflict harm and injury on their adherents, must be abandoned. Consider for comparative purposes the racial and religious discrimination that has been widely practiced around the world but that is not widely defended today. The reasons which may have once justified these practices are no longer accepted as valid. Specifically, the once widely held belief that Africans were brought to America from an uncivilized continent and were sub-human savages fit to be nothing more than slaves, as well as the belief that Jews in Nazi Germany were less human and less deserving of the rights endowed to all human beings than non-Jewish German citizens, are and always have been myths. The depth of the tradition of chattel slavery in American history or anti-Semitism in Nazi Germany would be no defense for the maintenance of these atrocities today.

Similarly, the fact that female circumcision is an age-old custom practiced for generations by several ethnic groups does not legitimate its persistence today. Arguments based on the control of female sexuality, aesthetics, and cleanliness do not reinforce ideals and beliefs that are widely held in modern society. The arguments that espouse the adherence to religious requirements and the enhancement of fertility are based on myths that cannot validate either the initial existence or the continued persistence of an undeniably harmful tradition. Thus, although in other contexts there are legitimate claims to ethnicity and cultural continuity, arguments along these lines in defense of female circumcision more likely cloak pretextual justifications based on manipulations of a dying, lost, or even mythical cultural past.

NOTES

1. Harriet Lawrence, Excising a Harmful Tradition, *Guardian*, June 11, 1992, p. 9.

2. See Berhane Ras-Work, "Traditional Practices That Inflict Disability," in *Women and Disability* 23, (1991) note 8, p. 23 ed. Esther Boylan.

3. It is estimated that at least 50% of the women in Nigeria have undergone some form of circumcision.

4. Sam Eferaro, "Why We Circumcise Our Pregnant Women," *Vanguard*, Jan. 19, 1993, p. 11.

5. Id., p. 10.

6. Nawal El Saadawi, *The Hidden Face of Eve: Women in the Arab World* 41, ed. and trans. Sherif Hetata (1980).

7. Constitution of the Federal Republic of Nig. (Enactment) Act ch. IV, p. 30(1).

8. Id., p. 31(1)(a).

9. See International Comm'n. of Jurists, Human and Peoples' Rights in Africa and the African Charter 94 (1986) [hereinafter Human and Peoples' Rights].

10. African Charter on Human and Peoples' Rights, June 27, 1981, 21 I.L.M. 58 [hereinafter African Charter], reprinted in *Basic Documents Supplement to International Law* 509, ed. Louis Henkin, Richard C. Pugh, Oscar Schachter, and Hans Smit (1987) [hereinafter Basic Documents], p. 511.

11. Id. art. 5, reprinted in Basic Documents, supra note 11, p. 511.

12. Id. art. 16(1), reprinted in Basic Documents, supra note 11, p. 513.

13. Id. art. 18(3), reprinted in Basic Documents, supra note 11, p. 514.

14. Id. art. 17(2), (3), reprinted in *Basic Documents,* supra note 10, p. 514.

15. Id. art. 29(7), reprinted in *Basic Documents,* supra note 11, p. 517.

16. Id. pmbl., reprinted in *Basic Documents,* supra note 11, p. 509–10.

17. Id., reprinted in *Basic Documents,* supra note 11, p. 510.

18. Id. art. 29(7), reprinted in *Basic Documents,* supra note 11, p. 517 (emphasis added).

19. Rhoda E. Howard, *Human Rights In Commonwealth Africa* (1986), p. 16.

20. *Human and Peoples' Rights,* supra note 10, p. 25 (emphasis added) (internal quotations omitted).

REVIEW AND DISCUSSION QUESTIONS

1. What are the main arguments offered in defense of female circumcision?
2. How does the author respond to the arguments mentioned in the previous question?
3. Describe the strategy the author recommends to those who hope to eliminate the practice.
4. How does the author characterize the "relativist" argument offered on behalf of the Nigerian Traditionalist Female position?
5. Why does the author reject the cultural relativist's defense of circumcision?
6. What cultural practices does the author think should not be criticized? On what basis are these distinguished from female cricumcision?
7. Which moral theory does the author of this article most closely reflect? Explain.

Trying Out One's New Sword

Mary Midgley

Moral isolationism, according to Mary Midgley, is the familiar position that respect and tolerance demand that members of one culture not criticize other cultures. Rejecting that position, she argues that it is little more than an internally inconsistent version of "immoralism." Nor, she claims, does it accurately describe the ways in which cultures are formed and changed. Using an ancient Samurai custom as an example, she suggests various ways in which cultures can, in fact, be criticized.

All of us are, more or less, in trouble today about trying to understand cultures strange to us. We hear constantly of alien customs. We see changes in our lifetime which would have astonished our parents. I want to discuss here one very short way of dealing with this difficulty, a drastic way which many people now theoretically favor. It consists in simply denying that we can ever understand any culture except our own well enough to make judgments about it. Those who recommend this hold that the world is sharply divided into separate societies, sealed units, each with its own system of thought. They feel that the respect and tolerance due from one system to another forbids us ever

From Mary Midgley, *Heart and Mind* (New York: St. Martin's Press, 1981). © by M. Midgley.

to take up a critical position to any other culture. Moral judgment, they suggest, is a kind of coinage valid only in its country of origin.

I shall call this position "moral isolationism." I shall suggest that it is certainly not forced upon us, and indeed that it makes no sense at all. People usually take it up because they think it is a respectful attitude to other cultures. In fact, however, it is not respectful. Nobody can respect what is entirely unintelligible to them. To respect someone, we have to know enough about him to make a *favorable* judgment, however general and tentative. And we do understand people in other cultures to this extent. Otherwise a great mass of our most valuable thinking would be paralysed.

To show this, I shall take a remote example, because we shall probably find it easier to think calmly about it than we should with a contemporary one, such as female circumcision in Africa or the Chinese Cultural Revolution. The principles involved will still be the same. My example is this. There is, it seems, a verb in classical Japanese which means "to try out one's new sword on a chance wayfarer." (The word is *tsujigiri,* literally "crossroads-cut.") A samurai sword had to be tried out because, if it was to work properly, it had to slice through someone at a single blow, from the shoulder to the opposite flank. Otherwise, the warrior bungled his stroke. This could injure his honour, offend his ancestors, and even let down his emperor. So tests were needed, and wayfarers had to be expended. Any wayfarer would do—provided, of course, that he was not another Samurai. Scientists will recognize a familiar problem about the rights of experimental subjects.

Now when we hear of a custom like this, we may well reflect that we simply do not understand it; and therefore are not qualified to criticize it at all, because we are not members of that culture. But we are not members of any other culture either, except our own. So we extend the principle to cover all extraneous cultures, and we seem therefore to be moral isolationists. But this is, as we shall see, an impossible position. Let us ask what it would involve.

We must ask first, Does the isolating barrier work both ways? Are people in other cultures equally unable to criticize us? This question struck me sharply when I read a remark in *The Guardian*

by an anthropologist about a South American Indian who had been taken into a Brazilian town for an operation, which saved his life. When he came back to his village, he made several highly critical remarks about the white Brazilians' way of life. They may very well have been justified. But the interesting point was that the anthropologist called these remarks "a damning indictment of Western civilization." Now the Indian had been in that town about two weeks. Was he in a position to deliver a damning indictment? Would we ourselves be qualified to deliver such an indictment on the Samurai, provided we could spend two weeks in ancient Japan? What do we really think about this?

My own impression is that we believe that outsiders can, in principle, deliver perfectly good indictments—only, it usually takes more than two weeks to make them damning. Understanding has degrees. It is not a slapdash yes-or-no matter. Intelligent outsiders can progress in it, and in some ways will be at an advantage over the locals. But if this is so, it must clearly apply to ourselves as much as anybody else.

Our next question is this: Does the isolating barrier between cultures block praise as well as blame? If I want to say that the Samurai culture has many virtues, or to praise the South American Indians, am I prevented from doing *that* by my outside status? Now, we certainly do need to praise other societies in this way. But it is hardly possible that we could praise them effectively if we could not, in principle, criticize them. Our praise would be worthless if it rested on definite grounds, if it did not flow from some understanding. Certainly we may need to praise things which we do not *fully* understand. We say "there's something very good here, but I can't quite make out what it is yet." This happens when we want to learn from strangers. And we can learn from strangers. But to do this we have to distinguish between those strangers who are worth learning from and those who are not. Can we then judge which is which?

This brings us to our third question: What is involved in judging? Now plainly there is no question here of sitting on a bench in a red robe and sentencing people. Judging simply means forming an opinion, and expressing it if it is called for. Is there anything wrong about this? Naturally, we ought to avoid forming   and expressing—*crude* opinions, like that of a simple-minded missionary, who might dismiss the whole Samurai culture as entirely bad, because non-Christian. But this is a different objection. The trouble with crude opinions is that they are crude, whoever forms them, not that they are formed by the wrong people. Anthropologists, after all, are outsiders quite as much as missionaries. Moral isolationism forbids us to form *any* opinions on these matters. Its ground for doing so is that we don't understand them. But there is much that we don't understand in our own culture too. This brings us to our last question: If we can't judge other cultures, can we really judge our own? Our efforts to do so will be much damaged if we are really deprived of our opinions about other societies, because these provide the range of comparison, the spectrum of alternatives against which we set what we want to understand. We would have to stop using the mirror which anthropology so helpfully holds up to us.

In short, moral isolationism would lay down a general ban on moral reasoning. Essentially, this is the programme of immoralism, and it carries a distressing logical difficulty. Immoralists like Nietzsche are actually just a rather specialized sect of moralists. They can no more afford to put moralizing out of business than smugglers can afford to abolish customs regulations. The power of moral judgment is, in fact, not a luxury, not a perverse indulgence of the self-righteous. It is a necessity. When we judge something to be bad or good, better or worse than something else, we are taking it as an example to aim at or avoid. Without opinions of this sort, we would have no framework of comparison for our own policy, no chance of profiting by other people's insights or mistakes. In this vacuum, we could form no judgments on our own actions.

Now it would be odd if Homo sapiens had really got himself into a position as bad as this—a position where his main evolutionary asset, his brain, was so little use to him. None of us is going to accept this skeptical diagnosis. We cannot do so, because our involvement in moral isolationism does not flow from apathy, but from a rather acute concern about human hypocrisy and other forms of wickedness. But we polarize that concern around a few selected moral truths. We are rightly angry with those who despise, oppress or steamroll other cultures. We think that doing these things is actually *wrong*. But this is itself a moral judgment. We could not condemn oppression and insolence if we thought that all our condemnations were just a trivial local quirk of our own culture. We could still less do it if we tried to stop judging altogether.

Real moral skepticism, in fact, could lead only to inaction, to our losing all interest in moral questions, most of all in those which concern other societies. When we discuss these things, it becomes instantly clear how far we are from doing this. Suppose, for instance, that I criticize the bisecting Samurai, that I say his behavior is brutal. What will usually happen next is that someone will protest, will say that I have no right to make criticisms like that of another culture. But it is most unlikely that he will use this move to end the discussion of the subject. Instead, he will justify the Samurai. He will try to fill in the background, to make me understand the custom, by explaining the exalted ideals of discipline and devotion which produced it. He will probably talk of the lower value which the ancient Japanese placed on individual life generally. He may well suggest that this is a healthier attitude than our own obsession with security. He may add, too, that the wayfarers did not seriously mind being bisected, that in principle they accepted the whole arrangement.

Now an objector who talks like this is implying that it *is* possible to understand alien customs. That is just what he is trying to make me do. And he implies, too, that if I do succeed in understanding them, I shall do something better than giving up judging them. He expects me to change my present judgment to a truer one—namely, one that is favourable. And the standards I must use to do this cannot just be Samurai standards. They have to be ones current in my own culture. Ideals like discipline and devotion will not move anybody unless he himself accepts them. As it happens, neither discipline nor devotion is very popular in the West at present. Anyone who appeals to them may well have to do some more arguing to make *them* acceptable, before he can use them to explain the Samurai. But if he does succeed here, he will have persuaded us, not just that there was something to be said for them in ancient Japan, but that there would be here as well.

Isolating barriers simply cannot arise here. If we accept something as a serious moral truth about one culture, we can't refuse to apply it—in however different an outward form—to other cultures as well, wherever circumstances admit it. If we refuse to do this, we just are not taking the other culture seriously. This becomes clear if we look at the last argument used by my objector—that of justification by consent of the victim. It is suggested that sudden bisection is quite in order, *provided* that it takes place between consenting adults. I cannot now discuss how conclusive this justification is. What I am pointing out is simply that it can only work if we believe that *consent* can make such a transaction respectable—and this is a thoroughly modern and Western idea. It would probably never occur to a Samurai; if it did, it would surprise him very much. It is *our* standard. In applying it, too, we are likely to make another typically Western demand. We shall ask for good factual evidence that the wayfarers actually do have this rather surprising taste—that they are really willing to be bisected. In applying Western standards in this way, we are not being confused or irrelevant. We are asking the questions which arise *from where we stand,* questions which we can see the sense of. We do this because asking questions which you can't see the sense of is humbug. Certainly we can extend our questioning by imaginative effort. We can come to understand other societies better. By doing so, we may make their questions our own, or we may see that they are really forms of the questions which we are asking already. This is not impossible. It is just very hard work. The obstacles which often prevent it are simply those of ordinary ignorance, laziness and prejudice.

If there were really an isolating barrier, of course, our own culture could never have been formed. It is no sealed box, but a fertile jungle of different influences—Greek, Jewish, Roman, Norse, Celtic and so forth, into which further influences are still pouring—American, Indian, Japanese, Jamaican, you name it. The moral isolationist's picture of separate, unmixable cultures is quite unreal. People who talk about British history usually stress the value of this fertilizing mix, no doubt rightly. But this is not just an odd fact about Britain. Except for the very smallest and most remote, all cultures are formed out of many streams. All have the problem of digesting and assimilating things which, at the start, they do not understand. All have the choice of learning something from this challenge, or, alternatively, of refusing to learn, and fighting it mindlessly instead.

This universal predicament has been obscured by the fact that anthropologists used to concentrate largely on very small and remote cultures, which did not seem to have this problem. These tiny societies, which had often forgotten their own history, made neat, self-contained subjects for study. No doubt it was valuable to emphasize their remoteness, their extreme strangeness, their independence of our cultural tradition. This emphasis was, I think, the root of moral isolationism. But, as the tribal studies themselves showed, even there the anthropologists were able to interpret what they saw and make judgments—often favourable—about the tribesmen. And the tribesmen, too, were quite equal to making judgments about the anthropologists—and about the tourists and Coca-Cola salesmen who followed them. Both sets of judgments, no doubt, were somewhat hasty, both have been refined in the light of further experience. A similar transaction between us and the Samurai might take even longer. But that is no reason at all for deeming it impossible. Morally as well as physically, there is only one world, and we all have to live in it.

REVIEW AND DISCUSSION QUESTIONS

1. What is *moral isolationism?*
2. Why does Midgley reject moral isolationism?
3. Explain what Midgley means in saying there is "only one world." Do you agree with her? Explain.
4. How might Ake respond to this essay? Would he defend the idea of "trying out a new sword"?

5. "Moral views cannot be proven true or false, therefore whatever you think is right is right for you." Describe carefully what somebody might mean by each part of that statement. In what sense, if any, do you agree with it? In what sense(s) do you disagree?

Taking Rights Seriously

Ronald Dworkin

Rights are central to many of our political and moral discussions: we often find ourselves disagreeing about the limits of free speech and religion, as well as the rights of the unborn, the environment, minorities, the terminally ill, the victims of crimes, and animals, to mention only a few examples. The legitimate role of governments, we also often say, is in part defined by rights. But what does it mean to say that an individual has a right, as opposed to something being the right thing for that person to do? And what must government do if it is to respect the rights of its citizens? Ronald Dworkin discusses these questions in detail, arguing that rights are like trump cards citizens hold against their government. They can be played even when officials believe it is not in the public interest for citizens to exercise their rights. The notion of rights, he argues, rests on a model that places the dignity of the individual at center stage. Dworkin concludes with a discussion of whether it is wise for government to take rights seriously, given the social costs of doing so. Ronald Dworkin teaches philosophy and law at Oxford and New York University.

1. THE RIGHTS OF CITIZENS

The language of rights now dominates political debate in the United States. Does the Government respect the moral and political rights of its citizens? Or does the Government's foreign policy, or its race policy, fly in the face of these rights? Do the minorities whose rights have been violated have the right to violate the law in return? Or does the silent majority itself have rights, including the right that those who break the law be punished? It is not surprising that these questions are now prominent. The concept of rights, and particularly the concept of rights against the Government, has its most natural use when a political society is divided, and appeals to co-operation or a common goal are pointless.

The debate does not include the issue of whether citizens have *some* moral rights against their Government. It seems accepted on all sides that they do. Conventional lawyers and politicians take it as a point of pride that our legal system recognizes, for example, individual rights of free speech, equality, and due process. They base their claim that our law deserves respect, at least in part, on that fact, for they would not claim that totalitarian systems deserve the same loyalty.

I shall not be concerned, in this essay, to defend the thesis that citizens have moral rights against their governments; I want instead to explore the implications of that thesis for those, including the present United States Government, who profess to accept it.

It is much in dispute, of course, what *particular* rights citizens have. Does the acknowledged right to free speech, for example, include the right to participate in nuisance demonstrations?

From Ronald Dworkin, *Taking Rights Seriously* (Cambridge: Harvard University Press, 1977), pp. 184–205. Reprinted by permission of the author.

In practice the Government will have the last word on what an individual's rights are, because its police will do what its officials and courts say. But that does not mean that the Government's view is necessarily the correct view; anyone who thinks it does must believe that men and women have only such moral rights as Government chooses to grant, which means that they have no moral rights at all.

All this is sometimes obscured in the United States by the constitutional system. The American Constitution provides a set of individual *legal* rights in the First Amendment, and in the due process, equal protection, and similar clauses. Under present legal practice the Supreme Court has the power to declare an act of Congress or of a state legislature void if the Court finds that the act offends these provisions. This practice has led some commentators to suppose that individual moral rights are fully protected by this system, but that is hardly so, nor could it be so.

The Constitution fuses legal and moral issues, by making the validity of a law depend on the answer to complex moral problems, like the problem of whether a particular statute respects the inherent equality of all men. This fusion has important consequences for the debates about civil disobedience; I have described these elsewhere[1] and I shall refer to them later. But it leaves open two prominent questions. It does not tell us whether the Constitution, even properly interpreted, recognizes all the moral rights that citizens have, and it does not tell us whether, as many suppose, citizens would have a duty to obey the law even if it did invade their moral rights.

Even if the Constitution were perfect, of course, and the majority left it alone, it would not follow that the Supreme Court could guarantee the individual rights of citizens. A Supreme Court decision is still a legal decision, and it must take into account precedent and institutional considerations like relations between the Court and Congress, as well as morality. And no judicial decision is necessarily the right decision. Judges stand for different positions on controversial issues of law and morals and, as the fights over Nixon's Supreme Court nominations showed, a President is entitled to appoint judges of his own persuasion, provided that they are honest and capable.

So, though the Constitutional system adds something to the protection of moral rights against the Government, it falls far short of guaranteeing these rights, or even establishing what they are.

2. RIGHTS AND THE RIGHT TO BREAK THE LAW

In most cases when we say that someone has a 'right' to do something, we imply that it would be wrong to interfere with his doing it, or at least that some special grounds are needed for justifying any interference. I use this strong sense of right when I say that you have the right to spend your money gambling, if you wish, though you ought to spend it in a more worthwhile way. I mean it would be wrong for anyone to interfere with you even though you propose to spend your money in a way that I think is wrong.

There is a clear difference between saying that someone has a right to do something in this sense and saying that it is the 'right' thing for him to do, or that he does no 'wrong' in doing it. Someone may have the right to do something that is the wrong thing for him to do, as might be the case with gambling. Conversely, something may be the right thing for him to do and yet he may have no right to do it, in the sense that it would not be wrong for someone to interfere with his trying. If our army captures an enemy soldier, we might say that the right thing for him to do is to try to escape, but it would not follow that it is wrong for us to try to stop him. We might admire him for trying to escape, and perhaps even think less of him if he did not. But there is no suggestion here that it is wrong of us to stand in his way; on the contrary, if we think our cause is just, we think it right for us to do all we can to stop him. . . .

These distinctions enable us to see an ambiguity in the orthodox question: Does a man ever have a right to break the law? Does that question mean to ask whether he ever has a right to break the law in the strong sense, so that the Government would do wrong to stop him, by arresting and prosecuting him? Or does it mean to ask whether he ever does the right thing to break the law, so that we should all respect him even though the Government should jail him?

Conservatives and liberals do agree that some-times a man does not do the wrong thing to break a law, when his conscience so requires. They dis-agree, when they do, over the different issue of what the State's response should be. Both parties do think that sometimes the State should prose-cute. But this is not inconsistent with the proposi-tion that the man prosecuted did the right thing in breaking the law. . . .

I said that in the United States citizens are sup-posed to have certain fundamental rights against their Government, certain moral rights made into legal rights by the Constitution. If this idea is sig-nificant, and worth bragging about, then these rights must be rights in the strong sense I just de-scribed. The claim that citizens have a right to free speech must imply that it would be wrong for the Government to stop them from speaking, even when the Government believes that what they will say will cause more harm than good. The claim cannot mean, on the prisoner-of-war analogy, only that citizens do no wrong in speaking their minds, though the Government reserves the right to pre-vent them from doing so.

This is a crucial point, and I want to labour it. Of course a responsible government must be ready to justify anything it does, particularly when it limits the liberty of its citizens. But normally it is a sufficient justification, even for an act that lim-its liberty, that the act is calculated to increase what the philosophers call general utility—that it is calculated to produce more over-all benefit than harm. So, though the New York City Government needs a justification for forbidding motorists to drive up Lexington Avenue, it is sufficient justifi-cation if the proper officials believe, on sound ev-idence, that the gain to the many will outweigh the inconvenience to the few. When individual citi-zens are said to have rights against the Govern-ment, however, like the right of free speech, that must mean that this sort of justification is not enough. Otherwise the claim would not argue that individuals have special protection against the law when their rights are in play, and that is just the point of the claim.

Not all legal rights, or even Constitutional rights, represent moral rights against the Govern-ment. I now have the legal right to drive either way on Fifty-seventh Street, but the Government would do no wrong to make that street one-way if it thought it in the general interest to do so. I have a Constitutional right to vote for a congressman every two years, but the national and state govern-ments would do no wrong if, following the amend-ment procedure, they made a congressman's term four years instead of two, again on the basis of a judgment that this would be for the general good.

But those Constitutional rights that we call fun-damental, like the right of free speech, are sup-posed to represent rights against the Government in the strong sense; that is the point of the boast that our legal system respects the fundamental rights of the citizen. If citizens have a moral right of free speech, then governments would do wrong to repeal the First Amendment that guarantees it, even if they were persuaded that the majority would be better off if speech were curtailed.

I must not overstate the point. Someone who claims that citizens have a right against the Gov-ernment need not go so far as to say that the State is *never* justified in overriding that right. He might say, for example, that although citizens have a right to free speech, the Government may override that right when necessary to protect the rights of others, or to prevent a catastrophe, or even to ob-tain a clear and major public benefit (though if he acknowledged this last as a possible justification he would be treating the right in question as not among the most important or fundamental). What he cannot do is to say that the Government is jus-tified in overriding a right on the minimal grounds that would be sufficient if no such right existed. He cannot say that the Government is entitled to act on no more than a judgement that its act is likely to produce, overall, a benefit to the commu-nity. That admission would make his claim of a right pointless, and would show him to be using some sense of 'right' other than the strong sense necessary to give his claim the political impor-tance it is normally taken to have. . . .

I said that any society that claims to recognize rights at all must abandon the notion of a general duty to obey the law that holds in all cases. This is important, because it shows that there are no short cuts to meeting a citizen's claim to right. If a citi-zen argues that he has a moral right not to serve in the Army, or to protest in a way he finds effective, then an official who wants to answer him, and not simply bludgeon him into obedience, must respond to the particular point he makes, and cannot point to the draft law or a Supreme Court decision as having even special, let alone decisive, weight. Sometimes an official who considers the citizen's moral arguments in good faith will be persuaded that the citizen's claim is plausible, or even right. It does not follow, however, that he will always be persuaded or that he always should be.

I must emphasize that all these propositions concern the strong sense of right, and they therefore leave open important questions about the right thing to do. If a man believes he has the right to break the law, he must then ask whether he does the right thing to exercise that right. He must remember that reasonable men can differ about whether he has a right against the Government, and therefore the right to break the law, that he thinks he has; and therefore that reasonable men can oppose him in good faith. He must take into account the various consequences his acts will have, whether they involve violence, and such other considerations as the context makes relevant; he must not go beyond the rights he can in good faith claim, to acts that violate the rights of others. . . .

3. CONTROVERSIAL RIGHTS

The argument so far has been hypothetical: if a man has a particular moral right against the Government, that right survives contrary legislation or adjudication. But this does not tell us what rights he has, and it is notorious that reasonable men disagree about that. There is wide agreement on certain clearcut cases; almost everyone who believes in rights at all would admit, for example, that a man has a moral right to speak his mind in a non-provocative way on matters of political concern, and that this is an important right that the State must go to great pains to protect. But there is great controversy as to the limits of such paradigm rights, and the so-called 'anti-riot' law involved in the famous Chicago Seven trial of the last decade is a case in point.

The defendants were accused of conspiring to cross state lines with the intention of causing a riot. This charge is vague—perhaps unconstitutionally vague—but the law apparently defines as criminal emotional speeches which argue that violence is justified in order to secure political equality. Does the right of free speech protect this sort of speech? That, of course, is a legal issue, because it invokes the free-speech clause of the First Amendment of the Constitution. But it is also a moral issue, because, as I said, we must treat the First Amendment as an attempt to protect a moral right. It is part of the job of governing to 'define' moral rights through statutes and judicial decisions, that is, to declare officially the extent that moral rights will be taken to have in law. Congress faced this task in voting on the anti-riot bill, and the Supreme Court has faced it in countless cases. How should the different departments of government go about defining moral rights?

They should begin with a sense that whatever they decide might be wrong. History and their descendants may judge that they acted unjustly when they thought they were right. If they take their duty seriously, they must try to limit their mistakes, and they must therefore try to discover where the dangers of mistake lie.

They might choose one of two very different models for this purpose. The first model recommends striking a balance between the rights of the individual and the demands of society at large. If the Government *infringes* on a moral right (for example, by defining the right of free speech more narrowly than justice requires), then it has done the individual a wrong. On the other hand, if the Government *inflates* a right (by defining it more broadly than justice requires) then it cheats society of some general benefit, like safe streets, that there is no reason it should not have. So a mistake on one side is as serious as a mistake on the other. The course of government is to steer to the middle, to balance the general good and personal rights, giving to each its due. . . .

The first model, described in this way, has great plausibility, and most laymen and lawyers, I think, would respond to it warmly. The metaphor of balancing the public interest against personal claims is established in our political and judicial rhetoric, and this metaphor gives the model both familiarity and appeal. Nevertheless, the first model is a false one, certainly in the case of rights generally regarded as important, and the metaphor is the heart of its error.

The institution of rights against the Government is not a gift of God, or an ancient ritual, or a national sport. It is a complex and troublesome practice that makes the Government's job of securing the general benefit more difficult and more expensive, and it would be frivolous and wrongful practice unless it served some point. Anyone who professes to take rights seriously, and who praises our Government for respecting them, must have some sense of what that point is. He must accept, at the minimum, one or both of two important ideas. The first is the vague but powerful idea of human dignity. This idea, associated with Kant, but defended by philosophers of different schools, supposes that there are ways of treating a man that are inconsistent with recognizing him as a full member of the human community, and holds that such treatment is profoundly unjust.

The second is the more familiar idea of political equality. This supposes that the weaker members of a political community are entitled to the same concern and respect of their government as the more powerful members have secured for themselves, so that if some men have freedom of decision whatever the effect on the general good, then all men must have the same freedom. I do not want to defend or elaborate these ideas here, but only to insist that anyone who claims that citizens have rights must accept ideas very close to these.[2]

It makes sense to say that a man has a fundamental right against the Government, in the strong sense, like free speech, if that right is necessary to protect his dignity, or his standing as equally entitled to concern and respect, or some other personal value of like consequence. It does not make sense otherwise.

So if rights make sense at all, then the invasion of a relatively important right must be a very serious matter. It means treating a man as less than a man, or as less worthy of concern than other men. The institution of rights rests on the conviction that this is a grave injustice, and that it is worth paying the incremental cost in social policy or efficiency that is necessary to prevent it. But then it must be wrong to say that inflating rights is as serious as invading them. If the Government errs on the side of the individual, then it simply pays a little more in social efficiency than it has to pay; it

pays a little more, that is, of the same coin that it has already decided must be spent. But if it errs against the individual it inflicts an insult upon him that, on its own reckoning, it is worth a great deal of that coin to avoid.

So the first model is indefensible. It rests, in fact, on a mistake I discussed earlier, namely the confusion of society's rights with the rights of members of society. 'Balancing' is appropriate when the Government must choose between competing claims of right—between the Southerner's claim to freedom of association, for example, and the black man's claim to an equal education. The Government can do nothing but estimate the merits of the competing claims, and act on its estimate. The first model assumes that the 'right' of the majority is a competing right that must be balanced in this way; but that, as I argued before, is a confusion that threatens to destroy the concept of individual rights. It is worth noticing that the community rejects the first model in that area where the stakes for the individual are highest, the criminal process. We say that it is better that a great many guilty men go free than that one innocent man be punished, and that homily rests on the choice of the second model for government.

The second model treats abridging a right as much more serious than inflating one, and its recommendations follow from that judgment. It stipulates that once a right is recognized in clear-cut cases, then the Government should act to cut off that right only when some compelling reason is presented, some reason that is consistent with the suppositions on which the original right must be based. It cannot be an argument for curtailing a right, once granted, simply that society would pay a further price for extending it. There must be something special about that further cost, or there must be some other feature of the case, that makes it sensible to say that although great social cost is warranted to protect the original right, this particular cost is not necessary. Otherwise, the Government's failure to extend the right will show that its recognition of the right in the original case is a sham, a promise that it intends to keep only until that becomes inconvenient.

How can we show that a particular cost is not worth paying without taking back the initial recognition of a right? I can think of only three sorts of grounds that can consistently be used to limit the definition of a particular right. First, the Government might show that the values protected by the original right are not really at stake in the marginal case, or are at stake only in some attenuated form. Second, it might show that if the right is defined to include the marginal case, then some competing right, in the strong sense I described earlier, would be abridged. Third, it might show that if the right were so defined, then the cost to society would not be simply incremental, but would be of a degree far beyond the cost paid to grant the original right, a degree great enough to justify whatever assault on dignity or equality might be involved. . . .

But what of the individual rights of those who will be destroyed by a riot, of the passer-by who will be killed by a sniper's bullet or the shopkeeper who will be ruined by looting? To put the issue in this way, as a question of competing rights, suggests a principle that would undercut the effect of uncertainty. Shall we say that some rights to protection are so important that the Government is justified in doing all it can to maintain them? Shall we therefore say that the Government may abridge the rights of others to act when their acts might simply increase the risk, by however slight or speculative a margin, that some person's right to life or property will be violated?

Some such principle is relied on by those who oppose the Supreme Court's recent liberal rulings on police procedure. These rulings increase the chance that a guilty man will go free, and therefore marginally increase the risk that any particular member of the community will be murdered, raped, or robbed. Some critics believe that the Court's decision must therefore be wrong.

But no society that purports to recognize a variety of rights, on the ground that a man's dignity or equality may be invaded in a variety of ways, can accept such a principle. If forcing a man to testify against himself, or forbidding him to speak, does the damage that the rights against self-incrimination and the right of free speech assume, then it would be contemptuous for the State to tell a man that he must suffer this damage against the possibility that other men's risk of loss may be marginally reduced. If rights make sense, then the degrees of their importance can-

not be so different that some count not at all when others are mentioned.

Of course the Government may discriminate and may stop a man from exercising his right to speak when there is a clear and substantial risk that his speech will do great damage to the person or property of others, and no other means of preventing this are at hand, as in the case of the man shouting 'Fire!' in a theater. But we must reject the suggested principle that the Government can simply ignore rights to speak when life and property are in question. So long as the impact of speech on these other rights remains speculative and marginal, it must look elsewhere for levers to pull.

4. WHY TAKE RIGHTS SERIOUSLY?

I said at the beginning of this essay that I wanted to show what a government must do that professes to recognize individual rights. It must dispense with the claim that citizens never have a right to break its laws, and it must not define citizens' rights so that these are cut off for supposed reasons of the general good. Any Government's harsh treatment of civil disobedience, or campaign against vocal protest, may therefore be thought to count against its sincerity.

One might well ask, however, whether it is wise to take rights all that seriously after all. . . .

[Former Vice President] Spiro Agnew supposed that rights are divisive, and that national unity and a new respect for law may be developed by taking them more skeptically. But he [was] wrong. America will continue to be divided by its social and foreign policy, and if the economy grows weaker again the divisions will become more bitter. If we want our laws and our legal institutions to provide the ground rules within which these issues will be contested, then these ground rules must not be the conqueror's law that the dominant class imposes on the weaker, as Marx supposed the law of a capitalist society must be. The bulk of the law—that part which defines and implements social, economic, and foreign policy—cannot be neutral. It must state, in its greatest part, the majority's view of the common good. The institution of rights is therefore crucial, because it represents the majority's promise to the minorities that their dignity and equality will be respected. When the divisions among the groups are most violent, then this gesture, if law is to work, must be most sincere.

The institution requires an act of faith on the part of the minorities, because the scope of their rights will be controversial whenever they are important, and because the officers of the majority will act on their own notions of what these rights really are. Of course these officials will disagree with many of the claims that a minority makes. That makes it all the more important that they take their decisions gravely. They must show that they understand what rights are, and they must not cheat on the full implications of the doctrine. The Government will not re-establish respect for law without giving the law some claim to respect. It cannot do that if it neglects the one feature that distinguishes law from ordered brutality.

NOTES

1. See "Civil Disobedience and the Law," Section 12.
2. He need not consider these ideas to be axiomatic. He may, that is, have reasons for insisting that dignity or equality are important values, and these reasons may be utilitarian. He may believe, for example, that the general good will be advanced, in the long run, only if we treat indignity or inequality as very great injustices, and never allow our opinions about the general good to justify them. I do not know of any good arguments for or against this sort of 'institutional' utilitarianism, but it is consistent with my point, because it argues that we must treat violations of dignity and equality as special moral crimes, beyond the reach of ordinary utilitarian justification.

REVIEW AND DISCUSSION QUESTIONS

1. What does Dworkin mean by "right" in the "strong" sense? In what ways does the U.S. Constitution protect citizens' rights in that sense?
2. Do citizens have a general duty to obey the law, according to Dworkin? Explain.
3. Describe the two models that government might use in defining the rights of citizens. Which model does Dworkin find most appealing, and why?
4. Why does Dworkin hold that governments should take rights seriously? Consider especially carefully what he says in note 2, and compare it with Mill's position. Could Mill agree with Dworkin?
5. It is sometimes said that rights are "relative" to a particular culture. What might such a claim mean? How might Dworkin respond?
6. How would Claude Ake respond to Dworkin's article? Is that response sound, in your view? Explain.
7. How would Dworkin respond to the criticisms of female circumcision discussed in the earlier essay? Which of his two approaches to rights seems most similar to that of the author of that article?

Part II
ISSUES OF LIFE AND DEATH

5
Animals and the Environment

Readings in this and the other sections in Part II deal with a variety of topics associated with the value of life and the morality of killing. They include the environment, animals, abortion, euthanasia, and war. Whereas some of the readings highlight problems unique to the particular topics discussed, other readings point to common themes. Positions we may take on euthanasia, for example, often have implications for our treatment of animals and fetuses; decisions about killing in self-defense and the justification of war may affect our position on abortion to save the mother. Essays in this section address the value of nonhuman life, including both animals and nature generally.

All Animals Are Equal

Peter Singer

In this influential essay, taken from his book *Animal Liberation*, Peter Singer argues that equality applies to animals as well as humans and that our ordinary attitudes toward nonhuman animals betray a bias toward our species that is rather like the attitudes of a racist or sexist. Both our eating habits and our use of animals in experiments are, he argues, morally wrong. Peter Singer is professor of philosophy and director of the Centre for Human Bioethics at Monash University, Australia.

"Animal Liberation" may sound more like a parody of other liberation movements than a serious objective. The idea of "The Rights of Animals" actually was once used to parody the case for women's rights. When Mary Wollstonecraft, a forerunner of today's feminists, published her *Vindication of the Rights of Women* in 1792, her views were widely regarded as absurd, and before long

From Peter Singer, *Animal Liberation* (New York: Avon Books, 1977). Reprinted by permission. Section titles added.

an anonymous publication appeared entitled *A Vindication of the Rights of Brutes*. The author of this satirical work (now known to have been Thomas Taylor, a distinguished Cambridge philosopher) tried to refute Mary Wollstonecraft's arguments by showing that they could be carried one stage further. If the argument for equality was sound when applied to women, why should it not be applied to dogs, cats, and horses? The reasoning seemed to hold for these "brutes" too; yet to hold that brutes had rights was manifestly absurd; therefore the reasoning by which this conclusion had been reached must be unsound, and if unsound when applied to brutes, it must also be unsound when applied to women, since the very same arguments had been used in each case.

1. SEXUAL AND RACIAL EQUALITY

In order to explain the basis of the case for the equality of animals, it will be helpful to start with an examination of the case for the equality of women. . . . The extension of the basic principle of equality from one group to another does not imply that we must treat both groups in exactly the same way, or grant exactly the same rights to both groups. Whether we should do so will depend on the nature of the members of the two groups. The basic principle of equality does not require equal or identical *treatment;* it requires equal *consideration.* Equal consideration for different beings may lead to different treatment and different rights.

. . . At this point such a conclusion [that all animals are equal] may appear odd; but if we examine more deeply the basis on which our opposition to discrimination on grounds of race or sex ultimately rests, we will see that we would be on shaky ground if we were to demand equality for blacks, women, and other groups of oppressed humans while denying equal consideration to nonhumans. To make this clear we need to see, first, exactly why racism and sexism are wrong.

When we say that all human beings, whatever their race, creed, or sex, are equal, what is it that we are asserting? Those who wish to defend hierarchical, inegalitarian societies have often pointed out that by whatever test we choose it simply is not true that all humans are equal. Like it or not we must face the fact that humans come in different shapes and sizes; they come with different moral capacities, different intellectual abilities, different amounts of benevolent feeling and sensitivity to the needs of others, different abilities to communicate effectively, and different capacities to experience pleasure and pain. In short, if the demand for equality were based on the actual equality of all human beings, we would have to stop demanding equality.

Still, one might cling to the view that the demand for equality among human beings is based on the actual equality of different races and sexes. Although, it may be said, humans differ as individuals there are no such differences between races and sexes *as such.* From the mere fact that a person is black or a woman we cannot infer anything about that person's intellectual or moral capacities. This, it may be said, is why racism and sexism are wrong. The white racist claims that whites are superior to blacks, but this is false. . . . The opponent of sexism would say the same: a person's sex is no guide to his or her abilities, and this is why it is unjustifiable to discriminate on the basis of sex.

The existence of individual variations that cut across the lines of race or sex, however, provides us with no defense at all against a more sophisticated opponent of equality, one who proposes that, say, the interests of all those with IQ scores below 100 be given less consideration than the interests of those with ratings over 100. . . .

There is a second important reason why we ought not to base our opposition to racism and sexism on any kind of actual equality, even the limited kind that asserts that variations in capacities and abilities are spread evenly between the different races and sexes: we can have no absolute guarantee that these capacities and abilities really are distributed evenly, without regard to race or sex, among human beings. So far as actual abilities are concerned there do seem to be certain measurable differences between both races and sexes. These differences do not, of course, appear in each case, but only when averages are taken. More important still, we do not yet know how much of these differences is really due to different genetic endowments of the different races and sexes, and how much is due to poor schools, poor housing, and other factors that are the result of past and continuing discrimination. Perhaps all the important differences will eventually prove to be environmental rather than genetic. Anyone opposed to racism and sexism will certainly hope that this well be so, for it will make the task of ending discrimination a lot easier; nevertheless it would be dangerous to rest the case against racism and sexism on the belief that all significant differences are environmental in origin. The opponent of, say, racism who takes this line will be unable to avoid conceding that *if* differences in ability do after all prove to have some genetic connection with race, racism would in some way be defensible.

Fortunately there is no need to pin the case for equality to one particular outcome of a scientific investigation. The appropriate response to those who claim to have found evidence of genetically based differences in ability between the races or sexes is not to stick to the belief that the genetic explanation must be wrong, whatever evidence to the contrary may turn up: instead we should make it quite clear that the claim to equality does not depend on intelligence, moral capacity, physical strength, or similar matters of fact. Equality is a moral idea, not an assertion of fact. There is no logically compelling reason for assuming that a factual difference in ability between two people justifies any difference in the amount of consideration we give to their needs and interests. *The principle of equality of human beings is not a description of an alleged actual equality among humans: it is a prescription of how we should treat humans.*

Jeremy Bentham, the founder of the reforming utilitarian school of moral philosophy, incorporated the essential basis of moral equality into his system of ethics by means of the formula: "Each to count for one and none for more than one." In other words, the interests of every being affected by an action are to be taken into account and given the same weight as the like interests of any other being. A later utilitarian, Henry Sidgwick, put the point in this way: "The good of any one individual is of no more importance, from the point of view (if I may say so) of the Universe, than the good of any other."

It is an implication of this principle of equality that our concern for others and our readiness to consider their interests ought not to depend on what they are like or on what abilities they may possess. Precisely what this concern or consideration requires us to do may vary according to the characteristics of those affected by what we do: concern for the well-being of a child growing up in America would require that we teach him to read; concern for the well-being of a pig may require no more than that we leave him alone with other pigs in a place where there is adequate food and room to run freely. But the basic element—the taking into account of the interests of the being, whatever those interests may be—must, according to the principle of equality, be extended to all beings, black or white, masculine or feminine, human or nonhuman.

Thomas Jefferson, who was responsible for writing the principle of the equality of men into the American Declaration of Independence, saw this point. It led him to oppose slavery even though he was unable to free himself fully from his slaveholding background. He wrote in a letter to the author of a book that emphasized the notable intellectual achievements of Negroes in order to refute the then common view that they had limited intellectual capacities:

Be assured that no person living wishes more sincerely than I do, to see a complete refutation of the doubts I have myself entertained and expressed on the grade of understanding allotted to them by nature, and to find that they are on a par with ourselves but whatever be their degree of talent it is no measure of their rights. Because Sir Isaac Newton was superior to others in understanding, he was not therefore lord of the property or person of others.[1]

Similarly when in the 1850s the call for women's rights was raised in the United States a remarkable black feminist named Sojourner Truth made the same point in more robust terms at a feminist convention:

. . . they talk about this thing in the head; what do they call it? ["Intellect," whispered someone near by.] That's it. What's that got to do with women's rights or Negroe's rights? If my cup won't hold but a pint and yours holds a quart, wouldn't you be mean not to let me have my little half-measure full?[2]

It is on this basis that the case against racism and the case against sexism must both ultimately rest;

and it is in accordance with this principle that the attitude that we may call "speciesism," by analogy with racism, must also be condemned.

2. SPECIESISM AND THE EQUALITY OF ANIMALS

Speciesism—the word is not an attractive one, but I can think of no better term—is a prejudice or attitude of bias toward the interests of members of one's own species and against those of members of other species. It should be obvious that the fundamental objections to racism and sexism made by Thomas Jefferson and Sojourner Truth apply equally to speciesism. If possessing a higher degree of intelligence does not entitle one human to use another for his own ends, how can it entitle humans to exploit nonhumans for the same purpose?[3]

Many philosophers and other writers have proposed the principle of equal consideration of interests, in some form or other, as a basic moral principle; but not many of them have recognized that this principle applies to members of other species as well as to our own. Jeremy Bentham was one of the few who did realize this. In a forward-looking passage written at a time when black slaves had been freed by the French but in the British dominions were still being treated in the way we now treat animals, Bentham wrote:

The day *may* come when the rest of the animal creation may acquire those rights which never could have been withholden from them but by the hand of tyranny. The French have already discovered that the blackness of the skin is no reason why a human being should be abandoned without redress to the caprice of a tormentor. It may one day come to be recognized that the number of the legs, the villosity of the skin, or the termination of the *os sacrum* are reasons equally insufficient for abandoning a sensitive being to the same fate. What else is it that should trace the insuperable line? Is it the faculty of reason, or perhaps the faculty of discourse? But a full-grown horse or dog is beyond comparison a more rational, as well as a more conversable animal, than an infant of a day or a week or even a month, old. But suppose they were otherwise, what would it avail? The question is not, Can they *reason?* nor Can they *talk?* but, Can they *suffer?*[4]

In this passage Bentham points to the capacity for suffering as the vital characteristic that gives a being the right to equal consideration. The capacity for suffering—or more strictly, for suffering and/or enjoyment or happiness—is not just another characteristic like the capacity for language or higher mathematics. Bentham is not saying that those who try to mark "the insuperable line" that determines whether the interests of a being should be considered happen to have chosen the wrong characteristic. By saying that we must consider the interests of all beings with the capacity for suffering or enjoyment Bentham does not arbitrarily exclude from consideration any interests at all—as those who draw the line with reference to the possession of reason or language do. The capacity for suffering and enjoyment is *a prerequisite for having interests at all*, a condition that must be satisfied before we can speak of interests in a meaningful way. It would be nonsense to say that it was not in the interests of a stone to be kicked along the road by a schoolboy. A stone does not have interests because it cannot suffer. Nothing that we can do to it could possibly make any difference to its welfare. A mouse, on the other hand, does have an interest in not being kicked along the road, because it will suffer if it is.

If a being suffers there can be no moral justification for refusing to take that suffering into consideration. No matter what the nature of the being, the principle of equality requires that its suffering be counted equally with the like suffering—in so far as rough comparisons can be made—of any other being. If a being is not capable of suffering, or of experiencing enjoyment or happiness, there is nothing to be taken into account. So the limit of sentience (using the term as a convenient if not strictly accurate shorthand for the capacity to suffer and/or experience enjoyment) is the only defensible boundary of concern for the interests of others. To mark this boundary by some other characteristic like intelligence or rationality would be to mark it in an arbitrary manner. Why not choose some other characteristic, like skin color?

The racist violates the principle of equality by giving greater weight to the interests of members of his own race when there is a clash between their interests and the interests of those of another race. The sexist violates the principle of equality by favoring the interests of his own sex. Similarly the speciesist allows the interests of his own species to override the greater interests of members of other species. The pattern is identical in each case.

Most human beings are speciesists. Ordinary human beings—not a few exceptionally cruel or heartless humans, but the overwhelming majority of humans—take an active part in, acquiesce in, and allow their taxes to pay for practices that require the sacrifice of the most important interests of members of other species in order to promote the most trivial interests of our own species. . . .

3. SPECIESISM IN PRACTICE

For the great majority of human beings, especially in urban, industrialized societies, the most direct form of contact with members of other species is at mealtimes: We eat them. In doing so we treat them purely as means to our ends. We regard their life and well-being as subordinate to our taste for a particular kind of dish. I say "taste" deliberately—this is purely a matter of pleasing our palate. There can be no defense of eating flesh in terms of satisfying nutritional needs, since it has been established beyond doubt that we could satisfy our need for protein and other essential nutrients far more efficiently with a diet that replaced animal flesh by soy beans, or products derived from soy beans, and other high protein vegetable products.[5]

It is not merely the act of killing that indicates what we are ready to do to other species in order to gratify our tastes. The suffering we inflict on the animals while they are alive is perhaps an even clearer indication of our speciesism than the fact that we are prepared to kill them.[6] In order to have meat on the table at a price that people can afford, our society tolerates methods of meat production that confine sentient animals in cramped, unsuitable conditions for the entire duration of their lives. Animals are treated like machines that convert fodder into flesh, and any innovation that results in a higher "conversion ratio" is liable to be adopted. As one authority on the subject has said, "cruelty is acknowledged only when profitability ceases."[7] So hens are crowded four or five to a cage with a floor area of twenty inches by eighteen inches, or around the size of a single page of the

New York Times. The cages have wire floors, since this reduces cleaning costs, though wire is unsuitable for the hens' feet; the floors slope, since this makes the eggs roll down for easy collection, although this makes it difficult for the hens to rest comfortably. In these conditions all the birds' natural instincts are thwarted: They cannot stretch their wings fully, walk freely, dust-bathe, scratch the ground, or build a nest. Although they have never known other conditions, observers have noticed that the birds vainly try to perform these actions. Frustrated at their inability to do so, they often develop what farmers call "vices," and peck each other to death. To prevent this, the beaks of young birds are often cut off.

This kind of treatment is not limited to poultry. Pigs are now also being reared in cages inside sheds. These animals are comparable to dogs in intelligence, and need a varied, stimulating environment if they are not to suffer from stress and boredom. Anyone who kept a dog in the way in which pigs are frequently kept would be liable to prosecution, in England at least, but because our interest in exploiting pigs is greater than our interest in exploiting dogs, we object to cruelty to dogs while consuming the produce of cruelty to pigs. Of the other animals, the condition of veal calves is perhaps worst of all, since these animals are so closely confined that they cannot even turn around or get up and lie down freely. In this way they do not develop unpalatable muscle. They are also made anaemic and kept short of roughage, to keep their flesh pale, since white veal fetches a higher price; as a result they develop a craving for iron and roughage, and have been observed to gnaw wood off the sides of their stalls, and lick greedily at any rusty hinge that is within reach.

Since, as I have said, none of these practices cater to anything more than our pleasures of taste, our practice of rearing and killing other animals in order to eat them is a clear instance of the sacrifice of the most important interests of other beings in order to satisfy trivial interests of our own. To avoid speciesism we must stop this practice, and each of us has a moral obligation to cease supporting the practice. Our custom is all the support that the meat industry needs. The decision to cease giving it that support may be difficult, but it is no more difficult than it would have been for a white

Southerner to go against the traditions of his society and free his slaves; if we do not change our dietary habits, how can we censure those slaveholders who would not change their own way of living?

The same form of discrimination may be observed in the widespread practice of experimenting on other species in order to see if certain substances are safe for human beings, or to test some psychological theory about the effect of severe punishment on learning, or to try out various new compounds just in case something turns up. People sometimes think that all this experimentation is for vital medical purposes, and so will reduce suffering overall. This comfortable belief is very wide of the mark. Drug companies test new shampoos and cosmetics that they are intending to put on the market by dropping them into the eyes of rabbits, held open by metal clips, in order to observe what damage results. Food additives, like artificial colorings and preservatives, are tested by what is known as the "LD50"—a test designed to find the level of consumption at which 50 percent of a group of animals will die. In the process, nearly all of the animals are made very sick before some finally die, and others pull through. If the substance is relatively harmless, as it often is, huge doses have to be forcefed to the animals, until in some cases sheer volume or concentration of the substance causes death.

Much of this pointless cruelty goes on in the universities. In many areas of science, nonhuman animals are regarded as an item of laboratory equipment, to be used and expended as desired. In psychology laboratories experimenters devise endless variations and repetitions of experiments that were of little value in the first place. To quote just one example, from the experimenter's own account in a psychology journal: At the University of Pennsylvania, Perrin S. Cohen hung six dogs in hammocks with electrodes taped to their hind feet. Electric shock of varying intensity was then administered through the electrodes. If the dog learned to press its head against a panel on the left, the shock was turned off, but otherwise it remained on indefinitely. Three of the dogs, however, were required to wait periods varying from 2 to 7 seconds while being shocked before making the response that turned off the current. If they failed to

wait, they received further shocks. Each dog was given from 26 to 46 "sessions" in the hammock, each session consisting of 80 "trials" or shocks, administered at intervals of one minute. The experimenter reported that the dogs, who were unable to move in the hammock, barked or bobbed their heads when the current was applied. The reported findings of the experiment were that there was a delay in the dogs' responses that increased proportionately to the time the dogs were required to endure the shock, but a gradual increase in the intensity of the shock had no systematic effect in the timing of the response. The experiment was funded by the National Institutes of Health, and the United States Public Health Service.[8]

In this example, and countless cases like it, the possible benefits to mankind are either nonexistent or fantastically remote, while the certain losses to members of other species are very real. This is, again, a clear indication of speciesism. . . .

4. THE VALUE OF LIVES: HUMANS AND NONHUMANS

If I give a horse a hard slap across its rump with my open hand, the horse may start, but it presumably feels little pain. Its skin is thick enough to protect it against a mere slap. If I slap a baby in the same way, however, the baby will cry and presumably does feel pain, for its skin is more sensitive. So it is worse to slap a baby than a horse, if both slaps are administered with equal force. But there must be some kind of blow—I don't know exactly what it would be, but perhaps a blow with a heavy stick—that would cause the horse as much pain as we cause a baby by slapping it with our hand. That is what I mean by "the same amount of pain," and if we consider it wrong to inflict that much pain on a baby for no good reason then we must, unless we are speciesists, consider it equally wrong to inflict the same amount of pain on a horse for no good reason.

There are other differences between humans and animals that cause other complications. Normal adult human beings have mental capacities which will, in certain circumstances, lead them to suffer more than animals would in the same circumstances. If, for instance, we decided to perform extremely painful or lethal scientific experiments on normal adult humans, kidnapped at random from public parks for this purpose, every adult who entered a park would become fearful that he would be kidnapped. The resultant terror would be a form of suffering additional to the pain of the experiment. The same experiments performed on nonhuman animals would cause less suffering since the animals would not have the anticipatory dread of being kidnapped and experimented upon. This does not mean, of course, that it would be right to perform the experiment on animals, but only that there is a reason, which is *not* speciesist, for preferring to use animals rather than normal adult humans, if the experiment is to be done at all. It should be noted, however, that this same argument gives us a reason for preferring to use human infants—orphans perhaps—or retarded humans for experiments, rather than adults, since infants and retarded humans would also have no idea of what was going to happen to them. So far as this argument is concerned nonhuman animals and infants and retarded humans are in the same category; and if we use this argument to justify experiments on nonhuman animals we have to ask ourselves whether we are also prepared to allow experiments on human infants and retarded adults; and if we make a distinction between animals and these humans, on what basis can we do it, other than a barefaced—and morally indefensible—preference for members of our own species?

There are many areas in which the superior mental powers of normal adult humans make a difference: anticipation, more detailed memory, greater knowledge of what is happening, and so on. Yet these differences do not all point to greater suffering on the part of the normal human being. Sometimes an animal may suffer more because of his more limited understanding. If, for instance, we are taking prisoners in wartime we can explain to them that while they must submit to capture, search, and confinement they will not otherwise be harmed and will be set free at the conclusion of hostilities. If we capture a wild animal, however, we cannot explain that we are not threatening its life. A wild animal cannot distinguish an attempt to overpower and confine from an attempt to kill; the one causes as much terror as the other.

It may be objected that comparisons of the sufferings of different species are impossible to make, and that for this reason when the interests of animals and humans clash the principle of equality gives no guidance. It is probably true that comparisons of suffering between members of different species cannot be made precisely, but precision is not essential. Even if we were to prevent the infliction of suffering on animals only when it is quite certain that the interests of humans will not be affected to anything like the extent that animals are affected, we would be forced to make radical changes in our treatment of animals that would involve our diet, the farming methods we use, experimental procedures in many fields of science, our approach to wildlife and to hunting, trapping and the wearing of furs, and areas of entertainment like circuses, rodeos, and zoos. As a result, a vast amount of suffering would be avoided.

So far I have said a lot about the infliction of suffering on animals, but nothing about killing them. This omission has been deliberate. The application of the principle of equality to the infliction of suffering is, in theory at least, fairly straightforward. Pain and suffering are bad and should be prevented or minimized, irrespective of the race, sex, or species of the being that suffers. How bad a pain is depends on how intense it is and how long it lasts, but pains of the same intensity and duration are equally bad, whether felt by humans or animals.

The wrongness of killing a being is more complicated. I have kept, and shall continue to keep, the question of killing in the background because in the present state of human tyranny over other species the more simple, straightforward principle of equal consideration of pain or pleasure is a sufficient basis for identifying and protesting against all the major abuses of animals that humans practice. Nevertheless, it is necessary to say something about killing.

Just as most humans are speciesists in their readiness to cause pain to animals when they would not cause a similar pain to humans for the same reason, so most humans are speciesists in their readiness to kill other animals when they would not kill humans. We need to proceed more cautiously here, however, because people hold widely differing views about when it is legitimate to kill humans, as the continuing debates over abortion and euthanasia attest. Nor have moral philosophers been able to agree on exactly what it is that makes it wrong to kill humans, and under what circumstances killing a human being may be justifiable.

Let us consider first the view that it is always wrong to take an innocent human life. We may call this the "sanctity of life" view. People who take this view oppose abortion and euthanasia. They do not usually, however, oppose the killing of nonhumans—so perhaps it would be more accurate to describe this view as the "sanctity of *human* life" view.

The belief that human life, and only human life, is sacrosanct is a form of speciesism. To see this, consider the following example.

Assuming that, as sometimes happens, an infant has been born with massive and irreparable brain damage. The damage is so severe that the infant can never be any more than a "human vegetable," unable to talk, recognize other people, act independently of others, or develop a sense of self-awareness. The parents of the infant, realizing that they cannot hope for any improvement in their child's condition and being in any case unwilling to spend, or ask the state to spend, the thousands of dollars that would be needed annually for proper care of the infant, ask the doctor to kill the infant painlessly.

Should the doctor do what the parents ask? Legally, he should not, and in this respect the law reflects the sanctity of life view. The life of every human being is sacred. Yet people who would say this about the infant do not object to the killing of nonhuman animals. How can they justify their different judgments? Adult chimpanzees, dogs, pigs, and many other species far surpass the brain-damaged infant in their ability to relate to others, act independently, be self-aware, and any other capacity that could reasonably be said to give value to life. With the most intensive care possible, there are retarded infants who can never achieve the intelligence level of a dog. Nor can we appeal to the concern of the infant's parents, since they themselves, in this imaginary example (and in some actual cases), do not want the infant kept alive.

The only thing that distinguishes the infant from the animal, in the eyes of those who claim it has a "right to life," is that it is, biologically, a member of the species Homo sapiens, whereas chimpanzees, dogs, and pigs are not. But to use *this* difference as the basis for granting a right to life to the infant and not to the other animals is, of course, pure speciesism.[9] It is exactly the kind of arbitrary difference that the most crude and overt kind of racist uses in attempting to justify racial discrimination.

This does not mean that to avoid speciesism we must hold that it is as wrong to kill a dog as it is to kill a normal human being. The only position that is irredeemably speciesist is the one that tries to make the boundary of the right to life run exactly parallel to the boundary of our own species. Those who hold the sanctity of life view do this because while distinguishing sharply between humans and other animals they allow no distinctions to be made within our own species, objecting to the killing of the severely retarded and the hopelessly senile as strongly as they object to the killing of normal adults.

To avoid speciesism we must allow that beings which are similar in all relevant respects have a similar right to life—and mere membership in our own biological species cannot be a morally relevant criterion for this right. Within these limits we could still hold that, for instance, it is worse to kill a normal adult human, with a capacity for self-awareness, and the ability to plan for the future and have meaningful relations with others, than it is to kill a mouse, which presumably does not share all of these characteristics; or we might appeal to the close family and other personal ties which humans have but mice do not have to the same degree; or we might think that it is the consequences for other humans, who will be put in fear of their own lives, that makes the crucial difference; or we might think it is some combination of these factors, or other factors altogether.

Whatever criteria we choose, however, we will have to admit that they do not follow precisely the boundary of our own species. We may legitimately hold that there are some features of certain beings which make their lives more valuable than those of other beings; but there will surely be some nonhuman animals whose lives, by any standards, are more valuable than the lives of some humans. A chimpanzee, dog, or pig, for instance, will have a higher degree of self-awareness and a greater capacity for meaningful relations with others than a severely retarded infant or someone in a state of advanced senility. So if we base the right to life on these characteristics we must grant these animals a right to life as good as, or better than, such retarded or senile humans.

Now this argument cuts both ways. It could be taken as showing that chimpanzees, dogs, and pigs, along with some other species, have a right to life and we commit a grave moral offense whenever we kill them, even when they are old and suffering and our intention is to put them out of their misery. Alternatively one could take the argument as showing that the severely retarded and hopelessly senile have no right to life and may be killed for quite trivial reasons, as we now kill animals.

Since my focus here is on ethical questions concerning animals and not on the morality of euthanasia I shall not attempt to settle this issue finally. I think it is reasonably clear, though, that while both of the positions just described avoid speciesism, neither is entirely satisfactory. What we need is some middle position which would avoid speciesism but would not make the lives of the retarded and senile as cheap as the lives of pigs and dogs now are, nor make the lives of pigs and dogs so sacrosanct that we think it wrong to put them out of hopeless misery. What we must do is bring nonhuman animals within our sphere of moral concern and cease to treat their lives as expendable for whatever trivial purposes we may have. At the same time, once we realize that the fact that a being is a member of our own species is not in itself enough to make it always wrong to kill that being, we may come to reconsider our policy of preserving human lives at all costs, even when there is no prospect of a meaningful life or of existence without terrible pain.

I conclude, then, that a rejection of speciesism does not imply that all lives are of equal worth. While self-awareness, intelligence, the capacity for meaningful relations with others, and so on are not relevant to the question of inflicting pain—since pain is pain, whatever other capacities, beyond the capacity to feel pain, the being may have—these capacities may be relevant to the question of taking life. It is not arbitrary to hold that the life of a self-aware being, capable of abstract thought, of planning for the future, of complex acts of communication, and so on, is more valuable than the life of a being without these capacities. To see the

difference between the issues of inflicting pain and taking life, consider how we would choose within our own species. If we had to choose to save the life of a normal human or a mentally defective human, we would probably choose to save the life of the normal human; but if we had to choose between preventing pain in the normal human or the mental defective—imagine that both have received painful but superficial injuries, and we only have enough painkiller for one of them—it is not nearly so clear how we ought to choose. The same is true when we consider other species. The evil of pain is, in itself, unaffected by the other characteristics of the being that feels the pain; the value of life is affected by these other characteristics.

Normally this will mean that if we have to choose between the life of a human being and the life of another animal we should choose to save the life of the human, but there may be special cases in which the reverse holds true, because the human being in question does not have the capacities of a normal human being. . . .

5. A DISTINCTIVE HUMAN DIGNITY?

[The] idea of a distinctive human dignity and worth has a long history. Contemporary philosophers have cast off its original metaphysical and religious shackles, and freely invoke the idea of human dignity without feeling any need to justify the idea at all. Why should we not attribute "intrinsic dignity" or "intrinsic worth" to ourselves? Why should we not say that we are the only things in the universe that have intrinsic value?

The truth is that the appeal to the intrinsic dignity of human beings appears to solve the egalitarian philosopher's problems only as long as it goes unchallenged. Once we ask why it should be that all humans—including infants, mental defectives, criminal psychopaths, Hitler, Stalin, and the rest—have some kind of dignity or worth that no elephant, pig, or chimpanzee can ever achieve, we see that this question is as difficult to answer as our original request for some relevant fact that justifies the inequality of humans and other animals. In fact, these two questions are really one: talk of intrinsic dignity or moral worth does not help, because any satisfactory defense of the claim that all and only humans have intrinsic dignity would need to refer to some relevant capacities or characteristics that only human beings have, in virtue of which they have this unique dignity or worth. To introduce ideas of dignity and worth as a substitute for other reasons for distinguishing humans and animals is not good enough. Fine phrases are the last resource of those who have run out of arguments. . . .

NOTES

1. Letter to Henri Gregoire, February 25, 1809.

2. Reminiscences by Francis D. Gage, from Susan B. Anthony, *The History of Woman Suffrage,* vol. 1; the passage is to be found in the extract in Leslie Tanner, ed., *Voices from Women's Liberation* (New York: Signet, 1970).

3. I owe the term *speciesism* to Richard Ryder.

4. *Introduction to the Principles of Morals and Legislation,* chapter 17.

5. In order to produce 1 lb. of protein in the form of beef or veal, we must feed 21 lbs. of protein to the animal. Other forms of livestock are slightly less inefficient, but the average ratio in the U.S. is still 1:8. It has been estimated that the amount of protein lost to humans in this way is equivalent to 90 percent of the annual world protein deficit. For a brief account, see Frances Moore Lappe, *Diet for a Small Planet* (New York: Friends of the Earth/Ballantine, 1971), pp. 4–11.

6. Although one might think that killing a being is obviously the ultimate wrong one can do to it, I think that the infliction of suffering is a clearer indication of speciesism because it might be argued that at least part of what is wrong with killing a human is that most humans are conscious of their existence over time, and have desires and purposes that extend into the future. . . . Of course, if one took this view one would have to hold that killing a human infant or mental defective is not in itself wrong, and is less serious than killing certain higher mammals that probably do have a sense of their own existence over time.

7. Ruth Harrison, *Animal Machines* (London: Stuart, 1964). This book provides an eye-opening account of intensive farming methods for those unfamiliar with the subject.

8. *Journal of the Experimental Analysis of Behavior,* 13, no. 1 (1970). Any recent volume of this journal, or of other journals in the field, such as the *Journal of Comparative and Physiological Psychology,* will contain reports of equally cruel and trivial experiments.

9. I am here putting aside religious views, for example, the doctrine that all and only humans have immortal souls, or are made in the image of God. Historically these views have been very important, and no doubt are partly responsible for the idea that human life has a special sanctity. Logically, however, these religious views are unsatisfactory, since a reasoned explanation of why it should be that all humans and no nonhumans have immortal souls is not offered. This belief too, therefore, comes under suspicion as a form of speciesism. In any case, defenders of the "sanctity of life" view are generally reluctant to base their position on purely religious doctrines, since these doctrines are no longer as widely accepted as they once were.

REVIEW AND DISCUSSION QUESTIONS

1. What reasons does Singer give for rejecting the idea that human equality rests on factual similarities?

2. What does Singer think human equality does mean? What are the implications of that for our treatment of animals?

3. Describe the practices that most clearly demonstrate our speciesism.

4. What facts about humans might you point to in defending the notion that a living human has rights that other animals lack?

5. Suppose a meat eater argued that although factory farms do involve some suffering, the animals are still better off for having lived. How would that claim, if true, affect Singer's argument for vegetarianism?

6. Singer disputes the claim that humans have a special "dignity." How would Kant respond to that? Whose position do you think is more reasonable? Explain.

7. Describe what you think would be the implications for Singer's position for euthanasia and abortion.

Speciesism and the Idea of Equality

Bonnie Steinbock

In this essay, Bonnie Steinbock rejects Peter Singer's argument, defending instead the view that membership in the human species is in itself morally important. Human beings, she claims, have important characteristics that warrant treating them differently from nonhuman animals even though, she admits, animal suffering is also morally important. Bonnie Steinbock is professor of philosophy at Albany University, State University of New York.

Most of us believe that we are entitled to treat members of other species in ways which would be considered wrong if inflicted on members of our own species. We kill them for food, keep them confined, use them in painful experiments. The moral philosopher has to ask what relevant difference justifies this difference in treatment. A look at this question will lead us to re-examine the distinctions which we have assumed make a moral difference.

It has been suggested by Peter Singer[1] that our current attitudes are 'speciesist', a word intended to make one think of 'racist' or 'sexist'. The idea is that membership in a species is in itself not relevant to moral treatment, and that much of our behaviour and attitudes towards nonhuman animals is based simply on this irrelevant fact.

There is, however, an important difference between racism or sexism and 'speciesism'. We do not subject animals to different moral treatment simply because they have fur and feathers, but because they are in fact different from human beings in ways that could be morally relevant. It is false that women are incapable of being benefited by education, and therefore that claim cannot serve to justify preventing them from attending school. But this is not false of cows and dogs, even chimpanzees. Intelligence is thought to be a morally relevant capacity because of its relation to the capacity for moral responsibility.

What is Singer's response? He agrees that nonhuman animals lack certain capacities that human animals possess, and that this may justify different *treatment*. But it does not justify giving less consideration to their needs and interests. According to Singer, the moral mistake which the racist or sexist makes is not essentially the factual error of thinking that blacks or women are inferior to white men. For even if there were no factual error, even if it were true that blacks and women are less intelligent and responsible than whites and men, this would not justify giving less consideration to their needs and interests. It is important to note that the term 'speciesism' is in one way like, and in another way unlike, the terms 'racism' and 'sexism'. What the term 'speciesism' has in common with these terms is the reference to focusing on a characteristic which is, in itself, irrelevant to moral treatment. And it is worth reminding us of this. But Singer's real aim is to bring us to a new understanding of the idea of equality. The question is, on what do claims to equality rest? The demand for *human* equality is a demand that the interests of all human beings be considered equally, unless there is a moral justification for not doing so. But why should the interests of all human beings be considered equally? In order to answer this question, we have to give some sense to the phrase, 'All men (human beings) are created equal'. Human

From Bonnie Steinbock, "Speciesism and the Idea of Equality," *Philosophy* 53, no. 204 (April 1978). © 1978 Cambridge University Press. Reprinted with the permission of Cambridge University Press.

beings are manifestly *not* equal, differing greatly in intelligence, virtue and capacities. In virtue of what can the claim to equality be made?

It is Singer's contention that claims to equality do not rest on factual equality. Not only do human beings differ in their capacities, but it might even turn out that intelligence, the capacity for virtue, etc., are not distributed evenly among the races and sexes:

The appropriate response to those who claim to have found evidence of genetically based differences in ability between the races or sexes is not to stick to the belief that the genetic explanation must be wrong, whatever evidence to the contrary may turn up; instead we should make it quite clear that the claim to equality does not depend on intelligence, moral capacity, physical strength, or similar matters of fact. Equality is a moral ideal, not a simple assertion of fact. There is no logically compelling reason for assuming that a factual difference in ability between two people justifies any difference in the amount of consideration we give to satisfying their needs and interests. The principle of equality of human beings is not a description of an alleged actual equality among humans: it is a prescription of how we should treat humans.[2]

In so far as the subject is human equality, Singer's view is supported by other philosophers. Bernard Williams, for example, is concerned to show that demands for equality cannot rest on factual equality among people, for no such equality exists?[3] The only respect in which all men are equal, according to Williams, is that they are all equally men. This seems to be a platitude, but Williams denies that it is trivial. Membership in the species *Homo sapiens* in itself has no special moral significance, but rather the fact that all men are human serves as a *reminder* that being human involves the possession of characteristics that are morally relevant. But on what characteristics does Williams focus? Aside from the desire for self-respect (which I will discuss later), Williams is not concerned with uniquely human capacities. Rather, he focuses on the capacity to feel pain and the capacity to feel affection. It is in virtue of these capacities, it seems, that the idea of equality is to be justified.

Apparently Richard Wasserstrom has the same idea as he sets out the racist's 'logical and moral mistakes' in 'Rights, Human Rights and Racial Discrimination'.[4] The racist fails to acknowledge that the black person is as capable of suffering as the white person. According to Wasserstrom, the reason why a person is said to have a right not to be made to suffer acute physical pain is that we all do in fact value freedom from such pain. Therefore, if anyone has a right to be free from suffering acute physical pain, everyone has this right, for there is no possible basis of discrimination. Wasserstrom says, 'For, if all persons do have equal capacities of these sorts and if the existence of these capacities is the reason for ascribing these rights to anyone, then all persons ought to have the right to claim equality of treatment in respect to the possession and exercise of these rights'.[5] The basis of equality, for Wasserstrom as for Williams, lies not in some uniquely human capacity, but rather in the fact that all human beings are alike in their capacity to suffer. Writers on equality have focused on this capacity, I think, because it functions as some sort of lowest common denominator, so that whatever the other capacities of a human being, he is entitled to equal consideration because, like everyone else, he is capable of suffering.

If the capacity to suffer is the reason for ascribing a right to freedom from acute pain, or a right to well being, then it certainly looks as though these rights must be extended to animals as well. This is the conclusion Singer arrives at. The demand for human equality rests on the equal capacity of all human beings to suffer and to enjoy well being. But if this is the basis of the demand for equality, then this demand must include all beings which have an equal capacity to suffer and enjoy well being. That is why Singer places at the basis of the demand for equality, not intelligence or reason, but sentience. And equality will mean, not equality of treatment, but 'equal consideration of interests'. The equal consideration of interests will often mean quite different treatment, depending on the nature of the entity being considered. (It would be as absurd to talk of a dog's right to vote, Singer says, as to talk of a man's right to have an abortion.)

It might be thought that the issue of equality depends on a discussion of rights. According to this line of thought, animals do not merit equal consideration of interests because, unlike human beings, they do not, or cannot, have rights. But I am not going to discuss rights, important as the issue is. The fact that an entity does not have rights does not necessarily imply that its interests are going to count for less than the interests of entities which are right-bearers. According to the view of rights held by H. L. A. Hart and S. I. Benn, infants do not have rights, nor do the mentally defective, nor do the insane, in so far as they all lack certain minimal conceptual capabilities for having rights.[6] Yet is certainly does not seem that either Hart or Benn would agree that therefore their interests are to be counted for less, or that it is morally permissible to treat them in ways in which it would not be permissible to treat rightbearers. It seems to mean only that we must give different sorts of reasons for our obligations to take into consideration the interests of those who do not have rights.

We have reasons concerning the treatment of other people which are clearly independent of the notion of rights. We would say that it is wrong to punch someone because doing that infringes his rights. But we could also say that it is wrong because doing that hurts him, and that is, ordinarily, enough of a reason not to do it. Now this particular reason extends not only to human beings, but to all sentient creatures. One has a *prima facie* reason not to pull the cat's tail (whether or not the cat has rights) because it hurts the cat. And this is the only thing, normally, which is relevant in this case. The fact that the cat is not a 'rational being', that it is not capable of moral responsibility, that it cannot make free choices or shape its life—all of these differences from us have nothing to do with the justifiability of pulling its tail. Does this show that rationality and the rest of it are irrelevant to moral treatment?

I hope to show that this is not the case. But first I want to point out that the issue is not one of cruelty to animals. We all agree that cruelty is wrong, whether perpetrated on a moral or nonmoral, rational or nonrational agent. Cruelty is defined as the infliction of unnecessary pain or suffering. What is to count as necessary or unnecessary is determined, in part, by the nature of the end pursued. Torturing an animal is cruel, because although the pain is logically necessary for the action to be torture, the end (deriving enjoyment from seeing the animal suffer) is monstrous. Allowing animals to suffer from neglect or for the sake of large profits

may also be thought to be unnecessary and therefore cruel. But there may be some ends, which are very good (such as the advancement of medical knowledge), which can be accomplished by subjecting animals to pain in experiments. Although most people would agree that the pain inflicted on animals used in medical research ought to be kept to a minimum, they would consider pain that cannot be eliminated 'necessary' and therefore not cruel. It would probably not be so regarded if the subjects were non-voluntary human beings. Necessity, then, is defined in terms of human benefit, but this is just what is being called into question. The topic of cruelty to animals, while important from a practical viewpoint, because much of our present treatment of animals involves the infliction of suffering for no good reason, is not very interesting philosophically. What is philosophically interesting is whether we are justified in having different standards of necessity for human suffering and for animal suffering.

Singer says, quite rightly I think, 'If a being suffers, there can be no moral justification for refusing to take that suffering into consideration'.[7] But he thinks that the principle of equality requires that, no matter what the nature of the being, its suffering be counted equally with the like suffering of any other being. In other words sentience does not simply provide us with reasons for acting; it is the only relevant consideration for equal consideration of interests. It is this view that I wish to challenge.

I want to challenge it partly because it has such counter-intuitive results. It means, for example, that feeding starving children before feeding starving dogs is just like a Catholic charity's feeding hungry Catholics before feeding hungry non-Catholics. It is simply a matter of taking care of one's own, something which is usually morally permissible. But whereas we would admire the Catholic agency which did not discriminate, but fed all children, first come, first served, we would feel quite differently about someone who had this policy for dogs and children. Nor is this, it seems to me, simply a matter of a sentimental preference for our own species. I might feel much more love for my dog than for a strange child—and yet I might feel morally obliged to feed the child before I fed my dog. If I gave in to the feelings of love and fed my dog and let the child go hungry, I would probably feel guilty. This is not to say that we can simply rely on such feelings. Huck Finn felt guilty at helping Jim escape, which he viewed as stealing from a woman who had never done him any harm. But while the existence of such feelings does not settle the morality of an issue, it is not clear to me that they can be explained away. In any event, their existence can serve as a motivation for trying to find a rational justification for considering human interests above nonhuman ones.

However, it does seem to me that this requires a justification. Until now, common sense (and academic philosophy) have seen no such need. Benn says, 'No one claims equal consideration for all mammals—human beings count, mice do not, though it would not be easy to say why not. . . . Although we hesitate to inflict unnecessary pain on sentient creatures, such as mice or dogs, we are quite sure that we do not need to show good reasons for putting human interests before theirs.'8

I think we do have to justify counting our interests more heavily than those of animals. But how? Singer is right, I think, to point out that it will not do to refer vaguely to the greater value of human life, to human worth and dignity:

Faced with a situation in which they see a need for some basis for the moral gulf that is commonly thought to separate humans and animals, but can find no concrete difference that will do this without undermining the equality of humans, philosophers tend to waffle. They resort to high-sounding phrases like 'the intrinsic dignity of the human individual'. They talk of 'the intrinsic worth of all men' as if men had some worth that other beings do not have or they say that human beings, and only human beings, are 'ends in themselves', while 'everything other than a person can only have value for a person'. . . . Why should we not attribute 'intrinsic dignity' or 'intrinsic worth' to ourselves? Why should we not say that we are the only things in the universe that have intrinsic value? Our fellow human beings are unlikely to reject the accolades we so generously bestow upon them and those to whom we deny the honour are unable to object.9

Singer is right to be skeptical of terms like 'intrinsic dignity' and 'intrinsic worth'. These phrases are no substitute for a moral argument. But they may point to one. In trying to understand what is meant by these phrases, we may find a difference or differences between human beings and nonhuman animals that will justify different treatment while not undermining claims for human equality. While we are not compelled to discriminate among people because of different capacities, if we can find a significant difference in capacities between human and nonhuman animals, this could serve to justify regarding human interests as primary. It is not arbitrary or smug, I think, to maintain that human beings have a different moral status from members of other species because of certain capacities which are characteristic of being human. We may not all be equal in these capacities, but all human beings possess them to some measure, and nonhuman animals do not. For example, human beings are normally held to be responsible for what they do. In recognizing that someone is responsible for his or her actions, you accord that person a respect which is reserved for those possessed of moral autonomy, or capable of achieving such autonomy. Secondly, human beings can be expected to reciprocate in a way that nonhuman animals cannot. Nonhuman animals cannot be motivated by altruistic or moral reasons; they cannot treat you fairly or unfairly. This does not rule out the possibility of an animal being motivated by sympathy or pity. It does rule out altruistic motivation in the sense of motivation due to the recognition that the needs and interests of others provide one with certain reasons for acting.10 Human beings are capable of altruistic motivation in this sense. We are sometimes motivated simply by the recognition that someone else is in pain, and that pain is a bad thing, no matter who suffers it. It is this sort of reason that I claim cannot motivate an animal or any entity not possessed of fairly abstract concepts. (If some nonhuman animals do possess the requisite concepts—perhaps chimpanzees who have learned a language—they might well be capable of altruistic motivation.) This means that our moral dealings with animals are necessarily much more limited than our dealings with other human beings. If rats invade our houses, carrying disease and biting our children, we cannot reason with them, hoping to persuade them of the injustice they do us. We can only attempt to get rid of them. And it is this that makes it reasonable for us to accord them a separate and not equal moral status, even though their capacity to suffer provides us with some reason to kill them painlessly, if this can be done without too much sacrifice of human interests. Thirdly, as Williams points out, there is the 'desire for self-respect': 'a certain human desire to be identified with what one is doing, to be able to realize purposes of one's own, and not to be the instrument of another's will unless one has willingly accepted such a role'.[11] Some animals may have some form of this desire, and to the extent that they do, we ought to consider their interest in freedom and self-determination. (Such considerations might affect our attitudes toward zoos and circuses.) But the desire for self-respect *per se* requires the intellectual capacities of human beings, and this desire provides us with special reasons not to treat human beings in certain ways. It is an affront to the dignity of a human being to be a slave (even if a well-treated one); this cannot be true for a horse or a cow. To point this out is of course only to say that the justification for the treatment of an entity will depend on the sort of entity in question. In our treatment of other entities, we must consider the desire for autonomy, dignity and respect, but only where such a desire exists. Recognition of different desires and interests will often require different treatment, a point Singer himself makes.

But is the issue simply one of different desires and interests justifying and requiring different treatment? I would like to make a stronger claim, namely, that certain capacities, which seem to be unique to human beings, entitle their possessors to a privileged position in the moral community. Both rats and human beings dislike pain, and so we have a *prima facie* reason not to inflict pain on either. But if we can free human beings from crippling diseases, pain and death through experimentation which involves making animals suffer, and if this is the only way to achieve such results, then I think that such experimentation is justified because human lives are more valuable than animals lives. And this is because of certain capacities and abilities that normal human beings have which animals apparently do not, and which human beings cannot exercise if they are devastated by pain or disease.

My point is not that the lack of the sorts of capacities I have been discussing gives us a justification for treating animals just as we like, but rather that it is these differences between human

beings and nonhuman animals which provide a rational basis for different moral treatment and consideration. Singer focuses on sentience alone as the basis of equality, but we can justify the belief that human beings have a moral worth that nonhuman animals do not, in virtue of specific capacities, and without resorting to 'highsounding phrases'.

Singer thinks that intelligence, the capacity for moral responsibility, for virtue, etc., are irrelevant to equality, because we would not accept a hierarchy based on intelligence any more than one based on race. We do not think that those with greater capacities ought to have their interests weighed more heavily than those with lesser capacities, and this, he thinks, shows that differences is such capacities are irrelevant to equality. But it does not show this at all. Kevin Donaghy argues (rightly, I think) that what entitles us human beings to a privileged position in the moral community is a certain minimal level of intelligence, which is a prerequisite for morally relevant capacities.[12] The fact that we would reject a hierarchical society based on degree of intelligence does not show that a minimal level of intelligence cannot be used as a cut-off point, justifying giving greater consideration to the interests of those entities which meet this standard.

Interestingly enough, Singer concedes the rationality of valuing the lives of normal human beings over the lives of nonhuman animals.[13] We are not required to value equally the life of a normal human being and the life of an animal, he thinks, but only their suffering. But I doubt that the value of an entity's life can be separated from the value of its suffering in this way. If we value the lives of human beings more than the lives of animals, this is because we value certain capacities that human beings have and animals do not. But freedom from suffering is, in general, a minimal condition for exercising these capacities, for living a fully human life. So, valuing human life more involves regarding human interests as counting for more. That is why we regard human suffering as more deplorable than comparable animal suffering.

But there is one point of Singer's which I have not yet met. Some human beings (if only a very few) are less intelligent than some nonhuman animals. Some have less capacity for moral choice and responsibility. What status in the moral community are these members of our species to occupy? Are their interests to be considered equally with ours? Is experimenting on them permissible where such experiments are painful or injurious, but somehow necessary for human well being? If it is certain of our capacities which entitle us to a privileged position, it looks as if those lacking those capacities are not entitled to a privileged position. To think it is justifiable to experiment on an adult chimpanzee but not on a severely mentally incapacitated human being seems to be focusing on membership in a species where that has no moral relevance. (It is being 'speciesist' in a perfectly reasonable use of the word.) How are we to meet this challenge? . . .

I doubt that anyone will be able to come up with a concrete and morally relevant difference that would justify, say, using a chimpanzee in an experiment rather than a human being with less capacity for reasoning, moral responsibility, etc. Should we then experiment on the severely retarded? Utilitarian considerations aside (the difficulty of comparing intelligence between species, for example), we feel a special obligation to care for the handicapped members of our own species, who cannot survive in this world without such care. Nonhuman animals manage very well, despite their 'lower intelligence' and lesser capacities; most of them do not require special care from us. This does not, of course, justify experimenting on them. However, to subject to experimentation those people who depend on us seems even worse than subjecting members of other species to it. In addition, when we consider the severely retarded, we think, 'That could be me'. It makes sense to think that one might have been born retarded, but not to think that one might have been born a monkey. And so, although one can imagine oneself in the monkey's place, one feels a closer identification with the severely retarded human being. Here we are getting away from such things as 'morally relevant differences' and are talking about something much more difficult to articulate, namely, the role of feeling and sentiment in moral thinking. We would be horrified by the use of the retarded in medical research. But what are we to make of this horror? Has it moral significance or is it 'mere' sentiment, of no more importance than the sentiment of whites against blacks? It is terribly difficult to know how to evaluate such feelings.[14] I am not going to say more about this, because I think that the treatment of severely incapacitated human beings does not pose an insurmountable objection to the privileged status principle. I am willing to admit that my horror at the thought of experiments being performed on severely mentally incapacitated human beings in cases in which I would find it justifiable and preferable to perform the same experiments on nonhuman animals (capable of similar suffering) may not be a moral emotion. But it is certainly not wrong of us to extend special care to members of our own species, motivated by feelings of sympathy, protectiveness, etc. If this is speciesism, it is stripped of its tone of moral condemnation. It is not racist to provide special care to members of your own race; it is racist to fall below your moral obligation to a person because of his or her race. I have been arguing that we are morally obliged to consider the interests of all sentient creatures, but not to consider those interests equally with human interests. Nevertheless, even this recognition will mean some radical changes in our attitude toward and treatment of other species.[15]

NOTES

1. Peter Singer, *Animal Liberation* (New York: Avon Books, 1977).

2. Singer, p. 5.

3. Bernard Williams, 'The Idea of Equality', *Philosophy, Politics and Society* (Second Series), ed. Laslett and Runciman (Blackwell, 1962), pp. 110–13, reprinted in *Moral Concepts,* ed. Feinberg (Oxford, 1970), pp. 153–71.

4. Richard Wasserstrom, "Rights, Human Rights, and Racial Discrimination," *Journal of Philosophy* 61, no. 20 (1964), reprinted in *Human Rights*, ed. A. I. Melden (Wadsworth, 1970), pp. 96–110.

5. Ibid., p. 106.

6. H. L. A. Hart, "Are There Any Natural Rights?" *Philosophical Review* 64 (1955), and S. I. Benn, "Abortion, Infanticide, and Respect for Persons," in *The Problem of Abortion,* ed. Feinberg (Wadsworth, 1973), pp. 92–104.

7. Singer, p. 9.

8. Benn "Equality, Moral and Social," *The Encyclopedia of Philosophy* 3, no. 40.

9. Singer, pp. 266–7.

10. This conception of altruistic motivation comes from Thomas Nagel's *The Possibility of Altruism* (Oxford, 1970).

11. Williams, p. 157.

12. Kevin Donaghy, "Singer on Speciesism," *Philosophic Exchange* (Summer 1974).

13. Singer, p. 22.

14. We run into the same problem when discussing abortion. Of what significance are our feelings toward the unborn when discussing its status? Is it relevant or irrelevant that it looks like a human being?

15. I would like to acknowledge the help of, and offer thanks to, Professor Richard Arneson of the University of California, San Diego; Professor Sidney Gendin of Eastern Michigan University; and Professor Peter Singer of Monash University, all of whom read and commented on earlier drafts of this paper.

REVIEW AND DISCUSSION QUESTIONS

1. Describe how Peter Singer understands equality and the relevance of that understanding to how we should treat animals.

2. How does Steinbock distinguish racism and sexism from speciesism?

3. Why does Steinbock reject Singer's understanding of equality?

4. Why does Steinbock think it is acceptable to treat a human being's interests more seriously than those of nonhuman animals?

5. How might Singer respond to Steinbock's claim that it may be correct to give mentally defective humans greater moral concern than nonhuman animals? Is that response adequate? Explain.

People or Penguins

William F. Baxter

What sorts of beings have moral standing? How is that standing to be determined? In this essay, William F. Baxter opens the discussion by arguing that the question that always needs to be addressed is: What are our goals? Instead of seeking simply to protect natural life, he argues, we must constantly be aware of other, competing values and make choices accordingly. Baxter thus defends what he terms a "cost-benefit" approach to nature and the environment—a view that, he argues, is sound from the perspective of nature and human beings. It is also, he claims, the only approach that is realistic. The soundest policy is to take account of only the needs and interests of people, not penguins or pine trees. Nature itself has no independent moral standing and will receive sufficient protection through a wise, human-centered ethic. The question always to be asked is therefore the optimal amount of pollution, not how pollution can be eliminated. William F. Baxter is William Benjamin Scott and Luna M. Scott Professor of Law at Stanford University.

I start with the modest proposition that, in dealing with pollution, or indeed with any problem, it is helpful to know what one is attempting to accomplish. Agreement on how and whether to pursue a particular objective, such as pollution control, is not possible unless some more general objective has been identified and stated with reasonable precision. We talk loosely of having clean air and clean water, of preserving our wilderness areas, and so forth. But none of these is a sufficiently general objective: each is more accurately viewed as a means rather than as an end.

With regard to clean air, for example, one may ask, "how clean?" and "what does clean mean?" It is even reasonable to ask, "why have clean air?" Each of these questions is an implicit demand that a more general community goal be stated—a goal sufficiently general in its scope and enjoying sufficiently general assent among the community of actors that such "why" questions no longer seem admissible with respect to that goal.

If, for example, one states as a goal the proposition that "every person should be free to do whatever he wishes in contexts where his actions do not interfere with the interests of other human beings," the speaker is unlikely to be met with a response of "why"? The goal may be criticized as uncertain in its implications or difficult to implement, but it is so basic a tenet of our civilization— it reflects a cultural value so broadly shared, at least in the abstract—that the question "why" is seen as impertinent or imponderable or both.

I do not mean to suggest that everyone would agree with the "spheres of freedom" objective just stated. Still less do I mean to suggest that a society could subscribe to four or five such general objectives that would be adequate in their coverage to serve as testing criteria by which all other disagreements might be measured. One difficulty in the attempt to construct such a list is that each new goal added will conflict, in certain applications, with each prior goal listed; and thus each goal serves as a limited qualification on prior goals.

Without any expectation of obtaining unanimous consent to them, let me set forth four goals that I generally use as ultimate testing criteria in attempting to frame solutions to problems of human organization. My position regarding pollution stems from these four criteria. If the criteria appeal to you and any part of what appears hereafter does not, our disagreement will have a helpful focus: Which of us is correct, analytically, in supposing that his position on pollution would better serve these general goals? If the criteria do not seem acceptable to you, then it is to be expected that our more particular judgments will differ, and the task will then be yours to identify the basic set of criteria upon which your particular judgments rest.

My criteria are as follows:

1. The spheres of freedom criterion stated above.

2. Waste is a bad thing. The dominant feature of human existence is scarcity—our available resources, our aggregate labors, and our skill in employing both have always been, and will continue for some time to be, inadequate to yield to every man all the tangible and intangible satisfactions he would like to have. Hence, none of those resources, or labors, or skills, should be wasted— that is, employed so as to yield less than they might yield in human satisfactions.

3. Every human being should be regarded as an end rather than as a means to be used for the betterment of another. Each should be afforded dignity and regarded as having an absolute claim to an evenhanded application of such rules as the community may adopt for its governance.

4. Both the incentive and the opportunity to improve his share of satisfactions should be preserved to every individual. Preservation of incentive is dictated by the "no-waste" criterion and enjoins against the continuous, totally egalitarian redistribution of satisfactions, or wealth; but subject to that constraint, everyone should receive, by continuous redistribution if necessary, some minimal share of aggregate wealth so as to avoid a level of privation from which the opportunity to improve his situation becomes illusory.

The relationship of these highly general goals to the more specific environmental issues at hand may not be readily apparent, and I am not yet ready to demonstrate their pervasive implications. But let me give one indication of their implications. Recently scientists have informed us that use of DDT in food production is causing damage to the penguin population. For the present purposes let us accept that assertion as an indisputable scientific fact. The scientific fact is often asserted as if the correct implication— that we must stop agricultural use of DDT—followed from the mere statement of the fact of penguin damage. But plainly it does not follow if my criteria are employed.

My criteria are oriented to people, not penguins. Damage to penguins, or sugar pines, or geological marvels is, without more, simply irrelevant. One must go further, by my criteria, and say: Penguins are important because people enjoy seeing them walk about rocks; and furthermore, the well-being of people would be less impaired by halting use of DDT than by giving up penguins. In short, my observations about environmental problems will be people-oriented, as are my criteria. I have no interest in preserving penguins for their own sake.

It may be said by way of objection to this position, that it is very selfish of people to act as if each person represented one unit of importance and nothing else was of any importance. It is undeniably selfish. Nevertheless I think it is the only tenable starting place for analysis for several reasons. First, no other position corresponds to the way most people really think and act—i.e., corresponds to reality.

Second, this attitude does not portend any massive destruction of nonhuman flora and fauna, for people depend on them in many obvious ways, and they will be preserved because and to the degree that humans do depend on them.

Third, what is good for humans is, in many respects, good for penguins and pine trees—clean air for example. So that humans are, in these respects, surrogates for plant and animal life.

Fourth, I do not know how we could administer any other system. Our decisions are either private or collective. Insofar as Mr. Jones is free to act privately, he may give such preferences as he wishes to other forms of life: he may feed birds in winter and do with less himself, and he may even decline to resist an advancing polar bear on the ground that the bear's appetite is more important than those portions of himself that the bear may

choose to eat. In short my basic premise does not rule out private altruism to competing life-forms. It does rule out, however, Mr. Jones' inclination to feed Mr. Smith to the bear, however hungry the bear, however despicable Mr. Smith.

Insofar as we act collectively on the other hand, only humans can be afforded an opportunity to participate in the collective decisions. Penguins cannot vote now and are unlikely subjects for the franchise—pine trees more unlikely still. Again each individual is free to cast his vote so as to benefit sugar pines if that is his inclination. But many of the more extreme assertions that one hears from some conservationists amount to tacit assertions that they are specially appointed representatives of sugar pines, and hence that their preferences should be weighted more heavily than the preferences of other humans who do not enjoy equal rapport with "nature." The simplistic assertion that agricultural use of DDT must stop at once because it is harmful to penguins is of that type.

Fifth, if polar bears or pine trees or penguins, like men, are to be regarded as ends rather than means, if they are to count in our calculus of social organization, someone must tell me how much each one counts, and someone must tell me how these life-forms are to be permitted to express their preferences, for I do not know either answer. If the answer is that certain people are to hold their proxies, then I want to know how those proxy-holders are to be selected: self-appointment does not seem workable to me.

Sixth, and by way of summary of all the foregoing, let me point out that the set of environmental issues under discussion—although they raise very complex technical questions of how to achieve any objective—ultimately raise a normative question: what ought we to do. Questions of ought are unique to the human mind and world— they are meaningless as applied to a nonhuman situation.

I reject the proposition that we ought to respect the "balance of nature" or to "preserve the environment" unless the reason for doing so, express or implied, is the benefit of man.

I reject the idea that there is a "right" or "morally correct" state of nature to which we should return. The word "nature" has no normative connotation. Was it "right" or "wrong" for the earth's crust to heave in contortion and create mountains and seas? Was it "right" for the first amphibian to crawl up out of the primordial ooze? Was it "wrong" for plants to reproduce themselves and alter the atmospheric composition in favor of oxygen? For animals to alter the atmosphere in favor of carbon dioxide both by breathing oxygen and eating plants? No answers can be given to these questions because they are meaningless questions.

All this may seem obvious to the point of being tedious, but much of the present controversy over environment and pollution rests on tacit normative assumptions about just such nonnormative phenomena: that it is "wrong" to impair penguins with DDT, but not to slaughter cattle for prime rib roasts. That it is wrong to kill stands of sugar pines with industrial fumes, but not to cut sugar pines and build housing for the poor. Every man is entitled to his own preferred definition of Walden Pond, but there is no definition that has any moral superiority over another, except by reference to the selfish needs of the human race.

From the fact that there is no normative definition of the natural state, it follows that there is no normative definition of clean air or pure water—hence no definition of polluted air—or of pollution—except by reference to the needs of man. The "right" composition of the atmosphere is one which has some dust in it and some lead in it and some hydrogen sulfide in it—just those amounts that attend a sensibly organized society thoughtfully and knowledgeably pursuing the greatest possible satisfaction for its human members.

The first and most fundamental step toward solution of our environmental problems is a clear recognition that our objective is not pure air or water but rather some optimal state of pollution. That step immediately suggests the question: How do we define and attain the level of pollution that will yield the maximum possible amount of human satisfaction?

Low levels of pollution contribute to human satisfaction but so do food and shelter and education and music. To attain ever lower levels of pollution, we must pay the cost of having less of these other things. I contrast that view of the cost of pollution control with the more popular statement that pollution control will "cost" very large numbers of dollars. The popular statement is true in some senses, false in others; sorting out the true and false senses is of some importance. The first step in that sorting process is to achieve a clear understanding of the difference between dollars and resources. Resources are the wealth of our nation; dollars are merely claim checks upon those resources. Resources are of vital importance; dollars are comparatively trivial.

Four categories of resources are sufficient for our purposes: At any given time a nation, or a planet if you prefer, has a stock of labor, of technological skill, of capital goods, and of natural resources (such as mineral deposits, timber, water, land, etc.). These resources can be used in various combinations to yield goods and services of all kinds—in some limited quantity. The quantity will be larger if they are combined efficiently, smaller if combined inefficiently. But in either event the resource stock is limited, the goods and services that they can be made to yield are limited; even the most efficient use of them will yield less than our population, in the aggregate, would like to have.

If one considers building a new dam, it is appropriate to say that it will be costly in the sense that it will require x hours of labor, y tons of steel and concrete, and z amount of capital goods. If these resources are devoted to the dam, then they cannot be used to build hospitals, fishing rods, schools, or electric can openers. That is the meaningful sense in which the dam is costly.

Quite apart from the very important question of how wisely we can combine our resources to produce goods and services, is the very different question of how they get distributed—who gets how many goods? Dollars constitute the claim checks which are distributed among people and which control their share of national output. Dollars are nearly valueless pieces of paper except to the extent that they do represent claim checks to some fraction of the output of goods and services. Viewed as claim checks, all the dollars outstanding during any period of time are worth, in the aggregate, the goods and services that are available to be claimed with them during that period—neither more nor less.

It is far easier to increase the supply of dollars than to increase the production of goods and services—printing dollars is easy. But printing more dollars doesn't help because each dollar then simply becomes a claim to fewer goods, i.e., becomes worth less.

The point is this: many people fall into error upon hearing the statement that the decision to build a dam, or to clean up a river, will cost $X million. It is regrettably easy to say: "It's only money. This is a wealthy country, and we have lots of money." But you cannot build a dam or clean a river with $X million—unless you also have a match, you can't even make a fire. One builds a dam or cleans a river by diverting labor and steel and trucks and factories from making one kind of goods to making another. The cost in dollars is merely a shorthand way of describing the extent of the diversion necessary. If we build a dam for $X million, then we must recognize that we will have $X million less housing and food and medical care and electric can openers as a result.

Similarly, the costs of controlling pollution are best expressed in terms of the other goods we will have to give up to do the job. This is not to say the job should not be done. Badly as we need more housing, more medical care, and more can openers, and more symphony orchestras, we could do with somewhat less of them, in my judgment at least, in exchange for somewhat cleaner air and rivers. But that is the nature of the trade-off, and analysis of the problem is advanced if that unpleasant reality is kept in mind. Once the trade-off relationship is clearly perceived, it is possible to state in a very general way what the optimal level of pollution is. I would state it as follows:

People enjoy watching penguins. They enjoy relatively clean air and smog-free vistas. Their health is improved by relatively clean water and air. Each of these benefits is a type of good or service. As a society we would be well advised to give up one washing machine if the resources that would have gone into that washing machine can yield greater human satisfaction when diverted into pollution control. We should give up one hospital if the resources thereby freed would yield more human satisfaction when devoted to elimination of noise in our cities. And so on, trade-off by trade-off, we should divert our productive capacities from the production of existing goods and services to the production of a cleaner, quieter, more pastoral nation up to—and no further than—the point at which we value more highly the next washing machine or hospital that we would have to do without than we value the next unit of environmental improvement that the diverted resources would create.

Now this proposition seems to me unassailable but so general and abstract as to be unhelpful—at least unadministerable in the form stated. It assumes we can measure in some way the incremental units of human satisfaction yielded by very different types of goods. The proposition must remain a pious abstraction until I can explain how this measurement process can occur. But I insist that the proposition stated describes the result for which we should be striving—and again, that it is always useful to know what your target is even if your weapons are too crude to score a bull's eye.

REVIEW AND DISCUSSION QUESTIONS

1. What are the basic tests or criteria Baxter uses to assess human decisions and organizations?
2. What are the reasons Baxter gives for thinking that his is the best approach to environmental issues?
3. Why does he speak of the optimal amount of pollution instead of its elimination?
4. How, specifically, would Peter Singer respond to this essay? How would Baxter respond to Singer?
5. Would Steinbock be likely to agree or disagree with Baxter? Explain.
6. Compare Baxter's view of nature with those who criticize homosexuality as "unnatural."

The Land Ethic

J. Baird Callicott

In this essay, J. Baird Callicott distinguishes holders of three positions: *ethical humanists,* who defend the special status of humans, *humane moralists* (like Peter Singer), who reject the notion of a special status for human beings in favor of "animal liberation"; and defenders of the "*land ethic*" (as represented by Aldo Leopold in his book *A Sand County Almanac*), who focus on the good of the "biotic community" as a whole. Each position offers its own account of what is valuable, but it is the land ethic, he argues, that is the most creative, interesting, and practicable of the alternatives. This environmentalist position also offers a different perspective on such questions as hunting and meat eating, as well as on the value of nonanimal life. J. Baird Callicott is professor of philosophy at the University of Wisconsin, Stevens Point.

ENVIRONMENTAL ETHICS AND ANIMAL LIBERATION

Partly because it is so new to Western philosophy (or at least heretofore only scarcely represented) *environmental ethics* has no precisely fixed conventional definition in glossaries of philosophical terminology. Aldo Leopold, however, is universally recognized as the father or founding genius of recent environmental ethics. His "land ethic" has become a modern classic and may be treated as the standard example, the paradigm case, as it were, of what an environmental ethic is. *Environmental ethics* then can be defined ostensively by using Leopold's land ethic as the exemplary type. I do not mean to suggest that all environmental ethics should necessarily conform to Leopold's paradigm, but the extent to which an ethical system resembles Leopold's land ethic might be used, for want of anything better, as a criterion to measure the extent to which it is or is not of the environmental sort.

It is Leopold's opinion, and certainly an overall review of the prevailing traditions of Western ethics, both popular and philosophical, generally confirms it, that traditional Western systems of ethics have not accorded moral standing to non-

human beings.[1] Animals and plants, soils and waters, which Leopold includes in his community of ethical beneficiaries, have traditionally enjoyed no moral standing, no rights, no respect, in sharp contrast to human persons whose rights and interests ideally must be fairly and equally considered if our actions are to be considered "ethical" or "moral." One fundamental and novel feature of the Leopold land ethic, therefore, is the extension of direct ethical considerability from people to nonhuman natural entities.

At first glance, the recent ethical movement usually labeled "animal liberation" or "animal rights" seems to be squarely and centrally a kind of environmental ethics. The more uncompromising among the animal liberationists have demanded equal moral consideration on behalf of cows, pigs, chickens, and other apparently enslaved and oppressed nonhuman animals. The theoreticians of this new hyperegalitarianism have coined such terms as *speciesism* (on analogy with *racism* and *sexism*) and *human chauvinism* (on analogy with male chauvinism), and have made animal liberation seem, perhaps not improperly, the next and most daring development of political liberalism. Aldo Leopold also draws upon metaphors of political liberalism when he tells us

From J. Baird Callicott, "Animal Liberation: A Triangular Affair," *Environmental Ethics* 2, no. 4 (Winter 1980), pp. 311–38. Reprinted by permission.

that his land ethic "changes the role of *Homo sapiens* from conqueror of the land community to plain member and citizen of it."[2] For animal liberationists it is as if the ideological battles for equal rights and equal consideration for women and for racial minorities have been all but won, and the next and greatest challenge is to purchase equality, first theoretically and then practically, for all (actually only some) animals, regardless of species. This more rhetorically implied than fully articulated historical progression of moral rights from fewer to greater numbers of "persons" (allowing that animals may also be persons) as advocated by animal liberationists, also parallels Leopold's scenario in "The Land Ethic" of the historical extension of "ethical criteria" to more and more "fields of conduct" and to larger and larger groups of people during the past three thousand or so years.[3] As Leopold develops it, the land ethic is a cultural "evolutionary possibility," the next "step in a sequence."[4] For Leopold, however, the next step is much more sweeping, much more inclusive than the animal liberationists envision, since it "enlarges the boundaries of the [moral] community to include soils, waters, [and] plants . . ." as well as animals.[5] Thus, the animal liberation movement *could* be construed as partitioning Leopold's perhaps undigestible and totally inclusive environmental ethic into a series of more assimilable stages: today animal rights, tomorrow equal rights for plants, and after that full moral standing for rocks, soil, and other earthy compounds, and perhaps sometime in the still more remote future, liberty and equality for water and other elementary bodies.

Put just this way, however, there is something jarring about such a graduated progression in the exfoliation of a more inclusive environmental ethic, something that seems absurd. A more or less reasonable case might be made for rights for some animals, but when we come to plants, soils, and waters, the frontier between plausibility and absurdity appears to have been crossed. Yet, there is no doubt that Leopold sincerely proposes that *land* (in his inclusive sense) be ethically regarded. The beech and chestnut, for example, have in his view as much "biotic right" to life as the wolf and the deer, and the effects of human actions on mountains and streams for Leopold is an ethical concern

as genuine and serious as the comfort and longevity of brood hens.[6] In fact, Leopold to all appearances never considered the treatment of brood hens on a factory farm or steers in a feed lot to be a pressing moral issue. He seems much more concerned about the integrity of the farm wood lot and the effects of clear-cutting steep slopes on neighboring streams.

Animal liberationists put their ethic into practice (and display their devotion to it) by becoming vegetarians, and the moral complexities of vegetarianism have been thoroughly debated in the recent literature as an adjunct issue to animal rights. (No one however has yet expressed, as among Butler's Erewhonians, qualms about eating plants, though such sentiments might be expected to be latently present, if the rights of plants are next to be defended.) Aldo Leopold, by contrast did not even condemn hunting animals, let alone eating them, nor did he personally abandon hunting, for which he had had an enthusiasm since boyhood, upon becoming convinced that his ethical responsibilities extended beyond the human sphere. There are several interpretations for this behavioral peculiarity. One is that Leopold did not see that his land ethic actually ought to prohibit hunting, cruelly killing, and eating animals. A corollary of this interpretation is that Leopold was so unperspicacious as deservedly to be thought stupid—a conclusion hardly comporting with the intellectual subtlety he usually evinces in most other respects. If not stupid, then perhaps Leopold was hypocritical. But if a hypocrite, we should expect him to conceal his proclivity for blood sports and flesh eating and to treat them as shameful vices to be indulged secretly. As it is, bound together between the same covers with "The Land Ethic" are his unabashed reminiscences of killing and consuming *game*. This term (like *stock*) when used of animals, moreover, appears to be morally equivalent to referring to a sexually appealing young woman as a "piece" or to a strong, young black man as a "buck"—if animal rights, that is, are to be considered as on a par with women's rights and the rights of formerly enslaved races. A third interpretation of Leopold's approbation of regulated and disciplined sport hunting (and *a fortiori* meat eating) is that it is a form of human/animal behavior not inconsistent with the land ethic as he conceived it. A corollary of this interpretation is that Leopold's land ethic and the environmental ethic of the animal liberation movement rest upon very different theoretical foundations, and that they are thus two very different forms of environmental ethics.

The urgent concern of animal liberationists for the suffering of *domestic* animals, toward which Leopold manifests an attitude which can only be described as indifference, and the urgent concern of Leopold, on the other hand, for the disappearance of species of plants as well as animals and for soil erosion and stream pollution, appear to be symptoms not only of very different ethical perspectives, but profoundly different cosmic visions as well. The neat similarities, noted at the beginning of this discussion, between the environmental ethic of the animal liberation movement and the classical Leopoldian land ethic appear in light of these observations to be rather superficial and to conceal substrata of thought and value which are not at all similar. The theoretical foundations of the animal liberation movement and those of the Leopoldian land ethic may even turn out not to be companionable, complementary, or mutually consistent. The animal liberationists may thus find themselves not only engaged in controversy with the many conservative philosophers upholding *apartheid* between man and "beast," but also faced with an unexpected dissent from another, very different, system of environmental ethics. Animal liberation and animal rights may well prove to be a triangular rather than, as it has so far been represented in the philosophical community, a polar controversy.

ETHICAL HUMANISM
AND HUMANE MORALISM

The orthodox response of "ethical humanism" (as this philosophical perspective may be styled) to the suggestion that nonhuman animals should be accorded moral standing is that such animals are not worthy of this high perquisite. Only human beings are rational, or capable of having interests, or possess *self*-awareness, or have linguistic abilities, or can represent the future, it is variously ar-

gued. These essential attributes taken singly or in various combinations make people somehow exclusively deserving of moral consideration. The so-called "lower animals," it is insisted, lack the crucial qualification for ethical considerability and so may be treated (albeit humanely, according to some, so as not to brutalize man) as things or means, not as persons or as ends.

The theoreticians of the animal liberation movement ("humane moralists" as they may be called) typically reply as follows. Not all human beings qualify as worthy of moral regard, according to the various criteria specified. Therefore, by parity of reasoning, human persons who do not so qualify as moral patients may be treated, as animals often are, as mere things or means (e.g., used in vivisection experiments, disposed of if their existence is inconvenient, eaten, hunted, etc., etc.). But the ethical humanists would be morally outraged if irrational and inarticulate infants, for example, were used in painful or lethal medical experiments, or if severely retarded people were hunted for pleasure. Thus, the double-dealing, the hypocrisy, of ethical humanism appears to be exposed. Ethical humanism, though claiming to discriminate between worthy and unworthy ethical patients on the basis of objective criteria impartially applied, turns out after all, it seems, to be *speciesism*, a philosophically indefensible prejudice (analogous to racial prejudice) against animals. . . .

The humane moralists, for their part, insist upon *sentience* (*sensibility* would have been a more precise word choice) as the only relevant capacity a being need possess to enjoy full moral standing. If animals, they argue, are conscious entities who, though deprived of reason, speech, forethought or even *self*-awareness (however that may be judged), are capable of suffering, then their suffering should be as much a matter of ethical concern as that of our fellow human beings, or strictly speaking, as our very own. . . . As a *moral* agent, I should not consider my pleasure and pain to be of greater consequence in determining a course of action than that of other persons. Thus, by the same token, if animals suffer pain—and among philosophers only strict Cartesians would deny that they do—then we are morally obliged to consider their suffering as much an evil to be minimized by conscientious moral agents as human suffering. Certainly actions of ours which contribute to the suffering of animals, such as hunting them, butchering and eating them, experimenting on them, etc., are on these assumptions morally reprehensible. Hence, a person who regards himself or herself as not aiming in life to live most selfishly, conveniently, or profitably, but rightly and in accord with practical principle, if convinced by these arguments, should, among other things, cease to eat the flesh of animals, to hunt them, to wear fur and leather clothing and bone ornaments and other articles made from the bodies of animals, to eat eggs and drink milk, if the animal producers of these commodities are retained under inhumane circumstances, and to patronize zoos (as sources of psychological if not physical torment of animals). On the other hand, since certain very simple animals are almost certainly insensible to pleasure and pain, they may and indeed should be treated as morally inconsequential. Nor is there any *moral* reason why trees should be respected or rivers or mountains or anything which is, though living or tributary to life processes, unconscious. The humane moralists, like the moral humanists, draw a firm distinction between those beings worthy of moral consideration and those not. They simply insist upon a different but quite definite cut-off point on the spectrum of natural entities, and accompany their criterion with arguments to show that it is more ethically defensible (granting certain assumptions) and more consistently applicable than that of the moral humanists.

THE FIRST PRINCIPLE OF THE LAND ETHIC

The fundamental principle of humane moralism, as we see, is Benthamic. Good is equivalent to pleasure and, more pertinently, evil is equivalent to pain. The presently booming controversy between moral humanists and humane moralists appears, when all the learned dust has settled, to be essentially internecine; at least, the lines of battle are drawn along familiar watersheds of the conceptual terrain.* A classical ethical theory, Bentham's, has been refitted and pressed into service to meet relatively new and unprecedented ethically relevant situations—the problems raised especially by factory farming and ever more exotic and frequently ill-conceived scientific research employing animal subjects. Then, those with . . . Kantian ethical affiliation have heard the bugle and have risen to arms. . . . The familiar historical positions have simply been retrenched, applied, and exercised.

*John Rodman, "The Liberation of Nature," (p. 95), comments: "Why do our 'new ethics' seem so old? Because the attempt to produce a 'new ethics' by the process of 'extension' perpetuates the basic assumptions of the conventional modern paradigm, however much it fiddles with the boundaries." When the assumptions remain conventional, the boundaries are, in my view, scaler, but triangular when both positions are considered in opposition to the land ethic. The scaler relation is especially clear when two other positions, not specifically discussed in the text, the reverence-for-life ethic and pan-moralism, are considered. The reverence-for-life ethic (as I am calling it in deference to Albert Schweitzer) seems to be the next step on the scale after the humane ethic. William Frankena considers it so in "Ethics and the Environment," *Ethics and Problems of the 21st Century*, pp. 3–20. W. Murry Hunt ("*Are Mere Things* Morally Considerable," *Environmental Ethics* 2 [1980]: 59–65) has gone a step past Schweitzer, and made the bold suggestion that *everything* should be accorded moral standing, pan-moralism. Hunt's discussion shows clearly that there is a similar logic ("slippery slope" logic) involved in taking each downward step, and thus a certain commonality of underlying assumptions among all the ethical types to which the land ethic stands in opposition. Hunt is not unaware that his suggestion may be interpreted as a *reductio ad absurdum* of the whole matter, but insists that that is not his intent. The land ethic is not part of this linear series of steps and hence may be represented as a point off the scale. The principal difference . . . is that the land ethic is collective or "holistic" while the others are distributive or "atomistic." Another relevant difference is that moral humanism, humane moralism, reverence-for-life ethics, and the limiting case, pan-moralism, either openly or implicitly espouse a pecking-order model of nature. The land ethic, founded upon an ecological model of nature emphasizing the contributing roles played by various species in the economy of nature, abandons the "higher"/"lower" ontological and axiological schema, in favor of a functional system of value. The land ethic, in other words, is inclined to establish value distinctions not on the basis of higher and lower orders of being, but on the basis of the importance of organisms, minerals, and so on to the biotic community. Some bacteria, for example, may be of greater value to the health or economy of nature than dogs, and thus command more respect.

But what about the third (and certainly minority) party to the animal liberation debate? What sort of reasonable and coherent moral theory would at once urge that animals (and plants and soils and waters) be included in the same class with people as beings to whom ethical consideration is owed and yet not object to some of them being slaughtered (whether painlessly or not) and eaten, others hunted, trapped, and in various other ways seemingly cruelly used? Aldo Leopold provides a concise statement of what might be called the categorical imperative or principal precept of the land ethic: "A thing is right when it tends to preserve the integrity, stability, and beauty of the biotic community. It is wrong when it tends otherwise."[7] What is especially note-worthy, and that to which attention should be directed in this proposition, is the idea that the good of the biotic *community* is the ultimate measure of the moral value, the rightness or wrongness, of actions. Thus, to hunt and kill a white-tailed deer in certain districts may not only be ethically permissible, it might actually be a moral requirement, necessary to protect the local environment, taken as a whole, from the disintegrating effects of a cervid population explosion. On the other hand, rare and endangered animals like the lynx should be especially nurtured and preserved. The lynx, cougar, and other wild feline predators, from the neo-Benthamite perspective (if consistently and evenhandedly applied) should be regarded as merciless, wanton, and incorrigible murderers of their fellow creatures, who not only kill, it should be added, but cruelly toy with their victims, thus increasing the measure of pain in the world. From the perspective of the land ethic, predators generally should be nurtured and preserved as critically important members of the biotic communities to which they are native. Certain plants, similarly, may be overwhelmingly important to the stability, integrity, and beauty of biotic communities, while some animals, such as domestic sheep (allowed perhaps by egalitarian and humane herdspersons to graze freely and to reproduce themselves without being harvested for lamb and mutton) could be a pestilential threat to the natural floral community of a given locale. Thus, the land ethic is logically coherent in demanding at once that moral consideration be given to plants as well as to animals and

yet in permitting animals to be killed, trees felled, and so on. In every case the effect upon ecological systems is the decisive factor in the determination of the ethical quality of actions.

THE LAND ETHIC AND THE ECOLOGICAL POINT OF VIEW

. . . Since ecology focuses upon the relationships between and among things, it inclines its students toward a more holistic vision of the world. Before the rather recent emergence of ecology as a science the landscape appeared to be, one might say, a collection of objects, some of them alive, some conscious, but all the same, an aggregate, a plurality of separate individuals. With this "atomistic" representation of things it is no wonder that moral issues might be understood as competing and mutually contradictory clashes of the "rights" of separate individuals, each separately pursuing its "interests." Ecology has made it possible to apprehend the same landscape as an articulate unity (without the least hint of mysticism or ineffability). Ordinary organic bodies have articulated and discernible parts (limbs, various organs, myriad cells); yet, because of the character of the network of relations among those parts, they form in a perfectly familiar sense a second-order whole. Ecology makes it possible to see land, similarly, as a unified system of integrally related parts, as, so to speak, a third-order organic whole.

Another analogy that has helped ecologists to convey the particular holism which their science brings to reflective attention is that land is integrated as a human community is integrated. The various parts of the "biotic community" (individual animals and plants) depend upon one another *economically* so that the system as such acquires distinct characteristics of its own. Just as it is possible to characterize and define collectively peasant societies, agrarian communities, industrial complexes, capitalist, communist, and socialist economic systems, and so on, ecology characterizes and defines various biomes as desert, savanna, wetland, tundra, wood land, etc., communities, each with its particular "professions," "roles," or "niches."

Now we may think that among the duties we as moral agents have toward ourselves is the duty of self-preservation, which may be interpreted as a duty to maintain our own organic integrity. It is not uncommon in historical moral theory, further, to find that in addition to those peculiar responsibilities we have in relation both to ourselves and to other persons severally, we also have a duty to behave in ways that do not harm the fabric of society *per se*. The land ethic, in similar fashion, calls our attention to the recently discovered integrity—in other words, the unity—of the biota and posits duties binding upon moral agents in relation to that whole. . . . Hence, the representation of the natural environment as, in Leopold's terms, "one humming community" (or, less consistently in his discussion, a third-order organic being) brings into play, whether rationally or not, those stirrings of conscience which we feel in relation to delicately complex, functioning social and organic systems.

The neo-Benthamite humane moralists have, to be sure, digested one of the metaphysical implications of modern biology. They insist that human beings must be understood continuously with the rest of organic nature. People are (and are only) animals, and much of the rhetorical energy of the animal liberation movement is spent in fighting a rear guard action for this aspect of Darwinism against those philosophers who still cling to the dream of a special metaphysical status for people in the order of "creation." To this extent the animal liberation movement is biologically enlightened. . . . [B]ut the biological information of the animal liberation movement seems to extend no further than this—the continuity of human with other animal life forms. The more recent ecological perspective especially seems to be ignored by humane moralists. The holistic outlook of ecology and the associated value premium conferred upon the biotic community, its beauty, integrity, and stability may simply not have penetrated the thinking of the animal liberationists, or it could be that to include it would involve an intolerable contradiction with the Benthamite foundations of their ethical theory. Bentham's view of the "interests of the community" was bluntly reductive. With his characteristic bluster, Bentham wrote, "The community is a fictitious *body* composed of the individual persons who are considered as constituting

as it were its *members*. The interest of the community then is, what?—the sum of the interests of the several members who compose it."[8] Bentham's very simile—the community is like a body composed of members—gives the lie to his reduction of its interests to the sum of its parts taken severally. The interests of a person are not those of his or her cells summed up and averaged out. Our organic health and well-being, for example, require vigorous exercise and metabolic stimulation which cause stress and often pain to various parts of the body and a more rapid turnover in the life cycle of our individual cells. For the sake of the person taken as whole, some parts may be, as it were, unfairly sacrificed. On the level of social organization, the interests of society may not always coincide with the sum of the interests of its parts. Discipline, sacrifice, and individual restraint are often necessary in the social sphere to maintain social integrity as within the bodily organism. A society, indeed, is particularly vulnerable to disintegration when its members become preoccupied totally with their own particular interest, and ignore those distinct and independent interests of the community as a whole. One example, unfortunately, our own society, is altogether too close at hand to be examined with strict academic detachment. The United States seems to pursue uncritically a social policy of reductive utilitarianism, aimed at promoting the happiness of all its members severally. Each special interest accordingly clamors more loudly to be satisfied while the community as a whole becomes noticeably more and more infirm economically, environmentally, and politically. . . .

ETHICAL HOLISM

Before we take up this question, however, some points of interest remain to be considered on the matter of a holistic versus a reductive environmental ethic. To pit the one against the other as I have done without further qualification would be mistaken. A society is constituted by its members, an organic body by its cells, and the ecosystem by the plants, animals, minerals, fluids, and gases which compose it. One cannot affect a system as a whole without affecting at least some of its components. An environmental ethic which takes as its *summum bonum* the integrity, stability, and beauty of the biotic community is not conferring moral standing on something else besides plants, animals, soils, and waters. Rather, the former, the good of the community as a whole, serves as a standard for the assessment of the relative value and relative ordering of its constitutive parts and therefore provides a means of adjudicating the often mutually contradictory demands of the parts considered separately for equal consideration. If diversity does indeed contribute to stability (a classical "law" of ecology), then specimens of rare and endangered species, for example, have a *prima facie* claim to preferential consideration from the perspective of the land ethic. Animals of those species, which, like the honey bee, function in ways critically important to the economy of nature, moreover, would be granted a greater claim to moral attention than psychologically more complex and sensitive ones, say, rabbits and moles, which seem to be plentiful, globally distributed, reproductively efficient, and only routinely integrated into the natural economy. Animals and plants, mountains, rivers, seas, the atmosphere are the *immediate* practical beneficiaries of the land ethic. The well-being of the biotic community, the biosphere as a whole, cannot be logically separated from their survival and welfare.

Some suspicion may arise at this point that the land ethic is ultimately grounded in human interests, not in those of nonhuman natural entities. . . . It is my view that there can be no value apart from an evaluator, that all value is as it were in the eye of the beholder. The value that is attributed to the ecosystem, therefore, is humanly dependent or (allowing that other living things may take a certain delight in the well-being of the whole of things, or that the gods may) at least dependent upon some variety of morally and aesthetically sensitive consciousness. Granting this, however, there is a further, very crucial distinction to be drawn. It is possible that while things may only have value because we (or someone) values them, they may nonetheless be valued for themselves as well as for the contribution they might make to the realization of our (or someone's) interests. Children are valued for themselves by most parents. Money, on the other hand, has only an instrumental or indirect value. Which sort of value has the health of the biotic community and its members severally for Leopold and the land ethic? It is especially difficult to separate these two general sorts of value, the one of moral significance, the other merely selfish, when something that may be valued in both ways at once is the subject of consideration. Are pets, for example, well-treated, like children, for the sake of themselves, or, like mechanical appliances, because of the sort of services they provide their owners? Is a healthy biotic community something we value because we are so utterly and (to the biologically well-informed) so obviously dependent upon it not only for our happiness but for our very survival, or may we also perceive it disinterestedly as having an independent worth? Leopold insists upon a noninstrumental value for the biotic community and mutatis mutandis for its constituents. According to Leopold, collective enlightened self-interest on the part of human beings does not go far enough; the land ethic in his opinion (and no doubt this reflects his own moral intuitions) requires "love, respect, and admiration for land, and a high regard for its value." The land ethic, in Leopold's view, creates "obligations over and above self-interest." And "obligations have no meaning without conscience, and the problem we face is the extension of the social conscience from people to land."[9] If, in other words, any genuine ethic is possible, if it is possible to value *people* for the sake of themselves, then it is equally possible to value land in the same way. . . .

The biospheric perspective does not exempt *Homo sapiens* from moral evaluation in relation to the well-being of the community of nature taken as a whole. The preciousness of individual deer, as of any other specimen, is inversely proportional to the population of the species. Environmentalists, however reluctantly and painfully, do not omit to apply the same logic to their own kind. As omnivores, the population of human beings should, perhaps, be roughly twice that of bears, allowing for differences of size. A global population of more than four billion persons and showing no signs of an orderly decline presents an alarming prospect to humanists, but it is at present a global disaster (the more *per capita* prosperity, indeed, the more disastrous it appears) for the biotic community. . . . Edward Abbey in his enormously popular *Desert Solitaire* bluntly states that he would sooner shoot a man than a snake.[10] Abbey may not be simply depraved; this is perhaps only his way of dramatically making the point that the human population has become so disproportionate from the biological point of view that if one had to choose between a specimen of *Homo sapiens* and a specimen of a rare even if unattractive species, the choice would be moot. . . .

REAPPRAISING DOMESTICITY

Among the last philosophical remarks penned by Aldo Leopold before his untimely death in 1948 is the following: "Perhaps such a shift of values [as implied by the attempt to weld together the concepts of ethics and ecology] can be achieved by reappraising things unnatural, tame, and confined in terms of things natural, wild, and free."[11] John Muir, in a similar spirit of reappraisal, had noted earlier the difference between the wild mountain sheep of the Sierra and the ubiquitous domestic variety. The latter, which Muir described as "hooved locusts," were only, in his estimation, "half alive" in comparison with their natural and autonomous counterparts.[12] One of the more distressing aspects of the animal liberation movement is the failure of almost all its exponents to draw a sharp distinction between the very different plights (and rights) of wild and domestic animals. But this distinction lies at the very center of the land ethic. Domestic animals are creations of man. They are living artifacts, but artifacts nevertheless, and they constitute yet another mode of extension of the works of man into the ecosystem. From the perspective of the land ethic a herd of cattle, sheep, or pigs is as much or more a ruinous blight on the landscape as a fleet of four-wheel drive off-road vehicles. There is thus something profoundly incoherent (and insensitive as well) in the complaint of some animal liberationists that the "natural behavior" of chickens and bobby calves is cruelly frustrated on factory farms. It would make almost as much sense to speak of the natural behavior of tables and chairs.

Here a serious disanalogy (which no one to my knowledge has yet pointed out) becomes clearly evident between the liberation of blacks from slavery (and more recently, from civil inequality) and the liberation of animals from a similar sort of subordination and servitude. Black slaves remained, as it were, metaphysically autonomous: they were by nature if not by convention free beings quite capable of living on their own. They could not be enslaved for more than a historical interlude, for the strength of the force of their freedom was too great. They could, in other words, be retained only by a continuous counterforce, and only temporarily. This is equally true of caged wild animals. African cheetahs in American and European zoos are captive, not indentured, beings. But this is not true of cows, pigs, sheep, and chickens. They have been bred to docility, tractability, stupidity, and dependency. It is literally meaningless to suggest that they be liberated. It is, to speak in hyperbole, a logical impossibility.

Certainly it is a practical impossibility. Imagine what would happen if the people of the world became morally persuaded that domestic animals were to be regarded as oppressed and enslaved persons and accordingly set free. In one scenario we might imagine that like former American black slaves they would receive the equivalent of forty acres and a mule and be turned out to survive on their own. Feral cattle and sheep would hang around farm outbuildings waiting forlornly to be sheltered and fed, or would graze aimlessly through their abandoned and deteriorating pastures. Most would starve or freeze as soon as winter settled in. Reproduction which had been assisted over many countless generations by their former owners might be altogether impossible in the feral state for some varieties, and the care of infants would be an art not so much lost as never acquired. And so in a very short time, after much suffering and agony, these species would become abruptly extinct. Or, in another scenario beginning with the same simple emancipation from human association, survivors of the first massive die-off of untended livestock might begin to recover some of their remote wild ancestral genetic traits and become smaller, leaner, heartier, and smarter versions of their former selves. An actual contemporary example is afforded by the feral mustangs ranging over parts of the American West. In time such animals as these would become (just as the mustangs are now) competitors both with their former human masters and (with perhaps more tragic consequences) indigenous wildlife for food and living space.

Foreseeing these and other untoward consequences of immediate and unplanned liberation of livestock, a human population grown morally more perfect than at present might decide that they had a duty, accumulated over thousands of years, to continue to house and feed as before their former animal slaves (whom they had rendered genetically unfit to care for themselves), but not to butcher them or make other ill use of them, including frustrating their "natural" behavior, their right to copulate freely, reproduce, and enjoy the delights of being parents. People, no longer having meat to eat, would require more vegetables, cereals, and other plant foods, but the institutionalized animal incompetents would still consume all the hay and grains (and more since they would no longer be slaughtered) than they did formerly. This would require clearing more land and bringing it into agricultural production with further loss of wildlife habitat and ecological destruction. Another possible scenario might be a decision on the part of people not literally to liberate domestic animals but simply to cease to breed and raise them. When the last livestock have been killed and eaten (or permitted to die "natural" deaths), people would become vegetarians and domestic livestock species would thus be rendered deliberately extinct (just as they had been deliberately created). But there is surely some irony in an outcome in which the beneficiaries of a humane extension of conscience are destroyed in the process of being saved.

The land ethic, it should be emphasized, as Leopold has sketched it, provides for the *rights* of nonhuman natural beings to a share in the life processes of the biotic community. The conceptual foundation of such rights, however, is less conventional than natural, based upon, as one might say, evolutionary and ecological entitlement. Wild animals and native plants have a particular place in nature, according to the land ethic, which domestic animals (because they are products of human art and represent an extended presence of human beings in the natural world) do not have. The land ethic, in sum, is as much opposed,

though on different grounds, to commercial traffic in wildlife, zoos, the slaughter of whales and other marine mammals, etc., as is the humane ethic. Concern for animal (and plant) rights and well-being is as fundamental to the land ethic as to the humane ethic, but the difference between naturally evolved and humanly bred species is an essential consideration for the one, though not for the other.

The "shift of values" which results from our "reappraising things unnatural, tame, and confined in terms of things natural, wild, and free" is especially dramatic when we reflect upon the definitions of *good* and *evil* espoused by Bentham and Mill and uncritically accepted by their contemporary followers. Pain and pleasure seem to have nothing at all to do with good and evil if our appraisal is taken from the vantage point of ecological biology. Pain in particular is primarily information. In animals, it informs the central nervous system of stress, irritation, or trauma in outlying regions of the organism. A certain level of pain under optimal organic circumstances is indeed desirable as an indicator of exertion—of the degree of exertion needed to maintain fitness, to stay "in shape," and of a level of exertion beyond which it would be dangerous to go. An arctic wolf in pursuit of a caribou may experience pain in her feet or chest because of the rigors of the chase. There is nothing bad or wrong in that. Or, consider a case of injury. Suppose that a person in the course of a wilderness excursion sprains an ankle. Pain informs him or her of the injury and by its intensity the amount of further stress the ankle may endure in the course of getting to safety. Would it be better if pain were not experienced upon injury or, taking advantage of recent technology, anaesthetized? Pleasure appears to be, for the most part (unfortunately it is not always so) a reward accompanying those activities which contribute to organic maintenance, such as the pleasures associated with eating, drinking, grooming, and so on, or those which contribute to social solidarity like the pleasures of dancing, conversation, teasing, etc., or those which contribute to the continuation of the species, such as the pleasures of sexual activity and of being parents. The doctrine that life is the happier the freer it is from pain and that the happiest life conceivable is one in which there is continuous pleasure uninterrupted by pain is biologically preposterous. A living mammal which experienced no pain would be one which had a lethal dysfunction of the nervous system. The idea that pain is evil and ought to be minimized or eliminated is as primitive a notion as that of a tyrant who puts to death messengers bearing bad news on the supposition that thus his well-being and security is improved.

More seriously still, the value commitments of the humane movement seem at bottom to betray a world-denying or rather a life-loathing philosophy. The natural world as actually constituted is one in which one being lives at the expense of others. Each organism, in Darwin's metaphor, struggles to maintain its own organic integrity. The more complex animals seem to experience (judging from our own case, and reasoning from analogy) appropriate and adaptive psychological accompaniments to organic existence. There is a palpable passion for self-preservation. There are desire, pleasure in the satisfaction of desires, acute agony attending injury, frustration, and chronic dread of death. But these experiences are the psychological substance of living. To live is to be anxious about life, to feel pain and pleasure in a fitting mixture, and sooner or later to die. That is the way the system works. If nature as a whole is good, then pain and death are also good. Environmental ethics in general require people to play fair in the natural system. The neo-Benthamites have in a sense taken the uncourageous approach. People have attempted to exempt themselves from the life/death reciprocities of natural processes and from ecological limitations in the name of a prophylactic ethic of maximizing rewards (pleasure) and minimizing unwelcome information (pain). To be fair, the humane moralists seem to suggest that we should attempt to project the same values into the nonhuman animal world and to widen the charmed circle—no matter that it would be biologically unrealistic to do so or biologically ruinous if, per impossible, such an environmental ethic were implemented.

There is another approach. Rather than imposing our alienation from nature and natural processes and cycles of life on other animals, we human beings could reaffirm our participation in nature by accepting life as it is given without a sugar coating. Instead of imposing artificial legalities, rights, and so on on nature, we might take the opposite course and accept and affirm natural biological laws, principles, and limitations in the human personal and social spheres. Such appears to have been the posture toward life of tribal peoples in the past. The chase was relished with its dangers, rigors, and hardships as well as its rewards: animal flesh was respectfully consumed; a tolerance for pain was cultivated; virtue and magnanimity were prized; lithic, floral, and faunal spirits were worshipped; population was routinely optimized by sexual continency, abortion, infanticide, and stylized warfare; and other life forms, although certainly appropriated, were respected as fellow players in a magnificent and awesome, if not altogether idyllic, drama of life. It is impossible today to return to the symbiotic relationship of Stone Age man to the natural environment, but the ethos of this by far the longest era of human existence could be abstracted and integrated with a future human culture seeking a viable and mutually beneficial relationship with nature. Personal, social, and environmental *health* would, accordingly, receive a premium value rather than comfort, self-indulgent pleasure, and anaesthetic insulation from pain. Sickness would be regarded as a worse evil than death. The pursuit of health or wellness at the personal, social, and environmental levels would require self-discipline in the form of simple diet, vigorous exercise, conservation, and social responsibility.

Leopold's prescription for the realization and implementation of the land ethic—the reappraisal of things unnatural, tame, and confined in terms of things natural, wild, and free—does not stop, in other words, with a reappraisal of nonhuman domestic animals in terms of their wild (or willed) counterparts; the human ones should be similarly reappraised. This means, among other things, the reappraisal of the comparatively recent values and concerns of "civilized" *Homo sapiens* in terms of those of our "savage" ancestors. Civilization has insulated and alienated us from the rigors and challenges of the natural environment. The hidden agenda of the humane ethic is the imposition of the anti-natural prophylactic ethos of comfort and soft pleasure on an even wider scale. The land ethic, on the other hand, requires a shrinkage, if at all possible, of the domestic sphere; it rejoices in a recrudescence of wilderness and a renaissance of tribal cultural experience.

The converse of those goods and evils, axiomatic to the humane ethic, may be illustrated and focused by the consideration of a single issue raised by the humane morality: a vegetarian diet. Savage people seem to have had, if the attitudes and values of surviving tribal cultures are representative, something like an intuitive grasp of ecological relationships and certainly a morally charged appreciation of eating. There is nothing more intimate than eating, more symbolic of the connectedness of life, and more mysterious. What we eat and how we eat is by no means an insignificant ethical concern.

From the ecological point of view, for human beings universally to become vegetarians is tantamount to a shift of trophic niche from omnivore with carnivorous preferences to herbivore.... The human population would probably, as past trends overwhelmingly suggest, expand in accordance with the potential thus afforded. The net result would be fewer nonhuman beings and more human beings, who, of course, have requirements of life far more elaborate than even those of domestic animals, requirements which would tax other "natural resources" (trees for shelter, minerals mined at the expense of topsoil and its vegetation, etc.) more than under present circumstances. A vegetarian human population is therefore *probably* ecologically catastrophic.

Meat eating as implied by the foregoing remarks may be more *ecologically* responsible than a wholly vegetable diet. Meat, however, purchased at the supermarket, externally packaged and internally laced with petrochemicals, fattened in feed lots, slaughtered impersonally, and, in general, mechanically processed from artificial insemination to microwave roaster, is an affront not only to physical metabolism and bodily health but to conscience as well. From the perspective of the land ethic, the immoral aspect of the factory farm has to do far less with the suffering and killing of nonhuman animals than with the monstrous transformation of living things from an organic to a mechanical mode of being....

Ethical vegetarianism to all appearances insists upon the human consumption of plants (in a paradoxical moral gesture toward those animals whose very existence is dependent upon human carnivorousness), even when the tomatoes are grown hydroponically, the lettuce generously coated with chlorinated hydrocarbons, the potatoes pumped up with chemical fertilizers, and the cereals stored with the help of chemical preservatives. The land ethic takes as much exception to the transmogrification of plants by mechanico-chemical means as to that of animals. The important thing, I would think, is not to eat vegetables as opposed to animal flesh, but to resist factory farming in all its manifestations, including especially its liberal application of pesticides, herbicides, and chemical fertilizers to maximize the production of *vegetable* crops.

The land ethic, with its ecological perspective, helps us to recognize and affirm the organic integrity of self and the untenability of a firm distinction between self and environment. On the ethical question of what to eat, it answers, not vegetables instead of animals, but organically as opposed to mechanicochemically produced food. Purists like Leopold prefer, in his expression, to get their "meat from God," i.e., to hunt and consume wildlife and to gather wild plant foods, and thus to live within the parameters of the aboriginal human ecological niche. Second best is eating from one's own orchard, garden, henhouse, pigpen, and barnyard. Third best is buying or bartering organic foods from one's neighbors and friends.

CONCLUSION

Philosophical controversy concerning animal liberation/rights has been most frequently represented as a polar dispute between traditional moral humanists and seemingly *avant garde* humane moralists. Further, animal liberation has been assumed to be closely allied with environmental ethics, possibly because in Leopold's classical formulation moral standing and indeed rights (of some unspecified sort) is accorded nonhuman beings, among them animals. The purpose of this discussion has been to distinguish sharply environmental ethics from the animal liberation/rights movement both in theory and practical application and to suggest, thereupon, that there is an underrepresented, but very important, point of view respecting the problem of the moral status of non-human animals. The debate over animal liberation, in short, should be conceived as triangular, not polar, with land ethics or environmental ethics, the third and, in my judgment, the most creative, interesting, and practicable alternative. Indeed, from this third point of view moral humanism and humane moralism appear to have much more in common with one another than either have with environmental or land ethics. On reflection one might even be led to suspect that the noisy debate between these parties has served to drown out the much deeper challenge to "business-as-usual" ethical philosophy represented by Leopold and his exponents, and to keep ethical philosophy firmly anchored to familiar modern paradigms.

Moral humanism and humane moralism, to re-state succinctly the most salient conclusions of this essay, are *atomistic* or distributive in their theory of moral value, while environmental ethics (again, at least, as set out in Leopold's outline) is *holistic* or collective. Modern ethical theory, in other words, has consistently located moral value in individuals and set out certain metaphysical reasons for including some individuals and excluding others . . . while environmental ethics locates ultimate value in the "biotic community" and assigns differential moral value to the constitutive individuals relatively to that standard. This is perhaps the most fundamental theoretical difference between environmental ethics and the ethics of animal liberation.

Allied to this difference are many others. One of the more conspicuous is that in environmental ethics, plants are included within the parameters of the ethical theory as well as animals. Indeed, inanimate entities such as oceans and lakes, mountains, forests, and wetlands are assigned a greater value than individual animals and in a way quite different from systems which accord them moral considerability through a further multiplication of competing individual loci of value and holders of rights. . . .

Environmental ethics sets a very low priority on domestic animals as they very frequently contribute to the erosion of the integrity, stability, and beauty of the biotic communities into which they have been insinuated. On the other hand, animal liberation, if pursued at the practical as well as rhetorical level, would have ruinous consequences on plants, soils, and waters, consequences which could not be directly reckoned according to humane moral theory. As this last remark suggests, the animal liberation/animal rights movement is in the final analysis utterly unpracticable. An imagined society in which all animals capable of sensibility received equal consideration or held rights to equal consideration would be so ludicrous that it might be more appropriately and effectively treated in satire than in philosophical discussion. The land ethic, by contrast, even though its ethical purview is very much wider, is nevertheless eminently practicable, since, by reference to a single good, competing individual claims may be adjudicated and relative values and priorities assigned to the myriad components of the biotic community. This is not to suggest that the implementation of environmental ethics as social policy would be easy. Implementation of the land ethic would require discipline, sacrifice, retrenchment, and massive economic reform, tantamount to a virtual revolution in prevailing attitudes and life styles. Nevertheless, it provides a unified and coherent practical principle and thus a decision procedure at the practical level which a distributive or atomistic ethic may achieve only artificially and so imprecisely as to be practically indeterminate.

NOTES

1. Aldo Leopold, *A Sand County Almanac* (New York: Oxford University Press, 1949), pp. 202–3.
2. Ibid., p. 204.
3. Ibid, pp. 201–3.
4. Ibid., p. 203.
5. Ibid., p. 204.
6. Ibid., p. 221 (trees); pp. 129–33 (mountains); p. 209 (streams).
7. Ibid., pp. 224–25.
8. *An Introduction to the Principles of Morals and Legislation* (Oxford: Oxford University Press, 1823), chap. 1, sec. 4.

9. Leopold, *Sand County Almanac,* pp. 223 and 209.

10. Edward Abbey, *Desert Solitaire* (New York: Ballantine Books, 1968), p. 20.

11. Leopold, *Sand County Almanac,* p. ix.

12. See John Muir, "The Wild Sheep of California," *Overland Monthly* 12 (1874) p. 359.

REVIEW AND DISCUSSION QUESTIONS

1. How does Callicott think environmental ethics differs from animal liberation (humane moralism)?
2. What is the first principle of the land ethic?
3. What does Callicott mean in saying that animal liberationists like Bentham are "bluntly reductive"?
4. How does the environmental ethic differ from moral humanism?
5. Describe the reasons that seem to lead Callicott to conclude that the environmental ethic is superior to the others.
6. What practical implications do Callicott and you see from the adoption of the land ethic, as opposed to animal liberation?
7. How might Peter Singer most reasonably respond to Callicott's argument? Is that response adequate?
8. Which of Callicott's three positions is closest to Steinbock's? How might she respond to Callicott's essay?
9. Discuss the following claim: "Callicott argues that 'wild' animals have a 'place in nature' that domestic ones do not. But if humans are part of nature, then there is no reason to suppose our dependents are less valuable or less a part of nature than the dependents of non-human animals."

6
Euthanasia

Essays in Section 6 focus on euthanasia—that is, the killing of human beings who are either terminally ill, suffering tremendously, or severely retarded. Authors take varying positions, some rejecting virtually all forms of euthanasia and others arguing that it should be allowed much more often than current law permits. Another issue that runs through many of the readings is the debate about the merits of distinguishing, legally and morally, between actively killing and passively allowing a person to die. The readings begin with one of the U.S. Supreme Court's most important cases on the subject.

Removing Life-Support Systems:

Cruzan v. *Director, Missouri Department of Health*

In this case, the U.S. Supreme Court reviews a Missouri court's decision not to allow the parents of Nancy Cruzan, who was in a "persistent vegetative state" as a result of an auto accident, to remove feeding and hydration tubes that kept her alive. The Missouri court had required that there be "clear and convincing" proof that such a decision expresses Nancy Cruzan's desires and held that no such proof had been presented. In what follows, a majority of the U.S. Supreme Court agreed with the Missouri court, holding that the U.S. Constitution does not require Missouri to allow the parents to remove the tubes from their daughter, nor does it prevent a state from imposing such a heavy burden of proof on those who may wish not to be kept on life-support systems. Two justices, however, wrote strong dissents.

Chief Justice Rehnquist Delivered the Opinion of the Court: Petitioner Nancy Beth Cruzan was rendered incompetent as a result of severe injuries sustained during an automobile accident. Co-petitioners Lester and Joyce Cruzan, Nancy's parents and co-guardians, sought a court order directing the withdrawal of their daughter's artificial feeding and hydration equipment after it became apparent that she had virtually no chance of recovering her cognitive faculties. The Supreme

Court of Missouri held that because there was no clear and convincing evidence of Nancy's desire to have life-sustaining treatment withdrawn under such circumstances, her parents lacked authority to effectuate such a request. We granted certiorari, and now affirm. . . .

After it had become apparent that Nancy Cruzan had virtually no chance of regaining her mental faculties her parents asked hospital employees to terminate the artificial nutrition and hy-

496 U.S. (1990).

dration procedures. All agree that such a removal would cause her death. The employees refused to honor the request without court approval. The parents then sought and received authorization from the state trial court for termination. The court found that a person in Nancy's condition had a fundamental right under the State and Federal Constitutions to refuse or direct the withdrawal of "death prolonging procedures." The court also found that Nancy's "expressed thoughts at age twenty-five in somewhat serious conversation with a housemate friend that if sick or injured she would not wish to continue her life unless she could live at least halfway normally suggests that given her present condition she would not wish to continue on with her nutrition and hydration." . . .

We granted certiorari to consider the question of whether Cruzan has a right under the United States Constitution which would require the hospital to withdraw life-sustaining treatment from her under these circumstances.

At common law, even the touching of one person by another without consent and without legal justification was a battery. [This] notion of bodily integrity has been embodied in the requirement that informed consent is generally required for medical treatment. Justice Cardozo, while on the Court of Appeals of New York, aptly described this doctrine: "Every human being of adult years and sound mind has a right to determine what shall be done with his own body; and a surgeon who performs an operation without his patient's consent commits an assault, for which he is liable in damages." *Schloendorff* v. *Society of New York Hospital* (1914). The informed consent doctrine has become firmly entrenched in American tort law.

The logical corollary of the doctrine of informed consent is that the patient generally possesses the right not to consent, that is, to refuse treatment. . . .

The Fourteenth Amendment provides that no State shall "deprive any person of life, liberty, or property, without due process of law." . . . For purposes of this case, we assume that the United States Constitution would grant a competent person a constitutionally protected right to refuse lifesaving hydration and nutrition.

The difficulty with petitioners' claim is that in a sense it begs the question: an incompetent person is not able to make an informed and voluntary choice to exercise a hypothetical right to refuse treatment or any other right. Such a "right" must be exercised for her, if at all, by some sort of surrogate. Here, Missouri has in effect recognized that under certain circumstances a surrogate may act for the patient in electing to have hydration and nutrition withdrawn in such a way as to cause death, but it has established a procedural safeguard to assure that the action of the surrogate conforms as best it may to the wishes expressed by the patient while competent. Missouri requires that evidence of the incompetent's wishes as to the withdrawal of treatment be proved by clear and convincing evidence. The question, then, is whether the United States Constitution forbids the establishment of this procedural requirement by the State. We hold that it does not.

Whether or not Missouri's clear and convincing evidence requirement comports with the United States Constitution depends in part on what interests the State may properly seek to protect in this situation. Missouri relies on its interest in the protection and preservation of human life, and there can be no gainsaying this interest. As a general matter, the States—indeed, all civilized nations—demonstrate their commitment to life by treating homicide as serious crime. Moreover, the majority of States in this country have laws imposing criminal penalties on one who assists another to commit suicide. We do not think a State is required to remain neutral in the face of an informed and voluntary decision by a physically-able adult to starve to death.

But in the context presented here, a State has more particular interests at stake. The choice between life and death is a deeply personal decision of obvious and overwhelming finality. We believe Missouri may legitimately seek to safeguard the personal element of this choice through the imposition of heightened evidentiary requirements. . . . Finally, we think a State may properly decline to make judgments about the "quality" of life that a particular individual may enjoy, and simply assert an unqualified interest in the preservation of human life to be weighed against the constitutionally protected interests of the individual.

In our view, Missouri has permissibly sought to advance these interests through the adoption of a "clear and convincing" standard of proof to govern such proceedings. . . .

[N]ot only does the standard of proof reflect the importance of a particular adjudication, it also serves as "a societal judgment about how the risk of error should be distributed between litigants." *Santosky*. The more stringent the burden of proof a party must bear, the more that party bears the risk of an erroneous decision. We believe that Missouri may permissibly place an increased risk of an erroneous decision on those seeking to terminate an incompetent individual's life-sustaining treatment. An erroneous decision not to terminate results in a maintenance of the status quo; the possibility of subsequent developments such as advancements in medical science, the discovery of new evidence regarding the patient's intent, changes in the law, or simply the unexpected death of the patient despite the administration of life-sustaining treatment, at least create the potential that a wrong decision will eventually be corrected or its impact mitigated. An erroneous decision to withdraw life-sustaining treatment, however, is not susceptible of correction. . . .

In sum, we conclude that a State may apply a clear and convincing evidence standard in proceedings where a guardian seeks to discontinue nutrition and hydration of a person diagnosed to be in a persistent vegetative state. . . .

No doubt is engendered by anything in this record but that Nancy Cruzan's mother and father are loving and caring parents. If the State were required by the United States Constitution to repose a right of "substituted judgment" with anyone, the Cruzans would surely qualify. But we do not think the Due Process Clause requires the State to repose judgment on these matters with anyone but the patient herself. Close family members may have a strong feeling—a feeling not at all ignoble or unworthy, but not entirely disinterested, either—that they do not wish to witness the continuation of the life of a loved one which they regard as hopeless, meaningless, and even degrading. But there is no automatic assurance that the view of close family members will necessarily be the same as the patient's would have been had she been confronted with the prospect of her situation while competent. All of the reasons previously discussed for allowing Missouri to require clear and convincing evidence of the patient's wishes lead us to conclude that the State may choose to defer only to those wishes, rather than confide the decision to close family members.

Justice Brennan, with Whom Justice Marshall and Justice Blackmun Join, Dissenting: A grown woman at the time of [her] accident, Nancy Cruzan had previously expressed her wish to forgo continuing medical care under circumstances such as these. Her family and her friends are convinced that this is what she would want. A guardian ad litem appointed by the trial court is also convinced that this is what Nancy would want. . . .

Because I believe that Nancy Cruzan has a fundamental right to be free of unwanted artificial nutrition and hydration, which right is not outweighed by any interests of the State, and because I find that the improperly biased procedural obstacles imposed by the Missouri Supreme Court impermissibly burden that right, I respectfully dissent. Nancy Cruzan is entitled to choose to die with dignity. . . .

. . . [Although] the right to be free of unwanted medical intervention, like other constitutionally protected interests, may not be absolute, no State interest could outweigh the rights of an individual in Nancy Cruzan's position. . . .

The only state interest asserted here is a general interest in the preservation of life. But the State has no legitimate general interest in someone's life, completely abstracted from the interest of the person living that life, that could outweigh the person's choice to avoid medical treatment. . . . Thus, the State's general interest in life must accede to Nancy Cruzan's particularized and intense interest in self-determination in her choice of medical treatment. There is simply nothing legitimately within the State's purview to be gained by superseding her decision.

Moreover, there may be considerable danger that Missouri's rule of decision would impair rather than serve any interest the State does have in sustaining life. Current medical practice recommends use of heroic measures if there is a scintilla of a chance that the patient will recover, on the assumption that the measures will be discontinued should the patient improve. When the President's Commission [for the Study of Ethical Problems in

Medicine and Biomedical and Behavioral Research] in 1982 approved the withdrawal of life support equipment from irreversibly vegetative patients, it explained that "[a]n even more troubling wrong occurs when a treatment that might save life or improve health is not started because the health care personnel are afraid that they will find it very difficult to stop the treatment if, as is fairly likely, it proves to be of little benefit and greatly burdens the patient." . . .

. . . This is not to say that the State has no legitimate interests to assert here. As the majority recognizes, Missouri has a parens patriae interest in providing Nancy Cruzan, now incompetent, with as accurate as possible a determination of how she would exercise her rights under these circumstances. Second, if and when it is determined that Nancy Cruzan would want to continue treatment, the State may legitimately assert an interest in providing that treatment. But until Nancy's wishes have been determined, the only state interest that may be asserted is an interest in safeguarding the accuracy of that determination.

Accuracy, therefore, must be our touchstone. Missouri may constitutionally impose only those procedural requirements that serve to enhance the accuracy of a determination of Nancy Cruzan's wishes or are at least consistent with an accurate determination. The Missouri "safeguard" that the Court upholds today does not meet that standard. The determination needed in this context is whether the incompetent person would choose to live in a persistent vegetative state on life-support or to avoid this medical treatment. Missouri's rule of decision imposes a markedly asymmetrical evidentiary burden. Only evidence of specific statements of treatment choice made by the patient when competent is admissible to support a finding that the patient, now in a persistent vegetative state, would wish to avoid further medical treatment. Moreover, this evidence must be clear and convincing. No proof is required to support a finding that the incompetent person would wish to continue treatment. . . .

To be sure, courts have long erected clear and convincing evidence standards to place the greater risk of erroneous decisions on those bringing disfavored claims. In such cases, however, the choice to discourage certain claims was a legitimate, constitutional policy choice. In contrast, Missouri has no such power to disfavor a choice by Nancy Cruzan to avoid medical treatment, because Missouri has no legitimate interest in providing Nancy with treatment until it is established that this represents her choice. Just as a State may not override Nancy's choice directly, it may not do so indirectly through the imposition of a procedural rule. . . .

Even more than its heightened evidentiary standard, the Missouri court's categorical exclusion of relevant evidence dispenses with any semblance of accurate fact finding. The court adverted to no evidence supporting its decision, but held that no clear and convincing, inherently reliable evidence had been presented to show that Nancy would want to avoid further treatment. In doing so, the court failed to consider statements Nancy had made to family members and a close friend. The court also failed to consider testimony from Nancy's mother and sister that they were certain that Nancy would want to discontinue artificial nutrition and hydration, even after the court found that Nancy's family was loving and without malignant motive. The court also failed to consider the conclusions of the guardian ad litem, appointed by the trial court, that there was clear and convincing evidence that Nancy would want to discontinue medical treatment and that this was in her best interests. . . .

[The] Missouri court's disdain for Nancy's statements in serious conversations not long before her accident, for the opinions of Nancy's family and friends as to her values, beliefs and certain choice, and even for the opinion of an outside objective fact finder appointed by the State evinces a disdain for Nancy Cruzan's own right to choose. The rules by which an incompetent person's wishes are determined must represent every effort to determine those wishes. The rule that the Missouri court adopted and that this Court upholds, however, skews the result away from a determination that as accurately as possible reflects the individual's own preferences and beliefs. It is a rule that transforms human beings into passive subjects of medical technology. . . .

. . . As many as 10,000 patients are being maintained in persistent vegetative states in the United States, and the number is expected to increase significantly in the near future. Medical technology, developed over the past 20 or so years, is often capable of resuscitating people after they have stopped breathing or their hearts have stopped beating. Some of those people are brought fully back to life. Two decades ago, those who were not and could not swallow and digest food, died. Intravenous solutions could not provide sufficient calories to maintain people for more than a short time. Today, various forms of artificial feeding have been developed that are able to keep people metabolically alive for years, even decades. In addition, in this century, chronic or degenerative ailments have replaced communicable diseases as the primary causes of death. [A] fifth of all adults surviving to age 80 will suffer a progressive dementing disorder prior to death. . . .

[Missouri] and this Court have displaced Nancy's own assessment of the processes associated with dying. They have discarded evidence of her will, ignored her values, and deprived her of the right to a decision as closely approximating her own choice as humanly possible. They have done so disingenuously in her name, and openly in Missouri's own. That Missouri and this Court may truly be motivated only by concern for incompetent patients makes no matter. As one of our most prominent jurists warned us decades ago: "Experience should teach us to be most on our guard to protect liberty when the government's purposes are beneficent. . . . The greatest dangers to liberty lurk in insidious encroachment by men of zeal, well meaning but without understanding." *Olmstead* v. *United States* (1928) (Brandeis, J., dissenting).

I respectfully dissent.

Justice Stevens, Dissenting: Our Constitution is born of the proposition that all legitimate governments must secure the equal right of every person to "Life, Liberty, and the pursuit of Happiness." In the ordinary case we quite naturally assume that these three ends are compatible, mutually enhancing, and perhaps even coincident. . . .

[I]n my view, the Constitution requires the State to care for Nancy Cruzan's life in a way that gives appropriate respect to her own best interests. . . .

Nancy Cruzan's death, when it comes, cannot be an historic act of heroism; it will inevitably be the consequence of her tragic accident. But Nancy Cruzan's interest in life, no less than that of any other person, includes an interest in how she will be thought of after her death by those whose opinions mattered to her. There can be no doubt that her life made her dear to her family, and to others. How she dies will affect how that life is remembered. The trial court's order authorizing Nancy's parents to cease their daughter's treatment would have permitted the family that cares for Nancy to bring to a close her tragedy and her death. Missouri's objection to that order subordinates Nancy's body, her family, and the lasting significance of her life to the State's own interests. . . .

Missouri asserts that its policy is related to a state interest in the protection of life. In my view, however, it is an effort to define life, rather than to protect it, that is the heart of Missouri's policy. Missouri insists, without regard to Nancy Cruzan's own interests, upon equating her life with the biological persistence of her bodily functions. Nancy Cruzan, it must be remembered, is not now simply incompetent. She is in a persistent vegetative state, and has been so for seven years. The trial court found, and no party contested, that Nancy has no possibility of recovery and no consciousness.

It seems to me that the Court errs insofar as it characterizes this case as involving "judgments about the 'quality' of life that a particular individual may enjoy." Nancy Cruzan is obviously "alive" in a physiological sense. But for patients like Nancy Cruzan, who have no consciousness and no chance of recovery, there is a serious question as to whether the mere persistence of their bodies is "life" as that word is commonly understood, or as it is used in both the Constitution and the Declaration of Independence. The State's unflagging determination to perpetuate Nancy Cruzan's physical existence is comprehensible only as an effort to define life's meaning, not as an attempt to preserve its sanctity.

This much should be clear from the oddity of Missouri's definition alone. Life, particularly human life, is not commonly thought of as a merely physiological condition or function. Its sanctity is often thought to derive from the impossibility of any such reduction. When people speak of life, they often mean to describe the experiences that comprise a person's history, as when it is said that somebody "led a good life." They may also mean to refer to the practical manifestation of the human spirit, a meaning captured by the familiar observation that somebody "added life" to an assembly. If there is a shared thread among the various opinions on this subject, it may be that life is an activity which is at once the matrix for and an integration of a person's interest. In any event, absent some theological abstraction, the idea of life is not conceived separately from the idea of a living person. Yet, it is by precisely such a separation that Missouri asserts an interest in Nancy Cruzan's life in opposition to Nancy Cruzan's own interests. The resulting definition is uncommon indeed.

[My] disagreement with the Court is thus unrelated to its endorsement of the clear and convincing standard of proof for cases of this kind. Indeed, I agree that the controlling facts must be established with unmistakable clarity. The critical question, however, is not how to improve the controlling facts but rather what proven facts should be controlling. In my view, the constitutional answer is clear: the best interests of the individual, especially when buttressed by the interests of all related third parties, must prevail over any general state policy that simply ignores those interests. Indeed, the only apparent secular basis for the State's interest in life is the policy's persuasive impact upon people other than Nancy and her family. [The] failure of Missouri's policy to heed the interests of a dying individual with respect to matters so private is ample evidence of the policy's illegitimacy.

Only because Missouri has arrogated to itself the power to define life, and only because the Court permits this usurpation, are Nancy Cruzan's life and liberty put into disquieting conflict. If Nancy Cruzan's life were defined by reference to her own interests, so that her life expired when her biological existence ceased serving any of her own interests, then her constitutionally protected interest in freedom from unwanted treatment would not come into conflict with her constitutionally protected interest in life. Conversely, if there were any evidence that Nancy Cruzan herself defined life to encompass every form of biological persistence by a human being, so that the continuation of treatment would serve Nancy's own liberty, then once again there would be no conflict between life and liberty. The opposition of life and liberty in this case are thus not the result of Nancy Cruzan's tragic accident, but are instead the artificial consequence of Missouri's effort, and this Court's willingness, to abstract Nancy Cruzan's life from Nancy Cruzan's person.

Both this Court's majority and the state court's majority express great deference to the policy choice made by the state legislature. . . . [The] Court's deference seems ultimately to derive from the premise that chronically incompetent persons have no constitutionally cognizable interests at all, and so are not persons within the meaning of the Constitution. Deference of this sort is patently unconstitutional. It is also dangerous in ways that may not be immediately apparent. Today the State of Missouri has announced its intent to spend several hundred thousand dollars in preserving the life of Nancy Beth Cruzan in order to vindicate its general policy favoring the preservation of human life. Tomorrow, another State equally eager to champion an interest in the "quality of life" might favor a policy designed to ensure quick and comfortable deaths by denying treatment to categories of marginally hopeless cases. If the State in fact has an interest in defining life, and if the State's policy with respect to the termination of life-sustaining treatment commands deference from the judiciary, it is unclear how any resulting conflict between the best interests of the individual and the general policy of the State would be resolved. I believe the Constitution requires that the individual's vital interest in liberty should prevail over the general policy in that case, just as in this.

That a contrary result is readily imaginable under the majority's theory makes manifest that this Court cannot defer to any State policy that drives a theoretical wedge between a person's life, on the one hand, and that person's liberty or happiness, on the other. The consequence of such a theory is to deny the personhood of those whose lives are defined by the State's interests rather than their own. This consequence may be acceptable in theology or in speculative philosophy, but it is radically inconsistent with the foundation of all legitimate government. Our Constitution presupposes a respect for the personhood of every individual, and nowhere is strict adherence to that principle more essential than in the Judicial Branch.

[The] Cruzan family's continuing concern provides a concrete reminder that Nancy Cruzan's interests did not disappear with her vitality or her consciousness. However commendable may be the State's interest in human life, it cannot pursue that interest by appropriating Nancy Cruzan's life as a symbol for its own purposes. Lives do not exist in abstraction from persons, and to pretend otherwise is not to honor but to desecrate the State's responsibility for protecting life. A State that seeks to demonstrate its commitment to life may do so by aiding those who are actively struggling for life and health. In this endeavor, unfortunately, no State can lack for opportunities: there can be no need to make an example of tragic cases like that of Nancy Cruzan.

I respectfully dissent.

REVIEW AND DISCUSSION QUESTIONS

1. Explain how the majority opinion, written by Justice Rehnquist, places this case in the context of other common law decisions.
2. What "interests" does Justice Rehnquist think the state has in this case?
3. How does Justice Rehnquist defend the "standard of proof" required by Missouri law before a patient can be removed from life-support systems?
4. Summarize the grounds on which Justice Brennan dissents.
5. Justice Stevens wrote a separate dissent. Describe the similarities and differences between his analysis and the dissent by Justice Brennan.
6. If you were on the Court, how would you have ruled in this case? Explain.

An Alternative to the Ethic of Euthanasia

Arthur J. Dyck

In this selection, Arthur J. Dyck raises an array of objections to euthanasia, arguing that it is wrong for people to kill themselves, as occurs in euthanasia, and that euthanasia is a dangerous social policy.

The arguments for euthanasia focus upon two humane and significant concerns: compassion for those who are painfully and terminally ill; and concern for the human dignity associated with freedom of choice. Compassion and freedom are values that sustain and enhance the common good. The question here, however, is how these values affect our behavior toward the dying.

The argument for compassion usually occurs in the form of attacking the inhumanity of keeping dying people alive when they are in great pain or when they have lost almost all of their usual

From Arthur J. Dyck, "An Alternative to the Ethic of Euthanasia," in *To Live and to Let Die,* ed. R. H. Williams. (New York: Springer-Verlag, 1973), pp. 98–112. Reprinted by permission of the publisher.

functions, particularly when they have lost the ability or will to communicate with others. . . . The argument for compassion is supplemented by an argument for greater freedom for a patient to choose how and when he or she will die. For one thing, the patient should not be subjected to medical treatment to which that patient does not consent. Those who argue for voluntary euthanasia extend this notion by arguing that the choice to withhold techniques that would prolong life is a choice to shorten life. Hence, if one can choose to shorten one's life, why cannot one ask a physician by a simple and direct act of intervention to put an end to one's life? Here it is often argued that physicians already curtail life by means of pain-killing drugs, which in the doses administered, will hasten death. Why should not the law recognize and sanction a simple and direct hastening of death, should the patient wish it?

How do the proponents of euthanasia view the general prohibition against killing? First of all, they maintain that we are dealing here with people who will surely die regardless of the intervention of medicine. They advocate the termination of suffering and the lawful foreshortening of the dying process. Secondly, although the patient is committing suicide, and the physician is an accomplice in such a suicide, both acts are morally justifiable to cut short the suffering of one who is dying.

It is important to be very clear about the precise moral reasoning by which advocates of voluntary euthanasia justify suicide and assisting a suicide. They make no moral distinction between those instances when a patient or a physician chooses to have life shortened by failing to accept or use life-prolonging techniques and those instances when a patient or a physician shortens life by employing a death-dealing chemical or instrument. They make no moral distinction between a drug given to kill pain, which also shortens life, and a substance given precisely to shorten life and for no other reason. Presumably these distinctions are not honored, because regardless of the stratagem employed—regardless of whether one is permitting to die or killing directly—the result is the same, the patient's life is shortened. Hence, it is maintained that, if you can justify one kind of act that shortens the life of the dying, you can justify any act that shortens the life of the dying when this act is seen to be willed by the one who is dying. Moral reasoning of this sort is strictly utilitarian; it focuses solely on the consequences of acts, not on their intent. . . .

Because of this loss of a merely descriptive term for a happy death, it is necessary to invent a term for a happy or good death—namely, benemortasia. The familiar derivatives for this new term are *bene* (good) and *mors* (death). . . . An ethic of benemortasia does not stand in opposition to the values of compassion and human freedom. It differs, however, from the ethic of euthanasia in its understanding of how these values are best realized. In particular, certain constraints upon human freedom are recognized and emphasized as enabling human beings to increase compassion and freedom rather than diminish them. . . .

Our ethic of benemortasia acknowledges the freedom of patients who are incurably ill to refuse interventions that prolong dying and the freedom of physicians to honor such wishes. However, these actions are not acts of suicide and assisting in suicide. In our ethic of benemortasia, suicide and assisting in suicide are unjustifiable acts of killing. Unlike the ethic of those who would legalize voluntary euthanasia, our ethic makes a moral distinction between acts that permit death and acts that cause death. . . . From the point of view of the dying person, when could his or her decisions be called a deliberate act to end life, the act we usually designate as suicide? Only, it seems to me, when the dying person commits an act that has the immediate intent of ending life and has no other purpose. That act may be to use, or ask the physician to use, a chemical or an instrument that has no other immediate effect than to end the dying person's life. If, for the sake of relieving pain, a dying person chooses drugs administered in potent doses, the intent of this act is not to shorten life, even though it has that effect. It is a choice as to how to live while dying. Similarly, if a patient chooses to forego medical interventions that would have the effect of prolonging his or her life without in any way promising release from death, this also is a choice as to what is the most meaningful way to spend the remainder of life, however short that may be. The choice to use drugs to relieve pain and the choice not to use medical measures that cannot promise a cure for one's dying are no different in principle from the choices we make throughout our lives as to how much we will rest, how hard we will work, how little and how much medical intervention we will seek or tolerate, and the like. For society or physicians to map out life styles for individuals with respect to such decisions is surely beyond anything that we find in Stoic, Jewish, or Christian ethics. Such intervention in the liberty of individuals is far beyond what is required in any society whose rules are intended to constrain people against harming others.

But human freedom should not be extended to include the taking of one's own life. Causing one's own death cannot generally be justified, even when one is dying. To see why this is so, we have to consider how causing one's death does violence to one's self and harms others.

The person who causes his or her own death repudiates the meaningfulness and worth of his or her own life. To decide to initiate an act that has as its primary purpose to end one's life is to decide that that life has no worth to anyone, especially to oneself. It is an act that ends all choices regarding what one's life and whatever is left of it is to symbolize.

Suicide is the ultimately effective way of shutting out all other people from one's life. Psychologists have observed how hostility for others can be expressed through taking one's own life. People who might want access to the dying one to make restitution, offer reparation, bestow last kindnesses, or clarify misunderstandings are cut off by such an act. Every kind of potentially and actually meaningful contact and relation among persons is irrevocably severed except by means of memories and whatever life beyond death may offer. Certainly for those who are left behind by death, there can remain many years of suffering occasioned by that death. The sequence of dying an inevitable death can be much better accepted than the decision on the part of a dying one that he or she has no worth to anyone. An act that presupposes that final declaration leaves tragic overtones for anyone who participated in even the smallest way in that person's dying.

But the problem is even greater. If in principle a person can take his or her own life whenever he or she no longer finds it meaningful, there is nothing in principle that prevents anyone from taking his or her life, no matter what the circumstances. For if the decision hinges on whether one regards his or her own life as meaningful, anyone can regard his or her own life as meaningless even under circumstances that would appear to be most fortunate and opportune for an abundant life.

What about those who would commit suicide or request euthanasia in order to cease being a "burden" on those who are providing care for them? If it is a choice to accept death by refusing non-curative care that prolongs dying, the freedom to embrace death or give one's life in this way is honored by our ethic of benemortasia. What is rejected is the freedom to cause death whether by suicide or by assisting in one.

How a person dies has a definite meaning for those to whom that person is related. In the first year of bereavement, the rate of death among bereaved relatives of those who die in hospitals is twice that of bereaved relatives of those who die at home; sudden deaths away from hospital and home increase the death rate of the bereaved even more.

The courage to be, as expressed in Christian and Jewish thought, is more than the overcoming of the fear of death, although it includes that Stoic dimension. It is the courage to accept one's own life as having worth no matter what life may bring, including the threat of death, because that life remains meaningful and is regarded as worthy by God, regardless of what that life may be like. . . . The courage to be as a part recognizes that one is not merely one's own, that one's life is a gift bestowed and protected by the human community and by the ultimate forces that make up the cycle of birth and death. In the cycle of birth and death, there may be suffering, as there is joy, but suffering does not render a life meaningless or worthless. Suffering people need the support of others; suffering people should not be encouraged to commit suicide by their community, or that community ceases to be a community.

This consideration brings us to a further difficulty with voluntary euthanasia and its legalization. Not only does euthanasia involve suicide, but also, if legalized, it sanctions assistance in suicide by physicians. Legislation like the Voluntary Euthanasia Act of 1969 makes it a duty of the medical profession to take someone else's life for him. Here the principle not to kill is even further eroded and violated by giving the physician the power and the encouragement to decide that someone else's life is no longer worth living. The whole notion that a physician can engage in euthanasia implies acceptance of the principle that another person's life is no longer meaningful enough to sustain, a principle that does not afford protection for the lives of any of the most defenseless, voiceless, or otherwise dependent members of a community. Everyone in a community is potentially a victim of such a principle, particularly among members of racial minorities, the every young, and the very old.

Those who would argue that these consequences of a policy of voluntary euthanasia cannot be predicted fail to see two things: that we have already had an opportunity to observe what happens when the principle that sanctions euthanasia is accepted by a society; and that regardless of what the consequences may be of such acts, the acts themselves are wrong in principle.

With respect to the first point, Leo Alexander's (1949) very careful analysis of medical practices and attitudes of German physicians before and during the reign of Nazism in Germany should serve as a definite warning against the consequences of making euthanasia a public policy. He notes that the outlook of German physicians that led to their cooperation in what became a policy of mass murders,

started with the acceptance of that attitude, basic in the euthanasia movement, that there is such a thing as life not worthy to be lived. This attitude in its early stages concerned itself merely with the severely and chronically sick. Gradually the sphere of those to be included in this category was enlarged to include the socially unproductive, the racially unwanted, and finally all non-Germans. But it is important to realize that the infinitely small wedged-in lever from which this entire trend of mind received its impetus was the attitude toward the nonrehabilitable sick.

Those who reject out of hand any comparison of what happened in Nazi Germany with what we can expect here in the United States should consider current examples of medical practice in this nation. The treatment of mongoloids is a case in point. Now that the notion is gaining acceptance that a fetus diagnosed in the womb as mongoloid can, at the discretion of a couple or the pregnant woman, be justifiably aborted, instances of infanticide in hospitals are being reported. At Johns Hopkins Hospital, for example, an allegedly mongoloid infant whose parents would not permit an operation that is generally successful in securing normal physical health and development, was ordered to have "nothing by mouth," condemning that infant to a death that took 15 days. . . .

Someone may argue that the mongoloid was permitted to die, not killed. But this is faulty reasoning. In the case of an infant whose future life and happiness could be reasonably assured through surgery, we are not dealing with someone who is dying and with intervention that has no curative effect. The fact that some physicians refer to this as a case of permitting to die is an ominous portent of the dangers inherent in accepting the principle that a physician or another party can decide for a patient that his or her life is not worth living. Equally ominous is the assumption that this principle, once accepted, can easily be limited to cases of patients for whom no curative intervention is known to exist. . . .

The hesitation to commit suicide and the ambivalence of the dying about their worth should give one pause before one signs a declaration that empowers a physician to decide that at some point one can no longer be trusted as competent to judge whether or not one wants to die. Physicians are also frail humans, and mistaken diagnoses, research interests, and sometimes errors of judgment that stem from a desire for organs, are part of the practice of medicine.

Comatose patients pose special problems for an ethic of benemortasia as they do for the advocates of voluntary euthanasia. Where patients are judged to be irreversibly comatose and where sustained efforts have been made to restore such persons to consciousness, no clear case can be made for permitting to die, even though it seems merciful to do so. It seems that the best we can do is to develop some rough social and medical consensus about a reasonable length of time for keeping "alive" a person's organ systems after "brain death" has been decided. Because of the pressures to do research and to transplant organs, it may also be necessary to employ special patient advocates who are not physicians and nurses. These patient advocates, trained in medical ethics, would function as ombudsmen.

In summary, even if the practice of euthanasia were to be confined to those who voluntarily request an end to their lives, no physician could in good conscience participate in such an act. To decide directly to cause the death of a patient is to abandon a cardinal principle of medical practice— namely, to do no harm to one's patient. The relief of suffering, which is surely a time-honored role for the physician, does not extend to an act that presupposes that the life of a patient who is suffering is not worthy to be lived. As we have argued, not even the patient who is dying can justifiably and unilaterally universalize the principle by which a dying life would be declared to be worthless.

REVIEW AND DISCUSSION QUESTIONS

1. Describe the practical difficulties that Dyck envisions with euthanasia.
2. Explain Dyck's argument that euthanasia is wrong because it involves suicide. What does he think is wrong with suicide?
3. Most people feel better about euthanasia if there is informed consent from the person to be killed or allowed to die. What problems are there in being sure that the consent is truly voluntary? Truly informed?
4. Does suicide "repudiate the meaningfulness and worth of life"? Why or why not?
5. Do you agree that the distinction between causing and permitting death is important? Explain.
6. How would Dyck view the Cruzan opinion? Was it a euthanasia case? Was her life "meaningful" in Dyck's terms?
7. Is self-sacrifice (falling on a grenade to save a comrade, for example) suicide in Dyck's view? If not, then why is taking a pain-killing drug that leads to death also not suicide, assuming it is equally clear in both cases the person will die?

Active and Passive Euthanasia

James Rachels

In this essay, James Rachels does not defend euthanasia directly; instead, he argues that if we are going to use euthanasia, then we should use active rather than passive means to kill. Not only is it more humane, but the widely respected distinction between killing and letting die, he argues, makes no moral difference. Reliance on the distinction also encourages people to make medical decisions on irrelevant grounds, according to Rachels. James Rachels is University Professor of Philosophy at the University of Alabama, Birmingham.

Reprinted with permission from *The New England Journal of Medicine*, 292, no. 2 (Jan. 9, 1975), pp. 78–80.

The distinction between active and passive euthanasia is thought to be crucial for medical ethics. The idea is that it is permissible, at least in some cases, to withhold treatment and allow a patient to die, but it is never permissible to take any direct action designed to kill the patient. This doctrine seems to be accepted by most doctors, and is endorsed in a statement adopted by the House of Delegates of the American Medical Association on December 4, 1973:

The intentional termination of the life of one human being by another—mercy killing—is contrary to that for which the medical profession stands and is contrary to the policy of the American Medical Association.
The cessation of the employment of extraordinary means to prolong the life of the body when there is irrefutable evidence that biological death is imminent is the decision of the patient and/or his immediate family. The advice and judgment of the physician should be freely available to the patient and/or his immediate family.

However, a strong case can be made against this doctrine. In what follows I will set out some of the relevant arguments, and urge doctors to reconsider their views on this matter.

To begin with a familiar type of situation, a patient who is dying of incurable cancer of the throat is in terrible pain, which can no longer be satisfactorily alleviated. He is certain to die within a few days, even if present treatment is continued, but he does not want to go on living for those days since the pain is unbearable. So he asks the doctor for an end to it, and his family joins in the request.

Suppose the doctor agrees to withhold treatment, as the conventional doctrine says he may. The justification for his doing so is that the patient is in terrible agony, and since he is going to die anyway, it would be wrong to prolong his suffering needlessly. But now notice this. If one simply withholds treatment, it may take the patient longer to die, and so he may suffer more than he would if more direct action were taken and a lethal injection given. This fact provides strong reason for thinking that, once the initial decision not to prolong his agony has been made, active euthanasia is actually preferable to passive euthanasia, rather than the reverse. To say otherwise is to endorse the option that leads to more suffering rather than less, and is contrary to the humanitarian impulse that prompts the decision not to prolong his life in the first place.

Part of my point is that the process of being "allowed to die" can be relatively slow and painful, whereas being given a lethal injection is relatively quick and painless. Let me give a different sort of example. In the United States about one in 600 babies is born with Down's syndrome. Most of these babies are otherwise healthy—that is, with only the usual pediatric care, they will proceed to an otherwise normal infancy. Some, however, are born with congenital defects such as intestinal obstructions that require operations if they are to live. Sometimes, the parents and the doctor will decide not to operate, and let the infant die. Anthony Shaw describes what happens then.

. . . When surgery is denied [the doctor] must try to keep the infant from suffering while natural forces sap the baby's life away. As a surgeon whose natural inclination is to use the scalpel to fight off death, standing by and watching a salvageable baby die is the most emotionally exhausting experience I know. It is easy at a conference, in a theoretical discussion, to decide that such infants should be allowed to die. It is altogether different to stand by in the nursery and watch as dehydration and infection wither a tiny being over hours and days. This is a terrible ordeal for me and the hospital staff—much more so than for the parents who never set foot in the nursery.[1]

I can understand why some people are opposed to all euthanasia, and insist that such infants must be allowed to live. I think I can also understand why other people favor destroying these babies quickly and painlessly. But why should anyone favor letting "dehydration and infection wither a tiny being over hours and days?" The doctrine that says that a baby may be allowed to dehydrate and wither, but may not be given an injection that would end its life without suffering, seems so patently cruel as to require no further refutation. The strong language is not intended to offend, but only to put the point in the clearest possible way.

My second argument is that the conventional doctrine leads to decisions concerning life and death made on irrelevant grounds.

Consider again the case of the infants with Down's syndrome who need operations for congenital defects unrelated to the syndrome to live.

Sometimes, there is no operation, and the baby dies, but when there is no such defect, the baby lives on. Now, an operation such as that to remove an intestinal obstruction is not prohibitively difficult. The reason why such operations are not performed in these cases is, clearly, that the child has Down's syndrome and the parents and doctor judge that because of that fact it is better for the child to die.

But notice that this situation is absurd, no matter what view one takes of the lives and potentials of such babies. If the life of such an infant is worth preserving, what does it matter if it needs a simple operation? Or, if one thinks it better that such a baby should not live on, what difference does it make that it happens to have an unobstructed intestinal tract? In either case, the matter of life and death is being decided on irrelevant grounds. It is the Down's syndrome, and not the intestines, that is the issue. The matter should be decided, if at all, on that basis, and not be allowed to depend on the essentially irrelevant question of whether the intestinal tract is blocked.

What makes this situation possible, of course, is the idea that when there is an intestinal blockage, one can "let the baby die," but when there is no such defect there is nothing that can be done, for one must not "kill" it. The fact that this idea leads to such results as deciding life or death on irrelevant grounds is another good reason why the doctrine should be rejected.

One reason why so many people think that there is an important moral difference between active and passive euthanasia is that they think killing someone is morally worse than letting someone die. But is it? Is killing, in itself, worse than letting die? To investigate this issue, two cases may be considered that are exactly alike except that one involves killing whereas the other involves letting someone die. Then, it can be asked whether this difference makes any difference to the moral assessments. It is important that the cases be exactly alike, except for this one difference, since otherwise one cannot be confident that it is this difference, and not some other that accounts for any variation in the assessments of the two cases. So, let us consider this pair of cases:

In the first, Smith stands to gain a large inheritance if anything should happen to his six-year-old cousin. One evening while the child is taking his bath, Smith sneaks into the bathroom and drowns the child, and then arranges things so that it will look like an accident.

In the second, Jones also stands to gain if anything should happen to his six-year-old cousin. Like Smith, Jones sneaks in planning to drown the child in his bath. However, just as he enters the bathroom Jones sees the child slip and hit his head, and fall face down in the water. Jones is delighted; he stands by, ready to push the child's head back under if it is necessary, but it is not necessary. With only a little thrashing about, the child drowns all by himself, "accidentally," as Jones watches and does nothing.

Now Smith killed the child, whereas Jones "merely" let the child die. That is the only difference between them. Did either man behave better, from a moral point of view? If the difference between killing and letting die were in itself a morally important matter, one should say that Jones's behavior was less reprehensible than Smith's. But does one really want to say that? I think not. In the first place, both men acted from the same motive, personal gain, and both had exactly the same end in view when they acted. It may be inferred from Smith's conduct that he is a bad man, although that judgment may be withdrawn or modified if certain further facts are learned about him—for example, that he is mentally deranged. But would not the very same thing be inferred about Jones from his conduct? And would not the same further considerations also be relevant to any modification of this judgment? Moreover, suppose Jones pleaded, in his own defense, "After all, I didn't do anything except just stand there and watch the child drown. I didn't kill him; I only let him die." Again, if letting die were in itself less bad than killing, this defense should have at least some weight. But it does not. Such a "defense" can only be regarded as a grotesque perversion of moral reasoning. Morally speaking, it is no defense at all.

Now it may be pointed out, quite properly, that the cases of euthanasia with which doctors are concerned are not like this at all. They do not involve personal gain or the destruction of normal healthy children. Doctors are concerned only with cases in which the patient's life is of no further use to him, or in which the patient's life has become or will soon become a terrible burden. However, the point is the same in these cases: the bare difference between killing and letting die does not, in itself, make a moral difference. If a doctor lets a patient die, for humane reasons, he is in the same moral position as if he had given the patient a lethal injection for humane reasons. If his decision was wrong—if, for example, the patient's illness was in fact curable—the decision would be equally regrettable no matter which method was used to carry it out. And if the doctor's decision was the right one, the method used is not in itself important.

The AMA policy statement isolates the crucial issue very well; the crucial issue is "the intentional termination of the life of one human being by another." But after identifying this issue, and forbidding "mercy killing," the statement goes on to deny that the cessation of treatment is the intentional termination of a life. This is where the mistake comes in, for what is the cessation of treatment, in these circumstances, if it is not "the intentional termination of the life of one human being by another?" Of course it is exactly that, and if it were not, there would be no point to it.

Many people will find this judgment hard to accept. One reason, I think, is that it is very easy to conflate the question of whether killing is, in itself, worse than letting die, with the very different question of whether most actual cases of killing are more reprehensible than most actual cases of letting die. Most actual cases of killing are clearly terrible (think, for example, of all the murders reported in the newspapers), and one hears of such cases every day. On the other hand, one hardly ever hears of a case of letting die, except for the actions of doctors who are motivated by humanitarian reasons. So one learns to think of killing in a much worse light than of letting die. But this does not mean that there is something about killing that makes it in itself worse than letting die, for it is not the bare difference between killing and letting die that makes the difference in these cases. Rather, the other factors—the murderer's motive of personal gain, for example, contrasted with the doctor's humanitarian motivation—account for different reactions to the different cases.

I have argued that killing is not in itself any worse than letting die; if my contention is right, it follows that active euthanasia is not any worse than passive euthanasia. What arguments can be given on the other side? The most common, I believe, is the following:

"The important difference between active and passive euthanasia is that, in passive euthanasia, the doctor does not do anything to bring about the patient's death. The doctor does nothing, and the patient dies of whatever ills already afflict him. In active euthanasia, however, the doctor does something to bring about the patient's death; he kills him. The doctor who gives the patient with cancer a lethal injection has himself caused his patient's death; whereas if he merely ceases treatment, the cancer is the cause of the death."

A number of points need to be made here. The first is that it is not exactly correct to say that in passive euthanasia the doctor does nothing, for he does do one thing that is very important: he lets the patient die. "Letting someone die" is certainly different, in some respects, from other types of action—mainly in that it is a kind of action that one may perform by way of not performing certain other actions. For example, one may let a patient die by way of not giving medication, just as one may insult someone by way of not shaking his hand. But for any purpose of moral assessment, it is a type of action nonetheless. The decision to let a patient die is subject to moral appraisal in the same way that a decision to kill him would be subject to moral appraisal: it may be assessed as wise or unwise, compassionate or sadistic, right or wrong. If a doctor deliberately let a patient die who was suffering from a routinely curable illness, the doctor would certainly be to blame for what he had done, just as he would be to blame if he had needlessly killed the patient. Charges against him would then be appropriate. If so, it would be no defense at all for him to insist that he didn't "do anything." He would have done something very serious indeed, for he let his patient die.

Fixing the cause of death may be very important from a legal point of view, for it may determine whether criminal charges are brought against the doctor. But I do not think that this notion can be used to show a moral difference between active and passive euthanasia. The reason why it is considered bad to be the cause of someone's death is that death is regarded as a great evil—and so it is.

However, if it has been decided that euthanasia—even passive euthanasia—is desirable in a given case, it has also been decided that in this instance death is no greater an evil than the patient's continued existence. And if this is true, the usual reason for not wanting to be the cause of someone's death simply does not apply.

Finally, doctors may think that all of this is only of academic interest—the sort of thing that philosophers may worry about but that has no practical bearing on their own work. After all, doctors must be concerned about the legal consequences of what they do, and active euthanasia is clearly forbidden by the law. But even so, doctors should also be concerned with the fact that the law is forcing upon them a moral doctrine that may well be indefensible, and has a considerable effect on their practices. Of course, most doctors are not now in the position of being coerced in this matter, for they do not regard themselves as merely going along with what the law requires. Rather, in statements such as the AMA policy statement that I have quoted, they are endorsing this doctrine as a central point of medical ethics. In that statement, active euthanasia is condemned not merely as illegal but as "contrary to that for which the medical profession stands," whereas passive euthanasia is approved. However, the preceding considerations suggest that there is really no moral difference between the two, considered in themselves (there may be important moral differences in some cases in their consequences, but, as I pointed out, these differences may make active euthanasia, and not passive euthanasia, the morally preferable option). So, whereas doctors may have to discriminate between active and passive euthanasia to satisfy the law, they should not do any more than that. In particular, they should not give the distinction any added authority and weight by writing it into official statements of medical ethics.

NOTE

1. A. Shaw, "Doctor, Do We Have a Choice?" *The New York Times Magazine,* Jan. 30, 1972, p. 54.

REVIEW AND DISCUSSION QUESTIONS

1. How does Rachels explain the generally held belief that it is worse to kill than allow to die?
2. Describe the relevance of the Smith and Jones cases to Rachels's thesis.
3. What difference is there between the drowning-child case and euthanasia? Does that difference weaken Rachels's argument?
4. Are there arguments you think important that weaken Rachels's position that a doctor who lets a person die is in the same moral position as one who gives a lethal injection?
5. Compare the positions of Rachels and Dyck. How might Dyck respond to Rachels's central argument?

Defective Newborns
and the Morality of Termination

Richard B. Brandt

Whether done passively or actively, the decision to administer euthanasia to severely defective newborns is among the most difficult of all to make. Here Richard Brandt argues that each of four relevant considerations leads to the conclusion that in some cases, at least, euthanasia is the best thing to do. Richard B. Brandt is professor emeritus of philosophy of the University of Michigan.

One of the ethical issues uppermost in the minds of practicing physicians at the present time is what they should do, or recommend to be done, when a seriously defective infant is born. . . .

Historically, many writers, including Pope Pius XI in *Casti Connubii* (1930), have affirmed an absolute prohibition against killing anyone who is neither guilty of a capital crime, nor an unjust assailant threatening one's life (killing in self-defense), except in case of "extreme necessity." This view leaves some questions open. It certainly implies that a defective newborn may not be given a lethal injection. But it is far from clear that it requires complicated and expensive surgery and other treatment, over a period of years, in order to save a life. I wish merely to point out this ambiguity. Historically, I believe this tradition of absolute prohibition of "killing" derives from the Biblical injunction, "Thou shalt not kill," which itself seems to involve the same ambiguity. Does "not killing" mean saving a life by use of extraordinary means? However that may be, the Biblical injunction requires interpretation. Does it forbid suicide, killing of animals or even plants? If we ask ourselves, for instance, whether it is morally wrong for a terminally ill patient in great pain to terminate his own life, I think we feel that the Biblical injunction needs qualification, or at least reflection! And once we see that interpretation of the scope of a proposed moral principle must be un-

dertaken, we see that its force for the problem of interest to us must be reconsidered. My belief is that virtually all of us would think that there are circumstances in which it is morally not wrong for a person to terminate his own life. And I suggest that the Biblical injunction does not settle the question whether it is morally right or wrong, in the case of some defective newborns, not to perform surgery to prolong their lives, or even to terminate them painlessly.

I want now to consider four lines of thinking, which I believe bear on a reasonable answer to our problem. They all rest on what I take to be rather widespread moral convictions, which I imagine all of you will share.

1. THE PROSPECTIVE QUALITY OF LIFE OF DEFECTIVE NEWBORNS

Suppose that killing a defective newborn, or allowing it to die, would not be an *injury,* but would rather be doing the infant a favor. In that case we should feel intuitively less opposed to termination of newborns, and presumably rational persons would be more inclined to support a moral code permitting such an action. In that case we would feel rather as we do about frustrating a suicide attempt in order that the person be elaborately tor-

From Richard B. Brandt, "Defective Newborns and the Morality of Termination," in *Infanticide and the Value of Life*, ed. Marvin Kohl (Buffalo: Prometheus Books, 1978). Reprinted by permission.

tured to death at a later stage. André Malraux, in *Man's Fate,* describes an incident of the capture of a group of revolutionary soldiers by Chiang Kai-shek's army. There was no trial. One by one they were being taken to a nearby steam locomotive, with the firebox roaring, and they were executed by being thrust, headfirst, into the firebox. One of the captives had a few cyanide pills. He gave all but one of these to his friends, who accepted and used them gratefully. He kept one for himself. Then he spied a young boy, also one who was to be killed, shaking in terror. He gave his last pill to the young boy, electing to be killed in the firebox himself. I believe everybody would think he had done the young boy a favor, and that he performed a heroic act. Doubtless this is an extreme case, but we do sometimes do a person a favor by giving a person the means to shorten his own life. Are we doing something like this if we do not treat, or even painlessly terminate the life of, a severely defective newborn? A British physician, John Lorber, has claimed, on the basis of experience with over 1,000 *spina bifida* babies treated at Sheffield, England, that, in the words of Dr. Robert Reid's recent article in a Report of the Hastings Center, it is "possible to say with accuracy on the first day of life whether that baby would have an existence compatible with health, dignity and all other factors which contribute to a reasonable quality of life."

It may be said that we have no way of knowing what the conscious experiences of defective children are like, and that we have no competence in any case to decide when or what kind of life is bad or not worth living. Further, it may be said that predictions about a defective newborn's prospects for the future are precarious, in view of possible further advances of medicine. It does seem, however, that here as everywhere the rational person will follow the evidence about the present or future facts. But there is a serious question for philosophers, how to decide whether a life is bad or not worth living.

In the case of *some* defective newborns, it seems clear that their prospective life is bad. Suppose, as sometimes happens, a child is hydrocephalic with an extremely low I.Q., is blind and deaf, has no control over its body, and can only lie on its back all day and have all its needs taken care of by others, and even cries out with pain when it is touched or lifted. Infants born with *spina bifida*—and these number over 2 per 1,000 births—are normally not so badly off, but sometimes they are so.

But what criterion are we using if we say that such a life is bad? One criterion might be called a "happiness" criterion. If a person likes a moment of experience while he is having it, his life is so far good; if a person dislikes a moment of experience while he is having it, his life is so far bad. Based on such reactions, we might construct a "happiness curve" for a person, going up above the indifference axis when a moment of experience is liked—and how far above depending on how strongly it is liked—and dipping down below the line when a moment is disliked. Then this criterion would say that a life is worth living if there is a net balance of positive area. . . .

Is the prospective life of the seriously defective newborn, like the one described above, bad or good according to this criterion? One thing seems clear: that it is less good than is the prospective life of a normal infant. But is it bad?

We have to do some extrapolating from what we know. For instance, such a child will presumably suffer from severe sensory deprivation; he is simply not getting interesting stimuli. On the basis of laboratory data, it is plausible to think the child's experience is at best boring or uncomfortable. Insofar as the child's experience is painful, of course, its moments are on the negative side. One must suppose that such a child hardly suffers from disappointment, since it will not learn to expect anything exciting, beyond being fed and fondled, and these events will be regularly forthcoming. One might expect such a child to suffer from isolation and loneliness, but insofar as this is true the object of dislike probably should be classified as just sensory deprivation; dislike of loneliness seems to depend on the deprivation of past pleasure of human company. There are also some positive enjoyments: of eating, drinking, elimination, and so on. But the brief enjoyments can hardly balance the long stretches of boredom, discomfort, or even pain. I speculate that on the whole the lives of such children are bad, on the happiness criterion.

Naturally we cannot generalize about the cases of *all* "defective" newborns: there are all sorts of defects, and the cases I have described are about the worst. A child with moderately severe *spina bifida* may, if he survives the numerous operations, I suppose, adjust to the frustrations of immobility; he may become accustomed to the embarrassments of no bladder or bowel control; he may have some intellectual enjoyments like playing chess; he will suffer from observing what others have but he cannot, such as sexual satisfactions, in addition to the pain of repeated surgery. How does it all balance out? Surely not as very good, but perhaps above the indifference level.

It may fairly be said, I think, that the lives of some defective newborns are destined to be bad on the whole, and it would be a favor to them if their lives were terminated. Contrariwise, the prospective lives of many defective newborns are modestly pleasant, and it would be some injury to them to be terminated, albeit the lives they will live are ones some of us would prefer not to live at all.

2. CONSENT

Let us now leave the question whether termination of a defective newborn would be doing him a favor, and ask whether he might possibly be construed to *consent* to nontreatment or termination. The suggestion that the newborn might be so construed may seem absurd at the outset, but I wish to pursue the point. The reason I wish to pursue it is that intuitively we would all, I think, be *more* favorably inclined to conclude that it is right to let the defective die if we could think he did not object; and I think also that, in case he could be construed to consent, rational persons would be more ready to support a moral code permitting termination. Notice that we think that if an ill person has signified what we think a rational and deliberated desire to die, we are morally better justified in withdrawing life-supporting measures than we otherwise would be.

The newborn, however, is incapable of expressing his preference (giving consent) at all, much less expressing a rational deliberated preference. There could in theory be court-appointed guardians or proxies, presumably disinterested parties, authorized to give such consent on his behalf; but even so this would not be his consent.

Nevertheless, there is a fact about the mental life of the newborn (defective or not) such that, when we understand it, it seems to us clear that he would not *object*—even rationally or after deliberation if that were possible—to his life being terminated, or to his parents substituting another child in his place. This suggestion may seem absurd, but let us see. The explanation runs along the lines of an argument I once used to support the morality of abortion. I quote the paragraph in which this argument was introduced:[1]

Suppose I were seriously ill, and were told that, for a sizable fee, an operation to save "my life" could be performed, of the following sort: my brain would be removed to another body which could provide a normal life, but the unfortunate result of the operation would be that my memory and learned abilities would be wholly erased, and that the forming of memory brain traces must begin again from scratch, as in a newborn baby. Now, how large a fee would I be willing to pay for this operation, when the alternative is my peaceful demise? My own answer would be: None at all. I would take no interest in the continued existence of "myself" in that sense, and I would rather add the sizable fee to the inheritance of my children. I cannot see the point of forfeiting my children's inheritance in order to start off a person who is brand new except that he happens to enjoy the benefit of having my present brain, without the memory traces. It appears that some continuity of memory is a necessary condition for personal identity *in an important sense.*

My argument was that the position of a fetus, at the end of the first trimester, is essentially the same as that of the person contemplating this operation: he will consider that the baby born after six months will not be *he* in any *important* and *motivating* sense (there will be no continuity of memory, and indeed maybe nothing to have been remembered), and the later existence of this baby, in a sense bodily continuous with his present body, would be a matter of indifference to him. So, I argued, nothing is being done to the fetus that he would object to having done if he understood the situation.

What do I think is necessary in order for the continuation of my body with its conscious experiences to be worthwhile? One thing is that it be able to remember the events I can now remember; another is that it takes some interest in the projects I am now planning and remembers them as my projects; another is that it recognizes my friends and has warm feelings for them, and so on. Reflection on these states of a future continuation of my body with its experiences is what makes the idea motivating. Now such motivating reflection for a newborn is impossible: he has no memories that he wants recalled later; he has no plans to execute; he has no warm feelings for other persons. He has simply not had the length of life necessary for these to come about. Not only that: the conception of these things *cannot* be motivating because the prospect of some future state of affairs being motivating requires roughly a past experience in which similar states of affairs were satisfying, and he has not lived long enough for the requisite conditioning to have taken place. (The most one could say is that the image of warm milk in the child's mouth is attractive; he might answer affirmatively if it could be put to him whether he would be aversive to the idea of no more warm milk.) So we can say, not merely that the newborn does not *want the continuation of himself as a subject of experiences* (he has not the conceptual framework for this); he does not want *anything* which his own survival would promote. It is like the case of the operation: there is nothing I want which the survival of my brain with no memory would promote. Give the newborn as much *conceptual* framework as you like; the wants are not there, which could give significance to him of the continuance of his life.

The newborn, then, is bound to be *indifferent* to the idea of a continuation of the steam of his experiences, even if he has the idea of that clearly. It seems we can know this about him.

The fact that the newborn would be indifferent, however, is still not for it to be the case that the newborn, defective or not, gives *consent* to, or expresses a preference for, the termination of his life. *Consent* is a performance, normally linguistic, but always requiring some conventional *sign*. A newborn who has not yet learned how to signalize consent, cannot give consent. And it may be thought that this difference makes all the difference.

In order to see what difference it does make in this case, we should ask what makes adult consent morally important. Why is it that we think euthanasia can be practiced on an adult only if he gives his consent, at least his implied consent

(e.g., by previous statements)? There seem to be two reasons. The first is that a person is likely to be concerned with his own welfare, and to take steps to secure his own welfare, more than are others, even his good friends. Giving an individual control over his own life, and not permitting others to take control except when he consents, is normally to help secure his welfare. An individual may, of course, behave stupidly or shortsightedly, but we think that on the whole a person's welfare is best secured if decisions about it are in his hands; and it is *best for society in the normal case* if persons' own lives are well-served. There is a second reason. That is the feeling of security a person can have if he knows that major decisions about himself are in his own hands. When they are not, a person can easily, and in some cases very reasonably, suppose that other persons may well be able to do something to him which he would very much like them not to do. He does not have to worry about that if he knows they cannot do it without his consent.

Are things different with the newborn? At least he, like the fetus, is not yet able to suffer from insecurity; he cannot worry about what others may do to him. So the second reason for requiring consent cannot have any importance in his case. His situation is thus very unlike that of the senile adult; for an adult can worry about what others may do to him if they judge him senile. And this worry can well cast a shadow over a lot of life. But how about the first reason? Here matters are more complex. In the case of children, we think their own lives are better cared for if certain decisions are in the hands of *others:* the child may not want to visit the dentist, but the parents know that his best interests are served by going, and they make him go. The same for compulsory school attendance. And the same for the newborn. It seems that the newborn's interests may be as well served if other persons of goodwill, who know what his future is going to be like, make the decision for him.

But there is another point. This is that society in certain cases has a strong interest in what happens to a person, and in some of these cases we do not think that the individual's own consent is decisive. We do not think an individual must consent before he is inducted into the armed forces in a just war; nor do we think that we must have a criminal's consent before he is punished for a crime; nor do we think we need an aggressor's consent before we use force to repel his aggression. If there is only one kidney machine, and after careful reflection we think that Mr. A has a much better claim to its use than does Mr. B, must we get Mr. B's consent before we are justified in allocating its use to Mr. A? Now, we must ask whether the position of the seriously defective newborn, a full-scale treatment of which may consume the time of many people and cost millions of dollars, is perhaps somewhat similar.

Everything considered, then, it seems that explicit or even implied consent does not have the moral weight in the case of the newborn that it has in the case of the normal adult.

On the one hand, then, the newborn will not care whether his life is terminated, even if he understood his situation perfectly; and, on the other hand, it seems that there are various reasons casting doubt on whether explicit *consent* has in any case the moral weight in his case that it has for adults. So, while it seems true that we would feel better about permitting termination of defective newborns if only they could give rational and deliberated consent and gave it, nevertheless when we bear the foregoing points in mind, the absence of consent does not seem morally crucial in their case. We can understand why rational persons deciding which moral code to support for their society might not make the giving of consent a necessary condition of feeling free to terminate an infant's life when such action was morally indicated by the other features of the situation.

3. REPLACEMENT IN ORDER TO GET A BETTER LIFE

I now wish to call your attention to some convictions which I think most of us will share, which seem to bear on our problem. My attention was called to them by Derek Parfit.

Suppose a woman wants a child, but is told that if she conceives a child now it will be defective, whereas if she waits three months she will produce a normal child. Obviously we think it would be outrageous morally for the mother not to delay. Of course, if she delays, she will not have the *same*

child as the one she would have had if she had not delayed; but we do not think we need worry about any rights of the child she might have had, in view of the fact that the later-conceived child will have a better life.

Suppose, however, a woman conceives but discovers three months later, after amniocentesis, that the fetus will develop into a defective child, but that in all probability she can have a normal child later if she has an abortion and tries again. Now this time there is still the same reason for having the abortion that there was formerly for the delay: that she will produce another child with a better life. Ought she then to have the abortion? If the child's life is bad, he could well complain that he had been injured by being brought to term, and in fact some court suits along this line have actually been filed. Would the child about to be aborted in favor of the later normal child, be inclined to complain, if he could grasp the situation? Not if the argument stated earlier is correct. I have not really stated that the mother in this case should have an abortion; I have only asked a rhetorical question, and that is not an argument. I do believe, however, that the vast majority of persons would think she should, and it is for this reason that amniocentesis is becoming so widespread, when there are reasons to expect congenital defects.

But now suppose the woman cannot discover until after she gives birth, that her child is seriously defective. She learns then that, were she to conceive again, it is highly probable that she would have a normal child. Are things really different, in the first few days? One might think that a benevolent person would want, in each of these cases, the substitution of a normal child for the defective one, of the better life for the worse one.

4. THE PSYCHOLOGICAL AND MATERIAL COSTS AND THEIR RELEVANCE

It is agreed that the burden of care for a seriously defective infant, say one born with *spina bifida*, is huge. The cost of surgery alone for an infant with *spina bifida* has been estimated to be around $275,000. In many places this cost must be borne by the family of the child, and there is in addition the cost of care in an institution if the child's condition does not permit care at home—and a very modest estimate of the monthly cost at present is $1,100. To meet even the surgical costs, not to mention monthly payments for continuing care, the lives of members of the family may have to be lived at a spartan level, for many years. The siblings of the defective may have to be deprived of a college education, and so on.

The psychological effects of the situation, and probably the more so if care is provided at home, are far-reaching. Just what are these costs? Doubtless they vary from case to case. One knows of cases in which the suicide of a sibling seems very clearly to have been caused by the presence of the defective infant in the home. The life of the parents may come to revolve in a small circle around the child. The family may feel unable to have a social life because it is uncomfortable to have guests to a meal given the unpredictable behavior of the defective family member. If the child is in the home, either the parents must remain at home or they must put up with the continuing presence of a caretaker. One can go on and on in spelling out just what life in such a family may be like, in the case of a severely defective infant. In one way or another the continued existence of the child is apt to reduce dramatically the quality of life of the family as a whole.

It can be and has been argued that such costs, while real, are irrelevant to the moral problem of what should be done. (Professor Philippa Foot so argues in a recent article on "Euthanasia," in *Philosophy and Public Affairs* [6, 1977, 85–112].) She says: "So it is not for their sake but to avoid trouble to others that they are allowed to die. When brought out into the open this seems unacceptable; at least we do not easily accept the principle that adults who need special care should be counted too burdensome to be kept alive." I would think that "to avoid trouble to others" is hardly the terminology to describe the havoc that is apt to be produced. I agree that adults should not be allowed to die, or actively terminated, without their consent, except possibly when they cannot give consent but are in pain; but the reasons which justify different behavior in the two situations have already been discussed. It seems obvious, however, that rational persons, when deciding which

moral code to support, would take these human costs into account. As indeed they should: for the parents and siblings are also human beings with lives to live, and any sacrifices a given law or moral system might call on them to make must be taken into account in deciding between laws and moral codes. Everyone will feel sympathy for a helpless newborn; but everyone should also think equally vividly, of all the others who will suffer and just how they will suffer—and, of course, as indicated above, of just what kind of life the defective newborn will have in any case. There is a choice here between allowing a newborn to die (possibly a favor to it, and in any case not a serious loss), and imposing a very heavy burden on the family for many years to come.

Philosophers who think the cost to others is irrelevant to what should be done should reflect that we do not accept the general principle that lives should be saved at no matter what cost. For instance, ships are deliberately built with only a certain margin of safety; they could be built so that they would hardly sink in any storm, but to do so would be economically unfeasible. We do not think we should require a standard of safety for automobiles that goes beyond a certain point of expense and inconvenience; we are prepared to risk a few extra deaths. And how about the lives we are willing to lose in war, in order to assure a certain kind of economic order, or democracy or free speech? Surely there is a point at which the loss of a life (or rather the abbreviation of a life) and the cost to others become comparable. Is it obvious that the continuation of a marginal kind of life for a child takes moral precedence over providing a college education for one or more of his siblings? Some comparisons will be hard to make, but continuing even a marginally *pleasant* life hardly has *absolute* priority. . . .

5. DRAWING LINES

There are two final questions which must be answered in any complete account of what is the morally right thing to do about defective newborns.

The first is: If a decision to terminate is made, how soon must it be made and the conclusion effectuated? Obviously it could not be postponed to the age of five, or of three, or even a year and a half. At those ages, all the reasons for insisting on consent are already cogent. And at those ages, the child will already care what happens to him. But ten days is tolerable. Doubtless advances in medicine will permit detection of serious prospective defects early in pregnancy, and this issue of how many days will not arise.

Second, the argument from the quality of the prospective life of the defective newborn requires that we decide which defects are so serious that the kind of life the defective child can have gives it no serious claim as compared with the social costs. Obviously this issue must be thought through and some guidelines established. Some guidelines have been proposed, and used, for instance by Dr. Lorber in Sheffield. Roughly his guidelines are, to cite Dr. Reid's paper, "First, the site of the *spina bifida*: if this is on the lower half of the back then the baby will be severely paralysed and incontinent and probably have severe hydrocephalus. Second, paralysis: if a baby is paralysed at birth, it will never recover its muscle power. Third, gross distortion of the spine as a result of, for example,

kyphosis: those affected are among the most handicapped children and the consequences tend to worsen with time. Fourth, gross hydrocephalus: a simple tape measure round the baby's head can establish the extent of the problem. Fifth, other gross congenital malformations: along with *spina bifida*, conditions such as congenital heart disease and mongolism can occur together." Dr. Lorber's proposal was that a child with any of these characteristics should not be recommended for treatment.

Criteria of this sort can be thought through and established by the medical profession, rather in the way in which the American Law Institute has drawn up recommendations for the reform of the penal codes of the various states. This task of framing criteria is certainly not one for philosophers. As I see it, it is a task to be undertaken by thoughtful medical specialists with wide experience, who at the same time are familiar with the morally relevant considerations, such as those I have been discussing. We might criticize specific proposals, but it would seem that the framing of some is a step in the right direction, which it is to be hoped the medical profession will undertake.

NOTE

1. "The morality of abortion," in an earlier form in *The Monist* 56 (1972), 504–526, and in revised form in *Abortion: Pro and Con*, ed. R. L. Perkins (Cambridge, MA: Schenkman, 1974).

REVIEW AND DISCUSSION QUESTIONS

1. How would Brandt decide when a life is not worth living?
2. Why does Brandt argue that an infant (even a healthy one) would be indifferent to being killed?
3. Brandt argues that the reasons to seek consent generally do not apply to infants. Why?
4. Are there other reasons, besides the ones Brandt mentions, that make getting consent important?
5. Why does Brandt think active is better than passive euthanasia?
6. Suppose, after deciding not to have the brain transplant described in the reading, you find out that the body in which your brain is now located will be tortured. Would you still take no interest in the transfer?
7. How would Dyck respond to Brandt's essay? Which position do you find more reasonable? Explain.
8. Compare and contrast the positions of the authors in this section with those of the Justices who wrote the *Cruzan* decision.

7
Abortion

Readings in Section 7 represent a broad range of views on one of the most controversial moral and legal issues in the United States: abortion. Two themes run through these readings. The first, and most often discussed, is the moral status of the fetus. Is it, as some have suggested, no more valuable than any other piece of human tissue, like a tonsil? Or is it, as others passionately believe, the moral equivalent of a newborn baby and therefore entitled to the same moral and legal respect we give each other? The second question involves women's rights. Can a pregnant woman legitimately get an abortion, based on her right to control her body, even if there is another person inside her?

Abortion as Constitutionally Protected:

Roe v. *Wade*

Few constitutional cases have created more controversy, both moral and legal, than abortion. *Roe* v. *Wade* is the famous Supreme Court decision that guarantees women the right to get an abortion. The case began in August 1969 when Norma McCorvey discovered she was pregnant. Too poor to travel from Texas to California, the nearest state where abortions were legal, she sought help. A friend introduced her to two recent law school graduates, Sarah Weddington and Linda Coffee, and the three decided to challenge the constitutionality of Texas's law forbidding abortion.

Norma McCorvey never got her abortion, nor did she see her baby girl again after leaving the hospital. Hoping to remain anonymous, she became Jane Roe for purposes of the lawsuit she was bringing against Henry Wade, District Attorney for Dallas County, Texas. Four years later, the Supreme Court took the controversial step of extending the right to privacy to include the right to get an abortion. Justice Blackmun wrote the majority opinion in this famous case; Justice White wrote a dissenting opinion. Justice Blackmun continued for years after this decision to get hate mail and threats; once, a pro-life advocate fired a bullet into his house.

Justice Blackmun Delivered the Opinion of the Court: Three reasons have been advanced to explain historically the enactment of criminal abortion laws in the nineteenth century and to justify their continued existence.

It has been argued occasionally that these laws were the product of a Victorian social concern to discourage illicit sexual conduct. Texas, however, does not advance this justification in the present case, . . .

410 U.S. 113 (1973). Some citations and footnotes omitted.

A second reason is concerned with abortion as a medical procedure. When most criminal abortion laws were first enacted, the procedure was a hazardous one for the woman. . . .

Modern medical techniques have altered this situation. Appellants and various amici refer to medical data indicating that abortion in early pregnancy, that is, prior to the end of first trimester, although not without its risk, is now relatively safe. . . . The State has a legitimate interest in seeing to it that abortion, like any other medical procedure, is performed under circumstances that insure maximum safety for the patient. This interest obviously extends at least to the performing physician and his staff, to the facilities involved, to the availability of aftercare, and to adequate provision for any complication or emergency that might arise. The prevalence of high mortality rates at illegal "abortion mills" strengthens, rather than weakens, the State's interest in regulating the conditions under which abortions are performed. Moreover, the risk to the woman increases as her pregnancy continues. Thus the State retains a definite interest in protecting the woman's own health and safety when an abortion is proposed at a late stage of pregnancy.

The third reason is the State's interest—some phrase it in terms of duty—in protecting prenatal life. Some of the argument for this justification rests on the theory that a new human life is present from the moment of conception. The State's interest and general obligation to protect life then extends, it is argued, to prenatal life. Only when the life of the pregnant mother herself is at stake, balanced against the life she carries within her, should the interest of the embryo or fetus not prevail. Logically, of course, a legitimate state interest in this area need not stand or fall on acceptance of the belief that life begins at conception or at some other point prior to live birth. In assessing the State's interest, recognition may be given to the less rigid claim that as long as at least *potential* life is involved, the State may assert interests beyond the protection of the pregnant woman alone.

Parties challenging state abortion laws have sharply disputed in some courts the contention that a purpose of these laws, when enacted, was to protect prenatal life. . . . There is some scholarly support for this view of original purpose. The few state courts called upon to interpret their laws in the nineteenth and early twentieth centuries did focus on the State's interest in protecting the woman's health rather than in preserving the embryo and fetus. . . .

The Constitution does not explicitly mention any right of privacy. In a line of decisions, however, . . . the Court has recognized that a right of personal privacy, or a guarantee of certain areas or zones of privacy, does exist under the Constitution. . . .

This right of privacy, whether it be founded in the Fourteenth Amendment's concept of personal liberty and restrictions upon state action, as we feel it is, or, as the District Court determined, in the Ninth Amendment's reservation of rights to the people, is broad enough to encompass a woman's decision whether or not to terminate her pregnancy. The detriment that the State would impose upon the pregnant woman by denying this choice altogether is apparent. Specific and direct harm medically diagnosable even in early pregnancy may be involved. Maternity, or additional offspring, may force upon the woman a distressful life and future. Psychological harm may be imminent. Mental and physical health may be taxed by child care. There is also the distress, for all concerned, associated with the unwanted child, and there is the problem of bringing a child into a family already unable, psychologically and otherwise, to care for it. In other cases, as in this one, the additional difficulties and continuing stigma of unwed motherhood may be involved. All these are factors the woman and her responsible physician necessarily will consider in consultation.

On the basis of elements such as these, appellants and some *amici* argue that the woman's right is absolute and that she is entitled to terminate her pregnancy at whatever time, in whatever way, and for whatever reason she alone chooses. With this we do not agree. Appellants' arguments that Texas either has no valid interest at all in regulating the abortion decision, or no interest strong enough to support any limitation upon the woman's sole determination, is unpersuasive. The Court's decisions recognizing a right of privacy also acknowledge that some state regulation in areas protected by that right is appropriate. As noted above, a state may properly assert important interests in safe-guarding health, in maintaining medical standards, and in protecting potential life. At some point in pregnancy, these respective interests become sufficiently compelling to sustain regulation of the factors that govern the abortion decision. The privacy right involved, therefore, cannot be said to be absolute. In fact, it is not clear to us that the claim asserted by some *amici* that one has an unlimited right to do with one's body as one pleases bears a close relationship to the right of privacy previously articulated in the Court's decisions. . . .

Where certain "fundamental rights" are involved, the Court has held that regulation limiting these rights may be justified only by a "compelling state interest," . . . and that legislative enactments must be narrowly drawn to express only the legitimate state interests at stake. . . .

A. The appellee and certain *amici* argue that the fetus is a "person" within the language and meaning of the Fourteenth Amendment. In support of this they outline at length and in detail the well-known facts of fetal development. If this suggestion of personhood is established, the appellant's case, of course, collapses, for the fetus' right to life is then guaranteed specifically by the Amendment. The appellant conceded as much on reargument. On the other hand, the appellee conceded on reargument that no case should be cited that holds that a fetus is a person within the meaning of the Fourteenth Amendment.

The Constitution does not define "person" in so many words. . . . But in nearly all these instances, the use of the word is such that it has application only postnatally. None indicates with any assurance that it has any possible pre-natal application.[1]

All this, together with our observation, *supra,* that throughout the major portion of the nineteenth century prevailing legal abortion practices were far freer than they are today, persuades us that the word "person," as used in the Fourteenth Amendment, does not include the unborn. . . .

This conclusion, however, does not of itself fully answer the contentions raised by Texas, and we pass on to other considerations.

B. The pregnant woman cannot be isolated in her privacy. She carries an embryo and, later, a fe-

tus, if one accepts the medical definitions of the developing young in the human uterus. . . .

Texas urges that, apart from the Fourteenth Amendment, life begins at conception and is present throughout pregnancy, and that, therefore, the State has a compelling interest in protecting that life from and after conception. We need not resolve the difficult question of when life begins. When those trained in the respective disciplines of medicine, philosophy, and theology are unable to arrive at any consensus, the judiciary, at this point in the development of man's knowledge, is not in a position to speculate as to the answer.

It should be sufficient to note briefly the wide divergence of thinking on this most sensitive and difficult question. There has always been strong support for the view that life does not begin until live birth. This was the belief of the Stoics. It appears to be the predominant, though not the unanimous, attitude of the Jewish faith. It may be taken to represent also the position of a large segment of the Protestant community, insofar as that can be ascertained; organized groups that have taken a formal position on the abortion issue have generally regarded abortion as a matter for the conscience of the individual and her family. As we have noted, the common law found greater significance in quickening. Physicians and their scientific colleagues have regarded that event with less interest and have tended to focus either upon conception or upon live birth or upon the interim point at which the fetus becomes "viable," that is, potentially able to live outside the mother's womb, albeit with artificial aid. Viability is usually placed at about seven months (28 weeks) but may occur earlier, even at 24 weeks. The Aristotelian theory of "mediate animation," that held sway throughout the Middle Ages and the Renaissance in Europe, continued to be official Roman Catholic dogma until the nineteenth century, despite opposition to this "ensoulment" theory from those in the Church who would recognize the existence of life from the moment of conception. The latter is now, of course, the official belief of the Catholic Church. As one of the briefs *amicus* discloses, this is a view strongly held by many non-Catholics as well, and by many physicians. Substantial problems for precise definition of this view are posed, however, by new embryological data that purport to indicate that conception is a "process" over time, rather than an event, and by new medical techniques such as menstrual extraction, the "morning-after" pill, implantation of embryos, artificial insemination, and even artificial wombs.

In areas other than criminal abortion the law has been reluctant to endorse any theory that life, as we recognize it, begins before live birth or to accord legal rights to the unborn except in narrowly defined situations and except when the rights are contingent upon live birth. For example, the traditional rule of tort law had denied recovery for prenatal injuries even though the child was born alive. That rule has been changed in almost every jurisdiction. In most States recovery is said to be permitted only if the fetus was viable, or at least quick, when the injuries were sustained, though few courts have squarely so held. . . . [U]nborn children have been recognized as acquiring rights or interests by way of inheritance or other devolution of property, and have been represented by guardians. . . .

In view of all this, we do not agree that, by adopting one theory of life, Texas may override the rights of the pregnant woman that are at stake. We repeat, however, that the State does have an important and legitimate interest in preserving and protecting the health of the pregnant woman, whether she be a resident of the State or a non-resident who seeks medical consultation and treatment there, and that it has still another important and legitimate interest in protecting the potentiality of human life. These interests are separate and distinct. Each grows in substantiality as the woman approaches term and, at a point during pregnancy, each becomes "compelling."

With respect to the State's important and legitimate interest in the health of the mother, the "compelling" point, in the light of present medical knowledge, is at approximately the end of the first trimester. This is so because of the now established medical fact, referred to above, that until the end of the first trimester mortality in abortion is less than mortality in normal childbirth. It follows that, from and after this point, a State may regulate the abortion procedure to the extent that the regulation reasonably relates to the preservation and protection of maternal health. Examples of permissible state regulation in this area are requirements as to the qualifications of the person who is to perform the abortion; as to the licensure of that person; as to the facility in which the procedure is to be performed, that is, whether it must be a hospital or may be a clinic or some other place of less-than-hospital status; as to the licensing of the facility; and the like.

This means, on the other hand, that, for the period of pregnancy prior to this "compelling" point, the attending physician, in consultation with his patient, is free to determine, without regulation by the State, that in his medical judgment the patient's pregnancy should be terminated. If that decision is reached, the judgment may be effectuated by an abortion free of interference by the State.

With respect to the State's important and legitimate interest in potential life, the "compelling" point is at viability. This is so because the fetus then presumably has the capability of meaningful life outside the mother's womb. State regulation protective of fetal life after viability thus has both logical and biological justifications. If the State is interested in protecting fetal life after viability, it may go so far as to proscribe abortion during that period except when it is necessary to preserve the life or health of the mother.

Measured against these standards, Art. 1196 of the Texas Penal Code, in restricting legal abortions to those "procured or attempted by medical advice for the purpose of saving the life of the mother," sweeps too broadly. The statute makes no distinction between abortions performed early in pregnancy and those performed later, and it limits to a single reason, "saving" the mother's life, the legal justification for the procedure. The statute, therefore, cannot survive the constitutional attack made upon it here

Mr. Justice White, . . . Dissenting: At the heart of the controversy in these cases are those recurring pregnancies that pose no danger whatsoever to the life or health of the mother but are nevertheless unwanted for any one or more of a variety of reasons—convenience, family planning, economics, dislike of children, the embarrassment of illegitimacy, etc. The common claim before us is that for any one of such reasons, or for no reason at all, and without asserting or claiming any threat to life or health, any woman is entitled to an abortion at her request if she is able to find a medical advisor willing to undertake the procedure.

The Court for the most part sustains this position: During the period prior to the time the fetus becomes viable, the Constitution of the United States values the convenience, whim or caprice of the putative mother more than the life or potential life of the fetus; the Constitution, therefore, guarantees the right to an abortion as against any state law or policy seeking to protect the fetus from an abortion not prompted by more compelling reasons of the mother.

With all due respect, I dissent. I find nothing in the language or history of the Constitution to support the Court's judgment. The Court simply fashions and announces a new constitutional right for pregnant mothers and, with scarcely any reason or authority for its action, invests that right with sufficient substance to override most existing state abortion statutes. The upshot is that the people and the legislatures of the 50 States are constitutionally disentitled to weigh the relative importance of the continued existence and development of the fetus on the one hand against a spectrum of possible impacts on the mother on the other hand. As an exercise of raw judicial power, the Court per-

haps has authority to do what it does today; but in my view its judgment is an improvident and extravagant exercise of the power of judicial review which the Constitution extends to this Court.

The Court apparently values the convenience of the pregnant mother more than the continued existence and development of the life or potential life which she carries. Whether or not I might agree with that marshalling of values, I can in no event join the Court's judgment because I find no constitutional warrant for imposing such an order of priorities on the people and legislatures of the States. In a sensitive area such as this, involving as it does issues over which reasonable men may easily and heatedly differ, I cannot accept the Court's exercise of its clear power of choice by interposing a constitutional barrier to state efforts to protect human life and by investing mothers and doctors with the constitutionally protected right to exterminate it. This issue, for the most part, should be left with the people and to the political processes the people have devised to govern their affairs.

It is my view, therefore, that the Texas statute is not constitutionally infirm because it denies abortions to those who seek to serve only their convenience rather than to protect their life or health. . . .

NOTE

1. When Texas urges that a fetus is entitled to Fourteenth Amendment protection as a person, it faces a dilemma. Neither in Texas nor in any other State are all abortions prohibited. Despite broad proscription, an exception always exists. The exception contained in Art. 1196, for an abortion procured or attempted by medical advice for the purpose of saving the life of the mother, is typical. But if the fetus is a person who is not to be deprived of life without due process of law, and if the mother's condition is the sole determinant, does not the Texas exception appear to be out of line with the Amendment's command?

There are other inconsistencies between Fourteenth Amendment status and the typical abortion statute. It has already been pointed out, . . . that in Texas the woman is not a principal or an accomplice with respect to an abortion upon her. If the fetus is a person, why is the woman not a principal or an accomplice? Further, the penalty for criminal abortion specified by Art. 1195 is significantly less than the maximum penalty for murder prescribed by Art. 1257 of the Texas Penal Code. If the fetus is a person, may the penalties be different?

REVIEW AND DISCUSSION QUESTIONS

1. According to Justice Blackmun, what have been the state's reasons for preventing abortion?
2. Why does the Court reject the view that a fetus is a "person" within the meaning of the Constitution?
3. Explain the "trimester" approach taken by Justice Blackmun in this case.

4. On what basis does Justice White dissent?
5. Does Blackmun's majority opinion successfully avoid the issue of the moral status of a fetus, as he suggests? Explain.

A Defense of Abortion

Judith Jarvis Thomson

This article is one of the best known in recent philosophical writing; it is discussed in philosophy courses, law schools, as well as many other places. Part of the essay's appeal is that it attempts to avoid what is usually thought to be the central problem in the abortion debate, the status of the fetus. Thomson, however, defends the right to get an abortion even if it is assumed that the fetus has the same moral status as a child. It is often assumed that the morality of abortion depends entirely upon when a developing human is "alive" or becomes a "person." Thomson thus disputes this. Employing an ingenious set of analogies, including one about a violinist who requires the use of your kidneys for nine months, she argues that a mother's right to her body allows her to "unplug" from a fetus even if we assume it is a person. And this is true, she contends, not just in cases in which the woman is pregnant because of rape. Judith Jarvis Thomson is professor of philosophy at Massachusetts Institute of Technology.

Most opposition to abortion relies on the premise that the fetus is a human being, a person, from the moment of conception. The premise is argued for, but, as I think, not well. Take, for example, the most common argument. We are asked to notice that the development of a human being from conception through birth into childhood is continuous; then it is said that to draw a line, to choose a point in this development and say "before this point the thing is not a person, after this point it is a person" is to make an arbitrary choice, a choice for which in the nature of things no good reason can be given. It is concluded that the fetus is, or anyway that we had better say it is, a person from the moment of conception. But this conclusion does not follow. Similar things might be said about the development of an acorn into an oak tree, and it does not follow that acorns are oak trees, or that we had better say they are. Arguments of this form are sometimes called "slippery slope arguments"—the phrase is perhaps self-explanatory—and it is dismaying that opponents of abortion rely on them so heavily and uncritically.

I am inclined to agree, however, that the prospects for "drawing a line" in the development of the fetus look dim. I am inclined to think also that we shall probably have to agree that the fetus has already become a human person well before birth. Indeed, it comes as a surprise when one first learns how early in its life it begins to acquire human characteristics. By the tenth week, for example, it already has a face, arms and legs, fingers and toes; it has internal organs, and brain activity is detectable. On the other hand, I think that the premise is false, that the fetus is not a person from the moment of conception. A newly fertilized

Thomson, Judith Jarvis, "A Defense of Abortion," *Philosophy and Public Affairs,* 1, no. 1 (1971), 47–66. © 1971 by Princeton University Press. Reprinted by permission of Princeton University Press. Section titles added.

ovum, a newly implanted clump of cells, is no more a person than an acorn is an oak tree. But I shall not discuss any of this. For it seems to me to be of great interest to ask what happens if, for the sake of argument, we allow the premise. How, precisely, are we supposed to get from there to the conclusion that abortion is morally impermissible? Opponents of abortion commonly spend most of their time establishing that the fetus is a person, and hardly any time explaining the step from there to the impermissibility of abortion. Perhaps they think the step too simple and obvious to require much comment. Or perhaps instead they are simply being economical in argument. Many of those who defend abortion rely on the premise that the fetus is not a person, but only a bit of tissue that will become a person at birth; and why pay out more arguments than you have to? Whatever the explanation, I suggest that the step they take is neither easy nor obvious, that it calls for closer examination than it is commonly given, and that when we do give it this closer examination we shall feel inclined to reject it.

I propose, then, that we grant that the fetus is a person from the moment of conception. How does the argument go from here? Something like this, I take it. Every person has a right to life. So the fetus has a right to life. No doubt the mother has a right to decide what shall happen in and to her body; everyone would grant that. But surely a person's right to life is stronger and more stringent than the mother's right to decide what happens in and to her body, and so outweighs it. So the fetus may not be killed; an abortion may not be performed.

It sounds plausible. But now let me ask you to imagine this. You wake up in the morning and find yourself back to back in bed with an unconscious violinist. A famous unconscious violinist. He has been found to have a fatal kidney ailment, and the Society of Music Lovers has canvassed all the available medical records and found that you alone have the right blood type to help. They have therefore kidnapped you, and last night the violinist's circulatory system was plugged into yours, so that your kidneys can be used to extract poisons from his blood as well as your own. The director of the hospital now tells you, "Look, we're sorry the Society of Music Lovers did this to you—we

would never have permitted it if we had known. But still, they did it, and the violinist now is plugged into you. To unplug you would be to kill him. But never mind, it's only for nine months. By then he will have recovered from his ailment, and can safely be unplugged from you." Is it morally incumbent on you to accede to this situation? No doubt it would be very nice of you if you did, a great kindness. But do you have to accede to it? What if it were not nine months, but nine years? Or longer still? What if the director of the hospital says, "Tough luck, I agree, but you've now got to stay in bed, with the violinist plugged into you, for the rest of your life. Because remember this. All persons have a right to life, and violinists are persons. Granted you have a right to decide what happens in and to your body, but a person's right to life outweighs your right to decide what happens in and to your body. So you cannot ever be unplugged from him." I imagine you would regard this as outrageous, which suggests that something really is wrong with that plausible-sounding argument I mentioned a moment ago.

In this case, of course, you were kidnapped; you didn't volunteer for the operation that plugged the violinist into your kidneys. Can those who oppose abortion on the ground I mentioned make an exception for a pregnancy due to rape? Certainly. They can say that persons have a right to life only if they didn't come into existence because of rape; or they can say that all persons have a right to life, but that some have less of a right to life than others, in particular, that those who come into existence because of rape have less. But these statements have a rather unpleasant sound. Surely the question of whether you have a right to life at all, or how much of it you have, shouldn't turn on the question of whether or not you are the product of a rape. And in fact the people who oppose abortion on the ground I mentioned do not make this distinction, and hence do not make an exception in case of rape.

Nor do they make an exception for a case in which the mother has to spend the nine months of her pregnancy in bed. They would agree that would be a great pity, and hard on the mother; but all the same, all persons have a right to life, the fetus is a person, and so on. I suspect, in fact, that they would not make an exception for a case in which, miraculously enough, the pregnancy went on for nine years, or even the rest of the mother's life.

Some won't even make an exception for a case in which continuation of the pregnancy is likely to shorten the mother's life; they regard abortion as impermissible even to save the mother's life. Such cases are nowadays very rare, and many opponents of abortion do not accept this extreme view. All the same, it is a good place to begin: a number of points of interest come out in respect to it.

1. THE EXTREME ANTI-ABORTION VIEW

Let us call the view that abortion is impermissible even to save the mother's life "the extreme view." I want to suggest first that it does not issue from the argument I mentioned earlier without the addition of some fairly powerful premises. Suppose a woman has become pregnant, and now learns that she has a cardiac condition such that she will die if she carries the baby to term. What may be done for her? The fetus, being a person, has a right to life, but as the mother is a person too, so has she a right to life. Presumably they have an equal right to life. How is it supposed to come out that an abortion may not be performed? If mother and child have an equal right to life, shouldn't we perhaps flip a coin? Or should we add to the mother's right to life her right to decide what happens in and to her body, which everybody seems to be ready to grant—the sum of her rights now outweighing the fetus' right to life?

The most familiar argument here is the following. We are told that performing the abortion would be directly killing the child, whereas doing nothing would not be killing the mother, but only letting her die. Moreover, in killing the child, one would be killing an innocent person, for the child has committed no crime, and is not aiming at his mother's death. . . . If directly killing an innocent person is murder, and thus is impermissible, then the mother's directly killing the innocent person inside her is murder, and thus is impermissible. But it cannot seriously be thought to be murder if the mother performs an abortion on herself to save her life. It cannot seriously be said that she must

refrain, that she *must* sit passively by and wait for her death. Let us look again at the case of you and the violinist. There you are, in bed with the violinist, and the director of the hospital says to you, "It's all most distressing, and I deeply sympathize, but you see this is putting an additional strain on your kidneys, and you'll be dead within the month. But you *have* to stay where you are all the same. Because unplugging you would be directly killing an innocent violinist, and that's murder, and that's impermissible." If anything in the world is true, it is that you do not commit murder, you do not do what is impermissible, if you reach around to your back and unplug yourself from that violinist to save your life.

The main focus of attention in writings on abortion has been on what a third party may or may not do in answer to a request from a woman for an abortion. This is in a way understandable. Things being as they are, there isn't much a woman can safely do to abort herself. So the question asked is what a third party may do, and what the mother may do, if it is mentioned at all, is deduced, almost as an afterthought, from what it is concluded that third parties may do. But it seems to me that to treat the matter in this way is to refuse to grant to the mother that very status of person which is so firmly insisted on for the fetus. For we cannot simply read off what a person may do from what a third party may do. Suppose you find yourself trapped in a tiny house with a growing child. I mean a very tiny house, and a rapidly growing child—you are already up against the wall of the house and in a few minutes you'll be crushed to death. The child on the other hand won't be crushed to death; if nothing is done to stop him from growing he'll be hurt, but in the end he'll simply burst open the house and walk out a free man. Now I could well understand it if a bystander were to say, "There's nothing we can do for you. We cannot choose between your life and his, we cannot be the ones to decide who is to live, we cannot intervene." But it cannot be concluded that you too can do nothing, that you cannot attack it to save your life. However innocent the child may be, you do not have to wait passively while it crushes you to death. Perhaps a pregnant woman is vaguely felt to have the status of [a] house, to which we don't allow the right of self-defense. But if the woman houses the child, it should be remembered that she is a person who houses it.

I should perhaps stop to say explicitly that I am not claiming that people have a right to do anything whatever to save their lives. I think, rather, that there are drastic limits to the right of self-defense. If someone threatens you with death unless you torture someone else to death, I think you have not the right, even to save your life, to do so. But the case under consideration here is very different. In our case there are only two people involved, one whose life is threatened, and one who threatens it. Both are innocent: the one who is threatened is not threatened because of any fault, the one who threatens does not threaten because of any fault. For this reason we may feel that we bystanders cannot intervene. But the person threatened can.

In sum, a woman surely can defend her life against the threat to it posed by the unborn child, even if doing so involves its death. And this shows that the extreme view of abortion is false, and so we need not canvass any other possible ways of arriving at it from the argument I mentioned at the outset.

The extreme view could of course be weakened to say that while abortion is permissible to save the mother's life, it may not be performed by a third party, but only by the mother herself. But this cannot be right either. For what we have to keep in mind is that the mother and the unborn child are not like two tenants in a small house which has, by an unfortunate mistake, been rented to both: the mother owns the house. The fact that she does adds to the offensiveness of deducing that the mother can do nothing from the supposition that third parties can do nothing. But it does more than this: it casts a bright light on the supposition that third parties can do nothing. Certainly it lets us see that a third party who says "I cannot choose between you" is fooling himself if he thinks this is impartiality. If Jones has found and fastened on a certain coat, which he needs to keep from freezing, but which Smith also needs to keep him from freezing, then it is not impartiality that says "I cannot choose between you" when Smith owns the coat. Women have said again and again, "This body is my body!" and they have reason to feel angry, reason to feel that it has been like shouting into the wind. Smith, after all, is hardly likely to

bless us if we say to him, "Of course it's your coat, anybody would grant that it is. But no one may choose between you and Jones who is to have it."

We should really ask what it is that says "no one may choose" in the face of the fact that the body that houses the child is the mother's body. It may be simply a failure to appreciate this fact. But it may be something more interesting, namely the sense that one has a right to refuse to lay hands on people, even where it would be just and fair to do so, even where justice seems to require that somebody do so. Thus justice might call for somebody to get Smith's coat back from Jones, and yet you have a right to refuse to be the one to lay hands on Jones, a right to refuse to do physical violence to him. This, I think, must be granted. But then what should be said is not "no one may choose," but only "I cannot choose," and indeed not even this, but "I will not act," leaving it open that somebody else can or should, and in particular that anyone in a position of authority, with the job of securing people's rights, both can and should. So this is no difficulty. I have not been arguing that any given third party must accede to the mother's request that he perform an abortion to save her life, but only that he may. . . .

2. THE RIGHT TO LIFE

Where the mother's life is not at stake, the argument I mentioned at the outset seems to have a much stronger pull. "Everyone has a right to life, so the unborn person has a right to life." And isn't the child's right to life weightier than anything other than the mother's own right to life, which she might put forward as ground for an abortion?

This argument treats the right to life as if it were unproblematic. It is not, and this seems to me to be precisely the source of the mistake.

For we should now, at long last, ask what it comes to, to have a right to life. In some views having a right to life includes having a right to be given at least the bare minimum one needs for continued life. But suppose that what in fact is the bare minimum a man needs for continued life is something he has no right at all to be given? If I am sick unto death, and the only thing that will save my life is the touch of Henry Fonda's cool hand on my fevered brow, then all the same, I have no right to be given the touch of Henry Fonda's cool hand on my fevered brow. It would be frightfully nice of him to fly in from the West Coast to provide it. It would be less nice, though no doubt well meaning, if my friends flew out to the West Coast and carried Henry Fonda back with them. But I have no right at all against anybody that he should do this for me. Or again, to return to the story I told earlier, the fact that for continued life that violinist needs the continued use of your kidneys does not establish that he has a right to be given the continued use of your kidneys. He certainly has no right against you that you should give him continued use of your kidneys. For nobody has any right to use your kidneys unless you give him such a right; and nobody has the right against you that you shall give him this right—if you do allow him to go on using your kidneys, this is a kindness on your part, and not something he can claim from you as his due. Nor has he any right against anybody else that *they* should give him continued use of your kidneys. Certainly he had no right against the Society of Music Lovers that they should plug him into you in the first place. And if you now start to unplug yourself, having learned that you will otherwise have to spend nine years in bed with him, there is nobody in the world who must try to prevent you, in order to see to it that he is given something he has a right to be given.

Some people are rather stricter about the right to life. In their view, it does not include the right to be given anything, but amounts to, and only to, the right not to be killed by anybody. But here a related difficulty arises. If everybody is to refrain from killing that violinist, then everybody must refrain from doing a great many different sorts of things. Everybody must refrain from slitting his throat, everybody must refrain from shooting him—and everybody must refrain from unplugging you from him. But does he have a right against everybody that they shall refrain from unplugging you from him? To refrain from doing this is to allow him to continue to use your kidneys. It could be argued that he has a right against us that we should allow him to continue to use your kidneys. That is, while he had no right against us that we should give him the use of your kidneys, it might be argued that he anyway has a right against

us that we shall not now intervene and deprive him of the use of your kidneys. I shall come back to third-party interventions later. But certainly the violinist has no right against you that you shall allow him to continue to use your kidneys. As I said, if you do allow him to use them, it is a kindness on your part, and not something you owe him. . . .

3. THE RIGHT TO USE THE MOTHER'S BODY

There is another way to bring out the difficulty. In the most ordinary sort of case, to deprive someone of what he has a right to is to treat him unjustly. Suppose a boy and his small brother are jointly given a box of chocolates for Christmas. If the older boy takes the box and refuses to give his brother any of the chocolates, he is unjust to him, for the brother has been given a right to half of them. But suppose that, having learned that otherwise it means nine years in bed with that violinist, you unplug yourself from him. You surely are not being unjust to him for you gave him no right to use your kidneys, and no one else can have given him any such right. But we have to notice that in unplugging yourself, you are killing him; and violinists, like everybody else, have a right to life, and thus in the view we were considering just now, the right not to be killed. So here you do what he supposedly has a right you shall not do, but you do not act unjustly to him in doing it.

The emendation which may be made at this point is this: the right to life consists not in the right not to be killed, but rather in the right not to be killed unjustly. This runs a risk of circularity, but never mind; it would enable us to square the fact that the violinist has a right to life with the fact that you do not act unjustly toward him in unplugging yourself, thereby killing him. For if you do not kill him unjustly, you do not violate his right to life, and so it is no wonder you do him no injustice.

But if this emendation is accepted, the gap in the argument against abortion stares us plainly in the face: it is by no means enough to show that the fetus is a person, and to remind us that all persons have a right to life—we need to be shown also that killing the fetus violates its right to life, i.e., that abortion is unjust killing. And is it?

I suppose we may take it as a datum that in a case of pregnancy due to rape the mother has not given the unborn person a right to the use of her body for food and shelter. Indeed, in what pregnancy could it be supposed that the mother has given the unborn person such a right? It is not as if there were unborn persons drifting about the world, to whom a woman who wants a child says, "I invite you in."

But it might be argued that there are other ways one can have acquired a right to the use of another person's body than by having been invited to use it by that person. Suppose a woman voluntarily indulges in intercourse, knowing of the chance it will issue in pregnancy, and then she does become pregnant; is she not in part responsible for the presence, in fact the very existence, of the unborn person inside her? No doubt she did not invite it in. But doesn't her partial responsibility for its being there itself give it a right to the use of her body? If so, then her aborting it would be more like the boy's taking away the chocolates, and less like your unplugging yourself from the violinist— doing so would be depriving it of what it does have a right to, and thus would be doing it an injustice.

And then, too, it might be asked whether or not she can kill it even to save her own life: If she voluntarily called it into existence, how can she now kill it, even in self-defense?

The first thing to be said about this is that it is something new. Opponents of abortion have been so concerned to make out the independence of the fetus, in order to establish that it has a right to life, just as its mother does, that they have tended to overlook the possible support they might gain from making out that the fetus is *dependent* on the mother, in order to establish that she has a special kind of responsibility for it, a responsibility that gives it rights against her which are not possessed by any independent person—such as an ailing violinist who is a stranger to her.

On the other hand, this argument would give the unborn person a right to its mother's body only if her pregnancy resulted from a voluntary act, undertaken in full knowledge of the chance a pregnancy might result from it. It would leave out entirely the unborn person whose existence is due to rape. Pending the availability of some further argument, then, we would be left with the conclu-

sion that unborn persons whose existence is due to rape have no right to the use of their mothers' bodies, and thus that aborting them is not depriving them of anything they have a right to and hence is not unjust killing.

And we should also notice that it is not at all plain that this argument really does go even as far as it purports to. For there are cases and cases, and the details make a difference. If the room is stuffy, and I therefore open a window to air it, and a burglar climbs in, it would be absurd to say, "Ah, now he can stay, she's given him a right to the use of her house—for she is partially responsible for his presence there, having voluntarily done what enabled him to get in, in full knowledge that there are such things as burglars, and that burglars burgle." It would be still more absurd to say this if I had had bars installed outside my windows, precisely to prevent burglars from getting in, and a burglar got in only because of a defect in the bars. It remains equally absurd if we imagine it is not a burglar who climbs in, but an innocent person who blunders or falls in. Again, suppose it were like this: people-seeds drift about in the air like pollen, and if you open your windows, one may drift in and take root in your carpets or upholstery. You don't want children, so you fix up your windows with fine mesh screens, the very best you can buy. As can happen, however, and on very, very rare occasions does happen, one of the screens is defective; and a seed drifts in and takes root. Does the person-plant who now develops have a right to the use of your house? Surely not—despite the fact that you voluntarily opened your windows, you knowingly kept carpets and upholstered furniture, and you knew that screens were sometimes defective. Someone may argue that you are responsible for its rooting, that it does have a right to your house, because after all you could have lived out your life with bare floors and furniture, or with sealed windows and doors. But this won't do—for by the same token anyone can avoid a pregnancy due to rape by having a hysterectomy, or anyway by never leaving home without a (reliable!) army.

It seems to me that the argument we are looking at can establish at most that there are some cases in which the unborn person has a right to the use of its mother's body, and therefore some cases in which abortion is unjust killing. There is room for much discussion and argument as to precisely which, if any. But I think we should sidestep this issue and leave it open, for at any rate the argument certainly does not establish that all abortion is unjust killing.

4. RIGHTS AND THEIR LIMITS

There is room for yet another argument here, however. We surely must all grant that there may be cases in which it would be morally indecent to detach a person from your body at the cost of his life. Suppose you learn that what the violinist needs is not nine years of your life, but only one hour: all you need do to save his life is to spend one hour in that bed with him. Suppose also that letting him use your kidneys for that one hour would not affect your health in the slightest. Admittedly you were kidnapped. Admittedly you did not give anyone permission to plug him into you. Nevertheless it seems to me plain you *ought* to allow him to use your kidneys for that hour—it would be indecent to refuse.

Again, suppose pregnancy lasted only an hour, and constituted no threat to life or health. And suppose that a woman becomes pregnant as a result of rape. Admittedly she did not voluntarily do anything to bring about the existence of a child. Admittedly she did nothing at all which would give the unborn person a right to the use of her body. All the same it might well be said, as in the newly emended violinist story, that she *ought* to allow it to remain for that hour—that it would be indecent in her to refuse. . . .

Suppose that the box of chocolates I mentioned earlier was given only to the older boy. There he sits, stolidly eating his way through the box, his small brother watching enviously. Here we are likely to say "You ought not to be so mean. You ought to give your brother some of those chocolates." My own view is that it just does not follow from the truth of this that the brother has any right to any of the chocolates. If the boy refuses to give his brother any, he is greedy, stingy, callous—but not unjust. . . . Take the case of Henry Fonda again. I said earlier that I had no right to the touch of his cool hand on my

fevered brow, even though I needed it to save my life. I said it would be frightfully nice of him to fly in from the West Coast to provide me with it, but that I had no right against him that he should do so. But suppose he isn't on the West Coast. Suppose he has only to walk across the room, place a hand briefly on my brow—and low, my life is saved. Then surely he *ought* to do it, it would be indecent to refuse. . . .

So my own view is that even though you ought to let the violinist use your kidneys for the one hour he needs, we should not conclude that he has a right to do so—we would say that if you refuse, you are, like the boy who owns all the chocolates and will give none away, self-centered and callous, indecent in fact, but not unjust. And similarly, that even supposing a case in which a woman pregnant due to rape ought to allow the unborn person to use her body for the hour he needs, we should not conclude that he has a right to do so; we should conclude that she is self-centered, callous, indecent, but not unjust, if she refuses. The complaints are no less grave; they are just different. . . . And so it is for the mother and unborn child. Except in such cases as the unborn person has a right to demand it—and we are leaving open the possibility that there may be such cases—nobody is morally *required* to make large sacrifices, of health, of all other interests and concerns, of all other duties and commitments, for nine years, or even for nine months, in order to keep a person alive.

5. THE GOOD SAMARITAN AND THE RESPONSIBILITIES OF PARENTS

We have in fact to distinguish between two kinds of Samaritan: the Good Samaritan and what we might call the Minimally Decent Samaritan. . . . The Good Samaritan went out of his way, at some cost to himself, to help one in need of it. . . . These things are a matter of degree, of course, but there is a difference, and it comes out perhaps most clearly in the story of Kitty Genovese, who, as you will remember, was murdered while thirty-eight people watched or listened, and did nothing at all to help her. A Good Samaritan would have rushed out to give direct assistance against the murderer. Or perhaps we had better allow that it would have been a Splendid Samaritan who did this, on the ground that it would have involved a risk of death for himself. But the thirty-eight not only did not do this, they did not even trouble to pick up a phone to call the police. Minimally Decent Samaritanism would call for doing at least that, and their not having done it was monstrous. . . . It seems plain that it was not morally required of any of the thirty-eight that he rush out to give direct assistance at the risk of his own life, and that it is not morally required of anyone that he give long stretches of his life—nine years or nine months—to sustain the life of a person who has no special right (we were leaving open the possibility of this) to demand it. . . .

What we should ask is not whether anybody should be compelled by law to be a Good Samaritan, but whether we must accede to a situation in which somebody is being compelled—by nature, perhaps—to be a Good Samaritan. . . . There you are, you were kidnapped, and nine years in bed with that violinist lie ahead of you. You have your own life to lead. You are sorry, but you simply cannot see giving up so much of your life to the sustaining of his. You cannot extricate yourself, and ask us to do so. I should have thought that—in light of his having no right to the use of your body—it was obvious that we do not have to accede to your being forced to give up so much. We can do what you ask. There is no injustice to the violinist in our doing so. . . .

It may be said that what is important is not merely the fact that the fetus is a person, but that it is a person for whom the woman has a special kind of responsibility issuing from the fact that she is its mother. . . . Surely we do not have any such "special responsibility" for a person unless we have assumed it, explicitly or implicitly. If a set of parents do not try to prevent pregnancy, do not obtain an abortion, but rather take it home with them, then they have assumed responsibility for it, and have given it rights, and they cannot *now* withdraw support from it at the cost of its life because they now find it difficult to go on providing for it. But if they have taken all reasonable precautions against having a child, they do not simply by virtue of their biological relationship to the child who comes into existence have a special responsibility for it. . . .

I have argued that you are not morally required to spend nine months in bed, sustaining the life of that violinist; but to say this is by no means to say that if, when you unplug yourself, there is a miracle and he survives, you then have a right to turn around and slit his throat. You may detach yourself even if this costs him his life; you have no right to be guaranteed his death, by some other means, if unplugging yourself does not kill him. There are some people who will feel dissatisfied by this feature of my argument. A woman may be utterly devastated by the thought of a child, a bit of herself, put out for adoption and never seen or heard of again. . . . All the same, I agree that the desire for the child's death is not one which anybody may gratify, should it turn out to be possible to detach a child alive.

At this place, however, it should be remembered that we have only been pretending throughout that the fetus is a human being from the moment of conception. A very early abortion is surely not the killing of a person, and so is not dealt with by anything I have said.

REVIEW AND DISCUSSION QUESTIONS

1. How does Thomson understand the right to life? Why shouldn't the fetus's having such a right prevent the mother from getting an abortion?

2. Suppose the violinist needed your kidneys for only five minutes. Does Thomson think you should allow him to use them? Why?

3. "Abortions almost always occur in cases in which the mother voluntarily had sex, so the violinist analogy doesn't apply." How does Thomson respond to this claim? Is her response adequate?

4. Suppose you found a baby in your mountain cabin just after the winter snows arrived. Should you now let it share your cabin for nine months (assuming the only alternative is to put it outside to die)? Is this situation a good analogy to abortion? Is it if we assume that in each case the costs are the same?

5. Is it important that it is her own child the mother kills, while the violinist is a stranger? Explain how Thomson understands this issue. Do you agree?

6. How would Peter Singer ("Rich and Poor") respond to Thomson's argument?

Opposition to Abortion:
A Human Rights Approach

Baruch Brody

Baruch Brody begins with a brief critical analysis of Thomson's defense of abortion. He then turns to a discussion of the circumstances in which it is acceptable to take another's life. Starting with the justification of self-defense, Brody goes on to consider various cases of killing innocents. He concludes that if we assume a fetus is a person, then abortion is wrong unless both mother and baby will die anyway.

If Brody's arguments have merit, then much will depend on the moral status of a fetus: Is it a living human being? Is it a person? Many opponents of abortion believe that these questions can be answered as follows:

> At conception there is a life started; it is obviously human since it has a human genetic code. Indeed, each of us could trace our development to such a point. Furthermore, if left alone that being will likely develop to the point of birth. Given these facts, nothing will occur between conception and birth that could possibly be important enough to justify saying that before it occurred the human organism could be killed but not afterward. Birth, for example, amounts to no more than a change of location and the start of respiration and digestion. Neither location nor being on one's own respirative and digestive systems is necessary to be a living person, as we know from visiting any hospital. Viability, similarly, means nothing more than that the fetus is developed enough to survive on its own systems—a fact that cannot be the same thing as being a living person. So only conception (for the reasons just mentioned) provides a morally significant point in the continuous development of a person.

In the final section of his article Brody attempts to answer this sort of argument by developing an alternative, more moderate position on the question of when human life begins. His approach is to look at when human life ends (a topic of obvious relevance to euthanasia) and to use the answer to that question as a way of attacking the problem of when a life begins. His conclusion is that there are

From *Abortion and the Sanctity of Human Life: A Philosophical View* (Cambridge, MA: MIT Press, 1975) and "Fetal Humanity and the Theory of Essentialism," in *Philosophy and Sex,* ed. Robert Baker and Frederick Elliston (Buffalo, NY: Prometheus Books, 1975). Reprinted by permission. Parts have been revised by Baruch Brody. Titles added.

two plausible options, both of which would justify early abortions: (1) brain death and (2) the revised traditional position, which holds that a functioning heart, respiratory system, or brain is a sufficient condition for life. Baruch Brody is professor of philosophy at Rice University.

1. THE WOMAN'S RIGHT TO HER BODY

It is a common claim that a woman ought to be in control of what happens to her body to the greatest extent possible, that she ought to be able to use her body in ways that she wants to and refrain from using it in ways that she does not want to. This right is particularly pressed where certain uses of her body have deep and lasting effects upon the character of her life, personal, social, and economic. Therefore, it is argued, a woman should be free either to carry her fetus to term, thereby using her body to support it, or to abort the fetus, thereby not using her body for that purpose.

In some contexts in which this argument is advanced, it is clear that it is not addressed to the issue of the morality of abortion at all. Rather, it is made in opposition to laws against abortion on the ground that the choice to abort or not is a moral decision that should belong only to the mother. But that specific direction of the argument is irrelevant to our present purposes; I will consider it [later] when I deal with the issues raised by laws prohibiting abortions. For the moment, I am concerned solely with the use of this principle as a putative ground tending to show the permissibility of abortion, with the claim that because it is the woman's body that carries the fetus and upon which the fetus depends, she has certain rights to abort the fetus that no one else may have.

We may begin by remarking that it is obviously correct that, as carrier of the fetus, the mother has it within her power to choose whether or not to abort the fetus. And, as an autonomous and responsible agent, she must make this choice. But let us notice that this in no way entails either that whatever choice she makes is morally right or that no one else has the right to evaluate the decision that she makes.

At first glance, it would seem that this argument cannot be used by anyone who supposes, as we do for the moment, that there is a point in fetal development from which time on the fetus is a hu-

man being. After all, people do not have the right to do anything whatsoever that may be necessary for them to retain control over the uses of their bodies. In particular, it would seem wrong for them to kill another human being in order to do so.

In a recent article,[1] Professor Judith Thomson has, in effect, argued that this simple view is mistaken. How does Professor Thomson defend her claim that the mother has a right to abort the fetus, even if it is a human being, whether or not her life is threatened and whether or not she has consented to the act of intercourse in which the fetus is conceived? At one point, discussing just the case in which the mother's life is threatened, she makes the following suggestion:

> In [abortion], there are only two people involved, one whose life is threatened and one who threatens it. Both are innocent: the one who is threatened is not threatened because of any fault, the one who threatens does not threaten because of any fault. For this reason, we may feel that we bystanders cannot intervene. But the person threatened can.

But surely this description is equally applicable to the following case: A and B are adrift on a lifeboat, B has a disease that he can survive, but A, if he contracts it, will die, and the only way that A can avoid that is by killing B and pushing him overboard. Surely, A has no right to do this. So there must be some special reason why the mother has, if she does, the right to abort the fetus.

There is, to be sure, an important difference between our lifeboat case and abortion, one that leads us to the heart of Professor Thomson's argument. In the case that we envisaged, both A and B have equal rights to be in the lifeboat, but the mother's body is hers and not the fetus's and she has first rights to its use. The primacy of these rights allow an abortion whether or not her life is threatened. Professor Thomson summarizes this argument in the following way:

> I am arguing only that having a right to life does not guarantee having either a right to be given the use of, or

a right to be allowed continued use of, another person's body—even if one needs it for life itself.

One part of this claim is clearly correct. I have no duty to X to save X's life by giving him the use of my body (or my life savings, or the only home I have, and so on), and X has no right, even to save his life, to any of those things. Thus, the fetus conceived in the laboratory that will perish unless it is implanted into a woman's body has in fact no right to any woman's body. But this portion of the claim is irrelevant to the abortion issue, for in abortion of the fetus that is a human being the mother must kill X to get back the sole use of her body, and that is an entirely different matter.

This point can also be put as follows: . . . we must distinguish the taking of X's life from the saving of X's life, even if we assume that one has a duty not to do the former and to do the latter. Now that latter duty, if it exists at all, is much weaker than the first duty; many circumstances may relieve us from the latter duty that will not relieve us from the former one. Thus, I am certainly relieved from my duty to save X's life by the fact that fulfilling it means the loss of my life savings. It may be noble for me to save X's life at the cost of everything I have, but I certainly have no duty to do that. And the same observation may be made about cases in which I can save X's life by giving him the use of my body for an extended period of time. However, I am not relieved of my duty not to take X's life by the fact that fulfilling it means the loss of everything I have and not even by the fact that fulfilling it means the loss of my life. . . .

At one point in her paper, Professor Thomson does consider this objection. She has previously imagined the following case: a famous violinist, who is dying from a kidney ailment, has been, without your consent, plugged into you for a period of time so that his body can use your kidneys. Applying this argument to the case of abortion, we can see that Professor Thomson's argument would run as follows:

1. Assume that the fetus's right to life includes the right not to be killed by the woman carrying him.
2. But to refrain from killing the fetus is to allow him the continued use of the woman's body.
3. So our first assumption entails that the fetus's right to life includes the right to the continued use of the woman's body.
4. But we all grant that the fetus does not have the right to the continued use of the woman's body.
5. Therefore, the fetus's right to life cannot include the right not to be killed by the woman in question.

And it is also now clear what is wrong with this argument. When we granted that the fetus has no right to the continued use of the woman's body, all that we meant was that he does not have this right merely because the continued use saves his life. But, of course, there may be other reasons why he has this right. One would be that the only way to take the use of the woman's body away from the fetus is by killing him, and that is something that neither she nor we have the right to do. So, I submit, the way in which Assumption 4 is true is irrelevant, and cannot be used by Professor Thomson, for Assumption 4 is true only in cases where the saving of the life of the fetus is at stake and not in cases where the taking of his life is at stake.

I conclude therefore that Professor Thomson has not established the truth of her claims about abortion, primarily because she has not sufficiently attended to the distinction between our duty to save X's life and our duty not to take it. Once one attends to that distinction, it would seem that the mother, in order to regain control over her body, has no right to abort the fetus from the point at which it becomes a human being.

It may also be useful to say a few words about the larger and less rigorous context of the argument that the woman has a right to her own body. It is surely true that one way in which women have been oppressed is by their being denied authority over their own bodies. But it seems to me that, as the struggle is carried on for meaningful amelioration of such oppression, it ought not to be carried so far that it violates the steady responsibilities all people have to one another. Parents may not desert their children, one class may not oppress another, one race or nation may not exploit another. For parents, powerful groups in society, races or nations in ascendancy, there are penalties for refraining from these wrong actions, but those penalties can in no way be taken as the justification for such wrong actions. Similarly, if the fetus is a human being, the penalty of carrying it cannot, I believe, be used as the justification for destroying it. . . .

2. ABORTION TO SAVE THE MOTHER

Let us begin by considering the case in which the continued existence of the fetus threatens the life of the mother. This would seem to be the case in which she has the strongest claim for the right to abort the fetus even if it is a human being with a right to life. . . .

Why would it not be permissible for the mother to have an abortion in order to save her life even after that point at which the fetus becomes a human being? After all, the fetus's continued existence poses a threat to the life of the mother, and why can't she void that threat by taking the life of the fetus, as an ultimate act of defense?

To be sure, it may be the physician, or other agent, who will cause the abortion, and not the mother herself, but that difference seems to be irrelevant. Our intuition is that the person whose life is threatened (call that person A) may either take the life of the person (B) who threatens his life or call upon someone else (C) to do so. And more important, it seems permissible (and perhaps even obligatory in some cases) for C to take B's life in order to save A's life. Put in traditional terms, we were really speaking of the mother's right as the pursued, or anyone else's right as an onlooker, to take the life of the fetus who is the pursuer.

Pope Pius XI observed, in objecting to this argument from self-defense, that in the paradigm case of killing the pursuer B is unjustly attempting to take A's life and is responsible for this attempt. It is the resulting guilt, based in part on B's intention (found in the attempt to kill A), together with the fact that A will die unless B is stopped, which permits the taking of B's life. The reader will notice that the abortion situation is quite different. Leaving aside for now—we shall return to it later on—the question as to whether the fetus can properly be described as attempting to take the mother's life, we can certainly agree that the fetus is not responsible for such an attempt (if it is occurring), that the fetus is therefore innocent, not guilty, and that the taking of fetal life cannot be compared to the paradigm case of killing the pursuer.

There is another way of putting Pope Pius's point. Consider the following case: there is, let us imagine, a medicine that A needs to stay alive, C owns some, and C will give it to A only if A kills B. Moreover, A has no other way of getting the medicine. In this case, the continued existence of B certainly poses a threat to the life of A; A can survive only if B does not survive. Still, it is not permissible for A to kill B in order to save A's life. Why not? How does this case differ from the paradigm case of killing the pursuer? The simplest answer is that in this case, while B's continued existence poses a threat to the life of A, B is not guilty of attempting to take A's life because there is no attempt to be guilty about it in the first place. Now if we consider the case of a fetus whose continued existence poses a threat to the life of the mother, we see that it is like the medicine case and not like the paradigm case of killing the pursuer. The fetus does pose (in our imagined situation) a threat to the life of its mother, but it is not guilty of attempting to take its mother's life. Consequently, in an analogue to the medicine case, the mother (or her agent) could not justify destroying the fetus on the ground that it would be a permissible act of killing the pursuer.

The persuasiveness of both of the preceding arguments indicates that we have to analyze the whole issue of pursuit far more carefully before we can definitely decide whether an abortion to save the life of the mother could be viewed as a permissible act of killing the pursuer. If we look again at a paradigm case of pursuit, we see that there are three factors involved:

1. The continued existence of B poses a threat to the life of A, a threat that can be met only by the taking of B's life (we shall refer to this as the condition of *danger*).
2. B is unjustly attempting to take A's life (we shall refer to this as the condition of *attempt*).
3. B is responsible for his attempt to take A's life (we shall refer to this as the condition of *guilt*).

In the medicine case, only the danger condition was satisfied. Our intuitions that it would be wrong for A to take B's life in that case reflects our belief that the mere fact that *B* is a danger to *A* is not sufficient to establish that killing *B* will be a justifiable act of killing a pursuer. But it would be rash to conclude, as Pope Pius did, that all three conditions must be satisfied before the killing of *B* will be a justifiable act of killing a pursuer. What would happen, for example, if the first two conditions, but not the guilt condition, were satisfied?

There are good reasons for supposing that the satisfaction of the first two conditions is sufficient justification for taking *B*'s life as an act of killing the pursuer. Consider, for example, a variation of the pursuit paradigm—one in which *B* is about to shoot *A,* and the only way by which *A* can stop him is by killing him first—but one in which *B* is a minor who is not responsible for his attempt to take *A*'s life. In this case, the only condition not satisfied is the condition of guilt. Still, despite that fact, it seems that *A* may justifiably take *B*'s life as a permissible act of killing a pursuer. The guilt of the pursuer, then, is not a requirement for legitimacy in killing the pursuer. . . .

To summarize, then, our general discussion of killing the pursuer, we can say the following: the mere satisfaction of the danger condition is not sufficient to justify the killing of the pursuer. If, in addition . . . the attempt condition is satisfied, then one would be justified in killing the pursuer to save the life of the pursued. In any case, the condition of guilt, arising from full knowledge and intent, need not be satisfied. . . .

Is, then, the aborting of the fetus, when necessary to save the life of the mother, a permissible act of killing a pursuer? It is true that in such cases the fetus is a danger to his mother. But it is also clear that the condition of attempt is not satisfied. The fetus has neither the beliefs nor the intentions to which we have referred. Furthermore, there is on the part of the fetus no action that threatens the life of the mother. . . . It seems to follow, therefore, that aborting the fetus could not be a permissible act of killing a pursuer. . . .

[Professor Brody goes on to consider the one exception that he believes should be made to this conclusion: where both *the fetus and mother will die unless an abortion is performed. Since here there is no question of unfairly sacrificing one person for another (the fetus will die anyway),*

Brody argues that in this case alone abortion may be performed. This is because we cannot under ordinary circumstances kill one person to save another.—Editor]

3. TWO ADDITIONAL CASES

All of the arguments that we have looked at so far are attempts to show that there is something special about abortion that justifies its being treated differently from other cases of the taking of human life. We shall now consider claims that are confined to certain special cases of abortion: the case in which the mother has been raped. . . and the case in which having the child may cause a problem for the rest of her family. . . .

When the expectant mother has conceived after being raped, there are two different sorts of considerations that might support the claim that she has the right to take the life of the fetus. They are the following: (A) the woman in question has already suffered immensely from the act of rape and the physical and/or psychological aftereffects of that act. It would be particularly unjust, the argument runs, for her to have to live through an unwanted pregnancy owing to that act of rape. Therefore, even if we are at a stage at which the fetus is a human being, the mother has the right to abort it; (B) the fetus in question has no right to be in that woman. It was put there as a result of an act of aggression upon her by the rapist, and its continued presence is an act of aggression against the mother. She has right to repel that aggression by aborting the fetus.

The first argument is very compelling. We can all agree that a terrible injustice has been committed on the woman who is raped. The question that we have to consider, however, is whether it follows that it is morally permissible for her to abort the fetus. We must make that consideration reflecting that, however unjust the act of rape, it was not the fetus who committed or commissioned it. The injustice of the act, then, should in no way impinge upon the rights of the fetus, for it is innocent. What remains is the initial misfortune of the mother (and the injustice of her having to pass through the pregnancy, and, further, to assume responsibility of at least giving the child over for adoption or assuming the burden of its care.) However unfortunate that circumstance, however unjust, the misfortune and the injustice are not sufficient cause to justify the taking of the life of an innocent human being as a means of mitigation.

It is at this point that Argument B comes in, for its whole point is that the fetus, by its mere presence in the mother, is committing an act of aggression against her, one over and above the one committed by the rapist, and one that the mother has a right to repel by abortion. But . . . (1) the fetus is certainly innocent (in the sense of not responsible) for any act of aggression against the mother and that (2) the mere presence of the fetus in the mother, no matter how unfortunate for her, does not constitute an act of aggression by the fetus against the mother. Argument B fails then at just that point at which Argument A needs its support, and we can therefore conclude that the fact that pregnancy is the result of rape does not give the mother the right to abort the fetus. . . .

We come finally to those cases in which the continuation of the pregnancy would cause serious problems for the rest of the family. There are a variety of cases that we have to consider here together. Perhaps the health of the mother will be affected in such a way that she cannot function effectively as a wife and mother during, or even after, the pregnancy. Or perhaps the expenses incurred as a result of the pregnancy would be utterly beyond the financial resources of the family. The important point is that the continuation of the pregnancy raises a serious problem for other innocent people involved besides the mother and the fetus, and it may be argued that the mother has the right to abort the fetus to avoid that problem.

By now, the difficulties with this argument should be apparent. We have seen earlier that the mere fact that the continued existence of the fetus threatens to harm the mother does not, by itself, justify the aborting of the fetus. Why should anything be changed by the fact that the threatened harm will accrue to the other members of the family and not to the mother? Of course, it would be different if the fetus were committing an act of aggression against the other members of the family. But, once more, this is certainly not the case.

We conclude, therefore, that none of these special circumstances justifies an abortion from that point at which the fetus is a human being. . . .

4. FETAL HUMANITY AND BRAIN FUNCTION

The question which we must now consider is the question of fetal humanity. Some have argued that the fetus is a human being with a right to life (or, for convenience, just a human being) from the moment of conception. Others have argued that the fetus only becomes a human being at the moment of birth. Many positions in between these two extremes have also been suggested. How are we to decide which is correct?

The analysis which we will propose here rests upon certain metaphysical assumptions which I have defended elsewhere. These assumptions are: (a) the question is when has the fetus acquired all the properties essential (necessary) for being a human being, for when it has, it is a human being; (b) these properties are such that the loss of any one of them means that the human being in question has gone out of existence and not merely stopped being a human being; (c) human beings go out of existence when they die. It follows from these assumptions that the fetus becomes a human being when it acquires all those characteristics which are such that the loss of any one of them would result in the fetus's being dead. We must, therefore, turn to the analysis of death. . . .

We will first consider the question of what properties are essential to being human if we suppose that death and the passing out of existence occur only if there has been an irreparable cessation of brain function (keeping in mind that the condition itself, as we have noted, is a matter of medical judgment). We shall then consider the same question on the supposition that [Paul] Ramsey's more complicated theory of death (the modified traditional view) is correct.

According to what is called the brain-death theory, as long as there has not been an irreparable cessation of brain function the person in question continues to exist, no matter what else has happened to him. If so, it seems to follow that there is only one property—leaving aside those entailed by this one property—that is essential to humanity, namely, the possession of a brain that has not suffered an irreparable cessation of function.

Several consequences follow immediately from this conclusion. We can see that a variety of often advanced claims about the essence of humanity are false. For example, the claim that movement, or perhaps just the ability to move, is essential for being human is false. A human being who has stopped moving, and even one who has lost the ability to move, has not therefore stopped existing. Being able to move, and a fortiori moving, are not essential properties of human beings and therefore are not essential to being human. Similarly, the claim that being perceivable by other human beings is essential for being human is also false. A human being who has stopped being perceivable by other humans (for example, someone isolated on the other side of the moon, out of reach even of radio communication) has not stopped existing. Being perceivable by other human beings is not an essential property of human beings and is not essential to being human. And the same point can be made about the claims that viability is essential for being human, that independent existence is essential for being human, and that actual interaction with other human beings is essential for being human. The loss of any of these properties would not mean that the human being in question had gone out of existence, so none of them can be essential to that human being and none of them can be essential for being human.

Let us now look at the following argument: (1) A functioning brain (or at least, a brain that, if not functioning, is susceptible of function) is a property that every human being must have because it is essential for being human. (2) By the time an entity acquires that property, it has all the other properties that are essential for being human. Therefore, when the fetus acquires that property it becomes a human being. It is clear that the property in question is, according to the brain-death theory, one that is had essentially by all human beings. The question that we have to consider is whether the second premise is true. It might appear that its truth does follow from the brain-death theory. After all, we did see that the theory entails that only one property (together

with those entailed by it) is essential for being human. Nevertheless, rather than relying solely on my earlier argument, I shall adopt an alternative approach to strengthen the conviction that this second premise is true: I shall note the important ways in which the fetus resembles and differs from an ordinary human being by the time it definitely has a functioning brain (about the end of the sixth week of development). It shall then be evident, in light of our theory of essentialism, that none of these differences involves the lack of some property in the fetus that is essential for its being human.

Structurally, there are few features of the human being that are not fully present by the end of the sixth week. Not only are the familiar external features and all the internal organs present, but the contours of the body are nicely rounded. More important, the body is functioning. Not only is the brain functioning, but the heart is beating sturdily (the fetus by this time has its own completely developed vascular system), the stomach is producing digestive juices, the liver is manufacturing blood cells, the kidney is extracting uric acid from the blood, and the nerves and muscles are operating in concert, so that reflex reactions can begin.

What are the properties that a fetus acquires after the sixth week of its development? Certain structures do appear later. These include the fingernails (which appear in the third month), the completed vocal chords (which also appear then), taste buds and salivary glands (again, in the third month), and hair and eyelashes (in the fifth month). In addition, certain functions begin later than the sixth week. The fetus begins to urinate (in the third month), to move spontaneously (in the third month), to respond to external stimuli (at least in the fifth month), and to breathe (in the sixth month). Moreover, there is a constant growth in size. And finally, at the time of birth the fetus ceases to receive its oxygen and food through the placenta and starts receiving them through the mouth and nose.

I will not examine each of these properties (structures and functions) to show that they are not essential for being human. The procedure would be essentially the one used previously to show that various essentialist claims are in error. We might, therefore, conclude, on the supposition that the brain-death theory is correct, that the fetus becomes a human being about the end of the sixth week after its development.

There is, however, one complication that should be noted here. There are, after all, progressive stages in the physical development and in the functioning of the brain. For example, the fetal brain (and nervous system) does not develop sufficiently to support spontaneous motion until some time in the third month after conception. There is, of course, no doubt that that stage of development is sufficient for the fetus to be human. No one would be likely to maintain that a spontaneously moving human being has died; and similarly, a spontaneously moving fetus would seem to have become human. One might, however, want to claim that the fetus does not become a human being until the point of spontaneous movement. So then, on the supposition that the brain-death theory is correct, one ought to conclude that the fetus becomes a human being at some time between the sixth and twelfth week after its conception.

But what if we reject the brain-death theory, and replace it with its equally plausible contender, Ramsey's theory of death? According to that theory—which we can call the brain, heart, and lung theory of death—the human being does not die, does not go out of existence, until such time as the brain, heart and lungs have irreparably ceased functioning naturally. What are the essential features of being human according to this theory?

Actually, the adoption of Ramsey's theory requires no major modifications. According to that theory, what is essential to being human, what each human being must retain if he is to continue to exist, is the possession of a functioning (actually or potentially) heart, lung, or brain. It is only when a human being possesses none of these that he dies and goes out of existence; and the fetus comes into humanity, so to speak, when he acquires one of these.

On Ramsey's theory, the argument would now run as follows: (1) The property of having a functioning brain, heart, or lungs (or at least organs of the kind that, if not functioning, are susceptible of function) is one that every human being must have because it is essential for being human. (2) By the time that an entity acquires that property it has all the other properties that are essential for being human. Therefore, when the fetus acquires that property it becomes a human being. There remains, once more, the problem of the second premise. Since the fetal heart starts operating rather early, it is not clear that the second premise is correct. Many systems are not yet operating, and many structures are not yet present. Still, following our theory of essentialism, we should conclude that the fetus becomes a human being when it acquires a functioning heart (the first of the organs to function in the fetus).

There is, however, a further complication here, and it is analogous to the one encountered if we adopt the brain-death theory: When may we properly say that the fetal heart begins to function? At two weeks, when occasional contractions of the primitive fetal heart are present? In the fourth to fifth week, when the heart, although incomplete, is beating regularly and pumping blood cells through a closed vascular system, and when the tracings obtained by an ECG exhibit the classical elements of an adult tracing? Or after the end of the seventh week, when the fetal heart is functioning complete and "normal"?

We have not reached a precise conclusion in our study of the question of when the fetus becomes a human being. We do know that it does so some time between the end of the second week and the end of the third month. But it surely is not a human being at the moment of conception and it surely is one by the end of the third month. Though we have not come to a final answer to our question, we have narrowed the range of acceptable answers considerably.

[In summary] we have argued that the fetus becomes a human being with a right to life some time between the second and twelfth week after conception. We have also argued that abortions are morally impermissible after that point except in rather unusual circumstances. What is crucial to note is that neither of these arguments appeal to any theological considerations. We conclude, therefore, that there is a human rights basis for moral opposition to abortions. . . .

NOTE

1. J. Thomson, "A Defense of Abortion," *Philosophy and Public Affairs*, 1, no. 1 (1971). [See previous article.]

REVIEW AND DISCUSSION QUESTIONS

1. Explain Brody's response to Thomson's defense of abortion, indicating the important distinction that, he argues, she has overlooked.
2. What conditions, according to Brody, justify taking an innocent person's life in self-defense? Under those conditions, is it justifiable to take the life of a fetus?
3. Is the baby in some sense the "cause" of the mother's death? Is that relevant to Brody's analysis?
4. Explain Brody's response to those who defend abortion in the cases of rape and of family hardship.
5. How does Brody answer the question of the humanity of the fetus? When, in other words, does he think life begins, and why?
6. Assess the conservative argument given in the introduction to this selection. Why does Brody reject that argument?
7. What, if anything, does that conservative argument imply about contraception?
8. Compare the brain-death theory with Ramsey's. Does one seem more reasonable to you than the other? Why?
9. Consider what Brody has argued here in light of the discussions in the last section about animals and the environment. How would Singer and Callicott respond to Brody?

On the Moral and Legal Status of Abortion

Mary Anne Warren

In this essay, Mary Anne Warren begins by discussing Judith Jarvis Thomson's defense of abortion. But instead of focusing on the distinction between the duty to save a life and the duty not to take it, as Brody did, Warren worries that Thomson's violinist analogy can justify only a small proportion of abortions. Warren thus believes, like Brody but contrary to Thomson, that the status of the fetus is of central importance in assessing abortion.

Warren's approach rests on a fundamental distinction that, if she is correct, would undermine both the traditional pro-life position and Brody's somewhat more moderate one. That distinction, according to Warren, is between a biological human being, on one hand, and the "moral community," whose members enjoy full and equal moral rights, on the other. Merely being a member of the species *Homo*

From *The Monist*, 1973. © 1973 *The Monist*, La Salle, IL 61301. Reprinted by permission.

sapiens is not, she argues, sufficient to qualify as a moral person. Warren then goes on to discuss the circumstances in which a being should be regarded as having full moral rights; what, she asks, are the criteria for "personhood"? In the last sections of her paper, Warren explores some of the consequences of her theory. Even very late abortions do not take the life of a person, she contends, nor is it relevant that a (merely) potential person is killed in abortions since its rights cannot outweigh the rights of already existing women. Mary Anne Warren is professor of philosophy at San Francisco State University.

We will be concerned with both the moral status of abortion, which for our purposes we may define as the act which a woman performs in voluntarily terminating, or allowing another person to terminate, her pregnancy, and the legal status which is appropriate for this act. I will argue that, while it is not possible to produce a satisfactory defense of a woman's right to obtain an abortion without showing that a fetus is not a human being, in the morally relevant sense of that term, we ought not to conclude that the difficulties involved in determining whether or not a fetus is human make it impossible to produce any satisfactory solution to the problem of the moral status of abortion. For it is possible to show that, on the basis of intuitions which we may expect even the opponents of abortion to share, a fetus is not a person, and hence not the sort of entity to which it is proper to ascribe full moral rights.

Of course, while some philosophers would deny the possibility of any such proof,[1] others will deny that there is any need for it, since the moral permissibility of abortion appears to them to be too obvious to require proof. But the inadequacy of this attitude should be evident from the fact that both the friends and the foes of abortion consider their position to be morally self-evident. Because proabortionists have never adequately come to grips with the conceptual issues surrounding abortion, most if not all, of the arguments which they advance in opposition to laws restricting access to abortion fail to refute or even weaken the traditional antiabortion argument, i.e., that a fetus is a human being, and therefore abortion is murder.

These arguments are typically of one of two sorts. Either they point to the terrible side effects of the restrictive laws, e.g., the deaths due to illegal abortions, and the fact that it is poor women who suffer the most as a result of these laws, or else they state that to deny a woman access to abortion is to deprive her of her right to control her own body.

Unfortunately, however, the fact that restricting access to abortion has tragic side effects does not, in itself, show that the restrictions are unjustified, since murder is wrong regardless of the consequences of prohibiting it; and the appeal to the right to control one's body, which is generally construed as a property right, is at best a rather feeble argument for the permissibility of abortion. Mere ownership does not give me the right to kill innocent people whom I find on my property, and indeed I am apt to be held responsible if such people injure themselves while on my property. It is equally unclear that I have any moral right to expel an innocent person from my property when I know that doing so will result in his death.

Furthermore, it is probably inappropriate to describe a woman's body as her property, since it seems natural to hold that a person is something distinct from her property, but not from her body. Even those who would object to the identification of a person with his body, or with the conjunction of his body and his mind, must admit that it would be very odd to describe, say, breaking a leg, as damaging one's property, and much more appropriate to describe it as injuring *oneself*. Thus it is probably a mistake to argue that the right to obtain an abortion is in any way derived from the right to own and regulate property.

But however we wish to construe the right to abortion, we cannot hope to convince those who consider abortion a form of murder of the existence of any such right unless we are able to produce a clear and convincing refutation of the traditional antiabortion argument, and this has not, to my knowledge, been done. With respect to the two most vital issues which that argument involves, i.e., the humanity of the fetus and its implication for the moral status of abortion, confusion has prevailed on both sides of the dispute.

Thus, both proabortionists and antiabortionists have tended to abstract the question of whether abortion is wrong to that of whether it is wrong to destroy a fetus, just as though the rights of another person were not necessarily involved. This mistaken abstraction has led to the almost universal assumption that if a fetus is a human being, with a right to life, then it follows immediately that abortion is wrong (except perhaps when necessary to save the woman's life), and that it ought to be prohibited. It has also been generally assumed that unless the question about the status of the fetus is answered, the moral status of abortion cannot possibly be determined. . . .

The question which we must answer in order to produce a satisfactory solution to the problem of the moral status of abortion is this: How are we to define the moral community, the set of beings with full and equal moral rights, such that we can decide whether a human fetus is a member of this community or not? What sort of entity, exactly, has the inalienable rights to life, liberty, and the pursuit of happiness? Jefferson attributed these rights to all *men,* and it may or may not be fair to suggest that he intended to attribute them *only* to men. Perhaps he ought to have attributed them to all human beings. If so, then we arrive, first, at the problem of defining what makes a being human, and, second, at the equally vital question . . . namely, What reason is there for identifying the moral community with the set of all human beings, in whatever way we have chosen to define that term?

ON THE DEFINITION OF "HUMAN"

One reason why this vital second question is so frequently overlooked in the debate over the moral status of abortion is that the term "human" has two distinct, but not often distinguished, senses. This fact results in a slide of meaning, which serves to conceal the fallaciousness of the traditional argument that since (1) it is wrong to kill innocent human beings, and (2) fetuses are innocent human beings, then (3) it is wrong to kill fetuses. For if "human" is used in the same sense in both (1) and (2) then, whichever of the two senses is meant, one of these premises is question-begging. And if it is used in two different senses then of course the conclusion doesn't follow.

Thus, (1) is a self-evident moral truth,[2] and avoids begging the question about abortion, only if "human being" is used to mean something like "a full-fledged member of the moral community." (It may or may not also be meant to refer exclusively to members of the species *Homo sapiens.*) We may call this the *moral* sense of "human." It is not to be confused with what we will call the *genetic* sense, i.e., the sense in which *any* member of the species is a human being, and no member of any other species could be. If (1) is acceptable only if the moral sense is intended, (2) is non-question-begging only if what is intended is the genetic sense.

In "Deciding Who is Human," Noonan argues for the classification of fetuses with human beings by pointing to the presence of the full genetic code, and the potential capacity for rational thought.[3] It is clear that what he needs to show, for his version of the traditional argument to be valid, is that fetuses are human in the moral sense, the sense in which it is analytically true that all human beings have full moral rights. But, in the absence of any argument showing that whatever is genetically human is also morally human, and he gives none, nothing more than genetic humanity can be demonstrated by the presence of the human genetic code. And, as we will see, the *potential* capacity for rational thought can at most show that an entity has the potential for *becoming* human in the moral sense.

DEFINING THE MORAL COMMUNITY

Can it be established that genetic humanity is sufficient for moral humanity? I think that there are very good reasons for not defining the moral community in this way. I would like to suggest an alternative way of defining the moral community, which I will argue for only to the extent of explaining why it is, or should be, self-evident. The suggestion is simply that the moral community consists of all and only *people,* rather than all and only human beings;[4] and probably the best way of demonstrating its self-evidence is by considering the concept of personhood, to see what sorts of entity are and are not persons, and what the decision that a being is or is not a person implies about its moral rights.

What characteristics entitle an entity to be considered a person? This is obviously not the place to attempt a complete analysis of the concept of personhood, but we do not need such a fully adequate analysis just to determine whether and why a fetus is or isn't a person. All we need is a rough and approximate list of the most basic criteria of personhood, and some idea of which, or how many, of these an entity must satisfy in order to properly be considered a person.

In searching for such criteria, it is useful to look beyond the set of people with whom we are acquainted, and ask how we would decide whether a totally alien being was a person or not. (For we have no right to assume that genetic humanity is necessary for personhood.) Imagine a space traveler who lands on an unknown planet and encounters a race of beings utterly unlike any he has ever seen or heard of. If he wants to be sure of behaving morally toward these beings, he has to somehow decide whether they are people, and hence have full moral rights, or whether they are the sort of thing which he need not feel guilty about treating as, for example, a source of food.

How should he go about making this decision? If he has some anthropological background, he might look for such things as religion, art, and the manufacturing of tools, weapons, or shelters, since these factors have been used to distinguish our human from our prehuman ancestors, in what seems to be closer to the moral than the genetic sense of "human." And no doubt he would be right to consider the presence of such factors as good evidence that the alien beings were people, and morally human. It would, however, be overly anthropocentric of him to take the absence of these things as adequate evidence that they were not, since we can imagine people who have progressed beyond, or evolved without ever developing, these cultural characteristics.

I suggest that the traits which are most central to the concept of personhood, or humanity in the moral sense, are, very roughly, the following:

(1) consciousness (of objects and events external and/or internal to the being), and in particular the capacity to feel pain;

(2) reasoning (the *developed* capacity to solve new and relatively complex problems);

(3) self-motivated activity (activity which is relatively independent of either genetic or direct external control);

(4) the capacity to communicate, by whatever means, messages of an indefinite variety of types, that is, not just with an indefinite number of possible contents, but on indefinitely many possible topics;

(5) the presence of self-concepts, and self-awareness, either individual, or racial, or both.

Admittedly, there are apt to be a great many problems involved in formulating precise definitions of these criteria, let alone in developing universally valid behavioral criteria for deciding when they apply. But I will assume that both we and our explorer know approximately what (1)–(5) mean, and that he is also able to determine whether or not they apply. How, then, should he use his findings to decide whether or not the alien beings are people? We needn't suppose that an entity must have *all* of these attributes to be properly considered a person; (1) and (2) alone may well be sufficient for personhood, and quite probably (1)–(3) are sufficient. Neither do we need to insist that any one of these criteria is *necessary* for personhood, although once again (1) and (2) look like fairly good candidates for necessary conditions, as does (3), if "activity" is construed so as to include the activity of reasoning.

All we need to claim, to demonstrate that a fetus is not a person, is that any being which satisfies *none* of (1)–(5) is certainly not a person. I consider this claim to be so obvious that I think anyone who denied it, and claimed that a being which satisfied none of (1)–(5) was a person all the same, would thereby demonstrate that he had no notion at all of what a person is—perhaps because he had confused the concept of a person with that of genetic humanity. If the opponents of abortion were to deny the appropriateness of these five criteria, I do not know what further arguments would convince them. We would probably have to admit that our conceptual schemes were indeed irreconcilably different, and that our dispute could not be settled objectively.

I do not expect this to happen, however, since I think that the concept of a person is one which is very nearly universal (to people), and that it is common to both proabortionists and antiabortionists, even though neither group has fully realized the relevance of this concept to the resolution of their dispute. Furthermore, I think that on reflection even the antiabortionists ought to agree not only that (1)–(5) are central to the concept of personhood, but also that it is a part of this concept that all and only people have full moral rights. The concept of a person is in part a moral concept; once we have admitted that *x* is a person we have recognized, even if we have not agreed to respect, *x*'s right to be treated as a member of the moral community. It is true that the claim that *x* is a *human being* is more commonly voiced as part of an appeal to treat *x* decently than is the claim that *x* is a person, but this is either because "human being" is here used in the sense which implies personhood, or because the genetic and moral senses of "human" have been confused.

Now if (1)–(5) are indeed the primary criteria of personhood, then it is clear that genetic humanity is neither necessary nor sufficient for establishing that an entity is a person. Some human beings are not people, and there may well be people who are not human beings. A man or woman whose consciousness has been permanently obliterated but who remains alive is a human being which is no longer a person; defective human beings, with no appreciable mental capacity, are not and presumably never will be people; and a fetus is a human being which is not yet a person, and which therefore cannot coherently be said to have full moral rights. Citizens of the next century should be prepared to recognize highly advanced, self-aware robots or computers, should such be developed, and intelligent inhabitants of other worlds, should such be found, as people in the fullest sense, and to respect their moral rights. But to ascribe full moral rights to an entity which is not a person is as absurd as to ascribe moral obligations and responsibilities to such an entity.

FETAL DEVELOPMENT AND THE RIGHT TO LIFE

Two problems arise in the application of these suggestions for the definition of the moral com-

munity to the determination of the precise moral status of a human fetus. Given that the paradigm example of a person is a normal adult human being, then (1) How like this paradigm, in particular how far advanced since conception, does a human being need to be before it begins to have a right to life by virtue, not of being fully a person as of yet, but of being *like* a person? and (2) To what extent, if any, does the fact that a fetus has the *potential* for becoming a person endow it with some of the same rights? Each of these questions requires some comment.

In answering the first question, we need not attempt a detailed consideration of the moral rights of organisms which are not developed enough, aware enough, intelligent enough, etc., to be considered people, but which resemble people in some respects. It does seem reasonable to suggest that the more like a person, in the relevant respects, a being is, the stronger is the case for regarding it as having a right to life, and indeed the stronger its right to life is. Thus we ought to take seriously the suggestion that, insofar as "the human individual develops biologically in a continuous fashion . . . the rights of a human person might develop in the same way."[5] But we must keep in mind that the attributes which are relevant in determining whether or not an entity is enough like a person to be regarded as having some of the same moral rights are no different from those which are relevant to determining whether or not it is fully a person—i.e., are no different from (1)–(5)—and that being genetically human, or having recognizably human facial and other physical features, or detectable brain activity, or the capacity to survive outside the uterus, are simply not among these relevant attributes.

Thus it is clear that even though a seven- or eight-month fetus has features which make it apt to arouse in us almost the same powerful protective instinct as is commonly aroused by a small infant, nevertheless it is not significantly more personlike than is a very small embryo. It is *somewhat* more personlike; it can apparently feel and respond to pain, and it may even have a rudimentary form of consciousness, insofar as its brain is quite active. Nevertheless, it seems safe to say that it is not fully conscious, in the way that an infant of a few months is, and that it cannot reason, or communicate messages of indefinitely many sorts, does not engage in self-motivated activity, and has no self-awareness. Thus, in the *relevant* respects, a fetus, even a fully developed one, is considerably less personlike than is the average mature mammal, indeed the average fish. And I think that a rational person must conclude that if the right to life of a fetus is to be based upon its resemblance to a person, then it cannot be said to have any more right to life than, let us say, a newborn guppy (which also seems to be capable of feeling pain), and that a right of that magnitude could never override a woman's right to obtain an abortion, at any stage of her pregnancy.

There may, of course, be other arguments in favor of placing legal limits upon the stage of pregnancy in which an abortion may be performed. Given the relative safety of the new techniques of artificially inducing labor during the third trimester, the danger to the woman's life or health is no longer such an argument. Neither is the fact that people tend to respond to the thought of abortion in the later stages of pregnancy with emotional repulsion, since mere emotional responses cannot take the place of moral reasoning in determining what ought to be permitted. Nor, finally, is the frequently heard argument that legalizing abortion, especially late in the pregnancy, may erode the level of respect for human life, leading, perhaps, to an increase in unjustified euthanasia and other crimes. For this threat, if it is a threat, can be better met by educating people to the kinds of moral distinctions which we are making here than by limiting access to abortion (which limitation may, in its disregard for the rights of women, be just as damaging to the level of respect for human rights).

Thus, since the fact that even a fully developed fetus is not personlike enough to have any significant right to life on the basis of its personlikeness shows that no legal restrictions upon the stage of pregnancy in which an abortion may be performed can be justified on the grounds that we should protect the rights of the older fetus and since there is no other apparent justification for such restrictions, we may conclude that they are entirely unjustified. Whether or not it would be *indecent* (whatever that means) for a woman in her seventh month to obtain an abortion just to avoid having to postpone a trip to Europe, it would not, in itself, be *immoral*, and therefore it ought to be permitted.

POTENTIAL PERSONHOOD AND THE RIGHT TO LIFE

We have seen that a fetus does not resemble a person in any way which can support the claim that it has even some of the same rights. But what about its *potential,* the fact that if nurtured and allowed to develop naturally it will very probably become a person? Doesn't that alone give it at least some right to life? It is hard to deny that the fact that an entity is a potential person is a strong prima facie reason for not destroying it; but we need not conclude from this that a potential person has a right to life, by virtue of that potential. It may be that our feeling that it is better, other things being equal, not to destroy a potential person is better explained by the fact that potential people are still (felt to be) an invaluable resource, not to be lightly squandered. Surely, if every speck of dust were a potential person, we would be much less apt to conclude that every potential person has a right to become actual.

Still, we do not need to insist that a potential person has no right to life whatever. There may be something immoral, and not just imprudent, about wantonly destroying potential people, when doing so isn't necessary to protect anyone's rights. But even if a potential person does have some prima facie right to life, such a right could not possibly outweigh the right of a woman to obtain an abortion, since the rights of any actual person invariably outweigh those of any potential person, whenever the two conflict. Since this may not be immediately obvious in the case of a human fetus, let us look at another case.

Suppose that our space explorer falls into the hands of an alien culture, whose scientists decide to create a few hundred thousand or more human beings, by breaking his body into its component cells, and using these to create fully developed human beings, with, of course, his genetic code. We may imagine that each of these newly created men will have all of the original man's abilities, skills, knowledge, and so on, and also have an individual self-concept, in short that each of them will be a bona fide (though hardly unique) person. Imagine that the whole project will take only seconds, and that its chances of success are extremely high, and that our explorer knows all of this, and also knows that these people will be treated fairly. I maintain that in such a situation he would have every right to escape if he could, and thus to deprive all of these potential people of their potential lives; for his right to life outweighs all of theirs together, in spite of the fact that they are all genetically human, all innocent, and all have a very high probability of becoming people very soon, if only he refrains from acting.

Indeed, I think he would have a right to escape even if it were not his life which the alien scientists planned to take, but only a year of his freedom, or, indeed, only a day. Nor would he be obligated to stay if he had gotten captured (thus bringing all these people-potentials into existence) because of his own carelessness, or even if he had done so deliberately, knowing the consequences. Regardless of how he got captured, he is not morally obligated to remain in captivity for *any* period of time for the sake of permitting any number of potential people to come into actuality, so great is the margin by which one actual person's right to liberty outweighs whatever right to life even a hundred thousand potential people have. And it seems reasonable to conclude that the rights of a woman will outweigh by a similar margin whatever right to life a fetus may have by virtue of its potential personhood.

Thus, neither a fetus's resemblance to a person, nor its potential for becoming a person provides any basis whatever for the claim that it has any significant right to life. Consequently, a woman's right to protect her health, happiness, freedom, and even her life,[6] by terminating an unwanted pregnancy, will always override whatever right to life it may be appropriate to ascribe to a fetus, even a fully developed one. And thus, in the absence of any overwhelming social need for every possible child, the laws which restrict the right to obtain an abortion, or limit the period of pregnancy during which an abortion may be performed, are a wholly unjustified violation of a woman's most basic moral and constitutional rights.

NOTES

1. For example, Roger Wertheimer, who in "Understanding the Abortion Argument" (*Philosophy and Public Affairs,* 1, no. 1 [Fall 1971], 67–95), argues that the problem of the moral status of abortion is insoluble, in that the dispute over the status of the fetus is not a question of fact at all, but only a question of how one responds to the facts.

2. Of course, the principle that it is (always) wrong to kill innocent human beings is in need of many other modifications, e.g., that it may be permissible to do so to save a greater number of other innocent human beings, but we may safely ignore these complications here.

3. John Noonan, "Deciding Who Is Human," *Natural Law Forum,* 13 (1968), p. 135.

4. From here on, we will use "human" to mean genetically human, since the moral sense seems closely connected to, and perhaps derived from, the assumption that genetic humanity is sufficient for membership in the moral community.

5. Thomas L. Hayes, "A Biological View," *Commonweal,* 85 (March 17, 1967), 677–78; quoted by Daniel Callahan in *Abortion, Law, Choice, and Morality* (London: Macmillan, 1970).

6. That is, insofar as the death rate, for the woman, is higher for childbirth than for early abortion.

REVIEW AND DISCUSSION QUESTIONS

1. How does Warren answer those who defend the right to an abortion based on the "terrible side effects" of anti-abortion laws?

2. How does Warren respond to those who defend abortion on the ground that the woman "owns" her body?

3. Explain the biological or genetic sense of the term *human,* indicating how Warren thinks that sense differs from the "moral" sense of the term.

4. On what basis does Warren think a human fetus is not a moral person?

5. How does Warren respond to those who argue that even if a fetus isn't a person, it is still a potential one and for that reason should not be killed?

6. Do you agree that, in theory at least, it is possible for there to be a "person" who is not a biological human? Explain, indicating the significance of that position for abortion.

7. When, in the course of your development, would Warren say you became a moral "person"?

8. In response to those who point out her view might justify infanticide, Warren has responded that it does not since (1) other people, besides the mother, would like the infant to raise themselves and (2) others also value infants and would prefer they not be killed. Are those responses adequate, in your opinion? Explain.

9. "One virtue of Warren's approach is that it solves not only the abortion problem but also helps resolve cases in which a human being has become a 'human vegetable' and therefore should not be kept alive." Explain that comment, indicating whether or not you agree.

8
War and Violence

Essays in Section 8 consider another of the issues of life and death, killing in war. Articles represent different perspectives and look at a range of issues, including the question of whether morality is relevant to war at all, the justifications of going to war, the legitimacy of killing innocents in wartime, and the claims of the absolute pacifist. Woven into these essays is another issue, considered from various angles, which is the role of violence in human life and whether competitive sports, such as boxing and football, encourage violence—or, rather, provide the occasion to develop genuinely important moral virtues. Also included is a famous court case in which a deeply divided U.S. Supreme Court allowed internment of Japanese Americans in concentration camps during World War II, raising further questions about moral limits in the conduct of war.

The Moral Equivalent of War

William James

William James (1842–1910) is among the best known and most widely read American philosophers. Along with John Dewey and C. S. Peirce, James was among the founders of what has come to be known as *philosophical pragmatism*. In addition to his work as a philosopher, James was also a psychologist and wrote important books in that field as well as in the fields of religion, science, ethics, and other areas of philosophy. William James's brother was Henry James, the novelist. William James was a pacifist, though in this essay, printed posthumously, he begins with a description of present-day attitudes toward war and the disputes between pacificists and war's apologists. He then turns to the virtues that, he believes, are realized in war and preserved by militarism and to the fears of "degeneration" that will follow from the transition to a "pleasure economy." James then considers how these fears might be overcome and war avoided. It would require, he says, much more imagination than is normal for society. He concludes with a proposal: universal conscription for a war against *Nature*.

The war against war is going to be no holiday excursion or camping party. The military feelings are too deeply grounded to abdicate their place among our ideals until better substitutes are offered than the glory and shame that come to nations as well as to individuals from the ups and downs of politics and the vicissitudes of trade. There is something highly paradoxical in the modern man's

First published in leaflet form by the Association for International Conciliation (1910) and later in *McClure's* (August 1910) and *The Popular Science Monthly* (October 1910).

relation to war. Ask all our millions, north and south, whether they would vote now (were such a thing possible) to have our war for the Union expunged from history, and the record of a peaceful transition to the present time substituted for that of its marches and battles, and probably hardly a handful of eccentrics would say yes. Those ancestors, those efforts, those memories and legends, are the most ideal part of what we now own together, a sacred spiritual possession worth more than all the blood poured out. Yet ask those same people whether they would be willing in cold blood to start another civil war now to gain another similar possession, and not one man or woman would vote for the proposition. In modern eyes, precious though wars may be, they must not be waged solely for the sake of the ideal harvest. Only when forced upon one, only when an enemy's injustice leaves us no alternative, is a war now thought permissible.

It was not thus in ancient times. The earlier men were hunting men, and to hunt a neighboring tribe, kill the males, loot the village and possess the females, was the most profitable, as well as the most exciting, way of living. Thus were the more martial tribes selected, and in chiefs and peoples a pure pugnacity and love of glory came to mingle with the more fundamental appetite for plunder.

Modern war is so expensive that we feel trade to be a better avenue to plunder; but modern man inherits all the innate pugnacity and all the love of glory of his ancestors. Showing war's irrationality and horror is of no effect upon him. The horrors make the fascination. War is the *strong* life; it is life *in extremis;* war-taxes are the only ones men never hesitate to pay, as the budgets of all nations show us. . . .

. . . We inherit the warlike type; and for most of the capacities of heroism that the human race is full of we have to thank this cruel history. Dead men tell no tales, and if there were any tribes of other type than this they have left no survivors. Our ancestors have bred pugnacity into our bone and marrow, and thousands of years of peace won't breed it out of us. The popular imagination fairly fattens on the thought of wars. Let public opinion once reach a certain fighting pitch, and no ruler can withstand it. . . .

At the present day, civilized opinion is a curious mental mixture. The military instincts and ideals are as strong as ever, but are confronted by reflective criticisms which sorely curb their ancient freedom. Innumerable writers are showing up the bestial side of military service. Pure loot and mastery seem no longer morally avowable motives, and pretexts must be found for attributing them solely to the enemy. . . . It may even reasonably be said that the intensely sharp competitive *preparation* for war by the nations *is the real war,* permanent, unceasing; and that the battles are only a sort of public verification of the mastery gained during the "peace" interval.

It is plain that on this subject civilized man has developed a sort of double personality. If we take European nations, no legitimate interest of any one of them would seem to justify the tremendous destructions which a war to compass it would necessarily entail. It would seem as though common sense and reason ought to find a way to reach agreement in every conflict of honest interests. I myself think it our bounden duty to believe in such international rationality as possible. But, as things stand, I see how desperately hard it is to bring the peace-party and the war-party together, and I believe that the difficulty is due to certain deficiencies in the program of pacificism which set the militarist imagination strongly, and to a certain extent justifiably, against it. In the whole discussion both sides are on imaginative and sentimental ground. It is but one utopia against another, and everything one says must be abstract and hypothetical. Subject to this criticism and caution, I will try to characterize in abstract strokes the opposite imaginative forces, and point out what to my own very fallible mind seems the best utopian hypothesis, the most promising line of conciliation.

In my remarks, pacificist though I am, I will refuse to speak of the bestial side of the war-*regime* (already done justice to by many writers) and consider only the higher aspects of militaristic sentiment. Patriotism no one thinks discreditable; nor does any one deny that war is the romance of history. But inordinate ambitions are the soul of every patriotism, and the possibility of violent death the soul of all romance. The military patriotic and romantic-minded everywhere, and especially the professional military class, refuse to admit for a moment that war may be a transitory phenomenon in social evolution. The notion of a sheep's paradise like that revolts, they say, our higher imagination. Where then would be the steeps of life? If war had ever stopped, we should have to re-invent it, on this view, to redeem life from flat degeneration.

Reflective apologists for war at the present day all take it religiously. It is a sort of sacrament. Its profits are to the vanquished as well as to the victor; and quite apart from any question of profit, it is an absolute good, we are told, for it is human nature at its highest dynamic. Its "horrors" are a cheap price to pay for rescue from the only alternative supposed, of a world of clerks and teachers, of co-education and zo-ophily, of "consumer's leagues" and "associated charities," of industrialism unlimited, and feminism unabashed. No scorn, no hardness, no valor any more! Fie upon such a cattleyard of a planet!

So far as the central essence of this feeling goes, no healthy minded person, it seems to me, can help to some degree partaking of it. Militarism is the great preserver of our ideals of hardihood, and human life with no use for hardihood would be contemptible. Without risks or prizes for the darer, history would be insipid indeed; and there is a type of military character which every one feels that the race should never cease to breed, for every one is sensitive to its superiority. The duty is incumbent on mankind, of keeping military characters in stock—of keeping them, if not for use, then as ends in themselves and as pure pieces of perfection,—so that Roosevelt's weaklings and mollycoddles may not end by making everything else disappear from the face of nature.

This natural sort of feeling forms, I think, the innermost soul of army-writings. Without any exception known to me, militarist authors take a highly mystical view of their subject, and regard war as a biological or sociological necessity, uncontrolled by ordinary psychological checks and motives. When the time of development is ripe the war must come, reason or no reason, for the justifications pleaded are invariably fictitious. War is, in short, a permanent human obligation. General Homer Lea, in his recent book "The Valor of Ignorance," plants himself squarely on this

ground. Readiness for war is for him the essence of nationality, and ability in it the supreme measure of the health of nations. . . .

Other militarists are more complex and more moral in their considerations. The "Philosophie des Krieges," by S. R. Steinmetz is a good example. War, according to this author, is an ordeal instituted by God, who weighs the nations in its balance. It is the essential form of the State, and the only function in which peoples can employ all their powers at once and convergently. No victory is possible save as the resultant of a totality of virtues, no defeat for which some vice or weakness is not responsible. Fidelity, cohesiveness, tenacity, heroism, conscience, education, inventiveness, economy, wealth, physical health and vigor—there isn't a moral or intellectual point of superiority that doesn't tell, when God holds his assizes and hurls the peoples upon one another. *Die Weltgeschichte ist das Weltgericht;* [Schiller, "History Is the Last Judgment"—ed.] and Dr. Steinmetz does not believe that in the long run chance and luck play any part in apportioning the issues.

The virtues that prevail, it must be noted, are virtues anyhow, superiorities that count in peaceful as well as in military competition; but the strain on them, being infinitely intenser in the latter case, makes war infinitely more searching as a trial. No ordeal is comparable to its winnowings. Its dread hammer is the welder of men into cohesive states, and nowhere but in such states can human nature adequately develop its capacity. The only alternative is "degeneration."

Dr. Steinmetz is a conscientious thinker, and his book, short as it is, takes much into account. Its upshot can, it seems to me, be summed up in Simon Patten's word, that mankind was nursed in pain and fear, and that the transition to a "pleasure-economy" may be fatal to a being wielding no powers of defense against its disintegrative influences. If we speak of the *fear of emancipation from the fear-regime,* we put the whole situation into a single phrase; fear regarding ourselves now taking the place of the ancient fear of the enemy.

Turn the fear over as I will in my mind, it all seems to lead back to two unwillingnesses of the imagination, one aesthetic, and the other moral; unwillingness, first to envisage a future in which army-life, with its many elements of charm, shall be forever impossible, and in which the destinies of peoples shall nevermore be decided quickly, thrillingly, and tragically, by force, but only gradually and insipidly by "evolution"; and, secondly, unwillingness to see the supreme theatre of human strenuousness closed, and the splendid military aptitudes of men doomed to keep always in a state of latency and never show themselves in action. These insistent unwillingnesses, no less than other aesthetic and ethical insistencies, have, it seems to me, to be listened to and respected. One cannot meet them effectively by mere counter-insistency on war's expensiveness and horror. The horror makes the thrill; and when the question is of getting the extremest and supremest out of human nature, talk of expense sounds ignominious. The weakness of so much merely negative criticism is evident—pacificism makes no converts from the military party. The military party denies neither the bestiality nor the horror, nor the expense; it only says that these things tell but half the story. It only says that war is *worth* them; that, taking human nature as a whole, its wars are its best protection against its weaker and more cowardly self, and that mankind cannot *afford* to adopt a peace-economy.

Pacificists ought to enter more deeply into the aesthetical and ethical point of view of their opponents. . . . So long as anti-militarists propose no substitute for war's disciplinary function, no *moral equivalent* of war, analogous, as one might say, to the mechanical equivalent of heat, so long they fail to realize the full inwardness of the situation. And as a rule they do fail. The duties, penalties, and sanctions pictured in the utopias they paint are all too weak and tame to touch the military-minded. Tolstoy's pacificism is the only exception to this rule, for it is profoundly pessimistic as regards all this world's values, and makes the fear of the Lord furnish the moral spur provided elsewhere by the fear of the enemy. But our socialistic peace-advocates all believe absolutely in this world's values; and instead of the fear of the Lord and the fear of the enemy, the only fear they reckon with is the fear of poverty if one be lazy. This weakness pervades all the socialistic literature with which I am acquainted. . . . Meanwhile men at large still live as they always have

lived, under a pain-and-fear economy—for those of us who live in an ease-economy are but an island in the stormy ocean—and the whole atmosphere of present-day utopian literature tastes mawkish and dishwatery to people who still keep a sense for life's more bitter flavors. It suggests, in truth, ubiquitous inferiority. . . .

. . . All the qualities of a man acquire dignity when he knows that the service of the collectivity that owns him needs them. If proud of the collectivity, his own pride rises in proportion. No collectivity is like an army for nourishing such pride; but it has to be confessed that the only sentiment which the image of pacific cosmopolitan industrialism is capable of arousing in countless worthy breasts is shame at the idea of belonging to *such* a collectivity. It is obvious that the United States of America as they exist today impress a mind like General Lea's as so much human blubber. Where is the sharpness and precipitousness, the contempt for life, whether one's own, or another's? Where is the savage "yes" and "no," the unconditional duty? Where is the conscription? Where is the blood-tax? Where is anything that one feels honored by belonging to?

Having said thus much in preparation, I will now confess my own utopia. I devoutly believe in the reign of peace and in the gradual advent of some sort of a socialistic equilibrium. The fatalistic view of the war-function is to me nonsense, for I know that war-making is due to definite motives and subject to prudential checks and reasonable criticisms, just like any other form of enterprise. And when whole nations are the armies, and the science of destruction vies in intellectual refinement with the sciences of production, I see that war becomes absurd and impossible from its own monstrosity. Extravagant ambitions will have to be replaced by reasonable claims, and nations must make common cause against them. . . . I look forward to a future when acts of war shall be formally outlawed as between civilized peoples.

All these beliefs of mine put me squarely into the anti-militarist party. But I do not believe that peace either ought to be or will be permanent on this globe, unless the states pacifically organized preserve some of the old elements of army-discipline. A permanently successful peace-economy cannot be a simple pleasure-economy. In the more or less socialistic future towards which mankind seems drifting we must still subject ourselves collectively to those severities which answer to our real position upon this only partly hospitable globe. We must make new energies and hardihoods continue the manliness to which the military mind so faithfully clings. Martial virtues must be the enduring cement; intrepidity, contempt of softness, surrender of private interest, obedience to command, must still remain the rock upon which states are built—unless, indeed, we wish for dangerous reactions against commonwealths fit only for contempt, and liable to invite attack whenever a center of crystallization for military-minded enterprise gets formed anywhere in their neighborhood.

The war-party is assuredly right in affirming and reaffirming that the martial virtues, although originally gained by the race through war, are absolute and permanent human goods. Patriotic pride and ambition in their military form are, after all, only specifications of a more general competitive passion. They are its first form, but that is no reason for supposing them to be its last form. Men now are proud of belonging to a conquering nation, and without a murmur they lay down their persons and their wealth, if by so doing they may fend off subjection. But who can be sure that *other aspects of one's country* may not, with time and education and suggestion enough, come to be regarded with similarly effective feelings of pride and shame? Why should men not some day feel that it is worth a blood-tax to belong to a collectivity superior in *any* ideal respect? Why should they not blush with indignant shame if the community that owns them is vile in any way whatsoever? Individuals, daily more numerous, now feel this civic passion. It is only a question of blowing on the spark till the whole population gets incandescent, and on the ruins of the old morals of military honor, a stable system of morals of civic honor builds itself up. What the whole community comes to believe in grasps the individual as in a vise. The war-function has grasped us so far; but constructive interests may some day seem no less imperative, and impose on the individual a hardly lighter burden.

Let me illustrate my idea more concretely. There is nothing to make one indignant in the mere fact that life is hard, that men should toil and suffer pain. The planetary conditions once for all are such, and we can stand it. But that so many men, by mere accidents of birth and opportunity, should have a life of *nothing else* but toil and pain and hardness and inferiority imposed upon them, should have *no* vacation, while others natively no more deserving never get any taste of this campaigning life at all,—*this* is capable of arousing indignation in reflective minds. It may end by seeming shameful to all of us that some of us have nothing but campaigning, and others nothing but unmanly ease. If now—and this is my idea—there were, instead of military conscription a conscription of the whole youthful population to form for a certain number of years a part of the army enlisted against *Nature,* the injustice would tend to be evened out, and numerous other goods to the commonwealth would follow. The military ideals of hardihood and discipline would be wrought into the growing fiber of the people; no one would remain blind as the luxurious classes now are blind, to man's relations to the globe he lives on, and to the permanently sour and hard foundations of his higher life. To coal and iron mines, to freight trains, to fishing fleets in December, to dishwashing, clothes-washing, and window-washing, to road-building and tunnel-making, to foundries and stoke-holes, and to the frames of skyscrapers, would our gilded youths be drafted off, according to their choice, to get the childishness knocked out of them, and to come back into society with healthier sympathies and soberer ideas. They would have paid their blood-tax, done their own part in the immemorial human warfare against nature; they would tread the earth more proudly, the women would value them more highly, they would be better fathers and teachers of the following generation.

Such a conscription, with the state of public opinion that would have required it, and the many moral fruits it would bear, would preserve in the midst of a pacific civilization the manly virtues which the military party is so afraid of seeing disappear in peace. We should get toughness without callousness, authority with as little criminal cruelty as possible, and painful work done cheerily because the duty is temporary, and threatens not, as now, to degrade the whole remainder of one's life. I spoke of the "moral equivalent" of war. So far, war has been the only force that can discipline a whole community, and until an equivalent discipline is organized, I believe that war must have its way. But I have no serious doubt that the ordinary prides and shames of social man, once developed to a certain intensity, are capable of organizing such a moral equivalent as I have sketched, or some other just as effective for preserving manliness of type. It is but a question of time, of skillful propagandism, and of opinion-making men seizing historic opportunities.

The martial type of character can be bred without war. Strenuous honor and disinterestedness abound elsewhere. Priests and medical men are in a fashion educated to it, and we should all feel some degree of it imperative if we were conscious of our work as an obligatory service to the state. We should be owned, as soldiers are by the army, and our pride would rise accordingly. We could be poor, then, without humiliation, as army officers now are. The only thing needed henceforward is to inflame the civic temper as past history has inflamed the military temper. . . .

REVIEW AND DISCUSSION QUESTIONS

1. Why does James seem to think war is so popular?
2. What are the virtues that are realized in war? What is James's attitude toward them?
3. What "fears" motivate people to reject peace?
4. How does James propose to avoid war?
5. Compare James's essay with MacIntyre's discussion of patriotism in Section 3. Would James agree with MacIntyre?
6. Assess James's proposal to avoid war. What are its major advantages? Disadvantages?

On the Morality of War: A Preliminary Inquiry

Richard A. Wasserstrom

When is war justified, if at all? And what are the moral limits on how wars should be fought? Sometimes, it is believed, war itself is simply beyond the bounds of morality; if not everything is fair in love, at least it is in war. In this essay, Richard A. Wasserstrom discusses both the question of applying morality to war and the various issues that arise as one begins to think about the justification of war as well as the rules governing how wars should be fought. He also weighs the issues surrounding killing innocents. Richard A. Wasserstrom is professor of philosophy at the University of California at Santa Cruz.

From Richard Wasserstrom, "On the Morality of War: A Preliminary Inquiry," *Stanford Law Review,* 21, no. 6 (June 1969), pp. 1627–1656. © 1969 by the Board of Trustees of Leland Stanford Junior University. Reprinted by permission of the *Stanford Law Review* and the author. Some footnotes omitted.

1. WAR AND MORAL NIHILISM

Before we examine the moral criteria for assessing war, we must examine the claim that it is not possible to assess war in moral terms. . . . For want of a better name for this general view, I shall call it moral nihilism in respect to war. If it is correct, there is, of course, no point in going further.

. . . During the controversy over the rightness of the Vietnam War there have been any number of persons, including a large number in the university, who have claimed that in matters of war (but not in other matters) morality has no place. The war in Vietnam may, they readily concede, be stupid, unwise, or against the best interests of the United States, but it is neither immoral nor unjust—not because it is moral or right, but because these descriptions are *in this context* either naive or meaningless or inapplicable.

Nor is this view limited to the Vietnam war. Consider, for example, the following passage from a speech given only a few years ago by Dean Acheson:

[T]hose involved in the Cuban crisis of October, 1962, will remember the irrelevance of the supposed moral considerations brought out in the discussions. Judgment centered about the appraisal of dangers and risks, and weighing of the need for decisive and effective action against considerations of prudence; the need to do enough, against the consequences of doing too much. Moral talk did not bear on the problem. Nor did it bear upon the decision of those called upon to advise the President in 1949 whether and with what degree or urgency to press the attempt to produce a thermonuclear weapon. A respected colleague advised me that it would be better that our nation and people should perish rather than be party to a course so evil as producing that weapon. I told him that on the Day of Judgment his view might be confirmed and that he was free to go forth and preach the necessity for salvation. It was not, however, a view which I would entertain as a public servant.[1]

. . . Whatever may be the correct exegesis of this text, I want to treat it as illustrative of the position that morality has no place in the assessment of war. There are several things worth considering in respect to such a view. In the first place, the claim that in matters of war morality has no place is ambiguous. To put it somewhat loosely, the claim may be descriptive, or it may be analytic, or it may be prescriptive. Thus, it would be descriptive if it were merely the factual claim that matters relating to war uniformly turn out to be decided on grounds of national interest or expediency rather than by appeal to what is moral. This claim I will not consider further; it is an empirical one better answered by students of American (and foreign) diplomatic relations.

It would be a prescriptive claim were it taken to assert that matters relating to war ought always be decided by appeal to (say) national interest rather than an appeal to the moral point of view. For reasons which have yet to be elucidated, on this view the moral criteria are capable of being employed but it is undesirable to do so. I shall say something more about this view in a moment.

The analytic point is not that morality ought not be used, but rather that it cannot. On this view the statement "The United States is behaving immorally in the way it is waging war in Vietnam" (or, "in waging war in Vietnam") is not wrong but meaningless.

What are we to make of the analytic view? As I have indicated, it could, of course, be advanced simply as an instance of a more sweeping position concerning the general meaninglessness of the moral point of view. What I find particularly interesting, though, is the degree to which this thesis is advanced as a special view about war and not as a part of a more general claim that all morality is meaningless.

I think that there are at least [three] reasons why this special view may be held. First, the accusation that one's own country is involved in an immoral war is personally very threatening. For one thing, if the accusation is well-founded it may be thought to imply that certain types of socially cooperative behavior are forbidden to the citizen and that other kinds of socially deviant behavior are obligatory upon him. Yet, in a time of war it is following just this sort of dictate that will be treated more harshly by the actor's own government. Hence the morally responsible citizen is put in a most troublesome moral dilemma. If his country is engaged in an immoral war then he may have a duty to oppose and resist; yet opposition and resistance will typically carry extraordinarily severe penalties.

The pressure is, I suspect, simply too great for many of us. We are unwilling to pay the fantastically high personal price that goes with the moral point of view, and we are equally unwilling to plead guilty to this most serious charge of immorality. So we solve the problem by denying the possibility that war can be immoral. The relief is immediate; the moral "heat" is off. If war cannot be immoral, then one's country cannot be engaged in an immoral war, but only a stupid or unwise one. And whatever one's obligation to keep one's country from behaving stupidly or improvidently, they are vastly less stringent and troublesome than obligations imposed by the specter of complicity in an immoral war. We may, however, pay a price for such relief since we obliterate the moral distinctions between the Axis and the Allies in World War II at the same time as the distinctions between the conduct of the United States in 1941–45 and the conduct of the United States in 1967–68 in Vietnam.

Second, I think the view that moral judgments are meaningless sometimes seems plausible because of the differences between personal behavior and the behavior of states. There are not laws governing the behavior of states in the same way in which there are positive laws governing the behavior of citizens. International law is a troublesome notion just because it is both like and unlike our concept of positive law.

Now, how does skepticism about the law-like quality of international law lead to the claim that it is impossible for war to be either moral or immoral? It is far from obvious. Perhaps it is because there is at least one sense of justice that is intimately bound up with the notion of rule-violation; namely, that which relates justice to the following of rules and to the condemnation and punishment of those who break rules. In the absence of positive laws governing the behavior of states, it may be inferred (although I think mistakenly) that it is impossible for states to behave either justly or unjustly. But even if justice can be said to be analyzable solely in terms of following rules, morality certainly cannot. Hence the absence of international laws cannot serve to make the moral appraisal of war impossible.

. . . More plausible, is the view that says there can be no moral assessment of war just because there is, by definition, no morality in war. If war is an activity in which anything goes, moral judgments on war are just not possible.

To this there are two responses. To begin with, it is not, as our definitional discussion indicates, a necessary feature of war that it be an activity in which everything is morally permissible. There is a difference between the view that war is unique because killing and violence are morally permissible in contexts and circumstances where they otherwise would not be and the view that war is unique because everything is morally permissible.

A less absolutist argument for the absurdity of discussing the morality of war might be that at least today the prevailing (although not necessary) conception of war is one that as a practical matter rules out no behavior on moral grounds. After all, if flame throwers are deemed perfectly permissible, if the bombing of cities is applauded and not condemned, and if thermonuclear weapons are part of the arsenal of each of the major powers, then the remaining moral prohibitions on the conduct of war are sufficiently insignificant to be ignored.

The answer to this kind of an argument requires, I believe, that we distinguish the question of what is moral in war from that of the morality of war or of war generally. . . . Paradoxically, the more convincing the argument from war's conduct, the stronger is the moral argument *against* engaging in war at all. For the more it can be shown that engaging in war will inevitably lead to despicable behavior to which no moral predicates are deemed applicable, the more this also constitutes an argument against bringing such a state of affairs into being.

There is still another way to take the claim that in matters of war morality has no place. That is what I have called the prescriptive view: that national interest ought to determine policies in respect to war, not morality. This is surely one way to interpret the remarks of Dean Acheson reproduced earlier. It is also, perhaps, involved in President Truman's defense of the dropping of the atomic bomb on Hiroshima. What he said was this:

Having found the bomb, we have to use it. We have used it against those who attacked us without warning at Pearl Harbor, against those who have starved and beaten and executed American prisoners of war, against those who have abandoned all pretense of obeying international laws of warfare. We have used it in order to shorten the agony of war, in order to save the lives of thousands and thousands of young Americans.[2]

Although this passage has many interesting features, I am concerned only with President Truman's insistence that the dropping of the bomb was justified because it saved the lives "of thousands and thousands of young Americans."

Conceivably, this is merely an elliptical way of saying that on balance fewer lives were lost through the dropping of the bomb and the accelerated cessation of hostilities than through any alternative course of conduct. Suppose, though, that this were not the argument. Suppose, instead, that the justification were regarded as adequate provided only that it was reasonably clear that fewer *American* lives would be lost than through any alternative course of conduct. Thus, to quantify the example, we can imagine someone maintaining that Hiroshima was justified because 20,000 fewer Americans died in the Pacific theater than would have died if the bomb had not been dropped. And this is justified even though 30,000 more Japanese died than would have been killed had the war been fought to an end with conventional means. Thus, even though 10,000 more people died than would otherwise have been the case, the bombing was justified because of the greater number of American lives saved.

On this interpretation the argument depends upon valuing the lives of Americans higher than the lives of persons from other countries. As such, is there anything to be said for the argument? Its strongest statement, and the only one that I shall consider, might go like this: Truman was the President of the United States and as such had an obligation always to choose that course of conduct that appeared to offer the greatest chance of maximizing the interests of the United States. As President, he was obligated to prefer the lives of American soldiers over those from any other country, and he was obligated to prefer them just because they were Americans and he was their President.

Some might prove such a point by drawing an analogy to the situation of a lawyer, or a parent, or a corporation executive. A lawyer has a duty to present his client's case in the fashion most calculated to ensure his client's victory; and he has this obligation irrespective of the objective merits of his client's case. Similarly, we are neither surprised nor dismayed when a parent prefers the interests of his child over those of other children. A parent *qua* parent is certainly not behaving immorally when he acts so as to secure satisfactions for his child, again irrespective of the objective merits of the child's needs or wants. And, *mutatis mutandis,* a corporate executive has a duty to maximize profits for his company. Thus, as public servants, Dean Acheson and Harry Truman had no moral choice but to pursue those policies that appeared to them to be in the best interest of the United States. And to a lesser degree, all persons *qua* citizens of the United States have a similar, if slightly more attenuated, obligation. Therefore, morality has no real place in war.

The analogy, however, must not stop halfway. It is certainly both correct and important to observe that public officials, like parents, lawyers, and corporate executives, do have special moral obligations that are imposed by virtue of the position or role they fill. A lawyer does have a duty to prefer his client's interests in a way that would be improper were the person anyone other than a client. And the same sort of duty, I think, holds for a parent, an executive, a President, and a citizen in their respective roles. The point becomes distorted, however, when it is supposed that such an obligation always, under all circumstances, overrides any and all other obligations that the person might have. The case of the lawyer is instructive. While he has an obligation to attend to his client's interests in very special ways, there are many other things that it is impermissible for the lawyer to do in furtherance of his client's interests—irrespective, this time, of how significantly they might advance that interest.

The case for the President, or for public servants generally, is similar. While the President may indeed have an obligation to prefer and pursue the national interests, this obligation could only be justifiable—could only be a moral obligation—if it were enmeshed in a comparable range of limiting and competing obligations. If we concede that the President has certain obligations to prefer the national interest that no one else has, we must be equally sensitive to the fact that the President also has some of the same obligations to other persons that all other men have—if for no other reason than that all persons have the right to be treated or not treated in certain ways. So, whatever special obligations the President may have cannot by themselves support the view that in war morality ought have no place. . . .

But the major problem with the national-interest argument is its assumption that the national interest not only is something immutable and knowable but also that it limits national interest to narrowly national concerns. It is parochial to suppose that the American national interest really rules out solicitude for other states in order to encourage international stability.

Finally, national interest as a goal must itself be justified. The United States' position of international importance may have imposed on it a duty of more than national concern. The fact that such a statement has become hackneyed by constant use to justify American interference abroad should not blind us to the fact that it may be viable as an argument for a less aggressive international responsibility.

2. ASSESSING THE MORALITY OF WARS

If we turn now to confront more directly the question of the morality of wars, it is evident that there is a variety of different perspectives from which, or criteria in terms of which, particular wars may be assessed. First, to the extent to which the model of war as a game continues to have a place, wars can be evaluated in terms of the degree to which the laws of war—the rules for initiating and conducting war—are adhered to by the opposing countries. Second, the rightness or wrongness of wars is often thought to depend very much upon the cause for which a war is fought. And third, there is the independent justification for a war that is founded upon an appeal of some kind to a principle of self-defense.

In discussing the degree to which the laws of war are followed or disregarded there are two points that should be stressed. First, a skepticism as to the meaningfulness of any morality *within* war is extremely common. The gnomic statement

is Sherman's: "War is hell." The fuller argument depends upon a rejection of the notion of war as a game. It goes something like this. War is the antithesis of law or rules. It is violence, killing and all of the horror they imply. Even if moral distinctions can be made in respect to such things as the initiation and purposes of a war, it is absurd to suppose that moral distinctions can be drawn once a war has begun. All killing is bad, all destruction equally wanton.

Now, there does seem to me to be a fairly simple argument of sorts that can be made in response. Given the awfulness of war, it nonetheless appears plausible to discriminate among degrees of awfulness. A war in which a large number of innocent persons are killed is, all other things being equal, worse than one in which only a few die. A war in which few combatants are killed is, *ceteris paribus,* less immoral than one in which many are killed. And more to the point, perhaps, any unnecessary harm to others is surely unjustifiable. To some degree, at least, the "laws of war" can be construed as attempts to formalize these general notions and to define instances of unnecessary harm to others.

The second criterion, the notion of the cause that can be invoked to justify a war may involve two quite different inquiries. On the one hand, we may intend the sense in which cause refers to the *consequences* of waging war, to the forward-looking criteria of assessment. Thus, when a war is justified as a means by which to make the world safe for democracy, or on the grounds that a failure to fight now will lead to a loss of confidence on the part of one's allies, or as necessary to avoid fighting a larger, more destructive war later, when these sorts of appeals are made, the justification is primarily consequential or forward-looking in character. Here the distinction between morality and prudence—never a very easy one to maintain in international relations—is always on the verge of collapse. On the other hand, a war may be evaluated through recourse to what may be termed backward-looking criteria. Just as in the case of punishment or blame where what happened in the past is relevant to the justice of punishing or blaming someone, so in the case of war, what has already happened is, on this view, relevant to the justice or rightness of the war that is subsequently waged. The two backward-looking criteria that are most frequently invoked in respect to war are the question of whether the war involved a violation of some prior promise, typically expressed in the form of a treaty or concord.

Two sorts of assertions are often made concerning the role of the treaty in justifying resort to war. First, if a country has entered into a treaty not to go to war and if it violates that treaty, it is to be condemned for, in effect, having broken its promise. And second, if a country has entered into a treaty in which it has agreed to go to war under certain circumstances and if those circumstances come to pass, then the country is at least justified in going to war—although it is not in fact obligated to do so.

Once again . . . it is clear that treaties can be relevant but not decisive factors. This is so just because it is sometimes right to break our promises and sometimes wrong to keep them. The fact that a treaty is violated at best tends to make a war unjust or immoral in some degree, but it does not necessarily render the war unjustified.

The other backward-looking question, that of aggression, is often resolved by concluding that under no circumstances is the initiation of a war of aggression justified. This is a view that Americans and America have often embraced. Such a view was expounded at Nuremberg by Mr. Justice Jackson when he said:

[T]he wrong for which their [the German] fallen leaders are on trial is not that they lost the war, but that they started it. And we must not allow ourselves to be drawn into a trial of the causes of war, for our position is that no grievances or policies will justify resort to aggressive war. . . . Our position is that whatever grievances a nation may have, however objectionable it finds that *status quo,* aggressive warfare is an illegal means for settling those grievances or for altering those conditions.[3]

A position such as this is typically thought to imply two things: (1) the initiation of war is never justifiable; (2) the warlike response to aggressive war is justifiable. Both views are troublesome.

To begin with, it is hard to see how the two propositions go together very comfortably. Conceivably, there are powerful arguments against the waging of aggressive war. Almost surely, though,

the more persuasive of these will depend, at least in part, on the character of war itself—on such things as the supreme importance of human life, or the inevitable injustices committed in every war. If so, then the justifiability of meeting war with war will to that degree be called into question.

To take the first proposition alone, absent general arguments about the unjustifiability of all war, it is hard to see how aggressive war can be ruled out in a wholly a priori fashion. Even if we assume that no problems are presented in determining what is and is not aggression, it is doubtful that the quality of aggression could always be morally decisive in condemning the war. Would a war undertaken to free innocent persons from concentration camps or from slavery always be unjustifiable just because *it was aggressive?* Surely this is to rest too much upon only one of a number of relevant considerations.

From a backward-looking point of view, the claim that a warring response to aggressive war is always justified is even more perplexing. . . .

In order to understand the force of the doctrine of self-defense when invoked in respect to war, and to assess its degree of legitimate applicability, it is necessary that we look briefly at self-defense as it functions as a doctrine of municipal criminal law. . . .

[W]hat is important is that we keep in mind two of the respects in which the law qualifies resort to the claim of self-defense. On one hand, the doctrine cannot be invoked successfully if the intended victim could have avoided the encounter through a reasonable escape or retreat unless the attack takes place on one's own property. And on the other hand, the doctrine requires that no more force be employed than is reasonably necessary to prevent the infliction of comparable harm.

Now how does all of this apply to self-defense as a justification for engaging in war? In the first place, to the extent to which the basic doctrine serves as an excuse, the applicability to war seems doubtful. While it may make sense to regard self-defense of one's person as a natural, instinctive response to an attack, it is only a very anthropomorphic view of countries that would lead us to elaborate a comparable explanation here.

In the second place, it is not even clear that self-defense can function very persuasively as a justification. For it to do so it might be necessary, for example, to be able to make out a case that countries die in the same way in which persons do, or that a country can be harmed in the same way in which a person can be. Of course, persons in the country can be harmed and killed by war, and I shall return to this point in a moment, but we can also imagine an attack in which none of the inhabitants of the country will be killed or even physically harmed unless they fight back. But the country, as a separate political entity, might nonetheless disappear. Would we say that this should be regarded as the equivalent of human death? That it is less harmful? More harmful? These are issues to which those who readily invoke the doctrine of self-defense seldom address themselves.

Even if we were to decide, however, that there is no question but that a country is justified in relying upon a doctrine of self-defense that is essentially similar to that which obtains in the criminal law, it would be essential to observe the constraints that follow. Given even the unprovoked aggressive waging of war by one country against another, the doctrine of self-defense could not be invoked by the country so attacked to justify waging unlimited defensive war or insisting upon unconditional surrender. Each or both of these responses might be justifiable, but not simply because a country was wrongly attacked. It would, instead, have to be made out that something analogous to retreat was neither possible nor appropriate, and, even more, that no more force was used than was reasonably necessary to terminate the attack.

There is, to be sure, an answer to this. The restrictions that the criminal law puts upon self-defense are defensible, it could be maintained, chiefly because we have a municipal police force, municipal laws, and courts. If we use no more than reasonable force to repel attacks, we can at least be confident that the attacker will be apprehended and punished and, further, that we live in a society in which this sort of aggressive behavior is deterred by a variety of means. It is the absence of such a context that renders restrictions on an international doctrine of self-defense inappropriate.

I do not think this answer is convincing. It is relevant to the question of what sorts of constraints will be operative on the behavior of persons and countries, but it is not persuasive as to the invocation of *self*-defense as a justification for war. To use more force than is reasonably necessary to defend oneself is, in short, to do more than defend oneself. If such non-self-defensive behavior is to be justified, it must appeal to some different principle or set of principles.

There are, therefore, clearly cases in which a principle of self-defense does appear to justify engaging in a war: at a minimum, those cases in which one's country is attacked in such a way that the inhabitants are threatened with deadly force and in which no more force than is reasonably necessary is employed to terminate the attack.

3. WAR AND INNOCENTS

The strongest argument against war is that which rests upon the connection between the morality of war and the death of innocent persons. The specter of thermonuclear warfare makes examination of this point essential; yet the problem was both a genuine and an urgent one in the pre-atomic days of air warfare, particularly during the Second World War.

The argument based upon the death of innocent persons goes something like this: Even in war innocent people have a right to life and limb that should be respected. It is no less wrong and no more justifiable to kill innocent persons in war than at any other time. Therefore, if innocent persons are killed in a war, that war is to be condemned.

The argument can quite readily be converted into an attack upon all modern war. Imagine a thoroughly unprovoked attack upon another country—an attack committed, moreover, from the worst of motives and for the most despicable of ends. Assume too, for the moment, that under such circumstances there is nothing immoral about fighting back and even killing those who are attacking. Nonetheless, if in fighting back innocent persons will be killed, the defenders will be acting immorally. However, given any war fought today, innocent persons will inevitably be killed. Therefore, any war fought today will be immoral.

There are a variety of matters that require clarification before the strength of this argument can be adequately assessed. In particular, there are four questions that must be examined: (1) What is meant by "innocence" in this context? (2) Is it plausible to suppose that there are any innocents? (3) Under what circumstances is the death of innocent persons immoral? (4) What is the nature of the connection between the immorality of the killing of innocent persons and the immorality of the war in which this killing occurs?

It is anything but clear what precisely is meant by "innocence" or "the innocent" in an argument such as this. One possibility would be that all noncombatants are innocent. But then, of course, we would have to decide what was meant by "noncombatants." Here we might be tempted to claim that noncombatants are all of those persons who are not in the army—not actually doing the fighting; the combatants are those who are. There are, however, serious problems with this position. For it appears that persons can be noncombatants in this sense and yet indistinguishable in any apparently relevant sense from persons in the army. Thus, civilians may be manufacturing munitions, devising new weapons, writing propaganda, or doing any number of other things that make them indistinguishable from many combatants vis-à-vis their relationship to the war effort.

A second possibility would be to focus upon an individual's causal connection with the attempt to win the war rather than on his status as soldier or civilian. On this view only some noncombatants would be innocent and virtually no combatants would be. If the causal connection is what is relevant, meaningful distinctions might be made among civilians. One might distinguish between those whose activities or vocations help the war effort only indirectly, if at all, and those whose activities are more plausibly described as directly beneficial. Thus the distinctions would be between a typical grocer or a tailor on the one hand, and a worker in an armaments plant on the other. Similarly, children, the aged, and the infirm would normally not be in a position to play a role causally connected in this way with the waging of war.

There are, of course, other kinds of possible causal connections. In particular, someone might urge that attention should also be devoted to the existence of a causal connection between the individual's civic behavior and the war effort. Thus, for example, a person's voting behavior, or the de-

gree of his political opposition to the government, or his financial contributions to the war effort might all be deemed to be equally relevant to his status as an innocent.

Still a fourth possibility, closely related to those already discussed, would be that interpretation of innocence concerned with culpability rather than causality per se. On this view a person would properly be regarded an innocent if he could not fairly be held responsible for the war's initiation or conduct. Clearly, the notion of culpability is linked in important ways with that of causal connection, but they are by no means identical. So it is quite conceivable, for example, that under some principles of culpability many combatants might not be culpable and some noncombatants might be extremely culpable, particularly if culpability were to be defined largely in terms of state of mind and enthusiasm for the war. Thus, an aged or infirm person who cannot do very much to help the war effort but is an ardent proponent of its aims and objectives might be more culpable (and less innocent in this sense) than a conscriptee who is firing a machine gun only because the penalty for disobeying the command to do so is death.

But we need not propose an airtight definition of "innocence" in order to answer the question of whether, in any war, there will be a substantial number of innocent persons involved. For irrespective of which sense or senses of innocence are ultimately deemed most instructive or important, it does seem clear that there will be a number of persons in any country (children are probably the clearest example) who will meet any test of innocence that is proposed.

The third question enumerated earlier is: Under what circumstances is the death of innocent persons immoral? One possible view is that which asserts simply that it is unimportant which circumstances bring about the death of innocent persons. As long as we know that innocent persons will be killed as a result of war, we know all we need to know to condemn any such war.

Another, and perhaps more plausible, view is that which regards the death of innocent persons as increasingly unjustifiable if it was negligently, recklessly, knowingly, or intentionally brought about. Thus, if a country engages in acts of war with the intention of bringing about the death of children, perhaps to weaken the will of the enemy, it would be more immoral than if it were to engage in acts of war aimed at killing combatants but which through error also kill children.

A different sort of problem arises if someone asks how we are to differentiate the deaths of children in war from, for example, the deaths of children that accompany the use of highways or airplanes in times of peace. Someone might, that is, argue that we permit children to ride in cars on highways and to fly in airplanes even though we *know* that there will be accidents and that as a result of these accidents innocent children will die. And since we know this to be the case, the situation appears to be indistinguishable from that of engaging in acts of war where it is known that the death of children will be a direct, although not intended, consequence.

I think that there are three sorts of responses that can be made to an objection of this sort. In the first place, in a quite straightforward sense the highway does not, typically, cause the death of the innocent passenger; the careless driver or the defective tire does. But it is the intentional bombing of the heavily populated city that does cause the death of the children who live in the city.

In the second place, it is one thing to act where one knows that certain more or less identifiable persons will be killed (say, bombing a troop camp when one knows that those children who live in the vicinity of the camp will also be killed), and quite another thing to engage in conduct in which all one can say is that it can be predicted with a high degree of confidence that over a given period of time a certain number of persons (including children) will be killed. . . .

In the third place, there is certainly a difference in the two cases in respect to the possibility of deriving benefits from the conduct. That is to say, when a highway is used, one is participating in a system or set of arrangements in which benefits are derived from that use (even though risks, and hence costs, are also involved). It is not easy to see how a similar sort of analysis can as plausibly be proposed in connection with typical acts of war.

The final and most important issue that is raised by the argument concerning the killing of the innocent in time of war is that of the connection between the immorality of the killing of innocent persons and the immorality of the war in which this killing occurs. Writers in the area often fail to discuss the connection.

Miss Anscombe puts the point this way: "[I]t is murderous to attack [the innocent] or make them a target for an attack which [the attacker] judges will help him toward victory. For murder is the deliberate killing of the innocent, whether for its own sake or as a means to some further end." . . .

. . . It is likely that Miss Anscombe means to assert an absolutist view here—that there are no circumstances under which the intentional killing of innocent persons, even in time of war, can be justified. It is always immoral to do so. At least their arguments are phrased in absolutist terms. If this is the view that they intend to defend, it is, I think, a hard one to accept. This is so just because it ultimately depends upon too complete a rejection of the relevance of consequences to the moral character of action. It also requires too rigid a dichotomy between acts and omissions. It seems to misunderstand the character of our moral life to claim that, no matter what the consequences, the intentional killing of an innocent person could never be justifiable—even, for example, if a failure to do so would bring about the death of many more innocent persons. . . .

My own view is that as a theoretical matter an absolutist position is even less convincing here. Given the number of criteria that are relevant to the moral assessment of any war and given the great number of persons involved in and the extended duration of most wars, it would be false to the complexity of the issues to suppose that so immediately simple a solution were possible.

But having said all of this, the *practical,* as opposed to the theoretical, thrust of the argument is virtually unabated. If wars were conducted, or were likely to be conducted, so as to produce only the occasional intentional killing of the innocent, that would be one thing. We could then say with some confidence that on this ground at least wars can hardly be condemned out of hand. Unfortunately, though, mankind no longer lives in such a world and, as a result, the argument from the death of the innocent has become increasingly more convincing. The intentional, or at least knowing, killing of the innocent on a large scale became a practically necessary feature of war with the advent of air warfare. And the genuinely indiscriminate killing of very great numbers of innocent persons is the dominant legacy of the birth of thermonuclear weapons. At this stage the argument from the death of the innocent moves appreciably closer to becoming a decisive objection to war. For even if we reject, as I have argued we should, both absolutist interpretations of the argument, the core of truth that remains is the insistence that in war, no less than elsewhere, the knowing killing of the innocent is an evil that throws up the heaviest of justificatory burdens. My own view is that in any major war that can or will be fought today, none of those considerations that can sometimes justify engaging in war will in fact come close to meeting this burden. But even if I am wrong, the argument from the death of the innocent does, I believe, make it clear both where the burden is and how unlikely it is today to suppose that it can be honestly discharged.

NOTES

1. D. Acheson, "Ethics in International Relations Today," in *The Vietnam Reader,* ed. M. Raskin and B. Fall (1965), p. 13.
2. Address to the Nation by President Harry S. Truman, Aug. 9, 1945, quoted in R. Tucker, *The Just War* (1960), pp. 21–22, n. 14.
3. Quoted in R. Tucker, supra note 2, p. 12.

REVIEW AND DISCUSSION QUESTIONS

1. Describe and evaluate the argument that warfare is amoral.
2. What considerations does Wasserstrom think could justify war? Describe the limitations of each.
3. "War is wrong because it inevitably means the deaths of innocents." How does Wasserstrom assess this argument?
4. Under what circumstances would it be right to say that a war is unjust?
5. How would William James respond to Wasserstrom's views on "just war"?

Wartime Internment of Japanese Americans:

Korematsu v. *United States*

The Supreme Court has often had to face questions about the limits on governmental power in the conduct of war, but no cases were more controversial than this one. Fear of invasion and of the power of the Japanese army, as well as angry hatred of the Japanese for their surprise attack, were widespread after Japan destroyed most of the U.S. naval fleet at Pearl Harbor and conquered much of the

323 U.S. 214 (1944).

western Pacific. At the same time, there was growing pressure along the West Coast of the United States for the military to do something about the minority population of Japanese Americans. Some argued that they could aid an invading army; others feared for the welfare of people of Japanese descent at the hands of angry mobs; and, finally, there was also a fair amount of economic advantage to be gained if these successful, hard-working people were forced to sell or otherwise lose their businesses and homes. Although people in both military intelligence and the FBI disputed the claims that Japanese Americans posed a danger, Franklin Roosevelt nevertheless signed a bill into law allowing the military to establish "military zones" from which any persons could be excluded and which validated the military's already established curfew on both Japanese citizens and American citizens of Japanese descent living on the West Coast.

In *Hirabayashi* v. *United States* (1943), the Supreme Court had already upheld the conviction of a University of Washington student, Gordon Hirabayashi, for violating the curfew. Military leaders went on to aggressively enforce Roosevelt's order by requiring that persons of Japanese ancestry living on the West Coast be sent to concentration camps.

Fred Korematsu was a native-born citizen of the United States of Japanese ancestry. After Pearl Harbor, he volunteered to join the army but was rejected because of ill health. He then worked for the civilian defense industry as a welder. Korematsu was convicted of refusing to report to the authorities for eventual internment in a concentration camp. He appealed to the Supreme Court, which, after bitter internal disputes, refused to overturn the military's judgment and allowed the concentration camps. Some justices wanted to allow only the curfew but not the camps; others refused to second-guess the president, Congress, and the military.

The economic consequences of the internment policy on the Japanese were staggering. They lost both their homes and their livelihoods. But even more important, perhaps, were the emotional consequences of their treatment at the hands of fellow citizens.

Mr. Justice Black Delivered the Opinion of the Court: ... It should be noted, to begin with, that all legal restrictions which curtail the civil rights of a single racial group are immediately suspect. That is not to say that all such restrictions are unconstitutional. It is to say that courts must subject them to the most rigid scrutiny. Pressing public necessity may sometimes justify the existence of such restrictions; racial antagonism never can. ...

In the light of the principles we announced in the *Hirabayashi* case, we are unable to conclude that it was beyond the war power of Congress and the Executive to exclude those of Japanese ancestry from the West Coast war area at the time they did. True, exclusion from the area in which one's home is located is a far greater deprivation than constant confinement to the home from 8:00 P.M. to 6:00 A.M. Nothing short of apprehension by the proper military authorities of the gravest imminent danger to the public safety can constitutionally justify either. But exclusion from a threatened area, no less than curfew, has a definite and close relationship to the prevention of espionage and sabotage. The military authorities, charged with the primary responsibility of defending our shores,

concluded that curfew provided inadequate protection and ordered exclusion. They did so, as pointed out in our *Hirabayashi* opinion, in accordance with Congressional authority to the military to say who should, and who should not, remain in the threatened areas ...,

Like curfew, exclusion of those of Japanese origin was deemed necessary because of the presence of an unascertained number of disloyal members of the group, most of whom we have no doubt were loyal to this country. It was because we could not reject the finding of the military authorities that it was impossible to bring about an immediate segregation of the disloyal from the loyal that we sustained the validity of the curfew order as applying to the whole group. In the instant case, temporary exclusion of the entire group was rested by the military on the same ground. The judgment that exclusion of the whole group was for the same reason a military imperative answers the contention that the exclusion was in the nature of group punishment based on antagonism to those of Japanese origin. That there were members of the group who retained loyalties to Japan has been confirmed by investigations made subsequent to the exclusion. Approximately five thousand American citizens of Japanese ancestry refused to swear unqualified allegiance to the United States and to renounce allegiance to the Japanese Emperor, and several thousand evacuees requested repatriation to Japan.

We uphold the exclusion order as of the time it was made and when the petitioner violated it. . . . In doing so, we are not unmindful of the hardships imposed by it upon a large group of American citizens. . . . But hardships are part of war, and war is an aggregation of hardships. All citizens alike, both in and out of uniform, feel the impact of war in greater or lesser measure. Citizenship has its responsibilities as well as its privileges, and in time of war the burden is always heavier. Compulsory exclusion of large groups of citizens from their homes, except under circumstances of direst and emergency and peril, is inconsistent with our basic governmental institutions. But when under conditions of modern warfare our shores are threatened by hostile forces, the power to protect must be commensurate with the threatened danger. . . .

It is said that we are dealing here with the case of imprisonment of a citizen in a concentration camp solely because of his ancestry, without evidence or inquiry concerning his loyalty and good disposition towards the United States. Our task would be simple, our duty clear, were this a case involving the imprisonment of a loyal citizen in a concentration camp because of racial prejudice. Regardless of the true nature of the assembly and relocation centers—and we deem it unjustifiable to call them concentration camps with all the ugly connotations that term implies—we are dealing specifically with nothing but an exclusion order. To cast this case into outlines of racial prejudice, without reference to the real military dangers which were presented, merely confuses the issue. Korematsu was not excluded from the Military Areas because of hostility to him or his race. He was excluded because we are at war with the Japanese Empire, because the properly constituted military authorities feared an invasion of our West Coast and felt constrained to take proper security measures, because they decided that the military urgency of the situation demanded that all citizens of Japanese ancestry be segregated from the West Coast temporarily, and finally, because Congress,

reposing its confidence in this time of war in our military leaders—as inevitably it must—determined that they should have the power to do just this. There was evidence of disloyalty on the part of some, the military authorities considered that the need for action was great, and time was short. We cannot—by availing ourselves of the calm perspective of hindsight—now say that at that time these actions were unjustified.

Affirmed.

Mr. Justice Murphy, Dissenting: This exclusion of "all persons of Japanese ancestry, both alien and non-alien," from the Pacific Coast area on a plea of military necessity in the absence of martial law ought not to be approved. Such exclusion goes over "the very brink of constitutional power" and falls into the ugly abyss of racism.

In dealing with matters relating to the prosecution and progress of a war, we must accord great respect and consideration to the judgments of the military authorities who are on the scene and who have full knowledge of the military facts. . . .

At the same time, however, it is essential that there be definite limits to military discretion, especially where martial law has not been declared. . . .

That this forced exclusion was the result in good measure of this erroneous assumption of racial guilt rather than bona fide military necessity is evidenced by the Commanding General's Final Report on the evacuation. . . . In it he refers to all individuals of Japanese descent as "subversive," as belonging to "an enemy race" whose "racial strains are undiluted," and as constituting "over 112,000 potential enemies . . . at large today." In support of this blanket condemnation of all persons of Japanese descent, however, no reliable evidence is cited to show that such individuals were generally disloyal, or . . . constitute[d] a special menace to defense installations or war industries, or had otherwise by their behavior furnished reasonable ground for their exclusion as a group.

Justification for the exclusion is sought, instead, mainly upon questionable racial and sociological grounds not ordinarily within the realm of expert military judgment, supplemented by certain semi-military conclusions drawn from an unwarranted use of circumstantial evidence. Individuals of Japanese ancestry are condemned because they are said to be "a large, unassimilated, tightly knit racial group, bound to an enemy nation by strong ties of race, culture, custom and religion." They are claimed to be given to "emperor worshipping ceremonies" and to "dual citizenship." Japanese language schools and allegedly pro-Japanese organizations are cited as evidence of possible group disloyalty, together with facts as to certain persons being educated and residing at length in Japan. . . .

The main reasons relied upon by those responsible for the forced evacuation . . . [are] largely an accumulation of much of the misinformation, half-truths and insinuations that for years have been directed against Japanese Americans by people with racial and economic prejudices—the same people who have been among the foremost advocates of the evacuation. A military judgment based upon such racial and sociological considerations is not entitled to the great weight ordinarily given the judgments based upon strictly military considerations. Especially is this so when every charge relative to race, religion, culture, geographical location, and legal and economic status has been substantially discredited by independent studies made by experts in these matters.

No adequate reason is given for the failure to treat these Japanese Americans on an individual basis by holding investigations and hearings to separate the loyal from the disloyal, as was done in the case of persons of German and Italian ancestry. It is asserted merely that the loyalties of this group "were unknown and time was of the essence." Yet nearly four months elapsed after Pearl Harbor before the first exclusion order was issued; nearly eight months went by until the last order was issued; and the last of these "subversive" persons was not actually removed until almost eleven months had elapsed. Leisure and deliberation seem to have been more of the essence than speed. And the fact that conditions were not such as to warrant a declaration of martial law adds strength to the belief that the factors of time and military necessity were not as urgent as they have been represented to be.

Moreover, there was no adequate proof that the Federal Bureau of Investigation and the military and naval intelligence services did not have the es-

pionage and sabotage situation well in hand during this long period. Nor is there any denial of the fact that not one person of Japanese ancestry was accused or convicted of espionage or sabotage after Pearl Harbor while they were still free, a fact which is some evidence of the loyalty of the vast majority of those individuals and of the effectiveness of the established methods of combating these evils. It seems incredible that under these circumstances it would have been impossible to hold loyalty hearings for the mere 112,000 persons involved—or at least for the 70,000 American citizens—especially when a large part of this number represented children and elderly men and women. . . .

I dissent, therefore, from this legalization of racism. Racial discrimination in any form and in any degree has no justifiable part whatever in our democratic way of life. It is unattractive in any setting but it is utterly revolting among a free people who have embraced the principles set forth in the Constitution of the United States. All residents of this nation are kin in some way by blood or culture to a foreign land. Yet they are primarily and necessarily a part of the new and distinct civilization of the United States. They must accordingly be treated at all times as the heirs of the American experiment and as entitled to all the rights and freedoms guaranteed by the Constitution.

Mr. Justice Jackson, Dissenting: Korematsu was born on our soil, of parents born in Japan. The Constitution makes him a citizen of the United States by nativity and a citizen of California by residence. No claim is made that he is not loyal to this country. There is no suggestion that apart from the matter involved here he is not law-abiding and well disposed. Korematsu, however, has been convicted of an act not commonly a crime. It consists merely of being present in the state whereof he is a citizen, near the place where he was born, and where all his life he has lived.

Even more unusual is the series of military orders which made this conduct a crime. They forbid such a one to remain, and they also forbid him to leave. They were so drawn that the only way Korematsu could avoid violation was to give himself up to the military authority. This meant submission to custody, examination, and transportation out of the territory, to be followed by indeterminate confinement in detention camps.

A citizen's presence in the locality, however, was made a crime only if his parents were of Japanese birth. Had Korematsu been one of four—the others being, say, a German alien enemy, an Italian alien enemy, and a citizen of American-born ancestors, convicted of treason but out on parole—only Korematsu's presence would have violated the order. The difference between their innocence and his crime would result, not from anything he did, said or thought, different than they, but only in that he was born of different racial stock.

Now, if any fundamental assumption underlies our system, it is that guilt is personal and not inheritable. Even if all of one's antecedents had been convicted of treason, the Constitution forbids its penalties to be visited upon him, for it provides that "no attainder of treason shall work corruption of blood, or forfeiture except during the life of the person attainted." But here is an attempt to make an otherwise innocent act a crime merely because this prisoner is the son of parents as to whom he had no choice, and belongs to a race from which there is no way to resign. . . .

. . . [T]he "law" which this prisoner is convicted of disregarding is not found in an act of Congress, but in a military order. Neither the Act of Congress nor the Executive Order of the President, nor both together, would afford a basis for the conviction. . . . And it is said that if the military commander had reasonable military grounds for promulgating the orders, they are constitutional and become law, and the Court is required to enforce them. . . .

It would be impracticable and dangerous idealism to expect or insist that each specific military command in an area of probable operations will conform to conventional tests of constitutionality. . . . The armed services must protect a society, not merely its Constitution. The very essence of the military job is to marshal physical force, to remove every obstacle to its effectiveness, to give it every strategic advantage. Defense measures will not, and often should not, be held within the limits that bind civil authority in peace. . . .

But if we cannot confine military expedients by the Constitution, neither would I distort the Constitution to approve all that the military may deem expedient. . . . I cannot say that the orders of General DeWitt were not reasonably expedient military precautions, nor could I say that they were. But even if they were permissible military procedures, I deny that it follows that they are constitutional. If, as the Court holds, it does follow, then we may as well say that any military order will be constitutional and have done with it. . . .

Much is said of the danger to liberty from the Army program. . . . But a judicial construction of the due process clause that will sustain this order is a far more subtle blow to liberty. . . . A military order, however unconstitutional, is not apt to last longer than the military emergency. Even during that period a succeeding commander may revoke it all. But once a judicial opinion rationalizes such an order to show that it conforms to the Constitution, or rather rationalizes the Constitution to show that the Constitution sanctions such an order, the Court for all time has validated the principle of racial discrimination in criminal procedure and of transplanting American citizens. The principle then lies about like a loaded weapon ready for the hand of any authority that can bring forward a plausible claim of an urgent need. . . . All who observe the work of courts are familiar with what Judge Cardozo described as "the tendency of a principle to expand itself to the limit of its logic." A military commander may overstep the bounds of constitutionality, and it is an incident. But if we review and approve, that passing incident becomes the doctrine of the Constitution. There it has a generative power of its own, and all that it creates will be in its own image. Nothing better illustrates this danger than does the Court's opinion in this case.

It argues that we are bound to uphold the conviction of Korematsu because we upheld one in *Hirabayashi*. . . .

In that case we were urged to consider only the curfew feature. . . . We yielded, and the Chief Justice guarded the opinion as carefully as language will do. He said: " . . . We decide only the issue as we have defined it—we decide only that the *curfew order* as applied, and at the time it was applied, was within the boundaries of the war power." . . . Now the principle of racial discrimination is pushed from support of mild measures to very harsh ones, and from temporary deprivations to indeterminate ones. And the precedent which it is said requires us to do so is *Hirabayashi*. The Court is now saying that in *Hirabayashi* we did decide the very things we there said we were not deciding. Because we said that these citizens could be made to stay in their homes during the hours of dark, it is said we must require them to leave home entirely; and if that, we are told they may also be taken into custody for deportation; and if that, it is argued they may also be held for some undetermined time in detention camps. How far the principle of this case would be extended before plausible reasons would play out, I do not know.

I should hold that a civil court cannot be made to enforce an order which violates constitutional limitations even if it is a reasonable exercise of military authority. The courts can exercise only the judicial power, can apply only law, and must abide by the Constitution, or they cease to be civil courts and become instruments of military policy.

. . . I would not lead people to rely on this Court for a review that seems to me wholly delusive. . . . If the people ever let command of the war power fall into irresponsible and unscrupulous hands, the courts wield no power equal to its restraint. The chief restraint upon those who command the physical forces of the country must be their responsibility to the political judgments of their contemporaries and to the moral judgments of history.

My duties as a justice . . . do not require me to make a military judgment as to whether General DeWitt's evacuation and detention program was a reasonable military necessity. I do not suggest that the courts should have attempted to interfere with the Army in carrying out its task. But I do not think they may be asked to execute a military expedient that has no place in law under the Constitution. I would reverse the judgment and discharge the prisoner.

REVIEW AND DISCUSSION QUESTIONS

1. Explain the reasoning behind Justice Black's opinion for the Court.
2. Justice Black begins his opinion with a brief indication of how he approaches the case, mentioning both "suspect" restrictions and "rigid scrutiny." These have now become the centerpiece of equal protection analysis. Explain what he means.
3. Describe the basis of Justice Murphy's dissent.
4. Justice Jackson's dissent focuses on due process, rather than equal protection. Explain how that aspect of Justice Jackson's position differs from Justice Murphy's.
5. On whose shoulders does Justice Jackson think rests the possibility of avoiding future abuses of authority by the military? Explain.
6. Justice Jackson's conclusion has been described as an example of judicial "nihilism." Explain that comment, indicating whether or not you agree.
7. How do you think Richard Wasserstrom would have decided this case, given his discussion of the moral limits on those who conduct a war?
8. In later years, Justice Douglas, who had reluctantly gone along with the majority, came to regret his decision and believed *Korematsu* was a grave mistake. He also said, however, that he thought any of the many courts on which he served during his long career would have ruled the same way. Justice Black, on the other hand, continued to believe that Congress had not exceeded its power in delegating authority to the military to intern Japanese Americans. Many today think the case represents how far the Court and Congress are willing to go in bending the Constitution in time of war. Still others see it as an indication that the racism infecting society has not been limited to blacks. How would you assess the case?

The Morality of Pacifism

Cheyney Ryan

In this selection from his longer article "Self-defense, Pacifism, and the Possibility of Killing," Cheyney Ryan describes the pacifist's position as requiring respect for other human beings and appreciation of the bond shared by us all. Far from a simple dispute, he argues, the dispute between the pacifist and those who would commit violent acts is a deep, intractable one to which people must pay close attention. Cheyney Ryan teaches philosophy at the University of Oregon.

. . . George Orwell tells how early one morning [during the Spanish Civil War] he ventured out with another man to snipe at the fascists from the trenches outside their encampment. After having little success for several hours, they were suddenly alerted to the sound of Republican airplanes overhead. Orwell writes,

At this moment a man, presumably carrying a message to an officer, jumped out of the trench and ran along the top of the parapet in full view. He was half-dressed and holding up his trousers with both hands as he ran. I refrained from shooting at him. It is true that I am a poor shot and unlikely to hit a running man at a hundred yards. Still, I did not shoot partly because of that detail about the trousers. I had come here to shoot "Fascists"; but a man who is holding up his trousers isn't a "Fascist" he is *visibly a fellow creature,* similar to yourself, and you don't feel like shooting him.[1]

Orwell was not a pacifist, but the problem he finds in this particular act of killing is akin to the problem which the pacifist finds in all acts of killing. That problem, the example suggests, takes the following form.

The problem with shooting the half-clothed man does not arise from the rights involved, nor is it dispensed with by showing that, yes indeed, you are justified (by your rights) in killing him. But this does not mean, as some have suggested to me, that the problem is therefore not a *moral* problem at all ("sheer sentimentality" was an objection raised by one philosopher ex-marine). Surely if Orwell had gleefully blasted away here, if he had not at least felt the tug of the other's "fellow-creaturehood," then this would have reflected badly, if not on his action, then on *him,* as a human being. The problem, in the Orwell case, is that the man's dishabille made inescapable the fact that he was a "fellow creature," and in so doing it stripped away the labels and denied the distance so necessary to murderous actions (it is not for nothing that armies give us stereotypes in thinking about the enemy). The problem, I am tempted to say, involves not so much the justification as the *possibility* of killing in such circumstances ("How could you bring yourself to do it?" is a natural response to one who felt no problem in such situations). And therein lies the clue to the pacifist impulse.

The pacifist's problem is that he cannot create, or does not wish to create, the necessary distance between himself and another to make the act of killing possible. Moreover, the fact that others obviously can create that distance is taken by the pacifist to reflect badly on them; they move about in the world insensitive to the half-clothed status which all humans, qua fellow creatures, share. This latter point is important to showing that the

From Cheyney C. Ryan, "Self-Defense, Pacifism, and the Possibility of Killing," *Ethics,* 93, no. 3 (April 1983).

pacifist's position is indeed a moral position, and not just a personal idiosyncrasy. What should now be evident is the sense in which that moral position is motivated by a picture of the personal relationship and outlook one should maintain towards others, regardless of the actions they might take toward you. It is fitting in this regard that the debate over self-defense should come down to a personal relationship, the "negative bond" between Aggressor and Defender. For even if this negative bond renders killing in self-defense permissible, the pacifist will insist that the deeper bonds of fellow creaturehood should render it impossible. That such an outlook will be branded by others as sheer sentimentality comes to the pacifist as no surprise.

I am aware that this characterization of the pacifist's outlook may strike many as obscure, but the difficulties in characterizing that outlook themselves reflect, I think, how truly fundamental the disagreement between the pacifist and the nonpacifist really is. That disagreement far transcends the familiar problems of justice and equity; it is no surprise that the familiar terms should fail us. As to the accuracy of this characterization, I would offer as indirect support the following example of the aesthetic of fascism, which I take to be at polar ends from that of pacifism, and so illustrative in contrast of the pacifist outlook: "War is beautiful because it establishes man's dominion over the subjugated machinery by means of gas masks, terrifying megaphones, flame throwers, and small tanks. War is beautiful because it initiates the dreamt-of metalization of the human body. War is beautiful because it enriches the flowering meadow with the fiery orchids of machine guns." What the fascist rejoices in the pacifist rejects, in toto—the "metalization of the human body," the insensitivity to fellow creaturehood which the pacifist sees as the presupposition of killing.

This account of the pacifist's position suggests some obvious avenues of criticism of the more traditional sort. One could naturally ask whether killing necessarily presupposes objectification and distance, as the pacifist feels it does. It seems to me though that the differences between the pacifist and the nonpacifist are substantial enough that neither side is likely to produce a simple "refutation" along such lines which the other conceivably could, or logically need, accept. If any

criticism of pacifism is to be forthcoming which can make any real claim to the pacifist's attention, it will be one which questions the consistency of his conclusions with what I have described as his motivating impulse. Let me suggest how such a criticism might go.

If the pacifist's intent is to acknowledge through his attitudes and actions the other person's status as a fellow creature, the problem is that violence, and even killing, are at times a means of acknowledging this as well, a way of bridging the distance between oneself and another person, a way of acknowledging one's *own* status as a person. This is one of the underlying themes of Hegel's account of conflict in the master-slave dialectic, and the important truth it contains should not be lost in its seeming glorification of conflict. That the refusal to allow others to treat one as an object is an important step to defining one's own integrity is a point well understood by revolutionary theorists such as Fannon. It is a point apparently lost to pacifists like Gandhi, who suggested that the Jews in the Warsaw Ghetto would have made the superior moral statement by committing collective suicide, since their resistance proved futile anyway. What strikes us as positively bizarre in the pacifist's suggestion, for example, that we *not* defend our loved ones when attacked is not the fact that someone's rights might be abused by our refusal to so act. Our real concern is what the refusal to intervene would express about our relationships and ourselves, for one of the ways we acknowledge the importance of a relationship is through our willingness to take such actions, and that is why the problem in such cases is how we can bring ourselves *not* to intervene (how is passivity possible).

The willingness to commit violence is linked to our love and estimation for others, just as the capacity for jealousy is an integral part of affection. The pacifist may respond that this is just a sociological or psychological fact about how our community links violence and care, a questionable connection that expresses thousands of years of macho culture. But this connection is no *more* questionable than that which views acts of violence against an aggressor as expressing hatred, or indifference, or objectification. If the pacifist's problem is that he cannot consistently live out his initial impulse—the posture he wishes to assume toward others requires that he commit violence and that he not commit violence—does this reflect badly on his position? Well, if you find his goals attractive it may well reflect badly on the position—or *fix*—we are all in. Unraveling the pacifist's logic may lead us to see that our world of violence and killing is one in which regarding some as people requires we regard others as things and that this is not a fact that can be excused or absolved through the techniques of moral philosophy. If the pacifist's error arises from the desire to smooth this all over by hewing to one side of the dilemma, he is no worse than his opponent, whose "refutation" of pacifism serves to dismiss those very intractable problems of violence of which pacifism is the anxious expression. As long as this tragic element in violence persists, pacifism will remain with us as a response; we should not applaud its demise, for it may well mark that the dilemmas of violence have simply been forgotten.

Impatience will now ask: so do we kill or don't we? It should be clear that I do not have the sort of answer to this question that a philosopher, at least, might expect. One can attend to the problems involved in either choice, but the greatest problem is that the choice does not flow naturally from a desire to acknowledge in others and in ourselves their importance and weaknesses and worth.

NOTES

1. George Orwell, "Looking Back on the Spanish Civil War." In *A Collection of Essays by George Orwell* (New York: Doubleday, 1954), p. 199.

2. The quote is from Marinetti, a founder of Futurism, cited in Walter Benjamin's essay, "The Work of Art in the Age of Mechanical Reproduction," *Illuminations* (New York: Schocken Books, 1969), p. 241.

REVIEW AND DISCUSSION QUESTIONS

1. Describe how Ryan understands the pacifist's position.
2. How might Wasserstrom respond to the pacifist's position?
3. Compare Ryan's discussion of pacifism with James's view of war. Would Ryan disagree with James, do you think? Explain.
4. Are you a pacifist? Why or why not?

Sports, Competition, and Violence

Robert L. Simon

In this essay Robert L. Simon considers a variety of arguments against various sports, all of which suggest that sports competition encourages violence and selfishness rather than the virtues its defenders often claim. Robert L. Simon is professor of philosophy at Hamilton College, where he coaches the golf team.

Is competition in sport ethical? Participants and fans assert that competitive sport builds character, teaches important values such as discipline and hard work, and prepares us for the pressures in our work and careers. Skeptics are not so sure, however. They regard many sports, such as football, as predominantly violent and warlike, perhaps contributing to the emphasis on violence in our society. In addition, they question whether the emphasis on winning in competitive sport teaches us selfishness, or at best a kind of almost nationalist identity with a narrow group. "My team, right or wrong!" does not seem an appropriate basis for a defensible moral code.

Is competitive sport a kind of war of all against all? Does it encourage violence against opponents, whom we are taught to regard as "the enemy" to be bullied or dominated into submission on the field of play (or should we say field of battle)? On the other hand, is there more to be said for competitive sport than the critics recognize? Does sport simply reflect some of the worst values of our society, such as selfishness, a win at all costs attitude, and violence against opponents? Alternatively, might sport express or support a set values that not only are defensible but that also have moral standing independent of the surrounding culture? Are selfishness and violence intrinsic to competitive sport, or does sport, at least at its best, present us with a moral framework that not only is defensible but

also admirable? In what follows, we will examine the morality of competitive sport, particularly as it is practiced in organized athletics.

COMPETITION IN SPORTS

At first glance, competition seems almost built into the very nature of sport. We speak of sporting events as contests or competitions, describe athletes as good or bad competitors, and refer to those on other teams as opponents.

However, the connection between sport and competition is far looser than such an initial reaction might suggest. Fishing and skiing are sports but neither necessarily involves competition. Indeed, virtually any sport can be played noncompetitively. Men and women may participate to get away from work, to exercise, because they enjoy physical activity, to make friends and meet new people, or to enjoy fresh air. Another goal of participants might be improvement. Such players, often misleadingly described as "competing with themselves," aim not at defeating opponents but at improving their own personal performance. Still others may have the purely aesthetic goal of making the movements of their sport with skill and grace. For example, basketball players may value outstanding moves rather than defeat of opponents. A leading amateur golfer, after years of hard

This essay is a revised version of a chapter from Robert L. Simon's book *Sports and Social Values* (Englewood Cliffs, NJ: Prentice Hall, 1985). Professor Simon has since written *Fair Play* (Boulder, CO: Westview Press), in which he discusses many of the same issues. Reprinted by permission of Prentice Hall and Robert L. Simon. Notes omitted.

practice, describes her aim as "to make a swing that you know is as close to perfection as you can get. And you say, 'Boy, look at what I did.' That's all it is."

None of these goals necessarily [excludes] competitiveness or a desire to win. One can value exercise, try to improve, appreciate skilled moves, *and* compete. What must be added to clear examples of noncompetitive sport, however, in order to derive a clear case of competition in sport?

If we are to evaluate competition in the context of sports or athletics, we first must be able to identify it and distinguish it from noncompetitive sport. Are there any specific elements that distinguish competitive from noncompetitive participation in sports?

It is possible that no common features are present in all sports. Perhaps there is at most a family resemblance. Be that as it may, there do seem to be elements that are central to *clear* or *paradigm cases* of competition in sports. By focusing on such clear cases, we can insure that central aspects of competition are being dealt with and leave borderline or puzzling instances for case-by-case analysis.

What seems missing from participation in sport as a means to improvement, exercise, and aesthetic appreciation is the goal of defeating an opponent. In clear cases at least, competition seems to be a form of zero-sum game. The aim, defeat of an opponent, cannot be obtained by all and attainment of the goal by one player (or team) precludes its attainment by others. Competition in sports and athletics, *at its most clear,* is participation with the goal of defeating opponents. . . .

Competition in sports and athletics paradigmatically is to be thought of as the attempt to secure victory within the appropriate constitutive rules defining the contest. How is competition in sports to be evaluated? Is it good or bad, fair or unfair, beneficial or harmful? Should it be tolerated, encouraged, or forbidden? It is to such questions that we now turn.

THE CRITIQUE OF COMPETITION

Why is it necessary for us to morally evaluate competition in sports? Isn't it enough to say that participants and spectators alike enjoy such competition and voluntarily associate themselves with it? To critics of competition in sports, that is not enough. They argue that such competition is inherently immoral or, more cautiously, that it expresses and reinforces undesirable social values. Many persons, including some successful professional athletes, have criticized the overemphasis on winning which they believe the competitive attitude breeds, and have proposed a more relaxed attitude toward sports than that sanctioned by the competitive creed.

On the other hand, proponents of athletic competition have argued for its moral value. At their most extreme, they have held that the competitive spirit in sports is one foundation of the best elements of our national character. General Douglas MacArthur may have overstated the case when he maintained that participation in competitive sport "is a vital character builder" which "molds the youth of our country for their roles as custodians of the republic." Overstated or not, the view he expressed is a widely shared one.

A moral assessment of competition in sport is necessary if we are to evaluate these different views. It is not enough to defend competition in sport on the grounds that it is fun, without hearing the arguments of the critics. After all, racist members of a dominant majority may enjoy terrorizing a racial minority but that doesn't make their behavior right. We need to rationally evaluate the arguments for and against the morality of competition in sport. . . .

Proponents of competitive sport . . . frequently claim that participation promotes such desirable traits as loyalty, discipline, commitment, a concern for excellence, and a "never-say-die" attitude. These views are expressed by well-known slogans, sometimes posted on the locker room wall, like "A quitter never wins, a winner never quits" and "When the going gets tough, the tough get going." Strongly stated generalizations, such as the assertion that "Athletics offer the greatest opportunity for character development of any activity" are common. Unfortunately, even if we restrict ourselves to effects upon competitors under actual rather than ideal conditions, such claims are difficult to document. Thus, with regard to altruism, one recent study concludes that "Most athletes indicate low interest in receiving support and concern from others, low need to take care of others and low need for affiliation. Such a personality seems necessary to achieve victory over others." More generally, the authors report

We found no empirical support for the tradition that sport builds character. . . . It seems that the personality of the ideal athlete is not the result of any molding process, but comes out of the ruthless selection process that occurs at all levels of sport. . . . Horatio Alger success—in spoil or elsewhere—comes only to those who already are mentally fit, resilient and strong.

Although no single study is decisive, this passage does suggest a number of important methodological conclusions. Even if participants in athletics do manifest desirable character traits to an unusual degree, it does not follow that participation in sport *caused* such traits to develop. Rather, it may have been prior possession of those traits that led to successful participation. *Correlation* should not be confused with *causation*.

However, by the same token, negative effects often attributed to competition need not be caused by competition itself. Thus, it has been suggested that "athletes whose sense of identity and self-worth is entirely linked to athletic achievement often experience an identity crisis when the athletic career has ended, and it becomes necessary to move on to something else." However, this may be true generally of hard-driving individuals who face significant changes at the end of careers in other fields. Would anyone be surprised by the claim "executives whose sense of identity and self-worth is entirely linked to achievement in business often experience an identity crisis when their career has ended and it becomes necessary to move on to something else?" We need to distinguish causation from correlation in evaluating both the positive and negative aspects of competition in sport.

Moreover, empirical studies may fail to capture subtle indirect causal connections. Professor Harry Edwards, while acknowledging that competitive sports do not build character from scratch, suggests that participation in competitive sport may reinforce *and* encourage development of pre-existing character traits. Perhaps individuals with

certain kinds of personalities tend to participate in competitive sport *and* have the relevant features of their character reinforced as a result. This suggests that it is not easy to show that participation in competitive sport either clearly does or clearly does not promote specific character traits in participants. . . .

. . . Competitors need not have as their primary motive the desire to beat opponents. Although as good competitors they try their best to win, they may value the competition not primarily for its outcome but for the process of testing oneself against other athletes.

Consider the following description of a Yale-Princeton football game played in 1895. Princeton was winning 16–10 but Yale was right on the Princeton goal line with a chance to turn the tide on the very last play of the game.

The clamor ceased once absolutely, and the silence was even more impressive than the tumult that had preceded it. . . . While they (Yale) were lining up for that last effort the cheering died away, yells both measured and inarticulate stopped and the place was so still . . . you could hear the telegraph instruments chirping like crickets from the side.

Yale scores to win the game on a brilliant run.

It is not possible to describe that run. It would be as easy to explain how a snake disappears through the grass, or an eel slips from your fingers, or to say how a flash of linked lightning wriggles across the sky.

Is the important point here simply that Yale won and Princeton lost? Edwin Delattre, one of our wisest educators, draws a different lesson from this episode and the many like it that take place during all seasons and at different levels of athletic competition.

Such moments are what makes the game worth the candle. Whether amidst the soft lights and sparkling balls against the baize of a billiard table, or the rolling terrain of a lush fairway or in the violent and crashing pits where linemen struggle, it is the moments when no let up is possible, when there is virtually no tolerance for error, which make up the game. The best and most satisfying contests maximize these moments and minimize respite from pressure

According to Delattre, it is these moments of test rather than victory or defeat that are the source of the value of competition in sport.

The testing of one's mettle in competitive athletics is a form of self discovery. . . . The claim of competitive athletics to importance rests squarely on their providing us opportunities for self discovery which might otherwise have been missed. . . . They provide opportunities for self-discovery, for concentration and intensity of involvement, for being carried away by the demands of the contest . . . with a frequency seldom matched elsewhere. . . . This is why it is a far greater success in competitive athletics to have played well under pressure of a truly worthwhile opponent and lost than to have defeated a less worthy or unworthy one where no demands were made.

Delattre would argue, then, that although it is essential to good competition that the competitors try as hard as they can to achieve victory, the principal value of athletic competition lies not in the attainment of victory itself but in the process of trying to overcome a worthy opponent. This position suggests that we can view competition as significantly *cooperative* rather than as a purely selfish zero-sum game. Opponents are engaging in the *cooperative* enterprise of generating challenges against which they can test themselves. Each has the obligation to the other to try his or her best. Although one wins and the other loses, each gains by facing a test that each voluntarily chooses to undertake. . . .

Boxing and the Ethics of Competition

. . . [I]t was suggested that competition in sport should be conceived of as the mutual quest for challenge among competitors. It is as if each competitor has contracted to do his or her best so as to stimulate the others to do their best. What follows if we apply this model to boxing?

The most direct implication is that boxers should intend not to injure competitors but rather to box skillfully so as do their best and bring out the best in their opponents. Perhaps contemporary professional boxing encourages the formation of intentions to do violence. However, it was at one time true that the goal of fencers was to skewer their enemies. Fencers today need not have any

such desire. Why can't the same be true of a reformed sport of boxing?

If boxing is conceived of as a sport, its goal should be demonstration of certain martial skills, not the injuring of rival competitors. Proponents of boxing as a sport surely would argue that in boxing at its best, it is the skill of the athletes and not the scent of blood that would be of interest. Of course, particular boxers may want to harm their opponents, just as a particular pitcher may want to bean a particular batter, but it is hard to see why such intentions *must* be part of boxing any more than they must be part of baseball or any other sport.

Accordingly, as was argued earlier, boxing can be seen as a paradigm of the controlled use of force rather than as socially acceptable violence. Boxers, on such a view, should use force to demonstrate their skills and bring out those of competitors, not to intentionally injure opponents.

In addition, modifications which channel boxing in the direction of fencing and away from Mayhem should be adopted. The nature of the reforms undoubtedly will be controversial, but they surely must include the introduction of safer equipment, more stringent medical monitoring of fighters, greater emphasis on scoring rather than on knockouts, and perhaps the penalizing of punches to the head. While boxing will never be as sedate as modern fencing, it can be modified so as to more clearly distinguish it from Mayhem.

Of course, hard-nosed libertarians may be quite right to argue that *the state* has no business interfering even with boxing at its most violent on the grounds that liberty of consenting adults is inviolate. But even if this point is correct, which is controversial, it concerns only the permissibility of *legal* prohibition of boxing. It does not follow that boxing at its most violent is an *ethically* defensible sport. It is when athletic competition treats competitors as persons, by application of the model of the mutual quest for excellence, that it is ethically defensible.

Defenders of boxing might object that such sanitization of boxing removes those very qualities which make it such a fascinating sport. The opportunity to show courage, to do one's best in the face of pain, and to demonstrate skill in the use of brute power would all be lost if boxing were made more like fencing. On such a view, the loss would not be worth the gain.

This point merits serious consideration. But before it is accepted, we ought to ask whether the same argument could be made in behalf of Mayhem. If this defense of boxing is accepted, aren't we also committed by application of the ethical requirement of systematic consistency . . . to the view that society must allow gladiatorial contests, lest liberty be violated? Surely sports such as baseball, basketball, and soccer give ample opportunities for the demonstration of courage, the capacity to overcome injury and use force skillfully without essentially involving the intent to inflict injury upon an opponent.

Finally, a proponent of boxing may deny a key premise of the critics; the claim that boxers intentionally aim at injuring their opponents. "Boxers do aim at boxing skillfully," a proponent may maintain, "but it just so happens that a skillful punch often results in the unintentional infliction of injury."

Superficially, this claim resembles the suggestion that a football player who injures an opponent by throwing a clean block may not have intended to inflict harm. In such a case, the player may have wanted only to open a hole for the ball carrier. By doing so, he unintentionally inflicts an injury on a defender. But is this really analogous to the situation in boxing or is it different? After all, in boxing, the quickest way to win is through a knockout. Alternately, one can win by injuring an opponent so severely that although conscious, he cannot continue the bout. Unfortunately, the attempt to distinguish between the act of hitting and the unintended consequence of injuring an opponent seems suspiciously like the attempt to distinguish between pulling the trigger of a loaded gun one has aimed at an enemy and the victim's death. Where the effect is so closely linked to the action, the burden of proof surely does fall on those who want to distinguish the attempt to knock out an opponent from the attempt to injure him.

Our discussion suggests, then, that even if boxing should be immune from legal interference or prohibition on libertarian grounds, radical reform of the sport is morally warranted. Emphasis should be on scoring and fistic skill, not on infliction of injury. *Perhaps* society has no right to force

boxers to give up their sport or prevent spectators from watching bouts. (Does it have the right to prohibit gladiatorial contests?) But ethical concerns about the nature of good sport put the burden of proof on proponents of boxing to show why significant reforms should not be adopted.

VIOLENCE AND CONTACT SPORTS

Can arguments concerning violence in boxing be carried over to discussions of other contact sports? For example, if it can be successfully argued that boxing should be reformed or even prohibited because of the violence it involves, why can't the same be said of football as well?

Critics of football maintain that football is a violent sport. Coaches and fans urge players to "smash," "smear" or "bury" the opposition. Players are viewed as pieces of meat to be expended on neutralizing the warriors of the other side. On this view, football is a miniaturized version of war. All too often the intent of the participants and spectators is to win by any means possible, including the inflicting of injury on the other side. When a coach declares on national television that "anytime you get a chance to take 'em out . . . I expect and encourage you to do it," the chances are that the values being expressed are not isolated within the profession.

Even players who claim to stay within the rules admit that physical intimidation of opponents is a key part of their game. As Oakland Raider free safety Jack Tatum puts it in his, some would say aptly named, book *They Call Me Assassin,* "My idea of a good hit is when the victim wakes up on the sidelines with the train whistles blowing in his head and wondering who he is and what ran over him." Unfortunately, one of Tatum's hits in a game against the New England Patriots resulted in what appears to be the permanent paralysis of the Patriot's pass receiver, Darryl Stingley.

Tatum claims that although he hits hard, he plays within the rules and does not take illegal "shots" at opponents. On his view, he is paid to make sure pass receivers don't make catches in his territory. A good way to achieve this goal is to let them know they will get hit hard when running pass patterns in his area. Then, the next time a pass is thrown to them, they may think too much about what is about to hit them and concentrate less on making the catch. As Tatum puts it, "do I let the receiver have the edge and give him the chance to make catches around me because I'm a sensitive guy or do I do what I am paid to do?"

It is understandable, then, why to its many critics, football is a sport which glorifies violence, encourages militaristic attitudes, and amounts to a public celebration of many of our worst values. In effect, these critics hold that football, particularly big-time college and professional football, are to contemporary American society what gladiatorial contests were to the Romans.

Paul Hoch, author of *Rip Off the Big Game*, a highly ideological critique of American sport but one which raises many serious issues for consideration, sees football as an expression of suppressed violence in the American psyche. Thus, he suggests that because violence is rule-governed in football, as opposed to the random violence of racial disorders or radical political protests, it "provides powerful ideological support for the officialized, rule-governed violence in society, in which judges have the final say. In short, the fans are supposed to identify with the distorted framework of law and order, both on the football field and in society, irrespective of what that law and order is supposed to protect."

Unfortunately, an atmosphere of violence pervades a good deal of big-time American sport, with football perhaps constituting a paradigm example. Thus, Hoch maintains,

if the fans can be encouraged . . . to demand higher levels of gladiatorial violence, sports owners can easily supply it. Professional athletes are encouraged to maim one another, not only by the macho-minded sports writers and fans . . . but by the knowledge that if they're not tough enough there are literally thousands . . . of players around to take their jobs. . . . In a militarized society, gladiatorial combat brings in profits at the box office. So its all part of the game. But whose game?

In a similar vein, James Michener reports on brutality in some college football programs. In one case, smaller players on a university team "were forced to wrestle huge linemen under the chicken wire, and the losers had to keep wrestling until they won, always screaming and cursing and trying to draw blood like some kind of animals."

The Ethics of Violence in Football

The charges discussed above can be reduced to two major claims. First, football is held to be a violent sport. Second, because of its emphasis on disciplined violence within the rules, football encourages fan acceptance of official violence while discouraging external criticism of the rules themselves. In other words, football is not ideologically neutral, at least in our society. It encourages a positive attitude towards officially sanctioned violence and discourages social criticism and the use of violence for social change.

Many of the distinctions which arose in our discussion of boxing also apply to analysis of the charges against football. In particular, it is important to distinguish between violence that is *intrinsic* and violence that is *extrinsic* to football, and secondly, it is important to distinguish between violence and the use of force.

Surely, violence, in the sense of the use of force intended to harm an opponent, normally is indefensible in sport. With the possible exception of such sports as boxing, players have not consented to become targets of violence and there is little reason to think it would be rational for them to do so. From the high school player, who wants to keep a healthy body so he can participate in sports throughout a lifetime, to the pro star whose career and earnings can be cut short by a serious injury, players have a clear interest in keeping violence (as opposed to legitimate body contact) out of football. In the long run, so do coaches, since their own stars are just as vulnerable as the stars on opposing teams. Spectators would lose, too, if exciting players spent more time on crutches than on the field because of intentionally administered injuries.

In any case, violence directed by players against players is no more ethically defensible than violence directed against persons in other contexts. Violence directed against an opponent treats that person as a mere means or thing to be used for the gratification or advancement of the agent. It violates the ethic of competition, which requires that opponents be conceived of as partners in a mutual quest for excellence, as well as the deeper underlying moral requirement of respect for persons.

But is violence in the strong sense of the use of force intended to harm another really intrinsic to football? Is football essentially a violent game or is violence a *misuse* of force within the sport?

Football clearly is a contact sport which requires the use of bodily force. It does not follow, however, that football is intrinsically violent. If critics want to argue the opposite, they need to do more than simply point out that football is a contact sport. The most that has been established is that unfortunately violence is frequently part of football, not that football is intrinsically violent. As we have seen, the use of force is morally quite distinct from violence.

But how is the line between violence and the use of force to be drawn? When Jack Tatum attempts to intimidate an opposing receiver through "good hits," then is he being violent? Tatum himself might say that he does not want to injure his opponent but only to make him afraid, and only through moves permitted by the rules. But what is the opposing receiver afraid of if not getting hurt? On the other hand, what if we say Tatum is using violence? Does it follow that the huge linemen who try to physically wear down their opposite numbers through constant application of force are violent too? And if we say they are violent, what part of football isn't violent? Is such violence unethical?

Perhaps it will help if we turn away from football for a moment and consider examples of intimidation in other sports. In baseball, a pitch thrown with the intent of injuring the batter—a "beanball" thrown at the batter's head—clearly constitutes an act of reprehensible violence. No game justifies the attempt to maim or kill an opponent. But what if a batter continually leans over the inside corner of the plate, in an attempt to deprive the pitcher of a portion of the strike zone? If the pitcher throws some inside "brushback" pitches, which are designed not to hit the batter, but to force him to move back to a position which is strategically advantageous to the pitcher, is violence involved? What of the tennis player who sees an opponent charging the net and smashes a return directly at the opposing player, not with the intent to injure, but with the goal of scoring a quick point?

Suppose one thinks that the brushback pitch and the forehand smash at an opponent are permissible moves within sport, and that if they do involve violence at all, they do so in an ethically defensible way. What might an ethical defense of such practices look like? Are there any principles we might discover in formulating such a defense which can be applied to football?

To begin with, we might note that sports often do involve the use of force against opponents to achieve strategic goals. Not infrequently, this use of force will involve the risk of injury. Presumably, participants are willing to take such a risk because they believe the risks are outweighed by the benefits of participation. The key ethical question, it might be claimed, is whether the use of force in question takes unfair advantage of the *vulnerability* of one's opponent. Thus, major league batters are supposed to have the reflexes and ability to avoid brushback pitches. The pitcher is not throwing at a sitting duck. In contrast, a beanball thrown just behind a batter's head takes advantage of the hitter's superb reflexes to inflict injury. The batter sees the pitch is inside, and ducks backward right into the path on which the ball is thrown. On the other hand, a brushback pitch, which might be ethically defensible when thrown in a major league game, would be ethically indefensible if thrown by a big league pitcher against a 50-year-old, out of shape businessman who hasn't played ball in decades.

If these suggestions have force, they support what we might call the Vulnerability Principle, or VP. According to the VP, the use of force against an opponent in sport is ethically indefensible just when the opponent's physical position or condition is such that no effective strategic response is possible and as a result it is highly likely that injury will result.

If we apply the VP to football, we find that the use of force by linemen against one another is acceptable. Physical intimidation of one line by another is permissible if it amounts to wearing down the opposition by the constant infliction of force, so long as the opponents are in a position to respond with strategic countermoves, i.e. blocks, and are not in an unusual position of physical risk. On the other hand, a hit from the blind side by a free safety on a receiver who is not the target of a pass catches the receiver in a position of vulnerability where no effective countermove is possible. Such a blow, therefore, is ethically dubious. Indeed, defensive backs, including Jack Tatum, have suggested that the rules be rewritten so as to provide more protection for receivers. Unfortunately, it may be the belief that a wide-open, high risk game is what brings in the dollars that contributes as much to injuries in big-time football as the moves of the players on the field.

Although our discussion of violence in football has not been conclusive, we have seen that the use of force to deliberately harm an opponent has no place in the sport. If there is a moral difference between such behavior and criminal assault, we have yet to be told what it is. On the other hand, we have seen that it is difficult to draw the line between defensible and indefensible uses of force for strategic purposes. Perhaps the VP represents a first step toward the formulation of a useful principle in this area, although it clearly needs to be examined and reformulated more rigorously in the light of counterexample. In any case, we have seen that violence is not equivalent to the mere use of force. The challenge contact sports provide is in the skilled and controlled use of force for strategic ends, and they are not to be condemned for that alone.

Is Football Conservative?

What about the charge that football supports values such as deference to the powerful and the legitimacy of officially sanctioned violence? Does football function ideologically to support conservatism and the *status quo?*

In assessing the charge that football serves a conservative function in our society, the first thing to note is the ambiguity of the claim being made. Perhaps it means that the great attention given to big-time football, and to other major sports, *causes* people to tolerate an unjust situation, perhaps by distracting them from their more serious problems or perhaps by inducing them to identify with power, as Hoch suggests. Alternately, perhaps what is being claimed is that the values implicit in the play of football are themselves objectionable; football is warlike or football requires unquestioning acceptance of officially sanctioned violence. Here what we have is not an empirical claim about the effects of football on the American public but rather a moral analysis of the kind of values embedded in the play of the game. Let us examine each kind of claim in turn.

The causal theses, of course, ultimately must be confirmed or disconfirmed by empirical data, not by philosophizing. In fact, the existing data is difficult to interpret but can perhaps be read to provide modest support for the role of sport in reinforcing conventional values. Nevertheless, as interesting as the interpretation of empirical studies might be, we need to keep in mind the philosophical points which interpretation of any studies in this area presuppose.

To begin with, we must remember not to confuse correlation with causality. Suppose empirical studies show that football fans, or even players and coaches, tend to be more tolerant of officially sanctioned violence, less tempted to rock the boat to correct injustice, and more disposed to respect those in power, regardless of what they command, than those not involved with football. Can one conclude on the basis of such data that involvement with football produces such a personality? One cannot. For one thing, it is entirely possible that people with such traits become football fans and not that football fans become such people. Alternately, some as-yet-unknown third factor might produce both involvement in football and the associated traits.

There is another, perhaps more profound, philosophical issue at stake. If what we are trying to measure are such traits as "unquestioning obedience to authority," "tolerance of injustice," "acceptance of official violence," and "unwillingness to challenge the rules," we need to be careful that we do not beg the question in favor of our own values. What one investigator believes to be blind obedience, another may see as admirable loyalty. In addition, value judgments may be called for in estimating what counts as injustice, what counts as blind or uncritical obedience and what degree of acceptance of authority is normal or justified. Accordingly, although the critics are quite right to raise the question of the social effects of sports and their value, they may smuggle in moral conclusions that have not been adequately defended. For example, they may assume that football is essentially violent, an assumption which we have seen needs explication and defense and which is far from self-evident. Or they may assume that violence is "just part of the game," ignoring the distinction between violence and force.

What of the second thesis, based on moral analysis, that regardless of its causal effects, football expresses by its very nature the values of blind obedience, militarism, toleration of official violence, and fear of going outside the rules to promote change? Does football *express* an ideologically loaded set of conservative values, whether or not it causes others to adopt them?

It will be useful to approach this issue by asking what it *means* to say that football, or any other sport, *expresses* certain values. On one hand, it might mean that action based upon particular values is or ought to be rewarded within the context of the sport. Thus, football would be essentially violent, in this sense, if acts of violence were rewarded within the game. As we have seen, players, coaches, and fans all have strong reasons to support a system of rules prohibiting violence (in the sense of the intentional use of force designed to harm opponents), as well as a system of sanctions supporting such rules. While the temptation to cheat on particular occasions might be overwhelming, all those involved in the sport have incentives to keep such occasions few and far between, and to do their best to make sure isolated acts of violence do not pay off. Clearly, there are grounds for denying that violence *ought* to be rewarded within football and for condemning those who encourage it.

There is a second sense is which a sport can be said to express certain values. In this sense, a sport expresses values just when playing the sport well requires that the players exhibit the values in question. For example, it can be argued that basketball at its best expresses the value of teamwork. Thus, the good basketball coach will teach his players that a coordinated team performance is more valuable than uncoordinated individual achievement. While basketball is often exciting precisely because of the outstanding moves of individual players such as Dr. J., the sport is most pleasing when players employ their individual skills within a framework of team goals.

Does football express violence in the sense that to play well, players must aim at hurting oppo-

nents? While some coaches may encourage violent attitudes among their players, and some players may not need much encouragement, such an approach is hardly an essential element of good football. Toughness may be a valuable attribute of football players, but meanness is not. Moreover, while the line between the defensible and indefensible use of force in contact sports is not always easy to draw, principles such as the VP may be used to reform the rules so as to make them more closely conform to moral requirements.

What about the claim that excellence in football requires blind subservience to the coach, and hence expresses the value of uncritical acceptance of the dictates of those in power? What football teaches us, critics such as Hoch tend to assert, is that violence is permissible if it is ordered by those in the power structure. After all, players are expected to carry out orders and "execute" the coach's commands, or those of the quarterback, without question. This is direct opposition to the kind of questioning of those in power that is so necessary for the workings of democracy and the critical inquiry which gives it life.

While there are too many examples of authoritarianism in sport, it may go too far to criticize sport itself rather than those who misuse power within it. In addition, we need to be careful not to beg important questions by viewing sports through our own ideological blinders. Thus, one might argue that football is conservative because it teaches us to follow existing rules, or with equal force argue that it is liberal because it teaches us that authority figures who break the rules are open to moral criticism. After all, the notion that American Presidents are not above the law is hardly an illiberal notion. Surely, there is no more reason to say that a football coach who requires his players to practice hard is teaching "blind subservience to authority" any more than does the philosophy professor who expects students to read assignments.

To conclude, we have not been given reason to believe that football illustrates or expresses indifference to or tolerance of violence. We already have seen that there is reason to doubt that football is essentially violent in the first place. On the contrary, we can plausibly argue that at its best, it illustrates not violence but the controlled use of force. On the other hand, to the extent that the actual practice of football is violent, or involves the indefensible use of force, it is subject to moral criticism. Thus, while violence may often occur in football, its mere presence doesn't teach people to think of it as justified or reasonable.

Of course, owners of pro teams may think that violence sells tickets. The media may too often glorify violence in the attempt to secure a wider audience. But whether we tolerate such abuses in sport depends at least in part on the critical principles we accept and apply in evaluating athletics. If we are ethically required to view competitors as partners in a mutual quest for excellence through challenge, a violent attitude toward them is surely unjustified. The ethic of good sports requires that we distinguish hard but legitimate contact from violence. It is far from clear that football illustrates the value of the latter rather than providing grounds, based on the ethic of good competition, for its condemnation.

The Ideal and the Actual in Philosophy of Sports

It is understandable that some critics of violence in sports may be impatient with the discussion so far. In their view, the discussion has been an exercise in developing an ideal which has perhaps been too tolerant of actual abuses. "It is all too easy to say that football is not *necessarily* violent," such a critic might argue, "when the important task is to show what is wrong with actual practice and to promote change."

While much of our discussion has been concerned with developing an ideal of good sport, it hardly lacks practical implications. It is difficult to understand how we could even identify abuses in sport unless we had some grasp of what principles were being violated in the first place. In addition, without some standards at which to aim, we would not know the proper direction for moral change.

Of course, moral reform involves far more than efficiently implementing an ideal. At a minimum, the ideal must be implemented in a fair and just way. For example, would it be fair to simply prohibit boxing without making some provision for employment for boxers whose jobs we would be eliminating? It is possible that the moral and practical costs of implementing some reforms might

be so high that we are bound to settle for "second best" solutions. Be that as it may, unless we know what principles should apply in sport, how are we to even tell what needs to be corrected in current practice?

Against Violence in Sports

I have argued that violence in sport, in the sense of force directed at inflicting harm on others, is incompatible with the ethic of athletic competition as the mutual quest for excellence. Since ethical competitors view each other as cooperating in the posing of challenges, they do not view opponents as obstacles to be gotten out of the way. Rather, they encourage opponents to play their best so that new and better challenges can be faced by all.

While we have rejected the view that football is to be condemned as illegitimately violent, it is important to see that the argument of the chapter counts against many defenders of the "boys will be boys" school of thought as well. For example, those who defend constant fighting in hockey by claiming roughness is "part of the game" make the very same logical error as those who confuse the use of force with violence. While body checking may be a defensible part of hockey, at least insofar as its goal is to advance play rather than to injure opponents, hitting an opponent with a hockey stick with the desire to "take him out" surely is not. If it is, the "game" being played is not a morally defensible one. Similarly, the encouraging of hockey professionals to fight so as to sell more tickets is about on a moral par with the subsidization of Mayhem.

However, we should not confuse the thesis that violence often is a part of sport, and is even exploited for commercial reasons, with the stronger thesis that sports are essentially violent. It is because the latter thesis is so questionable that we have grounds for condemning violence and its exploitation in the name of good sport. . . .

Sports and Social Values

At its best, competitive sport emphasizes the values or personal virtues necessary to meet challenges successfully. The ethic of the quest for excellence in the face of challenge implies that we should respect opponents rather than view them as enemies or obstacles to be overcome. A sports contest, therefore, is not a war although it shares with war the need for such qualities as physical courage, stamina, endurance, and determination. Thus, the ethical sports contest has its own set of values, which not only do not simply mirror those of the broader culture, but which also come into conflict with broader social values. For example, if the broader society relaxes standards and tends to reward half-hearted efforts in a kind of social grade inflation, sport with its emphasis on achievement in a quest for excellence may stand for a conflicting ethic; one that arguably is more defensible than the looser standards prevailing off the playing field.

In particular, if competition in sport is conceived as governed by the ethic of mutual quest for excellence, which it should be if competitors are to be morally respected persons, then violence in the strong sense has no place in it. A defensible ethic of sport must avoid the twin errors of, on one hand, equating the mere use of force in sport with indefensible violence and, on the other, tolerating violence because of a mistaken belief that since sport is a kind of war of all against all, anything goes so long as it works in the pursuit of victory. Competition in sport, properly conceived, embodies and expresses an ethic that stresses the values and personal virtues necessary for meeting challenges, not selfishness, violence, and war.

REVIEW AND DISCUSSION QUESTIONS

1. Describe the argument that competitive sports are inherently wrong.
2. How might sports be thought to be cooperative rather than competitive?
3. Is boxing immoral, according to Simon? How does Simon respond to those who wish to abolish boxing?
4. Describe Simon's view of the argument that football is violent since people seek to harm their opponents.
5. Describe Simon's vision of ideals inherent in sports.
6. How might the critic of sport respond to Simon? Assess the merits of those responses.
7. Compare Simon's understanding of virtue with William James's and Cheyney Ryan's.

Part III
POLITICAL RELATIONSHIPS

9
Justice and Economic Distribution

How should economic wealth and income be distributed? Is there a right to property? What do we owe to people who are starving to death, when we have more than enough? These and other questions are at the center of this section. Readings include John Locke's famous defense of individual rights and property, an essay by a contemporary critic of all efforts to redistribute wealth, and an essay that argues we owe far more to those in need than is often assumed. The last reading is from what many regard as the most important work in political philosophy this century, in which John Rawls seeks to revive social contract theory in the service of a liberal, egalitarian vision of government and social justice.

The Second Treatise of Government

John Locke

Born in 1632, John Locke was an important figure in both British and American politics; indeed, there are few, if any, philosophers who were more influential in the development of American political institutions and beliefs than John Locke. Locke's father was a politically influential lawyer who supported Oliver Cromwell and the British Parliament against King Charles I. John Locke was sent to Oxford at fifteen, where he became friendly with noted chemist Robert Boyle as well as other scientists, all of whom exerted an important influence on young John. After graduation, Locke served as a tutor in Greek. Then, after serving a period as a diplomat, he returned to Oxford to study medicine. Locke was active throughout his life in political and public affairs. At one point he was forced into

From *The Second Treatise of Government: An Essay Concerning the Origin, Extent and End of Civil Government* (1690).

exile by the king, but he returned to England after the Glorious Revolution in 1688. He died in 1704 at the age of seventy-two.

Locke's influence is evident, among other places, in the U.S. Declaration of Independence. In his First Treatise of Government, Locke attacks the divine right of kings; in the Second Treatise, from which the following selection is taken, he addresses the legitimate role of government together with the limits on governmental power. Locke begins by imagining persons in a state of nature in which each is independently pursuing his or her own interests. In that situation, he argues, people possess natural moral rights to life, property, and liberty, rights that are not to be transgressed by others. Given the realities of such a state of nature, it is in the interests of people to move toward cooperation and trade and to establish common institutions to provide protection of life and property. Governmental action is severely limited, however, by people's natural rights—a topic to which he devotes considerable attention. Locke also considers the related and important question of how a previously unowned resource may justly become the property of one person.

OF THE STATE OF NATURE

To understand political power aright, and derive it from its original, we must consider what state all men are naturally in, and that is a state of perfect freedom to order their actions and dispose of their possessions and persons as they think fit, within the bounds of the law of nature, without asking leave, or depending upon the will of any other man.

A state also of equality, wherein all the power and jurisdiction is reciprocal, no one having more than another; there being nothing more evident than that creatures of the same species and rank, promiscuously born to all the same advantages of nature, and the use of the same faculties, should also be equal one amongst another without subordination or subjection, unless the Lord and Master of them all should by any manifest declaration of His will set one above another, and confer on him by an evident and clear appointment an undoubted right to domination and sovereignty.

But though this be a state of liberty, yet it is not a state of license; though man in that state have an uncontrollable liberty to dispose of his person or possessions, yet he has not liberty to destroy himself, or so much as any creature in his possession, but where some nobler use than its bare preservation calls for it. The state of nature has a law of nature to govern it, which obliges everyone; and reason, which is that law, teaches all mankind who will but consult it, that, being all equal and independent, no one ought to harm another in his life, health, liberty, or possessions. For men being all the workmanship of one omnipotent and infinitely wise Maker—all the servants of one sovereign Master, sent into the world by His order, and about His business—they are His property, whose workmanship they are, made to last during His, not one another's pleasure; and being furnished with like faculties, sharing all in one community of nature, there cannot be supposed any such subordination among us, that may authorize us to destroy one another, as if we were made for one another's uses, as the inferior ranks of creatures are for ours. Everyone, as he is bound to preserve himself, and not to quit his station willfully, so, by the like reason, when his own preservation comes not in competition, ought he, as much as he can, to preserve the rest of mankind, and not, unless it be to do justice on an offender, take away or impair the life, or what tends to the preservation of the life, the liberty, health, limb, or goods of another.

And that all men may be restrained from invading others' rights, and from doing hurt to one another, and the law of nature be observed, which willeth the peace and preservation of all mankind, the execution of the law of nature is in that state put into every man's hand, whereby everyone has a right to punish the transgressors of that law to such a degree as may hinder its violation. For the law of nature would, as all other laws that concern men in this world, be in vain if there were nobody that, in the state of nature, had a power to execute that law, and thereby preserve the innocent and restrain offenders. And if anyone in the state of nature may punish another for any evil he has done, everyone may do so. For in that state of perfect equality, where naturally there is no superiority or jurisdiction of one over another, what any may do in prosecution of that law, everyone must needs have a right to do.

And thus in the state of nature one man comes by a power over another; but yet no absolute or arbitrary power, to use a criminal, when he has got him in his hands, according to the passionate heats or boundless extravagance of his own will; but only to retribute to him so far as calm reason and conscience dictate what is proportionate to his transgression, which is so much as may serve for reparation and restraint. For these two are the only reasons why one man may lawfully do harm to another, which is that we call punishment. In transgressing the law of nature, the offender declares himself to live by another rule than that of common reason and equity, which is that measure God has set to the actions of men, for their mutual security; and so he becomes dangerous to mankind, the tie which is to secure them from injury and violence being slighted and broken by him. Which, being a trespass against the whole species, and the peace and safety of it, provided for by the law of nature, every man upon this score, by the right he hath to preserve mankind in general, may restrain, or, where it is necessary, destroy things noxious to them, and so may bring such evil on anyone who hath transgressed that law, as may make him repent the doing of it, and thereby deter him, and by his example others, from doing the like mischief. And in this case, and upon this ground, every man hath a right to punish the offender, and be executioner of the law of nature. . . .

Besides the crime which consists in violating the law, and varying from the right rule of reason, whereby a man so far becomes degenerate, and declares himself to quit the principles of human nature, and to be a noxious creature, there is commonly injury done, and some person or other, some other man receives damage by his transgression, in which case he who hath received any damage, has, besides the right of punishment common to him with other men, a particular right to seek reparation from him that has done it. And any other person who finds it just, may also join with him that is injured, and assist him in recovering from the offender so much as may make satisfaction for the harm he has suffered.

. . . The magistrate, who by being magistrate hath the common right of punishing put into his hands, can often, where the public good demands not the execution of the law, remit the punishment of criminal offenses by his own authority, but yet cannot remit the satisfaction due to any private man for the damage he has received. That he who has suffered the damage has a right to demand in his own name, and he alone can remit. The damnified person has this power of appropriating to himself the goods or service of the offender, by right of self-preservation, as every man has a power to punish the crime, to prevent its being committed again, by the right he has of preserving all mankind, and doing all reasonable things he can in order to that end. And thus it is that every man in the state of nature has a power to kill a murderer, both to deter others from doing the like injury, which no reparation can compensate, by the example of the punishment that attends it from everybody, and also to secure men from the attempts of a criminal who having renounced reason, the common rule and measure God hath given to mankind, hath by the unjust violence and slaughter he hath committed upon one, declared war against all mankind, and therefore may be destroyed as a lion or a tiger, one of those wild savage beasts with whom men can have no society nor security. . . . .

To this strange doctrine—viz., that in the state of nature everyone has the executive power of the law of nature—I doubt not but it will be objected that it is unreasonable for men to be judges in their own cases, that self-love will make men partial to themselves and their friends. And on the other side, that ill-nature, passion, and revenge will carry them too far in punishing others; and hence nothing but confusion and disorder will follow; and that therefore God hath certainly appointed government to restrain the partiality and violence of men. I easily grant that civil government is the proper remedy for the inconveniences of the state of nature, which must certainly be great where men may be judges in their own case, since 'tis easy to be imagined that he who was so unjust as to do his brother an injury, will scarce be so just as to condemn himself for it. But I shall desire those who make this objection, to remember that absolute monarchs are but men, and if government is to be the remedy of those evils which necessarily follow from men's being judges in their own cases, and the state of nature is therefore not to be endured, I desire to know what kind of government that is, and how much better it is than the state of nature, where one man commanding a multitude, has the liberty to be judge in his own case, and may do to all his subjects whatever he pleases, without the least question or control of those who execute his pleasure; and in whatsoever he doth, whether led by reason, mistake, or passion, must be submitted to, which men in the state of nature are not bound to do one to another? And if he that judges, judges amiss in his own or any other case, he is answerable for it to the rest of mankind.

'Tis often asked as a mighty objection, Where are, or ever were there, any men in such a state of nature? To which it may suffice as an answer at present: That since all princes and rulers of independent governments all through the world are in a state of nature, 'tis plain the world never was, nor ever will be, without numbers of men in that state. I have named all governors of independent communities, whether they are or are not in league with others. For 'tis not every compact that puts an end to the state of nature between men, but only this one of agreeing together mutually to enter into one community, and make one body politic; other promises and compacts men may make one with another, and yet still be in the state of nature. The promises and bargains for truck, etc., between the two men in Soldania, in or between a Swiss and an Indian, in the woods of America, are binding to them, though they are perfectly in a state of nature in reference to one another. For truth and keeping of faith belong to men as men, and not as members of society. . . .

OF PROPERTY

Whether we consider natural reason, which tells us that men being once born have a right to their preservation, and consequently to meat and drink and such other things as nature affords for their subsistence; or revelation, which gives us an account of those grants God made of the world to Adam, and to Noah and his sons, 'tis very clear that God, as King David says, Psalm cxv. 16, "has given the earth to the children of men," given it to

mankind in common. But this being supposed, it seems to some a very great difficulty how anyone should ever come to have a property in anything. I will not content myself to answer that if it be difficult to make out property upon a supposition that God gave the world to Adam and his posterity in common, it is impossible that any man but one universal monarch should have any property upon a supposition that God gave the world to Adam and his heirs in succession, exclusive of all the rest of his posterity. But I shall endeavor to show how men might come to have a property in several parts of that which God gave to mankind in common, and that without any express compact of all the commoners.

God, who hath given the world to men in common, hath also given them reason to make use of it to the best advantage of life and convenience. The earth and all that is therein is given to men for the support and comfort of their being. And though all the fruits it naturally produces, and beasts it feeds, belong to mankind in common, as they are produced by the spontaneous hand of nature; and nobody has originally a private dominion exclusive of the rest of mankind in any of them as they are thus in their natural state; yet being given for the use of men, there must of necessity be a means to appropriate them some way or other before they can be of any use or at all beneficial to any particular man. The fruit or venison which nourishes the wild Indian, who knows no enclosure, and is still a tenant in common, must be his, and so his, i.e., a part of him, that another can no longer have any right to it, before it can do any good for the support of his life.

Though the earth and all inferior creatures be common to all men, yet every man has a property in his own person; this nobody has any right to but himself. The labor of his body and the work of his hands we may say are properly his. Whatsoever, then, he removes out of the state that nature hath provided and left it in, he hath mixed his labor with, and joined to it something that is his own, and thereby makes it his property. It being by him removed from the common state nature placed it in, it hath by this labor something annexed to it that excludes the common right of other men. For this labor being the unquestionable property of the laborer, no man but he can have a right to what that is once joined to, at least where there is enough, and as good left in common for others.

He that is nourished by the acorns he picked up under an oak, or the apples he gathered from the trees in the wood, has certainly appropriated them to himself. Nobody can deny but the nourishment is his. I ask, then, When did they begin to be his—when he digested, or when he ate, or when he boiled, or when he brought them home, or when he picked them up? And 'tis plain if the first gathering made them not his, nothing else could. That labor put a distinction between them and common; that added something to them more than nature, the common mother of all, had done, and so they became his private right. And will anyone say he had no right to those acorns or apples he thus appropriated, because he had not the consent of all mankind to make them his? Was it a robbery thus to assume to himself what belonged to all in common? If such a consent as that was necessary, man had starved, notwithstanding the plenty God had given him. We see in commons which remain so by compact that 'tis the taking any part of what is common and removing it out of the state nature leaves it in, which begins the property; without which the common is of no use. And the taking of this or that part does not depend on the express consent of all the commoners. Thus the grass my horse has bit, the turfs my servant has cut, and the ore I have dug in any place where I have a right to them in common with others, become my property without the assignation or consent of anybody. The labor that was mine removing them out of that common state they were in, hath fixed my property in them. . . .

It will perhaps be objected to this, that if gathering the acorns, or other fruits of the earth, etc., makes a right to them, then anyone may engross as much as he will. To which I answer, Not so. The same law of nature that does by this means give us property, does also bound that property too. "God has given us all things richly" (1 Tim. vi. 17), is the voice of reason confirmed by inspiration. But how far has He given it to us? To enjoy. As much as anyone can make use of to any advantage of life before it spoils, so much he may by his labor fix a property in; whatever is beyond this, is more than his share, and belongs to others, Nothing was made by God for man to spoil or destroy. And thus consid-

ering the plenty of natural provisions there was a long time in the world, and the few spenders, and to how small a part of that provision the industry of one man could extend itself, and engross it to the prejudice of others—especially keeping within the bounds, set by reason, of what might serve for his use—there could be then little room for quarrels or contentions about property so established. . . .

OF THE BEGINNING OF POLITICAL SOCIETIES

Men being, as has been said, by nature all free, equal, and independent, no one can be put out of this estate, and subjected to the political power of another, without his own consent, which is done by agreeing with other men to join and unite into a community for their comfortable, safe, and peaceable living one amongst another, in a secure enjoyment of their properties, and a greater security against any that are not of it. This any number of men may do, because it injures not the freedom of the rest; they are left as they were in the liberty of the state of nature. When any number of men have so consented to make one community or government, they are thereby presently incorporated, and make one body politic, wherein the majority have a right to act and conclude the rest.

For when any number of men have, by the consent of every individual, made a community, they have thereby made that community one body, with a power to act as one body, which is only by the will and determination of the majority. For that which acts any community being only the consent of the individuals of it, and it being one body must move one way, it is necessary the body should move that way whither the greater force carries it, which is the consent of the majority; or else it is impossible it should act or continue one body, one community, which the consent of every individual that united into it agreed that it should; and so everyone is bound by that consent to be concluded by the majority. And therefore we see that in assemblies empowered to act by positive laws, where no number is set by that positive law which empowers them, the act of the majority passes for the act of the whole, and of course determines, as having by the law of nature and reason the power of the whole.

And thus every man, by consenting with others to make one body politic under one government, puts himself under an obligation to every one of that society, to submit to the determination of the majority, and to be concluded by it; or else this original compact, whereby he with others incorporates into one society, would signify nothing, and be no compact, if he be left free and under no other ties than he was in before in the state of nature. For what appearance would there be of any compact? What new engagement if he were no farther tied by any decrees of the society, than he himself thought fit, and did actually consent to? This would be still as great a liberty as he himself had before his compact, or anyone else in the state of nature hath, who may submit himself and consent to any acts of it if he thinks fit. . . .

Whosoever therefore out of a state of nature unite into a community must be understood to give up all the power necessary to the ends for which they unite into society, to the majority of the community, unless they expressly agreed in any number greater than the majority. And this is done by barely agreeing to unite into one political society, which is all the compact that is, or needs be, between the individuals that enter into or make up a commonwealth. . . .

Every man being, as has been shown, naturally free, and nothing being able to put him into subjection to any earthly power but only his own consent, it is to be considered what shall be understood to be sufficient declaration of a man's consent to make him subject to the laws of any government. There is a common distinction of an express and a tacit consent, which will concern our present case. Nobody doubts but an express consent of any man entering into any society makes him a perfect member of that society, a subject of that government. The difficulty is, what ought to be looked upon as a tacit consent, and how far it binds i.e., how far anyone shall be looked on to have consented, and thereby submitted to any government, where he has made no expressions of it at all. And to this I say that every man that hath any possession or enjoyment of any part of the dominions of any government doth thereby give his tacit consent, and is as far forth obliged to obedience to the laws of that government during such enjoyment as anyone under it; whether this his possession be of land to him and his heirs for ever, or a lodging only for a week; or whether it be barely traveling freely on the highway; and in effect it reaches as far as the very being of anyone within the territories of that government.

To understand this the better, it is fit to consider that every man when he at first incorporates himself into any commonwealth, he, by his uniting himself thereunto, annexed also, and submits to the community those possessions which he has or shall acquire that do not already belong to any other government; for it would be a direct contradiction for anyone to enter into society with others for the securing and regulating of property, and yet to suppose his land, whose property is to be regulated by the laws of the society, should be exempt from the jurisdiction of that government to which he himself, and the property of the land, is a subject. . . .

But since the government has a direct jurisdiction only over the land, and reaches the possessor of it (before he has actually incorporated himself in the society), only as he dwells upon, and enjoys that: the obligation anyone is under, by virtue of such enjoyment, to submit to the government, begins and ends with the enjoyment; so that whenever the owner, who has given nothing but such a tacit consent to the government, will by donation, sale, or otherwise, quit the said possession, he is at liberty to go and incorporate himself into any other commonwealth, or to agree with others to begin a new one . . . in any part of the world they can find free and unpossessed. . . .

. . . The reason why men enter into society is the preservation of their property; and the end why they choose and authorize a legislative is that there may be laws made, and rules set, as guards and fences to the properties of all the members of the society to limit the power and moderate the dominion of every part and member of the society. For since it can never by supposed to be the will of the society that the legislative should have a power to destroy that which everyone designs secure by entering into society, and for which the people submitted themselves to legislators of their own making, whenever the legislators endeavor to take away and destroy the property of the people, or to reduce them to slavery under arbitrary power, they put themselves into a state of war with the people, who are thereupon absolved from any further obedience, and are left to the common refuge which God hath provided for all men against force and violence. Whensoever, therefore, the legislative shall transgress this fundamental rule of society, and either by ambition, fear, folly, or corruption, endeavor to grasp themselves or put into the hands of any other an absolute power over the lives, liberties, and estates of the people, by this breach of trust they forfeit the power the people had put into their hands, for quite contrary ends, and it devolves to the people, who have a right to resume their original liberty, and by the establishment of the new legislative (such as they shall think fit) provide for their own safety and security, which is the end for which they are in society. . . .

REVIEW AND DISCUSSION QUESTIONS

1. Describe the "state of nature" as envisioned by Locke. In what sense(s) is everybody equal in it?
2. How does Locke view nature, and humankind's relationship to it?
3. Why are people motivated to leave the state of nature?
4. What justifies or makes legitimate a government? When may citizens revolt, according to Locke?
5. What justifies somebody's taking an unowned resource for his or her own use? What provisos or limitations does Locke place on the acquisition of unowned resources?
6. Why should laboring on something be important? What if my laboring actually decreased the value of the object? Would I own it?

The Entitlement Theory

Robert Nozick

Like John Locke, Robert Nozick begins with a strong commitment to prepolitical individual rights—rights that may not be transgressed by others, either as individuals or collectively as the state. Commonly called *negative rights,* they constitute "side constraints" on the actions of others, ensuring a person's freedom from interference in the pursuit of his or her own life. These rights are negative because they require only that others refrain from acting in certain ways; in particular, that they refrain from interfering with us. Beyond this, no one is obliged to do anything positive for us; we have no right, for example, to expect others to provide us with satisfying work or with any material goods we might need. Each individual is to be seen as autonomous and responsible and should be left to fashion his or her own life free from the interference of others—as long as this is compatible with the right

Selected excerpts from pages 149–157, 160–163, and 290–292 from *Anarchy, State, and Utopia* by Robert Nozick. Copyright © 1974 by Basic Books, Inc. Reprinted by permission of Basic Books, a division of HarperCollins Publishers, Inc. Footnotes omitted.

of others to do the same. Only the acknowledgment of this almost absolute right to be free from coercion, argues Nozick, fully respects the distinctiveness of persons, each with a unique life to lead.

This framework of individual rights and corresponding duties constitutes the basis of what power the government may legitimately have. In Nozick's view, the only morally legitimate state is the so-called night-watchman state, one whose functions are restricted to protecting the negative rights of citizens, that is, to protecting them against force, theft, fraud, and so on. In the selection that follows, Nozick is especially concerned with rejecting the claim that a larger state is necessary in order to achieve a just economic distribution.

In contrast to theories he calls *end-state* and *patterned,* Nozick proposes the *entitlement theory of justice.* According to this theory, a distribution is just if it arises from a prior just distribution by just means. For example, as Locke also argued, unowned resources may be acquired originally by one's taking something from nature, subject to certain provisos. And, once legitimately owned, there are a number of ways of legitimately transferring justly acquired objects—gifts and voluntary exchange are among them, theft and blackmail are not. There is, however, no pattern to which a just distribution should conform. In the absence of force and fraud, people may do what they wish with their holdings. They have a right to acquire and dispose of their property as they see fit, and individuals are entitled to their personal talents and characteristics and to whatever property they can obtain with them, as long as the negative rights of others are not violated in the process.

In the final section, "The Tale of a Slave" Nozick creates an imaginary series of events meant to illustrate and extend his argument that taking property is tantamount to slavery or forced labor. Robert Nozick teaches philosophy at Harvard University.

The term "distributive justice" is not a neutral one. Hearing the term "distribution," most people presume that some thing or mechanism uses some principle or criterion to give out a supply of things. Into this process of distributing shares some error may have crept. So it is an open question, at least, whether *re*distribution should take place; whether we should do again what has already been done once, though poorly. However, we are not in the position of children who have been given portions of pie by someone who now makes last minute adjustments to rectify careless cutting. There is no *central* distribution, no person or group entitled to control all the resources, jointly deciding how they are to be doled out. What each person gets, he gets from others who give to him in exchange for something, or as a gift. In a free society, diverse persons control different resources, and new holdings arise out of the voluntary exchanges and actions of persons. There is no more a distributing or distribution of shares than there is a distributing of mates in a society in which persons choose whom they shall marry. The total result is the product of many individual decisions which the different individuals involved are entitled to make. . . . We shall speak of people's holdings; a principle of justice in holdings describes (part of) what justice

tells us (requires) about holdings. I shall state first what I take to be the correct view about justice in holdings, and then turn to the discussion of alternate views.

THE ENTITLEMENT THEORY

The subject of justice in holdings consists of three major topics. The first is the *original acquisition of holdings,* the appropriation of unheld things. This includes the issues of how unheld things may come to be held, the process, or processes, by which unheld things may come to be held, the things that may come to be held by these processes, the extent of what comes to be held by a particular process, and so on. We shall refer to the complicated truth about this topic, which we shall not formulate here, as the principle of justice in acquisition. The second topic concerns the *transfer of holdings* from one person to another. By what processes may a person transfer holdings to another? How may a person acquire a holding from another who holds it? Under this topic come general descriptions of voluntary exchange, and gift and (on the other hand) fraud, as well as reference to particular conventional details fixed upon in a given society. The complicated truth about this subject (with place-holders for conventional details) we shall call the principle of justice in transfer. (And we shall sup-pose it also includes principles governing how a person may divest himself of a holding, passing it into an unheld state.)

If the world were wholly just, the following in-ductive definition would exhaustively cover the subject of justice in holdings.

1. A person who acquires a holding in accordance with the principle of justice in acquisition is enti-tled to that holding.
2. A person who acquires a holding in accordance with the principle of justice in transfer, from some-one else entitled to the holding, is entitled to the holding.
3. No one is entitled to a holding except by (repeated) applications of 1 and 2.

The complete principle of distributive justice would say simply that a distribution is just if everyone is entitled to the holdings they possess under the distribution.

A distribution is just if it arises from another just distribution by legitimate means. The legiti-mate means of moving from one distribution to another are specified by the principle of justice in transfer. The legitimate first "moves" are spec-ified by the principle of justice in acquisition. Whatever arises from a just situation by just steps is itself just. The means of change specified by the principle of justice in transfer preserve justice. . . .

Not all actual situations are generated in ac-cordance with the two principles of justice in holdings: the principle of justice in acquisition and the principle of justice in transfer. Some peo-ple steal from others, or defraud them, or enslave them, seizing their product and preventing them from living as they choose, or forcibly exclude others from competing in exchanges. None of these are permissible modes of transition from one situation to another. And some persons ac-quire holdings by means not sanctioned by the principle of justice in acquisition. The existence of past injustice (previous violations of the first two principles of justice in holdings) raises the third major topic under justice in holdings: the rectification of injustice in holdings. If past injus-tice has shaped present holdings in various ways, some identifiable and some not, what now, if any-thing, ought to be done to rectify these injustices? What obligations do the performers of injustice have toward those whose position is worse than it would have been had the injustice not been done? Or, than it would have been had compensation been paid promptly? How, if at all, do things change if the beneficiaries and those made worse off are not the direct parties in the act of injustice, but, for example, their descendants? Is an injus-tice done to someone whose holding was itself based upon an unrectified injustice? How far back must one go in wiping clean the historical slate of injustices? What may victims of injus-tice permissibly do in order to rectify the in-justices being done to them, including the many injustices done by persons acting through their government? I do not know of a thorough or the-oretically sophisticated treatment of such issues. Idealizing greatly, let us suppose theoretical in-vestigation will produce a principle of rectifica-tion. This principle uses historical information about previous situations and injustices done in them (as defined by the first two principles of jus-tice and rights against interference), and informa-tion about the actual course of events that flowed from these injustices, until the present, and it yields a description (or descriptions) of holdings in the society. The principle of rectification pre-sumably will make use of its best estimate of sub-junctive information about what would have occurred (or a probability distribution over what might have occurred, using the expected value) if the injustice had not taken place. If the actual de-scription of holdings turns out not to be one of the descriptions yielded by the principle, then one of the descriptions yielded must be realized.

The general outlines of the theory of justice in holdings are that the holdings of a person are just if he is entitled to them by the principles of justice in acquisition and transfer, or by the principle of rectification of injustice (as specified by the first two principles). If each person's holdings are just, then the total set (distribution) of holdings is just. . . .

HISTORICAL PRINCIPLES AND END-RESULT PRINCIPLES

The general outlines of the entitlement theory illuminate the nature and defects of other conceptions of distributive justice. The entitlement theory of justice in distribution is *historical;* whether a distribution is just depends upon how it came about. In contrast, *current time-slice principles* of justice hold that the justice of a distribution is determined by how things are distributed (who has what) as judged by some *structural* principle(s) of just distribution. A utilitarian who judges between any two distributions by seeing which has the greater sum of utility and, if the sums tie, applies some fixed equality criterion to choose the more equal distribution, would hold a current time-slice principle of justice. . . .

Most persons do not accept current time-slice principles as constituting the whole story about distributive shares. They think it relevant in assessing the justice of a situation to consider not only the distribution it embodies, but also how that distribution came about. If some persons are in prison for murder or war crimes, we do not say that to assess the justice of the distribution in the society we must look only at what this person has, and that person has, and that person has, . . . at the current time. We think it relevant to ask whether someone did something so that he *deserved* to be punished, deserved to have a lower share. Most will agree to the relevance of further information with regard to punishments and penalties. Consider also desired things. One traditional socialist view is that workers are entitled to the product and full fruits of their labor; they have earned it; a distribution is unjust if it does not give the workers what they are entitled to. Such entitlements are based upon some past history. No socialist holding this view would find it comforting to be told that because the actual distribution A happens to coincide structurally with the one he desires *D, A* therefore is no less just that *D;* it differs only in that the "parasitic" owners of capital receive under A what the workers are entitled to under D, and the workers receive under *A* what the owners are entitled to under *D,* namely very little. This socialist rightly, in my view, holds onto the notions of earning, producing, entitlement, desert, and so

forth, and he rejects current time-slice principles that look only to the structure of the resulting set of holdings. (The set of holdings resulting from what? Isn't it implausible that how holdings are produced and come to exist has no effect at all on who should hold what?) His mistake lies in his view of what entitlements arise out of what sorts of productive processes.

We construe the position we discuss too narrowly by speaking of *current* time-slice principles. Nothing is changed if structural principles operate upon a time sequence of current time-slice profiles and, for example, give someone more now to counterbalance the less he has had earlier. . . . Henceforth, we shall refer to such unhistorical principles of distributive justice, including the current time-slice principles, as *end-result principles* or *end-state principles.*

In contrast to end-result principles of justice, *historical principles* of justice hold that past circumstances or actions of people can create differential entitlements or differential deserts to things. . . .

PATTERNING

The entitlement principles of justice in holdings that we have sketched are historical principles of justice. To better understand their precise character, we shall distinguish them from another subclass of the historical principles. Consider, as an example, the principle of distribution according to moral merit. This principle requires that total distributive shares vary directly with moral merit; no person should have a greater share than anyone whose moral merit is greater. (If moral merit could be not merely ordered but measured on an interval or ratio scale, stronger principles could be formulated.) Or consider the principle that results by substituting "usefulness to society" for "moral merit" in the previous principle. . . . The principle of distribution in accordance with moral merit is a patterned historical principle, which specifies a patterned distribution. "Distribute according to I.Q." is a patterned principle that . . . is not historical, however, in that it does not look to any past actions creating differential entitlements to evaluate a distribution; it requires only distributional matrices whose columns are labeled by I.Q. scores. The distribution in a society, however, may be composed of such simple patterned distributions, without itself being simply patterned. Different sectors may operate different patterns, or some combination of patterns may operate in different proportions across a society. A distribution composed in this manner, from a small number of patterned distributions, we also shall term "patterned." And we extend the use of "pattern" to include the overall designs put forth by combinations of end-state principles.

Almost every suggested principle of distributive justice is patterned: to each according to his moral merit, or needs, or marginal product, or how hard he tries, or the weighted sum of the foregoing, and so on. The principle of entitlement we have sketched is *not* patterned. There is no one natural dimension or weighted sum or combination of a small number of natural dimensions that yields the distributions generated in accordance with the principle of entitlement. The set of holdings that results when some persons receive their marginal products, others win at gambling, others receive a share of their mate's income, others receive gifts from foundations, others receive interest on loans, others receive gifts from admirers, others receive returns on investment, others make for themselves much of what they have, others find things, and so on, will not be patterned. . . .

HOW LIBERTY UPSETS PATTERNS

It is not clear how those holding alternative conceptions of distributive justice can reject the entitlement conception of justice in holdings. For suppose a distribution favored by one of these nonentitlement conceptions is realized. Let us suppose it is your favorite one and let us call this distribution D_1; perhaps everyone has an equal share, perhaps shares vary in accordance with some dimension you treasure. Now suppose that Wilt Chamberlain is greatly in demand by basketball teams, being a great gate attraction. (Also suppose contracts run only for a year, with players being free agents.) He signs the following sort of contract with a team: In each home game, twenty-five cents from the price of each ticket of admis-

sion goes to him. (We ignore the question of whether he is "gouging" the owners, letting them look out for themselves.) The season starts, and people cheerfully attend his team's games; they buy their tickets, each time dropping a separate twenty-five cents of their admission price into a special box with Chamberlain's name on it. They are excited about seeing him play; it is worth the total admission price to them. Let us suppose that in one season one million persons attend his home games, and Wilt Chamberlain winds up with $250,000, a much larger sum than the average income and larger even than anyone else has. Is he entitled to this income? Is this new distribution D_2, unjust? If so, why? There is *no* question about whether each of the people was entitled to the control over the resources they held in D_1; because that was the distribution (your favorite) that (for the purposes of argument) we assumed was acceptable. Each of these persons chose to give twenty-five cents of their money to Chamberlain. They could have spent it on going to the movies, or on candy bars, or on copies of *Dissent* magazine, or of *Monthly Review*. But they all, at least one million of them, converged on giving it to Wilt Chamberlain in exchange for watching him play basketball. If D_1 was a just distribution, and people voluntarily moved from it to D_2, transferring parts of their shares they were given under D_1 (what was it for if not to do something with?), isn't D_2 also just? If the people were entitled to dispose of the resources to which they were entitled (under D_1), didn't this include their being entitled to give it to, or exchange it with, Wilt Chamberlain? Can anyone else complain on grounds of justice? Each other person already has his legitimate share under D_1. Under D_1, there is nothing that anyone has that anyone else has a claim of justice against. After someone transfers something to Wilt Chamberlain, third parties *still* have their legitimate shares; *their* shares are not changed. By what process could such a transfer among two persons give rise to a legitimate claim of distributive justice on a portion of what was transferred, by a third party who had no claim of justice on any holding of the others *before* the transfer? . . .

The general point illustrated by the Wilt Chamberlain example . . . is that no end-state principle or distributional-patterned principle of justice can be continuously realized without continuous interference with people's lives. Any favored pattern would be transformed into one unfavored by the principle, by people choosing to act in various ways; for example, by people exchanging goods and services with other people, or giving things to other people, things the transferrers are entitled to under the favored distributional pattern. To maintain a pattern one must either continually interfere to stop people from transferring resources as they wish to, or continually (or periodically) interfere to take from some persons resources that others for some reason chose to transfer to them. . . .

THE TALE OF THE SLAVE

Consider the following sequence of cases, which we shall call *The Tale of the Slave,* and imagine it is you.

1. There is a slave completely at the mercy of his brutal master's whims. He often is cruelly beaten, called out in the middle of the night, and so on.

2. The master is kindlier and beats the slave only for stated infractions of his rules (not fulfilling the work quota, and so on). He gives the slave some free time.

3. The master has a group of slaves, and he decides how things are to be allocated among them on nice grounds, taking into account their needs, merit, and so on.

4. The master allows his slaves four days on their own and requires them to work only three days a week on his land. The rest of the time is their own.

5. The master allows his slaves to go off and work in the city (or anywhere they wish) for wages. He requires only that they send back to him three-sevenths of their wages. He also retains the power to recall them to the plantation if some emergency threatens his land; and to raise or lower the three-sevenths amount required to be turned over to him. He further retains the right to restrict the slaves from participating in certain dangerous activities that threaten his financial return, for example, mountain climbing, cigarette smoking.

6. The master allows all of his 10,000 slaves, except you, to vote, and the joint decision is made by all of them. There is open discussion, and so forth, among them, and they have the power to determine to what uses to put whatever percentage of your (and their) earnings they decide to take; what activities may legitimately be forbidden to you, and so on.

Let us pause in this sequence of cases to take stock. If the master contracts this transfer of power so that he cannot withdraw it, you have a change of master. You now have 10,000 masters instead of just one; rather you have one 10,000-headed master. Perhaps the 10,000 even will be kindlier than the benevolent master in case 2. Still, they are your master. However, still more can be done. A kindly single master (as in case 2) might allow his slave(s) to speak up and try to persuade him to make a certain decision. The 10,000-headed master can do this too.

7. Though still not having the vote, you are at liberty (and are given the right) to enter into the discussions of the 10,000 to try to persuade them to adopt various policies and to treat you and themselves in a certain way. They then go off to vote to decide upon policies covering the *vast* range of their powers.

8. In appreciation of your useful contributions to discussion, the 10,000 allow you to vote if they are deadlocked; they commit themselves to this procedure. After the discussion you mark your vote on a slip of paper, and they go off and vote. In the eventuality that they divide evenly on some issue, 5,000 for and 5,000 against, they look at your ballot and count it. This has never yet happened; they have never yet had the occasion to open your ballot. (A single master also might commit himself to letting his slave decide any issue concerning about which he, the master, was absolutely indifferent.)

9. They throw your vote in with theirs. If they are exactly tied your vote carries the issue. Otherwise it makes no difference to the electoral outcome.

The question is: which transition from case 1 to case 9 made it no longer the tale of a slave?

REVIEW AND DISCUSSION QUESTIONS

1. Why does Nozick think that the notion of "distributive justice" is misleading?
2. What are the three topics that, he thinks, constitute the subject of justice in holdings?
3. Distinguish historical from end-result principles.
4. What is a *patterned principle?*
5. Using the Chamberlain example, explain Nozick's argument that no patterned principle is compatible with freedom.
6. Describe *The Tale of a Slave.* What point do you think Nozick is making?
7. How would you answer the question at the end of Nozick's essay?

Rich and Poor

Peter Singer

Death resulting from starvation, disease, and preventable violence are widely reported throughout the world. How much do those of us who are well-off owe those in need? Rejecting the Lockean vision of a state of nature and natural rights, Peter Singer argues that such a libertarian view of property is mistaken and that we all have a duty to provide far more aid than we now give. He then considers several objections to his position—that people should "take care of their own," that the right to property contradicts his position, and that we are relieved of the obligation to assist because helping now would only increase overpopulation and make the problem worse. Peter Singer is professor of philosophy and director of the Centre for Human Bioethics at Monash University, Australia.

SOME FACTS

Consider these facts: by the most cautious estimates, 400 million people lack the calories, protein, vitamins, and minerals needed for a normally healthy life. Millions are constantly hungry; others suffer from deficiency diseases and from infections they would be able to resist on a better diet. Children are worst affected. According to one estimate, 15 million children under five die every year from the combined effects of malnutrition and infection. In some areas, half the children born can be expected to die before their fifth birthday. . . .

Death and disease apart, absolute poverty remains a miserable condition of life, with inadequate food, shelter, clothing, sanitation, health services and education. According to World Bank estimates which define absolute poverty in terms of income levels insufficient to provide adequate nutrition, something like 800 million people—almost 40 percent of the people of developing countries—live in absolute poverty. Absolute poverty is probably the principal cause of human misery today. . . .

The problem is not that the world cannot produce enough to feed and shelter its people. People

From Peter Singer, *Practical Ethics,* New York: Cambridge University Press, 1979. © 1979. Reprinted with the permission of Cambridge University Press.

in the poor countries consume, on average, 400 lbs. of grain a year, while North Americans average more than 2,000 lbs. The difference is caused by the fact that in the rich countries we feed most of our grain to animals, converting it into meat, milk and eggs. Because this is an inefficient process, wasting up to 95 percent of the food value of the animal feed, people in rich countries are responsible for the consumption of far more food than those in poor countries who eat few animal products. If we stopped feeding animals on grains, soybeans and fishmeal the amount of food saved would—if distributed to those who need it—be more than enough to end hunger throughout the world.

These facts about animal food do not mean that we can easily solve the world food problem by cutting down on animal products, but they show that the problem is essentially one of distribution rather than production. The world does produce enough food. Moreover the poorer nations themselves could produce far more if they made more use of improved agricultural techniques. . . .

At this stage I am making no ethical judgments about absolute affluence, merely pointing out that it exists. Its defining characteristic is a significant amount of income above the level necessary to provide for the basic human needs of oneself and one's dependents. By this standard Western Europe, North America, Japan, Australia, New Zealand and the oil-rich Middle Eastern states are all absolutely affluent, and so are many, if not all, of their citizens. The [former] USSR and Eastern Europe might also be included on this list. To quote Robert McNamara . . . :

The average citizen of a developed country enjoys wealth beyond the wildest dreams of the one billion people in countries with per capita incomes under $200.

These, therefore, are the countries—and individuals—who have wealth which they could, without threatening their own basic welfare, transfer to the absolutely poor.

At present, very little is being transferred. Members of the Organization of Petroleum Exporting Countries lead the way, giving an average of 2.1 percent of their Gross National Product. Apart from them, only Sweden, The Netherlands and Norway have reached the modest UN target of 0.7 percent of GNP. Britain gives 0.38 percent of its GNP in official development assistance and a small additional amount in unofficial aid from voluntary organizations. The total comes to less than £1 per month per person, and compares with 5.5 percent of GNP spent on alcohol, and 3 percent on tobacco. Other, even wealthier nations, give still less: Germany gives 0.27 percent, the United States 0.22 percent and Japan 0.21 percent. . . .

THE MORAL EQUIVALENT OF MURDER?

If these are the facts, we cannot avoid concluding that by not giving more than we do, people in rich countries are allowing those in poor countries to suffer from absolute poverty, with consequent malnutrition, ill health and death. . . . If, then, allowing someone to die is not intrinsically different from killing someone, it would seem that we are all murderers.

Is this verdict too harsh? . . . [It might be said that the plight of the hungry is not my doing, and so I cannot be held responsible for it.] On the one hand we feel ourselves to be under a greater obligation to help those whose misfortunes we have caused. (It is for this reason that advocates of overseas aid often argue that Western nations have created the poverty of Third World nations, through forms of economic exploitation which go back to the colonial system.) On the other hand any consequentialist would insist that we are responsible for all the consequences of our actions, and if a consequence of my spending money on a luxury item is that someone dies, I am responsible for that death. It is true that the person would have died even if I had never existed, but what is the relevance of that? The fact is that I do exist, and the consequentialist will say that our responsibilities derive from the world as it is, not as it might have been.

One way of making sense of the non-consequentialist view of responsibility is by basing it on a theory of rights of the kind proposed by John Locke or, more recently, Robert Nozick. If everyone has a right to life, and this right is a right *against* others who might threaten my life, but not a right *to* assistance from others when my life is in danger, then we can understand the feeling that we are responsible for acting to kill but not for omitting to save. The former violates the rights of others, the latter does not.

Should we accept such a theory of rights? If we build up our theory of rights by imagining, as Locke and Nozick do, individuals living independently from each other in a 'state of nature', it may seem natural to adopt a conception of rights in which as long as each leaves the other alone, no rights are violated. I might, on this view, quite properly have maintained my independent existence if I had wished to do so. So if I do not make you any worse off than you would have been if I had had nothing at all to do with you, how can I have violated your rights? But why start from such an unhistorical, abstract and ultimately inexplicable idea as an independent individual? We now know that our ancestors were social beings long before they were human beings, and could not have developed the abilities and capacities of human beings if they had not been social beings first. In any case we are not, now, isolated individuals. If we consider people living together in a community, it is less easy to assume that rights must be restricted to rights against interference. We might, instead, adopt the view that taking rights to life seriously is incompatible with standing by and watching people die when one could easily save them. . . .

THE ARGUMENT FOR AN OBLIGATION TO ASSIST

The path from the library at my university to the Humanities lecture theatre passes a shallow ornamental pond. Suppose that on my way to give a lecture I notice that a small child has fallen in and is in danger of drowning. Would anyone deny that I ought to wade in and pull the child out? This will mean getting my clothes muddy, and either cancelling my lecture or delaying it until I can find something dry to change into; but compared with the avoidable death of a child this is insignificant.

A plausible principle that would support the judgment that I ought to pull the child out is this:

If it is in our power to prevent something very bad happening, without thereby sacrificing anything of comparable moral significance, we ought to do it. This principle seems uncontroversial. It will obviously win the assent of consequentialists; but non-consequentialists should accept it too, because the injunction to prevent what is bad applies only when nothing comparably significant is at stake. Thus the principle cannot lead to the kinds of actions of which non-consequentialists strongly disapprove—serious violations of individual rights, injustice, broken promises, and so on. If a non-consequentialist regards any of these as comparable in moral significance to the bad thing that is to be prevented, he will automatically regard the principle as not applying in those cases in which the bad thing can only be prevented by violating rights, doing injustice, breaking promises, or whatever else is at stake. Most non-consequentialists hold that we ought to prevent what is bad and promote what is good. Their dispute with consequentialists lies in their insistence that this is not the sole ultimate ethical principle: that it is an ethical principle is not denied by any plausible ethical theory.

Nevertheless the uncontroversial appearance of the principle that we ought to prevent what is bad when we can do so without sacrificing anything of comparable moral significance is deceptive. If it were taken seriously and acted upon, our lives and our world would be fundamentally changed. For the principle applies, not just to rare situations in which one can save a child from a pond, but to the everyday situation in which we can assist those living in absolute poverty. In saying this I assume that absolute poverty, with its hunger and malnutrition, lack of shelter, illiteracy, disease, high infant mortality and low life expectancy, is a bad thing. And I assume that it is within the power of the affluent to reduce absolute poverty, without sacrificing anything of comparable moral significance. If these two assumptions and the principle we have been discussing are correct, we have an obligation to help those in absolute poverty which is no less strong than our obligation to rescue a drowning child from a pond. Not to help would be wrong, whether or not it is intrinsically equivalent to killing. Helping is not, as conventionally thought, a charitable act which it is praiseworthy to do, but not wrong to omit; it is something that everyone ought to do. . . .

Our affluence means that we have income we can dispose of without giving up the basic necessities of life, and we can use this income to reduce absolute poverty. Just how much we will think ourselves obliged to give up will depend on what we consider to be of comparable moral significance to the poverty we could prevent: colour television, stylish clothes, expensive dinners, a sophisticated stereo system, overseas holidays, a (second?) car, a larger house, private schools for our children. . . .

OBJECTIONS TO THE ARGUMENT

Taking Care of Our Own

Anyone who has worked to increase overseas aid will have come across the argument that we should look after those near us, our families and then the poor in our own country, before we think about poverty in distant places.

No doubt we do instinctively prefer to help those who are close to us. Few could stand by and watch a child drown; many can ignore a famine in Africa. But the question is not what we usually do, but what we ought to do, and it is difficult to see any sound moral justification for the view that distance, or community membership, makes a crucial difference to our obligations.

Consider, for instance, racial affinities. Should whites help poor whites before helping poor blacks? Most of us would reject such a suggestion out of hand, and our discussion of equal consideration of interests [see "All Animals Are Equal," reprinted above—Ed.] has shown why we should reject if: people's need for food has nothing to do with their race, and if blacks need food more than whites, it would be a violation of the principle of equal consideration to give preference to whites.

The same point applies to citizenship or nationhood. Every affluent nation has some relatively poor citizens, but absolute poverty is limited largely to the poor nations. Those living on the streets of Calcutta, or in a drought-stricken region of the Sahel, are experiencing poverty unknown in the West. Under these circumstances it would be wrong to decide that only those fortunate enough to be citizens of our own community will share our abundance.

We feel obligations of kinship more strongly than those of citizenship. Which parents could give away their last bowl of rice if their own children were starving? To do so would seem unnatural, contrary to our nature as biologically evolved beings—although whether it would be wrong is another question altogether. In any case, we are not faced with that situation, but with one in which our own children are well-fed, well-clothed, well-educated, and would now like new bikes, a stereo set, or their own car. In these circumstances any special obligations we might have to our children have been fulfilled, and the needs of strangers make a stronger claim upon us.

The element of truth in the view that we should first take care of our own, lies in the advantage of a recognized system of responsibilities. When families and local communities look after their own poorer members, ties of affection and personal relationships achieve ends that would otherwise require a large, impersonal bureaucracy. Hence it would be absurd to propose that from now on we all regard ourselves as equally responsible for the welfare of everyone in the world; but the argument for an obligation to assist does not propose that. It applies only when some are in absolute poverty, and others can help without sacrificing anything of comparable moral significance. To allow one's own kin to sink into absolute poverty would be to sacrifice something of comparable significance; and before that point had been reached, the breakdown of the system of family and community responsibility would be a factor to weigh the balance in favour of a small degree of preference for family and community. This small degree of preference is, however, decisively outweighed by existing discrepancies in wealth and property.

Property Rights

Do people have a right to private property, a right which contradicts the view that they are under an obligation to give some of their wealth away to those in absolute poverty? According to some theories of rights (for instance, Robert Nozick's) provided one has acquired one's property without the use of unjust means like force and fraud, one may be entitled to enormous wealth while others starve. This individualistic conception of rights is in contrast to other views, like the early Christian doctrine to be found in the works of Thomas Aquinas, which holds that since property exists for the satisfaction of human needs, 'whatever a man has in superabundance is owed, of natural right, to the poor for their sustenance'. A socialist would also, of course, see wealth as belonging to the community rather than the individual, while utilitarians, whether socialist or not, would be prepared to override property rights to prevent great evils. . . .

The argument for an obligation to assist can survive, with only minor modifications, even if we accept the individualistic theory of property rights. In any case, however, I do not think we should accept such a theory. It leaves too much to chance to be an acceptable ethical view. For instance, those whose forefathers happened to inhabit some sandy wastes around the Persian Gulf are now fabulously wealthy, because oil lay under those sands; while those whose forefathers settled on better land south of the Sahara live in absolute poverty, because of drought and bad harvests. Can this distribution be acceptable from an impartial point of view? If we imagine ourselves about to begin life as a citizen of either Kuwait or Chad—but we do not know which—would we accept the principle that citizens of Kuwait are under no obligation to assist people living in Chad?

Population and the Ethics of Triage

Perhaps the most serious objection to the argument that we have an obligation to assist is that since the major cause of absolute poverty is overpopulation, helping those now in poverty will only ensure that yet more people are born to live in poverty in the future.

In its most extreme form, this objection is taken to show that we should adopt a policy of 'triage'. The term comes from medical policies adopted in wartime. With too few doctors to cope with all the casualties, the wounded were divided into three categories: those who would probably survive without medical assistance, those who might survive if they received assistance, but otherwise probably would not, and those who even with medical assistance probably would not survive. Only those in the middle category were given medical assistance. The idea, of course, was to use limited medical resources as effectively as possible. For those in the first category, medical treatment was not strictly necessary; for those in the third category, it was likely to be useless. It has been suggested that we should apply the same policies to countries, according to their prospects of becoming self-sustaining. We would not aid countries which even without our help will soon be able to feed their populations. We would not aid countries which, even with our help, will not be able to limit their population to a level they can feed. We would aid those countries where our help might make the difference between success and failure in bringing food and population into balance.

Advocates of this theory are understandably reluctant to give a complete list of the countries they would place into the 'hopeless' category; but Bangladesh is often cited as an example. Adopting the policy of triage would, then, mean cutting off assistance to Bangladesh and allowing famine, disease and natural disasters to reduce the population of that country (now around 80 million) to the level at which it can provide adequately for all.

In support of this view Garrett Hardin has offered a metaphor: we in the rich nations are like the occupants of a crowded lifeboat adrift in a sea full of drowning people. If we try to save the drowning by bringing them aboard our boat will be overloaded and we shall all drown. Since it is better that some survive than none, we should leave the others to drown. In the world today, according to Hardin, 'lifeboat ethics' apply. The rich should leave the poor to starve, for otherwise the poor will drag the rich down with them.

Against this view, some writers have argued that over-population is a myth. The world produces ample food to feed its population, and could, according to some estimates, feed ten times as many. People are hungry because of inequitable land distribution, the manipulation of Third World economies by the developing nations, wastage of food in the West, and so on. . . . [I]t is true, as we have already seen, that the world now produces enough to feed its inhabitants—the amount lost to animals itself being enough to meet existing grain shortages. Nevertheless population growth cannot be ignored. . . . [But] the consequences of triage on this scale are so horrible that we are inclined to reject it without further argument. How could we sit by our television sets, watching millions starve while we do nothing? Would not that (far more than the proposals for legalizing euthanasia) be the end of all notions of human equality and respect for human life? Don't people have a right to our assistance, irrespective of the consequences?

Anyone whose initial reaction to triage was not one of repugnance would be an unpleasant sort of person. Yet initial reactions based on strong feelings are not always reliable guides. Advocates of triage are rightly concerned with the long-term consequences of our actions. They say that helping the poor and starving now merely ensures more poor and starving in the future. When our capacity to help is finally unable to cope—as one day it must be—the suffering will be greater than it would be if we stopped helping now. If this is correct, there is nothing we can do to prevent absolute starvation and poverty, in the long run, and so we have no obligation to assist. Nor does it seem reasonable to hold that under these circumstances people have a right to our assistance. If we do accept such a right, irrespective of the consequences, we are saying that, in Hardin's metaphor, we would continue to haul the drowning into our lifeboat until the boat sank and we all drowned.

If triage is to be rejected it must be tackled on its own ground, within the framework of consequentialist ethics. Here it is vulnerable. Any consequentialist ethics must take probability of outcome into account. A course of action that will certainly produce some benefit is to be preferred to an alternative course that may lead to a slightly larger benefit, but is equally likely to result in no benefit at all. Only if the greater magnitude of the uncertain benefit outweighs its uncertainty should we choose it. Better one certain unit of benefit than a 10 percent chance of 5 units; but better a 50 percent chance of 3 units than a single certain unit. The same principle applies when we are trying to avoid evils.

The policy of triage involves a certain, very great evil: population control by famine and disease. Tens of millions would die slowly. Hundreds of millions would continue to live in absolute poverty, at the very margin of existence. Against this prospect, advocates of the policy place a possible evil which is greater still: the same process of famine and disease, taking place in, say, fifty years time, when the world's population may be three times its present level, and the number who will die from famine, or struggle on in absolute poverty, will be that much greater. The question is: how probable is this forecast that continued assistance now will lead to greater disasters in the future?

Forecasts of population growth are notoriously fallible, and theories about the factors which affect it remain speculative. One theory, at least as plausible as any other, is that countries pass through a 'demographic transition' as their standard of living rises. When people are very poor and have no access to modern medicine their fertility is high, but population is kept in check by high death rates. The introduction of sanitation, modern medical techniques and other improvements reduces the death rate, but initially has little effect on the birth rate. Then population grows rapidly. Most poor countries are now in this phase. If standards of living continue to rise, however, couples begin to realize that to have the same number of children surviving to maturity as in the past, they do not need to give birth to as many children as their parents did. The need for children to provide economic support in old age diminishes. Improved education and the emancipation and employment of women also reduce the birthrate, and so population growth begins to level off. Most rich nations have reached this stage, and their populations are growing only very slowly.

If this theory is right, there is an alternative to the disasters accepted as inevitable by supporters of triage. We can assist the poor countries to raise the living standards of the poorest members of their population. We can encourage the governments of these countries to enact land reform measures, improve education, and liberate women from a purely child-bearing role. We can also help other countries to make contraception and sterilization widely available. There is a fair chance that these measures will hasten the onset of the demographic transition and bring population growth down to a manageable level. Success cannot be guaranteed; but the evidence that improved economic security and education reduce population growth is strong enough to make triage ethically unacceptable. We cannot allow millions to die from starvation and disease when there is a reasonable probability that population can be brought under control without such horrors.

Population growth is therefore not a reason against giving overseas aid, although it should make us think about the kind of aid to give. Instead of food handouts, it may be better to give aid that hastens the demographic transition. This may mean agricultural assistance for the rural poor, or assistance with education, or the provision of contraceptive services. Whatever kind of aid proves most effective in specific circumstances, the obligation to assist is not reduced. . . .

REVIEW AND DISCUSSION QUESTIONS

1. Describe the analogy Singer uses to develop his argument. What principle does he say establishes the duty to prevent absolute poverty?
2. Singer rejects the Lockean view of property rights for two reasons. Explain each.
3. Describe triage and its relevance to Singer's position. On what grounds does Singer reject the triage argument?
4. Would Singer's principle demand that you give your second kidney to save another's life? Your savings? Explain why or why not.
5. How might Judith Jarvis Thomson ("A Defense of Abortion") respond to Singer's argument? Is her response sound?
6. Compare the views of Locke and Singer on the relationship between humans and the natural environment. How does each of them differ from other authors who wrote on the environment?
7. How would David Hume respond to Singer's underlying moral and psychological views? Is Hume correct?

A Theory of Justice

John Rawls

Political philosophy has experienced a renaissance in recent years, in large part because of the work of John Rawls. His book, *A Theory of Justice,* has been translated into Japanese, Chinese, and Korean, as well as every major European language. In it, Rawls revives the social contract tradition. The focus of social justice is what he terms society's *basic structure,* by which he means its constitution and its economic system, not the justice or injustice of individual acts. Rawls's social contract is hypothetical rather than historical: correct principles of justice are ones that *would be* chosen in a fair position of equality. That, in turn, requires us to imagine ourselves in an "original position" behind a "veil of ignorance" that prevents us from relying on such morally irrelevant factors as race, gender, social class, or even our particular talents. By forcing ourselves to choose under fair circumstances, he argues, justice is assured. Situated in such a position, he then argues, people would choose to construct their government according to principles that (1) respect basic liberties and (2) allow social and economic inequalities only if they benefit everybody, in particular society's least advantaged, and assure that everyone is given genuine (fair) equality of opportunity to seek various positions.

THE MAIN IDEA OF THE THEORY OF JUSTICE

My aim is to present a conception of justice which generalizes and carries to a higher level of abstraction the familiar theory of the social contract as found, say, in Locke, Rousseau, and Kant. In order to do this we are not to think of the original contract as one to enter a particular society or to set up a particular form of government. Rather, the guiding idea is that the principles of justice for the basic structure of society are the object of the original agreement. They are the principles that free and rational persons concerned to further their own interests would accept in an initial position of equality as defining the fundamental terms of their association. These principles are to regulate all further agreements; they specify the kinds of social cooperation that can be entered into and the forms of government that can be established. This way of regarding the principles of justice I shall call justice as fairness.

Thus we are to imagine that those who engage in social cooperation choose together, in one joint act, the principles which are to assign basic rights and duties and to determine the division of social benefits. Men are to decide in advance how they are to regulate their claims against one another and what is to be the foundation charter of their society. Just as each person must decide by rational reflection what constitutes his good, that is, the system of ends which it is rational for him to pursue, so a group of persons must decide once and for all what is to count among them as just and unjust. The choice which rational men would make in this hypothetical situation of equal liberty, assuming for the present that this choice problem has a solution, determines the principles of justice.

In justice as fairness the original position of equality corresponds to the state of nature in the traditional theory of the social contract. This original position is not, of course, thought of as an actual historical state of affairs, much less as a primitive condition of culture. It is understood as a purely hypothetical situation characterized so as to lead to a certain conception of justice. Among the essential features of this situation is that no one knows his place in society, his class position or social status, nor does any one know his fortune in the distribution of natural assets and abilities, his intelligence, strength, and the like. I shall even assume that the parties do not know their conceptions of the good or their special psychological propensities. The principles of justice are chosen behind a veil of ignorance. This ensures that no one is advantaged or disadvantaged in the choice of principles by the outcome of natural chance or the contingency of social circumstances. Since all are similarly situated and no one is able to design principles to favor his particular condition, the principles of justice are the result of a fair agreement or bargain. For given the circumstances of the original position, the symmetry of everyone's relations to each other, this initial situation is fair between individuals as moral persons, that is, as rational beings with their own ends and capable, I shall assume, of a sense of justice. The original position is, one might say, the appropriate initial status quo, and thus the fundamental agreements reached in it are fair. This explains the propriety of the name "justice as fairness": it conveys the idea that the principles of justice are agreed to in an initial situation that is fair. The name does not mean that the concepts of justice and fairness are the same, any more than the phrase "poetry as metaphor" means that the concepts of poetry and metaphor are the same.

Justice as fairness begins, as I have said, with one of the most general of all choices which persons might make together, namely, with the choice of the first principles of a conception of justice which is to regulate all subsequent criticism and reform of institutions. Then, having chosen a conception of justice, we can suppose that they are to choose a constitution and a legislature to enact laws, and so on, all in accordance with the principles of justice initially agreed upon. Our social situation is just if it is such that by this sequence of hypothetical agreements we would have contracted into the general system of rules which defines it. Moreover, assuming that the original position does determine a set of principles (that is, that a particular conception of justice would be chosen), it will then be true that whenever social institutions satisfy these principles those engaged in them can say to one another that they are cooperating on terms to which they would agree if they were free and equal persons whose relations with respect to one another were fair. They could all view their arrangements as meeting the stipulations which they would acknowledge in an initial situation that embodies widely accepted and reasonable constraints on the choice of principles. The general recognition of this fact would provide the basis for a public acceptance of the corresponding principles of justice. No society can, of course, be a scheme of cooperation which men enter voluntarily in a literal sense; each person finds himself placed at birth in some particular position in some particular society, and the nature of this position materially affects his life prospects. Yet a society satisfying the principles of justice as fairness comes as close as a society can to being a voluntary scheme, for it meets the principles which free and equal persons would assent to under circumstances that are fair. In this sense its members are autonomous and the obligations they recognize self-imposed.

One feature of justice as fairness is to think of the parties in the initial situation as rational and mutually disinterested. This does not mean that the parties are egoists, that is, individuals with only certain kinds of interests, say in wealth, prestige, and domination. But they are conceived as not taking an interest in one another's interests. They are to presume that even their spiritual aims

may be opposed, in the way that the aims of those of different religions may be opposed. Moreover, the concept of rationality must be interpreted as far as possible in the narrow sense, standard in economic theory, of taking the most effective means to given ends. . . . [O]ne must try to avoid introducing into it any controversial ethical elements. The initial situation must be characterized by stipulations that are widely accepted.

In working out the conception of justice as fairness one main task clearly is to determine which principles of justice would be chosen in the original position. To do this we must describe this situation in some detail and formulate with care the problem of choice which it presents. . . . It may be observed, however, that once the principles of justice are thought of as arising from an original agreement in a situation of equality, it is an open question whether the principle of utility would be acknowledged. Offhand it hardly seems likely that persons who view themselves as equals, entitled to press their claims upon one another, would agree to a principle which may require lesser life prospects for some simply for the sake of a greater sum of advantages enjoyed by others. Since each desires to protect his interests, his capacity to advance his conception of the good, no one has a reason to acquiesce in an enduring loss for himself in order to bring about a greater net balance of satisfaction. In the absence of strong and lasting benevolent impulses, a rational man would not accept a basic structure merely because it maximized the algebraic sum of advantages irrespective of its permanent effects on his own basic rights and interests. Thus it seems that the principle of utility is incompatible with the conception of social cooperation among equals for mutual advantage. It appears to be inconsistent with the idea of reciprocity implicit in the notion of a well-ordered society. Or, at any rate, so I shall argue.

I shall maintain instead that the persons in the initial situation would choose two rather different principles: the first requires equality in the assignment of basic rights and duties, while the second holds that social and economic inequalities, for example inequalities of wealth and authority, are just only if they result in compensating benefits for everyone, and in particular for the least advantaged members of society. These principles rule out justifying institutions on the grounds that the hardships of some are offset by a greater good in the aggregate. It may be expedient but it is not just that some should have less in order that others may prosper. But there is no injustice in the greater benefits earned by a few provided that the situation of persons not so fortunate is thereby improved. The intuitive idea is that since everyone's well-being depends upon a scheme of cooperation without which no one could have a satisfactory life, the division of advantages should be such as to draw forth the willing cooperation of everyone taking part in it, including those less well situated. Yet this can be expected only if reasonable terms are proposed. The two principles mentioned seem to be a fair agreement on the basis of which those better endowed, or more fortunate in their social position, neither of which we can be said to deserve, could expect the willing cooperation of others when some workable scheme is a necessary condition of the welfare of all. Once we decide to look for a conception of justice that nullifies the accidents of natural endowment and the contingencies of social circumstance as counters in quest for political and economic advantage, we are led to these principles. They express the result of leaving aside those aspects of the social world that seem arbitrary from a moral point of view. . . .

THE ORIGINAL POSITION AND JUSTIFICATION

I have said that the original position is the appropriate initial status quo which insures that the fundamental agreements reached in it are fair. This fact yields the name "justice as fairness." It is clear, then, that I want to say that one conception of justice is more reasonable than another, or justifiable with respect to it, if rational persons in the initial situation would choose its principles over those of the other for the role of justice. Conceptions of justice are to be ranked by their acceptability to persons so circumstanced. Understood in this way the question of justification is settled by working out a problem of deliberation: we have to ascertain which principles it would be rational to

adopt given the contractual situation. This connects the theory of justice with the theory of rational choice.

If this view of the problem of justification is to succeed, we must, of course, describe in some detail the nature of this choice problem. A problem of rational decision has a definite answer only if we know the beliefs and interests of the parties, their relations with respect to one another, the alternatives between which they are to choose, the procedure whereby they make up their minds, and so on. . . . The concept of the original position, as I shall refer to it, is that of the most philosophically favored interpretation of this initial choice situation for purposes of a theory of justice.

But how are we to decide on the most favored interpretation? . . . To justify a particular description of the initial situation one shows that it incorporates these commonly held presumptions. One argues from widely accepted but weak premises to more specific conclusions. Each of the presumptions should by itself be natural and plausible; some of them may seem innocuous or even trivial. The aim of the contract approach is to establish that taken together they impose significant bounds on acceptable principles of justice. . . .

One should not be misled, then, by the somewhat unusual conditions which characterize the original position. The idea here is simply to make vivid to ourselves the restrictions that it seems reasonable to impose on arguments for principles of justice, and therefore on these principles themselves. Thus it seems reasonable and generally acceptable that no one should be advantaged or disadvantaged by natural fortune or social circumstances in the choice of principles. [Rawls argues in a later section that it is reasonable in the original position to exclude knowledge of "natural talents" such as intelligence as well as inherited wealth and social class because all of these are "morally arbitrary." Social class and natural talents are not "deserved," and one's "character" also "depends in large part on fortunate family and social circumstances."—Ed.] It also seems widely agreed that it should be impossible to tailor principles to the circumstances of one's own case. We should insure further that particular inclinations and aspirations, and persons' conceptions of their good do not affect the principles adopted. The aim is to rule out those principles that it would be rational to propose for acceptance, however little the chance of success, only if one knew certain things that are irrelevant from the standpoint of justice. For example, if a man knew that he was wealthy, he might find it rational to advance the principle that various taxes for welfare measures be counted unjust; if he knew that he was poor, he would most likely propose the contrary principle. To represent the desired restrictions one imagines a situation in which everyone is deprived of this sort of information. One excludes the knowledge of those contingencies which sets men at odds and allows them to be guided by their prejudices. In this manner the veil of ignorance is arrived at in a natural way. This concept should cause no difficulty if we keep in mind the constraints on arguments that it is meant to express. At any time we can enter the original position, so to speak, simply by following a certain procedure, namely, by arguing for principles of justice in accordance with these restrictions.

It seems reasonable to suppose that the parties in the original position are equal. That is, all have the same rights in the procedure for choosing principles; each can make proposals, submit reasons for their acceptance, and so on. Obviously the purpose of these conditions is to represent equality between human beings as moral persons, as creatures having a conception of their good and capable of a sense of justice. The basis of equality is taken to be similarity in these two respects. Systems of ends are not ranked in value; and each man is presumed to have the requisite ability to understand and to act upon whatever principles are adopted. Together with the veil of ignorance, these conditions define the principles of justice as those which rational persons concerned to advance their interests would consent to as equals when none are known to be advantaged or disadvantaged by social and natural contingencies.

There is, however, another side to justifying a particular description of the original position. This is to see if the principles which would be chosen match our considered convictions of justice or extend them in an acceptable way. We can note whether applying these principles would lead us to make the same judgments about the basic structure of society which we now make intuitively and in which we have the greatest confidence; or whether, in cases where our present judgments are in doubt and given with hesitation, these principles offer a resolution which we can affirm on reflection. There are questions which we feel sure must be answered in a certain way. For example, we are confident that religious intolerance and racial discrimination are unjust. We think that we have examined these things with care and have reached what we believe is an impartial judgment not likely to be distorted by an excessive attention to our own interests. These convictions are provisional fixed points which we presume any conception of justice must fit. But we have much less assurance as to what is the correct distribution of wealth and authority. Here we may be looking for a way to remove our doubts. We can check an interpretation of the initial situation, then, by the capacity of its principles to accommodate our firmest convictions and to provide guidance where guidance is needed.

In searching for the most favored description of this situation we work from both ends. We begin by describing it so that it represents generally shared and preferably weak conditions. We then see if these conditions are strong enough to yield a significant set of principles. If not, we look for further premises equally reasonable. But if so, and these principles match our considered convictions of justice, then so far well and good. But presumably there will be discrepancies. In this case we have a choice. We can either modify the account of the initial situation or we can revise our existing judgments, for even the judgments we take provisionally as fixed points are liable to revision. By going back and forth, sometimes altering the conditions of the contractual circumstances, at others withdrawing our judgments and conforming them to principle. I assume that eventually we shall find a description of the initial situation that both expresses reasonable conditions and yields principles which match our considered judgments duly pruned and adjusted. This state of affairs I refer to as reflective equilibrium.[1] It is an equilibrium because at last our principles and judgments coincide; and it is reflective since we know to what principles our judgments conform and the premises of their derivation. At the moment everything is in order. But this equilibrium is not necessarily stable. It is liable to be upset by further examination of the conditions which should be imposed on the contractual situation and by particular cases which may lead us to revise our judgments. Yet for the time being we have done what we can to render coherent and to justify our convictions of social justice. We have reached a conception of the original position. . . .

In arriving at the favored interpretation of the initial situation there is no point at which an appeal is made to self-evidence. . . . A conception of justice cannot be deduced from self-evident premises or conditions on principles; instead, its justification is a matter of the mutual support of many considerations, of everything fitting together into one coherent view.

A final comment. We shall want to say that certain principles of justice are justified because they would be agreed to in an initial situation of equality. I have emphasized that this original position is purely hypothetical. It is natural to ask why, if this agreement is never actually entered into, we should take any interest in these principles, moral or otherwise. The answer is that the conditions embodied in the description of the original position are ones that we do in fact accept. Or if we do not, then perhaps we can be persuaded to do so by philosophical reflection. Each aspect of the contractual situation can be given supporting grounds. Thus what we shall do is to collect together into one conception a number of conditions on principles that we are ready upon due consideration to recognize as reasonable. These constraints express what we are prepared to regard as limits on fair terms of social cooperation. One way to look at the idea of the original position, therefore, is to see it as an expository device which sums up the meaning of these conditions and helps us to extract their consequences. On the other hand, this conception is also an intuitive notion that suggests its own elaboration, so that led on by it we are drawn to define more clearly the standpoint from which we can best interpret moral relationships. We need a conception that enables us to envision our objec-

tive from afar: the intuitive notion of the original position is to do this for us. . . .

TWO PRINCIPLES OF JUSTICE

I shall now state in a provisional form the two principles of justice that I believe would be chosen in the original position. . . .

The first statement of the two principles reads as follows.

First: each person is to have an equal right to the most extensive basic liberty compatible with a similar liberty for others.

Second: social and economic inequalities are to be arranged so that they are both (a) reasonably expected to be to everyone's advantage, and (b) attached to positions and offices open to all. . . .

By way of general comment, these principles primarily apply, as I have said, to the basic structure of society. They are to govern the assignment of rights and duties and to regulate the distribution of social and economic advantages. As their formulation suggests, these principles presuppose that the social structure can be divided into two more or less distinct parts, the first principle applying to the one, the second to the other. They distinguish between those aspects of the social system that define and secure the equal liberties of citizenship and those that specify and establish social and economic inequalities. The basic liberties of citizens are, roughly speaking, political liberty (the right to vote and to be eligible for public office) together with freedom of speech and assembly; liberty of conscience and freedom of thought; freedom of the person along with the right to hold (personal) property; and freedom from arbitrary arrest and seizure as defined by the concept of the rule of law. These liberties are all required to be equal by the first principle, since citizens of a just society are to have the same basic rights.

The second principle applies, in the first approximation, to the distribution of income and wealth and to the design of organizations that make use of differences in authority and responsibility, or chains of command. While the distribution of wealth and income need not be equal, it must be to everyone's advantage, and at the same time, positions of authority and offices of command must be accessible to all. One applies the second principle by holding positions open, and then, subject to this constraint, arranges social and economic inequalities so that everyone benefits.

These principles are to be arranged in a serial order with the first principle prior to the second. This ordering means that a departure from the institutions of equal liberty required by the first principle cannot be justified by, or compensated for, by greater social and economic advantages. The distribution of wealth and income, and the hierarchies of authority, must be consistent with both the liberties of equal citizenship and equality of opportunity.

It is clear that these principles are rather specific in their content, and their acceptance rests on certain assumptions that I must eventually try to explain and justify. A theory of justice depends upon a theory of society in ways that will become evident as we proceed. For the present, it should be observed that the two principles (and this holds for all formulations) are a special case of a more general conception of justice that can be expressed as follows.

All social values —liberty and opportunity, income and wealth, and the bases of self-respect—are to be distributed equally unless an unequal distribution of any, or all, of these values is to everyone's advantage.

Injustice, then, is simply inequalities that are not to the benefit of all. Of course, this conception is extremely vague and requires interpretation.

As a first step, suppose that the basic structure of society distributes certain primary goods, that is, things that every rational man is presumed to want. These goods normally have a use whatever a person's rational plan of life. For simplicity, assume that the chief primary goods at the disposition of society are rights and liberties, powers and opportunities, income and wealth. (Later on in Part Three the primary good of self-respect has a central place.) These are the social primary goods. Other primary goods such as health and vigor, intelligence and imagination, are natural goods; although their possession is influenced by the basic

structure, they are not so directly under its control. Imagine, then, a hypothetical initial arrangement in which all the social primary goods are equally distributed: everyone has similar rights and duties, and income and wealth are evenly shared. This state of affairs provides a benchmark for judging improvements. If certain inequalities of wealth and organizational powers would make everyone better off than in this hypothetical starting situation, then they accord with the general conception.

Now it is possible, at least theoretically, that by giving up some of their fundamental liberties men are sufficiently compensated by the resulting social and economic gains. . . . We need not suppose anything so drastic as consenting to a condition of slavery. Imagine instead that men forego certain political rights when the economic returns are significant and their capacity to influence the course of policy by the exercise of these rights would be marginal in any case. It is this kind of exchange which the two principles as stated rule out; being arranged in serial order they do not permit exchanges between basic liberties and economic and social gains. The serial ordering of principles expresses an underlying preference among primary goods [for liberty over wealth and income]. When this preference is rational [*as Rawls later argues it is when society has achieved a certain level of economic development—Ed.*] so likewise is the choice of these principles in this order. . . .

Now the second principle insists that each person benefit from permissible inequalities in the basic structure. This means that it must be reasonable for each relevant representative man defined by this structure, when he views it as a going concern, to prefer his prospects with the inequality to his prospects without it. One is not allowed to justify differences in income or organizational powers on the ground that the disadvantages of those in one position are outweighed by the greater advantages of those in another. Much less can infringements of liberty be counterbalanced in this way. Applied to the basic structure, the principle of utility would have us maximize the sum of expectations of representative men . . . ; and this would permit us to compensate for the losses of some by the gains of others. Instead, the two principles require that everyone benefit from social and economic inequalities.

THE REASONING LEADING TO THE TWO PRINCIPLES OF JUSTICE

. . . I [now] take up the choice between the two principles of justice and the principle of average utility. Determining the rational preference between these two options is perhaps the central problem in developing the conception of justice as fairness. . . .

It will be recalled that the general conception of justice as fairness requires that all primary social goods be distributed equally unless an unequal distribution would be to everyone's advantage. . . . Now looking at the situation from the standpoint of one person selected arbitrarily, there is no way for him to win special advantages for himself. Nor, on the other hand, are there grounds for his acquiescing in special disadvantages. Since it is not reasonable for him to expect more than an equal share in the division of social goods, and since it is not rational for him to agree to less, the sensible thing for him to do is to acknowledge as the first principle of justice one requiring an equal distribution. Indeed, this principle is so obvious that we would expect it to occur to anyone immediately.

Thus, the parties start with a principle establishing equal liberty for all, including equality of opportunity, as well as an equal distribution of income and wealth. But there is no reason why this acknowledgment should be final. If there are inequalities in the basic structure that work to make everyone better off in comparison with the benchmark of initial equality, why not permit them? The immediate gain which a greater equality might allow can be regarded as intelligently invested in view of its future return. If, for example, these inequalities set up various incentives which succeed in eliciting more productive efforts, a person in the original position may look upon them as necessary to cover the costs of training and to encourage effective performance. One might think that ideally individuals should want to serve one another. But since the parties are assumed not to take an interest in one another's interests, their acceptance of these inequalities is only the acceptance of the relations in which men stand in the circumstances of justice. They have no grounds for complaining of one another's motives. A person in the original position would, therefore, concede the justice of these inequalities. Indeed, it would be shortsighted of him not to do so. He would hesitate to agree to these regularities only if he would be dejected by the bare knowledge or perception that others were better situated; and I have assumed that the parties decide as if they are not moved by envy. In order to make the principle regulating inequalities determinate, one looks at the system from the standpoint of the least advantaged representative man. Inequalities are permissible when they maximize, or at least all contribute to, the long-term expectations of the least fortunate group in society.

Now this general conception imposes no constraints on what sorts of inequalities are allowed, whereas the special conception, by putting the two principles in serial order . . . forbids exchanges between basic liberties and economic and social benefits. . . . The idea underlying this ordering is that if the parties assume their basic liberties can be effectively exercised, they will not exchange a lesser liberty for an improvement in economic well-being. It is only when social conditions do not allow the effective establishment of these rights that one can concede their limitation; and these restrictions can be granted only to the extent that they are necessary to prepare the way for a free society. The denial of equal liberty can be defended only if it is necessary to raise the level of civilization so that in due course these freedoms can be enjoyed. Thus in adopting a serial order we are in effect making a special assumption in the original position, namely, that the parties know that the conditions of their society, whatever they are, admit the effective realization of equal liberties. . . .

It seems clear from these remarks that the two principles are at least a plausible conception of justice. The question, though, is how one is to argue for them more systematically. Now there are several things to do. One can work out their consequences for institutions and note their implications for fundamental social policy. In this way they are tested by a comparison with our considered judgments of justice. . . . But one can also try to find arguments in their favor that are decisive from the standpoint of the original position. In order to see how this might be done, it is useful as a heuristic device to think of the two principles as the maximin solution to the problem of social justice. There is an analogy between the two principles and the maximin rule for choice under uncertainty. This is evident from the fact that the two principles are those a person would choose for the design of a society in which his enemy is to assign him his place. The maximin rule tells us to rank alternatives by their worst possible outcomes: we are to adopt the alternative the worst outcome of which is superior to the worst outcomes of the others. The persons in the original position do not, of course, assume that their initial place in society is decided by a malevolent opponent. As I note below, they should not reason from false premises. The veil of ignorance does not violate this idea, since an absence of information is not misinformation. But that the two principles of justice would be chosen if the parties were forced to protect themselves against such a contingency explains the sense in which this conception is the maximin solution. And this analogy suggests that if the original position has been described so that it is rational for the parties to adopt the conservative attitude expressed by this rule, a conclusive argument can indeed be constructed for these principles. Clearly the maximin rule is not, in general, a suitable guide for choices under uncertainty. But it is attractive in situations marked by certain special features. My aim, then, is to show that a good case can be made for the two principles based on the fact that the original position manifests these features to the fullest possible degree, carrying them to the limit, so to speak.

Consider the gain-and-loss table below. It represents the gains and losses for a situation which is not a game of strategy. . . .

	Circumstances		
Decisions	C1	C2	C3
d_1	−7	8	12
d_2	−8	7	14
d_3	5	6	8

The maximin rule requires that we make the third decision. For in this case the worst that can happen is that one gains five hundred dollars, which is better than the worst for the other actions. . . . The

term "maximin" means the maximum minimorum: and the rule directs our attention to the worst that can happen under any proposed course of action, and to decide in the light of that.

Now there appear to be three chief features of situations that give plausibility to this unusual rule. First, since the rule takes no account of the likelihoods of the possible circumstances, there must be some reason for sharply discounting estimates of these probabilities. . . . Thus it must be, for example, that the situation is one in which a knowledge of likelihoods is impossible, or at best extremely insecure. In this case it is unreasonable not to be skeptical of probabilistic calculations unless there is no other way out, particularly if the decision is a fundamental one that needs to be justified to others.

The second feature that suggests the maximin rule is the following: the person choosing has a conception of the good such that he cares very little, if anything, for what he might gain above the minimum stipend that he can, in fact, be sure of by following the maximin rule. It is not worthwhile for him to take a chance for the sake of a further advantage, especially when it may turn out that he loses much that is important to him. This last provision brings in the third feature, namely, that the rejected alternatives have outcomes that one can hardly accept. The situation involves grave risks. Of course these features work most effectively in combination. The paradigm situation for following the maximin rule is when all three features are realized to the highest degree. This rule does not, then, generally apply, nor of course is it self-evident. Rather, it is a maxim, a rule of thumb, that comes into its own in special circumstances. Its application depends upon the qualitative structure of the possible gains and losses in relation to one's conception of the good, all this against a background in which it is reasonable to discount conjectural estimates of likelihoods.

It should be noted, as the comments on the gain-and-loss table say, that the entries in the table represent monetary values and not utilities. . . . The essential point is that in justice as fairness the parties do not know their conception of the good and cannot estimate their utility in the ordinary sense. In any case, we want go behind de facto preferences generated by given conditions. Therefore expectations are based on the index of primary goods and the parties make their choice accordingly. The entries in the example are in terms of money and not utility to indicate this aspect of the contract doctrine.

Now, as I have suggested, the original position has been defined so that it is a situation in which the maximin rule applies. In order to see this, let us review briefly the nature of this situation with these three special features in mind. To begin with, the veil of ignorance excludes all but the vaguest knowledge of likelihood. The parties have no basis for determining the probable nature of their society, or their place in it. Thus they have strong reasons for being wary of probability calculations if any other course is open to them. They must also take in account the fact that their choice of principles should seem reasonable to others, in particular their descendants, whose rights will be deeply affected by it. . . . [T]hese considerations are strengthened by the fact that the parties know very little about the gain-and-loss table. Not only are they unable to conjecture the likelihoods of the various possible circumstances, they cannot say much about what the various circumstances are. . . . Those deciding are much more in the dark than the illustration by a numerical table suggests. It is for this reason that I have spoken of the maximin rule.

Several kinds of arguments for the two principles of justice illustrate the second feature. Thus, if we can maintain that these principles provide a workable theory of social justice, and that they are compatible with reasonable demands of efficiency, then this conception guarantees a satisfactory minimum. There may be, on reflection, little reason for trying to do better. . . .

Finally, the third feature holds if we can assume that other conceptions of justice may lead to institutions that the parties would find intolerable. For example, it has sometimes been held that under some conditions the utility principle (in either form) justifies, if not slavery or serfdom, at any rate serious infractions of liberty for the sake of greater social benefits. We need not consider here the truth of this claim, or the likelihood that the requisite conditions obtain. For the moment, this contention is only to illustrate the way in which conceptions of justice may allow for outcomes which the parties may not be able to accept. And having the ready alternative of the two principles of justice which secure a satisfactory minimum, it seems unwise, if not irrational, for them to take a chance that these outcomes are not realized.

[Rawls later points out that the choice of principles of justice is assumed to be "final" and cannot be revoked. Thus, if one makes the wrong decision and does not provide for basic rights or fair equality of opportunity, for instance, then that would affect one's life chances and those of one's family. This fact, he argues, also leads people to "maximin" and select the two principles over more risky options such as the utilitarian principle—Ed.]

NOTE

1. The process of mutual adjustment of principles and considered judgments is not peculiar to moral philosophy. See Nelson Goodman, *Fact, Fiction, and Forecast* (Cambridge, MA: Harvard University Press, 1955), pp. 65–68, for parallel remarks concerning the justification of the principles of deductive and inductive inference.

REVIEW AND DISCUSSION QUESTIONS

1. What does Rawls mean by the "basic structure" of society?
2. Describe the original position: what do people know, and what do they not know? What reasons does Rawls give for placing these facts behind the veil of ignorance?
3. What are "social primary goods"?
4. In what sense are the social contractors equal? How does Rawls's theory express the idea that all persons are "created equal"?

5. What is the general conception of justice? What are the two principles in serial order?

6. What is the "maximin rule" and what three reasons does Rawls give for thinking it would be rational for people to follow it in the original position?

7. Explain why Rawls thinks people would choose his two principles instead of utilitarianism.

8. Why does Rawls term his theory "justice as fairness"?

9. How might Rawls respond to Nozick's Chamberlain example?

10. Compare Rawls's view with Locke's social contract, paying special attention to the justification of basic liberties.

11. Would Rawlsean contractors accept Nozick's entitlement principle? Explain.

12. Compare Rawls's view of equality with that of Peter Singer.

13. It is sometimes said that Rawls unreasonably assumes people can "forget" social class, natural talents, and conception of the good when, in fact, they cannot do so. How would Rawls respond to that objection? Describe other circumstances in which we expect people to ignore what they know.

14. Discuss the following statement: utilitarians like Hume and Mill emphasize the role of feeling and sympathy in morality, while Kant and Rawls emphasize impartiality and fairness.

10
Welfare

Readings in this section discuss one of the most controversial of all issues on the American political agenda: welfare. Often the issues here relate directly to questions raised in the last section on economic justice and property, and the discussion of welfare will therefore be enriched by keeping in mind the ways that disputes about economic justice show up in this context as well. But disputes about welfare also go beyond those issues, as the many proposals to reform welfare illustrate. Some proposals argue for the complete abolition of welfare; others would extend it to include medical care and other basic needs; still others would emphasize the fact that people often work hard and so deserve to be rewarded for it. Essays in this section explore all those topics, along with one more: the need to limit the amount of money society now spends on providing free medical care for the elderly.

Security, Welfare, and the Communal Provision

Michael Walzer

In this essay, Michael Walzer argues that every society, including our own, acknowledges that members of the community are entitled, just by virtue of membership, to their share of the "communal provision." Security and welfare are the basis of the provision, though disputes often arise over how these two are to be understood. Both are thought of as needs, though they are defined differently in different times, as the examples of Ancient Greece and Medieval Jewish communities illustrate. After exploring these examples, Walzer next considers how "fair shares" are determined, that is, which sorts of goods are to be regarded as part of the communal provision as well as how they are to be distributed once that decision is made. Walzer concludes with a discussion of the American welfare system and health care reform. Along the way, he also discusses the social contract, including especially the position of John Rawls. Michael Walzer is professor of politics at Harvard University.

Selected excerpts from pages 64–91 from *Spheres of Justice: A Defense of Pluralism and Equality* by Michael Walzer. Copyright © 1983 by Basic Books, Inc. Reprinted by permission of Basic Books, a division of Harper-Collins Publisher, Inc.

MEMBERSHIP AND NEED

Membership is important because of what the members of a political community owe to one another and to no one else, or to no one else in the same degree. And the first thing they owe is the communal provision of security and welfare. This claim might be reversed: communal provision is important because it teaches us the value of membership. If we did not provide for one another, if we recognized no distinction between members and strangers, we would have no reason to form and maintain political communities. "How shall men love their country," Rousseau asked, "if it is nothing more for them than for strangers, and bestows on them only that which it can refuse to none?"[1] Rousseau believed that citizens ought to love their country and therefore that their country ought to give them particular reasons to do so. Membership (like kinship) is a special relation. It's not enough to say, as Edmund Burke did, that "to make us love our country, our country ought to be lovely."[2] The crucial thing is that it be lovely for us—though we always hope that it will be lovely for others (we also love its reflected loveliness).

Political community for the sake of provision, provision for the sake of community: the process works both ways, and that is perhaps its crucial feature. Philosophers and political theorists have been too quick to turn it into a simple calculation. Indeed, we are rationalists of everyday life; we come together, we sign the social contract or reiterate the signing of it, in order to provide for our needs. And we value the contract insofar as those needs are met. But one of our needs is community itself: culture, religion, and politics. It is only under the aegis of these three that all the other things we need become *socially recognized needs*, take on historical and determinate form. The social contract is an agreement to reach decisions together about what goods are necessary to our common life, and then to provide those goods for one another. The signers owe one another more than mutual aid, for that they owe or can owe to anyone. They owe mutual provision of all those things for the sake of which they have separated themselves from mankind as a whole and joined forces in a particular community. *Amour social* is one of

those things; but though it is a distributed good—often unevenly distributed—it arises only in the course of other distributions (and of the political choices that the other distributions require). Mutual provision breeds mutuality. So the common life is simultaneously the prerequisite of provision and one of its products.

Men and women come together because they literally cannot live apart. But they can live together in many different ways. Their survival and then their well-being require a common effort: against the wrath of the gods, the hostility of other people, the indifference and malevolence of nature (famine, flood, fire, and disease), the brief transit of a human life. Not army camps alone, as David Hume wrote, but temples, storehouses, irrigation works, and burial grounds are the true mothers of cities.[3] As the list suggests, origins are not singular in character. Cities differ from one another, partly because of the natural environments in which they are built and the immediate dangers their builders encounter, partly because of the conceptions of social goods that the builders hold. They recognize but also create one another's needs and so give a particular shape to what I will call the "sphere of security and welfare." The sphere itself is as old as the oldest human community. Indeed, one might say that the original community is a sphere of security and welfare, a system of communal provision, distorted, no doubt, by gross inequalities of strength and cunning. But the system has, in any case, no natural form. Different experiences and different conceptions lead to different patterns of provision. Though there are some goods that are needed absolutely, there is no good such that once we see it, we know how it stands vis-à-vis all other goods and how much of it we owe to one another. The nature of a need is not self-evident.

Communal provision is both general and particular. It is general whenever public funds are spent so as to benefit all or most of the members without any distribution to individuals. It is particular whenever goods are actually handed over to all or any of the members.* Water, for example,

---

*I don't mean to reiterate here the technical distinction that economists make between public and private goods. General provision is always public, at least on the less stringent defi-

is one of "the bare requirements of civil life," and the building of reservoirs is a form of general provision.4 But the delivery of water to one rather than to another neighborhood (where, say, the wealthier citizens live) is particular. The securing of the food supply is general; the distribution of food to widows and orphans is particular. Public health is most often general, the care of the sick, most often particular. Sometimes the criteria for general and particular provision will differ radically. The building of temples and the organization of religious services is an example of general provision designed to meet the needs of the community as a whole, but communion with the gods may be allowed only to particularly meritorious members (or it may be sought privately in secret or in nonconformist sects). The system of justice is a general good, meeting common needs; but the actual distribution of rewards and punishments may serve the particular needs of a ruling class, or it may be organized, as we commonly think it should be, to give to individuals what they individually deserve. Simone Weil has argued that, with regard to justice, need operates at both the general and the particular levels, since criminals need to be punished.5 But that is an idiosyncratic use of the word *need*. More likely, the punishment of criminals is something only the rest of us need. But need does operate both generally and particularly for other goods: health care is an obvious example that I will later consider in some detail.

Despite the inherent forcefulness of the word, needs are elusive. People don't just have needs, they have ideas about their needs; they have priorities, they have degrees of need; and these priorities and degrees are related not only to their human nature but also to their history and culture. Since resources are always scarce, hard choices

have to be made. I suspect that these can only be political choices. They are subject to a certain philosophical elucidation, but the idea of need and the commitment to communal provision do not by themselves yield any clear determination of priorities or degrees. Clearly we can't meet, and we don't have to meet, every need to the same degree or any need to the ultimate degree. The ancient Athenians, for example, provided public baths and gymnasiums for the citizens but never provided anything remotely resembling unemployment insurance or social security. They made a choice about how to spend public funds, a choice shaped presumably by their understanding of what the common life required. It would be hard to argue that they made a mistake. I suppose there are notions of need that would yield such a conclusion, but these would not be notions acceptable to— they might not even be comprehensible to—the Athenians themselves.

The question of degree suggests even more clearly the importance of political choice and the irrelevance of any merely philosophical stipulation. Needs are not only elusive; they are also expansive. In the phrase of the contemporary philosopher Charles Fried, needs are voracious; they eat up resources.6 But it would be wrong to suggest that therefore need cannot be a distributive principle. It is, rather, a principle subject to political limitation; and the limits (within limits) can be arbitrary, fixed by some temporary coalition of interests or majority of voters. Consider the case of physical security in a modern American city. We could provide absolute security, eliminate every source of violence except domestic violence, if we put a street light every ten yards and stationed a policeman every thirty yards throughout the city. But that would be very expensive, and so we settle for something less. How much less can only be decided politically.* One can imagine the sorts of things that would figure in the debates. Above all, I think, there would be a certain understanding—more or less widely shared, controver-

---

nitions of that term (which specify only that public goods are those that can't be provided to some and not to other members of the community). So are most forms of particular provision, for even goods delivered to individuals generate non-exclusive benefits for the community as a whole. Scholarships to orphans, for example, are private to the orphans, public to the community of citizens within which the orphans will one day work and vote. But public goods of this latter sort, which depend upon prior distributions to particular persons or groups, have been controversial in many societies; and I have designed my categories so as to enable me to examine them closely.

---

*And should be decided politically: that is what democratic political arrangements are for. Any philosophical effort to stipulate in detail the rights or the entitlements of individuals would radically constrain the scope of democratic decision making. I have argued this point elsewhere.7

sial only at the margins—of what constitutes "enough" security or of what level of insecurity is simply intolerable. The decision would also be affected by other factors: alternate needs, the state of the economy, the agitation of the policemen's union, and so on. But whatever decision is ultimately reached, for whatever reasons, security is provided because the citizens need it. And because, at some level, they all need it, the criterion of need remains a critical standard (as we shall see) even though it cannot determine priority and degree.

COMMUNAL PROVISION

There has never been a political community that did not provide, or try to provide, or claim to provide, for the needs of its members as its members understood those needs. And there has never been a political community that did not engage its collective strength—its capacity to direct, regulate, pressure, and coerce—in this project. The modes of organization, the levels of taxation, the timing and reach of conscription: these have always been a focus of political controversy. But the use of political power has not, until very recently, been controversial. The building of fortresses, dams, and irrigation works; the mobilization of armies; the securing of the food supply and of trade generally—all these require coercion. The state is a tool that cannot be made without iron. And coercion, in turn, requires agents of coercion. Communal provision is always mediated by a set of officials (priests, soldiers, and bureaucrats) who introduce characteristic distortions into the process, siphoning off money and labor for their own purposes or using provision as a form of control. But these distortions are not my immediate concern. I want to stress instead the sense in which every political community is in principle a "welfare state." Every set of officials is at least putatively committed to the provision of security and welfare; every set of members is committed to bear the necessary burdens (and actually does bear them). The first commitment has to do with the duties of office; the second, with the dues of membership. Without some shared sense of the duty and the dues there would be no political community at all and no se-

curity or welfare—and the life of mankind "solitary, poor, nasty, brutish, and short."

But how much security and welfare is required? Of what sorts? Distributed how? Paid for how? These are the serious issues, and they can be resolved in many different ways. Since every resolution will be appropriate or inappropriate to a particular community, it will be best to turn now to some concrete examples. I have chosen two, from different historical periods, with very different general and particular distributive commitments. The two represent the two strands of our own cultural tradition, Hellenic and Hebraic; but I have not looked for anything like extreme points on the range of possibilities. Rather, I have chosen two communities that are, like our own, relatively democratic and generally respectful of private property. Neither of them, so far as I know, has ever figured significantly in histories of the welfare state; and yet the citizens of both understood well the meaning of communal provision.

Athens in the Fifth and Fourth Centuries

"The Hellenistic city-states were highly sensitive to what may be called the general welfare, that is, they were quite willing to take measures which looked to the benefit of the citizenry as a whole; to social welfare . . . in particular the benefit of the poor as such, they were, on the contrary, largely indifferent."[8] This comment by the contemporary classicist Louis Cohn-Haft occurs in the course of a study of the "public physicians" of ancient Greece, a minor institution but a useful starting point for my own account. In Athens, in the fifth century B.C. (and during the later Hellenistic period in many Greek cities), a small number of doctors were elected to public office, much as generals were elected, and paid a stipend from public funds. It's not clear what their duties were; the surviving evidence is fragmentary. They apparently charged fees for their services much as other doctors did, though it seems likely that "as stipendiaries of the whole citizen body [they] would be under considerable social pressure not to refuse a sick person who could not pay a fee." The purpose of the election and the stipend seems to have been to assure the presence of qualified doctors in the city—in time of plague, for example.

The provision was general, not particular; and the city apparently took little interest in the further distribution of medical care. It did honor public physicians who "gave themselves ungrudgingly to all who claimed to need them"; but this suggests that the giving was not a requirement of the office; the doctors were paid for something else.9

This was the common pattern at Athens, but the range of general provision was very wide. It began with defense: the fleet, the army, the walls down to Piraeus, were all the work of the citizens themselves under the direction of their magistrates and generals. Or, perhaps it began with food: the Assembly was required, at fixed intervals, to consider an agenda item that had a fixed form—"corn and the defense of the country." Actual distributions of corn occurred only rarely; but the import trade was closely watched, and the internal market regulated, by an impressive array of officials: ten commissioners of trade, ten superintendents of the markets, ten inspectors of weights and measures, thirty-five "corn guardians" who enforced a just price, and—in moments of crisis—a group of corn buyers "who sought supplies wherever it could find them, raised public subscriptions for the necessary funds, introduced price reductions and rationing."10 All of these officials were chosen by lot from among the citizens. Or, perhaps it began with religion: the major public buildings of Athens were temples, built with public money; priests were public officials who offered sacrifices on the city's behalf. Or, perhaps it began, as in Locke's account of the origins of the state, with justice: Athens was policed by a band of state slaves (eighteen hundred Scythian archers); the city's courts were intricately organized and always busy. And beyond all this, the city provided a variety of other goods. Five commissioners supervised the building and repair of the roads. A board of ten enforced a rather minimal set of public health measures: "they ensure that the dung collectors do not deposit dung within ten *stados* of the walls."11 As I have already noted, the city provided baths and gymnasiums, probably more for social than for hygienic reasons. The burial of corpses found lying on the streets was a public charge. So were the funerals of the war dead, like the one at which Pericles spoke in 431. Finally, the great drama festivals were publicly organized and paid for, through

a special kind of taxation, by wealthy citizens. Is this last an expense for security and welfare? We might think of it as a central feature of the religious and political education of the Athenian people. By contrast, there was no public expenditure for schools or teachers at any level: no subsidies for reading and writing or for philosophy.

Alongside all this, the particular distributions authorized by the Athenian Assembly—with one central exception—came to very little. "There is a law," Aristotle reported, "that anyone with property of less than three *minae* who suffers from a physical disability which prevents his undertaking any employment should come before the Council, and if his claim is approved he should receive two *obols* a day subsistence from public funds."12 These (very small) pensions could be challenged by any citizen, and then the pensioner had to defend himself before a jury. One of the surviving orations of Lycias was written for a crippled pensioner. "All fortune, good and bad," Lycias had the pensioner tell the jury, "is to be shared in common by the community as a whole."13 This was hardly an accurate description of the city's practices. But the citizens did recognize their obligations to orphans and also to the widows of fallen soldiers. Beyond that, particular provision was left to the families of those who needed it. The city took an interest but only at a distance: a law of Solon required fathers to teach their sons a trade and sons to maintain their parents in old age.

The central exception, of course, was the distribution of public funds to all those citizens who held an office, served on the Council, attended the Assembly, or sat on a jury. Here a particular distribution served a general purpose: the maintenance of a vigorous democracy. The monies paid out were designed to make it possible for artisans and farmers to miss a day's work. Public spirit was still required, for the amounts were small, less than the daily earnings even of an unskilled laborer. But the yearly total was considerable, coming to something like half of the internal revenue of the city in the fifth century and more than that at many points in the fourth.14 Since the revenue of the city was not raised from taxes on land or income (but from taxes on imports, court fines, rents, the income of the silver mines, and so on), it can't be said that these payments were redistributive. But they did distribute public funds so as to balance somewhat the inequalities of Athenian society. This was particularly the case with regard to payments to elderly citizens who would not have been working anyway. Professor M. I. Finley is inclined to attribute to this distributive effect the virtual absence of civil strife or class war throughout the history of democratic Athens.[15] Perhaps this was an intended result, but it seems more likely that what lay behind the payments was a certain conception of citizenship. To make it possible for each and every citizen to participate in political life, the citizens as a body were prepared to lay out large sums. Obviously, this appropriation benefited the poorest citizens the most, but of poverty itself the city took no direct notice.

A Medieval Jewish Community

I shall not refer here to any particular Jewish community but shall try to describe a typical community in Christian Europe during the high Middle Ages. I am concerned primarily to produce a list of goods generally or particularly provided; and the list doesn't vary significantly from one place to another. Jewish communities under Islamic rule, especially as these have been reconstructed in the remarkable books of Professor S. D. Goitein, undertook essentially the same sort of provision though under somewhat different circumstances.[16] In contrast to Athens, all these were autonomous but not sovereign communities. In Europe, they possessed full powers of taxation, though much of the money they raised had to be passed on to the secular—that is, Christian—king, prince, or lord, either in payment of his taxes or as bribes, subsidies, "loans," and so on. This can be thought of as the price of protection. In the Egyptian cities studied by Goitein, the largest part of the communal funds was raised through charitable appeals, but the standardized form of the gifts suggests that social pressure worked very much like political power. It was hardly possible to live in the Jewish community without contributing; and short of conversion to Christianity, a Jew had no alternative; there was no place else to go.

In principle, these were democratic communities, governed by an assembly of male members, meeting in the synagogue. External pressures tended to produce oligarchy or, more precisely, plutocracy—the rule of the heads of the wealthiest families, who were best able to deal with avaricious kings. But the rule of the wealthy was continually challenged by more ordinary members of the religious community, and was balanced by the authority of the rabbinic courts. The rabbis played a crucial role in the apportionment of taxes, a matter of ongoing and frequently bitter controversy. The rich preferred a *per capita* tax, though in moments of crisis they could hardly avoid contributing what was necessary to their own, as well as the community's, survival. The rabbis seem generally to have favored proportional (a few of them even raised the possibility of progressive) taxation.[17]

As one might expect in communities whose members were at best precariously established, subject to intermittent persecution and constant harassment, a high proportion of public funds was distributed to individuals in trouble. But though it was established early on that the poor of one's own community took precedence over "foreign" Jews, the larger solidarity of a persecuted people is revealed in the very strong commitment to the "ransom of captives"—an absolute obligation on any community to which an appeal was made, and a significant drain on communal resources. "The redemption of captives," wrote Maimonides, "has precedence over the feeding and clothing of the poor."[18] This priority derived from the immediate physical danger in which the captive found himself, but it probably also had to do with the fact that his danger was religious as well as physical. Forced conversion or slavery to a non-Jewish owner were threats to which the organized Jewish communities were especially sensitive; for these were above all religious communities, and their conceptions of public life and of the needs of individual men and women were alike shaped through centuries of religious discussion.

The major forms of general provision—excluding protection money—were religious in character, though these included services that we now think of as secular. The synagogue and its officials, the courts and their officials, were paid for out of public funds. The courts administered Talmudic law, and their jurisdiction was wide (though it did not extend to capital crimes). Economic dealings were closely regulated, especially dealings with non-Jews since these could have implications for the community as a whole. The pervasive sumptuary laws were also designed with non-Jews in mind, so as not to excite envy and resentment. The community provided public baths, more for religious than for hygienic reasons, and supervised the work of the slaughterers. Kosher meat was taxed (in the Egyptian communities, too), so this was both a form of provision and a source of revenue. There was also some effort made to keep the streets clear of rubbish and to avoid overcrowding in Jewish neighborhoods. Toward the end of the medieval period, many communities established hospitals and paid communal midwives and physicians.

Particular distributions commonly took the form of a dole: regular weekly or twice-weekly distributions of food; less frequent distributions of clothing; special allocations for sick people, stranded travelers, widows and orphans, and so on—all this on a remarkable scale given the size and resources of the communities. Maimonides had written that the highest form of charity was the gift or loan or partnership designed to make the recipient self-supporting. These words were often quoted but, as Goitein has argued, they did not shape the structure of social services in the Jewish community. Perhaps the poor were too numerous, the situation of the community itself too precarious, for anything more than relief. Goitein has calculated that among the Jews of Old Cairo, "there was one relief recipient to every four contributors to the charities."19 The contributors of money also contributed their time and energy: from their ranks came a host of minor officials involved in the endless work of collection and distribution. Hence, the dole was a large and continuous drain, accepted as a religious obligation, with no end in sight until the coming of the messiah. This was divine justice with a touch of Jewish irony: "You must help the poor in proportion to their needs, but you are not obligated to make them rich."20

Beyond the dole, there were additional forms of particular provision, most importantly for educational purposes. In fifteenth-century Spain, some sixty years before the expulsion, a remarkable effort was made to establish something like universal and compulsory public education. The Valladolid synod of 1432 established special taxes on meat and wine, and on weddings, circumcisions, and burials, and ordered

that every community of fifteen householders [or more] shall be obliged to maintain a qualified elementary teacher to instruct their children in Scripture. . . . The parents shall be obliged to send their children to that teacher, and each shall pay him in accordance with their means. If this revenue should prove inadequate, the community shall be obliged to supplement it.

More advanced schools were required in every community of forty or more householders. The chief rabbi of Castile was authorized to divert money from wealthy to impoverished communities in order to subsidize struggling schools.21 This was a program considerably more ambitious than anything attempted earlier on. But throughout the Jewish communities a great deal of attention was paid to education: the school fees of poor children were commonly paid; and there were greater or lesser public subsidies, as well as additional charitable support, for religious schools and academies. Jews went to school the way Greeks went to the theater or the assembly—as neither group could have done had these institutions been left entirely to private enterprise.

Together, the Jews and the Greeks suggest not only the range of communal activity but also, and more important, the way in which this activity is structured by collective values and political choices. In any political community where the members have something to say about their government, some such pattern will be worked out: a set of general and particular provisions designed to sustain and enhance a common culture. The point would hardly have to be made were it not for contemporary advocates of a minimal or libertarian state, who argue that all such matters (except for defense) should be left to the voluntary efforts of individuals.22 But individuals left to themselves, if that is a practical possibility, will necessarily seek out other individuals for the sake of collective provision. They need too much from one another—not only material goods, which might be provided through a system of free exchange, but material goods that have, so to speak, a moral and cultural shape. Certainly one can find examples—there are many—of states that failed to provide either the material goods or the morality or that provided them so badly, and did so much else, that ordinary men and women yearned for nothing so much as deliverance from their impositions. Having won deliverance, however, these same men and women don't set out simply to maintain it but go on to elaborate a pattern of provision suited to their own needs (their own conception of their needs). The arguments for a minimal state have never recommended themselves to any significant portion of mankind. Indeed, what is most common in the history of popular struggles is the demand not for deliverance but for performance: that the state actually serve the purposes it claims to serve, and that it do so for all its members. The political community grows by invasion as previously excluded groups, one after another—plebeians, slaves, women, minorities of all sorts –demand their share of security and welfare.

FAIR SHARES

What is their rightful share? There are, in fact, two different questions here. The first concerns the range of goods that ought to be shared, the boundaries of the sphere of security and welfare: that is the subject of the next section. The second concerns the distributive principles appropriate within the sphere, which I shall try now to tease out of the Greek and Jewish examples.

We can best begin with the Talmudic maxim that the poor must (the imperative is important) be helped in proportion to their needs. That is common sense, I suppose, but it has an important negative thrust: not in proportion to any personal quality—physical attractiveness, say, or religious orthodoxy. One of the persistent efforts of Jewish communal organization, never entirely successful, was the elimination of beggary. The beggar is rewarded for his skill in telling a story, for his pathos, often—in Jewish lore—for his audacity; and he is rewarded in accordance with the kindness, the self-importance, the *noblesse oblige* of his benefactor, but never simply in proportion to his needs. But if we tighten the link between need

and provision, we can free the distributive process from all these extraneous factors. When we give out food, we will attend directly to the purpose of the giving: the relief of hunger. Hungry men and women don't have to stage a performance, or pass an exam, or win an election.

This is the inner logic, the social and moral logic of provision. Once the community undertakes to provide some needed good, it must provide it to all the members who need it in proportion to their needs. The actual distribution will be limited by the available resources; but all other criteria, beyond need itself, are experienced as distortions and not as limitations of the distributive process. And the available resources of the community are simply the past and present product, the accumulated wealth of its members—not some "surplus" of that wealth. It is commonly argued that the welfare state "rests on the availability of some form of economic surplus."[23] But what can that mean? We can't subtract from the total social product the maintenance costs of men and machines, the price of social survival, and then finance the welfare state out of what is left, for we will already have financed the welfare state out of what we have subtracted. Surely the price of social survival includes state expenditures for military security, say, and public health, and education. Socially recognized needs are the first charge against the social product; there is no real surplus until they have been met. What the surplus finances is the production and exchange of commodities outside the sphere of need. Men and women who appropriate vast sums of money for themselves, while needs are still unmet, act like tyrants, dominating and distorting the distribution of security and welfare.

I should stress again that needs are not merely physical phenomena. Even the need for food takes different forms under different cultural conditions. Thus the general distributions of food before religious holidays in the Jewish communities: a ritual and not a physical need was being served. It was important not only that the poor should eat but also that they should eat the right sorts of food, for otherwise they would be cut off from the community—but they were helped in the first place only because they were members of the community. Similarly, if disability is a reason for providing a pension, then every disabled citizen is entitled to that pension; but it still remains to work out what constitutes disability. In Athens this was accomplished, characteristically, through litigation. One can readily imagine alternative means but not, given the initial recognition of disability, alternative reasons. In fact, Lycias's pensioner felt bound to tell the jury that he was really a good fellow: I don't mean to suggest that the inner logic of provision is always or immediately understood. But the crucial charge against the pensioner was that he wasn't seriously disabled, and his crucial response was that he indeed fell within the category of disabled citizens as it had always been understood.

Education raises harder questions of cultural definition, and so may serve to complicate our understanding of both the possibilities and the limits of distributive justice in the sphere of security and welfare. Ignorance is obviously a more ambiguous notion than hunger or disability, for it is always relative to some body of socially valued knowledge. The education that children need is relative to the life we expect or want them to have. Children are educated for some reason, and they are educated particularly, not generally ("general education" is a modern idea designed to meet the specific requirements of our own society). In the medieval Jewish communities, the purpose of education was to enable adult men to participate actively in religious services and in discussions of religious doctrine. Since women were religiously passive, the community undertook no commitment to their education. In every other area of particular provision—food, clothing, medical care—women were helped exactly as men were helped, in proportion to their needs. But women did not need an education, for they were in fact less than full members of the (religious) community. Their primary place was not the synagogue but the household. Male dominance was most immediately expressed in the synagogue services (as it was among the Athenians in the Assembly debates) and then converted into the concrete coinage of subsidized schooling.

That dominance was occasionally challenged by writers who pointed to the importance of religious observance in the household, or to the religious significance of childrearing, or (less often)

to the contributions women might make to religious knowledge.[24] The argument necessarily focused on religion, and its success depended upon some moral or intellectual enhancement of the role of women in religious life. Because there were tensions within the Jewish tradition, there was something to argue about. It was at most a marginal enhancement that was aimed at, however; and so far as I know the synagogue was never actually described as a tyranny of men. Educational equality waited upon the development of alternative communities within which women might more readily claim to be members: thus the contemporary arguments for equality that invoke, as I shall do, the idea of an inclusive citizenship.

The Jewish communities did aim at including all men, however, and so faced the problem of organizing an educational system that cut across class lines. This might be achieved in a variety of ways. The community could organize charity schools for the poor, like the special schools for orphans in Old Cairo. Or it could pay the fees of poor children attending schools established and largely paid for by the better-off: this was the most common practice among medieval Jews. Or it could provide an education for everyone through the tax system and bar any additional charges even for those children whose parents could afford to pay more than their taxes. There is some pressure, I think, to move from the first to the second of these arrangements and then to some version of the third. For any social designation of the poor as "charity cases" is likely to produce discriminatory treatment within the schools themselves. Or, it is likely to be experienced by the children (or by their parents) as so degrading that it inhibits their participation in school activities (or their support for those activities). These effects may not be common to all cultures, but they are obviously widespread. Among medieval Jews, there was a great reluctance to accept public charity and some stigma attached to those who did so. Indeed, it can be one of the purposes of communal provision to stigmatize the poor and teach them their proper place—in, but not wholly of, the community. But except in some rigidly hierarchical society, that will never be its formal or publicly proclaimed purpose, and it will never be its only purpose. And if the publicly proclaimed purpose is, for example, to educate (male) children to read and discuss Scripture, then a common education commonly provided would seem to be the best arrangement.

Goitein notes a movement in this direction in the communities he has studied, but thinks the reasons were largely financial.25 Perhaps the rabbis of Spain had grasped the value of the common school: hence the element of compulsion in the scheme they devised. In any case, whenever the purpose of communal provision is to open the way to communal participation, it will make sense to recommend a form of provision that is the same for all the members. And it might well be said that, in democratic regimes, all provision has this purpose. The Athenian decision to pay every citizen who attended the Assembly the same (small) amount of money probably derives from some recognition of this fact. It would not have been difficult to devise a means test. But the citizens were not paid in proportion to their means, or to their needs as individuals, because it was not as individuals but as citizens that they were paid, and as citizens they were equal to one another. On the other hand, the Athenians barred from public office those citizens to whom disability pensions were paid.26 That probably reflects a peculiar view of disability, but it may also be taken to symbolize the degrading effects that sometimes (though not always) follow when communal provision takes the form of public charity.

THE EXTENT OF PROVISION

Distributive justice in the sphere of welfare and security has a twofold meaning: it refers, first, to the recognition of need and, second, to the recognition of membership. Goods must be provided to needy members because of their neediness, but they must also be provided in such a way as to sustain their membership. It's not the case, however, that members have a claim on any specific set of goods. Welfare rights are fixed only when a community adopts some program of mutual provision. There are strong arguments to be made that, under given historical conditions, such-and-such a program should be adopted. But these are not arguments about individual rights; they are arguments about the character of a particular political community. No one's rights were violated because the Athenians did not allocate public funds for the education of children. Perhaps they believed, and perhaps they were right, that the public life of the city was education enough.

The right that members can legitimately claim is of a more general sort. It undoubtedly includes some version of the Hobbesian right to life, some claim on communal resources for bare subsistence. No community can allow its members to starve to death when there is food available to feed them; no government can stand passively by at such a time—not if it claims to be a government of or by or for the community. The indifference of Britain's rulers during the Irish potato famine in the 1840s is a sure sign that Ireland was a colony, a conquered land, no real part of Great Britain.27 This is not to justify the indifference—one has obligations to colonies and to conquered peoples— but only to suggest that the Irish would have been better served by a government, virtually any government, of their own. Perhaps Burke came closest to describing the fundamental right that is at stake here when he wrote: "Government is a contrivance of human wisdom to provide for human wants. Men have a right that these wants should be provided for by this wisdom."28 It only has to be said that the wisdom in question is the wisdom not of a ruling class, as Burke seems to have thought, but of the community as a whole. Only its culture, its character, its common understandings can define the "wants" that are to be provided for. But culture, character, and common understandings are not givens; they don't operate automatically; at any particular moment, the citizens must argue about the extent of mutual provision.

They argue about the meaning of the social contract, the original and reiterated conception of the sphere of security and welfare. This is not a hypothetical or an ideal contract of the sort John Rawls has described. Rational men and women in the original position, deprived of all particular knowledge of their social standing and cultural understanding, would probably opt, as Rawls has argued, for an equal distribution of whatever goods they were told they needed.29 But this formula doesn't help very much in determining what choices people will make, or what choices they should make, once they know who and where they are. In a world of particular cultures, competing conceptions of the good, scarce resources, elusive and expansive needs, there isn't going to be a single formula, universally applicable. There isn't going to be a single, universally approved path that carries us from a notion like, say, "fair shares" to a comprehensive list of the goods to which that notion applies. Fair shares of what?

Justice, tranquility, defense, welfare, and liberty: that is the list provided by the United States Constitution. One could construe it as an exhaustive list, but the terms are vague; they provide at best a starting point for public debate. The standard appeal in that debate is to a larger idea: the Burkeian general right, which takes on determinate force only under determinate conditions and requires different sorts of provision in different times and places. The idea is simply that we have come together, shaped a community, in order to cope with difficulties and dangers that we could not cope with alone. And so whenever we find ourselves confronted with difficulties and dangers of that sort, we look for communal assistance. As the balance of individual and collective capacity changes, so the kinds of assistance that are looked for change, too.

The history of public health in the West might usefully be told in these terms. Some minimal provision is very old, as the Greek and Jewish examples suggest; the measures adopted were a function of the community's sense of danger and the extent of its medical knowledge. Over the years, living arrangements on a larger scale bred new dangers, and scientific advance generated a new sense of danger and a new awareness of the possibilities of coping. And then groups of citizens pressed for a wider program of communal provision, exploiting the new science to reduce the risks of urban life. That, they might rightly say, is what the community is for. A similar argument can be made in the case of social security. The very success of general provision in the field of public health has greatly extended the span of a normal human life and then also the span of years during which men and women are unable to support themselves, during which they are physically but most often not socially, politically, or morally incapacitated. Once again, support for the disabled is one of the oldest and most common forms of

particular provision. But now it is required on a much larger scale than ever before. Families are overwhelmed by the costs of old age and look for help to the political community. Exactly what ought to be done will be a matter of dispute. Words like *health, danger, science,* even *old age,* have very different meanings in different cultures; no external specification is possible. But this is not to say that it won't be clear enough to the people involved that something—some particular set of things—ought to be done.

Perhaps these examples are too easy. Disease is a general threat; old age, a general prospect. Not so unemployment and poverty, which probably lie beyond the ken of many well-to-do people. The poor can always be isolated, locked into ghettos, blamed and punished for their own misfortune. At this point, it might be said, provision can no longer be defended by invoking anything like the "meaning" of the social contract. But let us look more closely at the easy cases; for, in fact, they involve all the difficulties of the difficult ones. Public health and social security invite us to think of the political community, in T. H. Marshall's phrase, as a "mutual benefit club."[30] All provision is reciprocal; the members take turns providing and being provided for, much as Aristotle's citizens take turns ruling and being ruled. This is a happy picture, and one that is readily understandable in contractualist terms. It is not only the case that rational agents, knowing nothing of their specific situation, would agree to these two forms of provision; the real agents, the ordinary citizens, of every modern democracy have in fact agreed to them. The two are, or so it appears, equally in the interests of hypothetical and of actual people. Coercion is only necessary in practice because some minority of actual people don't understand, or don't consistently understand, their real interests. Only the reckless and the improvident need to be forced to contribute—and it can always be said of them that they joined in the social contract precisely in order to protect themselves against their own recklessness and improvidence. In fact, however, the reasons for coercion go much deeper than this; the political community is something more than a mutual benefit club; and the extent of communal provision in any given case—what it is and what it should be—is determined by conceptions of need that are more problematic than the argument thus far suggests.

Consider again the case of public health. No communal provision is possible here without the constraint of a wide range of activities profitable to individual members of the community but threatening to some larger number. Even something so simple, for example, as the provision of uncontaminated milk to large urban populations requires extensive public control; and control is a political achievement, the result (in the United States) of bitter struggles, over many years, in one city after another.[31] When the farmers or the middlemen of the dairy industry defended free enterprise, they were certainly acting rationally in their own interests. The same thing can be said of other entrepreneurs who defend themselves against the constraints of inspection, regulation, and enforcement. Public activities of these sorts may be of the highest value to the rest of us; they are not of the highest value to all of us. Though I have taken public health as an example of general provision, it is provided only at the expense of some members of the community. Moreover, it benefits most the most vulnerable of the others: thus, the special importance of the building code for those who live in crowded tenements, and of anti-pollution laws for those who live in the immediate vicinity of factory smokestacks or water drains. Social security, too, benefits the most vulnerable members, even if, for reasons I have already suggested, the actual payments are the same for everyone. For the well-to-do can, or many of them think they can, help themselves even in time of trouble and would much prefer not to be forced to help anyone else. The truth is that every serious effort at communal provision (insofar as the income of the community derives from the wealth of its members) is redistributive in character.[32] The benefits it provides are not, strictly speaking, mutual.

Once again, rational agents ignorant of their own social standing would agree to such a redistribution. But they would agree too easily, and their agreement doesn't help us understand what sort of a redistribution is required: How much? For what purposes? In practice, redistribution is a political matter, and the coercion it involves is foreshadowed by the conflicts that rage over its character and extent. Every particular measure is pushed through by some coalition of particular interests. But the ultimate appeal in these conflicts is not to the particular interests, not even to a public interest conceived as their sum, but to collective values, shared understandings of membership, health, food and shelter, work and leisure. The conflicts themselves are often focused, at least overtly, on questions of fact; the understandings are assumed. Thus the entrepreneurs of the dairy industry denied as long as they could the connection between contaminated milk and tuberculosis. But once that connection was established, it was difficult for them to deny that milk should be inspected: *caveat emptor* was not, in such a case, a plausible doctrine. Similarly, in the debates over old-age pensions in Great Britain, politicians mostly agreed on the traditional British value of self-help but disagreed sharply about whether self-help was still possible through the established working-class friendly societies. These were real mutual-benefit clubs organized on a strictly voluntary basis, but they seemed about to be overwhelmed by the growing numbers of the aged. It became increasingly apparent that the members simply did not have the resources to protect themselves and one another from poverty in old age. And few British politicians were prepared to say that they should be left unprotected.[33]

Here, then, is a more precise account of the social contract: it is an agreement to redistribute the resources of the members in accordance with some shared understanding of their needs, subject to ongoing political determination in detail. The contract is a moral bond. It connects the strong and the weak, the lucky and the unlucky, the rich and the poor, creating a union that transcends all differences of interest, drawing its strength from history, culture, religion, language, and so on. Arguments about communal provision are, at the deepest level, interpretations of that union. The closer and more inclusive it is, the wider the recognition of needs, the greater the number of social goods that are drawn into the sphere of security and welfare.[34] I don't doubt that many political communities have redistributed resources on very different principles, not in accordance with the needs of the members generally but in accordance with the power of the wellborn or the wealthy. But that, as Rousseau suggested in his *Discourse on Inequality*, makes a fraud of the social contract.35 In any community, where resources are taken away from the poor and given to the rich, the rights of the poor are being violated. The wisdom of the community is not engaged in providing for their wants. Political debate about the nature of those wants will have to be repressed, else the fraud will quickly be exposed. When all the members share in the business of interpreting the social contract, the result will be a more or less extensive system of communal provision. If all states are in principle welfare states, democracies are most likely to be welfare states in practice. Even the imitation of democracy breeds welfarism, as in the "people's democracies," where the state protects the people against every disaster except those that it inflicts on them itself.

So democratic citizens argue among themselves and opt for many different sorts of security and welfare, extending far beyond my "easy" examples of public health and old-age pensions. The category of socially recognized needs is open-ended. For the people's sense of what they need encompasses not only life itself but also the good life, and the appropriate balance between these two is itself a matter of dispute. The Athenian drama and the Jewish academies were both financed with money that could have been spent on housing, say, or on medicine. But drama and education were taken by Greeks and Jews to be not merely enhancements of the common life but vital aspects of communal welfare. I want to stress again that these are not judgments that can easily be called incorrect.

AN AMERICAN WELFARE STATE

What sort of communal provision is appropriate in a society like our own? It's not my purpose here to anticipate the outcomes of democratic debate or to stipulate in detail the extent or the forms of provision. But it can be argued, I think, that the citizens of a modern industrial democracy owe a great deal to one another, and the argument will provide a useful opportunity to test the critical force of the principles I have defended up until now: that every political community must attend to the needs of its members as they collectively understand those needs; that the goods that are distributed must be distributed in proportion to need; and that the distribution must recognize and uphold the underlying equality of membership. These are very general principles; they are meant to apply to a wide range of communities—to any community, in fact, where the members are each other's equals (before God or the law), or where it can plausibly be said that, however they are treated in fact, they ought to be each other's equals. The principles probably don't apply to a community organized hierarchically, as in traditional India, where the fruits of the harvest are distributed not according to need but according to caste—or rather, as Louis Dumont has written, where "the needs of each are conceived to be different, depending on [his] caste." Everyone is guaranteed a share, so Dumont's Indian village is still a welfare state, "a sort of cooperative where the main aim is to ensure the subsistence of everyone in accordance with his social function," but not a welfare state or a cooperative whose principles we can readily understand.36 (But Dumont does not tell us how food is supposed to be distributed in time of scarcity. If the subsistence standard is the same for everyone, then we are back in a familiar world.)

Clearly, the three principles apply to the citizens of the United States; and they have considerable force here because of the affluence of the community and the expansive understanding of individual need. On the other hand, the United States currently maintains one of the shabbier systems of communal provision in the Western world. This is so for a variety of reasons: the community of citizens is loosely organized; various ethnic and religious groups run welfare programs of their own; the ideology of self-reliance and entrepreneurial opportunity is widely accepted; and the movements of the left, particularly the labor movement, are relatively weak.37 Democratic decision making reflects these realities, and there is nothing in principle wrong with that. Nevertheless, the established pattern of provision doesn't measure up to the internal requirements of the sphere of security and welfare, and the common understandings of the citizens point toward a more elaborate pattern. One might also argue that American citizens should work to build a stronger and more intensely experienced political community. But this argument, though it would have distributive consequences, is not, properly speaking, an argument about distributive justice. The question is, What do the citizens owe one another, given the community they actually inhabit?

Consider the example of criminal justice. The actual distribution of punishments is an issue I will take up in a later chapter. But the autonomy of punishment, the certainty that people are being punished for the right reasons (whatever those are), depends upon the distribution of resources within the legal system. If accused men and women are to receive their rightful share of justice, they must first have a rightful share of legal aid. Hence the institution of the public defender and the assigned counsel: just as the hungry must be fed, so the accused must be defended; and they must be defended in proportion to their needs. But no impartial observer of the American legal system today can doubt that the resources necessary to meet this standard are not generally available.38 The rich and the poor are treated differently in American courts, though it is the public commitment of the courts to treat them the same. The argument for a more generous provision follows from that commitment. If justice is to be provided at all, it must be provided equally for all accused citizens without regard to their wealth (or their race, religion, political partisanship, and so on). I don't mean to underestimate the practical difficulties here; but this, again, is the inner logic of provision, and it makes for an illuminating example of complex equality. For the inner logic of reward and punishment is different, requiring, as I shall argue later, that distributions be proportional to desert and not to need. Punishment is a negative good that ought to be monopolized by those who have acted badly—and who have been found guilty of acting badly (after a resourceful defense).

Legal aid raises no theoretical problems because the institutional structures for providing it already exist, and what is at stake is only the readiness of the community to live up to the logic of its own institutions. I want to turn now to an area where American institutions are relatively underdeveloped, and where communal commitment is problematic, the subject of continuing political debate: the area of medical care. But here the argu-

ment for a more extensive provision must move more slowly. It isn't enough to summon up a "right to treatment." I shall have to recount something of the history of medical care as a social good.

The Case of Medical Care

Until recent times, the practice of medicine was mostly a matter of free enterprise. Doctors made their diagnosis, gave their advice, healed or didn't heal their patients, for a fee. Perhaps the private character of the economic relationship was connected to the intimate character of the professional relationship. More likely, I think, it had to do with the relative marginality of medicine itself. Doctors could, in fact, do very little for their patients; and the common attitude in the face of disease (as in the face of poverty) was a stoical fatalism. Or, popular remedies were developed that were not much less effective, sometimes more effective, than those prescribed by established physicians. Folk medicine sometimes produced a kind of communal provision at the local level, but it was equally likely to generate new practitioners, charging fees in their turn. Faith healing followed a similar pattern.

Leaving these two aside, we can say that the distribution of medical care has historically rested in the hands of the medical profession, a guild of physicians that dates at least from the time of Hippocrates in the fifth century B.C. The guild has functioned to exclude unconventional practitioners and to regulate the number of physicians in any given community. A genuinely free market has never been in the interest of its members. But it is in the interest of the members to sell their services to individual patients; and thus, by and large, the well-to-do have been well cared for (in accordance with the current understanding of good care) and the poor hardly cared for at all. In a few urban communities—in the medieval Jewish communities, for example—medical services were more widely available. But they were virtually unknown for most people most of the time. Doctors were the servants of the rich, often attached to noble houses and royal courts. With regard to this practical outcome, however, the profession has always had a collective bad conscience. For the distributive logic of the practice of medicine seems to be this:

that care should be proportionate to illness and not to wealth. Hence, there have always been doctors, like those honored in ancient Greece, who served the poor on the side, as it were, even while they earned their living from paying patients. Most doctors, present in an emergency, still feel bound to help the victim without regard to his material status. It is a matter of professional Good Samaritanism that the call "Is there a doctor in the house?" should not go unanswered if there is a doctor to answer it. In ordinary times, however, there was little call for medical help, largely because there was little faith in its actual helpfulness. And so the bad conscience of the profession was not echoed by any political demand for the replacement of free enterprise by communal provision.

In Europe during the Middle Ages, the cure of souls was public, the cure of bodies private. Today, in most European countries, the situation is reversed. The reversal is best explained in terms of a major shift in the common understanding of souls and bodies: we have lost confidence in the cure of souls, and we have come increasingly to believe, even to be obsessed with, the cure of bodies. Descartes's famous declaration that the "preservation of health" was the "chief of all goods" may be taken to symbolize the shift—or to herald it, for in the history of popular attitudes, Descartes's *Discourse on Method* came very early.[39] Then, as eternity receded in the popular consciousness, longevity moved to the fore. Among medieval Christians, eternity was a socially recognized need; and every effort was made to see that it was widely and equally distributed, that every Christian had an equal chance at salvation and eternal life: hence, a church in every parish, regular services, catechism for the young, compulsory communion, and so on. Among modern citizens, longevity is a socially recognized need; and increasingly every effort is made to see that it is widely and equally distributed, that every citizen has an equal chance at a long and healthy life: hence doctors and hospitals in every district, regular check-ups, health education for the young, compulsory vaccination, and so on.

Parallel to the shift in attitudes, and following naturally from it, was a shift in institutions: from the church to the clinic and the hospital. But the shift has been gradual: a slow development of communal interest in medical care, a slow erosion of interest in religious care. The first major form of medical provision came in the area of prevention, not of treatment, probably because the former involved no interference with the prerogatives of the guild of physicians. But the beginnings of provision in the area of treatment were roughly simultaneous with the great public health campaigns of the late nineteenth century, and the two undoubtedly reflect the same sensitivity to questions of physical survival. The licensing of physicians, the establishment of state medical schools and urban clinics, the filtering of tax money into the great voluntary hospitals: these measures involved, perhaps, only marginal interference with the profession—some of them, in fact, reinforced its guildlike character; but they already represent an important public commitment.[40] Indeed, they represent a commitment that ultimately can be fulfilled only by turning physicians, or some substantial number of them, into public physicians (as a smaller number once turned themselves into court physicians) and by abolishing or constraining the market in medical care. But before I defend that transformation, I want to stress the unavoidability of the commitment from which it follows.

What has happened in the modern world is simply that disease itself, even when it is endemic rather than epidemic, has come to be seen as a plague. And since the plague can be dealt with, it *must* be dealt with. People will not endure what they no longer believe they have to endure. Dealing with tuberculosis, cancer, or heart failure, however, requires a common effort. Medical research is expensive, and the treatment of many particular diseases lies far beyond the resources of ordinary citizens. So the community must step in, and any democratic community will in fact step in, more or less vigorously, more or less effectively, depending on the outcome of particular political battles. Thus, the role of the American government (or governments, for much of the activity is at the state and local levels): subsidizing research, training doctors, providing hospitals and equipment, regulating voluntary insurance schemes, underwriting the treatment of the very old. All this represents "the contrivance of human wisdom to provide for human wants." And all that is required to make it morally necessary is the development of a "want" so widely and deeply felt that it can plausibly be said that it is the want not of this or that person alone but of the community generally—a "human want" even though culturally shaped and stressed.*

But once communal provision begins, it is subject to further moral constraints: it must provide what is "wanted" equally to all the members of the community; and it must do so in ways that respect their membership. Now, even the pattern of medical provision in the United States, though it stops far short of a national health service, is intended to provide minimally decent care to all who need it. Once public funds are committed, public officials can hardly intend anything less. At the same time, however, no political decision has yet been made to challenge directly the system of free enterprise in medical care. And so long as that system exists, wealth will be dominant in (this part of) the sphere of security and welfare; individuals will be cared for in proportion to their ability to pay and not to their need for care. In fact, the situation is more complex than that formula suggests, for communal provision already encroaches upon the free market, and the very sick and the very old sometimes receive exactly the treatment they should receive. But it is clear that poverty remains a significant bar to adequate and consistent treatment. Perhaps the most telling statistic about contemporary American medicine is the correlation of visits to doctors and hospitals with social class rather than with degree or incidence of illness. Middle- and upper-class Americans are considerably more likely to have a private physician and to see him often, and considerably less likely to be seriously ill, than are their poorer fellow citizens.[44] Were medical care a luxury, these discrepancies would not matter much; but as soon as medical care becomes a socially recognized need, and as soon as the community invests in its provision, they matter a great deal. For then deprivation is a double loss—to one's health and to one's social standing. Doctors and hospitals have become such massively important features of contemporary life that to be cut off from the help they provide is not only dangerous but also degrading.

But any fully developed system of medical provision will require the constraint of the guild of physicians. Indeed, this is more generally true: the provision of security and welfare requires the constraint of those men and women who had previously controlled the goods in question and sold them on the market (assuming, what is by no means always true, that the market predates communal provision). For what we do when we declare this or that good to be a needed good is to block or constrain its free exchange. We also block any other distributive procedure that doesn't attend to need—popular election, meritocratic competition, personal or familial preference, and so on. But the market is, at least in the United States today, the chief rival of the sphere of security and welfare; and it is most importantly the market that is pre-empted by the welfare state. Needed goods cannot be left to the whim, or distributed in the interest, of some powerful group of owners or practitioners.

Most often, ownership is abolished, and practitioners are effectively conscripted or, at least, "signed up" in the public service. They serve for the sake of the social need and not, or not simply, for their own sakes: thus, priests for the sake of eternal life, soldiers for the sake of national defense, public school teachers for the sake of their pupils' education. Priests act wrongly if they sell salvation; soldiers, if they set up as mercenaries; teachers, if they cater to the children of the

---

*Arguing against Bernard Williams's claim that the only proper criterion for the distribution of medical care is medical need,[41] Robert Nozick asks why it doesn't then follow "that the only proper criterion for the distribution of barbering services is barbering need"?[42] Perhaps it does follow if one attends only to the "internal goal" of the activity, conceived in universal terms. But it doesn't follow if one attends to the social meaning of the activity, the place of the good it distributes in the life of a particular group of people. One can conceive of a society in which haircuts took on such central cultural significance that communal provision would be morally required, but it is something more than an interesting fact that no such society has ever existed. I have been helped in thinking about these issues by an article of Thomas Scanlon's; I adopt here his "conventionalist" alternative.[43]

wealthy. Sometimes the conscription is only partial, as when lawyers are required to be officers of the court, serving the cause of justice even while they also serve their clients and themselves. Sometimes the conscription is occasional and temporary, as when lawyers are required to act as "assigned counsels" for defendants unable to pay. In these cases, a special effort is made to respect the personal character of the lawyer-client relationship. I would look for a similar effort in any fully developed national health service. But I see no reason to respect the doctor's market freedom. Needed goods are not commodities. Or, more precisely, they can be bought and sold only insofar as they are available above and beyond whatever level of provision is fixed by democratic decision making (and only insofar as the buying and selling doesn't distort distributions below that level).

It might be argued, however, that the refusal thus far to finance a national health service constitutes a political decision by the American people about the level of communal care (and about the relative importance of other goods): a minimal standard for everyone—namely, the standard of the urban clinics; and free enterprise beyond that. That would seem to me an inadequate standard, but it would not necessarily be an unjust decision. It is not, however, the decision the American people have made. The common appreciation of the importance of medical care has carried them well beyond that. In fact, federal, state, and local governments now subsidize different levels of care for different classes of citizens. This might be all right, too, if the classification were connected to the purposes of the care—if, for example, soldiers and defense workers were given special treatment in time of war. But the poor, the middle class, and the rich make an indefensible triage. So long as communal funds are spent, as they currently are, to finance research, build hospitals, and pay the fees of doctors in private practice, the services that these expenditures underwrite must be equally available to all citizens.

This, then, is the argument for an expanded American welfare state. It follows from the three principles with which I began, and it suggests that the tendency of those principles is to free security

and welfare from the prevailing patterns of dominance. Though a variety of institutional arrangements is possible, the three principles would seem to favor provision in kind; they suggest an important argument against current proposals to distribute money instead of education, legal aid, or medical care. The negative income tax, for example, is a plan to increase the purchasing power of the poor—a modified version of simple equality.[45] This plan would not, however, abolish the dominance of wealth in the sphere of need. Short of a radical equalization, men and women with greater purchasing power could still, and surely would, bid up the price of needed services. So the community would be investing, though now only indirectly, in individual welfare but without fitting provision to the shape of need. Even with equal incomes, health care delivered through the market would not be responsive to need; nor would the market provide adequately for medical research. This is not an argument against the negative income tax, however, for it may be the case that money itself, in a market economy, is one of the things that people need. And then it too, perhaps, should be provided in kind.

I want to stress again that no *a priori* stipulation of what needs ought to be recognized is possible; nor is there any *a priori* way of determining appropriate levels of provision. Our attitudes toward medical care have a history; they have been different; they will be different again. The forms of communal provision have changed in the past and will continue to change. But they don't change automatically as attitudes change. The old order has its clients; there is a lethargy in institutions as in individuals. Moreover, popular attitudes are rarely so clear as they are in the case of medical care. So change is always a matter of political argument, organization, and struggle. All that the philosopher can do is to describe the basic structure of the arguments and the constraints they entail. Hence the three principles, which can be summed up in a revised version of Marx's famous maxim: From each according to his ability (or his resources); to each according to his socially recognized needs. This, I think, is the deepest meaning of the social contract. It only remains to work out the details—but in everyday life, the details are everything.

NOTES

1. Jean-Jacques Rousseau, "A Discourse on Political Economy," in *The Social Contract and Discourses,* trans. G. D. H. Cole (New York, 1950), pp. 302–3.

2. Edmund Burke, *Reflections on the French Revolution* (London, 1910), p. 75.

3. Cf. David Hume, *A Treatise of Human Nature,* bk. III, part II, chap. 8.

4. The quotation is from the Greek geographer Pausanias, in George Rosen, *A History of Public Health* (New York, 1958), p. 41.

5. Simone Weil, *The Need for Roots,* trans. Arthur Wills (Boston, 1955), p. 21.

6. Charles Fried, *Right and Wrong* (Cambridge, MA, 1978), p. 122.

7. Michael Walzer, "Philosophy and Democracy," *Political Theory* 9 (1981): 379–99. See also the thoughtful discussion in Amy Gutmann, *Liberal Equality* (Cambridge, England, 1980) especially pages 197–202.

8. Louis Cohn-Haft, *The Public Physicians of Ancient Greece* (Smith College Studies in History, vol. 42, Northampton, MA, 1956), p. 40.

9. Ibid., p. 49.

10. Aristotle, *The Constitution of Athens,* in *Aristotle and Xenophon on Democracy and Oligarchy,* trans. J. M. Moore (Berkeley, 1975), pp. 190–92 (secs. 49–52); M. I. Finley, *The Ancient Economy* (Berkeley, 1973), p. 170.

11. Aristotle, *Constitution* [10], p. 191 (50.2).

12. Ibid., p. 190 (49.4).

13. Kathleen Freeman, *The Murder of Herodes, and Other Trials from the Athenian Law Courts* (New York, 1963), p. 167.

14. A. H. M. Jones, *Athenian Democracy* (Oxford, England, 1957), p. 6.

15. Finley, *Ancient Economy* [10], p. 173.

16. S. D. Goitein, *A Mediterranean Society,* vol. II: *The Community* (Berkeley, 1971).

17. Salo Wittmayer Baron, *The Jewish Community* (Philadelphia, 1942), pp. 248–56; H. H. Ben-Sasson, "The Middle Ages," in Ben-Sasson, ed., *A History of the Jewish People* (Cambridge, MA, 1976), p. 551.

18. Baron, *Jewish Community* [17], p. 333.

19. Goitein, *Mediterranean Society* [16], p. 142.

20. Ibid.

21. Baron, *Jewish Community* [17], p. 172; see also Ben-Sasson, "Middle Ages" [17], pp. 608–11.

22. The strongest philosophical defense of this position is Robert Nozick, *Anarchy, State, and Utopia* (New York, 1974).

23. Morris Janowitz, *Social Control of the Welfare State* (Chicago, 1977), p. 10.

24. See Baron, *Jewish Community* [17], pp. 177–79.

25. Goitein, *Community* [16], p. 186.

26. Freeman, *Murder of Herodes* [13], p. 169.

27. For an account of the famine and the British response, see C. B. Woodham-Smith, *The Great Hunger: Ireland 1845–1849* (London, 1962).

28. Burke, *French Revolution* [2], p. 57.

29. John Rawls, *A Theory of Justice* (Cambridge, MA, 1971), part I, chaps. 2 and 3.

30. T. H. Marshall, *Class, Citizenship, and Social Development* (Garden City, NY, 1965), p. 298.

31. See Judith Walzer Leavitt, *The Healthiest City: Milwaukee and the Politics of Health Reform* (Princeton, 1982), chap. 5.

32. See the careful discussion in Harold L. Wilensky, *The Welfare State and Equality* (Berkeley, 1975), pp. 87–96.

33. P. H. J. H. Gosden, *Self-Help: Voluntary Associations in the Nineteenth Century* (London, 1973), chap. 9.

34. See, for example, Harry Eckstein's discussion of conceptions of community and welfare policies in Norway: *Division and Cohesion in Democracy: A Study of Norway* (Princeton, 1966), pp. 85–87.

35. Rousseau, *Social Contract* [1], pp. 250–52.

36. Louis Dumont, *Homo Hierarchus: The Caste System and Its Implications* (rev. English ed., Chicago, 1980), p. 105.

37. Wilensky, *Welfare State* [32], chaps. 2 and 3.

38. See Whitney North Seymour, *Why Justice Fails* (New York, 1973), especially chap. 4.

39. René Descartes, *Discourse on Method,* trans. Arthur Wollaston (Harmondsworth, England, 1960), p. 85.

40. For a brief account of these developments, see Odin W. Anderson, *The Uneasy Equilibrium: Private and Public Financing of Health Services in the United States, 1875–1965* (New Haven, 1968).

41. Bernard Williams, "The Idea of Equality," in *Problems of the Self* (Cambridge, England, 1973), p. 240.

42. See Robert Nozick, *Anarchy, State, and Utopia* (New York, 1974), pp. 233–35.

43. Thomas Scanlon, "Preference and Urgency," *Journal of Philosophy* 57 (1975): 655–70.

44. Monroe Lerner, "Social Differences in Physical Health," John B. McKinley, "The Help-Seeking Behavior of the Poor," and Julius Roth, "The Treatment of the Sick," in *Poverty and Health: A Sociological Analysis,* ed. John Kosa and Irving Kenneth Zola (Cambridge, MA, 1969), summary statements at pp. 103, 265, and 280–81.

45. Also, supposedly, a cheaper form of welfare: see Colin Clark, *Poverty before Politics: A Proposal for a Reverse Income Tax* (Hobart Paper 73, London, 1977),

REVIEW AND DISCUSSION QUESTIONS

1. Explain how Walzer understands the "communal provision" and its connection to membership and to needs.
2. Describe how ancient Athens and medieval Jewish communities understood the communal provision.
3. Explain the basis on which Walzer thinks that goods, understood as part of the communal provision, are to be distributed.
4. How is it decided which goods are to be included in people's "rightful share"; that is, what is the extent of the communal provision? How is the idea of a social contract relevant here?
5. What does Walzer argue Americans owe each other in the context of criminal justice?
6. Explain Walzer's defense of idea that medical care is part of the communal provision.
7. How would Nozick respond to Walzer's argument? (Consider Walzer's comments on Williams and Nozick in the note discussing barbering.)
8. Describe what you see as the similarities and differences between Walzer's position and those of MacIntyre and Rawls.

A Proposal for Public Welfare

Charles Murray

In this essay, Charles Murray argues in favor of abolishing all federally funded or mandated welfare for working-age people and replacing it with temporary unemployment insurance. Most people would not be affected by such a proposal, he thinks, while the few that are would be forced to work. Those who do not work could then turn either to charity or to their own families. In addition, he claims, we would also reduce births to unwed women, provide better services to those who seek help, and reward those who are worthy rather than those who are not. Charles Murray is an author and fellow at the Manhattan Institute for Policy Research.

I begin with the proposition that it is within our resources to do enormous good for some people quickly. We have available to us a program that would convert a large proportion of the younger generation of hardcore unemployed into steady workers making a living wage. The same program would drastically reduce births to single teenage girls. It would reverse the trendline in the breakup of poor families. It would measurably increase the upward socioeconomic mobility of poor families. These improvements would affect some millions of persons.

All these are results that have eluded the efforts of the social programs installed since 1965, yet, from everything we know, there is no real question about whether they would occur under the pro-

Selected excerpts from pages 227–235 from *Losing Ground: American Social Policy, 1950–1980* by Charles Murray. Copyright © 1984 by Charles Murray. Reprinted by permission of Basic Books, a division of Harper-Collins Publishers, Inc.

gram I propose. A wide variety of persuasive evidence from our own culture and around the world, from experimental data and longitudinal studies, from theory and practice, suggests that the program would achieve such results.

The proposed program, our final and most ambitious thought experiment, consists of scrapping the entire federal welfare and income-support structure for working-aged persons, including AFDC, Medicaid, Food Stamps, Unemployment Insurance, Worker's Compensation, subsidized housing, disability insurance, and the rest. It would leave the working-aged person with no recourse whatsoever except the job market, family members, friends, and public or private locally funded services. It is the Alexandrian solution: cut the knot, for there is no way to untie it.

It is difficult to examine such a proposal dispassionately. Those who dislike paying for welfare are for it without thinking. Others reflexively imagine bread lines and people starving in the streets. But as a means of gaining fresh perspective on the problem of effective reform, let us consider what this hypothetical society might look like.

A large majority of the population is unaffected. A surprising number of the huge American middle and working classes go from birth to grave without using any social welfare benefits until they receive their first Social Security check. Another portion of the population is technically affected, but the change in income is so small or so sporadic that it makes no difference in quality of life. A third group comprises persons who have to make new arrangements and behave in different ways. Sons and daughters who fail to find work continue to live with their parents or relatives or friends. Teenage mothers have to rely on support from their parents or the father of the child and perhaps work as well. People laid off from work have to use their own savings or borrow from others to make do until the next job is found. All these changes involve great disruption in expectations and accustomed roles.

Along with the disruptions go other changes in behavior. Some parents do not want their young adult children continuing to live off their income, and become quite insistent about their children learning skills and getting jobs. This attitude is most prevalent among single mothers who have to

depend most critically on the earning power of their offspring.

Parents tend to become upset at the prospect of a daughter's bringing home a baby that must be entirely supported on an already inadequate income. Some become so upset that they spend considerable parental energy avoiding such an eventuality. Potential fathers of such babies find themselves under more pressure not to cause such a problem, or to help with its solution if it occurs.

Adolescents who are not job-ready find they are job-ready after all. It turns out that they can work for low wages and accept the discipline of the workplace if the alternative is grim enough. After a few years, many—not all, but many—find that they have acquired salable skills, or that they are at the right place at the right time, or otherwise find that the original entry-level job has gradually been transformed into a secure job paying a decent wage. A few—not a lot, but a few—find that the process leads to affluence.

Perhaps the most rightful, deserved benefit goes to the much larger population of low-income families who have been doing things right all along and have been punished for it: the young man who has taken responsibility for his wife and child even though his friends with the same choice have called him a fool; the single mother who has worked full time and forfeited her right to welfare for very little extra money; the parents who have set an example for their children even as the rules of the game have taught their children that the example is outmoded. For these millions of people the instantaneous result is that no one makes fun of them any longer. The longer-term result will be that they regain the status that is properly theirs. They will not only be the bedrock upon which the community is founded (which they always have been), they will be recognized as such. The process whereby they regain their position is not magical, but a matter of logic. When it becomes highly dysfunctional for a person to be dependent, status will accrue to being independent, and in fairly short order. Noneconomic rewards will once again reinforce the economic rewards of being a good parent and provider.

The prospective advantages are real and extremely plausible. In fact, if a government program of the traditional sort (one that would "do" something rather than simply get out of the way) could as plausibly promise these advantages, its passage would be a foregone conclusion. Congress, yearning for programs that are not retreads of failures, would be prepared to spend billions. Negative side-effects (as long as they were the traditionally acceptable negative side-effects) would be brushed aside as trivial in return for the benefits. For let me be quite clear: I am not suggesting that we dismantle income support for the working-aged to balance the budget or punish welfare cheats. I am hypothesizing, with the advantage of powerful collateral evidence, that the lives of large numbers of poor people would be radically changed for the better.

There is, however, a fourth segment of the population yet to be considered, those who are pauperized by the withdrawal of government supports and unable to make alternate arrangements: the teenaged mother who has no one to turn to; the incapacitated or the inept who are thrown out of the house; those to whom economic conditions have brought long periods in which there is no work to be had; those with illnesses not covered by insurance. What of these situations?

The first resort is the network of local services. Poor communities in our hypothetical society are still dotted with storefront health clinics, emergency relief agencies, employment services, legal services. They depend for support on local taxes or local philanthropy, and the local taxpayers and philanthropists tend to scrutinize them rather closely. But, by the same token, they also receive considerably more resources than they formerly did. The dismantling of the federal services has poured tens of billions of dollars back into the private economy. Some of that money no doubt has been spent on Mercedes and summer homes on the Cape. But some has been spent on capital investments that generate new jobs. And some has been spent on increased local services to the poor, voluntarily or as decreed by this municipality. In many cities, the coverage provided by this network of agencies is more generous, more humane, more wisely distributed, and more effective in its results than the services formerly subsidized by the federal government.

But we must expect that a large number of people will fall between the cracks. How might we

go about trying to retain the advantages of a zero-level welfare system and still address the residual needs?

As we think about the nature of the population still in need, it becomes apparent that their basic problem in the vast majority of the cases is the lack of a job, and this problem is temporary. What they need is something to tide them over while finding a new place in the economy. So our first step is to reinstall the Unemployment Insurance program in more or less its previous form. Properly administered, unemployment insurance makes sense. Even if it is restored with all the defects of current practice, the negative effects of Unemployment Insurance alone are relatively minor. Our objective is not to wipe out chicanery or to construct a theoretically unblemished system, but to meet legitimate human needs without doing more harm than good. Unemployment Insurance is one of the least harmful ways of contributing to such ends. Thus the system has been amended to take care of the victims of short-term swings in the economy.

Who is left? We are now down to the hardest of the hard core of the welfare-dependent. They have no jobs. They have been unable to find jobs (or have not tried to find jobs) for a longer period of time than the unemployment benefits cover. They have no families who will help. For some reason, they cannot get help from local services or private charities except for the soup kitchen and a bed in the Salvation Army hall.

What will be the size of this population? We have never tried a zero-level federal welfare system under conditions of late-twentieth-century national wealth, so we cannot do more than speculate. But we may speculate. Let us ask of whom the population might consist and how they might fare.

For any category of "needy" we may name, we find ourselves driven to one of two lines of thought. Either the person is in a category that is going to be at the top of the list of services that localities vote for themselves, and at the top of the list of private services, or the person is in a category where help really is not all that essential or desirable. The burden of the conclusion is that every single person will be taken care of, but that the extent of resources to deal with needs is likely to be very great—not based on wishful thinking, but on extrapolations from reality.

To illustrate, let us consider the plight of the stereotypical welfare mother—never married, no skills, small children, no steady help from a man. It is safe to say that, now as in the 1950s, there is no one who has less sympathy from the white middle class, which is to be the source of most of the money for the private and local services we envision. Yet this same white middle class is a soft touch for people trying to make it on their own, and a soft touch for "deserving" needy mothers—AFDC was one of the most widely popular of the New Deal welfare measures, intended as it was for widows with small children. Thus we may envision two quite different scenarios.

In one scenario, the woman is presenting the local or private service with this proposition: "Help me find a job and day-care for my children, and I will take care of the rest." In effect, she puts herself into the same category as the widow and the deserted wife—identifies herself as one of the most obviously deserving of the deserving poor. Welfare mothers who want to get into the labor force are likely to find a wide range of help. In the other scenario, she asks for an outright and indefinite cash grant—in effect, a private or local version of AFDC—so that she can stay with the children and not hold a job. In the latter case, it is very easy to imagine situations in which she will not be able to find a local service or a private philanthropy to provide the help she seeks. The question we must now ask is: What's so bad about that? If children were always better off being with their mother all day and if, by the act of giving birth, a mother acquired the inalienable right to be with the child, then her situation would be unjust to her and injurious to her children. Neither assertion can be defended, however—especially not in the 1980s, when more mothers of all classes work away from the home than ever before, and even more especially not in view of the empirical record for the children growing up under the current welfare system. Why should the mother be exempted by the system from the pressures that must affect everyone else's decision to work?

As we survey these prospects, important questions remain unresolved. The first of these is why, if federal social transfers are treacherous, should locally mandated transfers be less so? Why should a municipality be permitted to legislate its own AFDC or Food Stamp program if their results are so inherently bad?

Part of the answer lies in conceptions of freedom. I have deliberately avoided raising them—the discussion is about how to help the disadvantaged, not about how to help the advantaged cut their taxes, to which arguments for personal freedom somehow always get diverted. Nonetheless, the point is valid: Local or even state systems leave much more room than a federal system for everyone, donors and recipients alike, to exercise freedom of choice about the kind of system they live under. Laws are more easily made and changed, and people who find them unacceptable have much more latitude in going somewhere more to their liking.

But the freedom of choice argument, while legitimate, is not necessary: We may put the advantages of local systems in terms of the Law of Imperfect Selection. A federal system must inherently employ very crude, inaccurate rules for deciding who gets what kind of help. . . . At the opposite extreme—a neighbor helping a neighbor, a family member helping another family member—the law loses its validity nearly altogether. Very fine-grained judgments based on personal knowledge are being made about specific people and changing situations. In neighborhoods and small cities, the procedures can still bring much individualized information to bear on decisions. Even systems in large cities and states can do much better than a national system; a decaying industrial city in the Northeast and a booming sunbelt city of the same size can and probably should adopt much different rules about who gets what and how much.

A final and equally powerful argument for not impeding local systems is diversity. We know much more in the 1980s than we knew in the 1960s about what does not work. We have a lot to learn about what does work. Localities have been a rich source of experiments. Marva Collins in Chicago gives us an example of how a school can bring inner-city students up to national norms. Sister Falaka Fattah in Philadelphia shows us how homeless youths can be rescued from the streets. There are numberless such lessons waiting to be learned from the diversity of local efforts. By all means, let a hundred flowers bloom, and if the federal government can play a useful role in lending a hand and spreading the word of success, so much the better.

The ultimate unresolved question about our proposal to abolish income maintenance for the working-aged is how many people will fall through the cracks. In whatever detail we try to foresee the consequences, the objection may always be raised: We cannot be sure that everyone will be taken care of in the degree to which we would wish. But this observation by no means settles the question. If one may point in objection to the child now fed by Food Stamps who would go hungry, one may also point with satisfaction to the child who would have an entirely different and better future. Hungry children should be fed; there is no argument about that. It is no less urgent that children be allowed to grow up in a system free of the forces that encourage them to remain poor and dependent. If a strategy reasonably promises to remove those forces, after so many attempts to "help the poor" have failed, it is worth thinking about.

But the rationale is too vague. Let me step outside the persona I have employed and put the issue in terms of one last intensely personal hypothetical example. Let us suppose that you, a parent, could know that tomorrow your own child would be made an orphan. You have a choice. You may put your child with an extremely poor family, so poor that you child will be badly clothed and will indeed sometimes be hungry. But you also know that the parents have worked hard all their lives, will make sure your child goes to school and studies, and will teach your child that independence is a primary value. Or you may put your child with a family with parents who have never worked, who will be incapable of overseeing your child's education—but who have plenty of food and good clothes, provided by others. If the choice about where one would put one's own child is as clear to you as it is to me, on what grounds does one justify support of a system that, indirectly but without doubt, makes the other choice for other children? The answer that "What we really want is a world where that choice is not forced upon us" is no answer. We have tried to have it that way. We failed. Everything we know about why we failed

tells us that more of the same will not make the dilemma go away.

THE IDEAL OF OPPORTUNITY

Billions for equal opportunity, not one cent for equal outcome—such is the slogan to inscribe on the banner of whatever cause my proposals constitute. Their common theme is to make it possible to get as far as one can go on one's merit, hardly a new ideal in American thought.

The ideal itself has never lapsed. What did lapse was the recognition that practical merit exists. Some people are better than others. They deserve more of society's rewards, of which money is only one small part. A principal function of social policy is to make sure they have the opportunity to reap those rewards. Government cannot identify the worthy, but it can protect a society in which the worthy can identify themselves.

I am proposing a triage of a sort, triage by self-selection. In triage on the battlefield, the doctor makes the decision—this one gets treatment, that one waits, the other one is made comfortable while waiting to die. In our social triage, the decision is left up to the patient. The patient always has the right to say "I can do X" and get a chance to prove it. Society always has the right to hold him to that pledge. The patient always has the right to fail. Society always has the right to let him in.

There is in this stance no lack of compassion but a presumption of respect. People—all people, black or white, rich or poor—may be unequally responsible for what has happened to them in the past, but all are equally responsible for what they do next. Just as in our idealized educational system a student can come back a third, fourth or fifth time to a course, in our idealized society a person can fail repeatedly and always be qualified for another chance—to try again, to try something easier, to try something different. The options are always open. Opportunity is endless. There is no punishment for failure, only a total absence of rewards. Society—or our idealized society—should be preoccupied with making sure that achievement is rewarded.

There is no shortage of people to be rewarded. Go into any inner-city school and you will find students of extraordinary talent, kept from knowing how good they are by rules we imposed in the name of fairness. Go into any poor community, and you will find people of extraordinary imagination and perseverance, energy and pride, making tortured accommodations to the strange world we created in the name of generosity. The success stories of past generations of poor in this country are waiting to be repeated.

There is no shortage of institutions to provide the rewards. Our schools know how to educate students who want to be educated. Our industries know how to find productive people and reward them. Our police know how to protect people who are ready to cooperate in their own protection. Our system of justice knows how to protect the rights of individuals who know how to protect the rights of individuals who know what their rights are. Our philanthropic institutions know how to multiply the effectiveness of people who are already trying to help themselves. In short, American society is very good at reinforcing the investment of an individual in himself. For the affluent and for the middle-class, these mechanisms continue to work about as well as they ever have, and we enjoy their benefits. Not so for the poor. American government, in its recent social policy, has been ineffectual in trying to stage-manage the decision to invest, and it has been unintentionally punitive toward those who make the decision on their own. It is time to get out of the way.

REVIEW AND DISCUSSION QUESTIONS

1. What are the problems with the current welfare system?
2. Explain why Murray thinks most people would not be affected by abolishing federal welfare programs.
3. Describe the advantages Murray thinks would follow from his proposal, were it adopted.
4. Explain how Murray thinks his proposal would advance the "ideal of opportunity."
5. Explain what you think are the main weaknesses of Murray's proposal, from a practical standpoint.
6. How would Michael Walzer respond to Murray's proposal?
7. Do you think William James's proposal for a war against nature, described in Section 8, might be useful in dealing with the problems Murray has outlined here? Explain.
8. Write a critique of Murray's proposal from the perspective of John Rawls and "justice as fairness."

What People Deserve

James Rachels

Often, it is claimed, people should be rewarded by society with economic or other goods because they deserve them. But what, exactly, is "desert"? In this essay, James Rachels begins with a discussion of justice, arguing that desert is part, but only a part, of treating people justly. While Nozick and other are correct in thinking that justice demands respecting people's rights, including the right to hire and fire as one wishes, desert is also an important component of justice. To deserve something, he says, requires that we reward or punish people in virtue of their past actions. People ought to be treated according to their deserts, he further claims, because it increases their control over their lives and shows them respect. Rachels also indicates how he thinks these concerns are relevant for affirmative action, as people compete for jobs and educational opportunities. James Rachels is professor of philosophy at the University of Alabama at Birmingham.

1. THE RELATION BETWEEN JUSTICE AND DESERT

. . . The fact that people are, or are not, treated as they deserve to be treated is one kind of reason why an action or social policy may be just or unjust. I say "one kind of reason" because there are also other sorts of reasons relevant to supporting claims of justice. Besides requiring that people be treated as they deserve, justice may also require that people's rights be respected, which is different. . . .

The term "distributive justice" . . . can be misleading. It suggests that there is a central supply of things which some authority has to dole out; but for most goods, there is no such supply and no such authority. Goods are produced by diverse individuals and groups who then have rights with respect to them, and the "distribution" of holdings at any particular time will depend, at least in part, on the voluntary exchanges and agreements those people have made. Jobs, for example, do not come from some great stockpile, to be handed out by a master "distributor" who may or may not follow principles of "justice." Jobs are created by the independent decisions of countless business people,

who are entitled, within some limits of course, to operate their own businesses according to their own judgments. In a free society those people get to choose with whom they will make what sorts of agreements, and this means, among other things, that they get to choose who is hired from among the various job applicants.

These observations suggest an argument in defense of reverse discrimination: If private business people have a right to hire whomever they please, don't they have a right to hire blacks and women in preference to others? In her paper on "Preferential Hiring" Judith Jarvis Thomson[1] advances an argument based on exactly this idea. The argument begins with this principle:

No perfect stranger has a right to be given a benefit which is yours to dispose of; no perfect stranger even has a right to be given an equal chance at getting a benefit which is yours to dispose of.[2]

Since many jobs are benefits which private employers have a right to dispose of, those employers violate no one's rights in hiring whomever they wish. If they choose to hire blacks, or women, rather than other applicants, they have a perfect

James Rachels, "What People Deserve," from John Arthur and William H. Shaw, *Justice and Economic Distribution* (Englewood Cliffs, NJ: Prentice Hall, 1978). Reprinted by permission.

right to do so. Therefore, she concludes, "there is no problem about preferential hiring," at least in the case of private business.

Thomson's principle is plausible. If something is *yours,* then no one else has a right to it—at least, no perfect stranger who walks in off the street wanting it. Suppose you have a book which you don't need and decide to give away as a gift. Smith and Jones both want it, and you decide to give it to Smith. Is Jones entitled to complain? Apparently not, since he had no claim on it in the first place. If it was your book, you were entitled to give it to whomever you chose; you violated no right of Jones in giving it to Smith. Why shouldn't the same be true of jobs? If you start a business, on your own, why shouldn't you be free to hire whomever you please to work with you? You violate no one's rights in hiring whomever you please, since no one had a right to be hired by you in the first place.

This is an important and powerful argument because it calls attention to a fact that is often overlooked, that people do not naturally have claims of right to jobs and other benefits which are privately produced. However, the argument also depends on another assumption which is false, namely, the assumption that people are treated unjustly only if their rights are violated. In fact, a person may be treated unjustly even though no right of his is violated, because he is not treated as he deserves to be treated. Suppose one applicant for a job has worked very hard to qualify himself for it; he has gone to nightschool, at great personal sacrifice, to learn the business, and so on. Another applicant could have done all that, but chose not to; instead, he has frittered away his time and done nothing to prepare himself. In addition, the first applicant has worked hard at every previous job he has held, making a good record for himself, whereas the second is a notorious loafer—and it's his own fault; he has no good excuse. Now it may be true that neither applicant has a right to the job, in the sense that the employer has the right to give the job to whomever he pleases. However, the first man is clearly more deserving, and if the employer is concerned to treat job applicants fairly he will not hire the second man over the first.

Now let me return to Nozick.[3] In Part II of *Anarchy, State and Utopia* he defends capitalism, not merely as efficient or workable, but as the only moral economic system, because it is the only such system which respects individual rights. Under capitalism people's holdings are determined by the voluntary exchanges (of services and work as well as goods) they make with others. Their right to liberty requires that they be allowed to make such exchanges, providing that they violate no one else's rights in doing so. Having acquired their holdings by such exchanges, they have a right to them; so it violates their rights for the government (or anyone else) to seize their property and give it to others. It is impermissible, therefore, for governments to tax some citizens in order to provide benefits for others.

The obvious objection is that such an arrangement could produce a disastrously unfair distribution of goods. Some lucky entrepreneurs could become enormously rich, while other equally deserving people are poor, and orphans starve. In reply Nozick contends that even if unmodified capitalism did lead to such a distribution, that would not necessarily be unjust. The justice of a distribution, he says, can be determined only by considering the historical process which led to it. We cannot tell whether a distribution is just simply by checking whether it conforms to some nonhistorical pattern, for example the pattern of everyone having equal shares, or everyone having what he or she needs. To show this Nozick gives a now-famous argument starring the basketball player Wilt Chamberlain. First, he says, suppose the goods in a society are distributed according to some pattern which you think just. Call this distribution D_1. Since you regard D_1 as a just distribution, you will agree that under it each person has a right to the holdings in his or her possession. Now suppose a million of these people each decide to give Wilt Chamberlain twenty-five cents to watch him play basketball. Chamberlain becomes rich, and the original pattern is upset. But if the original distribution was just, mustn't we admit that the new distribution (D_2) is also just? . . .

Each of these persons *chose* to give twenty-five cents of their money to Chamberlain. They could have spent it on going to the movies, or on candy bars, or on copies of *Dissent* magazine, or of *Monthly Review*. But they all, at least one million of them, converged on giving it to Wilt Chamberlain in exchange for watching him play basketball. If D_1 was a just distribution, and people voluntarily moved from it to D_2, transferring parts of their shares they were given under D_1 (what was it for if not to do something with?), isn't D_2 also just? . . . Can anyone else complain on grounds of justice? . . . After someone transfers something to Wilt Chamberlain, third parties *still* have their legitimate shares; *their* shares are not changed.[4]

The main argument here seems to depend on the principle that *If D_1 is a just distribution, and D_2 arises from D_1 by a process in which no one's rights are violated, then D_2 is also just.* Now Nozick is surely right that the historical process which produces a situation is one of the things that must be taken into account in deciding whether it is just. But that need not be the only relevant consideration. The historical process *and* other considerations, such as desert, must be weighed together to determine what is just. Therefore, it would not follow that a distribution is just *simply* because it is the result of a certain process, even a process in which no one's rights are violated. So this argument cannot answer adequately the complaint against unmodified capitalism.

To make the point less abstract, consider the justice of inherited wealth. A common complaint about inherited wealth is that some people gain fortunes which they have done nothing to deserve, while others, of equal merit, have nothing. This seems unjust on the face of it. Nozick points out that if the testators legitimately own their property—if it is *theirs*—then they have a right to give it to others as a gift. (The holdings of third parties will not be changed, etc.) Bequests are gifts; therefore property owners have a right to pass on their property to their heirs. This is fair enough, but at most it shows only that there is more than one consideration to be taken into account here. That some people have more than others, without deserving it, counts against the justice of the distribution. That they came by their holdings in a certain way may count in favor of the justice of the same distribution. It should come as no surprise that in deciding questions of justice competing claims must often be weighed against one another, for that is the way it usually is in ethics.

2. DESERT AND PAST ACTIONS

Deserts may be positive or negative, that is, a person may deserve to be treated well or badly; and they may be general or specific, that is, a person may deserve to be treated in a generally good or bad way, or he may deserve some specific kind of good or bad treatment. An example may make the latter distinction clear. Suppose a woman has always been kind and generous with others. As a general way of dealing with her, she deserves that others be kind and generous in return. Here we need not specify any *particular* act of kindness to say what she deserves, although of course treating her kindly will involve some particular act or other. What she deserves is that people treat her decently in *whatever* situation might arise. By way of contrast, think of someone who has worked hard to earn promotion in his job. He may deserve, *specifically,* to be promoted.

I wish to argue that the basis of all desert is a person's own past actions. In the case of negative desert, this is generally conceded. In order for a person to deserve punishment, for example, he must have done something to deserve it. Moreover, he must have done it "voluntarily," in Aristotle's sense, without any excuse such as ignorance, mistake, or coercion. In allowing these excuses and others like them, the law attempts to restrict punishment to cases in which it is deserved.

But not every negative desert involves punishment, strictly speaking. They may involve more informal responses to other people's misconduct. Suppose Adams and Brown work at the same factory. One morning Adams' car breaks down and he calls Brown to ask for a ride to work. Brown refuses, not for any good reason, but simply because he won't be bothered. Later, Brown finds himself in the same fix: his car won't start, and he can't get to work; so he calls Adams to ask for a lift. Now if Adams is a kind and forgiving person, he may grant Brown's request. And perhaps we all ought to be kind and forgiving. However, if Adams does choose to help Brown, he will be treating Brown better than Brown deserves. Brown deserves to be left in the lurch. Here I am not arguing that we ought to treat people as they deserve—although I do think there are reasons for so treating people, which I will mention presently—here I am only describing what the concept of desert involves. What Brown *deserves,* as opposed to what kindness or any other value might decree, is to be treated as well, or as *badly,* as he himself chooses to treat others.

If I am right, then the familiar lament "What did I do to deserve this?," asked by a victim of misfortune, is more than a mournful cliché. If there is no satisfactory answer, then in fact one does *not* deserve the misfortune. And since there is always a presumption against treating people badly, if a person does not deserve bad treatment it is likely to be wrong to treat him in that way. On the other side, in the case of positive deserts, we may notice a corresponding connection between the concept of desert and the idea of *earning* one's way, which also supports my thesis.

To elaborate an example I used earlier, think of an employer who has to decide which of two employees to give a promotion. One has worked very hard for the company for several years. He has always been willing to do more than his share of work; he has put in a lot of overtime when no one else would; and so on. The other has always done the least he could get by with, never taking on any extra work or otherwise exerting himself beyond the necessary minimum. Clearly, if the choice is between these two candidates, it is the first who deserves the promotion. It is important to notice that this conclusion does not depend on any estimate of how the two candidates are likely to perform in the future. Even if the second candidate were to reform, so that he would work just as hard (and well) in the new position as the first candidate, the first is still more deserving. What one deserves depends on what one has done, not on what one will do.

Of course there may be any number of reasons for not giving the promotion to the most deserving candidate: perhaps it is a family business, and the second candidate is the boss's son, and he will be advanced simply because of who he is. But that does not make him the most deserving candidate; it only means that the promotion is to be awarded on grounds other than desert. Again, the boss might decide to give the position to the second candidate because he is extraordinarily smart and

talented, and the boss thinks for that reason he will do a better job (he has promised to work harder in the future). This is again to award the job on grounds other than desert, for no one deserves anything *simply* in virtue of superior intelligence and natural abilities. As Rawls emphasizes, a person no more deserves to be intelligent or talented than he deserves to be the boss's son—or, than he deserves to be born white in a society prejudiced against nonwhites. These things are all matters of chance, at least as far as the lucky individual himself is concerned.

Three questions naturally arise concerning this view. First, aren't there bases of desert *other than* a person's past actions, and if not, why not? Second, if a person may not deserve things in virtue of being naturally talented or intelligent or fortunate in some other way, how can he deserve things by working for them? After all, isn't it merely a matter of luck that one person grows up to be industrious—perhaps as the result of a rigorous upbringing by his parents—while another person is not encouraged, and ends up lazy for reasons beyond his control? And finally, even if I am right about the basis of desert, what reason is there actually to treat people according to their deserts? Why should desert matter? I will take up these questions in order. The answers, as we shall see, are interrelated.

(a) . . . Does the most skillful player deserve to win an athletic competition? It seems a natural enough thing to say. But suppose the less skilled player has worked very hard, for weeks, to prepare himself for the match. He has practiced nine hours a day, left off drinking, and kept to a strict regimen. Meanwhile, his opponent, who is a "natural athlete," has partied, stayed drunk, and done nothing in the way of training. *But he is still the most skilled,* and as a result can probably beat the other guy anyway. Does he *deserve* to win the game, simply because he is better endowed by nature? Does he *deserve* the acclaim and benefits which go with winning? Of course, skills are themselves usually the product of past efforts. People must work to sharpen and develop their natural abilities; therefore, when we think of the most skillful as the most deserving, it may be because we think of them as having worked hardest. (Ted Williams

practiced hitting more than anyone else on the Red Sox). But sometimes that assumption is not true.

Do the prettiest and most handsome deserve to win beauty contests? Again, it seems a natural enough thing to say. There is no doubt that the *correct* decision for the judges of such a competition to make is to award the prize to the best-looking. But this may have little to do with the contestants' deserts. Suppose a judge were to base his decision on desert; we might imagine him reasoning like this: "Miss Montana isn't the prettiest, but after all, she'd done her best with what nature provided. She's studied the use of make-up, had her teeth and nose fixed, and spent hours practicing walking down runways in high-heeled shoes. That smile didn't just happen; she had to learn it by spending hours before a mirror. Miss Alabama, on the other hand, is prettier, but she just entered the contest on a lark—walked in, put on a bathing suit, and here she is. Her make-up isn't even very good." If all this seems ridiculous, it is because the point of such contests is not to separate the more deserving from the less (and maybe because beauty contests are themselves a little ridiculous, too). The criterion is beauty, not desert, and the two have little to do with one another. The same goes for athletic games: the purpose is to see who is the best player, or at least who is able to defeat all the others, and not to discover who is the most deserving competitor.

There is a reason why past actions are the only bases of desert. A fair amount of our dealings with other people involves holding them responsible, formally or informally, for one thing or another. It is unfair to hold people responsible for things over which they have no control. People have no control over their native endowments—over how smart, or athletic, or beautiful they naturally are—and so we may not hold them responsible for those things. They are, however, in control of (at least some of) their own actions, and so they may rightly be held responsible for the situations they create, or allow to exist, by their voluntary behavior. But those are the only things for which they may rightly be held responsible. The concept of desert serves to signify the ways of treating people that are appropriate responses to them, given that they are responsible for those actions or states of affairs. That is the role played by desert in our moral vocabulary. And, as ordinary-language philosophers used to like to say, if there weren't such a term, we'd have to invent one. Thus the explanation of why past actions are the only bases of desert connects with the fact that if people were never responsible for their own conduct—if hard determinism were true—no one would ever deserve anything, good or bad.

(b) According to the view I am defending, we may deserve things by working for them, but not simply by being naturally intelligent or talented or lucky in some other way. Now it may be thought that this view is inconsistent, because whether someone is willing to work is just another matter of luck, in much the same way that intelligence and talent are matters of luck. Rawls takes this position when he says:

> Perhaps some will think that the person with greater natural endowments deserves those assets and the superior character that made their development possible. Because he is more worthy in this sense, he deserves the greater advantages that he could achieve with them. This view, however, is surely incorrect. It seems to be one of the fixed points of our considered judgments that no one deserves his place in the distribution of native endowments, any more than one deserves one's initial starting place in society. The assertion that a man deserves the superior character that enables him to make the effort to cultivate his abilities is equally problematic; for his character depends in large part upon fortunate family and social circumstances for which he can claim no credit. The notion of desert seems not to apply to these cases.[5]

So if a person does not deserve anything on account of his intelligence or natural abilities, how can he deserve anything on account of his industriousness? Isn't willingness to work just another matter of luck?

The first thing to notice here is that people do not deserve things on account of their willingness to work, but only on account of their actually having worked. The candidate for promotion does not deserve it because he has been willing to work hard in his old job, or because he is willing to work hard in the new job. Rather he deserves the promotion because he actually *has* worked hard. Therefore it is no objection to the view I am defending to say that willingness to work is a character trait that one does not merit. For, on this view, the basis of desert is not a character trait of any kind, not even industriousness. The basis of desert is a person's past actions.

Now it may be that some people have been so psychologically devastated by a combination of poor native endowment and unfortunate family and social circumstances that they no longer have the capacity for making anything of their lives. If one of these people has a job, for example, and doesn't work very hard at it, it's no use blaming him because, as we would say, he just hasn't got it in him to do any better. On the other hand, there are those in whom the capacity for effort has not been extinguished. Among these, some choose to work hard, and others, who *could* so choose, do not. It is true of everyone in this latter class that he is *able,* as Rawls puts it, "to strive conscientiously." The explanation of why some strive, while others don't, has to do with their own choices. When I say that those who work hard are more deserving of success, promotions, etc., than those who don't, I have in mind comparisons made among people in this latter class, in whom the capacity for effort has not been extinguished.6

There is an important formal difference between industriousness, considered as a lucky asset, and other lucky assets such as intelligence. For only by exercising this asset—i.e., by working—can one utilize his other assets, and achieve anything with them. Intelligence alone produces nothing; intelligence plus work can produce something. And the same relation holds between industriousness and every other natural talent or asset. Thus "willingness to work," if it is a lucky asset, is a sort of superasset which enables one's other assets to be utilized. Working is simply the way one uses whatever else one has. This point may help to explain why the concept of desert is tied to work in a way in which it is not tied to intelligence or talents. And at the same time it may also provide a rationale for the following distinction: if a person displays intelligence and talent in his work, and earns a certain benefit by it, then he deserves the benefit not because of the intelligence or talent shown, but only on account of the work done.

(c) Finally, we must ask why people ought to be treated according to their deserts. Why should desert matter? In one way, it is an odd question. The reason why the conscientious employee ought to be promoted is precisely that he has earned the promotion by working for it. That is a full and sufficient justification for promoting him, which does not require supplementation of any sort. If we want to know why he should be treated in that way, that is the answer. It is not easy to see what else, by way of justification, is required.

Nevertheless, something more may be said. Treating people as they deserve is one way of treating them as autonomous beings, responsible for their own conduct. A person who is punished for his misdeeds is *held responsible* for them in a concrete way. He is not treated as a mindless automaton, whose defective performance must be "corrected," or whose good performance promoted, but as a responsible agent whose actions merit approval or resentment. The recognition of deserts is bound up with this way of regarding people. Moreover, treating people as they deserve *increases* their control over their own lives and fortunes, for it allows people to determine, through their own actions, how others will respond to them. It can be argued on grounds of kindness that people should not always be treated as they deserve, when they deserve ill. But this should not be taken to imply that deserts count for nothing. They can count for something, and still be overridden in some cases. To deny categorically that desert matters would not only excuse the malefactors; it would leave all of us impotent to earn the good treatment and other benefits which others have to bestow, and thus would deprive us of the ability to control our own destinies as social beings. [*Rachels pursues these issues further in the last section of this article, which I have included in the section on Affirmative Action—Ed.*]

NOTES

1. Judith Jarvis Thomson, "Preferential Hiring," *Philosophy and Public Affairs*, 2, no. 4 (Summer 1973), pp. 364–384.

2. Ibid., p. 369.

3. The following is from my review of *Anarchy, State and Utopia* in *Philosophia,* 7 (1977).

4. Robert Nozick, *Anarchy, State and Utopia* (New York: Basic Books, 1974), p. 161.

5. John Rawls, *A Theory of Justice* (Cambridge, MA: Harvard University Press, 1971), pp. 103–104.

6. What I am resisting—and what I think Rawls' view leads us towards—is a kind of determinism that would make all moral evaluation of persons meaningless. On this tendency in Rawls, see Nozick, pp. 213–214.

REVIEW AND DISCUSSION QUESTIONS

1. What are the two parts of justice, according to Rachels?
2. Describe the Wilt Chamberlain example and how it might be relevant to the distribution of income.
3. How does Rachels understand desert? Why does he think people should be given what they deserve?
4. How is desert relevant to affirmative action, according to Rachels?
5. Explain the significance of Rachels's position on the importance of desert for the debate over welfare.
6. How would Charles Murray respond to Rachels's ideas about desert and economic income?
7. Would Michael Walzer accept Rachels's claim that economic income should be distributed according to desert? Explain.
8. Discuss the criticism Rachels makes of Rawls. How might Rawls respond?

Aging and the Ends of Medicine

Daniel Callahan

One of the major sources of federal expenditure is Medicare, the program that provides all eligible senior citizens with medical care. Yet its costs, along with those of other medical programs, are skyrocketing, both in terms of real dollars and as a percentage of our total expenditures. At the same time that the elderly are consuming ever-greater amounts of our health care resources, the poor, and especially children, often suffer from malnutrition and lack of even basic medical care, including vaccinations. In this essay, Daniel Callahan addresses the problems of health care for the elderly, arguing that those who have lived a natural life span should be denied expensive new medical technologies, at least when they are given at government expense. This leads Callahan to consider the objectives of medicine, along with the notion of what constitutes a natural life span. Daniel Callahan is co-founder and president of the Hastings Center.

Reprinted with permission of the author and the publisher from *Annals of the New York Academy of Sciences,* 530 (June 15, 1988), pp. 125–132.

In October of 1986, Dr. Thomas Starzl of the Presbyterian-University Hospital in Pittsburgh successfully transplanted a liver into a 76-year-old woman. The typical cost of such an operation is over $200,000. He thereby accelerated the extension to the elderly of the most expensive and most demanding form of high-technology medicine. Not long after that, Congress brought organ transplantation under Medicare coverage, thus guaranteeing an even greater extension of this form of life-saving care to older age groups.

This is, on the face of it, the kind of medical progress we have long grown to hail, a triumph of medical technology and a new-found benefit to be provided by an established entitlement program. But now an oddity. At the same time those events were taking place, a parallel government campaign for cost containment was under way, with a special targeting of health care to the aged under the Medicare program.

It was not hard to understand why. In 1980, the 11% of the population over age 65 consumed some 29% of the total American health care expenditures of $219.4 billion. By 1986, the percentage of consumption by the elderly had increased to 31% and total expenditures to $450 billion. Medicare costs are projected to rise from $75 billion in 1986 to $114 billion in the year 2000, and in real not inflated dollars.

There is every incentive for politicians, for those who care for the aged, and for those of us on the way to becoming old to avert our eyes from figures of that kind. We have tried as a society to see if we can simply muddle our way through. That, however, is no longer sufficient. The time has come, I am convinced, for a full and open reconsideration of our future direction. We can not for much longer continue on our present course. Even if we could find a way to radically increase the proportion of our health care dollar going to the elderly, it is not clear that that would be a good social investment.

Is it sensible, in the face of a rapidly increasing burden of health care costs for the elderly, to press forward with new and expensive ways of extending their lives? Is it possible to even hope to control costs while, simultaneously, supporting the innovative research that generates ever-new ways to spend money? These are now unavoidable

questions. Medicare costs rise at an extraordinary pace, fueled by an ever-increasing number and proportion of the elderly. The fastest-growing age group in the United States are those over the age of 85, increasing at a rate of about 10% every two years. By the year 2040, it has been projected that the elderly will represent 21% of the population and consume 45% of all health care expenditures. Could costs of that magnitude be borne?

Yet even as this intimidating trend reveals itself, anyone who works closely with the elderly recognizes that the present Medicare and Medicaid programs are grossly inadequate in meeting the real and full needs of the elderly. They fail, most notably, in providing decent long-term care and medical care that does not constitute a heavy out-of-pocket drain. Members of minority groups, and single or widowed women, are particularly disadvantaged. How will it be possible, then, to keep pace with the growing number of elderly in even providing present levels of care, much less in ridding the system of its present inadequacies and inequities—and, at the same time, furiously adding expensive new technologies?

The straight answer is that it will not be possible to do all of those things and that, worse still, it may be harmful to even try. It may be harmful because of the economic burdens it will impose on younger age groups, and because of the skewing of national social priorities too heavily toward health care that it is coming to require. But it may also be harmful because it suggests to both the young and the old that the key to a happy old age is good health care. That may not be true.

It is not pleasant to raise possibilities of that kind. The struggle against what Dr. Robert Butler aptly and brilliantly called "ageism" in 1968 has been a difficult one. It has meant trying to persuade the public that not all the elderly are sick and senile. It has meant trying to convince Congress and state legislatures to provide more help for the old. It has meant trying to educate the elderly themselves to look upon their old age as a time of new, open possibilities. That campaign has met with only partial success. Despite great progress, the elderly are still subject to discrimination and stereotyping. The struggle against ageism is hardly over.

Three major concerns have, nonetheless, surfaced over the past few years. They are symptoms that a new era has arrived. The first is that an increasingly large share of health care is going to the elderly in comparison with benefits for children. The federal government, for instance, spends six times as much on health care for those over 65 as for those under 18. As the demographer Samuel Preston observed in a provocative 1984 presidential address to the Population Association of America:

There is surely something to be said for a system in which things get better as we pass through life rather than worse. The great leveling off of age curves of psychological distress, suicide and income in the past two decades might simply reflect the fact that we have decided in some fundamental sense that we don't want to face futures that become continually bleaker. But let's be clear that the transfers from the working-age population to the elderly are also transfers away from children, since the working ages bear far more responsibility for childrearing than do the elderly.[1]

Preston's address had an immediate impact. The mainline aging advocacy groups responded with pained indignation, accusing Preston of fomenting a war between the generations. But led by Dave Durenberger, Republican Senator from Minnesota, it also stimulated the formation of Americans for Generational Equity (AGE), an organization created to promote debate on the burden to future generations, but particularly the Baby Boom generation, of "our major social insurance programs."[2] These two developments signalled the outburst of a struggle over what has come to be called "Intergenerational equity" that is only now gaining momentum.

The second concern is that the elderly dying consume a disproportionate share of health care costs. Stanford economist Victor Fuchs has noted:

At present, the United States spends about 1 percent of the gross national product on health care for elderly persons who are in their last year of life. . . . One of the biggest challenges facing policy makers for the rest of this century will be how to strike an appropriate balance between care of the [elderly] dying and health services for the rest of the population.[3]

The third concern is summed up in an observation by Jerome L. Avorn, M.D., of the Harvard Medical School:

With the exception of the birth-control pill, each of the medical-technology interventions developed since the 1950s has its most widespread impact on people who are past their fifties—the further past their fifties, the greater the impact.[4]

Many of these interventions were not intended for the elderly. Kidney dialysis, for example, was originally developed for those between the age of 15 and 45. Now some 30% of its recipients are over 65.

These three concerns have not gone unchallenged. They have, on the contrary, been strongly resisted, as has the more general assertion that some form of rationing of health care for the elderly might become necessary. To the charge that the elderly receive a disproportionate share of resources, the response has been that what helps the elderly helps every other age group. It both relieves the young of the burden of care for elderly parents they would otherwise have to bear and, since they too will eventually become old, promises them similar care when they come to need it. There is no guarantee, moreover, that any cutback in health care for the elderly would result in a transfer of the savings directly to the young. Our system is not that rational or that organized. And why, others ask, should we contemplate restricting care for the elderly when we wastefully spend hundreds of millions of dollars on an inflated defense budget?

The charge that the elderly dying receive a large share of funds hardly proves that it is an unjust or unreasonable amount. They are, after all, the most in need. As some important studies have shown, moreover, it is exceedingly difficult to know that someone is dying; the most expensive patients, it turns out, are those who are expected to live but who actually die. That most new technologies benefit the old more than the young is perfectly sensible: most of the killer diseases of the young have now been conquered.

These are reasonable responses. It would no doubt be possible to ignore the symptoms that the raising of such concerns represents, and to put off for at least a few more years any full confrontation with the overpowering tide of elderly now on the way. There is little incentive for politicians to think about, much less talk about, limits of any kind on health care for the aged; it is a politically hazardous topic. Perhaps also, as Dean Guido Calabresi of the Yale Law School and his colleague Philip Bobbitt observed in their thoughtful 1978 book *Tragic Choices,* when we are forced to make painful allocation choices, "Evasion, disguise, temporizing . . . [and] averting our eyes enables us to save some lives even when we will not save all."5

Yet however slight the incentives to take on this highly troubling issue, I believe it is inevitable that we must. Already rationing of health care under Medicare is a fact of life, though rarely labeled as such. The requirement that Medicare recipients pay the first $500 of the costs of hospital care, that there is a cutoff of reimbursement of care beyond 60 days, and a failure to cover long-term care, are nothing other than allocation and cost-saving devices. As sensitive as it is to the votes of the elderly, The Reagan administration only grudgingly agreed to support catastrophic health care costs of the elderly (a benefit that will not, in any event, help many of the aged). It is bound to be far more resistant to long-term care coverage, as will any administration.

But there are other reasons than economics to think about health care for the elderly. The coming economic crisis provides a much-needed opportunity to ask some deeper questions. Just what is it that we want medicine to do for us as we age? Earlier cultures believed that aging should be accepted, and that it should be in part a time of preparation for death. Our culture seems increasingly to reject that view, preferring instead, it often seems, to think of aging as hardly more than another disease, to be fought and rejected. Which view is correct? To ask that question is only to note that disturbing puzzles about the ends of medicine and the ends of aging lie behind the more immediate financing worries. Without some kind of answer to them, there is no hope of finding a reasonable, and possibly even a humane, solution to the growing problem of health care for the elderly.

Let me put my own view directly. The future goal of medicine in the care of the aged should be that of improving the quality of their life, not in seeking ways to extend that life. In its longstanding ambition to forestall death, medicine has in the care of the aged reached its last frontier. That is hardly because death is absent elsewhere—children and young adults obviously still die of maladies that are open to potential cure—but because the largest number of deaths (some 70%) now occur among those over the age of 65, with the highest proportion in those over 85. If death is ever to be humbled, that is where the essentially endless work remains to be done. But however tempting that challenge, medicine should now restrain its ambition at that frontier. To do otherwise will, I believe, be to court harm to the needs of other age groups and to the old themselves.

Yet to ask medicine to restrain itself in the face of aging and death is to ask more than it, or the public that sustains it, is likely to find agreeable. Only a fresh understanding of the ends and meaning of aging, encompassing two conditions, are likely to make that a plausible stance. The first is that we—both young and old—need to understand that it is possible to live out a meaningful old age that is limited in time, one that does not require a compulsive effort to turn to medicine for more life to make it bearable. The second condition is that, as a culture, we need a more supportive context for aging and death, one that cherishes and respects the elderly while at the same time recognizing that their primary orientation should be to the young and the generations to come, not to their own age group. It will be no less necessary to recognize that in the passing of the generations lies the constant reinvigoration of biological life.

Neither of these conditions will be easy to realize. Our culture has, for one thing, worked hard to redefine old age as a time of liberation, not decline. The terms "modern maturity" or "prime time" have, after all, come to connote a time of travel, new ventures in education and self-discovery, the ever-accessible tennis court or golf course, and delightfully periodic but gratefully brief visits from well-behaved grandchildren.

This is, to be sure, an idealized picture. Its attraction lies not in its literal truth but as a widely-accepted utopian reference point. It projects the vision of an old age to which more and more believe they can aspire and which its proponents think an affluent country can afford if it so chooses. That it requires a medicine that is single-minded in its aggressiveness against the infirmities of old age is of a piece with its hopes. But as we have come to discover, the costs of that kind of war are prohibitive. No matter how much is spent the ultimate problem will still remain: people age and die. Worse still, by pretending that old age can be turned into a kind of endless middle age, we rob it of meaning and significance for the elderly themselves. It is a way of saying that old age can be acceptable only to the extent that it can mimic the vitality of the younger years.

There is a plausible alternative: that of a fresh vision of what it means to live a decently long and adequate life, what might be called a natural life span. Earlier generations accepted the idea that there was a natural life span—the biblical norm of three score years and ten captures that notion (even though, in fact, that was a much longer life span than was then typically the case). It is an idea well worth reconsidering, and would provide us with a meaningful and realizable goal. Modern medicine and biology have done much, however, to wean us away from that kind of thinking. They have insinuated the belief that the average life span is not a natural fact at all, but instead one that is strictly dependent upon the state of medical knowledge and skill. And there is much to that belief as a statistical fact: the average life expectancy continues to increase, with no end in sight.

But that is not what I think we ought to mean by a natural life span. We need a notion of a full life that is based on some deeper understanding of human need and sensible possibility, not the latest state of medical technology or medical possibility. We should instead think of a natural life span as the achievement of a life long enough to accomplish for the most part those opportunities that life typically affords people and which we ordinarily take to be the prime benefits of enjoying a life at all—that of loving and living, of raising a family, of finding and carrying out work that is satisfying, of reading and thinking, and of cherishing our friends and families.

If we envisioned a natural life span that way, then we could begin to intensify the devising of ways to get people to that stage of life, and to work to make certain they do so in good health and social dignity. People will differ on what they might count as a natural life span determining its appropriate range for social policy purposes would need extended thought and debate. My own view is that it can now be achieved by the late 70s or early 80s.

That many of the elderly discover new interests and new facets of themselves late in life—my mother took up painting in her seventies and was selling her paintings up until her death at 86—does not mean that we should necessarily encourage a kind of medicine that would make that the norm. Nor does it mean that we should base social and welfare policy on possibilities of that kind. A more reasonable approach is to ask how medicine can help most people live out a decently long life, and how that life can be enhanced along the way.

A longer life does not guarantee a better life—there is no inherent connection between the two. No matter how long medicine enabled people to live, death at any time—at age 90, or 100, or 110—would frustrate some possibility, some as-yet-unrealized goal. There is sadness in that realization, but not tragedy. An easily preventable death of a young child is an outrage. The death from an incurable disease of someone in the prime of young adulthood is a tragedy. But death at an old age, after a long and full life, is simply sad, a part of life itself.

As it confronts aging, medicine should have as its specific goal that of averting premature death, understood as death prior to a natural life span, and the relief of suffering thereafter. It should pursue those goals in order that the elderly can finish out their years with as little needless pain as possible, and with as much vigor as can be generated in contributing to the welfare of younger age groups and to the community of which they are a part. Above all, the elderly need to have a sense of the meaning and significance of their stage in life, one that is not dependent for its human value on economic productivity or physical vigor.

What would a medicine oriented toward the relief of suffering rather than the deliberate extension of life be like? We do not yet have a clear and ready answer to that question, so longstanding, central, and persistent has been the struggle against death as part of the self-conception of medicine. But the Hospice movement is providing us with much helpful evidence. It knows how to distinguish between the relief of suffering and the extension of life. A greater control by the elderly over their dying—and particularly a more readily respected and enforceable right to deny aggressive life-extending treatment—is a long-sought, minimally necessary goal.

What does this have to do with the rising cost of health care for the elderly? Everything. The indefinite extension of life combined with a never-satisfied improvement in the health of the elderly is a recipe for monomania and limitless spending. It fails to put health in its proper place as only one among many human goods. It fails to accept aging and death as part of the human condition. It fails to present to younger generations a model of wise stewardship.

How might we devise a plan to limit health care for the aged under public entitlement programs that is fair, humane, and sensitive to their special requirements and dignity? Let me suggest three principles to undergird a quest for limits. First, government has a duty, based on our collective social obligations to each other, to help people live out a natural life span, but not actively to help medically extend life beyond that point. Second, government is obliged to develop under its research subsidies, and pay for, under its entitlement programs, only that kind and degree of life-extending technology necessary for medicine to achieve and serve the end of a natural life span. The question is not whether a technology is available that can save the life of someone who has lived out a natural life span, but whether there is an obligation for society to provide them with that technology. I think not. Third, beyond the point of natural life span, government should provide only the means necessary for the relief of suffering, not life-extending technology. By proposing that we use age as a specific criterion for the limitation of life-extending health care, I am challenging one of the most revered norms of contemporary geriatrics: that medical need and not age should be the standard of care. Yet the use of age as a principle for the allocation of resources can be perfectly valid, both a necessary and legitimate basis for providing health care to the elderly. There is not likely to be any better or less arbitrary criterion for the limiting of resources in the face of the open-ended possibilities of medical advancement in therapy for the aged.

Medical "need," in particular, can no longer work as an allocation principle. It is too elastic a concept, too much a function of the state of medical art. A person of 100 dying from congestive heart failure "needs" a heart transplant no less than someone who is 30. Are we to treat both needs as equal? That is not economically feasible or, I would argue, a sensible way to allocate scarce resources. But it would be required by a strict need-based standard.

Age is also a legitimate basis for allocation because it is a meaningful and universal category. It can be understood at the level of common sense. It is concrete enough to be employed for policy purposes. It can also, most importantly, be of value to the aged themselves if combined with an ideal of old age that focuses on its quality rather than its indefinite extension.

I have become impressed with the philosophy underlying the British health care system and the way it meets the needs of the old and the chronically ill. It has, to begin with, a tacit allocation policy. It emphasizes improving the quality of life through primary care medicine and well-subsidized home care and institutional programs for the elderly rather than through life-extending acute care medicine. The well-known difficulty in getting dialysis after 55 is matched by like restrictions on access to open heart surgery, intensive care units, and other forms of expensive technology. An undergirding skepticism toward technology makes that a viable option. That attitude, together with a powerful drive for equity, "explains," as two commentators have noted, "why most British put a higher value on primary care for the population as a whole than on an abundance of sophisticated technology for the few who may benefit from it."[6]

That the British spend a significantly smaller proportion of their GNP (6.2%) on health care than Americans (10.8%) for an almost identical outcome in health status is itself a good advertisement for its priorities. Life expectancies are, for men, 70.0 years in the U.S. and 70.4 years in Great Britain; and, for women, 77.8 in the U.S. and 76.7 in Great Britain. There is, of course, a great difference in the U.S. and Britain, and our individualism and love of technology stand in the way of a quick shift of priorities.

Yet our present American expectations about aging and death, it turns out, may not be all that reassuring. How many of us are really so certain that high-technology American medicine promises us all that much better an aging and death, even if some features appear improved and the process begins later than in earlier times? Between the widespread fear of death in an impersonal ICU, cozened about machines and invaded by tubes, on the one hand, or wasting away in the back ward of a nursing home, on the other, not many of us seem comforted.

Once we have reflected on those fears, it is not impossible that most people could be persuaded that a different, more limited set of expectations for health care could be made tolerable. That would be all the more possible if there was a greater assurance than at present that one could live out a full life span, that one's chronic illnesses would be better supported, and that long-term care and home care would be given a more powerful societal backing than is now the case. Though they would face a denial of life-extending medical care beyond a certain age, the old would not necessarily fear their aging anymore than they now do. They would, on the contrary, know that a better balance had been struck between making our later years as good as possible rather than simply trying to add more years.

This direction would not immediately bring down the costs of care of the elderly; it would add new costs. But it would set in place the beginning of a new understanding of old age, one that would admit of eventual stabilization and limits. The time has come to admit we can not go on much longer on the present course of open-ended health care for the elderly. Neither confident assertions about American affluence, nor tinkering with entitlement provisions and cost-containment strategies will work for more than a few more years. It is time for the dream that old age can be an infinite and open frontier to end, and for the unflagging, but self-deceptive, optimism that we can do anything we want with our economic system to be put aside.

The elderly will not be served by a belief that only a lack of resources, or better financing mechanisms, or political power, stand between them and the limitations of their bodies. The good of younger age groups will not be served by inspiring in them a desire to live to an old age that will simply extend the vitality of youth indefinitely, as if old age is nothing but a sign that medicine has failed in its mission. The future of our society will not be served by allowing expenditures on health care for the elderly endlessly and uncontrollably to escalate, fueled by a false altruism that thinks anything less is to deny the elderly their dignity. Nor will it be served by that pervasive kind of self-serving that urges the young to support such a crusade because they will eventually benefit from it also.

We require instead an understanding of the process of aging and death that looks to our obligation to the young and to the future, that recognizes the necessity of limits and the acceptance of decline and death, and that values the old for their age and not for their continuing youthful vitality. In the name of accepting the elderly and repudiating discrimination against them, we have mainly succeeded in pretending that, with enough will and money, the unpleasant part of old age can be abolished. In the name of medical progress we have carried out a relentless war against death and decline, failing to ask in any probing way if that will give us a better society for all age groups.

The proper question is not whether we are succeeding in giving a longer life to the aged. It is whether we are making of old age a decent and honorable time of life. Neither a longer lifetime nor more life-extending technology are the way to that goal. The elderly themselves ask for greater financial security, for as much self-determination and independence as possible, for a decent quality of life and not just more life, and for a respected place in society.

The best way to achieve those goals is not simply to say more money and better programs are needed, however much they have their important place. We would do better to begin with a sense of limits, of the meaning of the human life cycle, and of the necessary coming and going of the generations. From that kind of starting point, we could devise a new understanding of old age.

NOTES

1. S. H. Preston, "Children and the Elderly: Divergent Paths for America's Dependents," *Demography*, 21 (1984), 491–495.

2. Americans for Generational Equity, "Case Statement," May 1986.

3. V. R. Fuchs, "Though Much Is Taken: Reflections on Aging, Health, and Medical Care, "*Milbank Memorial Fund Quarterly,* 62 (1984), 464–465.

4. J. L. Avorn, "Medicine, Health, and the Geriatric Transformation," *Daedalus,* 115 (1986), 211–225.

5. G. Calabresi and P. Bobbitt, *Tragic Choices.* (New York: W. W. Norton, 1978).

6. F. H. Miller and G. A. H. Miller, "The Painful Prescription: A Procrustean Perspective," *N. Engl. J. Med.,* 314 (1986), 1385.

REVIEW AND DISCUSSION QUESTIONS

1. Describe the problems with health care that Callahan identifies.
2. What should be the goal of medicine for the aged, according to Callahan?
3. What principles does he recommend for limiting public health care for the aged?
4. Which of the different positions on economic justice and welfare you have studied seems closest to the one Callahan relies on here? Explain.
5. Would Walzer agree with Callahan about the need to reform our health care system? Explain.
6. Explain whether James Rachels would think free medical care is just.
7. What do you think is the major weakness in Callahan's proposals?
8. Is Medicare a "welfare" program? Explain.
9. Compare Callahan's position on the value of life with authors you read on the problems of euthanasia, animals, and the environment.

11
Liberty and Its Limits

Liberty, we all tend to assume, is valuable and important. But why is that the case? Philosophers have offered different answers to that question. But perhaps the classic defense of individual liberty comes from John Stuart Mill and the utilitarian tradition, for it is Mill who famously claims that people have a right to act however they wish as long as they do not harm others. Following Mill's classic essay *On Liberty* are four readings, each addressing the problem of legal paternalism. Under what circumstances, they ask, may government interfere with liberty in the name of keeping a person from harming herself? Topics discussed here include people who refuse medical treatment or take various types of addictive drugs, alcohol, and tobacco.

On Liberty

John Stuart Mill

None of Mill's works has had a greater impact than *On Liberty;* its ideas are often discussed by academics, politicians, and the general public, even by people who have never heard of him. According to letters and other material from Mill's life, *On Liberty* should be thought of as a joint work authored by Mill himself and his long-time friend Harriet Taylor. Mill even said in a letter that there was not a sentence in the book that the two did not go over together many times. (Harriet Taylor also had a major role in other works, including *The Subjection of Women,* also reprinted here.) For a brief description of John Stuart Mill's life, see the introduction to his essay in Section 2; for a description of his relationship with Taylor, see the introduction to *The Subjection of Women* in Section 15.

In *On Liberty,* Mill examines a fundamental question of political philosophy: What are the limits of society's power over the individual? Mill's answer is that society may interfere with an individual's speech or actions only on the grounds of self-protection. Accordingly, Mill first discusses the history of the fight of the individual against tyrannical government. He next turns to the realm of freedom of thought, vigorously upholding freedom of opinion regardless of whether the belief is true or false. Indeed, he argues, it is essential that all opinions, including false ones, be freely expressed. Then Mill discusses the importance of individuality to a person's overall well-being, and, finally, he considers his famous "harm principle"—government is justified in interfering with a citizen's liberty only if the action involves a threat of harm to others.

From John Stuart Mill, *On Liberty* (1859).

INTRODUCTORY

The subject of this essay is . . . civil, or social liberty: the nature and limits of power which can be legitimately exercised by society over the individual. . . .

The struggle between liberty and authority is the most conspicuous feature in the portions of history with which we are earliest familiar, particularly in that of Greece, Rome, and England. But in old times this contest was between subjects, or some classes of subjects, and the government. By liberty, was meant protection against the tyranny of the political rulers. The rulers were conceived (except in some of the popular governments of Greece) as in a necessarily antagonistic position to the people whom they ruled. . . .

A time, however, came, in the progress of human affairs, when men ceased to think it a necessity of nature that their governors should be an independent power, opposed in interest to themselves. It appeared to them much better that the various magistrates of the State should be their tenants or delegates, revocable at their pleasure. In that way alone, it seemed, could they have complete security that the powers of government would never be abused to their disadvantage. By degrees this new demand for elective and temporary rulers became the prominent object of the exertions of the popular party, wherever any such party existed; and superseded, to a considerable extent, the previous efforts to limit the power of rulers. . . .

But in political and philosophical theories, as well as in persons, success discloses faults and infirmities which failure might have concealed from observation. . . . It was now perceived that such phrases as "self-government," and "the power of the people over themselves," do not express the true state of the case. The "people" who exercise the power are not always the same people with those over whom it is exercised; and the "self-government" spoken of is not the government of each by himself, but of each by all the rest. The will of the people, moreover, practically means the will of the most numerous or the most active *part* of the people—the majority, or those who succeed in making themselves accepted as the majority;

the people, consequently, may desire to oppress a part of their number, and precautions are as much needed against this as against any other abuse of power. The limitation, therefore, of the power of government over individuals loses none of its importance when the holders of power are regularly accountable to the community, that is, to the strongest party therein. . . .

The object of this essay is to assert one very simple principle, as entitled to govern absolutely the dealings of society with the individual in the way of compulsion and control, whether the means used be physical force in the form of legal penalties or the moral coercion of public opinion. That principle is, that the sole end for which mankind are warranted, individually or collectively, in interfering with the liberty of action of any of their number, is self-protection. That the only purpose for which power can be rightfully exercised over any member of a civilized community, against his will, is to prevent harm to others. His own good, either physical or moral, is not a sufficient warrant. He cannot rightfully be compelled to do or forbear because it will be better for him to do so, because it will make him happier, because, in the opinions of others, to do so would be wise or even right. These are good reasons for remonstrating with him, or reasoning with him, or persuading him, or entreating him, but not for compelling him or visiting him with any evil in case he do otherwise. To justify that, the conduct from which it is desired to deter him must be calculated to produce evil to someone else. The only part of the conduct of anyone, for which he is amenable to society, is that which concerns others. In the part which merely concerns himself, his independence is, of right, absolute. Over himself, over his own body and mind, the individual is sovereign.

It is, perhaps, hardly necessary to say that this doctrine is meant to apply only to human beings in the maturity of their faculties. We are not speaking of children, or of young persons below the age which the law may fix as that of manhood or womanhood. Those who are still in a state to require being taken care of by others, must be protected against their own actions as well as against external injury. For the same reason, we may leave out of consideration those backward states of society in which the race itself may be considered as in its nonage. The early difficulties in the way of spontaneous progress are so great, and there is seldom any choice of means for overcoming them; and a ruler full of the spirit of improvement is warranted in the use of any expedients that will attain an end, perhaps otherwise unattainable. Despotism is a legitimate mode of government in dealing with barbarians, provided the end be their improvement, and the means justified by actually effecting that end. Liberty, as a principle, has no application to any state of things anterior to the time when mankind have become capable of being improved by free and equal discussion. Until then, there is nothing for them but implicit obedience to an Akbar or a Charlemagne, if they are so fortunate as to find one. But as soon as mankind have attained the capacity of being guided to their own improvement by conviction or persuasion (a period long since reached in all nations with whom we need here concern ourselves), compulsion, either in the direct form or in that of pains and penalties for noncompliance, is no longer admissible as a means to their own good, and justifiable only for the security of others.

It is proper to state that I forego any advantage which could be derived to my argument from the idea of abstract right, as a thing independent of utility. I regard utility as the ultimate appeal on all ethical questions; but it must be utility in the largest sense, grounded on the permanent interests of a man as a progressive being. These interests, I contend, authorized the subjection of individual spontaneity to external control, only in respect to those actions of each which concern the interest of other people. If anyone does an act hurtful to others, there is a *prima facie* case for punishing him, by law, or, where legal penalties are not safely applicable, by general disapprobation. There are also many positive acts for the benefit of others, which he may rightfully be compelled to perform: such as to give evidence in a court of justice; to bear his fair share in the common defense, or in any other joint work necessary to the interest of the society of which he enjoys the protection; and to perform certain acts of individual beneficence, such as saving a fellow-creature's life, or interposing to protect the defenseless against ill-usage, things which

whenever it is obviously a man's duty to do, he may rightfully be made responsible to society for not doing. A person may cause evil to others not only by his actions but by his inaction, and in either case he is justly accountable to them for the injury. The latter case, it is true, requires a much more cautious exercise of compulsion than the former. . . .

. . . This, then is the appropriate region of human liberty. It comprises, *first,* the inward domain of consciousness; demanding liberty of conscience in the most comprehensive sense; liberty of thought and feeling; absolute freedom of opinion and sentiment on all subjects, practical or speculative, scientific, moral or theological. . . . *Secondly,* the principle requires liberty of tastes and pursuits; of framing the plan of our life to suit our own character; of doing as we like, subject to such consequences as may follow: without impediment from our fellow-creatures, so long as what we do does not harm them, even though they should think our conduct foolish, perverse, or wrong. *Thirdly,* from this liberty of each individual, follows the liberty, within the same limits, of combinations among individuals; freedom to unite, for any purpose not involving harm to others: the persons combining being supposed to be of full age, and not forced or deceived.

No society in which these liberties are not, on the whole, respected, is free, whatever may be its form of government; and none is completely free in which they do not exist absolute and unqualified. The only freedom which deserves the name, is that of pursuing our own good in our own way, as long as we do not attempt to deprive others of theirs, or impede their efforts to obtain it. Each is the proper guardian of his own health, whether bodily, or mental and spiritual. . . . *[Mill next discussed liberty of thought and discussion, an essay which is reprinted below—Ed.]*

OF INDIVIDUALITY, AS ONE OF THE ELEMENTS OF WELL-BEING

. . . No one pretends that actions should be as free as opinions. On the contrary, even opinions lose their immunity when the circumstances in which they are expressed are such as to constitute their expression a positive instigation to some mischievous act. An opinion that corn-dealers are starvers of the poor, or that private property is robbery, ought to be unmolested when simply circulated through the press, but may justly incur punishment when delivered orally to an excited mob assembled before the house of a corn-dealer, or when handed about among the same mob in the form of a placard. . . . It is desirable, in short, that in things which do not primarily concern others, individuality should assert itself. Where not the person's own character, but the traditions or customs of other people are the rule of conduct, there is wanting one of the principal ingredients of human happiness, and quite the chief ingredient of individual and social progress.

In maintaining this principle, the greatest difficulty to be encountered does not lie in the appreciation of means towards an acknowledged end, but in the indifference of persons in general to the end itself. If it were felt that the free development of individuality is one of the leading essentials of well-being; that it is not only a co-ordinate element with all that is designated by the terms civilization, instruction, education, culture, but is itself a necessary part and condition of all those things; there would be no danger that liberty should be undervalued, and the adjustment of the boundaries between it and social control would present no extraordinary difficulty. But the evil is, that individual spontaneity is hardly recognized by the common modes of thinking as having any intrinsic worth, or deserving any regard on its own account. . . . Few persons, out of Germany, even comprehend the meaning of the doctrine which Wilhelm von Humboldt, so eminent both as a savant and as a politician, made the text of a treatise—that "the end of man, or that which is prescribed by the eternal or immutable dictates of reason, and not suggested by vague and transient desires, is the highest and most harmonious development of his powers to a complete and consistent whole," that, therefore, the object "towards which every human being must ceaselessly direct his efforts, and on which especially those who design to influence their fellow-men must ever keep their eyes, is the individuality of power and development;" that for this there are two requisites, "freedom, and variety of situations;" and that from

the union of these arise "individual vigor and manifold diversity," which combine themselves in "originality." . . .

He who lets the world, or his own portion of it, choose his plan of life for him, has no need of any other faculty than the ape-like one of imitation. He who chooses his plan for himself, employs all his faculties. He must use observation to see, reasoning and judgments to foresee, activity to gather materials for decision, discrimination to decide, and when he has decided, firmness and self-control to hold to his deliberate decision. And these qualities he requires and exercises exactly in proportion as the part of his conduct which he determines according to his own judgment and feelings is a large one. It is possible that he might be guided in some good path, and kept out of harm's way, without any of these things. But what will be his comparative worth as a human being? It really is of importance, not only what men do, but also what manner of men they are that do it. Among the works of man which human life is rightly employed in perfecting and beautifying, the first in importance surely is man himself. . . . Human nature is not a machine to be built after a model, and set to do exactly the work prescribed for it, but a tree, which requires to grow and develop itself on all sides, according to the tendency of the inward forces which make it a living thing, . . .

But society has now fairly got the better of individuality. . . . In our times, from the highest class of society down to the lowest, everyone lives as under the eye of a hostile and dreaded censorship. Not only in what concerns others, but in what concerns only themselves, the individual or the family do not ask themselves—what do I prefer? or, what would suit my character and disposition? or, what would allow the best and highest in me to have fair play, and enable it to grow and thrive? They ask themselves, what is suitable to my position? what is usually done by persons of my station and pecuniary circumstances? or (worse still) what is usually done by persons of a station and circumstances superior to mine? I do not mean that they choose what is customary in preference to what suits their own inclination. It does not occur to them to have any inclination, except for what is customary. Thus the mind itself is bowed to the yoke: even in what people do for pleasure, conformity is the first thing thought of; they like crowds; they exercise choice only among things commonly done: peculiarity of taste, eccentricity of conduct, are shunned equally with crimes: until by dint of not following their own nature they have no nature to follow: their human capacities are withered and starved: they become incapable of any strong wishes or native pleasures, and are generally without either opinions or feelings of home growth, or properly their own. Now is this, or is it not, the desirable condition of human nature? . . .

OF THE LIMITS TO THE AUTHORITY OF SOCIETY OVER THE INDIVIDUAL

. . . Though society is not founded on a contract, and though no good purpose is answered by inventing a contract in order to deduce social obligations from it, everyone who receives the protection of society owes a return for the benefit, and the fact of living in society renders it indispensable that each should be bound to observe a certain line of conduct towards the rest. This conduct consists, *first,* in not injuring the interests of one another; or rather certain interests, which either by express legal provision or by tacit understanding, ought to be considered as rights; and *secondly,* in each person's bearing his share (to be fixed on some equitable principle) of the labors and sacrifices incurred for defending the society or its members from injury and molestation. These conditions society is justified in enforcing, at all costs to those who endeavor to withhold fulfillment. Nor is this all that society may do. The acts of an individual may be hurtful to others, or wanting in due consideration for their welfare, without going to the length of violating any of their constituted rights. The offender may then be justly punished by opinion, though not by law. As soon as any part of a person's conduct affects prejudicially the interests of others, society has jurisdiction over it, and the question whether the general welfare will or will not be promoted by interfering with it, becomes open to discussion. But there is no room for entertaining any such question when a person's conduct affects the interests of no persons besides himself, or need not affect them un-

less they like (all the persons concerned being of full age, and the ordinary amount of understanding). In all such cases, there should be perfect freedom, legal and social, to do the action and stand the consequences.

It would be a great misunderstanding of this doctrine to suppose that it is one of selfish indifference, which pretends that human beings have no business with each other's conduct in life, and that they should not concern themselves about the well-doing or well-being of one another, unless their own interest is involved. Instead of any diminution, there is need of a great increase of disinterested exertion to promote the good of others. But disinterested benevolence can find other instruments to persuade people to their good than whips and scourges, either of the literal or the metaphorical sort. I am the last person to undervalue the self-regarding virtues: they are only second in importance, if even second, to the social. It is equally the business of education to cultivate both. But even education works by conviction and persuasion as well as by compulsion, and it is by the former only that, when the period of education is passed, the self-regarding virtues should be inculcated. Human beings owe to each other help to distinguish the better from the worse, and encouragement to choose the former and avoid the latter. They should be forever stimulating each other to increased exercise of their higher faculties, and increased direction of their feelings and aims towards wise instead of foolish, elevating instead of degrading, objects and contemplations. But neither one person, nor any number of persons, is warranted in saying to another human creature of ripe years, that he shall not do with his life for his own benefit what he chooses to do with it. He is the person most interested in his own well-being: the interest which any other person, except in cases of strong personal attachment, can have in it, is trifling, compared with that which he himself has; the interest which society has in him individually (except as to conduct to others) is fractional, and altogether indirect; while with respect to his own feelings and circumstances, the most ordinary man or woman has means of knowledge immeasurably surpassing those that can be possessed by anyone else. The interference of society to overrule his judgment and purposes in what only regards himself must be grounded on general presumptions; which may be altogether wrong, and even if right, are as likely as not to be misapplied to individual cases, by persons no better acquainted with the circumstances of such cases than those are who look at them merely from without. In this department, therefore, of human affairs, individuality has its proper field of action. In the conduct of human beings towards one another it is necessary that general rules should for the most part be observed, in order that people may know what they have to expect; but in each person's own concerns his individual spontaneity is entitled to free exercise. Considerations to aid his judgment, exhortations to strengthen his will, may be offered to him, even obtruded on him, by others: but he himself is the final judge. All errors which he is likely to commit against advice and warning are far outweighed by the evil of allowing others to constrain him to what they deem his good. . . .

Though doing no wrong to anyone, a person may so act as to compel us to judge him, and feel to him, as a fool, or as a being of an inferior order; and since this judgment and feeling are a fact which he would prefer to avoid, it is doing him a service to warn him of it beforehand, as of any other disagreeable consequence to which he exposes himself. . . . We have a right, also, in various ways, to act upon our unfavorable opinion of anyone, not to the oppression of his individuality, but in the exercise of ours. We are not bound, for example, to seek his society; we have a right to avoid it (though not to parade the avoidance), for we have a right to choose the society most acceptable to us. We have a right, and it may be our duty, to caution others against him, if we think his example or conversation likely to have a pernicious effect on those with whom he associates. We may give others a preference over him in optional good offices, except those which tend to his improvement. In these various modes a person may suffer very severe penalties at the hands of others for faults which directly concern only himself; but he suffers these penalties only in so far as they are the natural and, as it were, the spontaneous consequences of the faults themselves, not because they are purposely inflicted on him for the sake of punishment. . . .

What I contend for is, that the inconveniences which are strictly inseparable from the unfavorable judgment of others, are the only ones to which a person should ever be subjected for that portion of his conduct and character which concerns his own good, but which does not affect the interest of others in their relations with him. Acts injurious to others require a totally different treatment. Encroachment on their rights; infliction on them of any loss or damage not justified by his own rights; falsehood or duplicity in dealing with them; unfair or ungenerous use of advantages over them; even selfish abstinence from defending them against injury—these are fit objects of moral reprobation, and, in grave cases, of moral retribution and punishment. And not only these acts, but the dispositions which lead to them, are properly immoral, and fit subjects of disapprobation which may rise to abhorrence. . . .

The distinction here pointed out between the part of a person's life which concerns only himself, and that which concerns others, many persons will refuse to admit. How (it may be asked)—can any part of the conduct of a member of society be a matter of indifference to the other members? No person is an entirely isolated being; it is impossible for a person to do anything seriously or permanently hurtful to himself, without mischief reaching at least to his near connections, and often far beyond them. If he injures his property, he does harm to those who directly or indirectly derived support from it, and usually diminishes, by a greater or less amount, the general resources of the community. If he deteriorates his bodily or mental faculties, he not only brings evil upon all who depended on him for any portion of their happiness, but disqualifies himself for rendering the services which he owes to his fellow-creatures generally; perhaps becomes a burden on their affection or benevolence; and if such conduct were very frequent, hardly an offense that is committed would detract more from the general sum of good. Finally, if by his vices or follies a person does not direct harm to others, he is nevertheless (it may be said) injurious by his example; and ought to be compelled to control himself, for the sake of those whom the sight or knowledge of his conduct might corrupt or mislead.

And even (it will be added) if the consequences of misconduct could be confined to the vicious or thoughtless individual, ought society to abandon to their own guidance those who are manifestly unfit for it? If protection against themselves is confessedly due to children and persons under age, is not society equally bound to afford it to persons of mature years who are equally incapable of self-government? If gambling, or drunkenness, or incontinence, or idleness, or uncleanliness, are as injurious to happiness, and as great a hindrance to improvement, as many or most of the acts prohibited by law, why (it may be asked) should not law, so far as is consistent with practicability and social convenience, endeavor to repress these also? And as a supplement to the unavoidable imperfections of law, ought not opinion at least to organize a powerful police against these vices, and visit rigidly with social penalties those who are known to practice them? There is no question here (it may be said) about restricting individuality, or impeding the trial of new and original experiments in living. The only things it is sought to prevent are things which have been tried and condemned from the beginning of the world until now; things which experience has shown not to be useful or suitable to any person's individuality. There must be some length of time and amount of experience after which a moral or prudential truth may be regarded as established: and it is merely desired to prevent generation after generation from falling over the same precipice which has been fatal to their predecessors.

I fully admit that the mischief which a person does to himself may seriously affect, both through their sympathies and their interests, those nearly connected with him and, in a minor degree, society at large. When, by conduct of this sort, a person is led to violate a distinct and assignable obligation to any other person or persons, the case is taken out of the self-regarding class and becomes amenable to moral disapprobation in the proper sense of the term. If, for example, a man, through intemperance or extravagance, becomes unable to pay his debts, or, having undertaken the moral responsibility of a family, becomes from the same cause incapable of supporting or educating them, he is deservedly reprobated, and might be justly punished; but it is for the breach of duty to

his family or creditors, not for the extravagance. If the resources which ought to have been devoted to them, had been diverted from them for the most prudent investment, the moral culpability would have been the same. George Barnwell murdered his uncle to get money for his mistress, but if he had done it to set himself up in business he would equally have been hanged. Again, in the frequent case of a man who causes grief to his family by addiction to bad habits, he deserves reproach for his unkindness or ingratitude; but so he may for cultivating habits not in themselves vicious, if they are painful to those with whom he passes his life, or who from personal ties are dependent on him for their comfort. Whoever fails in the consideration generally due to the interests and feelings of others, not being compelled by some more imperative duty, or justified by allowable self-preference, is a subject of moral disapprobation for that failure, but not for the cause of it, nor for the errors, merely personal to himself, which may have remotely led to it. In like manner, when a person disables himself, by conduct purely self-regarding, from the performance of some definite duty incumbent on him to the public, he is guilty of a social offense. No person ought to be punished simply for being drunk; but a soldier or policeman should be punished for being drunk on duty. Whenever, in short, there is a definite damage, or a definite risk of damage, either to an individual or to the public, the case is taken out of the province of liberty and placed in that of morality or law.

But with regard to the merely contingent or, as it may be called, constructive injury which a person causes to society by conduct which neither violates any specific duty to the public, nor occasions perceptible hurt to any assignable individual except himself, the inconvenience is one which society can afford to bear, for the sake of the greater good of human freedom. If grown persons are to be punished for not taking proper care of themselves, I would rather it were for their own sake than under pretense of preventing them from impairing their capacity or rendering to society benefits which society does not pretend it has a right to exact. But I cannot consent to argue the point as if society had no means of bringing its weaker members up to its ordinary standard of rational conduct, except waiting till they do something irrational, and then punishing them, legally or morally, for it. Society has had absolute power over them during all the early portion of their existence; it has had the whole period of childhood and nonage in which to try whether it could make them capable of rational conduct in life. The existing generation is master both of the training and the entire circumstances of the generation to come; it cannot indeed make them perfectly wise and good, because it is itself so lamentably deficient in goodness and wisdom; and its best efforts are not always, in individual cases, its most successful ones; but it is perfectly well able to make the rising generation, as a whole, as good as, and a little better than, itself. If society lets any considerable number of its members grow up mere children, incapable of being acted on by rational consideration of distant motives, society has itself to blame for the consequences. Armed not only with all the powers of education, but with the ascendancy which the authority of a received opinion always exercises over the minds who are least fitted to judge for themselves, and aided by the *natural* penalties which cannot be prevented from falling on those who incur the distaste or the contempt of those who know them—let not society pretend that it needs, besides all this, the power to issue commands and enforce obedience in the personal concerns of individuals in which, on all principles of justice and policy, the decision ought to rest with those who are to abide the consequences. Nor is there anything which tends more to discredit and frustrate the better means of influencing conduct than a resort to the worse. If there be among those whom it is attempted to coerce into prudence or temperance any of the material of which vigorous and independent characters are made, they will infallibly rebel against the yoke. No such person will ever feel that others have a right to control him in his concerns, such as they have to prevent him from injuring them in theirs; and it easily comes to be considered a mark of spirit and courage to fly in the face of such usurped authority and do with ostentation the exact opposite of what it enjoins, as in the fashion of grossness which succeeded, in the time of Charles II, to the fanatical moral intolerance of the Puritans. With respect to what is said of the necessity of protecting society from the bad example set to others

by the vicious or the self-indulgent, it is true that bad example may have a pernicious effect, especially the example of doing wrong to others with impunity to the wrongdoer. But we are now speaking of conduct which, while it does no wrong to others, is supposed to do great harm to the agent himself; and I do not see how those who believe this can think otherwise than that the example, on the whole, must be more salutary than hurtful, since, if it displays the misconduct, it displays also the painful or degrading consequences which, if the conduct is justly censured, must be supposed to be in all or most cases attendant on it.

But the strongest of all the arguments against the interference of the public with purely personal conduct is that, when it does interfere, the odds are that it interferes wrongly and in the wrong place. On questions of social morality, of duty to others, the opinion of the public, that is, of an overruling majority, though often wrong, is likely to be still oftener right, because on such questions they are only required to judge of their own interests, of the manner in which some mode of conduct, if allowed to be practiced, would affect themselves. But the opinion of a similar majority, imposed as a law on the minority, on questions of self-regarding conduct is quite as likely to be wrong as right, for in these cases public opinion means, at the best, some people's opinion of what is good or bad for other people, while very often it does not even mean that—the public, with the most perfect indifference, passing over the pleasure or convenience of those whose conduct they censure and considering only their own preference. There are many who consider as an injury to themselves any conduct which they have a distaste for, and resent it as an outrage to their feelings; as a religious bigot, when charged with disregarding the religious feelings of others, has been known to retort that they disregard his feelings by persisting in their abominable worship or creed. But there is no parity between the feeling of a person for his own opinion and the feeling of another who is offended at his holding it, no more than between the desire of a thief to take a purse and the desire of the right owner to keep it. And a person's taste is as much his own peculiar concern as his opinion or his purse. It is easy for anyone to imagine an ideal public which leaves the freedom and choice of individuals in all uncertain matters undisturbed and only requires them to abstain from modes of conduct which universal experience has condemned. But where has there been seen a public which set any such limit to its censorship? Or when does the public trouble itself about universal experience? In its interferences with personal conduct it is seldom thinking of anything but the enormity of acting or feeling differently from itself. . . .

APPLICATIONS

. . . It is a proper office of public authority to guard against accidents. If either a public officer or anyone else saw a person attempting to cross a bridge which had been ascertained to be unsafe, and there were no time to warn him of his danger, they might seize him and turn him back, without any real infringement of his liberty; for liberty consists in doing what one desires, and he does not desire to fall into the river. Nevertheless, when there is not a certainty, but only a danger of mischief, no one but the person himself can judge of the sufficiency of the motive which may prompt him to incur the risk; in this case, therefore (unless he is a child, or delirious, or in some state of ex-citement or absorption incompatible with the full use of the reflecting faculty), he ought, I conceive, to be only warned of the danger; not forcibly prevented from exposing himself to it. . . .

. . . In this and most other civilized countries an engagement by which a person should sell himself, or allow himself to be sold, as a slave, would be null and void; neither enforced by law nor by opinion. The ground for thus limiting his power of voluntarily disposing of his own lot in life, is apparent, and is very clearly seen in this extreme case. The reason for not interfering unless for the sake of others, with a person's voluntary acts, is consideration for his liberty. His voluntary choice is evidence that what he so chooses is desirable, or at least endurable, to him, and his good is on the whole best provided for by allowing him to take his own means of pursuing it. But by selling himself for a slave, he abdicates his liberty; he foregoes any future use of it beyond that single act. He therefore defeats, in his own case, the very purpose which is the justification of allowing him to dispose of himself. He is no longer free; but is thenceforth in a position which has no longer the presumption in its favor, that would be afforded by his voluntarily remaining in it. The principle of freedom cannot require that he should be free not to be free. It is not freedom to be allowed to alienate his freedom. . . .

REVIEW AND DISCUSSION QUESTIONS

1. Mill argues that the good life involves more than mere contentment. Of what else, specifically, does true well-being consist?

2. What "faculties" does Mill believe people living truly worthwhile and valuable lives will employ?

3. Mill admits that many acts may affect others, but he insists that unless they also harm others, government may not intervene. How does Mill define *harm?*

4. Describe how Mill thinks society may try to influence people whose actions are harmless to others, yet either immoral or not in their true interest.

5. What reasons does Mill give to support his claim that harming others is necessary to justify punishment?

6. Sometimes, Mill says, society is wise not to interfere even though an act is harmful to another. Give an example of such an act; then explain why Mill thinks society should nevertheless not interfere.

7. What does Mill say may be done if somebody is about to walk off a bridge? May society prevent suicide? Explain.

8. Why may a person not sell himself or herself into slavery, according to Mill? Is this position consistent with the rest of his essay? Explain.

9. Compare Mill's discussion of individuality in this selection with his description of the "higher" pleasures in *Utilitarianism,* and with Aristotle's discussion of happiness in *Nicomachean Ethics.*

Requiring Medical Treatment:

JFK Memorial Hospital v. *Heston*

Legal paternalism is the position that legal coercion may be used to protect individuals from self-inflicted harm; it therefore implies that sometimes the state knows the interests of individual citizens better than they themselves do. The following case, argued before the New Jersey Supreme Court, concerns a young woman who for religious reasons tried to refuse a blood transfusion deemed medically necessary to save her life.

The Opinion of the Court Was Delivered by Weintraub, C. J.: Delores Heston, age 22 and unmarried, was severely injured in an automobile accident. She was taken to the plaintiff's hospital where it was determined that she would expire unless operated upon for a ruptured spleen and that if operated upon she would expire unless whole blood was administered. Miss Heston and her parents are Jehovah's Witnesses and a tenet of their faith forbids blood transfusions. Miss Heston insists she expressed her refusal to accept blood, but the evidence indicates she was in shock on admittance to the hospital and in the judgment of the attending physicians and nurses was then or soon became disoriented and incoherent. Her mother remained adamant in her opposition to a transfusion, and signed a release of liability for the hospital and medical personnel. Miss Heston did not execute a release; presumably she could not. Her father could not be located.

Death being imminent, plaintiff on notice to the mother made application at 1:30 A.M. to a judge of the Superior Court for the appointment of a guardian for Miss Heston with directions to consent to transfusions as needed to save her life. At the hearing, the mother and her friends thought a certain doctor would pursue surgery without a transfusion, but the doctor, in response to the judge's telephone call, declined the case. The court appointed a guardian with authority to consent to blood transfusions "for the preservation of the life of Delores Heston." Surgery was performed at 4:00 A.M. the same morning. Blood was administered. Miss Heston survived.

Defendants then moved to vacate the order. Affidavits were submitted by both sides. The trial court declined to vacate the order. This appeal followed. We certified it before argument in the Appellate Division.

The controversy is moot. Miss Heston is well and no longer in plaintiff's hospital. The prospect of her return at some future day in like circumstances is too remote to warrant a declaratory judgment as between the parties. Nonetheless, the public interest warrants a resolution of the cause, and for that reason we accept the issue. . . .

58 N.J. 576 (1971).

In *Perricone*, we sustained an order for compulsory blood transfusion for an infant despite the objection of the parents who were Jehovah's Witnesses. In *Raleigh Fitkin-Paul Morgan Memorial Hospital* v. *Anderson, N. J.* (1964), it appeared that both the mother, a Jehovah's Witness, and the child she was bearing would die if blood were not transfused should she hemorrhage. We held that a blood transfusion could be ordered if necessary to save the lives of the mother and the unborn child. We said:

We have no difficulty in so deciding with respect to the infant child. The more difficult question is whether an adult may be compelled to submit to such medical procedures when necessary to save his life. Here we think it is unnecessary to decide that question in broad terms because the welfare of the child and the mother are so intertwined and inseparable that it would be impracticable to attempt to distinguish between them with respect to the sundry factual patterns which may develop. The blood transfusions (including transfusions made necessary by the delivery) may be administered if necessary to save her life or the life of her child, as the physician in charge at the time may determine.

The case at hand presents the question we thus reserved in *Raleigh Fitkin-Paul Morgan Memorial Hospital.*

It seems correct to say there is no constitutional right to choose to die. Attempted suicide was a crime at common law and was held to be a crime under N.J.S.A. 2A:85–1. It is now denounced as a disorderly persons offense. N.J.S.A. 2A:170–25.6. Ordinarily nothing would be gained by a prosecution, and hence the offense is rarely charged. Nonetheless the Constitution does not deny the State an interest in the subject. It is commonplace for the police and other citizens, often at great risk to themselves, to use force or stratagem to defeat efforts at suicide, and it could hardly be said that thus to save someone from himself violated a right of his under the Constitution subjecting the rescuer to civil or penal consequences.

Nor is constitutional right established by adding that one's religious faith ordains his death. Religious beliefs are absolute, but conduct in pursuance of religious beliefs is not wholly immune from governmental restraint. *Mountain Lakes Bd. of Educ.* v. *Maas, N. J.* (1960) (vaccination of children); *Bunn* v. *North Carolina* (1949) (the use of snakes in a religious ritual); *Baer* v. *City of Bend, Or.* (1956) (fluoridation of drinking water). Of immediate interest is *Reynolds* v. *United States* (1878), in which it was held that Congress could punish polygamy in a territory notwithstanding that polygamy was permitted or demanded by religious tenet, and in which the Court said:

Laws are made for the government of actions, and while they cannot interfere with mere religious belief and opinions, they may with practices. Suppose one believed that human sacrifices were a necessary part of religious worship, would it be seriously contended that the civil government under which he lived could not interfere to prevent a sacrifice? Or if a wife religiously believed it was her duty to burn herself upon the funeral pile of her dead husband, would it be beyond the power of the civil government to prevent her carrying her belief into practice?

Complicating the subject of suicide is the difficulty of knowing whether a decision to die is firmly held. Psychiatrists may find that beneath it all a person bent on self-destruction is hoping to be rescued, and most who are rescued do not repeat the attempt, at least not at once. Then, too, there is the question whether in any event the person was and continues to be competent (a difficult concept in this area) to choose to die. And of course there is no opportunity for a trial of these questions in advance of intervention by the State or a citizen.

Appellant suggests there is a difference between passively submitting to death and actively seeking it. The distinction may be merely verbal, as it would be if an adult sought death by starvation instead of a drug. If the State may interrupt one mode of self-destruction, it may with equal authority interfere with the other. It is arguably different when an individual, overtaken by illness, decides to let it run a fatal course. But unless the medical option itself is laden with the risk of death or of serious infirmity, the State's interest in sustaining life in such circumstances is hardly distinguishable from its interest in the case of suicide.

Here we are not dealing with deadly options. The risk of death or permanent injury because of a transfusion is not a serious factor. Indeed, Miss Heston did not resist a transfusion on that basis.

Nor did she wish to die. She wanted to live, but her faith demanded that she refuse blood even at the price of her life. The question is not whether the State could punish her for refusing a transfusion. It may be granted that it would serve no State interest to deal criminally with one who resisted a transfusion on the basis of religious faith. The question is whether the State may authorize force to prevent death or may tolerate the use of force by others to that end. Indeed, the issue is not solely between the State and Miss Heston, for the controversy is also between Miss Heston and a hospital and staff who did not seek her out and upon whom the dictates of her faith will fall as a burden.

Hospitals exist to aid the sick and the injured. The medical and nursing professions are consecrated to preserving life. That is their professional creed. To them, a failure to use a simple, established procedure in the circumstances of this case would be malpractice, however the law may characterize that failure because of the patient's private convictions. A surgeon should not be asked to operate under the strain of knowing that a transfusion may not be administered even though medically required to save this patient. The hospital and its staff should not be required to decide whether the patient is or continues to be competent to make a judgment upon the subject, or whether the re-lease tendered by the patient or a member of his family will protect them from civil responsibility. The hospital could hardly avoid the problem by compelling the removal of a dying patient, and Miss Heston's family made no effort to take her elsewhere.

When the hospital and staff are thus involuntary hosts and their interests are pitted against the belief of the patient, we think it reasonable to resolve the problem by permitting the hospital and its staff to pursue their functions according to their professional standards. The solution sides with life, the conservation of which is, we think, a matter of State interest. A prior application to a court is appropriate if time permits it, although in the nature of the emergency the only question that can be explored satisfactorily is whether death will probably ensue if medical procedures are not followed. If a court finds, as the trial court did, that death will likely follow unless a transfusion is administered, the hospital and the physician should be permitted to follow that medical procedure.

For the reasons already given, we find that the interest of the hospital and its staff, as well as the State's interest in life, warranted the transfusion of blood under the circumstances of this case. The judgment is accordingly affirmed.

REVIEW AND DISCUSSION QUESTIONS

1. On what ground does the court reach its opinion that Delores Heston should be forced to accept the transfusion?
2. How would Mill respond to this case? Explain.
3. If the woman's reasons were not based on established religious doctrine, do you think the courts would have had so much difficulty with these decisions? Would you? Explain.
4. In Michigan, a court considered the question whether a law requiring motorcycle helmets was constitutional. Using the essays that you have read in this section, explain whether or not you think such a law is philosophically justified. (The Michigan court in fact held that the law was unconstitutional and invalidated it, saying that it could not find a strong enough relationship between the law and public health, safety, or welfare.)

The Ethics of Addiction: An Argument in Favor of Letting Americans Take Any Drug They Want

Thomas Szasz

Relying explicitly on John Stuart Mill's theory of liberty, Thomas Szasz defends legalization of drugs. After reviewing the historical effects of prohibition, he argues that prohibition leads to socially harmful consequences and also fails to respect the legitimate control citizens may exercise over their own lives. A decent regard for individual liberty demands that government respect its citizens' right to "life, liberty, and the pursuit of highs." Thomas Szasz is a psychiatrist and the author of many books.

To avoid clichés about "drug abuse," let us analyze its official definition. According to the World Health Organization, "Drug addiction is a state of periodic or chronic intoxication detrimental to the individual and to society, produced by the repeated consumption of a drug (natural or synthetic). Its characteristics include: (1) an overpowering desire or need (compulsion) to continue taking the drug and to obtain it by any means, (2) a tendency to increase the dosage, and (3) a psychic (psychological) and sometimes physical dependence on the effects of the drug."

Since this definition hinges on the harm done to both the individual and society, it is clearly an ethical one. Moreover, by not specifying what is "detrimental," it consigns the problem of addiction to psychiatrists who define the patient's "dangerousness to himself and others."

Next, we come to the effort to obtain the addictive substance "by any means." This suggests that the substance must be prohibited, or is very expensive, and is hence difficult for the ordinary person to obtain (rather than that the person who wants it has an inordinate craving for it). If there were an abundant and inexpensive supply of what the "addict" wants, there would be no reason for him to go to "any means" to obtain it. Thus by the WHO's definition, one can be addicted only to a substance that is illegal or otherwise difficult to obtain. This surely removes the problem of addiction from the realm of medicine and psychiatry, and puts it squarely into that of morals and law.

In short, drug addiction or drug abuse cannot be defined without specifying the proper and improper uses of certain pharmacologically active agents. The regular administration of morphine by a physician to a patient dying of cancer is the paradigm of the proper use of a narcotic; whereas even its occasional self-administration by a physically healthy person for the purpose of "pharmacological pleasure" is the paradigm of drug abuse.

I submit that these judgments have nothing whatever to do with medicine, pharmacology, or psychiatry. They are moral judgments. Indeed, our present views on addiction are astonishingly similar to some of our former views on sex. Until recently, masturbation—or self-abuse, as it was called—was professionally declared, and popularly accepted, as both the cause and the symptom of a variety of illnesses. Even today, homosexuality—called a "sexual perversion"—is regarded as a disease by medical and psychiatric experts as well as by "well-informed" laymen.

To be sure, it is now virtually impossible to cite a contemporary medical authority to support the concept of self-abuse. Medical opinion holds that whether a person masturbates or not is medically irrelevant:and that engaging in the practice or refraining from it is a matter of personal morals or life-style. On the other hand, it is virtually impossible to cite a contemporary medical authority to oppose the concept of drug abuse. Medical opinion holds that drug abuse is a major medical, psychiatric, and public health problem; that drug addiction is a disease similar to diabetes, requiring prolonged (or lifelong) and careful, medically supervised treatment; and that taking or not taking drugs is primarily, if not solely, a matter of medical responsibility.

Thus the man on the street can only believe what he hears from all sides—that drug addiction is a disease, "like any other," which has now reached "epidemic proportions," and whose "medical" containment justifies the limitless expenditure of tax monies and the corresponding aggrandizement and enrichment of noble medical warriors against this "plague."

PROPAGANDA TO JUSTIFY PROHIBITION

Like any social policy, our drug laws may be examined from two entirely different points of view: technical and moral. Our present inclination is either to ignore the moral perspective or to mistake the technical for the moral.

Since most of the propagandists against drug abuse seek to justify certain repressive policies because of the alleged dangerousness of various drugs, they often falsify the facts about the true pharmacological properties of the drugs they seek to prohibit. They do so for two reasons: first, because many substances in daily use are just as harmful as the substances they want to prohibit: second, because they realize that dangerousness alone is never a sufficiently persuasive argument to justify the prohibition of any drug, substance, or artifact. Accordingly, the more they ignore the moral dimensions of the problem, the more they must escalate their fraudulent claims about the dangers of drugs.

To be sure, some drugs are more dangerous than others. It is easier to kill oneself with heroin than with aspirin. But it is also easier to kill one-self by jumping off a high building than a low one. In the case of drugs, we regard their potentiality for self-injury as justification for their prohibition: in the case of buildings, we do not.

Furthermore, we systematically blur and confuse the two quite different ways in which narcotics may cause death: by a deliberate act of suicide or by accidental overdosage.

Every individual is capable of injuring or killing himself. This potentiality is a fundamental expression of human freedom. Self-destructive behavior may be regarded as sinful and penalized by means of informal sanctions. But it should not be regarded as a crime or (mental) disease, justifying or warranting the use of the police powers of the state for its control.

Therefore, it is absurd to deprive an adult of a drug (or of anything else) because he might use it to kill himself. To do so is to treat everyone the way institutional psychiatrists treat the so-called suicidal mental patient: they not only imprison such a person but take everything away from him—shoelaces, belts, razor blades, eating utensils, and so forth—until the "patient" lies naked on a mattress in a padded cell—lest he kill himself. The result is degrading tyrannization.

Death by accidental overdose is an altogether different matter. But can anyone doubt that this danger now looms so large precisely because the sale of narcotics and many other drugs is illegal? Those who buy illicit drugs cannot be sure what drug they are getting or how much of it. Free trade in drugs, with governmental action limited to safeguarding the purity of the product and the veracity of the labeling, should reduce the risk of accidental overdose with "dangerous drugs" to the same levels that prevail, and that we find acceptable, with respect to other chemical agents and physical artifacts that abound in our complex technological society.

This essay is not intended as an exposition on the pharmacological properties of narcotics and other mind-affecting drugs. However, I want to make it clear that in my view, *regardless* of their danger, all drugs should be "legalized" (a misleading term I employ reluctantly as a concession to common usage). Although I recognize that some drugs—notably heroin, the amphetamines, and LSD, among those now in vogue—may have undesirable or dangerous consequences, I favor free trade in drugs for the same reason the Founding Fathers favored free trade in ideas. In an open society, it is none of the government's business what idea a man puts into his mind; likewise, it should be none of the government's business what drug he puts into his body.

WITHDRAWAL PAINS FROM TRADITION

It is a fundamental characteristic of human beings that they get used to things: one becomes habituated, or "addicted," not only to narcotics, but to cigarettes, cocktails before dinner, orange juice for breakfast, comic strips, and so forth. It is similarly a fundamental characteristic of living organisms that they acquire increasing tolerance to various chemical agents and physical stimuli: the first cigarette may cause nothing but nausea and headache; a year later, smoking three packs a day may be pure joy. Both alcohol and opiates are "addictive" in the sense that the more regularly they are used, the more the user craves them and the greater his tolerance for them becomes. Yet none of this involves any mysterious process of "getting hooked." It is simply an aspect of the universal biological propensity for *learning*, which is especially well developed in man. The opiate habit, like the cigarette habit or food habit, can be broken—and without any medical assistance—provided the person wants to break it. Often he doesn't. And why, indeed, should he, if he has nothing better to do with his life? Or, as happens to be the case with morphine, if he can live an essentially normal life while under its influence?

Actually, opium is much less toxic than alcohol. Just as it is possible to be an "alcoholic" and work and be productive, so it is (or, rather, it used to be) possible to be an opium addict and work and be productive. According to a definitive study published by the American Medical Association in 1929, ". . . morphine addiction is not characterized by physical deterioration or impairment of physical fitness. . . . There is no evidence of change in the circulatory, hepatic, renal, or endocrine functions. When it is considered that these subjects had been addicted for at least five years,

some of them for as long as twenty years, these negative observations are highly significant." In a 1928 study, Lawrence Kolb, an Assistant Surgeon General of the United States Public Health Service, found that of 119 persons addicted to opiates through medical practice, "90 had good industrial records and only 29 had poor ones. . . . Judged by the output of labor and their own statements, none of the normal persons had [his] efficiency reduced by opium. Twenty-two of them worked regularly while taking opium for twenty-five years or more; one of them, a woman aged 81 and still alert mentally, had taken 3 grains of morphine daily for 65 years. [The usual therapeutic dose is one-quarter grain, three to four grains being fatal for the nonaddict.] She gave birth to and raised six children, and managed her household affairs with more than average efficiency. A widow, aged 66, had taken 17 grains of morphine daily for most of 37 years. She is alert mentally, does physical labor every day, and makes her own living."

I am not citing this evidence to recommend the opium habit. The point is that we must, in plain honesty, distinguish between pharmacological effects and personal inclinations. Some people take drugs to help them function and conform to social expectations; others take them for the very opposite reason, to ritualize their refusal to function and conform to social expectations. Much of the "drug abuse" we now witness—perhaps nearly all of it—is of the second type. But instead of acknowledging that "addicts" are unfit or unwilling to work and be "normal," we prefer to believe that they act as they do because certain drugs—especially heroin, LSD, and the amphetamines—make them "sick." If only we could get them "well," so runs this comforting view, they would become "productive" and "useful" citizens. To believe this is like believing that if an illiterate cigarette smoker would only stop smoking, he would become an Einstein. With a falsehood like this, one can go far. No wonder that politicians and psychiatrists love it.

The concept of free trade in drugs runs counter to our cherished notion that everyone must work and idleness is acceptable only under special conditions. . . . [Drug users] are, in principle at least, capable of working and supporting themselves. But they refuse: they "drop out"; and in doing so, they challenge the most basic values of our society.

The fear that free trade in narcotics would result in vast masses of our population spending their days and nights smoking opium or mainlining heroin, rather than working and taking care of their responsibilities, is a bugaboo that does not deserve to be taken seriously. Habits of work and idleness are deep-seated cultural patterns. Free trade in abortions has not made an industrious people like the Japanese give up work for fornication. Nor would free trade in drugs convert such a people from hustlers to hippies. Indeed, I think the opposite might be the case: it is questionable whether, or for how long, a responsible people can tolerate being treated as totally irresponsible with respect to drugs and drug-taking. In other words, how long can we live with the inconsistency of being expected to be responsible for operating cars and computers, but not for operating our own bodies?

Although my argument about drug-taking is moral and political, and does not depend upon showing that free trade in drugs would also have fiscal advantages over our present policies, let me indicate briefly some of its economic implications.

The war on addiction is not only astronomically expensive; it is also counterproductive. On April 1, 1967, New York State's narcotics addiction control program, hailed as "the most massive ever tried in the nation," went into effect. "The program, which may cost up to $400 million in three years," reported the *New York Times*, "was hailed by Governor Rockefeller as 'the start of an unending war.'" Three years later, it was conservatively estimated that the number of addicts in the state had tripled or quadrupled. New York State Senator John Hughes reports that the cost of caring for each addict during this time was $12,000 per year (as against $4,000 per year for patients in state mental hospitals). It's been a great time, though, for some of the ex-addicts. In New York City's Addiction Services Agency, one ex-addict started at $6,500 a year in 1967, and was making $16,000 seven months later. Another started at $6,500 and soon rose to $18,100. The salaries of the medical bureaucrats in charge of these programs are similarly attractive. In short, the detection and rehabilitation of addicts is good

business. We now know that the spread of witchcraft in the late Middle Ages was due more to the work of witchmongers than to the lure of witchcraft. Is it not possible that the spread of addiction in our day is due more to the work of addictmongers than to the lure of narcotics?

Let us see how far some of the monies spent on the war on addiction could go in supporting people who prefer to drop out of society and drug themselves. Their "habit" itself would cost next to nothing: free trade would bring the price of narcotics down to a negligible amount. During the 1969–70 fiscal year, the New York State Narcotics Addiction Control Commission had a budget of nearly $50 million, excluding capital construction. Using these figures as a tentative base for calculation, here is what we come to. $100 million will support 30,000 drug addicts at $3,300 per year. Since the population of New York State is roughly one-tenth that of the nation, if we multiply its operating budget for addiction control by ten, we arrive at a figure of $500 million, enough to support 150,000 addicts.

I am not advocating that we spend our hard-earned money in this way. I am only trying to show that free trade in narcotics would be more economical for those of us who work, even if we had to support legions of addicts, than is our present program of trying to "cure" them. Moreover, I have not even made use, in my economic estimates, of the incalculable sums we would save by reducing crimes now engendered by the illegal traffic in drugs.

THE RIGHT OF SELF-MEDICATION

Clearly, the argument that marijuana—or heroin, methadone, or morphine—is prohibited because it is addictive or dangerous cannot be supported by facts. For one thing, there are many drugs, from insulin to penicillin, that are neither addictive nor dangerous but are nevertheless also prohibited; they can be obtained only through a physician's prescription. For another, there are many things, from dynamite to guns, that are much more dangerous than narcotics (especially to others) but are not prohibited. As everyone knows, it is still possible in the United States to walk into a store and walk out with a shotgun. We enjoy this right not because we believe that guns are safe but because we believe even more strongly that civil liberties are precious. At the same time, it is not possible in the United States to walk into a store and walk out with a bottle of barbiturates, codeine, or other drugs.

I believe that just as we regard freedom of speech and religion as fundamental rights, so we should also regard freedom of self-medication as a fundamental right. Like most rights, the right of self-medication should apply only to adults; and it should not be an unqualified right. Since these are important qualifications, it is necessary to specify their precise range.

John Stuart Mill said (approximately) that a person's right to swing his arm ends where his neighbor's nose begins. And Oliver Wendell Holmes said that no one has a right to shout "Fire!" in a crowded theater. Similarly, the limiting condition with respect to self-medication should be the inflicting of actual (as against symbolic) harm on others.

Our present practices with respect to alcohol embody and reflect this individualistic ethic. We have the right to buy, possess, and consume alcoholic beverages. Regardless of how offensive drunkenness might be to a person, he cannot interfere with another person's "right" to become inebriated so long as that person drinks in the privacy of his own home or at some other appropriate location, and so long as he conducts himself in an otherwise law-abiding manner. In short, we have a right to be intoxicated—in private. Public intoxication is considered an offense to others and is therefore a violation of the criminal law. It makes sense that what is a "right" in one place may become, by virtue of its disruptive or disturbing effect on others, an offense somewhere else.

The right to self-medication should be hedged in by similar limits. Public intoxication, not only with alcohol but with any drug, should be an offense punishable by the criminal law. Furthermore, acts that may injure others—such as driving a car—should, when carried out in a drug-intoxicated state, be punished especially strictly and severely. The right to self-medication must thus entail unqualified responsibility for the ef-

fects of one's drug-intoxicated behavior on others. For unless we are willing to hold ourselves responsible for our own behavior, and hold others responsible for theirs, the liberty to use drugs (or to engage in other acts) degenerates into a license to hurt others.

Such, then, would be the situation of adults, if we regarded the freedom to take drugs as a fundamental right similar to the freedom to read and worship. What would be the situation of children? Since many people who are now said to be drug addicts or drug abusers are minors, it is especially important that we think clearly about this aspect of the problem.

I do not believe, and I do not advocate, that children should have a right to ingest, inject, or otherwise use any drug or substance they want. Children do not have the right to drive, drink, vote, marry, or make binding contracts. They acquire these rights at various ages, coming into their full possession at maturity, usually between the ages of eighteen and twenty-one. The right to self-medication should similarly be withheld until maturity.

In short, I suggest that "dangerous" drugs be treated, more or less, as alcohol is treated now. Neither the use of narcotics, nor their possession, should be prohibited, but only their sale to minors. Of course, this would result in the ready availability of all kinds of drugs among minors—though perhaps their availability would be no greater than it is now, but would only be more visible and hence more easily subject to proper controls. This arrangement would place responsibility for the use of all drugs by children where it belongs: on parents and their children. This is where the major responsibility rests for the use of alcohol. It is a tragic symptom of our refusal to take personal liberty and responsibility seriously that there appears to be no public desire to assume a similar stance toward other "dangerous" drugs.

Consider what would happen should a child bring a bottle of gin to school and get drunk there. Would the school authorities blame the local liquor stores as pushers? Or would they blame the parents and the child himself? There is liquor in practically every home in America and yet children rarely bring liquor to school. Whereas marijuana, Dexedrine, and heroin—substances children usually do not find at home and whose very possession is a criminal offense—frequently find their way into the school.

Our attitude toward sexual activity provides another model for our attitude toward drugs. Although we generally discourage children below a certain age from engaging in sexual activities with others, we do not prohibit such activities by law. What we do prohibit by law is the sexual seduction of children by adults. The "pharmacological seduction" of children by adults should be similarly punishable. In other words, adults who give or sell drugs to children should be regarded as offenders. Such a specific and limited prohibition—as against the kinds of generalized prohibitions that we had under the Volstead Act or have now with respect to countless drugs—would be relatively easy to enforce. Moreover, it would probably be rarely violated, for there would be little psychological interest and no economic profit in doing so.

THE TRUE FAITH: SCIENTIFIC MEDICINE

What I am suggesting is that while addiction is ostensibly a medical and pharmacological problem, actually it is a moral and political problem. We ought to know that there is no necessary connection between facts and values, between what is and what ought to be. Thus, objectively quite harmful acts, objects, or persons may be accepted and tolerated—by minimizing their dangerousness. Conversely, objectively quite harmless acts, objects, or persons may be prohibited and persecuted—by exaggerating their dangerousness. It is always necessary to distinguish—and especially so when dealing with social policy—between description and prescription, fact and rhetoric, truth and falsehood.

In our society, there are two principal methods of legitimizing policy: social tradition and scientific judgment. More than anything else, time is the supreme ethical arbiter. Whatever a social practice might be, if people engage in it, generation after generation, that practice becomes acceptable.

Many opponents of illegal drugs admit that nicotine may be more harmful to health than marijuana; nevertheless, they urge that smoking cigarettes should be legal but smoking marijuana should not be, because the former habit is socially accepted while the latter is not. This is a perfectly reasonable argument. But let us understand it for what it is—a plea for legitimizing old and accepted practices, and for illegitimizing novel and unaccepted ones. It is a justification that rests on precedent, not evidence.

The other method of legitimizing policy, ever more important in the modern world, is through the authority of science. In matters of health, a vast and increasingly elastic category, physicians play important roles as legitimizers and illegitimizers. This, in short, is why we regard being medicated by a doctor as drug use, and self-medication (especially with certain classes of drugs) as drug abuse.

This, too, is a perfectly reasonable arrangement. But we must understand that it is a plea for legitimizing what doctors do, because they do it with "good therapeutic" intent; and for illegitimizing what laymen do, because they do it with bad self-abusive ("masturbatory" or mind-altering) intent. This justification rests on the principles of professionalism, not of pharmacology. Hence we applaud the systematic medical use of methadone and call it "treatment for heroin addiction," but decry the occasional nonmedical use of marijuana and call it "dangerous drug abuse."

Our present concept of drug abuse articulates and symbolizes a fundamental policy of scientific medicine—namely, that a layman should not medicate his own body but should place its medical care under the supervision of a duly accredited physician. Before the Reformation, the practice of True Christianity rested on a similar policy—namely, that a layman should not himself commune with God but should place his spiritual care under the supervision of a duly accredited priest. The self-interests of the church and of medicine in such policies are obvious enough. What might be less obvious is the interest of the laity: by delegating responsibility for the spiritual and medical welfare of the people to a class of authoritatively accredited specialists, these policies—and the practices they ensure—relieve individuals from assuming the burdens of responsibility for themselves. As I see it, our present problems with drug use and drug abuse are just one of the consequences of our pervasive ambivalence about personal autonomy and responsibility.

I propose a medical reformation analogous to the Protestant Reformation: specifically, a "protest" against the systematic mystification of man's relationship to his body and his professionalized separation from it. The immediate aim of this reform would be to remove the physician as intermediary between man and his body and to give the layman direct access to the language and contents of the pharmacopoeia. If man had unencumbered access to his own body and the means of chemically altering it, it would spell the end of medicine, at least as we now know it. This is why, with faith in scientific medicine so strong, there is little interest in this kind of medical reform. Physicians fear the loss of their privileges: laymen, the loss of their protections.

Finally, since luckily we still do not live in the utopian perfection of "one world," our technical approach to the "drug problem" has led, and will undoubtedly continue to lead, to some curious attempts to combat it.

Here is one such attempt: the American government is now pressuring Turkey to restrict its farmers from growing poppies (the source of morphine and heroin). If turnabout is fair play, perhaps we should expect the Turkish government to pressure the United States to restrict its farmers from growing corn and wheat. Or should we assume that Muslims have enough self-control to leave alcohol alone, but Christians need all the controls that politicians, policemen, and physicians can bring to bear on them to enable them to leave opiates alone?

LIFE, LIBERTY, AND THE PURSUIT OF HIGHS

Sooner or later we shall have to confront the basic moral dilemma underlying this problem: does a person have the right to take a drug, any drug—not because he needs it to cure an illness, but because he wants to take it?

The Declaration of Independence speaks of our inalienable right to "life, liberty, and the pursuit of happiness." How are we to interpret this? By asserting that we ought to be free to pursue happiness by playing golf or watching television, but not by drinking alcohol, or smoking marijuana, or ingesting pep pills?

The Constitution and the Bill of Rights are silent on the subject of drugs. This would seem to imply that the adult citizen has, or ought to have, the right to medicate his own body as he sees fit. Were this not the case, why should there have been a need for a Constitutional Amendment to outlaw drinking? But if ingesting alcohol was, and is now again, a Constitutional right, is ingesting opium, or heroin, or barbiturates, or anything else, not also such a right? If it is, then the Harrison Narcotic Act is not only a bad law but is unconstitutional as well, because it prescribes in a legislative act what ought to be promulgated in a Constitutional Amendment.

The questions remain: as American citizens, should we have the right to take narcotics or other drugs? If we take drugs and conduct ourselves as responsible and law-abiding citizens, should we have a right to remain unmolested by the government? Lastly, if we take drugs and break the law, should we have a right to be treated as persons accused of crime, rather than as patients accused of mental illness?

These are fundamental questions that are conspicuous by their absence from all contemporary discussions of problems of drug addiction and drug abuse. The result is that instead of debating the use of drugs in moral and political terms, we define our task as the ostensibly narrow technical problem of protecting people from poisoning themselves with substances for whose use they cannot possibly assume responsibility. This, I think, best explains the frightening national consensus against personal responsibility for taking drugs and for one's conduct while under their influence. In 1965, for example, when President Johnson sought a bill imposing tight federal controls over pep pills and goof balls, the bill cleared the House by a unanimous vote, 402 to 0.

The failure of such measures to curb the "drug menace" has only served to inflame our legislators' enthusiasm for them. In October 1970 the

Senate passed, again by a unanimous vote (54 to 0), "a major narcotics crackdown bill."

To me, unanimity on an issue as basic and complex as this means a complete evasion of the actual problem and an attempt to master it by attacking and overpowering a scapegoat—"dangerous drugs" and "drug abusers." There is an ominous resemblance between the unanimity with which all "reasonable" men—and especially politicians, physicians, and priests—formerly supported the protective measures of society against witches and Jews, and that with which they now support them against drug addicts and drug abusers.

After all is said and done, the issue comes down to whether we accept or reject the ethical principle John Stuart Mill so clearly enunciated: "The only purpose [he wrote in *On Liberty*] for which power can be rightfully exercised over any member of a civilized community, against his will, is to prevent harm to others. His own good, either physical or moral, is not a sufficient warrant. He cannot rightfully be compelled to do or forbear because it will make him happier, because in the opinions of oth-ers, to do so would be wise, or even right. . . . In the part [of his conduct] which merely concerns himself, his independence is, of right, absolute. Over himself, over his own body and mind, the individual is sovereign."

By recognizing the problem of drug abuse for what it is—a moral and political question rather than a medical or therapeutic one—we can choose to maximize the sphere of action of the state at the expense of the individual, or of the individual at the expense of the state. In other words, we could commit ourselves to the view that the state, the representative of many, is more important than the individual; that it therefore has the right, indeed the duty, to regulate the life of the individual in the best interests of the group. Or we could commit ourselves to the view that individual dignity and liberty are the supreme values of life, and that the foremost duty of the state is to protect and promote these values.

In short, we must choose between the ethic of collectivism and individualism, and pay the price of either—or of both.

REVIEW AND DISCUSSION QUESTIONS

1. Describe the "myths" that Szasz says surround drug addiction.
2. What, specifically, does Szasz propose should be done about drug laws? What motivates him to make that proposal?
3. Is this proposal one that Mill would accept? Why?
4. How does Szasz understand addiction? Do you agree with Szasz's analysis? Explain.
5. This article was written over twenty years ago. What lessons can be learned from the events since then? Would Szasz be likely to feel vindicated, or refuted, by recent history? Explain.

In Search of a Factual Foundation for the "Disease Concept of Alcoholism"

Herbert Fingarette

In this essay, Herbert Fingarette discusses the question whether alcoholism is, as is often claimed, a disease, or whether it is rather a voluntary pattern of behavior. Arguing against the "disease" view, he considers the nature of addictions as well as the problem of whether alcoholics experience a "loss of control." He concludes with a discussion of the political and financial reasons why the "disease concept of alcoholism" has won such wide support. Herbert Fingarette is professor of philosophy at the University of California at Santa Barbara.

In *Powell* v. *Texas*[1] the United States Supreme Court addressed . . . the significance of the "disease concept of alcoholism" for the criminal law. Leroy Powell had been convicted of public intoxication under the Texas penal code. The theory for reversal was that . . . it is "cruel and unusual" under the eighth amendment, and therefore a violation of due process, to punish a person suffering from the "disease" of alcoholism for manifesting an "involuntary" symptom of his disease by appearing drunk in public. . . . Contrary to the utterly confident expectations of a number of specialists in this area of law, the Court rejected Powell's appeal, five to four. . . . Four Justices both accepted the "disease concept" and, in a vigorous dissent by Justice Fortas, urged reversal. . . .

It is my aim in this paper to point out inadequacies in the structure of the *Powell* dissent and to document in some detail that "involuntariness" and "disease" are dangerously slippery concepts in this context.

I.

One factual premise of the argument of . . . the *Powell* dissent is that alcoholism is a "disease" which is "involuntarily" and non-culpably caused and maintained. . . . I wish in . . . this paper to examine the factual content of the statements, central to the "disease concept of alcoholism," that alcoholism is a "disease" and that alcoholism, and the alcoholic's excessive drinking, are "involuntary." Specifically, I will first comment briefly on the *Powell* dissent's conception of those statements, and the factual support there offered, and then explore at greater length the relevant medical literature.

II.

The dissent accepts, without evaluative comment, the trial judge's "findings of fact":

(1) That chronic alcoholism is a disease which destroys the afflicted person's willpower to resist the constant, excessive consumption of alcohol.

(2) That a chronic alcoholic does not appear in public by his own volition but under a compulsion symptomatic of the disease of chronic alcoholism.

(3) That Leroy Powell . . . is a chronic alcoholic who is afflicted with the disease of chronic alcoholism.

From Herbert Fingarette, "The Perils of Powell: In Search of a Factual Foundation for the 'Disease Concept of Alcoholism,' " *Harvard Law Review* 83:793–812. Copyright © 1970 by the Harvard Law Review Association. Some notes have been omitted.

... The first two of the "findings" constitute sweepingly general assertions about a large class of alcoholics: it is asserted that chronic alcoholism is itself an involuntarily maintained status, and it is further asserted that medical science has demonstrated constant and inevitable relationships between this status and public drunkenness. . . .

A major portion of the dissent consists of an attempt to provide just such an appropriate medical background as a "context" which, as the dissenting opinion avers, an understanding of the case "requires."

With respect to the medical background concerning "chronic alcoholism," the *Powell* dissent acknowledges that "there is a great deal that remains to be discovered," that "many aspects of the disease remain obscure," and that we are "woefully deficient in our medical, diagnostic, and therapeutic knowledge" in both this area and that of "mental disease."[2] Although this admission alone takes much of the ground from beneath the sweeping "findings of fact" of the trial judge, the dissent maintains that there are "some hard facts—medical and, especially, legal facts—that are accessible to us and that provide a context in which the instant case may be analyzed."[3]

One such "hard fact" appears to be that alcoholism is medically recognized as a disease.[4] The dissent also believes it to be a fact that the "core meaning" of the disease concept of alcoholism

as agreed by authorities, is that alcoholism is caused and maintained by something other than the moral fault of the alcoholic, something that, to a greater or lesser extent depending upon the physiological or psychological makeup and history of the individual, cannot be controlled by him.[5]

It will be noted that neither of these "facts" mentions public intoxication. This is not because the "core meaning" merely happens to be formulated in the dissent as a very general statement, but because, as we shall see in detail later, its statement can only be a very general one.

Though the "core meaning" is silent with respect to the symptoms or effects of alcoholism, or their voluntariness, it does raise the issue of voluntariness with respect to the causes of the status of chronic alcoholism and with respect to the persistence of that status. However, what it says is not that an alcoholic's condition is involuntary, but that an alcoholic's control over what causes his "disease" will be a matter of "greater or lesser degree;" the degree cannot be assessed in general for all "chronic alcoholics" but will depend upon the individual alcoholic's physiology, psychological makeup, and personal history. Such cautiousness contrasts sharply with the blunt conclusions of the trial judge and of the dissenters themselves that alcoholism is "involuntary."

Even more injudiciously blunt is the judgment that however alcoholism be caused, it is in any event not attributable to "the moral fault of the alcoholic."[6] The pontifical tone may be due in part to the fact that while medical men do have a certain expertise in studying causation, it is not, as medical scientists are themselves prone to insist, moral expertise. Expertise generates a sensitivity to the complexity of issues and a consequent cautiousness when generalizing on those issues; beyond the area of our expertise we tend to be freer with wholesale judgments. In fact, of course, moral exculpation is hardly a proper part of medical theory, and to offer it as medically established "fact" is on its face unjustifiable.

III.

Such inconsistencies and logical difficulties indicate that there may be underlying, unacknowledged factors influencing the dissent's conclusions. We shall discuss some of these factors in section IV, when we examine the significance of the widespread medical acceptance of the proposition that "alcoholism is a disease." For the present, we shall focus on the "voluntariness" approach by looking to the medical literature.

Many of the leading health authorities view "loss of control" as the "hallmark" of alcoholism.[7] The assertion is sufficiently widespread to give the impression of substantial agreement among many authorities on a basic fact having near self-evident moral-legal implications to men of goodwill. . . .

However, concepts which center around voluntariness, like those centering around intent and other questions of psychological fact, present some of the most complex issues in both law and ethics. A phrase like "I couldn't control myself" or "I had no choice" could report variously a strictly physical incapacity, unconsciousness incapacity to conform due to mental illness, somnambulism, involuntary intoxication, extreme provocation, or the necessity to act to save life or to act with little time to reflect. Some of these circumstances could serve in some jurisdictions as a complete defense to criminal liability, others as complete defenses in certain factual contexts, or as "partial" defenses in some degree mitigating culpability; others would have no legal effect but might mitigate punishment. These very different senses of self-control by no means exhaust the range of meanings. In what sense, then, do the authorities on alcoholism speak of "loss of control" in connection with chronic alcoholism? The *Powell* dissent's categorical claim that alcoholism is not within the alcoholic's control dissolves when one discovers the very different things that authorities mean by the phrase, the different sorts of facts which purportedly justify it, the substantive qualifications ultimately appended, and the authoritative literature in which the phrase is conspicuously omitted or explicitly rejected.

In the first place, it is difficult to sustain *any* categorical statements about alcoholism in light of the multiplicity of diagnostic schemes.[8] Jellinek distinguishes and lists over one hundred hypotheses about the nature of alcoholism.[9] There is not even any substantial agreement about the region of knowledge from which the best understanding of alcoholism may be forthcoming. Hypotheses range from the genetic through the physiological and pharmacological to the psychological and sociological. More damaging to the "involuntariness" argument, probably no expert would dispute that "variations in the patterns of drinking [among alcoholics] are tremendous";[10] and most would also agree that what alcoholics have in common is simply "a heavy preoccupation with drinking"[11] which in *some* cultural groups often leads to serious disturbances in social adaptation.[12]

Thus it is not surprising that many authorities who use "loss of control" language ultimately introduce serious qualifications. It turns out, for example, that one of the leading authorities who holds "loss of control" to be the "pathognomonic symptom" of alcoholism does not mean by this phrase that the person cannot abstain or cannot stop once he has started drinking. Rather, we are told, the phrase means that "*it is not certain that* [the alcoholic] *will be able to stop at will.*"[13] . . . Still other authorities characterize "loss of control" as "not an all-or-none phenomenon"[14] and "a relative and variable phenomenon."[15]

In short, we are told not that the alcoholic has *no* control of his drinking, but that he has greater or lesser control, *widely* varying in degree according to the circumstances and the individual. This consensus . . . is inconsistent with the *Powell* dissent, . . . insofar as those opinions assume that chronic alcoholics as a group are, by virtue of their being such, without power to control their drinking.

Thus far we have noted ways in which the notion of an alcoholic's "lack of control" must be qualified. We have not examined just which of the many possible senses of "control" is at issue. As my earlier remarks have recalled, there are a number of reasonable uses of the "loss of control" idiom which exclude neither conscious choice with awareness of the relevant consequences nor legal responsibility.

The frequent reference to alcoholism as an "addiction" may seem to all but settle the volitional issue. Yet the World Health Organization's Expert Committee on Dependence-Producing Drugs recently abandoned the term "addiction,"[16] proposing instead a series of terms connoting various significantly different kinds and degrees of drug "dependence." The proposed terms range from mere "desire" through a "strong desire or need" to "overpowering desire or need."[17]

Since appeal to labels like "addiction" is not illuminating, we must ask in what way and in what degree an alcoholic is thought to be alcohol-dependent. Among those who incline to the "loss of control" characterization, a number hold for a "physical" or "physiological mechanism." As to the nature of this mechanism, there is a wide variety of opinion. The most one can say by way of generalizing is that these theories postulate genetic, neurological, metabolic, or allergic abnormalities which create a peculiar vulnerability to alcohol. And while the word "physical" would appear at least to exclude meaningful choice, the specific hypotheses, as we have begun to see, are never that simple. Far from excluding volition, most consist of complex models which include volition, more or less explicitly, along with the physical causes.

In fact, there is universal agreement that alcohol is not as physiologically addictive as the morphine narcotics.[18] Beyond this threshold agreement, some theories postulate a physically induced craving for alcohol, while others speak of craving for the state of intoxication rather than for the liquor. More significant, some theories hypothesize a physically induced craving to begin drinking, whereas others assume control over the taking of a first drink, but with some loss of control over further drinking. Moreover, while some theorists view compulsion to keep drinking as due to a destruction of certain control centers in the brain, or as an involuntary, conditioned response to incipient withdrawal symptoms, others view this compulsion as only a learned, somewhat controllable preference for continued drinking. Finally, many of the "physical" hypotheses suppose a gradual physical change in an alcoholic caused by his habit, implying that the strength of the compulsion to drink varies over time.

Obviously the moral and legal implications of these various hypotheses may be quite different. If, for example, a physical craving for alcohol triggers a specific, automatic reflex of drinking alcohol, then we exclude by hypothesis any significant volition. To the extent such a reflex cannot be demonstrated, then we deal with volitional response to a desire, more or less strong. With respect to the many hypotheses which postulate no initial physical craving, but only a physical mechanism that compels continued drinking, a relevant question may be whether the alcoholic himself believes he can stop, and to what extent that belief is reasonable. The expert in *Powell* testified that many alcoholics have such a belief but that the reasonableness of that belief will vary with particular circumstances. Finally, some hypotheses find volition throughout the drinking pattern, conceiving both the initiation and continuance of drinking as volitional responses to a more or less compelling desire.

Hypotheses which stress involuntariness must contend with the fact that many alcoholics do choose to abstain or control their drinking—whether only occasionally, as is often true with chronic alcoholics, or in some more permanent way, as by a personal decision to abstain, by seeking medical or psychological help, or by joining such groups as Alcoholics Anonymous or Synanon. Of course, capacity to resist the urge to drink on one occasion or for a period of time does not imply that the alcoholic will have such capacity at other times. However, it would at least be more difficult to find "cruel and unusual" the punishment of an alcoholic who enjoyed periods of abstinence or who could be supposed capable of voluntarily subjecting himself to a "cure." . . .

It remains a central feature of most of the "physical" hypotheses that the alcoholic, though in some way peculiarly sensitive physically to alcohol, is one who faces a *very difficult and painful choice*. How one wishes to assess this for moral and legal purposes is a matter which I will not attempt to resolve here. . . . My only purpose here is to indicate that "physical" hypotheses do not claim that there is no volition in the alcoholic's excess drinking but that, partly because of physical abnormality, the alcoholic is one who faces a choice which is (increasingly) more difficult than for most people.

Moreover, by no means do all the contemporary hypotheses which are influential in the health professions claim that there is a critical physical factor at work. Many, though they may speak of "loss of control" (quite a number do not), ascribe this to psychological or social conditions rather than physical ones. Here the term "compulsive" or the like may again be used . . . but again we must look behind the metaphor.

One authority speaks of chronic drunkenness as "a means of adapting to life conditions which are otherwise harsh, insecure, unrewarding and unproductive of the essentials of human dignity."[19] Or, as another physician puts it: "[A]lcoholism is . . . only a 'common path' in the way of problem solving to a number of adaptational issues. . . . "[20] We should not be misled by the technical psychological and sociological language. This (large) group of authorities is simply saying that, on the whole, the alcoholic has chosen this way to handle his problems in life. On this view, it may be further supposed that the more he does so, the more he has a stake in this approach and a deep fear of or deep dislike for any other. To say "he can't control it" amounts in this context to saying that mere moralistic appeals of the usual kind by family and friends are no more likely to succeed than sub-vocal or vocal "resolutions" by the person himself. Excessive drinking has become his "way of life" in spite of such appeals and resolutions. But this view does not suppose that other kinds of appeal or a change in life-setting may not successfully lead him to self-control. A way of life is not easily or casually changed; on the other hand, it is not something beyond volition.

The most persuasive testimony in support of this view comes, unwittingly at times, from the very advocates of the various "loss of control" hypotheses. For when we look to the therapeutic techniques they propose or acknowledge as most effective, we see that these involve appeals for the alcoholic to adopt voluntarily one or another course of conduct. They appeal to him to enter voluntarily a "protective setting" such as a hospital and to abide voluntarily by its rules, or they appeal to him to enter voluntarily and cooperatively on a course of Antabuse, or of "reconditioning," or to join Alcoholics Anonymous.[21] Thus the "psychological" and "sociological" hypotheses generally do not exclude volition but presume it both in their views of the "etiology" of alcoholism and in their attempts at therapy. Indeed, there are leading authorities who explicitly recommend coercive pressures to get the alcoholic to control his drinking. The effectiveness of nonphysical deterrent measures shows that drinking is to some degree volitional, and suggests that the threat of the criminal sanction may be a factor in controlling such drinking as is likely to lead to criminal offenses.

We may summarize, then, by saying that the *Powell* dissent's formulation of the "core meaning" of the disease concept of alcoholism, vague and cautious as it is with respect to voluntariness, . . . errs on the "control" issue because it implies too much in the way of current medical knowledge. And it errs in implying that the phrase "loss of control," as used in the medical literature, implies absence of volition.

I have tried—translating the technical language and including the necessary qualifications—to formulate a statement in harmony with a large number of the influential hypotheses about alcoholism:

Possibly partly due to some abnormal physical condition, the chronic alcoholic is one who for any of a variety of other reasons has increasingly preferred drinking as a way of adapting to his life-problems; he has reached the point where the personal and social consequences of his drinking are such that abandoning heavy drinking and the life that goes with it would require him to make a choice which, though usually genuinely practicable, is so very distressing and so very difficult, both physically and mentally, that he is unlikely to make that choice and carry it out, although he may make it with the aid of special encouragement, professional guidance, or coercive influences.

It is in part because of ambiguities and confusion inherent in the "loss of control" phraseology that a good many authorities avoid such language altogether.

IV.

The second "medical fact" that we shall consider, and the one which probably has done most to foster the intuitive notion that alcoholism is an inappropriate object for criminal punishment, is the simple formula "alcoholism is a disease." The dissenting opinion notes at the very outset of its presentation of "hard facts" about alcoholism that

[i]n 1956 the [AMA] for the first time designated alcoholism as a major medical problem. . . . This significant development marked the acceptance among the medical profession of the "disease concept of alcoholism."[22]

To anticipate, it is my conclusion that the widespread (but by no means universal) acceptance in the medical and health professions of the "disease concept of alcoholism" reflects a variety of considerations which are legitimate and important to the *health* professions, but that none of these considerations has any obvious bearing on the legal issue of punishability under the eighth amendment.

One such consideration is the underlying judgment, with which I certainly concur, that it is reasonable for the health professions to attempt to help with the problem of alcoholism. Another important consideration, suggested by the first, is the widespread hope and expectation that the medical profession will someday develop understanding of and remedies for alcoholism. While there is no doubt about the importance and inspirational efficacy of this expectation, and while the reasonableness of the effort is apparent, these considerations are not obviously relevant to the propriety of punishing alcoholics.

There are certain ancillary practical considerations which also motivate acceptance among doctors of the "disease concept." In the first place, it is evidently in the interest of the medical attack on alcoholism that large sums of money be reliably accessible to researchers and therapists. Adherence within the profession to such formulas as "alcoholism is a disease" (or an "illness," or a "medical problem") does much to provide assurance to such fund-granting organizations as government agencies and foundations that the enterprise is legitimate. . . .

It is extremely important to concerned doctors that the general public support their efforts. The official AMA announcement and wide professional use—especially in public discussion—of such formulas as "alcoholism is a disease" have been vital to the growing public support of medical research in the area. The doctors' public use of the phrase has been a powerful influence in combatting what many health professionals see as a major cultural obstacle to their efforts—the public's habitual allegiance to "moralistic" approaches. Many health authorities feel that moral, religious, and penal approaches have failed and are bound to fail, and tend to see public commitment to these approaches as a major diversion of effort, money, and resources from the medical effort. There is also a profound but usually tacit moral judgment on the part of many health professionals that the condemnatory and penal approach is inhumane.

I recognize that one may grant that all these considerations have been important and relevant to medical acceptance of the "disease concept of alcoholism," yet retain a nagging wonder whether there is not in addition some more legally relevant factual content implicit in the phrase. This is not the place to discuss the concept of "disease" in general. However, I do wish to direct attention to the well-known attempt by Jellinek to clarify the factual content of the disease concept of alcoholism,[23] an attempt which concludes almost as quickly as it begins. After noting the perfunctory circularity and unhelpful generality of the medical dictionary definitions of disease, Jellinek concludes:[24]

> [A] *disease is what the medical profession recognizes as such.* . . . [T]hrough this fact alone alcoholism becomes an illness, whether a part of the lay public likes it or not, and even if a minority of the medical profession is disinclined to accept the idea.

In general, I do not believe that anything I have said precludes in any way the many legislative options for establishing rational procedures and institutions, whether within penal or civil systems, for "detoxifying" the acutely intoxicated, for counselling, for treating, and for otherwise helping the alcoholic. Nor is there any support in anything I have said for the irrational, expensive, and inhumane harassment of the alcoholic, especially the impoverished and alienated alcoholic, an approach today still so prevalent. The burden of my remarks is, however, that one tempting road to reform—the building of new constitutional doctrine on the basis of purported medical knowledge of alcoholism—is also a very dangerous one.

NOTES

1. 392 U.S. 514 (1968).
2. *Id.* at 559–60. All of the Justices seem to agree that medical knowledge of alcoholism is deficient. *Id.* at 522–23, 539, 551 n.3.
3. *Id.* at 559.
4. *Id.*
5. *Id.* at 560–61.
6. 392 U.S. at 561.
7. See, e.g., *The Cooperative Commission on the Study of Alcoholism, Alcohol Problems* 39 (prepared by T. Plaut 1967) [hereinafter cited as Plaut]; C. Rip, *The Alcoholic and the Group* 17 (1966); A. Ullman, *To Know the Difference* 8 (1960); Keller, *The Definition of Alcoholism and the Estimation of Its Prevalence, in Society, Culture, and Drinking Patterns* 310, 312–13 (D. Pittman & C. Synder, eds., 1962) [hereinafter cited as Pittman & Synder].

8. Compare Plaut at 41:

    > [T]he term "alcoholism" should be used with the awareness that this condition is not always easy to diagnose or to be distinguished from other types of problem drinking. In addition, even those to whom the diagnosis is correctly given still differ greatly from one another and are likely to require different types of treatment and assistance.

9. E. Jellinek, *The Disease Concept of Alcoholism* 55–59, 83–86, 113–15 (1960).

10. M. Block, *Alcoholism* 23 (1965).

11. Chafetz, *Comment*, in *Who Is Qualified to Treat the Alcoholic?: Comment on the Krystal-Moore Discussion*, 25 *Q. J. Studies On Alcohol* 347, 358 (1964).

12. See the discussion in E. Jellinek, *supra* note 44, at 13–32. In France and other beer and wine drinking countries a predominant pattern of alcoholism is the constant, daily drinking of wine, with "inability to abstain," but with control over the amount drunk at any one time so that drunkenness or incapacity to carry on with the day's activities is rare. Cessation of drinking does produce withdrawal symptoms, however. *Id.* at 25–32.

13. Keller, *supra* note 39, at 313 (emphasis in original).

14. *Id.*

15. Glatt, *Normal Drinking in Recovered Alcohol Addicts*, 26 *Q. J. Studies On Alcohol* 116 (1965).

16. *World Health Organization Expert Committee on Addiction-Producing Drugs, Thirteenth Report* 9–10 (Tech. Rep. Ser. No. 273, 1964) [hereinafter cited as *Thirteenth Report*].

17. *Final Report* at 13–16.

18. See *World Health Organization Expert Committee on Alcohol, First Report* 5–7, 9–11 (Tech. Rep. Ser. No. 84, 1954). Aside from the controversial issue of the "compulsiveness" of the desire, it takes years as against weeks for any physical dependence to develop in the case of alcohol as compared to morphine derivatives, and toler-ance levels remain comparatively, very low with alcohol. Dr. Jack Mendelson, Chief of the National Center for the Prevention and Control of Alcoholism of the National Institute of Mental Health, refers to the "notion also of the purported "triggering" effect: "[o]nce an individual has one drink . . . he can't control his alcohol ingestion. . . . We do not believe this is the case." *U.S. Dep't. of Health, Education, & Welfare, Social Welfare and Alcoholism* 21 (1967).

19. Pittman, *Public Intoxication and the Alcoholic Offender in American Society*, in *Task Force Report* 13.

20. Forizs, *Comment*, in *Who Is Qualified to Treat the Alcoholic?: Comment on the Krystal-Moore Discussion*, 26 *Q. J. Studies on Alcohol* 510, 511 (1965).

21. Alcoholics Anonymous maintains that alcoholism is a "disease," but not that drinking is involuntary. On the contrary, the entire approach in Alcoholics Anonymous is to enlist the voluntary cooperation of the alcoholic, to appeal to him on moral-religious-pragmatic grounds to voluntarily abstain from drinking, and to engage in reciprocal self-help along these lines with his brother AA members. According to the U.S. Public Health Service, "[r]emarkable success . . . has been achieved" in this way. *Alcoholism* 10.

22. 392 U.S. at 560 (1968).

23. E. Jellinek, *supra* note 9, at 11–12.

24. Jellinek, *id.* at 55–59, cites seven authorities who explicitly reject the disease concept of alcoholism. He goes on to cite approvingly Leopold Wexberg's remarks based on the latter's studies of the physiology of alcoholism.

    > In no other area of research and social or medical endeavor have slogans so extensively replaced theoretical insight, as a basis for therapeutic action, as in alcoholism. The emotional impact of the statement, "Alcoholism is a sickness," is such that very few people care to stop to think what it actually means.

    Jellinek's list is by no means complete as an inventory of authorities who reject the disease concept of alcoholism.

REVIEW AND DISCUSSION QUESTIONS

1. What evidence has been suggested showing that "chronic alcoholism" is a disease? How does Fingarette respond to that claim?

2. Describe the various ways it could be argued that alcoholics have "lost control"?

3. Why does Fingarette think that those who claim alcoholics "lose control" in the medical sense have not proven they act involuntarily?

4. If it is unclear that alcoholism is a disease, how does Fingarette explain the medical community's acceptance of that conclusion?

5. How does Fingarette understand the idea of *voluntariness,* do you think? Is it compatible with having strong desires? Explain.

6. Mill says people cannot sell themselves into slavery. Explain his reason, and then indicate whether you think this argument could be used to limit the sale of alcohol.

The Ethics of Smoking

Robert E. Goodin

Unlike the previous authors, who often doubted whether alcohol and other drugs cause people to lose control, Robert Goodin claims that tobacco's addictive nature means people do not voluntarily choose to smoke and therefore do not freely accept its risks. Beyond these "Kantean style" questions about consent, he argues, lie other, more utilitarian issues about the social costs of smoking. Goodin describes those costs and then responds to two familiar arguments that defenders of smoking have offered in an attempt to show that smoking is not, in fact, economically costly. He concludes with a discussion of three proposals: mandatory warnings, bans, and "medicalization"—that is, making tobacco a prescription drug. Robert E. Goodin is professorial fellow in philosophy at the Australian National University.

1. DO SMOKERS VOLUNTARILY ACCEPT THE RISKS?

Given what we know of the health risks from smoking, we may well be tempted to "ban cigarette manufacturers from continuing to manufacture their product on the grounds that we are preventing them from causing illness to others in the same way that we prevent other manufacturers from releasing pollutants into the atmosphere, thereby causing danger to members of the community." That would be to move too quickly. As Dworkin (1972/1983, p. 22) continues, "The difference is . . . that in the former but not the latter case the harm is of such a nature that it could be avoided by those individuals affected, if they so chose. The incurring of the harm requires the active cooperation of the victim. It would be a mistake in theory and hypocritical in practice to assert that our interference in such cases is just like our interference in standard cases of protecting others from harm." Courts have been as sensitive to this distinction as moral philosophers, appealing to the venerable legal maxim, *volenti non fit injuria,* to hold that through their voluntary assumption of the risk smokers have waived any claims against

cigarette manufacturers. In perhaps one of the most dramatic cases (given the well-established synergism between smoking and asbestos inhalation) the Fifth Circuit refused to enjoin cigarette manufacturers as codefendants in a suit against Johns-Manville, saying that "the danger is to the smoker who willingly courts it."[1]

Certainly there is, morally speaking, a world of difference between the harms that others inflict upon you and the harms that you inflict upon yourself. The question is simply whether, in the case of smoking, the active cooperation of the smoker really is such as to constitute voluntary acceptance of the consequent risks of illness and death. This question is decomposable into two further ones. The first concerns the question of whether smokers knew the risks. The second concerns the question of whether, even if smoking in full knowledge of the risks, they could be said to have "accepted" the risks in a sense that was fully voluntary.

The first is essentially a question of "informed consent." People can be held to have consented

[1] *Johns-Manville Sales Corp.* v. *International Association of Machinists, Machinists Local 1609,* 621 F.2d 756 at 759 (5th Cir. 1980). . . .

From Robert E. Goodin, "The Ethics of Smoking," *Ethics,* 99, no. 3. © 1989 University of Chicago Press. Reprinted by permission. Some notes and references omitted.

only if they knew to what they were supposedly consenting. In the personalized context of medical encounters, this means that each and every person being treated is told, in terms he or she understands, by the attending physician what the risks of the treatment might be (Gorovitz 1982, chap. 3). For largely anonymous transactions in the market, such personalized standards are inappropriate. Instead, we are forced to infer consent from what people know or should have known (in the standard legal construct, what a "reasonable" person should have been expected to know) about the product. And in the anonymous world of the market, printed warnings necessarily take the place of face-to-face admonitions.

Cigarette manufacturers, in defending against product liability suits, have claimed on both these grounds that smokers should be construed as having consented to the risks that they have run. They claim, first, that any "reasonable" person should have known, and the "ordinary consumer" did indeed know, that smoking was an "inherently dangerous" activity. Their interrogatories constantly seek to establish that plaintiffs had, in their youth, consorted with people calling cigarettes "coffin nails," and so on. Manufacturers claim, second, that printing of government-mandated health warnings on cigarette packets from 1966 onward has constituted further, explicit warning to users.

Now, of course, there are some risks (e.g., Buerger's disease, a circulatory condition induced, often in quite young people, by smoking that can result in amputation of limbs) of which smokers were never warned, by grandmother or government health warnings either. Indeed, the warnings of both folk wisdom and cigarette packets in the 1960s and 1970s at least were desperately nonspecific; and there is a more general question whether an all-purpose warning that "X may be hazardous to your health," without specifying just how likely X is to cause just what sorts of harms, is adequate warning to secure people's informed consent at all.

Furthermore, cigarette manufacturers take back through their advertising what is given by way of warnings.[2] The problem is not so much one of

literally deceptive advertising—though there is evidence of that, too (U.S. FTC 1981, 1984, 1985)—as it is one of the widespread use of deceptively healthy imagery (U.S. FTC 1981, pp. 428a, 491a). The printed warnings may say "smoking kills," but the advertising images are the very picture of robust good health. Cowboys, sports, and the great outdoors figure centrally in the ads. The U.S. Federal Trade Commission has continually warned Congress that "current practices and methods of cigarette advertising" have the effect of "reducing anxieties about the health risks posed by cigarette smoking" (U.S. FTC 1984, p.5), "negat[ing] the effect of health warnings because they imply that smoking is a habit which is compatible with performing various outdoor activities and having a strong healthy body" (U.S. FTC 1985, p.5).[3] The point is not that advertising bypasses consumers' capacity to reason and somehow renders them unfree to choose intelligently whether or not to consume the product. The point is, rather, that tobacco companies in effect are giving out—and, more important, consumers are receiving—conflicting information. The implicit health claims of the advertising imagery conflict with the explicit health warnings and thus undercut any volenti or informed-consent defense companies might try to mount on the basis of those warnings.

Despite tobacco companies' best efforts, however, nearly everyone—smokers included—knows, in broad outline, the health risks that smoking entails. In a 1978 Gallup poll, only 24 percent of heavy smokers claimed they were unaware of or did not believe the evidence that

---

[2]Warnings that "smoking may be dangerous," when conjoined with pictures of people enjoying dangerous sports (white-water rafting, etc.), perversely serve to make smoking more attractive; warnings that "smoking may complicate pregnancy," when conjoined with sexually provocative photos in a magazine devoted to casual sex without procreation, again perversely undercut the health warnings.

[3]Literally, of course, it is—at least broadly speaking and in the short run. But in the medium to long term, participation even in purely recreational sport (not to mention serious sport, where peak performance is required) is impaired by the consequences of smoking. Insofar as young smokers are encouraged in the belief that they can always quit, should smoking become a problem later, that is a false belief (as shown by the addiction evidence, discussed below); and advertisements carrying any such implications once again would count as clearly deceptive advertising.

smoking is hazardous. How that recalcitrant residual should be handled is a hard question. Having smoked thousands of packets containing increasingly stern warnings, and having been exposed to hundreds of column inches of newspaper reporting and several hours of broadcasting about smoking's hazards, they are presumably incorrigible in their false beliefs in this regard. Providing them with still more information is likely to prove pointless.

Ordinarily it is not the business of public policy to prevent people from relying on false inferences from full information which would harm only themselves. Sometimes, however, it is. One such case comes when the false beliefs would lead to decisions that are "far-reaching, potentially dangerous, and irreversible"—as, for example, with people who believe that when they jump out of a tenth-story window they will float upward (Dworkin 1972/1983, p. 31).

We are particularly inclined toward intervention when false beliefs with such disastrous results are traceable to familiar, well-understood forms of cognitive defect. One is "wishful thinking": smokers believing the practice is safe because they smoke rather than smoking because they believe it to be safe (Pears 1984). There is substantial evidence that smokers believe, groundlessly, that they are less vulnerable to smoking-related diseases; there is also evidence that they came to acquire those beliefs, and to "forget" what they previously knew about the dangers of smoking, after they took up the habit (Leventhal, Glynn, and Fleming 1987). Another cognitive defect is the "anchoring" fallacy (Kahneman, Slovic, and Tversky 1982): people smoke many times without any (immediately perceptible) bad effects; and . . . extrapolating from their own experience, they therefore quite reasonably but quite wrongly conclude that smoking is safe for them. Yet another phenomenon, sometimes regarded as a cognitive defect, is "time-discounting": since young smokers will not suffer the full effects of smoking-related diseases for some years to come, they may puff away happily now with little regard for the consequences, if they attach relatively little importance to future pains relative to present pleasures in their utility functions (Fuchs 1982). All of these cognitive defects point to relatively weak

forms of irrationality. In and of themselves, they would not be enough to justify interference with people's liberty, perhaps. But when they lead people to make decisions that are far-reaching, potentially dangerous, and irreversible, perhaps intervention would be justified.

Interfering with people's choices in such cases is paternalistic, admittedly. But there are many different layers of paternalism. What is involved here is a relatively weak form of paternalism, working within the individual's own theory of the good and merely imposing upon him better means of achieving his own ends.[4] It is one thing to stop people who want to commit suicide from doing so, but quite another to stop people who want to live from acting in a way that they falsely believe to be safe. Smokers who deny the health risks fall into that latter, easier category.

The larger and harder question is how to deal with the great majority of smokers who, knowing the risks, continue smoking anyway. Of course, it might be said that they do not really know the risks. Although most acknowledge that smoking is "unhealthy," in some vague sense, few know exactly what chances they run of exactly what diseases. In one poll, 49 percent of smokers did not know that smoking causes most cases of lung cancer, 63 percent that it causes most cases of bronchitis, and 85 percent that it causes most cases of emphysema. Overestimating badly the risks of dying in other more dramatic ways (car crashes, etc.), people badly underestimate the relative risks of dying in the more mundane ways associated with smoking—thus allowing them to rationalize further their smoking behavior as being "not all that dangerous," compared to other things that they are also doing.[5] Besides all that, there is the distinction between "knowing intellectually" some statistic and "feeling in your guts" its full implications. Consent counts—morally, as well as legally—only if it is truly informed consent, only

[4]One of a person's ends—continued life—at least. Perhaps the person has other ends ("relaxation," or whatever) that are well served by smoking, and insofar as "people taking risks actually value the direct consequences associated with them . . . it is more difficult to intrude paternalistically" (Daniels 1985, pp. 158, 163). But assuming that smoking is not the only means to the other ends—not the only way to relax, etc.— the intrusion is only minimally difficult to justify.

if people know what it is to which they are consenting. That, in turn, requires not only that we can state the probabilities but also that we "appreciate them in an emotionally genuine manner" (Dworkin 1972/1983, p. 30). There is reason to believe that smokers do not.[5]

It may still be argued that, as long as people had the facts, they can and should be held responsible if they chose not to act upon them when they could have done so. It may be folly for utilitarian policymakers to rely upon people's such imperfect responses to facts for purposes of constructing social welfare functions, and framing public policies around them. But there is the separate matter of who ought to be blamed when some self-inflicted harm befalls people. There, arguably, responsibility ought to be on people's own shoulders (Knowles 1977; Wikler 1987). Arguably, we ought to stick to that judgment, even if people were "pressured" into smoking by the bullying of aggressive advertising or peer pressure.

What crucially transforms the "voluntary acceptance" argument is evidence of the addictive nature of cigarette smoking. Of course, saying that smoking is addictive is not to say that no one can ever give it up. Many have done so. By the same token, though, more than 70 percent of American servicemen addicted to heroin in Vietnam gave it up when returning to the United States; yet we still rightly regard heroin as an addictive drug. The test of addictiveness is not impossibility but rather difficulty of withdrawal. . . .

---

[5]Logically, it would be perfectly possible for people both to underestimate the extent of the risk and simultaneously to overreact to it. People might suppose the chances of snakebite are slight but live in mortal fear of it nonetheless. Psychologically, however, the reverse seems to happen. People's subjective probability estimates of an event's likelihood increase the more they dread it and the more "psychologically available" the event therefore is to them (Kahneman, Slovic, and Tversky 1982). Smoking-related diseases, in contrast, tend to be "quiet killers" of which people have little direct or indirect experience, which tend to be underreported in newspapers and which act on people one at a time rather than catastrophically killing many people at once (Lichtenstein et al. 1983, p. 567). Smoking-related diseases being psychologically less available to people in these ways, they underestimate their frequency dramatically—by a factor of eight, in the case of lung cancer, according to one study (Slovic, Fischhoff, and Lichtenstein 1982, p. 469).

To establish a substance as addictive, we require evidence of "physical need" for the substance among its users. That evidence is necessary to prove smoking is an addiction rather than just a "habit" (U.S. DHEW 1964, chaps. 13-14), a psychological dependence, or a matter of mere sociological pressure (Daniels 1985, p. 159)—none of which would undercut, in a way that addictiveness does, claims that the risks of smoking are voluntarily incurred. That physical link has now been established, though. Particular receptors for the active ingredients of tobacco smoke have been discovered in the brain; the physiological sites and mechanisms by which nicotine acts on the brain have now been well mapped, and its tendency to generate compulsive, repetitive behavior in consequence has been well established. Such evidence—summarized in the surgeon general's 1988 report—has been one of the crucial factors leading the World Health Organization and the American Psychiatric Association to classify "nicotine dependence" as an addiction.

None of that evidence proves that it would be literally impossible for smokers to resist the impulse to smoke. Through extraordinary acts of will, they might. Nor does any of that evidence prove that it is literally impossible for them to break their dependence altogether. Many have. Recall, however, that the issue is not one of impossibility but rather of how hard people should have to try before their will is said to be sufficiently impaired that their agreement does not count as genuine consent.

The evidence suggests that nicotine addicts have to try very hard indeed. This is the second crucial fact to establish in proving a substance addictive.[6] Central among the WHO/APA criteria for diagnosing nicotine dependence is the requirement of evidence of "continuous use of tobacco for at least one month with . . . unsuccessful at-

---

[6]There are other physical needs that we would have trouble renouncing—such as our need for food—that we would be loath to call "addictions." Be that as it may, we would also be loath, for precisely those reasons, to say that we eat "of our own free will" (we would have no hesitation that someone who makes a credible threat of preventing us from eating has "coerced" us, etc.). Since involuntariness and impairment of free will are what is really at issue here, those thus do seem to be the aspects of addictiveness that matter in the present context.

tempts to stop or significantly reduce the amount of tobacco use on a permanent basis." A vast majority of smokers do indeed find themselves in this position. The surgeon general reports that 90 percent of regular smokers have tried to quit. Another 1975 survey found that 84 percent of smokers had attempted to stop, but that only 36 percent of them had succeeded in maintaining their changed behavior for a whole year.[7]

Such evidence of smokers trying and failing to stop is rightly regarded as central to the issue of addiction, philosophically as well as diagnostically. Some describe free will in terms of "second-order volitions"—desires about desires—controlling "first-order" ones (Frankfurt 1971). Others talk of one's "evaluational structure" controlling one's "motivational structure," so one strives to obtain something if and only if one thinks it of value (Watson 1975, 1977). Addiction—the absence of free will—is thus a matter of first-order volitions winning out over second-order ones, and surface desires prevailing over the agent's own deeper values. In the case of smoking, trying to stop can be seen as a manifestation of one's second-order volitions or one's deeper values, and failing to stop as evidence of the triumph of first-order surface desires over them. The same criteria the WHO/APA use to diagnose nicotine dependence also establish the impairment of the smoker's free will, philosophically.

Various policy implications follow from evidence of addictiveness. One might be that over-the-counter sales of cigarettes should be banned. If the product is truly addictive, then we have no more reason to respect a person's voluntary choice (however well informed) to abandon his future volition to an addiction than we have for respecting

a person's voluntary choice (however well informed) to sell himself into slavery (Mill 1859/1975, pp. 126–27). I am unsure how far to press this argument. After all, we do permit people to bind their future selves (through contracts, e.g.). But if it is the size of the stakes or the difficulty of breaking out of the bonds that makes the crucial difference, then acquiring a lethal and hard-to-break addiction is much more like a slavery contract than it is like an ordinary commercial commitment.

In any case, addictiveness thus defined makes it far easier to justify interventions that on their face appear paternalistic. In some sense, they would then be not paternalistic at all. Where people "wish to stop smoking, but do not have the requisite willpower . . . we are not imposing a good on someone who rejects it. We are simply using coercion to enable people to carry out their own goals" (Dworkin 1972/1983, p. 32). It is, of course, genuinely difficult to decide which is the "authentic" self: with whom should we side, when the person who asks us to help him "enforce rules on himself" repudiates the rules at the time they need to be enforced? But at least we have more of a warrant for interference in such cases than if we were never asked for assistance at all. Much of the assistance we render in such situations will necessarily be of a very personal nature and outside the scope of public policy. There is nonetheless a substantial role for public policy in these realms. Banning or restricting smoking in public places (especially the workplace) can contribute crucially to an individual's own efforts at smoking cessation, for example.

The force of the addiction findings . . . is to undercut the claim that there is any continuing consent to the risks involved in smoking. There might have been consent in the very first instance—in smoking your first cigarette. But once you were hooked, you lost the capacity to consent in any meaningful sense on a continuing basis. As Hume (1760) says, to consent implies the possibility of doing otherwise; and addiction substantially deprives you of the capacity to do other than continue smoking. So once you have become addicted to nicotine, your subsequent smoking cannot be taken as indicating your consent to the risks.

---

[7]The graphs mapping the relapse rate after a given period of time are almost identical for nicotine and for heroin, although it might be wrong to make too much of that fact. (Perhaps heroin addicts find both that it is harder to give up and that they have more reason to do so: then relapse rates would appear the same, even though heroin is more addictive in the sense of being harder to give up.) Pointing to the addiction evidence, U.S. federal courts have decided that "smoking can be an involuntary act for some persons" and that social security disability benefits may not therefore be routinely withheld from victims of smoking-related diseases on the grounds that they are suffering from voluntarily self-inflicted injuries (*Gordon v. Schweiker*, 725 F.2d 231, 236 [1984]).

If there is to be consent at all, then, it can only be consent in the very first instance, that is, when you first began to smoke. That, in turn, seriously undercuts the extent to which cigarette manufacturers can rely upon *volenti* or informed-consent defenses in product liability litigation and its moral analogues. Many of those now dying from tobacco-induced diseases started smoking well before warnings began appearing on packets in 1966; their consent to the risks of smoking could only have been based on "common knowledge" and "folk wisdom."

That is a short-term problem, though, since that cohort of smokers will eventually die off. The more serious, continuing problem is this. A vast majority of smokers began smoking in their early to middle teens. Evidence suggests that "of those teenagers who smoke more than a single cigarette only 15 percent avoid becoming regular dependent smokers"; and a great majority, perhaps up to 95 percent, of regular adult smokers are thought to have been addicted before they were twenty-one years of age. Being below the age of consent, they were incapable of consenting in the first instance;[8] and being addicted by the time they reached the age of consent they were incapable of consenting later, either.

2. DO THE BENEFITS OUTWEIGH THE COSTS?

In addition to Kantian-style questions about informed consent, there are utilitarian-style questions of overall social welfare to be considered in this connection. Presumably it is in these latter terms that public health measures are ordinarily justified. We do not leave it to the discretion of consumers, however well informed, whether or not to drink grossly polluted water, ingest grossly contaminated foods, or inject grossly dangerous

drugs. We simply prohibit such things, on grounds of public health, by appeal to utilitarian calculations of one sort or another.

To some extent, the same considerations that lead us to believe such measures are justified on grounds of social utility might also give us grounds for presuming people's (at least hypothetical) consent to them, also. To some extent, we can appeal to externality arguments to justify the measures: contagious diseases and costly cures affect the community as a whole. But to some extent, the justification of public health measures must be baldly paternalistic, turning on the benefits accruing to the person himself from avoiding diseases that he might otherwise cavalierly court.

All those considerations are in play in the case of smoking. Paternalistic elements have been canvassed above. There are contagion effects, too: being among smokers exerts strong social pressure upon people to start smoking and makes it difficult for people to stop; and these contagion effects are particularly pronounced among young people, whose smoking behavior is strongly affected by that of parents and peers. As regards externalities, smoking is believed to cause at least half of residential fires, harming family and neighbors as well as the smokers themselves; treating smoking-induced illnesses is costly, and even in the United States some 40 percent of those costs are borne by the public; premature deaths cost the economy productive members and entail pain and suffering for family and friends; and so on.

Dealing just in those nonquantified terms of human costs, smoking must surely stand indicted. The U.S. surgeon general says it is "the chief, single, avoidable cause of death in our society and the most important public health problem of our time." Cigarettes kill 25 percent of their users, even when used as their manufacturers intended they be used. Suppose a toaster or lawnmower had a similar record. It would be whipped off the market forthwith. On utilitarian grounds, there would seem to be no reason why cigarettes should be treated any differently.

For those preferring hard, solid numbers, economists (focusing principally upon medical costs and lost productivity) calculate that smoking costs

---

[8]Strictly speaking, ability to consent is not predicated—legally or morally—upon attaining some arbitrary age but, rather, upon having attained the capacity to make reasoned choices in the matter at hand. The level of understanding manifested by teenagers about smoking clearly suggests that their decision to start smoking cannot be deemed an informed choice, however (Leventhal, Glynn, and Fleming 1987).

the American economy on net $52–$62 billion per year. By that reckoning, too, there is clearly a case to answer against smoking, on grounds of social utility.

There are, in fact, rejoinders available on two levels. One is a micro-level argument couched in terms of benefits to smokers themselves from the practice. The other is a macro-level argument, querying the real costs to society from the practice.

The first style of argument . . . is that cost-benefit calculations should take into account whatever subjective pleasures smokers derive from the practice. In the boldest statement of this very standard microeconomic proposition, Buchanan (1970) argues that, if fully informed people would be willing to buy the product in preference to all others on the market, then we would be making them worse off (in preference—which for him equates to welfare—terms) by banning that product from the market. . . .

The . . . way around the microeconomic argument . . . starts from the observation that cigarette sales are substantially price inelastic *[i.e., sales do not go up and down much as prices fluctuate—Ed.]*. Estimates of just how inelastic vary. But much evidence suggests that even rather large increases in the price of the product (induced, e.g., by increased excise taxes) result in only slight decreases in sales to adult consumers. We might infer either of two conclusions from that fact. One would be that there is an enormous "consumer's surplus" (subjective benefit, net of subjective cost) that smokers enjoy, which even large taxes would not extinguish. Price inelasticity would then be taken as evidence that there are substantial subjective gains to consumers from smoking, which ought to be set off against the calculated social costs in any utilitarian decision procedure. Which would predominate we cannot say in advance. But other things being equal, utilitarians ought be more inclined to allow smoking the more satisfaction consumers derive from it.

Alternatively, we might infer from price inelasticity that people are indeed addicted to the product. Present users will pay any price for cigarettes for the same reason they will pay any price for heroin: they cannot help themselves. Most of them would rather not, according to surveys. Most wish they were not hooked but backslide every time they try to get unhooked.

There is, admittedly, a bit of a problem in determining what should count as a "benefit" to addicts. In one sense, they benefit from having their habits serviced—certainly they would suffer in some obvious sense otherwise. So in a way, the implication of the addiction interpretation would be much the same as that of the consumer surplus interpretation, that is, present users benefit, as indicated by their willingness to pay, from smoking. In another way, however, they would benefit—even in terms of subjective preferences—if they were to stop. In the same terms, others would benefit if they were never to start.

Addictive substances are not ordinary economic goods. Ordinarily, cultivating new tastes (acquiring a taste for fine foods, e.g.) is thought to make you better off—able to derive more pleasure—than before. With addictions, however, you are worse off, even in your own eyes, than before; whatever momentary pleasures you derive from servicing the addiction, you would prefer to stop but find that you cannot. Thus, we should do whatever we can to prevent new addicts, who would be subjectively worse off once addicted than they were before. As regards existing addicts, there may be a utilitarian case for continuing to service their habits, though even they would be subjectively better off in the long run if they could be helped to break the habit.

Whereas the first rejoinder to the utilitarian argument for curbing smoking alleges an underestimate of consumer benefits from smoking, a second rejoinder alleges an overestimate of net social costs. The less interesting versions of this argument point to the tobacco industry's contribution to the aggregate economy—but a contribution of $3.3 billion to the Gross National Product, set off against the $52–$62 billion cost estimates described above, leave the industry's account well in the red.

A more interesting version of this argument alleges that the above procedures overstate true social costs. As regards the narrow question of health care costs, everyone dies of something sooner or later. For an accurate assessment of the medical costs of smoking-related diseases, then, we must deduct the costs that would have been incurred had the people killed by smoking died of something else later (Wilder 1978/1983, p. 46). In terms of hospital bed days and overall medical expenditure, over the course of their lives as a whole, there is some evidence to suggest that there may be no significant difference between smokers and nonsmokers.

Similarly, perhaps we need not worry too much about externalities, in the sense of the unfair imposition of burdens on others. Smokers could be refused treatment in public hospital beds and made to pay their own way. They could be required to carry complete insurance against smoking-related diseases; and to avoid unfairness to coinsureds, we could further require that risks to smokers be pooled only with those of other smokers (Wikler 1978/1983, p. 49), as is increasingly done by insurance companies for purely commercial reasons, anyway. Alternatively, and perhaps more practically, "users of cigarettes and alcohol . . . could be made to pay an excise tax, the proceeds of which would cover the costs of treatment for lung cancer and other resulting illnesses" (Wikler 1978/1983, p. 49).

In those narrow terms, at least, smokers already more than pay their own way. In the United Kingdom, the cigarette tax accounts for over 8 percent of total government revenue. It has been estimated that in Ontario it takes only 8 percent of tobacco tax revenues to pay for all public health care expenditure on smoking-related disease. Even in the United States, if we count only the share of health care costs borne by the federal government, that is almost exactly counterbalanced by the federal excise tax on cigarettes—although there, as in those other cases as well, matters would look very different if we were to count total costs to the economy and society (e.g., lost productivity) as well as just medical costs borne by the government.

In other ways, too, smokers save us money by dying early. Just think: "Smoking tends to cause few problems during a person's productive years and then to kill the individual before the need to provide years of social security and pension payments. From this perspective, the truly burdensome individual may be the unreasonably fit senior citizen who lives on for thirty years after retirement, contributing to the bankruptcy of the social security system, and using up savings that would have reverted to the public purse via inheritance taxes, had an immoderate life-style brought an early death" (Wikler 1978/1983, p. 46).

In the eyes of many, this will appear to be a reductio ad absurdum. What it seems to suggest is nothing less than a thinly veiled form of not-altogether-voluntary euthanasia. Many suppose it is unjust, if not necessarily uneconomic, to encourage people to die off promptly upon their ceasing to be productive members of the work force (cf. Battin 1987).

What this is a reductio of, however, is not the utilitarian calculus but, rather, an economic calculus that serves as such a poor proxy for it. Most people who are already retired would wish to enjoy a long and happy retirement; most people still in the work force would wish the same for themselves and, indeed, for their elders. Those preferences, too, must be factored into any proper calculus of social utility. Once they are, early deaths induced by smoking are almost certain to turn out to be costs rather than benefits in the broader social scale of values.

3. POLICY OPTIONS

Publicity

Mandatory health warnings on cigarette packages and advertisements, and public health campaigns more generally, are [a] popular government response to smoking. Some thirty-eight countries now require such warnings. Among the more important reasons for the popularity of this strategy is that health warnings and public information campaigns are seen as the least paternalistic forms of government intervention. Mill (1859/1975, p. 118) himself holds that "labelling [a] drug with some word expressive of its dangerous character, may be enforced without violation of liberty," since presumably "the buyer cannot wish not to know that the thing he possesses has poisonous qualities." In this judgment, Mill has been followed by a host of more recent commentators.

No doubt publicizing health risks reduces smoking. Publication of the two great official reports—by the Royal College of Physicians in 1962 and the surgeon general in 1964—produced long-term drops in cigarette consumption by between 7 percent and 14 percent. The antismoking television advertisements, allowed under the Fairness Doctrine in the United States until the 1970 legislation banning television advertising of cigarettes altogether, seemed to have an effect almost twice as strong.

There are reasons to believe that health campaigns cannot work in isolation from other policy initiatives, though. Specifically, allowing cigarette advertising undercuts health messages by inducing newspapers and magazines to engage in self-censorship of health reports that might offend their tobacco sponsors. Thus, a publicity campaign might not really succeed unless coupled with something stronger: an advertising ban. Otherwise the message simply might not get carried effectively.

Bans

There are, in fact, various regulatory options under this general heading. Most modestly, we might ban cigarette advertising, either in particular settings (e.g., on television) or in general. More dramatically, we might ban sales of cigarettes, either to a certain group (e.g., children) or in general. Most dramatically, we might ban use of tobacco, either in particular settings (e.g., where there is a particular fire hazard, as in elevators, theaters, and subways, or where there are synergistic effects with other substances in the immediate vicinity, such as asbestos) or in general.

These are separable policy options, any one of which can be pursued independently of any other. From 1975, Norway has banned advertising but not sale of cigarettes. Similarly, we can ban sale without banning consumption. (Most states allow you to eat game birds and fish you shoot or catch yourself but not to sell them.) Though there is no modern experience of a general ban on sale or use of tobacco, advertising bans are reasonably common: fifteen countries have total bans, and another twelve have strong partial bans.

Advertising bans can be particularly helpful in reducing cigarette consumption among adoles-

cents, with whom we should be especially concerned on grounds of "informed consent." There is good evidence that cigarette advertising in general, and sport sponsorship in particular, appeals to children. Conversely, banning advertising of cigarettes in Norway in 1975 led to a sharp decline in the percentage of teenagers who subsequently became daily smokers.

Against bans on the use or sale of tobacco, the Prohibition analogy is standardly urged. Already we have evidence of substantial "bootlegging" (or "buttlegging") of cigarettes between states with low cigarette taxes and those with high ones. Any more serious ban on sale or use of tobacco would no doubt lead to even more illicit activity of this sort. Even accepting such slippage, however, this strategy is still bound to reduce smoking substantially. Whether more would be lost in terms of respect for the law than would be gained in terms of public health remains an open question.

Medicalization

If smoking tobacco is addictive, then perhaps a medical rather than legal or economic response is indicated. The idea here would be to make tobacco a prescription drug, available to registered users only.[9] The model would be methadone maintenance programs for heroin addicts, perhaps. The aim in making tobacco a prescription drug would be to respond humanely to the needs of present addicts, while discouraging new users. Again, it would be impossible to stop all new users—they can always smoke the cigarettes of registered users illicitly, unless we require registered users to smoke only in the clinics. But again, such a policy would have a strong tendency in the desired direction.

---

[9]Ironically, nicotine-containing chewing gum is a controlled prescription drug in the United States, United Kingdom, Sweden, and Canada, whereas wet snuff (whose risks are, if anything, greater) is freely available over the counter to adult purchasers. Czechoslovakia now requires consumers of twenty or more cigarettes per day to register with the medical service that monitors respiratory diseases, perhaps as a first step in this "medicalization" direction (*Daily Express*, London, February 17, 1986).

REFERENCES

Battin, Margaret P., "Age Rationing and the Just Distribution of Health Care: Is There a Duty to Die?" *Ethics* 97 (1987): 317–40.

Buchanan, James M., "In Defense of Caveat Emptor," *University of Chicago Law Review* 38(1970):64–73.

Daniels, Norman, *Just Health Care*. Princeton, N.J.: Princeton University Press, 1985.

Dworkin, Gerald, "Paternalism," *Monist* 56, no. 1(1972): 64–84. Reprinted in *Sartorius*, ed., 1983, pp. 19–34.

Feinberg, Joel, "Legal Paternalism," *Canadian Journal of Philosophy* 1(1971):106–24. Reprinted in *Sartorius*, ed., 1983, pp. 3–18.

Frankfurt, Harry G., "Freedom of the Will and the Concept of a Person," *Journal of Philosophy* 68(1971):5–20.

Fuchs, Victor R., "Time Preference and Health: An Exploratory Study," in *Economic Aspects of Health*, ed. Victor R. Fuchs, pp. 93–120. Chicago: University of Chicago Press.

Gorovitz, Samuel, *Doctors' Dilemmas*. New York: Oxford University Press, 1982.

Hume, David, "Of the Original Contract," in *Essays, Literary, Moral and Political*. London: A. Millar, 1760.

Kahneman, D., P. Slovic, and A. Tversky, eds., *Judgment under Uncertainty*. Cambridge: Cambridge University Press, 1982.

Knowles, John H., "The Responsibility of the Individual," *Daedalus* 106, no. 1(1977):57–80.

Leventhal, Howard, Kathleen Glynn, and Raymond Fleming, "Is the Smoking Decision an 'Informed Choice'?" *Journal of the American Medical Association* 257(1987): 3373–76.

Lichtenstein, S., P. Slovic, B. Fischhoff, M. Layman, and B. Combs, "Judged Frequency of Lethal Events," *Journal of Experimental Psychology (Human Learning and Memory)* 4(1978):551–78.

Mill, John Stuart, *On Liberty. In Three Essays*, ed. Richard Wollheim, pp. 1–141. Oxford: Oxford University Press, 1975 (1859).

Pears, David, *Motivated Irrationality*. Oxford: Clarendon, 1984.

Sartorius, Rolf, ed., *Paternalism*. Minneapolis: University of Minnesota Press, 1983.

Slovic, P., B. Fischhoff, and S. Lichtenstein, "Fact vs. Fears: Understanding Perceived Risks," in Kahneman, Slovic, and Tversky, eds., 1982, pp. 463–89.

United States Department of Health, Education and Welfare (U.S. DHEW), *Smoking and Health*. Report of the Advisory Committee to the Surgeon General of the Public Health Service. Washington, DC: Government Printing Office. 1964.

United States Federal Trade Commission (U.S. FTC), *Staff Report on the Cigarette Advertising Investigation*, Matthew L. Meyers, chairman. Public version. Washington, DC: FTC, 1981.

U.S. FTC, *A Report to the Congress Pursuant to the Federal Cigarette Labelling and Advertising Act*. Washington, DC: Government Printing Office, 1984.

U.S. FTC, *A Report to the Congress Pursuant to the Federal Cigarette Labelling and Advertising Act*. Washington, DC: Government Printing Office, 1985.

Watson, Gary, "Free Agency," *Journal of Philosophy* 72(1975): 205–20.

Watson, Gary, "Skepticism about Weakness of Will," *Philosophical Review* 86(1977):316–39.

Wikler, Daniel, "Persuasion and Coercion for Health: Ethical Issues in Government Efforts to Change Lifestyles," *Health and Society* (now *Milbank Quarterly*) 56(1978):303–38. Reprinted in *Sartorius*, ed., 1983, pp. 35–59

Wikler, Daniel, "Personal Responsibility for Illness," in *Health Care Ethics*, ed. D. van de Veer and T. Regan, pp. 326–58. Philadelphia: Temple University Press, 1987.

REVIEW AND DISCUSSION QUESTIONS

1. What role do ads play in encouraging smoking, according to Goodin?
2. Describe the three "cognitive defects" that Goodin thinks are relevant in assessing smoking.
3. In what "weak" sense does Goodin agree that interfering with smoking is paternalistic?
4. Describe how Goodin responds to those who say people voluntarily accept the risks of smoking.
5. What are the costs of smoking, according to Goodin?
6. How does Goodin respond to those who claim the benefits of smoking are often underestimated?
7. How does Goodin respond to those who claim that the costs of smoking are often overestimated?
8. What response does Goodin give to each of the three policy options?
9. Compare Goodin's understanding of addiction with Szasz's and Fingarette's.
10. Assess Goodin's analysis of the public policy issues in light of Mill's position on paternalism. Which position is sounder? Explain.

12

Disobedience, Punishment, and the Rule of Law

Law surrounds us, from before we are born until long after we are dead. It limits what we may do to others, and what they may do to us. It decides if we are to be born, whether we attend school, what our jobs are like, who we marry, and how we die. It also punishes us when we violate the law, even though we may sometimes believe the law to be unjust. Essays in this section address a range of interrelated problems about legal obligation and punishment, including the basis of legal obligation, whether civil disobedience is justified, and the purposes of criminal punishment. The section begins with probably the most famous, and certainly one of the earliest, discussions of the duty to obey law; other, recent writers discuss the civil rights protests, war crimes, and executions.

Crito

Plato

Plato was born into an aristocratic family in Athens around 427 B.C. Socrates (470–399 B.C.) was a friend of Plato's family from the time Plato was a schoolboy. Although a young Athenian of Plato's class would normally have pursued a political career, Plato chose philosophy instead. He achieved great fame as Socrates' most talented student and one of the world's greatest philosophers. In 387 B.C., Plato founded the Academy, a school of higher education and research (which existed for over 900 years), and he was its head until his death in 347 B.C. at the age of eighty. Plato wrote some twenty-five dialogues, including "Crito" and the book-length *Republic*.

"Crito" begins after Socrates has been condemned to death for corrupting the youth of Athens through his teaching. Friends try to convince Socrates to allow them to save his life by breaking him out of jail, but Socrates will agree only if he can be convinced that violating the law would be just. "Crito" thus sets the stage for centuries of debate over the nature and extent of legal obligation. (Socrates, in fact, refused to disobey and was executed.)

From *The Dialogues of Plato*, 3rd ed., trans. Benjamin Jowett (London: Oxford University Press, 1892).

SCENE: THE PRISON OF SOCRATES

Socrates: Dear Crito, . . . I am and always have been one of those natures who must be guided by reason, whatever the reason may be which upon reflection appears to me to be the best; and now that this fortune has come upon me, I can not put away the reasons which I have before given: the principles which I have hitherto honored and revered I still honor, and unless we can find other and better principles on the instant, I am certain not to agree with you; no, not even if the power of the multitude could inflict many more imprisonments, confiscations, deaths, frightening us like children with hobgoblin terrors. But what will be the fairest way of considering the question? Shall I return to your old argument about the opinions of men some of which are to be regarded, and others, as we were saying, are not to be regarded? Now were we right in maintaining this before I was condemned? And has the argument which was once good now proved to be talk for the sake of talking;—in fact an amusement only, and altogether vanity? That is what I want to consider with your help, Crito:—whether, under my present circumstances, the argument appears to be in any way different or not; and is to be allowed by me or disallowed. That argument, which, as I believe, is maintained by many who assume to be authorities, was to the effect, as I was saying, that the opinions of some men are to be regarded, and of other men not to be regarded. Now you, Crito, are a disinterested person who are not going to die tomorrow—at least, there is no human probability of this, and you are therefore not liable to be deceived by the circumstances in which you are placed. Tell me then, whether I am right in saying that some opinions, and the opinions of some men only, are to be valued, and other opinions and the opinions of other men, are not to be valued. I ask you whether I was right in maintaining this?

Crito: Certainly.

Socrates: Very good; and is not this true, Crito, of other things which we need not separately enumerate? In the matter of just and unjust, fair and foul, good and evil, which are the subjects of our present consultation, ought we to follow the opinion of the many and to fear them; or the opinion of the one man who has understanding, and whom we ought to fear and reverence more than all the rest of the world: and whom deserting we shall destroy and injure that principle in us which may be assumed to be improved by justice and deteriorated by injustice;—is there not such a principle?

Crito: Certainly there is, Socrates.

Socrates: Take a parallel instance:—if, acting under the advice of men who have no understanding, we destroy that which is improvable by health and deteriorated by disease—when that has been destroyed, I say, would life be worth having? And that is—the body?

Crito: Yes.

Socrates: Could we live, having an evil and corrupted body?

Crito: Certainly not.

Socrates: And will life be worth having, if that higher part of man be depraved, which is improved by justice and deteriorated by injustice? Do we suppose that principle, whatever it may be in man, which has to do with justice and injustice, to be inferior to the body?

Crito: Certainly not.

Socrates: More honored, then?

Crito: Far more honored.

Socrates: Then, my friend, we must not regard what the many say of us; but what he, the one man who has understanding of just and unjust, will say, and what the truth will say. And therefore you begin in error when you suggest that we should regard the opinion of the many about just and unjust, good and evil, honorable and dishonorable.—Well, some one will say, "but the many can kill us."

Crito: Yes, Socrates; that will clearly be the answer.

Socrates: That is true: but still I find with surprise that the old argument is, as I conceive, unshaken as ever. And I should like to know whether I may say the same of another proposition—that not life, but a good life, is to be chiefly valued?

Crito: Yes, that also remains.

Socrates: And a good life is equivalent to a just and honorable one—that holds also?

Crito: Yes, that holds.

Socrates: From these premises I proceed to argue the question whether I ought not to try and escape without the consent of the Athenians: and if I am clearly right in escaping, then I will make the attempt; but if not, I will abstain. The other considerations which you mention, of money and loss of character and the duty of educating children, are, as I fear, only the doctrines of the multitude, who would be as ready to call people to life, if they were able, as they are to put them to death—and with as little reason. But now, since the argument has thus far prevailed, the only question which remains to be considered is, whether we shall do rightly either in escaping or in suffering others to aid in our escape and paying them in money and thanks, or whether we shall not do rightly; and if the latter, then death or any other calamity which may ensue on my remaining here must not be allowed to enter into the calculation.

Crito: I think that you are right, Socrates; how then shall we proceed?

Socrates: Let us consider the matter together, and do you either refute me if you can, and I will be convinced; or else cease, my dear friend, from repeating to me that I ought to escape against the wishes of the Athenians: for I am extremely desirous to be persuaded by you, but not against my own better judgment. And now please to consider my first position, and do your best to answer me.

Crito: I will do my best.

Socrates: Are we to say that we are never intentionally to do wrong, or that in one way we ought and in another way we ought not to do wrong, or is doing wrong always evil and dishonorable, as I was just now saying, and as has been already acknowledged by us? Are all our former admissions which were made within a few days to be thrown away? And have we, at our age, been earnestly discoursing with one another all our life long only to discover that we are no better than children? Or are we to rest assured, in spite of the opinion of the many, and in spite of consequences whether better or worse, of the truth of what was then said, that injustice is always an evil and dishonor to him who acts unjustly? Shall we affirm that?

Crito: Yes.

Socrates: Then we must do no wrong?

Crito: Certainly not.

Socrates: Nor when injured injure in return, as the many imagine; for we must injure no one at all?

Crito: Clearly not.

Socrates: Again, Crito, may we do evil?

Crito: Surely not, Socrates.

Socrates: And what of doing evil in return for evil, which is the morality of the many—is that just or not?

Crito: Not just.

Socrates: For doing evil to another is the same as injuring him?

Crito: Very true.

Socrates: Then we ought not to retaliate or render evil for evil to any one, whatever evil we may have suffered from him. But I would have you consider, Crito, whether you really mean what you are saying. For this opinion has never been held, and never will be held, by any considerable number of persons; and those who are agreed and those who are not agreed upon this point have no common ground, and can only despise one another when they see how widely they differ. Tell me, then, whether you agree with and assent to my first principle, that neither injury nor retaliation nor warding off evil by evil is ever right. And shall that be the premiss of our argument? Or do you decline and dissent from this? For this has been of old and is still my opinion; but, if you are of another opinion, let me hear what you have to say. If, however, you remain of the same mind as formerly, I will proceed to the next step.

Crito: You may proceed, for I have not changed my mind.

Socrates: Then I will proceed to the next step, which may be put in the form of a question:—Ought a man to do what he admits to be right, or ought he to betray the right?

Crito: He ought to do what he thinks right.

Socrates: But if this is true, what is the application? In leaving the prison against the will of the Athenians, do I wrong any? or rather do I not wrong those whom I ought least to wrong? Do I not desert the principles which were acknowledged by us to be just? What do you say?

Crito: I can not tell, Socrates, for I do not know.

Socrates: Then consider the matter in this way:—Imagine that I am about to play truant (you may call the proceeding by any name which you like), and the laws and the government come and interrogate me. "Tell us, Socrates," they say; "what are you about? are you going by an act of yours to overturn us—the laws and the whole state, as far as in you lies? Do you imagine that a state can subsist and not be overthrown, in which the decisions of law have no power, but are set aside and overthrown by individuals?" What will be our answer, Crito, to these and the like words? Any one, and especially a clever rhetorician, will have a good deal to urge about the evil of setting aside the law which requires a sentence to be carried out; and we might reply, "Yes; but the state has injured us and given an unjust sentence." Suppose I say that?

Crito: Very good, Socrates.

Socrates: "And was that our agreement with you?" the law would say; "or were you to abide by the sentence of the state?" And if I were to express astonishment at their saying this, the law would probably add: "Answer, Socrates, instead of opening your eyes: you are in the habit of asking and answering questions. Tell us what complaint you have to make against us which justifies you in attempting to destroy us and the state? In the first place did we not bring you into existence? Your father married your mother by our aid and begat you. Say whether you have any objection to urge against those of us who regulate marriage?" None, I should reply. "Or against those of us who regulate the system of nurture and education of children in which you were trained? Were not the laws, who have the charge of this, right in commanding your father to train you in music and gymnastic?" Right, I should reply, "Well then, since you were brought into the world and nurtured and educated by us, can you deny in the first place that you are our child and slave, as your fathers were before you? And if this is true you are not on equal terms with us; nor can you think that you have a right to do to us what we are doing to you. Would you have any right to strike or revile or do any other evil to a father or to your master, if you had one, when you have been struck or reviled by him, or received some other evil at his hands?—you would not say this? And because we think right to destroy you, do you think that you have any right to destroy us in return, and your country as far as in you lies? And will you, O professor of true virtue, say that you are justified in this? Has a philosopher like you failed to discover that our country is more to be valued and higher and holier far than mother or father or any ances-

tor, and more to be regarded in the eyes of the gods and of men of understanding? also to be soothed, and gently and reverently entreated when angry, even more than a father, and if not persuaded, obeyed? And when we are punished by her, whether with imprisonment or stripes, the punishment is to be endured in silence; and if she lead us to wounds or death in battle, thither we follow as is right; neither may any one yield or retreat or leave his rank, but whether in battle or in a court of law, or in any other place, he must do what his city and his country order him; or he must change their view of what is just: and if he may do no violence to his father or mother, much less may he do violence to his country." What answer shall we make to this, Crito? Do the laws speak truly, or do they not?

Crito: I think that they do.

Socrates: Then the laws will say: "Consider, Socrates, if this is true, that in your present attempt you are going to do us wrong. For, after having brought you into the world, and nurtured and educated you, and given you and every other citizen a share in every good that we had to give, we further proclaim and give the right to every Athenian, that if he does not like us when he has come of age and has seen the ways of the city, and made our acquaintance, he may go where he pleases and take his goods with him; and none of us laws will forbid him or interfere with him. Any of you who does not like us and the city, and who wants to go to a colony or to any other city, may go where he likes, and take his goods with him. But he who has experience of the manner in which we order justice and administer the state, and still remains, has entered into an implied contract that he will do as we command him. And he who disobeys us is, as we maintain, thrice wrong; first, because in disobeying us he is disobeying his parents; secondly, because we are the authors of his education; thirdly, because he has made an agreement with us that he will duly obey our commands; and he neither obeys them nor convinces us that our commands are wrong; and we do not rudely impose them, but give them the alternative of obeying or convincing us;—that is what we offer, and he does neither. These are the sort of accusations to which, as we were saying, you, Socrates, will be exposed if you accomplish your intentions; you, above all other Athenians." Suppose I ask, why is this? they will justly retort upon me that I above all other men have acknowledged the agreement. "There is clear proof," they will say, "Socrates, that we and the city were not displeasing to you. Of all Athenians you have been the most constant resident in the city, which, as you never leave, you may be supposed to love. For you never went out of the city either to see the games, except once when you went to the Isthmus, or to any other place unless you were on military service; nor did you travel as other men do. Nor had you any curiosity to know other states or their laws: your affections did not go beyond us and our state; we were your special favorites, and you acquiesced in our government of you; and this is the state in which you begat your children, which is a proof of your satisfaction. Moreover, you might, if you had liked, have fixed the penalty at banishment in the course of the trial—the state which refuses to let you go now would have let you go then. But you pretended that you preferred death to exile, and that you were not grieved at death. And now you have forgotten these fine sentiments, and pay no respect to us the laws, of whom you are the destroyer; and are doing what only a miserable slave would do, running away and turning your back upon the compacts and agreements which you made as a citizen. And first of all answer this very question: Are we right in saying that you agreed to be governed according to us in deed, and not in word only? Is that true or not?" How shall we answer that, Crito? Must we not agree?

Crito: There is no help, Socrates.

Socrates: Then will they not say: "You, Socrates, are breaking the covenants and agreements which you made with us at your leisure, not in any haste or under any compulsion or deception, but having had seventy years to think of them, during which time you were at liberty to leave the city, if we were not to your mind, or if our covenants appeared to you to be unfair. You had your choice, and might have gone either to Lacedaemon or Crete, which you often praise for their good government, or to some other Hellenic or foreign state. Whereas you, above all other Athenians, seemed to be so fond of the state, or, in other words, of us her laws (for who would like a state that has no laws), that you never stirred out of her; the halt, the blind, the maimed were not more stationary in her than you were. And now you run away and forsake your agreements. Not so, Socrates, if you will take our advice; do not make yourself ridiculous by escaping out of the city."

"Listen, then, Socrates, to us who have brought you up. Think not of life and children first, and of justice afterwards, but of justice first, that you may be justified before the princes of the world below. For neither will you nor any that belong to you be happier or holier or juster in this life, or happier in another, if you do as Crito bids. Now you depart in innocence, a sufferer and not a doer of evil; a victim, not of the laws, but of men. But if you go forth, returning evil for evil, and injury for injury, breaking the covenants and agreements which you have made with us, and wronging those whom you ought least to wrong, that is to say, yourself, your friends, your country, and us, we shall be angry with you while you live, and our brethren, and laws in the world below, will receive you as an enemy; for they will know that you have done your best to destroy us. Listen, then, to us and not to Crito."

This is the voice which I seem to hear murmuring in my ears, like the sound of the flute in the ears of the mystic; that voice, I say, is humming in my ears, and prevents me from hearing any other. And I know that anything more which you may say will be vain. Yet speak, if you have anything to say.

Crito: I have nothing to say, Socrates.

Socrates: Then let me follow the intimations of the will of God.

REVIEW AND DISCUSSION QUESTIONS

1. Elaborate on Socrates' notion that the law is like a parent and so deserves the respect of its citizens.
2. Socrates is concerned that he not break his implied contract to abide by the law. On what basis does he think he has agreed to obey the law? Do you think he is right? Explain.
3. Sometimes we can lead others to expect us to behave in a certain way even though we never overtly promise to do so. Give an example of such behavior, and then discuss whether Socrates has done anything that can fairly be interpreted as leading others to expect him to obey the law.
4. At his trial, Socrates made an argument in his own defense. Is that relevant to the present issue?
5. Obviously, Socrates has benefited from living in Athens, benefits that he gladly accepted. Does that constitute an "implied contract" to obey?
6. What is gratitude? Does Socrates think part of his obligation to remain is based on gratitude? Explain.
7. Was Socrates' death a suicide? Why or why not?

Civil Disobedience and the Social Contract

John Rawls

Ours is a multicultural, diverse society that includes many incompatible visions of the good life, of religion, and of the meaning and purposes of human existence. We also have a tradition of respecting individual rights, as well as a commitment to majority rule. Given that diversity and those commitments, it seems inevitable that there will be conflicts over the nature and extent of rights as well as about the limits on governmental power. Such conflicts often lead to disobedience, and thus to philosophical questions about the basis of legal obligation, the justification of civil disobedience and, ultimately, the nature of social justice itself.

Few twentieth-century philosophers have had as much influence on our thinking about these issues as John Rawls. His seminal work, *A Theory of Justice* (a selection of which is reprinted in Section 9) offers a new and important work in the social contract tradition. Rawls argues that principles governing a constitution and laws enacted under it should be chosen behind a "veil of ignorance" in which people ignore their social class, race, and religion, as well as any other facts that are morally arbitrary and that, if known, would allow the laws to be tailored so as to advantage one group over another. He calls the theory "justice as fairness" because the veil of ignorance (corresponding to the traditional social contract) assures that the chosen principles are fair. Forced to choose a constitution and laws behind such a veil of ignorance, Rawls argues that people would secure for themselves ba-

From *Civic Disobedience*, ed. Hugo Bedau (Pegasus, 1969) and *Law and Philosophy*, ed. Sidney Hook (New York: New York University Press, 1968). Reprinted by permission of the author.

sic rights, assure equality of opportunity, and allow economic inequality only if everybody benefits from it, including the least advantaged.

In the following essay, John Rawls discusses the related questions of legal obligation and civil disobedience, both within the context of social contract theory. Legal obligation, he argues, is based on the duty of fair play. Even assuming the constitution is just, there is no assurance laws enacted in accordance with its procedures will also be just. Nonetheless, Rawls argues, citizens may have an obligation to obey that is based on their having benefited from the (generally) just regime. He concludes with a discussion of the role of civil disobedience in a constitutional democracy, including the circumstances in which it would be justified. John Rawls is emeritus professor of philosophy at Harvard University.

INTRODUCTION

I should like to discuss briefly, and in an informal way, the grounds of civil disobedience in a constitutional democracy. Thus, I shall limit my remarks to the conditions under which we may, by civil disobedience, properly oppose legally established democratic authority; I am not concerned with the situation under other kinds of government nor, except incidentally, with other forms of resistance. My thought is that in a reasonably just (though of course not perfectly just) democratic regime, civil disobedience, when it is justified, is normally to be understood as a political action which addresses the sense of justice of the majority in order to urge reconsideration of the measures protested and to warn that in the firm opinion of the dissenters the conditions of social cooperation are not being honored. This characterization of civil disobedience is intended to apply to dissent on fundamental questions of internal policy, a limitation which I shall follow to simplify our question.

THE SOCIAL CONTRACT DOCTRINE

It is obvious that the justification of civil disobedience depends upon the theory of political obligation in general, and so we may appropriately begin with a few comments on this question. The two chief virtues of social institutions are justice and efficiency, where by the efficiency of institutions I understand their effectiveness for certain social conditions and ends the fulfillment of which is to everyone's advantage. We should comply with and do our part in just and efficient social arrangements for at least two reasons: first of all, we have a natural duty not to oppose the estab-

lishment of just and efficient institutions (when they do not yet exist) and to uphold and comply with them (when they do exist); and second, assuming that we have knowingly accepted the benefits of these institutions and plan to continue to do so, and that we have encouraged and expect others to do their part, we also have an obligation to do our share when, as the arrangement requires, it comes our turn. Thus, we often have both a natural duty as well as an obligation to support just and efficient institutions, the obligation arising from our voluntary acts while the duty does not.

Now all this is perhaps obvious enough, but it does not take us very far. Any more particular conclusions depend upon the conception of justice which is the basis of a theory of political obligation. I believe that the appropriate conception, at least for an account of political obligation in a constitutional democracy, is that of the social contract theory from which so much of our political thought derives. If we are careful to interpret it in a suitably general way, I hold that this doctrine provides a satisfactory basis for political theory, indeed even for ethical theory itself, but this is beyond our present concern.[1] The interpretation I suggest is the following: that the principles to which social arrangements must conform, and in particular the principles of justice, are those which free and rational men would agree to in an original position of equal liberty; and similarly, the principles which govern men's relations to institutions and define their natural duties and obligations are the principles to which they would consent when so situated. It should be noted straightway that in this interpretation of the contract theory the principles of justice are understood as the outcome of a hypothetical agreement. They are principles which would be agreed to if the situation of the original position were to arise. There is no mention of an actual agreement nor need such an agreement ever be made. Social arrangements are just or unjust according to whether they accord with the principles for assigning and securing fundamental rights and liberties which would be chosen in the original position. This position is, to be sure, the analytic analogue of the traditional notion of the state of nature, but it must not be mistaken for a historical occasion. Rather it is a hypothetical situation which embodies the basic ideas of the contract doctrine; the description of this situation enables us to work out which principles would be adopted. I must now say something about these matters.

The contract doctrine has always supposed that the persons in the original position have equal powers and rights, that is, that they are symmetrically situated with respect to any arrangements for reaching agreement, and that coalitions and the like are excluded. But it is an essential element (which has not been sufficiently observed although it is implicit in Kant's version of the theory) that there are very strong restrictions on what the contracting parties are presumed to know. In particular, I interpret the theory to hold that the parties do not know their position in society, past, present, or future; nor do they know which institutions exist. Again, they do not know their own place in the distribution of natural talents and abilities, whether they are intelligent or strong, man or woman, and so on. Finally, they do not know their own particular interests and preferences or the system of ends which they wish to advance: they do not know their conception of the good. In all these respects the parties are confronted with a veil of ignorance which prevents any one from being able to take advantage of his good fortune or particular interests or from being disadvantaged by them. What the parties do know (or assume) is that Hume's circumstances of justice obtain: namely, that the bounty of nature is not so generous as to render cooperative schemes superfluous nor so harsh as to make them impossible. Moreover, they assume that the extent of their altruism is limited and that, in general, they do not take an interest in one another's interests. Thus, given the special features of the original position, each man tries to do the best he can for himself by insisting on principles calculated to protect and advance his system of ends whatever it turns out to be.

I believe that as a consequence of the peculiar nature of the original position there would be an agreement on the following two principles for assigning rights and duties and for regulating distributive shares as these are determined by the fundamental institutions of society: first, each person is to have an equal right to the most extensive liberty compatible with a like liberty for all; second, social and economic inequalities (as defined by the institutional structure or fostered by it) are to be arranged so that they are both to everyone's advantage and attached to positions and offices open to all. In view of the content of these two principles and their application to the main institutions of society, and therefore to the social system as a whole, we may regard them as the two principles of justice. Basic social arrangements are just insofar as they conform to these principles, and we can, if we like, discuss questions of justice directly by reference to them. But a deeper understanding of the justification of civil disobedience requires, I think, an account of the derivation of these principles provided by the doctrine of the social contract. Part of our task is to show why this is so.

THE GROUNDS OF COMPLIANCE WITH AN UNJUST LAW

If we assume that in the original position men would agree both to the principle of doing their part when they have accepted and plan to continue to accept the benefits of just institutions (the principle of fairness), and also to the principle of not preventing the establishment of just institutions and of upholding and complying with them when they do exist, then the contract doctrine easily accounts for our having to conform to just institutions. But how does it account for the fact that we are normally required to comply with unjust laws as well? The injustice of a law is not a sufficient ground for not complying with it any more than the legal validity of legislation is always sufficient to require obedience to it. Sometimes one hears these extremes asserted, but I think that we need not take them seriously.

An answer to our question can be given by elaborating the social contract theory in the following way. I interpret it to hold that one is to envisage a series of agreements as follows: first, men are to agree upon the principles of justice in the original position. Then they are to move to a constitutional convention in which they choose a constitution that satisfies the principles of justice already chosen. Finally they assume the role of a legislative body and guided by the principles of justice enact laws subject to the constraints and procedures of the just constitution. The decisions reached in any stage are binding in all subsequent stages. Now whereas in the original position the contracting parties have no knowledge of their society or of their own position in it, in both a constitutional convention and a legislature they do know certain general facts about their institutions, for example, the statistics regarding employment and output required for fiscal and economic policy. But no one knows particular facts about his own social class or his place in the distribution of natural assets. On each occasion the contracting parties have the knowledge required to make their agreement rational from the appropriate point of view, but not so much as to make them prejudiced. They are unable to tailor principles and legislation to take advantage of their social or natural position; a veil of ignorance prevents their knowing what this position is. With this series of agreements in mind, we can characterize just laws and policies as those which would be enacted were this whole process correctly carried out.

In choosing a constitution the aim is to find among the just constitutions the one which is most likely, given the general facts about the society in question, to lead to just and effective legislation. The principles of justice provide a criterion for the laws desired; the problem is to find a set of political procedures that will give this outcome. I shall assume that, at least under the normal conditions of a modern state, the best constitution is some form of democratic regime affirming equal political liberty and using some sort of majority (or other plurality) rule. Thus it follows that on the contract theory a constitutional democracy of

some sort is required by the principles of justice. At the same time it is essential to observe that the constitutional process is always a case of what we may call imperfect procedural justice: that is, there is no feasible political procedure which guarantees that the enacted legislation is just even though we have (let us suppose) a standard for just legislation. In simple cases, such as games of fair division, there are procedures which always lead to the right outcome (assume that equal shares is fair and let the man who cuts the cake take the last piece). These situations are those of perfect procedural justice. In other cases it does not matter what the outcome is as long as the fair procedure is followed: fairness of the process is transferred to the result (fair gambling is an instance of this). These situations are those of pure procedural justice. The constitutional process, like a criminal trial, resembles neither of these; the result matters and we have a standard for it. The difficulty is that we cannot frame a procedure which guarantees that only just and effective legislation is enacted. Thus even under a just constitution unjust laws may be passed and unjust policies enforced. Some form of the majority principle is necessary but the majority may be mistaken, more or less willfully in what it legislates. . . .

LEGAL OBLIGATION
AND THE DUTY OF FAIR PLAY

. . . There is, then, the question as to how it can be morally justifiable to acknowledge a constitutional procedure for making legislative enactments when it is certain (for all practical purposes) that laws will be passed that by one's own principles are unjust. It would be impossible for a person to undertake to change his mind whenever he found himself in the minority; it is not impossible, but entirely reasonable, for him to undertake to abide by the enactments made, whatever they are, provided that they are within certain limits. But what more exactly are the conditions of this undertaking?

First of all, it means, as previously suggested, that the constitutional procedure is misinterpreted as a procedure for making legal rules. It is a process of social decision that does not produce a statement to be believed (that B is the best policy) but a rule to be followed. Such a procedure, say involving some form of majority rule, is necessary because it is certain that there will be disagreement on what is the best policy. . . . If one thinks of the constitution as a fundamental part of the scheme of social cooperation, then one can say that if the constitution is just, and if one has accepted the benefits of its working and intends to continue doing so, and if the rule enacted is within certain limits, then one has an obligation, based on the principle of fair play, to obey it when it comes one's turn. In accepting the benefits of a just constitution one becomes bound to it, and in particular one becomes bound to one of its fundamental rules: given a majority vote in behalf of a statute, it is to be enacted and properly implemented.

The principle of fair play may be defined as follows. Suppose there is a mutually beneficial and just scheme of social cooperation, and that the advantages it yields can only be obtained if everyone, or nearly everyone, cooperates. Suppose further that cooperation requires a certain sacrifice from each person, or at least involves a certain restriction of his liberty. Suppose finally that the benefits produced by cooperation are, up to a certain point, free: that is, the scheme of cooperation is unstable in the sense that if any one person knows that all (or nearly all) of the others will continue to do their part, he will still be able to share a gain from the scheme even if he does not do his part. Under these conditions a person who has accepted the benefits of the scheme is bound by a duty of fair play to do his part and not to take advantage of the free benefit by not cooperating. The reason one must abstain from this attempt is that the existence of the benefit is the result of everyone's effort, and prior to some understanding as to how it is to be shared, if it can be shared at all, it belongs in fairness to no one.

Now I want to hold that the obligation to obey the law, as enacted by a constitutional procedure, even when the law seems unjust to us, is a case of the duty of fair play as defined. It is, moreover, an obligation in the more limited sense in that it depends upon our having accepted and our intention to continue accepting the benefits of a just scheme of cooperation that the constitution defines. In this sense it depends on our own voluntary acts. . . .

THE PLACE OF CIVIL DISOBEDIENCE IN A CONSTITUTIONAL DEMOCRACY

We are now in a position to say a few things about civil disobedience. I shall understand it to be a public, nonviolent, and conscientious act contrary to law usually done with the intent to bring about a change in the policies or laws of the government.[2] Civil disobedience is a political act in the sense that it is an act justified by moral principles which define a conception of civil society and the public good. It rests, then, on political conviction as opposed to a search for self or group interest; and in the case of a constitutional democracy, we may assume that this conviction involves the conception of justice (say that expressed by the contract doctrine) which underlies the constitution itself. That is, in a viable democratic regime there is a common conception of justice by reference to which its citizens regulate their political affairs and interpret the constitution. Civil disobedience is a public act which the dissenter believes to be justified by this conception of justice and for this reason it may be understood as addressing the sense of justice of the majority in order to urge reconsideration of the measures protested and to warn that, in the sincere opinion of the dissenters, the conditions of social cooperation are not being honored. For the principles of justice express precisely such conditions, and their persistent and deliberate violation in regard to basic liberties over any extended period of time cuts the ties of community and invites either submission or forceful resistance. By engaging in civil disobedience a minority leads the majority to consider whether it wants to have its acts taken in this way, or whether, in view of the common sense of justice, it wishes to acknowledge the claims of the minority.

Civil disobedience is also civil in another sense. Not only is it the outcome of a sincere conviction based on principles which regulate civil life, but it is public and nonviolent, that is, it is done in a situation where arrest and punishment are expected and accepted without resistance. In this way it manifests a respect for legal procedures. Civil disobedience expresses disobedience to law within the limits of fidelity to law, and this feature of it helps to establish in the eyes of the majority that it is indeed conscientious and sincere, that it really is meant to address their sense of justice.[3] Being completely open about one's acts and being willing to accept the legal consequences of one's conduct is a bond given to make good one's sincerity, for that one's deeds are conscientious is not easy to demonstrate to another or even before oneself. No doubt it is possible to imagine a legal system in which conscientious belief that the law is unjust is accepted as a defense for noncompliance, and men of great honesty who are confident in one another might make such a system work. But as things are such a scheme would be unstable; we must pay a price in order to establish that we believe our actions have a moral basis in the convictions of the community.

The nonviolent nature of civil disobedience refers to the fact that it is intended to address the sense of justice of the majority and as such it is a form of speech, an expression of conviction. To engage in violent acts likely to injure and to hurt is incompatible with civil disobedience as a mode of address. Indeed, an interference with the basic rights of others tends to obscure the civilly disobedient quality of one's act. Civil disobedience is nonviolent in the further sense that the legal penalty for one's action is accepted and that resistance is not (at least for the moment) contemplated. Nonviolence in this sense is to be distinguished from nonviolence as a religious or pacifist principle. While those engaging in civil disobedience have often held some such principle, there is no necessary connection between it and civil disobedience. For on the interpretation suggested, civil disobedience in a democratic society is best understood as an appeal to the principles of justice, the fundamental conditions of willing social cooperation among free men, which in the view of the community as a whole are expressed in the constitution and guide its interpretation. Being an appeal to the moral basis of public life, civil disobedience is a political and not primarily a religious act. It addresses itself to the common principles of justice which men can require one another to follow and not to the aspirations of love

which they cannot. Moreover by taking part in civilly disobedient acts one does not foreswear indefinitely the idea of forceful resistance; for if the appeal against injustice is repeatedly denied, then the majority has declared its intention to invite submission or resistance and the latter may conceivably be justified even in a democratic regime. We are not required to acquiesce in the crushing of fundamental liberties by democratic majorities which have shown themselves blind to the principles of justice upon which justification of the constitution depends.

THE JUSTIFICATION OF CIVIL DISOBEDIENCE

So far we have said nothing about the justification of civil disobedience, that is, the conditions under which civil disobedience may be engaged in consistent with the principles of justice that support a democratic regime. Our task is to see how the characterization of civil disobedience as addressed to the sense of justice of the majority (or to the citizens as a body) determines when such action is justified.

First of all, we may suppose that the normal political appeals to the majority have already been made in good faith and have been rejected, and that the standard means of redress have been tried. Thus, for example, existing political parties are indifferent to the claims of the minority and attempts to repeal the laws protested have been met with further repression since legal institutions are in the control of the majority. While civil disobedience should be recognized, I think, as a form of political action within the limits of fidelity to the rule of law, at the same time it is a rather desperate act just within these limits, and therefore it should, in general, be undertaken as a last resort when standard democratic processes have failed. In this sense it is not a normal political action. When it is justified there has been a serious breakdown; not only is there grave injustice in the law but a refusal more or less deliberate to correct it.

Second, since civil disobedience is a political act addressed to the sense of justice of the majority, it should usually be limited to substantial and clear violations of justice and preferably to those which, if rectified, will establish a basis for doing away with remaining injustices. For this reason there is a presumption in favor of restricting civil disobedience to violations of the first principle of justice, the principle of equal liberty, and to barriers which contravene the second principle, the principle of open offices which protects equality of opportunity. It is not, of course, always easy to tell whether these principles are satisfied. But if we think of them as guaranteeing the fundamental equal political and civil liberties (including freedom of conscience and liberty of thought) and equality of opportunity, then it is often relatively clear whether their principles are being honored. After all, the equal liberties are defined by the visible structure of social institutions; they are to be incorporated into the recognized practice, if not the letter, of social arrangements. When minorities are denied the right to vote or to hold certain political offices, when certain religious groups are repressed and others denied equality of opportunity in the economy, this is often obvious and there is no doubt that justice is not being given. However, the first part of the second principle which requires that inequalities be to everyone's advantage is a much more imprecise and controversial matter. Not only is there a problem of assigning it a determinate and precise sense, but even if we do so and agree on what it should be, there is often a wide variety of reasonable opinion as to whether the principle is satisfied. The reason for this is that the principle applies primarily to fundamental economic and social policies. The choice of these depends upon theoretical and speculative beliefs as well as upon a wealth of concrete information, and all of this mixed with judgment and plain hunch, not to mention in actual cases prejudice and self-interest. Thus unless the laws of taxation are clearly designed to attack a basic equal liberty, they should not be protested by civil disobedience; the appeal to justice is not sufficiently clear and its resolution is best left to the political process. But violations of the equal liberties that define the common status of citizenship are another matter. The deliberate denial of these more or less over any extended period of time in the face of normal political protest is, in general, an appropriate object of civil disobedience. We may think of the social system as divided roughly into two parts, one which incorporates the fundamental equal liberties (including equality of opportunity) and another which embodies social and economic policies properly aimed at promoting the advantage of everyone. As a rule civil disobedience is best limited to the former where the appeal to justice is not only more definite and precise, but where, if it is effective, it tends to correct the injustices in the latter.

Third, civil disobedience should be restricted to those cases where the dissenter is willing to affirm that everyone else similarly subjected to the same degree of injustice has the right to protest in a similar way. That is, we must be prepared to authorize others to dissent in similar situations and in the same way, and to accept the consequences of their doing so. Thus, we may hold, for example, that the widespread disposition to disobey civilly clear violations of fundamental liberties more or less deliberate over an extended period of time would raise the degree of justice throughout society and would insure men's self-esteem as well as their respect for one another. Indeed, I believe this to be true, though certainly it is partly a matter of conjecture. As the contract doctrine emphasizes, since the principles of justice are principles which we would agree to in an original position of equality when we do not know our social position and the like, the refusal to grant justice is either the denial of the other as an equal (as one in regard to whom we are prepared to constrain our actions by principles which we would consent to) or the manifestation of a willingness to take advantage of natural contingencies and social fortune at his expense. In either case, injustice invites submission or resistance; but submission arouses the contempt of the oppressor and confirms him in his intention. If straightway, after a decent period of time to make reasonable political appeals in the normal way, men were in general to dissent by civil disobedience from infractions of the fundamental equal liberties, these liberties would, I believe, be more rather than less secure. Legitimate civil disobedience properly exercised is a stabilizing device in a constitutional regime, tending to make it more firmly just.

Sometimes, however, there may be a complication in connection with this third condition. It is possible, although perhaps unlikely, that there are so many persons or groups with a sound case for resorting to civil disobedience (as judged by the foregoing criteria) that disorder would follow if they all did so. There might be serious injury to the just constitution. Or again, a group might be so large that some extra precaution is necessary in the extent to which its members organize and engage in civil disobedience. Theoretically the case is one in which a number of persons or groups are equally entitled to and all want to resort to civil disobedience, yet if they all do this, grave consequences for everyone may result. The question, then, is who among them may exercise their right, and it falls under the general problem of fairness. I cannot discuss the complexities of the matter here. Often a lottery or a rationing system can be set up to handle the case; but unfortunately the circumstances of civil disobedience rule out this solution. It suffices to note that a problem of fairness may arise and that those who contemplate civil disobedience should take it into account. They may have to reach an understanding as to who can exercise their right in the immediate situation and to recognize the need for special constraint.

The final condition, of a different nature, is the following. We have been considering when one has a right to engage in civil disobedience, and our conclusion is that one has the right should three conditions hold: when one is subject to injustice more or less deliberate over an extended period of time in the face of normal political protests; where the injustice is a clear violation of the liberties of equal citizenship; and provided that the general disposition to protest similarly in similar cases would have acceptable consequences. These conditions are not, I think, exhaustive but they seem to cover the more obvious points; yet even when they are satisfied and one has the right to engage in civil disobedience, there is still the different question of whether one should exercise this right, that is, whether by doing so one is likely to further one's ends. Having established one's right to protest one is then free to consider these tactical questions. We may be acting within our rights but still foolishly if our action only serves to provoke the harsh retaliation of the majority; and it is likely to do so if the majority lacks a sense of justice or if the action is poorly timed or not well designed to make the appeal to the sense of justice effective.

It is easy to think of instances of this sort, and in each case these practical questions have to be faced. From the standpoint of the theory of political obligation we can only say that the exercise of the right should be rational and reasonably designed to advance the protester's aims, and that weighing tactical questions presupposes that one has already established one's right, since tactical advantages in themselves do not support it.

CONCLUSION: SEVERAL OBJECTIONS CONSIDERED

In a reasonably affluent democratic society justice becomes the first virtue of institutions. Social arrangements irrespective of their efficiency must be reformed if they are significantly unjust. No increase in efficiency in the form of greater advantages for many justifies the loss of liberty of a few. That we believe this is shown by the fact that in a democracy the fundamental liberties of citizenship are not understood as the outcome of political bargaining nor are they subject to the calculus of social interests. Rather these liberties are fixed points which serve to limit political transactions and which determine the scope of calculations of social advantage. It is this fundamental place of the equal liberties which makes their systematic violation over any extended period of time a proper object of civil disobedience. For to deny men these rights is to infringe the conditions of social cooperation among free and rational persons, a fact which is evident to the citizens of a constitutional regime since it follows from the principles of justice which underlie their institutions. The justification of civil disobedience rests on the priority of justice and the equal liberties which it guarantees.

It is natural to object to this view of civil disobedience that it relies too heavily upon the existence of a sense of justice. Some may hold that the feeling for justice is not a vital political force, and that what moves men are various other interests, the desire for wealth, power, prestige, and so on. Now this is a large question the answer to which is highly conjectural and each tends to have his own opinion. But there are two remarks which may clarify what I have said: first, I have assumed that there is in a constitutional regime a common sense of justice the principles of which are recognized to support the constitution and to guide its interpretation. In any given situation particular men may be tempted to violate these principles, but the collective force in their behalf is usually effective since they are seen as the necessary terms of cooperation among free men; and presumably the citizens of a democracy (or sufficiently many of them) want to see justice done. Where these assumptions fail, the justifying conditions for civil disobedience (the first three) are not affected, but the rationality of engaging in it certainly is. In this case, unless the costs of repressing civil dissent injures the economic self-interest (or whatever) of the majority, protest may simply make the position of the minority worse. No doubt as a tactical matter civil disobedience is more effective when its appeal coincides with other interests, but a constitutional regime is not viable in the long run without an attachment to the principles of justice of the sort which we have assumed.

Then, further, there may be a misapprehension about the manner in which a sense of justice manifests itself. There is a tendency to think that it is shown by professions of the relevant principles together with actions of an altruistic nature requiring a considerable degree of self-sacrifice. But these conditions are obviously too strong, for the majority's sense of justice may show itself simply in its being unable to undertake the measures required to suppress the minority and to punish as the law requires the various acts of civil disobedience. The sense of justice undermines the will to uphold unjust institutions, and so a majority despite its superior power may give way. It is unprepared to force the minority to be subject to injustice. Thus, although the majority's action is reluctant and grudging, the role of the sense of justice is nevertheless essential, for without it the majority would have been willing to enforce the law and to defend its position. Once we see the sense of justice as working in this negative way to make established injustices indefensible, then it is recognized as a central element of democratic politics.

Finally, it may be objected against this account that it does not settle the question of who is to say when the situation is such as to justify civil disobedience. And because it does not answer this question, it invites anarchy by encouraging every man to decide the matter for himself. Now the reply to this is that each man must indeed settle this question for himself, although he may, of course, decide wrongly. This is true on any theory of political duty and obligation, at least on any theory compatible with the principles of a democratic constitution. The citizen is responsible for what he does. If we usually think that we should comply with the law, this is because our political principles normally lead to this conclusion. There is a presumption in favor of compliance in the absence of good reasons to the contrary. But because each man is responsible and must decide for himself as best he can whether the circumstances justify civil disobedience, it does not follow that he may decide as he pleases. It is not by looking to our personal interests or to political allegiances narrowly construed, that we should make up our mind. The citizen must decide on the basis of the principles of justice that underlie and guide the interpretation of the constitution and in the light of his sincere conviction as to how these principles should be applied in the circumstances. If he concludes that conditions obtain which justify civil disobedience and conducts himself accordingly, he has acted conscientiously and perhaps mistakenly, but not in any case at his convenience.

In a democratic society each man must act as he thinks the principles of political right require him to. We are to follow our understanding of these principles, and we cannot do otherwise. There can be no morally binding legal interpretation of these principles, not even by a supreme court or legislature. Nor is there any infallible procedure for determining what or who is right. In our system the Supreme Court, Congress, and the President often put forward rival interpretations of the Constitution. Although the Court has the final say in settling any particular case, it is not immune from powerful political influence that may change its reading of the law of the land. The Court presents its point of view by reason and argument; its conception of the Constitution must, if it is to endure, persuade men of its soundness. The final court of appeal is not the Court, or Congress, or the President, but the electorate as a whole. The civilly disobedient appeal in effect to this body. There is no danger of anarchy as long as there is a sufficient working agreement in men's conceptions of political justice and what it requires. That men can achieve such an understanding when the essential political liberties are maintained is the assumption implicit in democratic institutions. There is no way to avoid entirely the risk of divisive strife. But if legitimate civil disobedience seems to threaten civil peace, the responsibility falls not so much on those who protest as upon those whose abuse of authority and power justifies such opposition.

NOTES

1. By the social contract theory, I have in mind the doctrine found in Locke, Rousseau, and Kant.
2. Here I follow H. A. Bedau's definition of civil disobedience. See his "On Civil Disobedience," *Journal of Philosophy* (October, 1961).
3. For a fuller discussion on this point to which I am indebted, see Charles Fried, "Moral Causation," *Harvard Law Review* (1964).

REVIEW AND DISCUSSION QUESTIONS

1. Describe what Rawls means by justice as "fairness."
2. Why does Rawls think that the basic principles used to select a constitution and laws governing citizens' rights and opportunities should be chosen behind a "veil of ignorance"?
3. "Even a just constitution can lead to unjust laws." Explain using the analogy of a criminal trial.
4. Rawls thinks that the obligation to obey the law (assuming a just constitution) rests on the duty of fair play. Explain what he means.
5. How does Rawls define civil disobedience?
6. What role does civil disobedience play in a constitutional democracy?
7. Under what circumstances does Rawls think civil disobedience is justified?
8. How does Rawls respond to those who suggest his view is naive because it is based on the view that civil disobedience is an appeal to a majority's "sense of justice"?
9. Compare Rawls's conception of civil disobedience with conscientious objection.
10. Compare Rawls's view of legal obligation with that of Plato.

Civil Disobedience and the Law

Ronald Dworkin

In addition to the nature of legal obligation, civil disobedience raises further philosophical questions about law itself, according to Ronald Dworkin. It is often argued, he points out, that since society could not function if everybody were allowed to pick and choose the laws that he or she wishes to obey, fairness demands prosecution of civil disobedience. But in order to assess the argument,

From Ronald Dworkin, *Taking Rights Seriously* (Cambridge: Harvard University Press, 1977), pp. 206–222. Reprinted by permission.

Dworkin points out, we must first ask ourselves what we expect fellow citizens to do when they sincerely believe a law is unjust or immoral. In the American constitutional system, he claims, law and morality are not easily separated, which means, in turn, that the validity of law is itself often an issue in civil disobedience cases. That fact, Dworkin concludes, means that government should think of civil disobedients differently from ordinary criminals and often should choose not to punish them. Ronald Dworkin teaches philosophy at Oxford University and New York University School of Law.

How should the government deal with those who disobey the draft laws out of conscience? Many people think the answer is obvious: the government must prosecute the dissenters, and if they are convicted it must punish them. Some people reach this conclusion easily, because they hold the mindless view that conscientious disobedience is the same as lawlessness. They think that the dissenters are anarchists who must be punished before their corruption spreads. Many lawyers and intellectuals come to the same conclusion, however, on what looks like a more sophisticated argument. They recognize that disobedience to law may be *morally* justified, but they insist that it cannot be *legally* justified, and they think that it follows from this truism that the law must be enforced. Erwin Griswold, the Solicitor General of the United States, and the former dean of the Harvard Law School, appears to have adopted this view in a recent statement. "[It] is of the essence of law," he said, "that it is equally applied to all, that it binds all alike, irrespective of personal motive. For this reason, one who contemplates civil disobedience out of moral conviction should not be surprised and must not be bitter if a criminal conviction ensues. And he must accept the fact that organized society cannot endure on any other basis." . . .

But the argument that, because the government believes a man has committed a crime, it must prosecute him is much weaker than it seems. Society "cannot endure" if it tolerates all disobedience; it does not follow, however, nor is there evidence, that it will collapse if it tolerates some. In the United States prosecutors have discretion whether to enforce criminal laws in particular cases. A prosecutor may properly decide not to press charges if the lawbreaker is young, or inexperienced, or the sole support of the family, or is repentant, or turns state's evidence, or if the law is unpopular or unworkable or generally disobeyed, or if the courts are clogged with more important

cases, or for dozens of other reasons. This discretion is not license—we expect prosecutors to have good reasons for exercising it—but there are, at least *prima facie*, some good reasons for not prosecuting those who disobey the draft laws out of conscience. One is the obvious reason that they act out of better motives than those who break the law out of greed or a desire to subvert government. Another is the practical reason that our society suffers a loss if it punishes a group that includes—as a group of draft dissenters does—some of its most thoughtful and loyal citizens. Jailing such men solidifies their alienation from society, and alienates many like them who are deterred by the threat.

Those who think that conscientious draft offenders . . . should always be punished must show that these are not good reasons for exercising discretion, or they must find contrary reasons that outweigh them. What arguments might they produce? . . . Dean Griswold and those who agree with him seem to rely on a fundamental moral argument that it would be unfair, not merely impractical, to let the dissenters go unpunished. They think it would be unfair, I gather, because society could not function if everyone disobeyed laws he disapproved of or found disadvantageous. If the government tolerates those few who will not "play the game," it allows them to secure the benefits of everyone else's deference to law, without shouldering the burdens, such as the burden of the draft.

This argument is a serious one. It cannot be answered simply by saying that the dissenters would allow everyone else the privilege of disobeying a law he believed immoral. In fact, few draft dissenters would accept a changed society in which sincere segregationists were free to break civil rights laws they hated. The majority want no such change, in any event, because they think that society would be worse off for it; until they are shown this is wrong, they will expect their officials to punish anyone who assumes a privilege which they, for the general benefit, do not assume.

There is, however, a flaw in the argument. The reasoning contains a hidden assumption that makes it almost entirely irrelevant to the draft cases, and indeed to any serious case of civil disobedience in the United States. The argument assumes that the dissenters know that they are breaking a valid law, and that the privilege they assert is the privilege to do that. Of course, almost everyone who discusses civil disobedience recognizes that in America a law may be invalid because it is unconstitutional. . . .

Doubtful law is by no means special or exotic in cases of civil disobedience. On the contrary. In the United States, at least, almost any law which a significant number of people would be tempted to disobey on moral grounds would be doubtful—if not clearly invalid—on constitutional grounds as well. The constitution makes our conventional political morality relevant to the question of validity; any statute that appears to compromise that morality raises constitutional questions, and if the compromise is serious, the constitutional doubts are serious also.

[Editor's Note: Dworkin illustrates this by pointing out that the moral objections to the Vietnam War—for example, that the U.S. was using immoral weapons, that Congress had never officially declared war, and that it had been made a crime to "counsel" draft resistance—also provide the legal basis for constitutional arguments that, in fact, the war and laws related to it are unconstitutional and therefore invalid.]

. . . We cannot conclude from these arguments that the draft (or any part of it) was unconstitutional. . . . But the arguments of unconstitutionality were at least plausible and a reasonable and competent lawyer might think that they present a stronger case, on balance, than the counterarguments. . . .

Therefore we cannot assume, in judging what should have been done with the draft dissenters, that they were asserting a privilege to disobey valid laws. We cannot decide that fairness demanded their punishment until we try to answer further questions: What should a citizen do when the law is unclear, and when he thinks it allows what others think it does not? I do not mean to ask, of course, what it is *legally* proper for him to do, or what his *legal* rights are—that would be begging the question, because it depends upon whether he is right or they are right. I mean to ask what his proper course is as a citizen, what, in other words, we would consider to be "playing the game." That is a crucial question, because it cannot be unfair not to punish him if he is acting as, given his opinions, we think he should.[1]

There is no obvious answer on which most citizens would readily agree, and that is itself significant. If we examine our legal institutions and practices, however, we shall discover some relevant underlying principles and policies. I shall set out three possible answers to the question, and then try to show which of these best fits our practices and expectations. The three possibilities I want to consider are these:

1. If the law is doubtful, and it is therefore unclear whether it permits someone to do what he wants, he should assume the worst, and act on the assumption that it does not. He should obey the executive authorities who command him, even though he thinks they are wrong, while using the political process, if he can, to change the law.

2. If the law is doubtful, he may follow his own judgment, that is, he may do what he wants if he believes that the case that the law permits this is stronger than the case that it does not. But he may follow his own judgment only until an authoritative institution, like a court, decides the other way in a case involving him or someone else. Once an institutional decision has been reached, he must abide by that decision, even though he thinks that it was wrong. (There are, in theory, many subdivisions of this second possibility. We may say that the individual's choice is foreclosed by the contrary decision of any court, including the lowest court in the system if the case is not appealed. Or we may require a decision of some particular court or institution. I shall discuss this second possibility in its most liberal form, namely that the individual may properly follow his own judgment until a contrary decision of the highest court competent to pass on the issue, which, in the case of the draft, was the United States Supreme Court.)

3. If the law is doubtful, he may follow his own judgment, even after a contrary decision by the highest competent court. Of course, he must take the con-

trary decision of any court into account in making his judgment of what the law requires. Otherwise the judgment would not be an honest or reasonable one, because the doctrine of precedent, which is an established part of our legal system, has the effect of allowing the decision of the courts to change the law. Suppose, for example, that a taxpayer believes that he is not required to pay tax on certain forms of income. If the Supreme Court decides to the contrary, he should, taking into account the practice of according great weight to the decisions of the Supreme Court on tax matters, decide that the Court's decision has itself tipped the balance, and that the law now requires him to pay the tax.

Someone might think that this qualification erases the difference between the third and the second models, but it does not. The doctrine of precedent gives different weights to the decisions of different courts, and greatest weight to the decisions of the Supreme Court, but it does not make the decisions of any court conclusive. Sometimes, even after a contrary Supreme Court decision, an individual may still reasonably believe that the law is on his side; such cases are rare, but they are most likely to occur in disputes over constitutional law when civil disobedience is involved. The Court has shown itself more likely to overrule its past decisions if these have limited important personal or political rights, and it is just these decisions that a dissenter might want to challenge.

We cannot assume, in other words, that the Constitution is always what the Supreme Court says it is. Oliver Wendell Holmes, for example, did not follow such a rule in his famous dissent in the *Gitlow* case. A few years before, in *Abrams*, he had lost his battle to persuade the court that the First Amendment protected an anarchist who had been urging general strikes against the government. A similar issue was presented in *Gitlow*, and Holmes once again dissented. "It is true," he said, "that in my opinion this criterion was departed from [in *Abrams*] but the convictions that I expressed in that case are too deep for it to be possible for me as yet to believe that it . . . settled the law." Holmes voted for acquitting Gitlow, on the ground that what Gitlow had done was no crime, even though the Supreme Court had recently held that it was.

Here then are three possible models for the behavior of dissenters who disagree with the executive authorities when the law is doubtful. Which of them best fits our legal and social practices?

I think it plain that we do not follow the first of these models, that is, that we do not expect citizens to assume the worst. If no court has decided the issue, and a man thinks, on balance, that the law is on his side, most of our lawyers and critics think it perfectly proper for him to follow his own judgment. Even when many disapprove of what he does—such as peddling pornography—they do not think he must desist just because the legality of his conduct is subject to doubt.

I think it plain that we do not follow the first of these models, that is, that we do not expect citizens to assume the worst . . . [and that] he must desist just because the legality of his conduct is subject to doubt.

It is worth pausing a moment to consider what society would lose if it did follow the first model or, to put the matter the other way, what society gains when people follow their own judgment in cases like this. When the law is uncertain, in the sense that lawyers can reasonably disagree on what a court ought to decide, the reason usually is that different legal principles and policies have collided, and it is unclear how best to accommodate these conflicting principles and policies.

Our practice, in which different parties are encouraged to pursue their own understanding, provides a means of testing relevant hypotheses. If the question is whether a particular rule would have certain undesirable consequences, or whether these consequences would have limited or broad ramifications, then, before the issue is decided, it is useful to know what does in fact take place when some people proceed on that rule. (Much anti-trust and business regulation law has developed through this kind of testing.) If the question is whether and to what degree a particular solution would offend principles of justice or fair play deeply respected by the community, it is useful, again, to experiment by testing the community's response. The extent of community indifference to anti-contraception laws, for example, would never have become established had not some organizations deliberately flouted those laws.

If the first model were followed, we would lose the advantages of these tests. The law would suffer, particularly if this model were applied to constitutional issues. When the validity of a criminal statute is in doubt, the statute will almost always strike some people as being unfair or unjust, because it will infringe some principle of liberty or justice or fairness which they take to be built into the Constitution. If our practice were that whenever a law is doubtful on these grounds, one must act as if it were valid, then the chief vehicle we have for challenging the law on moral grounds would be lost, and over time the law we obeyed would certainly become less fair and just, and the liberty of our citizens would certainly be diminished. . . .

We must also reject the second model, that if the law is unclear a citizen may properly follow his own judgment until the highest court has ruled that he is wrong. This fails to take into account the fact that any court, including the Supreme Court, may overrule itself. In 1940 the Court decided that a West Virginia law requiring students to salute the Flag was constitutional. In 1943 it reversed itself, and decided that such a statute was unconstitutional after all. What was the duty as citizens, of those people who in 1941 and 1942 objected to saluting the Flag on grounds of conscience, and thought that the Court's 1940 decision was wrong? We can hardly say that their duty was to follow the first decision. They believed that saluting the Flag was unconscionable, and they believed, reasonably, that no valid law required them to do so. The Supreme Court later decided that in this they were right. The court did not simply hold that after the second decision failing to salute would not be a crime; it held (as in a case like this it almost always would) that it was no crime after the first decision either.

Some will say that the flag-salute dissenters should have obeyed the Court's first decision, while they worked in the legislatures to have the law repealed, and tried in the courts to find some way to challenge the law again without actually violating it. That would be, perhaps, a plausible recommendation if conscience were not involved, because it would then be arguable that the gain in orderly procedure was worth the personal sacrifice of patience. But conscience was involved, and if the dissenters had obeyed the law while biding their time, they would have suffered the irreparable injury of having done what their conscience forbade them to do. It is one thing to say that an individual must sometimes violate his conscience when he knows that the law commands him to do it. It is quite another to say that he must violate his conscience even when he reasonably believes that the law does not require it, because it would inconvenience his fellow citizens if he took the most direct, and perhaps the only, method of attempting to show that he is right and they are wrong.

Since a court may overrule itself, the same reasons we listed for rejecting the first model count against the second as well. If we did not have the pressure of dissent, we would not have a dramatic statement of the degree to which a court decision against the dissenter is felt to be wrong, a demonstration that is surely pertinent to the question of whether it was right. We would increase the chance of being governed by rules that offend the principles we claim to serve. . . .

Thus the third model, or something close to it, seems to be the fairest statement of a man's social duty in our community. A citizen's allegiance is to the law, not to any particular person's view of what the law is, and he does not behave unfairly so long as he proceeds on his own considered and reasonable view of what the law requires. Let me repeat (because it is crucial) that this is not the same as saying that an individual may disregard what the courts have said. The doctrine of precedent lies near the core of our legal system, and no one can make a reasonable effort to follow the law unless he grants the courts the general power to alter it by their decisions. But if the issue is one touching fundamental personal or political rights, and it is arguable that the Supreme Court has made a mistake, a man is within his social rights in refusing to accept that decision as conclusive. . . .

. . . I have been talking about the case of a man who believes that the law is not what other people think, or what the courts have held. This description may fit some of those who disobey the draft laws out of conscience, but it does not fit most of them. Most of the dissenters are not lawyers or political philosophers; they believe that the laws on the books are immoral, and inconsistent with their country's legal ideals, but they have not considered the question of whether they may be invalid as well. Of what relevance to their situation, then, is the proposition that one may properly follow one's own view of the law?

To answer this, I shall have to return to the point I made earlier. The Constitution, through the due process clause [government cannot deprive citizens of "life, liberty, or property without due process of law"], the equal protection clause [states cannot deny citizens the "equal protection of the laws"], the First Amendment [government cannot "abridge freedom of speech" or make a law "respecting the establishment of religion, or prohibiting the free exercise thereof], and the other provisions I mentioned, injects an extraordinary amount of our political morality into the issue of whether a law is valid. The statement that most draft dissenters are unaware that the law is invalid therefore needs qualification. They hold beliefs that, if true, strongly support the view that the law is on their side; the fact that they have not reached that further conclusion can be traced, in at least most cases, to their lack of legal sophistication. If we believe that when the law is doubtful people who follow their own judgment of the law may be acting properly, it would seem wrong not to extend that view to those dissenters whose judgments come to the same thing. No part of the case that I made for the third model would entitle us to distinguish them from their more knowledgeable colleagues.

We can draw several tentative conclusions from the argument so far: When the law is uncertain, in the sense that a plausible case can be made on both sides, then a citizen who follows his own judgment is not behaving unfairly. Our practices permit and encourage him to follow his own judgment in such cases. For that reason, our government has a special responsibility to try to protect him, and soften his predicament, whenever it can do so without great damage to other policies. It does not follow that the government can guarantee him immunity—it cannot adopt the rule that it will prosecute no one who acts out of conscience, or convict no one who reasonably disagrees with the courts. That would paralyze the government's ability to carry out its policies; it would, moreover, throw away the most important benefit of following the third model. If the state never prosecuted, then the courts could not act on the experience and the arguments the dissent has generated. But it does follow that when the practical reasons for prosecuting are relatively weak in a particular case, or can be met in other ways, the path of fairness lies in tolerance. The popular view that the law is the law and must always be enforced refuses to distinguish the man who acts on his own judgment of a doubtful law, and thus behaves as our practices provide, from the common criminal. I know of no reason, short of moral blindness, for not drawing a distinction in principle between the two cases.

I anticipate a philosophical objection to these conclusions: that I am treating law as a "brooding omnipresence in the sky." I have spoken of people making judgments about what the law requires, even in cases in which the law is unclear and undemonstrable. I have spoken of cases in which a man might think that the law requires one thing, even though the Supreme Court has said that is requires another, and even when it was not likely that the Supreme Court would soon change its mind. I will therefore be charged with the view that there is always a "right answer" to a legal problem to be found in natural law or locked up in some transcendental strongbox.

The strongbox theory of law is, of course, nonsense. When I say that people hold views on the law when the law is doubtful, and that these views are not merely predictions of what the courts will hold, I intend no such metaphysics. I mean only to summarize as accurately as I can many of the practices that are part of our legal process.

Lawyers and judges make statements of legal right and duty, even when they know these are not demonstrable, and support them with arguments even when they know that these arguments will not appeal to everyone. They make these arguments to one another, in the professional journals, in the classrooms, and in the courts. They respond to these arguments, when others make them, by judging them good or bad or mediocre. In so doing they assume that some arguments for a given doubtful position are better than others. They also assume that the case on one side of a doubtful proposition may be stronger than the case on the other, which is what I take a claim of law in a doubtful case to mean. . . .

Our legal system pursues these goals (the development and testing of the law through experimentation by citizens and through the adversary process) by inviting citizens to decide the strengths and weaknesses of legal arguments for themselves, or through their own counsel, and to act on these judgments, although that permission is qualified by the limited threat that they may suffer if the courts do not agree. Success in this strategy depends on whether there is sufficient agreement within the community on what counts as a good or bad argument, so that, although different people will reach different judgments, these differences will be neither so profound nor so frequent as to make the system unworkable, or dangerous for those who act by their own lights. I believe there is sufficient agreement on the criteria of the argument to avoid these traps, although one of the main tasks of legal philosophy is to exhibit and clarify these criteria. In any event, the practices I have described have not yet been shown to be misguided; they therefore must count

in determining whether it is just and fair to be lenient to those who break what others think is the law.

I have said that the government has a special responsibility to those who act on a reasonable judgment that a law is invalid. It should make accommodation for them as far as possible, when this is consistent with other policies. It may be difficult to decide what the government ought to do, in the name of that responsibility, in particular cases. The decision will be a matter of balance, and flat rules will not help. . . .

Some lawyers will be shocked by my general conclusion that we have a responsibility toward those who disobey the draft laws out of conscience, and that we may be required not to prosecute them, but rather to change our laws or adjust our sentencing procedures to accommodate them. The simple Draconian propositions, that crime must be punished, and that he who misjudges the law must take the consequences, have an extraordinary hold on the professional as well as the popular imagination. But the rule of law is more complex and more intelligent than that and it is important that it survive.

NOTES

1. I do not mean to imply that the government should always punish a man who deliberately breaks a law he knows is valid. There may be reasons of fairness or practicality, like those I listed in the third paragraph, for not prosecuting such men. But cases like the draft cases present special arguments for tolerance; I want to concentrate on these arguments and therefore have isolated these cases.

REVIEW AND DISCUSSION QUESTIONS

1. Describe how Dworkin sees the relation between morality and law. Why is it often difficult to know whether a law is valid?
2. What service does he think civil disobedients provide in our system?
3. Dworkin argues that it is not unfair to refuse to prosecute civil disobedients. His argument relies on a discussion of three courses of action open to citizens who object to law. Explain his argument.
4. What does Dworkin mean in rejecting the "strongbox" view of law? If law and morality are connected, as he suggests, how is the law to be tested and legal arguments assessed?
5. In light of one or two of the cases you have read, is Dworkin's description of the connections between law and morality an accurate one?
6. Compare Dworkin's views of law with those of Thomas Hobbes.
7. Compare Dworkin's position on civil disobedience and law with that of Rawls.

The Problem of the Grudge Informer

Lon L. Fuller

As the previous essay showed, questions about what law requires are not always casily resolved; nor is it always easy to determine whether to punish violators. Using an issue that is now being confronted as societies in eastern Europe and elsewhere undergo rapid political change, Lon Fuller confronts the specific question of whether to prosecute grudge informers from a prior Nazi-like regime. But that issue, he shows, raises further questions about the importance of the rule of law, the purpose of punishment, and the nature of law itself. Lon Fuller was professor of law at Harvard Law School.

By a narrow margin you have been elected Minister of Justice of your country, a nation of some twenty million inhabitants. At the outset of your term of office you are confronted by a serious problem that will be described below. But first the background of this problem must be presented.

For many decades your country enjoyed a peaceful, constitutional and democratic government. However, some time ago it came upon bad times. Normal relations were disrupted by a deepening economic depression and by an increasing antagonism among various factional groups, formed along economic, political, and religious lines. The proverbial man on horseback appeared in the form of the Headman of a political party or society that called itself the Purple Shirts.

In a national election attended by much disorder the Headman was elected President of the Republic and his party obtained a majority of the seats in the General Assembly. The success of the party at the polls was partly brought about by a campaign of reckless promises and ingenious falsifications, and partly by the physical intimidation of night-riding Purple Shirts who frightened many people away from the polls who would have voted against the party.

When the Purple Shirts arrived in power they took no steps to repeal the ancient Constitution or any of its provisions. They also left intact the Civil and Criminal Codes and the Code of Procedure. No official action was taken to dismiss any government official or to remove any judge from the bench. Elections continued to be held at intervals and ballots were counted with apparent honesty. Nevertheless, the country lived under a reign of terror.

Judges who rendered decisions contrary to the wishes of the party were beaten and murdered. The accepted meaning of the Criminal Code was perverted to place political opponents in jail. Secret statutes were passed, the contents of which were known only to the upper levels of the party hierarchy. Retroactive statutes were enacted which made acts criminal that were legally innocent when committed. No attention was paid by the government to the restraints of the Constitution, of antecedent laws, or even of its own laws. All opposing political parties were disbanded. Thousands of political opponents were put to death, either methodically in prisons or in sporadic night forays of terror. A general amnesty was declared in favor of persons under sentence for acts "committed in defending the fatherland against subversion." Under this amnesty a general liberation of all prisoners who were members of the Purple Shirt party was effected. No one not a member of the party was released under the amnesty.

From Lon L. Fuller, *The Morality of Law*, rev. ed. (New Haven: Yale University Press, 1969). Reprinted by permission.

The Purple Shirts as a matter of deliberate policy preserved an element of flexibility in their operations by acting at times through the party "in the streets," and by acting at other times through the apparatus of the state which they controlled. Choice between the two methods of proceeding was purely a matter of expediency. For example, when the inner circle of the party decided to ruin all the former Socialist-Republicans (whose party put up a last-ditch resistance to the new regime), a dispute arose as to the best way of confiscating their property. One faction, perhaps still influenced by prerevolutionary conceptions, wanted to accomplish this by a statute declaring their goods forfeited for criminal acts. Another wanted to do it by compelling the owners to deed their property over at the point of a bayonet. This group argued against the proposed statute on the ground that it would attract unfavorable comment abroad. The Headman decided in favor of direct action through the party to be followed by a secret statute ratifying the party's action and confirming the titles obtained by threats of physical violence.

The Purple Shirts have now been overthrown and a democratic and constitutional government restored. Some difficult problems have, however, been left behind by the deposed regime. These you and your associates in the new government must find some way of solving. One of these problems is that of the "grudge informer."

During the Purple Shirt regime a great many people worked off grudges by reporting their enemies to the party or to the government authorities. The activities reported were such things as the private expression of views critical of the government, listening to foreign radio broadcasts, associating with known wreckers and hooligans, hoarding more than the permitted amount of dried eggs, failing to report a loss of identification papers within five days, etc. As things then stood with the administration of justice, any of these acts, if proved, could lead to a sentence of death. In some cases this sentence was authorized by "emergency" statutes; in others it was imposed without statutory warrant, though by judges duly appointed to their offices.

After the overthrow of the Purple Shirts, a strong public demand grew up that these grudge informers be punished. The interim government, which preceded that with which you are associated, temporized on this matter. Meanwhile it has become a burning issue and a decision concerning it can no longer be postponed. Accordingly, your first act as Minister of Justice has been to address yourself to it. You have asked your five Deputies to give thought to the matter and to bring their recommendations to conference. At the conference the five Deputies speak in turn as follows:

First Deputy: "It is perfectly clear to me that we can do nothing about these so-called grudge informers. The acts they reported were unlawful according to the rules of the government then in actual control of the nation's affairs. The sentences imposed on their victims were rendered in accordance with principles of law then obtaining. These principles differed from those familiar to us in ways that we consider detestable. Nevertheless they were then the law of the land. One of the principal differences between that law and our own lies in the much wider discretion it accorded to the judge in criminal matters. This rule and its consequences are as much entitled to respect by us as the reform which the Purple Shirts introduced into the law of wills, whereby only two witnesses were required instead of three. It is immaterial that the rule granting the judge a more or less uncontrolled discretion in criminal cases was never formally enacted but was a matter of tacit acceptance. Exactly the same thing can be said of the opposite rule which we accept that restricts the judge's discretion narrowly. The difference between ourselves and the Purple Shirts is not that theirs was an unlawful government—a contradiction in terms—but lies rather in the field of ideology. No one has a greater abhorrence than I for Purple Shirtism. Yet the fundamental difference between our philosophy and theirs is that we permit and tolerate differences in viewpoint, while they attempted to impose their monolithic code on everyone. Our whole system of government assumes that law is a flexible thing, capable of expressing and effectuating many different aims. The cardinal point of our creed is that when an objective has been duly incorporated into a law or judicial decree it must be provisionally accepted even by those that hate it, who must await their chance at the polls, or in another litigation, to secure a legal recognition for their own aims. The Purple Shirts, on the other hand, simply disregarded laws that incorporated objectives of which they did not approve, not even considering it worth the effort involved to repeal them. If we now seek to unscramble the acts of the Purple Shirt regime, declaring this judgment invalid, that statute void, this sentence excessive, we shall be doing exactly the thing we most condemn in them. I recognize that it will take courage to carry through with the program I recommend and we shall have to resist strong pressures of public opinion. We shall also have to be prepared to prevent the people from taking the law into their own hands. In the long run, however, I believe the course I recommend is the only one that will insure the triumph of the conceptions of law and government in which we believe."

Second Deputy: "Curiously, I arrive at the same conclusion as my colleague, by an exactly opposite route. To me it seems absurd to call the Purple Shirt regime a lawful government. A legal system does not exist simply because policemen continue to patrol the streets and wear uniforms or because a constitution and code are left on the shelf unrepealed. A legal system presupposes laws that are known, or can be known, by those subject to them. It presupposes some uniformity of action and that like cases will be given like treatment. It presupposes the absence of some lawless power, like the Purple Shirt Party, standing above the government and able at any time to interfere with the administration of justice whenever it does not function according to the whims of that power. All of these presuppositions enter into the very conception of an order of law and have nothing to do with political and economic ideologies. In my opinion law in any ordinary sense of the word ceased to exist when the Purple Shirts came to power. During their regime we had, in effect, an interregnum in the rule of law. Instead of a government of laws we had a war of all against all conducted behind barred doors, in dark alleyways, in palace intrigues, and prison yard conspiracies. The acts of these so-called grudge informers were just one phase of that war. For us to condemn these acts as criminal would involve as much incongruity as if we were to attempt to apply juristic conceptions to the struggle for existence that goes on in the jungle or beneath the surface of the sea. We must put this whole dark, lawless chapter of our history behind us like a bad dream. If we stir among its hatreds, we shall bring upon ourselves something of its evil spirit and risk infection from its miasmas. I therefore say with my colleague, let bygones be bygones. Let us do nothing about the so-called grudge informers. What they did do was neither lawful nor contrary to law, for they lived, not under a regime of law, but under one of anarchy and terror."

Third Deputy: "I have a profound suspicion of any kind of reasoning that proceeds by an 'either-or' alternative. I do not think we need to assume either, on the one hand, that in some manner the whole of the Purple Shirt regime was outside the realm of law, or, on the other, that all of its doings are entitled to full credence as the act of a lawful government. My two colleagues have unwittingly delivered powerful arguments against these extreme assumptions by demonstrating that both of them lead to the same absurd conclusion, a conclusion that is ethically and politically impossible. If one reflects about the matter without emotion it becomes clear that we did not have during the Purple Shirt regime a 'war of all against all.' Under the surface much of what we call normal human life went on—marriages were contracted, goods were sold, wills were drafted and executed. This life was attended by the usual dislocations—automobile accidents, bankruptcies, unwitnessed wills, defamatory misprints in the newspapers. Much of this normal life and most of these equally normal dislocations of it were unaffected by the Purple Shirt ideology. The legal questions that arose in this area were handled by the courts much as they had been formerly and much as they are being handled today. It would invite an intolerable chaos if we were to declare everything that happened under the Purple Shirts to be without legal basis. On the other hand, we certainly cannot say that the murders committed in the streets by members of the party acting under orders from the Headman were lawful simply because the party had achieved control of the government and its chief had become President of the Republic. If we must condemn the criminal acts of the party and its members, it would seem absurd to uphold every act which happened to be canalized through the apparatus of a government that had become, in effect, the alter ego of the Purple Shirt Party. We must therefore, in this situation, as in most human affairs, discriminate. Where the Purple Shirt philosophy intruded itself and perverted the administration of justice from its normal aims and uses, there we must interfere. Among these perversions of justice I would count, for example, the case of a man who was in love with another man's wife and brought about the death of the husband by informing against him for a wholly trivial offense, that is, for not reporting a loss of his identification papers within five days. This informer was a murderer under the Criminal Code which was in effect at the time of his act and which the Purple Shirts had not repealed. He encompassed the death of one who stood in the way of his illicit passions and utilized the courts for the realization of his murderous intent. He knew that the courts were themselves the pliant instruments of whatever policy the Purple Shirts might for the moment consider expedient. There are other cases that are equally clear. I admit that there are also some that are less clear. We shall be embarrassed, for example, by the cases of mere busybodies who reported to the authorities everything that looked suspect. Some of these persons acted not from desire to get rid of those they accused, but with a desire to curry favor with the party, to divert suspicions (perhaps ill-founded) raised against themselves, or through sheer officiousness. I don't know how these cases should be handled, and make no recommendation with regard to them. But the fact that these troublesome cases exist should not deter us from acting at once in the cases that are clear, of which there are far too many to permit us to disregard them."

Fourth Deputy: "Like my colleague I too distrust 'either-or' reasoning, but I think we need to reflect more than he has about where we are headed. This proposal to pick and choose among the acts of the deposed regime is thoroughly objectionable. It is, in fact, Purple Shirtism itself, pure and simple. We like this law, so let us enforce it. We like this judgment, let it stand. This law we don't like, therefore it never was a law at all. This governmental act

we disapprove, let it be deemed a nullity. If we proceed this way, we take toward the laws and acts of the Purple Shirt government precisely the unprincipled attitude they took toward the laws and acts of the government they supplanted. We shall have chaos, with every judge and every prosecuting attorney a law unto himself. Instead of ending the abuses of the Purple Shirt regime, my colleague's proposal would perpetuate them. There is only one way of dealing with this problem that is compatible with our philosophy of law and government and that is to deal with it by duly enacted law, I mean, by a special statute directed toward it. Let us study this whole problem of the grudge informer, get all the relevant facts, and draft a comprehensive law dealing with it. We shall not then be twisting old laws to purposes for which they were never intended. We shall furthermore provide penalties appropriate to the offense and not treat every informer as a murderer simply because the one he informed against was ultimately executed. I admit that we shall encounter some difficult problems of draftsmanship. Among other things, we shall have to assign a definite legal meaning to 'grudge' and that will not be easy. We should not be deterred by these difficulties, however, from adopting the only course that will lead us out of a condition of lawless, personal rule."

Fifth Deputy: "I find a considerable irony in the last proposal. It speaks of putting a definite end to the abuses of the Purple Shirtism, yet it proposes to do this by resorting to one of the most hated devices of the Purple Shirt regime, the ex post facto criminal statute. My colleague dreads the confusion that will result if we attempt without a statute to undo and redress 'wrong' acts of the departed order, while we uphold and enforce its 'right' acts. Yet he seems not to realize that his proposed statute is a wholly specious cure for this uncertainty. It is easy to make a plausible argument for an undrafted statute; we all agree it would be nice to have things down in black and white on paper. But just what would this statute provide? One of my colleagues speaks of someone who had failed for five days to report a loss of his identification papers. My colleague implies that the judicial sentence imposed for that offense, namely death, was so utterly disproportionate as to be clearly wrong.

But we must remember that at that time the underground movement against the Purple Shirts was mounting in intensity and that the Purple Shirts were being harassed constantly by people with false identification papers. From their point of view they had a real problem, and the only objection we can make to their solution of it (other than the fact that we didn't want them to solve it) was that they acted with somewhat more rigor than the occasion seemed to demand. How will my colleague deal with this case in his statute, and with all of its cousins and second cousins? Will he deny the existence of any need for law and order under the Purple Shirt regime? I will not go further into the difficulties involved in drafting this proposed statute, since they are evident enough to anyone who reflects. I shall instead turn to my own solution. It has been said on very respectable authority that the main purpose of the criminal law is to give an outlet to the human instinct for revenge. There are times, and I believe this is one of them, when we should allow that instinct to express itself directly without the intervention of forms of law. This matter of the grudge informers is already in process of straightening itself out. One reads almost every day that a former lackey of the Purple Shirt regime has met his just reward in some unguarded spot. The people are quietly handling this thing in their own way and if we leave them alone, and instruct our public prosecutors to do the same, there will soon be no problem left for us to solve. There will be some disorders, of course, and a few innocent heads will be broken. But our government and our legal system will not be involved in the affair and we shall not find ourselves hopelessly bogged down in an attempt to unscramble all the deeds and misdeeds of the Purple Shirts."

As Minister of Justice which of these recommendations would you adopt?

REVIEW AND DISCUSSION QUESTIONS

1. Describe the problem faced by the Minister of Justice.
2. Outline each of the five alternatives that the various deputies defend.
3. Fuller's dialogue raises two issues. The first is whether or not a state may legitimately punish someone whose acts were wrong but not illegal. How would you respond to that issue?
4. The second issue deals with the validity of laws during the reign of the Purple Shirts. In light of the deputies' arguments, is the law of the Purple Shirts valid? Were laws from the previous constitutional regime still valid? How does that question bear on the choice among the five deputies' positions?
5. How would you answer the question raised at the end of the article? Explain why you reject the advice of each deputy whose position you think is mistaken.
6. How might Ronald Dworkin resolve this dispute, in light of his views on civil disobedience?
7. Explain how you think Thomas Hobbes would resolve this dispute.

The Death Penalty:

Gregg v. *Georgia*

The act of punishing a person, whether a child or a convicted criminal, involves causing harm in some way—for example, by taking away liberty, property, or, in extreme cases, life. Philosophers have proposed different types of justification for punishment. Utilitarians stress the socially useful consequences of punishing people, while retributivists argue that the purpose of punishment is to achieve justice by giving people what they morally deserve. People who deserve punishment should be punished, they claim, and that is true whether or not punishment has other social advantages.

The Eighth Amendment to the United States Constitution says in part that no "cruel and unusual punishment" shall be inflicted. But what, precisely, does that mean? Some examples are clear enough, for instance drawing and quartering, burning at the stake, and other extreme forms of mutilation or torture. But what about executions? The Supreme Court has consistently held that the meaning of "cruel and unusual" is not fixed, but instead it must be adjusted as society evolves. In this case, the question before the Court is whether executions for murder are unconstitutional. In an earlier case, *Furman* v. *Georgia* (1972), the Court overturned a death sentence in part because the specific procedures used made imposition of the penalty "arbitrary." A minority of the justices had also argued in *Furman* that executions per se were unconstitutional. In this opinion, the Court again considers both questions: the constitutionality of executions and the constitutionality of the procedures by which it is determined who shall die. In doing so, it also considers the important philosophical issues surrounding punishment and its justification.

Mr. Justice Stewart, with Justices Powell and Stevens Concurring: We address initially the basic contention that the punishment of death for the crime of murder is, under all circumstances, "cruel and unusual" in violation of the Eighth and Fourteenth Amendments of the Constitution. [Later in] this opinion, we will consider the sentence of death imposed under the Georgia statutes at issue in this case. . . .

The substantive limits imposed by the Eighth Amendment on what can be made criminal and punished were discussed in *Robinson* v. *California* (1962). The Court found unconstitutional a state statute that made the status of being addicted to a narcotic drug a criminal offense. It held, in effect, that it is "cruel and unusual" to impose any punishment at all for the mere status of addiction. The cruelty in the abstract of the actual sentence imposed was irrelevant: "Even one day in prison would be a cruel and unusual punishment for the

'crime' of having a common cold." *Id.*, at 667. Most recently, in *Furman* v. *Georgia*, . . . three Justices in separate concurring opinions found the Eighth Amendment applicable to procedures employed to select convicted defendants for the sentence of death.

It is clear from the foregoing precedents that the Eighth Amendment has not been regarded as a static concept. As Mr. Chief Justice Warren said, in an oft-quoted phrase, "[t]he Amendment must draw its meaning from the evolving standards of decency that mark the progress of a maturing society." Thus, an assessment of contemporary values concerning the infliction of a challenged sanction is relevant to the application of the Eighth Amendment. As we develop below more fully, . . . this assessment does not call for a subjective judgment. It requires, rather, that we look to objective indicia that reflect the public attitude toward a given sanction.

But our cases also make clear that public perceptions of standards of decency with respect to criminal sanctions are not conclusive. A penalty also must accord with "the dignity of man," which is the "basic concept underlying the Eighth Amendment." *Trop* v. *Dulles*. This means, at least, that the punishment not be "excessive." When a form of punishment in the abstract (in this case, whether capital punishment may ever be imposed as a sanction for murder) rather than in the particular (the propriety of death as a penalty to be applied to a specific defendant for a specific crime) is under consideration, the inquiry into "excessiveness" has two aspects. First, the punishment must not involve the unnecessary and wanton infliction of pain. . . . Second, the punishment must not be grossly out of proportion to the severity of the crime. . . .

The imposition of the death penalty for the crime of murder has a long history of acceptance both in the United States and in England. The common-law rule imposed as mandatory death sentence on all convicted murderers. . . . And the penalty continued to be used into the 20th century by most American States, although the breadth of the common-law rule was diminished, initially by narrowing the class of murders to be punished by death and subsequently by widespread adoption of laws expressly granting juries the discretion to recommend mercy. . . .

It is apparent from the text of the Constitution itself that the existence of capital punishment was accepted by the Framers. At the time the Eighth Amendment was ratified, capital punishment was a common sanction in every State. Indeed, the First Congress of the United States enacted legislation providing death as the penalty for specified crimes. . . .

The most marked indication of society's endorsement of the death penalty for murder is the legislative response to *Furman*. The legislatures of at least 35 States have enacted new statutes that provide for the death penalty for at least some crimes that result in the death of another person. And the Congress of the United States, in 1974, enacted a statute providing the death penalty for aircraft piracy that results in death. These recently adopted statutes have attempted to address the concerns expressed by the Court in *Furman* primarily (i) by specifying the factors to be weighed and the procedures to be followed in deciding when to impose a capital sentence, or (ii) by making the death penalty mandatory for specified crimes. . . .

. . . [H]owever, the Eighth Amendment demands more than that a challenged punishment be acceptable to contemporary society. The Court also must ask whether it comports with the basic concept of human dignity at the core of the Amendment. . . . Although we cannot "invalidate a category of penalties because we deem less severe penalties adequate to serve the ends of penology," *Furman* v. *Georgia*, . . . at 451 (Powell, J., dissenting), the sanction imposed cannot be so totally without penological justification that it results in the gratuitous infliction of suffering. . . .

The death penalty is said to serve two principal social purposes: retribution and deterrence of capital crimes by prospective offenders.[1]

In part, capital punishment is an expression of society's moral outrage at particularly offensive conduct. This function may be unappealing to many, but it is essential in an ordered society that asks its citizens to rely on legal processes rather than self-help to vindicate their wrongs.

"The instinct for retribution is part of the nature of man, and channeling that instinct in the administration of criminal justice serves an important purpose in promoting the stability of a society governed by law. When people begin to believe that organized society is unwilling or unable to impose upon criminal offenders the punishment they 'deserve,' then there are sown the seeds of anarchy—of self-help, vigilante justice, and lynch law." *Furman* v. *Georgia*, . . . at 308 (Stewart, J., concurring).

"Retribution is no longer the dominant objective of the criminal law," *Williams* v. *New York*, (1949), but neither is it a forbidden objective nor one inconsistent with our respect for the dignity of men. . . . Indeed, the decision that capital punishment may be the appropriate sanction in extreme cases is an expression of the community's belief that certain crimes are themselves so grievous an affront to humanity that the only adequate response may be the penalty of death.

Statistical attempts to evaluate the worth of the death penalty as a deterrent to crimes by potential offenders have occasioned a great deal of debate. The results simply have been inconclusive. . . .

Although some of the studies suggest that the death penalty may not function as a significantly greater deterrent than lesser penalties, there is no convincing empirical evidence either supporting or refuting this view. We may nevertheless assume safely that there are murderers, such as those who act in passion, for whom the threat of death has little or no deterrent effect. But for many others, the death penalty undoubtedly is a significant deterrent. There are carefully contemplated murders, such as murders for hire, where the possible penalty of death may well enter into the cold calculus that precedes the decision to act.[2] And there are some categories of murder, such as murder by a life prisoner, where other sanctions may not be adequate.

The value of capital punishment as a deterrent of crime is a complex factual issue the resolution of which properly rests with the legislatures, which can evaluate the results of statistical studies in terms of their own local conditions and with a flexibility of approach that is not available to the courts. . . . Indeed, many of the post-*Furman* statutes reflect just such a responsible effort to define those crimes and those criminals for which capital punishment is most probably an effective deterrent.

In sum, we cannot say that the judgment of the Georgia Legislature that capital punishment may be necessary in some cases is clearly wrong. Considerations of federalism, as well as respect for the ability of a legislature to evaluate, in terms of its particular State, the moral consensus concerning the death penalty and its social utility as a sanction, require us to conclude, in the absence of more convincing evidence, that the infliction of death as a punishment for murder is not without justification and thus is not unconstitutionally severe.

Finally, we must consider whether the punishment of death is disproportionate in relation to the crime for which it is imposed. There is no question that death as a punishment is unique in its severity and irrevocability. . . . When a defendant's life is at stake, the Court has been particularly sensitive to insure that every safeguard is observed. . . . But we are concerned here only with the imposition of capital punishment for the crime of murder, and

when a life has been taken deliberately by the offender, we cannot say that the punishment is invariably disproportionate to the crime. It is an extreme sanction, suitable to the most extreme of crimes.

We hold that the death penalty is not a form of punishment that may never be imposed, regardless of the circumstances of the offense, regardless of the character of the offender, and regardless of the procedure followed in reaching the decision to impose it.

We now consider whether Georgia may impose the death penalty on the petitioner in this case. . . . Because of the uniqueness of the death penalty, *Furman* held that it could not be imposed under sentencing procedures that created a substantial risk that it would be inflicted in an arbitrary and capricious manner. Mr. Justice White concluded that "the death penalty is exacted with great infrequency even for the most atrocious crimes and there is no meaningful basis for distinguishing the few cases in which it is imposed from the many cases in which it is not." at 313 (concurring). Indeed, the death sentences examined by the Court in *Furman* were "cruel and unusual in the same way that being struck by lightning is cruel and unusual. For, of all the people convicted of [capital crimes], many just as reprehensible as these, the petitioners [in *Furman* were] among a capriciously selected random handful upon whom the sentence of death has in fact been imposed. . . . [T]he Eighth and Fourteenth Amendments cannot tolerate the infliction of a sentence of death under legal systems that permit this unique penalty to be so wantonly and so freakishly imposed." *Id.*, at 309–310 (Stewart, J., concurring). . . .

In summary, the concerns expressed in *Furman* that the penalty of death not be imposed in an arbitrary or capricious manner can be met by a carefully drafted statute that ensures that the sentencing authority is given adequate information and guidance. As a general proposition these concerns are best met by a system that provides for a bifurcated proceeding at which the sentencing authority is apprised of the information relevant to the imposition of sentence and provided with standards to guide its use of the information.

The basic concern of *Furman* centered on those defendants who were being condemned to death capriciously and arbitrarily. Under the procedures before the Court in that case, sentencing authorities were not directed to give attention to the nature or circumstances of the crime committed or to the character or record of the defendant. Left unguided, juries imposed the death sentence in a way that could only be called freakish. The new Georgia sentencing procedures, by contrast, focus the jury's attention on the particularized nature of the crime and the particularized characteristics of the individual defendant. While the jury is permitted to consider any aggravating or mitigating circumstances, it must find and identify at least one statutory aggravating factor before it may impose a penalty of death. In this way the jury's discretion is channeled. No longer can a jury wantonly and freakishly impose the death sentence; it is always circumscribed by the legislative guidelines. In addition, the review function of the Supreme Court of Georgia affords additional assurance that the concerns that prompted our decision in *Furman* are not present to any significant degree in the Georgia procedure applied here.

For the reasons expressed in this opinion, we hold that the statutory system under which Gregg was sentenced to death does not violate the Constitution. Accordingly, the judgment of the Georgia Supreme Court is affirmed.

It is so ordered.

Mr. Justice Brennan, Dissenting: The Cruel and Unusual Punishments Clause "must draw its meaning from the evolving standards of decency that mark the progress of a maturing society."3. . . .

In *Furman* v. *Georgia*, . . . I read "evolving standards of decency" as requiring focus upon the essence of the death penalty itself and not primarily or solely upon the procedures under which the determination to inflict the penalty upon a particular person was made. I there said:

"From the beginning of our Nation, the punishment of death has stirred acute public controversy. Although pragmatic arguments for and against the punishment have been frequently advanced, this longstanding and heated controversy cannot be explained solely as the result of differences over the practical wisdom of a particular government policy. At bottom, the battle has been waged on moral grounds. The country has debated whether a society for which the dignity of the individual is the supreme value can, without a fundamental inconsistency, follow the practice of deliberately putting some of its members to death. In the United States, as in other nations of the western world, 'the struggle about this punishment has been one between ancient and deeply rooted beliefs in retribution, atonement or vengeance on the one hand, and, on the other, beliefs in the personal value and dignity of the common man that were born of the democratic movement of the eighteenth century, as well as beliefs in the scientific approach to an understanding of the motive forces of human conduct, which are the result of the growth of the sciences of behavior during the nineteenth and twentieth centuries.' It is this essentially moral conflict that forms the backdrop for the past changes in and the present operation of our system of imposing death as a punishment for crime." *Id.*, at 296.4

That continues to be my view. For the Clause forbidding cruel and unusual punishments under our constitutional system of government embodies in unique degree moral principles restraining the punishments that our civilized society may impose on those persons who transgress its laws. Thus, I too say: "For myself, I do not hesitate to assert the proposition that the only way the law has progressed from the days of the rack, the screw and the wheel is the development of moral concepts, or, as stated by the Supreme Court the application of 'evolving standards of decency'. . . ."5

This Court inescapably has the duty, as the ultimate arbiter of the meaning of our Constitution, to say whether, when individuals condemned to death stand before our Bar, "moral concepts" require us to hold that the law has progressed to the point where we should declare that the punishment of death, like punishments on the rack, the screw, and the wheel, is no longer morally tolerable in our civilized society. . . . I emphasize only that foremost among the "moral concepts" recognized in our cases and inherent in the Clause is the primary moral principle that the State, even as it punishes, must treat its citizens in a manner consistent with their intrinsic worth as human beings—a punishment must not be so severe as to be degrading to human dignity. A judicial determination whether the punishment of death comports with human dignity is therefore not only permitted but compelled by the Clause. . . .

The fatal constitutional infirmity in the punishment of death is that it treats "members of the human race as nonhumans, as objects to be toyed with and discarded. [It is] thus inconsistent with the fundamental premise of the Clause that even the vilest criminal remains a human being possessed of common human dignity." *Id.,* at 273. As such it is a penalty that "subjects the individual to a fate forbidden by the principle of civilized treatment guaranteed by the [Clause]." I therefore would hold, on that ground alone, that death is today a cruel and unusual punishment prohibited by the Clause. "Justice of this kind is obviously no less shocking than the crime itself, and the new 'official' murder, far from offering redress for the offense committed against society, adds instead a second defilement to the first."[6]

Mr. Justice Marshall, Dissenting: In *Furman* I concluded that the death penalty is constitutionally invalid for two reasons. First, the death penalty is excessive. . . . And second, the American people, fully informed as to the purposes of the death penalty and its liabilities, would in my view reject it as morally unacceptable. . . .

Since the decision in *Furman,* the legislatures of 35 States have enacted new statutes authorizing the imposition of the death sentence for certain crimes, and Congress has enacted a law providing the death penalty for air piracy resulting in death. . . . I would be less than candid if I did not acknowledge that these developments have a significant bearing on a realistic assessment of the moral acceptability of the death penalty to the American people. But if the constitutionality of the death penalty turns, as I have urged, on the opinion of an *informed* citizenry, then even the enactment of new death statutes cannot be viewed as conclusive. In *Furman,* I observed that the American people are largely unaware of the information critical to a judgment on the morality of the death penalty, and concluded that if they were better informed they would consider it shocking, unjust, and unacceptable. . . . A recent study, conducted after the enactment of the post-*Furman* statutes, has confirmed that the American people know little about the death penalty, and that the opinions of an informed public would differ significantly from those of a public unaware of the consequences and effects of the death penalty.[7]

Even assuming, however, that the post-*Furman* enactment of statutes authorizing the death penalty renders the prediction of the views of an informed citizenry an uncertain basis for a constitutional decision, the enactment of those statutes has no bearing whatsoever on the conclusion that the death penalty is unconstitutional because it is excessive. An excessive penalty is invalid under the Cruel and Unusual Punishments Clause "even though popular sentiment may favor" it. . . . The inquiry here, then, is simply whether the death penalty is necessary to accomplish the legitimate legislative purposes in punishment, or whether a less severe penalty—life imprisonment—would do as well. . . .

The two purposes that sustain the death penalty as nonexcessive in the Court's view are general deterrence and retribution. In *Furman,* I canvassed the relevant data on the deterrent effect of capital punishment. . . . The state of knowledge at that point, after literally centuries of debate, was summarized as follows by a United Nations Committee:

"It is generally agreed between the retentionists and abolitionists, whatever their opinions about the validity of comparative studies of deterrence, that the data which now exist show no correlation between the existence of capital punishment and lower rates of capital crime."[8]

The available evidence, I concluded in *Furman,* was convincing that "capital punishment is not necessary as a deterrent to crime in our society." *Id.,* at 353. . . .

The other principal purpose said to be served by the death penalty is retribution. . . . It is this notion that I find to be the most disturbing aspect of today's unfortunate decisions.

The concept of retribution is a multifaceted one, and any discussion of its role in the criminal law must be undertaken with caution. On one level, it can be said that the notion of retribution or reprobation is the basis of our insistence that only those who have broken the law be punished, and in this sense the notion is quite obviously central to a just system of criminal sanctions. But our recognition that retribution plays a crucial role in determining who may be punished by no means requires approval of retribution as a general justification for punishment.9 It is the question whether retribution can provide a moral justification for punishment—in particular, capital punishment—that we must consider.

My Brothers Stewart, Powell, and Stevens offer the following explanation of the retributive justification for capital punishment:

"The instinct for retribution is part of the nature of man, and channeling that instinct in the administration of criminal justice serves an important purpose in promoting the stability of a society governed by law. When people begin to believe that organized society is unwilling or unable to impose upon criminal offenders the punishment they 'deserve,' then there are sown the seeds of anarchy—of self-help, vigilante justice, and lynch law."

This statement is wholly inadequate to justify the death penalty. As my Brother Brennan stated in *Furman*, "[t]here is no evidence whatever that utilization of imprisonment rather than death encourages private blood feuds and other disorders." . . . at 303 (concurring opinion). It simply defies belief to suggest that the death penalty is necessary to prevent the American people from taking the law into their own hands.

In a related vein, it may be suggested that the expression of moral outrage through the imposition of the death penalty serves to reinforce basic moral values—that it marks some crimes as particularly offensive and therefore to be avoided. The argument is akin to a deterrence argument, but differs in that it contemplates the individual's shrinking from antisocial conduct, not because he fears punishment, but because he has been told in the strongest possible way that the conduct is wrong. This contention, like the previous one, provides no support for the death penalty. It is inconceivable that any individual concerned about conforming his conduct to what society says is "right" would fail to realize that murder is "wrong" if the penalty were simply life imprisonment.

The foregoing contentions—that society's expression of moral outrage through the imposition of the death penalty preempts the citizenry from taking the law into its own hands and reinforces moral values—are not retributive in the purest sense. They are essentially utilitarian in that they portray the death penalty as valuable because of its beneficial results. These justifications for the death penalty are inadequate because the penalty is, quite clearly I think, not necessary to the accomplishment of those results.

There remains for consideration, however, what might be termed the purely retributive justification for the death penalty—that the death penalty is appropriate, not because of its beneficial effect on society, but because the taking of the murderer's life is itself morally good. Some of the language of the opinion of my Brothers Stewart, Powell, and Stevens . . . appears positively to embrace this notion of retribution for its own sake as a justification for capital punishment. They state:

"[T]he decision that capital punishment may be the appropriate sanction in extreme cases is an expression of the community's belief that certain crimes are themselves so grievous an affront to humanity that the only adequate response may be the penalty of death."

They then quote with approval from Lord Justice Denning's remarks before the British Royal Commission on Capital Punishment:

"The truth is that some crimes are so outrageous that society insists on adequate punishment, because the wrong-doer deserves it, irrespective of whether it is a deterrent or not."

Of course, it may be that these statements are intended as no more than observations as to the popular demands that it is thought must be responded to in order to prevent anarchy. But the implication of the statements appears to me to be quite different—namely, that society's judgment that the murderer "deserves" death must be respected not simply because the preservation of order requires it, but because it is appropriate that society make the judgment and carry it out. It is this latter notion, in particular, that I consider to be fundamentally at odds with the Eighth Amendment. . . . The mere fact that the community demands the murderer's life in return for the evil he has done cannot sustain the death penalty, for as Justices Stewart, Powell, and Stevens remind us, "the Eighth Amendment demands more than that a challenged punishment be acceptable to contemporary society." To be sustained under the Eighth Amendment, the death penalty must "comport with the basic concept of human dignity at the core of the Amendment," *ibid.*; the objective in imposing it must be "[consistent] with our respect for the dignity of [other] men."Under these standards, the taking of life "because the wrongdoer deserves it" surely must fall, for such a punishment has as its very basis the total denial of the wrongdoer's dignity and worth.

The death penalty, unnecessary to promote the goal of deterrence or to further any legitimate notion of retribution, is an excessive penalty forbidden by the Eighth and Fourteenth Amendments. I respectfully dissent from the Court's judgment upholding the sentences of death imposed upon the petitioners in these cases.

NOTES

1. Another purpose that has been discussed is the incapacitation of dangerous criminals and the consequent prevention of crimes that they may otherwise commit in the future.

2. Other types of calculated murders, apparently occurring with increasing frequency, include the use of bombs or other means of indiscriminate killings, the extortion murder of hostages or kidnap victims, and the execution-style killing of witnesses to a crime.

3. *Trop* v. *Dulles*, 356 U.S. 86, 101 (1958) (plurality opinion of Warren, C. J.).

4. Quoting T. Sellin, *The Death Penalty*, A Report for the Model Penal Code Project of the American Law Institute 15 (1959).

5. *Novak* v. *Beto*, 453 F. 2d 661, 672 (CA5 1971) (Tuttle, J., concurring in part and dissenting in part).

6. A. Camus, *Reflections on the Guillotine* 5–6 (Fridtjof-Karla Pub. 1960).

7. Sarat & Vidmar, "Public Opinion, The Death Penalty, and the Eighth Amendment: Testing the Marshall Hypothesis," 1976 *Wis. L. Rev.* 171.

8. United Nations, Department of Economic and Social Affairs, *Capital Punishment*, pt. II, ¶ 159, p. 123 (1968).

9. See, *e.g.*, H. Hart, *Punishment and Responsibility* 8–10, 71–83 (1968); H. Packer, *Limits of the Criminal Sanction* 38–39, 66 (1968).

REVIEW AND DISCUSSION QUESTIONS

1. How would you define *punishment?* How is it different from taxation?

2. The Court states that the Eighth Amendment means that punishment cannot be "excessive." What two reasons do the justices who defend executions give to prove that capital punishment is not excessive?

3. How do the two dissenters respond to the argument that executions are not excessive punishment?

4. Besides not being excessive, the death penalty must also be compatible with society's "evolving standards of decency." Why does Justice Stewart think it is not incompatible?

5. Why do the dissenters think executions are not compatible with evolving standards of decency? How does Justice Marshall respond to Justice Stewart's point about what state legislatures had done after the *Furman* decision?

6. Consider the following argument: The death penalty must deter, no matter what statistics say, because almost everybody would prefer life in prison to execution. Do you agree with that argument?

Executions

Jonathan Glover

In this essay, Jonathan Glover reviews a variety of positions on the morality of the death penalty, including the claims that it is required by justice, that it is legally sanctioned murder, and that it deters other potential murderers. Jonathan Glover is a fellow of New College, Oxford.

The debate about capital punishment for murder is, emotionally at least, dominated by two absolutist views. On the retributive view, the murderer must be given the punishment he deserves, which is death. On the other view, analogous to pacifism about war, there is in principle no possibility of justifying capital punishment: in execution there is only "the unspeakable wrongness of cutting a life short when it is in full tide." Supporters of these two approaches agree only in rejecting the serpent-windings of utilitarianism.

Let us look first at the retributive view. According to retributivism in its purest form, the aim of punishment is quite independent of any beneficial social consequences it may have. To quote Kant:

Even if a Civil Society resolved to dissolve itself with the consent of all its members—as might be supposed in the case of a people inhabiting an island resolving to separate and scatter themselves throughout the whole world—the last Murderer lying in the prison ought to be executed before the resolution was carried out. This ought to be done in order that everyone may realize the desert of his deeds, and that blood-guiltiness may not remain upon the people; for otherwise they might all be regarded as participators in the murder as a public violation of justice.

This view of punishment, according to which it has a value independent of its contribution to reducing the crime rate, is open to the objection that acting on it leads to what many consider to be pointless suffering. To impose suffering or depri-

vation on someone, or to take his life, is something that those of us who are not retributivists think needs very strong justification in terms of benefits, either to the person concerned or to other people. The retributivist has to say either that the claims of justice can make it right to harm someone where no one benefits, or else to cite the curiously metaphysical "benefits" of justice being done, such as Kant's concern that we should have "blood-guiltiness" removed. I have no way of refuting these positions, as they seem to involve no clear intellectual mistake. I do not expect to win the agreement of those who hold them, and I am simply presupposing the other view, that there is already enough misery in the world, and that adding to it requires a justification in terms of nonmetaphysical benefits to people.

This is not to rule out retributive moral principles perhaps playing a limiting role in a general theory of punishment. There is a lot to be said for the retributive restrictions that only those who deserve punishment should receive it and that they should never get more punishment than they deserve. (The case for this, which at least partly rests on utilitarian considerations, has been powerfully argued by H. L. A. Hart.)[1] But the approach to be adopted here rules out using retributive considerations to justify any punishment not already justifiable in terms of social benefits. In particular it rules out the argument that capital punishment can be justified, whether or not it reduces the crime rate, because the criminal deserves it.

This approach also has the effect of casting doubt on another way of defending capital punishment, which was forthrightly expressed by Lord Denning: "The ultimate justification of any punishment is not that it is a deterrent, but that it is the emphatic denunciation by the community of a crime: and from this point of view, there are some murders which, in the present state of public opinion, demand the most emphatic denunciation of all, namely the death penalty.[2] The question here is whether the point of the denunciation is to reduce the murder rate, in which case this turns out after all to be a utilitarian justification, or whether denunciation is an end in itself. If it is an end in itself, it starts to look like the retributive view in disguise, and should be rejected for the same reasons.

If we reject retribution for its own sake as a justification for capital punishment, we are left with two alternative general approaches to the question. One is an absolute rejection in principle of any possibility of capital punishment being justified. . . . The other is the rather more messy approach, broadly utilitarian in character, of weighing up likely social costs and benefits.

THE ABSOLUTIST REJECTION OF CAPITAL PUNISHMENT

To some people, it is impossible to justify the act of killing a fellow human being. They are absolute pacifists about war and are likely to think of capital punishment as "judicial murder." They will sympathize with Beccaria's question: "Is it not absurd that the laws which detest and punish homicide, in order to prevent murder, publicly commit murder themselves?"

The test of whether an opponent of capital punishment adopts this absolutist position is whether he would still oppose it if it could be shown to save many more lives than it cost: if, say, every execution deterred a dozen potential murderers. The absolutist, unlike the utilitarian opponent of the death penalty, would be unmoved by any such evidence. . . .

There is a variant on the absolutist position. . . . On this view, while saving a potential murder victim is in itself as important as not killing a murderer, there is something so cruel about the kind of

death involved in capital punishment that this rules out the possibility of its being justified. . . . When this view is taken of the cruelty of the death penalty, it is not usually the actual method of execution which is objected to, though this can seem important, as in the case where international pressure on General Franco led him to substitute shooting for the garrotte. What seems peculiarly cruel and horrible about capital punishment is that the condemned man has the period of waiting, knowing how and when he is to be killed. Many of us would rather die suddenly than linger for weeks or months knowing we were fatally ill, and the condemned man's position is several degrees worse than that of the person given a few months to live by doctors. He has the additional horror of knowing exactly when he will die, and of knowing that his death will be in a ritualized killing by other people, symbolizing his ultimate rejection by the members of his community. The whole of his life may seem to have a different and horrible meaning when he sees it leading up to this end.

For reasons of this kind, capital punishment can plausibly be claimed to fall under the United States constitution's ban on 'cruel and unusual punishments', so long as the word 'unusual' is not interpreted too strictly. The same reasons make the death penalty a plausible candidate for falling under a rather similar ethical ban, which has been expressed by H. L. A. Hart: "There are many different ways in which we think it morally incumbent on us to *qualify* or *limit* the pursuit of the utilitarian goal by methods of punishment. Some punishments are ruled out as too barbarous to use *whatever their social utility*"[3] (final italics mine). Because of the extreme cruelty of capital punishment, many of us would, if forced to make a choice between two horrors, prefer to be suddenly murdered rather than be sentenced to death and executed. This is what makes it seem reasonable to say that the absolutist rejection of the death penalty need not rest on the acts and omissions doctrine.

But this appearance is illusory. The special awfulness of capital punishment may make an execution even more undesirable than a murder (though many would disagree on the grounds that this is outweighed by the desirability that the guilty rather than the innocent should die). Even if we accept that an execution is worse than an average murder, it does not follow from this that capital punishment is too barbarous to use *whatever its social utility*. For supposing a single execution deterred many murders? Or suppose that some of the murders deterred would themselves have been as cruel as an execution? When we think of the suffering imposed in a famous kidnapping case, where the mother received her son's ear through the post, we may feel uncertain even that capital punishment is more cruel than some "lesser" crimes than murder. The view that some kinds of suffering are too great to impose, whatever their social utility, rules out the possibility of justifying them, however much more suffering they would prevent. And this does presuppose the acts and omissions doctrine, and so excludes some of us even from this version of absolutism.

A UTILITARIAN APPROACH

It is often supposed that the utilitarian alternative to absolutism is simply one of adopting an unqualified maximizing policy. On such a view, the death penalty would be justified if, and only if, it was reasonable to think the number of lives saved exceeded the number of executions. (The question of what to do where the numbers exactly balance presupposes a fineness of measurement that is unattainable in these matters.) On any utilitarian view, numbers of lives saved must be a very important consideration. But there are various special features that justify the substantial qualification of a maximizing policy.

The special horror of the period of waiting for execution may not justify the absolutist rejection of the death penalty, but it is a powerful reason for thinking that an execution may normally cause more misery than a murder, and so for thinking that, if capital punishment is to be justified, it must do better than break even when lives saved through deterrence are compared with lives taken by the executioner.

This view is reinforced when we think of some of the other side-effects of the death penalty. It must be appalling to be told that your husband, wife or child has been murdered, but this is surely less bad than the experience of waiting a month or

two for your husband, wife or child to be executed. And those who think that the suffering of the murderer himself matters less than that of an innocent victim will perhaps not be prepared to extend this view to the suffering of the murderer's parents, wife and children.

There is also the possibility of mistakenly executing an innocent man, something which it is very probable happened in the case of Timothy Evans. The German Federal Ministry of Justice is quoted in the Council of Europe's report on *The Death Penalty in European Countries* as saying that in the hundred years to 1953, there were twenty-seven death sentences "now established or presumed" to be miscarriages of justice. This point is often used as an argument against capital punishment, but what is often not noticed is that its force must depend on the special horrors of execution as compared with other forms of death, including being murdered. For the victim of murder is innocent too, and he also has no form of redress. It is only the (surely correct) assumption that an innocent man faces something much worse in execution than in murder that gives this argument its claim to prominence in this debate. For, otherwise, the rare cases of innocent men being executed would be completely overshadowed by the numbers of innocent men being murdered. (Unless, of course, the acts and omissions doctrine is again at work here, for execution is something that we, as a community, *do*, while a higher murder rate is something we at most *allow*.)

The death penalty also has harmful effects on people other than the condemned man and his family. For most normal people, to be professionally involved with executions, whether as judge, prison warder or chaplain, or executioner, must be highly disturbing. Arthur Koestler quotes the case of the executioner Ellis, who attempted suicide a few weeks after he executed a sick woman "whose insides fell out before she vanished through the trap".[4] (Though the chances must be very small of the experience of Mr Pierrepoint, who describes in his autobiography how he had to execute a friend with whom he often sang duets in a pub.[5]) And there are wider effects on society at large. When there is capital punishment, we are all involved in the horrible business of a long-premeditated killing, and most of us will to some degree share in the emotional response George Orwell had so strongly when he had to be present. It cannot be good for children at school to know that there is an execution at the prison down the road. And there is another bad effect, drily stated in the *Report of the Royal Commission on Capital Punishment:* "No doubt the ambition that prompts an average of five applications a week for the post of hangman, and the craving that draws a crowd to the prison where a notorious murderer is being executed, reveal psychological qualities that no state would wish to foster in its citizens."

Capital punishment is also likely to operate erratically. Some murderers are likely to go free because the death penalty makes juries less likely to convict. (Charles Dickens, in a newspaper article quoted in the 1868 Commons debate, gave the example of a forgery case, where a jury found a £10 note to be worth 39 shillings, in order to save the forger's life.) There are also great problems in operating a reprieve system without arbitrariness, say, in deciding whether being pregnant or having a young baby should qualify a woman for a reprieve.

Finally, there is the drawback that the retention or re-introduction of capital punishment contributes to a tradition of cruel and horrible punishment which we might hope would wither away. Nowadays we never think of disembowelling people or chopping off their hands as a punishment. Even if these punishments would be specially effective in deterring some very serious crimes, they are not regarded as a real possibility. To many of us, it seems that the utilitarian benefits from this situation outweigh the loss of any deterrent power they might have if re-introduced for some repulsive crime like kidnapping. And the longer we leave capital punishment in abeyance, the more its use will seem as out of the question as the no more cruel punishment of mutilation. (At this point, I come near to Hart's view that some punishments are too barbarous to use whatever their social utility. The difference is that I think that arguments for and against a punishment should be based on social utility, but that a widespread view that some things are unthinkable is itself of great social utility.)

For these reasons, a properly thought-out utilitarianism does not enjoin an unqualified policy of seeking the minimum loss of life, as the no trade-off view does. Capital punishment has its own special cruelties and horrors, which change the whole position. In order to be justified, it must be shown, with good evidence, that it has a deterrent effect not obtainable by less awful means, and one which is quite substantial rather than marginal.

DETERRENCE AND MURDER

The arguments over whether capital punishment deters murder more effectively than less drastic methods are of two kinds: statistical and intuitive. The statistical arguments are based on various kinds of comparisons of murder rates. Rates are compared before and after abolition in a country, and, where possible, further comparisons are made with rates after reintroduction of capital punishment. Rates are compared in neighbouring countries, or neighbouring states of the U.S.A., with and without the death penalty. I am not a statistician and have no special competence to discuss the issue, but will merely purvey the received opinion of those who have looked into the matter. Those who have studied the figures are agreed that there is no striking correlation between the absence of capital punishment and any alteration in the curve of the murder rate. Having agreed on this point, they then fall into two schools. On one view, we can conclude that capital punishment is not a greater deterrent to murder than the prison sentences that are substituted for it. On the other, more cautious, view, we can only conclude that we do not know that capital punishment is a deterrent. I shall not attempt to choose between these interpretations. For, given that capital punishment is justified only where there is good evidence that it is a substantial deterrent, either interpretation fails to support the case for it.

If the statistical evidence were conclusive that capital punishment did not deter more than milder punishments, this would leave no room for any further discussion. But, since the statistical evidence may be inconclusive, many people feel there is room left for intuitive arguments. Some of these deserve examination. The intuitive case was forcefully stated in 1864 by Sir James Fitzjames Stephen:[6]

No other punishment deters men so effectually from committing crimes as the punishment of death. This is one of those propositions which it is difficult to prove, simply because they are in themselves more obvious than any proof can make them. It is possible to display ingenuity in arguing against it, but that is all. The whole experience of mankind is in the other direction. The threat of instant death is the one to which resort has always been made when there was an absolute necessity for producing some result. . . . No one goes to certain inevitable death except by compulsion. Put the matter the other way. Was there ever yet a criminal who, when sentenced to death and brought out to die, would refuse the offer of a commutation of his sentence for the severest secondary punishment? Surely not. Why is this? It can only be because "All that a man has will he give for his life." In any secondary punishment, however terrible, there is hope; but death is death; its terrors cannot be described more forcibly.

These claims turn out when scrutinized to be much more speculative and doubtful than they at first sight appear.

The first doubt arises when Stephen talks of "certain inevitable death." The Royal Commission, in their *Report*, after quoting the passage from Stephen above, quote figures to show that, in the fifty years from 1900 to 1949, there was in England and Wales one execution for every twelve murders known to the police. In Scotland in the same period there was less than one execution for every twenty-five murders known to the police. Supporters of Stephen's view could supplement their case by advocating more death sentences and fewer reprieves, or by optimistic speculations about better police detection or greater willingness of juries to convict. But the reality of capital punishment as it was in these countries, unmodified by such recommendations and speculations, was not one where the potential murderer faced certain, inevitable death. This may incline us to modify Stephen's estimate of its deterrent effect, unless we buttress his view with the further speculation that a fair number of potential murderers falsely believed that what they would face was certain, inevitable death.

The second doubt concerns Stephen's talk of "the threat of instant death." The reality again does not quite fit this. By the time the police conclude their investigation, the case is brought to trial, and verdict and sentence are followed by appeal, petition for reprieve and then execution, many months have probably elapsed, and when this time factor is added to the low probability of the murderers being executed, the picture looks very different. For we often have a time bias, being less affected by threats of future catastrophes than by threats of instant ones. The certainty of immediate death is one thing; it is another thing merely to increase one's chances of death in the future. Unless this were so, no one would smoke or take on such high-risk jobs as diving in the North Sea.

There is another doubt when Stephen very plausibly says that virtually all criminals would prefer life imprisonment to execution. The difficulty is over whether this entitles us to conclude that it is therefore a more effective deterrent. For there is the possibility that, compared with the long term of imprisonment that is the alternative, capital punishment is what may appropriately be called an "overkill." It may be that, for those who will be deterred by threat of punishment, a long prison sentence is sufficient deterrent. I am not suggesting that this is so, but simply that it is an open question whether a worse alternative here generates any additional deterrent effect. The answer is *not* intuitively obvious.

Stephen's case rests on the speculative psychological assumptions that capital punishment is not an overkill compared with a prison sentence; and that its additional deterrent effect is not obliterated by time bias, nor by the low probability of execution, nor by a combination of these factors. Or else it must be assumed that, where the additional deterrent effect would be obliterated by the low probability of death, either on its own or in combination with time bias, the potential murderer thinks the probability is higher than it is. Some of these assumptions may be true, but, when they are brought out into the open, it is by no means obvious that the required combination of them can be relied upon.

Supporters of the death penalty also sometimes use what David A. Conway, in his valuable discussion of this issue, calls "the best-bet argument."[7] On this view, since there is no certainty whether or not capital punishment reduces the number of murders, either decision about it involves gambling with lives. It is suggested that it is better to gamble with the lives of murderers than with the lives of their innocent potential victims. This presupposes the attitude, rejected here, that a murder is a greater evil than the execution of a murderer. But, since this attitude probably has overwhelmingly widespread support, it is worth noting that, even if it is accepted, the best-bet argument is unconvincing. This is because, as Conway has pointed out, it overlooks the fact that we are not choosing between the chance of a murderer dying and the chance of a victim dying. In leaving the death penalty, we are opting for the certainty of the murderer dying which we hope will give us a chance of a potential victim being saved. This would look like a good bet only if we thought an execution substantially preferable to a murder and either the statistical evidence or the intuitive arguments made the effectiveness of the death penalty as a deterrent look reasonably likely.

Since the statistical studies do not give any clear indication that capital punishment makes any difference to the number of murders committed, the only chance of its supporters discharging the heavy burden of justification would be if the intuitive arguments were extremely powerful. We might then feel justified in supposing that other factors distorted the murder rate, masking the substantial deterrent effect of capital punishment. The intuitive arguments, presented as the merest platitudes, turn out to be speculative and unobvious. I conclude that the case for capital punishment as a substantial deterrent fails.

NOTES

1. H. L. A. Hart: "Prolegomenon to the Principles of Punishment," *Proceedings of the Aristotelian Society*, 1959–60.

2. Quoted in the *Report of the Royal Commission on Capital Punishment*, 1953.

3. H. L. A. Hart: "Murder and the Principles of Punishment," *Northwestern Law Review*, 1958.

4. Arthur Koestler: *Reflections on Hanging*, London, 1956.

5. Albert Pierrepoint: *Executioner: Pierrepoint*, London, 1974.

6. James Fitzjames Stephen: Capital Punishments, *Fraser's Magazine*, 1864.

7. David A. Conway: "Capital Punishment and Deterrence," *Philosophy and Public Affairs*, 1974.

REVIEW AND DISCUSSION QUESTIONS

1. Describe the retributive view of executions.
2. On what basis might the retributivist position be defended?
3. Describe the harm caused by execution compared with the murder. Do you agree with Glover's conclusion on this issue?
4. How might it be argued that despite the fact that people fear the death penalty more than life in prison, they would be worse off spending their lives in prison?
5. What are the various utilitarian considerations, pro and con, regarding executions?
6. Glover distinguishes "intuitive" and "statistical" arguments that capital punishment deters. What are these two types of arguments? What does he think about the statistical argument?
7. Explain Stephen's intuitive argument for capital punishment. Why does Glover reject it?
8. Describe the "best bet" argument. Why does Glover reject it? Do you find his rejection of it acceptable? Explain.

Desert and Capital Punishment

Martin Perlmutter

Martin Perlmutter argues that the utilitarian approach to punishment, emphasizing the usefulness of deterrence, protection, and rehabilitation, is inadequate, primarily because it views punishment as "forward looking." Rather, he claims, the proper focus of punishment is on the past; people are punished in virtue of past wrongdoing. If the wrongdoing is serious enough, he argues, then capital punishment is appropriate and the wrongdoer deserves death. Perlmutter concludes by arguing that, in a sense, the criminal has a right to be punished—that to fail to do so treats him or her as less than a person. Martin Perlmutter is professor of philosophy at the University of Charleston, South Carolina.

'Shall we receive good at the hand of God and shall we not receive evil?' In all this Job did not sin with his lips.

Job 2:10

Punishment is a form of harm or deprivation; in punishing somebody, we are making that person worse off than he was before. And since it seems that we have a *prima facie* obligation not to make others worse off, the practice of punishment needs a justification in virtue of which that *prima facie* obligation is overridden. Why are we entitled to harm persons when we punish them?

There are two general answers to this question. The first looks to the future and to the overall consequences of inflicting the harm; it maintains that one is entitled to make a person worse off if the consequences of doing so outweigh the harm done. Inflicting harm is justified when the harm done is part of a larger chain in which that harm results in yet greater good. The good produced by the harm might be the rehabilitation of the offender, the protection of others from the offender, or the deterrence of other future offenders. This answer is utilitarian; it looks to future goods, which outweigh the present harm, as the justification of the present harm. The second looks to the past and to the past deeds of the offender; it maintains that one is entitled to make a person worse

off if that person's past deeds are such that he deserves to be punished. Just as it is fitting to reward someone who does well with some goods, whether those be a trophy, a better job, or a salary increase, so it is appropriate to deprive someone who does poorly of those same goods. Of course, it would be nice if good consequences proceeded from the punishment, just as it would be nice if good consequences proceeded from giving the trophy to the winner rather than to the loser, but good consequences, like rehabilitation, protection, or deterrence, are not in any way integral to punishment. This answer is the retributive view of punishment; it looks to past deeds in virtue of which the harm is deserved as justification of the harm.[1]

In this paper I will argue that punishment focuses on the past; it is thus a retributive concept. Just as the concepts "praise," "blame," and, more importantly, "desert" have a backward focus, so too "punishment" looks to the past. The justification of punishment is another matter. I will argue that the practice of punishment is justified, because the individual who did the wrong also "chose" the punishment; in punishing the wrongdoer, we are honoring that individual's choice. The justification of punishment is to be found in the broader notion of desert, another backward-looking concept. I will also argue that capital punishment is defensible; there are some crimes that are so serious, so offensive to the moral community, that their perpetrators deserve death for committing them. As Justice Stewart points out in *Gregg* v. *Georgia*, "the decision that capital punishment may be the appropriate sanction in extreme cases is an expression of the community's belief that certain crimes are themselves so grievous an affront to humanity that the only adequate response may be the penalty of death." Finally, as a postscript, I will make some general remarks about treating somebody as a person. In doing so, I will try to make sense of the seemingly absurd Hegelian view that "in punishment the offender is honored as a rational being, since the punishment is looked on as his right."

1. THE CONCEPT OF PUNISHMENT

Before we ask questions about the justification of punishment, we should be clear about what punishment is. Otherwise, we would not know whether or not it is punishment that we are justifying. So, for example, justifying the reform or rehabilitation of an offender might not be a difficult task, but it would be a justification of punishment only if punishment were essentially a reformative or rehabilitative notion.

There are two features of punishment that are essential to it. First, punishment is inflicting harm; nothing can count as punishment unless it is a deprivation or causes pain or suffering to the person on whom it is inflicted. This is not quite right since a person might prefer his punishment to the alternatives available to him; on occasion, a drunkard might prefer a warm cell with a mattress to the cold outside, and a child might rather be banished to his room than continue to play with his friends. The intention in punishing, however, is to do harm; in punishing somebody, we intend to make the person worse off than he would be without the punishment.[2] So, punishment must involve pain or other consequences normally considered unpleasant.

Not every case of making a person worse off, however, is an instance of punishment. Confining a person who has an infectious disease, hitting somebody just for the fun of it, and taxing the wealthy might well be instances of harming persons, but they are not cases of punishment, even if they were deprivations that we were justified in imposing. For a deprivation to be a punishment, it has to be associated with past wrongdoing. A heavily taxed wealthy person would be overstating his case if he complained that he was being punished for being wealthy, for there is no presumption of any past wrongdoing in his case.

Second, then, a person may be punished if and only if there is some presumption of past wrongdoing. Again, this is a conceptual requirement; it is part of the meaning of "punishment." Imposing harm is not punishment unless the imposition of the harm is connected with a supposed past wrongdoing.

This connection between wrongdoing and the imposition of harm is so strong that some have maintained a conceptual link between them. It has been claimed that the very concept of wrongdoing must contain a reference to punishment; that is, an act is an instance of wrongdoing if and only if the agent is subject to punishment for performing it. In legal contexts, a natural home for the discussion of punishment, such a view has had some currency. An act is a legal offense just in case there is a sanction that attaches to performing it; a rule of law requires that a person perform or forbear from performing some act and promises harm in case of noncompliance. As a more general thesis, however, it is false; wrongdoing or offense cannot have liability to punishment in its explication, for there are many offenses that do not subject the offender to any penalty. Punishment, however, does require reference to both harm and wrongdoing.

The imposition of harm and past wrongdoing are closely related. The harm imposed is in virtue of the past wrongdoing; the person deserves to suffer because he committed an offense. It is appropriate that the person suffer harm or deprivation because of the person's past deeds; had the person not done wrong, he would not have deserved the suffering. This is central to punishment.

The connection can be seen in the nature of rules, whether they be the regulations of baseball, the laws of society, or the rules of bridge. Rules are constitutive of baseball, society, and bridge. The rules define the practice, they distribute the benefits and the burdens, and they determine acceptable behavior within the practice. In violating a rule, the person is competing unfairly; that is an improper way of gaining an advantage. Throwing a spitball, stealing a car, or surreptitiously signaling the ace of spades are all unacceptable ways of getting ahead. Persons who attempt to benefit by violating a rule are subject to a penalty for so doing because they are benefiting from the practice, but are participating unfairly in it. Typically, there are procedures for determining whether the rule has been violated, what the penalty should be, and who should administer the penalty.

The legitimate domain of punishment is restricted to special relationships. A state can legitimately punish its citizens; it is within a parent's province to punish his or her child; and a teacher has the authority to punish his or her students.

So too the tournament director at bridge, the umpire, and the baseball commissioner. Not everyone, however, is entitled to punish, even in response to past wrongdoing. As a general rule, a citizen cannot punish the state, a child cannot punish a parent, and a student cannot punish a teacher.

Although blame is similar to punishment in many ways—in blaming a person, we are causing that person a limited sort of harm in virtue of a past wrongdoing—blame is more general than punishment in this way.[3] The legitimate domain of blame is not restricted to special relationships. While it may be morally unacceptable to blame somebody, though he is blameworthy, that unacceptability is in virtue of considerations of the future. On occasion, the bad consequences of expressing the blame make such expressions unacceptable even to someone who is blameworthy. It might be unacceptable to blame somebody for past deeds if that person is on his deathbed; it might be silly for you to blame somebody if doing so would upset you a great deal; and there might be no point to blaming somebody who would enjoy the loss of your esteem. In each of these cases, it might be morally unacceptable or imprudent to blame him, even though he is blameworthy. But it is not a question of authority; blame, unlike punishment, is not restricted to special relationships. Each of these three cases would be a paradigmatic instance of blaming, just as a morally unacceptable case of telling the truth would be a paradigmatic instance of truth-telling.

2. A UTILITARIAN CRITIQUE OF PUNISHMENT

A utilitarian might focus on the analogy of punishment to blame to argue that though punishment has a backward focus, the moral acceptability of inflicting the harm must derive from the future consequences of the harm inflicted. If it is morally unacceptable to express blame to a person on his deathbed, though the person is blameworthy, then blameworthiness is not sufficient for the moral acceptability of blaming. And it is forward-looking considerations that make expressing the blame morally unacceptable; that is, since nothing good will be accomplished by expressing the blame and somebody will be worse off for it, the blame should not be expressed. Similarly, in punishment, past wrong-doing is not sufficient for the moral acceptability of inflicting the harm. Even if inflicting harm requires past wrongdoing for it to be punishment, it requires good consequences for it to be morally acceptable. As a result in the utilitarian view, it is the consequences of inflicting harm that determine whether or not it is morally acceptable to inflict the harm, though it is backward-looking considerations that determine whether or not it is punishment. Just as taxing the wealthy might be a morally acceptable way of harming the wealthy only if the consequences justify it, so too fining a traffic offender is morally acceptable only if the consequences justify it. Of course, taxing the wealthy is not based on past wrongdoing, so it is not punishment, whereas fining the traffic offender is punishment. But whether or not inflicting harm is punishment is only a detail and does not speak to the moral acceptability of inflicting it.

This utilitarian view is general and not restricted to punishment. According to it, one should always do what has the best consequences. What has already happened is relevant only insofar as the future is concerned. The fact that a person has committed an offense might be a reason for inflicting harm on the person, but only in virtue of the future benefits of the harm. Thus, a past offense might serve as evidence for future offenses and future offenses are to be avoided, so it might be best to protect his future victims by imprisoning him. Or, it might be best to discourage future offenders by inflicting harm on this offender for this offense. But unless there is a justification in the future, it would be morally unacceptable to inflict the harm. For if there were no such future benefits, then, all things considered, in punishing one is increasing the amount of suffering in the world and that is morally unacceptable.

This utilitarian challenge might require abandoning the practice of punishment. If punishment involves intending to make a person worse off because of past wrongdoing, then the only utilitarian defense of punishment could be deterrence. For reform of the offender or protection of society from the offender's future offenses does not involve intentionally making the offender worse off any more than curing a person of an infectious disease involves that intention. Were we able to cure a person of a disease without inconveniencing the victim, one would surely do so. Similarly, if reform were the aim of punishment, punishment would not necessarily involve making the offender worse off, even temporarily. The same holds true for societal protection as an aim of punishment; it too does not necessarily involve making a person worse off. Deterrence fares a little better, but even it does not require actually inflicting the harm as opposed to merely appearing to others to inflict the harm. Punishment necessarily involves harm or deprivation, whereas reform, deprivation, and even deterrence do not.

An example might help. Suppose my son lies to me and suppose also that I am persuaded that I have no evidence that sending him to his room will do any more good than not sending him to his room. I might still think that he deserves to be punished for what he did and send him to his room, thereby inflicting harm on him for what he did. A utilitarian would claim that I should not have done it, for no good will result from my harming my son in this way. If he is right, it is not because he has a different theory of punishment which yields a different result in this case. Rather, it is because punishment is not justified; it is because, on his view, I am not entitled to inflict harm unless a greater good will result. The utilitarian is giving a critique of punishment, not an alternative theory of punishment.

Even if the utilitarian does not provide an alternative theory of punishment, he might be right in his critique of punishment. My punishing my son for lying might be morally unacceptable, because reform, protection, or deterrence is not gained by it. It might be morally unacceptable to do anything whose foreseeable consequences involve more harm than good. And if it is, then the practice of punishment ought to be abandoned.

3. A CRITIQUE OF UTILITARIANISM

The utilitarian contention ignores the fact that many of our moral concepts are backward-looking. Most often, we are morally required to do things because of what happened in the past. It is that which makes social contract theories appealing; we are obligated to behave in accordance with an implicit contract, something which we already tacitly agreed to do. More simply, though, we are required to keep a promise because we made it, we are required to award the prize to the winner because he won the race, and we are required to repay a debt because we borrowed the money. Frequently, it is the past and not the future which determines the moral acceptability of an action. Of course, keeping a promise has consequences for the practice of promise-keeping and the fact that a promise was made also has consequences since the promise created expectations. But what makes it right to keep a promise is the past fact that a promise was made. So, the well-known example of a secret promise to a dying man to deliver a hoard of money, which he entrusts to me, to his already rich son is relevant. It is the promise, and not the consequences, which makes it right to give his son the money.

The utilitarian is correct in recognizing that, on occasion, we are morally required to look to the future and that the future sometimes affects what it is morally acceptable to do, even in the case of backward-looking concepts. Thus, though a promise was made, perhaps to meet somebody for lunch, it would be morally unacceptable to do so if it would result in somebody's death, because of the need to rush somebody to the hospital. But in cases such as this, it is not *merely* minimizing harm or maximizing benefit that is operative. Rather, a rational person would not expect the promise to be kept to him in a case such as this. The commitment involved in promises does not create an obligation in such a case.

So, even though the utilitarian contention about maximizing benefits and minimizing harm has some plausibility, it does not conform to our everyday moral intuitions about what is morally acceptable. Of course, a utilitarian might urge that it is unreasonable to take the past as seriously as we do. But until we become persuaded by such urgings, and it is not clear that we should become persuaded by them, we should continue to take our everyday moral notions seriously and reject the utilitarian contention. Promises should be kept because they were made, debts should be repaid because they were incurred, and awards should be given because they are deserved. Moral notions such as these show that the past plays a much larger role in justifying behavior than a utilitarian acknowledges.

The notion of desert is central to punishment. What a person deserves is most often determined by what he has done. Does a person ever deserve to have harm inflicted on him for what he has done? The answer seems straightforward. On occasion, when a person knowingly and intentionally does wrong, he should be punished for what he did. In much the same way as a person occasionally deserves to be blamed, deserves the loss of another's esteem, a person occasionally deserves to have harm inflicted upon him.

Even a view which emphasizes deterrence as the rationale for inflicting the harm requires such a notion of desert. Otherwise, harming an innocent person to deter others would be morally acceptable. A plausible deterrence view must insist that in doing wrong a person made it acceptable to have harm inflicted upon himself, thereby deterring others. That is, he deserves the harm; the punishment is morally acceptable because of the past misdeed. So, even a theory which emphasizes deterrence requires a retributive underpinning.

4. CAPITAL PUNISHMENT

The view that the severity of the punishment should be determined by the severity of the crime is a natural extension of the retributive view that punishment is a person's due in virtue of the wrong that the person committed. That is, the crime should not only legitimate that the person be punished, but it should also determine the extent of the punishment. Simply put, the more serious the crime, the more severe the penalty.

Lex talionis, literally the law of retaliation, is the custom of inflicting a similar injury on the person who injures another. The person who causes another to lose an eye must himself lose an eye; the person who murders another must himself be put to death. That was a common practice of punishment in earlier societies and is included in the Biblical corpus of laws (Exodus 21:23–25, for example). Most often, *lex talionis* is inapplicable, since most wrongs do not have analogous injuries applicable to the offender. But the view that the severity of the offense should determine the severity of the punishment remains a plausible view, one which many of us intuitively accept. The U.S. Supreme Court used this principle as a negative test when it upheld the death penalty in *Gregg* v. *Georgia*: "The punishment must not be grossly out of proportion to the severity of the crime."

Of course, one cannot grade wrongs with mathematical precision and there is no scientific procedure for ranking punishments. But some wrongs are worse than others. Missing an appointment altogether is worse than being five minutes late; robbing a bank is worse than not feeding a parking meter; marking the deck of cards is worse than neglecting to inform one's opponents of a bridge convention; and intentionally losing a baseball game is worse than questioning an umpire's third-strike call. More generally, a third offense is worse than a first offense, a premeditated act is worse than an impulsive or negligent one; and an altogether self-interested criminal act is worse than a criminal act designed to benefit another. Punishments are more easily ranked. A thousand dollar fine is worse than a hundred dollar fine; ten years in prison is worse than one year in prison; and solitary confinement is worse than imprisonment in a minimum security detention facility.

Are there any limits on the appropriate punishments? Is life imprisonment, capital punishment, bodily mutilation, or castration beyond the pale of acceptable punishment? Two issues need to be separated. First, the appropriateness of the punishment for the particular crime. Life imprisonment would be too severe a penalty for a parking violation, even though life imprisonment might be appropriate for other offenses. Second, the appropriateness of the punishment for any crime.[4] Some harms are unacceptable because they are not the sorts of thing that persons are ever entitled to do, even as a punishment. Maiming, bodily mutilation, and torture seem to be disqualified for this reason.

Clearly, there are cultural factors which are relevant as response to these questions. How serious the crime and what punishments are compatible with conceptions of human dignity vary from culture to culture. And there are objective criteria which can be used to determine both issues. Sexual relations between consenting adults is generally allowed in our culture, but is a serious wrong in others. In our cultural setting, bodily mutilation is a form of humiliation that is unacceptable; it is not compatible with our fundamental standards of human dignity and decency. Nobody should be allowed to mutilate another, even as a response to a serious crime (such as mutilating another). Imprisonment, even for a long term, is different, since our society clearly thinks that imprisonment is an appropriate response to wrongdoing. Depriving a person of his liberty is an acceptable response to wrongdoing; bodily mutilation is not.

A person might reasonably prefer an unacceptable punishment to an acceptable one. Having one's hand cut off or being castrated seems less severe as a punishment than life imprisonment; a person might well prefer a life without a hand or a life without some sexual pleasures to a life without liberty, even though our society allows the latter as a punishment and disallows the former. The issue is not a matter of preference or severity; the punishment has to accord with human dignity. In our society, bodily integrity and privacy are important values that preclude maiming, bodily mutilation, or castration.

What about capital punishment? Again, we need to separate two questions. First, is death too severe a penalty to impose for any offense? Are there any crimes that are so serious that death is an appropriate penalty for them? Second, is capital punishment compatible with our views of human dignity and decency?

In our society, murder is a crime for which death is a fitting punishment. Not only does murder result in the death of another, it undermines the very fabric of a moral community. A murderer should be altogether and completely cut off from the moral community which he sought to undermine. The murderer caused death and deserves death in response. Life imprisonment is not adequate because it makes the criminal a dependent of the community, a ward of the community he sought to undermine. The murderer's only claim is that he be treated in a way that is compatible with society's standards of human dignity.

Others might want to restrict capital punishment to other crimes—to mass murder, to the killing of a police officer, or to political assassination. There is no scientific way to determine what crimes are so egregious that capital punishment is appropriate for them and I need not argue for the appropriateness of capital punishment for any particular crime. But I do want to insist that if our standards of decency allow death as an acceptable punishment, then there are some crimes that warrant it as a punishment.

But does our view of human dignity allow for capital punishment? The legislature of most every state has enacted new statutes authorizing the death penalty for certain crimes, the Congress has made air piracy punishable by death, and the Supreme Court has ruled that the death penalty is not cruel and unusual punishment. Surveys indicate that the vast majority of Americans support the death penalty for some crimes, and seemingly rational persons occasionally choose death when their life prospects are sufficiently grim. So, there is excellent evidence that capital punishment is not humiliating in an unacceptable way and that capital punishment is compatible with standards of human dignity.

5. PUNISHMENT AND DESERT

We are now in a position to understand the Hegelian view that "in punishment the offender is honored as a rational being, since the punishment is looked on as his right." If the offender deserves to be punished in virtue of his past wrongdoing, then if we do not punish him, then we should have some reason for not treating him as he deserves. If we are in no way excusing what he did but merely exempting him from the harm, then we are not dealing with him as he deserves. In choosing to do wrong and in realizing the consequences of what he did, he brought the punishment upon himself. In punishing him, we are respecting his choice. The punishment is his due in much the same way as the prize is the due of the winner. If we refused the winner the prize merely because we did not want him to benefit, then we would be acting illegitimately by not giving him his desert. So too with punishment. In punishment we are honoring the integrity of the agent by giving him his due.

The right to be punished is a strange sort of right. Rights are generally associated with what is in one's interest, so we must say that it is in the offender's interest to be punished. Pain or suffering is undesirable, however, so people will ordinarily not claim their right to be punished. Nevertheless, persons do have an interest in being treated as persons, as genuine members of the moral community. Such treatment requires that one's choices are honored and that one is dealt with in a manner appropriate to those choices. The right to be punished, then, is derivative on the right to be treated as a person. Just as persons deserve to be rewarded, so too persons deserve to be punished. Both rewarding and punishing are instances of respecting persons.

On occasion, it is more appropriate to use a therapy model than the model of honoring the integrity of human beings. Wrongdoing is occasionally pathological and should be dealt with much as one deals with other pathological conditions. If the agent is himself a victim, then it is appropriate to treat him as a victim in the way that a therapy model does. If kleptomania is a disease, then the person should be treated for it, not punished for it. So, one might treat the person for this illness much as one would treat a person for a cancer. In treating a person in this way, however, one is treating him as a victim, not as an agent; one is not respecting his choices; and one is not honoring him as a human being.

Most often, the therapy model is inappropriate. When it is inappropriate, the person as a moral agent has a right to be punished, not treated. It is demeaning to have our choices treated as if they were something over which we have no control. It is in our interest to be treated as a person, as an autonomous moral agent; we ordinarily do want our choices to be respected as emanating from us, rather than to be dealt with as symptoms of an ailment over which we have no control.

A deathbed scenario is sometimes used to criticize this retributive view. Should we punish a person on his deathbed for a past wrongdoing? The retributive view suggests that we should, that in doing so we are honoring his choices as a human being, and that he deserves the punishment in virtue of the wrong that he did. A utilitarian disagrees. He thinks that such treatment is inhumane, that respecting him as a human being requires that we forego the punishment.

The correct answer depends on how the person on his deathbed is viewed. If the only interest, or the overwhelming interest, that we associate with a dying person is a peaceful death, then we should not punish him. A dying person would require special treatment in virtue of that dominant interest. If he wants a promise to be made, even an unreasonable promise, it might be best to make it, later to break it. If he is blameworthy, it might be unacceptable to blame him. It might even be acceptable to lie to him about his prospects for survival. But insofar as we are entitled to do all these things, we are compromising his status as a full-fledged member of the moral community. If the pressing interest to die comfortably and untroubled overrides his generally more important interest to be treated as a person, then our ordinary moral discourse fails. It is not, however, because we respect him as a person that we are willing to do these things. Rather, it is because his situation is so dire that it demands that his immediate needs be met. Issues of desert are overwhelmed by issues of immediate need.

Most often, however, it is desert that determines the moral acceptability of behavior. Occasionally, what one deserves is for harm to be inflicted. On those occasions, one deserves to be punished; it is one's right as a person.

NOTES

1. These two general answers do get a bit more complex. For the utilitarian might go on to maintain that inflicting harm can only be punishment if it is in virtue of a past deed that the harm is inflicted. Taking from the wealthy to feed starving children might be a morally acceptable way of harming the wealthy, but it is a conceptual mistake to view it as a punishment. Inflicting harm to prevent yet greater harm or to produce beneficial consequences might be morally acceptable, but it is not punishment unless it is backward-looking enough so that it is inflicted in virtue of some past misdeed. And the retributivist might not want to be saddled with punishing a person when no possible earthly benefit will derive from it. It seems severe to inflict harm on another in those cases when absolutely nothing will be gained from it, except perhaps a balancing of the moral scales. So, punishment may become a bit backward-looking for the utilitarian and a bit forward-looking for the retributivist.

   Thus, both views, when modified, seem to agree that both backward-looking and forward-looking considerations are relevant for determining the moral acceptability of punishment. Yet, the focus of the two views is different. For the retributivist thinks that it is the past wrongdoing which makes inflicting harm morally acceptable, whereas the utilitarian maintains that inflicting harm can be made morally acceptable only by considering the future consequences of the harm. Thus, the retributivist is not committed to the view that inflicting the harm is morally acceptable only if doing so produces better consequences than not inflicting it, for he believes that the justification lies in the past.

2. Again, this will not do. A judge might realize that the drunken defendant prefers the warm cell, yet punish him by sentencing him to a night in jail. Presumably, a night in jail is normally considered less pleasant than not spending a night in jail, even if it is not so in every case. In legal contexts, the penalty is determined by what is normally considered harmful or unpleasant.

3. There are two features associated with blame that need to be distinguished. First, there is blameworthiness. Blameworthiness is wholly backward-looking, focusing exclusively on the agent and his past deeds. Blameworthiness is analogous to responsibility, another backward-looking concept. Second, there is expressing the blame, typically to the blameworthy person. On occasion, it is morally unacceptable to express blame, though blame is appropriate. The deathbed case might be such a case. Clearly, the fact that a man is dying does not affect his blameworthiness, for it has nothing whatever to do with his being accountable for his past misdeeds.

4. In his provocative essay, "Why I Am Not A Christian," Bertrand Russell criticizes Christ's teaching of hell. He says, "I do not myself feel that any person who is really profoundly humane can believe in everlasting punishment." For Russell, eternal damnation is always an inappropriate punishment, never deserved by any misdeed. He thinks it altogether too severe.

REVIEW AND DISCUSSION QUESTIONS

1. Explain why Perlmutter thinks utilitarians miss the point of punishment.
2. Why does Perlmutter think that to punish someone is to honor him, while failing to punish may show disrespect?
3. Retributivists take the view that the *degree* of punishment should match the degree of moral blameworthiness of the act. How would such a view of punishment treat attempted crimes as compared with successful ones? Is that a reasonable approach?
4. How might a retributivist be expected to view punishment of drunk drivers? Drivers who kill when drunk? Drivers who kill after falling asleep?
5. Are there ever cases in which we should punish people who are not morally blameworthy? Explain.
6. Compare Perlmutter's view of punishment with earlier discussions of law and legal authority by Plato and Rawls.
7. Do utilitarians ignore the fact that some moral concepts are "backward looking," as Perlmutter says? How might Mill respond to that claim? Is his response adequate?

Part IV
PERSONAL RELATIONSHIPS

13
Sex, Love, and Marriage

Essays in this section discuss a range of subjects having to do with dating, sex, and marriage. It begins with two different views about date rape, though behind these lie deeper disagreements about sex and male/female relationships. Other topics include the morality of homosexuality and of adultery.

Date Rape: A Feminist Analysis

Lois Pineau

In this article, Lois Pineau discusses a range of issues associated with date rape, including myths about consent and sexuality that make conviction difficult. She defends what she terms a "communicative" mode of sexuality, which, she argues, better describes the mutuality of sexual relationships and provides a better test for consent than the contractualist model she believes is currently used in law. Lois Pineau is professor of philosophy at Kansas State University.

Date rape is nonaggravated sexual assault, nonconsensual sex that does not involve physical injury, or the explicit threat of physical injury. But because it does not involve physical injury, and because physical injury is often the only criterion that is accepted as evidence that the *actus reas* is nonconsensual, what is really sexual assault is often mistaken for seduction. . . .

[If] a man is to be convicted, it does not suffice to establish that the *actus reas* was nonconsensual. In order to be guilty of sexual assault a man must have the requisite *mens rea*, i.e., he must either have believed that his victim did not consent or that she was probably not consenting. . . .

The criteria for *mens rea*, for the reasonableness of belief, and for consent are closely related.

From Lois Pineau, "Date Rape: A Feminist Analysis," *Law and Philosophy* 8, pp. 217–243. © 1989, Kluwer Academic Publishers. Reprinted by permission of Kluwer Academic Publishers.

For although a man's sincere belief in the consent of his victim may be sufficient to defeat *mens rea*, the court is less likely to believe his belief is sincere if his belief is unreasonable. If his belief is reasonable, they are more likely to believe in the sincerity of his belief. But evidence of the reasonableness of his belief is also evidence that consent really did take place. For the very things that make it reasonable for him to believe that the defendant consented are often the very things that incline the court to believe that she consented. What is often missing is the voice of the woman herself, an account of what it would be reasonable for *her* to agree to, that is to say, an account of what is reasonable from *her* standpoint. . . .

The following statements by self-confessed date rapists reveal how our lack of a solution for dealing with date rape protects rapists by failing to provide their victims with legal recourse:

All of my rapes have been involved in a dating situation where I've been out with a woman I know. . . . I wouldn't take no for an answer. I think it had something to do with my acceptance of rejection. I had low self-esteem and not much self-confidence and when I was rejected for something which I considered to be rightly mine, I became angry and I went ahead anyway. And this was the same in any situation, whether it was rape or it was something else.[1]

There is, at this time, nothing to protect women from this kind of unscrupulous victimization. A woman on a casual date with a virtual stranger has almost no chance of bringing a complaint of sexual assault before the courts. One reason for this is the prevailing criterion for consent. According to this criterion, consent is implied unless some emphatic episodic sign of resistance occurred, and its occurrence can be established. But if no episodic act occurred, or if it did occur, and the defendant claims that it didn't, or if the defendant threatened the plaintiff but won't admit it in court, it is almost impossible to find any evidence that would support the plaintiff's word against the defendant. This difficulty is exacerbated by suspicion on the part of the courts, police, and legal educators that even where an act of resistance occurs, this act should not be interpreted as a withholding of consent, and this suspicion is especially upheld where

the accused is a man who is known to the female plaintiff.

In Glanville Williams's classic textbook on criminal law we are warned that where a man is unknown to a woman, she does not consent if she expresses her rejection in the form of an episodic and vigorous act at the "vital moment." But if the man is known to the woman she must, according to Williams, make use of "all means available to her to repel the man."[2] Williams warns that women often welcome a "mastery advance" and present a token resistance. He quotes Byron's couplet,

> A little still she strove, and much repented
> And whispering "I will ne'er consent"—
> consented

by way of altering law students to the difficulty of distinguishing real protest from pretence.[3] Thus, while in principle, a firm unambiguous stand, or a healthy show of temper ought to be sufficient, if established, to show nonconsent, in practice the forceful overriding of such a stance is apt to be taken as an indication that the resistance was not seriously intended, and that the seduction had succeeded. The consequence of this is that it is almost impossible to establish the defendant's guilt beyond a reasonable doubt.

Thus, on the one hand, we have a situation in which women are vulnerable to the most exploitive tactics at the hands of men who are known to them. On the other hand, almost nothing will count as evidence of their being assaulted, including their having taken an emphatic stance in withholding their consent. The new laws have done almost nothing to change this situation. Yet clearly, some solutions must be sought. Moreover, the road to that solution presents itself clearly enough as a need for a reformulation of the criterion of consent. It is patent that a criterion that collapses whenever the crime itself succeeds will not suffice. . . .

THE PROBLEM OF THE CRITERION

The reasoning that underlies the present criterion of consent is entangled in a number of mutually supportive mythologies which see sexual assault as masterful seduction, and silent submission as sexual enjoyment. Because the prevailing ideology has so much informed our conceptualization of sexual interaction, it is extraordinarily difficult for us to distinguish between assault and seduction, submission and enjoyment, or so we imagine. At the same time, this failure to distinguish has given rise to a network of rationalizations that support the conflation of assault with seduction, submission with enjoyment. I therefore want to begin my argument by providing an example which shows both why it is so difficult to make this distinction, and that it exists. Later, I will identify and attempt to unravel the lines of reasoning that reinforce this difficulty.

The woman I have in mind agrees to see someone because she feels an intimate attraction to him and believes that he feels the same way about her. She goes out with him in the hope that there will be mutual enjoyment and in the course of the day or evening an increase of mutual interest. Unfortunately, these hopes of mutual and reciprocal interest are not realized. We do not know how much interest she has in him by the end of their time together, but whatever her feelings she comes under pressure to have sex with him, and she does not want to have the kind of sex he wants. She may desire to hold hands and kiss, to engage in more intense caresses or in some form of foreplay, or she may not want to be touched. She may have reasons unrelated to desire for not wanting to engage in the kind of sex he is demanding. She may have religious reservations, concerns about pregnancy or disease, a disinclination to be just another conquest. She may be engaged in a seduction program of her own which sees abstaining from sexual activity as a means of building an important emotional bond. She feels she is desirable to him, and she knows, and he knows that he will have sex with her if he can. And while she feels she doesn't owe him anything, and that it is her prerogative to refuse him, this feeling is partly a defensive reaction against a deeply held belief that if he is in need, she should provide. If she buys into the myth of insistent male sexuality she may feel he is suffering from sexual frustration and that she is largely to blame.

We do not know how much he desires her, but we do know that his desire for erotic satisfaction can hardly be separated from his desire for conquest. He feels no dating obligation, but has a strong commitment to scoring. He uses the myth of "so hard to control" male desire as a rhetorical tactic, telling her how frustrated she will leave him. He becomes overbearing. She resists, voic-

ing her disinclination. He alternates between telling her how desirable she is and taking a hostile stance, charging her with misleading him, accusing her of wanting him, and being coy, in short of being deceitful, all the time engaging in rather aggressive body contact. It is late at night, she is tired and a bit queasy from too many drinks, and he is reaffirming her suspicion that perhaps she has misled him. She is having trouble disengaging his body from hers, and wishes he would just go away. She does not adopt a strident angry stance, partly because she feels she thinks he is acting normally and does not deserve it, partly because she feels she is partly to blame, and partly because there is always the danger that her anger will make him angry, possibly violent. It seems that the only thing to do, given his aggression, and her queasy fatigue, is to go along with him and get it over with, but this decision is so entangled with the events in process it is hard to know if it is not simply a recognition of what is actually happening. She finds the whole encounter a thoroughly disagreeable experience, but he does not take any notice, and wouldn't have changed course if he had. He congratulates himself on his sexual prowess and is confirmed in his opinion that aggressive tactics pay off. Later she feels that she has been raped, but paradoxically tells herself that she let herself be raped.

The paradoxical feelings of the woman in our example indicate her awareness that what she feels about the incident stands in contradiction to the prevailing cultural assessment of it. She knows that she did not want to have sex with her date. She is not so sure, however, about how much her own desires count, and she is uncertain that she has made her desires clear. Her uncertainty is reinforced by the cultural reading of this incident as an ordinary seduction.

As for us, we assume that the woman did not want to have sex, but just like her, we are unsure whether her mere reluctance, in the presence of high-pressure tactics, constitutes non-consent. We suspect that submission to an overbearing and insensitive lout is no way to go about attaining sexual enjoyment, and we further suspect that he felt no compunction about providing it, so that on the face of it, from the outside looking in, it looks like a pretty unreasonable proposition for her.

Let us look at this reasoning more closely. Assume that she was not attracted to the kind of sex offered by the sort of person offering it. Then it would be *prima facie* unreasonable for her to agree to have sex, unreasonable, that is, unless she were offered some pay-off of her stoic endurance, money perhaps, or tickets to the opera. The reason is that in sexual matters, agreement is closely connected to attraction. Thus, where the presumption is that she was not attracted, we should at the same time presume that she did not consent. Hence, the burden of proof should be on her alleged assailant to show that she had good reasons for consenting to an unattractive proposition.

This is not, however, the way such situations are interpreted. In the unlikely event that the example I have described should come before the courts, there is little doubt that the law would interpret the woman's eventual acquiescence or "going along with" the sexual encounter as consent. But along with this interpretation would go the implicit understanding that she had consented because when all was said and done, when the "token" resistances to the "masterful advances" had been made, she had wanted to after all. Once the courts have constructed this interpretation, they are then forced to conjure up some horror story of feminine revenge in order to explain why she should bring charges against her "seducer."

In the even more unlikely event that the courts agreed that the woman had not consented to the above encounter, there is little chance that her assailant would be convicted of sexual assault.[4] The belief that the man's aggressive tactics are a normal part of seduction means that *mens rea* cannot be established. Her eventual "going along" with his advances constitutes reasonable grounds for his believing in her consent. These "reasonable" grounds attest to the sincerity of his belief in her consent. This reasonableness means that *mens rea* would be defeated even in jurisdictions which make *mens rea* a function of objective standards of reasonableness. Moreover, the sympathy of the court is more likely to lie with the rapist than with his victim, since, if the court is typical, it will be strongly inclined to believe that the victim had in some way "asked for it."

The position of the courts is supported by the widespread belief that male aggression and female reluctance are normal parts of seduction. Given their appearance of this model, the logic of their response must be respected. For if sexual aggres-

sion is a part of ordinary seduction, then it cannot be inconsistent with the legitimate consent of the person allegedly seduced by this means. And if it is normal for a woman to be reluctant, then this reluctance must be consistent with her consent as well. The position of the courts is not inconsistent just so long as they allow that some sort of protest on the part of a woman counts as a refusal. As we have seen, however, it frequently happens that no sort of a protest would count as a refusal. Moreover, if no sort of protest, or at least if precious few count, then the failure to register these protests will amount to "asking for it," it will amount, in other words, to agreeing.

The court's belief in "natural" male aggression and "natural" female reluctance has increasingly come under attack by feminist critics who see quite correctly that the entire legal position would collapse if, for example, it were shown empirically that men were not aggressive, and that women, at least when they wanted sex, were. This strategy is of little help, however, so long as aggressive men can still be found, and relics of reluctant women continue to surface. Fortunately, there is another strategy. The position collapses through the weakness of its internal logic. The next section traces several lines of this logic.

RAPE MYTHS

The belief that the natural aggression of men and the natural reluctance of women somehow makes date rape understandable underlies a number of prevalent myths about rape and human sexuality. . . . These myths are not just popular, however, but often emerge in the arguments of judges who acquit date rapists, and policemen who refuse to lay charges.

The claim that the victim provoked a sexual incident, that "she asked for it," is by far the most common defense given by men who are accused of sexual assault. . . .

The least sophisticated of the "she asked for it" rationales, and in a sense, the easiest to deal with, appeals to an injunction against sexually provocative behaviour on the part of women. If women should not be sexually provocative, then, from this standpoint, a woman who is sexually provocative deserves to suffer the consequences. Now it will not do to respond that women get raped even when they are not sexually provocative, or that it is men who get to interpret (unfairly) what counts as sexually provocative. The question should be: Why shouldn't a woman be sexually provocative? Why should this behaviour warrant any kind of aggressive response whatsoever?

Attempts to explain that women have a right to behave in sexually provocative ways without suffering dire consequences still meet with surprisingly tough resistance. Even people who find nothing wrong or sinful with sex itself, in any of its forms, tend to suppose that women must not behave sexually unless they are prepared to carry through on some fuller course of sexual interaction. The logic of this response seems to be that at some point a woman's behavior commits her to following through on the full course of a sexual encounter as it is defined by her assailant. At some point she has made an agreement, or formed a contract, and once that is done, her contractor is entitled to demand that she satisfy the terms of that contract. Thus, this view about sexual responsibility and desert is supported by other assumptions about contracts and agreement. But we do not normally suppose that casual nonverbal behavior generates agreements. Nor do we normally grant private persons the right to enforce contracts. What rationale would support our conclusion in this case?

The rationale, I believe, comes in the form of a belief in the especially insistent nature of male sexuality, an insistence which lies at the root of natural male aggression, and which is extremely difficult, perhaps impossible, to contain. At a certain point in the arousal process, it is thought, a man's rational will gives way to the IOU of nature. His sexual need can and does reach a point where it is uncontrollable, and his natural masculine aggression kicks in to assure that this need is met. Women, however, are naturally more contained, and so it is their responsibility not to provoke the irrational in the male. If they do go so far as that, they have both failed in their responsibilities, and subjected themselves to the inevitable. One does not go into the lion's cage and expect not to be eaten. Natural feminine reluctance, it is thought, is no protection against a sexually aroused male.

The belief about the normal aggressiveness of male sexuality is complemented by common knowledge about female gender development. Once, women were taught to deny their sexuality and to aspire to ideals of chastity. Things have not changed so much. Women still tend to eschew conquest mentalities in favor of a combination of sex and affection. Insofar as this is thought to be merely a cultural requirement, however, there is an expectation that women will be coy about their sexual desire. The assumption that women both want to indulge sexually, and are inclined to sacrifice this desire for higher ends, gives rise to the myth that they want to be raped. After all, doesn't rape give them the sexual enjoyment they *really* want, at the same time that it relieves them of the responsibility for admitting to and acting upon what they want? And how then can we blame men, who have been socialized to be aggressively seductive precisely for the purpose of overriding female reserve? If we find fault at all, we are inclined to cast our suspicions on the motives of the woman. For it is on her that the contradictory roles of sexual desirer and sexual denier have been placed. Our awareness of the contradiction expected of her makes us suspect her honesty. In the past, she was expected to deny her complicity because of the shame and guilt she felt at having submitted. This expectation persists in many quarters today, and is carried over into a general suspicion about her character, and the fear that she might make a false accusation out of revenge, or some other low motive. . . .

DISPELLING THE MYTHS

. . . The belief that a woman generates some sort of contractual obligation whenever her behavior is interpreted as seductive is the most indefensible part of the mythology of rape. In law, contracts are not legitimate just because a promise has been made. In particular, the use of pressure tactics to extract agreement is frowned upon. . . .

Even if we assume that a woman has initially agreed to an encounter, her agreement does not automatically make all subsequent sexual activity to which she submits legitimate. If during coitus a woman should experience pain, be suddenly overcome with guilt or fear of pregnancy, or simply lose her initial desire, those are good reasons for her to change her mind. Having changed her mind, neither her partner nor the state has any right to force her to continue. But then if she is forced to continue she is assaulted. Thus, establishing that consent occurred at a particular point during a sexual encounter should not conclusively establish the legitimacy of the encounter. What is needed is a reading of whether she agreed throughout the encounter.

If the "she asked for it" contractual view of sexual interchange has any validity, it is because there is a point at which there is no stopping a sexual encounter, a point at which that encounter becomes the inexorable outcome of the unfolding of natural events. If a sexual encounter is like a slide on which I cannot stop halfway down, it will be relevant whether I enter the slide of my own free will, or am pushed.

But there is no evidence that the entire sexual act is like a slide. While there may be a few seconds in the "plateau" period just prior to orgasm in which people are "swept" away by sexual feelings to the point where we could justifiably understand their lack of heed for the comfort of their partner, the greater part of a sexual encounter comes well within the bounds of morally responsible control of our own actions. Indeed, the available evidence shows that most of the activity involved in sex has to do with building the requisite level of desire, a task that involves the proper use of foreplay, the possibility of which implies control over the form that foreplay will take. Modern sexual therapy assumes that such control is universally accessible, and so far there has been no reason to question that assumption. All are unanimous, moreover, in holding that mutual sexual enjoyment requires an atmosphere of comfort and communication, a minimum of pressure, and an ongoing check-up on one's partner's state. They maintain that different people have different predilections, and that what is pleasurable for one person is very often anathema to another. These findings show that the way to achieve sexual pleasure, at any time at all, let alone with a casual acquaintance, decidedly does not involve overriding the other person's express reservations and providing them with just any kind of sexual stimulus. . . . In this case science seems to concur with women's perception that aggressive incommunicative sex is not what they want. But if science and the voice of women concur, if aggressive seduction does not lead to good sex, if women do not like it or want it, then it is not rational to think that they would agree to it. Where such sex takes place, it is therefore rational to presume that the sex was not consensual. . . .

In conclusion, there are no grounds for the "she asked for it" defence. Sexually provocative behaviour does not generate sexual contracts. Even where there are sexual agreements, they cannot be legitimately enforced either by the State, or by private right, or by natural prerogative. Secondly, all the evidence suggests that neither women nor men find sexual enjoyment in rape or in any form of non-communicative sexuality. Thirdly, male sexual desire is containable, and can be subjected to moral and rational control. Fourthly, since there is no reason why women should not be sexually provocative, they do not "deserve" any sex they do not want. This last is a welcome discovery. The taboo on sexual provocativeness in women is a taboo both on sensuality and on teasing. But sensuality is a source of delight, and teasing is playful and inspires wit. What a relief to learn that it is not sexual provocativeness, but its enemies, that constitutes a danger to the world.

COMMUNICATIVE SEXUALITY: REINTERPRETING THE KANTIAN IMPERATIVE

The present criterion of consent sets up sexual encounters as contractual events in which sexual aggression is presumed to be consented to unless there is some vigorous act of refusal. As long as we view sexual interaction on a contractual model, the only possibility for finding fault is to point to the presence of such an act. But it is clear that whether or not we can determine such a presence, there is something strongly disagreeable about the sexual aggression described above.

In thinking about sex we must keep in mind its sensual ends, and the facts show that aggressive high-pressure sex contradicts those ends. Consensual sex in dating situations is presumed to aim at mutual enjoyment. It may not always do this, and when it does, it might not always succeed. There is no logical incompatibility between wanting to continue a sexual encounter, and failing to derive sexual pleasure from it.

But it seems to me that there is a presumption in favour of the connection between sex and sexual enjoyment, and that if a man wants to be sure that he is not forcing himself on a woman, he has an obligation either to ensure that the encounter really is mutually enjoyable, or to know the reasons why she would want to continue the encounter in spite of her lack of enjoyment. A closer investigation of the nature of this obligation will enable us to construct a more rational and a more plausible norm of sexual conduct. . . .

The obligation to promote the sexual ends of one's partner implies the obligation to know what those ends are, and also the obligation to know how those ends are attained. Thus, the problem comes down to a problem of epistemic responsibility, the responsibility to know. The solution, in my view, lies in the practice of a communicative sexuality, one which combines the appropriate knowledge of the other with respect for the dialectics of desire.

So let us, for a moment, conceive of sexual interaction on a communicative rather than a contractual model. Let us look at it the way I think it should be looked at, as if it were a proper conversation rather than an offer from the Mafia. . . .

The communicative interaction involved in conversation is concerned with a good deal more than didactic content and argument. Good conversationalists are intuitive, sympathetic, and charitable. Intuition and charity aid the conversationalist in her effort to interpret the words of the other correctly and sympathy enables her to enter into the other's point of view. Her sensitivity alerts her to the tone of the exchange. Has her point been taken good-humouredly or resentfully? Aggressively delivered responses are taken as a sign that *ad hominems* are at work, and that the respondent's self-worth has been called into question. Good conversationalists will know to suspend further discussion until this sense of self-worth has been reestablished. Angry responses, resentful re-

sponses, bored responses, even over-enthusiastic responses require that the emotional ground be cleared before the discussion be continued. Often it is better to change the topic, or to come back to it on another day under different circumstances. Good conversationalists do not overwhelm their respondents with a barrage of their own opinions. While they may be persuasive, the forcefulness of their persuasion does not lie in their being overbearing, but rather in their capacity to see the other's point of view, to understand what it depends on, and so to address the essential point, but with tact and clarity.

Just as communicative conversationalists are concerned with more than didactic content, persons engaged in communicative sexuality will be concerned with more than achieving coitus. They will be sensitive to the responses of their partners. They will, like good conversationalists, be intuitive, sympathetic, and charitable. Intuition will help them to interpret their partner's responses; sympathy will enable them to share what their partner is feeling; charity will enable them to care. Communicative sexual partners will not overwhelm each other with the barrage of their own desires. They will treat negative, bored, or angry responses as a sign that the erotic ground needs to be either cleared or abandoned. Their concern with fostering the desire of the other must involve an ongoing state of alertness in interpreting her responses.

Just as a conversationalist's prime concern is for the mutuality of the discussion, a person engaged in communicative sexuality will be most concerned with the mutuality of desire. As such, both will put into practice a regard for their respondent that is guaranteed no place in the contractual language of rights, duties, and consent. The *dialectics* of both activities reflect the dialectics of desire insofar as each person's interest in continuing is contingent upon the other person wishing to do so too, and each person's interest is as much fueled by the other's interest as it is by her own. . . .

CULTURAL PRESUMPTIONS

. . . Traditionally, the decision to date indicates that two people have an initial attraction to each other, that they are disposed to like each other, and look forward to enjoying each other's company. Dating derives its implicit meaning from this tradition. It retains this meaning unless other aims are explicitly stated, and even then it may not be possible to alienate this meaning. It is a rare woman who will not spurn a man who states explicitly, right at the onset, that he wants to go out with her solely on the condition that he have sexual intercourse with her at the end of the evening, and that he has no interest in her company apart from gaining that end, and no concern for mutual satisfaction.

Explicit protest to the contrary aside, the conventions of dating confer on it its social meaning, and this social meaning implies a relationship which is more like friendship than the cutthroat competition of opposing teams. As such, it requires that we do more than stand on our rights with regard to each other. As long as we are operating under the auspices of a dating relationship, it requires that we behave in the mode of friendship and trust. But if a date is more like friendship than a business contract, then clearly respect for the dialectics of desire is incompatible with the sort of sexual pressure that is inclined to end in date rape. And clearly, also, a conquest mentality which exploits a situation of trust and respect for purely selfish ends is morally pernicious. Failure to respect the dialectics of desire when operating under the auspices of friendship and trust is to act in flagrant disregard of the moral requirement to avoid manipulative, coercive, and exploitive behaviour. Respect for the dialectics of desire is *prima facie* inconsistent with the satisfaction of one person at the expense of the other. The proper end of friendship relations is mutual satisfaction. But the requirement of mutuality means that we must take a communicative approach to discovering the ends of the other, and this entails that we respect the dialectics of desire.

But now that we know what communicative sexuality is, and that it is morally required, and that it is the only feasible means to mutual sexual enjoyment, why not take this model as the norm of what is reasonable in sexual interaction? The evidence strongly indicates that women whose partners are aggressively uncommunicative have little chance of experiencing sexual pleasure. But it is not reasonable for women to consent to what they have little chance of enjoying. Hence it is not reasonable for women to consent to aggressive noncommunicative sex. Nor can we reasonably suppose that women have consented to sexual encounters which we know and they know they do not find enjoyable. With the communicative model as the norm, the aggressive contractual model should strike us as a model of deviant sexuality, and sexual encounters patterned on that model should strike us as encounters to which *prima facie* no one would reasonably agree. But if acquiescence to an encounter counts as consent only if the acquiescence is reasonable, something to which a reasonable person, in full possession of knowledge relevant to the encounter, would agree, then acquiescence to aggressive noncommunicative sex is not reasonable. Hence, acquiescence under such conditions should not count as consent.

Thus, where communicative sexuality does not occur, we lack the main ground for believing that the sex involved was consensual. Moreover, where a man does not engage in communicative sexuality, he acts either out of reckless disregard, or out of willful ignorance. For he cannot know, except through the practice of communicative sexuality, whether his partner has any sexual reason for continuing the encounter. And where she does not, he runs the risk of imposing on her what she is not willing to have. All that is needed then, in order to provide women with legal protection from "date rape," is to make both reckless indifference and willful ignorance a sufficient condition of *mens rea* and to make communicative sexuality the accepted norm of sex to which a reasonable woman would agree. Thus, the appeal to communicative sexuality as a norm for sexual encounters accomplishes two things. It brings the aggressive sex involved in "date rape" well within the realm of sexual assault, and it locates the guilt of date rapists in the failure to approach sexual relations on a communicative basis. . . .

NOTES

1. Sylvia Levine and Joseph Loenig, eds., *Why Men Rape* (Toronto: Macmillan, 1980), p. 83.
2. Williams, *Textbook of Criminal Law* (1983), p. 238.
3. Ibid.
4. See Jeanne C. Marsh, Allison Geist, and Nathan Caplan, *Rape and the Limits of Law Reform* (Boston: Auburn House, 1982), p. 32. According to Marsh's study on the impact on the Michigan reform of rape laws, convictions were increased for traditional conceptions of rape, i.e., aggravated assault. However, date rape, which has a much higher incidence than aggravated assault, has a very low rate of arrest and an even lower one of conviction.

REVIEW AND DISCUSSION QUESTIONS

1. What is Pineau's definition of date rape?
2. Describe the problems that prosecutors face in proving date rape.
3. In the example she discusses, why is it unlikely that the man would be convicted of rape?
4. Describe the myths that Pineau points to about sex and rape, indicating why she thinks they should be dispelled.
5. What is the "communicative" model of sexuality? How is it different from the alternative, more traditional view?
6. How does Pineau link communicative sexuality with consent?
7. Do you think the hypothetical case she describes is date rape? Explain.
8. It has been argued that "plain" sex sometimes involves nothing more than the desire for physical contact and the pleasure it brings, and that other definitions are either too narrow or too broad. Elaborate briefly on that position, then explain how Pineau would respond to that claim.

An Interview about Date Rape

Camille Paglia

In this two-part interview with Celia Farber for *SPIN* magazine, Camille Paglia defends a different view about sex and male-female relations than does Pineau, one that leads her to criticize the behavior of some who see themselves as victims of date rape. Rather than communication, Paglia sees in sex an inherent aggressiveness of males. Women, she thinks, must both acknowledge the true nature of sex and take responsibility for themselves and the risks they take. Camille Paglia is professor of humanities at the University of the Arts in Philadelphia.

From Celia Farber, "An Interview with Camille Paglia," *SPIN*, September–October 1991.

Paglia:　I'm noticing that many people coming into the media now are people whose minds have been poisoned by their training at Yale and other Ivy League places. For example, I see where this whole date-rape thing is coming from. I recognize the language of these smart girls who are entering the media; they are coming from these schools. They have this stupid, pathetic, completely-removed-from-reality view of things that they've gotten from these academics who are totally off the wall, totally removed. Whereas my views on sex are coming from the fact that I am a football fan and I am a rock fan. Rock and football are revealing something true and permanent and eternal about male energy and sexuality. They are revealing the fact that women, in fact, *like* the idea of flaunting, strutting, wild masculine energy. . . . This date-rape propaganda has been primarily coming out of the elite schools, where the guys are all these cooperative, literate, introspective, sit-on-their-ass guys, whereas you're not getting it that much down in the football schools where people accept the fact of the beauty and strength of masculinity. You see jocks on the campus all the time—they understand what manhood is down there. It's only up here where there is this idea that they can get men on a leash. It's these guys in the Ivy League schools who get used to obeying women. They're sedentary guys. It's ironic that you're getting the biggest bitching about men from the schools where the men are just eunuchs and bookworms.

SPIN:　That point about primordial male sexuality is also at odds with much contemporary pop psychology. I'm referring to the twelve-step, women-who-love-too-much school of thought, which insists that a woman's attraction to an "untamed" man, as it were, is necessarily a sign of sickness—a sign of a warped emotional life that invariably traces back to childhood, and the attention span of the father. It never considers such an attraction to be a naturally occurring phenomenon—a force of nature. I think the approach to remedying the problem is simplistic, even dangerously so at times.

Paglia:　I agree. I'm a Freudian. I like Freud very much, even though I adapt him and add things to him. But his system of analysis is extremely accurate. It's a conflict-based system that allows for paradox. It's also very self-critical and self-analytical. I've watched therapy getting more and more mushy in the past fifteen years in America. . . . It's become what I call coercive compassion. It's disgusting, it's condescending, it's insulting, it's coddling, it keeps everyone in an infantile condition rather than in the adult condition that was postulated as the ultimate goal of Freudian analysis. You were meant to be totally self-aware as a Freudian. Now, it's everyone who will help you, the group will help you. It's awful. It's a return to the Fifties conformist model of things. It's this victim-centered view of the world, which is very pernicious. We cannot have a world where everyone is a victim. "I'm this way because my father made me this way. I'm this way because my husband made me this way." Yes, we are indeed formed by traumas that happened to us. But then you must take charge, you must take over, you are responsible. Personal responsibility is at the heart of my system. But today's system is this whining thing, "Why won't you help me, Mommy and Daddy?" It's like this whole thing with date rape.

SPIN:　One point that hasn't been made in the whole rape debate is women's role over men, sexually. In the case of a rape, a man has to use brute force to obtain something that a woman has—her very sex. So naturally she's weaker physically, and will always be oppressed by him physically. But in that moment when he decides that the only way he can get what he wants from her emotionally, or sexually, or whatever, is to rape her, he is confessing to a weakness that is all-encompassing. She is abused, but he is utterly tragic and pathetic. One is temporary and the other is permanent. I was raped once and it helped me to think of it like that. Not at all to apologize for him, but to focus on my power instead of my helplessness. It was a horrible experience, but it certainly didn't destroy my whole life or my psyche, as much as contemporary wisdom insisted it must have.

Paglia:　Right, we *have* what they want. I think woman is the dominant sex. Men have to do all sorts of stuff to prove that they are worthy of a woman's attention. It's very interesting what you said about the rape, because one of the German magazine reporters who came to talk to me—she's been living in New York for ten years—she came to talk to me about two weeks ago and she told me a very interesting story, very similar to yours. She lives in Brooklyn, and she let this guy in whom she shouldn't have, and she got raped. She said that, because she's a feminist, of course she had to go for counseling. She said it was awful, that the minute she arrived there, the rape counselors were saying, "You will never recover from this, what's happened to you is so terrible." She said, what the hell, it was a terrible experience, but she was going to pick herself up, and it wasn't that big a deal. The whole system now is designed to make you feel that you are maimed and mutilated forever if something like that happens. She said it made her feel worse. It's absolutely American—it is not European—and the whole system is filled with these clichés about sex. I think there is a fundamental prudery about sex in all this. Rape is one of the risk factors in getting involved with men. It's a risk factor. It's like driving a car. My attitude is, it's like gambling. If you go to Atlantic City—these girls are going to Atlantic City, and when they lose, it's like "Oh, Mommy and Daddy, I lost." My answer is stay home and do your nails, if that's the kind of person you are. My Sixties attitude is, yes, go for it, take the risk, take the challenge—if you get raped, if you get beat up in a dark alley in a street, it's okay. That was part of the risk of freedom, that's part of what we've demanded as women. Go with it. Pick yourself up, dust yourself off, and go on. We cannot regulate male sexuality. The uncontrollable aspect of male sexuality is part of what makes sex interesting. And yes, it can lead to rape in some situations. What feminists are asking for is for men to be castrated, to make eunuchs out of them. The powerful, uncontrollable force of male sexuality has been censored out of white middle-class homes. But it's still there in black culture, and in Spanish culture.

SPIN: In the first part of our interview, the section about rape upset every single woman who read it—in the offices at *SPIN* and even at the typesetters. They all seemed to feel that you were defending the rapist.

Paglia: No, that's not it at all. The point is, these white, upper-middle-class feminists believe that a pain-free world is achievable. I'm saying that a pain-free world will be achievable only under totalitarianism. There is no such thing as risk-

free anything. In fact, all valuable human things come to us from risk and loss. Therefore we value beauty and youth because they are transient. Part of the sizzle of sex is the danger, the risk of loss of identity in love. That's part of the drama of love. My generation demanded no more overprotection of women. We wanted women to be able to freely choose sex, to freely have all the adventures that men could have. So women began to hike on mountain paths and do all sorts of dangerous things. That's the risk of freedom. If women break their legs on mountain bikes, that's the risk factor. I'm not defending the rapist—I'm defending the freedom to risk rape. I don't want sexual experience to be protected by society. A part of it is that since women are physically weaker than men, in our sexual freedom, women are going to get raped. We should be angry about it, but it's a woman's personal responsibility now, in this age of sexual liberation, to make herself physically fit, so that she can fight off as best she can man's advances. She needs to be alert in her own mind to any potential danger. It's up to the woman to give clear signals of what her wishes are. If she does not want to be out of control of the situation, she should not get drunk, she should not be in a private space with a man whom she does not know. Rape does not destroy you forever. It's like getting beaten up. Men get beat up all the time.

SPIN: But don't you think that people see a man getting beat up and a woman getting raped as completely different? Do you think rape should be considered as serious a crime as murder?

Paglia: That's absurd. I dislike anything that treats women as if they are special, frail little creatures. We don't need special protection. Rape is an assault. If it is a totally devastating psychological experience for a woman, then she doesn't have a proper attitude toward sex. It's this whole stupid feminist thing about how we are basically nurturing, benevolent people, and sex is a wonderful thing between two equals. With that kind of attitude, then of course rape is going to be a total violation of your entire life, because you have had a stupid, naive, Mary Poppins view of life to begin with. Sex is a turbulent power that we are not in control of; it's a dark force. The sexes are at war with each other. That's part of the excitement and interest of sex. It's the dark realm of the night.

When you enter the realm of the night, horrible things can happen there. You can be attacked on a dark street. Does that mean we should never go into dark streets? Part of my excitement as a college student in the Sixties was coming out of the very protective Fifties. I was wandering those dark streets understanding that not only could I be raped, I could be killed. It's like the gay men going down to the docks and having sex in alleyways and trucks; it's the danger. Feminists have no idea that some women like to flirt with danger because there is a sizzle in it. You know what gets me sick and tired? The battered-woman motif. It's so misinterpreted, the way we have to constantly look at it in terms of male oppression and tyranny, and female victimization. When, in fact, everyone knows throughout the world that many of these working-class relationships where women get beat up have hot sex. They ask why she won't leave him? Maybe she won't leave him because the sex is very hot. I say we should start looking at the battered-wife motif in terms of sex. If gay men go down to bars and like to get tied up, beaten up, and have their asses whipped, how come we can't allow that a lot of wives like the kind of sex they are getting in these battered-wife relationships? We can't consider that women might have kinky tastes, can we? No, because women are naturally benevolent and nurturing, aren't they? Everything is so damn Mary Poppins and sanitized.

SPIN: What do you think is the main quality that women have within them that they aren't using?

Paglia: What women have to realize is their dominance as a sex. That women's sexual powers are enormous. All cultures have seen it. Men know it. Women know it. The only people who don't know it are feminists. Desensualized, desexualized, neurotic women. I wouldn't have said this twenty years ago because I was militant feminist myself. But as the years have gone on, I begin to see more and more that the perverse, neurotic psychodrama projected by these women is coming from their own problems with sex.

REVIEW AND DISCUSSION QUESTIONS

1. Explain what Paglia means when she speaks of some women's "victim-centered" view. Who has that view? What is it?

2. What is the "fifties"view of sex that Paglia rejects, as contrasted with her own?

3. Paglia has claimed that all rape is erotic, for the man, and that people who claim rape is violence rather than sex are wrong. Do you agree?

4. In answering a question during another interview about whether a woman has a right to wear "sexually provocative" clothes in public, Paglia answered that "We have the *right* to leave our purse on a park bench in Central Park and go play twenty-five feet away and hope the purse is going to be there when we return, okay? Now, this is just simply stupid behavior. If someone steals the purse, we pursue the thief, we put him in jail. We also say to you, "That was really *stupid!*" Now, the same thing here. You may have the *right* to leave your purse there, you may have the *right* to dress in that way, but you are running a *risk!*" Do you agree with Paglia? Explain.

5. Paglia has also written that "Aggression and eroticism are deeply intertwined. Hunt, pursuit, and capture are biologically programmed into male sexuality." Compare her view of sexuality with Pineau's position.

6. What is wrong with rape, according to Paglia? According to Pineau?

Gay Basics: Some Questions, Facts, and Values

Richard D. Mohr

In this essay, Richard D. Mohr surveys the wide array of issues surrounding homosexuality. He begins with a discussion of some of the important facts about homosexuals and homosexuality, including a discussion of the most prominent stereotypes, which, he points out, are in fact contradictory. He then reviews different forms of discrimination experienced by gays, considers arguments that homosexuality is wrong, and concludes with a discussion of social policies that affect gays. Richard D. Mohr is professor of philosophy at the University of Illinois.

WHO ARE GAYS ANYWAY?

A recent Gallup poll found that only one in five Americans reports having a gay or lesbian acquaintance.[1] This finding is extraordinary given the number of practicing homosexuals in America. Alfred Kinsey's 1948 study of the sex lives of 5,000 white males shocked the nation: 37 percent had at least one homosexual experience to orgasm in their adult lives; an additional 13 percent had homosexual fantasies to orgasm; 4 percent were exclusively homosexual in their practices; another 5 percent had virtually no heterosexual experience; and nearly one-fifth had at least as many homosexual as heterosexual experiences.[2]

Two out of five men one passes on the street have had orgasmic sex with men. Every second family in the country has a member who is essentially homosexual, and many more people regularly have homosexual experiences. Who are homosexuals? They are your friends, your minister, your teacher, your bank teller, your doctor, your mail carrier, your secretary, your congressional representative, your sibling, parent, and spouse. They are everywhere, virtually all ordinary, virtually all unknown.

Several important consequences follow. First, the country is profoundly ignorant of the actual experience of gay people. Second, social attitudes and practices that are harmful to gays have a much greater overall harmful impact on society than is usually realized. Third, most gay people live in hiding—in the closet—making the "coming out" experience the central fixture of gay consciousness and invisibility the chief characteristic of the gay community.

IGNORANCE, STEREOTYPE, AND MORALITY

Ignorance about gays, however, has not stopped people from having strong opinions about them. The void which ignorance leaves has been filled with stereotypes. Society holds chiefly two groups of antigay stereotypes; the two are an oddly contradictory lot. One set of stereotypes revolves around alleged mistakes in an individual's gender identity: Lesbians are women that want to be, or at least look and act like, men—bulldykes, diesel dykes; while gay men are those who want to be, or at least look and act like, women—queens, fairies, limp-wrists, nellies. These stereotypes of mismatched genders provide the materials through which gays and lesbians become the butts of ethnic-like jokes. These stereotypes and jokes, though derisive, basically view gays and lesbians as ridiculous.

For Robert W. Switzer, © 1986 by Richard D. Mohr. Reprinted by permission.

Another set of stereotypes revolves around gays as a pervasive sinister conspiratorial threat. The core stereotype here is the gay person as child molester and, more generally, as sex-crazed maniac. These stereotypes carry with them fears of the very destruction of family and civilization itself. Now, that which is essentially ridiculous can hardly have such a staggering effect. Something must be afoot in this incoherent amalgam.

Sense can be made of this incoherence if the nature of stereotypes is clarified. Stereotypes are not *simply* false generalizations from a skewed sample of cases examined. Admittedly, false generalizing plays some part in the stereotypes a society holds. If, for instance, one takes as one's sample homosexuals who are in psychiatric hospitals or prisons, as was done in nearly all early investigations, not surprisingly one will probably find homosexuals to be of a crazed and criminal cast. Such false generalizations, though, simply confirm beliefs already held on independent grounds, ones that likely led the investigator to the prison and psychiatric ward to begin with. Evelyn Hooker, who in the late '50s carried out the first rigorous studies to use nonclinical gays, found that psychiatrists, when presented with case files including all the standard diagnostic psychological profiles—but omitting indications of sexual orientation—were unable to distinguish gay files from straight ones, even though they believed gays to be crazy and supposed themselves to be experts in detecting craziness.[3] These studies proved a profound embarrassment to the psychiatric establishment, the financial well-being of which has been substantially enhanced by "curing" allegedly insane gays. The studies led the way to the American Psychiatric Association finally dropping homosexuality from its registry of mental illnesses in 1973.[4] Nevertheless, the stereotype of gays as sick continues apace in the mind of America.

False generalizations *help maintain* stereotypes, they do not *form* them. As the history of Hooker's discoveries shows, stereotypes have a life beyond facts; their origin lies in a culture's ideology—the general system of beliefs by which it lives—and they are sustained across generations by diverse cultural transmissions, hardly any of which, including slang and jokes, even purport to

have a scientific basis. Stereotypes, then, are not the products of bad science but are social constructions that perform central functions in maintaining society's conception of itself.

On this understanding, it is easy to see that the antigay stereotypes surrounding gender identification are chiefly means of reinforcing still powerful gender roles in society. If, as this stereotype presumes and condemns, one is free to choose one's social roles independently of gender, many guiding social divisions, both domestic and commercial, might be threatened. The socially gender-linked distinctions between breadwinner and homemaker, boss and secretary, doctor and nurse, protector and protected would blur. The accusations "fag" and "dyke" exist in significant part to keep women in their place and to prevent men from breaking ranks and ceding away theirs.

The stereotypes of gays as child molesters, sex-crazed maniacs, and civilization destroyers function to displace (socially irresolvable) problems from their actual source to a foreign (and so, it is thought, manageable) one. Thus, the stereotype of child molester functions to give the family unit a false sheen of absolute innocence. It keeps the unit from being examined too closely for incest, child abuse, wife battering, and the terrorism of constant threats. The stereotype teaches that the problems of the family are not internal to it, but external.[5]

One can see these cultural forces at work in society's and the media's treatment of current reports of violence, especially domestic violence. When a mother kills her child or a father rapes his daughter—regular Section B fare even in major urban papers—this is never taken by reporters, columnists, or pundits as evidence that there is something wrong with heterosexuality or with traditional families. These issues are not even raised. But when a homosexual child molestation is reported, it is taken as confirming evidence of the way homosexuals are. One never hears of heterosexual murders, but one regularly hears of "homosexual" ones. Compare the social treatment of Richard Speck's sexually motivated mass murder of Chicago nurses with that of John Wayne Gacy's murders of Chicago youths. Gacy was in the culture's mind taken as symbolic of gay men in general. To prevent the possibility that "The Family" was viewed as anything but an innocent victim in this affair, the mainstream press knowingly failed to mention that most of Gacy's adolescent victims were homeless hustlers. That knowledge would be too much for the six o'clock news and for cherished beliefs.

Because "the facts" largely don't matter when it comes to the generation and maintenance of stereotypes, the effects of scientific and academic research and of enlightenment generally will be, at best, slight and gradual in the changing fortunes of lesbians and gay men. If this account of stereotypes holds, society has been profoundly immoral. For its treatment of gays is a grand scale rationalization, a moral sleight-of-hand. The problem is not that society's usual standards of evidence and procedure in coming to judgments of social policy have been misapplied to gays; rather, when it comes to gays, the standards themselves have simply been ruled out of court and disregarded in favor of mechanisms that encourage unexamined fear and hatred.

ARE GAYS DISCRIMINATED AGAINST? DOES IT MATTER?

Partly because lots of people suppose they don't know any gay people and partly through willful ignorance of its own workings, society at large is unaware of the many ways in which gays are subject to discrimination in consequence of widespread fear and hatred. Contributing to this social ignorance of discrimination is the difficulty for gay people, as an invisible minority, even to complain of discrimination. For if one is gay, to register a complaint would suddenly target one as a stigmatized person, and so in the absence of any protections against discrimination, would simply invite additional discrimination. Further, many people, especially those who are persistently downtrodden and so lack a firm sense of self to begin with, tend either to blame themselves for their troubles or to view injustice as a matter of bad luck rather than as indicating something wrong with society. The latter recognition would require doing something to rectify wrong, and most people, especially the already beleaguered, simply aren't up to that. So for a number of reasons discrimina-

tion against gays, like rape, goes seriously underreported.

First, gays are subject to violence and harassment based simply on their perceived status rather than because of any actions they have performed. A recent extensive study by the National Gay Task Force found that over 90 percent of gays and lesbians had been victimized in some form on the basis of their sexual orientation.[6] Greater than one in five gay men and nearly one in ten lesbians had been punched, hit, or kicked, a quarter of all gays had had objects thrown at them, a third had been chased, a third had been sexually harassed, and 14 percent had been spit on—all just for being perceived as gay.

The most extreme form of antigay violence is queerbashing—where groups of young men target a person who they suppose is a gay man and beat and kick him unconscious and sometimes to death amid a torrent of taunts and slurs. Such seemingly random but in reality socially encouraged violence has the same social origin and function as lynchings of blacks—to keep a whole stigmatized group in line. As with lynchings of the recent past, the police and courts have routinely averted their eyes, giving their implicit approval to the practice.

Few such cases with gay victims reach the courts. Those that do are marked by inequitable procedures and results. Frequently judges will describe queerbashers as "just all-American boys." Recently a District of Columbia judge handed suspended sentences to queerbashers whose victim had been stalked, beaten, stripped at knife-point, slashed, kicked, threatened with castration, and pissed on, because the judge thought the bashers were good boys at heart—after all, they went to a religious prep school.[7]

Police and juries will simply discount testimony from gays; they typically construe assaults on and murders of gays as "justified" self-defense—the killer need only claim his act was a panicked response to a sexual overture. Alternatively, when guilt seems patent, juries will accept highly implausible "diminished capacity" defenses, as in the case of Dan White's 1978 assassination of openly gay San Francisco city [supervisor] Harvey Milk—Hostess Twinkies made him do it.[8]

These inequitable procedures and results collectively show that the life and liberty of gays, like those of blacks, simply count for less than the life and liberty of members of the dominant culture.

The equitable rule of law is the heart of an orderly society. The collapse of the rule of law for gays shows that society is willing to perpetrate the worst possible injustices against them. Conceptually there is only a difference in degree between the collapse of the rule of law and systematic extermination of members of a population simply for having some group status independently of any act an individual has performed. In the Nazi concentration camps, gays were forced to wear pink triangles as identifying badges, just as Jews were forced to wear yellow stars. In remembrance of that collapse of the rule of law, the pink triangle has become the chief symbol of the gay rights movement.9

Gays are subject to widespread discrimination in employment—the very means by which one puts bread on one's table and one of the chief means by which individuals identify themselves to themselves and achieve personal dignity. Governments are leading offenders here. They do a lot of discriminating themselves, require that others do it ([such as] government contractors), and set precedents favoring discrimination in the private sector. The federal government explicitly discriminates against gays in the armed forces, the CIA, FBI, National Security Agency, and the State Department. The federal government refuses to give security clearances to gays and so forces the country's considerable private-sector military and aerospace contractors to fire known gay employees. State and local governments regularly fire gay teachers, policemen, firemen, social workers, and anyone who has contact with the public. Further, states through licensing laws officially bar gays from a vast array of occupations and professions—everything from doctors, lawyers, accountants, and nurses to hairdressers, morticians, and used car dealers. The American Civil Liberties Union's handbook *The Rights of Gay People* lists 307 such prohibited occupations.10

Gays are subject to discrimination in a wide variety of other ways, including private-sector employment, public accommodations, housing, immigration and naturalization, insurance of all types, custody and adoption, and zoning regulations that bar "singles" or "nonrelated" couples. All of these discriminations affect central components of a meaningful life; some even reach to the means by which life itself is sustained. In half the states, where gay sex is illegal, the central role of sex to meaningful life is officially denied to gays.

All these sorts of discriminations also affect the ability of people to have significant intimate relations. It is difficult for people to live together as couples without having their sexual orientation perceived in the public realm and so becoming targets for discrimination. Illegality, discrimination, and the absorption by gays of society's hatred of them all interact to impede or block altogether the ability of gays and lesbians to create and maintain significant personal relations with loved ones. So every facet of life is affected by discrimination. Only the most compelling reasons could justify it.

BUT AREN'T THEY IMMORAL?

Many people think society's treatment of gays is justified because they think gays are extremely immoral. To evaluate this claim, a different sense of *moral* must be distinguished. Sometimes by *morality* is meant the overall beliefs affecting behavior in a society—its mores, norms, and customs. On this understanding, gays certainly are not moral: Lots of people hate them and social customs are designed to register widespread disapproval of gays. The problem here is that this sense of morality is merely a *descriptive* one. On this understanding *every* society has a morality—even Nazi society, which had racism and mob rule as central features of its "morality" understood in this sense. What is needed in order to use the notion of morality to praise or condemn behavior is a sense of morality that is *prescriptive* or *normative*—a sense of morality whereby, for instance, the descriptive morality of the Nazis is found wanting.

As the Nazi example makes clear, that something is descriptively moral is nowhere near enough to make it normatively moral. [The fact that] a lot of people in a society say something is good, even over eons, does not make it so. Our rejection of the long history of socially approved and state-enforced slavery is another good example of this principle at work. Slavery would be wrong even if nearly everyone liked it. So consistency and fairness require that we abandon the belief that gays are immoral simply because most people dislike or disapprove of gays or gay acts, or even because gay sex acts are illegal.

Furthermore, recent historical and anthropological research has shown that opinion about gays has been by no means universally negative. Historically, it has varied widely even within the larger part of the Christian era and even within the church itself.[11] There are even societies—current ones—where homosexuality is not only tolerated but a universal compulsory part of social maturation.[12] Within the last thirty years, American society has undergone a grand turnabout from deeply ingrained, near total condemnation to near total acceptance on two emotionally charged "moral" or "family" issues: contraception and divorce. Society holds its current descriptive morality of gays not because it has to, but because it chooses to.

If popular opinion and custom are not enough to ground moral condemnation of homosexuality, perhaps religion can. Such argument[s] proceed along two lines. One claims that the condemnation is a direct revelation of God, usually through the Bible; the other claims to be able to detect condemnation in God's plan as manifested in nature.

One of the more remarkable discoveries of recent gay research is that the Bible may not be as univocal in its condemnation of homosexuality as has been usually believed.[13] Christ never mention[ed] homosexuality. Recent interpreters of the Old Testament have pointed out that the story of Lot at Sodom is probably intended to condemn inhospitality rather than homosexuality. Further, some of the Old Testament condemnations of homosexuality seem simply to be ways of tarring those of the Israelites' opponents who happen to accept homosexual practices when the Israelites themselves did not. If so, the condemnation is merely a quirk of history and rhetoric rather than a moral precept.

What does seem clear is that those who regularly cite the Bible to condemn an activity like homosexuality do so by reading it selectively. Do ministers who cite what they take to be condemnations of homosexuality in Leviticus maintain in their lives all the hygienic and dietary laws of Leviticus? If they cite the story of Lot at Sodom to condemn homosexuality, do they also cite the story of Lot in the cave to praise incestuous rape? It seems then not that the Bible is being used to ground condemnations of homosexuality as much as society's dislike of homosexuality is being used to interpret the Bible.[14]

Even if a consistent portrait of condemnation could be gleaned from the Bible, what social significance should it be given? One of the guiding principles of society, enshrined in the [U.S.] Constitution as a check against the government, is that decisions affecting social policy are not made on religious grounds. If the real ground of the alleged immorality invoked by governments to discriminate against gays is religious (as it has explicitly been even in some recent court cases involving teachers and guardians), then one of the major commitments of our nation is violated.

BUT AREN'T THEY UNNATURAL?

The most noteworthy feature of the accusation of something being unnatural (where a moral rather than an advertising point is being made) is that the plaint is so infrequently made. One used to hear the charge leveled against abortion, but that has pretty much faded as antiabortionists have come to lay all their chips on the hope that people will come to view abortion as murder. Incest used to be considered unnatural but discourse now usually assimilates it to the moral machinery of rape and violated trust. The charge comes up now in ordinary discourse only against homosexuality. This suggests that the charge is highly idiosyncratic and has little, if any, explanatory force. It fails to put homosexuality in a class with anything else so that one can learn by comparison with clear cases of the class just exactly what it is that is allegedly wrong with it.

Though the accusation of unnaturalness looks whimsical, in actual ordinary discourse when applied to homosexuality, it is usually delivered with venom of forethought. It carries a high emotional charge, usually expressing disgust and evincing queasiness. Probably it is nothing but an emotional charge. For people get equally disgusted and queasy at all sorts of things that are perfectly natural—to be expected in nature apart from artifice—and that could hardly be fit subjects for moral condemnation. Two typical examples in current American culture are some people's responses to mothers' suckling in public and to women who do not shave body hair. When people have strong emotional reactions, as they do in these cases, without being able to give good reasons for them, we think of them not as operating morally, but rather as being obsessed and manic. So the feelings of disgust that some people have to gays will hardly ground a charge of immorality. People fling the term *unnatural* against gays in the same breath and with the same force as when they call gays "sick" and "gross." When they do this, they give every appearance of being neurotically fearful and incapable of reasoned discourse.

When *nature* is taken in *technical* rather than ordinary usage, it looks like the notion also will not ground a charge of homosexual immorality. When *unnatural* means "by artifice" or "made by humans," it need only be pointed out that virtually everything that is good about life is unnatural in this sense, that the chief feature that distinguishes people from other animals is their very ability to make over the world to meet their needs and desires, and that their well-being depends upon these departures from nature. On this understanding of human nature and the natural, homosexuality is perfectly unobjectionable.

Another technical sense of *natural* is that something is natural, and so, good, if it fulfills some function in nature. Homosexuality on this view is unnatural because it allegedly violates the function of genitals, which is to produce babies. One problem with this view is that lots of bodily parts have lots of functions and just because some one activity can be fulfilled by only one organ (say, the mouth for eating) this activity does not condemn other functions of the organ to immorality (say, the mouth for talking, licking stamps, blowing bubbles, or having sex). So the possible use of the genitals to produce children does not, without more, condemn the use of the genitals for other purposes, say, achieving ecstasy and intimacy.

The functional view of nature will only provide a morally condemnatory sense to the unnatural if

a thing which might have many uses has but one proper function to the exclusion of other possible functions. But whether this is so cannot be established simply by looking at the thing. For what is seen is all its possible functions. The notion of function seemed like it might ground moral authority, but instead it turns out that moral authority is needed to define proper function. Some people try to fill in this moral authority by appeal to the "design" or "order" of an organ, saying, for instance, that the genitals are designed for the purpose of procreation. But these people cheat intellectually if they do not make explicit *who* the designer and orderer is. If it is God, we are back to square one—holding others accountable for religious beliefs.

Further, ordinary moral attitudes about child-rearing will not provide the needed supplement, which, in conjunction with the natural function view of bodily parts, would produce a positive obligation to use the genitals for procreation. Society's attitude toward a childless couple is that of pity not censure—even if the couple could have children. The pity may be an unsympathetic one, that is, not registering a course one would choose *for oneself*, but this does not make it a course one would *require* of others. The couple who discovers it cannot have children is viewed not as having thereby had a debt canceled, but rather as having to forgo some of the richness of life, just as a quadriplegic is not viewed as absolved from some moral obligation to hop, skip, and jump, but is viewed as missing some of the richness of life. Consistency requires then that, at most, gays who do not or cannot have children are to be pitied rather than condemned. What is immoral is the willful preventing of people from achieving the richness of life. Immorality in this regard lies with those social customs, regulations, and statutes that prevent lesbians and gay men from establishing blood or adoptive families, not with gays themselves.

Sometimes people attempt to establish authority for a moral obligation to use bodily parts in a certain fashion simply by claiming that moral laws are natural laws and vice versa. On this account, inanimate objects and plants are good in that they follow natural laws by necessity, animals by instinct, and persons by a rational will. People are special in that they must first discover the laws that govern them. Now, even if one believes the view—dubious in the post-Newtonian, post-Darwinian world—that natural laws in the usual sense ($e = mc^2$, for instance) have some moral content, it is not at all clear how one is to discover the laws in nature that apply to people.

If, on the one hand, one looks to people themselves for a model—and looks hard enough—one finds amazing variety, including homosexuality as a social ideal (upper-class 5th-century Athenians) and even as socially mandatory (Melanesia today). When one looks to people, one is simply unable to strip away the layers of social custom, history, and taboo in order to see what's really there to any degree more specific than that people are the creatures that make over their world and are capable of abstract thought. That this is so should raise doubts that neutral principles are to be found in human nature that will condemn homosexuality.

On the other hand, if one looks to nature apart from people for models, the possibilities are staggering. There are fish that change gender over their lifetimes: Should we "follow nature" and be operative transsexuals? Orangutans, genetically our next of kin, live completely solitary lives without social organization of any kind: Ought we to "follow nature" and be hermits? There are many species where only two members per generation reproduce: Shall we be bees? The search in nature for people's purpose—far from finding sure models for action—is likely to leave one morally rudderless.

BUT AREN'T GAYS WILLFULLY THE WAY THEY ARE?

It is generally conceded that if sexual orientation is something over which an individual—for whatever reason—has virtually no control, then discrimination against gays is especially deplorable, as it is against racial and ethnic classes, because it holds people accountable without regard for anything they themselves have done. And to hold a person accountable for that over which the person has no control is a central form of prejudice.

Attempts to answer the question whether or not sexual orientation is something that is reasonably thought to be within one's own control usually appeal simply to various claims of the biological or "mental" sciences. But the ensuing debate over genes, hormones, twins, early childhood development, and the like is as unnecessary as it is currently inconclusive.[15] All that is needed to answer the question is to look at the actual experience of gays in current society, and it becomes fairly clear that sexual orientation is not likely a matter of choice. For coming to have a homosexual identity simply does not have the same sort of structure that decision-making has.

On the one hand, the "choice" of the gender of a sexual partner does not seem to express a trivial desire which might be as easily well fulfilled by a simple substitution of the desired object. Picking the gender of a sex partner is decidedly dissimilar, that is, to such activities as picking a flavor of ice cream. If an ice-cream parlor is out of one's flavor, one simply picks another. And if people were persecuted, threatened with jail terms, shattered careers, loss of family and housing and the like for eating, say, Rocky Road ice cream, no one would ever eat it; everyone would pick another easily available flavor. That gay people abide in being gay even in the face of persecution shows that being gay is not a matter of easy choice.

On the other hand, even if establishing a sexual orientation is not like making a relatively trivial choice, perhaps it is nevertheless relevantly like making the central and serious life choices by which individuals try to establish themselves as being of some type. Again, if one examines gay experience, this seems not to be the case. For one never sees anyone setting out to become a homosexual, in the way one does see people setting out to become doctors, lawyers, and bricklayers. One does not find gays-to-be picking some end—"At some point in the future, I want to become a homosexual"—and then set[ting] about planning and acquiring the ways and means to that end, in the way one does see people deciding that they want to become lawyers, and then sees them plan[ning] what courses to take and what sort of temperaments, habits, and skills to develop in order to become lawyers. Typically gays-to-be simply find themselves having homosexual encounters and yet at least initially resisting quite strongly the identification of being homosexual. Such a person even very likely resists having such encounters but ends up having them anyway. Only with time, luck, and great personal effort, but sometimes never, does the person gradually come to accept her or his orientation, to view it as a given material condition of life, coming as materials do with certain capacities and limitations. The person begins to act in accordance with his or her orientation and its capacities, seeing its actualization as a requisite for an integrated personality and as a central component of personal well-being. As a result, the experience of coming out to oneself has for gays the basic structure of a discovery, not the structure of a choice. And far from signaling immorality, coming out to others affords one of the few remaining opportunities in ever more bureaucratic, mechanistic, and socialistic societies to manifest courage.

HOW WOULD SOCIETY AT LARGE BE CHANGED IF GAYS WERE SOCIALLY ACCEPTED?

Suggestions to change social policy with regard to gays are invariably met with claims that to do so would invite the destruction of civilization itself: After all, isn't that what did Rome in? Actually Rome's decay paralleled not the flourishing of homosexuality, but its repression under the later Christianized emperors.[16] Predictions of American civilization's imminent demise have been as premature as they have been frequent. Civilization has shown itself rather resilient here, in large part because of the country's traditional commitments to a respect for privacy, to individual liberties, and especially to people minding their own business. These all give society an open texture and the flexibility to try out things to see what works. And because of this one now need not speculate about what changes reforms in gay social policy might bring to society at large. For many reforms have already been tried.

Half the states have decriminalized homosexual acts. Can you guess which of the following states still have sodomy laws? Wisconsin, Minnesota; New Mexico, Arizona; Vermont, New Hampshire; Nebraska, Kansas. One from each pair does and one does not have sodomy laws. And yet one would be hard pressed to point out any substantial difference between the members of each pair. (If you're interested: It is the second of each pair with them.) Empirical studies have shown that there is no increase in other crimes in states that have decriminalized [homosexual acts].[17] Further, sodomy laws are virtually never enforced. They remain on the books not to "protect society" but to insult gays and, for that reason, need to be removed.

Neither has the passage of legislation barring discrimination against gays ushered in the end of civilization. Some 50 counties and municipalities, including some of the country's largest cities (like Los Angeles and Boston) have passed such statutes and among the states and [counties] Wisconsin and the District of Columbia have model protective codes. Again, no more brimstone has fallen in these places than elsewhere. Staunchly antigay cities, like Miami and Houston, have not been spared the AIDS crisis.

Berkeley, California, has even passed domestic partner legislation giving gay couples the same rights to city benefits as married couples, and yet Berkeley has not become more weird than it already was.

Seemingly hysterical predictions that the American family would collapse if such reforms would pass proved false, just as the same dire predictions that the availability of divorce would lessen the ideal and desirability of marriage proved completely unfounded. Indeed, if current discriminations, which drive gays into hiding and into anonymous relations, were lifted, far from seeing gays raze American families, one would see gays forming them.

Virtually all gays express a desire to have a permanent lover. Many would like to raise or foster children—perhaps [from among the] alarming number of gay kids who have been beaten up and thrown out of their "families" for being gay. But currently society makes gay coupling very difficult. A life of hiding is a pressure-cooker existence not easily shared with another. Members of nongay couples are here asked to imagine what it would take to erase every trace of their own sexual orientation for even just a week.

Even against oppressive odds, gays have shown an amazing tendency to nest. And those gay couples who have survived the odds show that the structure of more usual couplings is not a matter of destiny but of personal responsibility. The so-called basic unit of society turns out not to be a unique immutable atom but can adopt different parts, be adapted to different needs, and even be improved. Gays might even have a thing or two to teach others about divisions of labor, the relation of sensuality and intimacy, and stages of development in such relations.

If discrimination ceased, gay men and lesbians would enter the mainstream of the human community openly and with self-respect. The energies that the typical gay person wastes in the anxiety of leading a day-to-day existence of systematic disguise would be released for use in personal flourishing. From this release would be generated the many spin-off benefits that accrue to a society when its individual members thrive.

Society would be richer for acknowledging another aspect of human richness and diversity. Families with gay members would develop relations based on truth and trust rather than lies and fear. And the heterosexual majority would be better off for knowing that they are no longer trampling their gay friends and neighbors.

Finally and perhaps paradoxically, in extending to gays the rights and benefits it has reserved for its dominant culture, America would confirm its deeply held vision of itself as a morally progressing nation, a nation itself advancing and serving as a beacon for others—especially with regard to human rights. The words with which our national pledge ends—"with liberty and justice for all"—are not a description of the present but a call for the future. Ours is a nation given to a prophetic political rhetoric which acknowledges that morality is not arbitrary and that justice is not merely the expression of the current collective will. It is this vision that led the black civil rights movement to its successes. Those congressmen who opposed that movement and its centerpiece, the 1964 Civil Rights Act, on obscurantist grounds, but who lived long enough and were noble enough came in time to express their heartfelt regret and shame at what they had done. It is to be hoped and someday to be expected that those who now grasp at anything to oppose the extension of that which is best about America to gays will one day feel the same.

NOTES

1. "Public Fears—and Sympathies," *Newsweek*, August 12, 1985, p. 23.

2. Alfred C. Kinsey, *Sexual Behavior in the Human Male* (Philadelphia: Saunders, 1948), pp. 650–51. On the somewhat lower incidences of lesbianism, see Alfred C. Kinsey, *Sexual Behavior in the Human Female* (Philadelphia: Saunders, 1953), pp. 472–75.

3. Evelyn Hooker, "The Adjustment of the Male Overt Homosexual," *Journal of Projective Techniques* 21 (1957), pp. 18–31, reprinted in Hendrik M. Ruitenbeek, ed., *The Problem of Homosexuality* (New York: Dutton, 1963), pp. 141–61.

4. See Ronald Bayer, *Homosexuality and American Psychiatry* (New York: Basic Books, 1981).

5. For studies showing that gay men are no more likely—indeed, are less likely—than heterosexuals to be child molesters and that the largest classes and most persistent sexual abusers of children are the children's fathers, stepfathers, or mother's boyfriends, see Vincent De Francis, *Protecting the Child Victim of Sex Crimes Committed by Adults* (Denver: The American Humane Association, 1969), pp vii, 38, 69–70; A. Nicholas Groth, "Adult Sexual Orientation and Attraction to Underage Persons," *Archives of Sexual Behavior* 7 (1978), pp. 175–81; Mary J. Spencer, "Sexual Abuse of Boys," *Pediatrics* 78:1 (July 1986), pp. 133–38.

6. See National Gay Task Force, *Antigay/Lesbian Victimization* (New York: NGTF, 1984).

7. "2 St. John's Students Given Probation in Assault on Gay," *The Washington Post*, May 15, 1984, p. 1.

8. See Randy Shilts, *The Mayor of Castro Street: The Life and Times of Harvey Milk* (New York: St. Martin's, 1982), pp. 308–25.

9. See Richard Plant, *The Pink Triangle: The Nazi War Against Homosexuals* (New York: Holt, 1986).

10. E. Carrington Boggan, *The Rights of Gay People: The Basic ACLU Guide to a Gay Person's Rights* (New York: Avon, 1975), pp. 211–35.

11. John Boswell, *Christianity, Social Tolerance, and Homosexuality: Gay People in Western Europe from the Beginning of the Christian Era to the Fourteenth Century* (Chicago: The University of Chicago Press, 1980).

12. See Gilbert Herdt, *Guardians of the Flute: Idioms of Masculinity* (New York: McGraw-Hill, 1981), pp. 232–39, 284–88; and see generally Gilbert Herdt, ed., *Ritualized Homosexuality in Melanesia* (Berkeley: University of California Press, 1984). For another eye-opener, see Walter J. Williams, *The Spirit and the Flesh: Sexual Diversity in American Indian Culture* (Boston: Beacon, 1986).

13. See especially Boswell, op. cit., Chap. 4.

14. For Old Testament condemnations of homosexual acts, see Leviticus 18:22, 21:3. For hygienic and dietary codes, see, for example, Leviticus 15:19–27 (on the uncleanliness of women) and Leviticus 11:1–47 (on not eating rabbits, pigs, bats, finless water creatures, legless creeping creatures, and so on). For Lot at Sodom, see Genesis 19:1–25. For Lot in the cave, see Genesis 19:30–38.

15. The preponderance of the scientific evidence supports the view that homosexuality is either genetically determined or a permanent result of early childhood development. See the Kinsey Institute's study by Alan Bell, Martin Weinberg, and Sue Hammersmith, *Sexual Preference: Its Development in Men and Women* (Bloomington: Indiana University Press, 1981); Frederick Whitam and Robin Mathy, *Male Homosexuality in Four Societies* (New York: Praeger, 1986), Chap. 7.

16. See Boswell, op. cit., Chapter 3.

17. See Gilbert Geis, "Reported Consequences of Decriminalization of Consensual Adult Homosexuality in Seven American States," *Journal of Homosexuality* 1:4 (1976), pp. 419–26; Ken Sinclair and Michael Ross, "Consequences of Decriminalization of Homosexuality: A Study of Two Australian States," *Journal of Homosexuality* 12:1 (1985), pp. 119–27.

REVIEW AND DISCUSSION QUESTIONS

1. Who, according to Mohr, are gays? What are the consequences of the fact that homosexuality is commonplace, according to Mohr?

2. Describe the stereotypes Mohr finds about gays, along with the false generalizations he says lie behind them.

3. In what ways does he argue gays experience discrimination? Is it important, in this connection, that according to Mohr sexual orientation is not chosen?

4. How does Mohr respond to the argument that homosexuality is unnatural?

5. What policy changes does Mohr recommend, and why?

6. Do Mohr, Pineau, and Paglia disagree over the nature of sexuality? How would each respond to the claim that in reality all sex necessarily involves is the desire for pleasant physical contact?

Is Adultery Immoral?

Richard A. Wasserstrom

Richard Wasserstrom considers various reasons that might be given for supposing adultery is wrong, including claims that it involves promise breaking and deception. He concludes with a discussion of the importance of fidelity as a support for the institution of marriage and whether adultery may be wrong just because it constitutes an attack on marriage. Richard A. Wasserstrom is professor of philosophy at the University of California, Santa Cruz.

. . . I propose in this paper to think about the topic of sexual morality, and to do so in the following fashion. I shall consider just one kind of behavior that is often taken to be a case of sexual immorality—adultery. I am interested in pursuing at least two questions. First, I want to explore the question of in what respects adulterous behavior falls within the domain of morality at all: For this surely is one of the puzzles one encounters when considering the topic of sexual morality. It is often hard to see on what grounds much of the behavior is deemed to be either moral or immoral, for example, private homosexual behavior between consenting adults. I have purposely selected adultery because it seems a more plausible candidate for moral assessment than many other kinds of sexual behavior.

The second question I want to examine is that of what is to be said about adultery, without being especially concerned to stay within the area of morality. I shall endeavor, in other words, to identify and to assess a number of the major arguments that might be advanced against adultery. I believe that they are the chief arguments that would be given in support of the view that adultery is immoral, but I think they are worth considering even if some of them turn out to be nonmoral arguments and considerations.

A number of the issues involved seem to me to be complicated and difficult. In a number of places I have at best indicated where further philosophical exploration is required without having successfully conducted the exploration myself. The paper may very well be more useful as an illustration of how one might begin to think about the subject of sexual morality than as an elucidation of important truths about the topic.

Before I turn to the arguments themselves there are two preliminary points that require some clarification. Throughout the paper I shall refer to the immorality of such things as breaking a promise, deceiving someone, etc. In a very rough way, I mean by this that there is something morally wrong that is done in doing the action in question. I mean that the action is, in a strong sense of *"prima facie"* *prima facie* wrong or unjustified. I do not mean that it may never be right or justifiable to do the action; just that the fact that it is an action of this description always does count

against the rightness of the action. I leave entirely open the question of what it is that makes actions of this kind immoral in this sense of "immoral."

The second preliminary point concerns what is meant or implied by the concept of adultery. I mean by "adultery" any case of extramarital sex, and I want to explore the arguments for and against extramarital sex, undertaken in a variety of morally relevant situations. Someone might claim that the concept of adultery is conceptually connected with the concept of immorality, and that to characterize behavior as adulterous is already to characterize it as immoral or unjustified in the sense described above. There may be something to this. Hence the importance of making it clear that I want to talk about extramarital sexual relations. If they are always immoral, this is something that must be shown by argument. If the concept of adultery does in some sense entail or imply immorality, I want to ask whether that connection is a rationally based one. If not all cases of extramarital sex are immoral (again, in the sense described above), then the concept of adultery should either be weakened accordingly or restricted to those classes of extramarital sex for which the predication of immorality is warranted.

One argument for the immorality of adultery might go something like this: what makes adultery immoral is that it involves the breaking of a promise, and what makes adultery seriously wrong is that it involves the breaking of an important promise. For, so the argument might continue, one of the things the two parties promise each other when they get married is that they will abstain from sexual relationships with third persons. Because of this promise both spouses quite reasonably entertain the expectation that the other will behave in conformity with it. Hence, when one of the parties has sexual intercourse with a third person he or she breaks that promise about sexual relationships which was made when the marriage was entered into, and defeats the reasonable expectations of exclusivity entertained by the spouse.

In many cases the immorality involved in breaching the promise relating to extramarital sex may be a good deal more serious than that involved in the breach of other promises. This is so because adherence to this promise may be of much greater importance to the parties than is adherence to many of the other promises given or received by them in their lifetime. The breaking of this promise may be much more hurtful and painful than is typically the case.

Why is this so? To begin with, it may have been difficult for the nonadulterous spouse to have kept the promise. Hence that spouse may feel the unfairness of having restrained himself or herself in the absence of reciprocal restraint having been exercised by the adulterous spouse. In addition, the spouse may perceive the breaking of the promise as an indication of a kind of indifference on the part of the adulterous spouse. If you really cared about me and my feelings—the spouse might say—you would not have done this to me. And third, and related to the above, the spouse may see the act of sexual intercourse with another as a sign of affection for the other person and as an additional rejection of the nonadulterous spouse as the one who is loved by the adulterous spouse. It is not just that the adulterous spouse does not take the feelings of the spouse sufficiently into account, the adulterous spouse also indicates through the act of adultery affection for someone other than the spouse. I will return to these points later. For the present, it is sufficient to note that a set of arguments can be developed in support of the proposition that certain kinds of adultery are wrong just because they involve the breach of a serious promise which, among other things, leads to the intentional infliction of substantial pain by one spouse upon the other.

Another argument for the immorality of adultery focuses not on the existence of a promise of sexual exclusivity but on the connection between adultery and deception. According to this argument, adultery involves deception. And because deception is wrong, so is adultery.

Although it is certainly not obviously so, I shall simply assume in this paper that deception is always immoral. Thus the crucial issue for my purposes is the asserted connection between extramarital sex and deception. Is it plausible to maintain, as this argument does, that adultery always does involve deception and is on that basis to be condemned?

The most obvious person on whom deceptions might be practiced is the nonparticipating spouse;

and the most obvious thing about which the nonparticipating spouse can be deceived is the existence of the adulterous act. One clear case of deception is that of lying. Instead of saying that the afternoon was spent in bed with A, the adulterous spouse asserts that it was spent in the library with B, or on the golf course with C.

There can also be deception even when no lies are told. Suppose, for instance, that a person has sexual intercourse with someone other than his or her spouse and just does not tell the spouse about it. Is that deception? It may not be a case of lying if, for example, the spouse is never asked by the other about the situation. Still, we might say, it is surely deceptive because of the promises that were exchanged at marriage. As we saw earlier, these promises provide a foundation for the reasonable belief that neither spouse will engage in sexual relationships with any other persons. Hence the failure to bring the fact of extramarital sex to the attention of the other spouse deceives that spouse about the present state of the marital relationship.

Adultery, in other words, can involve both active and passive deception. An adulterous spouse may just keep silent or, as is often the fact, the spouse may engage in an increasingly complex way of life devoted to the concealment of the facts from the nonparticipating spouse. Lies, half-truths, clandestine meetings, and the like may become a central feature of the adulterous spouse's existence. These are things that can and do happen, and when they do they make the case against adultery an easy one. Still, neither active nor passive deception is inevitably a feature of an extramarital relationship.

It is possible, though, that a more subtle but pervasive kind of deceptiveness is a feature of adultery. It comes about because of the connection in our culture between sexual intimacy and certain feelings of love and affection. The point can be made indirectly at first by seeing that one way in which we can, in our culture, mark off our close friends from our mere acquaintances is through the kinds of intimacies that we are prepared to share with them. I may, for instance, be willing to reveal my very private thoughts and emotions to my closest friends or to my wife, but to no one else. My sharing of these intimate facts about myself is from one perspective a way of making a gift to those who mean the most to me. Revealing these things and sharing them with those who mean the most to me is one means by which I create, maintain, and confirm those interpersonal relationships that are of most importance to me.

Now in our culture, it might be claimed, sexual intimacy is one of the chief currencies through which gifts of this sort are exchanged. One way to tell someone—particularly someone of the opposite sex—that you have feelings of affection and love for them is by sharing with them sexual behaviors that one doesn't share with the rest of the world. This way of measuring affection was certainly very much a part of the culture in which I matured. It worked something like this. If you were a girl, you showed how much you liked someone by the degree of sexual intimacy you would allow. If you liked a boy only a little, you never did more than kiss—and even the kiss was not very passionate. If you liked the boy a lot and if your feeling was reciprocated, necking, and possibly petting, was permissible. If the attachment was still stronger and you thought it might even become a permanent relationship, the sexual activity was correspondingly more intense and more intimate, although whether it would ever lead to sexual intercourse depended on whether the parties (and particularly the girl) accepted fully the prohibition on nonmarital sex. The situation of the boy was related, but not exactly the same. The assumption was that males did not naturally link sex with affection in the way in which females did. However, since women did, males had to take this into account. That is to say, because a woman would permit sexual intimacies only if she had feelings of affection for the male and only if those feelings were reciprocated, the male had to have and express those feelings, too, before sexual intimacies of any sort would occur.

The result was that the importance of a correlation between sexual intimacy and feelings of love and affection was taught by the culture and assimilated by those growing up in the culture. The scale of possible positive feelings toward persons of the opposite sex ran from casual liking at the one end to the love that was deemed essential to and characteristic of marriage at the other. The scale of possible sexual behavior ran from brief, passionless kissing or hand-holding at the one end to sexual intercourse at the other. And the correlation between the two scales was quite precise. As a result, any act of sexual intimacy carried substantial meaning with it, and no act of sexual intimacy was simply a pleasurable set of bodily sensations. Many such acts were, of course, more pleasurable to the participants because they were a way of saying what the participants' feelings were. And sometimes they were less pleasurable for the same reason. The point is, however, that in any event sexual activity was much more than mere bodily enjoyment. It was not like eating a good meal, listening to good music, lying in the sun, or getting a pleasant back rub. It was behavior that meant a great deal concerning one's feelings for persons of the opposite sex in whom one was most interested and with whom one was most involved. It was among the most authoritative ways in which one could communicate to another the nature and degree of one's affection.

If this sketch is even roughly right, then several things become somewhat clearer. To begin with, a possible rationale for many of the rules of conventional sexual morality can be developed. If, for example, sexual intercourse is associated with the kind of affection and commitment to another that is regarded as characteristic of the marriage relationship, then it is natural that sexual intercourse should be thought properly to take place between persons who are married to each other. And if it is thought that this kind of affection and commitment is only to be found within the marriage relationship, then it is not surprising that sexual intercourse should only be thought to be proper within marriage.

Related to what has just been said is the idea that sexual intercourse ought to be restricted to those who are married to each other as a means by which to confirm the very special feelings that the spouses have for each other. Because the culture teaches that sexual intercourse means that the strongest of all feelings for each other are shared by the lovers, it is natural that persons who are married to each other should be able to say this to each other in this way. Revealing and confirming verbally that these feelings are present is one thing that helps to sustain the relationship; engaging in sexual intercourse is another.

In addition, this account would help to provide a framework within which to make sense of the notion that some sex is better than other sex. As I indicated earlier, the fact that sexual intimacy can be meaningful in the sense described tends to make it also the case that sexual intercourse can sometimes be more enjoyable than at other times. On this view, sexual intercourse will typically be more enjoyable where the strong feelings of affection are present than it will be where it is merely "mechanical." This is so in part because people enjoy being loved, especially by those whom they love. Just as we like to hear words of affection, so we like to receive affectionate behavior. And the meaning enhances the independently pleasurable behavior.

More to the point, moreover, an additional rationale for the prohibition on extramarital sex can now be developed. For given this way of viewing the sexual world, extramarital sex will almost always involve deception of a deeper sort. If the adulterous spouse does not in fact have the appropriate feelings of affection for the extramarital partner, then the adulterous spouse is deceiving that person about the presence of such feelings. If, on the other hand, the adulterous spouse does have the corresponding feelings for the extramarital partner but not toward the nonparticipating spouse, the adulterous spouse is very probably deceiving the nonparticipating spouse about the presence of such feelings toward that spouse. Indeed, it might be argued, whenever there is no longer love between the two persons who are married to each other, there is deception just because being married implies both to the participants and to the world that such a bond exists. Deception is inevitable, the argument might conclude, because the feelings of affection that ought to accompany any act of sexual intercourse can only be held toward one other person at any given time in one's life. And if this is so, then the adulterous spouse always deceives either the partner in adultery or the nonparticipating spouse about the existence of such feelings. Thus extramarital sex involves deception of this sort and is for this reason immoral even if no deception vis-à-vis the occurrence of the act of adultery takes place.

What might be said in response to the foregoing arguments? The first thing that might be said

is that the account of the connection between sexual intimacy and feelings of affection is inaccurate. Not inaccurate in the sense that no one thinks of things that way, but in the sense that there is substantially more divergence of opinion than that account suggests. For example, the view I have delineated may describe reasonably accurately the concepts of the sexual world in which I grew up, but it does not capture the sexual *weltanschauung* of today's youth at all. Thus, whether or not adultery implies deception in respect to feelings depends very much on the persons who are involved and the way they look at the "meaning" of sexual intimacy.

Second, the argument leaves to be answered the question of whether it is desirable for sexual intimacy to carry the sorts of messages described above. For those persons for whom sex does have these implications, there are special feelings and sensibilities that must be taken into account. But it is another question entirely whether any valuable end—moral or otherwise—is served by investing sexual behavior with such significance. That is something that must be shown and not just assumed. It might, for instance, be the case that substantially more good than harm would come from a kind of demystification of sexual behavior: one that would encourage the enjoyment of sex more for its own sake and one that would reject the centrality both of the association of sex with love and of love with only one other person.

I regard these as two of the more difficult, unresolved issues that our culture faces today in respect to thinking sensibly about the attitudes toward sex and love that we should try to develop in ourselves and in our children. Much of the contemporary literature that advocates sexual liberation of one sort or another embraces one or the other of two different views about the relationship between sex and love.

One view holds that sex should be separated from love and affection. To be sure sex is probably better when the partners genuinely like and enjoy each other. But sex is basically an intensive, exciting sensuous activity that can be enjoyed in a variety of suitable settings with a variety of suitable partners. The situation in respect to sexual pleasure is no different from that of the person who knows and appreciates fine food and who can have a very satisfying meal in any number of good restaurants with any number of congenial companions. One question that must be settled here is whether sex can be so demystified; another, more important question is whether it would be desirable to do so. What would we gain and what might we lose if we all lived in a world in which an act of sexual intercourse was no more or less significant or enjoyable than having a delicious meal in a nice setting with a good friend? The answer to this question lies beyond the scope of this paper.

The second view seeks to drive the wedge in a different place. It is not the link between sex and love that needs to be broken; rather, on this view, it is the connection between love and exclusivity that ought to be severed. For a number of the reasons already given, it is desirable, so this argument goes, that sexual intimacy continue to be reserved to and shared with only those for whom one has very great affection. The mistake lies in thinking that any "normal" adult will only have those feelings toward one other adult during his or her lifetime—or even at any time in his or her life. It is the concept of adult love, not ideas about sex, that, on this view, needs demystification. What are thought to be both unrealistic and unfortunate are the notions of exclusivity and possessiveness that attach to the dominant conception of love between adults in our and other cultures. Parents of four, five, six, or even ten children can certainly claim and sometimes claim correctly that they love all of their children, that they love them all equally, and that it is simply untrue to their feelings to insist that the numbers involved diminish either the quantity or the quality of their love. If this is an idea that is readily understandable in the case of parents and children, there is no necessary reason why it is an impossible or undesirable ideal in the case of adults. To be sure, there is probably a limit to the number of intimate, "primary" relationships that any person can maintain at any given time without the quality of the relationship being affected. But one adult ought surely to be able to love two, three, or even six other adults at any one time without that love being different in kind or degree from that of the traditional, monogamous, lifetime marriage. And as between the individuals in these relationships, whether within a marriage or without, sexual intimacy is fitting and good.

The issues raised by a position such as this one are also surely worth exploring in detail and with care. Is there something to be called "sexual love" which is different from parental love or the nonsexual love of close friends? Is there something about love in general that links it naturally and appropriately with feelings of exclusivity and possession? Or is there something about sexual love, whatever that may be, that makes these feelings especially fitting here? Once again the issues are conceptual, empirical, and normative all at once: What is love? How could it be different? Would it be a good thing or a bad thing if it were different?

Suppose, though, that having delineated these problems we were now to pass them by. Suppose, moreover, we were to be persuaded of the possibility and the desirability of weakening substantially either the links between sex and love or the links between sexual love and exclusivity. Would it not then be the case that adultery could be free from all of the morally objectionable features described so far? To be more specific, let us imagine that a husband and wife have what is today sometimes characterized as an "open marriage." Suppose, that is, that they have agreed in advance that extramarital sex is—under certain circumstances—acceptable behavior for each to engage in. Suppose, that as a result there is no impulse to deceive each other about the occurrence or nature of any such relationships, and that no deception in fact occurs. Suppose, too, that there is no deception in respect to the feelings involved between the adulterous spouse and the extramarital partner. And suppose, finally, that one or the other or both of the spouses then has sexual intercourse in circumstances consistent with these understandings. Under this description, so the argument might conclude, adultery is simply not immoral. At a minimum, adultery cannot very plausibly be condemned either on the ground that it involves deception or on the ground that it requires the breaking of a promise. . . .

The remaining argument seeks to justify the prohibition by virtue of the role that it plays in the development and maintenance of nuclear families. The argument, or set of arguments, might, I believe, go something like this.

Consider first a farfetched nonsexual example. Suppose a society were organized so that after some suitable age—say, 18, 19, or 20—persons were forbidden to eat anything but bread and water with anyone but their spouse. Persons might still choose in such a society not to get married. Good food just might not be very important to them because they have underdeveloped taste buds. Or good food might be bad for them because there is something wrong with their digestive system. Or good food might be important to them, but they might decide that the enjoyment of good food would get in the way of the attainment of other things that were more important. But most persons would, I think, be led to favor marriage in part because they preferred a richer, more varied, diet to one of bread and water. And they might remain married because the family was the only legitimate setting within which good food was obtainable. If it is important to have society organized so that persons will both get married and stay married, such an arrangement would be well suited to the preservation of the family, and the prohibitions relating to food consumption could be understood as fulfilling that function.

It is obvious that one of the more powerful human desires is the desire for sexual gratification. The desire is a natural one, like hunger and thirst, in the sense that it need not be learned in order to be present within us and operative upon us. But there is in addition much that we do learn about what the act of sexual intercourse is like. Once we experience sexual intercourse ourselves—and in particular once we experience orgasm—we discover that it is among the most intensive, short-term pleasures of the body.

Because this is so, it is easy to see how the prohibition upon extramarital sex helps to hold marriage together. At least during that period of life when the enjoyment of sexual intercourse is one of the desirable bodily pleasures, persons will wish to enjoy those pleasures. If one consequence of being married is that one is prohibited from having sexual intercourse with anyone but one's spouse, then the spouses in a marriage are in a position to provide an important source of pleasure for each other that is unavailable to them elsewhere in the society.

The point emerges still more clearly if this rule of sexual morality is seen as of a piece with the other rules of sexual morality. When this prohibition is coupled, for example, with the prohibition on nonmarital sexual intercourse, we are presented with the inducement both to get married and to stay married. For if sexual intercourse is only legitimate within marriage, then persons seeking that gratification which is a feature of sexual intercourse are furnished explicit social directions for its attainment; namely marriage.

Nor, to continue the argument, is it necessary to focus exclusively on the bodily enjoyment that is involved. Orgasm may be a significant part of what there is to sexual intercourse, but it is not the whole of it. We need only recall the earlier discussion of the meaning that sexual intimacy has in our own culture to begin to see some of the more intricate ways in which sexual exclusivity may be connected with the establishment and maintenance of marriage as the primary heterosexual, love relationship. Adultery is wrong, in other words, because a prohibition on extramarital sex is a way to help maintain the institutions of marriage and the nuclear family.

Now I am frankly not sure what we are to say about an argument such as this one. What I am convinced of is that, like the arguments discussed earlier, this one also reveals something of the difficulty and complexity of the issues that are involved. So, what I want now to do—in the brief and final portion of this paper—is to try to delineate with reasonable precision what I take several of the fundamental, unresolved issues to be.

The first is whether this last argument is an argument for the *immorality* of extramarital sexual intercourse. What does seem clear is that there are differences between this argument and the ones considered earlier. The earlier arguments condemned adulterous behavior because it was behavior that involved breaking of a promise, taking unfair advantage, or deceiving another. To the degree to which the prohibition on extramarital sex can be supported by arguments which invoke considerations such as these, there is little question but that violations of the prohibition are properly regarded as immoral. And such a claim could be defended on one or both of two distinct grounds. The first is that things like promise-breaking and deception are just wrong. The second is that adultery involving promise-breaking or deception is wrong because it involves the straightforward infliction of harm on another human being—typically the nonadulterous spouse—who has a strong claim not to have that harm so inflicted.

The argument that connects the prohibition on extramarital sex with the maintenance and preservation of the institution of marriage is an argument for the instrumental value of the prohibition. To some degree this counts, I think, against regarding all violations of the prohibition as obvious cases of immorality. This is so partly because hypothetical imperatives are less clearly within the domain of morality than are categorical ones, and even more because instrumental prohibitions are within the domain of morality only if the end they serve or the way they serve it is itself within the domain of morality.

What this should help us see, I think, is the fact that the argument that connects the prohibition on adultery with the preservation of marriage is at best seriously incomplete. Before we ought to be convinced by it, we ought to have reasons for believing that marriage is a morally desirable and just social institution. And this is not quite as easy or obvious a task as it may seem to be. For the concept of marriage is both a loosely structured and a complicated one. There may be all sorts of intimate, interpersonal relationships which will resemble but not be identical with the typical marriage relationship presupposed by the traditional sexual morality. There may be a number of distinguishable sexual and loving arrangements which can all legitimately claim to be called *marriages*. The prohibitions of the traditional sexual morality may be effective ways to maintain some marriages and ineffective ways to promote and preserve others. The prohibitions of the traditional sexual morality may make good psychological sense if certain psychological theories are true, and they may be purveyors of immense psychological mischief if other psychological theories are true. The prohibitions of the traditional sexual morality may seem obviously correct if sexual intimacy carries the meaning that the dominant culture has often ascribed to it, and they may seem equally bizarre when sex is viewed through the perspective of the counterculture. Irrespective of whether instrumental arguments of this sort are properly deemed moral arguments, they ought not to fully convince anyone until questions like these are answered.

REVIEW AND DISCUSSION QUESTIONS

1. Describe the various ways that adultery may involve deception.
2. How might one argue that adultery is wrong based on the importance of marriage? Does Wasserstrom accept this argument?
3. Suppose adultery does weaken the marriage institution. Does that mean it is wrong? Are people obligated never to weaken a useful institution?
4. Is "passive" deception always wrong? Explain, using examples, and then indicate if you think this is a problem for Wasserstrom's position.
5. Is Wasserstrom's argument relevant to the discussions of the nature of sex in the previous essays? Explain.

14
Parents and Children

Readings in this section focus on relations between parents and children. Beginning with a discussion of the moral issues surrounding surrogacy, essays that follow discuss related questions of allowing sale of babies, licensing parents, the powers of parents to control their children's upbringing, and, finally, the moral obligations of adult children to their parents.

Surrogate Motherhood as Prenatal Adoption

Bonnie Steinbock

In this essay, Bonnie Steinbock begins with a discussion of the famous Baby M case in which Mary Beth Whitehead originally agreed to serve as a surrogate mother but later changed her mind. Steinbock then considers different arguments in support of surrogacy and concludes with a discussion of the objections to surrogacy: that it involves exploitation, that it is incompatible with human dignity, that it violates the right to privacy of the birth mother, and that it harms the offspring resulting from the contract. Bonnie Steinbock is professor of philosophy at the State University of New York at Albany.

The recent case of "Baby M" has brought surrogate motherhood to the forefront of American attention. Ultimately, whether we permit or prohibit surrogacy depends on what we take to be good reasons for preventing people from acting as they wish. A growing number of people want to be, or hire, surrogates; are there legitimate reasons to prevent them? Apart from its intrinsic interest, the issue of surrogate motherhood provides us with an opportunity to examine different justifications for limiting individual freedom.

In the first section, I examine the Baby M case, and the lessons it offers. In the second section, I

examine claims that surrogacy is ethically unacceptable because exploitive, inconsistent with human dignity, or harmful to the children born of such arrangements. I conclude that these reasons justify restrictions on surrogate contracts, rather than an outright ban.

I. BABY M

Mary Beth Whitehead, a married mother of two, agreed to be inseminated with the sperm of William Stern, and to give up the child to him for

From Bonnie Steinbock, "Surrogate Motherhood as Prenatal Adoption," *Law, Medicine and Health Care*, 16, no. 1 (Spring/Summer 1988), 44–50.

a fee of $10,000. The baby (whom Mrs. Whitehead named Sara, and the Sterns named Melissa) was born on March 27, 1986. Three days later, Mrs. Whitehead took her home from the hospital, and turned her over to the Sterns.

Then Mrs. Whitehead changed her mind. She went to the Sterns' home, distraught, and pleaded to have the baby temporarily. Afraid that she would kill herself, the Sterns agreed. The next week, Mrs. Whitehead informed the Sterns that she had decided to keep the child, and threatened to leave the country if court action was taken.

At that point, the situation deteriorated into a cross between the Keystone Kops and Nazi stormtroopers. Accompanied by five policemen, the Sterns went to the Whitehead residence armed with a court order giving them temporary custody of the child. Mrs. Whitehead managed to slip the baby out of a window to her husband, and the following morning the Whiteheads fled with the child to Florida, where Mrs. Whitehead's parents lived. During the next three months, the Whiteheads lived in roughly twenty different hotels, motels, and homes to avoid apprehension. From time to time, Mrs. Whitehead telephoned Mr. Stern to discuss the matter: He taped these conversations on advice of counsel. Mrs. Whitehead threatened to kill herself, to kill the child, and falsely to accuse Mr. Stern of sexually molesting her older daughter.

At the end of July 1986, while Mrs. Whitehead was hospitalized with a kidney infection, Florida police raided her mother's home, knocking her down, and seized the child. Baby M was placed in the custody of Mr. Stern, and the Whiteheads returned to New Jersey, where they attempted to regain custody. After a long and emotional court battle, Judge Harvey R. Sorkow ruled on March 31, 1987, that the surrogacy contract was valid, and that specific performance was justified in the best interests of the child. Immediately after reading his decision, he called the Sterns into his chambers so that Mr. Stern's wife, Dr. Elizabeth Stern, could legally adopt the child.

This outcome was unexpected and unprecedented. Most commentators had thought that a court would be unlikely to order a reluctant surrogate to give up an infant merely on the basis of a contract. Indeed, if Mrs. Whitehead had never surrendered the child to the Sterns, but had simply taken her home and kept her there, the outcome undoubtedly would have been different. It is also likely that Mrs. Whitehead's failure to obey the initial custody order angered Judge Sorkow, and affected his decision.

The decision was appealed to the New Jersey Supreme Court, which issued its decision on February 3, 1988. Writing for a unanimous court, Chief Justice Wilentz reversed the lower court's ruling that the surrogacy contract was valid. The court held that a surrogacy contract which provides money for the surrogate mother, and which includes her irrevocable agreement to surrender her child at birth, is invalid and unenforceable. Since the contract was invalid, Mrs. Whitehead did not relinquish, nor were there any other grounds for terminating, her parental rights. Therefore, the adoption of Baby M by Mrs. Stern was improperly granted, and Mrs. Whitehead remains the child's legal mother.

The Court further held that the issue of custody is determined solely by the child's best interests, and it agreed with the lower court that it was in Melissa's best interests to remain with the Sterns. However, Mrs. Whitehead, as Baby M's legal as well as natural mother, is entitled to have her own interest in visitation considered. The determination of what kind of visitation rights should be granted to her, and under what conditions, was remanded to the trial court.

The distressing details of this case have led many people to reject surrogacy altogether. Do we really want police officers wrenching infants from their mothers' arms, and prolonged custody battles when surrogates find they are unable to surrender their children, as agreed? Advocates of surrogacy say that to reject the practice wholesale, because of one unfortunate instance, is an example of a "hard case" making bad policy. Opponents reply that it is entirely reasonable to focus on the worst potential outcomes when deciding public policy. Everyone can agree on at least one thing: This particular case seems to have been mismanaged from start to finish, and could serve as a manual of how not to arrange a surrogate birth.

First, it is now clear that Mary Beth Whitehead was not a suitable candidate for surrogate motherhood. Her ambivalence about giving up the child was recognized early on, although this information was not passed on to the Sterns.[1] Second, she had contact with the baby after birth, which is usually avoided in "successful" cases. Typically, the adoptive mother is actively involved in the pregnancy, often serving as the pregnant woman's coach in labor. At birth, the baby is given to the adoptive, not the biological, mother. The joy of the adoptive parents in holding their child serves both to promote their bonding, and to lessen the pain of separation of the biological mother.

At Mrs. Whitehead's request, no one at the hospital was aware of the surrogacy arrangement. She and her husband appeared as the proud parents of "Sara Elizabeth Whitehead," the name on her birth certificate. Mrs. Whitehead held her baby, nursed her, and took her home from the hospital—just as she would have done in a normal pregnancy and birth. Not surprisingly, she thought of Sara as her child, and she fought with every weapon at her disposal, honorable and dishonorable, to prevent her being taken away. She can hardly be blamed for doing so.[2]

Why did Dr. Stern, who supposedly had a very good relation with Mrs. Whitehead before the birth, not act as her labor coach? One possibility is that Mrs. Whitehead, ambivalent about giving up her baby, did not want Dr. Stern involved. At her request, the Sterns' visits to the hospital to see the newborn baby were unobtrusive. It is also possible that Dr. Stern was ambivalent about having a child. The original idea of hiring a surrogate was not hers, but her husband's. It was Mr. Stern who felt a "compelling" need to have a child related to him by blood, having lost all his relatives to the Nazis.

Furthermore, Dr. Stern was not infertile, as was stated in the surrogacy agreement. Rather, in 1979 she was diagnosed by two eye specialists as suffering from optic neuritis, which meant that she "probably" had multiple sclerosis. (This was confirmed by all four experts who testified.) Normal conception was ruled out by the Sterns in late 1982, when a medical colleague told Dr. Stern that his wife, a victim of multiple sclerosis, had suffered a temporary paralysis during pregnancy. "We decided the risk wasn't worth it," Mr. Stern said.[3]

Mrs. Whitehead's lawyer, Harold J. Cassidy, dismissed the suggestion that Dr. Stern's "mildest case" of multiple sclerosis determined their decision to seek a surrogate. He noted that she was not even treated for multiple sclerosis until after the Baby M dispute had started. "It's almost as though it's an afterthought," he said.[4]

Judge Sorkow deemed the decision to avoid conception "medically reasonable and understandable." The Supreme Court did not go so far, noting that "her anxiety appears to have exceeded the actual risk, which current medical authorities assess as minimal."[5] Nonetheless the court acknowledged that her anxiety, including fears that pregnancy might precipitate blindness and paraplegia, was "quite real." Certainly, even a woman who wants a child very much, may reasonably wish to avoid becoming blind and paralyzed as a result of pregnancy. Yet is it believable that a woman who really wanted a child would decide against pregnancy solely on the basis of someone else's medical experience? Would she not consult at least one specialist on her own medical condition before deciding it wasn't worth the risk? The conclusion that she was at best ambivalent about bearing a child seems irresistible.

This possibility conjures up many people's worst fears about surrogacy: That prosperous women, who do not want to interrupt their careers, will use poor and educationally disadvantaged women to bear their children. I will return shortly to the question of whether this is exploitive. The issue here is psychological: What kind of mother is Dr. Stern likely to be? If she is unwilling to undergo pregnancy, with its discomforts, inconveniences, and risks, will she be willing to make the considerable sacrifices which good parenting requires? Mrs. Whitehead's ability to be a good mother was repeatedly questioned during the trial. She was portrayed as immature, untruthful, hysterical, overly identified with her children, and prone to smothering their independence. Even if all this is true—and I think that Mrs. Whitehead's inadequacies were exaggerated—Dr. Stern may not be such a prize either. The choice for Baby M may have been between a highly strung, emotional, over-involved mother, and a remote, detached, even cold one.

The assessment of Mrs. Whitehead's ability to be a good mother was biased by the middle-class prejudices of the judge and mental health officials who testified. Mrs. Whitehead left school at 15, and is not conversant with the latest theories on child rearing: She made the egregious error of giving Sara teddy bears to play with, instead of the more "age-appropriate," expert-approved pans and spoons. She proved to be a total failure at patty-cake. If this is evidence of parental inadequacy, we're all in danger of losing our children.

The Supreme Court felt that Mrs. Whitehead was "rather harshly judged" and acknowledged the possibility that the trial court was wrong in its initial award of custody. Nevertheless, it affirmed Judge Sorkow's decision to allow the Sterns to retain custody, as being in Melissa's best interests. George Annas disagrees with the "best interests" approach. He points out that Judge Sorkow awarded temporary custody of Baby M to the Sterns in May 1986 without giving the Whiteheads notice or an opportunity to obtain legal representation. That was a serious wrong and injustice to the Whiteheads. To allow the Sterns to keep the child compounds the original unfairness: ". . . justice requires that reasonable consideration be given to returning Baby M to the permanent custody of the Whiteheads."[6]

But a child is not a possession, to be returned to the rightful owner. It is not fairness to all parties that should determine a child's fate, but what is best for her. As Chief Justice Wilentz rightly stated, "The child's interests come first: We will not punish it for judicial errors, assuming any were made."[7]

Subsequent events have substantiated the claim that giving custody to the Sterns was in Melissa's best interests. After losing custody, Mrs. Whitehead, whose husband had undergone a vasectomy, became pregnant by another man. She divorced her husband and married Dean R. Gould last November. These developments indicate that the Whiteheads were not able to offer a stable home, although the argument can be made that their marriage might have survived, but for the strains introduced by the court battle, and the loss of Baby M. But even if Judge Sorkow had no reason to pre-

fer the Sterns to the Whiteheads back in May 1986, he was still right to give the Sterns custody in March 1987. To take her away then, at nearly eighteen months of age, from the only parents she had ever known, would have been disruptive, cruel, and unfair to her.

Annas' preference for a just solution is premised partly on his belief that there is no "best interest" solution to this "tragic custody case." I take it that he means that however custody is resolved, Baby M is the loser. Either way, she will be deprived of one parent. However, a best interests solution is not a perfect solution. It is simply the solution which is on balance best for the child, given the realities of the situation. Applying this standard, Judge Sorkow was right to give the Sterns custody, and the Supreme Court was right to uphold the decision.

The best interests argument is based on the assumption that Mr. Stern has at least a *prima facie* claim to Baby M. We certainly would not consider allowing a stranger who kidnapped a baby, and managed to elude the police for a year, to retain custody on the grounds that he was providing a good home to a child who had known no other parent. However, the Baby M case is not analogous. First, Mr. Stern is Baby M's biological father and, as such, has at least some claim to raise her, which no non-parental kidnapper has. Second, Mary Beth Whitehead *agreed* to give him their baby. Unlike the miller's daughter in *Rumpelstiltskin*, the fairy tale to which the Baby M case is sometimes compared, she was not forced into the agreement. Because both Mary Beth Whitehead and Mr. Stern have *prima facie* claims to Baby M, the decision as to who should raise her should be based on her present best interests. Therefore we must, regretfully, tolerate the injustice to Mrs. Whitehead, and try to avoid such problems in the future.

It is unfortunate that the Court did not decide the issue of visitation on the same basis as custody. By declaring Mrs. Whitehead Gould the legal mother, and maintaining that she is entitled to visitation, the Court has prolonged the fight over Baby M. It is hard to see how this can be in her best interests. This is no ordinary divorce case, where the child has a relation with both parents which it is desirable to maintain. As Mr. Stern said at the start of the court hearing to determine visitation, "Melissa has a right to grow and be happy and not be torn between two parents."[8]

The court's decision was well-meaning but internally inconsistent. Out of concern for the best interests of the child, it granted the Sterns custody. At the same time, by holding Mrs. Whitehead Gould to be the legal mother, with visitation rights, it precluded precisely what is most in Melissa's interest, a resolution of the situation. Further, the decision leaves open the distressing possibility that a Baby M situation could happen again. Legislative efforts should be directed toward ensuring that this worst-case scenario never occurs.

II. SHOULD SURROGACY BE PROHIBITED?

On June 27, 1988, Michigan became the first state to outlaw commercial contracts for women to bear children for others. Yet making a practice illegal does not necessarily make it go away: Witness black market adoption. The legitimate concerns which support a ban on surrogacy might be better served by careful regulation. However, some practices, such as slavery, are ethically unacceptable, regardless of how carefully regulated they are. Let us consider the arguments that surrogacy is intrinsically unacceptable.

A. PATERNALISTIC ARGUMENTS

These arguments against surrogacy take the form of protecting a potential surrogate from a choice she may later regret. As an argument for banning surrogacy, as opposed to providing safeguards to ensure that contracts are freely and knowledgeably undertaken, this is a form of paternalism.

At one time, the characterization of a prohibition as paternalistic was a sufficient reason to reject it. The pendulum has swung back, and many people are willing to accept at least some paternalistic restrictions on freedom. Gerald Dworkin points out that even Mill made one exception to his otherwise absolute rejection of paternalism: He thought that no one should be allowed to sell himself into slavery, because to do so would be to destroy his future autonomy.

This provides a narrow principle to justify some paternalistic interventions. To preserve freedom in the long run, we give up the freedom to make certain choices, those which have results which are "far-reaching, potentially dangerous and irreversible."[9] An example would be a ban on the sale of crack. Virtually everyone who uses crack becomes addicted and, once addicted, a slave to its use. We reasonably and willingly give up our freedom to buy the drug, to protect our ability to make free decisions in the future.

Can a Dworkinian argument be made to rule out surrogacy agreements? Admittedly, the decision to give up a child is permanent, and may have disastrous effects on the surrogate mother. However, many decisions may have long-term, disastrous effects (e.g., postponing childbirth for a career, having an abortion, giving a child up for adoption). Clearly we do not want the state to make decisions for us in all these matters. Dworkin's argument is rightly restricted to paternalistic interferences which protect the individual's autonomy or ability to make decisions in the future. Surrogacy does not involve giving up one's autonomy, which distinguishes it from both the crack and selling-oneself-into-slavery examples. Respect for individual freedom requires us to permit people to make choices which they may later regret.

B. MORAL OBJECTIONS

Four main moral objections to surrogacy were outlined in the Warnock Report.[10]

1. It is inconsistent with human dignity that a woman should use her uterus for financial profit.
2. To deliberately become pregnant with the intention of giving up the child distorts the relationship between mother and child.
3. Surrogacy is degrading because it amounts to child-selling.
4. Since there are some risks attached to pregnancy, no woman ought to be asked to undertake pregnancy for another in order to earn money.

We must all agree that a practice which exploits people or violates human dignity is immoral.

However, it is not clear that surrogacy is guilty on either count.

1. Exploitation.   The mere fact that pregnancy is risky does not make surrogate agreements exploitive, and therefore morally wrong. People often do risky things for money; why should the line be drawn at undergoing pregnancy? The usual response is to compare surrogacy and kidney-selling. The selling of organs is prohibited because of the potential for coercion and exploitation. But why should kidney-selling be viewed as intrinsically coercive? A possible explanation is that no one would do it, unless driven by poverty. The choice is both forced and dangerous, and hence coercive.

The situation is quite different in the case of the race car driver or stuntman. We do not think that they are *forced* to perform risky activities for money: They freely choose to do so. Unlike selling one's kidneys, these are activities which we can understand (intellectually, anyway) someone choosing to do. Movie stuntmen, for example, often enjoy their work, and derive satisfaction from doing it well. Of course they "do it for the money," in the sense that they would not do it without compensation; few people are willing to work "for free." The element of coercion is missing, however, because they enjoy the job, despite the risks, and could do something else if they chose.

The same is apparently true of most surrogates. "They choose the surrogate role primarily because the fee provides a better economic opportunity than alternative occupations, but also because they enjoy being pregnant and the respect and attention that it draws."[11] Some may derive a feeling of self-worth from an act they regard as highly altruistic: Providing a couple with a child they could not otherwise have. If these motives are present, it is far from clear that the surrogate is being exploited. Indeed, it seems objectionably paternalistic to insist that she is.

2. Human Dignity.   It may be argued that even if womb-leasing is not necessarily exploitive, it should still be rejected as inconsistent with human dignity. But why? As John Harris points out, hair, blood and other tissue is often donated or sold; what is so special about the uterus?[12]

Human dignity is more plausibly invoked in the strongest argument against surrogacy, namely, that it is the sale of a child. Children are not property, nor can they be bought or sold. It could be argued that surrogacy is wrong because it is analogous to slavery, and so is inconsistent with human dignity.

However, there are important differences between slavery and a surrogate agreement. The child born of a surrogate is not treated cruelly or deprived of freedom or resold; none of the things which make slavery so awful are part of surrogacy. Still, it may be thought that simply putting a market value on a child is wrong. Human life has intrinsic value; it is literally priceless. Arrangements which ignore this violate our deepest notions of the value of human life. It is profoundly disturbing to hear the boyfriend of a surrogate say, quite candidly in a television documentary on surrogacy, "We're in it for the money."

Judge Sorkow accepted the premise that producing a child for money denigrates human dignity, but he denied that this happens in a surrogate agreement. Mrs. Whitehead was not paid for the surrender of the child to the father: She was paid for her willingness to be impregnated and carry Mr. Stern's child to term. The child, once born, is his biological child. "He cannot purchase what is already his."

This is misleading, and not merely because Baby M is as much Mrs. Whitehead's child as Mr. Stern's. It is misleading because it glosses over the fact that the surrender of the child was part—indeed, the whole point—of the agreement. If the surrogate were paid merely for being willing to be impregnated and carrying the child to term, then she would fulfill the contract upon giving birth. She could take the money *and* the child. Mr. Stern did not agree to pay Mrs. Whitehead merely to *have* his child, but to provide him with a child. The New Jersey Supreme Court held that this violated New Jersey's laws prohibiting the payment or acceptance of money in connection with adoption.

One way to remove the taint of baby-selling would be to limit payment to medical expenses associated with the birth or incurred by the surrogate during pregnancy (as is allowed in many jurisdictions, including New Jersey, in ordinary adoptions). Surrogacy could be seen, not as baby-selling, but as a form of adoption. Nowhere did the Supreme Court find any legal prohibition against surrogacy when there is no payment, and when the surrogate has the right to change her mind and keep the child. However, this solution effectively prohibits surrogacy, since few women would become surrogates solely for self-fulfillment or reasons of altruism.

The question, then, is whether we can reconcile paying the surrogate, beyond her medical expenses, with the idea of surrogacy as prenatal adoption. We can do this by separating the terms of the agreement, which include surrendering the infant at birth to the biological father, from the justification for payment. The payment should be seen as compensation for the risks, sacrifice, and discomfort the surrogate undergoes during pregnancy. This means that if, through no fault on the part of the surrogate, the baby is stillborn, she should still be paid in full, since she has kept her part of the bargain. (By contrast, in the Stern-Whitehead agreement, Mrs. Whitehead was to receive only $1,000 for a stillbirth.) If, on the other hand, the surrogate changes her mind and decides to keep the child, she would break the agreement, and would not be entitled to any fee, or compensation for expenses incurred during pregnancy.

C. THE RIGHT OF PRIVACY

Most commentators who invoke the right of privacy do so in support of surrogacy. However, George Annas makes the novel argument that the right to rear a child you have borne is also a privacy right, which cannot be prospectively waived. He says:

[Judge Sorkow] grudgingly concedes that [Mrs. Whitehead] could not prospectively give up her right to have an abortion during pregnancy. . . . This would be an intolerable restriction on her liberty and under *Roe* v. *Wade*, the state has no constitutional authority to enforce a contract that prohibits her from terminating her pregnancy.

But why isn't the same logic applicable to the right to rear a child you have given birth to? Her constitutional rights to rear the child she has given birth to are even stronger since they involve even more intimately, and

over a lifetime, her privacy rights to reproduce and rear a child in a family setting.[13]

Absent a compelling state interest (such as protecting a child from unfit parents), it certainly would be an intolerable invasion of privacy for the state to take children from their parents. But Baby M has two parents, both of whom now want her. It is not clear why only people who can give birth (i.e., women) should enjoy the right to rear their children.

Moreover, we do allow women to give their children up for adoption after birth. The state enforces those agreements, even if the natural mother, after the prescribed waiting period, changes her mind. Why should the right to rear a child be unwaivable before, but not after, birth? Why should the state have the constitutional authority to uphold postnatal, but not prenatal, adoption agreements? It is not clear why birth should affect the waivability of this right, or have the constitutional significance which Annas attributes to it.

Nevertheless, there are sound moral and policy, if not constitutional, reasons to provide a postnatal waiting period in surrogate agreements. As the Baby M case makes painfully clear, the surrogate may underestimate the bond created by gestation, and the emotional trauma caused by relinquishing the baby. Compassion requires that we acknowledge these feelings, and not deprive a woman of the baby she has carried because, before conception, she underestimated the strength of her feelings for it. Providing a waiting period, as in ordinary postnatal adoptions, will help protect women from making irrevocable mistakes, without banning the practice.

Some may object that this gives too little protection to the prospective adoptive parents. They cannot be sure that the baby is theirs until the waiting period is over. While this is hard on them, a similar burden is placed on other adoptive parents. If the absence of a guarantee serves to discourage people from entering surrogacy agreements, that is not necessarily a bad thing, given all the risks inherent in such contracts. In addition, this requirement would make stricter screening and counselling of surrogates essential, a desirable side effect.

D. HARM TO OTHERS

Paternalistic and moral objections to surrogacy do not seem to justify an outright ban. What about the effect on the offspring of such contracts? We do not yet have solid data on the effects of being a "surrogate child." Any claim that surrogacy creates psychological problems in the children is purely speculative. But what if we did discover that such children have deep feelings of worthlessness from learning that their natural mothers deliberately created them with the intention of giving them away? Might we ban surrogacy as posing an unacceptable risk of psychological harm to the resulting children?

Feelings of worthlessness are harmful. They can prevent people from living happy, fulfilling lives. However, a surrogate child, even one whose life is miserable because of these feelings, cannot claim to have been harmed by the surrogate agreement. Without the agreement, the child would never have existed. Unless she is willing to say that her life is not worth living because of these feelings, that she would be better off never having been born, she cannot claim to have been harmed by being born of a surrogate mother.

Children can be *wronged* by being brought into existence, even if they are not, strictly speaking, *harmed*. They are wronged if they are deprived of the minimally decent existence to which all citizens are entitled. We owe it to our children to see that they are not born with such serious impairments that their most basic interests will be doomed in advance. If being born to a surrogate is a handicap of this magnitude, comparable to being born blind or deaf or severely mentally retarded, then surrogacy can be seen as wronging the offspring. This would be a strong reason against permitting such contracts. However, it does not seem likely. Probably the problems arising from surrogacy will be like those faced by adopted children and children whose parents divorce. Such problems are not trivial, but neither are they so serious that the child's very existence can be seen as wrongful.

If surrogate children are neither harmed nor wronged by surrogacy, it may seem that the argument for banning surrogacy on grounds of its harmfulness to the offspring evaporates. After all,

if the children themselves have no cause for complaint, how can anyone else claim to reject it on their behalf? Yet it seems extremely counterintuitive to suggest that the risk of emotional damage to the children born of such arrangements is not even relevant to our deliberations. It seems quite reasonable and proper—even morally obligatory—for policymakers to think about the possible detrimental effects of new reproductive technologies, and to reject those likely to create physically or emotionally damaged people. The explanation for this must involve the idea that it is wrong to bring people into the world in a harmful condition, even if they are not, strictly speaking, harmed by having been brought into existence. Should evidence emerge that surrogacy produces children with serious psychological problems, that would be a strong reason for banning the practice.

There is some evidence on the effect of surrogacy on the other children of the surrogate mother. One woman reported that her daughter, now 17, who was 11 at the time of the surrogate birth, ". . . is still having problems with what I did, and as a result she is still angry with me." She explains, "Nobody told me that a child could bond with a baby while you're still pregnant. I didn't realize then that all the times she listened to his heartbeat and felt his legs kick that she was becoming attached to him."14

A less sentimental explanation is possible. It seems likely that her daughter, seeing one child given away, was fearful that the same might be done to her. We can expect anxiety and resentment on the part of children whose mothers give away a brother or sister. The psychological harm to these children is clearly relevant to a determination of whether surrogacy is contrary to public policy. At the same time, it should be remembered that many things, including divorce, remarriage, and even moving to a new neighborhood, create anxiety and resentment in children. We should not use the effect on children as an excuse for banning a practice we find bizarre or offensive.

CONCLUSION

There are many reasons to be extremely cautious of surrogacy. I cannot imagine becoming a surrogate, nor would I advise anyone else to enter into a contract so fraught with peril. But the fact that a practice is risky, foolish, or even morally distasteful is not sufficient reason to outlaw it. It would be better for the state to regulate the practice, and minimize the potential for harm, without infringing on the liberty of citizens.

NOTES

1. Had the Sterns been informed of the psychologist's concerns as to Mrs. Whitehead's suitability to be a surrogate, they might have ended the arrangement, costing the Infertility Center its fee. As Chief Justice Wilentz said, "It is apparent that the profit motive got the better of the Infertility Center." In the matter of Baby M, Supreme Court of New Jersey, A-39, at 45.

2. "[W]e think it is expecting something well beyond normal human capabilities to suggest that this mother should have parted with her newly born infant without a struggle. . . . We . . . cannot conceive of any other case where a perfectly fit mother was expected to surrender her newly born infant, perhaps forever, and was then told she was a bad mother because she did not." *Id.* at 79.

3. Father Recalls Surrogate Was "Perfect," *New York Times*, January 6, 1987, p. B2.

4. *Id.*

5. In the matter of Baby M, *supra* note 1 at 8.

6. G. J. Annas, "Baby M: Babies (and Justice) for Sale," *Hastings Center Report* 17 (3): 15, 1987.

7. In the matter of Baby M, *supra* note 1, at 75.

8. "Anger and Anguish at Baby M Visitation Hearing," *New York Times*, March 29, 1988, p. 17.

9. G. Dworkin, "Paternalism," in ed. R. A. Wasserstrom, *Morality and the Law* (Belmont, CA: Wadsworth, 1971) reprinted in J. Feinberg, and H. Gross, eds., *Philosophy of Law*, 3rd ed. (Belmont, CA: Wadsworth, 1986) p. 265.

10. M. Warnock, chair, *Report of the Committee of Inquiry into Human Fertilization and Embryology* (London, Her Majesty's Stationery Office, 1984).

11. J. A. Robertson, "Surrogate Mothers: Not So Novel after All," *Hastings Center Report* 13 (5): 29, 1983. Citing P. Parker, "Surrogate Mother's Motivations: Initial Findings," *American Journal of Psychiatry* (140): 1, 1983.

12. J. Harris, *The Value of Life* (London: Routledge & Kegan Paul, 1985) p. 144.

13. Annas, *supra* note 6.

14. "Baby M Case Stirs Feelings of Surrogate Mothers," *New York Times*, March 2, 1987, p. B1.

REVIEW AND DISCUSSION QUESTIONS

1. Describe the factual and legal situation surrounding the Baby M case.

2. How might it be argued that laws banning surrogacy are paternalistic? Are they? Explain.

3. What is exploitation, and how might it be argued that surrogacy is an instance of it?

4. In what sense(s) might surrogacy involve the right to privacy?

5. Does surrogacy harm anybody? Explain.

6. What sorts of regulations does Steinbock suggest are appropriate? Do you agree with her that surrogacy should only be regulated, not banned? Explain.

7. How would you have decided the Baby M case? Explain your position, including your response to the main argument for reaching the conclusion opposite to yours.

Selling Babies

Richard A. Posner

Judge Richard A. Posner criticizes current adoption practices that outlaw baby selling. A freer market (though one that is still regulated in important respects) would have many advantages, he claims, including lower prices and higher quality. Nor, he concludes, should we be persuaded by "symbolic" claims that baby selling might lead to abuses or slavery. Indeed, we already have in place something of a market in babies, although it is highly regulated and often hidden from view. Richard A. Posner is a judge of the U.S. Court of Appeals for the Seventh Circuit and a senior lecturer at the University of Chicago Law School.

I. CHARACTERISTICS OF AND DESIRABLE CONSTRAINTS ON THE BABY MARKET

A. The Question of Price

For heuristic purposes (only!) it is useful to analogize the sale of babies to the sale of an ordinary good, such as an automobile or a television set. We observe, for example, that although the supply of automobiles and of television sets is rationed by price, not all the automobiles and television sets are owned by wealthy people. On the contrary, the free market in these goods has lowered prices, through competition and innovation, to the point where the goods are available to a lot more people than in highly controlled economies such as that of the Soviet Union. There is even less reason for thinking that if babies could be sold to adoptive parents the wealthy would come to monopolize babies. Wealthy people (other than those few who owe their wealth to savings or inheritance rather than to a high income) have high costs of time. It therefore costs them more to raise a child— child rearing still being a time-intensive activity— than it costs the nonwealthy. As a result, wealthy couples tend to have few rather than many children. This pattern would not change if babies could be bought. Moreover, since most people have a strong preference for natural, as distinct from adopted, children, wealthy couples able to have natural children are unlikely (to say the least) to substitute adopted ones.

It is also unlikely that allowing people to bid for babies with dollars would drive up the price of babies, thereby allocating the supply to wealthy demanders. Today we observe a high black-market price conjoined with an artificially low price for babies obtained from adoption agencies and through lawful independent adoptions. The "blended" or average price is hard to calculate; but probably it is very high. The low price in the lawful market is deceptive. It ignores the considerable queuing costs— most people would pay a considerable premium to get their adopted baby now, not five or ten years from now. And for people unable to maneuver successfully in the complex market created by the laws against baby selling, the price is infinite. Quality-adjusted prices in free markets normally are lower than black market prices, and there is no reason to doubt that this would be true in a free market for adoptions. Thus, ... the words "black market" ought to be italicized. It is not the free market, but unwarranted restrictions on the operation of that market, that has raised the black market price of babies beyond the reach of ordinary people.

From Richard A. Posner, "The Regulation of the Market in Adoption," *Boston University Law Review*, January 1987. Reprinted by permission. © Richard A. Posner.

Thus far I have implicitly been speaking only of the market for healthy white infants. There is no shortage of nonwhite and of handicapped infants, and of any children who are no longer infants, available for adoption. Such children are substitutes for healthy white infants, and the higher price of the latter, the greater will be the demand for the former. The network of regulations that has driven up the full price (including such nonmonetary components of price as delay) of adopting a healthy, white infant may have increased the willingness of childless couples to consider adopting a child of a type not in short supply, though how much (if at all) no one knows. The present system is, in any event, a grossly inefficient, as well as covert, method of encouraging the adoption of the hard-to-place child. If society wants to subsidize these unfortunate children, the burden of the subsidies should be borne, if not by the natural parents of these children, then by the taxpaying population at large—rather than by just the nation's childless white couples, who under the present unsystematic system bear the lion's share of the burden by being denied the benefits of an efficient method of allocating healthy white infants for adoption in the hope that this will induce them to adopt nonwhite, handicapped, or older children.

B. The Question of Quality

As soon as one mentions quality, people's hackles rise and they remind you that one is talking about a traffic in human beings, not in inanimate objects. The observation is pertinent, and at least five limitations might have to be placed on the operation of the market in babies for adoption. The first, already mentioned and already in place, is that the buyers can have no right to abuse the thing bought, as they would if the thing were a piece of steel or electronics. This really should go without saying. The laws against child abuse have never distinguished among different methods of acquiring custody of the child. Natural parents are not permitted to abuse a child because they are natural rather than adoptive parents; and people who acquire their children illegally through the black market are no more exempt from the child-abuse laws than people with illegal income are exempt from paying income tax on it. If I were arrested for

torturing my cat and charged with violation of the laws forbidding cruelty to animals, it would be no defense that I had bought the cat for forty dollars.

If the laws against child abuse were perfectly efficacious, nothing more would have to be said on the subject. But they are not. The abuse occurs in secret, and the victim may be too young and too dependent to bring it to the attention of the authorities—or indeed to know what is going on. In addition, many child abusers may be so mentally or psychologically abnormal that they cannot be deterred even by very harsh penalties. In such a setting, preventive as well as punitive measures may be justified. Today, all adoptive parents are, in theory anyway, screened for fitness. Adoption agencies are charged with this responsibility, and if we moved toward a freer market in babies the agencies could be given the additional function of investigating and certifying prospective purchasers, who would pay the price of the service.

But let us not make too much of screening. The idea that a significant number of people are lurking about who if given the chance would buy babies for criminal purposes is a bogeyman. Most child abuse occurs as a result either of stresses arising from the experience of parenthood or from the sexual maturing of the child; it is not planned in advance when a baby is conceived or when steps are initiated to adopt a baby. As I will note in a moment, a market in babies for adoption should only be allowed to operate with regard to infants; a couple should not be allowed to sell its thirteen-year-old daughter for immoral (or any other) purposes.

Moreover, since we do not screen natural parents, and any proposal to do so would be met with justifiable protests against governmental intrusion into private matters, the case for screening adoptive parents can hardly be considered self-evident. Maybe, since people like their own children more than strangers' children, the child molester is less likely to molest his own children than other people's children. But people who adopt children do so not out of a mild affection toward children in general, which might easily be overborne by a tendency to abuse children, but in the hope of creating the same close bonds of affection with the adopted child as natural parents have with their children. Allowing price to play a bigger role in adoptions is not likely to change this. But whether screening adoptive parents is a good or a bad idea is not the issue in this article. Whatever screening is deemed necessary for persons who adopt through an agency or by independent adoption would also be necessary for persons who adopted children in a free(r) market. Freeing the adoption market from price regulation would leave the case for or against screening largely, perhaps entirely, unaffected.

The third limitation on a baby market concerns remedies for breach of contract. In an ordinary market a buyer can both reject defective goods and, if the seller refuses to deliver and damages would be an inadequate remedy for the refusal, get specific performance of the contract. Natural parents are not permitted to reject their baby, either when it is born or afterward, because it turns out to be handicapped or otherwise not in conformity with their expectations; no more should adoptive parents who buy their babies. Nor should the adoptive parents be able to force the natural mother to surrender the baby to them if she changes her mind, unless some competent authority determines that the baby would be better off adopted. For the welfare of the baby must be considered along with that of the contracting parties. Refusing to grant specific performance in circumstances in which it appears that forcing the sale to go through would harm the baby is consistent with the basic equity principle that the third-party effects of equitable remedies must be considered in deciding whether to grant such a remedy or confine the plaintiff to damage remedies. The child is an interested third party whose welfare would be disserved by a mechanical application of the remedies available to buyers in the market for inanimate goods.

For the same reason (the child's welfare) neither natural nor adopting parents should be allowed to sell their children after infancy, that is, after the child has established a bond with its parents. Nor should the natural mother be allowed to take back the baby after adoption, any more than a seller of a conventional good or service can (except in extraordinary circumstances) rescind the sale after delivery and payment in accordance with his contract with the buyer, unless, once again, a competent authority decides that the

baby's welfare would be increased. I shall not try to resolve the question whether, in any of these remedial settings, the welfare of the child should be paramount or should be balanced with that of the adult parties.

The last limitation on the baby market that I shall discuss relates to eugenic breeding. Although prospects still seem remote, one can imagine an entrepreneur in the baby market trying to breed a race of *Übermenschen* who would command premium prices. The external effects of such an endeavor could be very harmful, and would provide an appropriate basis for governmental regulation.

I am not so sanguine about the operation of a baby market, even with the limitations I have discussed, that I am prepared to advocate the complete and immediate repeal of the laws forbidding the sale of babies for adoption. That such a market might give somewhat greater scope for child abusers and might encourage weird and potentially quite harmful experiments in eugenic breeding should be enough to give anyone pause. But to concentrate entirely on the downside would be a mistake. One million abortions a year is a serious social problem regardless of where one stands on the underlying ethical issues; so is a flourishing black market in babies combined with a severe shortage in the lawful market. The severity of the shortage is, admittedly, a matter of fair debate. In our 1978 article Dr. Landes and I estimated that about 130,000 married couples who at present are childless might adopt a child under free-market conditions. More recent research suggests this estimate is reasonable. A study conducted by the National Center for Health Statistics found that 46% of the estimated 274,000 currently married women who are between 30 and 44 years of age and sterile have adopted a child. If all those who have not adopted would like to, and would be willing to pay a free-market price, then the 148,000 married couples in the relevant population who have not yet adopted a child are unsatisfied demanders. But some unknown fraction of this number either do not want to have children at all or do not want to have adopted children. Dr. Landes and I noted that 96% of couples marrying in 1975 in which the wife was between 18 and 24 years old expected to have a child. Since most people who marry young do not know whether they have a fertility problem, it seems a fair guess that almost all of the 274,000 married couples who are sterile planned when they got married to have children, and hence that most of the 148,000 who have not yet adopted a child would like, or at some time in the past would have liked, to adopt a child. Of course, wanting something and being willing to pay for it are two different things, and it might seem that many childless couples would be unwilling or unable to pay for a baby if they had to pay free market prices. But this seems unlikely. The purchase price on the free market would probably be lower than under the present system (for reasons discussed earlier), and in any event only a small fraction of the total cost (even discounted to present value) of raising a child. Bear in mind, too, that adoptive parents save the medical and opportunity costs of pregnancy. Marrying couples who expected to have a child, notwithstanding the cost, are unlikely to be deterred by the small, probably zero or even negative, incremental cost of adopting a child in a free market.

True, some couples decide after marriage that they don't want to have a child. This is particularly likely if the couple anticipates a high probability of divorce. About half of American marriages end in divorce, and some of these divorces are anticipated before children enter the picture. Another consideration is that some couples do not consider an adopted child a good substitute for the natural child they cannot have, and they may therefore decide to remain childless even if the price of an adopted child is low and the quality high.* Although these factors suggest a downward adjust-

*The potential importance of this point is brought out by a 1977 study that found that, of then-married women who had no children and wanted to have one or more, only 62% said they would adopt a child. See Bonham, "Who Adopts: The Relationship of Adoption and Social-Demographic Characteristics of Women," *Journal of Marriage and Family* 39, 295, 300 tab. 3 (1977). If 46% of sterile couples have adopted a child, and 62% would like to, it might seem that the fraction of unsatisfied demanders (to be multiplied by 274,000 to yield an estimate of their number) would be 16% rather than 54%. But apart from other factors mentioned in the text, a statement of nonintention to adopt a child may simply reflect awareness of the obstacles to adoption under the present system. As we shall see, the nonintending 38% (100% − 62%) is almost twice the percentage of couples who become sterile after having one child and then adopt—suggesting a very large unsatisfied demand among this group.

ment in my estimates, there are three offsetting factors to consider. First, some unknown fraction of adoptions is of babies bought in the black market, and the part of the demand for a good that is satisfied in a black market reflects the shortage in the lawful market. Second, the 148,000 figure excludes married couples who become sterile after having one or more children and who would like to adopt. In fact, 20% of married couples who become sterile after having one child go on to adopt a child, and 42% of married couples with one child say that they would adopt a second child if they became sterile. Finally, and bearing particularly on the experiment that Dr. Landes and I proposed, ten times as many premarital pregnancies end in "pregnancy loss" (miscarriage, stillbirth, and no doubt the biggest category, abortion) as in putting the baby up for adoption.

One reason people fear the operation of a free market in babies for adoption is that they extrapolate from experience with the illegal market. Critics who suggest that baby selling offers the promise of huge profits to middlemen—the dreaded "baby brokers"—fail to distinguish between an illegal market, in which sellers demand a heavy premium (an apparent, though not real, profit) in order to defray the expected costs of punishment, and a legal market, in which the premium is eliminated. Seemingly exorbitant profits, low quality, poor information, involvement of criminal elements—these widely asserted characteristics of the black market in babies are no more indicative of the behavior of a lawful market than the tactics of the bootleggers and rum-runners during Prohibition were indicative of the behavior of the liquor industry after Prohibition was repealed. . . .

II. THE OBJECTION FROM SYMBOLISM AND THE ISSUE OF SEMANTICS

Even if partial deregulation of the baby market might make practical utilitarian sense along the lines just suggested, some will resist on symbolic grounds. If we acknowledge that babies can be sold, the argument goes, we open the door to all sorts of monstrous institutions—including slavery. We regularly resist this type of argument in analogous contexts, and I have difficulty understanding why it stubbornly persists in this one. Some people argue that military conscription is wrong because it legitimates government coercion of the civilian labor force, or because it is a form of slavery; others that the sale of blood should be forbidden because it treats human life as a commodity; others that medicine should be socialized so that the wealthy can't use their wealth to increase their chances of a long and healthy life, relative to the poor; others that parents should not be allowed to spank their children because that is treating the children like slaves; others that capital punishment should be outlawed because it implicates the state in murder. The common thread in these arguments is the reprobating of social practices not because of any demonstrable or even probable bad effects, but because the practices have a symbolic affinity with practices that do have horrible effects. Allowing parents to sell their children into slavery would be a monstrous idea. Allowing the prospective mother of an illegitimate child to receive money in exchange for giving up the child for adoption, when described in shorthand as "baby selling," seems to many people uncomfortably close to the type of real baby selling that is found in slave societies—that was found in the slave societies of the South before the Civil War. No doubt it requires more thought than most people are willing to give to the problem to hold these quite different concepts separate in their minds. But if they are not held separate we may find ourselves condemned to perpetuate the painful spectacle of mass abortion and illegitimacy in a society in which, to a significant extent, children are not available for adoption by persons unwilling to violate the law.

One should always be suspicious of arguments against the market when they are made by people who have no desire to participate in it themselves, people who want to restrict the availability of goods to other people. Most people who invoke vague symbols in opposition to "baby selling" have no interest in or expectation of either adopting a child or conceiving one out of wedlock. They have little empathy with the needs of people who find themselves involuntarily childless or involuntarily pregnant.

The opponents of "baby selling" are unwilling to acknowledge that what we have today, even apart from the black market, is closer to a free market in babies than a free market in babies would be to slavery or torture (always bearing in mind that a free market in an economic sense is one in which due consideration is given the welfare of affected third parties, here the babies themselves). As I said at the outset, adoption agencies do lawfully "sell" babies, and many charge thousands of dollars. Moreover, in independent adoptions, the mother herself may "sell" her baby, for it is not considered unlawful to use a part of the fee paid by the adoptive parents to defray the medical and other maintenance costs of the mother during pregnancy. It seems that to obtain lawfully a healthy, white infant (rarely available through adoption agencies), a couple must be prepared to lay out at least $5,000. Black-market prices of $25,000, even $50,000, have been rumored, but the equilibrium baby price in a free market (by which I do not mean an entirely unregulated market, for I suggested that the market should be regulated in various ways) might not exceed $5,000. As a matter of fact, though baby selling is everywhere unlawful, almost half the states have no specific restrictions on fees payable for adoption, and in many other states the restrictions are porous. No doubt many lawful and semi-lawful "baby sales" are taking place today at approximately free-market prices.

Two other important examples of legal baby selling should be mentioned. One is the "family compact" doctrine, which allows a woman to enter into an enforceable contract to give up her baby for adoption by a close relative. The other is surrogate motherhood, by which (at least in some states) a married couple in which the wife is infertile can make an enforceable contract with another woman whereby the latter agrees to be artificially inseminated with the husband's sperm and to carry the baby to term and give it up to the couple. In the first case the close family relative "buys" the baby, in the second the father (and his wife) "buys out" the natural mother's "share" in their joint product.

So we have legal baby selling today; the question of public policy is not whether baby selling should be forbidden or allowed but how extensively it should be regulated. I simply think it should be regulated less stringently than is done today.

REVIEW AND DISCUSSION QUESTIONS

1. Why would a market in babies improve the (current) price structure, according to Posner?
2. What impact does Posner think a freer market would have on "quality"? Explain why.
3. Explain the limitations Posner would place on the baby market.
4. Describe the "objection from symbolism," along with Posner's response to it.
5. What is your overall assessment of Posner's proposal? What are its major strengths? Major weaknesses?

Licensing Parents

Hugh LaFollette

To undertake the raising of a child is an act with vast consequences, for good or ill. Indeed, they are potentially far greater than those that result from driving a car, for example. Yet society requires a license to make certain that people are at least minimally capable of driving safely before they are allowed on the street, let alone practice medicine and law or give psychological counseling. Why, then, shouldn't parenting be an activity that also requires some sort of assurances of minimal competence? Hugh LaFollette argues that it should, and that neither the theoretical nor the practical objections that might be brought against licensing parents are sufficiently strong to justify allowing people to have children when they are incapable of raising them competently. Hugh LaFollette teaches philosophy at East Tennessee State University.

In this essay I shall argue that the state should require all parents to be licensed. My main goal is to demonstrate that the licensing of parents is theoretically desirable, though I shall also argue that a workable and just licensing program actually could be established.

My strategy is simple. After developing the basic rationale for the licensing of parents, I shall consider several objections to the proposal and argue that these objections fail to undermine it. I shall then isolate some striking similarities between this licensing program and our present policies on the adoption of children. If we retain these adoption policies—as we surely should—then, I argue, a general licensing program should also be established. Finally, I shall briefly suggest that the reason many people object to licensing is that they think parents, particularly biological parents, own or have natural sovereignty over their children.

REGULATING POTENTIALLY HARMFUL ACTIVITIES

Our society normally regulates a certain range of activities; it is illegal to perform these activities unless one has received prior permission to do so. We require automobile operators to have licenses. We forbid people from practicing medicine, law, pharmacy, or psychiatry unless they have satisfied certain licensing requirements.

Society's decision to regulate just these activities is not ad hoc. The decision to restrict admission to certain vocations and to forbid some people from driving is based on an eminently plausible, though not often explicitly formulated, rationale. We require drivers to be licensed because driving an auto is an activity which is potentially harmful to others, safe performance of the activity requires a certain competence, and we have a moderately reliable procedure for determining that competence. The potential harm is obvious: incompetent drivers can and do maim and kill people. The best way we have of limiting this harm without sacrificing the benefits of automobile travel is to require that all drivers demonstrate at least minimal competence. We likewise license doctors, lawyers, and psychologists because they perform activities which can harm others. Obviously they must be proficient if they are to perform these activities properly, and we have moderately reliable procedures for determining proficiency. Imagine a world in which everyone could legally drive a car, in which everyone could legally perform surgery, prescribe medications, dispense drugs, or offer legal advice. Such a world would hardly be desirable.

Consequently, any activity that is potentially harmful to others and requires certain demonstrated competence for its safe performance, is subject to regulation—that is, it is theoretically desirable that we regulate it. If we also have a reliable procedure for determining whether someone has the requisite competence, then the action is not only subject to regulation but ought, all things considered, to be regulated.

It is particularly significant that we license these hazardous activities, even though denying a license to someone can severely inconvenience and even harm that person. Furthermore, available competency tests are not 100 percent accurate. Denying someone a driver's license in our society, for example, would inconvenience that person acutely. In effect that person would be prohibited from working, shopping, or visiting in places reachable only by car. Similarly, people denied vocational licenses are inconvenienced, even devastated. We have all heard of individuals who had the "life-long dream" of becoming physicians or lawyers, yet were denied that dream. However, the realization that some people are disappointed or inconvenienced does not diminish our conviction that we must regulate occupations or activities that are potentially dangerous to others. Innocent people must be protected even if it means that others cannot pursue activities they deem highly desirable.

Furthermore, we maintain licensing procedures even though our competency tests are sometimes inaccurate. Some people competent to perform the licensed activity (for example, driving a car) will be unable to demonstrate competence (they freeze up on the driver's test). Others may be incompetent, yet pass the test (they are lucky or certain aspects of competence—for example, the sense of responsibility—are not tested). We recognize clearly—or should recognize clearly—that no test will pick out all and only competent drivers, physicians, lawyers, and so on. Mistakes are inevitable. This does not mean we should forget that innocent people may be harmed by faulty regulatory procedures. In fact, if the procedures are sufficiently faulty, we should cease regulating that activity entirely until more reliable tests are available. I only want to emphasize here that tests need not be perfect. Where moderately reliable tests are available, licensing procedures should be used to protect innocent people from incompetents.

These general criteria for regulatory licensing can certainly be applied to parents. First, parenting is an activity potentially very harmful to children. The potential for harm is apparent: each year more than half a million children are physically abused or neglected by their parents.[1] Many millions more are psychologically abused or neglected—not given love, respect, or a sense of self-worth. The results of this maltreatment are obvious. Abused children bear the physical and psychological scars of maltreatment throughout their lives. Far too often they turn to crime.[2] They are far more likely than others to abuse their own children.[3] Even if these maltreated children never harm anyone, they will probably never be well-adjusted, happy adults. Therefore, parenting clearly satisfies the first criterion of activities subject to regulation.

The second criterion is also incontestably satisfied. A parent must be competent if he is to avoid harming his children; even greater competence is required if he is to do the "job" well. But not everyone has this minimal competence. Many people lack the knowledge needed to rear children adequately. Many others lack the requisite energy, temperament, or stability. Therefore, child-rearing manifestly satisfies both criteria of activities subject ot regulation. In fact, I dare say that parenting is a paradigm of such activities since the potential for harm is so great (both in the extent of harm any one person can suffer and in the number of people potentially harmed) and the need for competence is so evident. Consequently, there is good reason to believe that all parents should be licensed. The only ways to avoid this conclusion are to deny the need for licensing any potentially harmful activity; to deny that I have identified the standard criteria of activities which should be regulated; to deny that parenting satisfies the standard criteria; to show that even though parenting satisfies the standard criteria there are special reasons why licensing parents is not theoretically desirable; or to show that there is no reliable and just procedure for implementing this program.

While developing my argument for licensing I have already identified the standard criteria for activities that should be regulated, and I have shown that they can properly be applied to parenting. One could deny the legitimacy of regulation by licensing, but in doing so one would condemn not only the regulation of parenting, but also the regulation of drivers, physicians, druggists, and doctors. Furthermore, regulation of hazardous activities appears to be a fundamental task of any stable society.

Thus only two objections remain. In the next section I shall see if there are any special reasons why licensing parents is not theoretically desirable. Then, in the following section, I shall examine several practical objections designed to demonstrate that even if licensing were theoretically desirable, it could not be justly implemented.

THEORETICAL OBJECTIONS TO LICENSING

Licensing is unacceptable, someone might say, since people have a right to have children, just as they have rights to free speech and free religious expression. They do not need a license to speak freely or to worship as they wish. Why? Because they have a right to engage in these activities. Similarly, since people have a right to have children, any attempt to license parents would be unjust.

This is an important objection since many people find it plausible, if not self-evident. However, it is not as convincing as it appears. The specific rights appealed to in this analogy are not without limitations. Both slander and human sacrifice are prohibited by law; both could result from the unrestricted exercise of freedom of speech and freedom of religion. Thus, even if people have these rights, they may sometimes be limited in order to protect innocent people. Consequently, even if people had a right to have children, that right might also be limited in order to protect innocent people, in this case children. Secondly, the phrase "right to have children" is ambiguous; hence, it is important to isolate its most plausible meaning in this context. Two possible interpretations are not credible and can be dismissed summarily. It is implausible to claim either that infertile people have rights to be *given* children or that people have rights to intentionally create children biologically without incurring any subsequent responsibility to them.

A third interpretation, however, is more plausible, particularly when coupled with observations about the degree of intrusion into one's life that the licensing scheme represents. On this interpretation people have a right to rear children if they make good-faith efforts to rear procreated children the best way they see fit. One might defend this claim on the ground that licensing would require too much intrusion into the lives of sincere applicants.

Undoubtedly one should be wary of unnecessary governmental intervention into individuals' lives. In this case, though, the intrusion would not often be substantial, and when it is, it would be warranted. Those granted licenses would face merely minor intervention; only those denied licenses would encounter marked intrusion. This encroachment, however, is a necessary side-effect of licensing parents—just as it is for automobile and vocational licensing. In addition, as I shall argue in more detail later, the degree of intrusion arising from a general licensing program would be no more than, and probably less than, the present (and presumably justifiable) encroachment into the lives of people who apply to adopt children. Furthermore, since some people hold unacceptable views about what is best for children (they think children should be abused regularly), people do not automatically have rights to rear children just because they will rear them in a way they deem appropriate.

Consequently, we come to a somewhat weaker interpretation of this right claim: a person has a right to rear children if he meets certain minimal standards of child rearing. Parents must not abuse or neglect their children and must also provide for the basic needs of the children. This claim of right is certainly more credible than the previously canvassed alternatives, though some people might still reject this claim in situations where exercise of the right would lead to negative consequences, for example, to overpopulation. More to the point, though, this conditional right is compatible with licensing. On this interpretation one has a right to have children only if one is not going to abuse or neglect them. Of course the very purpose of licensing is just to determine whether people *are* going to abuse or neglect their children. If the determination is made that someone will maltreat children, then that person is subject to the limitations of the right to have children and can legitimately be denied a parenting license.

In fact, this conditional way of formulating the right to have children provides a model for formulating all alleged rights to engage in hazardous activities. Consider, for example, the right to drive a car. People do not have an unconditional right to drive, although they do have a right to drive if they are competent. Similarly, people do not have an unconditional right to practice medicine; they have a right only if they are demonstrably competent. Hence, denying a driver's or physician's license to someone who has not demonstrated the requisite competence does not deny that person's

rights. Likewise, on this model, denying a parenting license to someone who is not competent does not violate that person's rights.

Of course someone might object that the right is conditional on actually being a person who will abuse or neglect children, whereas my proposal only picks out those we can reasonably predict will abuse children. Hence, this conditional right would be incompatible with licensing.

There are two ways to interpret this objection and it is important to distinguish these divergent formulations. First, the objection could be a way of questioning our ability to predict reasonably and accurately whether people would maltreat their own children. This is an important practical objection, but I will defer discussion of it until the next section. Second, this objection could be a way of expressing doubt about the moral propriety of the prior restraint licensing requires. A parental licensing program would deny licenses to applicants judged to be incompetent even though they had never maltreated any children. This practice would be in tension with our normal skepticism about the propriety of prior restraint.

Despite this healthy skepticism, we do sometimes use prior restraint. In extreme circumstances we may hospitalize or imprison people judged insane, even though they are not legally guilty of any crime, simply because we predict they are likely to harm others. More typically, though prior restraint is used only if the restriction is not terribly onerous and the restricted activity is one which could lead easily to serious harm. Most types of licensing (for example, those for doctors, drivers, and druggists) fall into this latter category. They require prior restraint to prevent serious harm, and generally the restraint is minor—though it is important to remember that some individuals will find it oppressive. The same is true of parental licensing. The purpose of licensing is to prevent serious harm to children. Moreover, the prior restraint required by licensing would not be terribly onerous for many people. Certainly the restraint would be far less extensive than the presumably justifiable prior restraint of, say, insane criminals. Criminals preventively detained and mentally ill people forcibly hospitalized are denied most basic liberties, while those denied parental licenses would be denied only that one specific opportunity. They could still vote, work for political candidates, speak on controversial topics, and so on. Doubtless some individuals would find the restraint onerous. But when compared to other types of restraint currently practiced, and when judged in light of the severity of harm maltreated children suffer, the restraint appears *relatively* minor.

Furthermore, we could make certain, as we do with most licensing programs, that individuals denied licenses are given the opportunity to reapply easily and repeatedly for a license. Thus, many people correctly denied licenses (because they are incompetent) would choose (perhaps it would be provided) to take counseling or therapy to improve their chances of passing the next test. On the other hand, most of those mistakenly denied licenses would probably be able to demonstrate in a later test that they would be competent parents.

Consequently, even though one needs to be wary of prior restraint, if the potential for harm is great and the restraint is minor relative to the harm we are trying to prevent—as it would be with parental licensing—then such restraint is justified. This objection, like all the theoretical objections reviewed, has failed.

PRACTICAL OBJECTIONS TO LICENSING

I shall now consider five practical objections to licensing. Each objection focuses on the problems or difficulties of implementing this proposal. According to these objections, licensing is (or may be) theoretically desirable; nevertheless, it cannot be efficiently and justly implemented.

The first objection is that there may not be, or we may not be able to discover, adequate criteria of "a good parent." We simply do not have the knowledge, and it is unlikely that we could ever obtain the knowledge, that would enable us to distinguish adequate from inadequate parents.

Clearly there is some force to this objection. It is highly improbable that we can formulate criteria that would distinguish precisely between good and less than good parents. There is too much we

do not know about child development and adult psychology. My proposal, however, does not demand that we make these fine distinctions. It does not demand that we license only the best parents; rather it is designed to exclude only the very bad ones. This is not just a semantic difference, but a substantive one. Although we do not have infallible criteria for picking out good parents, we undoubtedly can identify bad ones—those who will abuse or neglect their children. Even though we could have a lively debate about the range of freedom a child should be given or the appropriateness of corporal punishment, we do not wonder if a parent who severely beats or neglects a child is adequate. We know that person isn't. Consequently, we do have reliable and useable criteria for determining who is a bad parent; we have the criteria necessary to make a licensing program work.

The second practical objection to licensing is that there is no reliable way to predict who will maltreat their children. Without an accurate predictive test, licensing would be not only unjust, but also a waste of time. Now I recognize that as a philosopher (and not a psychologist, sociologist, or social worker), I am on shaky ground if I make sweeping claims about the present or future abilities of professionals to produce such predictive tests. Nevertheless, there are some relevant observations I can offer.

Initially, we need to be certain that the demands on predictive tests are not unreasonable. For example, it would be improper to require that tests be 100 precent accurate. Procedures for licensing drivers, physicians, lawyers, druggists, etc., plainly are not 100 percent (or anywhere near 100 percent) accurate. Presumably we recognize these deficiencies yet embrace the procedures anyway. Consequently, it would be imprudent to demand considerably more exacting standards for the tests used in licensing parents.

In addition, from what I can piece together, the practical possibilities for constructing a reliable predictive test are not all that gloomy. Since my proposal does not require that we make fine-line distinctions between good and less than good parents, but rather that we weed out those who are potentially very bad, we can use existing tests that claim to isolate relevant predictive characteristics—whether a person is violence-prone, easily frustrated, or unduly self-centered. In fact researchers at Nashville General Hospital have developed a brief interview questionnaire which seems to have significant predictive value. Based on their data, the researchers identified 20 percent of the interviewees as a "risk group"—those having great potential for serious problems. After one year they found "the incidence of major breakdown in parent-child interaction in the risk group was approximately four to five times as great as in the low risk group."[4] We also know that parents who maltreat children often have certain identifiable experiences; for example, most of them were themselves maltreated as children. Consequently, if we combined our information about these parents with certain psychological test results, we would probably be able to predict with reasonable accuracy which people will maltreat their children.

However, my point is not to argue about the precise reliability of present tests. I cannot say emphatically that we now have accurate predictive tests. Nevertheless, even if such tests are not available, we could undoubtedly develop them. For example, we could begin a longitudinal study in which all potential parents would be required to take a specified battery of tests. Then these parents could be "followed" to discover which ones abused or neglected their children. By correlating the test scores with information on maltreatment, a usable, accurate test could be fashioned. Therefore, I do not think that the present unavailability of such tests (if they are unavailable) would count against the legitimacy of licensing parents.

The third practical objection is that even if a reliable test for ascertaining who would be an acceptable parent were available, administrators would unintentionally misuse that test. These unintentional mistakes would clearly harm innocent individuals. Therefore, so the argument goes, this proposal ought to be scrapped. This objection can be dispensed with fairly easily unless one assumes there is some special reason to believe that more mistakes will be made in administering parenting licenses than in other regulatory activities. No matter how reliable our proceedings are, there will always be mistakes. We may license a physician who, through incompetence, would cause the

death of a patient; or we may mistakenly deny a physician's license to someone who would be competent. But the fact that mistakes are made does not and should not lead us to abandon attempts to determine competence. The harm done in these cases could be far worse than the harm of mistakenly denying a person a parenting license. As far as I can tell, there is no reason to believe that more mistakes will be made here than elsewhere.

The fourth proposed practical objection claims that any testing procedure will be intentionally abused. People administering the process will disqualify people they dislike, or people who espouse views they dislike, from rearing children.

The response to this objection is parallel to the response to the previous objection, namely, that there is no reason to believe that the licensing of parents is more likely to be abused than driver's license tests or other regulatory procedures. In addition, individuals can be protected from prejudicial treatment by pursuing appeals available to them. Since the licensing test can be taken on numerous occasions, the likelihood of the applicant's working with different administrative personnel increases and therefore the likelihood decreases that intentional abuse could ultimately stop a qualified person from rearing children. Consequently, since the probability of such abuse is not more than, and may even be less than, the intentional abuse of judicial and other regulatory authority, this objection does not give us any reason to reject the licensing of parents.

The fifth objection is that we could never adequately, reasonably, and fairly enforce such a program. That is, even if we could establish a reasonable and fair way of determining which people would be inadequate parents, it would be difficult, if not impossible, to enforce the program. How would one deal with violators and what could we do with babies so conceived? There are difficult problems here, no doubt, but they are not insurmountable. We might not punish parents at all—we might just remove the children and put them up for adoption. However, even if we are presently uncertain about the precise way to establish a just and effective form of enforcement, I do not see why this should undermine my licensing proposal. If it is important enough to protect children from being maltreated by parents, then surely a reasonable enforcement procedure can be secured. At least we should assume one can be unless someone shows that it cannot.

AN ANALOGY WITH ADOPTION

So far I have argued that parents should be licensed. Undoubtedly many readers find this claim extremely radical. It is revealing to notice, however, that this program is not as radical as it seems. Our moral and legal systems already recognize that not everyone is capable of rearing children well. In fact, well-entrenched laws require adoptive parents to be investigated—in much the same ways and for much the same reasons as in the general licensing program advocated here. For example, we do not allow just anyone to adopt a child; nor do we let someone adopt without first estimating the likelihood of the person's being a good parent. In fact, the adoptive process is far more rigorous than the general licensing procedures I envision. Prior to adoption the candidates must first formally apply to adopt a child. The applicants are then subjected to an exacting home study to determine whether they really want to have children and whether they are capable of caring for and rearing them adequately. No one is allowed to adopt a child until the administrators can reasonably predict that the person will be an adequate parent. The results of these procedures are impressive. Despite the trauma children often face before they are finally adopted, they are five times less likely to be abused than children reared by their biological parents.5

Nevertheless we recognize, or should recognize, that these demanding procedures exclude some people who would be adequate parents. The selection criteria may be inadequate; the testing procedures may be somewhat unreliable. We may make mistakes. Probably there is some intentional abuse of the system. Adoption procedures intrude directly in the applicants' lives. Yet we continue the present adoption policies becaues we think it better to mistakenly deny some people the opportunity to adopt than to let just anyone adopt.

Once these features of our adoption policies are clearly identified, it becomes quite apparent that

there are striking parallels between the general licensing program I have advocated and our present adoption system. Both programs have the same aim—protecting children. Both have the same drawbacks and are subject to the same abuses. The only obvious dissimilarity is that the adoption requirements are *more* rigorous than those proposed for the general licensing program. Consequently, if we think it is so important to protect adopted children, even though people who want to adopt are less likely than biological parents to maltreat their children, then we should likewise afford the same protection to children reared by their biological parents.

I suspect, though, that many people will think the cases are not analogous. The cases are relevantly different, someone might retort, because biological parents have a natural affection for their children and the strength of this affection makes it unlikely that parents would maltreat their biologically produced children.

Even if it were generally true that parents have special natural affections for their biological offspring, that does not mean that all parents have enough affection to keep them from maltreating their children. This should be apparent given the number of children abused each year by their biological parents. Therefore, even if there is generally such a bond, that does not explain why we should not have licensing procedures to protect children of parents who do not have a sufficiently strong bond. Consequently, if we continue our practice of regulating the adoption of children, and certainly we should, we are rationally compelled to establish a licensing program for all parents.

However, I am not wedded to a strict form of licensing. It may well be that there are alternative ways of regulating parents which would achieve the desired results—the protection of children—without strictly prohibiting nonlicensed people from rearing children. For example, a system of tax incentives for licensed parents, and protective services scrutiny of nonlicensed parents, might adequately protect children. If it would, I would endorse the less drastic measure. My principal concern is to protect children from maltreatment by parents. I begin by advocating the more strict form of licensing since that is the standard method of regulating hazardous activities.

I have argued that all parents should be licensed by the state. This licensing program is attractive, not because state intrusion is inherently judicious and efficacious, but simply because it seems to be the best way to prevent children from being reared by incompetent parents. Nonetheless, even after considering the previous arguments, many people will find the proposal a useful academic exercise, probably silly, and possibly even morally perverse. But why? Why do most of us find this proposal unpalatable, particularly when the arguments supporting it are good and the objections to it are philosophically flimsy?

I suspect the answer is found in a long-held, deeply ingrained attitude toward children, repeatedly reaffirmed in recent court decisions, and present, at least to some degree, in almost all of us. The belief is that parents own, or at least have natural sovereignty over, their children. It does not matter precisely how this belief is described, since on both views parents legitimately exercise extensive and virtually unlimited control over their children. Others can properly interfere with or criticize parental decisions only in unusual and tightly prescribed circumstances—for example, when parents severely and repeatedly abuse their children. In all other cases, the parents reign supreme.

This belief is abhorrent and needs to be supplanted with a more child-centered view. Why? Briefly put, this attitude has adverse effects on children and on the adults these children will become. Parents who hold this view may well maltreat the children. If these parents happen to treat their children well, it is only because they want to, not because they think their children deserve or have a right to good treatment. Moreover, this belief is manifestly at odds with the conviction that parents should prepare children for life as adults. Children subject to parents who perceive children in this way are likely to be adequately prepared for adulthood. Hence, to prepare children for life as adults and to protect them from maltreatment, this attitude toward children must be dislodged. As I have argued, licensing is a viable way to protect children. Furthermore, it would increase the likelihood that more children will be inadequately prepared for life as adults than is now the case.

NOTES

1. The statistics on the incidence of child abuse vary. Probably the most recent detailed study [Saad Nagi, *Child Maltreatment in the United States* (Columbia University Press, 1977)] suggests that between 400,000 and 1 million children are abused or neglected each year. Other experts claim the incidence is considerably higher.

2. According to the National Committee for the Prevention of Child Abuse, more than 80 percent of incarcerated criminals were, as children, abused by their parents. In addition, a study in the *Journal of the American Medical Association* 168, no. 3: 1755–1758, reported that first-degree murderers from middle-class homes and who have "no history of addiction to drugs, alcoholism, organic disease of the brain, or epilepsy" were frequently found to have been subject to "remorseless physical brutality at the hands of the parents."

3. "A review of the literature points out that abusive parents were raised in the same style that they have recreated in the pattern of rearing children. . . . An individual who was raised by parents who used physical force to train their children and who grew up in a violent household has had as a role model the use of force and violence as a means of family problem solving." R. J. Gelles, "Child Abuse as Psychopathology—A Sociological Critique and Reformulation," *American Journal of Orthopsychiatry* 43, no. 4 (1973): 618–19.

4. The research gathered by Altemeir was reported by Ray Helfer in "Review of the Concepts and a Sampling of the Research Relating to Screening for the Potential to Abuse and/or Neglect One's Child." Helfer's paper was presented at a workshop sponsored by the National Committee for the Prevention of Child Abuse, 3–6 December 1978.

5. According to a study published by the Child Welfare League of America, at least 51 percent of the adopted children had suffered, prior to adoption, more than minimal emotional deprivation. See Elizabeth A. Lawder et al., *A Follow-up Study of Adoptions: Post-Placement Functioning of Adoption Families* (New York, 1969).

   According to a study by David Gil [*Violence Against Children* (Cambridge: Harvard University Press, 1970)] only .4 percent of abused children were abused by adoptive parents. Since at least 2 percent of the children in the United States are adopted (*Encyclopedia of Social Work*, National Association of Social Workers, New York, 1977), that means the rate of abuse by biological parents is five times that of adoptive parents.

REVIEW AND DISCUSSION QUESTIONS

1. What provides the motivation behind LaFollette's proposal? Is his concern legitimate?
2. Describe LaFollette's response to the claim that parents have a right to raise children.
3. Describe the practical objections LaFollette discusses, along with his response.
4. On balance, do you think LaFollette's arguments are sufficiently sound to overcome the objections he considers? Explain.

Who Controls a Child's Education?

Wisconsin v. *Yoder*

This well-known case arose in response to a Wisconsin law requiring all children to be sent to school until the age of sixteen. The Amish parents of two children, ages fourteen and fifteen, refused to comply, arguing that compulsory school attendance beyond eighth grade violated their constitutional right of free exercise of religion protected by the First Amendment to the United States Constitution. The case went all the way to the Supreme Court, and the Court overturned the law, upholding the right of the Amish parents to guide the religious future and education of their children. In his dissenting opinion, Justice Douglas discusses problems associated with allowing parents to impose their religious notions on children as well as the possible effects of the Court's ruling on the children's educational development.

Mr. Chief Justice Burger: On complaint of the school district administrator for the public schools, respondents [Mr. and Mrs. Yoder] were charged, tried, and convicted of violating the compulsory-attendance law in Green County Court and were fined the sum of $5 each. Respondents defended on the ground that the application of the compulsory-attendance law violated their rights under the First and Fourteenth Amendments. The trial testimony showed that respondents believed, in accordance with the tenets of Old Order Amish communities generally, that their children's attendance at high school, public or private, was contrary to the Amish religion and way of life. . . . The State stipulated that respondents' religious beliefs were sincere.

In support of their position, respondents presented as expert witnesses scholars on religion and education whose testimony is uncontradicted. They expressed their opinions on the relationship of the Amish belief concerning school attendance to the more general tenets of their religion, and described the impact that compulsory high school attendance could have on the continued survival of Amish communities as they exist in the United States today. . . .

Amish beliefs require members of the community to make their living by farming or closely related activities. Broadly speaking, the Old Order Amish religion pervades and determines the entire mode of life of its adherents. . . .

406 U.S. 205 (1972).

Amish objection to formal education beyond the eighth grade is firmly grounded in these central religious concepts. They object to the high school, and higher education generally, because the values they teach are in marked variance with Amish values and the Amish way of life; they view secondary school education as an impermissible exposure of their children to a "worldly" influence in conflict with their beliefs. The high school tends to emphasize intellectual and scientific accomplishments, self-distinction, competitiveness, worldly success, and social life with other students. Amish society emphasizes informal learning-through-doing; a life of "goodness," rather than a life of intellect; wisdom, rather than technical knowledge; community welfare, rather than competition; and separation from, rather than integration with, contemporary worldly society.

Formal high school education takes [Amish children] away from their community, physically and emotionally, during the crucial and formative adolescent period of life. During this period, the children must acquire Amish attitudes favoring manual work and self-reliance and the specific skills needed to perform the adult role of an Amish farmer or housewife. They must learn to enjoy physical labor. . . . And, at this time in life, the Amish child must also grow in his faith and his relationship to the Amish community if he is to be prepared to accept the heavy obligations imposed by adult baptism. . . .

The Amish do not object to elementary education through the first eight grades as a general proposition because they agree that their children must have basic skills in the "three R's" in order to read the Bible, to be good farmers and citizens, and to be able to deal with non-Amish people when necessary in the course of daily affairs. They view such a basic education as acceptable because it does not significantly expose their children to worldly values or interfere with their development in the Amish community during the crucial adolescent period. . . .

On the basis of such considerations, [an expert] testified that compulsory high school attendance could not only result in great psychological harm to Amish children, because of the conflicts it would produce, but would also, in his opinion, ultimately result in the destruction of the Old Order

Amish church community as it exists in the United States today. . . .

In order for Wisconsin to compel school attendance beyond the eighth grade against a claim that such attendance interferes with the practice of a legitimate religious belief, it must appear either that the State does not deny the free exercise of religious belief by its requirement, or that there is a state interest of sufficient magnitude to override the interest claiming protection under the Free Exercise Clause. . . .

A way of life, however virtuous and admirable, may not be interposed as a barrier to reasonable state regulation of education if it is based on purely secular considerations; to have the protection of the Religion Clauses, the claims must be rooted in religious belief. Although a determination of what is a "religious" belief or practice entitled to constitutional protection may present a most delicate question, the very concept of ordered liberty precludes allowing every person to make his own standards on matters of conduct in which society as a whole has important interests. Thus, if the Amish asserted their claims because of their subjective evaluation and rejection of the contemporary secular values accepted by the majority, much as Thoreau rejected the social values of his time and isolated himself at Walden Pond, their claims would not rest on a religious basis. Thoreau's choice was philosophical and personal rather than religious, and such belief does not rise to the demands of the Religion Clauses.

Giving no weight to such secular considerations, however, we see that the record in this case abundantly supports the claim that the traditional way of life of the Amish is not merely a matter of personal preference, but one of deep religious conviction, shared by an organized group, and intimately related to daily living. That the Old Order Amish daily life and religious practice stem from their faith is shown by the fact that it is in response to their literal interpretation of the Biblical injunction from the Epistle of Paul to the Romans, "be not conformed to this world. . . ."

Their way of life in a church-oriented community, separated from the outside world and "worldly" influences, their attachment to nature and the soil, is a way inherently simple and uncomplicated, albeit difficult to preserve against the pressure to conform. Their rejection of telephones, automobiles, radios, and television, their mode of dress, of speech, their habits of manual work do indeed set them apart from much of contemporary society; these customs are both symbolic and practical. . . .

The State advances two primary arguments in support of its system of compulsory education. It notes, as Thomas Jefferson pointed out early in our history, that some degree of education is necessary to prepare citizens to participate effectively and intelligently in our open political system if we are to preserve freedom and independence. Further, education prepares individuals to be self-reliant and self-sufficient participants in society. We accept these propositions.

However, the evidence adduced by the Amish in this case is persuasively to the effect that an additional one or two years of formal high school for Amish children in place of their long-established program of informal vocational education would do little to serve those interests. . . . It is one thing to say that compulsory education for a year or two beyond the eighth grade may be necessary when its goal is the preparation of the child for life in modern society as the majority live, but it is quite another if the goal of education be viewed as the preparation of the child for life in the separated agrarian community that is the keystone of the Amish faith. . . .

Whatever their idiosyncrasies as seen by the majority, the Amish community has been a highly successful social unit within our society, even if apart from the conventional "mainstream." Its members are productive and very law-abiding members of society; they reject public welfare in any of its usual modern forms. . . .

This case involves the fundamental interest of parents, as contrasted with that of the State, to guide the religious future and education of their children. The history and culture of Western civilization reflect a strong tradition of parental concern for the nurture and upbringing of their children. This primary role of the parents in the upbringing of their children is now established beyond debate as an enduring American tradition. . . .

To be sure, the power of the parent, even when linked to a free exercise claim, may be subject to

limitation if it appears that parental decisions will jeopardize the health or safety of the child, or have a potential for significant social burdens. But in this case, the Amish have introduced persuasive evidence undermining the arguments the State has advanced to support its claims in terms of the welfare of the child and society as a whole.

Mr. Justice Douglas, Dissenting in Part: The Court's analysis assumes that the only interests at stake in the case are those of the Amish parents on the one hand, and those of the State on the other. The difficulty with this approach is that, despite the Court's claim, the parents are seeking to vindicate not only their own free exercise claims, but also those of their high-school-age children. . . .

No analysis of religious-liberty claims can take place in a vacuum. If the parents in this case are allowed a religious exemption, the inevitable effect is to impose the parents' notions of religious duty upon their children. Where the child is mature enough to express potentially conflicting desires, it would be an invasion of the child's rights to permit such an imposition without canvassing his views. . . . As the child has no other effective forum, it is in this litigation that his rights should be considered. And, if an Amish child desires to attend high school, and is mature enough to have that desire respected, the State may well be able to override the parents' religiously motivated objections.

This issue has never been squarely presented before today. Our opinions are full of talk about the power of the parents over the child's education. . . . And we have in the past analyzed similar conflicts between parent and State with little regard for the views of the child. . . . Recent cases, however, have clearly held that the children themselves have constitutionally protectible interests.

These children are "persons" within the meaning of the Bill of Rights. . . . While the parents, absent dissent, normally speak for the entire family, the education of the child is a matter on which the child will often have decided views. He may want to be a pianist or an astronaut or an oceanographer. To do so he will have to break from the Amish tradition. . . .

If a parent keeps his child out of school beyond the grade school, then the child will be forever barred from entry into the new and amazing world of diversity that we have today. . . .

[In the cases in which the Court held anti-polygamy laws constitutional,] action which the Court deemed to be antisocial could be punished even though it was grounded on deeply held and sincere religious convictions. What we do today, at least in this respect, opens the way to give organized religion a broader base than it has ever enjoyed.

In another way, however, the Court retreats when in reference to Henry Thoreau it says his "choice was philosophical and personal rather than religious, and such belief does not rise to the demands of the Religion Clauses." That is contrary to what we held in *United States* v. *Seeger*, where we were concerned with the meaning of the words "religious training and belief" in the Selective Service Act, which were the basis of many conscientious objector claims. We said: "Within that phrase would come all sincere religious beliefs which are based upon a power or being, or upon a faith, to which all else is subordinate or upon which all else is ultimately dependent. The test might be stated in these words: A sincere and meaningful belief which occupies in the life of its possessor a place parallel to that filled by the God of those admittedly qualifying for the exemption comes within the statutory definition. This construction avoids imputing to Congress an intent to classify different religious beliefs, exempting some and excluding others, and is in accord with the well-established congressional policy of equal treatment for those whose opposition to service is grounded in their religious tenets."

REVIEW AND DISCUSSION QUESTIONS

1. Describe the issue being addressed by the Court in this case.
2. Does Justice Burger seem to rely more on religious freedom or the rights of parents over children? Explain.
3. On what basis does Justice Douglas dissent?
4. Does Justice Burger think the Constitution should be "neutral" among different religions? Explain.
5. Children will eventually have the right to make decisions for themselves in many areas, independently of what government or others may think. Can parents sometimes damage their children's future right to self-determination? Explain, giving examples.
6. "This case allows parents to violate their own children's basic rights and deny their children's good." Explain how that statement might be defended. Do you agree?
7. How would LaFollette respond to this case? Do you agree with that position?

What Do Grown Children Owe Their Parents?

Jane English

One way to view the responsibilities of grown children to their parents is to suppose that children owe their parents love, respect, and financial or other help on the basis of past sacrifices parents have made. Jane English rejects this form of argument, claiming instead that friendship is a better model for understanding the parent-child relationship than debts owed.

What do grown children owe their parents? I will contend that the answer is "nothing." Although I agree that there are many things that children ought to do for their parents, I will argue that it is inappropriate and misleading to describe them as things "owed." I will maintain that parents' voluntary sacrifices, rather than creating "debts" to be "repaid," tend to create love or "friendship." The duties of grown children are those of friends and result from love between them and their parents, rather than being things owed in repayment for the parents' earlier sacrifices. Thus, I will oppose those philosophers who use the word "owe" whenever a duty or obligation exists. Although the "debt" metaphor is appropriate in some moral circumstances, my argument is that a love relationship is not such a case.

Misunderstandings about the proper relationship between parents and their grown children have resulted from reliance on the "owing" terminology. For instance, we hear parents complain, "You owe it to us to write home (keep up your piano playing, not adopt a hippie lifestyle), because of all we sacrificed for you (paying for piano lessons, sending you to college)." The child is sometimes even heard to reply, "I didn't ask to be born (to be given piano lessons, to be sent to college)." This inappropriate idiom of ordinary language tends to obscure, or even to undermine, the love that is the correct ground of filial obligation.

1. FAVORS CREATE DEBTS

There are some cases, other than literal debts, in which talk of "owing," though metaphorical, is apt. New to the neighborhood, Max barely knows his neighbor, Nina, but he asks her if she will take in his mail while he is gone for a month's vacation. She agrees. If, subsequently, Nina asks Max to do the same for her, it seems that Max has a moral obligation to agree (greater than the one he would have had if Nina had not done the same for him), unless for some reason it would be a burden far out of proportion to the one Nina bore for him. I will call this a *favor*: when A, at B's request, bears some burden for B, then B incurs an obligation to reciprocate. Here the metaphor of Max's "owing" Nina is appropriate. It is not literally a debt, of course, nor can Nina pass this IOU on to heirs, demand payment in the form of Max's taking out her garbage, or sue Max. Nonetheless, since Max ought to perform one act of similar nature and amount of sacrifice in return, the term is suggestive. Once he reciprocates, the debt is "discharged"—that is, their obligations revert to the condition they were in before Max's initial request.

Contrast a situation in which Max simply goes on vacation and, to his surprise, finds upon his return that his neighbor has mowed his grass twice weekly in his absence. This is a voluntary sacrifice

From Jane English, "What Do Grown Children Owe Their Parents?" in *Having Children*, Onora O'Neill and William Ruddick, eds. (New York: Oxford University Press, 1979). Reprinted by permission.

rather than a favor, and Max has no duty to reciprocate. It would be nice for him to volunteer to do so, but this would be supererogatory on his part. Rather than a favor, Nina's action is a friendly gesture. As a result, she might expect Max to chat over the back fence, help her catch her straying dog, or something similar—she might expect the development of a friendship. But Max would be chatting (or whatever) out of friendship, rather than in repayment for mown grass. If he did not return her gesture, she might feel rebuffed or miffed, but not unjustly treated or indignant, since Max has not failed to perform a duty. Talk of "owing" would be out of place in this case.

It is sometimes difficult to distinguish between favors and non-favors, because friends tend to do favors for each other, and those who exchange favors tend to become friends. But one test is to ask how Max is motivated. Is it "to be nice to Nina" or "because she did x for me"? Favors are frequently performed by total strangers without any friendship developing. Nevertheless, a temporary obligation is created, even if the chance for repayment never arises. For instance, suppose that Oscar and Matilda, total strangers, are waiting in a long checkout line at the supermarket. Oscar, having forgotten the oregano, asks Matilda to watch his cart for a second. She does. If Matilda now asks Oscar to return the favor while she picks up some tomato sauce, he is obliged to agree. Even if she had not watched his cart, it would be inconsiderate of him to refuse, claiming he was too busy reading the magazines. He may have a duty to help others, but he would not "owe" it to her. But if she had done the same for him, he incurs an additional obligation to help, and talk of "owing" is apt. It suggests an agreement to perform equal, reciprocal, canceling sacrifices.

2. THE DUTIES OF FRIENDSHIP VERSUS DEBTS

The terms "owe" and "repay" are helpful in the case of favors, because the sameness of the amount of sacrifice on the two sides is important; the monetary metaphor suggests equal quantities of sacrifice. But friendship ought to be characterized by *mutuality* rather than reciprocity: friends

offer what they can give and accept what they need, without regard for the total amounts of benefits exchanged. And friends are motivated by love rather than by the prospect of repayment. Hence, talk of "owing" is singularly out of place in friendship.

For example, suppose Alfred takes Beatrice out for an expensive dinner and a movie. Beatrice incurs no obligation to "repay" him with a goodnight kiss or a return engagement. If Alfred complains that she "owes" him something, he is operating under the assumption that she should repay a favor, but on the contrary his was a generous gesture done in the hopes of developing a friendship. We hope that he would not want her repayment in the form of sex or attention if this was done to discharge a debt rather than from friendship. Since, if Alfred is prone to reasoning in this way, Beatrice may well decline the invitation or request to pay for her own dinner, his attitude of expecting a "return" on his "investment" could hinder the development of a friendship. Beatrice should return the gesture only if she is motivated by friendship.

Another common misuse of the "owing" idiom occurs when the Smiths have dined at the Joneses' four times, but the Joneses at the Smiths' only once. People often say, "We owe them three dinners." This line of thinking may be appropriate between business acquaintances, but not between friends. After all, the Joneses invited the Smiths not in order to feed them or to be fed in turn, but because of the friendly contact presumably enjoyed by all on such occasions. If the Smiths do not feel friendship toward the Joneses, they can decline future invitations and not invite the Joneses; they owe them nothing. Of course, between friends of equal resources and needs, roughly equal sacrifices (though not necessarily roughly equal dinners) will typically occur. If the sacrifices are highly out of proportion to the resources, the relationship is closer to servility than to friendship.

Another difference between favors and friendship is that after a friendship ends, the duties of friendship end. The party that has sacrificed less owes the other nothing. For instance, suppose Elmer donated a pint of blood that his wife Doris needed during an operation. Years after their divorce, Elmer is in an accident and needs one pint of blood. His new wife, Cora, is also of the same blood type. It seems that Doris not only does not "owe" Elmer blood, but that she should actually refrain from coming forward if Cora has volunteered to donate. To insist on donating not only interferes with the newlyweds' friendship, but it belittles Doris and Elmer's former relationship by suggesting that Elmer gave blood in hopes of favors returned instead of simply out of love for Doris. It is one of the heart-rending features of divorce that it attends to quantity in a relationship previously characterized by mutuality. If Cora could not donate, Doris's obligation is the same as that for any former spouse in need of blood; it is not increased by the fact that Elmer similarly aided her. It is affected by the degree to which they are still friends, which in turn may (or may not) have been influenced by Elmer's donation.

In short, unlike the debts created by favors, the duties of friendship do not require equal quantities of sacrifice. Performing equal sacrifices does not cancel the duties of friendship, as it does the debts of favors. Unrequested sacrifices do not themselves create debts, but friends have duties regardless of whether they requested or initiated the friendship. Those who perform favors may be motivated by mutual gain, whereas friends should be motivated by affection. These characteristics of the friendship relation are distorted by talk of "owing."

3. PARENTS AND CHILDREN

The relationship between children and their parents should be one of friendship characterized by mutuality rather than one of reciprocal favors. The quantity of parental sacrifice is not relevant in determining what duties the grown child has. The medical assistance grown children ought to offer their ill mothers in old age depends upon the mothers' need, not upon whether they endured a difficult pregnancy, for example. Nor do one's duties to one's parents cease once an equal quantity of sacrifice has been performed, as the phrase "discharging a debt" may lead us to think.

Rather, what children ought to do for their parents (and parents for children) depends upon

(1) their respective needs, abilities, and resources and (2) the extent to which there is an ongoing friendship between them. Thus, regardless of the quantity of childhood sacrifices, an able, wealthy child has an obligation to help his needy parents more than does a needy child. To illustrate, suppose sisters Cecile and Dana are equally loved by their parents, even though Cecile was an easy child to care for, seldom ill, while Dana was often sick and caused some trouble as a juvenile delinquent. As adults, Dana is a struggling artist living far away, while Cecile is a wealthy lawyer living nearby. When the parents need visits and financial aid, Cecile has an obligation to bear a higher proportion of these burdens than her sister. This results from her abilities, rather than from the quantities of sacrifice made by the parents earlier.

Sacrifices have an important causal role in creating an ongoing friendship, which may lead us to assume incorrectly that it is the sacrifices that are the source of the obligation. That the source is the friendship instead can be seen by examining cases in which the sacrifices occurred but the friendship, for some reason, did not develop or persist. For example, if a woman gives up her newborn child for adoption, and if no feelings of love ever develop on either side, it seems that the grown child does not have an obligation to "repay" her for her sacrifices in pregnancy. For that matter, if the adopted child has an unimpaired love relationship with the adoptive parents, he or she has the same obligations to help them as a natural child would have.

The filial obligations of grown children are a result of friendship, rather than owed for services rendered. Suppose that Vance married Lola despite his parents' strong wish that he marry within their religion, and that as a result, the parents refuse to speak to him again. As the years pass, the parents are unaware of Vance's problems, his accomplishments, the birth of his children. The love that once existed between them, let us suppose, has been completely destroyed by this event and thirty years of desuetude. At this point, it seems, Vance is under no obligation to pay his parents' medical bills in their old age, beyond his general duty to help those in need. An additional, filial obligation would only arise from whatever love he may still feel for them. It would be irrelevant for his parents to argue, "But look how much we sacrificed for you when you were young," for that sacrifice was not a favor but occurred as part of a friendship which existed at that time but is now, we have supposed, defunct. A more appropriate message would be, "We still love you, and we would like to renew our friendship."

I hope this helps to set the question of what children ought to do for their parents in a new light. The parental argument, "You ought to do x because we did y for you," should be replaced by, "We love you and you will be happier if you do x," or "We believe you love us, and anyone who loved us would do x." If the parents' sacrifice had been a favor, the child's reply, "I never asked you to do y for me," would have been relevant; to the revised parental remarks, this reply is clearly irrelevant. The child can either do x or dispute one of the parents' claims: by showing that a love relationship does not exist, or that love for someone does not motivate doing x, or that he or she will not be happier doing x.

Seen in this light, parental requests for children to write home, visit, and offer them a reasonable amount of emotional and financial support in life's crises are well founded, so long as a friendship still exists. Love for others does call for caring about and caring for them. Some other parental requests, such as for more sweeping changes in the child's lifestyle or life goals, can be seen to be insupportable, once we shift the justification from debts owed to love. The terminology of favors suggests the reasoning, "Since we paid for your college education, you owe it to us to make a career of engineering, rather than becoming a rock musician." This tends to alienate affection even further, since the tuition payments are depicted as investments for a return rather than done from love, as though the child's life goals could be "bought." Basing the argument on love leads to different reasoning patterns. The suppressed premise, "If A loves B, then A follows B's wishes as to A's lifelong career" is simply false. Love does not even dictate that the child adopt the parents' values as to the desirability of alternative life goals. So the parents' strongest available argument here is, "We love you, we are deeply concerned about your happiness, and in the long run you will be happier as an engineer." This makes it clear that an empirical claim is really the subject of the debate.

The function of these examples is to draw out our considered judgments as to the proper relation between parents and their grown children, and to show how poorly they fit the model of favors. What is relevant is the ongoing friendship that exists between parents and children. Although that relationship developed partly as a result of parental sacrifices for the child, the duties that grown children have to their parents result from the friendship rather than from the sacrifices. The idiom of owing favors to one's parents can actually be destructive if it undermines the role of mutuality and leads us to think in terms of quantitative reciprocal favors.

REVIEW AND DISCUSSION QUESTIONS

1. What differences does English find between duties to friends and the obligation to repay debts?
2. Why does English advocate the model of friendship rather than of reciprocal favors in describing the parent-child relationship?
3. Does the friendship model exhaust the duties of children? Is the mere fact of a biological connection between parent and child morally irrelevant? Explain.
4. Suppose a parent has not been a "friend" to the child, but instead has been strict, remote, and uncompromising but also self-sacrificing. Does the adult child then owe the parent nothing?
5. Compare English's position with the view of parent-child relationships described by Judith Jarvis Thomson in her article on abortion.

Part V

GENDER, RACE, AND MULTICULTURALISM

15
Sexual Equality
and Discrimination

What, exactly, is sexual equality? Do women live in a world of sexual domination and oppression? Are women who choose traditional roles doing so "freely" or are they conditioned by society in ways that destroy their capacity to choose freely? Do biological differences show that inequalities between the sexes are "natural" and therefore undermine feminists' criticisims of society? Essays in this section offer a variety of perspectives on these controversial and much discussed issues. The first reading in this section, written by John Stuart Mill and Harriet Taylor, is perhaps the most important early work on women's rights and equality. Other readings explore the strengths and weakness of Mill's and Taylor's vision of sexual equality along with the alternative, "dominance" approach advocated by some feminists.

The Subjection of Women

John Stuart Mill and Harriet Taylor

As noted in the introduction to Mill's essay on utilitarianism, John Stuart Mill and Harriet Taylor enjoyed a lengthy and profoundly rewarding relationship. Her influence on Mill was extraordinary; indeed, there are many who believe it was she, as much or more than he, who was responsible for the following essay. In any event, this is a prescient essay on the subject of women's rights, and even today, more than a century later, it speaks to many issues still very much in the forefront of our discussions of sexual equality.

From John Stuart Mill and Harriet Taylor, *The Subjection of Women* (1869).

Mill and Taylor begin with an analysis of the situation faced by women, along with the possible causes of their plight. They then respond to those who would argue that the observed differences between the sexes are natural and those who believe women willingly accept their lot. They conclude with a discussion of the various reasons why women's equality should be advanced.

It is interesting to note that before Mill and Taylor were married, Mill signed an agreement renouncing all of the powers the law would normally bestow on him, asserting instead that his prospective wife was to retain the same rights to her property and personal freedom as if they had never married. When she died, Mill bought a house near the graveyard in France in order to spend his last years near his wife's grave. The description of an ideal marriage appearing near the end of the essay mirrors Mill's own description of their relationship. (Because the essay was originally published under Mill's name alone, it is written using the first-person singular. Nonetheless, I have included Taylor as co-author, as I believe Mill would have wished.)

Chapter 1.   The object of this Essay is to explain as clearly as I am able, the grounds of an opinion which I have held from the very earliest period when I had formed any opinions at all on social or political matters, and which, instead of being weakened or modified, has been constantly growing stronger by the progress of reflection and the experience of life: That the principle which regulates the existing social relations between the two sexes—the legal subordination of one sex to the other—is wrong in itself, and now one of the chief hindrances to human improvement; and that it ought to be replaced by a principle of perfect equality, admitting no power or privilege on the one side, no disability on the other. . . .

The generality of a practice is in some cases a strong presumption that it is, or at all events once was, conducive to laudable ends. This is the case, when the practice was first adopted, or afterwards kept up, as a means to such ends, and was grounded on experience of the mode in which they could be most effectually attained. If the authority of men over women, when first established, had been the result of a conscientious comparison between different modes of constituting the government of society; if, after trying various other modes of social organization—the government of women over men, equality between the two, and such mixed and divided modes of government as might be invented—it had been decided, on the testimony of experience, that the mode in which women are wholly under the rule of men, having no share at all in public concerns, and each in private being under the legal obligation of obedience to the man with whom she has associated her destiny, was the arrangement most conducive to the happiness and well being of both; its general adoption might then be fairly thought to be some evidence that, at the time when it was adopted, it was the best: though even then the considerations which recommended it may, like so many other primeval social facts of the greatest importance, have subsequently, in the course of ages, ceased to exist. But the state of the case is in every respect the reverse of this. In the first place, the opinion in favour of the present system, which entirely subordinates the weaker sex to the stronger, rests upon theory only; for there never has been trial made of any other: so that experience, in the sense in which it is vulgarly opposed to theory, cannot be pretended to have pronounced any verdict. And in the second place, the adoption of this system of inequality never was the result of deliberation, or forethought, or any social ideas, or any notion whatever of what conduced to the benefit of humanity or the good order of society. It arose simply from the fact that from the very earliest twilight of human society, every woman (owing to the value attached to her by men, combined with her inferiority in muscular strength) was found in a state of bondage to some man. Laws and systems of polity always begin by recognising the relations they find already existing between individuals. They convert what was a mere physical fact into a legal right, give it the sanction of society, and principally aim at the substitution of public and organized means of asserting and protecting these rights, instead of the irregular and lawless conflict of physical strength. Those who had already been compelled to obedience became in this manner legally bound to it. . . . But this dependence, as it exists at present, is not an original institution, taking a fresh start from considerations of justice and social expediency—it is the primitive state of slavery lasting on, through successive mitigations and modifications occasioned by the same causes which have softened the general manners, and brought all human relations more under the control of justice and the influence of humanity. It has not lost the taint of its brutal origin. No presumption in its favour, therefore, can be drawn from the fact of its existence. . . . The inequality of rights between men and women has no other source than the law of the strongest.

But, it will be said, the rule of men over women differs from all these others in not being a rule of force: it is accepted voluntarily; women make no complaint, and are consenting parties to it. In the first place, a great number of women do not accept it. Ever since there have been women able to make their sentiments known by their writings (the only mode of publicity which society permits to them), an increasing number of them have recorded protests against their present social condition. . . .

All causes, social and natural, combine to make it unlikely that women should be collectively rebellious to the power of men. They are so far in a position different from all other subject classes, that their masters require something more from them than actual service. Men do not want solely the obedience of women, they want their sentiments. All men, except the most brutish, desire to have, in the woman most nearly connected with them, not a forced slave but a willing one, not a slave merely, but a favourite. They have therefore put everything in practice to enslave their minds. The masters of all other slaves rely, for maintaining obedience, on fear; either fear of themselves, or religious fears. The masters of women wanted more than simple obedience, and they turned the whole force of education to effect their purpose. All women are brought up from the very earliest years in the belief that their ideal of character is the very opposite to that of men; not self-will, and government by self-control, but submission, and yielding to the control of others. All the moralities tell them that it is the duty of women, and all the current sentimentalities that it is their nature, to live for others; to make complete abnegation of themselves, and to have no life but in their affections. And by their affections are meant the only ones they are allowed to have—those to the men with whom they are connected, or to the children who constitute an additional and indefeasible tie between them and a man. When we put together three things—first, the natural attraction between opposite sexes; secondly, the wife's entire dependence on the husband, every privilege or pleasure she has being either his gift, or depending entirely on his will; and lastly, that the principal object of human pursuit, consideration, and all objects of social ambition, can in general be sought or obtained by her only through him, it would be a miracle if the object of being attractive to men had not become the polar star of feminine education and formation of character. And, this great means of influence over the minds of women having been acquired, an instinct of selfishness made men avail themselves of it to the upmost as a means of holding women in subjection, by representing to them meekness, submissiveness, and resignation of all individual will into the hands of a man, as an essential part of sexual attractiveness. Can it be doubted that any of the other yokes which mankind have succeeded in breaking, would have subsisted till now if the same means had existed, and had been as sedulously used, to bow down their minds to it? . . .

Neither does it avail anything to say that the *nature* of the two sexes adapts them to their present functions and position, and renders these appropriate to them. Standing on the ground of common sense and the constitution of the human mind, I deny that any one knows, or can know, the nature of the two sexes, as long as they have only been seen in their present relation to one another. . . .

One thing we may be certain of—that what is contrary to women's nature to do, they never will be made to do by simply giving their nature free play. The anxiety of mankind to interfere in behalf of nature, for fear lest nature should not succeed in effecting its purpose, is an altogether unnecessary solicitude. . . .

Chapter 2. . . . Marriage being the destination appointed by society for women, the prospect they are brought up to, and the object which it is intended should be sought by all of them, except those who are too little attractive to be chosen by any man as his companion; one might have supposed that everything would have been done to make this condition as eligible to them as possible, that they might have no cause to regret being denied the option of any other. Society, however, both in this, and, at first, in all other cases, has preferred to attain its object by foul rather than fair means: but this is the only case in which it has substantially persisted in them even to the present day. Originally women were taken by force, or regularly sold by their father to the husband. . . .

[Today] the wife is the actual bondservant of her husband: no less so, as far as legal obligation goes, than slaves commonly so called. She vows a life-long obedience to him at the altar, and is held to it all through her life by law. Casuists may say that the obligation of obedience stops short of participation in crime, but it certainly extends to everything else. She can do no act whatever but by his permission, at least tacit. She can acquire no property but for him; the instant it becomes hers, even if by inheritance, it becomes *ipso facto* his. In this respect the wife's position under the common law of England is worse than that of slaves in the laws of many countries. . . . The two are called "one person in law," for the purpose of inferring that whatever is hers is his, but the parallel inference is never drawn that whatever is his is hers; the maxim is not applied against the man, except to make him responsible to third parties for her acts, as a master is for the acts of his slaves or of his cattle. I am far from pretending that wives are in general no better treated than slaves; but no slave is a slave to the same lengths, and in so full a sense of the word, as a wife is. Hardly any slave, except one immediately attached to the master's person, is a slave at all hours and all minutes; in general he has, like a soldier, his fixed task, and when it is done, or when he is off duty, he disposes, within certain limits, of his own time, and has a family life into which the master rarely intrudes. "Uncle Tom" under his first master had his own life in his "cabin," almost as much as any man whose work takes him away from home, is able to have in his own family. But it cannot be so with the wife. Above all, a female slave has (in Christian countries) an admitted right, and is considered under a moral obligation, to refuse to her master the last familiarity. Not so the wife: however brutal a tyrant she may unfortunately be chained to—

though she may know that he hates her, though it may be his daily pleasure to torture her, and though she may feel it impossible not to loathe him—he can claim from her and enforce the lowest degradation of a human being, that of being made the instrument of an animal function contrary to her inclinations. While she is held in this worst description of slavery as to her own person, what is her position in regard to the children in whom she and her master have a joint interest? They are by law his children. He alone has any legal rights over them. Not one act can she do towards or in relation to them, except by delegation from him. Even after he is dead she is not their legal guardian, unless he by will has made her so. He could even send them away from her, and deprive her of the means of seeing or corresponding with them, until this power was in some degree restricted by Serjeant Talfourd's Act. This is her legal state. And from this state she has no means of withdrawing herself. If she leaves her husband, she can take nothing with her, neither her children nor anything which is rightfully her own. If he chooses, he can compel her to return, by law, or by physical force; or he may content himself with seizing for his own use anything which she may earn, or which may be given to her by her relations. . . .

When we consider how vast is the number of men, in any great country, who are little higher than brutes, and that this never prevents them from being able, through the law of marriage, to obtain a victim, the breadth and depth of human misery caused in this shape alone by the abuse of the institution swells to something appalling. . . . I grant that the wife, if she cannot effectually resist, can at least retaliate; she, too, can make the man's life extremely uncomfortable, and by that power is able to carry many points which she ought, and many which she ought not, to prevail in. But this instrument of self-protection—which may be called the power of the scold, or the shrewish sanction—has the fatal defect, that it avails most against the least tyrannical superiors, and in favour of the least deserving dependents. It is the weapon of irritable and self-willed women; of those who would make the worst use of power if they themselves had it, and who generally turn this power to a bad use. . . .

But how, it will be asked, can any society exist without government? In a family, as in a state, some one person must be the ultimate ruler. Who shall decide when married people differ in opinion? Both cannot have their way, yet a decision one way or the other must be come to.

It is true that in all voluntary association between two people, one of them must be absolute master: still less that the law must determine which of them it shall be. . . .

It is quite true that things which have to be decided every day, and cannot adjust themselves gradually, or wait for a compromise, ought to depend on one will: one person must have their sole control. But it does not follow that this should always be the same person. The natural arrangement is a division of powers between the two; each being absolute in the executive branch of their own department, and any change of system and principle requiring the consent of both. . . .

The real practical decision of affairs, to whichever may be given the legal authority, will greatly depend, as it even now does, upon comparative qualifications. The mere fact that he is usually the eldest, will in most cases give the preponderance to the man; at least until they both attain a time of life at which the difference in their years is of no importance. There will naturally also be a more potential voice on the side, whichever it is, that brings the means of support. . . .

After what has been said respecting the obligation of obedience, it is almost superfluous to say anything concerning the more special point included in the general one—a woman's right to her own property; for I need not hope that this treatise can make any impression upon those who need anything to convince them that a woman's inheritance or gains ought to be as much her own after marriage as before. The rule is simple: whatever would be the husband's or wife's if they were not married, should be under their exclusive control during marriage. . . .

When the support of the family depends, not on property, but on earnings, the common arrangement, by which the man earns the income and the wife superintends the domestic expenditure, seems to me in general the most suitable division of labour between the two persons. If, in addition to the physical suffering of bearing children, and

the whole responsibility of their care and education in early years, the wife undertakes the careful and economical application of the husband's earnings to the general comfort of the family; she takes not only her fair share, but usually the larger share, of the bodily and mental exertion required by their joint existence. If she undertakes any additional portion, it seldom relieves her from this, but only prevents her from performing it properly. The care which she is herself disabled from taking of the children and the household, nobody else takes; those of the children who do not die, grow up as they best can, and the management of the household is likely to be so bad, as even in point of economy to be a great drawback from the value of the wife's earnings. In an otherwise just state of things, it is not, therefore, I think, a desirable custom, that the wife should contribute by her labour to the income of the family. In an unjust state of things, her doing so may be useful to her, by making her of more value in the eyes of the man who is legally her master; but, on the other hand, it enables him still farther to abuse his power, by forcing her to work, and leaving the support of the family to her exertions, while he spends most of his time in drinking and idleness. The *power* of earning is essential to the dignity of a woman, if she has not independent property. But if marriage were an equal contract, not implying the obligation of obedience; if the connexion were no longer enforced to the oppression of those to whom it is purely a mischief, but a separation, on just terms (I do not now speak of a divorce), could be obtained by any woman who was morally entitled to it; and if she would then find all honourable employments as freely open to her as to men; it would not be necessary for her protection, that during marriage she should make this particular use of her faculties. Like a man when he chooses a profession, so, when a woman marries, it may in general be understood that she makes choice of the management of a household, and the bringing up of a family, as the first call upon her exertions, during as many years of her life as may be required for the purpose; and that she renounces, not all other objects and occupations, but all which are not consistent with the requirements of this. The actual exercise, in a habitual or systematic manner, of outdoor occupations, or such as cannot be carried on at home, would by this principle be practically interdicted to the greater number of married women. But the utmost latitude ought to exist for the adaptation of general rules to individual suitabilities; and there ought to be nothing to prevent faculties exceptionally adapted to any other pursuit, from obeying their vocation notwithstanding marriage: due provision being made for supplying otherwise any falling-short which might become inevitable, in her full performance of the ordinary functions of mistress of a family. These things, if once opinion were rightly directed on the subject, might with perfect safety be left to be regulated by opinion, without any interference of law.

Chapter 3.   On the other point which is involved in the just equality of women, their admissibility to all the functions and occupations hitherto retained as the monopoly of the stronger sex, I should anticipate no difficulty in convincing any one who has gone with me on the subject of the equality of women in the family. I believe that their disabilities elsewhere are only clung to in order to maintain their subordination in domestic life. . . . It is not sufficient to maintain that women on the average are less gifted than men on the average, with certain of the higher mental faculties, or that a smaller number of women than of men are fit for occupations and functions of the highest intellectual character. It is necessary to maintain that no women at all are fit for them, and that the most eminent women are inferior in mental faculties to the most mediocre of the men on whom those functions at present devolve. . . . Is there so great a superfluity of men fit for high duties, that society can afford to reject the service of any competent person? Are we so certain of always finding a man made to our hands for any duty or function of social importance which falls vacant, that we lose nothing by putting a ban upon one-half of mankind, and refusing beforehand to make their faculties available, however distinguished they may be? And even if we could do without them, would it be consistent with justice to refuse to them their fair share of honour and distinction, or to deny to them the equal moral right of all human beings to choose their occupation (short of injury to others) according to their own preferences, at

their own risk? Nor is the injustice confined to them: it is shared by those who are in a position to benefit by their services. . . .

But (it is said) there is anatomical evidence of the superior mental capacity of men compared with women: they have a larger brain. I reply, that in the first place the fact itself is doubtful. It is by no means established that the brain of a woman is smaller than that of a man. . . . Next, I must observe that the precise relation which exists between the brain and the intellectual powers is not yet well understood, but is a subject of great dispute. . . . It would not be surprising—it is indeed an hypothesis which accords well with the differences actually observed between the mental operations of the two sexes—if men on the average should have the advantage in the size of the brain, and women in activity of cerebral circulation. The results which conjecture, founded on analogy, would lead us to expect from this difference of organization, would correspond to some of those which we most commonly see. In the first place, the mental operations of men might be expected to be slower. They would neither be so prompt as women in thinking, nor so quick to feel. Large bodies take more time to get into full action. On the other hand, when once got thoroughly into play, men's brains would bear more work. It would be more persistent in the line first taken; it would have more difficulty in changing from one mode of action to another, but, in the one thing it was doing, it could go on longer without loss of power or sense of fatigue. And do we not find that the things in which men most excel women are those which require most plodding and long hammering at a single thought, while women do best what must be done rapidly? A woman's brain is sooner fatigued, sooner exhausted; but given the degree of exhaustion, we should expect to find that it would recover itself sooner. I repeat that this speculation is entirely hypothetical. . . .

Let us take, then, the only marked case which observation affords, of apparent inferiority of women to men, if we except the merely physical one of bodily strength. No production in philosophy, science, or art, entitled to the first rank, has been the work of a woman. Is there any mode of accounting for this, without supposing that women are naturally incapable of producing them?

In the first place, we may fairly question whether experience has afforded sufficient grounds for an induction. It is scarcely three generations since women, saving very rare exceptions, have begun to try their capacity in philosophy, science, or art. It is only in the present generation that their attempts have been at all numerous; and they are even now extremely few, everywhere but in England and France. It is a relevant question, whether a mind possessing the requisites of first-rate eminence in speculation or creative art could have been expected, on the mere calculation of chances, to turn up during that lapse of time, among the women whose tastes and personal position admitted of their devoting themselves to these pursuits. . . .

Chapter 4.   There remains a question, not of less importance than those already discussed, and which will be asked the most importunately by those opponents whose conviction is somewhat shaken on the main point. What good are we to expect from the changes proposed in our customs and institutions? Would mankind be at all better off if women were free? If not, why disturb their minds, and attempt to make a social revolution in the name of an abstract right? . . .

To which let me first answer, [there is] the advantage of having the most universal and pervading of all human relations regulated by justice instead of injustice. The vast amount of this gain to human nature, it is hardly possible, by any explanation or illustration, to place in a stronger light than it is placed by the bare statement, to any one who attaches a moral meaning to words. All the selfish propensities, the self-worship, the unjust self-preference, which exist among mankind, have their source and root in, and derive their principal nourishment from, the present constitution of the relation between men and women. Think what it is to a boy, to grow up to manhood in the belief that without any merit or any exertion of his own, though he may be the most frivolous and empty or the most ignorant and stolid of mankind, by the mere fact of being born a male he is by right the superior of all and every one of an entire half of the human race. . . . What must be the effect on his character, of this lesson? And men of the cultivated classes are often not aware how deeply it

sinks into the immense majority of male minds. For, among right-feeling and well-bred people, the inequality is kept as much as possible out of sight; above all, out of sight of the children. As much obedience is required from boys to their mother as to their father: they are not permitted to domineer over their sisters, nor are they accustomed to see these postponed to them, but the contrary; the compensations of the chivalrous feeling being made prominent, while the servitude which requires them is kept in the background. . . .

The second benefit to be expected from giving to women the free use of their faculties, by leaving them the free choice of their employments, and opening to them the same field of occupation and the same prizes and encouragements as to other human beings, would be that of doubling the mass of mental faculties available for the higher service of humanity. . . . This great accession to the intellectual power of the species, and to the amount of intellect available for the good management of its affairs, would be obtained, partly, through the better and more complete intellectual education of women. . . .

The opinion of women would then possess a more beneficial, rather than a greater, influence upon the general mass of human belief and sentiment. I say a more beneficial, rather than a greater influence; for the influence of women over the general tone of opinion has always, or at least from the earliest known period, been very considerable. . . .

. . . The wife's influence tends, as far as it goes, to prevent the husband from falling below the common standard of approbation of the country. It tends quite as strongly to hinder him from rising above it. The wife is the auxiliary of the common public opinion. A man who is married to a woman his inferior in intelligence, finds her a perpetual dead weight, or, worse than a dead weight, a drag, upon every aspiration of his to be better than public opinion requires him to be. It is hardly possible for one who is in these bonds, to attain exalted virtue. . . .

Though it may stimulate the amatory propensities of men, it does not conduce to married happiness, to exaggerate by differences of education whatever may be the native differences of the sexes. If the married pair are well-bred and well-behaved people, they tolerate each other's tastes; but is mutual toleration what people look forward to, when they enter into marriage? . . .

What marriage may be in the case of two persons of cultivated faculties, identical in opinions and purposes, between whom there exists that best kind of equality, similarity of powers and capacities with reciprocal superiority in them—so that each can enjoy the luxury of looking up to the other, and can have alternately the pleasure of leading and of being led in the path of development—I will not attempt to describe. To those who can conceive it, there is no need; to those who cannot, it would appear the dream of an enthusiast.

But I maintain, with the profoundest conviction, that this, and this only, is the ideal of marriage; and that all opinions, customs, and institutions which favour any other notion of it, or turn the conceptions and aspirations connected with it into any other direction, by whatever pretences they may be coloured, are relics of primitive barbarism. The moral regeneration of mankind will only really commence, when the most fundamental of the social relations is placed under the rule of equal justice, and when human beings learn to cultivate their strongest sympathy with an equal in rights and in cultivation.

REVIEW AND DISCUSSION QUESTIONS

1. Describe the situation of English women at the time Mill and Taylor were writing.
2. To what do the authors attribute the situation of women?
3. How do Mill and Taylor answer the claim that women are naturally inferior? That they willingly accept their status?
4. Describe the reasons the authors give for concluding that the current situation is intolerable.
5. What do Mill and Taylor see as the ideal marriage? Do you agree? Explain.
6. How does Mill's discussion of happiness and the good life, described in *Utilitarianism* and *On Liberty*, inform this essay on women and their plight?
7. Describe the connections you see between this essay and the limits on government that Mill defends in *On Liberty*. Are women who are raised in the environment he has described likely to be able to make truly "autonomous" choices?

Sexual Harassment:

Ellison v. *Brady*

The U.S. Senate Judiciary Committee hearings involving Anita Hill and Clarence Thomas brought the problem of sexual harassment before the public in a way that had never been done before, convincing many that such harassment is a serious problem. Yet until recently it was ignored by society

924 F.2d. 872 (1991).

and law alike. Legally, the debate has revolved around whether sexual harassment is a form of sex discrimination, which is prohibited under Title VII of the 1964 Civil Rights Act. That act makes it illegal for an employer to "discriminate" against any individual in "compensation, terms, conditions of privileges of employment" based on "race, color, religion, sex, or national origin." In *Meritor Savings Bank* v. *Vinson* (1986), the Supreme Court held that sexual harassment of a female employee constitutes "discrimination" based on "sex" within the meaning of that statute. The Court stated in *Meritor* that women could demand compensation for psychological as well as purely economic consequences of a "hostile workplace environment." Such harassment can include "unwelcome sexual advances, requests for sexual favors, and other verbal or physical conduct of a sexual nature."

Having established in *Meritor* that sexual harassment is a form of sex discrimination, the courts then faced a variety of questions. What, precisely, are the bounds of sexual conduct in the workplace? From whose perspective should questions concerning the hostility of a work environment be judged: the average person, the man, or the woman? *Ellison v. Brady* addresses these further questions about sexual harassment.

Beezer, Circuit Judge: Kerry Ellison worked as a revenue agent for the Internal Revenue Service in San Mateo, California. During her initial training in 1984 she met Sterling Gray, another trainee, who was also assigned to the San Mateo office. The two co-workers never became friends, and they did not work closely together.

Gray's desk was twenty feet from Ellison's desk, two rows behind and one row over. Revenue agents in the San Mateo office often went to lunch in groups. In June of 1986 when no one else was in the office, Gray asked Ellison to lunch. She accepted. Gray had to pick up his son's forgotten lunch, so they stopped by Gray's house. He gave Ellison a tour of his house.

Ellison alleges that after the June lunch Gray started to pester her with unnecessary questions and hang around her desk. On October 9, 1986, Gray asked Ellison out for a drink after work. She declined, but she suggested that they have lunch the following week. She did not want to have lunch alone with him, and she tried to stay away from the office during lunch time. One day during the following week, Gray uncharacteristically dressed in a three-piece suit and asked Ellison out for lunch. Again, she did not accept.

On October 22, 1986 Gray handed Ellison a note he wrote on a telephone message slip which read:

I cried over you last night and I'm totally drained today. I have never been in such constant term oil (sic). Thank you for talking with me. I could not stand to feel your hatred for another day.

When Ellison realized that Gray wrote the note, she became shocked and frightened and left the room. Gray followed her into the hallway and demanded that she talk to him, but she left the building.

Ellison later showed the note to Bonnie Miller, who supervised both Ellison and Gray. Miller said "this is sexual harassment." Ellison asked Miller not to do anything about it. She wanted to try to handle it herself. Ellison asked a male co-worker to talk to Gray, to tell him that she was not interested in him and to leave her alone. The next day, Thursday, Gray called in sick.

Ellison did not work on Friday, and on the following Monday, she started four weeks of training in St. Louis, Missouri. Gray mailed her a card and a typed, single-spaced, three-page letter. She describes this letter as "twenty times, a hundred times weirder" than the prior note. Gray wrote, in part:

I know that you are worth knowing with or without sex. . . . Leaving aside the hassles and disasters of recent weeks. I have enjoyed you so much over these past few months. Watching you. Experiencing you from O so far away. Admiring your style and elan. . . . Don't you think it odd that two people who have never even talked together, alone, are striking off such intense sparks. . . . I will [write] another letter in the near future.[1]

Explaining her reaction, Ellison stated: "I just thought he was crazy. I thought he was nuts. I didn't know what he would do next. I was frightened."

She immediately telephoned Miller. Ellison told her supervisor that she was frightened and really upset. She requested that Miller transfer either her or Gray because she would not be comfortable working in the same office with him. . . .

Gray subsequently transferred to the San Francisco office. . . . After three weeks in San Francisco, Gray filed union grievances requesting a return to the San Mateo office. The IRS and the union settled the grievances in Gray's favor, agreeing to allow him to transfer back to the San Mateo office provided that he spend four more months in San Francisco and promise not to bother Ellison. On January 28, 1987, Ellison first learned of Gray's request in a letter from Miller. . . . After receiving the letter, Ellison was "frantic." She filed a formal complaint alleging sexual harassment on January 30, 1987 with the IRS. She also obtained permission to transfer to San Francisco temporarily when Gray returned.

Gray sought joint counseling. He wrote Ellison another letter which still sought to maintain the idea that he and Ellison had some type of relationship.

The IRS employee investigating the allegation agreed with Ellison's supervisor that Gray's conduct constituted sexual harassment. In its final decision, however, the Treasury Department rejected Ellison's complaint because it believed that the complaint did not describe a pattern or practice of sexual harassment covered by the EEOC regulations. After an appeal, the EEOC . . . concluded that the agency took adequate action to prevent the repetition of Gray's conduct.

Ellison filed a complaint in September of 1987 in federal district court. The court granted the government's motion for summary judgment on the ground that Ellison had failed to state a prima facie case of sexual harassment due to a hostile working environment. Ellison appeals. . . .

The government asks us to apply the reasoning of other courts which have declined to find Title VII violations on more egregious facts. In *Scott* v. *Sears, Roebuck & Co.* (7th Cir. 1986), the Seventh Circuit analyzed a female employee's working conditions for sexual harassment. It noted that she was repeatedly propositioned and winked at by her supervisor. When she asked for assistance, he asked "what will I get for it?" Co-workers slapped

her buttocks and commented that she must moan and groan during sex. The court examined the evidence to see if "the demeaning conduct and sexual stereotyping cause[d] such anxiety and debilitation to the plaintiff that working conditions were 'poisoned' within the meaning of Title VII." The court did not consider the environment sufficiently hostile.

Similarly, in *Rabidue* v. *Osceola Refining Co.* (6th Cir. 1986), the Sixth Circuit refused to find a hostile environment where the workplace contained posters of naked and partially dressed women, and where a male employee customarily called women "whores," "cunt," "pussy," and "tits," referred to plaintiff as "fat ass," and specifically stated, "All that bitch needs is a good lay." Over a strong dissent, the majority held that the sexist remarks and the pin-up posters had only a de minimis effect and did not seriously affect the plaintiff's psychological well-being.

We do not agree with the standards set forth in *Scott* and *Rabidue*, and we choose not to follow those decisions. Neither *Scott*'s search for "anxiety and debilitation" sufficient to "poison" a working environment nor *Rabidue*'s requirement that a plaintiff's psychological well-being be "seriously affected" follows directly from language in *Meritor*. It is the harasser's conduct which must be pervasive or severe, not the alteration in the conditions of employment. Surely, employees need not endure sexual harassment until their psychological well-being is seriously affected to the extent that they suffer anxiety and debilitation. Although an isolated epithet by itself fails to support a cause of action for a hostile environment, Title VII's protection of employees from sex discrimination comes into play long before the point where victims of sexual harassment require psychiatric assistance.

We have closely examined *Meritor* and our previous cases, and we believe that Gray's conduct was sufficiently severe and pervasive to alter the conditions of Ellison's employment and create an abusive working environment. We first note that the required showing of severity or seriousness of the harassing conduct varies inversely with the pervasiveness or frequency of the conduct. . . .

Next, we believe that in evaluating the severity and pervasiveness of sexual harassment, we should focus on the perspective of the victim. If we only examined whether a reasonable person would engage in allegedly harassing conduct, we would run the risk of reinforcing the prevailing level of discrimination. Harassers could continue to harass merely because a particular discriminatory practice was common, and victims of harassment would have no remedy.

We therefore prefer to analyze harassment from the victim's perspective. A complete understanding of the victim's view requires, among other things, an analysis of the different perspectives of men and women. Conduct that many men consider unobjectionable may offend many women.

We realize that there is a broad range of viewpoints among women as a group, but we believe that many women share common concerns which men do not necessarily share. For example, because women are disproportionately victims of rape and sexual assault, women have a stronger incentive to be concerned with sexual behavior. Women who are victims of mild forms of sexual harassment may understandably worry whether a harasser's conduct is merely a prelude to violent sexual assault. Men, who are rarely victims of sexual assault, may view sexual conduct in a vacuum without a full appreciation of the social setting or the underlying threat of violence that a woman may perceive.

In order to shield employers from having to accommodate the idiosyncratic concerns of the rare hyper-sensitive employee, we hold that a female plaintiff states a prima facie case of hostile environment sexual harassment when she alleges conduct which a reasonable woman[2] would consider sufficiently severe or pervasive to alter the conditions of employment and create an abusive working environment.[3]

We adopt the perspective of a reasonable woman primarily because we believe that a sex-blind reasonable person standard tends to be male-biased and tends to systematically ignore the experiences of women. The reasonable woman standard does not establish a higher level of protection for women than men. Instead, a gender-conscious examination of sexual harassment enables women to participate in the workplace on an equal footing with men. By acknowledging and not trivializing the effects of sexual harassment on

reasonable women, courts can work towards ensuring that neither men nor women will have to "run a gauntlet of sexual abuse in return for the privilege of being allowed to work and make a living." *Henson* v. *Dundee* (11th Cir. 1982).

We note that the reasonable victim standard we adopt today classifies conduct as unlawful sexual harassment even when harassers do not realize that their conduct creates a hostile working environment. Well-intentioned compliments by co-workers or supervisors can form the basis of a sexual harassment cause of action if a reasonable victim of the same sex as the plaintiff would consider the comments sufficiently severe or pervasive to alter a condition of employment and create an abusive working environment.[4] That is because Title VII is not a fault-based tort scheme. . . .

The facts of this case illustrate the importance of considering the victim's perspective. Analyzing the facts from the alleged harasser's viewpoint, Gray could be portrayed as a modern-day Cyrano de Bergerac wishing no more than to woo Ellison with his words. There is no evidence that Gray harbored ill will toward Ellison. He even offered in his "love letter" to leave her alone if she wished. Examined in this light, it is not difficult to see why the district court characterized Gray's conduct as isolated and trivial.

Ellison, however, did not consider the acts to be trivial. Gray's first note shocked and frightened her. After receiving the three-page letter, she became really upset and frightened again. She immediately requested that she or Gray be transferred. Her supervisor's prompt response suggests that she too did not consider the conduct trivial. When Ellison learned that Gray arranged to return to San Mateo, she immediately asked to transfer, and she immediately filed an official complaint.

We cannot say as a matter of law that Ellison's reaction was idiosyncratic or hyper-sensitive. We believe that a reasonable woman could have had a similar reaction. After receiving the first bizarre note from Gray, a person she barely knew, Ellison asked a co-worker to tell Gray to leave her alone. Despite her request, Gray sent her a long, passionate, disturbing letter. He told her he had been "watching" and "experiencing" her; he made repeated references to sex; he said he would write again. Ellison had no way of knowing what Gray would do next. A reasonable woman could consider Gray's conduct, as alleged by Ellison, sufficiently severe and pervasive to alter a condition of employment and create an abusive working environment. . . .

We hope that over time both men and women will learn what conduct offends reasonable members of the other sex. When employers and employees internalize the standard of workplace conduct we establish today, the current gap in perception between the sexes will be bridged. . . .

Stephens, District Judge, Dissenting: . . . Nowhere in section 2000e of Title VII, the section under which the plaintiff in this case brought suit, is there any indication that Congress intended to provide for any other than equal treatment in the area of civil rights. The legislation is designed to achieve a balanced and generally gender neutral and harmonious workplace which would improve production and the quality of the employees' lives. In fact, the Supreme Court has shown a preference against systems that are not gender or race neutral, such as hiring quotas. . . . While women may be the most frequent targets of this type of conduct that is at issue in this case, they are not the only targets. I believe that it is incumbent upon the court in this case to use terminol-

ogy that will meet the needs of all who seek recourse under this section of Title VII. Possible alternatives that are more in line with a gender neutral approach include "victim," "target," or "person."

The term "reasonable man" as it is used in the law of torts, traditionally refers to the average adult person, regardless of gender, and the conduct that can reasonably be expected of him or her. For the purposes of the legal issues that are being addressed, such a term assumes that it is applicable to all persons. . . . It is clear that the authors of the majority opinion intend a difference between the "reasonable woman" and the "reasonable man" in Title VII cases on the assumption that men do not have the same sensibilities as women. This is not necessarily true. A man's response to circumstances faced by women and their effect upon women can be and in given circumstances may be expected to be understood by men. . . .

The creation of the proposed "new standard" which applies only to women will not necessarily come to the aid of all potential victims of the type of misconduct that is at issue in this case. I believe that a gender neutral standard would greatly contribute to the clarity of this and future cases in the same area. . . .

NOTES

1. In the middle of the long letter, Gray did say "I am obligated to you so much that if you want me to leave you alone I will. . . . If you want me to forget you entirely, I can not do that."

2. Of course, where male employees allege that co-workers engage in conduct which creates a hostile environment, the appropriate victim's perspective would be that of a reasonable man.

3. We realize that the reasonable woman standard will not address conduct which some women find offensive. Conduct considered harmless by many today may be considered discriminatory in the future. Fortunately, the reasonableness inquiry which we adopt today is not static. As the views of reasonable women change, so too does the Title VII standard of acceptable behavior.

4. If sexual comments or sexual advances are in fact welcomed by the recipient, they, of course, do not constitute sexual harassment. Title VII's prohibition of sex discrimination in employment does not require a totally desexualized work place.

REVIEW AND DISCUSSION QUESTIONS

1. Describe the events leading to Ms. Ellison's claim that she was sexually harassed. Was her work environment "hostile"?
2. On what basis does the court reject the *Scott* and *Rabidue* decisions?
3. What is the "reasonable woman" standard? Why does the Court adopt it?
4. Explain the reason Judge Stephens dissents.
5. "This decision is unfair to men." Do you agree or disagree? Explain.
6. How do you think Mill and Taylor would respond to this case?

Sexual Equality and Discrimination: Difference vs. Dominance

Will Kymlicka

According to Will Kymlicka, sex discrimination is commonly interpreted as the arbitrary or irrational use of gender in the awarding of benefits or positions. That is, sex discrimination is unequal treatment that cannot be justified by reference to some sexual difference. This "difference approach" to discrimination perceives sexual equality in terms of the ability of women to compete under gender-neutral rules for various roles and positions. The problem, Kymlicka argues, is that these roles and positions may be defined in such a way as to make men more suited to them, even under gender-neutral competition. Will Kymlicka is a policy analyst with the Canadian Royal Commission on New Productive Technologies. He has taught philosophy at the University of Toronto, Princeton University, and Queen's University in Kingston, Ontario.

Until well into this century, most male theorists on all points of the political spectrum accepted the belief that there was a 'foundation in nature' for the confinement of women to the family, and for the 'legal and customary subjection of women to their husbands' within the family (Okin 1979: 200).[1] Restrictions on women's civil and political rights were said to be justified by the fact that women are, by nature, unsuited for political and economic activities outside the home. Contemporary theorists have progressively abandoned this assumption of women's natural inferiority. They have accepted that women, like men, should be viewed as 'free and equal beings', capable of self-determination and a sense of justice, and hence free to enter the public realm. And liberal democracies have progressively adopted anti-discrimination statutes intended to ensure that women have equal access to education, employment, political office, etc.

But these anti-discrimination statutes have not brought about sexual equality. In the United States and Canada, the extent of job segregation in the lowest-paying occupations is increasing. Indeed, if present trends continue, all of the people below the poverty line in America in the year 2000 will be women or children (Wietzman 1985: 350). Moreover, domestic violence and sexual assault are increasing, as are other forms of violence and degradation aimed at women. Catharine MacKinnon summarizes her survey of the effects of equal rights in the United States by saying that 'sex equality law has been utterly ineffective at getting women what we need and are socially prevented from having on the basis of a condition of birth: a chance at productive lives of reasonable physical security, self-expression, individuation, and minimal respect and dignity' (MacKinnon, 1987:32).

Why is this? Sex discrimination, as commonly interpreted, involves the arbitrary or irrational use of gender in the awarding of benefits or positions. On this view, the most blatant forms of sex discrimination are those where, for example, someone refuses to hire a woman for a job even though gender has no rational relationship to the task being performed. MacKinnon calls this the 'difference approach' to sexual discrimination, for it views as discriminatory unequal treatment that cannot be justified by reference to some sexual difference.

Sex discrimination law of this sort was modelled on race discrimination law. And just as race equality legislation aims at a 'colour-blind' society, so sex equality law aims at a sex-blind society. A society would be non-discriminatory if race or gender never entered into the awarding of benefits. Of course, while it is conceivable that political and economic decisions could entirely disregard race, it is difficult to see how a society could be entirely sex-blind. A society which provides for pregnancy benefits, or for sexually segregated sports, taking sex into account, but this does not seem unjust. And while racially segregated washrooms are clearly discriminatory, most people do not feel that way about sex-segregated washrooms. So the 'difference approach' accepts that there are legitimate instances of differential treatment of the sexes. These are not discriminatory, however, so long as there is a genuine sexual difference which explains and justifies the differential treatment. Opponents of equal rights for women often invoked the spectre of sexually integrated sports (or washrooms) as

evidence that sex equality is misguided. But defenders of the difference approach respond that the cases of legitimate differentiation are sufficiently rare, and the cases of arbitrary differentiation so common, that the burden of proof rests on those who claim that sex is a relevant ground for assigning benefits or positions.

This difference approach, as the standard interpretation of sex equality law in most Western countries, has had some successes. Its 'moral thrust' is to 'grant women access to what men have access to', and it has indeed 'gotten women some access to employment and education, the public pursuits, including academic, professional, and blue-collar work, the military, and more than nominal access to athletics' (MacKinnon 1987: 33, 35). The difference approach has helped create gender-neutral access to, or competition for, existing social benefits and positions.

But its successes are limited, for it ignores the gender inequalities which are built into the very definition of these positions. The difference approach sees sex equality in terms of the ability of women to compete under gender-neutral rules for the roles that men have defined. But equality cannot be achieved by allowing men to build social institutions according to their interests, and then ignoring the gender of the candidates when deciding who fills the roles in these institutions. The problem is that the roles may be defined in such a way as to make men more suited to them, even under gender-neural competition.

Consider that fact that most jobs 'require that the person, gender neutral, who is qualified for them will be someone who is not the primary caretaker of a preschool child' (MacKinnon 1987: 37). Given that women are still expected to take care of children in our society, men will tend to do better than women in competing for such jobs. This is not because women applicants are discriminated against. Employers may pay no attention to the gender of the applicants, or may in fact wish to hire more women. The problem is that many women lack a relevant qualification for the job—i.e. being free from child-care responsibilities. There is gender-neutrality, in that employers do not attend to the gender of applicants, but there is no sexual equality, for the job was defined under the assumption that it would be filled by men who had wives at home taking care of the children. The difference approach insists that gender should not be taken into account in deciding who should have a job, but it ignores the fact 'that day one of taking gender into account was the day the job was structured with the expectation that its occupant would have no child care responsibilities' (MacKinnon 1987:37).

Whether or not gender-neutrality yields sexual equality depends on whether and how gender was taken into account earlier. As Janet Radcliffe Richards says,

If a group is kept out of something for long enough, it is overwhelmingly likely that activities of that sort will develop in a way unsuited to the excluded group. We know for certain that women have been kept out of many kinds of work, and this means that the work is quite likely to be unsuited to them. The most obvious example of this is the incompatibility of most work with the bearing and raising of children; I am firmly convinced that if women had been fully involved in the running of society from the start they would have found a way of arranging work and children to fit each other. Men have had no such motivation, and we can see the results. (Radcliffe Richards 1980: 113–14)

This incompatibility that men have created between child-rearing and paid labour has profoundly unequal results for women. The result is not only that the most valued positions in society are filled by men, while women are disproportionately concentrated into lower-paying part-time work, but also that many women become economically dependent on men. Where most of the 'household income' comes from the man's paid work, the woman who does the unpaid domestic work is rendered dependent on him for access to resources. The consequences of this dependence have become more apparent with the rising divorce rate. While married couples may share the same standard of living during marriage, regardless of who earns the income, the effects of divorce are catastrophically unequal. In California, men's average standard of living goes up 42 per cent after divorce, women's goes down 73 per cent, and similar results have been found in other states (Okin 1989b: 161). However, none of these unequal consequences of the incompatibility of child care and paid work are discriminatory, according to the difference approach, for they do not involve arbitrary discrimination. The fact is that freedom from child-care responsibilities is relevant to most existing jobs, and employers are not being arbitrary in insisting on it. Because it is a relevant qualification, the difference approach says that it is not discriminatory to insist upon it, regardless of the disadvantages it creates for women. Indeed, the difference approach sees the concern with child-care responsibilities, rather than irrelevant criteria like gender, as evidence that sex discrimination has been eliminated. It cannot see that the relevance of child-care responsibilities is itself a profound source of sexual inequality, one that has arisen from the way men have historically structured the economy to suit their interests.

So before we decide whether gender should be taken into account, we need to know how it has already been taken into account. And the fact is that almost all important roles and positions have been structured in gender-biased ways:

virtually every quality that distinguishes men from women is already affirmatively compensated in this society. Men's physiology defines most sports, their needs define auto and health insurance coverage, their socially-designed biographies define workplace expectations and successful career patterns, their perspectives and concerns define quality in scholarship, their experiences and obsessions define merit, their objectification of life defines art, their military service defines citizenship, their presence defines family, their inability to get along with each other—their wars and rulerships—defines history, their image defines god, and their genitals define sex. For each of their differences from women, what amounts to an affirmative action plan is in effect, otherwise known as the structure and values of American society. (MacKinnon 1987: 36)

All of this is 'gender-neutral', in the sense that women are not arbitrarily excluded from pursuing the things society defines as valuable. But it is sexist, because the things being pursued in a gender-neutral way are based on men's interests and values. Women are disadvantaged, not because chauvinists arbitrarily favour men in the awarding of jobs, but because the entire society systematically favours men in the defining of jobs, merits, etc.

Indeed, the more society defines positions in a gendered way, the less the difference approach is able to detect an inequality. Consider a society which restricts access to contraception and abortion, which defines paying jobs in such a way as to make them incompatible with child-bearing and child-rearing, and which does not provide economic compensation for domestic labour. Every woman who faces an unplanned pregnancy, and who cannot both raise children and work for wages, is rendered economically dependent on someone who is a stable income-earner (i.e. a man). In order to ensure that she acquires this support, she must become sexually attractive to men. Knowing that this is their likely fate, many girls do not try as hard as boys to acquire employment skills which can only be exercised by those who avoid pregnancy. Where boys pursue personal security by increasing their employment skills, girls pursue security by increasing their attractiveness to men. This, in turn, results in a system of cultural identifications in which masculinity is associated with income-earning, and femininity is defined in terms of sexual and domestic service for men, and the nurturing of children. So men and women enter marriage with different income-earning potential, and this disparity widens during marriage, as the man acquires valuable job experience. Since the woman faces greater difficulty supporting herself outside of the marriage, she is more dependent on maintaining the marriage, which allows the man to exercise greater control within it.

In such a society, men as a group exercise control over women's general life-chances (through political decisions about abortion, and economic decisions concerning job requirements), and individual men exercise control over economically vulnerable women within marriages. Yet there need be no arbitrary discrimination. All of this is gender-neutral, in that one's gender does not necessarily affect how one is treated by those in charge of distributing contraception, jobs, or domestic pay. By whereas the difference approach takes the absence of arbitrary discrimination as evidence of the absence of sexual inequality, it may in fact be evidence of its pervasiveness. It is precisely because women are dominated in this society that there is no need for them to be discriminated against. Arbitrary discrimination in employment is not only unnecessary for the maintenance of male privilege, it is unlikely to occur, for most women will never be in a position to be arbitrarily discriminated against in employment. Perhaps the occasional woman can overcome the social pressures supporting traditional sex-roles. But the greater the domination, the less the likelihood that any women will be in a position to compete for employment, and hence the less room for arbitrary discrimination. The more sexual inequality there is in society, the more that social institutions reflect male interests, the less arbitrary discrimination there will be.

None of the contemporary Western democracies correspond exactly to his model of a patriarchal society, but they all share some of its essential features. And if we are to confront these forms of injustice, we need to reconceptualize sexual inequality as a problem, not of arbitrary discrimination, but of domination. As MacKinnon puts it,

> to require that one be the same as those who set the standard—those which one is already socially defined as different from—simply means that sex equality is conceptually designed never to be achieved. Those who most need equal treatment will be the least similar, socially, to those whose situation sets the standard as against which one's entitlement to be equally treated is measured. Doctrinally speaking, the deepest problems of sex inequality will not find women 'similarly situated' to men. Far less will practices of sex inequality require that acts be intentionally discriminatory. (MacKinnon 1987:44; cf. Taub and Schneider 1982:134)

The subordination of women is not fundamentally a matter of irrational differentiation on the basis of sex, but of male supremacy, under which gender differences are made relevant to the distribution of benefits, to the systematic disadvantage of women (MacKinnon 1987:42; Frye 1983:38).

Since the problem is domination, the solution is not only the absence of discrimination, but the presence of power. Equality requires not only equal opportunity to pursue male-defined roles, but also equal power to create female-defined roles, or to create androgynous roles men and women have an equal interest in filling. The result of such empowerment could be very different from our society, or from the equal-opportunity-to-enter-male-institutions that is favoured by contemporary sex-discrimination theory. From a position of equal power, we would not have created a system of social roles that defines 'male' jobs as superior to 'female' jobs. For example, the roles of male and female health practitioners were redefined by men against the will of women in the field. With the professionalization of medicine, women were squeezed out of their traditional health care roles as midwives and healers, and relegated to the role of nurse—a position which is subservient to, and financially less rewarding than, the role of doctor. That redefinition would not have happened had women been in a position of equality, and will have to be rethought now if women are to achieve equality.

NOTE

1. In accepting this prevailing view that there is 'a Foundation in Nature' for the rule of the husband 'as the abler and the stronger' (Locke, in Okin 1979:200), classical liberals created a serious contradiction for themselves. For they also argued that all humans are by nature equal, that nature provides no grounds for an inequality of rights. This, we have seen, was the point of their state-of-nature theories. . . . Why should the supposed fact that men are 'abler and stronger' justify unequal rights for women when, as Locke himself says, 'differences in excellence of parts or ability' do not justify unequal rights? One cannot both maintain equality amongst men as a class, on the grounds that differences in ability do not justify different rights, and also exclude women as a class, on the grounds that they are less able. If women are excluded on the grounds that the average woman is less able than the average man, then all men who are less able than the average man must also be excluded. As Okin puts it, 'If the basis of his individualism was to be firm, he needed to argue that individual women were equal with individual men, just as weaker men were with stronger ones' (Okin 1979:199).

REFERENCES

Eisenstein, Z. (1981). *The Radical Future of Liberal Feminism.* Longman, New York.

Frye, M. (1983). *The Politics of Reality: Essays in Feminist Theory.* Crossing Press, Trumansburg.

Gross, E. (1986). "What Is Feminist Theory?," in C. Pateman and E. Gross (eds.), *Feminist Challenges, Social and Political Theory.* Northeastern University Press, Boston MA.

MacKinnon, C. (1987). *Feminism Unmodified: Discourses on Life and Law.* Harvard University Press, Cambridge MA.

Okin, S. (1979). *Women in Western Political Thought.* Princeton University Press, Princeton, NJ.

Radcliffe Richards, J. (1980). *The Skeptical Feminist: A Philosophical Enquiry.* Routledge and Kegan Paul, London.

Weitzman, L. (1985). *The Divorce Revolution.* The Free Press, New York.

REVIEW AND DISCUSSION QUESTIONS

1. Why does Kymlicka think anti-discrimination laws have not achieved sex equality?
2. What is the "difference" approach to sex equality? Give an example of this approach.
3. What is the "dominance" approach to sex equality? How does it differ from the "difference" approach?
4. What specific proposals would be necessary to achieve genuine sex equality?
5. How would Mill and Taylor respond to this essay?

Freedom, Conditioning, and the Real Woman

Janet Radcliffe Richards

In this selection from her book, *The Skeptical Feminist,* Janet Radcliffe Richards argues that we are free to the extent others' desires do not keep us from realizing our own, and that freedom is valuable as an end in itself. Some feminists, however, seem to doubt this. Contending that women have been conditioned by male society, they believe that a truly liberated woman is not one who is free to choose without restraints but, rather, a woman who makes certain choices. In response, Richards argues that the fact that women are as they are because of social influences does not show that their choices are not their own. She explores carefully the relation between freedom and conditioning and discusses the ways in which conditioning ought to be properly attacked. Janet Radcliffe Richards is lecturer in philosophy at the Open University in England.

A DEFENCE OF LIBERTY

Here, then, is [my account] of freedom as a possession: you are free to the extent that other people's desires do not come between you and your own. Another, apparently rival, account will appear later in the chapter, but for now we shall concentrate on this one. If this is freedom, what is its value?

One obvious and common defence of freedom is that it is a means to happiness. People who approve of freedom say that it leads to happiness because we are made unhappy if we know that other people control what we do, or because we know better than anyone else what we want and will be made happiest by being left to decide for ourselves, or because freedom leads to strength and self reliance which in turn lead to happiness. Other people are doubtful about these arguments, and say that, on the contrary, too much freedom makes people unhappy. People do not really know what is best for them, it is argued, so they may be happier if other people make the decisions. Midge Decter, for instance, in her arguments against Women's Liberation, says that what is making

women dissatisfied is not a lack of freedom but a surfeit of it.[1]

All these arguments are of course important, but here they are beside the point. Here the issue is not whether freedom is an effective means to some *other* end like happiness, but whether it is good *as an end in itself.* Can we argue that freedom is good irrespective of whether it leads to happiness or anything else we value? And if so, how valuable is it in comparison with these other things?

In some sense there can be very little argument on subjects like this one, because with questions of ultimate values there does not seem to be any common ground for discussion between people who disagree. If people really, in the last analysis, value different things, there is nothing more to be said. However it is possible to do something not unlike arguing. It does seem possible to make it clear by illustration that a great many people, whether they realize it or not, do in fact value freedom as an end in itself, and that many value it even more than happiness. . . .

Suppose, for instance, you were an outstandingly gifted but miserably neurotic artist or musi-

From Janet Radcliffe Richards, *The Skeptical Feminist* (Harmondsworth, England: Penguin, 1982). Reprinted by permission.

cian, and someone offered you a drug which would make you happy, but would result in your losing all your ability. There are already drugs along these lines, but we are to think of one so entirely effective that once having taken it the patient would not even regret having lost the desire or ability to compose or paint. Suppose also that you had complete faith in its efficacy, and in the intentions of the person who offered it. Would you take it? Some people would no doubt be very happy to, but there must be many who in such a situation would rather remain unhappy than achieve happiness at the cost of losing a skill they valued far more than any prospect of happiness.

Suppose, again, you lived in a country with a political regime you disliked intensely, with no way of escaping and not much hope of making things more to your liking. Suppose also that the government had a programme of 're-education' which you believed would be completely effective and which would make you entirely happy with the political situation afterwards. Would you be willing to undergo this programme? Many people would certainly not. They would rather remain unhappy than be so radically changed. Or suppose that you were very dissatisfied with your life as it was. Would you welcome the opportunity (to take a classic example) to become a satisfied pig? Again, probably not.

Of course these thought experiments are all rather artificial. They presuppose impossibilities, and anyway are not specific enough: whether we should be willing to become satisfied pigs would probably depend a good deal on the degree of our unhappiness as human beings. Nevertheless, the arguments are useful because they do suggest that to many people there are things which are more important than happiness.

So far, of course, this does not prove that anyone prefers *freedom* to happiness because the discussion has only been about which of two things we should take if we were in a position to choose, and as long as there is a question of choice some freedom is built into the example. All this shows is that there are occasions where people would choose to cling to what might be called their identities, rather than lose them for the sake of happiness. No doubt they would like happiness as well, but given the necessity of choice, happiness might

well be abandoned first. However, it is possible to look at the question of freedom by considering similar cases which involve other people.

Why is it, for instance, that so many people object to Soviet dissidents' being put in psychiatric hospitals? Of course there are several reasons. We may not think the 'treatment' will work, and we may not like the system the patients' minds are being changed to fit. However, even supposing we did approve of the political system, and supposing we did believe that after treatment the dissidents would fit happily into Russian society and regard their former activities and attitudes as absurd, would we then approve of the practice? Probably not. We might be happy for people to be offered such treatment if they wanted it, but still think that they should be allowed to choose for themselves whether they would rather be altered and made happy, or remain unhappy but still themselves. And if we think that it is more important to give people this choice than to force happiness on them, it means we are in favour of freedom, and regard it as more important than happiness.

There are many other examples of this sort of attitude. For instance, most of us would be shocked by this advertisement described by Sheila Rowbotham:[2] 'There was a picture of a young mother with a pram in front of a big block of flats and the heading "She can't change her environment but you can change her mood with Serenid-D".' There are all kinds of reasons for being upset about putting people on happiness drugs, including being afraid of side effects and long-term consequences. Nevertheless, part of the objection is to the idea of making women happy *without fulfilling their desires*. If we were concerned only with happiness for people we should not worry about putting them on effective happiness drugs. If happiness is all that matters there is nothing intrinsically wrong with brainwashing, or forcible medication, or giving people sedatives and tranquilizers instead of coping with their emotional problems. Most of us do care about allowing people to determine the course of their own lives, rather than having other people make them happy in ways they do not want. Since there can hardly be a feminist in existence who would regard it as an acceptable solution to women's problems that someone should invent some kind of medication or special process of re-education which would make women happy in their present lot, but had to be administered against their wills, we must think that most feminists value freedom more than happiness for women. The firm feminist rejection of male paternalism comes not only through the recognition that men's apparent concern for women's well-being is by some curious coincidence remarkably well adapted to the interests of men. Even if men's dominance were wholly good for women, we should still reject its being forced on them. As Kant said, paternalism is the worst despotism imaginable'. And as Mill said, 'the only purpose for which power can be rightfully exercised over any member of a civilized community, against his will, is to prevent harm to others. His own good, either physical or moral, is not a sufficient warrant.[3]

There is probably no way of arguing with any feminist who disagrees with all this, as doubtless some must. However, the principle of freedom will be taken as fundamental to feminism throughout this book, and where it produces statements with which feminists disagree, at least it will be obvious where the disagreement stems from. Freedom is being taken as a fundamental good in its own right, and a thing of which we should, therefore, all have as much as possible. How much each individual should have when the claims of other people are taken into consideration is a question of distributive justice. . . .

INNER FREEDOM

Two main propositions have been argued for in the previous two sections. One is that we are free to the extent that we can do as we like (which means that we are not properly described as free or not-free, only as more or less free). The other is that freedom, understood in this way, is good in itself. We should all have as much of it as possible, and if our freedom is to be curtailed it is to be for the sake only of other people, not ourselves.

However, we now have to look at the question of whether feminists do indeed think that freedom is a good thing, and want it for women. If freedom is the ability to fulfill one's desires, and if feminists do want it for women, they should surely be

trying to make the world as much as possible as women would like it to be. However, it is a most conspicuous fact about some feminists that they seem to include among their aims things which not only men find objectionable, but which women do too. There are all kinds of things which women seem to want and have no wish to change, and yet which many feminists apparently want to abolish. Traditional marriage and division of labour seem to be happily chosen by many women; many enjoy making themselves attractive to men, and giving men certain kinds of service in return for being protected by them. Many would rather look after a home and family than do anything else. And many, with the appearance of total freedom, choose to enter beauty competitions (which are watched as willingly by millions more women), or to become striptease artists, 'hostesses' of various sorts, and prostitutes.

Of course, you can argue here that some of these apparently free choices are not very free at all, because choosing the best of a bad lot does not give women what they really want. They probably not choose to become housewives or prostitutes if better things were readily available to them. There is much truth in that, no doubt, but it does not provide the slightest reason for taking away the best there is and leaving these women with something which must, in their eyes, be still worse. The true liberator can always be recognized by her wanting to increase the options open to the people who are to be liberated, and there is never any justification for taking a choice away from a group you want to liberate unless it is demonstrable beyond all reasonable doubt that removing it will bring other, more important, options into existence. To give women freedom we must give them more choice, and then if they really do not want the things they are choosing now, like homes and families, those things will just die out without our having to push them.

Of course there are many feminists who do want to increase the options open to women. Consider, for instance, the programme for the picketing of a Miss America Pageant, which stated 'There will be . . . Lobbying Visits to the contestants urging our sisters to reject the Pageant Farce and join us . . . we do not plan heavy disruptive tactics. . . .'[4] That was genuinely liberating. The women entering the competition might not have thought of other routes to success, or they might not have realized that there were groups of people where different things were valued. However that is, or at least seems (it is not always easy to know how literally things are to be taken) a very different matter from the demonstrations at the Miss World competition in London where feminist protestors would apparently have liked to disrupt the whole proceedings. To prevent women from doing what they have chosen to do is not to be concerned with their freedom. Nevertheless, that does seem to be the aim of some feminists.

But that is not the end of the matter. This kind of feminist need not accept yet the accusation that she is not really offering women freedom. In general, when the liberators of women or anyone else take the view that they know better than the beneficiaries of their efforts what should be done for them, they will argue that these people are *conditioned*, and therefore not in a state of mind to be able to choose freely no matter how many alternatives are open to them. *That* is why the liberators sometimes have to make choices on their behalf.

This kind of view certainly has intuitive plausibility about it. However, it does present many problems, and in particular the immediate one of seeming to call for (at least) a modification of the account of freedom so far given. It has been argued so far that an individual's freedom is a function mainly of how many choices there are available. If we are to accept, however, that it may sometimes be acceptable to restrict such choices in the name of freedom, on the grounds that the person to be liberated is conditioned and therefore unable to choose, a new element seems to have entered into the idea of liberty. It seems that to be free it is not enough to have a wide range of options open. As well as, or perhaps even instead of, having such options, the free individual must be in a certain state of mind. Freedom must be at least in part an internal thing.

There certainly is no doubt that some such view is widespread in feminism. Perhaps the most striking indication of it is the use of the word 'liberated' when applied to women. To the outsider as well as to the feminist a liberated woman is not one who is free to choose among a great many options, but one who makes *certain kinds of choices*;

she is not a woman with a tolerant and helpful husband who encourages her to achieve all her ambitions, but one who would not stand any nonsense from her husband if he tried any.

Now there is indeed a long philosophical tradition of saying that true freedom does not consist in being in an environment which permits you to do as you please, but consists (at least partly, depending on the theory) in being in a particular state of mind. Theories like these still do keep to the basic idea of freedom as the satisfaction of desire, but it is differently interpreted and analyzed. There are innumerable variants on the theme, but we need consider only two, and without too much detail.

The first and more extreme, is the idea that freedom is contained entirely within the mind of the free person, with outside circumstances irrelevant. According to this view you are truly free when your desires have been so adjusted that you desire nothing you cannot get. According to the Stoic idea, for instance, if the slave reaches total tranquility of mind while the master is in the grips of unrealized desire, the slave is the freer of the two. And in Christianity, the reason for saying that perfect freedom is to be found in the service of God is that once the Christian has achieved a state of mind in which nothing is desired but to do the will of God, that desire need never be unfulfilled: the will of God can be done in any circumstances whatever. This extreme idea of freedom is not much found in feminism, although there are traces of it. The woman who determines that she will no longer care about things which previously obsessed her, like the approval of men, may be looking for freedom in this way. If she ceases to care about what men think she can act to please herself rather than men, and so lessen the extent of her unfulfilled desire.

The second, more moderate, view of internal freedom is one more commonly found in feminism. This idea is that being in the right state of mind is not enough on its own to make you free: to be free you also need the kind of freedom we have been discussing . . . which involves being able to do as you like. However, that is not enough on its own, and a necessary condition of your choosing freely is that you should be in the right state of mind before deciding among the options which are open to you. There are all kinds of variants on his idea, but common to them all is something like the view that each individual has a *true self* which should be doing the choosing, but that its activities are obstructed by various contaminants which have got into the person in some way, and which prevent real choice as effectively as obstructions in the environment do. Plato, for instance, thought that there were parts of the soul, and that the lower parts were always trying to pull the highest part from its chosen path. A common idea in religion is that the uncontaminated soul would choose what was good, but that evil powers may take possession of it and force evil choices. More recently, there is the psychoanalytic idea that you cannot be truly free without getting rid of the neuroses which come between yourself and your real desires. Of course, an idea along these lines is very common in feminism. The domination of men has been so complete that the male has entered women's souls, making them choose on behalf of men and against their own interests. That they think themselves free is beside the point: all that shows is how well the work of conditioning has been done.

Now it is quite clear that however difficult all this may be to work out in detail, there is something in it. It is also true that (risky as it may sound) it is *sometimes* reasonable to override people's immediate wishes in the cause of their greater freedom, even when the earlier definition of freedom is taken and we say that people are free to the extent that they can do as they like. For instance, if a friend wanted to achieve something which was very important to her, and we knew beyond any doubt that she was setting about it the wrong way but could not persuade her to change, we might override her immediate wishes because we wanted her to get something which we knew she wanted more. Or again, since freedom is not simply a matter of how many immediate choices there are, but also of *scope* of choice, we might override some trivial choice to make sure that there was a greater range of choices later on. This is always being done in the case of children. Parents are not (necessarily) working against their children's freedom if, for instance, they do not let the children decide which schools they should go to. If a school is so much better than another that it will allow the children far more important choices later on in life, it is in the interests of the children's freedom that they should not be allowed to choose now.

Nevertheless, it is obvious that if we are going to take this sort of line, we have to take *great care*. If women's wishes are to be ignored in the name of their freedom, on the grounds that they are conditioned, it is essential to know exactly what is meant by conditioning, why it is supposed to impair freedom, to what extent it is legitimate to ignore what people want if they are conditioned, and how to distinguish women who are conditioned from the ones who are not. If we do not take care, we run the risk of planning a scheme in which the only freedom women get is the freedom to do what their liberators want them to do.

That is a tempting line anyway. As an early feminist Margaret Rhondda said, 'the passion to decide to look after your fellowmen, to do good to them in your way, is far more common than the desire to put into everyone's hand the power to look after themselves.[5] The danger becomes intensified a thousand times when you can do this but still be able to convince yourself that you are offering freedom because the whole issue has been obscured under more or less indiscriminate accusations of conditioning. If the idea of conditioning is to be used to enhance freedom, and not as a general device by which a liberation movement can do as it likes in the name of freedom, it must be pinned down more precisely.

CONDITIONING AND THE REAL WOMAN

There is one point which must be made quite clear before going any further. The conditioning which was referred to in the previous section is supposed to be a sort of thing which is *actually a constraint* on a woman; something which comes between herself and her true desires. Now the word 'conditioning' is one which is extremely commonly used in feminism, in all kinds of circumstances, and what must on no account be presumed is that whenever the word is used the so-called conditioned desires, attitudes and responses are things which actually do prevent the real woman from fulfilling her real desires.

In feminist contexts the usual ground for making an accusation of conditioning is to point to the social root of the habit of mind in question (which is, of course, always one which is disapproved of). Women want to make themselves beautiful only because society has made them want to; they think that their mission in life is to be mothers because everyone has been drumming it into them since the age of two; they lack ambition because they have been brought up from birth to think that the female is the natural servant of the male and on no account to compete with him. This may all be true. However, to establish that a woman is conditioned in *that* sense of the word is nothing like enough to show that she is conditioned in the very different sense of having something in her personality which gets between herself and the fulfillment of her real desires, and therefore that these environmentally produced characteristics limit her freedom.

The reason why conditioning in the sense of 'coming from a (disapproved of) social influence' cannot be the same as conditioning in the sense of 'getting in the way of the true woman's desires' is obvious from the discussion of the nature of woman. . . . You cannot distinguish between the woman as she now is and what is supposed to be the 'true' woman by pointing to the way society has shaped her. It is absolutely inevitable that the adult woman should be as she is partly as a result of social influence, and it is a thing we cannot possibly object to unless we are to suggest that people should be sent to grow up among wolves (and anyway there are social pressures even among wolves). We cannot say of social pressures *in general* that they turn the woman into something which is not her true self; on the contrary, they cannot be anything other than a contribution to what she actually is.

Of course we may not *like* the way women are at present, and if we do not we can argue that their upbringing ought to be changed. Very obviously, for instance, feminists are bound to disapprove of any upbringing which is so much at odds with women's intrinsic natures that they are bound to be unhappy. They can also reasonably object to women's being brought up to depend on men in the achievement of what they want, because that is unreliable and their success in life should be

more firmly based. They can disapprove of women's being encouraged to see their main aim in life as relationships with men, and all their ambitions directed towards pleasing men in one way or another, because it is undignified and they want women to be dignified. They can say that women ought not to be brought up to confine their interests and activities to domestic matters and concentrate their energies on trivia, because they would prefer them to be well-educated, ambitious and serious-minded. Since there is no neutral way to bring children up (they must be surrounded by influences of one kind or another) we have a good deal of choice about how adults eventually turn out. We certainly could make women other than they are now, and it is not surprising that feminists would like to see a good many changes.

On the other hand, none of this provides any reason at all for saying that women as they are now, with the desires they have now, are not *free*. We may think it a good thing that women should be brought up to be happy, dignified, independent, serious and useful, but, once again, everything is what it is. Happiness is happiness, dignity is dignity, independence is independence: none of these things is freedom. Even though there may be some difficulty about finding a definitive account of freedom there are limits to what we can reasonably decide to adopt, and it really would be travesty of the language (as well as potentially treacherous) to say that people were not free just because we did not like the way they were, or that in making them into something we liked better we should be giving them freedom. We may argue with perfect justice that women are as they are because of social influences, but that is not enough to show that the choices they are making are not their own real choices. And if by 'conditioned' we want to mean 'not in a state to make free choices' we must mean something more than 'influenced by social pressures we disapprove of'.

Of course we can still, if we want to, say that 'conditioned' does just refer to socially induced characteristics in women, rather than aspects of a woman's character which somehow do get in the way of her real desires. However, this is dangerous. The word has now such deeply entrenched connotations of interference with freedom that if we take a definition which does not include those connotations we open the floodgates to mistakes and double dealing. I shall therefore take it that 'conditioning' is properly used only when it does refer to a real restriction on freedom. The problem is, now that we have decided that a woman brought up one way is no less her real self than a woman brought up any other way, to work out what form conditioning might take.

FREEDOM AND CONDITIONING

Since we are trying to distinguish the social pressures which condition a woman from the ones which simply form her character, one obvious starting point is the fact that from the point of view of each individual there is a great difference between different kinds of social pressure. Whereas some are congenial and easily conformed to, others are not: some social pressures push people towards doing things for which they have an intrinsic dislike.

Nevertheless, people often go along even with these, because doing so is less unpleasant than suffering the social consequences of resistance. So a woman who has no natural interest in beauty may make herself as beautiful as she can; or one who is not interested in children may do her best to absorb herself in the concerns of a family; or a woman by nature apt to explore jungles may become a secretary, because that is the feminine thing to do and that way she will get social approval. None of this shows conditioning. The environment is constricting, but nevertheless a woman who makes the best choice among the limited set available to her is behaving perfectly rationally and choosing in her own interest, and as long as she is doing that the only restrictions on her freedom are external, not internal.

However, what happens to these women who go along with uncongenial social pressures when liberators appear on the scene, and suggest to them that the world would be a better place if women did not spend so much time on their appearance, or that children are not necessarily the ideal object of every woman's devotion? Or what happens if they find themselves in a situation where the uncongenial social pressures are beginning to lessen, and following their natural inclinations would bring down less social censure?

If they thoroughly understand the situation in which they have grown up there may be no difficulty. They may instantly join in the campaign to change the things which are alien to their natures, or at least take advantage of any changes which come about. But this may well not happen. Usually when children are subjected to pressures in growing up they do not think separately about what they would like to do and what adult pressures and encouragements compel them to do; they just get into habits of doing what produces the least unacceptable consequences. The result is that when the situation changes, or when there is some prospect of its changing, they may not rush to embrace the new but cling to the habits they have grown up with. Probably they do not understand that their present preferences came about by the forcible suppression of their natural (that is, inherent) inclinations, but even if they do they may well have difficulty in ridding themselves of the habits they have gathered. These habits may then come between the adults and their real desires.

A simple analogy can be drawn from an entirely different context. When you learn to drive you rapidly pick up the skills of braking and steering, and your responses to various situations become so automatic that you can usually do the right thing without thinking. But you may well learn these habits without knowing much about how braking and steering work, and the result is that the first time you skid you react in the way you always have reacted when the car moves too fast in the wrong direction, by braking as hard as possible and hauling the steering wheel round. The consequences are exactly the opposite of what you want. In order to avoid the situation in future you have to do two things. The first is to understand the theory, so that you know under what conditions the usual methods will and will not work, and the second is to free yourself of your habitual actions.

As a motorist you have very definite desires (to move in particular directions), but you yourself may interfere with their fulfillment through ignorance, or bad habits, or both. Much the same may happen with women. Their failure to understand the situation they are in, and the persistence of deeply entrenched habits, may get in the way of what they want to do. And where this happens we can say that a woman's state of mind is obstructing her desires, *without having to resort to dubious theories about hidden desires in the core of her imaginary real self.*

Failure to understand the nature of the world and the structure of possibilities within it acts against women in all kinds of ways. For instance, many women (if not all) are by nature as inclined as men to seek fame and fortune, but the traditional restricted upbringing of a woman means that in most cases there is only a limited number of forms in which she is capable of casting this ambition: she may think as a matter of course that success for a woman must take the form of being pursued by men, envied by women and renowned for beauty. But if that is the only way in which she can imagine making an impact on the world she is likely to have condemned herself to failure before even setting out. Few women succeed in being renowned for beauty, and anyway beauty does not last. Or she may have more specific ambitions, and look for political power, but may automatically presume that political success for a woman must take the form of being the wife of a politician, and in that case her potential for success is restricted from the start by the casting of her ambitions in a form which sets a low upper limit on possible success. If women squeeze their desires into a conventionally feminine mould they are likely to be doomed to failure from the first. But even if they succeed in it, [they] may still fail because of habits of mind which interfere: perhaps she cannot avoid feeling that she ought to take care with her dress, or feeling guilty if she lets her husband do his fair share of the housework, however clearly she may understand the unreasonableness of such feelings. Her ingrained habits of mind prevent the fulfillment of her strongest desires.

This analysis seems to provide a very good account of what it is to be conditioned, and there is no difficulty at all about seeing it as an internal lack of freedom: something about the woman which prevents her from doing as she really wants. One aspect of conditioning is *ignorance*, probably the greatest curtailer of freedom there is, because if someone does not know or fully grasp that the world contains certain possibilities, as far as that person is concerned they might just as well not exist. The other aspect is the inability to change unwelcome aspects of oneself, which is as much a restriction on the fulfillment of desire as the inability to change anything in the outside world. If you want to be more beautiful, or run faster, or be stronger, or be able to charm people, but cannot do whatever it is, you are as curtailed in your desires as you would be through not having money, or influence, or a car, or tools for a trade.

The upshot of all this is that feminists are indeed right in thinking that lack of freedom can be internal: a woman may be in a state where her own mind prevents her from achieving what she really wants (a matter which must not be confused with her mind preventing what she would have wanted if she had been someone else). However, although the comparisons drawn in the last paragraph between internal and external restrictions on freedom do show that freedom can be limited by aspects of the mind, what they also show at the same time is that there is no intrinsic difference between external and internal lack of freedom; they are essentially the same sort of thing. Internal lack of freedom does not consist in being in a special state of mind or having a particular set of desires, only in having within oneself (rather than in surrounding circumstances) the things which prevent fulfillment of desire. This means that, in fact, there is no problem about reconciling the concept of internal freedom with the first account of freedom given in this chapter. The only acceptable interpretation of 'internal freedom' (the only account of it which does not involve calling something quite different by the name of freedom, or presuming that the real woman is something uninfluenced by society) is one which makes it essentially a matter of being unimpeded in one's desires by one's own ignorance and habits. This is important. Once it is clear people will be less likely to be confused by the vague way in which 'conditioned' is often used, or lured into thinking that if women have socially induced desires which the liberators disapprove of, they are necessarily not free.

THE ATTACK ON CONDITIONING

When women are really conditioned, their preconceptions and immediate desires do get in the way of what, in some perfectly obvious way, they really want. If they are conditioned, therefore, it does seem that other people may be justified in overriding their immediate desires in order to produce not what the liberators think they should want, but what they actually do want.

However, there is an obvious danger in taking this attitude, because the only case in which it would be reasonable to override a woman's wishes in the name of her freedom would be where it was absolutely certain that she was conditioned, and equally certain what she really wanted and how it could be brought about. And the simple fact of the matter is that it is virtually impossible even to approach certainty in cases like this, let alone reach it. It is very hard to tell when, and to what extent, people are conditioned.

The main reason why this must be so is probably obvious from what has gone before. The point is that it is quite impossible to tell conditioned women from unconditioned ones[6] by their preferences. The pressures on women to be beautiful and maternal and domestic and deferential to men have no doubt left in many women habits of mind which will prevent their ever achieving what they really want to achieve, but we are not entitled to presume that the pressures which produced these mental blocks in some women did the same for all. For the women to whom these pressures were congenial, as they must have been for some, the desires produced became their own most basic desires, and not obstacles to the fulfillment of others. If a woman is interested mainly in dress or nursery design it is no doubt true to say that it can be attributed to her background to some extent: if she had been brought up differently she would have had different interests. However, these may be genuinely hers, and ideally suited to her nature. The 'conditioned' responses may be genuinely her own. It is therefore impossible to tell whether or not a woman is conditioned just by knowing about her likes and dislikes, or about her formative influences.

What that means is that the only attack which can be safely mounted against conditioning must be directed to its source. It is too dangerous to try to 'free' women who are regarded as conditioned by forcing them to do what the prevailing feminist ideology presumes they must want, because with that method there is always the danger of ignoring women's real wishes. They may not be conditioned at all. The only thing to do is start from the beginning and try, even at this late stage, to remove the cause of the trouble, and give conditioned women a chance to become unconditioned in a way which runs no risk of damaging those who are not, because it still leaves women to make their own choices.

There are two stages to this process, corresponding to the two aspects of conditioning. The first is to increase understanding of how the present state of things came about and how it works, so that women who have been doing what does not suit them can understand why, and at the same time what alternatives are possible. The second is to make help available to women who decide as a result of this that they do want to change their habits.

There are all kinds of ways in which advances could be made on these two fronts. The key to the first is *diversity*. Women must be exposed to kinds of new influences and information (in addition to the old, of course, not instead of them) to make them fully aware of the possibilities the world contains. Some people, no doubt, will try to turn the freedom argument against this procedure by saying that if people have new alternatives thrust before them they are *forced to choose,* and that in itself is an infringement of liberty because people ought to have the freedom not to choose if that is what they would prefer. However, that argument cannot possibly work. This is because it is true as a matter of *logic* that people cannot be the ultimate determiners of their own degree of freedom. Whatever anyone chooses to do, that choice comes from among alternatives which already exist, and those alternatives were not themselves chosen. Since, therefore, the ultimate degree of freedom is always out of the hands of the individual we are right to insist that the choice given should always be as great as possible. We cannot, in the name of liberty for women, force them to do anything against their wills or bring about states of society they do not like, but we are bound to give them more knowledge of possibilities.

The second part of the attack on conditioning is to reinforce this for women who do decide that they would like to change their lives by giving them every help in overcoming unwelcome habits of mind: help ranging from the support of other women who understand the position to full-scale psychotherapy. As long as this was directed to bringing about what women themselves wanted, and not to persuading them into something they did not want, it would be genuinely liberating.

Still, however energetically we pursued such a programme, we should have to be hopelessly optimistic to think that we should actually eliminate all existing conditioning as a result of it, and perhaps this seems to justify the wish of some feminists to make a firm attack on the symptoms of conditioning, rather than going in this gently way for its cause. However much we may want freedom for women, they could argue, even the freedom to stay conditioned, can we allow them this freedom if the price of it is to trap other women in the same bonds? Can we allow a conditioned mother to bring up her daughter in the same way? Surely for the sake of the daughters we ought to be willing to run the risk of attacking directly what we believe to be the mothers' conditioned desires, even though we may run some risk of going against their real wishes? Surely we should work directly against bad influences, and deliberately get rid of (for instance), beauty competitions, sexist literature in schools, and anything else we think objectionable, whatever the conditioned mothers may think of the matter?

However, even though conditioned mothers will certainly tend to bring up conditioned daughters, and although we certainly cannot allow that, this conclusion is not the proper one to draw. The way to prevent the daughters from becoming conditioned is not to keep them out of the range of influence of the things which are believed to have conditioned their mothers, because it was not *being in the range of those influences* which did the

harm, but *being out of the range of others*. If we bring the daughters up on a diet of so-called non-sexist literature (much of what is around at present is actually *female* sexist) to think that there should be no sex roles, that does not free them from conditioning: it only brings them up with a different sort. If to get feminist approval a little girl is forced to sneer at the idea of beauty competitions, she is as much coerced as her mother was by parents who expected her to look pleased when she was given dolls and pretty party frocks. Once again, whether or not a girl is conditioned cannot be judged by which slogans she grows up chanting, because in theory she could be conditioned into chanting any.

The solution to the problem, as always with questions of freedom, is once again diversity. We can perhaps summarize the conditioned mothers and those of daughters who are to be rescued from conditioning by proposing a solution to the widely debated problem of how free a parent should be to determine a child's education. We can put it this way. Within practicable limits, the parent should be allowed to say that the child *must* learn certain things, and have lessons from people of particular political, moral or religious views. On the other hand, no parent should have the right to *prevent* the child's learning anything (going to scripture classes in the wrong religion or having sex education) or being exposed to other people's views. The education authorities should have a positive duty to diversify influences, since in that way the parents' wishes are respected but the child's freedom is not impaired. That should be what feminists want. As Germaine Greer said of a similar problem, 'censorship is the weapon of the opposition, not ours'.7

NOTES

1. Midge Decter, *The New Chastity*, p. 51.
2. Sheila Rowbotham, *Woman's Consciousness, Man's World*, pp. 75–6.
3. John Stuart Mill, "On Liberty," in *The Essential Works of John Stuart Mill*, ed. Lerner, p. 263.
4. "No More Miss America!" in *Sisterhood is Powerful*, ed. Morgan, p. 584.
5. Margaret Rhondda, quoted in Firestone, *The Dialectic of Sex*, p. 20.
6. More accurately, of course, *more* or *less* conditioned, and in certain ways rather than just in general. Throughout arguments of this sort it must not be forgotten that freedom is a matter of degree.
7. Germaine Greer, *The Female Eunuch*, p. 309.

REVIEW AND DISCUSSION QUESTIONS

1. How does Radcliffe Richards define freedom?
2. What is the alternative, "inner" way of understanding freedom that she discusses?
3. In what ways does Radcliffe Richards agree with those who advocate "inner" freedom?
4. How does Radcliffe Richards distinguish pressures that "condition"—that is, restrict freedom—from those that merely play a part in the general formation of a person?
5. Why is Radcliffe Richards skeptical of those who argue that women who dress for men or participate in beauty pageants are not truly free?
6. What solutions does Radcliffe Richards think will help assure women are not, in fact, choosing in accord with conditioning rather than choosing freely?
7. Explain how censorship can damage women's freedom, according to Radcliffe Richards. How can education help women?
8. How might Radcliffe Richards react to the legal case of *Wisconsin* v. *Yoder*?
9. How would Radcliffe Richards respond to Catharine MacKinnon who has written that women's choices are "structured" and that marriage, prostitution, and sexual harassment are "indistinguishable"? Which view seems most reasonable to you? Explain.
10. Discuss the following claim: "Radcliffe Richards understates the importance of society and culture in forming people but overestimates either the power of individual choice or the role of biology."
11. Compare this essay with Jaggar's discussion of feminist ethics.

The Female Mind: Feminists, Meet Mr. Darwin

Robert Wright

In this essay, Robert Wright argues that feminists, although they often ignore or even despise Darwinian evolutionary theory, in fact have much to learn, and gain, from its results. Using recent discoveries of biologists about reproduction and other patterns of behavior, he argues that "difference," "radical," and "equity" feminists as well as anybody else interested in understanding male-female relationships can benefit from the deeper understanding of human nature that biology provides. Topics Wright discusses include sexual harassment, monogamy, rape, affirmative action, and the "ethics of care." Robert Wright is an editor and writer at *The New Republic* and the author of *The Moral Animal*.

From Robert Wright, "Feminists, Meet Mr. Darwin," *The New Republic,* November 28, 1994. Reprinted by permission.

History has not been kind to ideologies that rested on patently false beliefs about human nature. Communism, for example, isn't looking very robust these days. From the beginning communists held that human selfishness, the great crippler of communal utopias, was eradicable. They shaped scientific theory accordingly. Marx insisted that traits acquired through education—a more generous disposition, say—were biologically inherited by offspring. Up until 1964, long after Western geneticists had dismissed this idea, it was still an official doctrine of Soviet biology. Occasionally Soviet geneticists who failed to appreciate the doctrine were sent to prison.

It would be melodramatic to say that today feminism is where communism was at midcentury. Still, it's tempting. Once again an ideology clings to a doctrine that, for better or worse, isn't true—in this case the idea that "gender" is essentially a "construct": that male and female nature are inherently more or less identical. Once again, the falseness of the doctrine is increasingly evident. And, once again, adherents of the ideology can admit this falseness only at some risk—not imprisonment, maybe, but an extremely chilly reception from fellow feminists.

Of course, there are the much-discussed "difference feminists." But even they don't believe—or, at least, don't admit to believing—that men and women are inherently different. They either stay silent on the question of where the differences come from or trace them to early social influences.

There has been much talk about the fragmentation of modern feminism. In addition to the difference feminists (e.g., psychologist Carol Gilligan, linguist Deborah Tannen), there are the "radical feminists" (e.g., Catharine MacKinnon, Andrea Dworkin), the liberal "equity feminists" (e.g., Supreme Court Justice Ruth Bader Ginsburg, writer Katha Pollitt) and assorted others. But as diverse as these thinkers seem, they are bound by a common thread: none is interested in the well-grounded study of human nature, of the male and female minds.

By "well-grounded study of human nature" I don't *just* mean, "grounded the way I think the study of human nature should be grounded" (al-though I do, of course, mean that). I mean grounded in comprehension of the process that designed human beings: natural selection. Specifically, the field of inquiry that I commend to feminists, and that they seem loath to explore, is a science called evolutionary psychology. Evolutionary psychology sees (among other things) some clear differences between the male and female minds. These differences aren't wholly immutable. The difference feminists are right to sense that culture matters; we are a pretty plastic species. Still, many of the differences between men and women are more stubborn than most feminists would like, and complicate the quest for—even the definition of—social equality between the sexes.

The feminist aversion to the Darwinian study of difference has as much to do with Darwinism as with difference. Traditionally, after all, Darwinism has been most potently wielded by the right wing. Feminists fear that it will again be used to justify oppression as "natural," as "in our genes," as beyond our control. That's certainly a danger, but it's not inevitable. And besides, it's not necessarily worse than the alternative danger: that feminism, like communism, will falter under the weight of its doctrinal absurdities; and that the laudable ideals it started with, rather than reaching a gritty compromise with reality, will begin to wither for lack of honest support.

It would be misleading to say that feminists casually disregard Darwinism. A fair amount of effort goes into the disregard. A few feminists have actually studied and then dismissed the Darwinian view of human nature. Unfortunately, they seem to have expended more energy on the dismissal than on the study.

A typical dismissal begins by mocking Darwin's observation that in species after species, "the differences between the sexes follow almost exactly the same rules; the males are almost always the wooers. . . ." The female, "with the rarest exception, is less eager than the male. . . . [S]he is coy. . . . The exertion of some choice on the part of the female seems almost as general a law as the eagerness of the male." This is a vital observation, for the evolutionary logic behind it (which wasn't grasped until a century after Darwin) underlies many psychological differences between men and women.

Darwin's observation has been ridiculed by Carol Tavris in her much-praised (by feminists) book *The Mismeasure of Woman*. Tavris calls it the "myth of the coy female." The pattern Darwin thought he saw, she asserts, isn't really there. We can no longer explain sex roles by "appealing to the universality of such behavior in other species" because "other species aren't cooperating."

Actually, they are. To be sure, there are many species whose females are less than devoutly monogamous. There are even species whose females are as sexually assertive as males, or more so. What Tavris doesn't seem to appreciate is how all this variety can specifically reinforce our belief that the general rule of *relative* female sexual reserve has a genetic basis.

To see this crucial point, you have to first see the modern Darwinian explanation for that reserve. A female can reproduce much less often than a male, because she is stuck with the time-sapping job of birthing and maybe even rearing the young. Thus it makes Darwinian sense for her to appraise carefully the quality of aspiring mates—both their genetic quality and, in species with "high male parental investment," like ours, their ability and willingness to help provide for the young after birth. This quality control helps keep the female from wasting one of her rare and arduous reproductive episodes creating offspring with poor survival prospects. (A woman needn't think about these things; rather, her genetically based impulses of attraction have been shaped by this logic over millions of years; genes encouraging selectivity have flourished, while genes allowing females to squander precious reproductive episodes have not.)

For a male, in contrast, reproduction can be a frequent and low-cost affair; the more sex partners, the more chances to get genes into the next generation. Hence the massively documented fact that males in our species, when sizing up sheerly *sexual* (not marital) opportunities, are on average less choosy than females. (Among the documentation are male and female tastes in pornography and prostitution, as well as the oft-noted fact that gay males are on average more promiscuous than gay females; both homosexual cultures are a de facto experiment in how one sex behaves when it doesn't have to compromise with the other.)

Now, as it happens, in a few eccentric "sex-reversed" species the *males* assume much of the burden of giving birth. Male sea horses have an incubation pouch in which the female deposits the eggs. Male phalaropes (sea snipes) sit in the nest and incubate the eggs, taking themselves one of commission and leaving their mates free to embark on another round of reproduction. And these are the species in which stereotypes of courtship behavior most reliably break down; female sea horses and phalaropes are quite sexually assertive. Thus these ostensible "exceptions" to Darwinian logic in fact comply with and bolster it. They are yet more evidence that the sex that can reproduce more often will typically be the randier sex. They are yet more reason to believe that *human* females, whose reproductive episodes are rare and arduous, are indeed genetically, inclined to be more discriminating about sex partners than human males are.

The feminist Anne Fausto-Sterling, author of *Myths of Gender*, is thus missing the point by 180 degrees when she cites the phalaropes, with their reversed sex roles, and says sarcastically, "You name your animal species and make your political point." You name your animal species and it complies with evolutionary theory. Politics will have to adjust accordingly.

It turns out that females in our species are not, by nature, utterly coy or utterly monogamous. There is physiological evidence that they are "naturally" prone to promiscuity and infidelity under some circumstances. But they are not nearly so prone as males. More to the point: figuring out how naturally adventurous women are, and why, has depended on careful study of various species whose females, for various reasons, don't precisely fit the coy stereotype. (Some of the pioneering work was done by the anthropologist Sarah Blaffer Ilrdy, author of *The Woman That Never Evolved*.)

So, while Tavris is in one sense right to say the "myth of the coy female" is dead, she is exactly wrong to imply that this means women aren't by nature more sexually reserved than men, or that recent zoology has sapped confidence in the Darwinian comprehension of the human mind. For

Tavris and Fausto-Sterling to note that the crudest stereotypes about human sex roles aren't found throughout the animal kingdom, and then end the discussion there, is to get a C− in Evolutionary Biology 101. And these are the two most commonly cited feminist "experts" on Darwinism.

I cannot, in the space of this article, try to convince skeptics that men are "naturally" less discriminating about sex partners than women—or that men and women inherently differ in the various other ways I'll discuss. I would direct readers who seek deeper immersion in the arguments for modern Darwinism to various books, including Matt Ridley's *The Red Queen,* David Buss's *The Evolution of Desire* and (got a pencil handy?) my own recently published *The Moral Animal.* (Or, at a more academic level: Donald Symons's *The Evolution of Human Sexuality;* Martin Daly and Margo Wilson's *Sex, Evolution, and Behavior;* and *The Adapted Mind,* edited by Jerome Barkow, Leda Cosmides and John Tooby.)

In lieu of persuasion, I'll mostly confine my assertions about human nature to beliefs that are widely accepted within evolutionary psychology—doctrines subscribed to by, among others, many female (and male) Darwinians who would call themselves feminists. When discussing more speculative theories, I'll so label them. Of course, detached from the larger body of cross-cultural and cross-species evidence in which they're embedded, all these claims will strike any determined skeptic as "just-so stories." But do not excuse yourself from confronting them on grounds that they are just tired Darwinian doctrines, scrutinized by feminists and judiciously rejected. There is not a single well-known feminist who has learned enough about modern Darwinism to pass judgment on it.

Some of them would be well advised to. Though it is simplistic to say that evolutionary psychology vindicates one feminist school or another, some schools could use the field to support at least part of their platform. At the same time, every school can find something in the field that threatens cherished beliefs. Most feminists should have a love-hate relationship with modern Darwinism.

Oddly, given Darwinism's historical (and confused) association with right-wing politics, evolutionary psychology lends a kind of support to some of the most radical feminists, such as MacKinnon and Dworkin. Both have gotten lots of ink for saying genuinely nutty things (such as Dworkin's theatrical suggestion that all heterosexual sex is rape)—pronouncements that defy all attempts at justification. But both have other positions, of more measured extremity, that, if they can be justified at all, are best justified in Darwinian terms.

Consider sexual harassment. MacKinnon helped establish the "hostile environment" test for harassment, and she defines such environments broadly; by her reckoning, two-thirds of working women have been harassed. Whereas some feminists consider the Anita Hill affair a borderline harassment case (if a clear-cut indictment of Clarence Thomas's character), MacKinnon jumped vehemently to Hill's defense.

I can see why: a man who held power over Hill was alleged to have made persistent, if not explicit, sexual overtures. Naturally, Hill would feel great distress. But I can only take this view by thinking of Hill as a woman, with the kind of mind natural selection designed for women. A man might feel uncomfortable with a comparable undercurrent of sexual advance from a female boss, but it would be strange for him to feel deep distress.

Again, the logic goes back to the fact that for women reproductive opportunities are precious. Thus during evolution it was costly (genetically) for a woman to have sex with a man she didn't want to have sex with—often a man who (a) evidently had genes not conducive to viable and fertile offspring or (b) had no evident inclination to stick around and help provide for the offspring. The abhorrence women feel at the prospect of sex with a man they find unattractive is an expression of this logic.

For men, the logic is different. Being coerced into sex with a woman (a) wasn't an issue during evolution, since men can't have sex unless physiologically aroused; and (b) would have had no large ill effects; the worst likely outcome for the man (in genetic terms) is that pregnancy would not ensue. And spending fifteen minutes failing to get a woman pregnant is hardly a major Darwinian disaster. There is no reason for evolution to have instilled in the male mind an aversion to coerced sex with women.

So, yes, I'd say Anita Hill was sexually harassed. She was under coercive, if subtle, pressure to have sex. But that judgment depends on her mind being a female mind, with female vulnerabilities.

Many feminists, even without any help from Darwin, have discerned the tension here: the more protection you want to provide women, the harder it is to argue that they don't by their nature need special protection; the more often you see them victimized, the stronger the implication that they are by nature victims, weaker than men. That is why some feminists resist MacKinnon's broader definitions of sexual harassment and of rape, and her view of pornography as an assault on women. That is why she is called a "victim" feminist—and not just by conservatives such as Christina Hoff Sommers, but by feminists further to the left, such as Naomi Wolf. Justice Ruth Bader Ginsburg, who as a liberal equity feminist professes to seek only equal treatment for women, remarked after hearing MacKinnon speak, "That woman has bad karma."

Yet the equity feminists have failed just as surely as MacKinnon to resolve the tension between protecting women and patronizing them. Consider the Supreme Court's unanimous ruling in the latest sexual harassment case. It concerned a woman at a forklift company and her creepy boss. He would joke about large breasts, ask female employees to fish through his pockets for coins and so on. The straw that broke the camel's back was his asking a subordinate if she had landed one of her accounts by meeting with the client at a Holiday Inn.

Ruling in support of the female worker, the Supreme Court tried to sustain a broad definition of "hostile environment." The victim, it said, needn't prove that she had been psychologically damaged—only that she might "reasonably" have found the comments hostile. But, in a bow to Ginsburg and the equity feminists, the Court cast its ruling in terms of a "reasonable person," not a "reasonable woman."

This simply won't wash. How does a "reasonable person" feel about the implication that he or she closed a deal by sleeping with a customer? Well, the average woman feels quite insulted, and the average man feels somewhere between mildly insulted and quite flattered. She is being called a whore. He is being called a stud.

It is tempting to dismiss these value-laden labels as file residue of centuries of patriarchy, or as echoes of the Victorian Madonna-whore dichotomy—ephemeral cultural pathologies that the Court needn't stoop to accommodate. But there is another explanation: these moral judgments may have a genetic basis.

To begin with, men tend to find a history of extreme promiscuity an exceedingly undesirable feature in a wife, and this makes perfect Darwinian sense. The more promiscuous the wife, the less likely that the children in which the man invests his time and energy are in fact carrying his genes. In other words, genes inclining men to abhor promiscuous long-term mates would do better at getting into ensuing generations than less discriminating genes. The logic isn't the same for women, since the children they give birth to always carry their genes (or, at least, did during evolution, before high technology—and that's what counts).

This isn't to say men don't find loose women sexy. From a Darwinian standpoint, loose women are in some ways great *sex* partners, because they're so easy to get—and for purposes of a man's genetic proliferation, remember, the more gettable women there are the better. (Contraception has now short-circuited this logic, too, but again: we're stuck with the minds the logic shaped.) A loose woman just isn't the genetically optimal woman to fall in *love* with; investing in her children is ill-advised.

Hence, it seems, the Madonna-whore distinction. Men appear to be designed by natural selection to feel merely lust for fast women but to feel love as well for (some) slower ones. They won't always insist on marrying a Madonna, of course, virgins being scarce, and, besides, the choice of a mate being a complex unconscious calculus full of tradeoffs. Still, men do often draw a morally colored distinction among their romantic prospects, viewing some kinds of women as full-fledged human beings, warranting extensive psychological exploration, and other kinds as something more like pieces of meat. And one of various features that can put a woman in the latter camp is a reputation for extreme promiscuity. Men seldom admit this to either kind of woman, and some men don't admit it to themselves. But if you listen carefully to men talking to one another, the attitude is there.

It is not surprising, then, that the average woman resists being publicly labeled "easy," regardless of her actual degree of promiscuity. During evolution, that label would have cut the chances of a man's investing in her offspring. (A general theme of evolutionary psychology is that we all naturally burnish our reputations in all kinds of ways, regardless of whether the gloss reflects our actual behavior.)

This idea of an inherent and morally charged male mental distinction between fast and slow women is just a theory. And, while it probably commands majority allegiance within evolutionary psychology (though only when given more nuance than space here permits), it is not as solidly established as, say, the idea of sex differences in promiscuity. Even more tentative is the idea that women have some natural aversion to accusations of extreme sexual looseness (though certainly women do, in general, resist them more than men). Still, the closer we look at the evidence, the better things look for the theory. Various culturally deterministic anthropologists, notably Margaret Mead, claimed to have found exotic cultures in which women were as prone to promiscuity as men and no one cared. These claims have collapsed upon reexamination. Mead's favorite example, Samoa, turns out to have featured a virtual male obsession with the virginity of mates. (In Samoan lore, as Derek Freeman noted in *Margaret Mead and Samoa*, a deflowered woman is called a "wanton woman, like an empty shell exposed by the ebbing tide." A song performed at defloration ceremonies went like this: "All others have failed to achieve entry. . . . Being first, he is foremost, O to be foremost.")

All of this explains what for almost everyone is the commonsense reaction to the forklift case, yet what few feminists will admit: the reason the remark about the Holiday Inn was offensive was because it was made to a woman. What evolutionary psychology suggests is that this relevance of gender to law is no fleeting creation of culture; jurists might as well reckon with it.

In the end, the problem with the Ginsburgian "reasonable person" formulation is not that it leads to a narrow definition of harassment, but that it leads to no definition at all. Asking what a "reasonable person" finds offensive is like asking what color a typical fruit is. The answer depends on whether you're talking apples or oranges.

The general truth suggested here is that we can either give women broad protection against sexual harassment that is grounded specifically in an understanding of the female mind, or we can ignore sex differences and give women much less protection. Or we can do what the Supreme Court did: carefully craft tortured legal doctrines that defy both common sense and our emerging comprehension of human nature—doctrines that are unlikely to withstand the test of time.

Evolutionary psychology's tendency to provide at least some support for radical feminism goes beyond sexual harassment. Dworkin's contention that "dehumanization is a basic part of the content of all pornography" is characteristically overstated, but in Darwinian light it looks far from crazy. Certainly most pornography rivets the "whore," not the "Madonna," part of the male mind. The women in *Hustler* aren't women a man would want to marry. They're women whose appeal has nothing to do with getting to know them. Indeed, they're women who are exciting partly because they're portrayed as not demanding that he get to know them; they seem willing to be treated as meat, as optimally efficient sex objects.

To say that men objectify loose women isn't to say, alas, that men never see the lucky recipients of their lasting affection as objects. The male tendency to "possessively" guard mates against the advances of rivals may be more than mere metaphor. For men, "the same mental algorithms are apparently activated in the marital and mercantile spheres," write the evolutionary psychologists Martin Daly and Margo Wilson. Again, the reason seems to be the high genetic costs cuckoldry brings the male victim. As evolutionary psychologists have shown, the average woman isn't as threatened as the average man by the purely sexual infidelity of a mate, apparently because it doesn't so immediately threaten her genes.

Even the radical feminists' famously expansive definitions of rape have *some* Darwinian merit. One of MacKinnon's more moderate utterances on the subject is this: "Politically, I call it rape whenever a woman has sex and feels violated."

Psychologically, too, you might call it that. When a woman has sex under a man's pretenses of enduring affection (Darwinian translation: pretenses of commitment to ensuing offspring) and then he never calls again, the evolutionary source of her anguish is the same as for the anguish following rape: she has had sex with a man she (unconsciously) deemed unworthy of her eggs, even though in this case the deeming was done after the fact, once evidence of his unworthiness surfaced.

Again, though, if you really want to claim such a broad realm of moral protection for women, you have to admit they're different from men and in some ways uniquely vulnerable. Men, after all, virtually never feel "violated" by sex with a woman. A man may feel crushed if a woman he loves leaves him, but it is an odd man indeed who regrets the sex.

Dworkin has distinguished between rape and seduction as follows: "In seduction, the rapist bothers to buy a bottle of wine." Another feminist has opined that rape is "on a continuum" with normal male sexual behavior. Some Darwinians would agree. They'd say rape is something men do when other forms of manipulation fail. It may be "natural" when men with a manifest inability to legitimately obtain a mate resort to sex with aggression. Hence the profile of the typical rapist: lacking the material and personal resources to attract women.

Dworkin has written, "A man wants what a woman has—sex. He can steal it (rape), persuade her to give it away (seduction), rent it (prostitution), lease it over the long term (marriage in the United States) or own it outright (marriage in most societies)." However depressing, this would strike some Darwinians as a fair thumbnail sketch of the situation. This doesn't mean men think of their pursuits this way (in general the radical feminists attribute too much conscious calculation to men); but it is a fairly apt functional analysis of the emotions men feel—from lust to love to the selective evaporation of affection upon conquest.

Plainly, the resonance between radical feminism and Darwinism isn't just that the former's implicit depiction of female vulnerabilities is explicit in the latter. Darwinism also depicts men as something like the animals that MacKinnon and Dworkin say they are. Human males are by nature oppressive, possessive, flesh-obsessed pigs. They're not beyond cultural improvement, thanks to the fact that love, compassion, guilt, remorse and the conscience are evolved parts of the mind, just like lust and jealous rage. Still, MacKinnon and Dworkin are probably right to suggest that the current cultural climate does a lackluster job of improving men.

I won't spend the next few weeks waiting for MacKinnon and Dworkin to call and thank me for empowering their worldview. For they don't want its power to run quite so deep. Dworkin denounces "Female" supremacists—some of the difference feminists—as being "biological determinists." (Remarkably, she does this one paragraph after asserting that "men as a class are moral cretins.") MacKinnon, hit by less radical feminists with the entirely apt label "victim feminist," tries to fob it off on the difference feminists. Her reaction to Gilligan's book *In a Different Voice*, which depicted women as more empathetic and less abstractly logical than men in their moral thinking, was to call this "different" voice "the voice of a victim."

This aversion to "biological determinism" (a misnomer) is one thing all major brands of feminism have in common. Even the difference feminists don't want to talk about *deep* differences. Tannen, in her bestseller *You Just Don't Understand* and her recent *Talking From 9 to 5*, says men are on average more concerned than women with status and hierarchy. This undeniable fact begs to be placed on its proper Darwinian foundation. During evolution, high male status seems to have expanded sexual access to females (as it does in many species, including our nearest relatives, chimpanzees). This Darwinian perk has been documented in "hunter-gatherer" societies, the closest living model of the social context of human evolution. Given this distinctively male link between social achievement and genetic proliferation, it is plausible, to say the least, that millions of years of evolution would endow males with a distinctive thirst for power.

Yet Tannen couches her explanation for this thirst in cultural terms. The tendency of boys to "jockey for center stage, challenge those who get it and deflect challenges" is "learned" by boys and not girls because boys' groups "tend to be more obviously hierarchical." Well, yes, lots of learning goes on, and every child has a range of flexibility whose bounds still aren't precisely known. Culture matters. But does that explain why the boys' groups are always more hierarchical in the first place? Tannen's overriding emphasis on culture would make more sense if she could point to a single one of the 1,200 societies on the anthropological record and show women, on average, pursuing social status and political power as fiercely and opportunistically as the average man. She can't.

Poor Tannen. Her evasion of Darwinism fails to keep her safe from the wrath of even the mild-mannered equity feminists. Katha Pollitt says Tannen and Gilligan "massage their findings to fit their theories," and that their prominence just proves that social science is "one part science and nine parts social. They say what people want to hear: women really are different, just the ways we always thought." Maybe so. But did you ever wonder why it is that we've always thought that?

It's logical that liberal feminists would fear the idea of innate sex differences in ambition. For it imperils two liberal feminist legal principles. One is sex discrimination—in particular, the claim that a gross underrepresentation of women in high-paying jobs is by itself evidence of discrimination. This logic assumes not just that men and women are equally qualified, but that they pursue a given job or promotion with equal intensity. If men are on average more ambitious than women, this assumption falters.

The second legal doctrine imperiled by evolutionary psychology is affirmative action for women. It is sometimes (not always) justified on similar grounds: that, in the absence of discrimination, men and women would be equally represented at the higher levels of corporate and government life. But if men on average work harder at self-advancement, this rationale won't work.

As Ridley notes in *The Red Queen*, there are other possible rationales for affirmative action. Our emerging knowledge of male-female differences might lead us to favor quotas for women on grounds that they are less inclined than men to sacrifice the organization's welfare to personal advancement. In other words: if a meritocracy is a

place where people are promoted according to their actual value to the employer, then affirmative action may be needed to make the workplace a meritocracy. (The business pages are full of tales of male primates who follow their impulses to no good corporate end. How much money did Barry Diller waste trying vainly to outbid his old rival, Sumner Redstone, in the battle over—as it were—Paramount? A lot, but maybe not as much as Redstone wasted by "winning.")

Evolutionary psychology suggests that if affirmative action for women is to rest on coherent logic, the subject of sex differences will have to come into play. Once again: if women want broad protection, they can most cogently seek it as women, not as persons.

The deepest source of the feminist aversion to Darwinism is larger and vaguer than specific policy issues. Evolutionary psychology seems to paint a generally grim view of the "natural" order. Some of the ugliest things about the word—the very things that stirred modern feminist indignation to begin with—have biological roots. These include the male "patriarchy" that the radicals see everywhere they look, and men's attempts to control the sexuality of women. Even the classically reviled male hypocrisy over promiscuity—the "double standard"—appears to be a legacy of natural selection. Men not only are naturally inclined to cheat on their mates; men are also inclined to abhor, and thus fiercely condemn, the philandering of a mate. Women share both inclinations, but they aren't as strong as the male versions. Indeed, a woman may actually reinforce the double standard when she finds herself able to forgive a husband's sexual infidelity in order to head off what for her female ancestors was a much bigger threat—a male's desertion, his withdrawal of resources.

None of this is great news for feminism (or, really, for humankind). But it isn't *quite* as bad as it seems. By getting clear on what the word "natural" does and doesn't mean, we can isolate the parts of evolutionary psychology that should most worry feminists.

To infer that what's "natural" is morally "good" is an elementary logical error, famously labeled the "naturalistic fallacy" by the turn-of-the-century British ethicist G. E. Moore. Indeed, I would go further, Darwinism not only doesn't tell us that the double standard is morally right; it tells us that any intuitive sense men have of its rightness is untrustworthy. This sense is a mere vestige of natural selection, morally arbitrary so far as we know. A central lesson of evolutionary psychology by my lights is that we should cast a wary eye on our moral intuitions generally (including, for example, the sense that retribution is just); they are a voice not from God but from our genes, echoes of our amoral creator, natural selection. What's natural may or may not be good, but it's certainly not good *by virtue of the fact* that it's natural.

Another thing "natural" doesn't mean is unchangeable. There are cultures in which the "natural" male impulse to control female sexuality is expressed as ritual genital mutilation. There are cultures, like ours, in which men don't do such things. And there is no reason to think we've reached the biological limit of male malleability. Evolutionary psychologists aren't genetic determinists, and they aren't "biological determinists" except in a sense so broad as to encompass both genes and culture.

So much for the good news. The bad news is (a) The average beer-drinking, two-timing, wife-beating lout isn't going to change his moral views after being handed a copy of G. E. Moore's *Principia Ethica*. He is more likely to conveniently see modern Darwinism as a divine embrace of his loutishness, And (b) People, though malleable, aren't simply and infinitely malleable. They aren't malleable enough to make communism a productive economic system, and they aren't malleable enough to create a society of perfect behavioral symmetry between men and women. Some changes simply can't be made, and others will come only at some cost.

Here is where the word "natural" assumes a second import that is not so easily dismissed as the first, and that feminists may find uncomfortable. Here we can expect men to turn the tables and use evolutionary psychology to talk about *their* vulnerabilities, to make *their* appeals for special treatment on grounds of peculiar biological predicament. Thus, for example, a man could urge for the double standard by saying (a) that his own philandering is hard to control, and (b) that he is more "vulnerable" than his wife to the pain of a mate's sexual infidelity.

Obviously, this is a self-serving argument. And it can be combated in two ways: by pointing to the social costs of male infidelity (which, I would argue, are extremely high in the current social environment); and by noting that "hard to control" doesn't mean "impossible to control." Still, this argument, though combatable, isn't laughable in the way the naturalistic fallacy is. It uses our understanding of "natural" impulses not to justify them as being *right*, strictly speaking, but to excuse them by stressing the psychic costs of defying them. Feminists are right to dread some of the rhetorical resistance Darwinism will abet.

Men seeking to stress their victim status can also lay claim to being "objectified" much as women are. Feminists complain about women's beauty and youth counting for so much in the eyes of men. (And this male obsession, according to evolutionary psychologists, isn't merely a product of Madison Avenue.) But men could just as easily complain about being viewed as walking wallets—about the fact that women place so much value on the social status and/or wealth of a mate. (This emphasis, too, appears to be a legacy of evolution, a deep aesthetic impulse that lives on after its evolutionary logic has been broken by a modern world in which women can earn their own wealth and status.) One reason you don't hear more about this male grievance is that low-status men have trouble getting their grievances heard. They aren't a very prominent group.

In the end, Darwinism's proper place in moral discourse is not to aid simplistic assertions about some natural order that is supposedly good or supposedly inevitable, but, rather to inform arguments about the social costs and benefits of alternative norms in light of human nature, with heightened awareness of which groups the costs and benefits fall on. The issue of what's "natural" will enter the debate, but by itself should confer no justification for anything.

Feminists' fear of the word "natural," and their attendant reluctance to confront sex differences, has left open a gaping intellectual niche. Perhaps it is poetic justice that the void is being semi-occupied by the scourge of name-brand feminism, the dreaded Camille Paglia. At least, Paglia professes to be a Darwinian; she talks about "instinctual drives" and says primal things like "sex crime means back to nature." Still, she has no evident grasp of evolutionary theory and prefers free-form literary explanation. For example, when men kill mates or ex-mates, it is usually out of jealousy, and many evolutionary psychologists would call this an extreme, pathological expression of a "natural" impulse to punish a woman for real or suspected infidelity. But Paglia has a different explanation: "Men who kill the women they love have reverted to pagan cult. She whom a man cannot live without has become a goddess, an avatar of his half-divinized, half-demonized mother, a magic fountain of cosmic creativity." Thanks for clearing that up.

For all her impressionistic excess, Paglia does tell a few simple, crude truths about sex differences, and this is one reason she's gotten where she is today (the other being the impressionistic excess). If name-brand feminists don't like the moral spin she puts on her comic-book Darwinism, there's one solution: to learn real Darwinism and put their own moral spin on it. It is certainly spinnable; like all theories of human behavior, evolutionary psychology has no inherent moral upshot. It merely limits the range of realistic moral and political discourse. Within the arena thus defined, interest groups will contest, each trying to shape the moral and legal codes to its ends. And the groups that aren't in the arena will lose.

In retrospect, much of the recent history of feminism might have been predicted with the help of evolutionary psychology. To begin with, the prime mover of modern feminism, the discontent of the 1950s suburban housewife, was entirely natural. To see this, you need only look at a hunter-gatherer society, which, being a rough approximation of the social context of human evolution, is a rough guide to the patterns of behavior "natural" to us, absent the influence of modern technological society. In hunter-gatherer societies, women have a career: gathering. This may sound to an upper-middle-class feminist like menial labor; but it gets them out of the house. (And besides, menial compared to what—hunting?)

But women in such societies are also mothers, the primary caregivers. And reconciling their home and work lives is surprisingly practical. When they go out to gather food, child care is barely an issue; their children may go with them

or, instead, stay with relatives. And when mothers, back from work, do care for children, the context is social, even communal. As the anthropologist Marjorie Shostak wrote after observing the !Kung San hunter-gatherers, "The isolated mother burdened with bored small children is not a scene that has parallels in !Kung daily life." Women weren't designed to be suburban housewives.

The generic suburban habitat of the '50s was more "natural," more congenial, for men. Like many hunter-gatherers, vintage suburban husbands spent a little time with children and a lot of time out bonding with males, in work, play or ritual. Thus the grievance that drove 1950s housewives toward feminism was solidly grounded: suburbia let men behave naturally while forcing mothers into artificial isolation—removed from their kin, often lacking close friends and devoid of purpose beyond child-rearing.

If this inequity is clear from a Darwinian vantage point, so is the reason that redressing it has been hard. It is no surprise that many working mothers feel not just harried by their dual identity but guilty about it—guilty about, say, spending forty hours a week away from a 1- or 2-year-old child while the child is in the hands of someone who is neither kin nor close friend. To judge by hunter-gatherer societies, this is quite an unnatural predicament. That doesn't mean women can't adapt to it. But anecdotal evidence suggests that they don't easily do so, and that some working mothers today aren't dramatically happier than the lonely suburban mothers of the 1950s.

This is one of the most pressing issues now facing women. Various partial solutions are possible, such as job-sharing and workplace-based child care. But if these are to be pursued vigorously *as feminist issues*, it would help to acknowledge that they are fundamentally the concerns of women; that, although men can certainly play a large role in child-rearing, it's much easier for the average man than for the average woman to be away from young offspring—and that it always will be.

Many feminists will admit no such thing. The reason women have always been primary caregivers, Pollitt writes, has nothing in particular to do with their psychology. "Historically, women have taken care of children because high fertility and lack of other options left most of them no choice." Well, yes, that's been going on for a while—throughout human evolution, in fact. That's why any evolutionary psychologist finds it hard to believe that natural selection wouldn't have molded the female mind to this task. The task, after all, is pretty vital: protecting the vessel that carries the genes into the next generation.

Some consider the liberal equity feminists the most sober of the major schools of feminism, and Pollitt in particular has become known as the voice of calm reason. Yet she and the other mainstream liberals may have the most warped vision in all of feminism. Quite unlike the difference feminists, and more than the radical feminists, they are committed to ignoring basic features of reality. Imagine a social observer as acute as Pollitt not sensing how deeply—well, for lack of a better term—*maternal* women are compared with men. That must take a lot of perceptual restraint.

When Pollitt, under the pressure of overwhelming evidence, does concede some distinctive female feature, she seems disappointed, no matter how ostensibly laudable it is, and hastens to predict its demise. Thus she grants that "social scientists who look for it can find traces of empathy, caring and so on in some women who have risen in the world of work and power." But that's just because "we are in a transition period" and working women haven't yet learned the ropes. Thus, it seems, we can look forward to a day when working women will have been stripped of the last trace of empathy and caring. Then they'll be just like men. Congratulations.

The reductio ad absurdum of Pollitt's attitude has been performed by the feminist novelist Katherine Dunn. When she isn't celebrating the several women who have taken up boxing (equal opportunity brain damage!) Dunn spends her time trying to dispel some of the fuss about wife-beating. In both [*The New Republic*] and *Mother Jones*, she has touted some study that found that women strike their husbands about as often as men strike their wives. Well, maybe so (though probably not). But getting hit is not the essence of being an abused spouse. Chronic intimidation is. How many husbands live in fear of assault by their wives? How many husbands, while out with their wives, desperately avoid eye contact with the opposite sex lest they be beaten upon returning to their cage? That major liberal magazines are publishing articles whose predictable effect is to downplay the plight of battered wives is a sure sign that equity feminism's denial of harsh Darwinian truths is reaching pathological extremes.

To be sure, neither the difference feminists nor the radical feminists come close to getting the whole picture. The difference feminists often stress ways women are good, and the radical feminists always stress ways men are bad; both tend to ignore female badness and male goodness. Also, of course, both schools deny any important role for biology. Still, at least the larger project of the radical feminists and, especially, of the difference feminists, is quietly eroding that denial; the fit between Darwinian theory and the social reality they're documenting is too neat to go unnoticed. That these feminists are emphatically not Darwinians makes their database even more valuable as objective corroboration.

The radical feminists' penetrating perception of social reality, paired with delusion about its deepest roots, is reminiscent of Marxism. Though Marx fooled himself about human nature, his view of the way the upper classes exploit their power, manipulating ideology to the detriment of the less fortunate, is acute (and, actually, quite Darwinian, much like the radical feminists' keen attention to the levers of male sexual power. (Though the radical feminists tend to ignore the often subtler means by which women use their sexuality to control men.) And the parallels don't end there. Like the Marxists, the radical feminists are marginalizing themselves by the hyperbole of their indictment and by their dreams of a perfect post-revolution world. They depict an enemy of overwhelming force and envision its unconditional surrender.

With both Marxism and feminism, the struggle against the forces of oppression is worthy and, up to a point, practical. But in both cases, the struggle is best conducted with thorough comprehension of those forces and of their bases in human nature. If feminists—of all stripes—want to know their enemy, it is now available for inspection.

REVIEW AND DISCUSSION QUESTIONS

1. Why does Wright compare many contemporary feminists with communists?
2. How do biologists explain the relatively greater sexual reserve of females?
3. Why do men distinguish between "fast" and "slow" women, according to Wright?
4. Describe Wright's position on sexual harassment, and why he thinks the Supreme Court's approach is mistaken.
5. In what ways does Darwinian theory agree and disagree with the Dworkin-MacKinnon view of men?
6. Why does Wright think affirmative action for women is incompatible with biology?
7. Does Wright agree that what is "natural" is also "morally good"? Explain.
8. How can evolutionary theory explain the emergence of feminism out of the 1950s, according to Wright?
9. Compare Wright's view of sex differences with those of Camille Paglia and Lois Pineau. Is Pineau's "communicative" understanding of sex compatible with Wright's position?
10. Discuss the significance of evolutionary theory and its claims about what is "natural" for how society and individuals "ought" to behave.
11. How might "dominance" feminists respond to this essay? Which view seems most reasonable to you? Explain.
12. How would Alison Jaggar (Section 3) respond to Wright's essay? Was she wrong in ignoring evolutionary theory in discussing the issues feminists should concern themselves with? Explain.

16
Race, Identity, and Difference

Essays in this section address issues having to do with racial, ethnic, and religious differences, focusing especially on political issues involving assimilation, personal identity, and group consciousness. The first three selections look briefly at the history of racism and efforts to end legal segregation. Two are legal cases that are now seen to be central landmarks in the struggle for equality, one holding legal segregation consistent with the Constitution and the other requiring integration of public schools. Also included is a letter from one of America's most influential judges, Learned Hand, on the subject of allowing Jews into Harvard College. With this as background, the next three articles in the section address issues of race, ethnicity, and gender in the contemporary context, asking, among other things, how a just society would treat those categories. Are people inevitably defined by their ethnicity, race, and gender? And what are the similarities and differences between sexism, on one hand, and racism on the other? Political issues are also in the foreground of these discussions as the authors weigh the advantages and disadvantages of using ethnic and racial categories in defining legal rights and responsibilities. Is assimilation the ideal, so that race and gender are treated no differently from eye color, or should society acknowledge and even encourage group identity?

Separate but Equal:

Plessy v. *Ferguson*

Few American legal opinions on race are more notorious than this one, in which the U.S. Supreme Court accepted legally imposed segregation. After the Civil War, three constitutional amendments were adopted dealing with race. The Thirteenth Amendment abolished slavery; the Fifteenth Amendment promised that the right to vote will not be denied on account of race, color, or previous condition of servitude; and the Fourteenth Amendment stated that the states cannot deny "equal protection" of the laws, abridge the "privileges or immunities of citizens of the United States," or deprive citizens of life, liberty, or property without "due process of law." Some of the early cases interpreting the Fourteenth Amendment suggested the Court might work to enforce the ideal of equality embedded in it, but soon the Court backtracked, allowing southern radicals committed to removing federal troops and resegregating and disenfranchising blacks to gain firm control. "Jim Crow" laws mandating segregation were soon in force throughout the South. This case arose after Homer Plessy was prosecuted for refusing to give up his railroad seat to a white, as required by law. Plessy claimed the law denied him "equal protection," but the Supreme Court upheld such laws.

163 U.S. 537 (1896).

Mr. Justice Brown: The distinction between laws interfering with the political equality of the negro and those requiring the separation of the two races in schools, theatres and railway carriages has been frequently drawn by this court.... [W]e think the enforced separation of the races, as applied to the internal commerce of the State, neither abridges the privileges or immunities of the colored man, deprives him of his property without due process of law, nor denies him the equal protection of the laws, within the meaning of the Fourteenth Amendment.... [I]t is suggested ... that the same argument that will justify the state legislature in requiring railways to provide separate accommodations for the two races will also authorize them to require separate cars to be provided for people whose hair is of a certain color, or who are aliens, or who belong to certain nationalities, or to enact laws requiring colored people to walk upon one side of the street, and white people upon the other, or requiring white men's houses to be painted white, and colored men's black, or their vehicles or business signs to be of different colors, upon the theory that one side of the street is as good as the other, or that a house or vehicle of one color is as good as one of another color. The reply to all this is that every exercise of the police power must be reasonable, and extend only to such law as are enacted in good faith for the promotion for the public good, and not for the annoyance or oppression of a particular class....

So far, then, as a conflict with the Fourteenth Amendment is concerned, the case reduces itself to the question whether the statute of Louisiana is a reasonable regulation, and with respect to this there must necessarily be a large discretion on the part of the legislature. In determining the question of reasonableness it is at liberty to act with reference to the established usages, customs and traditions of the people, and with a view to the promotion of their comfort, and the preservation of the public peace and good order. Gauged by this standard, we cannot say that a law which authorizes or even requires the separation of the two races in public conveyances is unreasonable, or more obnoxious to the Fourteenth Amendment than the acts of Congress requiring separate schools for colored children in the District of Columbia, the constitutionality of which does not seem to have been questioned, or the corresponding acts of state legislatures.

We consider the underlying fallacy of the plaintiff's argument to consist in the assumption that the enforced separation of the two races stamps the colored race with a badge of inferiority. If this be so, it is not by reason of anything found in the act, but solely because the colored race chooses to put that construction upon it. The argument necessarily assumes that if, as has been more than once the case, and is not unlikely to be so again, the colored race should become the dominant power in the state legislature, and should enact a law in precisely similar terms, it would thereby relegate the white race to an inferior position. We imagine that the white race, at least, would not acquiesce in this assumption. The argument also assumes that social prejudices may be overcome by legislation, and that equal rights cannot be secured to the negro except by an enforced commingling of the two races. We cannot accept this proposition. If the two races are to meet upon terms of social equality, it must be the result of natural affinities, a mutual appreciation of each other's merits and a voluntary consent of individuals.... Legislation is powerless to eradicate racial instincts or to abolish distinctions based upon physical differences, and the attempt to do so can only result in accentuating the difficulties of the present situation. If the civil and political rights of both races be equal one cannot be inferior to the other civilly or politically. If one race be inferior to the other socially, the Constitution of the United States cannot put them upon the same plane.

Mr. Justice Harlan, Dissenting: The white race deems itself to be the dominant race in this country. And so it is, in prestige, in achievements, in education, in wealth and in power. So, I doubt not, it will continue to be for all time, if it remains true to its great heritage and holds fast to the principles of constitutional liberty. But in view of the Constitution, in the eye of the law, there is in this country no superior, dominant, ruling class of citizens. There is no caste here. Our Constitution is color-blind, and neither knows nor tolerates classes among citizens. In respect of civil rights, all citizens are equal before the law. The humblest is the peer of the most powerful. The law regards man as man, and takes no account of his surroundings or of his color when his civil rights as guaranteed by the supreme law of the land are involved. It is, therefore, to be regretted that this high tribunal, the final expositor of the fundamental law of the land, has reached the conclusion that it is competent for a State to regulate the enjoyment by citizens of their civil rights solely upon the basis of race.

In my opinion, the judgment this day rendered will, in time, prove to be quite as pernicious as the decision made by this tribunal in the *Dred Scott* case [1857]. . . . The destinies of the two races, in this country, are indissolubly linked together, and the interests of both require that the common government of all shall not permit the seeds of race hate to be planted under the sanction of law. What can more certainly arouse race hate, what more certainly create and perpetuate a feeling of distrust between these races, than state enactments, which, in fact, proceed on the ground that colored citizens are so inferior and degraded that they cannot be allowed to sit in public coaches occupied by white citizens? That, as all will admit, is the real meaning of such legislation as was enacted in Louisiana.

The sure guarantee of the peace and security of each race is the clear, distinct, unconditional recognition by our governments, National and State, of every right that inheres in civil freedom, and of the equality before the law of all citizens of the United States without regard to race. State enactments regulating the enjoyment of civil rights, upon the basis of race and cunningly devised to defeat legitimate results of the war, under the pretence of recognizing equality of rights, can have no other result than to render permanent peace impossible, and to keep alive a conflict of races, the continuance of which must do harm to all concerned. This question is not met by the suggestion that social equality cannot exist between the white and black races in this country . . . ; for social equality no more exists between two races when travelling in a passenger coach or a public highway than when members of the same races sit by each other in a street car or in the jury box, or stand or sit with each other in a political assembly, or when they use in common the streets of a city or town. . . .

The arbitrary separation of citizens, on the basis of race, while they are on a public highway, is a badge of servitude wholly inconsistent with the civil freedom and the equality before the law established by the Constitution. It cannot be justified upon any legal grounds. . . .

We boast of the freedom enjoyed by our people above all other peoples. But it is difficult to reconcile that boast with a state of the law which, practically, puts the brand of servitude and degradation upon a large class of our fellow-citizens, our equals before the law. The thin disguise of "equal" accommodations for passengers in railroad coaches will not mislead any one, nor atone for the wrong this day done.

REVIEW AND DISCUSSION QUESTIONS

1. Describe the basic argument offered by Justice Brown in defense of the Louisiana law's constitutionality.
2. What does he see as the "underlying fallacy" of Plessy's argument?
3. Has history proved Justice Brown right in his claim about the limits of legislation?
4. Justice Harlan wrote a famous dissent. Explain briefly his reasoning. Do you agree that the Constitution is "color-blind," as he famously stated?
5. Did those laws treat all citizens equally, as the Court claimed? Explain.

The Great School Desegregation Case:

Brown v. *Board of Education*

In a few cases during the 1930s, the Supreme Court began to show some concern for the way states habitually treated black citizens. One case, *Brown* v. *Mississippi* (1936), involved three blacks who had been arrested for murder. The deputy sheriff hanged one of them by the neck from a tree, occasionally lowering him only to ask if he were ready to confess, which he eventually did. All three were found guilty after a brief trial before an all-white jury, without the benefit of a lawyer. Even the rope scars did not sway the jurors, who sentenced all three to death. The Supreme Court reversed the conviction, saying the defendants had been denied their rights under the due process clause of the Fourteenth Amendment.

But by far the biggest victories came in the area of education. From its founding in 1909, the National Association for the Advancement of Colored People (NAACP) fought to overturn *Plessy*. Then, in 1938, a young civil rights lawyer named Thurgood Marshall was named director of the NAACP Legal Defense and Education Fund, and for the next eighteen years he and others won an extraordinary series of legal victories that slowly but surely undermined the legal basis of state-enforced segregation. In 1954, the NAACP attacked *Plessy* directly in a case that involved the segregated educational systems of four states plus the District of Columbia. After hearing the initial arguments, the Justices tentatively voted five to four in favor of the NAACP's position. Chief Justice Vinson soon died, and President Eisenhower appointed Earl Warren to replace him (a decision Eisenhower later said was a mistake). Warren worked hard to persuade the remaining dissenters, winning over the last holdout, Justice Reed, arguing that unanimity was crucial if the order was to be carried out and that his love of the Court should take precedence over his personal views.

The opinion was widely hated; calls for Warren's impeachment could be seen on billboards throughout the South. Prince Edward County, Virginia, went as far as closing its public schools rather than integrate them, and it was not until the Civil Rights Act of 1964, along with more aggressive efforts by the Courts to enforce *Brown*, that progress was made. Nonetheless, most agree that *Brown* v. *Board of Education* is among the Supreme Court's greatest achievements.

Chief Justice Warren Delivered the Opinion of the Court: The plaintiffs contend that segregated public schools are not "equal" and cannot be made "equal," and that hence they are deprived of the equal protection of the laws. . . .

Reargument [in an additional hearing asked for by the Court—Ed.] was largely devoted to the circumstances surrounding the adoption of the Fourteenth Amendment in 1868. . . . This discussion and our own investigation convince us that, although these sources cast some light, it is not enough to resolve the problem with which we are faced. At best, they are inconclusive. The most

avid proponents of the post-War Amendments undoubtedly intended them to remove all legal distinctions among "all persons born or naturalized in the United States." Their opponents, just as certainly, were antagonistic to both the letter and the spirit of the Amendments and wished them to have the most limited effect. . . .

An additional reason for the inclusive nature of the Amendment's history, with respect to segregated schools, is the status of public education at that time. In the South, the movement toward free common schools, supported by general taxation, had not yet taken hold. Education of white chil-

347 U.S. 483 (1954). Some citations omitted.

dren was largely in the hands of private groups. Education of Negroes was almost nonexistent, and practically all of the race were illiterate. In fact, any education of Negroes was forbidden by law in some states. . . .

In the first cases in this Court construing the Fourteenth Amendment, decided shortly after its adoption, the Court interpreted it as proscribing all state-imposed discriminations against the Negro race. The doctrine of "separate but equal" did not make its appearance in this Court until 1896 in the case of *Plessy* v. *Ferguson*, involving not education but transportation. American courts have since labored with the doctrine for over half a century. . . .

In more recent cases, all on the graduate school level, inequality was found in that specific benefits enjoyed by white students were denied to Negro students of the same educational qualifications. . . .

In the instant cases, that question is directly presented. Here, unlike *Sweatt* v. *Painter* (1950), there are findings below that the Negro and white schools involved have been equalized, or are being equalized, with respect to buildings, curricula, qualifications and salaries of teachers, and other "tangible" factors. Our decision, therefore, cannot turn on merely a comparison of these tangible factors in the Negro and white schools involved in each of the cases. We must look instead to the effect of segregation itself on public education.

In approaching this problem, we cannot turn the clock back to 1868 when the Amendment was adopted, or even to 1896 when *Plessy* was written. We must consider public education in the light of its full development and its present place in American life throughout the Nation. Only in this way can it be determined if segregation in public schools deprives these plaintiffs of the equal protection of the laws.

Today, education is perhaps the most important function of state and local governments. Compulsory school attendance laws and the great expenditures for education both demonstrate our recognition of the importance of education to our democratic society. . . . In these days, it is doubtful that any child may reasonably be expected to succeed in life if he is denied the opportunity of an education. Such an opportunity, where the state has undertaken to provide it, is a right which must be made available to all on equal terms.

We come then to the question presented: Does segregation of children in public schools solely on the basis of race, even though the physical facilities and other "tangible" factors may be equal, deprive the children of the minority group of equal educational opportunities? We believe that it does.

In *Sweatt*, in finding that a segregated law school for Negroes could not provide them equal educational opportunities, this Court relied in large part on "those qualities which are incapable of objective measurement but which make for greatness in a law school." In *McLaurin* v. *Oklahoma* (1950), the Court, in requiring that a Negro admitted to a white graduate school be treated like all other students, again resorted to intangible considerations: ". . . . his ability to study, to engage in discussions and exchange views with other students, and; in general, to learn his profession." Such considerations apply with added force to children in grade and high schools. To separate them from others of similar age and qualifications solely because of their race generates a feeling of inferiority as to their status in the community that may affect their hearts and minds in a way unlikely ever to be undone. The effect of this separation on their educational opportunities was well stated by a finding in the Kansas case by a court which nevertheless felt compelled to rule against the Negro plaintiffs: "Segregation of white and colored children in public schools has a detrimental effect upon the colored children. The impact is greater when it has the sanction of the law; for the policy of separating the races is usually interpreted as denoting the inferiority of the negro group. A sense of inferiority affects the motivation of a child to learn. Segregation with the sanction of law, therefore, has a tendency to [retard] the educational and mental development of Negro children and to deprive them of some of the benefits they would receive in a racial[ly] integrated school system."

Whatever may have been the extent of psychological knowledge at the time of *Plessy*, this finding is amply supported by modern authority. [Citing various studies, including ones showing that black and white children prefer white dolls.] Any language in *Plessy* contrary to this finding is rejected.

We conclude that in the field of public education the doctrine of "separate but equal" has no place. Separate educational facilities are inherently unequal. Therefore, we hold that the plaintiffs and others similarly situated for whom the actions have been brought are, by reason of the segregation complained of, deprived of the equal protection of the laws guaranteed by the Fourteenth Amendment.

Because these are class actions, because of the wide applicability of this decision, and because of the great variety of local conditions, the formulation of decrees in these cases presents problems of considerable complexity. On reargument, the consideration of appropriate relief was necessarily subordinated to the primary question—the constitutionality of segregation in public education. We have now announced that such segregation is a denial of the equal protection of the laws.

REVIEW AND DISCUSSION QUESTIONS

1. The Court did not explicitly overrule *Plessy* in *Brown*. Explain just what the Court did do.

2. What is the sociological basis of the Court's claim?

3. Why do you think the Court expected desegregation would improve the educational opportunities for black children?

4. Judging from the Court's opinion in *Brown* alone, what would you have predicted it would do with cases involving segregated public swimming pools and legal bans on interracial marriage? (Later decisions, in fact, struck these down as well, using *Brown* as a precedent.)

5. This has been described as a conservative opinion because the country had no real choice at the time but to desegregate. Describe the historical, social, economic, and international factors that might be used to make that argument.

6. Compare this decision with Justice Harlan's dissent in *Plessy*.

7. Later Courts, responding to the refusal of school districts to abide by the decision in *Brown*, ordered school busing both within and across district lines to eliminate the vestiges of past discrimination. Are those remedies consistent with this decision? Are they required by *Brown*?

8. Though state-supported women's and men's colleges have been ruled unconstitutional [as Justice Sandra Day O'Connor held in *Mississippi University for Women v. Hogan* (1982)], there are still many public "historically black" universities in the United States, most of which were created during the time of segregation. Though they allow whites to attend, few whites choose to do so, and the schools remain overwhelmingly black. Should courts now force them to integrate, even though many black colleges resist? Is the fact that blacks choose to attend relevant? ("Freedom of choice" plans were struck down by the Court for primary and secondary schools, which described them as a means to avoid integration.)

Jewish Quotas at Harvard College

Learned Hand

Jews have faced quotas in education and employment in the United States and throughout the world. In this letter, written in 1922 by one of this nation's great judges, Learned Hand discusses the controversy over the number of Jewish students that should be allowed to enter Harvard College.

New York
November 14, 1922

Charles H. Grandgent, Esq.
Harvard College
Cambridge, Mass.

Dear Sir:

I have understood that your committee welcomes the opinion of alumni on the question of limiting the numbers of Jewish undergraduates. This is my excuse for writing you. The difficulties are no doubt real in a sense that a graduate of thirty years ago would find it hard to realize. I have been told that the college now contains large numbers of Jews, insensitive, aggressive and ill-conditioned, whose presence causes much hostility among the Christians. I shall assume this to be true, and that their increase, to say nothing of their present numbers, will be likely to drive away many students of the kind to which we have been accustomed.

Notwithstanding, I cannot agree that a limitation based upon race will in the end work out any good purpose. If the Jew does not mix well with the Christian, it is no answer to segregate him. Most of those qualities which the Christian dislikes in him are, I believe, the direct result of that very policy in the past. Both Christian and Jew are here; they must in some way learn to live on tolerable terms, and disabilities have never proved tolerable. It seems hardly necessary to argue that they intensify on both sides the very feelings which they are designed to relieve on one. If after acquaintance the two races are irretrievably alien, which I believe unproven, we are, it is true, in a bad case, but even so not as bad as if we separate them on race lines. Along that path lie only bitterness and distraction.

But the proposal is not segregation or exclusion but to limit the number of Jews. That, however, is if anything worse. Those who are in fact shut out are of course segregated; those who are let in are effectively marked as racially undesirable. Intercourse with them is with social inferiors; there can be no other conceivable explanation for the limitation. The results of that will be deplorable to both sides. The argument is put somewhat differently; that the effort is to prevent Jews from concentrating in too great numbers in any one college. They must be spread about in equal proportions. This does not escape the same vice, I think. They are spread involuntarily, which must mean that some are excluded and all are only tolerated wherever they eventually come to rest; the same objections remain.

If anyone could devise an honest test for character, perhaps it would serve well. I doubt its feasibility except to detect formal and obvious delinquencies. Short of it, it seems to me that students can only be chosen by tests of scholarship, unsatisfactory as those no doubt are. A raw, ill-bred and barbarous student will be offensive; he will in the end feel it, perhaps he will improve. At least one may hope for it. A sensitive, well-nurtured student will dislike him; if he has no humanity in him, it will rest there; if he has any, he will see something more. At least let him learn decent toleration, and if he will not, we should not fear to lose him. I cannot feel that college should be a retreat from what he must learn somehow to live with.

After all, the Jews who can qualify among the increasingly limited numbers that get in at all, must excel in scholarly tests. If there are better ways of testing scholarship, let us by all means have them, but whatever they are, success in them is success in the chief aim of a college, an interest in, and aptitude for, learning. The rest is secondary, and so far as there are any who will be turned away because they find themselves in too great a company of the uncouth, their prime pur-

pose is not scholarship. Perhaps it is here that the real difference lies between those who would limit and those who would not. A college may gather together men of a common tradition, or it may put its faith in learning. If so, it will I suppose take its chance that in learning lies the best hope, and that a company of scholars will prove better than any other company. Our tests do not indeed go far to produce such a company but they are all we have.

Sincerely yours,
Learned Hand

REVIEW AND DISCUSSION QUESTIONS

1. What seem to be the reasons that those who defend quotas were offering, to which Hand is responding?
2. Describe Hand's argument against the quotas.
3. Compare the quotas discussed in this letter with the segregation laws that were at first allowed and then struck down in the *Plessy* and *Brown* cases.

On Racism and Sexism: Realities and Ideals

Richard A. Wasserstrom

Richard A. Wasserstrom discusses two important problems. One is the degree to which modern social realities continue to reflect racism and sexism. The second concerns the ideal: How would a decent society treat race and sex? The first topic, realities, leads Wasserstrom to describe a variety of important features of modern society, including its institutions, practices, and attitudes. In considering social ideals, Wasserstrom distinguishes the assimilationist ideal from those of diversity and tolerance. He then defends the ideal of assimilation, that is, the view that race and sex should have no more institutional significance than eye color. Richard A. Wasserstrom is professor of philosophy at the University of California at Santa Cruz.

From Parts I and II of Richard A. Wasserstrom, "Racism, Sexism, and Preferential Treatment: An Approach to the Topics," *UCLA Law Review,* 24, (1977), 581–622. © 1977 by Richard A. Wasserstrom. Some footnotes have been deleted and the remaining ones renumbered. Reprinted by permission of the author.

INTRODUCTION

Racism and sexism are two central issues that engage the attention of many persons living within the United States today. But while there is relatively little disagreement about their importance as topics, there is substantial, vehement, and apparently intractable disagreement about what individuals, practices, ideas, and institutions are either racist or sexist—and for what reasons. In dispute are a number of related questions concerning how individuals ought to regard and respond to matters relating to race or sex. . . .

What I want to do in this essay is first propose a general way of looking at issues of racism and sexism, then look at several of the respects in which racism and sexism are alike and different, and then, finally, examine one somewhat neglected but fundamental issue; namely that of what a genuinely nonracist or nonsexist society might look like. . . .

1. SOCIAL REALITIES

A. The Position of Blacks and Women

Methodologically, the first thing it is important to note is that to talk about social realities is to talk about a particular social and cultural context. And in our particular social and cultural context race and sex are socially very important categories. They are so in virtue of the fact that we live in a culture which has, throughout its existence, made race and sex extremely important characteristics of and for all the people living in the culture.

It is surely possible to imagine a culture in which race would be an unimportant, insignificant characteristic of individuals. In such a culture race would be largely if not exclusively a matter of superficial physiology; a matter, we might say, simply of the way one looked. And if it were, then any analysis of race and racism would necessarily assume very different dimensions from what they do in our society. In such a culture, the meaning of the term "race" would itself have to change substantially. This can be seen by the fact that in such a culture it would literally make no sense to say of a person that he or she was "passing."[1] This is

something that can be said and understood in our own culture and it shows at least that to talk of race is to talk of more than the way one looks.[2]

Sometimes when people talk about what is wrong with affirmative action programs, or programs of preferential hiring, they say that what is wrong with such programs is that they take a thing as superficial as an individual's race and turn it into something important. They say that a person's race doesn't matter; other things do, such as qualifications. Whatever else may be said of statements such as these, as descriptions of the social realities they seem to be simply false. One complex but true empirical fact about our society is that the race of an individual is much more than a fact of superficial physiology. It is, instead, one of the dominant characteristics that affects both the way the individual looks at the world and the way the world looks at the individual. As I have said, that need not be the case. It may in fact be very important that we work toward a society in which that would not be the case, but it is the case now and it must be understood in any adequate and complete discussion of racism. That is why, too, it does not make much sense when people sometimes say, in talking about the fact that they are not racists, that they would not care if an individual were green and came from Mars, they would treat that individual the same way they treat people exactly like themselves. For part of our social and cultural history is to treat people of certain races in a certain way, and we do not have a social or cultural history of treating green people from Mars in any particular way. To put it simply, it is to misunderstand the social realities of race and racism to think of them simply as questions of how some people respond to other people whose skins are of different hues, irrespective of the social context.

I can put the point another way: Race does not function in our culture as does eye color. Eye color is an irrelevant category; nobody cares what color people's eyes are; it is not an important cultural fact; nothing turns on what eye color you have. It is important to see that race is not like that at all. And this truth affects what will and will not count as cases of racism. In our culture to be nonwhite—especially to be black—is to be treated and seen to be a member of a group that is different from and inferior to the group of standard, fully developed persons, the adult white males. To be black is to be a member of what was a despised minority and what is still a disliked and oppressed one. That is simply part of the awful truth of our cultural and social history, and a significant feature of the social reality of our culture today.

We can see fairly easily that the two sexual categories, like the racial ones, are themselves in important respects products of the society. Like one's race, one's sex is not merely or even primarily a matter of physiology. To see this we need only realize that we can understand the idea of a transsexual. A transsexual is someone who would describe himself or herself as a person who is essentially a female but through some accident of nature is trapped in a male body, or a person who is essentially a male but through some accident of nature is trapped in the body of a female. His (or her) description is some kind of a shorthand way of saying that he (or she) is more comfortable with the role allocated by the culture to people who are physiologically of the opposite sex. The fact that we regard this assertion of the transsexual as intelligible seems to me to show how deep the notion of sexual identity is in our culture and how little it has to do with physiological differences between males and females. Because people do pass in the context of race and because we can understand what passing means; because people are transsexuals and because we can understand what transsexuality means, we can see that the existing social categories of both race and sex are in this sense creations of the culture.

It is even clearer in the case of sex than in the case of race that one's sexual identity is a centrally important, crucially relevant category within our culture. I think, in fact, that it is more important and more fundamental than one's race. It is evident that there are substantially different role expectations and role assignments to persons in accordance with their sexual physiology, and that the positions of the two sexes in the culture are distinct. We do have a patriarchal society in which it matters enormously whether one is a male or a female. By almost all important measures it is more advantageous to be a male rather than a female. . . .

As is true for race, it is also a significant social fact that to be a female is to be an entity or creature viewed as different from the standard, fully developed person who is male as well as white. But to be female, as opposed to being black, is not to be conceived of as simply a creature of less worth. That is one important thing that differentiates sexism from racism: The ideology of sex, as opposed to the ideology of race, is a good deal more complex and confusing. Women are both put on a pedestal and deemed not fully developed persons. They are idealized; their approval and admiration is sought; and they are at the same time regarded as less competent than men and less able to live fully developed, fully human lives—for that is what men do. At best, they are viewed and treated as having properties and attributes that are valuable and admirable for humans of this type. For example, they may be viewed as especially empathetic, intuitive, loving, and nurturing. At best, these qualities are viewed as good properties for women to have, and, provided they are properly muted, are sometimes valued within the more well-rounded male. Because the sexual ideology is complex, confusing, and variable, it does not unambiguously proclaim the lesser value attached to being female rather than being male, nor does it unambiguously correspond to the existing social realities. For these, among other reasons, sexism could plausibly be regarded as a deeper phenomenon than racism. It is more deeply embedded in the culture, and thus less visible. . . .

Viewed from the perspective of social reality it should be clear, too, that racism and sexism should not be thought of as phenomena that consist simply in taking a person's race or sex into account, or even simply in taking a person's race or sex into account in an arbitrary way. Instead, racism and sexism consist in taking race and sex into account in a certain way, in the context of a specific set of institutional arrangements and a specific ideology which together create and maintain a specific system of institutions, role assignments, beliefs and attitudes. That system is one, and has been one, in which political, economic, and social power and advantage is concentrated in the hands of those who are white and male. . . .

. . . Take, for instance, the most hideous of the practices, human slavery. The primary thing that was wrong with the institution was not that the particular individuals who were assigned the place of slaves were assigned there arbitrarily because the assignment was made in virtue of an irrelevant characteristic, i.e., their race. Rather, it seems to me clear that the primary thing that was and is wrong with slavery is the practice itself—the fact of some individuals being able to own other individuals and all that goes with that practice. It would not matter by what criterion individuals were assigned; human slavery would still be wrong. And the same can be said for many of the other discrete practices and institutions that comprised the system of racial discrimination even after human slavery was abolished. The practices were unjustifiable—they were oppressive—and they would have been so no matter how the assignment of victims had been made. What made it worse, still, was that the institutions and ideology all interlocked to create a system of human oppression whose effects on those living under it were as devastating as they were unjustifiable.

Some features of the system of sexual oppression are like this and others are different. For example, if it is true that women are socialized to play the role of servers of men and if they are in general assigned that position in the society, what is objectionable about that practice is the practice itself. It is not that women are being arbitrarily or capriciously assigned the social role of server, but rather that such a role is at least *prima facie* unjustifiable as a role in a decent society. As a result, the assignment on any basis of individuals to such a role is objectionable.

The assignment of women to primary responsibility for child rearing and household maintenance may be different; it may be objectionable on grounds of unfairness of another sort. That is to say, if we assume that these are important but undesirable aspects of social existence—if we assume that they are, relatively speaking, unsatisfying and unfulfilling ways to spend one's time, then the objection is that women are unduly and unfairly allocated a disproportionate share of unpleasant, unrewarding work. Here the objection, if it is proper, is to the degree to which the necessary burden is placed to a greater degree than is fair on women, rather than shared equally by persons of both sexes. . . .

[T]he primary evil of the various schemes of racial segregation against blacks that the courts were being called upon to assess was not that such schemes were a capricious and irrational way of allocating public benefits and burdens. That might well be the primary wrong with racial segregation if we lived in a society very different from the one we have. The primary evil of these schemes was instead that they designedly and effectively marked off all black persons as degraded, dirty, less than fully developed persons who were unfit for full membership in the political, social, and moral community.

It is worth observing that the social reality of sexually segregated bathrooms appears to be different. The idea behind such sexual segregation seems to have more to do with the mutual undesirability of the use by both sexes of the same bathroom at the same time. There is no notion of the possibility of contamination; or even directly of inferiority and superiority. What seems to be involved—at least in part—is the importance of inculcating and preserving a sense of secrecy concerning the genitalia of the opposite sex. What seems to be at stake is the maintenance of that same sense of mystery or forbiddenness about the other sex's sexuality which is fostered by the general prohibition upon public nudity and the unashamed viewing of genitalia.

Sexually segregated bathrooms simply play a different role in our culture than did racially segregated ones. But that is not to say that the role they play is either benign or unobjectionable—only that it is different. Sexually segregated bathrooms may well be objectionable, but here too, the objection is not on the ground that they are prima facie capricious or arbitrary. Rather, the case against them now would rest on the ground that they are, perhaps, one small part of that scheme of sex-role differentiation which uses the mystery of sexual anatomy, among other things, to maintain the primacy of heterosexual sexual attraction central to that version of the patriarchal system of power relationships we have today.[3] Once again, whether sexually segregated bathrooms would be objectionable, because irrational, in the good society depends once again upon what the good society would look like in respect to sexual differentiation.

B. Types of Racism or Sexism

Another recurring question that can profitably be examined within the perspective of social realities is whether the legal system is racist or sexist. Indeed, it seems to me essential that the social realities of the relationships and ideologies concerning race and sex be kept in mind whenever one is trying to assess claims that are made about the racism or sexism of important institutions such as the legal system. It is also of considerable importance in assessing such claims to understand that even within the perspective of social reality, racism or sexism can manifest itself, or be understood, in different ways. That these are both important points can be seen through a brief examination of the different, distinctive ways in which our own legal system might plausibly be understood to be racist. The mode of analysis I propose serves as well, I believe, for an analogous analysis of the sexism of the legal system, although I do not undertake the latter analysis in this paper.

The first type of racism is the simplest and the least controversial. It is the case of overt racism, in which a law or a legal institution expressly takes into account the race of individuals in order to assign benefits and burdens in such a way as to bestow an unjustified benefit upon a member or members of the racially dominant group or an unjustified burden upon members of the racial groups that are oppressed. We no longer have many, if any, cases of overt racism in our legal system today, although we certainly had a number in the past. Indeed, the historical system of formal, racial segregation was both buttressed by, and constituted of, a number of overtly racist laws and practices. At different times in our history, racism included laws and practices which dealt with such things as the exclusion of nonwhites from the franchise, from decent primary and secondary schools and most professional schools, and the prohibition against interracial marriages.

The second type of racism is very similar to overt racism. It is covert, but intentional, racism, in which a law or a legal institution has as its purpose the allocation of benefits and burdens in order to support the power of the dominant race, but does not use race specifically as a basis for allocating these benefits and burdens. One particularly good historical example involves the use of grandfather clauses which were inserted in statutes governing voter registration in a number of states after passage of the fifteenth amendment.

Covert racism within the law is not entirely a thing of the past. Many instances of de facto school segregation in the North and West are cases of covert racism. At times certain school boards—virtually all of which are overwhelmingly white in composition—quite consciously try to maintain exclusively or predominantly white schools within a school district. . . .

I believe it is a mistake to think about the problem of racism in terms of overt or covert racial discrimination by state action, which is now banished, and racial prejudice, which still lingers, but only in the hearts of persons. For there is another, more subtle kind of racism—unintentional, perhaps, but effective—which is as much a part of the legal system as are overt and covert racist laws and practices. It is what some critics of the legal system probably mean when they talk about the "institutional racism" of the legal system.

There are at least two kinds of institutional racism. The first is the racism of sub-institutions within the legal system such as the jury, or the racism of practices built upon or countenanced by the law. These institutions and practices very often, if not always, reflect in important and serious ways a variety of dominant values in the operation of what is apparently a neutral legal mechanism. The result is the maintenance and reinforcement of a system in which whites dominate over nonwhites. One relatively uninteresting (because familiar) example is the case of de facto school segregation. As observed above, some cases of de facto segregation are examples of covert racism. But even in school districts where there is no intention to divide pupils on grounds of race so as to maintain existing power relationships along racial lines, school attendance zones are utilized which are based on the geographical location of the pupil. Because it is a fact in our culture that there is racial discrimination against black people in respect to housing, it is also a fact that any geographical allocation of pupils—unless one pays a lot of attention to housing patterns—will have the effect of continuing to segregate minority pupils very largely on grounds of race. It is perfectly appropriate to regard this effect as a case of racism in public education. . . .

The second type of institutional racism is what I will call "conceptual" institutional racism. . . .

We use concepts. Quite often without realizing it, the concepts used take for granted certain objectionable aspects of racist ideology without our being aware of it. The second *Brown* case (*Brown II*) provides an example.[4] There was a second *Brown* case because, having decided that the existing system of racially segregated public education was unconstitutional (*Brown I*),[5] the Supreme Court gave legitimacy to a second issue—the nature of the relief to be granted—by treating it as a distinct question to be considered and decided separately. That in itself was striking because in most cases, once the Supreme Court has found unconstitutionality, there has been no problem about relief (apart from questions of retroactivity): The unconstitutional practices and acts are to cease. As is well known, the Court in *Brown II* concluded that the desegregation of public education had to proceed "with all deliberate speed."[6] The Court said that there were "complexities arising from the transition to a system of public education freed from racial discrimination."[7] More specifically, time might be necessary to carry out the ruling because of

problems related to administration, arising from the physical condition of the school plant, the school transportation system personnel, revision of school districts and attendance areas into compact units to achieve a system of determining admission to the public school on a non-racial basis, and revision of local laws and regulations which may be necessary in solving the foregoing problems.[8]

Now, I do not know whether the Court believed what it said in this passage, but it is a fantastic bit of nonsense that is, for my purposes, most instructive. Why? Because there was nothing complicated about most of the dual school systems of the southern states. . . . There was nothing difficult about deciding that—as of the day after the decision—half of the children in the country, say all those who lived in the southern part of the county, would go to "Robert E. Lee High School," and all those who lived in the northern half would go to "Booker T. Washington High School." *Brown I* could have been implemented the day after the Court reached its decision. But it was also true that the black schools throughout the South were utterly wretched when compared to the white

schools. There never had been any system of separate but equal education. In almost every measurable respect, the black schools were inferior. One possibility is that, without being explicitly aware of it, the members of the Supreme Court made use of some assumptions that were a significant feature of the dominant racist ideology. If the assumptions had been made explicit, the reasoning would have gone something like this: Those black schools are wretched. We cannot order white children to go to those schools, especially when they have gone to better schools in the past. So while it is unfair to deprive blacks, to make them go to these awful, segregated schools, they will have to wait until the black schools either are eliminated or are sufficiently improved so that there are good schools for everybody to attend.

What seems to me to be most objectionable, and racist, about *Brown II* is the uncritical acceptance of the idea that during this process of change, black schoolchildren would have to suffer by continuing to attend inadequate schools. The Supreme Court's solution assumed that the correct way to deal with this problem was to continue to have the black children go to their schools until the black schools were brought up to par or eliminated. That is a kind of conceptual racism in which the legal system accepts the dominant racist ideology, which holds that the claims of black children are worth less than the claims of white children in those cases in which conflict is inevitable. It seems to me that any minimally fair solution would have required that during the interim process, if anybody had to go to an inadequate school, it would have been the white children, since they were the ones who had previously had the benefit of the good schools. But this is simply not the way racial matters are thought about within the dominant ideology.

A study of *Brown II* is instructive because it is a good illustration of conceptual racism within the legal system. It also reflects another kind of conceptual racism—conceptual racism about the system. . . . [T]he fact that we have, as well as inculcate, attitudes of effusive praise toward *Brown I* and *II* and its progeny reveals a kind of persistent conceptual racism in talk about the character of the legal system, and what constitutes the right way to have dealt with the social reality of American racial oppression of black people.

2. IDEALS

The second perspective . . . which is also important for an understanding and analysis of racism and sexism, is the perspective of the ideal. Just as we can and must ask what is involved today in our culture in being of one race or of one sex rather than the other, and how individuals are in fact viewed and treated, we can also ask different questions: namely, what would the good or just society make of race and sex, and to what degree, if at all, would racial and sexual distinctions ever be taken into account? Indeed, it could plausibly be argued that we could not have an adequate idea of whether a society was racist or sexist unless we had some conception of what a thoroughly nonracist or nonsexist society would look like. This perspective is an extremely instructive as well as an often neglected one. Comparatively little theoretical literature that deals with either racism or sexism has concerned itself in a systematic way with this perspective.

In order to ask more precisely what some of the possible ideals are of desirable racial or sexual differentiation, it is necessary to see that we must ask: "In respect to what?" And one way to do this is to distinguish in a crude way among three levels or areas of social and political arrangements and activities. . . . First, there is the area of basic political rights and obligations, including the rights to vote and to travel, and the obligation to pay income taxes. Second, there is the area of important, nongovernmental institutional benefits and burdens. Examples are access to and employment in the significant economic markets, the opportunity to acquire and enjoy housing in the setting of one's choice, the right of persons who want to marry each other to do so, and the duties (nonlegal as well as legal) that persons acquire in getting married. And third, there is the area of individual, social interaction, including such matters as whom one will have as friends, and what aesthetic preferences one will cultivate and enjoy.

As to each of these three areas we can ask, for example, whether in a nonracist society it would be thought appropriate ever to take the race of the individuals into account. Thus, one picture of a nonracist society is that which is captured by what I call the assimilationist ideal: a nonracist society would be one in which the race of an individual would be the functional equivalent of the eye color of individuals in our society today.[9] In our society no basic political rights and obligations are determined on the basis of eye color. No important institutional benefits and burdens are connected with eye color. Indeed, except for the mildest sort of aesthetic preferences, a person would be thought odd who even made private, social decisions by taking eye color into account. And for reasons that we could fairly readily state we could explain why it would be wrong to permit anything but the mildest, most trivial aesthetic preference to turn on eye color. The reasons would concern the irrelevance of eye color for any political or social institution, practice or arrangement. According to the assimilationist ideal, a nonracist society would be one in which an individual's race was of no more significance in any of these three areas than is eye color today.

The assimilationist ideal in respect to sex does not seem to be as readily plausible and obviously attractive here as it is in the case of race. In fact, many persons invoke the possible realization of the assimilationist ideal as a reason for rejecting the Equal Rights Amendment and indeed the idea of women's liberation itself. My own view is that the assimilationist ideal may be just as good and just as important an ideal in respect to sex as it is in respect to race. But many persons think there are good reasons why an assimilationist society in respect to sex would not be desirable.

To be sure, to make the assimilationist ideal a reality in respect to sex would involve more profound and fundamental revisions of our institutions and our attitudes than would be the case in respect to race. On the institutional level we would have to alter radically our practices concerning the family and marriage. If a nonsexist society is a society in which one's sex is no more significant than eye color in our society today, then laws that require the persons who are getting married to be of different sexes would clearly be sexist laws.

And on the attitudinal and conceptual level, the assimilationist ideal would require the eradication of all sex-role differentiation. It would never teach about the inevitable or essential attributes of masculinity or femininity; it would never encourage or discourage the ideas of sisterhood or brotherhood;

and it would be unintelligible to talk about the virtues as well as disabilities of being a woman or a man. Were sex like eye color, these things would make no sense. Just as the normal, typical adult is virtually oblivious to the eye color of other persons for all major interpersonal relationships, so the normal, typical adult in this kind of nonsexist society would be indifferent to the sexual, physiological differences of other persons for all interpersonal relationships.

To acknowledge that things would be very different is, of course, hardly to concede that they would be undesirable. But still, perhaps the problem is with the assimilationist ideal. And the assimilationist ideal is certainly not the only possible, plausible ideal.

There are, for instance, two others that are closely related, but distinguishable. One I call the ideal of diversity; the other, the ideal of tolerance. Both can be understood by considering how religion, rather than eye color, tends to be thought about in our culture. According to the ideal of diversity, heterodoxy in respect to religious belief and practice is regarded as a positive good. On this view there would be a loss—it would be a worse society—were everyone to be a member of the same religion. According to the other view, the ideal of tolerance, heterodoxy in respect to religious belief and practice would be seen more as a necessary, lesser evil. On this view there is nothing intrinsically better about diversity in respect to religion, but the evils of achieving anything like homogeneity far outweigh the possible benefits.

Now, whatever differences there might be between the ideals of diversity and tolerance, the similarities are more striking. Under neither ideal would it be thought that the allocation of basic political rights and duties should take an individual's religion into account. And we would want equalitarianism even in respect to most important institutional benefits and burdens—for example, access to employment in the desirable vocations. Nonetheless, on both views it would be deemed appropriate to have some institutions (typically those that are connected in an intimate way with these religions) that do in a variety of ways take the religion of members of the society into account. For example, it might be thought permissible and appropriate for members of a religious group to join together in collective associations which have religious, educational and social dimensions. And on the individual, interpersonal level, it might be thought unobjectionable, or on the diversity view, even admirable, were persons to select their associates, friends, and mates on the basis of their religious orientation. So there are two possible and plausible ideals of what the good society would look like in respect to religion in which religious differences would be to some degree maintained because the diversity of religions was seen either as an admirable, valuable feature of the society, or as one to be tolerated. The picture is a more complex, less easily describable one than that of the assimilationist ideal.

It may be that in respect to sex (and conceivably, even in respect to race) something more like either of these ideals in respect to religion is the right one. But one problem then—and it is a very substantial one—is to specify with a good deal of precision and care what that ideal really comes to. Which legal, institutional and personal differentiations are permissible and which are not? Which attitudes and beliefs concerning sexual identification and difference are properly introduced and maintained and which are not? Part, but by no means all, of the attractiveness of the assimilationist ideal is its clarity and simplicity. In the good society of the assimilationist sort we would be able to tell easily and unequivocally whether any law, practice, or attitude was in any respect either racist or sexist. Part, but by no means all, of the unattractiveness of any pluralistic ideal is that it makes the question of what is racist or sexist a much more difficult and complicated one to answer. But although simplicity and lack of ambiguity may be virtues, they are not the only virtues to be taken into account in deciding among competing ideals. We quite appropriately take other considerations to be relevant to an assessment of the value and worth of alternative nonracist and nonsexist societies.

Nor do I even mean to suggest that all persons who reject the assimilationist ideal in respect to sex would necessarily embrace either something like the ideal of tolerance or the ideal of diversity. Some persons might think the right ideal was one in which substantially greater sexual differentiation and sex-role identification was retained than would be the case under either of these conceptions. Thus, someone might believe that the good society was, perhaps, essentially like the one they think we now have in respect to sex: equality of political rights, such as the right to vote, but all of the sexual differentiation in both legal and non-legal institutions that is characteristic of the way in which our society has been and still is ordered. And someone might also believe that the usual ideological justifications for these arrangements are the correct and appropriate ones. . . .

The next question, of course, is that of how a choice is rationally to be made among these different, possible ideals. One place to begin is with the empirical world. For the question of whether something is a plausible and attractive ideal does turn in part on the nature of the empirical world. If it is true, for example, that any particular characteristic, such as sex, is not only a socially significant category in our culture but that it is largely a socially created one as well, then many ostensible objections to the assimilationist ideal appear immediately to disappear.

What I mean is this: It is obvious that we could formulate and use some sort of a crude, incredibly imprecise physiological concept of race. In this sense we could even say that race is a naturally occurring rather than a socially created feature of the world. There are diverse skin colors and related physiological characteristics distributed among human beings. But the fact is that except for skin hue and the related physiological characteristics, race is a socially created category. And skin hue, as I have shown, is neither a necessary nor a sufficient condition for being classified as black in our culture. Race as a naturally occurring characteristic is also a socially irrelevant category. There do not in fact appear to be any characteristics that are part of this natural concept of race and that are in any plausible way even relevant to the appropriate distribution of any political, institutional, or interpersonal concerns in the good society. Because in this sense race is like eye color, there is no plausible case to be made on this ground against the assimilationist ideal.[10]

There is, of course, the social reality of race. In creating and tolerating a society in which race matters, we must recognize that we have created a vastly more complex concept of race which includes what might be called the idea of ethnicity

as well—a set of attitudes, traditions, beliefs, etc., which the society has made part of what it means to be of a race. It may be, therefore, that one could argue that a form of the pluralist ideal ought to be preserved in respect to race, in the socially created sense, for reasons similar to those that might be offered in support of the desirability of some version of the pluralist ideal in respect to religion. As I have indicated, I am skeptical, but for the purposes of this essay it can well be left an open question.

Despite appearances, the case of sex is more like that of race than is often thought. What opponents of assimilationism seize upon is that sexual difference appears to be a naturally occurring category of obvious and inevitable social relevance in a way, or to a degree, which race is not. The problems with this way of thinking are twofold. To begin with, an analysis of the social realities reveals that it is the socially created sexual differences which tend in fact to matter the most. It is sex-role differentiation, not gender per se, that makes men and women as different as they are from each other, and it is sex-role differences which are invoked to justify most sexual differentiation at any of the levels of society.[11]

More importantly, even if naturally occurring sexual differences were of such a nature that they were of obvious prima facie social relevance, this would by no means settle the question of whether in the good society sex should or should not be as minimally significant as eye color. Even though there are biological differences between men and women in nature, this fact does not determine the question of what the good society can and should make of these differences. . . . For there appear to be very few, if any, respects in which the ineradicable, naturally occurring differences between males and females must be taken into account. The industrial revolution has certainly made any of the general differences in strength between the sexes capable of being ignored by the good society in virtually all activities. And it is sex-role acculturation, not biology, that mistakenly leads many persons to the view that women are both naturally and necessarily better suited than men to be assigned the primary responsibilities of child rearing. Indeed, the only fact that seems required to be taken into account is the fact that reproduction of the human species requires that the fetus develop in utero for a period of months. Sexual intercourse is not necessary, for artificial insemination is available. Neither marriage nor the family is required for conception or child rearing. Given the present state of medical knowledge and the natural realities of female pregnancy, it is difficult to see why any important institutional or interpersonal arrangements *must* take the existing gender difference of *in utero* pregnancy into account. . . .

There is, however, at least one more argument based upon nature, or at least the "natural," that is worth mentioning. Someone might argue that significant sex-role differentiation is natural not in the sense that it is biologically determined but only in the sense that it is a virtually universal phenomenon in human culture. By itself, this claim of virtual universality, even if accurate, does not directly establish anything about the desirability or undesirability of any particular ideal. But it can be made into an argument by the addition of the proposition that where there is a virtually universal social practice, there is probably some good or important purpose served by the practice. . . . The straightforward way to think about that . . . is to ask what would be good and what would be bad about a society in which sex functioned like eye color does in our society. We can imagine what such a society would look like and how it would work. It is hard to see how our thinking is substantially advanced by reference to what has typically or always been the case. If it is true, as I think it is, that the sex-role differentiated societies we have had so far have tended to concentrate power in the hands of males, have developed institutions and ideologies that have perpetuated that concentration and have restricted and prevented women from living the kinds of lives that persons ought to be able to live for themselves, then this says far more about what may be wrong with any nonassimilationist ideal than does the conservative premise say what may be right about any nonassimilationist ideal.

Nor is this all that can be said in favor of the assimilationist ideal. For it seems to me that the strongest affirmative moral argument on its be-

half is that it provides for a kind of individual autonomy that a nonassimilationist society cannot attain. Any nonassimilationist society will have sex roles. Any nonassimilationist society will have some institutions that distinguish between individuals by virtue of their gender, and any such society will necessarily teach the desirability of doing so. Any substantially nonassimilationist society will make one's sexual identity an important characteristic, so that there are substantial psychological, role, and status differences between persons who are males and those who are females. Even if these could be attained without systemic dominance of one sex over the other, they would, I think, be objectionable on the ground that they necessarily impaired an individual's ability to develop his or her own characteristics, talents and capacities to the fullest extent to which he or she might desire. Sex roles, and all that accompany them, necessarily impose limits—restrictions on what one can do, be or become. As such, they are, I think at least *prima facie* wrong.

To some degree, all role-differentiated living is restrictive in this sense. Perhaps, therefore, all role-differentiation in society is to some degree troublesome, and perhaps all strongly role-differentiated societies are objectionable. . . .

I do not believe that all I have said in this section shows in any conclusive fashion the desirability of the assimilationist ideal in respect to sex. I have tried to show why some typical arguments against the assimilationist ideal are not persuasive, and why some of the central ones in support of that ideal are persuasive. But I have not provided a complete account, or a complete analysis. At a minimum, what I have shown is how thinking about this topic ought to proceed, and what kinds of arguments need to be marshalled and considered before a serious and informed discussion of alternative conceptions of a nonsexist society can even take place. Once assembled, these arguments need to be individually and carefully assessed before any final, reflective choice among the competing ideals can be made. There does, however, seem to me to be a strong presumptive case for something very close to, if not identical with, the assimilationist ideal.

NOTES

1. Passing is the phenomenon in which a person who in some sense knows himself or herself to be black "passes" as white because he or she looks white. A version of this is described in Sinclair Lewis' novel *Kingsblood Royal* (1947), where the protagonist discovers when he is an adult that he, his father, and his father's mother are black (or, in the idiom of the late 1940's, Negro) in virtue of the fact that his great grandfather was black. His grandmother knew this and was consciously passing. When he learns about his ancestry, one decision he has to make is whether to continue to pass, or to acknowledge to the world that he is in fact "Negro."

2. That looking black is not in our culture a necessary condition for being black can be seen from the phenomenon of passing. That it is not a sufficient condition can be seen from the book *Black Like Me* (1960), by John Howard Griffin, where "looking black" is easily understood by the reader to be different from being black. I suspect that the concept of being black is, in our culture, one which combines both physiological and ancestral criteria in some moderately complex fashion.

3. This conjecture about the role of sexually segregated bathrooms may well be inaccurate or incomplete. The sexual segregation of bathrooms may have more to do with privacy than with patriarchy. However, if so, it is at least odd that what the institution makes relevant is sex rather than merely the ability to perform the eliminatory acts in private.

4. *Brown* v. *Board of Educ.*, 349 U.S. 294 (1955).

5. *Brown* v. *Board of Educ.*, 347 U.S. 483 (1954).

6. 349 U.S. at 301.

7. *Id.* at 299.

8. *Id.* at 300–01.

9. There is a danger in calling this ideal the "assimilationist" ideal. That term suggests the idea of incorporating oneself, one's values, and the like into the dominant group and its practices and values. I want to make it clear that no part of that idea is meant to be captured by my use of this term. Mine is a stipulative definition.

10. This is not to deny that certain people believe that race is linked with characteristics that *prima facie* are relevant. Such beliefs persist. They are, however, unjustified by the evidence. More to the point, even if it were true that such a linkage existed, none of the characteristics suggested would require that political or social institutions, or interpersonal relationships, would have to be structured in a certain way.

11. See, e.g., M. Mead, *Sex and Temperament in Three Primitive Societies* (1935): "These three situations [the cultures of the Anapesh, the Mundugumor, and the Tchambuli] suggest, then, a very definite conclusion. If those temperamental attitudes which we have traditionally regarded as feminine—such as passivity, responsiveness, and a willingness to cherish children—can so easily be set up as the masculine pattern in one tribe, and in another to be outlawed for the majority of women as well as for the majority of men, we no longer have any basis for regarding such aspects of behavior as sex-linked. . . . We are forced to conclude that human nature is almost unbelievably malleable, responding accurately and contrastingly to contrasting cultural conditions. . . . Standardized personality differences between the sexes are of this order, cultural creations to which each generation, male and female is trained to conform." *Id.* at 190–91.

A somewhat different view is expressed in J. Sherman, *On the Psychology of Women* (1971). There, the author suggests that there are "natural" differences of a psychological sort between men and women, the chief ones being aggressiveness and strength of sex drive. See *id.* at 238. However, even if she is correct as to these biologically based differences, this does little to establish what the good society should look like.

Almost certainly the most complete discussion of this topic is E. Maccoby & C. Jacklin, *The Psychology of Sex Differences* (1974). The authors conclude that the sex differences which are, in their words, "fairly well established," are: (1) that girls have greater verbal ability than boys; (2) that boys excel in visual-spatial ability; (3) that boys excel in mathematical ability; and (4) that males are more aggressive. *Id.* at 351–52. They conclude, in respect to the etiology of these psychological sex differences, that there appears to be a biological component to the greater visual-spatial ability of males and to their greater aggressiveness. *Id.* at 360.

REVIEW AND DISCUSSION QUESTIONS

1. What point about race does Wasserstrom make in his discussion of "passing"?

2. How does Wasserstrom understand racism and sexism? What is their connection with social realities?

3. In what ways are racism and sexism similar? Different?

4. Describe the different types of racism and sexism Wasserstrom notes.

5. How do the Supreme Court's rulings in *Brown* v. *Board of Education* illustrate institutional racism, according to Wasserstrom?

6. Identify and explain briefly the three "ideals."

7. Why does Wasserstrom think the assimilationist ideal is preferable?

8. Assess the assimilationist ideal, indicating whether you agree that it is preferable to the other two. Is there another alternative that might be better? Explain.

9. Have events in recent years given us reason to question Wasserstrom's assessment of social realities? Explain.

10. Compare Wasserstrom's understanding of racism and sexism with Peter Singer's discussion of equality in Section 5.

Social Movements and the Politics of Difference

Iris Marion Young

In this essay, Iris Marion Young offers a wide-ranging and important discussion of the significance of group differences and personal identity to contemporary politics. Beginning with a critique of Wasserstrom's assimilationist ideal, she goes on to outline an alternative, "relational" ideal and defend the "politics of difference" as the best means to achieve genuine emancipation. She then considers various group conscious policies for women, involving pregnancy, childbirth, and the workplace. Iris Marion Young is professor of Public and International Affairs at the University of Pittsburgh.

In this chapter I criticize an ideal of justice that defines liberation as the transcendence of group difference, which I refer to as an ideal of assimilation. This ideal usually promotes equal treatment as a primary principle of justice. Recent social movements of oppressed groups challenge this ideal. Many in these movements argue that a positive self-definition of group difference is in fact more liberatory.

I endorse this politics of difference, and argue that at stake is the meaning of social difference itself. Traditional politics that excludes or devalues some persons on account of their group attributes assumes an essentialist meaning of difference; it defines groups as having different natures. An egalitarian politics of difference, on the other hand, defines difference more fluidly and relationally as the product of social processes.

An emancipatory politics that affirms group difference involves a reconception of the meaning of equality. The assimilationist ideal assumes that equal social status for all persons requires treating everyone according to the same principles, rules, and standards. A politics of difference argues, on the other hand, that equality as the participation and inclusion of all groups sometimes requires different treatment for oppressed or disadvantaged groups. To promote social justice,

I argue, social policy should sometimes accord special treatment to groups. . . .

COMPETING PARADIGMS OF LIBERATION

In "On Racism and Sexism," Richard Wasserstrom (1980) develops a classic statement of the ideal of liberation from group-based oppression as involving the elimination of group-based difference itself. A truly nonracist, nonsexist society, he suggests, would be one in which the race or sex of an individual would be the functional equivalent of eye color in our society today. While physiological differences in skin color or genitals would remain, they would have no significance for a person's sense of identity or how others regard him or her. No political rights or obligations would be connected to race or sex, and no important institutional benefits would be associated with either. People would see no reason to consider race or gender in policy or everyday interactions. In such a society, social group differences would have ceased to exist.

Wasserstrom contrasts this ideal of assimilation with an ideal of diversity much like the one I will argue for, which he agrees is compelling. He offers three primary reasons, however, for choosing the assimilationist ideal of liberation over the ideal of diversity. First, the assimilationist ideal exposes the arbitrariness of group-based social distinctions which are thought natural and necessary. By imagining a society in which race and sex have no social significance, one sees more clearly how pervasively these group categories unnecessarily limit possibilities for some in existing society. Second, the assimilationist ideal presents a clear and unambiguous standard of equality and justice. According to such a standard, any group-related differentiation or discrimination is suspect. Whenever laws or rules, the division of labor, or other social practices allocate benefits differently according to group membership, this is a sign of injustice. The principle of justice is simple: treat everyone according to the same principles, rules, and standards. Third, the assimilationist ideal maximizes choice. In a society where differences make no social difference people can develop themselves as individuals, unconstrained by group norms and expectations.

There is no question that the ideal of liberation as the elimination of group difference has been enormously important in the history of emancipatory politics. The ideal of universal humanity that denies natural differences has been a crucial historical development in the struggle against exclusion and status differentiation. It has made possible the assertion of the equal moral worth of all persons, and thus the right of all to participate and be included in all institutions and positions of power and privilege. The assimilationist ideal retains significant rhetorical power in the face of continued beliefs in the essentially different and inferior natures of women, Blacks, and other groups.

The power of this assimilationist ideal has inspired the struggle of oppressed groups and the supporters against the exclusion and denigration of these groups, and continues to inspire many. Periodically in American history, however, movements of the oppressed have questioned and rejected this "path to belonging." . . . Instead they have seen self-organization and the assertion of a positive group cultural identity as a better strategy for achieving power and participation in dominant institutions. Recent decades have witnessed a resurgence of this "politics of difference" not only among racial and ethnic groups, but also among women, gay men and lesbians, old people, and the disabled. . . .

None of the social movements asserting positive group specificity is in fact a unity. All have group differences within them. The Black movement, for example, includes middle-class Blacks and working-class Blacks, gays and straight people, men and women, and so it is with any other group. The implications of group differences within a social group have been most systematically discussed in the women's movement. Feminist conferences and publications have generated particularly fruitful, though often emotionally wrenching, discussions of the oppression of racial and ethnic blindness and importance of attending to group differences among women. . . . From such discussions emerged principled efforts to provide autonomously organized forums for Black women, Latinas, Jewish women, lesbians, differently abled women, old women, and any other women who see reason for claiming that they have as a group a distinctive voice that might be silenced in a general feminist discourse. Those discussions, along with the practices feminists instituted structure discussion and interaction among differently identifying groups of women, offer some beginning models for the development of a heterogeneous public. Each of the other social movements has also generated discussion of group differences that cut across their identities, leading to other possibilities of coalition and alliance.

EMANCIPATION THROUGH THE POLITICS OF DIFFERENCE

Implicit in emancipatory movements asserting a positive sense of group difference is a different ideal of liberation, which might be called democratic cultural pluralism. In this vision the good society does not eliminate or transcend group difference. Rather, there is equality among socially and culturally differentiated groups, who mutually respect one another and affirm one another in their differences. What are the reasons for rejecting the assimilationist ideal and promoting a politics of difference?

. . . Some deny the reality of social groups. For them, group difference is an invidious fiction produced and perpetuated in order to preserve the privilege of the few. Others, such as Wasserstrom, may agree that social groups do now exist and have real social consequences for the way people identify themselves and one another, but assert that such social group differences are undesirable. The assimilationist ideal involves denying either the reality or the desirability of social groups.

Those promoting a politics of difference doubt that a society without group differences is either possible or desirable. Contrary to the assumption of modernization theory, increased urbanization and the extension of equal formal rights to all groups has not led to a decline in particularist affiliations. If anything, the urban concentration and interactions among groups that modernizing social processes introduce tend to reinforce group solidarity and differentiation. Attachment to specific traditions, practices, languages, and other culturally specific forms is a crucial aspect of so-

cial existence. People do not usually give up their social group identifications, even when they are oppressed.

Whether eliminating social group difference is possible or desirable in the long run, however, is an academic issue. Today and for the foreseeable future societies are certainly structured by groups, and some are privileged while others are oppressed. New social movements of group specificity do not deny the official story's claim that the ideal of liberation as eliminating difference and treating everyone the same has brought significant improvement in the status of excluded groups. Its main quarrel is with the story's conclusion, namely, that since we have achieved formal equality, only vestiges and holdovers of differential privilege remain, which will die out with the continued persistent assertion of an ideal of social relations that make differences irrelevant to a person's life prospects. The achievement of formal equality does not eliminate social differences, and rhetorical commitment to the sameness of persons makes it impossible even to name how those differences presently structure privilege and oppression.

Though in many respects the law is now blind to group differences, some groups continue to be marked as deviant, as the Other. In everyday interactions, images, and decisions, assumptions about women, Blacks, Hispanics, gay men and lesbians, old people, and other marked groups continue to justify exclusion, avoidance, paternalism, and authoritarian treatment. Continued racist, sexist, homophobic, ageist, and ableist institutions and behavior create particular circumstances for these groups, usually disadvantaging them in their opportunity to develop their capacities. Finally, in part because they have been segregated from one another, and in part because they have particular histories and traditions, there are cultural differences among social groups—differences in language, style of living, body comportment and gestures, values, and perspectives on society.

Today in American society, as in many other societies, there is widespread agreement that no person should be excluded from political and economic activities because of ascribed characteristics. Group differences nevertheless continue to exist, and certain groups continue to be privileged. Under these circumstances, insisting that equality and liberation entail ignoring difference has oppressive consequences in three respects.

First, blindness to difference disadvantages groups whose experience, culture, and socialized capacities differ from those of privileged groups. The strategy of assimilation aims to bring formerly excluded groups into the mainstream. So assimilation always implies coming into the game after it is already begun, after the rules and standards have already been set, and having to prove oneself according to those rules and standards. In the assimilationist strategy, the privileged groups implicitly define the standards according to which all will be measured. Because their privilege involves not recognizing these standards as culturally and experientially specific, the ideal of a common humanity in which all can participate without regard to race, gender, religion, or sexuality poses as neutral and universal. The real differences between oppressed groups and the dominant norm, however, tend to put them at a disadvantage in measuring up to these standards, and for that reason assimilationist policies perpetuate their disadvantage. . . .

Second, the ideal of a universal humanity without social group differences allows privileged groups to ignore their own group specificity. Blindness to difference perpetuates cultural imperialism by allowing norms expressing the point of view and experience of privileged groups to appear neutral and universal. The assimilationist ideal presumes that there is a humanity in general, an unsituated group-neutral human capacity for self-making that left to itself would make individuality flower, thus guaranteeing that each individual will be different. . . . Because there is no such unsituated group-neutral point of view, the situation and experience of dominant groups tend to define the norms of such a humanity in general. Against such a supposedly neutral humanist ideal, only the oppressed groups come to be marked with particularity; they, and not the privileged groups, are marked, objectified as the Others.

Thus, third, this denigration of groups that deviate from an allegedly neutral standard often produces an internalized devaluation by members of those groups themselves. When there is an ideal of general human standards according to which everyone should be evaluated equally, then Puerto

Ricans or Chinese Americans are ashamed of their accents or their parents, Black children despise the female-dominated kith and kin networks of their neighborhoods, and feminists seek to root out their tendency to cry, or to feel compassion for a frustrated stranger. The aspiration to assimilate helps produce the self-loathing and double consciousness characteristic of oppression. The goal of assimilation holds up to people a demand that they "fit," be like the mainstream, in behavior, values, and goals. At the same time, as long as group differences exist, group members will be marked as different—as Black, Jewish, gay—and thus as unable simply to fit. When participation is taken to imply assimilation the oppressed person is caught in an irresolvable dilemma: to participate means to accept and adopt an identity one is not, and to try to participate means to be reminded by oneself and others of the identity one is.

A more subtle analysis of the assimilationist ideal might distinguish between a conformist and a transformational ideal of assimilation. In the conformist ideal, status quo institutions and norms are assumed as given, and disadvantaged groups who differ from those norms are expected to conform to them. A transformational ideal of assimilation, on the other hand, recognizes that institutions as given express the interests and perspective of the dominant groups. Achieving assimilation therefore requires altering many institutions and practices in accordance with neutral rules that truly do not disadvantage or stigmatize any person, so that group membership really is irrelevant to how persons are treated. Wasserstrom's ideal fits a transformational assimilation, as does the group-neutral ideal advocated by some feminists (Taub and Williams, 1985). Unlike the conformist assimilationist, the transformational assimilationist may allow that group-specific policies, such as affirmative action, are necessary and appropriate means for transforming institutions to fit the assimilationist ideal. Whether conformist or transformational, however, the assimilationist ideal still denies that group difference can be positive and desirable; thus any form of the ideal of assimilation constructs group difference as a liability or disadvantage.

Under these circumstances, a politics that asserts the positivity of group difference is liberating and empowering. In the act of reclaiming the identity the dominant culture has taught them to despise and affirming it as an identity to celebrate, the oppressed remove double consciousness. I am just what they say I am—a Jewboy, a colored girl, a fag, a dyke, or a hag—and proud of it. No longer does one have the impossible project of trying to become something one is not under circumstances where the very trying reminds one of who one is. This politics asserts that oppressed groups have distinct cultures, experiences, and perspectives on social life with humanly positive meaning, some of which may even be superior to the culture and perspectives of mainstream society. The rejection and devaluation of one's culture and perspective should not be a condition of full participation in social life.

Asserting the value and specificity of the culture and attributes of oppressed groups, moreover, results in a relativizing of the dominant culture. When feminists assert the validity of feminine sensitivity and the positive value of nurturing behavior, when gays describe the prejudice of heterosexuals as homophobic and their own sexuality as positive and self-developing, when Blacks affirm a distinct Afro-American tradition, then the dominant culture is forced to discover itself for the first time as specific: as Anglo, European, Christian, masculine, straight. In a political struggle where oppressed groups insist on the positive value of their specific culture and experience, it becomes increasingly difficult for dominant groups to parade their norms as neutral and universal, and to construct the values and behavior of the oppressed as deviant, perverted, or inferior. By puncturing the universalist claim to unity that expels some groups and turns them into the Other, the assertion of positive group specificity introduces the possibility of understanding the relation between groups as merely difference, instead of exclusion, opposition, or dominance.

The politics of difference also promotes a notion of group solidarity against the individualism of liberal humanism. Liberal humanism treats each person as an individual, ignoring differences of race, sex, religion, and ethnicity. Each person should be evaluated only according to her or his individual efforts and achievements. With the institutionalization of formal equality some

members of formerly excluded groups have indeed succeeded, by mainstream standards. Structural patterns of group privilege and oppression nevertheless remain. When political leaders of oppressed groups reject assimilation they are often affirming group solidarity. Where the dominant culture refuses to see anything but the achievement of autonomous individuals, the oppressed assert that we shall not separate from the people with whom we identify in order to "make it" in a white Anglo male world. The politics of difference insists on liberation of the whole group of Blacks, women, American Indians, and that this can be accomplished only through basic institutional changes. These changes must include group representation in policymaking and an elimination of the hierarchy of rewards that forces everyone to compete for scarce positions at the top.

Thus the assertion of a positive sense of group difference provides a standpoint from which to criticize prevailing institutions and norms. Black Americans find in their traditional communities, which refer to their members as "brother" and "sister," a sense of solidarity absent from the calculating individualism of white professional capitalist society. Feminists find in the traditional female values of nurturing a challenge to a militarist world-view, and lesbians find in their relationships a confrontation with the assumption of complementary gender roles in sexual relationships. From their experience of a culture tied to the land American Indians formulate a critique of the instrumental rationality of European culture that results in pollution and ecological destruction. Having revealed the specificity of the dominant norms which claim universality and neutrality, social movements of the oppressed are in a position to inquire how the dominant institutions must be changed so that they will no longer reproduce the patterns of privilege and oppression.

From the assertion of positive difference the self-organization of oppressed groups follows. Both liberal humanist and leftist political organizations and movements have found it difficult to accept this principle of group autonomy. In a humanist emancipatory politics, if a group is subject to injustice, then all those interested in a just society should unite to combat the powers that perpetuate that injustice. If many groups are subject to injustice, moreover, then they should unite to work for a just society. The politics of difference is certainly not against coalition, nor does it hold that, for example, whites should not work against racial injustice or men against sexist injustice. This politics of group assertion, however, takes as a basic principle that members of oppressed groups need separate organizations that exclude others, especially those from more privileged groups. Separate organization is probably necessary in order for these groups to discover and reinforce the positivity of their specific experience, to collapse and eliminate double consciousness. In discussions within autonomous organizations, group members can determine their specific needs and interests. Separation and self-organization risk creating pressures toward homogenization of the groups themselves, creating new privileges and exclusions. . . . But contemporary emancipatory social movements have found group autonomy an important vehicle for empowerment and the development of a group-specific voice and perspective.

Integration into the full life of the society should not have to imply assimilation to dominant norms and abandonment of group affiliation and culture. If the only alternative to the oppressive exclusion of some groups defined as Other by dominant ideologies is the assertion that they are the same as everybody else, then they will continue to be excluded because they are not the same.

Some might object to the way I have drawn the distinction between an assimilationist ideal of liberation and a radical democratic pluralism. They might claim that I have not painted the ideal of a society that transcends group differences fairly, representing it as homogeneous and conformist. The free society envisaged by liberalism, they might say, is certainly pluralistic. In it persons can affiliate with whomever they choose; liberty encourages a proliferation of life styles, activities, and associations. While I have no quarrel with social diversity in this sense, this vision of liberal pluralism does not touch on the primary issues that give rise to the politics of difference. The vision of liberation as the transcendence of group difference seeks to abolish the public and political significance of group difference, while retaining and promoting both individual and group diversity in

private, or nonpolitical, social contexts. . . . This way of distinguishing public and private spheres, where the public represents universal citizenship and the private individual differences, tends to result in group exclusion from the public. Radical democratic pluralism acknowledges and affirms the public and political significance of social group differences as a means of ensuring the participation and inclusion of everyone in social and political institutions.

RECLAIMING THE MEANING OF DIFFERENCE

Many people inside and outside the movements I have discussed find the rejection of the liberal humanist ideal and the assertion of a positive sense of group difference both confusing and controversial. They fear that any admission by oppressed groups that they are different from the dominant groups risks justifying anew the subordination, special marking, and exclusion of those groups. Since calls for a return of women to the kitchen, Blacks to servant roles and separate schools, and disabled people to nursing homes are not absent from contemporary politics, the danger is real.

It may be true that the assimilationist ideal that treats everyone the same and applies the same standards to all perpetuates disadvantage because real group differences remain that make it unfair to compare the unequals. But this is far preferable to a reestablishment of separate and unequal spheres for different groups justified on the basis of group difference.

Since those asserting group specificity certainly wish to affirm the liberal humanist principle that all persons are of equal moral worth, they appear to be faced with a dilemma. Analyzing W.E.B. Du Bois's arguments for cultural pluralism, Bernard Boxill poses the dilemma this way: "On the one hand, we must overcome segregation because it denies the idea of human brotherhood; on the other hand, to overcome segregation we must self-segregate and therefore also deny the idea of human brotherhood" (Boxill, 1984, p. 174). . . .

These dilemmas are genuine, and exhibit the risks of collective life, where the consequences of one's claims, actions, and policies may not turn out as one intended because others have understood them differently or turned them to different ends. Since ignoring group differences in public policy does not mean that people ignore them in everyday life and interaction, however, oppression continues even when law and policy declare that all are equal. Thus I think for many groups and in many circumstances it is more empowering to affirm and acknowledge in political life the group differences that already exist in social life. One is more likely to avoid the dilemma of difference in doing this if the meaning of difference itself becomes a terrain of political struggle. Social movements asserting the positivity of group difference have established this terrain, offering an emancipatory meaning of difference to replace the old exclusionary meaning.

The oppressive meaning of group difference defines it as absolute otherness, mutual exclusion, categorical opposition. This essentialist meaning of difference submits to the logic of identity. One group occupies the position of a norm, against which all others are measured. The attempt to reduce all persons to the unity of a common measure constructs as deviant those whose attributes differ from the group-specific attributes implicitly presumed in the norm. The drive to unify the particularity and multiplicity of practices, cultural symbols, and ways of relating in clear and distinct categories turns difference into exclusion. . . .

The attempt to measure all against some universal standard generates a logic of difference as hierarchical dichotomy—masculine/feminine, civilized/savage, and so on. The second term is defined negatively as a lack of the truly human qualities; at the same time it is defined as the complement to the valued term, the object correlating with its subject, that which brings it to completion, wholeness, and identity. By loving and affirming him, a woman serves as a mirror to a man, holding up his virtues for him to see. By carrying the white man's burden to tame and educate the savage peoples, the civilized will realize universal humanity. The exotic orientals are there to know and master, to be the completion of reason's progress in history, which seeks the unity of the world. In every case the valued term achieves its value by its determinately negative relation to the Other.

In the objectifying ideologies of racism, sexism, anti-Semitism, and homophobia, only the oppressed and excluded groups are defined as different. Whereas the privileged groups are neutral and exhibit free and malleable subjectivity, the excluded groups are marked with an essence, imprisoned in a given set of possibilities. By virtue of the characteristics the group is alleged to have by nature, the ideologies allege that group members have specific dispositions that suit them for some activities and not others. Difference in these ideologies always means exclusionary opposition to a norm. There are rational men, and then there are women; there are civilized men, and then there are wild and savage peoples. The marking of difference always implies a good/bad opposition; it is always a devaluation, the naming of an inferiority in relation to a superior standard of humanity.

Difference here always means absolute otherness; the group marked as different has no common nature with the normal or neutral ones. The categorical opposition of groups essentializes them, repressing the differences within groups. In this way the definition of difference as exclusion and opposition actually denies difference. This essentializing categorization also denies difference in that its universalizing norms preclude recognizing and affirming a group's specificity in its own terms.

Essentializing difference expresses a fear of specificity, and a fear of making permeable the categorical border between oneself and the others. . . . The politics of difference confronts this fear, and aims for an understanding of group difference as indeed ambiguous, relational, shifting, without clear borders that keep people straight—as entailing neither amorphous unity nor pure individuality. By asserting a positive meaning for their own identity, oppressed groups seek to seize the power of naming difference itself, and explode the implicit definition of difference as deviance in relation to a norm, which freezes some groups into a self-enclosed nature. Difference now comes to mean not otherness, exclusive opposition, but specificity, variation, heterogeneity. Difference names relations of similarity and dissimilarity that can be reduced to neither coextensive identity nor nonoverlapping otherness.

The alternative to an essentializing, stigmatizing meaning of difference as opposition is an understanding of difference as . . . relational rather than defined by substantive categories and attributes. A relational understanding of difference relativizes the previously universal position of privileged groups, which allows only the oppressed to be marked as different. When group difference appears as a function of comparison between groups, whites are just as specific as Blacks or Latinos, men just as specific as women, able-bodied people just as specific as disabled people. Difference thus emerges not as a description of the attributes of a group, but as a function of the relations between groups and the interaction of groups with institutions.

In this relational understanding, the meaning of difference also becomes contextualized. Group differences will be more or less salient depending on the groups compared, the purposes of the comparison, and the point of view of the comparers. Such contextualized understandings of difference undermine essentialist assumptions. For example, in the context of athletics, health care, social service support, and so on, wheelchair-bound people are different from others, but they are not different in many other respects. Traditional treatment of the disabled entailed exclusion and segregation because the differences between the disabled and the able-bodied were conceptualized as extending to all or most capacities.

In general, then, a relational understanding of group difference rejects exclusion. Difference no longer implies that groups lie outside one another. To say that there are differences among groups does not imply that there are not overlapping experiences, or that two groups have nothing in common. The assumption that real differences in affinity, culture, or privilege imply oppositional categorization must be challenged. Different groups are always similar in some respects, and always potentially share some attributes, experiences, and goals.

Such a relational understanding of difference entails revising the meaning of group identity as well. In asserting the positive difference of their experience, culture, and social perspective, social movements of groups that have experienced cultural imperialism deny that they have a common identity, a set of fixed attributes that clearly mark who belongs and who doesn't. Rather, what makes a group a group is a social process of interaction and differentiation in which some people come to have a particular *affinity* for others. My "affinity group" in a given social situation comprises those people with whom I feel the most comfortable, who are more familiar. Affinity names the manner of sharing assumptions, affective bonding, and networking that recognizably differentiates groups from one another, but not according to some common nature. The salience of a particular person's group affinities may shift according to the social situation or according to changes in her or his life. Membership in a social group is a function not of satisfying some objective criteria, but of a subjective affirmation of affinity with that group, the affirmation of that affinity by other members of the group, and the attribution of membership in that group by persons identifying with other groups. Group identity is constructed from a flowing process in which individuals identify themselves and others in terms of groups, and thus group identity itself flows and shifts with changes in social process.

Groups experiencing cultural imperialism have found themselves objectified and marked with a devalued essence from the outside, by a dominant culture they are excluded from making. The assertion of a positive sense of group difference by these groups is emancipatory because it reclaims the definition of the group by the group, as a creation and construction, rather than a given essence. To be sure, it is difficult to articulate positive elements of group affinity without essentializing them, and these movements do not always succeed in doing so. But they are developing a language to describe their similar social situation and relations to one another, and their similar perceptions and perspectives on social life. These movements engage in the project of cultural revolution, . . . insofar as they take culture as in part a matter of collective choice. While their ideas of women's culture, Afro-American culture, and American Indian culture rely on past cultural expressions, to a significant degree these movements have self-consciously constructed the culture that they claim defines the distinctiveness of their groups.

Contextualizing both the meaning of difference and identity thus allows the acknowledgment of difference within affinity groups. In our complex, plural society, every social group has group differences cutting across it, which are potential sources of wisdom, excitement, conflict, and oppression. Gay men, for example, may be Black, rich, homeless, or old, and these differences produce different identifications and potential conflicts among gay men, as well as affinities with some straight men.

RESPECTING DIFFERENCE IN POLICY

A goal of social justice, I will assume, is social equality. Equality refers not primarily to the distribution of social goods, though distributions are certainly entailed by social equality. It refers primarily to the full participation and inclusion of everyone in a society's major institutions, and the socially supported substantive opportunity for all to develop and exercise their capacities and realize their choices. American society has enacted formal legal equality for members of all groups, with the important and shameful exception of gay men and lesbians. But for many groups social equality is barely on the horizon. Those seeking social equality disagree about whether group-neutral or group-conscious policies best suit that goal, and their disagreement often turns on whether they hold an assimilationist or culturally pluralist ideal. . . .

The issue of formally equal versus group-conscious policies arises primarily in the context of workplace relations and access to political power. I have already discussed one of the primary reasons for preferring group-conscious to neutral policies: policies that are universally formulated and thus blind to differences of race, culture, gender, age, or disability often perpetuate rather than undermine oppression. Universally formulated standards or norms, for example, according to which all competitors for social positions are evaluated, often presume as the norm capacities, values, and cognitive and behavioral styles typical of dominant groups, thus disadvantaging others. Racist, sexist, homophobic, ageist, and ableist aversions and stereotypes, moreover, continue to devalue or render invisible some people, often disadvantaging them in economic and political interactions. Policies that take notice of the specific situation of oppressed groups can offset these disadvantages.

It might be objected that when facially neutral standards or policies disadvantage a group, the standards or policies should simply be restructured so as to be genuinely neutral, rather than replaced by group-conscious policies. For some situations this may be appropriate, but in many the group-related differences allow no neutral formulation. . . .

More important, however, some of the disadvantages that oppressed groups suffer can be remedied in policy only by an affirmative acknowledgment of the group's specificity. . . . Group-conscious polices are sometimes necessary in order to affirm the solidarity of groups, to allow them to affirm their group affinities without suffering disadvantage in the wider society.

Some group-conscious policies are consistent with an assimilationist ideal in which group difference has no social significance, as long as such policies are understood as means to that end, and thus as temporary divergences from group-neutral norms. . . . A culturally pluralist democratic ideal . . . supports group-conscious policies not only as means to the end of equality, but also as intrinsic to the ideal of social equality itself. Groups cannot be socially equal unless their specific experience, culture, and social contributions are publicly affirmed and recognized.

The dilemma of difference exposes the risks involved both in attending to and in ignoring differences. The danger in affirming difference is that the implementation of group-conscious policies will reinstate stigma and exclusion. In the past, group-conscious policies were used to separate those defined as different and exclude them from access to the rights and privileges enjoyed by dominant groups. A crucial principle of democratic cultural pluralism, then, is that group-specific rights and policies should stand together with general civic and political rights of participation and inclusion. Group-conscious policies cannot be used to justify exclusion of or discrimination against members of a group in the exercise of general political and civil rights. A democratic cultural pluralism thus requires a dual system of rights: a general system of rights which are the same for all, and a more specific system of group-conscious policies and rights. . . . In the words of Kenneth Karst:

When the promise of equal citizenship is fulfilled, the paths to belonging are opened in two directions for members of cultural minorities. As full members of larger society, they have the option to participate to whatever degree they choose. They also may look inward, seeking solidarity within their cultural group, without being penalized for that choice. (Karst, 1986, p. 337)

If "cultural minority" is interpreted to mean any group subject to cultural imperialism, then this statement applies to women, old people, disabled people, gay men and lesbians, and working-class people as much as it applies to ethnic or national groups. I will now briefly consider . . . cases in which group-specific policies are necessary to support [women's] social equality.

Are women's interests best promoted through gender-neutral or group-conscious rules and policies? This question has been fiercely debated by feminists in recent years. The resulting literature raises crucial questions about dominant models of law and policy that take equality to mean sameness, and offers some subtle analyses of the meaning of equality that do not assume identity (see Vogel, 1990). Most of this discussion has focused on the question of pregnancy and childbirth rights in the workplace.

Advocates of an equal treatment approach to pregnancy argue that women's interests are best served by vigorously pressing for the inclusion of pregnancy leaves and benefits within gender-neutral leave and benefit policies relevant to any physical condition that renders men or women unable to work. The history of protective legislation shows that women cannot trust employers and courts not to use special classification as an excuse for excluding and disadvantaging women, and we are best protected from such exclusion by neutral policies (Williams, 1983). Even such proponents of equal treatment, however, agree that gender-neutral policies that take male lives as the norm will disadvantage women. The answer, according to Nadine Taub and Wendy Williams, is a model of equality in the workplace that recognizes and accommodates the specific needs of all workers;

such a model requires significant restructuring of most workplace policy (Taub and Williams, 1986).

In my view an equal treatment approach to pregnancy and childbirth is inadequate because it either implies that women do not have any right to leave and job security when having babies, or assimilates such guarantees under the supposedly gender-neutral category of "disability." Such assimilation is unacceptable because pregnancy and childbirth are usually normal conditions of normal women, because pregnancy and childbirth themselves count as socially necessary work, and because they have unique and variable characteristics and needs (Scales, 1981; Littleton, 1987). Assimilating pregnancy and childbirth to disability tends to stigmatize these processes as "unhealthy." It suggests, moreover, that the primary or only reason that a woman has a right to leave and job security is that she is physically unable to work at her job, or that doing so would be more difficult that when she is not pregnant and recovering from childbirth. While these are important considerations, another reason is that she ought to have the time to establish breast-feeding and develop a relationship and routine with her child, if she chooses. At issue is more than eliminating the disadvantage women suffer because of male models of uninterrupted work. It is also a question of establishing and confirming positive public recognition of the social contribution of childbearing. Such recognition can and should be given without either reducing women to childbearers or suggesting that all women ought to bear children and are lacking if they do not.

Feminists who depart from a gender-neutral model of women's rights generally restrict this departure to the biological situation of childbirth. Most demand that parental leave from a job, for example, should be gender-neutral, in order not to perpetuate the connection of women with the care of children, and in order not to penalize those men who choose more than average childrearing responsibilities. I myself agree with gender-neutral policy on this issue.

Restricting the issue of group-conscious policies for women to childbirth, however, avoids some of the hardest questions involved in promoting women's equality in the workplace. Women suffer workplace disadvantage not only or even primarily because of their birthing capacity, but because their gender socialization and identity orients the desires, temperaments, and capacities of many women toward certain activities and away from others, because many men regard women in inappropriately sexual terms, and because women's clothes, comportment, voices, and so on sometimes disrupt the disembodied ideal of masculinist bureaucracy. Differences between women and men are not only biological, but also socially gendered. Such gender differences are multiple, variable, and do not reduce men and women to segregating essences. Perhaps such differences should not exist, but without doubt they do now. Ignoring these differences sometimes disadvantages women in public settings where masculine norms and styles predominate.

In a model she calls "equality as acceptance," Christine Littleton argues for a gender-conscious approach to policy directed at rendering femininely gendered cultural attributes costless for women. This model begins with the assumption of structured social gender differences—for example, gender-dominated occupational categories, woman-dominated childrearing and other family member caretaking, and gender differences in the sports people wish to pursue. None of these are essences; it is not as though all men or all women follow the gendered patterns, but the patterns are identifiable and apply broadly to many people's lives. Littleton's model of equality as acceptance supports policies which not only will not disadvantage women who engage in traditionally feminine activity or behavior, but which value the feminine as much as the masculine:

The focus of equality as acceptance, therefore, is not on the question of whether women are different, but rather on the question of how the social fact of gender asymmetry can be dealt with so as to create some symmetry in the lived-out experience of all members of the community. I do not think it matters so much whether differences are "natural" or not; they are built into our structures and selves in either event. As social facts, differences are created by the interaction of person with person or person with institution; they inhere in the relationship, not in the person. On this view, the function of equality is to make gender differences, perceived or actual, costless relative to each other, so that anyone may follow a male, female, or androgynous lifestyle accord-

ing to their natural inclination or choice without being punished for following a female lifestyle or rewarded for following a male one. (Littleton, 1987, p. 1297)

The acceptance model of equality, then, publicly acknowledges culturally based gender differences, and takes steps to ensure that these differences do not disadvantage. Though Littleton does not emphasize it, this model implies, first, that gender differences must not be used implicitly or explicitly as a basis for excluding persons from institutions, positions, or opportunities. That is, general rights to equal opportunity, as well as other civil and political rights, must obtain. Over and above this, equality as acceptance explicitly revalues femininely coded activity and behavior as the equal of masculine-coded activity.

Comparable worth policies are a widely discussed strategy for revaluing the culturally feminine. Schemes of equal pay for work of comparable worth require that predominantly male and predominantly female jobs have similar wage structures if they involve similar degrees of skill, difficulty, stress, and so on. The problem in implementing these policies, of course, lies in designing methods of comparing different jobs. Most schemes of comparison still choose to minimize sex differences by using supposedly gender-neutral criteria, such as educational attainment, speed of work, whether the work involves manipulation of symbols, pleasantness of work conditions, decisionmaking ability, and so on. Some writers have suggested, however, that standard classifications of job traits may be systematically biased to keep specific kinds of tasks involved in many female-dominated occupations hidden. . . . Many female-dominated occupations involve gender-specific kinds of labor—such as nurturing, smoothing over social relations, or the exhibition of sexuality—which most task observation ignores. . . . A fair assessment of the skills and complexity of many female-dominated jobs may therefore involve paying explicit attention to gender differences rather than applying gender-blind categories of comparison (cf. Littleton, 1987, p. 1312).

Littleton offers sports as another area of revaluation. An "equality as acceptance" approach, she suggests, would support an equal division of resources between male and female programs rather than divide up the available sports budget per capita (Littleton, 1987, p. 1313). If the disparities in numbers of people involved were too great, I do not think this proposal would be fair, but I agree with the general principle Littleton is aiming at. Women who wish to participate in athletic activities should not be disadvantaged because there are not more women who currently wish to;

they should have as many well-paid coaches, for example, as do men, their locker room facilities should be as good, and they should have access to all the equipment they need to excel. More importantly, femininely stereotyped sports, such as synchronized swimming or field hockey, should receive a level of support comparable to more masculine sports like football or baseball. . . .

BIBLIOGRAPHY

Bastian, Ann, et al., *Choosing Equality: the Case for Democratic Schooling.* (Philadelphia: Temple University Press, 1986).

Boxill, Bernard, *Blacks and Social Justice.* (Totowa, NJ: Rowman and Allenheld, 1984).

Canter, Norma V, "Testimony from Mexican American Legal Defense and Education Fund," *Congressional Digest* (March 1987).

Karst, Kenneth, "Paths to Belonging: The Constitution and Cultural Identity," *North Carolina Law Review* 64 (1986), 303–77.

Littleton, Christine, "Reconstructing Sexual Equality," *California Law Review* 75 (July 1987), 1279–1377.

Sears, David O., and Leonia Huddy, "Bilingual Education: Symbolic Meaning and Support Among Non-Hispanics." Paper presented at the annual meeting of the American Political Science Association, Chicago, September 1987.

Taub, Nadine, and Wendy Williams, "Will Equality Require More than Assimilation, Accommodation or Separation from the Existing Social Structure?" *Rutgers Law Review* 31 (1985) 825–44.

Wasserstrom, Richard, "On Racism and Sexism," in *Philosophy and Social Issues* (Notre Dame, IN: Notre Dame University Press, 1980).

REVIEW AND DISCUSSION QUESTIONS

1. How does Young characterize Wasserstrom's ideal of "assimilation"? Is it an accurate description of his position? Explain.

2. What objections does Young raise against the ideal of assimilation?

3. What is the difference between the "conformist" and the "transformational" versions of assimilation?

4. How does Young distinguish those who "essentialize difference" from the "relational" understanding of difference?

5. Why does Young think that equality for women and others is best achieved by group conscious policies instead of neutral ones that rely on "formal" equality? Give some examples of the policies she defends, indicating the basis on which she makes her argument.

6. How would Richard Wasserstrom respond to Young's critique? Are his responses sound? Explain.

17
Affirmative Action

Readings in this section deal with one of the most hotly debated subjects in American politics: affirmative action policies that give preference to members of racial or ethnic minorities and women applying for admission to universities and seeking employment. The essays explore a wide range of positions on the subject. Some argue it is a sound policy; others think its effects have been disastrous. Other times, the issue turns from policy to justice, raising two different problems. First, is it unjust to white males who are passed over on the basis of race? Are they being treated unequally by such policies, for example, or does it deny their right not to be refused admission based on race? Others contend, on the other hand, that justice actually requires that preferences be given to minorities. Is this because of past injustices? All these questions and more are explored in the following essays.

The term *affirmative action* was first used by President John Kennedy in 1961. His Executive Order 10295 required that contractors working for the federal government take "affirmative action to ensure that applicants are employed without regard to their race, creed, color, or national origin." Over the next decade, however, this requirement moved slowly away from racial neutrality and toward preferences and quotas as the government tried to expand opportunities for minorities. In 1965, President Lyndon Johnson's secretary of labor issued guidelines for federal contractors that included "goals and timetables" to increase minority employment, and, today, preferences based on race, ethnicity, and gender are commonplace. The focus of discussion is often admission policies at universities, although the implications of the debate extend far beyond that.

Reverse Discrimination

James Rachels

In this essay, James Rachels considers affirmative action from two perspectives. First, he asks whether it is a wise policy. Is society better off giving preferences to minorities than it would be without it? Rachels then considers the claim that under certain circumstances, affirmative action is required by considerations of justice. James Rachels teaches philosophy at the University of Alabama at Birmingham.

This is Part 3 of James Rachels, "What People Deserve," originally printed in John Arthur and William H. Shaw, Eds., *Justice and Economic Distribution* (Prentice-Hall, 1978). Reprinted by permission. Parts 1 and 2 are reprinted in Section 10.

... Is it right to give preferential treatment to blacks, women, or members of other groups who have been discriminated against in the past? I will approach this issue by considering the deserts of the individuals involved. "Reverse Discrimination" is not a particularly good label for the practices in question because the word "discrimination" has come to have such unsavory connotations. Given the way that word is now used, to ask whether reverse *discrimination* is justified already prejudices the question in favor of a negative answer. But in other ways the term is apt: the most distinctive thing about reverse discrimination is that it *reverses* past patterns, so that those who have been discriminated against are now given preferential treatment. At any rate, the label is now part of our common vocabulary, so I will stay with it.

The following example incorporates the essential elements of reverse discrimination. The admissions committee of a certain law school assesses the qualifications of applicants by assigning numerical values to their college grades, letters of recommendation, and test scores, according to some acceptable formula. (The better the grades, etc., the higher the numerical values assigned.) From past experience the committee judges that a combined score of 600 is necessary for a student to have a reasonable chance of succeeding in the school's program. Thus in order to be minimally qualified for admission an applicant must score at least 600. However, because there are more qualified applicants than places available, many who score over 600 are nevertheless rejected.

Against this background two students, one black and one white, apply for admission. The black student's credentials are rated at 700, and the white student's credentials are rated at 720. So although both exceed the minimum requirement by a comfortable margin, the white student's qualifications are somewhat better. But the white applicant is rejected and the black applicant is accepted. The officials of the school explain that this decision is part of a policy designed to bring more blacks into the legal profession. The scores of the white applicants are generally higher than those of the blacks; so, some blacks with lower scores must be admitted in order to have a fair number of black students in the entering class. . . .

Now a number of arguments can be given in support of the law school's policy, and other policies like it. Black people have been, and still are, the victims of racist discrimination. One result is that they are poorly represented in the professions. In order to remedy this it is not enough that we simply stop discriminating against them. For, so long as there are not enough "role models" available—i.e., black people visibly successful in the professions, whom young blacks can recognize as models to emulate—young blacks cannot be expected to aspire to the professions and prepare for careers in the way that young whites do. It is a vicious cycle: while there are relatively few black lawyers, relatively few young blacks will take seriously the possibility of becoming lawyers, and so they will not be prepared for law school. But if relatively few young blacks are well-prepared for law school, and admissions committees hold them to the same high standards as the white applicants, there will be relatively few black lawyers. Law school admissions committees may try to help set things right, and break this cycle, by temporarily giving preferential treatment to black applicants.

Moreover, although many people now recognize that racist discrimination is wrong, prejudice against blacks is still widespread. One aspect of the problem is that a disproportionate number of blacks are still poor and hold only menial jobs, while the most prestigious jobs are occupied mostly by whites. So long as this is so, it will be easy for the white majority to continue with their old stereotyped ideas about black people. But if there were more black people holding prestigious jobs, it would be much more difficult to sustain the old prejudices. So in the long run law school admissions policies favoring black applicants will help reduce racism throughout the society.

I believe these arguments, and others like them, show that policies of reverse discrimination can be socially useful, although this is certainly a debatable point. For one thing, the resentment of those who disapprove of such policies will diminish their net utility. For another, less qualified persons will not perform as well in the positions they attain. However, I will not discuss these issues any further. I will concentrate instead on the more fundamental question of whether policies of reverse discrimination are unjust. After all, the rejected white student may concede the utility of such policies and nevertheless still complain that he has been treated unjustly. He may point out that he has been turned down simply because of his race. If he had been black, and had had exactly the same qualifications, he would have been accepted. This, he may argue, is equally as unjust as discriminating against black people on account of their race. Moreover, he can argue that, even if black people have been mistreated, he was not responsible for it, and so it is unfair to penalize him for it now. These are impressive arguments and, if they cannot be answered, the rightness of reverse discrimination will remain in doubt regardless of its utility.

I will argue that whether the white applicant has been treated unjustly depends on why he has better credentials than the black, that is, it depends on what accounts for the 20-point difference in their qualifications.

Suppose, for example, that his higher qualifications are due entirely to the fact that he has worked harder. Suppose the two applicants are equally intelligent, and have had the same opportunities. But the black student has spent a lot of time enjoying himself, going to the movies, and so forth, while the white student has passed by such pleasures to devote himself to his studies. If *this* is what accounts for the difference in their qualifications, then it seems that the white applicant really has been treated unjustly. For he has earned his superior qualifications; he deserves to be admitted ahead of the black student because he has worked harder for it.

But now suppose a different explanation is given as to why the white student has ended up with a 20-point advantage in qualifications. Suppose the applicants are equally intelligent and they have worked equally hard. However, the black student has had to contend with obstacles which his white competitor has not had to face. For example, his early education was at the hands of ill-trained teachers in crowded, inadequate schools, so that by the time he reached college he was far behind the other students and despite his best efforts he never quite caught up. If *this* is what accounts for the difference in qualifications, things look very different. For now the white student has not earned his superior qualifications. He has done nothing to deserve them. His record is, of course,

the result of things he's done, just as the black student's record is the result of things the black student has done. But the fact that he has a *better* record than the black student is not due to anything he has done. That difference is due only to his good luck in having been born into a more advantaged social position. Surely he cannot deserve to be admitted into law school ahead of the black simply because of *that*.

Now in fact black people in the United States have been, and are, systematically discriminated against, and it is reasonable to believe that this mistreatment does make a difference to black people's ability to compete with whites for such goods as law school admission. Therefore, at least some actual cases probably do correspond to the description of my example. Some white students have better qualifications for law school only because they have not had to contend with the obstacles faced by their black competitors. If so, their better qualifications do not automatically entitle them to prior admission.

Thus it is not the fact that the applicant is black that matters. What is important is that, as a result of past discriminatory practices, he has been unfairly handicapped in trying to achieve the sort of academic standing required for admission. If he has a claim to "preferential" treatment now, it is for *that* reason.

It follows that, even though a system of reverse discrimination might involve injustice for some whites, in many cases no injustice will be done. In fact, the reverse is true: If no such system is employed—if, for example, law school admissions are granted purely on the basis of "qualifications"—*that* may involve injustice for the disadvantaged who have been unfairly handicapped in the competition for qualifications.

It also follows that the most common arguments against reverse discrimination are not valid. The white student in our example cannot complain that he is being rejected simply because he is white. The effect of the policy is only to *neutralize an advantage* that he has had because he is white, and that is very different.[1] Nor will it do any good for the white to complain that, while blacks may have suffered unjust hardships, *he* is not responsible for it and so should not be penalized for it. The white applicant is not being penalized, or being made to pay reparations, for the wrongs that have been done to blacks. He is simply not being allowed to *profit* from the fact that those wrongs were done, by now besting the black in a competition that is "fair" only if we ignore the obstacles which one competitor, but not the other, has had to face.

NOTE

1. See George Sher, "Justifying Reverse Discrimination in Employment," *Philosophy and Public Affairs*, 4, no. 2 (Winter 1975), 159–170. Sher also argues that "reverse discrimination is justified insofar as it neutralizes competitive disadvantages caused by past privations" (p. 165). I have learned a lot from Sher's paper.

REVIEW AND DISCUSSION QUESTIONS

1. What are the potential advantages of affirmative action that Rachels identifies?
2. What are the potential costs to society of affirmative action, according to Rachels?
3. Describe the factors that could mean that preference in hiring or admission is deserved, as a matter of justice.
4. "Reverse discrimination only serves to prevent some people from cashing in on an unfair system; it's rather like awarding a prize to a horse that came in second but would have won had the race been fair." Does Rachels agree or disagree with this statement, do you think? Explain.
5. Since many minorities enjoy education and economic advantages while many whites are poor and suffer educational and other disadvantages, it is arguable that Rachels has not shown that affirmative action is justified. Do you agree? Explain.

Affirmative Action in Universities:

Regents of the University of California v. *Bakke*

Affirmative action programs are often defended as efforts to help rectify the racial, sexual, and socioeconomic inequalities in our society. Yet critics of affirmative action contend that it violates the principle of equality by showing preference to members of certain groups. The controversy over affirmative action came to a head in the famous Supreme Court case, *Regents of the University of California* v. *Bakke*.

Allan Bakke applied for admission to the medical school at the University of California at Davis. Only a tiny percentage of doctors are not white, and in order to help remedy this situation, the University of California at Davis had an affirmative action program that set aside 16 out of its 100 entrance places for minority students. If qualified minority students could not be found, those places were not to be filled. In addition to the special admission process, minority students were free to

438 U.S. 265 (1978).

compete through the regular admission process for one of the unrestricted 84 positions. Bakke was refused admission, but he sued the University of California, contending that he had been discriminated against in violation of both the 1964 Civil Rights Act and the equal protection clause of the Constitution. He argued that he would have won admission if those 16 places had not been withdrawn from open competition and reserved for minority students. The University of California did not deny this but contended that its program was legally permissible and socially necessary. (The Court reported that Bakke scored in the 97th percentile on the MCAT, whereas the average of the minority students admitted under the quota system was the 30th; Bakke's GPA was 3.44, whereas the GPA for the minority students who were admitted was 2.42.)

A badly divided Supreme Court reached a compromise. Although striking down rigid quotas for minority applicants, it also held that universities need not be color-blind in their admissions policies but may instead consider racial diversity as a goal in selecting students. Justice Powell delivered the opinion of the Court, while Justice Brennan dissented in part.

Mr. Justice Powell: Although many of the Framers of the Fourteenth Amendment conceived of its primary function as bridging the vast distance between members of the Negro race and the white "majority," the Amendment itself was framed in universal terms, without reference to color, ethnic origin, or condition of prior [servitude.]. . .

Over the past 30 years, this Court has embarked upon the crucial mission of interpreting the Equal Protection Clause with the view of assuring to all persons "the protection of equal laws" in a Nation confronting a legacy of slavery and racial discrimination. . . .

Petitioner [U.C. Davis] urges us to adopt for the first time a more restrictive view [and] hold that discrimination against members of the white "majority" cannot be suspect if its purpose can be characterized as "benign." [But it] is far too late to argue that the guarantee of equal protection to all persons permits the recognition of special wards entitled to a degree of protection greater than that accorded others. . . .

The concepts of "majority" and "minority" necessarily reflect temporary arrangements and political judgments. The white "majority" itself is composed of various minority groups, most of which can lay claim to a history of prior discrimination at the hands of the state and private individuals. Not all of these groups can receive preferential treatment and corresponding judicial tolerance of distinctions drawn in terms of race and nationality, for then the only "majority" left would be a new minority of White Anglo-Saxon Protestants. There is no principled basis for decid-

ing which groups would merit "heightened judicial solicitude" and which would not. . . .

Moreover, there are serious problems of justice connected with the idea of preference itself. . . . Preferential programs may only reinforce common stereotypes holding that certain groups are unable to achieve success without special protection based on a factor having no relationship to individual worth. . . . There is [also] a measure of inequity in forcing innocent persons in respondent's position to bear the burdens of redressing grievances not of their making.

In this case, [there] has been no determination by the legislature or a responsible administrative agency that the University engaged in a discriminatory practice requiring remedial efforts. . . . [When] a classification denies an individual opportunities or benefits enjoyed by others solely because of his race or ethnic background, it must be regarded as suspect.

[The] special admissions program purports to serve the purposes of: (i) "reducing the historic deficit of traditionally disfavored minorities in medical schools and the medical profession"; (ii) countering the effects of societal discrimination; (iii) increasing the number of physicians who will practice in communities currently underserved; and (iv) obtaining the educational benefits that flow from an ethnically diverse student body. It is necessary to decide which, if any, of these purposes is substantial enough to support the use of a suspect classification.

A. If petitioner's purpose is to assure within its student body some specified percentage of a particular group merely because of its race or ethnic origin, such preferential purpose must be rejected not as insubstantial but as facially invalid. Preferring members of any one group for no reason other than race or ethnic origin is discrimination for its own sake. This the Constitution forbids.

B. The State certainly has a legitimate and substantial interest in ameliorating, or eliminating where feasible, the disabling effects of identified discrimination. . . . We have never approved a classification that aids persons perceived as members of relatively victimized groups at the expense of other innocent individuals in the absence of judicial, legislative, or administrative findings of constitutional or statutory violations. . . . Petitioner does not purport to have made, and is in no position to make, such findings. . . .

Hence, the purpose of helping certain groups whom the faculty of the Davis Medical School perceived as victims of "societal discrimination" does not justify a classification that imposes disadvantages upon persons like respondent, who bear no responsibility for whatever harm the beneficiaries of the special admissions program are thought to have suffered. . . .

C. Petitioner identifies, as another purpose of its program, improving the delivery of health care services to communities currently underserved. . . . It may be correct to assume that some of them will carry out this intention, and that it is more likely they will practice in minority communities than the average white doctor. . . . An applicant of whatever race who has demonstrated his concern for disadvantaged minorities in the past and who declares that practice in such a community is his primary professional goal would be more likely to contribute to alleviation of the medical shortage than one who is chosen entirely on the basis of race and disadvantage. . . .

D. The fourth goal asserted by petitioner is the attainment of a diverse student body. . . . Physicians serve a heterogeneous population. An otherwise qualified medical student with a particular background—whether it be ethnic, geographic, culturally advantaged or disadvantaged—may bring to a professional school of medicine experiences, outlooks and ideas that enrich the training of its student body and better equip its graduates to render with understanding their vital service to humanity.

Ethnic diversity, however, is only one element in a range of factors a university properly may consider in attaining the goal of a heterogeneous student body. . . . [The] diversity that furthers a compelling state interest encompasses a far broader array of qualifications and characteristics of which racial or ethnic origin is but a single though important element. Petitioner's special admissions program, focused *solely* on ethnic diversity, would hinder rather than further attainment of genuine diversity. . . .

The experience of other university admissions programs, which take race into account in achieving the educational diversity valued by the First Amendment, demonstrates that the assignment of a fixed number of places to a minority group is not a necessary means toward that end. An illuminating example is found in the Harvard College program.

In such an admissions program, race or ethnic background may be deemed a "plus" in a particular applicant's file, yet it does not insulate the individual from comparison with all [others]. . . . This kind of program treats each applicant as an individual in the admissions process. The applicant who loses out [to] another candidate receiving a "plus" on the basis of ethnic background will not have been foreclosed from all consideration [simply] because he was not the right color or had the wrong surname. . . .

It has been suggested that an admissions program which considers race only as one factor is simply a subtle and more sophisticated—but no less effective—means of according racial preference than the Davis program. A facial intent to discriminate, however, is evident [in] this case. No such facial infirmity exists in an admissions program where race or ethnic background is simply one element—to be weighed fairly against other elements—in the selection process. . . .

[W]hen a State's distribution of benefits or imposition of burden hinges on the color of a person's skin or ancestry, that individual is entitled to a demonstration that the challenged classification is necessary to promote a substantial state interest. Petitioner has failed to carry this burden. . . .

In enjoining petitioner from ever considering the race of any applicant, however, the courts below failed to recognize that the State has a substantial interest that legitimately may be served by a properly devised admissions program involving the competitive consideration of race and ethnic origin. For this reason, so much of the California court's judgment as enjoins petitioner from any consideration of the race of any applicant must be reversed.

Mr. Justice Brennan, Concurring in the Judgment and Dissenting in Part: Since we conclude that the [program] is constitutional, we would reverse the judgment below in all respects. Mr. Justice Powell agrees that some uses of race in university admissions are permissible and, therefore, he joins with us to make five votes reversing the judgment below insofar as it prohibits the University from establishing race-conscious programs in the future. . . .

[E]ven today officially sanctioned discrimination is not a thing of the past. Against this background, claims that law must be "color-blind" or that the datum of race is no longer relevant to public policy must be seen as aspiration rather than as description of reality. This is not to denigrate aspiration; for reality rebukes us that race has too often been used by those who would stigmatize and oppress minorities. Yet we cannot [let] color blindness become myopia which masks the reality that many "created equal" have been treated within our lifetimes as inferior both by the law and by their fellow citizens. . . .

[A] government practice or statute which restricts "fundamental rights" or which contain "suspect classifications" is to be subjected to "strict scrutiny."But no fundamental right is involved here. . . . Nor do whites as a class have any of the "traditional indicia of suspectedness: the class is not saddled with such disabilities, or subjected to such a history of purposeful unequal treatment, or relegated to such a position of political powerlessness as to command extraordinary protection from the majoritarian political process." . . .

Moreover, [this] is not a case where racial classifications are "irrelevant and therefore prohibited." Nor has anyone suggested that the University's purposes contravene the cardinal principle that racial classifications that stigmatize—because they are drawn on the presumption that one race is inferior to another or because they

put the weight of government behind racial hatred and separatism—are invalid without more. . . .

Davis had a sound basis for believing that the problem of underrepresentation of minorities was substantial and chronic and that the problem was attributable to handicaps imposed on minority applicants by past and present racial discrimination. Until at least 1973, the practice of medicine in this country [was] largely the prerogative of whites. . . .

Davis clearly could conclude that the serious and persistent underrepresentation [is] the result of handicaps under which minority applicants labor as a consequence of a background of deliberate, purposeful discrimination against minorities in education and in society generally, as well as in the medical profession. . . .

The habit of discrimination and the cultural tradition of race prejudice [were] not immediately dissipated [*by Brown I*]. Rather, massive official and private resistance prevented, and to a lesser extent still prevents, attainment of equal opportunity in education at all levels and in the professions. The generation of minority students applying to Davis Medical School since it opened in 1968—most of whom were born before or about the time *Brown I* was decided—clearly have been victims of this discrimination. Judicial decrees recognizing discrimination in public education in California testify to the fact of widespread discrimination suffered by California-born minority applicants; many minority group members living in California, moreover, were born and reared in school districts in southern States segregated by law. [T]he conclusion is inescapable that applicants to medical school must be few indeed who endured the effects of de jure segregation, the resistance to *Brown I,* or the equally debilitating pervasive private discrimination fostered by our long history of official discrimination, and yet come to the starting line with an education equal to whites.

It is not even claimed that Davis' program in any way operates to stigmatize or single out any discrete and insular, or even any identifiable, nonminority group. Nor will harm comparable to that imposed upon racial minorities by exclusion or separation on grounds of race be the likely result of the program. It does not, for example, establish an exclusive preserve for minority [students].

Rather, its purpose is to overcome the effects of segregation by bringing the races together. True, whites are excluded from participation in the special admissions program, but this fact only operates to reduce the number of whites to be admitted in the regular admissions program in order to permit admission of a reasonable percentage—less than their proportion of the California population—of otherwise underrepresented qualified minority applicants.

Nor was Bakke in any sense stamped as inferior by [rejection].

Unlike discrimination against racial minorities, the use of racial preferences for remedial purposes does not inflict a pervasive injury upon individual whites in the sense that wherever they go or whatever they do there is a significant likelihood that they will be treated as second-class citizens because of their color. This distinction does not mean that the exclusion of a white resulting from the preferential use of race is not sufficiently serious to require justification; but it does mean that the injury inflicted by such a policy is not distinguishable from disadvantages caused by a wide range of government actions, none of which has ever been thought impermissible for that reason alone.

In addition, there is simply no evidence that the Davis program discriminates intentionally or unintentionally against any minority group which it purports to benefit. The program does not establish a quota in the invidious sense of a ceiling on the number of minority applicants to be admitted. Nor can the program reasonably be regarded as stigmatizing the program's beneficiaries or their race as inferior. The Davis program does not simply advance less qualified applicants; rather, it compensates applicants, whom it is uncontested are fully qualified to study medicine, for educational disadvantage which it was reasonable to conclude was a product of state-fostered discrimination. Once admitted, these students must satisfy the same degree [requirements]; they are taught by the same faculty in the same classes; and their performance is evaluated by the same standards by which regularly admitted students are judged. . . . We disagree with the lower courts' conclusion that the Davis program's use of race was unreasonable in light of its objectives. First, as petitioner argues, there are no practical means by which it could achieve its ends in the foreseeable future without the use of race-conscious measures. . . .

Second, [the] program does not simply equate minority status with disadvantage. Rather, Davis considers [each] applicant's personal history to determine whether he or she has likely been disadvantaged by racial discrimination. The record makes clear that only minority applicants likely to have been isolated from the mainstream of American life are considered in the special [program].

Finally, Davis' special admissions program cannot be said to violate the Constitution simply because it has set aside a predetermined number of places for qualified minority applicants rather than using minority status as a positive factor to be considered in evaluating the applications of disadvantaged minority applicants. For purposes of constitutional adjudication, there is no difference between the two approaches.

REVIEW AND DISCUSSION QUESTIONS

1. This was a somewhat unusual case. Four of the justices wanted to hold the California program constitutional along the lines described by Justice Brennan. Four others thought that the California program violated the 1964 Civil Rights Act's promise that no person shall be "discriminated against" on the basis of race and, following usual practice, did not address the constitutional question of whether it also denied Bakke equal protection of the law under the Fourteenth Amendment. The ninth judge, Justice Powell, said that the policy did, in fact, trigger "strict scrutiny" because a fundamental constitutional right was at stake. What is that right? Why does Justice Brennan disagree?

2. Which of the university's reasons for having the program does Justice Powell reject, and why?

3. What reason(s) for the program does Justice Powell accept?

4. Summarize the reasoning behind Justice Brennan's dissent.
5. How might it be argued that affirmative action programs are owed, as a matter of right, to minorities?
6. Defend the claim that the program violated Bakke's fundamental right to equal protection.
7. Compare the justification Rachels gives for affirmative action with that offered by the Court in the *Bakke* case. Which seems to have the stronger position?

The Rights of Allan Bakke

Ronald Dworkin

Do quotas requiring that a certain number of minority applicants get into medical school violate the moral or constitutional rights of white males who would have gotten in had race not been taken into account? That question was raised by Allan Bakke, who, having been refused admission to medical school, filed suit claiming that his rights under the 1964 Civil Rights Act and the Equal Protection Clause of the Fourteenth Amendment (which applies to all governmental agencies) had been violated. Soon after this article was published, the Supreme Court ruled five to four that the quota system at Davis was unconstitutional. (See the previous opinion.) The Court also held, however, that preferential admissions are not per se unconstitutional as long as quotas are avoided. The "fatal flaw" in the Davis program, according to Justice Powell, is that it tells applicants "who are not Negro, Asian, or Chicano that they are totally excluded from a specific percentage of seats in an entering class." Interestingly, four of the justices argued that the Davis policy was a violation of the 1964 Civil Rights Act, while four others contended that it violated neither that act nor the Constitution. The outcome was therefore a compromise that only one of the Justices supported in total. In the following article, Ronald Dworkin argues that Bakke's rights were not violated by the Davis policy. Ronald Dworkin teaches philosophy and jurisprudence at New York University and Oxford University.

On October 1, 1977 the Supreme Court heard oral argument in the case of *The Regents of the University of California* v. *Allan Bakke*. No lawsuit has ever been more widely watched or more thoroughly debated in the national and international press before the Court's decision. Still, some of the most pertinent facts set before the Court have not been clearly summarized.

The medical school of the University of California at Davis has an affirmative action program (called the "task force program") designed to admit more black and other minority students. It sets sixteen places aside for which only members of "educationally and economically disadvantaged minorities" compete. Allan Bakke, white, applied for one of the remaining eighty-four places; he was rejected but, since his test scores were relatively high, the medical school has conceded that it could not prove that he would have been rejected if the sixteen places reserved had been open to him. Bakke sued, arguing that the task force program deprived him of his constitutional rights.

This article originally appeared as "Why Bakke Has No Case" in *The New York Review of Books*, November 10, 1977. Reprinted with the permission from The New York Review of Books. © 1977 Nyrev, Inc.

The California Supreme Court agreed, and ordered the medical school to admit him. The university appealed to the Supreme Court.

The Davis program for minorities is in certain respects more forthright (some would say cruder) than similar plans now in force in many other American universities and professional schools. Such programs aim to increase the enrollment of black and other minority students by allowing the fact of their race to count affirmatively as part of the case for admitting them. Some schools set a "target" of a particular number of minority places instead of setting aside a flat number of places. But Davis would not fill the number of places set aside unless there were sixteen minority candidates it considered clearly qualified for medical education. The difference is therefore one of administrative strategy and not of principle.

So the constitutional question raised by Bakke is of capital importance for higher education in America, and a large number of universities and schools have entered briefs amicus curiae urging the Court to reverse the California decision. They believe that if the decision is affirmed then they will no longer be free to use explicit racial criteria in any part of their admissions programs, and that they will therefore be unable to fulfill what they take to be their responsibilities to the nation.

It is often said that affirmative action programs aim to achieve a racially conscious society divided into racial and ethnic groups, each entitled, as a group, to some proportionable share of resources, careers, or opportunities. That is a perverse description. American society is currently a racially conscious society; that is the inevitable and evident consequence of a history of slavery, repression, and prejudice. Black men and women, boys and girls, are not free to choose for themselves in what roles—or as members of which social groups—others will characterize them. They are black, and no other feature of personality or allegiance or ambition will so thoroughly influence how they will be perceived and treated by others, and the range and character of the lives that will be open to them.

The tiny number of black doctors and professionals is both a consequence and a continuing cause of American racial consciousness, one link in a long and self-fueling chain reaction. Affirma-

tive action programs use racially explicit criteria because their immediate goal is to increase the number of members of certain races in these professions. But their long-term goal is to reduce the degree to which American society is overall a racially conscious society.

The programs rest on two judgments. The first is a judgment of social theory: that America will continue to be pervaded by racial divisions as long as the most lucrative, satisfying, and important careers remain mainly the prerogative of members of the white race, while others feel themselves systematically excluded from a professional and social elite. The second is a calculation of strategy: that increasing the number of blacks who are at work in the professions will, in the long run, reduce the sense of frustration and injustice and racial self-consciousness in the black community to the point at which blacks may begin to think of themselves as individuals who can succeed like others through talent and initiative. At that future point the consequences of nonracial admissions programs, whatever these consequences might be, could be accepted with no sense of racial barriers or injustice.

It is therefore the worst possible misunderstanding to suppose that affirmative action programs are designed to produce a balkanized America, divided into racial and ethnic subnations. They use strong measures because weaker ones will fail; but their ultimate goal is to lessen not to increase the importance of race in American social and professional life.

According to the 1970 census, only 2.1 percent of US doctors were black. Affirmative action programs aim to provide more black doctors to serve black patients. This is not because it is desirable that blacks treat blacks and whites treat whites, but because blacks, for no fault of their own, are now unlikely to be well served by whites, and because a failure to provide the doctors they trust will exacerbate rather than reduce the resentment that now leads them to trust only their own. Affirmative action tries to provide more blacks as classmates for white doctors, not because it is desirable that a medical school class reflect the racial makeup of the community as a whole, but because professional association between blacks and whites will decrease the degree to which whites think of blacks as a race rather than as people, and thus the degree to which blacks think of themselves that way. It tries to provide "role models" for future black doctors, not because it is desirable for a black boy or girl to find adult models only among blacks, but because our history has made them so conscious of their race that the success of whites, for now, is likely to mean little or nothing for them.

The history of the campaign against racial injustice since 1954, when the Supreme Court decided *Brown* v. *Board of Education,* is a history in large part of failure. We have not succeeded in reforming the racial consciousness of our society by racially neutral means. We are therefore obliged to look upon the arguments for affirmative action with sympathy and an open mind. Of course, if Bakke is right that such programs, no matter how effective they may be, violate his constitutional rights then they cannot be permitted to continue. But we must not forbid them in the name of some mindless maxim, like the maxim that it cannot be right to fight fire with fire, or that the end cannot justify the means. If the strategic claims for affirmative action are cogent, they cannot be dismissed simply on the ground that racially explicit tests are distasteful. If such tests are distasteful it can only be for reasons that make the underlying social realities the programs attack more distasteful still.

The New Republic, in a recent editorial opposing affirmative action, missed that point. "It is critical to the success of a liberal pluralism," it said, "that group membership itself is not among the permissible criteria of inclusion and exclusion." But group membership is in fact, as a matter of social reality rather than formal admission standards, part of what determines inclusion or exclusion for us now. If we must choose between a society that is in fact liberal and an illiberal society that scrupulously avoids formal racial criteria, we can hardly appeal to the ideals of liberal pluralism to prefer the latter.

Professor Archibald Cox of Harvard Law School, speaking for the University of California in oral argument, told the Supreme Court that this is the choice the United States must make. As things stand, he said, affirmative action programs are the only effective means of increasing the absurdly small number of black doctors. The California Supreme Court, in approving Bakke's

claim, had urged the university to pursue that goal by methods that do not explicitly take race into account. But that is unrealistic. We must distinguish, as Cox said, between two interpretations of what the California court's recommendation means. It might mean that the university should aim at the same immediate goal, of increasing the proportion of black and other minority students in the medical school, by an admissions procedure that on the surface is not racially conscious.

That is a recommendation of hypocrisy. If those who administer the admissions standards, however these are phrased, understand that their immediate goal is to increase the number of blacks in the school, then they will use race as a criterion in making the various subjective judgments the explicit criteria will require, because that will be, given the goal, the only right way to make those judgments. The recommendation might mean, on the other hand, that the school should adopt some nonracially conscious goal, like increasing the number of disadvantaged students of all races, and then hope that that goal will produce an increase in the number of blacks as a by-product. But even if that strategy is less hypocritical (which is far from plain), it will almost certainly fail because no different goal, scrupulously administered in a nonracially conscious way, will in fact significantly increase the number of black medical students.

Cox offered powerful evidence for that conclusion, and it is supported by the recent and comprehensive report of the Carnegie Council on Policy Studies in Higher Education. Suppose, for example, that the medical school sets aside separate places for applicants "disadvantaged" on some racially neutral test, like poverty, allowing only those disadvantaged in that way to compete for these places. If the school selected these from that group who scored best on standard medical school aptitude tests, then it will take almost no blacks, because blacks score relatively low even among the economically disadvantaged. But if the school chooses among the disadvantaged on some basis other than test scores, just so that more blacks will succeed, then it will not be administering the special procedure in a nonracially conscious way.

So Cox was able to put his case in the form of two simple propositions. A racially conscious test for admission, even one that sets aside certain places for qualified minority applicants exclusively, serves goals that are in themselves unobjectionable and even urgent. Such programs are, moreover, the only means that offer any significant promise of achieving these goals. If these programs are halted, then no more than a trickle of black students will enter medical or other professional schools for another generation at least.

If these propositions are sound, then on what ground can it be thought that such programs are either wrong or unconstitutional? We must notice an important distinction between two different sorts of objections that might be made. These programs are intended, as I said, to decrease the importance of race in the United States in the long run. It may be objected, first, that the programs will in fact harm that goal more than they will advance it. There is no way now to prove that that is so. Cox conceded, in his argument, that there are costs and risks in these programs.

Affirmative action programs seem to encourage, for example, a popular misunderstanding, which is that they assume that racial or ethnic groups are entitled to proportionate shares of opportunities, so that Italian or Polish ethnic minorities are, in theory, as entitled to their proportionate shares as blacks or Chicanos or American Indians are entitled to the shares the present programs give them. That is a plain mistake: the programs are not based on the idea that those who are aided are entitled to aid, but only on the strategic hypothesis that helping them is now an effective way of attacking a national problem. Some medical schools may well make that judgment, under certain circumstances, about a white ethnic minority. Indeed it seems likely that some medical schools are even now attempting to help white Appalachian applicants, for example, under programs of regional distribution.

So the popular understanding is wrong, but so long as it persists it is a cost of the program because the attitudes it encourages tend to a degree to make people more rather than less conscious of race. There are other possible costs. It is said, for example, that some blacks find affirmative action degrading; they find that it makes them more rather than less conscious of prejudice against their race as such. This attitude is also based on a misperception, I think, but for a small minority of blacks at least it is a genuine cost.

In the view of the many important universities who have such programs, however, the gains will very probably exceed the losses in reducing racial consciousness overall. This view is hardly so implausible that it is wrong for these universities to seek to acquire the experience that will allow us to judge whether they are right. It would be particularly silly to forbid these experiments if we know that the failure to try will mean, as the evidence shows, that the status quo will almost certainly continue. In any case, this first objection could provide no argument that would justify a decision by the Supreme Court holding the programs unconstitutional. The Court has no business substituting its speculative judgment about the probable consequences of educational policies for the judgment of professional educators.

So the acknowledged uncertainties about the long-term results of such programs could not justify a Supreme Court decision making them illegal. But there is a second and very different form of objection. It may be argued that even if the programs *are* effective in making our society less a society dominated by race, they are nevertheless unconstitutional because they violate the individual constitutional rights of those, like Allan Bakke, who lose places in consequence. In the oral argument Reynold H. Colvin of San Francisco, who is Bakke's lawyer, made plain that his objection takes this second form. Mr. Justice White asked him whether he accepted that the goals affirmative action programs seek are important goals. Mr. Colvin acknowledged that they were. Suppose, Justice White continued, that affirmative action programs are, as Cox had argued, the only effective means of seeking such goals. Would Mr. Colvin nevertheless maintain that the programs are unconstitutional? Yes, he insisted, they would be, because his client has a constitutional right that the programs be abandoned, no matter what the consequences.

Mr. Colvin was wise to put his objections on this second ground; he was wise to claim that his client has rights that do not depend on any judgment about the likely consequences of affirmative action for society as a whole, because if he makes out that claim then the Court must give him the relief he seeks.

But can he be right? If Allan Bakke has a constitutional right so important that the urgent goals of affirmative action must yield, then this must be because affirmative action violates some fundamental principle of political morality. This is not a case in which what might be called formal or technical law requires a decision one way or the other. There is no language in the Constitution whose plain meaning forbids affirmative action. Only the most na[greek symbol]au[greek symbol]dive theories of statutory construction could argue that such a result is required by the language of any earlier Supreme Court decision or of the Civil Rights Act of 1964 or of any other congressional enactment. If Mr. Colvin is right it must be because Allan Bakke has not simply some technical legal right but an important moral right as well.

What could that right be? The popular argument frequently made on editorial pages is that Bakke has a right to be judged on his merit. Or that he has a right to be judged as an individual rather than as a member of a social group. Or that he has a right, as much as any black man, not to be sacrificed or excluded from any opportunity because of his race alone. But these catch phrases are deceptive here, because, as reflection demonstrates, the only genuine principle they describe is the principle that no one should suffer from the prejudice or contempt of others. And that principle is not at stake in this case at all. In spite of popular opinion, the idea that the Bakke case presents a conflict between a desirable social goal and important individual rights is a piece of intellectual confusion.

Consider, for example, the claim that individuals applying for places in medical school should be judged on merit, and merit alone. If that slogan means that admissions committees should take nothing into account but scores on some particular intelligence test, then it is arbitrary and, in any case, contradicted by the long-standing practice of every medical school. If it means, on the other hand, that a medical school should choose candidates that it supposes will make the most useful doctors, then everything turns on the judgment of what factors make different doctors useful. The Davis medical school assigned to each regular applicant, as well as to each minority applicant, what it called a "benchmark score." This reflected not only the results of aptitude tests and college grade averages, but a subjective evaluation of the applicant's chances of functioning as an effective doc-

tor, in view of society's present needs for medical service. Presumably the qualities deemed important were different from the qualities that a law school or engineering school or business school would seek, just as the intelligence tests a medical school might use would be different from the tests these other schools would find appropriate.

There is no combination of abilities and skills and traits that constitutes "merit" in the abstract; if quick hands count as "merit" in the case of a prospective surgeon, this is because quick hands will enable him to serve the public better and for no other reason. If a black skin will, as a matter of regrettable fact, enable another doctor to do a different medical job better, then that black skin is by the same token "merit" as well. That argument may strike some as dangerous; but only because they confuse its conclusion—that black skin may be a socially useful trait in particular circumstances—with the very different and despicable idea that one race may be inherently more worthy than another.

Consider the second of the catch phrases I have mentioned. It is said that Bakke has a right to be judged as an "individual," in deciding whether he is to be admitted to medical school and thus to the medical profession, and not as a member of some group that is being judged as a whole. What can that mean? Any admissions procedure must rely on generalizations about groups that are justified only statistically. The regular admissions process at Davis, for example, set a cutoff figure for college grade-point averages. Applicants whose averages fell below that figure were not invited to any interview, and therefore rejected out of hand.

An applicant whose average fell one point below the cutoff might well have had personal qualities of dedication or sympathy that would have been revealed at an interview, and that would have made him or her a better doctor than some applicant whose average rose one point above the line. But the former is excluded from the process on the basis of a decision taken for administrative convenience and grounded in the generalization, unlikely to hold true for every individual, that those with grade averages below the cutoff will not have other qualities sufficiently persuasive. Indeed, even the use of standard Medical College Aptitude tests (MCAT) as part of the admissions procedure requires judging people as part of groups because it assumes that test scores are a guide to medical intelligence which is in turn a guide to medical ability. Though this judgment is no doubt true statistically, it hardly holds true for every individual.

Allan Bakke was himself refused admission to two other medical schools, not because of his race but because of his age: these schools thought that a student entering medical school at the age of thirty-three was likely to make less of a contribution to medical care over his career than someone entering at the standard age of twenty-one. Suppose these schools relied, not on any detailed investigation of whether Bakke himself had abilities that would contradict the generalization in his specific case, but on a rule of thumb that allowed only the most cursory look at applicants over (say) the age of thirty. Did these two medical schools violate his right to be judged as an individual rather than as a member of a group?

The Davis Medical School permitted whites to apply for the sixteen places reserved for members of "educationally or economically disadvantaged minorities," a phrase whose meaning might well include white ethnic minorities. In fact several whites have applied, though none has been accepted, and the California Court found that the special committee charged with administering the program had decided, in advance, against admitting any. Suppose that decision had been based on the following administrative theory: it is so unlikely that any white doctor can do as much to counteract racial imbalance in the medical professions as a well-qualified and trained black doctor can do that the committee should for reasons of convenience proceed on the presumption no white doctor could. That presumption is, as a matter of fact, more plausible than the corresponding presumption about medical students over the age of thirty, or even the presumption about applicants whose grade-point averages fall below the cutoff line. If the latter presumptions do not deny the alleged right of individuals to be judged as individuals in an admissions procedure, then neither can the former.

Mr. Colvin, in oral argument, argued the third of the catch phrases I mentioned. He said that his client had a right not to be excluded from medical school because of his race alone, and this as a statement of constitutional right sounds more plausible than claims about the right to be judged on merit or as an individual. It sounds plausible, however, because it suggests the following more complex principle. Every citizen has a constitutional right that he not suffer disadvantage, at least in the competition for any public benefit, because the race or religion or sect or region or other natural or artificial group to which he belongs is the object of prejudice or contempt.

That is a fundamentally important constitutional right, and it is that right that was systematically violated for many years by racist exclusions and anti-Semitic quotas. Color bars and Jewish quotas were not unfair just because they made race or religion relevant or because they fixed on qualities beyond individual control. It is true that blacks or Jews do not choose to be blacks or Jews. But it is also true that those who score low in aptitude or admissions tests do not choose their levels of intelligence. Nor do those denied admission because they are too old, or because they do not come from a part of the country underrepresented in the school, or because they cannot play basketball well, choose not to have the qualities that made the difference.

Race seems different because exclusions based on race have historically been motivated not by some instrumental calculation, as in the case of intelligence or age or regional distribution or athletic ability, but because of contempt for the excluded race or religion as such. Exclusion by race was in itself an insult, because it was generated by and signaled contempt.

Bakke's claim, therefore, must be made more specific than it is. He says he was kept out of medical school because of his race. Does he mean that he was kept out because his race is the object of prejudice or contempt? That suggestion is absurd. A very high proportion of those who were accepted (and, presumably, of those who run the admissions program) were members of the same race. He therefore means simply that if he had been black he would have been accepted, with no suggestion that this would have been so because blacks are thought more worthy or honorable than whites.

That is true: no doubt he would have been accepted if he were black. But it is also true, and in exactly the same sense, that he would have been accepted if he had been more intelligent, or made a better impression in his interview, or, in the case of other schools, if he had been younger when he decided to become a doctor. Race is not, in his case, a different matter from these other factors equally beyond his control. It is not a different matter because in his case race is not distinguished by the special character of public insult. On the contrary; the program presupposes that his race is still widely if wrongly thought to be superior to others.

In the past, it made sense to say that an excluded black or Jewish student was being sacrificed because of his race or religion; that meant that his or her exclusion was treated as desirable in itself, not because it contributed to any goal in which he as well as the rest of society might take pride. Allan Bakke is being "sacrificed" because of his race only in a very artificial sense of the word. He is being "sacrificed" in the same artificial sense because of his level of intelligence, since he would have been accepted if he were more clever than he is. In both cases he is being excluded not by prejudice but because of a rational calculation about the socially most beneficial use of limited resources for medical education.

It may now be said that this distinction is too subtle, and that if racial classifications have been and may still be used for malign purposes, then everyone has a flat right that racial classifications not be used at all. This is the familiar appeal to the lazy virtue of simplicity. It supposes that if a line is difficult to draw, or might be difficult to administer if drawn, then there is wisdom in not making the attempt to draw it. There may be cases in which that is wise, but those would be cases in which nothing of great value would as a consequence be lost. If racially conscious admissions policies now offer the only substantial hope for bringing more qualified black and other minority doctors into the profession, then a great loss is suffered if medical schools are not allowed voluntarily to pursue such programs. We should then be trading away a chance to attack certain and present injustice in order to gain protection we may not need against speculative abuses we have other means to prevent. And such abuses cannot, in any case, be worse than the injustice to which we would then surrender.

We have now considered three familiar slogans, each widely thought to name a constitutional right that enables Allan Bakke to stop programs of affirmative action no matter how effective or necessary these might be. When we inspect these slogans, we find that they can stand for no genuine principle except one. This is the important principle that no one in our society should suffer because he is a member of a group thought less worthy of respect, as a group, than other groups. We have different aspects of that principle in mind when we say that individuals should be judged on merit, that they should be judged as individuals, and that they should not suffer disadvantages because of their race. The spirit of that fundamental principle is the spirit of the goal that affirmative action is intended to serve. The principle furnishes no support for those who find, as Bakke does, that their own interests conflict with that goal.

It is of course regrettable when any citizen's expectations are defeated by new programs serving some more general concern. It is regrettable, for example, when established small businesses fail because new and superior roads are built; in that case people have invested more than Bakke has. And they have more reason to believe their businesses will continue than Bakke had to suppose he could have entered the Davis medical school at thirty-three even without a task force program.

There is, of course, no suggestion in that program that Bakke shares in any collective or individual guilt for racial injustice in America; or that he is any less entitled to concern or respect than any black student accepted in the program. He has been disappointed, and he must have the sympathy due that disappointment, just as any other disappointed applicant—even one with much worse test scores who would not have been accepted in any event—must have sympathy. Each is disappointed because places in medical schools are scarce resources and must be used to provide what the more general society most needs. It is hardly Bakke's fault that racial justice is now a special need—but he has no right to prevent the most effective measures of securing that justice from being used.

REVIEW AND DISCUSSION QUESTIONS

1. Dworkin says that affirmative action programs rest on two premises. Explain them.
2. How does Dworkin answer critics of those two premises?
3. How does Dworkin respond to the claim that Bakke's right to be judged on the basis of merit was infringed?
4. How does he respond to the claim that Bakke was not "judged as an individual"?
5. In fact, Bakke's lawyer claimed he had a right not to be excluded from medical school because of race. How does Dworkin answer that charge?
6. Setting aside questions of justice or rights, describe the potential social and economic advantages and disadvantages of affirmative action policies.
7. How might it be argued that some people have a right to affirmative action programs? Are those you mention the same groups that benefit from such a program? Explain.
8. The *Journal of the American Medical Association* reported that in 1988, medical school graduates passed the National Board of Medical Examiners certifying test at the following rates: white males, 89 percent; while females, 84 percent; black males, 54 percent; black females, 44 percent. It also reported that the large majority of those who first fail will eventually pass the exam. Are those figures significant for this debate? Explain.

Affirmative Racism

Charles Murray

Even the most well-intentioned social policies sometimes have unforeseen results. In this essay, Charles Murray offers a broad-based attack on affirmative action, arguing, among other things, that preferential treatment for blacks has actually worked against their interests by encouraging a new form of racism.

A few years ago, I got into an argument with a lawyer friend who is a partner in a New York firm. I was being the conservative, arguing that preferential treatment of blacks was immoral; he was being the liberal, urging that it was the only way to bring blacks to full equality. In the middle of all this he abruptly said, "But you know, let's face it. We must have hired at least ten blacks in the last few years, and none of them has really worked out." He then returned to his case for still stronger affirmative action, while I wondered what it had been like for those ten blacks. And if he could make a remark like that so casually, what remarks would he be able to make some years down the road, if by that time it had been fifty blacks who hadn't "really worked out"?

My friend's comment was an outcropping of a new racism that is emerging to take its place alongside the old. It grows out of preferential treatment for blacks, and it is not just the much-publicized reactions, for example, of the white policemen or firemen who are passed over for promotion because of an affirmative action court order. The new racism that is potentially most damaging is located among the white elites—educated, affluent, and occupying the positions in education, business, and government from which this country is run. It currently focuses on blacks; whether it will eventually extend to include Hispanics and other minorities remains to be seen.

The new racists do not think blacks are inferior. They are typically longtime supporters of civil rights. But they exhibit the classic behavioral symptom of racism: they treat blacks differently from whites, because of their race. The results can be as concretely bad and unjust as any that the old racism produces. Sometimes the effect is that blacks are refused an education they otherwise could have gotten. Sometimes blacks are shunted into dead-end jobs. Always, blacks are denied the right to compete as equals.

The new racists also exhibit another characteristic of racism: they *think* about blacks differently from the way they think about whites. Their global view of blacks and civil rights is impeccable. Blacks must be enabled to achieve full equality. They are still unequal, through no fault of their own (it is the fault of racism, it is the fault of inadequate opportunity, it is the legacy of history). But the new racists' local view is that the blacks they run across professionally are not, on the average, up to the white standard. Among the new racists, lawyers have gotten used to the idea that the brief a black colleague turns in will be a little less well-rehearsed and argued than the one they would have done. Businessmen expect that a black colleague will not read a balance sheet as subtly as they do. Teachers expect black students to wind up toward the bottom of the class.

The new racists also tend to think of blacks as a commodity. The office must have a sufficient supply of blacks, who must be treated with special delicacy. The personnel problems this creates are more difficult than most because whites barely admit to themselves what's going on.

What follows is a foray into very poorly mapped territory. I will present a few numbers that explain much about how the process gets started. But the ways that the numbers get translated into behavior are even more important. The cases I present are composites constructed from my own observations and taken from firsthand accounts. All are based on real events and real people, stripped of their particularities. But the individual cases are not intended as evidence, because I cannot tell you how often they happen. They have not been the kind of thing that social scientists or journalists have wanted to count. I am writing this because so many people, both white and black, to whom I tell such stories know immediately what I am talking about. It is apparent that a problem exists. How significant is it? What follows is as much an attempt to elicit evidence as to present it.

As in so many of the crusades of the 1960s, the nation began with a good idea. It was called "affirmative action," initiated by Lyndon Johnson through Executive Order 11246 in September 1965. It was an attractive label and a natural corrective to past racism: actively seek out black candidates for jobs, college, or promotions, without treating them differently in the actual decision to hire, admit, or promote. The term originally evoked both the letter and the spirit of the order.

Then, gradually, affirmative action came to mean something quite different. In 1970 a federal court established the legitimacy of quotas as a means of implementing Johnson's executive order. In 1971 the Supreme Court ruled that an employer could not use minimum credentials as a prerequisite for hiring if the credential acted as a "built-in headwind" for minority groups—even when there was no discriminatory intent and even when the hiring procedures were "fair in form." In 1972 the Equal Employment Opportunity Commission acquired broad, independent enforcement powers.

Thus by the early 1970s it had become generally recognized that a good-faith effort to recruit qualified blacks was not enough—especially if one's school depended on federal grants or one's business depended on federal contracts. Even for businesses and schools not directly dependent on the government, the simplest way to withstand an accusation of violating Title VII of the Civil Rights Act of 1964 was to make sure not that they had not just interviewed enough minority candidates, but that they had actually hired or admitted enough of them. Employers and admissions committees arrived at a rule of thumb: if the blacks who are available happen to be the best candidates, fine; if not, the best available black candidate will be given some sort of edge in the selection process. Sometimes the edge will be small; sometimes it will be predetermined that a black candidate is essential, and the edge will be very large.

Perhaps the first crucial place where the edge applies is in admission to college. Consider the cases of the following three students: John, William, and Carol, 17 years old and applying to college, are all equal on paper. Each has a score of 520 in the mathematics section of the Scholastic Aptitude Test, which puts them in the top third—at the 67th percentile—of all students who took the test. (Figures are based on 1983 data.)

John is white. A score of 520 gets him into the state university. Against the advice of his high school counselor, he applies to a prestigious school, Ivy U., where his application is rejected in the first cut—its average white applicant has math scores in the high 600s.

William is black, from a middle-class family who sent him to good schools. His score of 520 puts him at the 95th percentile of all blacks who took the test. William's high school counselor points out that he could probably get into Ivy U. William applies and is admitted—Ivy U. uses separate standards for admission of whites and blacks, and William is among the top blacks who applied.

Carol is black, educated at an inner-city school, and her score of 520 represents an extraordinary achievement in the face of terrible schooling. An alumnus of Ivy U. who regularly looks for promising inner-city candidates finds her, recruits her, and sends her off with a full scholarship to Ivy U.

When American universities embarked on policies of preferential admissions by race, they had the Carols in mind. They had good reason to be optimistic that preferential treatment would work—for many years, the best universities had been weighting the test scores of applicants from small-town public schools when they were compared against those of applicants from the top private schools, and had been giving special breaks to students from distant states to ensure geo-

graphic distribution. The differences in preparation tended to even out after the first year or so. Blacks were being brought into a long-standing and successful tradition of preferential treatment.

In the case of blacks, however, preferential treatment ran up against a large black-white gap in academic performance combined with ambitious goals for proportional representation. This gap has been the hardest for whites to confront. But though it is not necessary or even plausible to believe that such differences are innate, it is necessary to recognize openly that the differences exist. By pretending they don't, we begin the process whereby both the real differences and the racial factor are exaggerated.

The black-white gap that applies most directly to this discussion is the one that separates blacks and whites who go to college. In 1983, for example, the mean Scholastic Aptitude Test score for all blacks who took the examination was more than 100 points below the white score on both the verbal and the math sections. Statistically, it is an extremely wide gap. To convert the gap into more concrete terms, think of it this way: in 1983, the same Scholastic Aptitude Test math score that put a black at the 50th percentile of all blacks who took the test put him at the 16th percentile of all whites who took the test.

These results clearly mean we ought to be making an all-out effort to improve elementary and secondary education for blacks. But that doesn't help much now, when an academic discrepancy of this magnitude is fed into a preferential admissions process. As universities scramble to make sure they are admitting enough blacks, the results feed the new racism. Here's how it works:

In 1983, only 66 black students nationwide scored above 700 in the verbal section of the Scholastic Aptitude Test, and only 205 scored above 700 in the mathematics section. This handful of students cannot begin to meet the demand for blacks with such scores. For example, Harvard, Yale, and Princeton have in recent years been bringing an aggregate of about 270 blacks into each entering class. If the black students entering these schools had the same distribution of scores as that of the freshman class as a whole, then every black student in the nation with a verbal score in the 700s, and roughly 70 percent of the ones with a math score in the 700s, would be in their freshman classes.

The main problem is not that a few schools monopolize the very top black applicants, but that these same schools have much larger implicit quotas than they can fill with those applicants. They fill out the rest with the next students in line—students who would not have gotten into these schools if they were not black, who otherwise would have been showing up in the classrooms of the nation's less glamorous colleges and universities. But the size of the black pool does not expand appreciably at the next levels. The number of blacks scoring in the 600s on the math section in 1983, for example, was 1,531. Meanwhile, 31,704 nonblack students in 1983 scored in the 700s on the math section and 121,640 scored in the 600s. The prestige schools cannot begin to absorb these numbers of other highly qualified freshmen, and they are perforce spread widely throughout the system.

At schools that draw most broadly from the student population, such as the large state universities, the effects of this skimming produce a situation that confirms the old racists in everything they want most to believe. There are plenty of outstanding students in such student bodies (at the University of Colorado, for example, 6 percent of the freshmen in 1981 had math scores in the 700s and 28 percent had scores in the 600s), but the skimming process combined with the very small raw numbers means that almost none of them are black. What students and instructors see in their day-to-day experience in the classroom is a disproportionate number of blacks who are below the white average, relatively few blacks who are at the white average, and virtually none who are in the first rank. The image that the white student carries away is that blacks are less able than whites.

I am not exalting the SAT as an infallible measure of academic ability, or pointing to test scores to try to convince anyone that blacks are performing below the level of whites. I am simply using them to explain what instructors and students already notice, and talk about, among themselves.

They do not talk openly about such matters. One characteristic of the new racism is that whites deny in public but acknowledge in private that there are significant differences in black and white academic performance. Another is that they dis-

miss the importance of tests when black scores are at issue, blaming cultural bias and saying that test scores are not good predictors of college performance. At the same time, they watch anxiously over their own children's test scores.

The differences in academic performance do not disappear by the end of college. Far from narrowing, the gap separating black and white academic achievement appears to get larger. Various studies, most recently at Harvard, have found that during the 1970s blacks did worse in college (as measured by grade point average) than their test scores would have predicted. Moreover, the black-white gap in the Graduate Record Examination is larger than the gap in the Scholastic Aptitude Test. The gap between black and white freshmen is a bit less than one standard deviation (the technical measure for comparing scores). Black and white seniors who take the Graduate Record Examination reveal a gap of about one and a quarter standard deviations.

Why should the gap grow wider? Perhaps it is an illusion—for example, perhaps a disproportionate number of the best black students never take the examination. But there are also reasons for suspecting that in fact blacks get a worse education in college than whites do. Here are a few of the hypotheses that deserve full exploration.

Take the situation of William—a slightly above-average student who, because he is black, gets into a highly competitive school. William studies very hard during the first year. He nonetheless gets mediocre grades. He has a choice. He can continue to study hard and continue to get mediocre grades, and be seen by his classmates as a black who cannot do very well. Or he can explicitly refuse to engage in the academic game. He decides to opt out, and his performance gets worse as time goes on. He emerges from college with a poor education and is further behind the whites than he was as a freshman.

If large numbers of other black students at the institution are in the same situation as William, the result can be group pressure not to compete academically. (At Harvard, it is said, the current term among black students for a black who studies like a white is "incognegro.") The response is not hard to understand. If one subpopulation of students is conspicuously behind another population and is visibly identifiable, then the population that is behind must come up with a good excuse for doing poorly. "Not wanting to do better" is as good as any.

But there is another crucial reason why blacks might not close the gap with whites during college: they are not taught as well as whites are. Racist teachers impeding the progress of students? Perhaps, but most college faculty members I know tend to bend over backward to be "fair" to black students—and that may be the problem. I suggest that inferior instruction is more likely to be a manifestation of the new racism than the old.

Consider the case of Carol, with outstanding abilities but deprived of decent prior schooling: she struggles the first year, but she gets by. Her academic skills still show the aftereffects of her inferior preparation. Her instructors diplomatically point out the more flagrant mistakes, but they ignore minor lapses, and never push her in the aggressive way they push white students who have her intellectual capacity. Some of them are being patronizing (she is doing quite well, considering). Others are being prudent: teachers who criticize black students can find themselves being called racists in the classroom, in the campus newspaper, or in complaints to the administration.

The same process continues in graduate school. Indeed, because there are even fewer blacks in graduate schools than in undergraduate schools, the pressure to get black students through to the degree, no matter what, can be still greater. But apart from differences in preparation and ability that have accumulated by the end of schooling, the process whereby we foster the appearance of black inferiority continues. Let's assume that William did not give up during college. He goes to business school, where he gets his Masters degree. He signs up for interviews with the corporate recruiters. There are 100 persons in his class, and William is ranked near the middle. But of the 5 blacks in his class, he ranks first (remember that he was at the 95th percentile of blacks taking the Scholastic Aptitude Test). He is hired on his first interview by his first-choice company, which also attracted the very best of the white students. He is hired alongside 5 of the top-ranking white members of the class.

William's situation as one of 5 blacks in a class of 100 illustrates the proportions that prevail in business schools, and business schools are by no means one of the more extreme examples. The pool of black candidates for any given profession is a small fraction of the white pool. This works out to a 20-to-1 edge in business; it is even greater in most of the other professions. The result, when many hiring institutions are competing, is that a major gap between the abilities of new black and white employees in any given workplace is highly likely. Everyone needs to hire a few blacks, and the edge that "being black" confers in the hiring decision warps the sequence of hiring in such a way that a scarce resource (the blacks with a given set of qualifications) is exhausted at an artificially high rate, producing a widening gap in comparison with the remaining whites from which an employer can choose.

The more aggressively affirmative action is enforced, the greater the imbalance. In general, the first companies to hire can pursue strategies that minimize or even eliminate the difference in ability between the new black and white employees. IBM and Park Avenue law firms can do very well, just as Harvard does quite well in attracting the top black students. But the more effectively they pursue these strategies, the more quickly they strip the population of the best black candidates.

To this point I have been discussing problems that are more or less driven by realities we have very little hope of manipulating in the short term except by discarding the laws regarding preferential treatment. People do differ in acquiring abilities. Currently, acquired abilities in the white and black populations are distributed differently. Schools and firms do form a rough hierarchy when they draw from these distributions. The results follow ineluctably. The dangers they represent are not a matter of statistical probabilities, but of day-to-day human reactions we see around us.

The damage caused by these mechanistic forces should be much less in the world of work than in the schools, however. Schools deal in a relatively narrow domain of skills, and "talent" tends to be assigned specific meanings and specific measures. Workplaces deal in highly complex sets of skills, and "talent" consists of all sorts of combinations of qualities. A successful career depends in large part upon finding jobs that elicit and develop one's strengths.

At this point the young black professional must sidestep a new series of traps laid by whites who need to be ostentatiously nonracist. Let's say that William goes to work for the XYZ Corporation, where he is assigned with another management trainee (white) to a department where much of the time is spent preparing proposals for government contracts. The white trainee is assigned a variety of scud work—proofreading drafts, calculating the costs of minor items in the bid, making photocopies, taking notes at conferences. William gets more dignified work. He is assigned portions of the draft to write (which are later rewritten by more experienced staff), sits in on planning sessions, and even goes to Washington as a highly visible part of the team to present the bid. As time goes on, the white trainee learns a great deal about how the company operates, and is seen as a go-getting young member of the team. William is perceived to be a bright enough fellow, but not much of a detail man and not really much of a self-starter.

Even if a black is hired under terms that put him on a par with his white peers, the subtler forms of differential treatment work against him. Particularly for any corporation that does business with the government, the new employee has a specific, immediate value purely because he is black. There are a variety of requirements to be met and rituals to be observed for which a black face is helpful. These have very little to do with the long-term career interests of the new employee; on the contrary, they often lead to a dead end as head of the minority-relations section of the personnel department.

Added to this is another problem that has nothing to do with the government. When the old racism was at fault (as it often still is), the newly hired black employee was excluded from the socialization process because the whites did not want him to become part of the group. When the new racism is at fault, it is because many whites are embarrassed to treat black employees as badly as they are willing to treat whites. Hence another reason that whites get on-the-job training that blacks do not: much of the early training of an employee is intertwined with menial assignments and mild hazing. Blacks who are put through these routines often see themselves as racially abused (and when a black is involved, old-racist responses may well have crept in). But even if the black is not unhappy

about the process, the whites are afraid that he is, and so protect him from it. There are many variations, all having the same effect: the black is denied an apprenticeship that the white has no way of escaping. Without serving the apprenticeship, there is no way of becoming part of the team.

Carol suffers a slightly different fate. She and a white woman are hired as reporters by a major newspaper. They both work hard, but after a few months there is no denying it: neither one of them can write. The white woman is let go. Carol is kept on, because the paper cannot afford to have any fewer blacks than it already has. She is kept busy with reportorial work, even though they have to work around the writing problem. She is told not to worry—there's lots more to being a journalist than writing.

It is the mascot syndrome. A white performing at a comparable level would be fired. The black is kept on, perhaps to avoid complications with the Equal Employment Opportunity Commission (it can be very expensive to fire a black), perhaps out of a more diffuse wish not to appear discriminatory. Everybody pretends that nothing is wrong—but the black's career is at a dead end. The irony, of course, is that the white who gets fired and has to try something else has been forced into accepting a chance of making a success in some other line of work whereas the black is seduced into *not* taking the same chance.

Sometimes differential treatment takes an even more pernicious form: the conspiracy to promote a problem out of existence. As part of keeping Carol busy, the newspaper gives her some administrative responsibilities. They do not amount to much. But she has an impressive title on a prominent newspaper and she is black—a potent combination. She gets an offer from a lesser paper in another part of the country to take a senior editorial post. Her current employer is happy to be rid of an awkward situation and sends along glowing references. She gets a job that she is unequipped to handle—only this time, she is in a highly visible position, and within a few weeks the deficiencies that were covered up at the old job have become the subject of jokes all over the office. Most of the jokes are openly racist.

It is important to pause and remember who Carol is: an extremely bright young woman, not (in other circumstances) a likely object of condescension. But being bright is no protection. Whites can usually count on the market to help us recognize egregious career mistakes and to prevent us from being promoted too far from a career line that fits our strengths, and too far above our level of readiness. One of the most prevalent characteristics of white differential treatment of blacks has been to exempt blacks from these market considerations, substituting for them a market premium attached to race.

The most obvious consequence of preferential treatment is that every black professional, no matter how able, is tainted. Every black who is hired by a white-run organization that hires blacks preferentially has to put up with the knowledge that many of his coworkers believe he was hired because of his race; and he has to put up with the suspicion in his own mind that they might be right.

Whites are curiously reluctant to consider this a real problem—it is an abstraction, I am told, much less important than the problem that blacks face in getting a job in the first place. But black professionals talk about it, and they tell stories of mental breakdowns; of people who had to leave the job altogether; of long-term professional paralysis. What white would want to be put in such a situation? Of course it would be a constant humiliation to be resented by some of your coworkers and condescended to by others. Of course it would affect your perceptions of yourself and your self-confidence. No system that produces such side effects—as preferential treatment must do—can be defended unless it is producing some extremely important benefits.

And that brings us to the decisive question. If the alternative were no job at all, as it was for so many blacks for so long, the resentment and condescension are part of the price of getting blacks into the positions they deserve. But is that the alternative today? If the institutions of this country were left to their own devices now, to what extent would they refuse to admit, hire, and promote people because they were black? To what extent are American institutions kept from being racist by the government's intervention?

It is another one of those questions that are seldom investigated aggressively, and I have no evidence. Let me suggest a hypothesis that bears

looking into: that the signal event in the struggle for black equality during the last thirty years, the one with real impact, was not the Civil Rights Act of 1964 or Executive Order 11246 or any other governmental act. It was the civil rights movement itself. It raised to a pitch of acute and lasting discomfort the racial consciousness of the generations of white Americans who are now running the country. I will not argue that the old racism is dead at any level of society. I will argue, however, that in the typical corporation or in the typical admissions office, there is an abiding desire to be not-racist. This need not be construed as brotherly love. Guilt will do as well. But the civil rights movement did its job. I suggest that the laws and the court decisions and the continuing intellectual respectability behind preferential treatment are not holding many doors open to qualified blacks that would otherwise be closed.

Suppose for a moment that I am right. Suppose that, for practical purposes, racism would not get in the way of blacks if preferential treatment were abandoned. How, in my most optimistic view, would the world look different?

There would be fewer blacks at Harvard and Yale; but they would all be fully competitive with the whites who were there. White students at the state university would encounter a cross-section of blacks who span the full range of ability, including the top levels, just as whites do. College remedial courses would no longer be disproportionately black. Whites rejected by the school they wanted would quit assuming they were kept out because a less-qualified black was admitted in their place. Blacks in big corporations would no longer be shunted off to personnel-relations positions, but would be left on the mainline tracks toward becoming comptrollers and sales managers and chief executive officers. Whites would quit assuming that black colleagues had been hired because they were black. Blacks would quit worrying that they had been hired because they were black.

Would blacks still lag behind? As a population, yes, for a time, and the nation should be mounting a far more effective program to improve elementary and secondary education for blacks than it has mounted in the last few decades. But in years past virtually every ethnic group in America has at one time or another lagged behind as a population, and has eventually caught up. In the process of catching up, the ones who breached the barriers were evidence of the success of that group. Now blacks who breach the barriers tend to be seen as evidence of the inferiority of that group.

And that is the evil of preferential treatment. It perpetuates an impression of inferiority. The system segments whites and blacks who come in contact with each other so as to maximize the likelihood that whites have the advantage in experience and ability. The system then encourages both whites and blacks to behave in ways that create self-fulfilling prophecies even when no real differences exist.

It is here that the new racism links up with the old. The old racism has always openly held that blacks are permanently less competent than whites. The new racism tacitly accepts that, in the course of overcoming the legacy of the old racism, blacks are temporarily less competent than whites. It is an extremely fine distinction. As time goes on, fine distinctions tend to be lost. Preferential treatment is providing persuasive evidence for the old racists, and we can already hear it *sotto voce:* "We gave you your chance, we let you educate them

and push them into jobs they couldn't have gotten on their own and coddle them every way you could. And see: they still aren't as good as whites, and you are beginning to admit it yourselves." Sooner or later this message is going to be heard by a white elite that needs to excuse its failure to achieve black equality.

The only happy aspect of the new racism is that the corrective—to get rid of the policies encouraging preferential treatment—is so natural. Deliberate preferential treatment by race has sat as uneasily with America's equal-opportunity ideal during the post-1965 period as it did during the days of legalized segregation. We had to construct tortuous rationalizations when we permitted blacks to be kept on the back of the bus—and the rationalizations to justify sending blacks to the head of the line have been just as tortuous. Both kinds of rationalization say that sometimes it is all right to treat people of different races in different ways. For years, we have instinctively sensed this was wrong in principle but intellectualized our support for it as an expedient. I submit that our instincts were right. There is no such thing as good racial discrimination.

REVIEW AND DISCUSSION QUESTIONS

1. How, according to Murray, does reverse discrimination encourage racism?
2. What is the "mascot syndrome," according to Murray?
3. Are the dangers Murray emphasizes outweighed by the longer term advantages of preferential admission and hiring? What are those advantages?
4. How would Ronald Dworkin respond to Murray's argument?
5. How accurate is Murray's description of the world without preferential treatment? Are there features of that world that he overlooks?
6. Are the responses of those whites whom Murray describes as racist reasonable, given their circumstances? Should their feelings be given significant weight in assessing affirmative action?
7. Affirmative action is sometimes defended as an attempt to compensate for society's failure to provide fair equality of opportunity. Is that a sound argument for such policies? Explain.
8. Sociologist Charles Moskos wrote in *The Atlantic Monthly* in May 1986 that nearly 10 percent of the army's officers are black, and although they believe they must work harder than whites to succeed, they oppose introduction of affirmative action programs into the army. How would Murray explain such opposition to affirmative action programs? Do you think his explanation is reasonable?
9. How might Iris Marion Young view affirmative action, given her defense of the "politics of difference"?

18

Political Correctness: Free Speech and the Multicultural Curriculum

Freedom of speech is thought to be among the most important rights. Yet all rights have limits, and speech is no exception. Two areas, in particular, have created controversy: racist speech and pornography. This section begins with a chapter from Mill's *On Liberty* that is widely regarded as one of the most important and articulate defenses of free expression ever written. The next two selections focus on racist speech. The first is a famous court opinion defending the rights of Nazis to march in a Jewish community; it is followed by a debate over speech codes on campus by two constitutional law professors. Turning to pornography, the next selection is a legal opinion striking down an attempt by feminists to limit pornography, followed by a discussion of the philosophical issues raised by those who argue that pornography should be banned based on its implicit messages about women. The section concludes with two selections that extend the discussion of free speech to include another, related area that has also been much debated on college campuses: the efforts by racial, ethnic, religious, and other groups to revise the intellectual "canon" in order to include their perspectives and traditions. In the final reading, the U.S. Supreme Court considers the rights of religious fundamentalists who objected to the teaching of "secular humanism" in their children's school curriculum.

Of the Liberty of Thought and Discussion

John Stuart Mill

In the following selection, taken from his classic work *On Liberty,* Mill examines freedom of conscience and speech. Mill vigorously upholds freedom of opinion, regardless of whether the belief is true or false. Indeed, he argues, it is especially important that false and evil opinions be freely expressed. For a brief description of John Stuart Mill's life, see the introduction to *Utilitarianism.*

From John Stuart Mill, *On Liberty* (1859).

The time, it is to be hoped, is gone by, when any defense would be necessary of the "liberty of the press" as one of the securities against corrupt or tyrannical government. No argument, we may suppose, can now be needed against permitting a legislature or an executive, not identified in interest with the people, to prescribe opinions to them, and determine what doctrines or what arguments they shall be allowed to hear. . . . Let us suppose . . . that government is entirely at one with the people, and never thinks of exerting any power of coercion unless in agreement with what it conceives to be their voice. But I deny the right of the people to exercise such coercion, either by themselves or by their government. The power itself is illegitimate. The best government has no more title to it than the worst. It is as noxious, or more noxious, when exerted in accordance with public opinion than when in opposition to it. If all mankind minus one were of one opinion, mankind would be no more justified in silencing that one person than he, if he had the power, would be justified in silencing mankind. Were an opinion a personal possession of no value except to the owner, if to be obstructed in the enjoyment of it were simply a private injury, it would make some difference whether the injury was inflicted only on a few persons or on many. But the peculiar evil of silencing the expression of an opinion is that it is robbing the human race, posterity as well as the existing generation—those who dissent from the opinion, still more than those who hold it. If the opinion is right, they are deprived of the opportunity of exchanging error for truth; if wrong, they lose, what is almost as great a benefit, the clearer perception and livelier impression of truth produced by its collision with error.

It is necessary to consider separately these two hypotheses, each of which has a distinct branch of the argument corresponding to it. We can never be sure that the opinion we are endeavoring to stifle is a false opinion; and if we were sure, stifling it would be an evil still.

First, the opinion which it is attempted to suppress by authority may possibly be true. Those who desire to suppress it, of course, deny its truth; but they are not infallible. They have no authority to decide the question for all mankind and exclude every other person from the means of judging. To refuse a hearing to an opinion because they are sure that it is false to assume that *their* certainty is the same thing as *absolute* certainty. All silencing of discussion is an assumption of infallibility. Its condemnation may be allowed to rest on this common argument, not the worse for being common.

Unfortunately for the good sense of mankind, the fact of their fallibility is far from carrying the weight in their practical judgment which is always allowed to it in theory; for while everyone well knows himself to be fallible, few think it necessary to take any precautions against their own fallibility, or admit the supposition that any opinion of which they feel very certain may be one of the examples of the error to which they acknowledge themselves to be liable. . . .

The objection likely to be made to this argument would probably take some such form as the following. There is no greater assumption of infallibility in forbidding the propagation of error than in any other thing which is done by public authority on its own judgment and responsibility. . . . It is the duty of governments, and of individuals, to form the truest opinions they can; to form them carefully, and never impose them upon others unless they are quite sure of being right. But when they are sure (such reasoners may say), it is not conscientiousness but cowardice to shrink from acting on their opinions and allow doctrines which they honestly think dangerous to the welfare of mankind, either in this life or in another, to be scattered abroad without restraint, because other people, in less enlightened times, have persecuted opinions now believed to be true. . . . There is no such thing as absolute certainty, but there is assurance sufficient for the purposes of human life. We may, and must, assume our opinion to be true for the guidance of our own conduct; and it is assuming no more when we forbid bad men to pervert society by the propagation of opinions which we regard as false and pernicious.

I answer, that it is assuming very much more. There is the greatest difference between presuming an opinion to be true because, with every opportunity for contesting it, it has not been refuted, and assuming its truth for the purpose of not permitting its refutation. Complete liberty of contradicting and disproving our opinion is the very condition which justifies us in assuming its truth for purposes of action; and on no other terms can a being with human faculties have any rational assurance of being right. . . .

Let us now pass to the second division of the argument, and dismissing the supposition that any of the received opinions may be false, let us assume them to be true and examine into the worth of the manner in which they are likely to be held when their truth is not freely and openly canvassed. However unwillingly a person who has a strong opinion may admit the possibility that his opinion may be false, he ought to be moved by the consideration that, however true it may be, if it is not fully, frequently, and fearlessly discussed, it will be held as a dead dogma, not a living truth. . . .

If the cultivation of the understanding consists in one thing more than in another, it is surely in learning the grounds of one's own opinions. Whatever people believe, on subjects on which it is of the first importance to believe rightly, they ought to be able to defend against at least the common objections. . . . The greatest orator, save one, of antiquity, has left it on record that he always studied his adversary's case with as great, if not still greater, intensity than even his own. What Cicero practiced as the means of forensic success requires to be imitated by all who study any subject in order to arrive at the truth. He who knows only his own side of the case knows little of that. His reasons may be good, and no one may have been able to refute them. But if he is equally unable to refute the reasons on the opposite side, if he does not so much as know what they are, he has no ground for preferring either opinion. The rational position for him would be suspension of judgment, and unless he contents himself with that, he is either led by authority or adopts, like the generality of the world, the side to which he feels most inclination. Nor is it enough that he should hear the arguments of adversaries from his own teachers, presented as they state them, and accompanied by what they offer as refutations. That is not the way to do justice to the arguments or bring them into real contact with his own mind. He must be able to hear them from persons who actually believe them, who defend them in earnest and do their very utmost for them. He must know them in their most plausible and persuasive form; he must feel the whole force of the difficulty which the true view of the subject has to encounter and dispose of, else he will never

really possess himself of the portion of truth which meets and removes that difficulty. . . .

The fact . . . is that not only the grounds of the opinion are forgotten in the absence of discussion, but too often the meaning of the opinion itself. The words which convey it cease to suggest ideas, or suggest only a small portion of those they were originally employed to communicate. Instead of a vivid conception and a living belief, there remain only a few phrases retained by rote; or, if any part, the shell and husk only of the meanings is retained, the finer essence being lost. The great chapter in human history which this fact occupies and fills cannot be too earnestly studied and meditated on. . . .

We have hitherto considered only two possibilities: that the received opinion may be false, and some other opinion, consequently, true; or that, the received opinion being true, a conflict with the opposite error is essential to a clear apprehension and deep feeling of its truth. But there is a commoner case than either of these: when the conflicting doctrines, instead of being one true and the other false, share the truth between them, and the nonconforming opinion is needed to supply the remainder of the truth of which the received doctrine embodies only a part. Popular opinions, on subjects not palpable to sense, are often true, but seldom or never the whole truth. They are a part of the truth, sometimes a greater, sometimes a smaller part, but exaggerated, distorted, and disjointed from the truths by which they ought to be accompanied and limited. Heretical opinions, on the other hand, are generally some of these suppressed and neglected truths, bursting the bonds which kept them down, and either seeking reconciliation with the truth contained in the common opinion, or fronting it as enemies, and setting themselves up, with similar exclusiveness, as the whole truth. The latter case is hitherto the most frequent, as, in the human mind, one-sidedness has always been the rule, and many-sidedness the exception. . . . Such being the partial character of prevailing opinions, even when resting on a true foundation, every opinion which embodies somewhat of the portion of truth which the common opinion omits ought to be considered precious, with whatever amount of error and confusion that truth may be blended. . . .

We have now recognized the necessity to the mental well-being of mankind (on which all their other well-being depends) of freedom of opinion, and freedom of the expression of opinion, on four distinct grounds, which we will now briefly recapitulate:

First, if any opinion is compelled to silence, that opinion may, for aught we can certainly know, be true. To deny this is to assume our own infallibility.

Secondly, although the silenced opinion be an error, it may, and very commonly does, contain a portion of truth; and since the general or prevailing opinion on any subject is rarely or never the whole truth, it is only by the collision of adverse opinions that the remainder of the truth has any chance of being supplied.

Thirdly, even if the received opinion be not only true, but the whole truth; unless it is suffered to be, and actually is, vigorously and earnestly contested, it will, by most of those who receive it, be held in the manner of a prejudice, with little comprehension or feeling of its rational grounds. And not only this, but fourthly, the meaning of the doctrine itself will be in danger of being lost or enfeebled, and deprived of its vital effect on the character and conduct: the dogma becoming a mere formal profession, inefficacious for good, but cumbering the ground and preventing the growth of any real and heartfelt conviction from reason or personal experience. . . .

REVIEW AND DISCUSSION QUESTIONS

1. What values or purposes does Mill think are served by freedom of speech?
2. Why does Mill think that false speech should be tolerated or even encouraged?
3. Explain why Mill thinks those who would censor speech are assuming, falsely, that they are "infallible."
4. How does Mill respond to those who say that "offensive" speech may be banned?
5. Describe how Mill's discussion of free speech fits into his larger discussion of liberty and individuality in *On Liberty*.
6. Suppose somebody defends censorship of Nazi propaganda based on the risk that Nazis will eventually gain power, as occurred in post–World War I Germany. How would Mill respond to such an argument? Is that response sound?

Nazi Marches:

Village of Skokie v. *National Socialist Party*

Skokie, Illinois, was the home of over forty thousand Jews and five to seven thousand survivors of Nazi concentration camps. When the National Socialist Party (the American Nazi Party) tried to march in Skokie, the village won an injunction preventing various forms of conduct. An appeals court modified that injunction but allowed the ban on displaying the swastika to stand. Here the Supreme Court of Illinois considers an appeal by the Nazi leader, Frank Collin, of the lower court's ban. (The U.S. Supreme Court later refused to reconsider this decision of the Illinois Supreme Court.)

373 N.E. 2d 21 (Ill. 1978).

Per Curiam: [D]efendant Frank Collin, who testified that he was "party leader," stated that on or about March 20, 1977, he sent officials of the plaintiff village a letter stating that the party members and supporters would hold a peaceable, public assembly in the village on May 1, 1977, to protest the Skokie Park District's requirement that the party procure $350,000 of insurance prior to the party's use of the Skokie public parks for public assemblies. The demonstration was to begin at 3 P.M., last 20 to 30 minutes, and consist of 30 to 50 demonstrators marching in single file, back and forth, in front of the village hall. The marchers were to wear uniforms which include a swastika emblem or armband. They were to carry a party banner containing a swastika emblem and signs containing such statements as "White Free Speech," "Free Speech for the White Man," and "Free Speech for White America." The demonstrators would not distribute handbills, make any derogatory statements directed to any ethnic or religious group, or obstruct traffic. They would cooperate with any reasonable police instructions or requests.

At the hearing on plaintiff's motion for an "emergency injunction" a resident of Skokie testified that he was a survivor of the Nazi holocaust. He further testified that the Jewish community in and around Skokie feels the purpose of the march in the "heart of the Jewish population" is to remind the two million survivors "that we are not through with you" and to show "that the Nazi threat is not over, it can happen again." Another resident of Skokie testified that as the result of defendants' announced intention to march in Skokie, 15 to 18 Jewish organizations, within the village and surrounding area, were called and a counterdemonstration of an estimated 12,000 to 15,000 people was scheduled for the same day. There was opinion evidence that defendants' planned demonstration in Skokie would result in violence. . . .

In defining the constitutional rights of the parties who come before this court, we are, of course, bound by the pronouncements of the United States Supreme Court in its interpretation of the United States Constitution. The decisions of that court, particularly *Cohen* v. *California*. . . in our opinion compel us to permit the demonstration as proposed, including display of the swastika.

"It is firmly settled that under our Constitution the public expression of ideas may not be prohibited merely because the ideas are themselves offensive to some of their hearers". . . and it is entirely clear that the wearing of distinctive clothing can be symbolic expression of a thought or philosophy. The symbolic expression of thought falls within the free speech clause of the first amendment . . . and the plaintiff village has the heavy burden of justifying the imposition of a prior restraint upon defendants' right to freedom of speech . . . . The village of Skokie seeks to meet this burden by application of the "fighting words" doctrine first enunciated in *Chaplinsky* v. *New Hampshire* (1942). . . . That doctrine was designed to permit punishment of extremely hostile personal communication likely to cause immediate physical response, "no words being 'forbidden except such as have a direct tendency to cause acts of violence by the persons to whom, individually, the remark is addressed'". . . . In *Cohen* the Supreme Court restated the description of fighting words as "those personally abusive epithets which, when addressed to the ordinary citizen, are, as a matter of common knowledge, inherently likely to provoke violent reaction. . . . Plaintiff urges, and the appellate court has held, that the exhibition of the Nazi symbol, the swastika, addresses to ordinary citizens a message which is tantamount of fighting words. Plaintiff further asks this court to extend *Chaplinsky*, which upheld a statute punishing the use of such words, and hold that the fighting-words doctrine permits a prior restraint on defendants' symbolic speech. In our judgment we are precluded from doing so.

In *Cohen,* defendant's conviction stemmed from wearing a jacket bearing the words "Fuck the Draft" in a Los Angeles County courthouse corridor. The Supreme Court for reasons we believe applicable here refused to find that the jacket inscription constituted fighting words. That court stated:

"The constitutional right of free expression is powerful medicine in a society as diverse and populous as ours. It is designed and intended to remove governmental restraints from the arena of public discussion, putting the decision as to what views shall be voiced largely into the hands of each of us, in the hope that use of such freedom will ultimately produce a more capable citizenry and more perfect polity and in the belief that no other approach would comport with the premise of individual dignity and choice upon which our political system rests. . . .

To many, the immediate consequence of this freedom may often appear to be only verbal tumult, discord, and even offensive utterance. These are, however, within established limits, in truth necessary side effects of the broader enduring values which the process of open debate permits us to achieve. That the air may at times seem filled with verbal cacophony is, in this sense not a sign of weakness but of strength. We cannot lose sight of the fact that, in what otherwise might seem a trifling and annoying instance of individual distasteful abuse of a privilege, these fundamental societal values are truly implicated. . . . 'so long as the means are peaceful, the communication need not meet standards of acceptability,' . . .

Against this perception of the constitutional policies involved, we discern certain more particularized considerations that peculiarly call for reversal of this conviction. First, the principle contended for by the State seems inherently boundless. How is one to distinguish this from any other offensive word [emblem]? Surely the State has no right to cleanse public debate to the point where it is grammatically palatable to the most squeamish among us. Yet no readily ascertainable general principle exists for stopping short of that result were we to affirm the judgment below. For, while the particular four-letter word [emblem] being litigated here is perhaps more distasteful than most others of its genre, it is nevertheless often true that one man's vulgarity is another's lyric. Indeed, we think it is largely because governmental officials cannot make principled distinctions in this area that the Constitution leaves matters of taste and style so largely to the individual. . . .

Finally, and in the same vein, we cannot indulge the facile assumption that one can forbid particular words without also running a substantial risk of suppressing ideas in the process. Indeed, governments might soon seize upon the censorship of particular words [emblems] as a convenient guise for banning the expression of unpopular views. We have been able, as noted above, to discern little social benefit that might result from running the risk of opening the door to such grave results". . . .

The display of the swastika, as offensive to the principles of a free nation as the memories it recalls may be, is symbolic political speech intended to convey to the public the beliefs of those who display it. It does not, in our opinion, fall within the definition of "fighting words," and that doctrine cannot be used here to overcome the heavy presumption against the constitutional validity of a prior restraint.

Nor can we find that the swastika, while not representing fighting words, is nevertheless so offensive and peace threatening to the public that its display can be enjoined. We do not doubt that the sight of this symbol is abhorrent to the Jewish citizens of Skokie, and that the survivors of the Nazi persecutions, tormented by their recollections, may have strong feelings regarding its display. Yet it is entirely clear that this factor does not justify enjoining defendants' speech. The *Cohen* court spoke to this subject.

"Finally, in arguments before this Court much has been made of the claim that Cohen's distasteful mode of expression was thrust upon unwilling or unsuspecting viewers, and that the State might therefore legitimately act as it did in order to protect the sensitive from otherwise unavoidable exposure to appellant's crude form of protest. Of course, the mere presumed presence of unwitting listeners or viewers does not serve automatically to justify curtailing all speech capable of giving offense. . . . While this Court has recognized that government may properly act in many situations to prohibit intrusion into the privacy of the home of unwelcome views and ideas which cannot be totally banned from the public dialogue we have at the same time consistently stressed that 'we are often "captives" outside the sanctuary of the home and subject to objectionable speech.' The ability of government, consonant with the Constitution, to shut off discourse solely to protect others from hearing it is, in other words, dependent upon a showing that substantial privacy interests are being invaded in an essentially intolerable manner. Any broader view of this authority would effectively empower a majority to silence dissidents simply as a matter of personal predilections."

Rockwell v. *Morris* . . . also involved an American Nazi leader, George Lincoln Rockwell, who challenged a bar to his use of a New York City park to hold a public demonstration where anti-Semitic speeches would be made. Although approximately 2 1/2 million Jewish New Yorkers were hostile to Rockwell's message, the court ordered that a permit to speak be granted, stating:

"A community need not wait to be subverted by street riots and storm troopers; but, also, it cannot, by its policemen or commissioners, suppress a speaker, in prior

restraint, on the basis of news reports, hysteria, or inference that what he did yesterday, he will do today.
Thus, too, if the speaker incites others to immediate unlawful action he may be punished—in a proper case,
stopped when disorder actually impends; but this is not
to be confused with unlawful action from others who
seek unlawfully to suppress or punish the speaker.

So, the unpopularity of views, their shocking quality,
their obnoxiousness, and even their alarming impact
is not enough. Otherwise, the preacher of any strange
doctrine could be stopped; the anti-racist himself could
be suppressed, if he undertakes to speak in 'restricted'
areas; and one who asks that public schools be open indiscriminately to all ethnic groups could be lawfully
suppressed, if only he choose to speak where persuasion
is needed most." . . .

In summary, as we read the controlling Supreme
Court opinions, use of the swastika is a symbolic
form of free speech entitled to first amendment
protections. Its display on uniforms or banners by
those engaged in peaceful demonstrations cannot
be totally precluded solely because that display
may provoke a violent reaction by those who view
it. Particularly is this true where, as here, there has
been advance notice by the demonstrators of their
plans so that they have become, as the complaint
alleges, "common knowledge" and those to whom
sight of the swastika banner or uniforms would be
offense are forewarned and need not view them.
A speaker who gives prior notice of his message
has not compelled a confrontation with those who
voluntarily listen.

As to those who happen to be in a position to
be involuntarily confronted with the swastika, the
following observations from *Erznoznik* v. *City of
Jacksonville* . . . are appropriate:

"The plain, if at all times disquieting, truth is that in
our pluralistic society, constantly proliferating new
and ingenious forms of expression, 'we are inescapably
captive audiences for many purposes.' . . . Much that
we encounter offends our esthetic, if not our political
and moral, sensibilities. Nevertheless, the Constitution does not permit government to decide which types
of otherwise protected speech are sufficiently offensive to require protection for the unwilling listener or
viewer. Rather, absent the narrow circumstances described above [home intrusion or captive audience], the
burden normally falls upon the viewer to 'avoid further
bombardment of [his] sensibilities simply by averting
[his] eyes.' . . .

REVIEW AND DISCUSSION QUESTIONS

1. Describe the factual background and legal issues in this case.
2. The court relied on an earlier U.S. Supreme Court case, *Cohen* v. *California*, in deciding
   this one. What happened in *Cohen?* Why does the court think it is relevant to Skokie?
3. What do you think the intention of the Nazis was in deciding to march in Skokie, if not to
   win political converts to their cause? Should the court have considered their purposes?
4. How does the court distinguish this case from *Chaplinsky* and the "fighting words"
   exception?
5. It is sometimes said that this case was rightly decided because for the court to rule otherwise would put it on a slippery slope of trying to balance the offensiveness of speech
   against the First Amendment rights of the speaker, with the result that civil rights marches
   would have been jeopardized. Do you agree? Explain.
6. How would Mill respond to this case?

Prohibiting Racist Speech on Campus: A Debate

Charles Lawrence and Gerald Gunther

This selection includes two essays written by two law professors in response to Stanford University's speech code. One supported the code; the other opposed it. (In 1990, Stanford revised the code, along the lines described in the questions after the reading.) Charles Lawrence is professor of law at Georgetown University, and Gerald Gunther is professor of law at Stanford University.

BY CHARLES LAWRENCE

I have spent the better part of my life as a dissenter. As a high-school student, I was threatened with suspension for my refusal to participate in a civil-defense drill, and I have been a conspicuous consumer of my First Amendment liberties ever since. There are very strong reasons for protecting even speech that is racist. Perhaps the most important is that such protection reinforces our society's commitment to tolerance as a value. By protecting bad speech from government regulation, we will be forced to combat it as a community.

I have, however, a deeply felt apprehension about the resurgence of racial violence and the corresponding increase in the incidence of verbal and symbolic assault and harassment to which blacks and other traditionally excluded groups are subjected. I am troubled by the way the debate has been framed in response to the recent surge of racist incidents on college and university campuses and in response to some universities' attempts to regulate harassing speech. The problem has been framed as one in which the liberty of free speech is in conflict with the elimination of racism. I believe this has placed the bigot on the moral high ground and fanned the rising flames of racism.

Above all, I am troubled that we have not listened to the real victims—that we have shown so little understanding of their injury, and that we have abandoned those whose race, gender, or sexual orientation continues to make them second-class citizens. It seems to me a very sad irony that the first instinct of civil libertarians has been to challenge even the smallest, most narrowly framed efforts by universities to provide black and other minority students with the protection the Constitution, in my opinion, guarantees them.

The landmark case of *Brown* v. *Board of Education* is not a case that we normally think of as a case about speech. But *Brown* can be broadly read as articulating the principle of equal citizenship. *Brown* held that segregated schools were inherently unequal because of the message that segregation conveyed: that black children were an untouchable caste, unfit to go to school with white children. If we understand the necessity of eliminating the system of signs and symbols that signal the inferiority of blacks, then we should hesitate before proclaiming that all racist speech that stops short of physical violence must be defended.

University officials who have formulated policies to respond to incidents of racial harassment have been characterized in the press as "thought police," even though such policies generally do nothing more than impose sanctions against intentional face-to-face insults. Racist speech takes the form of face-to-face insults, catcalls, or other assaultive speech aimed at an individual or small

From Charles Lawrence and Gerald Gunther, "Good Speech, Bad Speech—Yes," and "Good Speech, Bad Speech—No," *Stanford Lawyer,* 24 (1990), pp. 6, 8, 40, and 7, 9, 41. Reprinted with permission.

group of persons falls directly within the "fighting words" exception to the First Amendment protection. The Supreme Court has held in *Chaplinsky* v. *New Hampshire* that words which "by their very utterance inflict injury or tend to incite an immediate breach of the peace" are not protected by the First Amendment.

If the purpose of the First Amendment is to foster the greatest amount of speech, racial insults disserve that purpose. Assaultive racist speech functions as a preemptive strike. The invective is experienced as a blow, not as a proffered idea. And once the blow is struck, a dialogue is unlikely to follow. Racial insults are particularly undeserving of First Amendment protection, because the perpetrator's intention is not to discover truth or initiate dialogue but to injure the victim. In most situations, members of minority groups realize that they are likely to lose if they fight back, and are forced to remain silent and submissive.

Courts have held that offensive speech may not be regulated in public forums (such as streets, where the listener may avoid the speech by moving on). But the regulation of otherwise protected speech has been permitted when the speech invades the privacy of the unwilling listener's home, or when the unwilling listener cannot avoid the speech. Racist posters, fliers, and graffiti in dormitories, bathrooms, and other common living spaces would seem to fall within the reasoning of these cases. Minority students should not be required to remain in their rooms in order to avoid racial insult. Minimally, they should find a safe haven in their dorms and in all other common rooms that are a part of their daily routine.

I would also argue that the university's responsibility for ensuring that these students receive an equal educational opportunity provides a compelling justification for regulations that ensure them safe passage in all common areas. A minority student should not have to risk becoming the target of racially assaulting speech every time he or she chooses to walk across campus. Regulating vilifying speech that cannot be anticipated or avoided need not preclude announced speeches and rallies—situations that would give minority-group members and their allies the opportunity to organize counterdemonstrations or avoid the speech altogether.

The most commonly advanced argument against the regulation of racist speech proceeds something like this: We recognize that minority groups suffer pain and injury as the result of racist speech, but we must allow this hate mongering for the benefit of society as a whole. Freedom of speech is the lifeblood of our democratic system. It is especially important for minorities, because often it is their only vehicle for rallying support for the redress of their grievances. It will be impossible to formulate a prohibition so precise that it will prevent the racist speech you want to suppress, without catching in the same net all kinds of speech that it would be unconscionable for a democratic society to suppress.

Such arguments seek to strike a balance between our concern, on the one hand, for the continued free flow of ideas and the democratic process dependent on that flow, and, on the other, our desire to further the cause of equality. There can, however, be no meaningful discussion of how we should reconcile our commitment to equality with our commitment to free speech, until it is acknowledged that racist speech inflicts real harm, and that this harm is far from trivial.

To engage in a debate about the First Amendment and racist speech without a full understanding of the nature and extent of that harm is to risk making the First Amendment an instrument of domination rather than a vehicle of liberation. We have not all known the experience of victimization by racist, misogynist, and homophobic speech, nor do we equally share the burden of the harm it inflicts. We are often quick to say that we have heard the cry of the victims when we have not.

The *Brown* case is again instructive, because it speaks directly to the psychic injury inflicted by racist speech by noting that the symbolic message of segregation affected "the hearts and minds" of Negro children "in a way unlikely ever to be undone." Racial epithets and harassment often cause deep emotional scarring and feelings of anxiety and fear that pervade every aspect of a victim's life.

Brown also recognized that black children did not have an equal opportunity to learn and participate in the school community when they bore the additional burden of being subjected to the humiliation and psychic assault contained in the message of segregation. University students bear an analogous burden when they are forced to live and work in an environment where at any moment they may be subjected to denigrating verbal harassment and assault. The same injury was addressed by the Supreme Court when it held that, under Title VII of the Civil Rights Act of 1964, sexual harassment which creates a hostile or abusive work environment violates the ban on sex discrimination in employment.

Carefully drafted university regulations could bar the use of words as assault weapons while at the same time leaving unregulated even the most heinous of ideas provided those ideas are presented at times and places and in manners that provide an opportunity for reasoned rebuttal or escape from immediate insult. The history of the development of the right to free speech has been one of carefully evaluating the importance of free expression and its effects on other important societal interests. We have drawn the line between protected and unprotected speech before without dire results. (Courts have, for example, exempted from the protection of the First Amendment obscene speech and speech that disseminates official secrets, defames or libels another person, or is used to form a conspiracy or monopoly.)

Blacks and other people of color are skeptical about the argument that even the most injurious speech must remain unregulated because, in an unregulated marketplace of ideas, the best ones will rise to the top and gain acceptance. Experience tells quite the opposite. People of color have seen too many demagogues elected by appealing to America's racism, and too many sympathetic politicians shy away from issues that might brand them as being too closely allied with disparaged groups.

Whenever we decide that racist speech must be tolerated because of the importance of maintaining societal tolerance for all unpopular speech, we are asking blacks and other subordinated groups to bear the burden for the good of all. We must be careful that the ease with which we strike the balance against the regulation of racist speech is in no way influenced by the fact that the cost will be borne by others. We must be certain that those who will pay that price are fairly represented in our deliberations and that they are heard.

At the core of the argument that we should resist all government regulation of speech is the ideal that the best cure for bad speech is good—that ideas that affirm equality and the worth of all individuals will ultimately prevail. This is an empty ideal unless those of us who would fight racism are vigilant and unequivocal in that fight. We must look for ways to offer assistance and support to students whose speech and political participation are chilled in a climate of racial harassment.

Civil rights lawyers might consider suing on behalf of blacks whose right to an equal education is denied by a university's failure to ensure a nondiscriminatory educational climate or conditions of employment. We must embark upon the development of a First Amendment jurisprudence grounded in the reality of our history and our contemporary experience. We must think hard about how best to launch legal attacks against the most indefensible forms of hate speech. Good lawyers can create exceptions and narrow interpretations that limit the harm of hate speech without opening the floodgates of censorship.

Everyone concerned with these issues must find ways to engage actively in actions that resist and counter the racist ideas that we would have the First Amendment protect. If we fail in this, the victims of hate speech must rightly assume that we are on the bigots' side.

BY GERALD GUNTHER

I am deeply troubled by current efforts—however well-intentioned—to place new limits on freedom of expression at this and other campuses. Such limits are not only incompatible with the mission and meaning of a university; they also send exactly the wrong message from academia to society as a whole. University campuses should exhibit greater, not less, freedom of expression than prevails in society at large.

Proponents of new limits argue that historic First Amendment rights must be balanced against "Stanford's commitment to the diversity of ideas and persons." Clearly, there is ample room and need for vigorous University action to combat racial and other discrimination. But curbing freedom of speech is the wrong way to do so. The proper answer to bad speech is usually more and better speech—not new laws, litigation, and repression.

Lest it be thought that I am insensitive to the pain imposed by expressions of racial or religious hatred, let me say that I have suffered that pain and empathize with others under similar verbal assault. My deep belief in the principles of the First Amendment arises in part from my own experiences.

I received my elementary education in a public school in a very small town in Nazi Germany. There I was subjected to vehement anti-Semitic remarks from my teacher, classmates and others— "Judensau" (Jew pig) was far from the harshest. I can assure you that they hurt. More generally, I lived in a country where ideological orthodoxy reigned and where the opportunity for dissent was severely limited.

The lesson I have drawn from my childhood in Nazi Germany and my happier adult life in this country is the need to walk the sometimes difficult path of denouncing the bigots' hateful ideas with all my power, yet at the same time challenging any community's attempt to suppress hateful ideas by force of law.

Obviously, given my own experience, I do not quarrel with the claim that words can do harm. But I firmly deny that a showing of harm suffices to deny First Amendment protection, and I insist on the elementary First Amendment principle that our Constitution usually protects even offensive, harmful expression.

That is why—at the risk of being thought callous or doctrinaire—I feel compelled to speak out against the attempt by some members of the Stanford community to enlarge the area of forbidden speech under the Fundamental Standard. Such proposals, in my view, seriously undervalue the First Amendment and far too readily endanger its precious content. Limitations on free expression beyond those established by law should be eschewed in an institution committed to diversity and the First Amendment.

In explaining my position, I will avoid extensive legal arguments. Instead, I want to speak from the heart, on the basis of my own background and of my understanding of First Amendment principles—principles supported by an even larger number of scholars and Supreme Court justices, especially since the days of the Warren Court.

Among the core principles is that any official effort to suppress expression must be viewed with the greatest skepticism and suspicion. Only in very narrow, urgent circumstances should government or similar institutions be permitted to inhibit speech. True, there are certain categories of speech that may be prohibited; but the number and scope of these categories has steadily shrunk over the last fifty years. Face-to-face insults are one such category; incitement to immediate illegal action is another. But opinions expressed in debates and arguments about a wide range of political and social issues should not be suppressed simply because of disagreement with those views, with the content of the expression.

Similarly, speech should not and cannot be banned simply because it is "offensive" to substantial parts or a majority of a community. The refusal to suppress offensive speech is one of the most difficult obligations the free speech principle imposes upon all of us; yet it is also one of the First Amendment's greatest glories—indeed it is a central test of a community's commitment to free speech.

The Supreme Court's 1989 decision to allow flag-burning as a form of political protest, in *Texas* v. *Johnson,* warrants careful pondering by all those who continue to advocate campus restraints on "racist speech." As Justice Brennan's majority opinion in Johnson reminded, "If there is a bedrock principle underlying the First Amendment, it is that the Government may not prohibit the expression of an idea simply because society finds the idea itself offensive or disagreeable." In refusing to place flag-burning outside the First Amendment, moreover, the *Johnson* majority insisted (in words especially apt for the "racist speech" debate): "The First Amendment does not guarantee that other concepts virtually sacred to our Nation as a whole—*such as the principle that discrimination on the basis of race is odious and destructive*—will go unquestioned in the marketplace of ideas. We decline, therefore, to create for the flag an exception to the joust of principles protected by the First Amendment." (Italics added.)

Campus proponents of restricting offensive speech are currently relying for justification on the Supreme Court's allegedly repeated reiteration that "fighting words" constitute an exception to the First Amendment. Such an exception has indeed been recognized in a number of lower court cases. However, there has only been one case in the history of the Supreme Court in which a majority of the Justices has ever found a statement to be a punishable resort to "fighting words." That was *Chaplinsky* v. *New Hampshire,* a nearly fifty-year-old case involving words which would very likely not be found punishable today.

More significant is what has happened in the nearly half-century since: Despite repeated appeals to the Supreme Court to recognize the applicability of the "fighting words" exception by affirming challenged convictions, the Court has in every instance refused. One must wonder about the strength of an exception that, while theoretically recognized, has for so long not been found apt in practice. (Moreover, the proposed Stanford rules are not limited to face-to-face insults to an addressee, and thus go well beyond the traditional, albeit fragile, "fighting words" exception.)

The phenomenon of racist and other offensive speech that Stanford now faces is not a new one in the history of the First Amendment. In recent decades, for example, well-meaning but in my view misguided majorities have sought to suppress not only racist speech but also antiwar and antidraft speech, civil rights demonstrators, the Nazis and the Ku Klux Klan, and left-wing groups.

Typically, it is people on the extremes of the political spectrum (including those who advocate overthrow of our constitutional system and those who would not protect their opponents' right to dissent were they the majority) who feel the brunt of repression and have found protection in the First Amendment; typically, it is well-meaning people in the majority who believe that their "community standards," their sensibilities, their sense of outrage, justify restraints.

Those in power in a community recurrently seek to repress speech they find abhorrent; and their efforts are understandable human impulses. Yet freedom of expression—and especially the protection of dissident speech, the most important function of the First Amendment—is an anti-majoritarian principle. Is it too much to hope that, especially on a university campus, a majority can be persuaded of the value of freedom of expression and of the resultant need to curb our impulses to repress dissident views?

The principles to which I appeal are not new. They have been expressed, for example, by the most distinguished Supreme Court justices ever since the beginning of the Court's confrontations with First Amendment issues nearly seventy years ago. These principles are reflected in the words of so imperfect a First Amendment defender as Justice Oliver Wendell Holmes: "If there is any principle of the Constitution that more imperatively calls for attachment than any other it is the principle of free thought—not free thought for those who agree with us but freedom for the thought that we hate."

This is the principle most elaborately and eloquently addressed by Justice Louis D. Brandeis, who reminded us that the First Amendment rests on a belief "in the power of reason as applied through public discussion" and therefore bars "silence coerced by law—the argument of force in its worst form."

This theme, first articulated in dissents, has repeatedly been voiced in majority opinions in more recent decades. It underlies Justice Douglas's remark in striking down a conviction under a law banning speech that "stirs the public to anger": "A function of free speech [is] to invite dispute. . . . Speech is often provocative and challenging. That is why freedom of speech [is ordinarily] protected against censorship or punishment."

It also underlies Justice William J. Brennan's comment about our "profound national commitment to the principle that debate on public issues should be uninhibited, robust and wide-open, and that it may well include vehement, caustic and sometimes unpleasantly sharp attacks"—a comment he followed with a reminder that constitutional protection "does not turn upon the truth, popularity or social utility of the ideas and beliefs which are offered."

These principles underlie as well the repeated insistence by Justice John Marshall Harlan, again in majority opinions, that the mere "inutility or immorality" of a message cannot justify its repression, and that the state may not punish because of "the underlying content of the message." Moreover, Justice Harlan, in one of the finest First Amendment opinions on the books, noted, in words that Stanford would ignore at its peril at this time:

The constitutional right of free expression is powerful medicine in a society as diverse and populous as ours. . . . To many, the immediate consequence of this freedom may often appear to be only verbal tumult, discord and even offensive utterance. These are, however, within established limits, in truth necessary side effects of the broader enduring values which the process of open debate permits us to achieve. That the air may at times seem filled with verbal cacophony is, in this sense, not a sign of weakness but of strength.

In this same passage, Justice Harlan warned that a power to ban speech merely because it is offensive is an "inherently boundless" notion, and added that "we think it is largely because governmental officials cannot make principled distinctions in this area that the Constitution leaves matters of taste and style so largely to the individual." (The Justice made these comments while overturning the conviction of an antiwar protestor for "offensive conduct." The defendant had worn, in a courthouse corridor, a jacket bearing the words "Fuck the Draft." It bears noting, in light of the ongoing campus debate, that Justice Harlan's majority opinion also warned that "we cannot indulge in the facile assumption that one can forbid particular words without also running the substantial risk of suppressing ideas in the process.")

I restate these principles and repeat these words for reasons going far beyond the fact that they are familiar to me as a First Amendment scholar. I believe—in my heart as well as my mind—that these principles and ideals are not only established but right. I hope that the entire Stanford community will seriously reflect upon the risks to free expression, lest we weaken hard-won liberties at Stanford and, by example, in this nation.

REVIEW AND DISCUSSION QUESTIONS

1. Explain why Lawrence supports the code. What values does he argue are at stake?
2. Why does Gunther oppose the code? How does he address the concerns raised by Lawrence?
3. How might Lawrence respond to Gunther, if he were given the opportunity?
4. Stanford's new policy is directed at either verbal or symbolic harassment, and it must be "intended to stigmatize an individual or small number of individuals." Harassment is defined as behavior "commonly understood to convey direct and visceral hatred or contempt for human beings on the basis of their sex, race, color, handicap, religion, sexual orientation, or national or ethnic origin." Would this definition answer the objections raised by Gunther?
5. How would Lawrence be likely to view a racist attack by a member of a minority against a white male? Against a woman?

Pornography and Respect for Women

Ann Garry

Pornography, along with racist speech, is often thought a good candidate for censorship. Some argue that pornography is harmful because it endangers the welfare of women by encouraging violence and rape. But while studies do tend to show that *violent* pornography does influence people's attitudes by making them less sensitive to violence, there is no evidence that explicit depictions of sex by themselves have that effect. (Furthermore, all violent works seem to have the same result, not just sexually explicit material.) It has not been clearly shown, however, that these measurable changes in people's attitudes resulting from seeing violence carries over to crime. But whatever the truth in this difficult area, pornography is sometimes condemned on different, though no less important grounds that it constitutes objectionable treatment of women by seeing them as mere objects. Ann Garry defends this thesis, arguing that pornography is wrong because it evidences a particular form of disrespect toward women, encouraging discriminatory and other harmful patterns of behavior that disadvantages women generally. Then, in the final section, she asks whether it is possible that some pornography might not treat women in this fashion. Ann Garry is professor of philosophy at California State University, Los Angeles.

Pornography, like rape, is a male invention, designed to dehumanize women, to reduce the female to an object of sexual access, not to free sensuality from moralistic or parental inhibition. . . . Pornography is the undiluted essence of anti-female propaganda.

Susan Brownmiller,
Against Our Will: Men, Women and Rape[1]

It is often asserted that a distinguishing characteristic of sexually explicit material is the degrading and demeaning portrayal of the role and status of the human female. It has been argued that erotic materials describe the female as a mere sexual object to be exploited and manipulated sexually. . . . A recent survey shows that 41 percent of American males and 46 percent of the females believe that "sexual materials lead people to lose respect for women." . . . Recent experiments suggest that such fears are probably unwarranted.

Presidential Commission on Obscenity
and Pornography[2]

The kind of apparent conflict illustrated in these passages is easy to find in one's own thinking as well. For example, I have been inclined to think that pornography is innocuous and to dismiss traditional "moral" arguments for censoring it because many such arguments rest on an assumption I do not share—that sex is an evil to be controlled. At the same time I believe that it is wrong to exploit or degrade human beings, particularly women and others who are especially susceptible. So if pornography degrades human beings, then even if I would oppose its censorship I surely cannot find it morally innocuous.

In an attempt to resolve this apparent conflict I discuss three questions: Does pornography degrade (or exploit or dehumanize) human beings? If so, does it degrade women in ways or to an extent that it does not degrade men? If so, must pornography degrade women, as Brownmiller

This article first appeared in *Social Theory and Practice,* 4 (Summer 1978): 395–442. It is reprinted here by permission of the author, with minor revisions, as it appeared in *Philosophy and Women,* edited by Sharon Bishop and Marjorie Weinzweig (Belmont, CA: Wadsworth, 1979). Some footnotes omitted.

thinks, or could genuinely innocuous, nonsexist pornography exist? Although much current pornography does degrade women, I will argue that it is possible to have nondegrading, nonsexist pornography. However, this possibility rests on our making certain fundamental changes in our conceptions of sex and sex roles.

What interests me is not whether pornography should be censored but whether one can object to it on moral grounds. The only moral ground I consider is whether pornography degrades people; obviously, other possible grounds exist, but I find this one to be the most plausible.[3]

The argument I will consider is that pornography is morally objectionable, whether or not it leads people to show disrespect for women, because pornography itself exemplifies and recommends behavior that violates the moral principle to respect persons. The content of pornography is what one objects to. It treats women as mere sex objects "to be exploited and manipulated" and degrades the role and status of women. In order to evaluate this argument, I will first clarify what it would mean for pornography itself to treat someone as a sex object in a degrading manner. I will then deal with three issues central to the discussion of pornography and respect for women: how "losing respect" for a woman is connected with treating her as a sex object; what is wrong with treating someone as a sex object; and why it is worse to treat women rather than men as sex objects. I will argue that the current content of pornography sometimes violates the moral principle to respect persons. Then . . . I will suggest that pornography need not violate this principle if certain fundamental changes were to occur in attitudes about sex.

To many people, including Brownmiller and some other feminists, it appears to be an obvious truth that pornography treats people, especially women, as sex objects in a degrading manner. And if we omit "in a degrading manner," the statement seems hard to dispute: How could pornography *not* treat people as sex objects?

First, is it permissible to say that either the content of pornography or pornography itself degrades people or treats people as sex objects? It is not difficult to find examples of degrading content in which women are treated as sex objects. Some pornographic films convey the message that all

women really want to be raped, that their resisting struggle is not to be believed. By portraying women in this manner, the content of the movie degrades women. Degrading women is morally objectionable. While seeing the movie need not cause anyone to imitate the behavior shown, we can call the content degrading to women because of the character of the behavior and attitudes it recommends. The same kind of point can be made about films (or books or TV commercials) with other kinds of degrading, thus morally objectionable, content—for example, racist messages.

The next step in the argument is to infer that, because the content or message of pornography is morally objectionable, we can call pornography itself morally objectionable. Support for this step can be found in an analogy. If a person takes every opportunity to recommend that men rape women, we would think not only that his recommendation is immoral but that he is immoral too. In the case of pornography, the objection to making an inference from recommended behavior to the person who recommends is that we ascribe predicates such as "immoral" differently to people than to films or books. A film vehicle for an objectionable message is still an object independent of its message, its director, its producer, those who act in it, and those who respond to it. Hence one cannot make an unsupported inference from "the content of the film is morally objectionable" to "the film is morally objectionable." Because the central points in this paper do not depend on whether pornography itself (in addition to its content) is morally objectionable, I will not try to support this inference. (The question about the relation of content to the work itself is, of course, extremely interesting; but in part because I cannot decide which side of the argument is more persuasive, I will pass.) Certainly one appropriate way to evaluate pornography is in terms of the moral features of its content. If a pornographic film exemplifies and recommends morally objectionable attitudes or behavior, then its content is morally objectionable.

Let us now turn to the first of our three questions about respect and sex objects: What is the connection between losing respect for a woman and treating her as a sex object? Some people who have lived through the era in which women were taught to worry about men "losing respect" for them if they engaged in sex in inappropriate circumstances find it troublesome (or at least amusing) that feminists—supposedly "liberated" women—are outraged at being treated as sex objects, either by pornography or in any other way. The apparent alignment between feminists and traditionally "proper" women need not surprise us when we look at it more closely.

The "respect" that men have traditionally believed they have for women—hence a respect they can lose—is not a general respect for persons as autonomous beings; nor is it respect that is earned because of one's personal merits or achievements. It is respect that is an outgrowth of the "double standard." Women are to be respected because they are more pure, delicate, and fragile than men, have more refined sensibilities, and so on. Because some women clearly do not have these qualities, thus do not deserve respect, women must be divided into two groups—the good ones on the pedestal and the bad ones who have fallen from it. One's mother, grandmother, Sunday School teacher, and usually one's wife are "good" women. The appropriate behavior by which to express respect for good women would be, for example, not swearing or telling dirty jokes in front of them, giving them seats on buses, and other "chivalrous" acts. This kind of "respect" for good women is the same sort that adolescent boys in the back seats of cars used to "promise" not to lose. Note that men define, display, and lose this kind of respect. If women lose respect for women, it is not typically a loss of respect for (other) women as a class but a loss of self-respect.

It has now become commonplace to acknowledge that, although a place on the pedestal might have advantages over a place in the "gutter" beneath it, a place on the pedestal is not at all equal to the place occupied by other people (i.e., men). "Respect" for those on the pedestal was not respect for whole, full-fledged people but for a special class of inferior beings.

If a person makes two traditional assumptions—that (at least some) sex is dirty and that women fall into two classes, good and bad—it is easy to see how that person might think that pornography could lead people to lose respect for women or that pornography is itself disrespectful to women. Pornography describes or shows women engaging in activities inappropriate for good women to engage in—or at least inappropriate for them to be seen by strangers engaging in. If one sees these women as symbolic representatives of all women, then all women fall from grace with these women. This fall is possible, I believe, because the traditional "respect" that men have had for women is not genuine, wholehearted respect for full-fledged human beings but half-hearted respect for lesser beings, some of whom they feel the need to glorify and purify. It is easy to fall from a pedestal. Can we imagine 41 percent of men and 46 percent of women answering "yes" to the question, "Do movies showing men engaging in violent acts lead people to lose respect for men?"

Two interesting asymmetries appear. The first is that losing respect for men as a class (men with power, typically Anglo men) is more difficult than losing respect for women or ethnic minorities as a class. Anglo men whose behavior warrants disrespect are more likely to be seen as exceptional cases than are women or minorities (whose "transgressions" may be far less serious). Think of the following: women are temptresses; Blacks cheat the welfare system; Italians are gangsters; but the men of the Nixon administration are exceptions—Anglo men as a class did not lose respect because of Watergate and related scandals.

The second asymmetry concerns the active and passive roles of the sexes. Men are seen in the active role. If men lose respect for women because of something "evil" done by women (such as appearing in pornography), the fear is that men will then do harm to women—not that women will do harm to men. Whereas if women lose respect for male politicians because of Watergate, the fear is still that male politicians will do harm, not that women will do harm to male politicians. This asymmetry might be a result of one way in which our society thinks of sex as bad—as harm that men do to women (or to the person playing a female role, as in a homosexual rape). Robert Baker calls attention to this point in " 'Pricks' and 'Chicks': A Plea for 'Persons'."[4] Our slang words for sexual intercourse—'fuck,' 'screw,' or older words such as 'take' or 'have'—not only can mean harm but have traditionally taken a male subject and a female object. The active male screws (harms) the passive female. A "bad" woman only tempts men to hurt her further.

It is easy to understand why one's proper grandmother would not want men to see pornography or lose respect for women. But feminists reject these "proper" assumptions: good and bad classes of women do not exist; and sex is not dirty (though many people believe it is). Why then are feminists angry at the treatment of women as sex objects, and why are some feminists opposed to pornography?

The answer is that feminists as well as proper grandparents are concerned with respect. However, there are differences. A feminist's distinction between treating a woman as a full-fledged person and treating her as merely a sex object does not correspond to the good-bad woman distinction. In the latter distinction, "good" and "bad" are properties applicable to groups of women. In the feminist view, all women are full-fledged people—some, however, are treated as sex objects and perhaps think of themselves as sex objects. A further difference is that, although "bad" women correspond to those thought to deserve treatment as sex objects, good women have not corresponded to full-fledged people; only men have been full-fledged people. Given the feminist's distinction, she has no difficulty whatever in saying that pornography treats women as sex objects, not as full-fledged people. She can morally object to pornography or anything else that treats women as sex objects.

One might wonder whether any objection to treatment as a sex object implies that the person objecting still believes, deep down, that sex is dirty. I don't think so. Several other possibilities emerge. First, even if I believe intellectually and emotionally that sex is healthy, I might object to being treated *only* as a sex object. In the same spirit, I would object to being treated *only* as a maker of chocolate chip cookies or *only* as a tennis partner, because only one of my talents is being valued. Second, perhaps I feel that sex is healthy, but it is apparent to me that you think sex is dirty; so I don't want you to treat me as a sex object. Third, being treated as any kind of object, not just as a sex object, is unappealing. I would rather be a partner (sexual or otherwise) than an object. Fourth, and more plausible than the first three possibilities, is Robert Baker's view mentioned

above. Both (i) our traditional double standard of sexual behavior for men and women and (ii) the linguistic evidence that we connect the concept of sex with the concept of harm point to what is wrong with treating women as sex objects. As I said earlier, 'fuck' and 'screw,' in their traditional uses, have taken a male subject, a female object, and have had at least two meanings: harm and have sexual intercourse with. (In addition, a prick is a man who harms people ruthlessly; and a motherfucker is so low that he would do something very harmful to his own dear mother.)[5] Because in our culture we connect sex with harm that men do to women, and because we think of the female role in sex as that of harmed object, we can see that to treat a woman as a sex object is automatically to treat her as less than fully human. To say this does not imply that no healthy sexual relationships exist; nor does it say anything about individual men's conscious intentions to degrade women by desiring them sexually (though no doubt some men have these intentions). It is merely to make a point about the concepts embodied in our language.

Psychoanalytic support for the connection between sex and harm comes from Robert J. Stoller. Stoller thinks that sexual excitement is linked with a wish to harm someone (and with at least a whisper of hostility). The key process of sexual excitement can be seen as dehumanization (fetishization) in fantasy of the desired person. He speculates that this is true in some degree of everyone, both men and women, with "normal" or "perverted" activities and fantasies.[6]

Thinking of sex objects as harmed objects enables us to explain some of the first three reasons why one wouldn't want to be treated as a sex object: (1) I may object to being treated only as a tennis partner, but being a tennis partner is not connected in our culture with being a harmed object; and (2) I may not think that sex is dirty and that I would be a harmed object; I may not know what your view is; but what bothers me is that this is the view embodied in our language and culture.

Awareness of the connection between sex and harm helps explain other interesting points. Women are angry about being treated as sex objects in situations or roles in which they do not intend to be regarded in that manner—for example, while serving on a committee or attending a discussion. It is not merely that a sexual role is inappropriate for the circumstances; it is thought to be a less fully human role than the one in which they intended to function.

Finally, the sex-harm connection makes clear why it is worse to treat women as sex objects than to treat men as sex objects, and why assume the role of "harmed object" in sex; for men have the self-concept of sexual agents, not of passive objects. This is also related to my earlier point concerning the difference in the solidity of respect for men and for women; respect for women is more fragile. Despite exceptions, it is generally harder for people to degrade men, either sexually or nonsexually, than to degrade women. Men and women have grown up with different patterns of self-respect and expectations regarding the extent to which they deserve and will receive respect or degradation. The man who doesn't understand why women do not want to be treated as sex objects (because he'd sure like to be) would not think of himself as being harmed by that treatment; a woman might. Pornography, probably more than any other contemporary institution, succeeds in treating men as sex objects.

Having seen that the connection between sex and harm helps explain both what is wrong with treating someone as a sex object and why it is worse to treat a woman in this way, I want to use the sex-harm connection to try to resolve a dispute about pornography and women. Brownmiller's view, remember, was that pornography is "the undiluted essence of anti-female propaganda" whose purpose is to degrade women. Some people object to Brownmiller's view by saying that, since pornography treats both men and women as sex objects for the purpose of arousing the viewer, it is neither sexist, antifemale, nor designed to degrade women; it just happens that degrading of women arouses some men. How can this dispute be resolved?

Suppose we were to rate the content of all pornography from most morally objectionable to least morally objectionable. Among the most objectionable would be the most degrading—for example, "snuff" films and movies which recommend that men rape women, molest children and puppies, and treat nonmasochists very sadistically.

Next we would find a large amount of material (probably most pornography) not quite so blatantly offensive. With this material it is relevant to use the analysis of sex objects given above. As long as sex is connected with harm done to women, it will be very difficult not to see pornography as degrading to women. We can agree with Brownmiller's opponent that pornography treats men as sex objects, too, but we maintain that this is only pseudoequality: such treatment is still more degrading to women.

In addition, pornography often exemplifies the active/passive, harmer/harmed object roles in a very obvious way. Because pornography today is male-oriented and is supposed to make a profit, the content is designed to appeal to male fantasies. Judging from the content of the most popular legally available pornography, male fantasies still run along the lines of stereotypical sex roles—and, if Stoller is right, include elements of hostility. In much pornography the women's purpose is to cater to male desires, to service the man or men. Her own pleasure is rarely emphasized for its own sake; she is merely allowed a little heavy breathing, perhaps in order to show her dependence on the great male "lover" who produces her pleasure. In addition, women are clearly made into passive objects in still photographs showing only close-ups of their genitals. Even in movies marketed to appeal to heterosexual couples, such as *Behind the Green Door*, the woman is passive and undemanding (and in this case kidnapped and hypnotized as well). Although many kinds of specialty magazines and films are gauged for different sexual tastes, very little contemporary pornography goes against traditional sex roles. There is certainly no significant attempt to replace the harmer/harmed distinction with anything more positive and healthy. In some stag movies, of course, men are treated sadistically by women; but this is an attempt to turn the tables on degradation, not a positive improvement.

What would cases toward the least objectionable end of the spectrum be like? They would be increasingly less degrading and sexist. The genuinely nonobjectionable cases would be nonsexist and nondegrading; but commercial examples do not readily spring to mind.7 The question is: does or could any pornography have nonsexist, nondegrading content?

I want to start with the easier question: Is it possible for pornography to have nonsexist, morally acceptable content? Then I will consider whether any pornography of this sort currently exists.

Imagine the following situation, which exists only rarely today: Two fairly conventional people who love each other enjoy playing tennis and bridge together, cooking good food together, and having sex together. In all these activities they are free from hang-ups, guilt, and tendencies to dominate or objectify each other. These two people like to watch tennis matches and old romantic movies on TV, like to watch Julia Child cook, like to read the bridge column in the newspaper, and like to watch pornographic movies. Imagine further that this couple is not at all uncommon in society and that nonsexist pornography is as common as this kind of nonsexist sexual relationship. This situation sounds fine and healthy to me. I see no reason to think that an interest in pornography would disappear in these circumstances. People seem to enjoy watching others experience or do (especially do well) what they enjoy experiencing, doing or wish they could do themselves. We do not morally object to people watching tennis on TV; why would we object to these hypothetical people watching pornography?

Can we go from the situation today to the situation just imagined? In much current pornography, people are treated in morally objectionable ways. In the scene just imagined, however, pornography would be nonsexist, nondegrading, morally acceptable. The key to making the change is to break the connection between sex and harm. If Stoller is right, this task may be impossible without changing the scenarios of our sexual lives—scenarios that we have been writing since early childhood. (Stoller does not indicate whether he thinks it possible for adults to rewrite their scenarios or for social change to bring about the possibility of new scenarios in future generations.) But even if we believe that people can change their sexual scenarios, the sex-harm connection is deeply entrenched and has widespread implications. What

is needed is a thorough change in people's deep-seated attitudes and feelings about sex roles in general, as well as about sex and roles in sex (sexual roles). Although I cannot even sketch a general outline of such changes here, changes in pornography should be part of a comprehensive program. Television, children's educational material, and nonpornographic movies and novels may be far better avenues for attempting to change attitudes; but one does not want to take the chance that pornography is working against one.

What can be done about pornography in particular? If one wanted to work within the current institutions, one's attempt to use pornography as a tool for the education of male pornography audiences would have to be fairly subtle at first; nonsexist pornography must become familiar enough to sell and be watched. One should realize too that any positive educational value that nonsexist pornography might have may well be as short-lived as most of the effects of pornography. But given these limitations, what could one do?

Two kinds of films must be considered. First is the short film with no plot or character development, just depicting sexual activity in which nonsexist pornography would treat men and women as equal sex partners. The man would not control the circumstances in which the partners had sex or the choice of positions or acts; the woman's preference would be counted equally. There would be no suggestion of a power play or conquest on the man's part, no suggestion that "she likes it when I hurt her." Sexual intercourse would not be portrayed as primarily for the purpose of male ejaculation—his orgasm is not "the best part" of the movie. In addition, both the man and woman would express their enjoyment; the man need not be cool and detached.

The film with a plot provides even more opportunity for nonsexist education. Today's pornography often portrays the female characters as playthings even when not engaging in sexual activity. Nonsexist pornography could show women and men in roles equally valued by society, and sex equality would amount to more than possession of equally functional genitalia. Characters would customarily treat each other with respect and consideration, with no attempt to treat men or women brutally or thoughtlessly. The local Pussycat Theater showed a film written and directed by a woman (*The Passions of Carol*), which exhibited a few of the features just mentioned. The main female character in it was the editor of a magazine parody of *Viva*. The fact that some of the characters treated each other very nicely, warmly, and tenderly did not detract from the pornographic features of the movie. This should not surprise us, for even in traditional male-oriented films, lesbian scenes usually exhibit tenderness and kindness.

Plots for nonsexist films could include women in traditionally male jobs (e.g., long-distance truckdriver) or in positions usually held in respect by pornography audiences. For example, a high-ranking female Army officer, treated with respect by men and women alike, could be shown not only in various sexual encounters with other people but also carrying out her job in a humane manner. Or perhaps the main character could be a female urologist. She could interact with nurses and other medical personnel, diagnose illnesses brilliantly, and treat patients with great sympathy as well as have sex with them. When the Army officer or the urologist engage in sexual activities, they will treat their partners and be treated by them in some of the considerate ways described above.

In the circumstances we imagined, our nonsexist films could be appreciated in the proper spirit. Under these conditions the content of our new pornography would clearly be nonsexist and morally acceptable. But would the content of such a film be morally acceptable if shown to a typical pornography audience today? It might seem strange for us to change our moral evaluation of the content on the basis of a different audience, but an audience today is likely to see the "respected" urologist and Army officer as playthings or unusual prostitutes—even if our intention in showing the film is to counteract this view. The effect is that, although the content of the film seems morally acceptable and our intention in showing it is morally flawless, women are still degraded. The fact that audience attitude is so important makes one wary of giving whole-hearted approval to any pornography seen today.

The fact that good intentions and content are insufficient does not imply that one's effort toward change would be entirely in vain. Of course, I could not deny that anyone who tries to change an institution from within faces serious difficulties. This is particularly evident when one is trying to change both pornography and a whole set of related attitudes, feelings, and institutions concerning sex and sex roles. But in conjunction with other attempts to change this set of attitudes, it seems preferable to try to change pornography instead of closing one's eyes in the hope that it will go away. For I suspect that pornography is here to stay.

NOTES

1. (New York: Simon and Schuster, 1975), p. 394.

2. *The Report of the Commission on Obscenity and Pornography* (Washington, DC, 1970), p. 201. Hereinafter, *Report*.

3. To degrade someone in this situation is to lower her/his rank or status in humanity. This is morally objectionable because it is incompatible with showing respect for a person. Some of the other moral grounds for objecting to pornography have been considered by the Supreme Court: Pornography invades our privacy and hurts the moral tone of the community. See *Paris Adult Theatre* v. *Slaton*, 413 U.S. 49 (1973). Even less plausible than the Court's position is to say that pornography is immoral because it depicts sex, depicts an immoral kind of sex, or caters to voyeuristic tendencies. I believe that even if moral objections to pornography exist, one must preclude any simple inference from "pornography is immoral" to "pornography should be censored" because of other important values and principles such as freedom of expression and self-determination.

4. Richard Wasserstrom, ed., *Today's Moral Problems* (New York: Macmillan, 1975), pp. 152–71; see pp. 167–71.

5. Baker, in Wasserstrom, *Today's Moral Problems*, pp. 168–69.

6. "Sexual Excitement," *Archives of General Psychiatry* 33 (1976):899–909, especially 903.

7. Virginia Wright Wexman uses the film *Group Marriage* (Stephanie Rothman, 1973) as an example of "more enlightened erotica." Wexman also asks the following questions in an attempt to point out sexism in pornographic films: *Does it [the film] portray rape as pleasurable to women? Does it consistently show females nude but present men fully clothed? Does it present women as childlike creatures whose sexual in-*

terests must be guided by knowing experienced men? Does it show sexually aggressive women as castrating viragos? Does it pretend that sex is exclusively the prerogative of women under twenty-five? Does it focus on the physical aspects of love-making rather than the emotional ones? Does it portray women as purely sexual beings? ("Sexism of X-rated Films," *Chicago Sun-Times*, 28 March 1976.)

REVIEW AND DISCUSSION QUESTIONS

1. How does Garry define "pornography"?
2. In what way does Garry think pornography degrades people?
3. What two "asymmetries" between men and women does Garry point to? How are they relevant to the question of whether pornography degrades women, but not men?
4. How does Garry distinguish her position from that of a censor who opposes pornography because sex is "dirty"? Do you agree that her view is distinct?
5. Is it possible to have nonsexist, nondegrading pornography? Explain your view, comparing it with Garry's.
6. Does it follow from Garry's argument that pornography should be censored? Explain why or why not.
7. Given her position on pornography and how it degrades women, do you think Garry would support the *Skokie* decision or not? Explain.
8. Compare Garry's view of sex with that of Pineau and Paglia in their discussions of date rape, reprinted in Section 13. Which view seems most reasonable?

Pornography:

American Booksellers v. *Hudnut*

This case arose when the Indianapolis City Council passed an ordinance outlawing the production, sale, exhibition, and distribution of pornography. The ordinance defined pornography as any "graphic sexually explicit subordination of women" that also presented women as sexual objects

> who enjoy rape, pain, or humiliation; enjoy being penetrated by objects or animals; in scenarios of degradation, injury, debasement, torture, shown as filthy or inferior; or presented as sexual objects for domination, conquest, violation, exploitation, possession, or use.

The ordinance allowed women who can show they have been injured as a direct result of pornography to win private damages from the person who produced, sold, exhibited, or distributed it. Earlier Supreme Court decisions had held that "obscenity" is not protected by the First Amendment's guarantee of freedom of speech. In those cases the Court defined obscenity as work that (1) appeals to the "prurient" interest, (2) depicts sex in a "patently offensive way," and (3) lacks "serious literary, artis-

771 F.2d 323 (1985).

tic, political, or scientific value" (*Miller* v. *California*). Here, however, the issue is pornography, not obscenity, and Judge Easterbrook, of the court of appeals, affirms a lower court's decision that, unlike obscenity, pornography is constitutionally protected speech.

Judge Easterbrook: We do not try to balance the arguments for and against an ordinance such as this. The ordinance discriminates on the ground of the content of the speech. Speech treating women in the approved way—in sexual encounters "premised on equality" is lawful no matter how sexually explicit. Speech treating women in the disapproved way—as submissive in matters sexual or as enjoying humiliation—is unlawful no matter how significant the literary, artistic, or political qualities of the work taken as a whole. The state may not ordain preferred viewpoints in this way. The Constitution forbids the state to declare one perspective right and silence opponents. . . .

"If there is any fixed star in our constitutional constellation, it is that no official, high or petty, can prescribe what shall be orthodox in politics, nationalism, religion, or other matters of opinion or force citizens to confess by word or act their faith therein." *West Virginia State Board of Education* v. *Barnette,* 319 U.S. 624, 642 (1943). Under the First Amendment the government must leave to the people the evaluation of ideas. Bald or subtle, an idea is as powerful as the audience allows it to be. . . . A belief may be pernicious—the beliefs of Nazis led to the death of millions, those of the Klan to the repression of millions. A pernicious belief may prevail. Totalitarian governments today rule much of the planet, practicing suppression of billions and spreading dogma that may enslave others. One of the things that separates our society from theirs is our absolute right to propagate opinions that the government finds wrong or even hateful. . . .

Under the ordinance graphic sexually explicit speech is "pornography" or not depending on the perspective the author adopts. Speech that "subordinates" women and also, for example, presents women as enjoying pain, humiliation, or rape, or even simply presents women in "positions of servility or submission or display" is forbidden, no matter how great the literary or political value of the work taken as a whole. Speech that portrays women in positions of equality is lawful, no mat-

ter how graphic the sexual content. This is thought control. It establishes an "approved" view of women, of how they may react to sexual encounters, of how the sexes may relate to each other. Those who espouse the approved view may use sexual images; those who do not, may not.

Indianapolis justifies the ordinance on the ground that pornography affects thoughts. Men who see women depicted as subordinate are more likely to treat them so. Pornography is an aspect of dominance. It does not persuade people so much as change them. It works by socializing, by establishing the expected and the permissible. In this view pornography is not an idea; pornography is the injury.

There is much to this perspective. Beliefs are also facts. People often act in accordance with the images and patterns they find around them. People raised in a religion tend to accept the tenets of that religion, often without independent examination. People taught from birth that black people are fit only for slavery rarely rebelled against that creed; beliefs coupled with the self-interest of the masters established a social structure that inflicted great harm while enduring for centuries. Words and images act at the level of the subconscious before they persuade at the level of the conscious. Even the truth has little chance unless a statement fits within the framework of beliefs that may never have been subjected to rational study.

Therefore we accept the premises or this legislation. Depictions of subordination tend to perpetuate subordination. The subordinate status of women in turn leads to affront and lower pay at work, insult and injury at home, battery and rape on the streets. . . .

Yet this simply demonstrates the power of pornography as speech. All of these unhappy effects depend on mental intermediation. Pornography affects how people see the world, their fellows, and social relations. If pornography is what pornography does, so is other speech. Hitler's orations affected how some Germans saw Jews. Communism is a world view, not simply a Manifesto by

Marx and Engels or a set of speeches. Efforts to suppress communist speech in the United States were based on the belief that the public acceptability of such ideas wound increase the likelihood of totalitarian government. Religions affect socialization in the most pervasive way. The opinion in *Wisconsin* v. *Yoder* shows how a religion can dominate an entire approach to life, governing much more than the relation between the sexes. . . .

Racial bigotry, anti-semitism, violence on television, reporters' biases—these and many more influence the culture and shape our socialization. None is directly answerable by more speech, unless that speech too finds its place in the popular culture. Yet all is protected as speech, however insidious. Any other answer leaves the government in control of all of the institutions of culture, the great censor and director of which thoughts are good for us.

Sexual responses often are unthinking responses, and the association of sexual arousal with the subordination of women therefore may have a substantial effect. But almost all cultural stimuli provoke unconscious responses. Religious ceremonies condition their participants. Teachers convey messages by selecting what not to cover; the implicit message about what is off limits or unthinkable may be more powerful than the messages for which they present rational argument. Television scripts contain unarticulated assumptions. People may be conditioned in subtle ways. If the fact that speech plays a role in a process of conditioning were enough to permit governmental regulation, that would be the end of freedom of speech. . . .

Much of Indianapolis's argument rests on the belief that when speech is "unanswerable," and the metaphor that there is a "marketplace of ideas" does not apply, the First Amendment does not apply either. The metaphor is honored; Milton's *Areopagitica* and John Stewart Mill's *On Liberty*

defend freedom of speech on the ground that the truth will prevail, and many of the most important cases under the First Amendment recite this position. The Framers undoubtedly believed it. As a general matter it is true. But the Constitution does not make the dominance of truth a necessary condition of freedom of speech. To say that it does would be to confuse an outcome of free speech with a necessary condition for the application of the amendment.

A power to limit speech on the ground that truth has not yet prevailed and is not likely to prevail implies the power to declare truth. At some point the government must be able to say (as Indianapolis has said): "We know what the truth is, yet a free exchange of speech has not driven out falsity, so that we must now prohibit falsity." If the government may declare the truth, why wait for the failure of speech? Under the First Amendment, however, there is no such thing as a false idea. . . . The government may not restrict speech on the ground that in a free exchange truth is not yet dominant. . . .

We come, finally, to the argument that pornography is "low value" speech, that it is enough like obscenity that Indianapolis may prohibit it. Some cases hold that speech far removed from politics and other subjects at the core of the Framers' concerns may be subjected to special regulation. . . .

In *Pacifica* the FCC sought to keep vile language off the air during certain times. The Court held that it may; but the Court would not have sustained a regulation prohibiting scatological descriptions of Republicans but not scatological descriptions of Democrats, or any other form of selection among viewpoints. . . .

At all events, "pornography" is not low value speech within the meaning of these cases. . . . True, pornography and obscenity have sex in common. But Indianapolis left out of its definition any reference to literary, artistic, political, or scientific value. . . .

REVIEW AND DISCUSSION QUESTIONS

1. What did the law that is being challenged in this case do, exactly?
2. What is the difference between obscenity and pornography?
3. Describe the justification that judge Easterbrook gives for overturning the statute. What precedents and principles does he rely on?

4. Explain why the Court might have thought obscenity is not protected speech, while pornography is protected. Do you think this position is reasonable? Explain.

5. How do you think Mill would have reacted to this opinion, given his position on free speech?

6. Would Mill's view of individual liberty, especially the "harm principle," lead him to agree or disagree with this opinion? Explain.

7. Would Garry approve of this decision? Explain.

Multiculturalism

Amy Gutmann

In this essay, Amy Gutmann directs the discussion toward recent controversies over multiculturalism and the university curriculum. Many groups are now arguing that the core curriculum should be broadened, or even replaced, with works written by non-Western and third-world authors. She begins by comparing the positions of "essentialists" who oppose any dilution in the traditional "canon" with "deconstructionists" who claim that the canon perpetuates sexism, racism, Eurocentrism, and the tyranny of the Truth. While essentialists misunderstand the importance of adding new perspectives to those seeking a liberal education, she argues, deconstructionists undermine education by rejecting the possibility or desirability of intellectual standards in favor of relativism. Rejecting both positions, Gutmann defends a "moderate" position that, she contends, is compatible with the purposes of liberal education. She concludes by considering the implications of her essay for efforts to ban racist, sexist, and homophobic speech at some campuses. Amy Gutmann is professor of politics at Princeton University and director of the University Center for Human Values.

... Public controversy over multiculturalism has hit the campuses of American colleges and universities, where we have witnessed some of the most acrimonious arguments. Even though life and death do not hang on the outcome, the political identity of Americans, the quality of our collective intellectual life, and the nature and value of higher education are all at issue. So the stakes are rightly perceived as high. Consider the opening lines of an op-ed piece that ran in the *Wall Street Journal* in the midst of the controversy that raged over Stanford University's core curriculum: "The intellectual heritage of the West goes on trial at Stanford University today. Most predict it will lose." The controversy referred to by the author of the piece, Isaac Barchas, a Stanford classics major, revolved around the content of Stanford's only year-long requirement in "Western Culture." Students were required to choose one of eight courses, all of which shared a core reading list of fifteen works by classical thinkers such as Plato, Homer, Dante, and Darwin.

If Barchas's characterization is correct, the intellectual heritage of the West lost at Stanford three years ago, with remarkably little opposition from the faculty. The faculty voted, 39 to 4, to replace the requirement in Western Culture with one called "Culture, Ideas, and Values" that adds works of some non-European cultures and works by women, African-Americans, Hispanics, Asians, and Native Americans to a contracted core of the classics. The Old and New Testament, Plato, Saint Augustine, Machiavelli, Rousseau, and Marx remain in the new core.

In the ensuing public debate over whether to change the content of such core courses, one side—call them "essentialists"—argued that to dilute the core with new works for the sake of including previously unheard voices would be to forsake the values of Western civilization for the standardlessness of relativism, the tyranny of the social sciences, lightweight trendiness, and a host of related intellectual and political evils. Another, diametrically opposed side—call them "deconstructionists"—argued that to preserve the core by excluding contributions to civilization by women, African-Americans, Hispanics, Asians, and Native Americans as if the classical canon were sacred, unchanging, and unchangeable would be to denigrate the identities of members of these previously excluded groups and to close off Western civilization from the influences of unorthodox and challenging ideas for the sake of perpetuating sexism, racism, Eurocentrism, closed-mindedness, the tyranny of Truth (with a capital "T"), and a host of related intellectual and political evils.

Much more is at issue, and of value, here than meets the ear in the public debate between essentialists and deconstructionists. If the intellectual heritage of the West went on trial at Stanford and other campuses that have considered changing their core curricula, then the intellectual heritage of the West lost before the trials began. Neither the intellectual heritage of the West nor the liberal democratic ideal of higher education can be preserved by a decision to require or not to require of every university student several courses in fifteen, thirty, or even a hundred great books. Nor can our heritage be eradicated by a decision to decrease the number of canonical books to make room for newer, less established, less widely esteemed or even less lasting works that speak more explicitly to the experiences or better express the sense of social alienation of women and minorities. The reason is not that Western civilization will not stand or fall on such small decisions. A long train of seemingly small abuses can create a large revolution, as we Americans, of all people, should know.

There is another reason, which has been lost in the public debate. Liberal education, an education adequate to serve the life of a free and equal citizen in any modern democracy, requires far more than the reading of great books, although great books are an indispensable aid. We also need to read and think about books, and therefore to teach them, in a spirit of free and open inquiry, the spirit of both democratic citizenship and individual freedom. The cultivation of that spirit is aided by immersion in profound and influential books, like Plato's *Republic*, which expose us to eloquently original, systematically well-reasoned, intimidating, and unfamiliar visions of the good life and good society. But liberal education fails if intimidation leads to blind acceptance of those visions or if unfamiliarity leads us to blind rejection.

These two signs of failure are too often reflected in the public debate over multiculturalism on college and university campuses. In resisting the substitution of new works for old ones, essentialists suggest that the insights and truths of the old will be lost by even partial substitution, which is typically is at stake in controversies like the one at Stanford. But preservation of tried-and-true verities is not among the best reasons for including the classics in any list of required reading at the university level. Why not say that great books like Plato's *Republic* or Aristotle's *Politics* are among the most challenging to anyone who wants to think carefully, systematically, and critically about politics? It is intellectual idolatry, and not philosophical openness and acuity, that supports the claim, frequently articulated but rarely defended, that the greatest philosophical works—judged by such standards as originality and eloquence, systematic reasoning, depth of moral, psychological, or political understanding, and influence on our inherited social understandings—contain the greatest wisdom now available to us on all significant subjects.

Is Aristotle's understanding of slavery more enlightening than Frederick Douglass's? Is Aquinas's argument about civil disobedience more defensible than Martin Luther King's or John Rawls's? If not, then why not assign students *The Autobiography of Frederick Douglass*, "Letter from

Birmingham City Jail," and *A Theory of Justice* alongside the *Politics* and *Summa Theologica*? Although Rousseau's understanding of women challenges contemporary feminism, it is far less credible or compelling on intellectual grounds than Virginia Woolf's, Simone de Beauvoir's, or Toni Morrison's insights on women. Similarly, Hannah Arendt offers a perspective on political evil that goes beyond that of any canonical political philosopher. Were essentialists explicitly to open their public argument to the possibility that the classics do not contain comprehensive or timeless truths on all significant subjects, they could moderate their critique and recognize the reasonableness of some proposed reforms that create more multicultural curricula.

A significant internal obstacle that stands in the way of moderation is the belief held in reserve by some essentialists that the classics, especially the works of Plato and Aristotle, are the key to timeless moral and political truths, the truths of human nature. In the spirit of Robert Maynard Hutchins, essentialists often invoke Plato, Aristotle, and "nature" as critical standards. The argument, explicitly made by Hutchins but only intimated by Allan Bloom and other contemporary critics, goes roughly as follows: The highest form of human nature is the same in America as in Athens, as should be the content of higher education, if it is to be true to the highest in human nature, the intellectual virtues cultivated to their greatest perfection. Here is Hutchins' succinct formulation: "Education implies teaching. Teaching implies knowledge. Knowledge is truth. The truth is everywhere the same. Hence education should be everywhere the same. I do not overlook the possibilities of differences in organization, in administration, in local habits and customs. These are details."[1] Essentialists honor and invoke the great books as the critical standard for judging both "lesser" works and societies that inevitably fail to live up to Platonic or Aristotelian standards.

One need not in any way denigrate the great books or defend a standardless relativism to worry about the way in which the essentialist critique of multiculturalism partakes of intellectual idol worship. Compare the essentialist defense of the canon to Ralph Waldo Emerson's approach to books, as argued in "The American Scholar."

Emerson's perspective serves as an important challenge to essentialism, and yet no contemporary critic takes up this challenge: "The theory of books is noble. . . . But none is quite perfect. As no airpump can by any means make a perfect vacuum, so neither can any artist entirely exclude the conventional, the local, the perishable from his book, or write a book of pure thought, that shall be as efficient, in all respects, to a remote posterity, as to contemporaries, or rather to the second age."[2] Emerson is not saying that because even the best books are to some significant extent conventional and rooted in a particular social context, we should read them primarily for what they reflect about their own times rather than what they can say to us and our times. We can still learn a lot about the human condition from Plato's *Republic*, or about our obligation to the state from the *Crito*. But we cannot learn everything profound about obligation, let alone everything worth knowing about the human condition, from reading Plato, Aristotle, or the entire corpus of canonical works.

"Each age," Emerson concludes, "must write its own books."[3] Why? Because well-educated, open-minded people and liberal democratic citizens must think for themselves. In liberal democracies, a primary aim of liberal arts universities is not to create bookworms, but to cultivate people who are willing and able to be self-governing in both their political and personal lives. "Books are the best of things, well used," Emerson argues, "abused, among the worst. What is the right use?. . . They are for nothing but to inspire."[4]

It would also be a form of intellectual idolatry to take Emerson's words as gospel. Books do more than inspire. They also unite us in a community, or communities, of learning. They teach us about our intellectual heritage, our culture, as well as about foreign cultures. American universities may aspire to be more international, but to the extent that our liberal arts curriculum along with our student body is still primarily American, it is crucial, as Wolf suggests in her comments, that universities recognize who "we" are when they defend a core curriculum that speaks to "our" circumstances, culture, and intellectual heritage. Not because students can identify only with works written by authors of the same race, ethnicity, or gender, but because there are books by and about women, African-Americans, Asian-Americans, and Native Americans that speak to neglected parts of our heritage and human condition, and speak more wisely than do some of the canonical works. Although social injustices concern us all, neglect of noncanonical literature is more acutely perceived by people who identify themselves with the neglected, and the exclusion of such works is not unreasonably thought to reflect lack of respect for members of these groups, or disregard for part of their cultural identities. Criticism of the canon per se should not therefore be equated with tribalism or particularism. Emerson was guilty of neither when he argued that each age must write, and presumably also read, its own books.

Radically opposed to essentialism, deconstructionists erect a different obstacle to liberal democratic education when they deny the desirability of shared intellectual standards, which scholars and students of diverse cultural backgrounds might use to evaluate our common education. Although deconstructionists do not deny the possibility of shared standards, they view common standards as masks for the will to political power of dominant, hegemonic groups. This reductionist argument about intellectual standards is often made on behalf of groups that are underrepresented in the university and disadvantaged in society, but it is hard to see how it can come to the aid of anyone. The argument is self-undermining, both logically and practically. By its internal logic, deconstructionism has nothing more to say for the view that intellectual standards are masks for the will to political power than that it too reflects the will to power of deconstructionists. But why then bother with intellectual life at all, which is not the fastest, surest, or even most satisfying path to political power, if it is political power that one is really after?

Deconstructionism is also impractical. If intellectual standards are political in the sense of reflecting the antagonistic interests and will to power of particular groups, then disadvantaged groups have no choice but to accept the hegemonic standards that society imposes on the academy and the academy in turn imposes on them. The less powerful cannot possibly hope to have their standards win out, especially if their academic spokespersons publicize the view that intellectual standards

are nothing more than assertions or reflections of the will to power.

The deconstructionist outlook on the academy not only deconstructs itself, it does so in a dangerous way. Deconstructionists do not *act* as if they believed that common standards are impossible. They act, and often speak, as if they believed that the university curriculum *should* include works by and about disadvantaged groups. And some version of this position, as we have seen, is defensible on universalistic grounds. But the reduction of all intellectual disagreements to conflicts of group interests is not. It does not stand up to evidence or reasoned argument. Anyone who doubts this conclusion might try to demonstrate in a nontautological way that the *strongest* arguments for and against legalizing abortion, not the arguments offered by politicians but the most careful and compelling philosophical arguments, simply reflect the will to power, class and gender interests of their proponents.

Reductionism of intellect and argument to political interest threatens to politicize the university more profoundly and destructively than ever before. I say "threatens" because deconstructionism has not actually "taken over" the academy, as some critics claim. But the anti-intellectual, politicizing threat it poses is nonetheless real. A great deal of intellectual life, especially in the humanities and the "soft" social sciences, depends upon dialogue among reasonable people who disagree on the answers to some fundamental questions about the value of various literary, political, economic, religious, educational, scientific, and aesthetic understandings and achievements. Colleges and universities are the only major social institutions dedicated to fostering knowledge, understanding, intellectual dialogue, and the pursuit of reasoned argument in the many directions that it may lead. The threat of deconstructionism to intellectual life in the academy is twofold: (1) it denies *a priori* that there are any reasonable answers to fundamental questions, and (2) it reduces every answer to an exercise of political power.

Taken seriously, on its own terms, the deconstructionist defense of a more multicultural curriculum itself appears as an assertion of political power in the name of the exploited and oppressed, rather than as an intellectually defensible reform. And deconstructionism represents critics and criticisms of multiculturalism, however reasonable, as politically retrograde and unworthy of intellectual respect. Whereas essentialists react to reasonable uncertainty and disagreement by invoking rather than defending timeless truths, deconstructionists react by explaining away our different viewpoints, presuming they are equally indefensible on intellectual grounds. Intellectual life is deconstructed into a political battlefield of class, gender, and racial interests, an analogy that does not do justice to democratic politics at its best, which is not merely a contest of competing interest groups. But the image conveyed of academic life, the real arena of deconstructionist activity, is more dangerous still because it can create its own reality, converting universities into political battlefields rather than mutually respectful communities of substantial, sometimes even fundamental, intellectual disagreement.

Deconstructionists and essentialists disagree about the value and content of a multicultural curriculum. The disagreement is exacerbated by the zero-sum nature of the choice between canonical and newer works, when a few required core courses become the focus in academic and public discussions of what constitutes a good education. But disagreement about what books should be required and how they should be read is not in itself terribly troubling. No university curriculum can possibly include all the books or represent all the cultures worthy of recognition in a liberal democratic education. Nor can any free society, let alone any university of independent scholars and teachers, expect to agree on hard choices between competing goods. The cause for concern about the ongoing controversies over multiculturalism and the curriculum is rather that the most vocal parties to these disputes appear unwilling to defend their views before people with whom they disagree, and to entertain seriously the possibility of change in the face of well-reasoned criticism. Instead, in an equal and opposite reaction, essentialists and deconstructionists express mutual disdain rather than respect for their differences. And so they create two mutually exclusive and disrespecting intellectual cultures in academic life, evincing an attitude of unwillingness to learn anything from

the other or recognize any value in the other. In political life writ large, there is a parallel problem of disrespect and lack of constructive communication among the spokespersons for ethnic, religious, and racial groups, a problem that all too often leads to violence.

The survival of many mutually exclusive and disrespecting cultures is not the moral promise of multiculturalism, in politics or in education. Nor is it a realistic vision: neither universities nor polities can effectively pursue their valued ends without mutual respect among the various cultures they contain. But not every aspect of cultural diversity is worthy of respect. Some differences—racism and anti-Semitism are obvious examples ought not to be *respected*, even if expressions of racist and anti-Semitic views must be *tolerated*.

The controversy on college campuses over racist, ethnic, sexist, homophobic, and other forms of offensive speech directed against members of disadvantaged groups exemplifies the need for a shared moral vocabulary that is richer than our rights to free speech. Suppose one grants that members of a university community should have the right to express racist, anti-Semitic, sexist, and homophobic views provided they do not threaten anyone. What is left to say about the racist, anti-Semitic, sexist, and homophobic remarks that have become increasingly common on college campuses? Nothing, if our shared moral vocabulary is limited to the right of free speech, unless one challenges racist and anti-Semitic statements on free speech grounds. But then the public issue will quickly shift from the pernicious content of the speech to the speaker's right of free speech.

Everything is left to say, however, if we can distinguish between tolerating and respecting differences. Toleration extends to the widest range of views, so long as they stop short of threats and other direct and discernible harms to individuals. Respect is far more discriminating. Although we need not agree with a position to respect it, we must understand it as reflecting a moral point of view. Someone with a pro-choice position on abortion, for example, should be able to understand how a morally serious person without ulterior motives might be opposed to legalizing abortion. There are serious moral arguments to be made against legalization. And vice versa. A multicultural society is bound to include a wide range of such respectable moral disagreements, which offers us the opportunity to defend our views before morally serious people with whom we disagree and thereby learn from our differences. In this way, we can make a virtue out of the necessity of our moral disagreements.

There is no virtue in misogyny, racial and ethnic hatred, or rationalizations of self-interest and group interest parading as historical or scientific knowledge. Undeserving of respect are views that flagrantly disregard the interests of others and therefore do not take a genuine moral position at all, or that make radically implausible empirical claims (of racial inferiority, for example) that are not grounded upon publicly shared or accessible standards of evidence. Incidents of hate speech on college campuses fall into this category of disrespectable speech. Racist and anti-Semitic slogans are indefensible on moral and empirical grounds, and add nothing valuable to democratic deliberation or intellectual life. They reflect a refusal to treat people as equals, along with an unwillingness or inability to provide publicly accessible evidence for presuming other groups of people fundamentally inferior to oneself and one's group. Hate speech violates the most elementary moral injunction to respect the dignity of all human beings, and simply *presumes* the fundamental inferiority of others.

As communities dedicated to intellectual inquiry, universities should give the broadest protection to free speech. But, having protected everyone's right to speak, university communities need not and should not be silent when faced with racist, anti-Semitic, or other disrespectable speech. Members of academic communities—faculty, students, and administrators—can use our right to free speech to denounce disrespectable speech by exposing it for what it is, flagrant disregard for the interests of other people, rationalization of self-interest or group interest, prejudice, or sheer hatred of humanity. There is no valuable understanding to be gained directly from the content of disrespectable speech. Even so, incidents of hate speech challenge members of liberal democratic communities to articulate the most fundamental moral presuppositions that unite us. We fail ourselves and, more importantly, the targets of hate speech if we do not respond to the often unthinking, sometimes drunken disregard for the most elementary standards of human decency.

Respectable moral disagreements, on the other hand, call for deliberation, not denunciation. Colleges and universities can serve as models for deliberation, by encouraging rigorous, honest, open, and intense intellectual discussions, both inside and outside the classroom. The willingness and ability to deliberate about our respectable differences is also part of the democratic political ideal. Multicultural societies and communities that stand for the freedom and equality of all people rest upon mutual respect for reasonable intellectual, political, and cultural differences. Mutual respect requires a widespread willingness and ability to articulate our disagreements, to defend them before people with whom we disagree, to discern the difference between respectable and disrespectable disagreement, and to be open to changing our own minds when faced with well-reasoned criticism. The moral promise of multiculturalism depends on the exercise of these deliberative virtues.

NOTES

1. Robert Maynard Hutchins, *The Higher Learning in America* (New Haven: Yale University Press, 1936), p. 66.
2. Ralph Waldo Emerson, "The American Scholar," in *Selected Essays,* ed. Larzer Ziff (New York: Viking Penguin, 1982), p. 87.
3. Ibid.
4. Ibid., p. 88.

REVIEW AND DISCUSSION QUESTIONS

1. Describe the view of *essentialists* and why Gutmann thinks they are mistaken.
2. What is *deconstructionism* and why does Gutmann think it "deconstructs itself"?
3. In what sense does Gutmann argue deconstructionists are inconsistent in their beliefs and actions?
4. What does Gutmann mean by a "shared moral vocabulary" and why does she think it is important?
5. What is the difference between tolerating and respecting differences? Which does Gutmann think is owed to all views?
6. Why does Gutmann say that the "moral promise of multiculturalism" depends on rejecting deconstructionism?
7. Compare Gutmann's position on free speech and the campus with those of Mill and Garry. Does speech serve the same ends on campus and off? Are its limits similar? Explain.
8. How would Gutmann react to the debate about speech codes on campus, do you think? On what basis does she criticize racist and sexist speech? Does she seem to think it should be banned? Explain.

Public Education and Religious Fundamentalism:

Smith v. Board of Education of Mobile

The First Amendment guarantees citizens the right to exercise their religion and prevents government from "establishing" an official religion. But if religion is broadly enough defined, then it is possible to argue that by teaching "secular humanism" schools establish secular humanism as a religion. U.S. District Court Judge Brevard Hand makes that argument in the case below, *Smith* v. *Board of Education of Mobile*. The impetus for the case came in 1982 when the Supreme Court overruled an earlier decision by Judge Hand in which he had argued that a one-minute period of silent prayer in schools was not a violation of the establishment clause. Having lost that argument, Judge Hand did not let the issue die, suggesting in his opinion that should he be overruled (as he later was), he would then be willing to consider arguments that the school board had established another religion—secular humanism—in violation of the establishment clause. A group of religious conservatives took up the judge's offer and filed this case, *Smith* v. *Board of Education of Mobile*. After the trial, which included many expert witnesses on both sides, Judge Hand wrote a lengthy opinion contending that secular humanism is a religion and that the Mobile school board "established" it by requiring students to read certain textbooks. Although this decision was later overturned as well, Judge Hand's opinion in *Smith* raises important and difficult issues concerning the extent to which school texts that have the effect of undermining the values and religious beliefs of a community can be required.

655 F. Supp. 939 (S.D. Ala. 1987).

I. A FIRST AMENDMENT DEFINITION OF RELIGION

The Supreme Court has never stated an absolute definition of religion under the first amendment. . . .

The application of these principles to the question of what constitutes a religion under the first amendment indicates that the state may not decide the question by reference to the validity of the beliefs or practices involved. . . . The state must instead look to factors common to all religious movements to decide how to distinguish those ideologies worthy of the protection of the religious clauses from those which must seek refuge under other constitutional provisions.

Any definition of religion must not be limited, therefore, to traditional religions, but must encompass systems of belief that are equivalent to them for the believer. . . . The Supreme Court has focused on such factors as a person's "ultimate concern," organization and social structure, and on equivalency to belief in a Supreme Deity. All of these are evidence of the type of belief a person holds. But all religious beliefs may be classified by the questions they raise and issues they address. Some of these matters overlap with non-religious governmental concerns. A religion, however, approaches them on the basis of certain fundamental assumptions with which governments are unconcerned. These assumptions may be grouped as about: (1) the existence of supernatural and/or transcendent reality; (2) the nature of man; (3) the ultimate end, or goal or purpose of man's existence, both individually and collectively; (4) the purpose and nature of the universe. . . .

Whenever a belief system deals with fundamental questions of the nature of reality and man's relationship to reality, it deals with essentially religious questions. A religion need not posit a belief *in* a deity, or a belief *in* supernatural existence. A religious person adheres to some position on whether supernatural and/or transcendent reality exists at all, and if so, how, and if not, why. A mere "comprehensive world-view" or "way of life" is not by itself enough to identify a belief system as religious. A world-view may be merely economic, or sociological, and a person might choose to follow a "way of life" that ignores ultimate issues addressed by religions. . . .

There are also a number of characteristics exhibited by most known religious groups to which courts can look when trying to determine if a set of theories or system of ideas is religious in nature. First would be the sincerity of the adherents' claims. . . . Another factor is group organization and hierarchial structure, which evidence the social characteristics of a movement, and show that the adherents sincerely follow a theory of human relationship. Literary manifestations of a movement may also be important, particularly if they take the form of an authoritative text. Ritual and worship also would be significant because they would be evidence of the religion's belief about supernatural or transcendent reality. . . .

II. HUMANISM A RELIGION?

In the present case, the plaintiffs contend that a particular belief system fits within the first amendment definition of religion. . . . All of the experts, and the class representatives, agreed that this belief system [humanism] is a religion which: "makes a statement about supernatural existence a central pillar of its logic; defines the nature of man; and sets forth a goal or purpose for individual and collective human existence; and defines the nature of the universe, and thereby delimits its purpose."

It purports to establish a closed definition of reality; not closed in that adherents know everything, but in that everything is knowable: can be recognized by human intellect aided only by the devices of that intellect's own creation or discovery. The most important belief of this religion is its denial of the transcendent and/or supernatural: there is no God, no creator, no divinity. By force of logic the universe is thus self-existing, completely physical and hence, essentially knowable. Man is the product of evolutionary, physical forces. He is purely biological and has no supernatural or transcendent spiritual component or quality. Man's individual purpose is to seek and obtain personal fulfillment by freely developing every talent and ability, especially his rational intellect, to the highest level. Man's collective purpose is to seek the good life by the increase of every person's freedom and potential for personal development.

In addition, humanism, as a belief system, erects a moral code and identifies the source of morality. This source is claimed to exist in humans and the social relationships of humans. Again, there is no spiritual or supernatural origin for morals: man is merely physical, and morals, the rules governing his private and social conduct, are founded only on man's actions, situation and environment. In addition to a moral code, certain attitudes and conduct are proscribed since they interfere with personal freedom and fulfillment. In particular any belief in a deity or adherence to a religious system that is theistic in any way is discouraged.

Secular humanism, or humanism in the sense of a religious belief system, (as opposed to humanism as just an interest in the humanities), has organizational characteristics. . . .

These organizations publish magazines, newsletters and other periodicals, including *Free Inquiry, The Humanist* and *Progressive World.* The entire body of thought has three key documents that furnish the text upon which the belief system rests as on a platform: *Humanist Manifesto I, Humanist Manifesto II,* and the *Secular Humanist Declaration.* . . .

To say that science is only concerned with data collected by the five senses as enhanced by technological devices of man's creation is to define science's limits. These are the parameters within which scientists function. However, to claim that there is nothing real beyond observable data is to make an assumption based not on science, but on faith, faith that observable data is all that is real. A statement that there is no transcendent or supernatural reality is a *religious* statement. . . .

This Court is holding that the promotion and advancement of a religious system occurs when one faith-theory is taught to the exclusion of others and this is prohibited by the first amendment religion clauses.

For purposes of the first amendment, secular humanism is a religious belief system, entitled to the protections of, and subject to the prohibitions of, the religion clauses. It is not a mere scientific methodology that may be promoted and advanced in the public schools.

III. RELIGIOUS PROMOTION IN TEXTBOOKS?

. . . [T]he Supreme Court has declared that teaching religious tenets in such a way as to promote or encourage a religion violates the religion clauses. This prohibition is not implicated by mere coincidence of ideas with religious tenets. Rather, there must be systematic, whether explicit or implicit, promotion of a belief system as a whole. The facts showed that the State of Alabama has on its state textbook list certain volumes that are being used by school systems in this state, which engage in such promotion. . . .

The virtually unanimous conclusion of the numerous witnesses, both expert and lay, party and non-party, was that textbooks in the fields examined were poor from an educational perspective. Mere rotten and inadequate textbooks, however, have not yet been determined to violate any constitutional provision, much less the religion clauses. . . . Their expert opinion was that religion was so deliberately underemphasized and ignored that theistic religions were effectively discriminated against and made to seem irrelevant and unimportant within the context of American history. . . . The religious influence on the abolitionist, woman's suffrage, temperance, modern civil rights and peace movements is ignored or diminished to insignificance. The role of religion in the lives of immigrants and minorities, especially southern blacks, is rarely mentioned. After the Civil War, religion is given almost no play. . . .

In addition to omitting particular historical events which religious significance, these books uniformly ignore the religious aspect of most American culture. The vast majority of Americans, for most of our history, have lived in a society in which religion was a part of daily life. . . . For many people, religion is still this important. One would never know it by reading these books. Religion, where treated at all, is generally represented as a private matter, only influencing American public life at some extraordinary moments. This view of religion is one humanists have been seeking to instill for fifty years. These books assist that effort by perpetuating an inaccurate historical picture. . . .

According to humanistic psychology, as with humanism generally, man is the center of the universe and all existence. Morals are a matter of taste, dependent upon whether the consequences of actions satisfy human "needs." These needs are always defined as purely temporal and non-supernatural. . . .

The [social studies] books do not state that this is a *theory* of the way humans make choices, they teach the student that things *are* this way. . . . The books teach that the student must determine right and wrong based only on his own experience, feelings and "values." These "values" are described as originating from within. A description of the origin of morals must be based on a faith assumption: a religious dogma. The books are not simply claiming that a moral rule must be internally accepted before it becomes meaningful, because this is true of *all* facts *and* beliefs. . . . The books repeat, over and over, that the decision is "yours alone," or is "purely personal" or that "only you can decide." The emphasis and overall approach implies, and would cause any reasonable, thinking student to infer, that the book is teaching that moral choices

are just a matter of preference, because, as the books say, "you are the most important person in your life." . . . This faith assumes that self-actualization is the goal of every human being, that man has no supernatural attributes or component, that there are only temporal and physical consequences for man's actions, and that these results, alone, determine the morality of an action. This belief strikes at the heart of many theistic religions' beliefs that certain actions are in and of themselves immoral, *whatever the consequences*, and that, in addition, actions will have extratemporal consequences. The Court is not holding that high school . . . books must not discuss various theories of human psychology. But it must not present faith based systems to the exclusion of other faith based systems, it must not present one as true and the other as false, and it *must* use a comparative approach to withstand constitutional scrutiny. . . .

With these [history and social studies] books, the State of Alabama has overstepped its mark, and must withdraw to perform its proper nonreligious functions. . . . The Court will enter an order to prohibit further use of the books.

REVIEW AND DISCUSSION QUESTIONS

1. Describe the legal issue that is before the court in this case.
2. How does Judge Hand understand the legal definition of *religion?*
3. Why does he think humanism is a religion?
4. What does Judge Hand find in the textbooks that leads him to believe that they "establish" a religion?
5. The court of appeals overturned Judge Hand's decision, and the Supreme Court agreed with the appeals court. Is Judge Hand's opinion consistent with the Supreme Court's ruling in *Wisconsin* v. *Yoder?* Explain.
6. Are the religious groups who brought this case raising issues about the curriculum similar to those Gutmann has raised? Explain.
7. In another, related case, the Supreme Court ruled that schools can teach evolutionary theory despite the fact that it is incompatible with some students' religious views. How would you decide such a case? Explain.